William Adolphus Wheeler, Noah Webster, William Greenleaf Webster

A high-school dictionary of the English language explanatory, pronouncing, and synonymous

William Adolphus Wheeler, Noah Webster, William Greenleaf Webster

A high-school dictionary of the English language explanatory, pronouncing, and synonymous

ISBN/EAN: 9783337157265

Printed in Europe, USA, Canada, Australia, Japan

Cover: Foto ©Paul-Georg Meister /pixelio.de

More available books at **www.hansebooks.com**

A

HIGH-SCHOOL
DICTIONARY

OF THE

ENGLISH LANGUAGE

EXPLANATORY, PRONOUNCING, AND SYNONYMOUS
,—WITH AN APPENDIX CONTAINING VARIOUS USEFUL TABLES.

MAINLY ABRIDGED FROM THE LATEST EDITION OF THE
QUARTO DICTIONARY OF

NOAH WEBSTER, LL.D.,

By WILLIAM G. WEBSTER

AND

WILLIAM A. WHEELER.

𝔍llustrated with more than 𝔗hree 𝔥undred 𝔈ngrabings on 𝔚ood.

IVISON, BLAKEMAN, TAYLOR & CO.
NEW YORK AND CHICAGO.
PHILADELPHIA: J. B. LIPPINCOTT & CO.   CINCINNATI: WILSON, HINKLE
& CO.   SPRINGFIELD, MASS.: G. & C. MERRIAM.
1878.

PREFACE.

The first edition of this work, which is mainly an abridgment of the AMERICAN DICTIONARY of Dr. WEBSTER, was published in 1848, under the editorial care of Dr. Webster's son, Mr. WILLIAM G. WEBSTER, who, nine years later, or in 1857, prepared a very careful revision and improvement of the same. The design, as stated by Mr. Webster in the Preface to the latter edition, was "to furnish a vocabulary of the more common words which constitute the body of our language, with many technical terms in the sciences and arts."

With the view of bringing it in all important respects into conformity with the revised edition of the American Dictionary published in 1864, the work has now been reviewed and corrected throughout by the subscriber, who has availed himself of the opportunity thus presented to introduce several new features, although he has adhered to the general plan of the previous editions. Of the additions which have been made, the most important are the Principles of Pronunciation and the Rules for Spelling, in the Introduction, and, in the Appendix, the pronouncing vocabularies of Greek and Latin Names, of Scripture Names, and of Modern Biographical Names, the pronouncing and explanatory list of Christian Names, the explanatory table of Arbitrary Signs used in Writing and Printing, and the list of Prefixes and Suffixes. Distributed throughout the Dictionary are upward of 300 wood-cuts, skillfully engraved, and designed to serve not as mere embellishments of the book, but as veritable illustrations of the words under which they are given. The vocabulary has been considerably enlarged, and now comprises an aggregate of nearly 27,000 words, all of which are in current or occasional use at the present day. To many of the words are attached numerical references to the principles of pronunciation or the rules of orthography which these words exemplify. Etymologies have now and then been introduced in the hope of attracting the attention of young students, and of stimulating in them a desire to learn more of the origin, structure, and affinities of our language.

In the hands of an accomplished teacher, this volume may be made highly useful in schools, since it furnishes material for a valuable course of exercises on words, including their orthography, pronunciation, definition, composition, syllabication, and the like.

WILLIAM A. WHEELER.

DORCHESTER, MASSACHUSETTS, *March*, 1868.

CONTENTS.

KEY TO THE PRONUNCIATION v
PRINCIPLES OF PRONUNCIATION . . . . vi–xix
RULES FOR SPELLING CERTAIN CLASSES OF WORDS . . . . xx–xxiv
ABBREVIATIONS AND EXPLANATIONS xxiv

A DICTIONARY OF THE ENGLISH LANGUAGE 25 to 338.

APPENDIX.

GREEK AND LATIN PROPER NAMES 339–346
SCRIPTURE PROPER NAMES 347–354
CHRISTIAN NAMES OF MEN AND WOMEN 355–360
MODERN GEOGRAPHICAL NAMES 361–370
MODERN BIOGRAPHICAL NAMES 371–376
PREFIXES AND SUFFIXES 377–383
ABBREVIATIONS 384–387
METRIC SYSTEM OF WEIGHTS AND MEASURES 388, 389
ARBITRARY SIGNS 390, 391
WORDS, PHRASES, ETC., FROM THE GREEK, THE LATIN, AND MODERN
    FOREIGN LANGUAGES 392–397
PICTORIAL ILLUSTRATIONS 399–411

KEY TO THE PRONUNCIATION.

VOWELS.

REGULAR LONG AND SHORT SOUNDS.

Ā, ā, *long*, as in . . Āle, Fāte, Grāy.
Ă, ă, *short*, as in . . Ădd, Făt, Răndom.
Ē, ē, *long*, as in . . Ēve, Mēte, Sēizure.
Ĕ, ĕ, *short*, as in . . Ĕnd, Mĕt, Lĕopard.
Ī, ī, *long*, as in . . . Īce, Fīne, Thrīve.
Ĭ, ĭ, *short*, as in . . . Ĭll, Fĭn, Trĭbute.

Ō, ō, *long*, as in . . . Ōld, Nōte, Depōse.
Ŏ, ŏ, *short*, as in . . Ŏdd, Nŏt, Tŏrrid.
Ū, ū, *long*, as in . . . Ūse, Tūbe, Feūdal.
Ŭ, ŭ, *short*, as in . . Ŭs, Tŭb, Stŭdy.
Ȳ, ȳ, *long*, as in . . . Flȳ, Stȳle, Edifȳ.
Y̆, y̆, *short*, as in . . Nўmph, Lўric.

OCCASIONAL SOUNDS.

Â, â, as in . . . . . Âir, Shâre, Pâir.
Ä, ä, *Italian*, as in . . Ärm, Fäther, Fär.
Á, á, as in . . . . Ásk, Gráss, Dánce.
A̤, a̤, *broad*, as in . . A̤ll, Ta̤lk, Ha̤ul.
Ȧ, ȧ, *like short e*, as in Whȧt, Wȧnder.

Ê, ê, *like á*, as in . . Êre, Thêre, Hêir.
E̟, e̟, *like long a*, as in E̟ight, Pre̟y, Obe̟y.
Ẽ, ẽ, as in . . . . Ẽrmine, Vẽrge.

Ï, ï, *like long e*, as in . Pïque, Machïne.
Ĩ, ĩ, *like e*, as in . . . Ĩrksome, Vĩrgin.

Ȯ, ȯ, like short *u*, as in Ȯther, Dȯne, Sȯn.
Ǫ, ǫ, like long *oo*, as in Prǫve, Dǫ, Mǫve.
O̬, o̬, like short *oo*, as in Bo̬som, Wo̬man.
Ô, ô, like broad *a*, as in Ôrder, Fôrm, Stôrk.
OO, oo, as in . . . Moon, Food, Booty.
Oo, oo, as in . . . Wool, Foot, Good.

Ū, ū, preceded by *r*, as in Rūde, Rūle, Rūmor.
U̬, u̬, like short *oo*, as in Bu̬ll, Pu̬t, Pu̬sh.
Û, û, as in . . . . Ûrge, Bûrn, Fûrl.

e, i, o, (Italic) silent, Fall*e*n, Tok*e*n, Cous*i*n.

REGULAR DIPHTHONGAL SOUNDS.

Oi, oi, or Oy, oy (unmarked), as in . . . . . . Oil, Join, Oyster, Toy.
Ou, ou, or Ow, ow (unmarked), as in . . . . . Out, Hound, Owl, Vowel.

CONSONANTS.

Ç, ç, *soft*, like *s* sharp, as in . Çede,Aççept.
€, c, *hard*, like *k*, as in . . €all, €on€ur.
Ch, ch (unmarked), as in . . Child, Touch.
Çh, çh, *soft*, like *sh*, as in . Çhaise, Maçhine.
€h, €h, *hard*, like *k*, as in . €horus, E€ho.
G̣, g̣, *hard*, as in . . . . G̣et, Tig̣er.
G, g, *soft*, like *j*, as in . . Gem, Engine.
S, s, *sharp* (unmarked), as in Same; Rest.
Ṣ, ṣ, *flat or vocal*, like *z*, as in Haṣ, Amuṣe.

Th, th, *sharp* (unmarked) as in Thirtieth.
T͟h, t͟h, *flat or vocal*, as in . T͟hit͟her.
Ng, ng (unmarked), as in . Singing.
N̈, n̈, as in . . . . . . An̈ger, In̈k.
X̱, x̱, like *gz*, as in . . . . Ex̱ample.
Ph, ph, like *f* (unmarked), as in Seraphic.
Qu, qu, like *kw* (unmarked), as in Quantity.
Wh, wh, like *hw* (unmk'd), as in Awhile.
Zh, zh, as in . . . . Vision (vĭzh'un).

⁂ When one letter of an improper diphthong, or of a triphthong, is marked, it is to be taken as representing the sound of the combination, and the letter or letters which are not marked are to be regarded as silent; as in ā̆im, clēan, cēil, pēople, ro̤ute, so̤ul, jo̤ũrnal, tōw, &c. The combined letters *ce, ci, sci, se, si*, or *ti*, occurring before a vowel in a syllable immediately preceded by an accented syllable, are generally equivalent to *sh*; as in o′cean, ceta′ceous, so′cial, logi′cian, suspi′cion, auspi′cious, con′science, nau′seous, controver′sial, dissen′sion, ini′tial, ora′tion, ficti′tious, &c. Such syllables are not always respelled, as, in general, they will naturally be pronounced correctly by an English speaker. But in all exceptional, doubtful, or difficult cases, the appropriate respelling is used.

ACCENT. — The principal accent is denoted by a heavy mark; the secondary, by a lighter mark; as in Su′perintend′ent. In the division of words into syllables, these marks, besides performing their proper office, supply the place of the hyphen, except in some compound and derivative words.

PRINCIPLES OF PRONUNCIATION,

WITH EXPLANATIONS OF THE KEY.

VOWELS.

I. VOWELS IN MONOSYLLABLES AND ACCENTED SYLLABLES.

A.

§ 1. Regular long sound, marked Ā, ā, as in *āle*; heard also in *pāin, dāy, gāol, gāuge, āye, brēak, rēil, whēy*, &c.

NOTE. — This sound of *a* is in most cases diphthongal, having a slight "vanish" in *ĕ* annexed to its "radical" or initial sound, as in *pay*, where the *y* may be regarded as representing the vanish. Writers are not agreed as to the nature of the radical part, some considering it to be the sound of short *e*, while others assert that it is a distinct, though very similar, element, being like the other long vowels as compared with their true corresponding short sounds, of a slightly less open quality. — See § 9.

§ 2. Regular short sound, marked Ă, ă, as in *ădd*; heard also in *plăid, bădĕ*, &c.

NOTE. — This is a distinct element from the *long a*. With respect to its position in the scale of sounds, it is a palatal vowel, intermediate between *ä* and *ĕ*, the tongue being raised higher than for *ä*, and not so high as for *ĕ*.

OCCASIONAL SOUNDS OF A.

§ 3. Sound of *a* before *r*, in such words as *air, care, fare, bear, prayer, parent*, marked Â, â.

According to Smart, this element is our long *a* in *fate*, and owes all its peculiarity to the subsequent *r*. Such, also, is the statement of Dr. Webster and of most English orthoëpists. The sound of *r* in these words is what Smart calls a "guttural vibration," — a sound which he represents by *ur*, and Dr. Webster by *er*. In *care* we touch lightly on the *ā* sound (*the radical alone, without the vanish; see* § 1), and then pass fully and strongly into the guttural vibration (câ'ur or câ'er), drawing the two as closely as possible into the same syllable. Another mode of identifying the sound in question is that of prolonging our short *e* before *r*. Thus, *ther* (with the *e* as in *thĕn*), drawn out into long quantity, gives us *there* (thâr); and *er* (the first syllable in *ĕrror*) gives us *ere* or *e'er* (âr). Thus, in the view here presented, the *initial* sound should always be that of *a* in *fate* (the *radical* without the vanish; see § 1), though the final impression upon the ear is that of an open or broad sound, in consequence of the "opening power" of the *r*.

Some, however, especially in New England, give to words of this class a slightly different sound; namely, that of our *short a* before *r*, as in *air*, pronounced *äer*, with a somewhat lengthened sound of the *ä*. This sound is rather more open than the one mentioned above, and is apt, in the mouths of our common people, to become too broad and coarse. If well executed, however, it is scarcely at all inferior to the other in smoothness and grace.

§ 4. Sound of the Italian *a*, marked Ä, ä, as in *ärm, fäther, fär*; heard also in *äh, heärth, dauni, guärd, äre*, &c.

NOTE. — The Italian *a* is the most open of all the vowel sounds, and is one of the extremes of the vowel scale, the other extremes being *ē* and *ōō*. In its formation, the mouth and throat are opened widely, and the tongue is left in its natural position of rest.

§ 5. Sound of *a* in certain words (chiefly monosyllables) ending in *ff, ft, ss, st, sk, sp*, with a few in *nce*, and *nt*, marked A̍, a̍, as in *sta̍ff, gra̍ft, pa̍ss, la̍st, a̍sk, ga̍sp, cha̍nce, cha̍nt*, &c.

NOTE. — This is *a shortened* or *brief form* of the Italian *a*. A majority of good speakers, both in England and America, give this sound to words of the class under consideration. Many speakers, particularly in London and in the Middle States, pronounce the *a* in such words with its short, flat sound (see § 2), saying *stăff, grăft, păss*, &c., — a practice which is not to be commended, though it is too general to be condemned as unsupported by good usage.

§ 6. Sound of broad *a*, marked A̧, a̧, as in *a̧ll, ta̧lk, ha̧ul, swa̧rm*; heard also in *sa̧uce, a̧we, gȩorgic, fo̧rk, gro̧at, bo̧ught*, &c.

NOTE. — This sound is formed by a depression of the larynx, and a consequent retraction of the tongue, which enlarges the cavity of the mouth posteriorly.

§ 7. Short sound of broad *a*, marked A̤, a̤, as in *wha̤t, wa̤nder*, &c.; heard also in *kno̤wledge*

(vi)

PRINCIPLES OF PRONUNCIATION. vii

NOTE. — This is the extreme short sound of broad *a*, and coincides with the sound of *o* in *not*. It differs, however, in quality as well as quantity from broad *a*, being a more open sound; that is to say, the aperture of the lips and the internal cavity of the mouth, though of the same shape in both cases, are somewhat larger for the former (*a*) than for the latter (*ǒ*), while the position of the tongue remains unaltered throughout.

There is a sound of *a*, as heard in *salt*, *although*, &c., which is intermediate between that in *awe* and that in *what*. — See § 19, NOTE.

E.

§ 8. Regular long sound, marked E, ē, as in *ēve*, *mēte*, &c.; heard also in *Cæsar*, *bēard*, *feet*, *lēisure*, *key*, *machīne*, *fīeld*, *œsophagus*, &c.

NOTE. — In the formation of this element, the tongue is raised convexly within the dome of the palate, pressing against its sides, and leaving only the smallest possible passage through which a vowel sound can be uttered.

§ 9. Regular short sound, marked Ĕ, ĕ, as in *ĕnd*, *mĕt*; heard also in *many*, *aphæresis*, *said*, *feather*, *heifer*, *friend*, *asafœtida*, *bury*, *guess*.

NOTE. — This is not a short sound of the long *e*. It has usually been considered as the shut or extreme short sound of the *a* in *fate*; but most orthoëpists at the present day, while allowing it to be a nearly related sound, regard it as distinct, it being slightly more open than the radical part of *ā*, and lacking the vanish: both are intermediate between *ă* and *ē*, the tongue not being so much depressed as for the former, nor raised so high toward the palate as for the latter. — See § 1.

OCCASIONAL SOUNDS OF E.

§ 10. Sound of *e* like *ă* (as in *care*, *fair*, *bear*, &c.), marked Ê, ê, as in *êre*, *thêre*, *hêir*, *ê'er*, &c. This is the same sound with that of *a* in *care*. — See § 3.

§ 11. Sound of *e* like *ă*, marked E, ȩ, as in *sh*, *sight*, *prȩy*, *vȩin*, &c. — See § 1.

§ 12. Sound of *e* before *r*, verging toward the sound of *u* in *urge*, marked Ẽ, ẽ, as in *ẽrmine*, *vẽrge*, *prefẽr*; heard also in *ẽarnest*, *mȳrth*, *myrtle*, &c.

NOTE. — The vulgar universally, and many cultivated speakers both in England and America, give the *e* in such words the full sound of *u* in *urge*, as, *murcy* for *mercy*, *turm* for *term*, &c. But, in the most approved style of pronunciation, the organs are placed in a position intermediate between that requisite for sounding *ŭ* and that for sounding *ē*, thus making (as Smart observes) "a *compromise* between the two." In other words, this element is radically distinct from both *ŭ* and *ē*, being less guttural than the former and less palatal than the latter, from which it was doubtless originally evolved.

I.

§ 13. Regular long sound, marked Ī, ī, as in *īce*; heard also in *aisle*, *hēight*, *ēying*, *ēye*, *vīe*,

guīle, *buȳ*, *thȳ*, *rȳe*, &c.; in *pīnt*, in *chīld*, *mīld*, *wīld*; and in most monosyllables ending with *nd*, as *bīnd*, *fīnd*, *kīnd*, &c.

NOTE. — This sound, though represented by a single character, is not a simple element, but a diphthong. It is composed of *ä* and *ē* as extremes, with the *ä* accented, but made so very brief that the ear with difficulty recognizes the precise character of the sound.

§ 14. Regular short sound, marked Ĭ, ĭ, as in *ĭll*; heard also in *English*, *beaufin*, *been*, *sieve*, *women*, *busy*, *guinea*, *nȳmph*, &c.

NOTE. — This is not a short sound of long *i*. Many have considered it as the shut or extreme short sound of long *e*; but it is really a distinct, though closely allied, element. In its formation, the tongue is slightly relaxed from the position assumed for producing *ē*; this is the only difference between the two sounds.

OCCASIONAL SOUNDS OF I.

§ 15. Sound of *i* like long *e*, marked Ī, ī, as in *pīque*, *machīne*, *caprīce*, &c. — See § 8.

NOTE. — Most of the English words in which this sound is represented by this letter are from the French.

§ 16. Sound of *i* before *r*, verging toward *u* in *urge*, marked Ĩ, ĩ, as in *ĩrksome*, *vĩrgin*, &c., identical with that of *ẽ* in *ẽrmine*. — See § 12.

O.

§ 17. Regular long sound, marked Ō, ō, as in *ōld*; heard also in *hautboy*, *beau*, *yeōman*, *sew*, *rōam*, *hōe*, *dōor*, *shōulder*, *grōw*, *ōwe*, &c.

NOTE. — This sound of *o* is in most cases diphthongal, having a slight "vanish" in *oo* annexed to the "radical" or initial sound, as in *below*. The radical part of the sound is a simple element, intermediate with respect to the mode of its formation, between *a* and *oo*, the tongue being less depressed than for *a*, and the labial aperture greater than for *oo*. It is essentially the same element as that described in the next section, but is of a slightly less open quality.

§ 18. It is exceedingly common, in some parts of the United States, to shorten the long *o* of certain words, as *bolt*, *most*, *only*, &c., by dropping the vanishing element which belongs to the vowel, and giving to the radical portion a somewhat more open quality; but this practice is wholly opposed to English usage. The provincialism here pointed out obtains, more or less widely, in respect to the following words; namely, *boat*, *bolster*, *bolt*, *bone*, *both*, *broke*, *broken*, *choke*, *cloak*, *close*, a., *coach*, *coat*, *coax*, *colt*, *colter*, *comb*, *don't*, *folks*, *goad*, *hold*, *holm*, *holster*, *home*, *homely*, *hope*, *jolt*, *load*, *molten*, *most*, *molt*, *none*, *only*, *open*, *pole*, *polka*, *poultice*, *poultry*, *revolt*, *road*, *rode*, *rogue*, *soap*, *sloth*, *smoke*, *sofa*, *spoke*, v., *spoken*, *stone*, *story*, *swollen* (or *swoln*), *throat*, *toad*, *upholsterer*, *upholstery*, *whole*, *wholly*, *wholesome*, *wrote*, *yoke*, *yolk*, and possibly a few others. Most persons

PRINCIPLES OF PRONUNCIATION.

in New England sound the *o* in a part or all of these words without the vanish, while some among the vulgar go further, and give to a number of them almost the sound of short *u*, as *hum* for *home*, &c. They should all, however, have the full sound of the *o* as heard in accented syllables, though not in all cases with quite the same prolongation of the sound.

§ 19. Regular short sound, marked Ŏ, ŏ, as in *ŏdd*, *nŏt*; heard also in *wŏnder*, *knŏwledge*, &c. — See § 7.

NOTE. — This is the *shut* or extreme short sound of broad *a*, and coincides with the sound of *a* in *what*. There is a medium sound of this letter which is neither so short as in *not*, nor so long as in *naught*. This medium sound is usually given to the short *o* when directly followed by *ss*, *st*, and *th*, as in *cross*, *cost*, *broth*; also, in *gone*, *cough*, *trough*, *off*, and some other words.

OCCASIONAL SOUNDS OF O.

§ 20. Sound of *o* like short *u*, marked Ó, ó, as in *óther*, *dóve*, &c.; heard also in *dóes*, *gŭn*, *flŏod*, *dŏuble*, &c. — See § 23.

§ 21. Sound of *o* like *oo* long, marked Ǫ, ǫ, as in *prǫve*, *dǫ*, *mǫve*, *tǫmb*, &c. — See § 24.

§ 22. Sound of *o* like *oo* short, marked Ọ, ọ, as in *bọsom*, *wọlf*, *wọman*, &c. — See § 25.

NOTE. — This sound coincides with that of *u* in *bull*, which is also used for *oo* short. — See § 30.

§ 23. Sound of *o* like *ạ* (broad *a*), marked Ô, ô, as in *ôrder*, *fôrm*, *stôrk*, &c. — See § 6.

OO.

§ 24. Regular long or open sound, marked OO, ōō, as in *mōōn*, *fōōd*; heard also in *rheum*, *drew*, *tǫ*, *canǫe*, *grǫup*, *ryde*, *rye*, *recruit*, &c.

NOTE. — This is the closest labial vowel; that is to say, in forming it the lips are more nearly closed than for any other vowel, the sides being brought into contact with each other so as to leave only a small central aperture for the escape of the voice.

§ 25. Regular short sound of *oo*, marked ŎŎ, ŏŏ, as in *wŏŏl*, *fŏŏt*; heard also in *wọlf*, *shọuld*, *bụll*, &c.

U.

§ 26. Regular long sound, marked Ū, ū, as in *mūte*, *ūnit*, &c.; heard also in *beauty*, *feodal*, *feūd*, *pew*, *ewe*, *lieū*, *view*, *cūe*, *sūit*, *yew*, *you*, *yule*, &c.

NOTE. — This is a compound sound, formed of the vowel *oo*, with a slight sound of the consonant *y* or of the vowel *ĕ* or *ĭ* before it. When the *u* begins a syllable, or is preceded by any one of the palatal or labial sounds *k*, *g*, *p*, *b*, *f*, *v*, *m*, the sound of *y* is clearly perceived, as in the words *usage*, *cube*, *gules*, *puny*, *burin*, *futile*, *mule*.

§ 27. When the long *u* is preceded, in the same syllable, by any one of the consonants *d*, *t*, *l*, *n*, *s*, and *th*, it is peculiarly difficult to introduce the sound of *y*; and hence negligent speakers omit it entirely, pronouncing *duty*, *dooty*; *tune*, *toon*; *lute*, *loot*; *nuisance*, *noosance*; *suit*, *soot*; *thurible*, *thoorible*, &c. The reason is, that, in forming these consonants, the organs are in a position to pass with perfect ease to the sound of *oo*, while it is very difficult in doing so to touch the intermediate *y*; hence the *y* in such cases is very apt to be dropped. The practice of good society, however, is to let the *y* sink into a *very brief* sound of long *e* or of short *i*, both of which have a very close organic relationship to consonant *y*. Special care must be taken not only to make this sound as brief as possible, but to pronounce it in the same syllable with the *oo*.

It ought to be added that wherever the sound of *sh*, *zh*, or *y* consonant precedes the *u*, the *y* is omitted, as in *sure*, sounded *shoor*; *sugar*, *shoogar*; *azure*, *azh'oor*; *yule*, *yool*, &c.

§ 28. Regular short sound, marked Ŭ, ŭ, as in *bŭt*; heard also in *dŏes*, *blŏod*, *tŏuch*, &c.

NOTE. — This is not the short sound of long *u*. In its organic formation, it is essentially the same sound as *u* in *urge*, but is shorter in quantity, and of a rather more open quality.

OCCASIONAL SOUNDS OF U.

§ 29. Sound of *u* preceded by *r* in the same syllable, marked Ụ, ụ, as in *rụde*, *rụmor*, &c.

NOTE. — All the English orthoëpists agree that the *u* in this case drops the *y* or *i* which is generally an element of its compound sound when preceded, in the same syllable, by any other consonant than *r*, and becomes simply *oo*, so that *rue* is pronounced rōō; *rule*, rōōl; *ruby*, rōōby, &c.

§ 30. Sound of *u* like that of short *oo* (ŏŏ), marked Ų, ų, as in *bųll*, *pųt*, *pųsh*, *pųll*, &c. — See § 25.

§ 31. Sound of *u* before *r* in such words as *ûrge*, *bûrn*, *fûrl*, *concûr*, &c., marked Û, û; heard also in *worm*, *journey*, &c.

NOTE. — This has been termed *the neutral vowel*, with reference to its want of any strongly-marked, distinctive character. The sound differs from that of short *u* (with which it has often been identified) in length, and in a somewhat greater degree of closeness.

Y.

§ 32. Regular long sound, marked Ȳ, ȳ, as in *flȳ*, *stȳle*, *skȳ*, *edifȳ*, &c.

NOTE. — This is the same sound as long *i*. — See § 13.

§ 33. Regular short sound, marked Y̆, y̆, as in *cy̆st*, *ny̆mph*, *ly̆ric*, *aby̆ss*, coinciding with the sound of short *i*. — See § 14.

OCCASIONAL SOUND OF Y.

§ 34. Y has only one occasional sound;

PRINCIPLES OF PRONUNCIATION.

namely, in such words as *myrrh*, *myrtle*, in which it has, like the *e* and *i* in similar circumstances (see § 12 and § 16), very nearly the sound of *u* in *urge*.

II. REGULAR OR PROPER DIPHTHONGS.

OI or OY.

§ 35. The sound of *oi* or *oy* (unmarked), as heard in *oil*, *join*, *oyster*, &c.

NOTE.—The elements of this diphthong are *ŏ* as in *cord* (the same as broad *a*), and *ĭ* as in *fin* (short *i*), with the accent on the former. *Oy* is always regular in English words, and *oi* is regular also, except in the following cases; namely, avoirdupois (av-*ur*-du-poiz′), connoisseur (kon-*is*-soor′), chamois (sham′my), choir (kwire), tortoise (tor′tis), tur-quois (sometimes pronounced tur-*keez*′).

OW.

§ 36. The sound of *ow* (unmarked), as heard in *owl*, *vowel*, *flower*, &c.

NOTE.—This diphthong is compounded of the elements *ä* and *oo*, the former of which is accented, but made extremely brief. In a considerable number of words, *ow* represents the sound of long *o*; in the single word *knowledge* and in its derivatives, it has the sound of short *o*. These are accordingly distinguished by the proper mark, as *blōw*, *knōw*, *knŏwledge*, &c.

OU.

§ 37. This diphthong has two leading sounds.

(1.) That of *ow* in words derived from the Anglo-Saxon, as in *out*, *hound*, &c.

(2.) That of *oo* in words derived from the French, as in *soup*, *group*, &c.

§ 38. The diphthong *ou* has also, in a number of words, the sound of long *o*, as in *sōul*; in a few cases, the sound of the broad *a*, as in *bought* (bawt); sometimes that of short *u*, as in *couple*; sometimes that of *u* in *urge*, as in *adjourn* (adjurn); and, in the three words *could*, *would*, *should*, that of *oo* as in *foot*. These peculiarities are indicated in this Dictionary by the appropriate mark over the significant or sounded vowel, or by respelling.

III. VOWELS IN UNACCENTED SYLLABLES.

§ 39. When an unaccented syllable ends in a consonant, its vowel, if single, has, in strict theory, its regular short or shut sound, though uttered somewhat more faintly, or with a less proportionate force, than in an accented syllable; as in *ds*-sign′, con′dйct, con′flict, &c. In many words of this class, however, the vowel is apt to suffer a change or corruption of its distinctive quality, passing over into some sound of easier utterance. Thus the vowel sounds in the unaccented syllables *ar*, *er*, *ir*, or,

yr (as in *altar*, *offer*, *tapir*, *mirror*, *zephyr*), are coincident with that of the second *u* in *sulphur*. As a general rule, *a* and *o*, in unaccented syllables ending in a consonant, verge toward, or fall into, the sound of short *u*, particularly in colloquial discourse, as in bal′lad, bar′rack, ver′bal, bed′lam, cap′stan, jal′ap, bi′as, bal′last, hav′oc, meth′od, pis′tol, ven′om, compel′, flag′on, bish′op, pi′lot, prov′ost. In such words, it would ordinarily be pedantic or affected to give the vowel its regular short sound.

The vowel *e*, in unaccented syllables ending in a consonant, is, in some words, liable to be sounded like short *i* (as in *barrel*), and, in others, like short *u* (as in *silent*); but these changes are usually avoided by good speakers.

It may here be remarked, that some of the diphthongs are similarly affected by the absence of accent. Thus *ai*, which, in an accented syllable, is usually sounded like long *a* (as in *com-plāin*′), sinks into *ĕ* or *ĭ* in an unaccented syllable, as in *mountain*, pronounced moun′tĕn or moun′tĭn. So *ei*, *ey*, and *ie* become changed in pronunciation into *ĭ* (as in *sur′feit*, hon′ey, car′ried), and *ou* is sounded as *ŭ* (as in griev′ous).

§ 40. When the unaccented syllable does not end in a consonant, two cases arise; namely,—

(1.) The syllable may consist of, or may end in, a vowel, as in the words *a*-bound′, *di*-rect′, *e*-vent′, *mo*-lest′, &c.

(2.) The syllable may end in a consonant, with final *e* mute at the close of words, as in ul′ti-mate, fi′nite, rep′tile, &c.

The former of these will, for the sake of brevity, be called No. 1, the latter No. 2. These will now be considered under each of the vowels.

A.

§ 41. (No. 1. See § 40.) Here the *a* has properly a brief sound of the Italian *a*, as in Cu′ba, *a*-muse′, *A*-mer′i-ca; but, in familiar speech, it is almost always so slighted and obscured as to be indistinguishable from the neutral vowel, or *u* in *urge*, *murmur*, &c. In some words, like *ā*-e′ri-al, chā-ot′ic, &c., the *a* has its regular long or name sound, somewhat shortened by the omission of the "vanish." This is due to the influence of the subsequent vowel, which, in fluent utterance, refuses to take the Italian *a* before it without the intervention of one or more consonants. Some speakers in this country give the same brief sound of long *a* to this letter when it occurs in an initial unaccented syllable followed by a consonant in an accented syllable, as in *a*-bound′, *fa*-tal′i-ty; but this practice is not sanctioned by the best orthoëpists. In the terminations -*a-ny* and -*a-ry*, the *a* has usually the same

PRINCIPLES OF PRONUNCIATION.

sound as short *e* unaccented, as in mis′cel-la-ny, mo′ment-a-ry, &c.

§ 42. (No. 2. See § 40.) Here the *a* has sometimes its long sound, particularly in verbs ending in *ate* ; as, ded′i-cāte, ed′u-cāte, &c. In other parts of speech, the sound of the *a* is more obscure, verging toward short *e*, as in ul′ti-mate, night′in-gale, pref′ace, &c. In some instances it is apt to verge toward short *i*, as in vil′lage.

E.

§ 43. (No. 1. See § 40.) Here the *e* has its long sound, slightly obscure or abridged, as in *e*-vent′, *e*-mo′tion, so-ci′e-ty, &c.

§ 44. (No. 2. See § 40.) Here, also, the *e* has usually its long sound a little shortened and slighted, as in ob′so-lete.

I.

There is great diversity in the case of this letter. Hence it is difficult to lay down general rules ; and, as Smart remarks, " The inquirer must be sent to the Dictionary to learn, in each particular case, the true pronunciation."

§ 45. (No. 1. See § 40.) *I*, when final in a syllable, has more commonly its short sound, as in phī-los′o-phy, dī-rect′, &c. But the *i* is usually long in the *initial* syllables *i, bi, chi, cli, cri, pri, tri*, as in ī-de′a, bī-ol′o-gy, crī-te′ri-on, prī-me′val, &c.

§ 46. (No. 2. See § 40.) In these terminations, usage is greatly divided. On the whole, the *i* is more generally short, as in ac-com′plĭce, in′fi-nīte, fer′tĭle, mar′i-tĭme, ad-a-man′tĭne, pos′i-tĭve, &c. ; but there are some important exceptions, as, cock′a-trīce, ex′īle, gen′tīle, con′cubīne, ar′chīve, &c. ; also, all names of minerals ending in *lite* or *ite* ; as chrys′o-līte, ste′a-tīte, &c.

O.

§ 47. (No. 1. See § 40.) Here the *o* has usually its long sound slightly abbreviated, and without its " vanish " (see § 19), as in *o*-plu′ion, croc′o-dīle, to-bac′co, &c. — See § 107.

§ 48. (No. 2. See § 40.) The *o* in these terminations has usually its regular long sound, as in tel′e-scōpe, ep′ōde, &c. Sometimes it has the sound of short *o*, as in di′a-logue : in other cases, it verges toward short *u*, as in pur′pose.

U.

§ 49. (No. 1. See § 40.) Here the *u* generally has its long sound slightly abridged, as in ac′cu-rate, e-mol′u-ment, man-u-mit′, an′nu-al, dep′u-tize, u-til′i-ty. But when the *u* is preceded by *d, t,* or *s*, these combinations, *du, tu,* and *su*, are by the great majority of speakers changed into *joo, choo,* and *shoo* or *zhoo*, respectively, as in ed′u-cate (ĕj′oo-kate), ha-bit′u-al (ha-bĭch′-oo-al), sen′su-ous (sĕn′shoo-us), vis′u-al (vĭzh′-oo-al). (See §§ 63, 74, 89, 90, 92, and 104.) In the notation of words of this class in the Dictionary, the regular pronunciation is generally given instead of the irregular, in conformity with the views of Dr. Webster. When the *u* is preceded by *r*, it simply drops the *y* sound, and is pronounced *oo*, as in er-u-di′tion (er-oo-dish′un). (See § 29.)

§ 50. (No. 2. See § 40.) The *u* in these terminations should generally retain its regular long sound (see §§ 26, 27) slightly abridged, as in grat′i-tūde, in′sti-tūte, rĭd′i-cūle, trĭb′ute, &c. There are a few exceptions, as min′u*t*e (min′it), *n.*, and let′tuce (let′tis). If the letter *r* precedes the *u*, the initial element of the vowel is dropped, as in ce′ruse (se′roos), per′uke (pẽr′ook), &c. — See § 29.

The terminations *dure, ture,* and *sure*, though sometimes pronounced with the regular sounds of the letters, are more commonly pronounced *joor, choor,* and *shoor* or *zhoor*, respectively, as in the words tem′per-a-tūre (tem′per-a-choor), ver′dure (ver′joor), cy′no-sure (si′no-shoor), ex-po′sure (eks-po′zhoor). (See §§ 63, 74, 89, 90, 104.) When these terminations are immediately preceded by an accented syllable, many speakers change them still further into *chur, jur,* and *shur*, or *zhur*, as in na′ture (na′chur), ver′dure (ver′jur), cen′sure (sen′shur), ex-po′sure (eks-po′zhur). The Dictionary follows the practice of Dr. Webster in giving to *dure* and *ture* the regular sounds of *d, t,* and *u* (pronouncing *verdure*, vẽrd′yoor, *creature*, kreet′yoor, &c.)

Y.

§ 51. (No. 1. See § 40.) Here *y* has usually its short sound, as in bȳ-poc′ri-sȳ, mȳ-thol′o-gȳ, van′i-tȳ, mer′ri lȳ, proph′e-cȳ, &c. ; but verbs ending in *fy* have the *y* long, as in jus′ti-fȳ, mag′ni-fȳ, &c. ; also the three verbs, oc′cu-pȳ, mul′ti-plȳ, proph′e-sȳ.

§ 52. (No. 2. See § 40.) The *y* in these terminations (which are few in number) is generally long, as in an′o-dȳne, per′i-stȳle, ne′o-phȳte, pros′e-lȳte, &c.

IV. SILENT VOWELS.

§ 53. Vowels which are printed in Italics are not to be sounded ; as the *e* in us*e*d, burd*e*n, the *i* in cous*i*n, &c. Some of these cases require a more particular consideration.

E *final.*

§ 54. The letter *e* is always mute when final, except in monosyllables containing no other vowel, in classical words, and in some words from modern foreign languages : but in a monosyllable or in an accented syllable of a word, though silent, it generally serves the purpose of indicating that a preceding single vowel followed by a single consonant, a conso-

PRINCIPLES OF PRONUNCIATION.

nant digraph, or the combined letters *st* or *ng*, has its regular long sound, as in *plane, hope, cube, inscribe, paste, change*. When a silent *e* follows *c* or *g* at the end of a word, it serves also to show that the consonant is to have its soft, and not its hard, sound, as in *ace, nice, age, huge, oblige*. In a number of monosyllables (as *bide, come, give, wīre, done, &c.*) and in the accented syllables of a few words derived from them (as *forbade', become', forgive'*), the *e* does not have its usual effect of lengthening the sound of the preceding vowel. In unaccented syllables, it sometimes keeps the vowel in its long sound, as in *gen'tile, su'pine, fi'nite, ar'chive*; but in a great many instances it exercises no such influence, as in *jus'tice, hos'tile, mar i-time, doc'trine, an'ise, gran'ite, plain'tive*.

EN with E silent.

§ 55. Most words ending in *en* drop the *e* in pronunciation, as, *often* (of'n), *heaven* (heav'n), *even* (ev'n). &c. The following are nearly all the words in which the *e* should be sounded: aspen, chicken, hyphen, kitchen, jerken, latten, lichen, marten, mynchen, paten, patten, platen, rowen, wicken, and yewen. The *e* is also sounded when preceded by the liquids *l, m, n, r*, as in woolen, omen, linen, siren, &c., though fallen, stolen, and swollen omit the *e* in pronunciation. With regard to *Eden, bounden, heathen, mitten, sudden*, and *sloven*, there is a diversity of usage among good speakers, some suppressing, and some sounding, the *e*.

ON with O silent.

§ 56. Many words ending in *on* preceded by *c, ck, s*, and *t*, omit the *o* in pronunciation, as in *reckon* (reck'n), *bacon* (bak'n), *treason* (treas'n), *mutton* (mutt'n), &c.

ED with E silent.

§ 57. The termination *ed* is usually shortened in pronunciation by dropping the sound of the *e* (as in *loved* (lov'd), *aimed* (aim'd), *diffused* (diffus'd), &c.), unless this letter is preceded by *d* or *t* (as in *am-nded, contented, &c.*), when its omission is organically impossible. But in adverbs formed by adding *ly*, and in nouns formed by adding *ness* to words ending in *ed*, the *e* of this termination is uniformly sounded, as in *assuredly, confusedly, renewedly, amazedness, composedness*, &c. There are also some participial adjectives, and some adjectives not derived from verbs, in which the *e* is commonly sounded; as, *aged, beloved, blessed, crabbed, cragged, cronked, crutched, cursed, cusped, deuced, dogged, hooked, jagged, learned, legged, naked, peaked, picked* (sharp), *ragged, rugged, stubbed, wicked, winged, wretched*. The *e* is also pronounced in the derivatives formed from such adjectives, as, *learnedly, blessedness*; but

is generally omitted in the compounds, as, *full-aged* (ūjd).

EL with E silent.

§ 58. As a general rule, the *e* is sounded in these terminations, as in *gravel, level, vessel, chapel*, &c. The following are nearly or quite all the words of this kind in which the *e* is properly omitted; namely, barbel, betel, chattel, drazel, drivel, easel, grovel, hazel, mangel-wurzel, mantel, mispickel, mussel, navel, ousel, ravel, rivel, scovel, shekel, shovel, shrivel, snivel, swingel, swivel, teasel, toggel, towsel, weasel.

CONSONANTS.

B.

§ 59. The sound represented by this letter (which is unmarked) is heard in the words *barn, rob, labor, table*, &c.

NOTE.—This sound is formed by the compression of vocalized breath or voice, within the mouth, while the lips are shut and the back nostrils are closed by covering them with the soft palate. When preceded by *m*, or followed by *t*, in the same syllable, *b* is generally silent, as in *bomb, climb, tomb, debt, doubt, subtile*, &c. *Accumb, dithyramb, iamb, succumb, rhomb, rhumb*, are said to be exceptions.

C.

§ 60. *C* marked thus, Ç, ç (soft *c*), has the sound of *s*, as in *çede, traçe, açid, çypress*, &c.

NOTE.—It takes this sound whenever it occurs before *e* (even if silent), *i*, or *y*.—See § 87.

When the letters *ce* or *ci* are immediately preceded by an accented syllable, and are followed by a vowel in the next syllable, the *c* combines in pronunciation with the *e* or *i* to form the sound *sh*, as in *ocean, social, saponaceous*, &c. In some words, *c* alone has this sound, or, rather, the *c* or *i* is used twice, first combining with the *c* to represent the sound of *sh*, and then, in the same syllable, taking on its customary vowel sound, as in *so-ci-al'i-ty*.—See §II, § 92.

§ 61. *C* marked thus, Ꞓ, ꞓ (hard *c*), has the sound of *k* when it comes before *a, o, u, l*, or *r*, before *k, s*, or *t*, and when it ends a word or a syllable, as in *call, cot, cut, clot, crown, black, act, zinc, traffic, picture, flac'cid, eth'ics*.—See K, § 75.

§ 62. *C* has the sound of *z* in the words *sacrifice, sice, suffice*, and *discern*, and in their derivatives. It is silent in the words *czar, victuals, indict*, and their derivatives; also in the termination *scle*, as in *muscle, corpuscle*, &c.

CH.

§ 63. *Ch* unmarked (English *ch*) has very nearly the sound of *tsh*, as in *child, much, richer, speechless*, &c.

NOTE.—When the letter *t* comes before *u*

PRINCIPLES OF PRONUNCIATION.

(= yoo) in an unaccented syllable, and is at the same time preceded by an accented syllable (as in *nature*), or when it is preceded by *s* or *z* in an accented syllable, and is immediately followed by *ia* (= ya) or *io* (= yo) in an unaccented syllable (as in *Christian*, *question*, *admixtion*), both this letter and the *y* virtually following it are, by some speakers, preserved in their usual and appropriate sounds; thus, *nature* (nāt′yoor), *Christian* (krĭst′yŭn), *question* (kwĕst′yŭn), *admixtion* (ad-mĭkst′yŭn), &c. But by others they are suffered to sink into the easier and closely allied sound of *ch* in *church;* thus, *nature* (nā-choor), *Christian* (krĭs′chan), *question* (kwĕs′chun), *admixtion* (ad-mĭks′chun), &c.

§ 64. *Ch* marked thus, Çh, çh (French *ch*), has the sound of *sh*, as in *chaise*, *marchioness*, *machine*, &c. — See SH, § 92. Most words of this kind are derived from the French.

§ 65. *Ch* marked thus, €h, єh (Latin *ch*,) has the sound of *k*, as in *chorus*, *epoch*, *distich*, &c. This is the usual sound in words derived from the ancient languages; but *cherub* and *charity*, with their derivatives, are exceptions *Ch* is always hard (like *k*) before *l* and *r*, as in *chlorine*, *chrism*.

NOTE. — The prefix *arch*, denoting *chief*, is pronounced *ark* in *archangel* and its derivatives, and in words from foreign languages in which the other component part is not separately current in English, as *architecture*, *archipelago*, *architrave*, &c. In all other cases, it is pronounced *artch*, as in *arch*-bishop, *arch*-enemy, *arch*-fiend, &c.

§ 66. *Ch* is silent in the word *drachm* (though not in *drachma*, drăk′ma), and also in *schism*, *yacht* (yot), and their derivatives.

D.

§ 67. The sound of *d* (unmarked), as in *dale*, *sad*, *rider*, *tradesman*, &c.

NOTE. — The sound of this letter is formed by pressing the end of the tongue against the upper gums, and then forcing up vocalized breath, or voice, into the mouth, the soft palate being raised to prevent its escape through the nose.

D is silent only in the words *Wednesday* and *handkerchief*.

F.

§ 68. The sound of *f* (unmarked), as in *fame*, *leaf*, *definite*, *softly*, &c.

NOTE. — This letter, which is never silent, is uttered by applying the lower lip to the upper front teeth, and emitting the breath. *F* has only this one sound, except in the single word *of*, in which it has the power of *v*.

G.

§ 69. *G* marked thus, Ġ, ġ (*g* hard), has the sound of that letter in the word *go;* as in *get*, *gave*, *give*, *begun*, *keg*, *sluggish*, *smuggle*, &c.

NOTE. — This sound is produced by a compression of intonated breath, or voice, confined within the mouth by a contact of the root of the tongue with the posterior part of the palate, which is at the same time raised sufficiently to cover the back nostrils, or openings from the pharynx into the nose.

G is hard before *a* (except in the single word *gaol* and its derivatives), *o*, *u*, *h*, *l*, and *r*, as in *gate*, *gore*, *gum*, *ghastly*, *glad*, *grain*. It is sometimes, though not usually, hard before *e*, *i*, and *y*, as in *get*, *give*, *gibbous*, *muggy*. It is also, and always, hard at the end of words, and in the derivatives of such words, even when the *g* is doubled and followed by *e*, *i*, or *y*, as in *crag*, *drug*, *fog*, *cragged*, *druggist*, *foggy*.

When *a*, *i*, or *i*, is preceded in the same syllable by the sound of *g*, or of *k*, very many speakers, particularly in England, interpose a slight sound of *ĕ*, as in *card*, *kind*, *garden*, *guard*, *girl*, *guile*, *guise*, *sky*. The practice of a very large portion, if not a majority, of the best speakers in the United States, and also of many educated persons in England, is to join the sound of the *g* or *k* to that of the *ä* or *ī*, without suffering any other sound to slip in between them.

§ 70. *G* marked thus, Ǥ, ǥ (*g* soft), has the compound sound of *j*, as in *gem*, *rage*, *engine*, *caged*, &c. — See § 74.

NOTE. — The letter *g* generally takes this sound when it comes before *e*, *i*, or *y;* but there are some exceptions. (See the preceding section.)

§ 71. In a few words from the French, *g* retains the sound of *zh*, which it has before *e* and *i* in that language, as in *rouge* (roozh), *mirage* (mī-räzh′), &c.

G is silent before *m* and *n* final, and also when initial before *n*, as in *phlegm*, *sign*, *gnat*.

For the office which *g* performs in such words as *longer*, *stronger*, &c., see § 79.

GH.

§ 72. This digraph (which is unmarked) is sounded, at the beginning of a word, like *g* hard, as in *ghastly*, *ghost*, *gherkin*, &c. It is silent after the vowel *i*, as in *high*, *sigh*, *weigh;* and it is generally silent before *t*, as in *bough*, *fraught*, *taught*, &c. The words *draught* and *laughter*, where it has the sound of *f*, are exceptions. In other cases, *gh* is generally pronounced like *f*, as in *chough*, *cough*, *rough*, *tough*, *trough*, *enough*, &c.; but it sometimes has the sound of *k*, as in *hough*, *lough*, *shough*. In the word *hiccough*, it is usually pronounced like *p*.

H.

§ 73. This letter (which is unmarked) is a mere aspiration or breathing, and represents no fixed configuration of the vocal organs.

NOTE. — It is an emission of unvocalized breath through whatever position of the mouth-organs is required by the succeeding element, the organs being always placed to form the next

PRINCIPLES OF PRONUNCIATION. xiii

following letter before the *h* is pronounced. Thus, in *he* the tongue is put in a position to sound the *e* before the *h* is uttered; and similarly in *hall, hard, home*, &c.

In the following words, *heir, heiress, herb, herbage, honest, honor, honorable, hour*, with their derivatives, and also in *hostler* (also spelt *ostler*), *h* is silent. It is also marked as silent by most orthoëpists in *hospital, humor*, and *humble*, with their derivatives. There is, however, an increasing tendency to sound the *h* in these words. *H* is silent after *g* initial, as in *ghost, gherkin*, &c.; after *r*, as in *rhyme, myrrh*, &c.; and also when preceded by a vowel in the same syllable, as in *ah, eh, oh, buhl, Jehovah*, &c. In many parts of England, the sound of this letter is almost always omitted where it ought to be uttered, and uttered where it ought to be omitted; as *'ouse* for *house, happle* for *apple*, &c. This very gross and vulgar error is rarely, if ever, heard among natives of the United States.

J.

§ 74. This letter (which is unmarked) has very nearly the sound of *dzh*, being precisely the same as that of *g* soft, as in *jar, jeer, joke*, &c. — See § 70.

NOTE. — *J* is never silent. In the word *hallelujah*, it has the sound of consonant *y*.

In words in which *d* precedes a letter having regularly the sound of *y*, and occurring in an unaccented syllable, as in *modulate* (mod′u-late), *soldier* (sōld′yer), the sound of *j* is very often substituted for the combined sounds of the *d* and *y* (thus, mōj′oo-late, sōl′jer); — just as the sound of *ch* is substituted for the combined sounds of *t* and *y* in *nature, question, righteous*, &c. (See § 63, NOTE.)

K.

§ 75. This letter (which is unmarked) has one uniform sound, as heard in *keep, king, kitchen*, &c., and is precisely equivalent to *c* hard. — See § 61.

NOTE. — The sound represented by this letter differs from that of *g* in *go* (hard *g*) only in being a whispered and not a vocal utterance; the organs are placed in the same position for forming both sounds. Before *n*, in the same syllable, *k* is silent, as in *knack, knell, knit, know*, &c. It is also silent after *c*, as in *back, barrack*, &c. In regard to the pronunciation sometimes given to such words as *kind, sky*, &c., see § 60, NOTE.

L.

§ 76. The sound of *l* (unmarked), as heard in *left, bell, chalice, melting*, &c.

NOTE. — This letter has only one sound, which consists of an efflux of vocalized breath, or voice, over the sides of the tongue, while its tip is pressed against the gums of the upper front teeth. *L* is silent in many words, especially before a final consonant, as in *almond, malmsey, palmer, alms, calm, walk, half, could, would, should*, &c.

M.

§ 77. The sound of *m* (unmarked), as heard in *make, aim, clamor, armed*, &c.

NOTE. — This letter has one uniform sound, produced by closing the lips, and letting the voice issue through the nose. It is silent when it precedes *n* in the same syllable, as in *mnemonics*.

N.

§ 78. The sound of *n* (unmarked), as heard in *nail, ten, panel, entry*, &c.

NOTE. — In the production of this sound, the tip of the tongue is pressed against the upper gums, as for *d*; but the voice, instead of being confined within the mouth, is suffered to escape uninterruptedly through the nose, the nasal passages being uncovered for that purpose.

When final after *l* or *m*, *n* is uniformly silent, as in *kiln, condemn, solemn, hymn, limn*, &c.; but it is generally sounded in the derivatives formed from such words by adding to them a termination beginning with a vowel, as in *condemnatory, solemnize, hymnic, limner*, &c. In the present participles of verbs ending in *mn*, as *contemn, hymn*, &c., the *n*, though often unpronounced, is more properly sounded, as, *contemning, hymning*, &c.

§ 79. The sound of *n* as heard in *linger, link, uncle*, &c. (marked N̦, ņ).

NOTE. — This is essentially the same sound as that represented by *ng*; but its length varies greatly according as it is followed by a whispered or a vocal consonant. When it is followed in the same syllable by the sound of *k*, as in *link*, it is cut so short by the instantaneous and perfect closure of the organs which form this pure mute as to add almost nothing to the length of the syllable. But when this sound of *n* is followed by that of *g* in a separate syllable, as in the primitive words *anger, finger, conger, hunger*, it is long and sonorous, and increases the duration of the syllabic utterance very perceptibly. As a general rule, the change of *n* into ņ takes place only before *g* and *k* (or before the equivalents of *k*, namely, *c, q*, and *x=ks*). It takes place before *k* or its equivalents when any one of these letters follows *n* in the same syllable, as in *link, cinque, minx, bethink′, adunque′, phar′ynx;* and before *g* or *k*, or an equivalent of *k*, when any one of these letters begins an unaccented syllable and the *n* ends a preceding accented one, as in con′cord, con′gress, un′cle, &c. Pen′guin and a few other words are exceptions; also words beginning with the prefixes *in, non, quinque*, and *un;* as, in′come, non′-con-form′ity, quin′quevalve, un′com-pound′ed, &c. It is to be observed that, if the *n* ends an *unaccented* syllable, and the *g* or *k* begins an *accented* one, the *n* invariably retains its regular sound; as in con-cord′ant, con-gres′sional.

It is also to be observed that there is a small class of words in which the *n* has its ordinary sound, as in *nail*, and the *g* its soft sound, as in *gem*. Of this class, the words, *danger, stranger, ginger*, and *plunger* are examples.

PRINCIPLES OF PRONUNCIATION.

and at the end of words; but there are some exceptions.

§ 96. *Th* marked thus, Ŧħ, *th*, has its soft, flat, or vocal sound, as in *thine*, *then*, *with*, *mother*, *writhed*, &c.

NOTE.—This sound differs from the foregoing only in being an utterance of voice instead of simple breath. It occurs chiefly between two vowels in words purely English, as in *leather*, *wither*, *heathen*; also at the end of the verbs *mouth*, *bequeath*, and *smooth*; and when followed by a final *e* mute, as in *breathe*, *clothe*, &c.

Nouns which, in the singular, end in *th* sharp, usually preserve the same sound in the plural, as *death*, *deaths*; *sabbath*, *sabbaths*, &c.; but in the plurals of the following seven words the *th* is vocal; namely, *bath*, *cloth*, *lath*, *mouth*, *oath*, *path*, and *wreath*, as, *baths*, *cloths*, *laths*, *paths*, &c. Some pronounce *truths*, in the plural, with the vocal sound (*trudhs*), but this is sanctioned by no orthoëpist.

§ 97. *Th* has the sound of *t* in *phthisic* (tiz'ik), *thyme* (tīm), and their derivatives; and also in the proper names *Thomas* (tom'as) and *Thames* (temz.)—See § 105.

V.

§ 98. The sound of *v* (unmarked), as in *vane*, *leave*, *civil*, &c.

NOTE.—This sound differs from that of *f* only in being an utterance of the voice instead of the breath, the organs assuming precisely the same position for both sounds.

V is never silent, except in *sevennight* (sen'nĭt), which is also written *sennight*.

W.

§ 99. At the beginning of a word or of a syllable, as *wet*, *worse*, *inward*, this letter (which is unmarked) is a consonant, formed from, and nearly resembling, the vowel *oo*, but requiring for its utterance a closer position, or greater contraction, of the labial aperture; and this compression of the lips changes the quality of the sound, giving it a buzzing and articulative instead of a smooth and purely vocal character.

NOTE.—After a vowel in the same syllable, *w* is generally silent, as in *glōw*, *thrōwn*, &c., though sometimes significant, as in *flaw*. With *e* it unites to form a diphthong, which is generally sounded like long *u*, as in *dew*, *few*, *new*; but it is sounded like *oo*, or like *u* in *rude*, if the letter *r* stands before it, as in *crew*, *shrew*. It is often joined with a preceding *o* to represent the diphthongal sound otherwise expressed by *ou*, as in *brow*, *cow*, *town*.—See § 36.

W is always silent before *r* in the same syllable, as in *wring* (ring), *wrote* (rōt), *awry* (a-rȳ'); also in the words *answer* (an'ser), *sword* (sōrd), *toward* (to'ard), *two* (too).

It is often represented by *u* occurring before another vowel in the same syllable, as *quail*, *query*, *languid*, *assuage*, &c.

Wh.

§ 100. The true sound of these letters is in the reverse order, namely, *hw*, as they were written by the Anglo-Saxons; e. g., *whet* is pronounced *hwet*. The *h* is here a free emission of breath through the position taken by the lips in the formation of *w*, the vocal cords being all the while completely relaxed. (See § 73.) In *who*, *whole*, *whoop*, *whore*, and their derivatives, the *w* is silent.

X.

§ 101. This letter has two sounds; namely, its regular sharp sound (unmarked) like *ks*, as in *expect*, *tax*, &c., and its soft or flat sound (marked X̱, x̱,) like *gz*, as in *exist*, *example*, &c.

NOTE.—This latter sound usually occurs when the syllable which immediately follows the *x* begins with an accented vowel, as in *auxiliary*, *exert*, *luxurious*, and sometimes also in the derivatives of such words, even though the *x* is under the accent, as in *exemplary*, *exhalation*, &c.

In *anxious*, *noxious*, *luxury*, and a few other words, the *s* which is the second element of the *x*, and the following *i* or the first element of the following *u*, instead of retaining their usual sound of *y*, are generally exchanged for the sound of *sh*; thus, *ank'shus*, *nok'shus*, *luk'shoo-ry*, &c.

At the beginning of words, *x* has the sound of *z*, as in *xanthic* (zan'-), *xebec* (ze'-), *zylography* (zī'-), &c.

Y.

§ 102. The sound of Y (unmarked), as in *yawn*, *year*, *young*, *beyond*, &c.

NOTE.—This sound—heard in English only at the beginning of a word or a syllable—is formed from the vowel *e* by a closer approximation of the tongue to the roof of the mouth, which destroys the pure vocality of the *e*.

In the middle or at the end of a syllable, *y* is a vowel, and has precisely the sound that *i* would have in the same situation.—See §§ 13, 14, 32, 45, 51, &c.

Y is often represented by *i*, when this letter occurs in an unaccented syllable before another vowel, and, at the same time, follows an accented syllable, as in *familiar*, *minion*, &c.

Z.

§ 103. The regular and leading sound of this letter (which is unmarked) is heard in *zone*, *maze*, *hazy*, *frozen*, &c. It is the vocal or sonant form of *s*. (See § 87.) In a few words it takes the sound of *zh*; as in *seizure* (sē'zhoor). (See § 104.) In *rendezvous* it is silent.

Zh.

§ 104. This sound is the vocal correspondent of *sh*, and is uttered with the organs in precisely the same position.

NOTE.—It has arisen, in all English words, from an attempt to pronounce the sound of *z* in *maze* (see § 103) and that of consonant *y* (see § 102) in immediate succession. Thus, *fusion* may be supposed to have been originally pro-

PRINCIPLES OF PRONUNCIATION. xv

and in the English and American pronunciation of such words as *poorer*, *boring*, &c., consists in the interposition between the *r* and the preceding vowel of an obscure vowel sound like that of *u* in *urge*.

S.

§ 87. *S* unmarked has its regular sharp or hissing sound, as in *same*, *yes*, *resting*, &c.

NOTE. — This sound is an utterance of unvocal breath forced between the tip of the tongue and the upper gum, the tongue being placed in the proper position for sounding *t* and *d*. *S* always has this sound at the beginning, and frequently in the middle and at the end, of words. — See § 105.

§ 88. *S*, when marked thus, $\underline{S}$, $\underline{s}$, has the buzzing sound of *z* in *zeal*, as in *ha$\underline{s}$*, *amu$\underline{s}$e*, *ro$\underline{s}$y*, &c. — See § 105.

NOTE. — There are a few verbs ending in *se*, which are also used as nouns or adjectives. To distinguish between them, the *s* is vocalized in the verb, and whispered in the noun or adjective; as *close*, a., and *clo$\underline{s}$e*, v.; *house*, n., and *hou$\underline{s}$e*, v.; *use*, n., and *u$\underline{s}$e*, v.; *diffuse*, a., and *diffu$\underline{s}$e*, v.

§ 89. When the letter *s*, having regularly its sharp or hissing sound, follows a liquid or another *s*, and precedes a letter having the sound of consonant *y*, as *i* in *reversion*, *mansion*, *passion*, and, in a few cases, when it precedes *u* (= yoo), as in *sure*, *sugar*, *censure*, *sensual*, the sounds represented by these letters are exchanged for that of the simple but very similar element represented by *sh*. Thus the examples just given are actually pronounced *re-ver'shun*, *man'shun*, *pash'un*, *shoor*, *shoog'ar*, *cen'shoor*, *sen'shoo-al*, though the theoretical pronunciation would be *re-vers'yun*, *mans'yun*, *pass'yun*, *s-yoor*, *s-yoog'ar*, *cens'yoor*, *sens'yoo-al*.

In a few words, *s* alone takes the sound of *sh*, as in *nausea*, *Asiatic;* or rather the *e* or *i*, in such cases, does double duty, uniting with the *s* to signify the sound of *sh*, and at the same time retaining its usual vowel character.

§ 90. When *s* is preceded by a vowel in an accented syllable, and is followed by a vowel having regularly or theoretically the sound of consonant *y*, these two letters are commonly pronounced like *zh*, as in *a-lhesion*, *revision*, *explosion*, *confusion*, *pleasure*, *visual*, *usury*, &c. (See § 104.) So also in *scission*, *abscission*, *rescission*, though the *s* is not preceded by a vowel in the accented syllable.

§ 91. *S* is silent in the words *aisle*, *isle*, *island*, *demesne*, *puisne*, *viscount*, and generally at the end of French words adopted into English, as *chamois*, *corps*, *vis-a-vis*, &c.

Sh.

§ 92. This digraph (which is unmarked) represents the simple sound heard in *shelf*, *flesh*, *usher*, &c.

NOTE. — This element is formed by a partial contact of the upper surface of the tongue, near the tip, with that side of the arch or dome of the palate which is just above the gums of the front teeth, and by an effusion of unvocal breath through the narrow aperture left for its escape. This sound has been evolved from the combination of those of *s* and consonant *y* which, in rapid utterance, do not easily maintain their distinct character. Thus, if we pronounce the word *special* in three syllables, *spec'i-al*, and then try to reduce it to two, we shall find that it is difficult to articulate the *c* (= s) and the *i* (= y) by one continuous effort of the organs, and that the intermediate *sh* is naturally substituted as an easier and a closely allied sound. So with *version*, *mission*, *sure*, &c.

Sh is never silent. It is expressed: 1. By *c*, as in *o-ce-an'ic*, *e-ma-ci-a'tion*; 2. By *s*, as in *nau'se-ate*, *A-si-at'ic*; 3. By *t*, as in *ne-go-ti-a'tion*; 4. By *ce*, as in *o'cean*; 5. By *ci*, as in *so'cial*; 6. By *se*, as in *nau'seous*; 7. By *si*, as in *ten'sion*; 8. By *ti*, as in *cap'tious*; 9. By the *si* implied in *xi* (= ksi), as in *noxious*; 10. By the *sy* implied in *su* (= syoo), as in *men-su-ra'tion* (men-*shoo*-ra/shun); 11. By the *sy* implied in *xu* (= ksyoo), as in *lux'ury* (luk/*shoo*-ry); 12. By *ch*, as in *chaise*, *char'la-tan*, *ma-chine'*; 13. By *chs*, as in *fu'chsi-a*; 14. By *sc*, as in *con-sci-en'tious*; 15. By *sch*, as in *schorl*; 16. By *sci*, as in *con'science*. — See §§ 60, 89, 94, 101.

T.

§ 93. The sound of *t* (unmarked) as heard in *tone*, *note*, *noted*, *assets*, &c.

NOTE. — This sound differs from that of *d* (see § 67) only in being a whispered and not a vocal utterance.

T is silent in the terminations *ten* and *tle* after *s*, as in *fasten*, *listen*, *often*, *castle*, *gristle*, *throstle*, &c. It is also silent in the words *chestnut*, *Christmas*, *hostler*, or *ostler*, *mistletoe*, and *mortgage*.

§ 94. When *t* precedes any one of the diphthongs *ia*, *ie*, and *io*, and at the same time follows an accented syllable not ending in *s* or *x*, it assumes, in some words, the sound of *sh*, as in *negotiation;* but, in most cases, the compound sound resulting from the coalescence of *t* and *i* is exchanged for that of *sh*, as in *patient*, *station*, *partial*, &c. When *s* or *x* precedes the *t*, this letter and the *i* following it either preserve their own sounds pure, or exchange them for the sound of *ch* in *chin*, as in *question* (kwest'yun or kwes'chun), *mixtion* (mikst'yun or miks'chun), &c. — See § 63, NOTE, and § 92.

Th.

§ 95. *Th* unmarked has its sharp or whispered sound, as in *thing*, *breath*, *author*, &c.

NOTE. — This is the sound made in lisping. It is produced by putting the point of the tongue between the teeth, or by placing it against the back of the upper front teeth, and forcing out unintonated breath.

Th has this sound generally at the beginning

PRINCIPLES OF PRONUNCIATION.

§ 80. The sound of *ng* (unmarked), as in *sing, singer, singly*, &c.

NOTE.—This is a simple elementary sound, and is not (as might be supposed) a compound sound made up of the sound of *n* in conjunction with that of *g*. In forming *ng*, the tongue is placed in the same position as for forming *g*; the nostrils, however, are not completely closed, but yet so much so as to produce a marked resonance (somewhat similar to the sound of *n*), which may be continued to any length, as in *sing, bring*, &c.—See § 79.

P.

§ 81. The sound of *p* (unmarked), as heard in *pay, ape, paper, aptly*, &c.

NOTE.—The position of the organs necessary for forming this sound is the same as for *b*, but the sound itself differs from that of *b* in being an utterance of breath instead of voice.

P has but one sound; it is silent when initial before *n*, *s*, and *t*, as in *pneumatics, psalm, pshaw, ptarmigan*. It is also silent or very indistinct when it occurs between *m* and *t* in the same syllable, as in *tempt, exempt*, &c.; but when preceded by *m* in the same syllable, and followed by *t* or by *k* in the next syllable, it is more properly sounded; as in *temp-ta'tion, ex-emp'tion, redemp'tion, con-sump'tive, sump'-tuous, bump'kin, pump'kin*, &c., though, in colloquial utterance, it is very often suppressed in words of this class. It is also mute in the following words, and in their derivatives; namely, *raspberry, receipt, sempstress, accompt*, and *corps*.

PH.

§ 82. This digraph (which is unmarked) occurs chiefly in words of Greek derivation, and has usually the sound of *f*, as in *phantom, sylph, philosophy*, &c. In *Stephen* it has the sound of *v*; and, according to most orthoëpists, it has the same sound in *nephew* (nev'ew).

Before *th* initial, *ph* is silent, as in *phthisis*; it is also silent in apop'thegm. In *diphthong, triphthong, ophtha'my, naph'tha*, and other allied words, together with their derivatives, the *ph* is often sounded as *p*, or the *h* may be regarded as silent.

Q.

§ 83. *Q* is followed in all cases by *u*, and these two letters, taken together, have usually the sound of *kw*, as in *queen* (kween), *conquest* (kong'west), &c. In a few words derived from the French, *qu* is sounded like *k*, as in *coquette, quadrille*, &c. It has the same sound in the common termination *que*, as in *antique, oblique, burlesque*, &c.

R.

§ 84. This letter (which is unmarked) may be viewed under three aspects:—

(1.) *R* as in *rip, trip, carol*, &c. (sometimes called *rough, trilled, dental*, or *initial r*).

In forming this sound, the tongue assumes nearly the same position as for *d*; but the voice, instead of being confined within the mouth, is suffered to flow freely over the tip of the tongue, producing a very slightly trilled and peculiarly liquid sound which is heard in the two following cases: 1. When *r* is not preceded by a vowel, as in *ream, dream, prompt, spring*; 2. When it stands between two vowels of which the first is short, as in *baron, merit, spirit, florid*. Often the *r* is doubled in the written word, as in *barren, merry, torrid*; but, in these cases, only one *r* is heard in the pronunciation, providing the preceding vowel is short.—See § 109.

(2.) *R* as in *far, form, terse, surge*, &c. (sometimes called *smooth, palatal, guttural, obscure*, or *final r*).

By most orthoëpists at the present day, the letter *r*, when it occurs before any consonant, or when final, is regarded as a distinct element from the last, and as formed by a slight vibration of the back part, or root, of the tongue against the extremity of the soft palate. Many writers, however, do not admit any such distinction in the sound of *r*, maintaining that the value of the letter (apart from the obscure vowel element described in No. 3) is uniform in all situations.

(3.) *R*, connected with a guttural vowel sound, as heard in such words as *fare, mere, ire, ore, cure, poor, pure*, &c. Here the character *r* represents two sounds; namely, an obscure vowel sound resembling that of *u* in *urge*, and a smooth or palatal *r*, so that the above words are pronounced fāur (see § 4), mēur, iur, &c.

§ 85. In the pronunciation of accurate speakers, *r* is never silent; but when it occurs after a long vowel or a diphthong in the same syllable, as in *here, fur, murmur, our, mire*, &c., it is commonly and entirely suppressed, both in the United States and the south of England.

§ 86 In English usage, when the letter *r* is preceded in an accented syllable by a long vowel or a diphthong, and is followed by a vowel in the next syllable, it uniformly represents both the palatal, or smooth, and the dental, or trilled, sound of this letter, as in *hero, iris, glory, lurid*, pronounced hēr'ro, ir'ris, glōr'ry, lūr'rid. In the United States, this double power of the letter *r* is chiefly, though not invariably, restricted to the *derivatives* of words ending in *r* or *re* preceded by a long vowel or a diphthong, as in *poorer* (poōr'rer), from *poor*; *boring* (bōr'ring), from *bore*; *airy* (ār'ry), from *air*; *peerage* (peer'rage) from *peer*; *wiry* (wir'ry), from *wire*; *securing* (secūr'ring), from *secure*; but, on the other hand, we say *he'ro, i'ris, glo'ry, lu'rid*, &c., because these words are not derived from any other words in the language.

It is to be observed that those orthoëpists who maintain that *r* has one invariable sound, assert that the only peculiarity in the English pronunciation of such words as *hero, iris*, &c.,

PRINCIPLES OF PRONUNCIATION.

nounced *fŭz'yun*, and then *fŭ'zhun; grazier*, first *grāz'yer*, and then *grāzh'er*. — See § 92.

The combination *zh* is used in works on pronunciation to indicate the sound here described, on account of the relationship of this sound to that commonly expressed by the digraph *sh*. But the two letters *zh* never come together in the proper orthography of any English word. The sound for which they stand is represented by *zi* (when the *z* occurs in, or is immediately preceded by, an accented syllable, and the *i* is followed by another vowel, and occurs in an unaccented syllable, as in *glazier*); by the *zy* implied in *zu* (= *zyoo*), as in *azure*; by *s* in *symposium*, &c.; by *si* in certain situations (see § 90); by *ti* in the single word *transition*, as sometimes pronounced; and by *g* in one or two words adopted from the French, as *rouge*.

ASSIMILATION OF CONSONANTS.

§ 105. When a whispered and a vocal consonant come together in the same syllable, it is generally very difficult, in fluent pronunciation, to preserve each in its regular and appropriate sound. Hence it frequently becomes necessary to change the character of the one or of the other, in order to make the combination readily pronounceable. This is generally done, in English, by assimilating the sound of the second consonant, whether whispered or vocal, to that of the first. Thus, in *chintz*, the vocal consonant *z* assumes the sound of its whispered correspondent *s*, in order to unite with the whispered *t*. On the other hand, the *s* in *winds* is vocalized, or assumes the sound of *z*, for the sake of corresponding with the vocal *d*. Sometimes, though rarely, the sound of the first consonant is assimilated to that of the second, as in *spasm* (spazm).

This affinity between these two classes of consonants is an important fact, and one which needs to be familiarly known. For there are four very common inflectional terminations which invariably come under its influence, namely : 1. Possessive forms in *s*, as *maid's* (maidz) ; 2. Plurals in *s*, as *tubs* (tubz), *groves* (grōvz); 3. *S* in the third person singular of verbs, as *loads* (lodz), *smooths* (smoothz); 4. Preterits and participles in *d* preceded by *e* mute, as in *dashed* (dasht), *ingulfed* (ingulft).

DUPLICATION OF CONSONANTS.

§ 106. In many words, a consonant is doubled between two vowels; yet, in such cases, no more than one articulation is ever used in speaking. In *banner*, for example, we close the organs but once between the first and second syllables; nor is it possible to use both of the letters *n* without pronouncing *ban*, then intermitting the voice entirely, opening the organs, and closing them a second time. Hence, in all cases, when the same consonant is written twice between vowels, as in *banner, robbing*, &c., one of them only is represented by an articulation of the organs; and the only reason for repeating the consonant is to indicate the fact that the preceding vowel has its short sound.

But although only one articulation is ever used, or in fluent speech possibly can be used, where a consonant is written twice, yet in some words the articulation is dwelt upon for an appreciable space of time, producing an *apparent* duplication of the *sound*. This effect takes place in many derived words in which the primitive ends or begins with the same letter as that with which a superadded suffix or prefix of English origin respectively begins or ends, as in *soulless, foully, keenness, misstep, outtravel, unnatural*. The same effect takes place in most compound words, in which the second part begins with the same sound as that with which the first part ends, as in *post-town, head-dress, half-filled*. — See § 121.

ACCENT.

§ 107. Accent is a particular stress or effort of voice upon certain syllables of words, which distinguishes them from the others by a greater distinctness and loudness of pronunciation. Accent is of two kinds, *primary*, as in in-tend', where the full force of the voice is on the last syllable, and *secondary*, as in su'per-in-tend', where the first syllable is distinguished by a stress greater than that laid on the second and third syllables, though less than that laid on the last. In some words there are two secondary or subordinate accents, as in in-com'pre-hen'si-bil'i-ty.

NOTE. — (1.) The general tendency of accent, whether primary or secondary, is to shorten all vowels but *u*, when further back than the penultimate syllable, as in *ten'ement, nec'essariness, an'atom'ical, person'ifica'tion*, &c.; but we say *lu'bricate*, and not *lĭb'ricate; tru'culency*, and not *trŭc'ulency; su'perabun'dant*, and not *sŭp'erabun'dant*, &c. This tendency generally fails, if the accented syllable is followed by two unaccented vowels, as in *pe'ri-od, ma'ni-ac*,; or by two vowels of which the former only is unaccented, as in *de'vi-a'tion, o'ri-en'tal*.

(2.) The primary and secondary accents are, in certain cases, so nearly equal that we interchange them freely, "making," as Walker remarks, "the secondary principal and the principal secondary." Examples are *ambuscade, cavalcade, caricature, etiquette, reverie, confidante, governante, invalid,* n., *parachute*, &c.

(3.) Many in America give a marked secondary accent in certain words which properly have but one accent, and that on a pre-antepenultimate syllable, as in *ter'ri-tō'ry, diffi-cŭl'ty, cir'cum-stăn'ces, in'ter-est'ing*, &c. This droning fault may be corrected by giving the accented syllable a sharp percussion, which carries the voice lightly through the rest of the word.

DIVIDED USAGE.

§ 108. In quite a large number of words, there is a diversity of practice among good speakers as to the place of the primary accent. This arises mainly from a *conflict* between certain great principles which affect the seat of the accent. A few of these will now be mentioned, with a view to account for this diversity.

§ 109. FIRST PRINCIPLE. — *Derivatives* take for a time, if not permanently, the accent of the original words from which they are formed, as *resolve'*, from *resol'vo*, *aspect'* (Shakespeare, Milton), from *aspectus*, *Hin/los!an'ee*, from *Hindostan'*, &c. So also words derived from other English words by adding one or more syllables to their beginning or end; as, *within'* from *in*, *improp'er* from *prop'er*, *po'etess* from *po'et*, *serviceable* from *serv'ice*, *re-adjust'ment* from *adjust'*, &c.

§ 110. SECOND PRINCIPLE. — *Ease of utterance* has some influence in deciding the place of the accent. *Ac'ceptable*, *rec'eptacle*, and *u'tensil*, fashionable in the days of Walker, have now taken the easier accentuation of *accept'able*, *recept'acle*, and *uten'sil*. *Dyspep'sy* has taken the place of *dys'pepsy* in the marking of Webster, Smart, Cull, Wright, Clarke, Cooley, &c., and is now the prevailing accentuation. On the same ground, *ances'tral* is preferred to *an'cestral* by Jameson, Webster, Boag, Clarke, and Cull, in conformity with *campes'tral*, and other similar words. These may serve as instances of the application of this principle.

DISSYLLABLES.

§ 111. THIRD PRINCIPLE. — In words of two syllables, there is a tendency (though with numerous exceptions) to accent the former or *penultimate* syllable, as in *a'gue*, *bar'on*, *com'mon*, *dis'cord*, &c.

NOTE. — (1.) This tendency meets with a powerful counteraction in Principle No. 1, namely, that of *derivatives* retaining the accent of their primitives, as in *amuse'*, *deter'*, *offend'*, &c. It is natural, in such formatives, to place the accent on the radical part of the word; and hence some hundreds of our dissyllables, especially verbs and adverbs, have their accent on the last syllable.

(2.) Still, there is a constant struggle (especially among the common people, who are unacquainted with the derivation of words) to draw back the accent to the first syllable. Here arises another conflict, which produces a diversity of accent; and the common people, being a majority, are, on the whole, slowly gaining upon those who are tenacious of Principle No. 1. Thus, *con'nate* and *in'nate* (instead of *connate'* and *innate'*) are generally prevalent in America, and are now sanctioned by recent English orthoëpists. *Re'tail* (for *retail'*) is now the marking of a majority of the orthoëpists. *De'tail* (for *detail'*) is less prevalent, but is sanctioned by Smart, Clarke, Cull, Cooley, &c.

Pro'lix and *pre'text* (for *prolix'* and *pretext'*) are widely prevalent (especially the former), and are authorized by some recent lexicographers. *Bom'bast* (for *bombast'*) is the accentuation of Walker, Barclay, Richardson, Cull, and Webster; it is admitted by Worcester, and is extensively used in the United States. *Bu'reau* (for *bureau'*) was admitted by Dr. Webster, and is very generally applied to the article of furniture, while *bureau'* is sometimes used in reference to a department of the government.

§ 112. We have about eighty cases among our dissyllables in which the same word is used for a verb on the one hand, and a noun or an adjective on the other. To distinguish between them, we accent the nouns and the adjectives on the *first* syllable, and the verbs on the *last*, as, a *con'vert*, to *convert'*; a *con'tract*, to *contract'*, &c. It is unnecessary to give the list in full, since the accent of nearly all these words has been long settled by general usage.

NOTE. — There are a few cases of divided use in nouns, which will sooner or later be made to conform to the general rule. For example, usage will probably soon fix permanently on *per'fect* for the adjective, and *perfect'* for the verb; *per'mit* for the noun, and *permit'* for the verb; *pro'test* for the noun, and *protest'* for the verb; *per'fume* for the noun, and *perfume'* for the verb; *pro'ceeds* for the noun, and *proceed'* for the verb; *de'tail* for the noun, and *detail'* for the verb; *in'crease* for the noun, and *increase'* for the verb; *re'tail* for the noun, and *retail'* for the verb; *sur'vey* for the noun, and *survey'* for the verb.

There is a tendency among many to accent the *first* syllable of the noun *ally*, *allies*; and, although without sanction as yet from a single orthoëpist, it would not be surprising if this tendency should prevail, making the noun *al'ly*, *al'lies*, and the verb *ally'*.

§ 113. We have a few dissyllables which are at once nouns and adjectives. These are distinguished by accenting the nouns on the *first* syllable, and the adjectives on the *last*.

NOUNS.	ADJECTIVES.
Au'gust, the month.	August', noble.
Com'pact, an engagement.	Compact', close.
Ex'ile, banishment.	Exile', small, slender.
In'stinct, an impulse.	Instinct', animated.
Min'ute (of time).	Minute', very small.
Su'pine (in grammar).	Supine', indolent.

TRISYLLABLES AND POLYSYLLABLES.

§ 114. FOURTH PRINCIPLE. — In words of three or more syllables, there is a strong tendency to accent the *antepenult*, or third syllable from the end, as in *el'oquent*, *ac'cident*, *opportu'nity*.

NOTE. — This tendency is counteracted by that of *derivation* (Principle No. 1. See § 109); and here arises another "conflict," which, to some extent, arrays our scholars on the one side, and the body of the people on the other. Many scholars, for example, are strongly in-

PRINCIPLES OF PRONUNCIATION.

clined to say *contem'plate, demon'strate, confis'- cate, obdu'rate*, &c. (forgetting that they come from participles, *contempla'tus, demonstra'tus*, &c.), because by Latin rules their second syllable is long; while the mass of the people, who know nothing of Latin, and are governed by English analogies, are equally bent on saying *con'template, dem'onstrate, ob'durate*, &c. The latter pronunciation is now very extensively heard, and thus we have a "divided usage" in respect to these and similar words.

§ 115. It is a just principle, laid down by Walker, that "when words come to us *whole* from the Greek or Latin, the same accent ought to be preserved as in the original." Hence the following words ought to be accented as here marked: namely, *Ab'do'men, hori'zon, deco'rum, diplo'ma, muse'um, sono'rous, acu'men, bitu'men*, and, on like grounds, *farra'go*, and others. Yet the strong tendency of our language to accent the antepenultimate in all words of three or more syllables has caused this principle to be violated in some cases, as in *am'azon, min'ister, or'ator*, &c.

§ 116. Words of more than two syllables having the same orthography are generally distinguished by a difference of accent, as *at'tribute*, n., and *attrib'ute*, v.; *miscon'duct*, n., and *miscon'duct*, v.; *o'verthrow*, n., and *overthrow'*, v. In such cases, the nouns have the accent further from the end.

§ 117. With a very few exceptions, words of more than two syllables having the following terminations take the accent on the antepenult, or last syllable but two:—

-*racy*; as, *democ'racy, theoc'racy*;
-*ferous*; as, *somnif'erous, umbellif'erous*;
-*fluent*; as, *af'fluent, circum'fluent*;
-*fluous*; as, *mellif'luous, super'fluous*;
-*gonal*; as, *diag'onal, hexag'onal*;
-*gony*; as, *cosmog'ony, theog'ony*;
-*grapher*; as, *lexicog'rapher, stenog'rapher*;
-*graphy*; as, *photog'raphy, typog'raphy*;
-*loger*; as, *philol'oger, astrol'oger*;
-*logist*; as, *entomol'ogist, physiol'ogist*;
-*logy*; as, *chronol'ogy, mythol'ogy*;
-*loquy*; as, *col'loquy, solil'oquy*;
-*meter*; as, *barom'eter, hygrom'eter*;
-*metry*; as, *altim'etry, geom'etry*;
-*nomy*; as, *astron'omy, econ'omy*;
-*parous*; as, *ovip'arous, vivip'arous*;
-*pathy*; as, *ap'athy, antip'athy*;
-*strophe*; as, *apos'trophe, catas'trophe*;
-*tomy*; as, *anat'omy, lithot'omy*;
-*trophy*; as, *at'rophy, hyper'trophy*;
-*vorous*; as, *carniv'orous, graminiv'orous*.

§ 118. Words of more than two syllables, ending in -*cate*, -*date*, -*gate*, -*fy*, -*tude*, and -*ly*, preceded by a vowel, have, for the most part, the accent on the antepenult; as *dep'recate, rus'ticate, recip'rocate; an'tedate, elu'cidate, accom'modate; prop'agate, del'egate, fu'migate;* *rar'efy, sanc'tify; qui'etude, lat'itude; soci'ety, acid'ity, dep'uty*.

§ 119. The penultimate syllable is to be accented in almost all words having the sound of *sh*, or *zh*, or of consonant *y* immediately before the last vowel or diphthong; e. g., *dona'tion, conces'sion, illu'sion, controver'sial, vermil'ion, opin'ion*.

THE TERMINATIONS IC AND ICS.

§ 120. Words ending in *ic* and *ics* (derivatives from words in ικος or *icus*, in Greek or Latin, or formed after the same analogy) have their accent on the penult: as, *epidem'ic, scientif'ic*, &c. The following words are exceptions, having the accent on the antepenult; namely, *ag'aric, Ar'abic, arith'metic, ar'senic*, n., *cath'olic, chol'eric, ephem'eric, her'etic, lu'natic, pleth'oric, pol'itic, rhet'oric*, and *tur'meric. Climacteric* has usually the antepenultimate accent, though some pronounce it *climacter'ic*. In like manner, the nouns *empiric* and *schismatic*, and the noun and adjective *splenetic*, are sometimes accented on the penult, and sometimes on the antepenult.

---

§ 121. When two words of similar formation and the same accentuation are contrasted with each other, the accent is transferred to the *syllable of difference* (unless this is already accented, as in *em'inent, im'minent*), and the regularly accented syllable takes a secondary accent; thus, *undo'* is pronounced *un'do'* when opposed to *do* or to *out'do'*, and *in'tervene'* is pronounced *in'tervene'* when used antithetically to *su'per-vene'*. So also with *am'puta'tion* and *im'puta'tion, bien'nial* and *triten'nial, op'pose'* and *sup'pose'; ex'ercise* and *ex'orcise'; proph'et'* and *prof'it'; do'nor'* and *do'nee'*.

§ 122. When separately pronounced, all monosyllabic words have their vowel as distinctly sounded as if under accent. But in connected discourse, certain classes of monosyllables, such as articles, prepositions, pronouns, conjunctions, and auxiliary verbs, are usually unemphasized, and their vowel is liable to the same corruption of quality as that in an unaccented syllable of a word. But when used antithetically to other words, they are emphasized, receiving a full and distinct stress of voice. Thus, we say ă, yŭr, thăt, thĕ, frŏm, fŏr, &c., when we pronounce the words by themselves; but in actual use they become nearly or quite ŭ, yur, thŭt, thŭ, frŭm, fur, &c. The following passage from the "Spectator," No. 80, well illustrates this tendency to a corruption of the vowel sound in unemphasized monosyllables:—"My lords, with humble submission thăt that I say is this, that thăt that thăt gentleman has advanced is not thăt that he should have proved to your lordships."

RULES FOR SPELLING CERTAIN CLASSES OF WORDS.

FOUNDED ON THE ORTHOGRAPHY OF DR. WEBSTER, AS EXHIBITED IN THIS VOLUME.

§ 123 (1). The letters *f* and *l*, at the end of monosyllables, and standing immediately after single vowels, are generally doubled; as in *staff, cliff, doff, puff; all, bell, hill, toll, null*. The words *clef, if, of,* and *sol*, are exceptions.

§ 124 (2). The letter *s*, at the end of a monosyllable, and standing immediately after a single vowel, is generally doubled, except when it is used to form the possessive case or plural of a noun, or the third person singular of a verb; as in *grass, press, hiss, moss, truss*. The only important exceptions are *as, gas, has, was, yes, his, is, thus,* and *us*.

§ 125 (3). Besides *f, l,* and *s*, the only consonants that are ever doubled at the end of a word are *b, d, g, m, n, r, t,* and *z*. The following list contains all, or nearly all, the words in which these letters are doubled; namely, *abb, ebb; add, odd, rudd; egg; lamm; inn, bunn; err, shirr, burr, purr; mitt, butt; fizz, frizz, fuzz, buzz*.

§ 126 (4). A consonant standing at the end of a word immediately after a diphthong or double vowel is never doubled. The words *ail, peat, haul, door,* and *maim*, are examples.

§ 127 (5). Monosyllables ending with the sound of *k*, and in which *e* follows the vowel, have usually *k* added after the *c*; as in *black, fleck, click, knock,* and *buck*. *Lac, sac, talc, zinc, soe, are, marc, orc,* and *fisc*, are exceptions.

Words of more than one syllable, ending in *ic* or *iac*, which formerly ended in *k*, also words derived from the Latin or Greek, or from other sources, and similar to these, or formed in an analogous manner, are now written without the *k*; as, *maniac, elegiac, cubic, music, public*. The word *derrick* is an exception. Words of more than one syllable, in which *c* is preceded by other vowels than *i* or *ia*, commonly end in *ck*; as, *arrack, barrack, hammock, hillock, wedlock*. The words *almanae, sandarac, limbec, rebec, zebec, manioc,* and *havoc*, are exceptions. *Almanac, limbec,* and *havoc*, however, are sometimes written with *k* after the *c*, especially in England.

§ 128 (6). In derivatives formed from words ending in *c*, by adding a termination beginning with *e, i,* or *y*, the letter *k* is inserted after the *c*, in order that the latter may not be inaccurately pronounced like *s* before the following vowel; as, *traffic, trafficked, trafficking, trafficker; zinc, zincky*.

§ 129 (7). In derivatives formed by adding a termination beginning with a vowel to monosyllables, and words accented on the last syllable, when these words end in a single consonant (except *x*) preceded by a single vowel, that consonant is doubled; as, *plan, planned, planning, planner; bag, baggage; hot, hotter, hottest; eaball, caballer; begin', begin'ning, begin'ner*. The consonant is doubled in these words in order to preserve the short sound of the vowel, as otherwise the latter would be liable to be pronounced long. Words of this class, in which the final consonant is preceded by *qu* followed by a single vowel, form no exception to the rule, since the *u* performs the office of the consonant *w*; as, *quit, quitted, quitting*.

The derivatives of the word *gas* (except *gassed, gassing,* and *gassy*) are written with but one *s*; as, *gaseous, gaseity, gasify. Ex'cellence*, as being from the Latin *excellens*, retains the double *l*, though one *l* has been dropped from the termination of *excel'*. Besides these, the only exceptions to the rule are those derivatives in which the accent of the primitive is thrown back upon another syllable; as, *prefer', pref'erence*. It is no exception to this rule that *chancellor*, and the derivatives of *metal* and *crystal*, as *metalloid, metallurgy, crystalline, crystallize,* and the like, are written with the *l* doubled, since they are derived respectively from the Latin *chancellarius* (through the French), and *metallum*, and the Greek κρύσταλλος. So also the word *tranquillity* retains the double *l* as being from the Latin *tranquillitas*, while the English derivatives of *tranquil*, though often written with two *l*'s, are more properly written with only one; as, *tranquilize, tranquilizer,* &c.

§ 130 (8). When a diphthong, or a digraph representing a vowel sound, precedes the final consonant of a word, or the accent of a word ending in a single consonant falls on any other syllable than the last, or when the word ends in two different consonants, the final consonant is not doubled in derivatives formed by the addition of a termination beginning with a vowel; as, *daub, daubed, dauber; brief, briefer, briefest; trav'el, trav'eling, trav'eler; act, acted, actor*.

The final consonant is doubled in the derivatives of a few words ending in *g*, in order to diminish the liability to its being pronounced like *j*, before *e* or *i*; as *humbug, humbugged, humbugging; periwig, periwigged*. The word *woolen* is more generally thus written, in the United States, with one *l*; but in England it is written *woollen*.

NOTE. — There is a large class of words end-

RULES FOR SPELLING.

ing in a single consonant, and accented on some other syllable than the last, the final consonants of which are, by very many writers and lexicographers, doubled in their derivatives, unnecessarily and contrarily to analogy. This practice appears to have arisen from a desire to prevent the vowel of the final syllable of the primitive from being inaccurately pronounced long in the derivatives. These words are chiefly those ending in *l*, with also a few of other terminations. The following list, tho words in which are chiefly verbs, includes the most important of those in regard to which usage varies; namely, *apparel, barrel, bevel, bias, bowel, cancel, carburet* (and all similar words ending in *uret*), *cavil, carol, channel, chisel, compromit, counsel, cudgel, dial, dishevel, dowel, drivel, duel, empanel, enamel, equal, funnel, gambol, gravel, grovel, handsel, hatchel, imperil, jewel, kennel, kidnap, label, laurel, level, libel, marshal, marvel, medal, metal, model, panel, parallel, parcel, pencil, peril, pistol, pommel, quarrel, ravel, revel, rival, rowel, shovel, shrivel, snivel, tassel, tinsel, trammel, travel, tunnel, unravel, vial, victual, worship.* In this Dictionary, the derivatives of these words are made to conform to tho rule, as recommended by Walker, Lowth, and other eminent scholars.

§ 131 (9). Derivatives formed from words ending in a double consonant, by adding one or more syllables, commonly retain both consonants; as, *ebb, ebbing; stiff, stiffness; skill, skillful, skillfulness; will, willful, willfullness; dull, dullness; full, fullness.* So also the double *l* is retained in the words *installment, inthrallment, thralldom,* and *enrollment* (from *install, inthrall, thrall,* and *enroll*), in order to prevent the false pronunciation they might receive if spelled with one *l*. Many writers and lexicographers, especially in England, omit one *l* in these words, as also in the derivatives of *skill, will, dull,* and *full,* formed by adding the syllables *ly* and *ness.* The derivatives of *pontiff* are exceptions to the rule, being written with only one *f*; as, *pontific, pontifical, pontificial,* and the like. One *l* also is dropped in a few words formed by adding the termination *ly* to words ending in *ll*, in order to prevent the concurrence of three *l*'s; as, *dull, dully; full, fully.*

§ 132 (10). In derivatives formed from words ending with silent *e*, the *e* is generally retained when the termination begins with a consonant; as, *pale, paleness; hate, hateful; incite, incitement.* When, however, the *e* is immediately preceded by another vowel (except *el*), it is often dropped from the derivative; as, *due, duly; argue, argument; true, truly; awe, awful;* and the derivatives and compounds of these words. The words *wholly, nursling, wisdom, abridgment, acknowledgment, lodgment, judgment,* and the compounds of some of these, are exceptions. The last four, however, are written, by many authors, *abridgement, acknowledgement, lodgement, judgement.*

§ 133 (11). In derivatives formed from words ending with silent *e*, when the termination begins with a vowel, the *e* is generally omitted, except in the cases mentioned in the next paragraph; as, *bride, bridal; plume, plumage; come, coming; move, movable; fleece, fleecy; force, forcible; true, truism.*
The *e* is retained in the words *hoeing, shoeing,* and *toeing* (from *hoe, shoe,* and *toe*), in order to prevent a doubt as to the pronunciation, that might arise in case it were omitted. It is retained, also, in the words *dyeing, singeing, springeing, swingeing, tingeing* (from *die, singe, springe, swinge, tinge*), to distinguish them from *dying, singing, springing, swinging, tinging* (from *die, sing, spring, swing, ting.*) The word *mileage,* as commonly written, does not omit the *e*, though it is sometimes, and more correctly, spelled *milage.* The *e*, standing, in a derivative, before a termination beginning with *a* or *o*, and immediately after *c* or *g*, is retained in order to preserve the soft sounds of these consonants; as, *peace, peaceable; notice, noticeable; manage, manageable; change, changeable; advantage, advantageous; mortgage, mortgageor.*

§ 134 (12). In derivatives formed from words ending in *ie*, by adding the termination *ing*, the *e* is dropped, and the *i* changed to *y*, in order to prevent two *i*'s from coming together; as, *die, dying; hie, hying; lie, lying; tie, tying; vie, vying.*

§ 135 (13). In derivatives of words ending in *y*, preceded by a consonant, and formed by appending any termination except one beginning with *i*, the *y* is usually changed into *i*; as, *mercy, merciless; tidy, tidiness; modify, modifies; foggy, fogginess; pity, pitiful.*
The derivatives of adjectives of one syllable, ending in *y*, preceded by a consonant, are exceptions, and usually retain the *y*; as, *shy, shyness; sly, slyest; dry, dryly; wry, wryness.* But the adjectives *drier* and *driest,* from *dry,* are commonly written with *i* instead of *y*. Derivatives formed by adding the termination *ship,* as *secretaryship, suretyship, ladyship,* and tho like, also retain the *y*, though some authors write them with *i*, according to the rule. *Babyhood* and *ladykin* are likewise exceptions.

§ 136 (14). Derivatives formed by affixing a termination to words ending in *y*, preceded by a vowel, generally retain the *y* unchanged; as, *gay, gayety, gayly; play, player, plays; sway, swayed; obey, obeying; joy, joyful.*
The words *daily, laid, paid, said, saith, slain,* and *staid* (from *day, lay, pay, say, slay,* and *stay*), with their compounds, are exceptions. *Staid,* however, is sometimes written *stayed.* Derivatives from words ending in *uy,* as *colloquies,* from *colloquy,* are not exceptions to the rule, as *u,* in such cases, is not strictly a vowel, but stands for the consonant *w*.

§ 137 (15). Derivatives formed by appending

a syllable beginning with a vowel to words ending with a vowel sound, generally retain the letter or letters representing such sound; as, *huzza, huzzaed; agree, agreeable, agreeing; weigh, weighing; echo, echoed; woo, wooes.*

Derivatives of words of this class ending in silent *e*, as also those formed from words ending in double *e*, by adding a termination beginning with *e*, drop the final *e*; as, *hoe, hoed; sue, sued; owe, owed; free, freer, freest; agree, agreed.* The cases mentioned in sections 11, 12, and 13 are also exceptions.

§ 138 (16). Derivatives formed by prefixing one or more syllables to words ending in a double consonant commonly retain both consonants; as, *rebuff, befall, inthrall, foretell, fulfill, enroll, emboss* (from *buff, fall, thrall, tell, fill, roll, boss*).

The word *until* is an exception, being always written with one *l*. Those words of this class which end in *ll* are written by some authors, especially in England, with one *l*; as, *befal, inthral, foretel, fulfil, enrol.* The words *distill* and *instill* should be written with the *l* doubled, though they are often written *distil* and *instil*, with only one *l*.

§ 139 (17). Compound words formed by joining two or more words commonly retain all the letters of the simple words; as, *stiff-necked, well-bred, dull-eyed, save-all.*

There are numerous exceptions to this rule, many of them compounds which by long use have acquired the force of single words. They are the following; namely, some compounds of *all* and *well*; as, *almighty, almost, alone, already, also, although, altogether, always, withal, therewithal, wherewithal, welcome, welfare;*—compounds of *mass*; as, *Candlemas, Christmas, Lammas, Michaelmas,* &c. ;—words of which the second part is the adjective *full*; as, *artful, hateful, rueful, woeful;*—also, the words *chilblain, fulfill, namesake, neckerchief, numskull, pastime, standish,* and *wherever.*

§ 140 (18). The plural of nouns regularly ends in *s*, or, in certain classes of words, in *es*.

When the noun in the singular ends with such a sound that the sound of *s* can unite with it, and be pronounced without forming a separate syllable, *s* only is added in forming the plural; as, *sea, seas; tree, trees; woe, woes; canto, cantos; virtue, virtues; cab, cabs; bead, beads; chief, chiefs: bag, bags; path, paths; lock, locks; gem, gems; jam, jams; ear, ears; art, arts.* A few plurals from nouns ending in *o* preceded by a consonant, end in *es*: as, *echo, echoes; cargo, cargoes; embargo, embargoes; motto, mottoes; potato, potatoes.* Other nouns of this class generally form their plurals regularly, though usage differs with regard to some of them. Those in which final *o* is preceded by a vowel form their plurals regularly. With regard to nouns ending in *i*, usage differs, though they are more properly written with the termination *is*.

When the noun in the singular ends with such a sound (as that of *ch, sh, j, s, x,* or *z*) that the sound of *s* can not unite with it in pronunciation, but must form a separate syllable, *e* is inserted before *s* in forming the plural, unless the word ends with silent *e*, in which case the latter serves to form a separate syllable with *s*; as, *church, churches; rush, rushes; age, ages; lace, laces; gas, gases; box, boxes; maze, mazes.*

To express the plural of a letter, figure, or any character or sign, or of a word mentioned without regard to its meaning, the letter *s*, generally preceded by the apostrophe, is appended, as in the phrases, " The two *l*'s in *all*; " " The *why*'s and *wherefore*'s of the question."

§ 141 (19). Nouns ending in *y* preceded by a consonant form their plural by adding *es* and changing *y* into *i*; as, *mercy, mercies; lady, ladies.* This rule includes words ending in *quy*, in which *u*, being pronounced like *w*, is strictly a consonant; as, *colloquy, colloquies.*

When the singular of a noun ends in *y* preceded by a vowel (except *u* having the power of *w*), the plural is regularly formed by adding *s* only: as, *day, days; key, keys; money, moneys; attorney, attorneys; alloy, alloys.*

§ 142 (20). The plurals of a few nouns ending in *f* or *fe* are irregularly formed by changing *f* or *fe* into *ves*. The following words, with their compounds, are the principal examples; namely, *life, lives; knife, knives; wife, wives; leaf, leaves; sheaf, sheaves; loaf, loaves; beef, beeves; thief, thieves; calf, calves; half, halves; elf, elves; self, selves; shelf, shelves; wolf, wolves.* The plural of *staff* is sometimes written *staffs*, but more commonly *staves*, except when it means a corps of officers, either military or civil, in which sense it is always written *staffs.* The plural of *wharf* is generally written *wharfs* in England; in the United States it is more commonly, but improperly, written *wharves.* The plurals of other nouns ending in *f, fe,* or *ff*, are formed regularly by the addition of *s* only.

§ 143 (21). In the following nouns, the plural is distinguished from the singular only by a change of the vowel or vowel sound of the word; namely, *man, men; woman, women; goose, geese; foot, feet; tooth, teeth; brother, brethren; louse, lice ; mouse, mice.* Compounds ending with these words form their plurals in the same manner; as, *foeman, foemen; dormouse, dormice.* Words which end-in the syllable *man*, and are not compounds, form their plurals regularly, by adding *s* only; as, *cayman, caymans; firman, firmans; talisman, talismans; German, Germans; Mussulman, Mussulmans.*

§ 144 (22). A few plurals end in *en* ; namely, *brother, brethren; child, children; ox, oxen.*

§ 145 (23). The words *brother, die, pea,* and *penny,* have each two plurals of different forms and with different significations; as, *brothers,* male children of the same parent, also, members of the same society, association, class, or profession; *brethren,* members of the same religious or ecclesiastical body, the word in this form being rarely used except in religious writings, or in scriptural language, where it also has the same meaning that *brother* has in ordinary language; *dies,* implements for making impressions by stamping, or for making screws, also the cubical parts of pedestals; *dice,* the cubical blocks used in games of chance; *peas,* seeds of the pea-plant, when a definite number is mentioned; *pease,* the same in bulk, or spoken of collectively; *pennies,* the coins, especially when a definite number is mentioned; *pence,* the amount reckoned by these coins.

§ 146 (24). A few words, mostly names of animals, have the same form in the plural as in the singular; as, *deer, sheep, trout,* &c.

§ 147 (25). Many words adopted from foreign languages retain their original plurals; as, *datum, data; criterion, criteria; genus, genera; larva, larvæ; crisis, crises; matrix, matrices; focus, foci; monsieur, messieurs.*

Many words of this class, while retaining the original plurals, have also a second, formed after the analogy of English words of similar termination; as, *formula, formulæ* or *formulas; beau, beaux* or *beaus; stratum, strata* or *stratums; bandit, banditti* or *bandits; cherub, cherubim* or *cherubs; seraph, seraphim* or *seraphs.* The plurals of the last two words are sometimes incorrectly written *cherubims* and *seraphims,* with double plural terminations.

§ 148 (26). In certain loose compounds consisting of a noun followed by an adjective or other qualifying expression, the plural is commonly formed by making the same change in the noun as when it stands alone; as, *court-martial, courts-martial; cousin-german, cousins-german; son-in-law, sons-in-law.* When, however, the adjective is so closely joined to the noun that the compound has the force of a simple word, the plural of the compound is commonly formed like that of any other word of the same termination; as, *cupful, cupfuls.*

§ 149 (27). There are many words, besides those mentioned in the preceding paragraphs, in respect to which good usage is variable. The most important of these words are mentioned in this and the succeeding sections.

The derivatives of the word *villain,* as *villainous, villainy,* &c., though often written *villanous, villany,* &c., properly retain the *i,* according to the practice of many writers, like those of other words similarly ending in *ain,* as *mountainous,* from *mountain.*

The words *connection, deflection, inflection,* and *reflection,* follow the spelling of the words *connect, deflect, inflect,* and *reflect,* though often written, especially in England, *connexion, deflexion, inflexion,* and *reflexion.*

The word *woe,* though often written without the final *e,* should retain it, like most other nouns of one syllable and of similar form; as, *doe, floe, foe, hoe, sloe, toe,* &c. Monosyllables other than nouns, and words of more than one syllable, having a similar termination, omit the *e;* as, *do, go, no, so, canto, motto, potato.*

The words *defense, expense, offense,* and *pretense,* are properly written thus, though often spelled with *c* instead of *s;* for the *s* belongs to the words from which they are derived, and is also used in all their derivatives.

The words *drought* and *height* were formerly written *drouth* and *hight,* and are still very often thus written in America.

The verb *practice* is thus written like the noun, in preference to *practise,* though the latter spelling is used by many writers, especially in England. The difference in spelling between the noun and the verb is properly observed, in words of this kind, only in such as are accented on the last syllable, as *device, devise.*

§ 150 (28). There is a class of words beginning with *en* or *in* — as, *enclose* or *inclose, enquire,* or *inquire, ensure,* or *insure,* and the like, — many of which take either form of the prefix indifferently. They are chiefly derived from the Latin, either directly or through the French, the prefix *in* belonging to the former language, and *en* to the latter. In some of these words, *en* is to be preferred; in others, *in;* in many of them, either may be used.

§ 151 (29). There is a class of words ending in *er,* some of which are written by most authors with the termination *re;* as, *center, meter, theater,* &c., which are often written *centre, metre, theatre,* &c. *Acre, chancre, lucre, nacre, massacre,* and *ogre,* retain the termination *re,* so as to preserve the hard sound of the *c* and the *g.*

§ 152 (30). There are two classes of chemical words ending respectively, as more commonly written, in *ide* and *ine,* in regard to which usage has been variable. Most of them were formerly written without the final *e,* but it is now the almost universal practice to retain it: as, *bromide, iodide, chlorine, fluorine,* &c. The word *tannin* is always written without the final *e. Oxide* is now generally written with the termination *ide,* though formerly by many written *oxyd,* from the supposition that the *y* of the last syllable represented the *υ* of the Greek ὀξύς, from which the word is derived; whereas the last syllable is simply the same as the termination *c* the words *bromide, sulphide,* &c.

§ 153 (31). There is a class of words ending, as pronounced, with the sound of long *i,* followed by z, some of which are differently written, by different authors, with either *ise* or *ize* to represent this sound; as, *criticize* or *criticise*; *civilize* or *civilise*; *naturalize* or *naturalise*; *patronize* or *patronise*. These words are mostly verbs, and are chiefly derived from Greek words ending in ιζω, or from French words ending in *iser* or *ise*. There are a few from other sources, but formed in analogy with those derived from these languages. Those formed from Greek words have the termination *ize*; as, *characterize*, *dramatize*, *tantalize*. The words *catechise* and *exorcise* are exceptions. Those formed in an analogous manner from English words are likewise written with *ize*; as, *memorize*. Those derived from the French verb *prendre* (participle *pris*, or *prise*) end in *ise*; as, *apprise*, *comprise*, *emprise*, *enterprise*, *surprise*. Of those formed from French words other than *prendre*, or which have corresponding forms in the French, a majority end in *ize*, though in respect to some of them usage is variable; as, *civilize*, *organize*, *satirize*. The following are the principal English verbs ending in *ise*; namely, *advertise, advise, apprise, catechise, chastise, circumcise, comprise, compromise, criticise, demise, despise, devise, disfranchise, disguise, divertise, emprise, enfranchise, enterprise, exercise, exorcise, franchise, misprise, premise, reprise, revise, supervise, surmise, surprise*. It may be remarked that most of those in respect to which usage varies are more frequently written in England with the termination *ise*, and in the United States with the termination *ize*.

§ 154 (32). The words *mold* and *molt*, and their compounds and derivatives, are written in this Dictionary with *o* instead of *ou*, in analogy with the words *bold, bolt, colt, gold*, &c., from which the *u* has been dropped. Most authors, however, write these words *mould* and *moult*, and their derivatives in like manner.

§ 155 (33). There is a numerous class of words almost universally written, in the United States, with the termination *or*, many of which are written, in England, with the termination *our*; as, *candor, favor, honor, labor, rumor, vigor*. English usage, however, is far from being uniform with respect to these words, many of them being written with *or* in English books.

ABBREVIATIONS AND EXPLANATIONS.

a. adjective.
adv. adverb.
Amer. America.
Ar. Arabic.
A.-S. Anglo-Saxon.
Celt. Celtic.
colloq. colloquially.
compar. comparative.
conj. conjunction.
D. Dutch.
Dan. Danish. [flsh.
Eng. England, Eng-
esp. especially.

f. feminine.
Fr. French.
Gael. Gaelic.
Ger. German.
Goth. Gothic.
Gr. Greek.
Gram. Grammar.
Heb. Hebrew.
Hung. Hungarian.
imp. imperfect.
interj. interjection.
It. Italian. *Ir.* Irish.
Lat. Latin.

L. Lat. Low Latin.
m. masculine.
Mus. Music.
n. noun.
obs. obsolete. [jective.
p. a. participial ad-
Per. Persian.
Pg. Portuguese.
pl. plural.
p. p. participle past.
p. pr. participle present.
prep. preposition.

pron. pronoun; pronounced.
sing. singular.
Skr. Sanskrit.
Slav. Slavonic.
Sp. Spanish.
Sw. Swedish.
SYN. Synonyms.
Turk. Turkish.
v. verb.
v. i. verb intransitive.
v. t. verb transitive.
W. Welsh.

⁎ Compound words, which, in ordinary writing and printing, have their constituent parts separated by a hyphen, are here distinguished from those which are usually and properly written and printed without one, by the use of a longer hyphen than that employed for the mere division of words into syllables; as, Able-bodied. Words having prefixes or initial syllables which are commonly separated from the other syllables by a hyphen, are distinguished in the same way; as, Re-enforce, Electro-magnetism.

⁎ For the "KEY TO THE PRONUNCIATION," see page v. It is desirable that those who use this Dictionary should make themselves familiar with the Key, as they will then find it easy to understand the notation by which the pronunciation of every word is expressed.

⁎ The figures which immediately follow certain words in the Vocabulary refer to corresponding sections in the Principles of Pronunciation on pp. vi.-xix, or to the Rules for Spelling on pp. xx.-xxiv.

⁎ A dagger [†] prefixed to a word shows that it is from the *Latin* or *Greek*, or from some *modern foreign language*, and is not fully Anglicized.

A DICTIONARY

OF THE

ENGLISH LANGUAGE.

A.

A (122), called the *indefinite article*, is a contraction of *an*, and is used before words beginning with the sound of a consonant; any; one.
A-băck' (41), *adv.* Backward; by surprise.
Ăb'a-cus, *n.* An instrument for performing arithmetical calculations; uppermost member of a column.
A-bäft' (5), *adv.* Toward the stern; astern.
Ab-āl'ien-ate (-yen-), *v. t.* To transfer the title of.
A-băn'don, *v. t.* To forsake wholly; to renounce.
A-băn'doned, *a.* Given up entirely; very wicked.— SYN. Forsaken; profligate; depraved; reprobate.
A-băn'don-ment, *n.* Entire desertion; a final giving up.
A-bāse', *v. t.* [From Lat. *basis*, base.] To bring low; to humble; to depress.
A-bāse'ment (132), *n.* State of being brought low; humiliation; degradation.
A-băsh', *v. t.* To make ashamed; to confuse.
A-hăt'a-ble (133), *a.* Capable of being abated.
A-bāte', *v. t.* To lessen; to diminish in price. — *v. i.* To grow less; to decrease.
A-bāte'ment, *n.* Act of abating; decrease; sum or quantity taken away.
Ăb'a-tĭs, *n.* Branches of trees turned outward for defense.
Ăb'bā, *n.* Father; religious superior.
Ăb'ba-cy, *n.* Condition, rights, or privileges of an abbot.
Ab-bā'tial, *a.* Relating to an abbey.

†**Ab-bé** (Ăb'bā), *n.* An ecclesiastic without office or rights.
Ăb'bess (140), *n.* Governess of a nunnery.
Ăb'bey (141), *n.* A monastery or convent.
Ăb'bot, *n.* [Lat. *abba* (genitive *abbatis*). See ABBA.] Head of a society of monks; chief of an abbey.
Ab-brē'vi-āte, *v. t.* To shorten; to abridge; to contract.
Ab-brē'vi-ā'tion (107), *n.* Act of shortening; contraction.
Ab-brē'vi-ā'tor, *n.* One who abbreviates or shortens.
Ăb'di-cāte, *v. t.* To relinquish; to resign. — *v. i.* To give up an office.
Ăb'di-cā'tion, *n.* Act of abdicating.
Ăb'di-eā'tive, *n.* Causing or implying abdication.
Ab-dō'men (115), *n.* The belly, or upper part of the belly.
Ab-dŏm'i-nal, *a.* Pertaining to the abdomen.
Ab-dūçe', *v. t.* To draw away.
Ab-dūçt', *v. t.* To kidnap.
Ab-dŭc'tion, *n.* Act of carrying a person away by force or fraud.
Ā'be-çe-dā'ri-an, *n.* A teacher or a learner of the alphabet.
A-bĕd', *adv.* In bed; on the bed.
Ab-ĕr'rançe, *n.* A straying from the right way; aberration.
Ab-ĕr'rant, *a.* Wandering.
Ăb'er-rā'tion, *n.* Act of wandering from the right way.
A-bĕt' (129), *v. t.* To encourage; to help. [ting.
A-bĕt'ment, *n.* Act of abet-
A-bĕt'tor, *n.* One who abets.
A-bey'ançe, *n.* A state of suspense.
Ab-hŏr' (129), *v. t.* To dislike or hate bitterly; to detest.

ABOLISH

Ab-hŏr'rençe, *n.* Extreme hatred; detestation.
Ab-hŏr'rent, *a.* Inconsistent; detesting; odious.
†**Ā'bib**, *n.* The first month of the Jewish year.
A-bīde', *v. i.* [*imp. & p. p.* ABODE.] To stay or dwell in a place; to wait for. — *v. t.* To bear or endure.
Ăb'i-gail (-ḡel), *n.* A lady's waiting-woman.
A-bĭl'i-ty, *n.* Power; means; skill; (*pl.*) mental powers.
Ăb'ject, *a.* Mean; worthless; base; despicable. [basely.
Ăb'ject-ly, *adv.* Meanly;
Ăb'ject-ness, *n.* Meanness of spirit; baseness. [juring.
Ăb'ju-rā'tion, *n.* Act of abjuring.
Ab-jūr'a-to-ry, *a.* Containing abjuration.
Ab-jūre', *v. t.* To renounce upon oath; to retract; to recant.
Ăb'la-tĭve, *a.* Denoting what takes away; — applied to the sixth case of Latin nouns.
A-blāze', *adv.* On fire; in a blaze. [capable.
Ā'ble (Ā'bl), *a.* Having power;
Ā'ble-bŏd'ied, *a.* Having strength of body.
Ab-lū'tion, *n.* Act of washing.
Ā'bly, *adv.* With ability.
Ăb'ne-gāte, *v. t.* To deny; to renounce.
Ăb'ne-gā'tion, *n.* Self-denial.
Ab-nŏr'mal, *a.* [Lat. *ab*, from, and *norma*, a rule.] Not conformed to rule; irregular.
A-bōard', *adv.* On board; in a ship or boat. — *prep.* On board of.
A-bōde', *n.* State or place of residence. — SYN. Dwelling; habitation; domicile. — *v., imp. & p. p.* of *Abide*.
A-bŏl'ish, *v. t.* To repeal; to make void; to annul.

ABOLISHABLE — ACADEMICAL

A-bŏl′ish-a-ble, *a.* Capable of being destroyed.
A-bŏl′ish-ment, *n.* Act of abolishing; abolition.
Ăb′o-lī′tion (-lĭsh′un, 119), *n.* The act of abolishing.
Ăb′o-lī′tion-ĭşm, *n.* Principles or measures of abolitionists.
Ăb′o-lī′tion-ĭst, *n.* One who favors abolitionism.
A-bŏm′i-na-ble, *a.* Detestable.
A-bŏm′i-nāte, *v. t.* To hate utterly; to abhor.
A-bŏm′i-nā′tion, *n.* Extreme hatred; object of hatred.
Ăb′o-rĭg′i-nal, *a.* First, or primitive. — *n.* Original inhabitant.
†**Ăb′o-rĭg′i-nēş,** *n. pl.* First inhabitants of a country.
A-bŏr′tion, *n.* A miscarriage; an untimely birth.
A-bŏr′tĭve, *a.* Unsuccessful; untimely; premature.
A-bŏr′tĭve-ly, *adv.* Immaturely; without success.
A-bŏr′tĭve-ness, *n.* State of being abortive.
A-bound′, *v. i.* To be in great plenty; to be prevalent.
A-bout′, *prep.* Round; encircling; on every side of; near to; concerning. — *adv.* Around; here and there; every way.
A-bŏve′ (a-bŭv′), *prep.* Higher than; more than. — *adv.* In a higher place.
Ăb′ra-ca-dăb′ra, *n.* A superstitious charm against certain diseases.
A-brāde′, *v. t.* [Lat. *ab*, from, and *radere*, to scrape.] To rub or wear off; to grate.
A-brā′sion, *n.* A wearing or rubbing off. [in a line.
A-brēast′, *adv.* Side by side;
†**A-breu-voir′ (vwŏr′),** *n.* The joint between two stones in masonry.
A-brĭdġe′, *v. t.* To make shorter; to contract; to cut short; to abbreviate.
A-brĭdġ′ment (122), *n.* A work abridged; a summary; epitome; compend; compendium.
A-brōach′, *adv.* In a posture to let out liquor.
A-brŏad′ (a-brawd′), *adv.* At large; out of doors; in another country. [annul.
Ăb′ro-gāte, *v. t.* To repeal; to
Ăb′ro-gā′tion, *n.* Act of repealing, as a law.
A-brŭpt′, *a.* [Lat. *abruptus*, broken off.] Sudden; steep; broken.

Ab-rŭp′tion, *n.* Violent separation of bodies.
Ab-rŭpt′ly, *adv.* In an abrupt manner; suddenly.
Ab-rŭpt′ness, *n.* An abrupt manner; suddenness.
Ăb′sçess, *n.* A tumor filled with purulent matter.
Ab-sçīnd′, *v. t.* To cut off.
Ab-sçĭş′gion (-sĭzh′un), *n.* The act of cutting off; removal; separation.
Ab-seŏnd′, *v. i.* To secrete one's self; to hide.
Ăb′sençe, *n.* State of being absent; inattention.
Ăb′sent, *a.* Not present; inattentive; lost in thought.
Ab-sĕnt′, *v. t.* To keep away.
Ăb′sen-tee′, } *n.* One who absents himself.
Ăb-sĕnt′er, }
Ăb′so-lūte, *a.* Not limited; unconditional; complete; arbitrary; despotic; positive; peremptory.
Ăb′so-lūte-ly, *adv.* Positively; arbitrarily.
Ăb′so-lūte-ness, *n.* Completeness; arbitrary power.
Ăb′so-lū′tion, *n.* Act of absolving; forgiveness; pardon; remission of sins.
Ăb′so-lū′tĭşm, *n.* Principles of absolute government.
Ab-sŏl′u-to-ry, *adv.* Absolving.
Ab-ṣōlve′ (-zŏlv′), *v. t.* To free from; to pardon.
Ăb-sŏrb′, *v. t.* [Lat. *ab*, from, and *sorbere*, to suck in.] To suck up; to imbibe; to engross.
Ab-sŏrb′a-ble, *a.* Capable of being absorbed.
Ab-sŏrb′ent, *n.* A substance that absorbs. — *a.* Sucking or drying up; imbibing.
Ab-sŏrp′tion, *n.* Act of absorbing; sucking up.
Ab-sŏrp′tĭve, *a.* Having power to absorb. [forbear.
Ab-stāin′, *v. i.* To refrain; to
Ab-stē′mi-oŭs, *a.* Temperate in diet; abstinent.
Ab-stē′mi-oŭs-ly, *adv.* Temperately.
Ab-stē′mi-oŭs-ness, *n.* A sparing use of food, &c.
Ab-stērġe′, *v. t.* To cleanse by wiping; to purify.
Ab-stēr′ġent, *a.* Having a cleansing quality. [cleansing.
Ab-stēr′sion, *n.* The act of
Ab-stēr′sĭve, *a.* Serving to cleanse; abstergent.
Ăb′sti-nençe, *n.* A refraining from food, or from any action.

Ăb′sti-nent, *a.* Practicing abstinence; fasting.
Ab-strāct′, *v. t.* To draw from; to separate; to remove; to purloin.
Ab′strāct, *a.* Separate; existing in the mind only; abstruse; difficult. — *n.* An abridgment or epitome.
Ab-strāct′ed-ness, *n.* State of being abstracted.
Ab-strāc′tion, *n.* Act of abstracting; separation; absence of mind.
Ab-strāct′ĭve, *a.* Having the power of abstracting.
Ăb′strāct-ly, *adv.* By itself.
Ăb′strāct-ness, *n.* State of being abstract.
Ab-strūse′ (29), *a.* Difficult to be understood; obscure.
Ab-strūse′ness, *n.* Obscurity or difficulty of meaning.
Ab-strūse′ly, *adv.* Obscurely; darkly.
Ab-sŭrd′, *a.* Contrary to reason or to manifest truth. — SYN. Foolish; irrational; ridiculous.
Ab-sŭrd′i-ty, } *n.* Quality of
Ab-sŭrd′ness, } being absurd; that which is absurd.
A-bŭn′dançe, *n.* Great plenty; exuberance.
A-bŭn′dant, *a.* Very plentiful; ample; exuberant.
A-bŭn′dant-ly, *adv.* Plentifully. [or use ill.
A-būşe′ (-būz′), *v. t.* To treat
A-būşe′, *n.* Ill use of any thing; corrupt practice; contumely.
A-bū′sĭve, *a.* Marked by abuse. — SYN. Reproachful; injurious; opprobrious.
A-bū′sĭve-ly, *adv.* In an abusive manner; by a wrong use.
A-bū′sĭve-ness, *n.* State of being abusive.
A-bŭt′, *v. i.* To end or border upon; to be contiguous to.
A-bŭt′ment, *n.* That which borders upon or adjoins; the solid part of a bridge next the land.
A-bŭt′tal, *n.* The butting or boundary of land.
A-byss′, *n.* [Gr. *a*, without, and *bussos*, bottom.] A bottomless gulf or depth.
Ăç′a-dē′mi-an, } *n.* A
Ăç′a-dĕm′ic, } member
Ăç′a-de-mĭ′cian, } of an a-
A-căd′e-mĭst, } cademy; an academic philosopher.
Ăç′a-dĕm′ic, } *a.* Pertain-
Ăç′a-dĕm′ic-al, } ing to an

ā, ā, ī, ō, ū, y̆, *long*; ă, ĕ, ĭ, ŏ, ŭ, ў, *short*: cāre, cär, ȧsk, ạll, whạt; ẽre, vẽil, tẽrm; p″que, fĭrm;

academy, college, or university.

A-cad'e-my, n. A school of arts and sciences; a school holding a place intermediate between the common school and college.

Ac-cēde', v. i. To be added to; to assent; to agree.

Ac-cĕl'er-āte, v. t. To hasten the motion of; to quicken.

Ac-cĕl'er-ā'tion, n. Act of accelerating, or hastening.

Ac-cĕl'er-a-tīve, } a. Increasing
Ac-cĕl'er-a-to-ry, } the speed.

Ac'cent, n. Modulation of voice; superior stress of voice on a syllable; a mark to regulate pronunciation, distinguish magnitudes, &c.

Ac-cĕnt', v. t. To express or note the accent.

Ac-cĕnt'u-al, a. Relating to accent.

Ac-cĕnt'u-āte, v. t. To mark or pronounce with an accent.

Ac-cĕnt'u-ā'tion, n. Act or mode of uttering or marking accents.

Ac-cĕpt', v. t. To receive; to admit; to subscribe and become liable for.

Ac-cĕpt'a-ble, a. Likely to be accepted; agreeable; welcome; pleasing; grateful.

Ac-cĕpt'a-bĭl'ĭ-ty, } n. The
Ac-cĕpt'a-ble-ness, } quality of being acceptable.

Ac-cĕpt'a-bly, adv. In an acceptable manner; agreeably.

Ac-cĕpt'ançe, n. Reception with approbation; a bill accepted.

Ac'çep-tā'tion, n. Acceptance; the commonly received meaning of a word.

Ac-cĕpt'er, n. One who accepts.

Ac-çĕss', or Ac'çess, n. Approach; admission; increase.

Ac-çĕs'sa-ry, a. Additional; acceding. — n. One who accedes to an offense.

Ac-çĕs'sĭ-bĭl'ĭ-ty, n. Quality of being accessible.

Ac-çĕss'ĭ-ble, a. Capable of being approached.

Ac-çĕs'sion (-sĕsh'un), n. Act of acceding to; addition; increase.

Ac'çes-sō'rĭ-al, a. Pertaining to an accessory.

Ac-çĕs'so-rĭ-ly, adv. In the manner of an accessory.

Ac-çĕs'so-ry, n. One who helps to commit a crime; an accomplice — a. Contributing; aiding.

Ac'ci-dençe, n. A book containing the rudiments of grammar.

Ac'ci-dent, n. An unforeseen or unexpected event; chance; casualty; contingency.

Ac'ci-dĕnt'al, a. Happening by chance; not essential. — SYN. Casual; fortuitous; incidental.

Ac'ci-dĕnt'al-ly, adv. By accident; by chance.

Ac-claim', } n. A shout
Ac'cla-mā'tion, } of applause.

Ac-clăm'a-to-ry, a. Expressing joy or applause.

Ac-clī'māte, v. t. To habituate to a climate not native.

Ac'cli-mā'tion, n. Process or state of being acclimated.

Ac-clĭv'ĭ-ty, n. Ascending slope or inclination.

Ac-clī'vous, a. Rising with a slope, as a hill.

Ac-cŏm'mo-dāte, v. t. To supply with conveniences; to adapt; to suit; to adjust.

Ac-cŏm'mo-dā'ting, a. Disposed to oblige; kind.

Ac-cŏm'mo-dā'tion, n. Provision of conveniences; fitness; reconciliation; (pl.) conveniences.

Ac-cŏm'pa-ni-ment (135), n. That which accompanies, or is added as ornament.

Ac-cŏm'pa-nĭst, n. The performer in music who takes the accompanying part.

Ac-cŏm'pa-ny (-kŭm'-), v. t. To go or be with; to attend.

Ac-cŏm'plĭçe, n. An associate in a crime; an accessory.

Ac-cŏm'plish, v. t. To finish entirely; to bring to pass. — SYN. To execute; effect; fulfill.

Ac-cŏm'plished (-plĭsht), p. a. Finished; completed; refined; well-educated.

Ac-cŏm'plish-ment, n. A completion; an acquirement which adds grace.

Ac-cŏmpt'ant (-kount'-), n. See Accountant.

Ac-cŏrd', n. [From Lat. cor, cordis, the heart.] Agreement; concurrence; consent; union. — v. i. To agree; to harmonize.

Ac-cŏrd'ançe, n. Agreement; harmony; conformity.

Ac-cŏrd'ant, a. Corresponding; agreeing; consonant; agreeable.

Ac-cŏrd'ing to. In accordance with.

Ac-cŏrd'ing-ly, adv. Agreeably; suitably; consequently.

Ac-cōr'dĭ-on, n. A small musical instrument, with keys and bellows.

Ac-cŏst', v. t. To speak first; to address.

†Accouchement (ăk'kōōsh'-mŏng'), n. [Fr.] Delivery in child-bed.

Ac-count', v. t. To reckon; to compute; to esteem; to assign the causes of. — n. Computation; estimation; regard; explanation; narration.

Ac-count'a-bĭl'ĭ-ty, n. Liability to give account.

Ac-count'a-ble, a. Liable to be called to account; responsible.

Ac-count'a-ble-ness, n. A being liable to answer for; accountability.

Ac-count'ant, n. One employed, or skillful, in keeping accounts.

Ac-coŭ'ple (-kŭp'pl), v. t. To couple; to join together.

Ac-çoū'ter } (ak-kōō'ter, 151),
Ac-çoū'tre } v. t. To equip; to furnish.

Ac-çoū'ter-ments } (-kōō'-
Ac-çoū'tre-ments } ter-), n. Equipage; trappings; ornaments.

Ac-crĕd'ĭt, v. t. To furnish with credentials; to give credit to.

Ac-crĕs'çent, a. Growing; increasing.

Ac-crē'tion, n. The act of growing to; increase.

Ac-crē'tīve, a. Increasing by growth.

Ac-crŭe', v. i. To arise; to be added; to increase.

Ac-cŭm'ben-çy, n. State of reclining.

Ac-cŭm'bent, a. Reclining; leaning.

Ac-cū'mu-lāte, v. t. To heap together. — v. i. To increase; to be augmented.

Ac-cū'mu-lā'tion, n. Act of accumulating; a heap.

Ac-cū'mu-lā'tĭve, a. Causing accumulation.

Ac-cū'mu-lā'tor, n. One who accumulates.

Ăc'cu-ra-çy, } n. Exact-
Ăc'cu-rate-ness, } ness; correctness; closeness.

Ăc'cu-rate (42), a. Done with care; without error. — SYN. Correct; precise; just.

sŏn, ôr, dọ, wọlf, tōō, tŏŏk; ûrn, rụe, pụll; ç, ġ, soft; c, g, hard; aş; eẋist; ṇ as ng; this.

ACCURATELY 28 ACUPUNCTURE

Ac'cu-rate-ly, *adv.* Exactly; correctly; nicely.
Ac-curse', *v. t.* To doom to misery; to curse.
Ac-cûrs'ed, *p. p.* or *a.* [*p. p.* pron. *ak-kurst'*, and *a. ak-kurs'ed.*] Cursed; execrable.
Ac'cu-sa'tion, *n.* Act of accusing; charge of a crime.
Ac-cū'sa-tive, *a.* Accusing—applied to a case in grammar.
Ac-cūse', *v. t.* To charge with a crime; to blame; to censure; to impeach. [cuses.
Ac-cūs'er, *n.* One who accuses.
Ac-cūs'tom, *v. t.* To make habitual or familiar by use.
Açe, *n.* A unit on cards or dice.
A-çěl'da-mà, *n.* A field of blood.
A-çĕph'a-loŭs, *a.* [Gr. *a*, without, and *kephale*, a head.] Headless.
A-çĕrb'i-ty, *n.* Bitterness of taste or of spirit.
A-çĕs'çen-çy, *n.* A tendency to sourness.
A-çĕs'çent, *a.* Tending to sourness.
Aç'e-tate, *n.* A salt formed by acetic acid united to a base.
A-çĕt'ic, or **A-çē'tic,** *a.* [Lat. *acetum*, vinegar.] Having the properties of vinegar.
A-çĕt'i-fi-cā'tion, *n.* Act of turning into acid or vinegar.
A-çĕt'i-fȳ, *v. t.* or *i.* To turn acid; to make or become acid.
Aç'e-tim'e-ter, *n.* An instrument for ascertaining the strength of acids.
Aç'e-tim'e-try, *n.* Art of ascertaining the strength of acids.
A-çē'toŭs, *a.* Having the quality of vinegar; sour.
Ache (āk), *v. i.* To be in pain.
— *n.* A continued pain.
A-chiev'a-ble, *a.* Capable of being achieved.
A-chiēve', *v. t.* To do; to perform; to obtain.
A-chieve'ment, *n.* A performance; an action.
Ach'ing (āk'ing), *n.* Continued pain.
Ach'ro-măt'ic, *a.* [Gr. *a*, without, and *chroma*, color.] Destitute of color.
Aç'id (ăs'id), *a.* Sour; like vinegar. — *n.* A sour substance; a substance by which salts are formed.
A-çid'i-fī'a-ble, *a.* Capable of being acidified.
A-çid'i-fi-cā'tion, *n.* Act of acidifying.
A-çid'i-fȳ (51), *v. t.* To convert into acid. — *v. i.* To become acid or sour.
A-çid'i-ty, } *n.* Acid taste;
Aç'id-ness, } sourness; sharpness.
A-çĭd'u-late (42), *v. t.* To tinge with acids.
A-çĭd'u-loŭs, *a.* Slightly sour.
Ac-knŏwl'edge (ak-nŏl'ej), *v. t.* To own; to confess; to avow.
Ac-knŏwl'edg-ment (-nŏl'ej-ment, 132), *n.* The owning of a thing; avowal; thanks.
Ac'me, *n.* The highest point; summit; crisis of a disease.
Ā'corn, *n.* [A.-S. *æc*, oak, and *corn*, grain.] Fruit or seed of an oak.
A-cŏt'y-lē'don, *n.* A plant in which the seed-lobes are not present.
A-cous'tic (-kow'-), *a.* Pertaining to hearing.
A-cous'tics, *n. pl.* The theory or science of sounds.
Ac-quāint', *v. t.* To inform; to make familiar with.
Ac-quāint'ance, *n.* Knowledge; familiarity; one well known.
Ac'qui-ĕsçe' (ăk'wī-ĕss'), *v. ĭ.* To assent; to be satisfied with; to comply.
Ac'qui-ĕs'çençe, *n.* Consent; compliance.
Ac'qui-ĕs'çent, *a.* Submitting or disposed to submit.
Ac-quīr'a-ble (133), *a.* Capable of being acquired.
Ac-quīre', *v. t.* To gain; to obtain; to come to; to attain.
Ac-quīre'ment, *n.* That which is acquired; gain; acquisition.
Ac'qui-şi'tion (-zĭsh'un), *n.* Act of acquiring; the thing acquired.
Ac-quĭş'i-tive, *a.* Disposed to make acquisitions.
Ac-quĭş'i-tive-ness, *n.* Desire of possession.
Ac-quĭt', *v. t.* To discharge; to set free; to clear; to release; to absolve.
Ac-quĭt'tal (129), *n.* Formal release from a charge.
Ac-quĭt'tançe, *n.* A receipt in full for debt; discharge.
Ā'cre (ā'ker, 151), *n.* [A.-S. *æcer*, an open field.] A piece of land containing 160 square rods or 4840 square yards.
Ā'crid, *a.* Hot and biting to the taste; pungent.
Ā'crid-ness, *n.* A sharp, harsh quality; pungency.
Ac'ri-mō'ni-oŭs, *a.* Full of acrimony; bitter; sarcastic; censorious; severe.
Ac'ri-mo-ny, *n.* Bitterness of feeling or language. — SYN. Asperity; sharpness; severity; harshness.
Ac'ro-băt, *n.* One who practices high-vaulting, rope-dancing, &c.
A-crŏn'y-cal, *a.* Rising at sunset, and setting at sunrise.
A-crŏp'o-lis, *n.* A citadel.
A-crŏss', *prep.* From side to side of; athwart; over.
A-crŏs'tic, *n.* A poem in which certain letters taken successively, one in each line, form a name. [acrostics.
A-crŏs'tic-al, *a.* Pertaining to
Act, *v. t.* To perform; to do; to move; to feign. — *v. i.* To be in action; to imitate; to conduct or behave. — *n.* A deed; exploit; action; division of a play.
Act'ing, *n.* Act of performing; action.
Ac'tion, *n.* Deed; feat; battle; suit at law; gesture; gesticulation.
Ac'tion-a-ble, *a.* Admitting an action at law.
Act'ive, *a.* Causing or communicating action or motion; engaged in action; transitive. — SYN. Brisk; alert; nimble; quick.
Act'ive-ly, *adv.* In an active manner.
Ac-tiv'i-ty, *n.* Quality of being active; nimbleness; agility.
Act'or, *n.* One who acts; a stage-player.
Act'ress, *n.* A female actor.
Act'u-al, *a.* Existing in act; real; certain.
Ac'tu-ăl'i-ty, *n.* State of being actual. [actual.
Act'u-al-īze, *v. t.* To make
Act'u-al-ly, *adv.* In act or in fact; really; truly.
Act'u-a-ry, *n.* A registrar or clerk.
Act'u-āte (42), *v. t.* To put in action; to excite.
A-cūle'-ate, *a.* Prickly.
A-cū'men, *n.* Quickness of perception; acuteness.
A-cū'mi-nate, *a.* Having a long, tapering point.
A-cū'mi-nāte, *v. i.* To rise to a point.
A-cū'mi-nā'tion, *n.* Act of sharpening; a sharp point; quickness.
Ac'u-pŭnçt'ūre, *n.* Introduction of needles into the

ACUTE — 29 — ADMIRABLE

living tissues for remedial purposes.

A-cūte′, a. Sharp; ingenious; penetrating; keen.

A·cūte′ly, adv. Sharply; keenly; ingeniously.

A·cūte′ness, n. Sharpness; quickness of intellect.

Ăd′age, n. A proverb; maxim; an old saying.

†**Ad-ä′ġio, n.** (Mus.) A mark of slow time. — adv. Slowly.

Ăd′a-mant, n. A very hard stone; a diamond.

Ăd′a-mant-ē′an, | a. Ex-
Ad/a-mant′īne, | tremely hard; hard as adamant.

A-dăpt′, v. t. To fit; to suit.

A-pt′a-bĭl′ĭ-ty, n. Quality adaptation.

A-dăpt′a-ble, a. Capable of being adapted.

Ad-ap-tā′tion, n. The act of adapting or fitting; suitableness; fitness.

A dăpt′ed-ness, n. State of being adapted.

Add (125), v. t. [Lat. ad, to, and dare, to give.] To join; to augment or increase.

†**Ad-dĕn′dum, n.** (pl. Ad-dĕn′da, 147.) [Lat.] Thing added.

Ăd′der, n. A kind of venomous serpent. [added.

Ăd′dĭ-ble, a. Capable of being

Ad-dĭct′, v. t. To give up habitually; to apply. — SYN. To devote; to dedicate.

Ad-dĭct′ed-ness, | n. State of
Ad-dĭc′tion, | being addicted.

Ad-dĭ′tion (-dĭsh′un), n. Act of adding; thing added; increase; part of arithmetic which treats of adding numbers.

†**Ad-dĭ′tion-al (-dĭsh′un-), n.** Added.

Ad-dĭ′tion-al-ly (-dĭsh′un-), adv. By way of addition.

Ăd′dle, v. t. To make addle or corrupt. — a. Diseased, as eggs; putrid; corrupt; barren; empty.

Ad-drĕss′, v. t. To speak or apply to; to prepare for; to direct; to make love to. — n. Application; petition; dexterity; skill; courtship; direction of a letter.

Ad-dūçe′, v. t. To bring forward; to allege. [ward.

Ad-dūçent, a. Bringing for-

Ad-dū′çĭ-ble, a. Capable of being adduced.

Ad-dūc′tion, n. The act of adducing, or bringing forward.

Ad-dŭct′ĭve, a. Serving to bring forward.

A-dĕpt′, n. A person skilled in any art. — a. Well-versed; skillful.

Ăd′e-qua-çy, n. State of being adequate; sufficiency.

Ăd′e-quate, a. Fully sufficient; equal; proportionate; correspondent.

Ăd′e-quate-ly, adv. In proportion; sufficiently; fitly.

Ad-hēre′, v. i. To stick close; to remain fixed or firm.

Ad-hēr′ençe, | n. Quality or
Ad-hēr′en-çy, | state of adhering; tenacity; fidelity; constancy.

Ad-hēr′ent, a. United with or to; sticking to.

Ad-hēr′ent, | n. One who ad-
Ad-hēr′er, | heres; a follower; a partisan.

Ad-hē′sion, n. Act or state of sticking; adherence.

Ad-hē′sĭve, a. Sticking; tenacious.

Ad-hē′sĭve-ly, adv. With adhesion.

Ad-hē′sĭve-ness, n. Quality of sticking; tenacity.

Ad-hŏr′ta-to-ry, a. Containing counsel; advisory.

A-dieū′ (a-dū′, 27), adv. Farewell; good-by. — n. Act of taking leave.

Ăd′ĭ-po-çēre′, n. A waxy substance into which fat is sometimes converted.

Ăd′ĭ-pōse, a. Consisting of fat; fat; fatty.

Ăd′ĭt, n. [Lat. aditus, entrance.] A horizontal entrance into a pit.

Ad-jā′çen-çy, n. State of lying close to; contiguity.

Ad-jā′çent, a. Lying near; contiguous.

Ăd′jec-tī′val, a. Pertaining to, or partaking of, an adjective.

Ăd′jec-tĭve, n. A word added to a noun to express some quality, attribute, or property.

Ăd′jec-tĭve-ly, adv. In the manner of an adjective.

Ad-join′, v. t. To join or unite to. — v. i. To be contiguous.

Ad-join′ing, a. Joining; adjacent; near; contiguous.

Ad-jŏurn′ (37), v. t. To put off to another time. — SYN. To postpone; delay; defer; prorogue.

Ad-jŏurn′ment, n. Act of adjourning; postponement; delay.

Ad-jūdge′, v. t. To sentence; to decide judicially.

Ad-jū′dĭ-cāte, v. t. To determine by law.

Ad-jū′dĭ-cā′tion, n. Judicial trial or sentence.

Ăd′junçt, n. Something joined to another. — a. Added to, or united with.

Ad-jūnç′tion, n. Act of adjoining.

Ad-jūnçt′ĭve, n. That which is joined. — a. Tending to join.

Ad′ju-rā′tion, n. Act of charging solemnly; form of oath.

Ad-jūre′, v. t. To charge on oath; to enjoin earnestly or solemnly.

Ad-jūr′er, n. One who adjures.

Ad-jŭst′, v. t. To make exact or conformable; to set right. — SYN. To adapt; suit; fit.

Ad-jŭst′a-ble, a. Capable of being adjusted.

Ad-jŭst′ment, n. A setting in order; regulation; settlement.

Ăd′ju-tan-çy, n. Office of an adjutant.

Ăd′ju-tant, n. A military officer who assists a superior officer.

Ăd′ju-vant, a. Helping; helpful. — n. A helper; an assistant.

Ad-mĕas′ūre (-mĕzh′ụr), v. t. To take the dimensions or capacity of.

Ad-mĕas′ūre-ment (-mĕzh′ụr-), n. Act or result of measuring; measurement.

Ad-mĕn′su-rā′tion, n. Act of measuring; mensuration.

Ad-mĭn′ĭs-tẽr, v. t. To manage; to direct; to supply; to settle, as an estate. — v. t. To contribute; to act as administrator.

Ad-mĭn′ĭs-tō′rĭ-al, a. Pertaining to administration.

Ad-mĭn′ĭs-tra-ble, a. Capable of being administered.

Ad-mĭn′ĭs-trā′tion, n. Act of administering; executive part of government.

Ad-mĭn′ĭs-trā′tĭve, a. Administering.

Ad-mĭn′ĭs-trā′tor, n. A man who manages an intestate estate.

Ad-mĭn′ĭs-trā′tor-ship, n. Office of an administrator.

Ad-mĭn′ĭs-trā′trĭx, n. A woman who administers an estate.

Ăd′mĭ-ra-ble, a. Worthy of admiration. — SYN. Wonderful; rare; excellent.

---

sŏn, ôr, dọ, wǫlf, tōō, tŏŏk; ûrn, ruẹ, pụll; ç, ġ, soft; c, ḡ, hard; aẓ; ex̣ist; ṇ as ng; this.

ADMIRABLY 30 ADVERT

Ad'mi-ra-bly, *adv.* Wonderfully; excellently.

Ad'mi-ral, *n.* [Ar. *amir-al-(bāhr)*, commander of (the sea).] Principal officer of a fleet or navy.

Ad'mi-ral-ship, *n.* Office of admiral.

Ad'mi-ral-ty, *n.* The power or the court for administering naval affairs.

Ad'mi-rā'tion, *n.* Wonder mingled with pleasure; astonishment; esteem.

Ad-mīre', *v. t.* To regard with wonder or love.—*v. i.* To wonder.

Ad-mīr'er, *n.* One who admires; a lover.

Ad-mis'si-bil'i-ty, *n.* Quality of being admissible.

Ad-mis'si-ble, *a.* Capable of being admitted.

Ad-mis'sion (-mĭsh'un), *n.* Act of admitting; admittance; allowance.

Ad-mĭt', *v. t.* To let in; to receive as true; to allow.

Ad-mĭt'tance (129), *n.* Act or power of entering.

Ad-mĭx', *v. t.* To mingle.

Ad-mĭx'tion (-mĭkst'yun, 63), *n.* A mingling.

Ad-mĭxt'ūre (-mĭkst'yụr), *n.* Act of mixing; the substance mixed.

Ad-mŏn'ish, *v. t.* To warn; to reprove gently; to advise.

Ad-mŏn'ish-er, *n.* One who admonishes.

Ad'mo-nī'tion (-nĭsh'un), *n.* Gentle reproof; counsel; warning.

Ad-mŏn'i-tīve, } *a.* Containing admonition; monitory; warning.
Ad-mŏn'i-to-ry, }

Ad-mŏn'i-tor, *n.* One who admonishes.

Ad-nās'cent, *a.* Growing to something else. [thing.

Ad'nate, *a.* Growing on some-

A-dō'(-dōō'), *n.* Trouble; difficulty; bustle; stir.

†A-dō'be, *n.* [Sp.] An unburnt brick dried in the sun.

Ăd'o-lĕs'cence, *n.* State of growing; youth.

Ăd'o-lĕs'cent, *a.* Growing; advancing to manhood.

A-dŏpt', *v. t.* To take as one's own. [ing.

A-dŏp'tion, *n.* Act of adopting.

A-dŏpt'ĭve, *a.* Adopting; adopted.

A-dōr'a-ble, *a.* Worthy of adoration; divine.

A-dōr'a-ble-ness, *n.* Quality of being adorable.

Ăd'o-rā'tion, *n.* Divine worship; homage; profound reverence.

A-dōre', *v. t.* [Lat. *ad*, to, and *orare*, to pray.] To worship; to venerate; to reverence; to revere; to love intensely.

A-dōr'er, *n.* One who adores; a worshiper; a lover.

A-dōrn', *v. t.* To deck; to embellish; to decorate.

A-dōrn'ment, *n.* Embellishment; decoration.

A-down', *adv.* Down.—*prep.* Downward.

A-drift', *a.* or *adv.* Floating at random.

A-droit', *a.* Skillful; expert; dexterous; ingenious.

A-droit'ly, *adv.* Ingeniously.

A-droit'ness, *n.* Dexterity; skill.

A-drȳ', *a.* In want of drink.

Ăd'scĭ-tī'tiŏŭs (-tĭsh'ŭs), *a.* Additional; supplemental.

Ăd'u-lā'tion, *n.* Excessive or servile flattery.

Ăd'u-lā'tor, *n.* A servile flatterer. [excess.

Ăd'u-lā'to-ry, *a.* Flattering to

A-dŭlt', *n.* A person grown.—*a.* Grown to maturity.

A-dŭl'ter-ant, *n.* A person or thing that adulterates.

A-dŭl'ter-āte, *v. t.* To debase or corrupt by mixture.

A-dŭl'ter-ate, *a.* Debased; corrupted; tainted with adultery.

A-dŭl'ter-ā'tion, *n.* Act of adulterating, or state of being adulterated.

A-dŭl'ter-er, *n.* A man who is guilty of adultery.

A-dŭl'ter-ess, *n.* A woman guilty of adultery.

A-dŭl'ter-ŏŭs, *a.* Guilty of adultery; spurious; corrupt.

A-dŭl'ter-y, *n.* A violation of the marriage bed. [adult.

A-dŭlt'ness, *n.* State of being

Ad-ŭm'brant, *a.* Giving a faint shadow.

Ad-ŭm'brāte, *v. t.* To shadow out faintly.

Ăd'um-brā'tion, *n.* A shadow or faint resemblance.

Ad-ŭn'çi-ty, *n.* A bending in the form of a hook.

A-ŭnçe'ŏŭs, *a.* Hooked; bent.

A-dŭst', *a.* Burnt or scorched, or looking so.

A-dŭs'tion (-dŭst'yun), *n.* The act of burning up.

A-vănçe', *n.* A going forward; promotion; payment beforehand.—*v. t.* To bring forward or higher; to raise; to promote; to pay beforehand.—*v. i.* To go on; to improve; to rise in rank.

Ad-vănçe'ment, *n.* Act of advancing or moving forward; progress; promotion; preferment.

Ad-văn'tage (5, 183), *n.* Favorable circumstances; superiority; gain; benefit; profit.—*v. t.* To benefit; to promote.

Ăd'van-tā'geŏŭs, *a.* Being of advantage; profitable; useful.

Ăd'van-tā'geŏŭs-ly, *adv.* Profitably; conveniently.

Ăd'van-tā'geŏŭs-ness, *n.* Quality or state of being advantageous.

Ad'vent, *n.* A coming; the season of four weeks before Christmas.

Ăd'ven-tī'tiŏŭs (-tĭsh'ŭs), *a.* Added; accidental; incidental; not essentially inherent.

Ăd'ven-tī'tiŏŭs-ly (-tĭsh'ŭs-), *adv.* In an adventitious manner.

Ad-věn'tĭve, *a.* Accidental; adventitious.

Ad-věnt'u-al, *a.* Relating to the advent.

Ad-věnt'ūre (-věnt'yụr), *n.* An extraordinary event; an enterprise; chance; hazard.—*v. t.* To try the chance; to risk.—*v. i.* To venture.

Ad-věnt'ūr-er, *n.* One who adventures.

Ad-věnt'ūre-sŏme (132), *a.* Bold; daring; enterprising.

Ad-věnt'ūr-ŏŭs (133), *a.* Daring; bold; enterprising; venturesome.

Ăd'vẽrb, *n.* A word used to modify a verb, adjective, or other adverb.

Ad-vẽrb'i-al, *a.* Relating to, or like, an adverb.

Ad-vẽrb'i-al-ly, *adv.* In the manner of an adverb.

Ăd'ver-sa-ry, *n.* An opponent; enemy; antagonist.

Ad-vẽr'sa-tĭve, *a.* Expressing contrariety or opposition.

Ăd'vẽrse, *a.* Contrary; calamitous; afflictive.

Ăd'vẽrse-ly, *adv.* In an adverse manner; unfortunately.

Ad-vẽr'si-ty, *n.* Misfortune; affliction; calamity.

Ad-vẽrt', *v. i.* [Lat. *advertere*, to turn to.] To turn the mind.—SYN. To attend; regard; observe; refer.

ā, ē, ī, ō, ū, ÿ, *long*; ă, ĕ, ĭ, ŏ, ŭ, ў, *short*; câre, cär, ȧsk, ąll, whąt; ẽre, vẽil, tẽrm; pīque, fĩrm;

ADVERTENCE 31 AFFLATUS

Ad-vẽrt'ençe, } n. Direction
Ad-vẽrt'en-çy, } of the mind;
  attention; heed.
Ad-vẽrt'ent, a. Attentive; heedful.
Ad'ver-tīṣe' (153), v. t. To inform; to give public notice of.
Ad-vẽr'tīṣe-ment, or Ad'ver-tīṣe'ment, n. A public notice; information.
Ad'ver-tīṣ'er, n. One who advertises.
Ad-vīçe', n. Counsel; instruction; notice; intelligence.
Ad-vīṣ'a-ble, a. Fit to be advised or done; prudent; expedient.
Ad-vīṣ'a-ble-ness, n. Fitness; propriety; expediency.
Ad-vīṣe' (153), v. t. To give advice to; to counsel; to inform; to apprise. — v. i. To consider.
Ad-vīṣ'ed-ly (57), adv. With deliberation or advice; prudently.
Ad-vīṣ'ed-ness, n. Deliberate consideration.
Ad-vīṣe'ment, n. Caution; advice; counsel.
Ad-vīṣ'er, n. One who advises: a counselor.
Ad-vī'ṣo-ry, a. Having power to advise; giving advice.
Ad'vo-ca-çy, n. Act of pleading; intercession; support.
Ad'vo-cate, n. One who pleads for another; a defender.
Ad'vo-cāte, v. t. To plead in favor of; to support; to vindicate.
Ad'vo-cā'tion, n. Act of pleading; a plea.
Ad'vow-ee', n. One who has the right of advowson.
Ad-vow'ṣon, n. The right of presenting a priest to a vacant benefice.
A'dy-nâm'ic, a. Pertaining to debility; weak; feeble.
†Ad'y-tŭm, n. [Lat.] A secret apartment in a temple.
Adz, } n.
Adze, } A tool with an arched blade or chipping. Adz.
Æ-ō'li-an, a. Pertaining to, or produced by, the wind. — Eolian harp, a stringed instrument played on by the wind.
A-ē'ri-al (41), a. [Lat. aër, air.] Belonging to the air; high.

Aē'rie (ē'rỹ or ā'rỹ), n. The nest of an eagle or other bird of prey. [acrifying.
A'er-i-fi-cā'tion, n. Act of
A'er-i-fôrm, a. Having the form of air, as gas.
A'er-i-fỹ, v. t. To combine or fill with air.
A'er-ŏg'ra-phy, n. Description of the air.
A'er-o-līte, n. [Gr. aēr, air, and lithos, stone.] A meteoric stone.
A'er-ŏl'o-ġy, n. The science which treats of the air.
A'er-o-mân'çy, n. Divination by means of the air, or of substances found in it.
A'er-ŏm'e-ter, n. An instrument for measuring the weight or density of air and gases.
A'er-ŏm'e-try, n. Art or science of ascertaining the mean bulk of gases.
A'er-o-naut', n. An aerial navigator; a balloonist.
A'er-o-naut'ic (120), a. Pertaining to, or practicing, aërial sailing.
A'er-o-naut'ics, n. sing. The art of sailing in the air.
A'er-o-naut'iṣm, n. Practice of ascending in balloons.
A'er-ŏs'co-py, n. Observation of the state and variations of the atmosphere.
A'er-o-stăt'ic, } a. Relating to
A'er-o-stăt'ic-al, } aërostatics.
A'er-o-stăt'ics, n. sing. The science that treats of the equilibrium of elastic fluids.
A'er-os-tā'tion, n. Aërial navigation; aëronautics.
Æs-thĕt'ic, a. Pertaining to æsthetics.
Æs-thĕt'ics, n. sing. The theory or philosophy of taste; the science of the beautiful.
A-fär', adv. At a great distance; far.
A-fēard', a. Affected with fear.
Af'fa-bĭl'i-ty, n. Readiness to converse; civility.
Af'fa-ble, a. Easy of manners or conversation; courteous.
Af'fa-bly, adv. In an affable manner; courteously.
Af-fâir', n. Business; a partial or minor engagement.
Af-fĕct', v. t. To act upon; to influence; to dispose or incline; to aim at; to make a show of.
Af'fec-tā'tion, n. False show;

artificial appearance; insincerity; pretense.
Af-fĕct'ed, a. Disposed; full of affectation.
Af-fĕct'ed-ly, adv. With affectation.
Af-fĕct'ing, a. Moving the feelings; pathetic.
Af-fĕc'tion, n. Love; fondness; inseparable attribute or quality; disease.
Af-fĕc'tion-ate, a. Fond; tender; loving; kind.
Af-fĕc'tion-ate-ly, adv. With affection; tenderly.
Af-fĕct'ive, a. Affecting or exciting emotion.
Af-fī'ançe, n. A marriage contract; confidence; trust. — v. t. To betroth; to contract.
Af-fī'an-çer, n. One who affiances.
Af-fī'ant, n. One who makes an affidavit.
Af'fi-dā'vit, n. A sworn statement in writing.
Af-fĭl'i-āte, v. t. To adopt; to receive as a member.
Af-fĭl'i-ā'tion, n. Adoption; legal assignment of a child to its father.
Af'fi-nage, n. Art of refining metals by the cupel.
Af-fĭn'i-ty, n. Relation by marriage; close agreement; chemical attraction.
Af-fĭrm', v. t. To establish or ratify; to declare positively. — SYN. To aver; protest; assert; asseverate.
Af-fĭrm'a-ble, a. Capable of being affirmed.
Af-fĭrm'ançe, n. Confirmation; declaration.
Af-fĭrm'ant, n. One who affirms.
Af'fir-mā'tion, n. A solemn declaration; confirmation; ratification.
Af-fĭrm'a-tive, a. Affirming; declaratory; confirmative. — n. That which contains an affirmation.
Af-fĭrm'a-tive-ly, adv. Positively; absolutely.
Af-fĭx', v. t. [Lat. affigere, affixus, to fasten to.] To attach; to fasten to the end; to annex; to fix.
Af'fĭx, n. A syllable or letter joined to the end of a word.
Af-fĭxt'ûre, n. That which is affixed or annexed.
Af-flā'tion, n. A blowing or breathing upon.
Af-flā'tus, n. Breath; blast; inspiration.

sŏn, ôr, dọ, wǫlf, tōō, tǒǒk; ûrn, rụe, pụll; ç, ġ, soft; c, g, hard; aṣ; ex̱ist; ɳ as ng; this.

AFFLICT 32 AGONISM

Af-flict', *v. t.* To give pain to; to trouble; to distress.
Af-flict'ed, *a.* Troubled; suffering distress.
Af-flict'ing, *a.* Grievous; distressing.
Af-flic'tion, *n.* State of being afflicted; sorrow; calamity; distress.
Af-flict'ive, *a.* Distressing; painful.
Af'flu-ençe, *n.* Abundance; wealth; riches.
Af'flu-ent, *a.* Wealthy; rich; plentiful; abundant.
Af'flux, } *n.* The act of
Af-flūx'ion, } flowing to; that which flows to.
Af-fōrd', *v. t.* To yield; to confer; to supply; to furnish; to be able to sell, exchange, or expend.
Af-fōr'est, *v. t.* To turn into forest.
A-foul', *adv.* Not free; entangled.
Af-frăn'chiṣe (-chīz), *v. t.* To make free; to enfranchise.
Af-frāy', *n.* A tumultuous quarrel; brawl; fray.
Af-fright' (-frīt'), *v. t.* To frighten; to terrify; to alarm. — *n.* Sudden fear.
Af-frŏnt' (-frŭnt'), *n.* Open disrespect or ill-treatment. — *v. t.* To insult; to offend.
Af-frŏnt'ive, *a.* Giving offense.
Af-fūṣe', *v. t.* To pour upon.
Af-fū'sion, *n.* Act of pouring upon.
A-field', *adv.* To, in, or on the field.
A-flōat', *adv.* or *a.* Swimming; in a floating state.
A-foot', *adv.* On foot; in action.
A-fōre', *adv.* or *prep.* Before.
A-fōre'said (-sĕd), *a.* Named before.
A-fōre'tīme, *adv.* In time past.
A-fraid', *a.* Struck with fear. — SYN. Fearful; apprehensive; timid; alarmed; frightened; appalled.
A-frĕsh', *adv.* Anew; again.
Aft, *adv.* or *a.* Near the stern; astern; abaft.
Aft'er, *prep.* Later in time; behind; in search or imitation of; concerning. — *a.* Subsequent; more aft. — *adv.* Subsequently in time or place.
Aft'er-bĭrth, *n.* The membrane inclosing the fetus, coming away after delivery.

Aft'er-clăp, *n.* An unexpected subsequent event.
Aft'er-crŏp, *n.* A second crop.
Aft'er-măth, *n.* Second crop of grass.
Aft'er-mōst, *a.* Hindmost; nearest the stern.
Aft'er-nōon', *n.* The time from noon to evening.
Aft'er-pāinş, *n. pl.* Pains succeeding childbirth.
Aft'er-pièçe, *n.* A piece performed after a play.
Aft'er-thôught (-thawt), *n.* Reflection after an act.
Aft'er-ward, } *adv.* In time
Aft'er-wardṣ, } subsequent.
A-gain' (-gĕn'), *adv.* Another time; once more; in return.
A-gainst' (-gĕnst'), *prep.* Opposite to; in opposition to; in provision for.
A-gāpe', *adv.* With the mouth wide open; with staring surprise.
Ăg'ate, *n.* [From the river *Achates*, in Sicily.] A kind of quartz; a kind of type; thus,
☞ Agate type.
Ăg'a-tine, *a.* Pertaining to, or resembling, agate.
A-gā've, *n.* The great American aloe.
Āge, *n.* Any period of time; a particular period; decline of life; mature years; a generation; a century.
Āged (57), *a.* Advanced in age; old; being of the age of.
Ā'gen-çy, *n.* Quality of acting or state of action; office of an agent or factor.
Ā'gent, *n.* One who acts as a deputy; an active cause or power.
Ag-glŏm'er-āte, *v. t.* To gather into a ball or mass.
Ag-glŏm'er-ate, *a.* Collected into a ball or heap.
Ag-glŏm'er-ā'tion, *n.* Act of gathering into a ball; close collection.
Ag-glū'ti-nant, *a.* Uniting as glue; causing adhesion. — *n.* Any viscous or adhesive substance.
Ag-glū'ti-nāte, *v. t.* To cause to adhere or unite.
Ag-glū'ti-nā'tion, *n.* Act of uniting, as by glue; adhesion. [to unite.
Ag-glū'ti-na-tive, *a.* Tending
Ăg'grand-īze, *v. t.* To make great; to enlarge; to exalt.
Ăg-grăn'dīze-ment, or **Ăg'-grăn-dīze'ment**, *n.* Act of aggrandizing, or state of being aggrandized; exaltation.

Ăg'gra-vāte, *v. t.* To make worse; to exaggerate; to enhance; to provoke.
Ăg'gra-vā'tion, *n.* The act of aggravating.
Ăg'gre-gāte, *v. t.* To collect.
Ăg'gre-gate, *a.* Formed of parts collected. — *n.* A sum or assemblage of particulars.
Ăg'gre-gate-ly, *adv.* In a mass.
Ăg'gre-gā'tion, *n.* The act of collecting into a mass; mass formed by collection of parts or particulars.
Ăg'gre-gā'tive, *a.* Causing aggregation; collective.
Ag-grĕss', *v. i.* To attack or assault first.
Ag-grĕs'sion (-grĕsh'un), *n.* First attack; invasion, or encroachment.
Ag-grĕss'ive, *a.* Making the first attack.
Ag-grĕss'or, *n.* One who begins to attack, or injure.
Ag-griēv'ançe, *n.* Injury.
Ag-griēve', *v. t.* To afflict; to oppress or injure; to harass.
Ag-group' (-groop'), *v. t.* To bring together; to group.
A-ghäst', *adv.* Amazed; stupefied with horror.
Ăg'ĭle, *a.* Quick of motion. — SYN. Nimble; active; lively; brisk.
Ăg'ĭle-ness, } *n.* Activity
A-gĭl'ĭ-ty, } quickness.
Ā'gĭ-o (140), *n.* Difference in value between metallic and paper money; premium.
Ăg'ĭ-ta-ble, *a.* Capable of being agitated.
Ăg'ĭ-tāte, *v. t.* To disturb; to perturb; to discuss.
Ăg'ĭ-tā'tion, *n.* Disturbance; discussion.
Ăg'ĭ-tā'tor, *n.* One who agitates.
Ăg'let, *n.* A tag; a point at the end of a fringe.
Ăg'nāil, *n.* A disease of the nails; a whitlow.
Ăg'nāte, *a.* Related or akin by the father's side.
Ag-nā'tion, *n.* Relation by the father's side.
Ag-nō'men, *n.* An additional name given on account of some exploit.
A-gō', *adv.* In time past; past.
A-gŏg', *adv.* In a state of eager desire or curiosity.
A-gō'ing, *p. pr.* In motion.
Ăg'o-niṣm, *n.* Contention for a prize.

Ag'o-nist, *n.* One who contends for the prize in public games.

Ag'o-nist'ic, *a.* Relating
Ag'o-nist'ic-al, to any violent contest, bodily or mental.

Ag'o-nize, *v. i.* To writhe with agony; to suffer anguish.— *v. t.* To cause to suffer agony; to torture.

Ag'o-ny, *n.* Excessive pain of body or mind.— SYN. Anguish; pang.

A-grā'ri-an, *a.* Relating to an equal division of lands or property.— *n.* One who favors an equal division of property.

A-grā'ri-an-ĭşm, *n.* An equal division of land or property

A-gree', *v. i.* To be of one mind; to be in concord; to harmonize; to yield assent; to suit; to correspond in gender, number, case, or person.

A-gree'a-ble (137), *a.* Agreeing or suitable; in conformity; pleasing to the mind or senses.

A-gree'a-bly, *adv.* In an agreeable manner; conformably.

A-gree'ment, *n.* Act or state of agreeing; concord; harmony; bargain; compact.

A-grĕs'tic, *a.* Relating to the country; rustic; rural.

Ag'ri-cŭlt'ūr-al, *a.* Relating to agriculture.

Ag'ri-cŭlt'ūre, *n.* Art of cultivating the ground; husbandry; tillage.

Ag'ri-cŭlt'ūr-ist, *n.* A farmer.

A-ground', *adv.* On the ground; stranded.

Ā'gue (ā'gū), *n.* Chilliness; an intermitting fever.

Ā'gu-ĭsh (133), *a.* Shivering; chilly; partaking of ague.

Äh, *interj.* An exclamation expressive of surprise, triumph, &c., according to the mode of utterance.

Ä-hä', *interj.* An exclamation denoting triumph, contempt, surprise, &c. [forward.

A-hĕad', *adv.* Further on;

Aid, *v. t.* To help; to assist.— *n.* Help; assistance; succor.

Aid'-de-camp (ăd'-de-kŏng),
Ā-de-de-camp *n.* (*pl.* **Aids'-de-camp** or **Aides-de-camp**;.) An officer who assists a general.

Ail, *n.* Disorder; indisposition.— *v. t.* To affect with pain or uneasiness; to be the matter with; to trouble.

Ail'ment, *n.* Illness; morbid affection.

Aim, *n.* Direction; endeavor; design; purpose; intention.
— *v. i.* or *t.* To point, or direct as a weapon.

Aim'less, *a.* Without aim.

Air (3), *n.* The fluid we breathe; atmosphere; a tune; peculiar manner or appearance; mien; show of pride. — *v. t.* To expose to the air; to ventilate; to dry by air and warmth.

Air'-blăd'der, *n.* An organ in some fishes, filled with air, enabling them to maintain their equilibrium in water.

Air'-çĕllş, *n. pl.* Cavities containing air.

Air'-gŭn, *n.* A gun discharged by means of compressed air.

Air'-hōle, *n.* A hole to admit or discharge air.

Air'i-ly, *adv.* Gayly; merrily.

Air'i-ness, *n.* Openness to the air; gayety; levity.

Air'ing, *n.* An excursion in the open air; exposure to air.

Air'less, *a.* Void of air; close.

Air'-pŭmp, *n.* A machine for exhausting the air from a closed vessel. Air-pump.

Air'-shăft, *n.* A passage for air into a mine.

Air'-tight (-tit), *a.* So tight as not to admit air.

Air'y, *a.* Open to the air; gay; unsubstantial.

Aisle (īl), *n.* Wing of a building; a passage in a church.

A-jär', *adv.* Partly open.

A-kĭm'bo, *adv.* With a crook.

A-kĭn', *a.* Related by blood; allied by nature.

Al'a-băs'ter, *n.* A soft, translucent variety of sulphate or carbonate of lime.

A-lăck', *interj.* An exclamation expressive of sorrow.

A-lăck'a-dāy, *interj.* An exclamation denoting sorrow.

A-lăc'ri-ty, *n.* Cheerful readiness or willingness; liveliness.

Al'a-mōde', *adv.* In the fashion.— *n.* A kind of thin glossy black silk.

A-lärm', *n.* [It. *all' arme,* to arms!] A notice of danger; sudden surprise and fear. — *v. t.* To give notice of danger; to disturb; to terrify.

A-lärm'-clŏck, *n.* A clock made to sound an alarm.

A-lärm'ist, *n.* One who intentionally excites alarm.

A-lăs', *interj.* An exclamation expressive of sorrow.

A-lāte', *a.* Winged; having expansions like wings.
A-lāt'ed,

Ălb, *n.* [Lat. *albus,* white.] A vestment of white linen worn by Roman Catholic priests.

Ăl'ba-trŏss, *n.* A large, web-footed sea-bird found in the Southern Ocean.

Al-bē'it, *adv.* Although; notwithstanding.

Al-bĕs'çent, *a.* Becoming white or whitish.

Al-bī'no, *n.* (*pl.* **Al-bī'nŏs,** 140). A person or animal preternaturally white; especially, a white negro.

Ăl'bu-gĭn'e-oŭs, *a.* Relating to the white of an egg, or to the white of an eye.

Ăl'bum, *n.* A blank book for autographs, &c.

Al-bū'men, *n.* A peculiar animal substance found nearly pure in the white of an egg.

Al-bûr'num, *n.* White soft part of wood.

Ăl'ca-hĕst, *n.* A universal
Ăl'ka-hĕst, solvent.

Al-caïd', *n.* A Spanish governor or warden.

Al-chĕm'ic-al, Relating to, or produced by, alchemy.

Ăl'che-mist, *n.* One who practices alchemy.

Ăl'che-my, *n.* Occult chemistry; the art of changing base metals into gold.

Ăl'co-hŏl, *n.* Pure or highly rectified spirit.

Ăl'co-hŏl'ic, *a.* Pertaining to, or partaking of, alcohol.

Ăl'co-rän, *n.* The sacred book of the Mohammedans.

Ăl'cove, or **Al-cōve'** (111), *n.* A recess in a library or other room. [varieties.

Ăl'der, *n.* A tree of several

Ăl'der-man (143), *n.* A magistrate ranking below a mayor.

Āle, *n.* [A.-S. *eale,* fr. *alan,* to nourish.] A fermented malt liquor.

Āle'-house, *n.* A place where ale is retailed.

A-lĕm'bic, *n.* Chemical vessel used in distilling.

A-lẽrt', *a.* [It. *all' erta,* on one's guard.] On the watch; vigilant; brisk; prompt.

A-lẽrt'ness, *n.* Watchfulness; briskness; activity.

són, ôr, dọ, wọlf, tōō, tōŏk; ûrn, rye, pụll; ç, ġ, *soft;* c, ġ, *hard;* aş; eẋist; ŋ *as* ng; this.

Āle′wīfe (142), n. A kind of fish resembling the herring.

Al′ex-an′drine, n. A verse of twelve syllables.

A-lex′i-phär′mic,) n. A med-
A-lex′i-tĕr′ic,   ) icine that expels or resists poison.

Al′ge-brā, n. A branch of mathematics that investigates the relations of numbers by means of letters and other symbols.

Al′ge-brā′ic,   ) a. Pertain-
Al′ge-brā′ic-al,) ing to, or performed by, algebra.

Al′go-brā′ist, n. One who is skilled in algebra.

A′li-as, adv. Otherwise. — n. A second writ; an assumed name.

'Al′i-bī, n. [Lat., elsewhere.] Another place.

Al′ien (āl′yen), a. Foreign; adverse. — n. A foreigner.

Al′ien-a-ble, a. Capable of being alienated.

Al′ien-āte, v. t. To transfer to another; to estrange.

Al′ien-ā′tion, n. Transfer; legal conveyance; estrangement.

Al′ien-ā′tor, n. One who alienates.

Al′ien-ee′, n. One to whom the title of property is transferred.

Al′i-fôrm, a. Having the shape of a wing.

A-līght′ (a-līt′), v. i. To get down; to dismount; to fall; to descend and settle.

A-līgn′ment (-līn′-), n. The adjusting of a line; the line of adjustment; ground-plan of a road.

A-līke′, adv. In the same manner. — a. Similar; without difference.

Al′i-ment, n. [Lat. alimentum, from alere, to feed.] That which nourishes. — SYN. Food; nourishment.

Al′i-mĕnt′al,   ) a. Pertain-
Al′i-mĕnt′a-ry,) ing to, or supplying, food; nutritious.

Al′i-ment-ā′tion, n. Act or power of affording nutriment.

Al′i-mĕnt′ive-ness, n. Appetite for food.

Al′i-mo-ny, n. A separate maintenance allowed a wife out of her husband's estate, on her divorce or separation from him.

Al′i-quănt, a. Not dividing without a remainder.

Al′i-quŏt, a. Dividing without a remainder.

A-līve′, a. Having life; living; active; lively; susceptible.

Al′ka-hĕst, n. A pretended universal solvent.

Al′ka-lĕs′cent, a. Tending to the properties of an alkali.

Al′ka-li, or Al′ka-lī, n. (pl. Al′ka-lies, -līz or -līz.) A caustic substance which neutralizes acids.

Al-kăl′i-fȳ, or Al′ka-li-fȳ, v. t. To convert into an alkali. — v. i. To become changed into an alkali.

Al′ka-line (-lĭn or -līn), a. Having the qualities of alkali.

Al′ka-līze, v. t. To make alkaline.

Al′ka-loid, a. A vegetable principle possessing alkaline properties.

Al′ko-răn, n. The Koran; the Mohammedan Bible.

All, a. Every one; comprising the whole number. — n. The whole; everything; the total. — adv. Wholly; completely; entirely; quite.

Al′lah, n. The Arabic name for God.

Al-lāy′, v. t. To make quiet; to put at rest or bring down. — SYN. To check; appease; calm; pacify; assuage; mitigate; repress.

Al-lāy′ment, n. Act of allaying or state of being allayed; that which allays.

Al′le-gā′tion, n. Positive affirmation or assertion; declaration.

Al-lēge′ (al-lĕj′), v. t. To assert positively; to declare; to plead in excuse; to cite.

Al-lē′giance, n. The duty of fidelity which a subject owes to his government; loyalty; fealty.

Al′le-gŏr′ic,   ) a. In the
Al′le-gŏr′ic-al,) manner of allegory; figurative.

Al′le-gŏr′ic-al-ly, adv. In an allegorical manner.

Al′le-go-rīze, v. t. To form or turn into allegory. — v. i. To use allegory.

Al′le-go-ry, n. A figurative sentence or discourse; a parable.

Al-lē′gro, adv. Quick; lively. — n. A quick, sprightly movement in music.

Al′le-lū′iă (-lū′yȧ),) n. Praise
Al′le-lū′iah,   ) Jehovah; a song or ascription of praise to God.

Al-lē′vi-āte, v. t. To make light; to ease; to lessen.

Al-lē′vi-ā′tion, n. Act of alleviating or making light.

Al-lē′vi-a-tive, n. Something that alleviates or mitigates.

Al′ley (141), n. A narrow walk or passage. [April.

All-fōōls′-dāy, n. The first of

All-fōurs′, n. A game at cards.

All-hāil′, interj. All health; a phrase of salutation.

All-hăl′lōws, n. All-Saints day, the first of November.

Al-lī′ance, n. Union by treaty or marriage; confederacy; league; parties allied.

Al′li-gāte, v. t. To tie or join together.

Al′li-gā′tion, n. A rule of arithmetic.

Al′li-gā′tor, n. [Sp. el lagarto, the lizard.] A large amphibious reptile; the American crocodile. Alligator.

Al-lī′sion (al-līzh′un), n. Act of striking or dashing.

Al-lit′er-ā′tion, n. Repetition of the same letter at the beginning of two or more successive words.

Al-lit′er-a-tive, a. Pertaining to, or consisting in, alliteration.

Al′lo-cā′tion, n. A putting one thing to another.

Al′lo-cū′tion, n. Act or manner of addressing; address.

Al-lō′di-al, a. Free of rent or service; freehold.

Al-lō′di-um, n. Land which is the absolute property of the owner: freehold estate.

Al-lônge′ (-lŭnj′), n. A pass or thrust made in fencing.

Al′lo-păth′ic, a. Pertaining to allopathy.

Al-lŏp′a-thy (117), n. The ordinary theory and practice of medicine as opposed to homeopathy. [lot; to distribute.

Al-lŏt′ (129), v. t. To give by

Al-lŏt′ment. n. Act of allotting: share allotted.

Al-lōw′, v. t. To permit; to grant; to yield; to make abatement.

Al-lōw′a-ble, a. Proper to be allowed; permissible.

Al-lōw′a-bly, adv. In an allowable manner.

Al-lōw′ance, n Act of allowing; that which is allowed; permission; sanction; abatement: — v. t. To limit to a

ALLOY 35 ALUMINOUS

certain quantity of food or drink.

Al-loy', n. A compound of two or more metals; a baser metal mixed with a fine. — v. t. To debase by mixing.

Al-loy'age, n. Act of alloying or mixing metals.

All-saints'-day, n. The first day of November.

All-souls'-day, n. The second day of November.

All'spiçe, n. The berry of the pimento.

Al-lūde', v. i. To refer to without direct mention. — SYN. To hint; to insinuate; to suggest.

Al-lūre', v. t. To attempt to draw to. — SYN. To entice; decoy; seduce.

Al-lūre'ment, n. That which allures or entices.

Al-lūr'ing (133), a. Having power to allure; enticing.

Al-lū'gion, n. Reference; properly, indirect reference.

Al-lū'sive, a. Having allusion, or indirect reference.

Al-lū'vi-al, a. Pertaining to, or composed of, alluvium.

Al-lū'vi-on,) n. (pl. †Al-lū'-
Al-lū'vi-um,) vi-â.) Earth deposited by water.

Al-ly' (19), n. [Lat ad, to, and ligare, to bind.] One united to another by treaty, or by any tie; a confederate. — v. t. To unite by compact.

†Ăl'ma Mā'ter. [Lat., fostering mother.] A college or seminary where one is educated.

Al'ma-nae (127), n. A calendar of months, weeks, days, &c.

Al-mīght'i-ness (-mīt'-), n. Power to do all things; omnipotence.

Al-mīght'y (-mīt'-), a. All-powerful; omnipotent. — n. The omnipotent God.

Ăl'mond (ä'mund), n. The fruit of the almond-tree, a tree much resembling the peach; one of two glands in the throat; tonsil.

Ăl'mon-er, n. A distributer of alms for another.

Ăl'mon-ry, n. Place for distributing alms.

Al-mōst' (139), adv. Nearly; well-nigh: for the most part.

Ălms (ämz), n. sing. and pl. Any thing given to relieve the poor. [of charity.

Ălms'-deed (ämz'-), n. Act

Ălms'-ġiv'ing, n. Bestowment of charity.

Ălms'-house, n. A house for the use of the poor.

Ăl'ōe (140), n. A tree of several species; the inspissated juice of the tree, used as a drug.

Ăl'o-ēt'ic,) a. Pertaining
Ăl'o-ēt'ic-al,) to, or partaking of the qualities of, aloes.

A-lŏft', adv. On high; above.

A-lōne', a. Single; solitary. — adv. Separately.

A-lŏng', adv. Lengthwise; onward; forward; together. — All along, the whole way; throughout. — prep. By the length of. [side.

A-lŏng-sīde', adv. Side by

A-lŏŏf', adv. At or from a distance; apart. — prep. At a distance from; away from.

A-loud', adv. Loudly.

Ăl-pāe'ä (140), n. The Peruvian sheep, or llama, and the cloth made of its wool.

†Ăl'phä, n. First letter of the Greek alphabet, answering to A in English; the beginning.

Ăl'pha-bet. n. [Gr. alpha, beta, the two first Greek letters.] The letters of a language arranged in order. — v. t. To arrange in the order of an alphabet.

Ăl'pha-bĕt'ic,) a. Pertain-
Ăl'pha-bĕt'ic-al,) ing to, or in the order of, an alphabet.

Ăl'pha-bĕt'ic-al-ly, adv. In alphabetic order.

Ăl'pīne, a. Pertaining to the Alps, or to any lofty mountain; very high.

Al-rĕad'y (139), adv. At or before this time; now.

Ăl'sō, adv. or conj. In the same manner; likewise; too.

Ăl'tar, n. A place for offerings to some deity; the communion table.

Ăl'tar-piēçe, n. A painting or piece of sculpture over or behind the altar.

Alpaca.

Ăl'ter, v. t. To make some change in. — v. i. To change; to vary.

Ăl'ter-a-ble, a. Capable of being altered. [ably.

Ăl'ter-a-bly, adv. Change-

Ăl'ter-ant, a. Producing a gradual change. — n. An alterative. [ing; change.

Ăl'ter-ā'tion, n. Act of alter-

Ăl'ter-a-tive, a. Causing alteration. — n. A medicine that gradually produces a change in the habit or constitution.

Ăl'ter-cāte, v. i. To contend in words; to wrangle.

Ăl'ter-cā'tion, n. Warm contention in words; controversy; wrangle; dispute.

Al-tēr'nate, a. Being by turns. — n. That which happens by turns; a vicissitude.

Ăl'ter-nāte, or Al-tēr'nāte (114), v. t. To perform by turns. — v. i. To happen or to act by turns.

Al-tēr'nate-ly, adv. By turns.

Ăl'ter-nā'tion, n. Act of alternating; reciprocal succession.

Al-tēr'na-tive, n. Choice of two things. — a. Offering a choice of two things.

Al-tēr'na-tive-ly, adv. Reciprocally; by turns.

Al-thē'ä, n. A shrub.

Ăl-though' (ąl-thō'), conj. Grant; allow or admit that; notwithstanding.

Al-tĭm'e-ter, n. An instrument for taking altitudes by geometrical principles.

Al-tĭm'e-try, n. Art of measuring heights.

Al-tĭs'o-nant,) a. High-
Al-tĭs'o-noŭs,) sounding; lofty; pompous.

Ăl'ti-tūde, n. The height of an object; elevation.

Ăl'to, adv. High. — n. The counter tenor.

Ăl'to-ġĕth'er (139), adv. Wholly; entirely; without exception; conjointly.

Ăl'u-del, n. A chemical pot for sublimation of mercury.

Al'um, n. A peculiar astringent mineral substance.

A-lū'mi-nä,) n. One of the
Al'u-mīne,) earths. When pure it is called sapphire.

Ăl'u-mĭn'i-um,) n. A light,
A-lū'mi-num,) white metal, the metallic base of alumina.

A-lū'mi-noŭs, a. Containing or resembling alum.

†A-lŭm'nus, n. (pl. A-lŭm'nī, 147). A pupil; a graduate.
Al've-o-late, a. Pitted like a honey-comb. [belly.
Al'vine, a. Belonging to the
Al'way ¦ (139), adv. Forever;
Al'ways ¦ perpetually; constantly.
Am. The first person of To be.
A-māin', adv. With all force; suddenly.
A-măl'gam, n. A compound of quicksilver with another metal.
A-măl'gam-āte, v. t. To combine with quicksilver; to unite or absorb.
A-măl'gam-ā'tion, n. The act of amalgamating.
A-măn'u-ĕn'sis, n. (pl. †A-măn'u-ĕn'sēs.) A writer of what another dictates; a copyist.
Ăm'a-ranth, n. [Gr. amarantos, not withering.] An ornamental plant with showy flowers; an imaginary flower that never fades.
Ăm'a-ranth'ĭne, a. Like amaranth; unfading.
A-măss', v. t. To collect into a heap; to accumulate.
A-măss'ment, n. A heap; collection; accumulation.
Ăm'a-teur' (-tur'), n. A lover of any one of the fine arts, not a professor.
Ăm'a-tive-ness, n. Propensity to love.
Ăm'a-to-ry; a. Relating to, or induced by, love.
†Ăm'au-rō'sis, n. Loss or decay of sight, without any visible defect in the eye.
A-māze', v. t. To astonish; to confound. — n. A mingled feeling of surprise and wonder; astonishment.
A-māze'ment (132), n. Astonishment; confusion.
A-māz'ing, a. Wonderful.
Ăm'a-zon (115), n. A warlike woman; a virago.
Ăm'a-zō'ni-an, a. Relating to, or resembling, an Amazon. [bassador.
Am-băs'sa-dor, n. See Em-
Ăm'ber, n. A yellowish fossil resin, used for ornamental purposes, varnishes, &c.
Ăm'ber-gris, n. A fragrant waxy secretion of the sperm whale.
Ăm'bi-dĕx'ter, n. One who uses both hands with equal dexterity; a double-dealer.
Ăm'bi-dex-tĕr'i-ty, n. The power of using both hands with equal ease; doublc-dealing.
Ăm'bi-dĕx'trous, a. Using both hands with equal facility.
Ăm'bi-ent. a. Encompassing; surrounding; investing.
Ăm'bi-gū'i-ty, n. Doubtfulness of meaning.
Ăm-bĭg'u-oŭs, a. Of uncertain meaning; doubtful; equivocal.
Ăm-bĭg'u-oŭs-ly, adv. Equivocally; doubtfully. [cult.
Ăm'bit, n. Compass or cir-
Am-bĭ'tion (-bĭsh'un), n. Eager desire of fame or power.
Am-bĭ'tioŭs (-bĭsh'us), a. Controlled by, or indicating, ambition; desirous of superiority.
Ăm'ble, v. t. To move with an amble. — n. Peculiar gait of a horse in which the two legs on the same side move together. [ambles or paces.
Ăm'bler, n. A horse which
Am-brō'sĭa (-brō'zhà), n. The imaginary food of the gods; genus of plants.
Am-brō'sial, ¦ a. Having the
Am-brō'sian, ¦ qualities of ambrosia; delicious.
Ăm'bro-tȳpe, n. [Gr. ambrotos, immortal, and tupos, impression.] A photographic picture taken on a plate of prepared glass.
Ămbs'-āce (āmz'ās), n. A double ace.
Ăm'bu-lance, n. A kind of moving hospital; a four-wheeled vehicle for conveying the wounded from a battle-field.
Ăm'bu-lant, a. Walking; moving from place to place.
Ăm'bu-lā'tion, n. Act of walking about.
Ăm'bu-la-to-ry, a. Able to walk; walking; movable. — n. Any part of a building intended for walking in.
Ăm'bus-cāde', n. A concealed place in which troops lie hid to attack an enemy; the troops themselves.
Ăm'bush, n. The act or place of lying in wait; troops posted in a concealed place to attack an enemy; an ambuscade.
A-měl'io-rāte, v. t. To make better. — v. i. To grow better.
A-měl'io-rā'tion, n. Act of making or growing better; improvement; melioration.
Ā'mĕn'. [Heb., firm, true.] So be it; verily; truly. —
n. Truth; one who is true.
A-mē'na-ble. a. Liable to give account; responsible; answerable.
A-mĕnd', v. t. To change in any way for the better. —
v. i. To grow better. — SYN. To correct; reform; rectify.
A-mĕnd'a-ble, a. Capable of being amended.
A-mĕnd'a-to-ry, a. Containing amendment; corrective.
†A-mende' (ä-möngd'), n. [Fr. A pecuniary fine; reparation; retraction.
A-mĕnd'ment, n. A change for the better; improvement.
A-mĕnds', n. sing. and pl. Compensation; recompense; satisfaction.
A-mĕn'i-ty, n. Pleasantness; agreeableness of situation or of manners.
A-mĕrçe' (12), v. t. To punish with a fine; to mulct.
A-mĕrçe'a-ble, a. Capable of being amerced; liable to a fine. [fine.
A-mĕrçe'ment, n. Arbitrary
A-mĕr'çer, n. One who amerces, or imposes a fine.
A-mĕr'i-can, a. Pertaining to America, and, specifically, to the United States. — n. A native of America; a native of the United States.
A-mĕr'i-can-ĭsm, n. A word, phrase, or idiom peculiar to America, or to the United States.
A-mĕr'i-can-īze, v. t. To render American.
Ăm'e-thȳst, n. A precious stone of a violet-blue color.
Ăm'e-thȳst'ĭne, a. Pertaining to, or like, amethyst.
Ā'mi-a-bĭl'i-ty, n. Amiableness; lovableness.
Ā'mi-a-ble, a. Worthy of love; lovely; lovable.
Ā'mi-a-ble-ness, n. Quality of being amiable; sweetness of disposition.
Ā'mi-a-bly, adv. In an amiable manner.
Ăm'i-ăn'thus, n. An incombustible fibrous mineral substance; earth-flax.
Ăm'i-ca-ble, a. Friendly; peaceable; harmonious; kind.
A-mid', ¦ prep. In the midst
A-mĭdst', ¦ or middle of; among.
A-mĭss', a. Wrong; improper.
— adv. Improperly.

AMITY 37 ANCHORITE

Ăm'i-ty, n. Friendship; harmony; agreement; goodwill. [alkali.
Am-mō'ni-à, n. A volatile
Am-mō'ni-ăe, n. A peculiar concrete juice used in medicine.
Am-mō'ni-ăc,) a. Pertain-
Ăm'mo-ni'ae-al,) ing to, or containing, ammonia.
Ăm'mu-ni'tion (-nĭsh'un), n. Military stores, as powder, balls, bombs, &c.
Ăm'nes-ty, n. An act of general pardon.
A-mŏng', A-mŏngst', prep. Mingled or associated with.
Ăm'o-rō'so, n. A lover.
Ăm'o-roŭs, a. [Lat. amor, love.] Pertaining to love; inclined to love; enamored; passionate.
A-mŏr'phoŭs, a. Having no determinate form.
A-mŏr'ti-zā'tion,) n. Act or
A-mŏr'tize-ment,) right of alienating lands to a corporation. [a corporation.
A-mŏr'tīze, v. t. To convey to
A-moŭnt', v. i. To come in the aggregate; to be equivalent. — n. The sum total; aggregate.
A-moŭr', n. A love intrigue; an affair of gallantry.
Ăm-phĭb'i-an, n. An animal that lives on land or in water.
Am-phĭb'I-oŭs, a. Living in two different elements.
Am-phĭb'i-oŭs-ness, n. Quality of being amphibious.
Ăm'phi-bŏl'o-ġy, n. Discourse or proposition of doubtful meaning.
Ăm'phi-brăch, n. A metrical foot of three syllables, the middle one long, the others short.
Ăm'phi-thē'a-ter,) n. (151)
Ăm'phi-thē'a-tre,) An edifice of a circular or oval form, used for public sports.
Ăm'phi-the-ăt'ric-al, a. Pertaining to an amphitheater.
Ăm'ple. a. Large; extended; liberal; diffusive; wide.
Am-plĕx'i-caul, a. Surrounding, or clasping, the stem.
Ăm'pli-fi-cā'tion, n. Enlargement; diffusive description or discourse. [amplifies.
Ăm'pli-fī'er (135), n. One who
Ăm'pli-fy, v. t. To enlarge; to treat copiously. — v. i. To become large; to dilute.
Ăm'pli-tūde, n. Largeness; extent; capacity. [ly.
Ăm'ply, adv. Largely; liberal-

Ăm'pul-lā'ceoŭs, a. Swelling, as a bottle. [as a limb.
Ăm'pu-tāte, v. t. To cut off,
Ăm'pu-tā'tion, n. Act of cutting off a limb.
A-mŭck', n. Act of killing. —
To run amuck, to rush out frantically, attacking all that come in the way.
Ăm'u-let, n. Something worn to prevent evil; a charm.
A-mūṣe', v. t. To entertain agreeably; to delude. — SYN. To divert; entertain.
A-mūṣe'ment, n. That which amuses. [amusement.
A-mūṣ'ing (133), a. Affording
A-mū'sive, a. Having power to amuse.
A-mȳg'da-late, a. Pertaining to, or made of, almonds. — n. An emulsion made of almonds.
A-mȳg'da-līne, a. Pertaining to, or like, almonds.
Ăm'y-lā'ceoŭs, a. Pertaining to, or resembling, starch.
Ăn. [A.-S. an, ane, one.] One; any; — the same as a, the indefinite article.
Ăn'a-băp'tist, n. [Gr. ana, again, and baptizein, to baptize.] One who holds that infant baptism is not valid, and that adults should be baptized again.
A-năch'ro-niṣm (-năk'-), n. An error in chronology.
Ăn'a-cŏn'dà (140), n. A large serpent of the Boa family.
A-năc're-ŏn'tic, a. Pertaining to Anacreon, a Greek poet; amatory; convivial.
Ăn'a-glyph, n. An embossed or chased ornament.
Ăn'a-gŏg'ic-al, a. Mysterious; mystical; spiritual.
Ăn'a-gram, n. Transposition of the letters of a name or word.
Ăn'a-lĕp'tic, a. Giving strength after disease. — n. A restorative medicine.
Ăn'a-lŏġ'ic-al, a. According to analogy.
Ăn'a-lŏġ'ic-al-ly, adv. By way of analogy.
A-năl'o-ġīze, v. t. To explain by analogy.
A-năl'o-goŭs, a. Having analogy or resemblance.
A-năl'o-ġy, n. Agreement between things which are in most respects entirely unlike; proportion.
A-năl'y-sĭs, n. (pl. A-năl'y-sēṣ.) Resolution of any thing into its constituent elements.

Ăn'a-lȳst, n. One who analyzes.
Ăn'a-lȳt'ic,) a. Pertaining
Ăn'a-lȳt'ic-al,) to analysis; resolving into elements.
Ăn'a-lȳt'ics, n. sing. The science of analysis.
Ăn'a-lȳze, v. t. To resolve into first principles or elements. [alyzes.
Ăn'a-lȳz'er, n. One who an-
Ăn'a-pest, n. A metrical foot of one long and two short, or one accented and two unaccented, syllables.
Ăn'a-pĕst'ic, a. Pertaining to the anapest. [archy.
Ăn'areh, n. Author of an-
A-närch'ic,) a. Being
A-närch'ie-al,) without government; lawless; disorderly.
Ăn'areh-y, n. Want of government; lawlessness.
A-năth'e-mà (140), n. An ecclesiastical curse and excommunication.
A-năth'e-ma-tīze, v. t. To pronounce an anathema against.
Ăn'a-tŏm'ic-al, a. Belonging to anatomy or dissection.
A-năt'o-mĭst, n. One skilled in anatomy.
A-năt'o-my, n. [Gr. ana, up, and tome, a cutting.] Art of dissection; doctrine of the structure of the body learned by dissection; thing dissected.
Ăn'bu-ry, n. Soft tumor on horses and cows; excrescence on the roots of turnips, &c.
Ăn'ces-tor, n. One from whom a person descends; progenitor; forefather.
An-çĕs'tral (110), a. Pertaining to, or descending from, ancestors.
Ăn'çes-try, n. Series of ancestors; lineage, honorable descent.
Ăneh'or,
An iron instrument for holding a ship at rest. — v. t. To place at Anchor. anchor.— v. i. To cast anchor.
Ăneh'or-age, n. Ground for anchoring; duty paid for anchoring. [anchoret.
Ăneh'o-rĕss, n. A female
Ăneh'o-rĕt,) n. A religious
Ăneh'o-rīte,) solitary; a hermit; a recluse.

són, ôr, dọ, wọlf, tǒo, tǒok; ûrn, rụe, pụll; ç, ġ, soft; c, g̃, hard; aș; eẋist; n as ng; this.

An-cho'vy, *n.* A small sea-fish used in seasoning.
An'cient (ān'shent), *a.* Of former times; not modern; old; of great age.
An'cient-ly, *adv.* In old times; formerly.
An'cient-ry, *n.* The honor of ancient lineage.
An'cients (ān'shents), *n. pl.* Men of former times; old men.
An'cil-la-ry, *a.* Subservient or subordinate, like a handmaid.
And, *conj.* A particle expressing the relation of addition, and serving to connect words or sentences.
†**An-dān'te,** *a.* (*Mus.*) Rather slow; moderate. — *n.* A movement or piece in *andante* time.
And'i-ron (-I-urn), *n.* A utensil for supporting wood in a fire-place.
An-drŏg'y-nal, } *a.* Having
An-drŏg'y-nous, } the characteristics of both sexes; hermaphroditic.
An-ec-dōte, *n.* A short story or incident. [to anecdotes.
An'ec-dŏt'ic-al, *a.* Pertaining
An'e-mŏl'o-ġy, *n.* The doctrine of winds, or a treatise on them.
An-e-mŏm'e-ter, *n.* An instrument for measuring the force and velocity of the wind.
A-nĕm'o-ne, *n.* (Gr., from *anemos,* wind.) A plant of the crowfoot family; the wind flower.
A-nĕm'o-scōpe, *n.* An instrument for showing on a dial the course or direction of the wind.
An'eū-rĭsm, *n.* A soft pulsating tumor formed by a morbid enlargement of an artery.
A-new' (27), *adv.* Afresh; newly; over again.
An'ġel, *n.* A divine messenger; a ministering spirit; a beautiful person.
An-ġĕl'ic, } *a.* Belonging
An-ġĕl'ic-al, } to, or resembling, angels. [angel.
An-ġĕl'ic-al-ly, *adv.* Like an
An'ġel-ŏl'o-ġy, *n.* [Gr. *aggelos,* angel, and *logos,* discourse.] The doctrine respecting angels.
An'ġer, *n.* A strong passion excited by injury; resentment; rage; wrath. — *v. t.* To make angry; to provoke; to enrage.

An'ġle, *n.* A point where two lines meet; a corner; difference of direction of two lines or planes; fishing tackle. — *v. i.* To fish with a line and hook.

CAE, right angle; DAE, acute angle; BAE, obtuse angle.

An'ġler, *n.* One who angles or fishes.
An'gli-ean, *a.* English.
An'gli-çĭsm, *n.* An English idiom.
An'gli-çīze, *v. t.* To render into English.
An'gling, *n.* Act of fishing with a line and hook.
An'gri-ly (185), *adv.* With anger.
An'gry, *a.* Moved with anger; exasperated; provoked.
An-guĭn'e-al, *a.* Pertaining to a snake.
An'guish, *n.* Excessive pain.
An'gu-lar, *a.* Having angles.
An'gu-lăr'i-ty, *n.* Quality of being angular.
An'gu-lar-ly, *adv.* In an angular manner. [angles.
An'gu-lā'ted, *a.* Formed with
An'he-lā'tion, *n.* Shortness of breath. [bccile.
An'īle, *a.* Old-womanish; im-
A-nĭl'i-ty, *n.* Old age of a woman; dotage.
An'i-mad-vĕr'sion, *n.* Remarks by way of criticism or reproof. — SYN. Strictures; comment; blame.
An'i-mad-vĕrt', *v. t.* To turn the mind; to remark by way of criticism.
An'i-mal, *n.* An organized living being, endowed with sensation and voluntary motion; an irrational being. — *a.* Pertaining to animals.
An'i-măl'cu-lar, *a.* Relating to, or resembling, animalcules.
An'i-măl'cūle, *n.* (*pl.* **An'i-măl'cūles.**) An invisible or very minute animal.
An'i-măl'eu-line, *a.* Animalcular.
†**An'i-măl'eu-lum** *n.* (*pl.* **An'i-măl'eu-lă,** 147.) An animalcule.
An'i-mal-ĭsm, *n.* Animal nature; brutishness; sensuality.
An'i-măl'i-ty, *n.* Animal existence or nature.

An'i-mal-i-zā'tion, *n.* Act of giving animal life.
An'i-mal-īze (153), *v. t.* To give animal life to.
An'i-māte, *v. t.* To give life to; to quicken; to enliven.
An'i-māte (42). *a.* Possessing animal life; alive.
An'i-māt'ed, *a.* Full of life or spirit.
An'i-mā'tion, *n.* Quality of being animated; life; spirit; vigor.
An'i-mŏs'i-ty, *n.* Extreme hatred; malevolence; malignity.
†**An'i-mus,** *n.* [Lat.] Intention; purpose; spirit.
An'īse, *n.* An aromatic plant.
An'kle (ăŋk'l), *n.* The joint between the foot and the leg.
An'nal-ist, *n.* A writer of annals.
An'nals, *n. pl.* A chronological history; chronicles.
An'nats. *n. pl.* First fruits or profits of a spiritual preferment.
An-neal', *v. t.* To temper, as glass or metals, by first heating and then cooling.
An-nĕx', *v. t.* To join at the end; to subjoin; to add.
An'nex-ā'tion, *n.* Conjunction; addition; union.
An-nī'hi-la-ble. *a.* Capable of being annihilated.
An-nī'hi-lāte, *v. t.* [Lat. *ad,* to, and *nihil,* nothing.] To reduce to nothing; to destroy the specific form of a thing.
An-nī'hi-lā'tion, *n.* Act of annihilating, or reducing to nothing.
An'ni-vĕr'sa-ry, *a.* Returning with the year; annual; yearly. — *n.* A day celebrated as it returns each year.
An'no-tāte, *v. i.* To make comments or notes.
An'no-tā'tion, *n.* An explanatory note.
An'no-tā'tor, *n.* A writer of notes: a commentator.
An-nŏt'to, *n.* A kind of reddish dyeing material.
An-nounçe', *v. t.* To give notice of; to proclaim; to publish.
An-nounçe'ment, *n.* A declaration or advertisement; publication.
An-noy', *v. t.* To incommode; to vex; to molest: to pester.
An-noy'ançe, *n.* That which annoys or molests.
An'nu-al (ăn'u-al), *a.* Coming

yearly. — *n.* A plant whose root dies yearly; a yearly publication. [year.
An'nu-al-ly, *adv.* Year by
An-nū'i-tant, *n.* A person who has an annuity.
An-nū'i-ty, *n.* A yearly allowance of money.
An-nūl' (129), *v. t.* To make void; to abrogate; to abolish; to nullify.
An'nu-lar } (ăn'u-), *a.*
An'nu-la-ry } Having the form of a ring; round.
An'nu-lā-ted, *a.* Having rings or belts.
An'nu-lĕt, *n.* A little ring.
An-nŭl'ment, *n.* Act of annulling.
An'nu-lōse', *a.* Furnished with, or composed of, rings.
An-nū'mer-āte, *v. t.* To add.
An-nū'mer-ā'tion, *n.* Addition to a former number.
An-nŭn'ci-āte (-shĭ-āt), *v. t.* To announce.
An-nŭn'ci-ā'tion (-shĭ-ā'shun), *n.* The act of announcing; thing announced.
An'o-dyne, *n.* Medicine to assuage pain. — *a.* Mitigating pain.
A-noint', *v. t.* To rub, as with oil; to consecrate by the use of oil.
A-noint'ed, *n.* The Messiah.
A-noint'ment, *n.* Act of anointing.
A-nŏm'a-lism, *n.* A deviation from rule; irregularity; anomaly.
A-nŏm'a-list'ic, *a.* Irregular.
A-nŏm'a-loŭs, *a.* Deviating from rule or analogy; irregular.
A-nŏm'a-ly, *n.* That which deviates from rule; irregularity.
A-nŏn', *adv.* Soon; quickly. — *Ever and anon*, now and then.
A-nŏn'y-moŭs, *a.* [Gr. *an*, without, and *onoma*, a name.] Wanting a name; nameless.
A-nŏn'y-moŭs-ly, *adv.* Without a name.
An-ŏth'er, *a.* Some other; not the same; one more; any other.
Ăn'sāt-ed, *a.* Having a handle.
Ăn'ser-ĭne, *a.* Pertaining to, or resembling, a goose.
Ăn'swer (ăn'ser), *v. t.* To speak in reply to; to refute; to face; to suit: to atone for. — *v. i.* To reply; to account; to suit. — *n.* A reply; something done in consequence of something else; a solution.
Ăn'swer-a-ble (ăn'ser-a-bl), *a.* Capable of being answered; liable to answer; accountable; suitable.
Ăn'swer-a-bly (-ser-), *adv.* Suitably; agreeably.
Ăn'swer-er (ăn'ser-er), *n.* One who answers.
Ant, *n.* A small insect; emmet; pismire.
An-tăg'o-nĭsm, *n.* Opposition of action; contest.
An-tăg'o-nĭst, *n.* An opponent; a competitor; a contender. — *a.* Counteracting; opposing.
An-tăg'o-nĭst'ic, *a.* Opposing; antagonist.
An-tăg'o-nīze, *v. i.* To act in opposition; to strive against.
An-tăl'gĭe, *a.* Alleviating pain. — *n.* Medicine to relieve pain.
Ant-ărc'tic, *a.* Opposite to the arctic zone; relating to the southern polar region.
Ănt'ar-thrīt'ic, *a.* Counteracting the gout.
Ănt'-ēat'er, *n.* A tropical animal that lives on ants.
Ăn'te-çēd'ençe, *n.* Act of preceding in time.
Ăn'te-çēd'ent, *n.* That which goes before. — *a.* Going before in time. — SYN. Prior; preceding; previous; anterior; foregoing.
Ăn'te-çēd'ent-ly, *adv.* Previously.
Ăn'te-çēs'sor, *n.* One who goes before; predecessor.
Ăn'te-chăm'ber, *n.* A room leading into the chief apartment.
Ăn'te-dāte, *v. t.* To date before the true time; to anticipate. — *n.* A prior date; anticipation.
Ăn'te-dĭ-lū'vĭ-al, } *a.* Being
Ăn'te-dĭ-lū'vĭ-an, } before the flood in Noah's days.
Ăn'te-dĭ-lū'vĭ-an, *n.* One who lived before the flood.
Ăn'te-lōpe, *n.* A genus of animals, between the goat and the deer.
Ăn'tĕ-lū'cän, *a.* Being before light.
Ăn'te-me-rĭd'i-an, *a.* Being before noon.
Ăn'te-mŭn'dāne, *a.* Being before the creation.
†An-tĕn'nă *n. a.* (*pl.* An-tĕn'-nae, 147.) One of the feelers of an insect. *a a*, Antennae.
Ăn'te-nŭp'tial (-nŭp'shal), *a.* Being before marriage.
Ăn'te-pās'chal, *a.* Pertaining to the time before Easter.
Ăn'te-pāst, *n.* Foretaste; anticipation.
Ăn'te-pe-nŭlt', *n.* The last syllable of a word but two.
Ăn'te-pe-nŭlt'i-mate, *a.* Relating to the last syllable but two.
An-tē'ri-or, *a.* [Lat., comparative of *ante*, before.] Before in time or place; previous.
An-tē'ri-ŏr'i-ty, *n.* State of being anterior, or before in time or place.
Ăn'te-room, *n.* A room leading to the principal apartment.
Ăn'thel-mĭn'tie, *a.* Destroying or expelling worms. — *n.* A remedy for worms; a vermifuge.
Ăn'them, *n.* Church music adapted to passages from the Scriptures.
Ăn'ther, *n.* The tip of the stamen, containing the pollen.
Ăn'tho-lŏg'ic-al, *a.* Pertaining to anthology.
An-thŏl'o-gy, *n.* A collection of flowers A, Anther. or of poems.
Ăn'tho-ny's-fīre (ăn'to-), *n.* The erysipelas.
Ăn'thra-çĭte, *n.* A hard, compact kind of mineral coal.
Ăn'thra-çĭt'ic, *a.* Pertaining to anthracite.
Ăn'thro-pŏl'o-gy, *n.* Natural history of man; science of man considered in his entire nature.
Ăn'thro-po-mōr'phĭsm, *n.* Representation of God under a human form.
Ăn'thro-pŏph'a-gy, *n.* The feeding on human flesh; cannibalism.
Ăn'tic, *a.* Odd; fanciful; fantastic. — *n.* A buffoon or merry-andrew.
Ăn'tĭ-christ, *n.* A great adversary of Christ.

An'ti-chris'tian (-krĭst'yan), a. Opposing Christianity.
An-tic'i-pāte, v. t. To take or do before; to foretaste.
An-tic'i-pā'tion, n. Act of anticipating; foretaste.
An-tic'i-pā'tor, n. One who anticipates.
An'ti-cli'max, n. A sentence in which the ideas become less striking at the close.
An'ti-dō'tal, a. Efficacious
An'ti-dō'ta-ry, against poison.
An'ti-dōte, n. A remedy for
An ti-fĕb'rīle, or An'ti-fā'brĭle, a. Good against fever.
An'ti-mā'son (-sn), n. One opposed to freemasonry.
An'ti-mo-nārch'ic-al, a. Opposed to monarchy.
An'ti-mō'ni-al, a. Pertaining to, or composed of, antimony. — n. A preparation of antimony.
An'ti-mo-ny, n. A brittle white metal, and an ore of the same.
An'ti-nō'mi-an, n. One who holds good works to be not necessary to salvation. — a. Pertaining to the Antinomians.
An'ti-nō'mi-an-ĭşm, n. Tenets of the Antinomians.
An'ti-no-my, or An-tin'o-my, n. Contradiction between two laws. [Pope.
An'ti-pā'pal, a. Opposing the
An'ti-pär'a-lyt'ic, a. Good against paralysis.
An'ti-pa-thĕt'ic, a. Having antipathy.
An-tip'a-thy, n. Aversion or dislike.
An'ti-pĕs'ti-lĕn'tial, a. Counteracting infection.
An'ti-phlo-gĭst'ic, a. Counteracting inflammation. -- n. Medicine or diet to check in flammation.
An-tiph'o-nal, n. Book of antiphons. — a. Relating to, or consisting of, alternate singing.
An'ti-phon, n. Alternate
An-tiph'o-ny, or responsive singing.
An-tiph'ra-sis, n. Use of words in a sense opposite to the true one.
An-tip'o-dal, a. Pertaining to the antipodes.
An'ti-pōde, n. (pl. † An-tip'o-dēş.) [Gr. anti, opposite, and pous, podos, foot.] One living on the opposite side of the globe.

An'ti-pōpe, n. One who usurps the papal power.
An'ti-quā'ri-an, a. Pertaining to antiquity. — n. An antiquary.
An'ti-qua-ry, n. One versed in antiquities.
An'ti-quāte, v. t. To make obsolete, old, or void.
An'ti-quāt'ed, p. a. Grown old; obsolete.
An-tīque' (-teek'), a. Ancient; old. — n. A remnant of antiquity.
An-tĭq'ui-ty, n. Old times; a relic of old times.
A'ti-scor-bū'tic, a.
A'ti-scor-bū'tic-al, Good against the scurvy.
An'ti-script'ur-al, a. Not according to the Scriptures.
An'ti-sĕp'tic, a. Counteracting putrefaction.
An'ti-slāv'er-y, n. Opposition to slavery.
An'ti-spas-mŏd'ic, a. Opposing spasm.
An'ti-spăst'ic, a. Causing a revulsion of fluids or humors.
An-tĭs'tro-phe, n. A stanza alternating with another called the strophe, in ancient lyric poetry.
An-tĭth'e-sis, n. (pl. † An-tĭth'e-sēş.) Opposition of words or sentiments; contrast.
An'ti-thĕt'ic, a. Pertain-
An'ti-thĕt'ic-al, ing to, or containing, antithesis; placed in contrast.
An'ti-type, n. That which is prefigured by the type; thus the paschal lamb was a type, of which Christ is the antitype.
An'ti-tȳp'ic-al, a. Relating to, or of the nature of, an antitype.
Ant'ler, n. Branch of a stag's horn.
An'vil, n. An iron block for hammering metals on.
Anx-ī'e-ty (ang-zī'e-ty̆), n. Trouble of mind; solicitude; concern; disquietude.
Anx'ioŭs (ăŋk'shus), a. Greatly solicitous; uneasy.
Anx'ioŭs-ly (ăŋk'shus-), adv. With solicitude.
A'ny (ĕn'ny), a. One, indefinitely; every; whoever.
Ā'o-rĭst, n. A Greek tense expressing indeterminate past time.
A-ôr'tä, n. The great artery
A-pāçe', adv. Quickly; hastily; fast; with speed.
Ap'a-gŏg'ic-al, a. Proving in-

directly by showing the absurdity of the contrary.
A-pärt', adv. Separately; aside; asunder; to pieces.
A-pärt'ment, n. A room.
Ap'a-thĕt'ic, a. Without feeling; insensible.
Ap'a-thy, n. Want of feeling; insensibility.
Āpe, n. A kind of tailless monkey; a mimic or imitator. - v. t. To imitate as an ape; to mimic.
A-pēak', adv. On the point; perpendicularly.
A-pē'ri-ent (86), a. [Lat. aperiens, opening.] Gently purgative; laxative. — n. A laxative.
Ap'er-tūre, n. An opening; a hole.
Āp'er-y, n. Practice of aping; mimicry. [petals.
A-pĕt'al-oŭs, a. Having no
Ā'pex, n. (pl. Ā'pex-eş, or † Ap'i-çēş.) The tip, point, or summit of a thing; top.
A-phær'e-sis, n. The taking
A-phĕr'e-sis, of a letter or syllable from the beginning of a word.
A-phēl'ion (a-fēl'yun), n. (pl. † A-phē'li-ä.) The point of a planet's orbit most distant from the sun.
Āph'o-rĭşm, n. A precept or principle expressed in a few words. — SYN. Axiom; maxim; adage; apothegm.
Āph'o-rĭst, n. A writer of aphorisms.
Āph'o-rĭst'ic, a. Having
Āph'o-rĭst'ic-al, the form of an aphorism.
Āph'thŏŋg (ăf- or ăp'-), n. A letter having no sound.
Ā'pi-a-ry, n. A place for bees.
A-piēçe', adv. To each one's share; each by itself.
Āp'ish, a. Like an ape. — SYN. Silly; foppish; affected.
Āp'ish-ness, n. Buffoonery.
A-pŏc'a-lypse, n. The book of Revelation.
A-pŏc'a-lyp'tic, a. Relat-
A-pŏc'a-lyp'tic-al, ing to the Apocalypse; containing revelation; mysterious.
A-pŏc'o-pāte, v. t. To cut off or drop the last letter or syllable of.
A-pŏc'o-pe, n. Omission of the last letter or syllable of a word.

APOCRYPHA 41 APPOINT

A-pŏc′ry-phả, *n.* Books of doubtful authenticity, appended to the Old Testament.
A-pŏc′ry-phal, *a.* Not authentic; doubtful.
Ap′o-dal, *a.* Having no feet.
Ap′o-gee, *n.* [Gr. *apo*, from, and *gē*, the earth.] The point in the moon's orbit most distant from the earth.
Ap′o-grăph, *n.* A copy.
A-pŏl′o-gĕt′ic, *a.* Said by
A-pŏl′o-gĕt′ic-al, way of defense or excuse.
A-pŏl′o-gĭst, *n.* One who makes an apology.
A-pŏl′o-gīze, *v. i.* To plead or make excuse.
Ap′o-lōgue (-lŏg), *n.* A moral fable. [excuse.
A-pŏl′o-ġy, *n.* A defense; an
Ap′oph-thĕgm (ăp′o-thĕm). See *Apothegm.* [apoplexy.
Ap′o-plĕc′tic, *a.* Relating to
Ap′o-plĕx′y, *n.* A disease characterized by sudden loss of sense and motion.
A-pŏs′ta-sy, *n.* A departure from professed principles.
A-pŏs′tate, *n.* One who forsakes his principles or religion. — *a.* Falling from faith.
A-pŏs′ta-tīze, *v. i.* To abandon one's faith or party.
A-pŏs′te-māte, *v. i.* To form into an abscess.
Ap′os-tēme, *n.* An abscess.
A-pŏs′tle (a-pŏs′sl), *n.* A messenger sent to execute some important business; one of the twelve disciples sent forth by Christ to preach the gospel. [apostle.
A-pŏs′tle-shĭp, *n.* Office of an
A-pŏs′to-late, *n.* Mission; apostleship.
Ap′os-tŏl′ic, *a.* Relating
Ap′os-tŏl′ic-al, to, or resembling, an apostle; taught by the apostles.
A-pŏs′to-lĭç′i-ty, *n.* State or quality of being apostolical.
A-pŏs′tro-phe, *n.* [Gr. *apo*, from, and *strophē*, a turning.] A turning from real auditors to an imagined one; contraction of a word, or the mark [′] used to denote such contraction.
Ap′o-strŏph′ic, *a.* Pertaining to, or denoting an apostrophe. [address.
A-pŏs′tro-phīze (153), *v. t.* To
A-pŏth′e-ca-ry, *n.* A compounder of medicines; a druggist.
Ap′o-thĕgm (ăp′o-thĕm),
Ap′oph-thĕgm *n.* A re-

markable saying; a maxim; an aphorism.
Ap′o-thĕg-măt′ic, *a.* Being in the manner of an apothegm.
Ap′o-thē′o-sĭs, *n.* Act of placing among the gods; deification. [deify.
Ap′o-thē′o-sīze, *v. t.* To
Ap-pall′, *v. t.* To smite with terror. — SYN. To dismay; daunt; terrify; intimidate.
Ap′pa-nage, *n.* Portion of land assigned by a prince for the subsistence of his younger son.
Ap′pa-rā′tus, *n.* (*pl.* **Ap′pa-rā′tus,** or **Ap′pa-rā′tus-es**.) Collection of implements or organs; furniture; utensils.
Ap-păr′el, *n.* Clothing; dress; vesture; raiment; equipment. — *v. t.* (130) To dress; to clothe; to attire; to deck.
Ap-păr′ent (3), *a.* Visible to the eye; seeming. — SYN. Obvious; clear; evident.
Ap-păr′ent-ly, *adv.* Plainly; clearly; in appearance.
Ap′pa-rĭ′tion (-rĭsh′un), *n.* Appearance; thing appearing; ghost; specter.
Ap-păr′i-tor, *n.* A messenger of a spiritual court.
Ap-pēal′, *n.* Removal of a cause to a higher court; reference to another as witness; resort; recourse. — *v. t.* To remove to a higher court; to accuse. — *v. i.* To remove a cause to a higher tribunal; to refer to another for decision.
Ap-pēal′a-ble, *a.* Capable of being appealed.
Ap-pēar′, *v. i.* To be in sight; to become visible; to seem.
Ap-pēar′ançe, *n.* A coming in sight; things seen; semblance; mien; a coming into court.
Ap-pēas′a-ble, *a.* Capable of being appeased.
Ap-pēase′, *v. t.* To quiet; to pacify. [quieting.
Ap-pēas′ive, *a.* Mitigating;
Ap-pēase′ment, *n.* Act of appeasing.
Ap-pĕl′lant, *n.* One who appeals. [peals.
Ap-pĕl′late. *a.* Relating to ap-
Ap′pel-lā′tion, *n.* A name by which a thing is called. — SYN. Title; address; style.
Ap-pĕl′la-tĭve, *a.* Pertaining to a common or general name. — *n.* A common, as

distinguished from a proper, name.
Ap′pel-lee′, *n.* The defendant in an appeal; one who is prosecuted by a private man for a crime.
Ap′pel-lôr′, *n.* One who prosecutes another for a crime.
Ap-pĕnd′, *v. t.* To hang or attach to; to add; to annex.
Ap-pĕnd′age, *n.* An addition; adjunct; concomitant.
Ap-pĕnd′ant, *a.* Hanging to; annexed; appended by prescription. — *n.* Something incidental or subordinate belonging to a thing.
Ap-pĕn′dix, *n.* (*pl.* **Ap-pĕn′dix-es** or †**Ap-pĕn′di-çēs**.) Something annexed; literary matter added to a book.
Ap′per-çĕp′tion, *n.* Self-consciousness.
Ap′per-tāin′, *v. i.* To belong; to relate.
Ap′pe-tençe, *n.* Strong nat-
Ap′pe-ten-çy, ural desire; eager appetite.
Ap′pe-tent, *a.* Very desirous.
Ap′pe-tīte. *n.* Desire, especially of food or drink.
Ap′pe-tīze, *v. t.* To whet the appetite.
Ap′pe-tīz′er, *n.* Something that creates or whets an appetite.
Ap-plạud′, *v. t.* To praise by clapping of hands, &c.; to commend. [plauds.
Ap-plạud′er, *n.* One who ap-
Ap-plạuse′, *n.* Approbation loudly expressed; public praise; acclamation.
Ap′ple, *n.* A tree and its fruit; the pupil of the eye.
Ap-plī′ançe, *n.* Act of applying; thing applied.
Ap′pli-ca-bĭl′i-ty, *n.* Quality of being applicable.
Ap′pli-ca-ble (135), *a.* Capable of being applied.
Ap′pli-cant, *n.* One who applies; a petitioner.
Ap′pli-cā′tion, *n.* Act of applying; entreaty; persevering industry; assiduity; request.
Ap-plȳ′, *v. t.* To lay or place; to put or bring; to devote; to address. — *v. i.* To suit; to agree; to make request.
†**Ap-pŏġ′gia-tu′rȧ,** *n.* [It.] A small note in music, indicating a passing tone.
Ap-point′, *v. t.* To fix, establish, or ordain; to set apart; to equip; to designate; to direct.

---

sŏn, ôr, dọ, wọlf, tọo, tọ̆ok; ûrn, rụe, pụll; ç, ġ, *soft*; c, ġ, *hard*; ạs; ęxist; ŋ *as* ng; this.

APPOINTABLE 42 ARCANUM

Ap-point'a-ble, *a.* Capable of being appointed.

Ap'point-ee', *n.* A person appointed.

Ap-point'ment, *n.* Act of appointing; equipment; direction.

Ap-pōr'tion, *v. t.* [Lat. *ad,* to, and *portio,* portion.] To divide and assign fairly; to allot; to distribute.

Ap-pōr'tion-ment, *n.* A dividing into just shares or proportions.

Ap'po-site, *a.* Very applicable; proper; suitable.

Ap'po-site-ly, *adv.* Properly; suitably; fitly.

Ap'po-site-ness, *n.* Fitness; suitableness.

Ap'po-si'tion (-zish'un), *n.* State of two nouns put in the same case without a connecting word.

Ap-prais'al, *n.* Valuation by authority; appraisement.

Ap-praise', *v. t.* To set a price on.

Ap-praise'ment (132), *n.* Act of appraising.

Ap-prais'er, *n.* A person appointed to appraise.

Ap-prē'cia-ble (-prē'shĭ-), *a.* Capable of being estimated.

Ap-prē'ci-āte (-shī-), *v. t.* To value; to raise the value of. — *v. i.* To rise in value.

Ap-prē'ci-ā'tion (-shĭ-ā'-shun), *n.* Act of appreciating or valuing; a just estimate.

Ap'pre-hēnd', *v. t.* To seize; to conceive by the mind; to fear.

Ap'pre-hēn'si-ble, *a.* Capable of being apprehended.

Ap'pre-hēn'sion, *n.* Act of apprehending; conception of ideas; fear; distrust.

Ap'pre-hēn'sive, *a.* Quick to apprehend; fearful.

Ap'pre-hēn'sive-ness, *n.* Quality or state of being apprehensive; fearfulness.

Ap-prēn'tice, *n.* One bound by indentures to learn a trade or art. — *v. t.* To bind as an apprentice.

Ap-prēn'tice-ship, *n.* The time an apprentice serves.

Ap-prīse' (153), *v. t.* To give notice; to inform.

Ap-prīze', *v. t.* See *Appraise.*

Ap-prōach', *v. t.* To draw near to; to approximate. — *v. i.* To draw near. — *n.* Act of drawing near; access; advance; admittance.

Ap-prōach'a-ble, *a.* Capable of being approached; accessible.

Ap-pro-bā'tion, *n.* Act of approving; liking; support.

Ap'pro-bā'tive, } *a.* Approv-

Ap'pro-bā'to-ry, } ing or implying approbation.

Ap-prō'pri-a-ble, *a.* Capable of being appropriated.

Ap-prō'pri-āte, *v. t.* To set apart for a purpose, or for one's self; to assign.

Ap-prō'pri-ate(42), *a.* Belonging peculiarly. — SYN. Fit; adapted; pertinent; suitable; proper. [erly.

Ap-prō'pri-ate-ly, *adv.* Prop-

Ap-prō'pri-ate-ness, *n.* Peculiar fitness.

Ap-prō'pri-ā'tion, *n.* Act of appropriating; a setting apart to a particular use; any thing set apart.

Ap-prŏv'a-ble, *a.* Worthy of approbation.

Ap-prŏv'al, *n.* Approbation.

Ap-prŏve', *v. t.* To like or allow of; to commend; to justify.

Ap-prŏx'i-māte, *v. t.* To bring near; to cause to approach. — *v. i.* To draw near; to approach.

Ap-prŏx'i-mate (42), *a.* Near; nigh. [proach.

Ap-prŏx'i-mā'tion, *n.* Ap-

Ap-prŏx'i-mā'tive, *a.* Approaching.

Ap'pulse, or Ap-pŭlse', } *n.*

Ap-pŭl'sion (-shun), } Act of striking against.

Ap-pūr'te-nançe, *n.* That which appertains or belongs to something else. [by right.

Ap-pūr'te-nant, *a.* Belonging

Ā'pri-cōt. *n.* A kind of plum, very delicious.

Ā'pril, *n.* [Lat. *Aprilis,* from *aperire,* to open.] Fourth month of the year.

Ā'pron (ā'purn or ā'prun), *n.* A part of dress worn in front.

Ăp'ro-pōs' (-pō'), *adv.* By the way.

Apt, *a.* Fit; suitable; liable; ready; qualified.

Ăp'ter-al, *a.* Having columns only in front.

Ăp'ter-oŭs, *a.* Without wings.

Ăpt'i-tūde (50), *n.* Fitness; adaptation; tendency.

Ăpt'ly, *adv.* Properly; fitly.

Ăpt'ness, *n.* Fitness; readiness; tendency.

†**A-quā-fōr'tis,** *n.* Nitric acid.

A-quăt'ic, *a.* Living in water.

†**A'quā-vī'tæ,** *n.* Brandy.

Ăq'ue-dŭct (ăk'we-dŭkt), *n.* An artificial channel for conveying water; a conduit.

Ā'que-oŭs, *a.* Pertaining to water; watery.

A'qui-fōrm, *a.* Having the form of water.

Ăq'ui-līne (ăk'wĭ-līn *or* -lĭn), *a.* Like an eagle or its beak; hooked.

Ăr'ab, *n.* A native of Arabia.

Ăr'a-bĕsque (-bĕsk), *a.* Pertaining to, or in the manner of, Arabian architecture.

A-rā'bi-an, } *a.* Pertaining to

Ăr'a-bic, } Arabia.

Ăr'a-bic (120), *n.* The language of Arabians. [tillage.

Ăr'a-ble, *a.* Fit for plowing or

A-rā'ne-oŭs, *a.* Resembling a cobweb. [judge.

Ăr'bi-ter, *n.* An umpire; a

Ăr'bi-tra-ble, *a.* Arbitrary; determinable.

Ar-bĭt'ra-ment, *n.* Will; determination; award of arbitrators.

Ăr'bi-tra-ri-ly, *adv.* By will only; absolutely.

Ăr'bi-tra-ry, *a.* Dictated by, or depending on, will; bound by no law; absolute in power. — SYN. Tyrannical; imperious; unlimited; absolute; despotic.

Ăr'bi-trāte, *v. i. or t.* To hear and judge as an arbitrator; to decide or determine generally.

Ăr'bi-trā'tion, *n.* A hearing and decision by arbitrators.

Ăr'bi-trā'tor, *n.* An umpire; arbiter. [biter.

Ăr'bi-tress, *n.* A female ar-

Ăr'bor, *n.* A shady bower; a spindle or axis.

Ăr'bor-al, } *a.* Belonging

Ăr-bō're-oŭs, } to trees.

Ăr'bo-rĕs'çençe, *n.* The figure or resemblance of a tree.

Ăr'bo-rĕs'çent, *a.* Growing like a tree.

Ăr'bor-ĭst, *n.* One who makes trees his study.

Ăr'bor-ī-zā'tion, *n.* A tree-like appearance, especially in minerals. [a tree.

Ăr'bo-roŭs, *a.* Pertaining to

Ărc (4), *n.* Part of the circumference of a circle or curve.   Arc.

Ar-cāde', *n.* A series of arches and columns; a long arched building or gallery.

†**Ar-cā'num,** *n.* (*pl.* **Ar-cā'na.**) [Lat.] A secret.

ā, ē, ī, ō, ū, y, *long;* ă, ĕ, ĭ, ŏ, ŭ, ў, *short;* cāre, cär, ȧsk, ąll, whạt; ẽre, vẽil, tẽrm; pīque, fīrm;

Ärch, *a.* Chief; principal; waggish; sly. — *n.* A part of a circle; arc; curved or vaulted structure. **Arch.**
— *v. t.* To form into an arch. — *v. i.* To form an arch.

Är'chæ-ŏl'o-ġy, *n.* The science of antiquities.

Ar-cha'ic, *a.* Ancient; antiquated; obsolete.

Är'cha-ism, *n.* An obsolete word, expression, or style.

Ärch-ăn'ġel (ärk-), *n.* A chief angel. [op.

Ärch-bĭsh'op, *n.* A chief bishop.

Ärch-bĭsh'op-rĭe, *n.* Jurisdiction or office of an archbishop.

Ärch-dēa'con (-dē'kn), *n.* A bishop's deputy.

Ärch-dēa'con-ry, *n.* Office of an archdeacon.

Ärch-dū'cal, *a.* Pertaining to an archduke.

Ärch-dŭch'ess, *n.* Wife of an archduke; daughter of the emperor of Austria.

Ärch-dūke', *n.* A grand duke of the house of Austria.

Ärched (ärcht), *a.* In form of an arch. [with a bow.

Ärch'er, *n.* One who shoots

Ärch'er-y, *n.* Art of shooting with a bow.

Ärch'e-tȳp'al, *a.* Belonging to an archetype; original.

Ärch'e-tȳpe, *n.* An original; a pattern; a model.

Ärch'fiĕnd, *n.* The chief of the fiends.

Är'chi-e-pĭs'co-pal, *a.* Relating to an archbishop or an archbishopric.

Är'chi-pĕl'a-go, *n.* A sea with many small islands in it.

Är'chi-tĕct, *n.* One skilled in the art of building; a contriver.

Är'chi-tĕct'ĭve, *a.* Belonging to architecture.

Är'chi-tĕct'ūr-al, *a.* Pertaining to architecture.

Är'chi-tĕct'ūre, *n.* The art or science of building.

Är'chi-trāve, *n.* That part of the entablature resting immediately on the column.

Är'chives, *n. pl.* Records, or places where they are kept.

Är'chi-vĭst, *n.* Keeper of archives.

Är'chi-vŏlt, *n.* Inner contour of an arch.

Ärch'ness, *n.* Sly humor.

Ärch'wāy, *n.* A passage under an arch.

Āre'tic, *a.* Lying far north.

Ăr'cu-āte, *a.* Bent like a bow.

Ăr'cu-ā'tion, *n.* A bending; convexity; incurvation.

Är'den-çy, *n.* Eagerness; zeal; ardor; heat.

Är'dent, *a.* [Lat. *ardens,* burning.] Hot; fervid; vehement; zealous.

Är'dor, *n.* Heat; warmth; affection; zeal.

Ärd'u-oŭs (26, 49), *a.* High; lofty; hard to climb; laborious.

Ärd'u-oŭs-ness, *n.* Height; difficulty of execution.

Ā're-à (140), *n.* An open surface; inclosed space; superficial contents.

Ăr'e-făe'tion, *n.* The act of drying; dryness.

Ā-rē'nà, *n.* [Lat., sand, a sandy place.] An open space for combats; any place of public exertion.

Ăr'e-nā'ceoŭs, *a.* Consisting of sand; sandy.

A-rē'o-là, *n.* Colored ring around a nipple or vesicle.

Ā're-ŏm'o-ter, *n.* An instrument for measuring the specific gravity of fluids.

Ā're-ŏm'e-try, *n.* Art of measuring the specific gravity of liquids.

Ăr'e-ŏp'a-gŭs, *n.* The supreme tribunal at ancient Athens.

Är'gal, *n.* Crude tartar.

Är'ġent, *a.* Silvery; white and shining, like silver.

Är'ġent-ine, *a.* Relating to, or resembling, silver. [clay.

Är'ġil, *n.* Potter's earth; pure

Är'ġil-lā'ceoŭs, *a.* Of the nature of clay; clayey.

Ar-ġĭl'loŭs, *a.* Clayey.

Är'go-sȳ, *n.* A large ship either for merchandise or war.

Är'gūe, *v. i.* or *t.* To debate or discuss; to persuade.

Är'gū-er, *n.* One who argues.

Är'gu-ment (132), *n.* Reason alleged to induce belief; plea.

Är'gu-mĕnt'al (132), *a.* Belonging to argument.

Är'gu-mĕn-tā'tion, *n.* Act or process of reasoning.

Är'gu-mĕnt'a-tĭve, *a.* Consisting of argument.

Ā'ri-an, *n.* One who denies the deity of Christ. — *a.* Pertaining to Arianism.

Ā'ri-an-ism, *n.* The doctrine of Arius, who denied the deity of Christ.

Ăr'id, *a.* Dry; parched.

Ăr'id-ness,) *n.* Dryness; absence of moisture.

A-rĭd'i-ty,)

†Ā'rĭ-ēs, *n.* [Lat.] The Ram; one of the twelve signs of the zodiac.

A-right' (-rīt), *adv.* Rightly.

A-rīse', *v. i.* [*imp.* AROSE.; *p. p.* ARISEN.] To rise; to mount; to ascend.

Ăr'is-tŏc'ra-çy, *n.* Government by nobles; nobility.

A-rĭs'to-crăt, or **Ăr'is-to-crăt,** *n.* One who favors aristocracy.

Ăr'is-to-crăt'ic,) *a.* Relating to aristocracy.

Ăr'is-to-crăt'ic-al,)

Ăr'ith-măn'çy, or **A-rĭth'-man-çy,** *n.* Divination by the use of numbers.

A-rĭth'me-tic, *n.* The science of numbers.

Ăr'ith-mĕt'ic-al, *a.* Relating to, or according to, arithmetic.

A-rĭth'me-tĭ'cian (-tĭsh'an), *n.* One skilled in arithmetic.

Ärk, *n.* [Lat. *arca,* fr. *arcere,* to inclose.] A chest or coffer; a large vessel or boat.

Ärm, *n.* Limb of the body from the shoulder to the wrist; a branch; an inlet of water. — *v. t.* To furnish with arms. — *v. i.* To take arms.

Ar-mā'dà (140), *n.* A large fleet of armed ships.

Är'ma-ment, *n.* A force equipped for war.

Är'ma-tūre (50), *n.* Armor; a piece of iron to connect the poles of a magnet. [arms.

Ärm'-châir, *n.* A chair with

Ärm'ful (148), *n.* As much as the arms can hold.

Ärm'hōle, *n.* A hole for the arm.

Ar-mĭġ'er-oŭs, *a.* Bearing arms.

Är'mil-la-ry, *a.* Resembling a bracelet; consisting of rings.

Ar-mĭn'ian (-yan), *n.* One who denies predestination, and holds to a provision for universal redemption.

Ar-mĭn'ian-ism (-yan-), *n.* The tenets of Arminians.

Ar-mĭp'o-tent, *a.* Powerful in arms.

són, ôr, dọ, wọlf, tōō, tŏŏk; ûrn · rụe, pụll; ç, ġ, *soft*; c, ğ, *hard*; a̤; exist; ɴ *as* ng; this.

Ar'mis-tiçe, *n.* A cessation from arms; truce.
Arm'let, *n.* A little arm; ornament for the arm.
Arm'or (155), *n.* Defensive arms or covering.
Ar'mo-rer, *n.* One who makes, sells, or has the care of, arms.
Ar-mō'ri-al, *a.* Belonging to armor. [arms.
Ar'mo-ry, *n.* A repository for
Arm'pit, *n.* The hollow or cavity under the shoulder.
Arms, *n. pl.* Weapons; ensigns armorial.
Ar'my, *n.* A large body of armed men; great number.
A-rō'mȧ, *n.* The fragrant principle of plants.
Ar'o-măt'ic, *a.* Spicy; fragrant; odoriferous.
Ar'o-măt'ics, *n. pl.* Fragrant spices or perfumes.
A-rō'ma-tīze, or **Ar'o-ma-tīze,** *v. t.* To impregnate with aroma.
A-rōṡe', *imp.* of *Arise.*
A-round', *prep.* On all sides of; about; from one part to another of. — *adv.* In a circle; on every side; here and there.
A-rouṡe', *v. t.* To excite to action; to awaken suddenly; to animate. [hand-gun.
Ar'que-būse, *n.* A sort of
Ar'que-būs-iēr, *n.* A soldier armed with an arquebuse.
Ar'rack, *n.* A spirit obtained from the cocoanut, rice, or sugar-cane.
Ar-rāign' (ar-rān'), *v. t.* To call to answer in court; to call in question; to accuse.
Ar-rāign'ment (ar-rān'-), *n.* Act of arraigning.
Ar-rānġe', *v. t.* To set in order; to adjust; to prepare.
Ar-rānġe'ment, *n.* Act of arranging; adjustment.
Ar'rant, *a.* Notoriously bad; infamous.
Ar'ras, *n.* Tapestry; figured hangings.
Ar-rāy', *n.* Order of battle; dress; raiment. — *v. t.* To put in order; to dress. — SYN. To dispose: deck; arrange: clothe; envelop.
Ar-rēar'aġe (142), *n.* The part of a debt unpaid.
Ar-rēarṡ', *n. pl.* That which remains unpaid.
Ar-rĕct', *a.* Lifted up; erect.
Ar-rĕst', *v. t.* To seize by authority of law; to detain; to obstruct. — *n.* A seizure by legal authority; staying

or stopping after verdict, as of a judgment.
†Ar-rĕt' (*or* ar-rā'), *n.* [Fr.] A decree of a court, &c.
Ar-rĭv'al (133), *n.* Act of arriving or coming; person or thing arriving. [reach.
Ar-rīve', *v. i.* To come; to
Ar'ro-ġançe, *n.* Insolence of bearing; proud contempt of others; haughtiness.
Ar'ro-gant, *a.* Haughty; proud; insolent.
Ar'ro-gant-ly, *adv.* Very proudly; haughtily.
Ar'ro-gāte, *v. t.* To claim unjustly; to assume. [gating.
Ar'ro-gā'tion, *n.* Act of arro-
Ar'ro-gā'tive, *a.* Arrogant.
Ar'rōw, *n.* A weapon for a bow.
Ar'rōw-rōōt, *n.* A plant and a nutritive starch from it.
Ar'se-nal, *n.* [Ar. *dárcinah*, house of industry.] A magazine of arms and military stores.
Ar'se-nĭc (129), *n.* A metal and a white oxide of it, both very poisonous.
Ar-sĕn'ic-al, *a.* Pertaining to, or containing, arsenic.
Ar-sē'ni-oŭs, *a.* Composed of, or containing, arsenic.
Ar'son (56), *n.* The malicious burning of a house.
Art, 2d person of the verb *To be.* — *n.* Acquired skill; dexterity; system of rules; cunning; artifice. [artery.
Ar-tē'ri-al, *a.* Belonging to an
Ar-tē'ri-al-īze, *v. t.* To communicate the qualities of arterial blood to.
Ar'te-ry, *n.* A vessel conveying blood from the heart.
Art'ful (130), *a.* Skillful; cunning; sly; crafty.
Art'ful-ness, *n.* Cunning; craft; dexterity.
Ar-thrĭt'ic, *a.* Pertaining to the joints or to the gout.
†Ar-thrī'tis, *n.* The gout.
Ar'ti-chōke, *n.* A garden vegetable.
Ar'ti-cle, *n.* [Lat. *articulus,* a little joint.] A particular item, clause, condition, part, thing, or the like; a certain part of speech. — *v. t.* To bind by articles.
Ar-tĭc'u-lar, *a.* Belonging to articulations or joints.
Ar-tĭc'u-lāte (42), *a.* Having joints; distinctly uttered.
Ar-tĭc'u-lāte, *v. t.* To pronounce distinctly; to unite by means of joints. — *v. i.* To utter elementary sounds.

Ar-tĭc'u-lā'tion, *n.* Connection by joints; a joint; distinct utterance.
Ar'ti-fiçe, *n.* Artful contrivance; device. — SYN. Stratagem; finesse; deception; fraud; deceit; trick.
Ar-tĭf'i-çer, *n.* A skillful workman in some art.
Ar'ti-fĭ'cial (är'ti-fish'al), *a.* Made by art; not natural; fictitious.
Ar'ti-fĭ'cial-ly (-fish'al-lỹ), *adv.* By art or skill.
Ar-tĭl'ler-ist, *n.* One skilled in gunnery.
Ar-tĭl'ler-ỹ, *n.* Weapons for war; ordnance; troops who manage ordnance.
Ar'ti-ṡan, *n.* A mechanic.
Art'ist, *n.* A professor and practicer of one of the fine arts.
†Artiste (är-tēest'), *n.* [Fr.] One skilled in almost any art.
Ar-tĭst'ic, *a.* Pertaining to art.
Art'less, *a.* Without art; simple; guileless.
Art'less-ly, *adv.* Without art.
Art'less-ness, *n.* Want of art.
A-rŭn'di-nā'ceoŭs, *a.* Pertaining to, or resembling, a reed or cane.
A-rŭn-dĭn'e-oŭs, *a.* Abounding in reeds.
A-rŭs'pĭçe, *n.* A priest or soothsayer in ancient Rome.
Aṡ (ăz), *adv.* In like manner to; while; in the idea, character, or condition of; for example; thus.
Aṡ'a-fœt'i-dȧ, *n.* A fetid in-
Aṡ'a-fĕt'i-dȧ, spissated sap, used in medicine.
As-bĕs'tĭne, *a.* Pertaining to asbestus.
As-bĕs'tus, *n.* A mineral
As-bĕs'tos, which is fibrous and incombustible.
As-çĕnd', *v. i.* To move upward; to mount; to rise. — *v. t.* To go upward on; to climb.
As-çĕnd'ant, *a.* Above the horizon; superior. — *n.* Superior influence; height; elevation.
As-çĕnd'en-çy, *n.* Controlling influence. — SYN. Authority; prevalence; control.
As-çĕn'sion, *n.* The act of ascending; a rising.
As-çĕn'sion-dāy, *n.* The day on which our Savior's ascension is commemorated.
As-çĕnt', *n.* Act of rising; rise; an eminence; acclivity.

ASCERTAIN 45 ASSOCIABLE

Ăs'çer-tāin', v. t. To make certain; to find out; to make confident.

Ăs'çer-tāin'a-ble, a. Capable of being ascertained.

Ăs'çer-tāin'ment, n. Act of ascertaining.

As-çĕt'ic, n. A devout recluse: a hermit. — a. Austere; recluse.

As-çĕt'i-çişm, n. The practice of ascetics.

As-çĭt'ic, a. Tending to dropsy of the abdomen.

As-crīb'a-ble (133), a. Capable of being ascribed.

As-crībe', v. t. To attribute; to assign; to impute.

As-crĭp'tion, n. Act of ascribing; thing ascribed.

Ăsh, n. A well-known tree and its wood. [shame.

Ȧ-shāmed', a. Covered with

Ăsh'en, a. Made of ash-wood; resembling ashes.

Ăsh'eş, n. pl. The incombustible remains of what is burnt; figuratively, a dead body that is burnt.

Ȧ-shore', adv. On or to shore.

Ăsh'-Wĕdneş'day (wĕnz'dȳ), n. The first day of Lent.

Ăsh'y, a. Ash-colored; like ashes.

Ȧ'si-ăt'ic (-shĭ-ät'ĭk), a. Pertaining to Asia. [side.

Ȧ-sīde', adv. On or to one

Ăs'i-nīne, a. Pertaining to an ass; stupid.

Ȧsk (5), v. t. or i. To make request; to question; to beg; to invite; to demand.

Ȧ-skănçe', } adv. Toward
Ȧ-skănt', } one corner of the eye; sidewise; obliquely.

Ȧ-skew' (a-skū'), adv. Obliquely.

Ȧ-slănt', adv. Obliquely.

Ȧ-slēep', a. In a state of sleep or of death. — adv. In a sleeping state.

Ȧ-slōpe', adv. In a slanting manner; with declivity.

Ăsp, n. A small hooded and poisonous serpent of Egypt.

As-pär'a-gŭs, n. A garden plant.

Ăs'peet, n. Look; air; countenance; appearance. [har.

Ȧsp'en, n. A species of pop-

As-pĕr'i-ty, n. Roughness; harshness: moroseness.

As-pẽrse' (12), v. t. To attack with slander. — SYN. To calumniate; slander; defame; vilify; censure.

As-pẽrs'er, n. One who asperses.

As-pẽr'sion, n. A sprinkling; calumny; slander; censure.

As-phält', } n. A bituminous substance.
As-phält'um, }

As-phält'ic, a. Bituminous.

Ăs'pho-del, n. A perennial plant having beautiful flowers.

As-phўx'i-à, } n. Suspended
As-phўx'y, } animation; fainting.

Ăsp'ic, n. The asp. [pires.

As-pīr'ant, n. One who aspires.

Ȧs'pi-rāte, n. A letter which is aspirated; a mark of aspiration; a whispered consonant. — a. Pronounced with a rough breathing.

Ȧs'pi-rāte, v. t. To pronounce with a breathing.

Ȧs'pi-rā'tion, n. Act of aspirating or breathing; an ardent wish.

As-pīre', v. i. To desire eagerly; to ascend; to rise.

As-pīr'er, n. One who aspires.

As-pīr'ing, a. Aiming at something great; ambitious; emulous. [askance.

A-squint', adv. Obliquely;

Ȧss, n. An animal of burden; a dolt. [assault.

As-sāil', v. t. To attack; to

As-sāil'a-ble, a. Capable of being assailed. [sails.

As-sāil'ant, n. One who assails.

As-sās'sin, n. One who kills by secret assault.

As-sās'sin-āte, v. t. To murder by secret assault.

As-sās'sin-ā'tion, n. Act of assassinating.

As-sault', n. [Lat. ad, to, and saltus, a leaping.] Violent onset or attack. — v. t. To attack with violence; to storm.

As-sāy', v. t. To examine chemically, as metals. — v. i. To attempt; to endeavor; to try. — n. A trial; attempt; examination, as of metals. [says.

As-sāy'er, n. One who assays.

As-sĕm'blage, n. A collection of individuals, or of particular things.

As-sĕm'ble, v. To bring or meet together.

As-sĕm'bly, n. A company assembled; a legislature.

As-sĕnt', v. i. To admit a thing as true. — n. The act of agreeing: consent.

As-sĕn'tiĕnt (-shent), a. Giving assent: agreeing.

As-sẽrt' (12), v. t. To affirm positively; to maintain; to aver; to asseverate.

As-sẽr'tion, n. Act of asserting; declaration.

As-sẽrt'ive, a. Positive; affirming confidently.

As-sẽrt'or, n. One who asserts.

As-sĕss', v. t. To tax; to value; to determine.

As-sĕss'a-ble, a. Liable to be assessed.

As-sĕss'ment, n. Act of assessing; the sum assessed.

As-sĕss'or, n. An associate; one appointed to apportion taxes.

Ȧs'sets, n. pl. Effects of a deceased or insolvent person.

Ȧs-sĕv'er-āte, v. t. To affirm solemnly.

As-sĕv'er-ā'tion, n. Solemn affirmation.

Ȧs'si-dū'i-ty, n. Closeness of application; diligence.

As-sĭd'u-oŭs, a. Constant in application; diligent; busy.

As-sīgn' (as-sīn'), v. t. To mark out; to appropriate; to make over. — n. An assignee.

As-sīgn'a-ble (-sīn'-) a. Capable of being assigned.

Ȧs'sig-nā'tion, n. Appointment for a meeting.

Ȧs'sign-ee' (as'sĭn-ee'), n. One to whom something is assigned.

Ȧs-sīgn'er (-sīn'-), } n. One
Ȧs'sign-ôr' (-sĭn-), } who assigns: one who makes a transfer to another.

As-sīgn'ment (as-sīn'-), n. Act of assigning, transfer of title or interest.

As-sĭm'i-lāte, v. t. To make similar. — v. i. To become similar.

As-sĭm'i-lā'tion, n. Act of assimilating.

As-sĭm'i-la-tĭve, a. Having power to assimilate.

As-sĭst', v. t. To help; to succor; to relieve; to aid.

As-sĭst'ançe, n. Help; aid; relief; succor; support.

As-sĭst'ant, n. One who assists. — a. Helping.

As-sīze', n. A court, or session of a court, for the trial of processes: time or place of holding such court. [Usually in the pl.] — v. t. To fix the measure, rate, price, or weight of, by authority.

As-sīz'er, n. One who assizes.

As-sō'cia-ble (-sō'sha-), a. Capable of being associated.

---

sŏn, ôr, do, wọlf, too, tŏŏk; ûrn, rụe, pụll; ç, ġ, soft; c, ġ, hard; aş; eẋist; ŋ as ng; this

ASSOCIATE — ATRAMENTOUS

As-sō'ci-āte (-shī-āt), *v. t.* To join in company; to unit with. — *v. i.* To unite in company or action. — *a.* Joined in interest; united.

As-sō'ci-ate, *n.* A companion; partner; partaker.

As-sō'ci ā'tion (-shī-ā'shun), *n.* Union; connection; a society.

As-sō'ci-ā'tion-al (-sō'shī-), *a.* Of, or pertaining to, an association.

As-sō'ci-ā-tive (-sō'shī-), *a.* Tending or pertaining to association.

As'so-nance, *n.* Resemblance of sound without rhyme.

As'so-nant, *a.* Having a resemblance of sounds without rhyme.

As-sŏrt', *v. t.* To arrange or distribute in classes; to class.

As-sŏrt'ment, *n.* Quantity selected or arranged; collection assorted.

As-suāge', *v. t.* To soften or reduce, as pain or grief. — SYN. To pacify; mitigate; alleviate; allay.

As-suāge'ment (132), *n.* Mitigation. [allaying.

As-suā'sive, *a.* Mitigating;

As'sue-tūde (ăs'swe-tūd), *n.* Custom; habitual use.

As-sūme', *v. t.* [Lat. *ad,* to, and *sumere,* to take.] To take; to take for granted; to pretend to possess. — *v. i.* To be arrogant. [haughty.

As-sūm'ing, *p. a.* Arrogant;

As-sūmp'sit, *n.* (*Law.*) A promise or undertaking; action to recover damages for breach of promise or contract.

As-sŭmp'tion (81), *n.* Act of assuming; supposition; thing supposed.

As-sur'ançe (a-shụr'ans), *n.* Certain expectation; confidence; want of modesty; insurance.

As-sure' (a-shụr', 29), *v. t.* To make secure; to assert positively; to insure. [sures.

As-sur'er, *n.* One who assures.

As'ter, *n.* A plant called also star-wort. [printing.

As'ter-isk, *n.* A mark [*] in

As'ter-ism, *n.* A constellation of fixed stars; an asterisk.

A-stĕrn', *adv.* In the hinder part of a ship; behind a ship; in the rear.

As'ter-oid, *n.* One of the small planets between Mars and Jupiter.

Ăsth'mă (ăst'mă, ăz'mă, *or* ăs'mă), *n.* Shortness of breath.

Asth-măt'ic (ast-, az-, *or* as-), *a.* Pertaining to asthma; troubled with asthma.

A̍s-tŏn'ish, *v. t.* To amaze; to surprise; to confound.

As-tŏn'ish-ing, *a.* Very wonderful.

As-tŏn'ish-ment, *n.* Emotion created by a sudden or extraordinary event. — SYN. Amazement; wonder; surprise.

As-tound', *v. t.* To strike with fear and wonder; to astonish.

A-străd'dle, *adv.* With the legs across a thing.

Ăs'tra-gal, *n.* A little round molding at the top or bottom of a column or cannon.

Ăs'tral, *a.* Belonging to the stars; starry. [right way.

A-strāy', *adv.* Out of the

As-trīc'tion, *n.* Act of binding; restraint; contraction.

A-strīde', *adv.* Across; with the legs apart.

As-trīnge', *v. t.* To draw together; to brace; to bind.

As-trĭn'gen-çy, *n.* The power of binding or contracting.

As-trĭn'gent, *a.* Binding; contracting. — *n.* A medicine which binds.

Ăs'tro-lābe, *n.* An instrument for taking the altitude of the sun or stars at sea.

As-trŏl'o-ger, *n.* One who foretells events by the stars.

Ăs'tro-lŏg'ic, } *a.* Relating
Ăs'tro-lŏg'ic-al, } to astrology.

As-trŏl'o-gy, *n.* The art of predicting events by the aspects of the stars.

As-trŏn'o-mer, *n.* One skilled in astronomy.

Ăs'tro-nŏm'ic-al, *n.* Belonging to astronomy.

Ăs'tro-nŏm'ic-al-ly, *adv.* In the manner of astronomy.

As-trŏn'o-my, *n.* [Gr. *astron,* star, and *nomos,* law, rule.] The science of the heavenly bodies.

As-tūte' (26), *a.* Shrewd; sagacious; discerning; acute.

As-tūte'ness, *n.* Shrewdness; sagacity; cunning. [parts.

A-sŭn'der, *adv.* Apart; into

A-sȳ'lum, *n.* A refuge; sanctuary; a charitable institution.

Ăs'ymp-tōte (-im-), *n.* A line which continually approaches a curve, but never reaches it.

Ăt, *prep.* Near to; in; by; on; with; toward.

Ăt'a-ghăn (-gan), *n.* A kind of Turkish dagger.

Āte, *imp.* of EAT.

Ā'the-ĭṣm, *n.* Disbelief in the existence of a God.

Ā'the-ĭst, *n.* [Gr. *a,* without, and *theos,* a god.] One who denies the existence of a God.

Ā'the-ĭst'ic, } *a.* Pertain
Ā'the-ĭst'ic-al, } ing to atheism; denying a God.

Ā'the-ĭst'ic-al-ly, *adv.* In an atheistical manner.

Ăth'e-næ'um (147), *n.* A literary or scientific association; a public reading-room furnished with papers and periodicals.
Ăth'e-nē'um }

A-thĭrst', *a.* Thirsty.

Ăth'lēte, *n.* A contender for a prize in public games; a wrestler.

Ath-lĕt'ic, *a.* Belonging to wrestling; strong; vigorous.

A-thwart', *adv.* Sidewise; obliquely. — *prep.* Across; from side to side of.

A-tĭlt', *adv.* As if about to make a thrust; with one end raised.

Ăt'lan-tē'an, *a.* Pertaining to, or resembling, Atlas, a fabulous giant.

†At-lan'tēṣ, *n. pl.* Figures or half-figures of men used instead of columns.

At-lăn'tic, *a.* Pertaining to the ocean between Europe and America.

Ăt'las (140), *n.* A collection of maps bound in a volume.

Ăt'mos-phēre, *n.* The air that surrounds the earth.

Ăt'mos-phĕr'ic, } *a.* Be
Ăt'mos-phĕr'ic-al, } longing to the atmosphere.

Ăt'om, *n.* A minute particle.

A-tŏm'ic, } *a.* Relating to,
A-tŏm'ic-al, } or consisting of, atoms. [of atoms.

Ăt'om-ĭṣm, *n.* The doctrine

A-tōne', *v. i.* To expiate; to make satisfaction for; to reconcile.

A-tōne'ment (132), *n.* Satisfaction; expiation; reconciliation.

A-tōn'ic, *a.* Wanting tone or tension; destitute of vocality.

A-tŏp', *adv.* At or on the top; above.

Ăt'ra-bĭl-ā'ri-oŭs, *a.* Affected with melancholy.

Ăt'ra-mĕnt'al, } *a.* Black
Ăt'ra-mĕnt'oŭs, } like ink; inky.

ATROCIOUS 47 AURA

A-trō'cioŭs, *a.* Wicked in a high degree; enormous; flagitious.

A-trō'cioŭs-ly, *adv.* Very wickedly; flagitiously.

A-trōç'i-ty, *n.* Horrible wickedness.

Ăt'ro-phy, *n.* A wasting away; emaciation.

At-tăch', *v. t.* To take by legal process; to win or gain over.

At-tăch'a-ble, *a.* Capable of being taken by attachment.

Attaché (ăt'a-shā'), *n.* One attached to the suite of an ambassador.

At-tăch'ment, *n.* Act of attaching; state of being attached; thing attached; seizure by legal process in a civil suit; affection.

At-tăck', *v. t.* To assault; to assail. — *n.* An assault; onset; invasion.

At-tāin', *v. i.* To reach by efforts; to arrive at. — SYN. To obtain; to acquire.

At-tāin'a-ble, *a.* Capable of being attained.

At-tāin'der, *n.* Act of attainting in law.

At-tāin'ment, *n.* Act of attaining; thing attained; acquisition.

At-tāint', *v. t.* To corrupt; to disgrace; to taint, as blood, when one is found guilty of treason. — *n.* A stain; spot; taint; a kind of writ.

At-tāint'ment, *n.* State of being attainted.

Ăt'tar, *a.* A fragrant oil obtained from the petals of roses.

At-tĕm'per, *v. t.* To qualify by mixture; to soften; to temper.

At-tĕmpt', *n.* A trial; effort; essay. — т. *t.* To try; to endeavor; to essay; to attack.

At-tĕmpt'a-ble, *a.* Capable of being attempted.

At-tĕnd', *v. t.* To wait on; to serve; to accompany. — *v. i.* To give heed; to be in waiting.

At-tĕnd'ançe, *n.* Act of waiting; service; retinue; train; attention.

At-tĕnd'ant, *a.* Accompanying; connected. — *n.* One who attends or accompanies.

At-tĕn'tion, *n.* Act of attending or heeding; civility.

At-tĕnt'ĭve, *a.* Paying attention; heedful; regardful.

At-tĕnt'ĭve-ly, *adv.* Heedfully.

At-tĕn'u-ant, *a.* Making less viscid; making thin.

At-tĕn'u-āte, *v. t.* To thin; to subtilize; to make slender; to draw out.

At-tĕn'u-ā'tion, *n.* A making thin or slender.

At-tĕst', *v. t.* [Lat. *ad*, to, and *testis*, a witness.] To bear witness to. [timony; witness.

Ăt'tĕs-tā'tion, *n.* Official testimony.

At-tĕst'or, *n.* One who attests.

Ăt'tie, *a.* Pertaining to Attica; pure; classical. — *n.* An upper story.

Ăt'ti-çĭşm, *n.* Elegant Greek.

Ăt'ti-çīze, *v. t.* To conform to the Greek idiom — *v. i.* To use Atticisms.

At-tīre', *v. t.* To dress; to array. — *n.* Clothes; apparel; dress; habit. [position.

Ăt'ti-tūde (50), *n.* Posture;

Ăt'ti-tūd'i-nal, *a.* Pertaining to attitude.

Ăt'ti-tūd'i-nīze, *v. t.* To assume affected attitudes.

At-tŏl'lent, *a.* Lifting up.

At-tor'ney (-tŭr'-, 141), *n.* One legally appointed by another to act for him.

At-trăet', *v. t.* To draw; to allure; to win; to invite.

At-trăet'a-ble, *a.* Capable of being attracted.

At-trăc'tion, *n.* Act or power of attracting; allurement; an object that attracts.

At-trăet'ĭve, *a.* Drawing; alluring; inviting. — *n.* That which draws.

At-trăet'ĭve-ness, *n.* The quality which draws.

At-trăet'or, *n.* One who attracts.

Ăt'tra-hent, *a.* Attracting. — *n.* That which attracts, as a magnet.

At-trĭb'u-ta-ble, *a.* Capable of being attributed; ascribable.

At-trĭb'ute, *v. t.* To ascribe; to impute. [quality.

Ăt'tri-būte, *n.* An inherent

At'tri-bū'tion, *n.* The act of attributing.

At-trĭb'u-tĭve, *a.* Relating to, or expressing, an attribute. — *n.* A word denoting an attribute.

At-trīte', *a.* Worn by rubbing.

At-trī'tion (-trĭsh'un), *n.* Act of wearing or rubbing.

At-tūnc', *v. t.* To put in tune.

Au'burn, *a.* Reddish brown.

Aue'tion, *n.* [From Lat. *augere*, to increase.] A public sale to the highest bidder.

Aue'tion-eer', *n.* Manager of an auction.

Au-dā'cioŭs, *a.* Bold; impudent; presumptuous.

Au-dā'cioŭs-ly, *adv.* Impudently.

Au-dăç'i-ty, *n.* Boldness; daring spirit; presumptuous impudence.

Au'di-ble, *a.* Capable of being heard.

Au'di-bly, *adv.* In a manner to be heard.

Au'di-ençe, *n.* A hearing; assembly of hearers; auditory.

Au'dit, *n.* An examination of accounts under authority. — *v. t.* To examine and adjust, as accounts.

Au'dit-or, *n.* A hearer; a listener; one who audits accounts.

Au'dit-o-ry, *n.* An assembly of hearers. — *a.* Having the power of hearing.

Au'ğer, *n.* A tool to bore holes.

Aught (awt), *n.* Any thing; any part.

Aug-mĕnt', *v. t.* To make larger; to increase. — *v. i.* To grow larger.

Aug'ment, *n.* An increase or state of increase; enlargement; a sign of past time, in grammar.

Aug'men-tā'tion, *n.* Act of augmenting or increasing; thing added.

Aug-mĕnt'a-tive, *a.* Having the quality of augmenting.

Au'gur, *n.* A diviner by the flight of birds; a soothsayer. — *v. t.* To predict by signs; to prognosticate. — *v. i.* To conjecture by signs or omens.

Au-gū'ri-al, *a.* Relating to augurs or augury.

Au'gu-ry, *n.* A prediction founded on the flight of birds, &c.; an omen; prognostication.

Au'gust, *n.* Eighth month of the year.

Au-gŭst', *a.* Impressing reverence or awe. — SYN. Grand; great; imposing; majestic.

Au-gŭst'ness, *n.* Quality of being august; majesty.

Au-lĕt'ie, *a.* Pertaining to pipes.

Au'lie, *a.* Pertaining to a royal court.

Aunt (änt), *n.* A father's or mother's sister.

Au'ra, *n.* Any invisible fluid,

especially that supposed to flow from the body.
Au-rē'o-lå,) n. A halo of
Au're-ōle,) light or luminous rays.
Au'ri-cle, n. The external ear.
Au-ric'u-lar, a. Pertaining to the ear or to the sense of hearing; recognized by the ear.
Au-ric'u-late, a. Shaped like an ear.
Au-rif'er-ous, a. [Lat. *aurum*, gold, and *ferre*, to bear.] Producing gold.
Au'rist, n. One skilled in disorders of the ear.
Au-rō'rå, n. The dawning light. — *Aurora borealis*, a luminous meteoric phenomenon; the northern lights.
Au-rō'ral, a. Pertaining to the aurora.
Aus'cul-tā'tion, n. Mode of detecting lung-diseases by listening to sounds within the chest.
Au'spiçe, n. sing.) Omen; influence.
Au'spi-çeş, n. pl.)
Au-spi'cial (-spish'al), a. Relating to auspices.
Au-spi'cioŭs (-spĭsh'us), a. Having omens of success. — SYN. Prosperous; propitious.
Au-spi'cioŭs-ly (-spish'us-), adv. Prosperously.
Au-spi'cioŭs-ness (-spĭsh'us), n. Quality of being auspicious.
Au-stēre', a. Severe; rigid.
Au-stēre'ly, adv. Severely.
Au-stēr'i-ty, n. Severity; harsh discipline; rigor.
Aus'tral, a. Southern.
Au-thĕn'tic, a. Genuine; original; not counterfeit or fictitious.
Au-thĕn'tic-al-ly, adv. With marks of credibility.
Au-thĕn'ti-cāte, v. t. To establish by proof.
Au-thĕn'ti-cā'tion, n. Establishment by proof.
Au'then-tiç'i-ty, n. State of being authentic; genuineness.
Au'thor, n. [Lat. *auctor*, fr. *augere*, to increase, produce.] One who produces any thing, a writer. [thor.
Au'thor-ess, n. A female author.
Au-thōr'i-ta-tĭve, a. Having authority.
Au-thōr'i-ta-tĭve-ly, adv. With authority; positively.
Au-thōr'i-ty, n. Legal power; warrant; rule; support; testimony.

Au'thor-i-zā'tion, n. Establishment by authority.
Au'thor-īze, v. t. To give authority to; to make legal; to justify.
Au'thor-shĭp, n. The state of being an author.
Au'to-bī-ŏg'ra-pher, n. One who writes a history of his own life.
Au'to-bī-ŏg'ra-phy, n. The writing of one's own life.
Au'to-bī'o-grăph'ic-al, a. Relating to autobiography.
Au-tŏc'ra-cy, n. Supreme independent power.
Au'to-crăt, n. An absolute sovereign.
Au'to-crăt'ic,) a. Pertaining to autocracy or to an autocrat.
Au'to-crăt'ic-al,)
†Au'to-dá-fe' (-dä-fā'), n. Punishment of a heretic by burning; also, the sentence then read.
Au'to-grăph, n. A person's own handwriting; signature.
Au'to-grăph'ic,) a. Consisting of one's own handwriting.
Au'to-grăph'ic-al,)
Au'to-măt'ic, a. Belonging to, or resembling, an automaton.
Au-tŏm'a-ton, n. (pl. Au-tŏm'a-tons; Lat. pl. Au-tŏm'a-tá, 147.) A self-moving machine, especially one which imitates the motions of men or animals.
Au'top-sy, n. A post-mortem examination.
Au'tumn (aw'tum), n. Third season of the year; fall.
Au-tŭm'nal, a. Of, or belonging to, autumn.
Aux-ĭl'ia-ry, a. Helping; assisting. — n. A verb that helps to form the moods and tenses of other verbs.
Aux-ĭl'ia-rieş, n. pl. Troops assisting another nation.
A-vāil', v. t. To turn to the advantage of; to profit; to assist; to promote. — v. i. To be of use or advantage. — n. Advantage; profit; (pl.) proceeds of property sold.
A-vāil'a-ble, a. Profitable; valid.
A vāil'a-ble-ness, n. Quality of being available.
Av'a-lănche, n. Body of snow, earth, &c., sliding down a mountain. [gain.
Av'a-riçe, n. Excessive love of
Av'a-ri'cious (-rĭsh'us), a. Greedy of wealth. — SYN.

Covetous; miserly; penurious; niggardly.
Av'a-ri'cioŭs-ly (-rĭsh'us-), adv. With avarice.
A-väst', interj. Cease; hold.
A-väunt', interj. Get away; hence; begone.
Ā've-Mā'ry,) n. A prayer to the Virgin Mary.
Ā've-Ma-rī'å,)
Av'e-nā'ceoŭs, a. Relating to oats.
A-vĕnge', v. t. To take just satisfaction for; to take vengeance on. [avenges.
A-vĕng'er, n. One who
Ăv'e-nūe (140), n. An entrance; passage; shaded alley in a garden; wide street.
A-vĕr' (12), v. t. To declare positively; to affirm; to assert.
Av'er-age (42), n. A mean proportion; medium. — a. Relating to a mean. — v. t. To reduce to a mean. — v. i. To be or form a medial sum or quantity. [tion.
A-vĕr'ment, n. Positive assertion.
A-vĕrse' (12), n. Having a strong dislike; disinclined; unwilling; reluctant.
A-vĕr'sion, n. Hatred; dislike; the cause of aversion.
A-vĕrt', v. t. or i. [Lat. *a*, from, and *vertere*, to turn.] To turn aside.
Ā'vi-a-ry, n. A place for keeping birds in.
A-vĭd'i-ty, n. Greediness; eagerness; intense desire.
Av'o-cā'tion, n. Business that calls away.
A-void', v. t. To keep at a distance from; to make void; to defeat or evade. — v. i. To become void or vacant.
A-void'a-ble, a. Capable of being avoided. [ing
A-void'ançe, n. Act of avoiding.
A-void'er, n. One who avoids.
A-void'less, a. Inevitable.
Av'oir-du-pois' (ăv'er-), n. A weight which has sixteen ounces to the pound.
A-vouch', v. t. To declare positively; to affirm; to maintain. [avouching.
A-vouch'ment, n. Act of
A-vow', v. t. To declare openly; to own and justify.
A-vow'a-ble, a. Capable of being avowed. [tion.
A-vow'al, n. A frank declaration.
A-vow'ed-ly, adv. In an open manner.
A-vow'er, n. One who avows.
A-vŭl'sion, n. A tearing asunder.

AWAIT 49 BADINAGE

A-wāit', v. t. To wait for; to expect; to be in store for.
A-wāke', a. Not sleeping. — v. t. [imp. & p. p. AWAKED or AWOKE.] To rouse from sleep; to wake. — v. i. To cease to sleep.
A-wāk'en (-wāk'n), v. t. or i. To awake; to put in action.
A-wārd', v. t. To adjudge; to decree. — n. A judgment; a sentence.
A-ward'er, n. One who awards.
A-wāre', a. Foreseeing; vigilant; watchful; apprised.
A-wāy', adv. At a distance.
Awe, n. Reverential fear. — v. t. To strike with awe or dread.
Aw'ful (132), a. Striking awe.
Aw'ful-ly, adv. So as to fill with awe.
Aw'ful-ness, n. Quality of striking with awe.
A-while', adv. For some time; for a short time.
Awk'ward, a. Clumsy; unhandy; inelegant; ungraceful.
Awk'ward-ly, adv. Ungracefully; clumsily.
Awk'ward-ness, n. Ungracefulness; clumsiness.
Awl, n. A tool to pierce holes.
Awn, n. The beard of grasses and grain.
Awn'ing, n. A covering from the sun or weather.
A-wōke', imp. & p. p. from Awake.
A-wry' (-rī'), a. or adv. Oblique or obliquely; aside.
Ax, } n. An iron tool with a
Axe, } steel edge, for hewing and chopping.
Ax'i-al, a. Pertaining to an axis.
Ax'i-form, a. Having the shape of an ax.
Ax'il-la-ry, a. Belonging to the armpit.
Ax'i-om, n. A self-evident proposition or truth. — SYN. Maxim; adage.
Ax'i-om-ăt'ic, } a. Pertaining to axioms; of the nature of an axiom.
Ax'i-om-ăt'ic-al, }
Ax'is, n. (pl. †Ax'ēs.) The line on which a thing revolves; stem of a plant.
Ax'le (ăks'l), } n.
Ax'le-tree, } A shaft on which a wheel turns.
Ay, or Aye, adv. Yes.
Āye (ā), adv. Always; ever; continually.
C, Axle.
Az'i-muth, n. An arc of the horizon intercepted between the meridian of the place and a vertical circle passing through the center of any object.
A-zōte', n. Nitrogen gas.
A-zōt'ic, a. Relating to azote.
Az'ure (āzh'ur or ā'zhur), a. Blue; sky-colored; cerulean.
— n. A light blue; the sky.

B.

BÄÄ, n. The cry or bleating of sheep. — v. i. To cry like a sheep.
Băb'ble, v. t. To talk idly: to prattle. — n. Senseless prattle; idle talk. [prater.
Băb'bler, n. An idle talker; a
Bābe, n. An infant; a young child; a baby.
Bā'bel, n. Confusion; disorder.
Bab-ōon', n. A large species of monkey.
Bā'by (141), n. An infant; a young child; a babe.
Bā'by-hood, n. State of being a baby. Baboon.
Bā'by-ish, a. Like a baby; childish.
Băc'ca-lau're-ate, n. The degree of Bachelor of Arts
Băc'cate, a. Pulpy, like a berry. [berries.
Băc'ca-ted, a. Having many
Băc'cha-nal, n. A drunkard; a reveler; (pl.) feasts in honor of Bacchus; revels.
Băc'cha-nā'li-an, a. Reveling in intemperance; drunken; riotous. — n. A drunken reveler. [berries.
Bac-cĭf'er-oŭs, a. Producing
Bac-cĭv'o-roŭs, a. Subsisting on berries.
Băch'e-lor, n. An unmarried man; one who has taken the first degree in any of the liberal arts. [a bachelor.
Băch'e-lor-shĭp, n. State of
Băck, n. The hinder part in man and the upper part in beasts; the rear; outward or upper part of a thing. — adv. To, in, or toward the rear; backward; behind; again. — v. t. To mount; to support; to furnish with a back.
Băck'bīte, v. t. To slander in the absence of the person traduced. [luminator.
Băck'bīt-er, n. A secret ca-
Băck'bōne, n. The bone of the back; the spine.
Băck'dōor, n. A door behind a house.
Băck-găm'mon, n. [W. bach, little, and cammawn, combat.] A game with dice, played on a kind of table or board.
Băck'ground, n. Ground or part behind; shade.
Băck'hănd-ed, adv. With the hand turned backward; indirectly.
Băck'-piēce, n. Armor for the back.
Băck'sīde, n. The hinder part.
Băck-slīde', v. i. To fall off; to apostatize.
Băck-slīd'er, n. An apostate.
Băck'sword (-sōrd), n. A sword with one sharp edge.
Băck'ward, } a. Unwilling;
Băck'wards, } slow; late; dull. [ingly.
Băck'ward-ly, adv. Unwill-
Băck'ward-ness, n. State or quality of being backward.
Băck-wŏŏds'man (143), n. An inhabitant of the forest in new settlements.
Bā'con (bā'kn), n. Hog's flesh salted, or pickled and dried, usually in smoke.
Băd, a. Wanting good qualities; ill; evil; wicked; vicious.
Bāde, imp. of Bid. [tion.
Bădge, n. A mark of distinc-
Bădg'er, n. A quadruped. — v. t. To tease; to worry.
†Băd'i-nāge (băd'i-nāsh), n. Light or playful discourse.

Băd′ly, *adv.* In a bad manner; not well; ill.
Băd′ness, *n.* State of being bad; want of good qualities.
Băf′fle, *v. t.* To elude or defeat by artifice. — SYN. To balk; frustrate; disappoint.
Băf′fler, *n.* One who baffles.
Băg, *n.* A sack; pouch; purse. — *v. t.* To put into a bag. — *v. i.* To swell like a bag.
Bĭg′a-tĕlle′, *n.* A thing of no importance; a trifle.
Bĭg′gage, *n.* Utensils and other necessaries of an army; clothing; luggage.
Băg′ging, *n.* Cloth for bags.
Băgn′io (băn′yo), *n.* A hot bath; a brothel.
Băg′pīpe, *n.* A musical wind instrument.
Băg′pīp-er, *n.* One who plays on a bagpipe.
Bāil, *n.* A surety for another's appearance; a handle. — *v. t.* To give security; to set free on security; to release or deliver by bail; to free from water. [ing bailed.
Bāil′a-ble, *a.* Capable of being
Bāil′bŏnd, *n.* A bond given by a prisoner and his surety to insure the prisoner's appearance in court, at the return of the writ.
Bail-ee′, *n.* One to whom goods are bailed, or delivered in trust.
Bāil′ie, *n.* A Scotch municipal officer.
Bāil′iff, *n.* A sheriff's deputy; an under-steward.
Bāil′i-wick, *n.* Jurisdiction of a bailiff.
Bāil′ment, *n.* Delivery of goods in trust.
Bāil′or,) *n.* One who delivers
Bāil′er,) goods in trust.
Bāirn, or Bärn, *n.* A child.
Bāit, *v. t.* To put food on, as on a hook; to give refreshment to. — *v. i.* To stop for refreshment on a journey. — *n.* A lure; temptation; enticement; refreshment.
Bāize, *n.* A kind of coarse woolen stuff.
Bāke, *v. t.* To heat or harden by heat; to cook in a close heated place. — *v. i.* To do the work of baking; to dry and harden in heat.
Bāke′house, *n.* A place for baking bread, cakes, &c.
Bāk′er, *n.* A person whose trade is to bake.
Bāk′er-y, *n.* Trade of a baker.

Bāk′ing (133), *n.* A drying by heat; quantity baked at once.
Băl′ance, *n.* A pair of scales; the difference of accounts; equipoise; a sign in the zodiac. — *v. t.* To make equal; to weigh; to estimate; to adjust and settle. — *v. i.* To hesitate; to fluctuate.
Băl′ance-sheet, *n.* A paper exhibiting a summary and balance of accounts.
Băl′co-ny, *n.* A kind of gallery on the outer wall of a building.
Bāld, *a.* Without hair; naked.
Băl′der-dăsh, *n.* A worthless mixture; jargon; nonsense.
Bāld′ness, *n.* A want of hair.
Bāld′pāte, *n.* A pate or person without hair.
Băl′drie, *n.* A girdle; a belt.
Bāle, *n.* Misery; sorrow; calamity; a bundle of goods. — *v. t.* To put into, or make up into, bales; to pack up.
Bāle′-fīre, *n.* A signal fire.
Bāle′ful (139), *a.* Full of bale; sorrowful; sad.
Ba-līze′, *n.* A pole on a bank for a sea-mark.
Balk (bawk), *n.* An unplowed ridge of laud; a great beam or rafter; hindrance; disappointment. — *v. t.* To disappoint. — *v. i.* To stop abruptly.
Bāll, *n.* Any round body; a globe; a bullet; a social assembly for dancing; a game. — *v. i.* To form into a ball; to gather balls of snow on the feet.
Băl′lad, *n.* A simple popular song of the narrative kind.
Băl′last, *n.* Any heavy substance to steady a ship. — *v. t.* To load with ballast.
Băl′let (or băl′lā), *n.* Theatrical exhibition of dancing, &c.
Băl′lis-ter, or Bal-lis′ter, *n.* A cross-bow.
Bal-lōōn′, *n.* A hollow vessel filled with gas for sailing in the air.
Băl′lot, *n.* A ball or ticket used in voting. — *v. i.* To vote by ballot. Balloon.
Băl′lot-bŏx, *n.* A box for receiving ballots.

Bălm (bäm), *n.* An odoriferous plant; an ointment.
Bălm′y (bäm′y), *a.* Sweet; fragrant.
Băl′sam, *n.* An aromatic resinous substance.
Băl-săm′ic, *a.* Having the qualities of balsam; soft; healing. — *n.* That which has the properties of a balsam
Băl′us-ter, *n.* A small pillar to support a rail.
Băl′us-trāde, *n.* A row of balusters topped by a rail.
Bam-bōō′, *n.* A kind of tropical reed.
Bam-bōō′zle, *v. t.* To deceive.
Băn, *n.* A public notice; interdict; curse.
Ba-nā′na, *n.* A kind of plantain tree, and its fruit.
Bănd, *n.* [A.-S. *bunda,* fr. *bindan,* to bind.] Any thing that binds; a company. — *v. t.* or *i.* To unite together.
Bănd′age, *n.* A fillet.
Ban-dăn′ă,) *n.* A kind of
Ban-dăn′nă,) silk.
Bănd′bŏx, *n.* A light box for bands, bonnets, &c.
Băn′dĭt (pl. Băn′dits or †Ban-dĭt′ti, 147), *n.* An outlaw; a robber.
Bănd′let,) *n.* (*Arch.*) Any
Bănd′e-let,) little band or flat molding.
Băn′dŏg, *n.* A fierce dog
Băn′do-leer′, *n.* A leathern belt thrown over the right shoulder; a case for musket charges.
Băn′dore, or Ban-dōre′, *n.* A stringed musical instrument.
Bănd′rŏl, *n.* A little flag.
Băn′dy, *n.* A club for striking a ball. — *v. t.* To beat to and fro, as a ball; to exchange. — *v. i.* To contend.
Băn′dy-lĕg, *n.* A crooked leg.
Băn′dy-lĕgged, *a.* Having crooked legs.
Bāne, *n.* Deadly poison; mischief; ruin. [ious; hurtful.
Bāne′ful, *a.* Poisonous; nox-
Băng, *v. t.* To beat; to thump. — *n.* A blow; a thump.
Băn′ian, *n.* A morning gown; Indian fig-tree.
Băn′ish, *v. t.* To exile from one's country; to drive away.
Băn′ĭsh-ment, *n.* Expulsion from one's own country.
Băn′is-ter, *n.* A baluster.
Bănk (79), *n.* A ridge of earth; steep acclivity; side of a

ă, ĕ, ĭ, ŏ, ŭ, y̆, *long*; ă, ĕ, ĭ, ŏ, ŭ, y̆, *short*; câre, cär, àsk, ąll, whạt; ēre, vẽil, tẽrm; pïque, fĭrm;

stream ; a shoal or shelf; place where money is deposited. — *v. t.* To raise a bank about.
Bank'a-ble, *a.* Receivable by a bank.
Bank'-bill,) *n.* A promissory note issued by a banking company.
Bank'-note,)
Bank'-book, *n.* A small book for private bank accounts.
Bank'er, *n.* One who deals in money or discounts notes.
Bank'ing, *n.* The business of a banker.
Bank'rupt, *n.* One who can not pay his debts; an insolvent. — *a.* Unable to pay debts; insolvent. — *v. t.* To make insolvent.
Bank'rupt-cy, *n.* State of a bankrupt; failure in trade.
Bank'-stock, *n.* Shares in a banking capital.
Ban'ner, *n.* A military standard; a flag. [meal.
Ban'nock, *n.* A cake of oat-
Ban'quet (bănk'wet), *n.* A grand entertainment; a feast. — *v. t.* To give a feast to. — *v. i.* To regale one's self with a feast.
Bans. *n. pl.* Proclamation in church of an intended marriage.
Ban'tam, *n.* A small variety of fowl, with feathered legs.
Ban'ter, *v. t.* To rally ; to ridicule; to joke or jest with. — *n.* Raillery; joke.
Bant'ling, *n.* An infant.
Ban'yan, or **Ban-yăn'**, *n.* A kind of fig-tree, called the Indian fig.
Bā'o-băb, *n.* An African tree, the largest in the world.
Bap'tism, *n.* Application of water to the body as a sacrament or religious ceremony.
Bap-tĭṣ'mal, *a.* Pertaining to baptism.
Bap'tist, *n.* One who holds to baptism of adults only, and that by immersion.
Bap'tis-ter-y, *n.* A place for baptizing.
Bap-tīze', *v. t.* To administer baptism to by sprinkling or immersion. [tizes.
Bap-tīz'er, *n.* One who bap-
Bar, *n.* A bolt; obstruction; inclosure in an inn or courtroom; division in music; bank of sand in a river; body of lawyers; a tribunal. — *v. t.* To fasten; to shut out.
Barb, *n.* Any thing resembling a beard; a point standing backward, as in a fish-hook; horse-armor; a Barbary horse. — *v. t.* To furnish with barbs; to clothe with armor, as a horse.
Bar-bā'ri-an (86), *n.* A savage; a man uncivilized. — *a.* Savage; uncivilized.
Bar-băr'ic, *a.* Foreign; rude; barbarous.
Bar'ba-riṣm, *n.* Savageness.
Bar-băr'i-ty, *n.* A savage state ; cruelty; barbarism.
Bär'ba-rīze, *v. t.* To make barbarous.
Bär'ba-roŭs, *a.* Uncivilized ; savage ; rude; cruel.
Bär'ba-roŭs-ly, *adv.* Inhumanly.
Bär'be-cŭe, *n.* [Fr. *barbe-á-queue*, lit. from snout to tail.] A hog, &c., roasted whole ; a feast in the open air. — *v. t.* To dress and roast whole.
Bär'ba-ted, *a.* Having barbed points. [fresh-water fish.
Bär'bel, *n.* A kind of large
Bär'ber, *n.* One whose business is to shave beards.
Bär'ber-ry, *n.* A shrubby plant, and its fruit.
Bär'bet, *n.* A variety of shaggy dog.
Bärd, *n.* A Celtic minstrel; a poet. [bards.
Bärd'ic, *a.* Pertaining to
Bāre, *a.* Naked ; uncovered ; destitute ; mere; raw. — *v. t.* To make naked ; to uncover.
Bāre'fāçed (-fāst), *a.* Shameless; impudent.
Bāre'foot, *a.* and *adv.* Without shoes or stockings.
Bāre' head-ed, *a.* With the head uncovered.
Bāre'ly, *adv.* Nakedly ; only; merely.
Bāre'ness, *n.* State of being bare; nakedness; poverty.
Bär'gain (39,) *n.* Agreement; a thing bought or sold. — *v. t.* To make a contract with ; to sell. — *v. i.* To agree.
Bär'gain-ee', *n.* The party in a contract who agrees to receive the property sold.
Bär'gain-er, *n.* The party in a contract who stipulates to sell and convey property to another.
Bärge, *n.* A large boat for pleasure, &c. [barge.
Bärge'man. *n.* Master of a
Ba-rĭl'lȧ, *n.* A sea-shore plant; impure carbonate of soda.

Bär'i-tōne, *n.* See *Barytone*.
Bärk, *n.* Rind of a tree ; the noise made by a dog. — *v. t.* To strip of bark. — *v. i.* To make the noise of a dog.
Bärk,) *n.* A ship with
Bärque,) three masts, without a mizzen top-mast.
Bär'ley, *n.* A kind of grain that malt is made of.
Bär'ley-cörn, *n.* A grain of barley; third part of an inch.
Bärm, *n.* The foam on malt liquors when fermenting ; yeast.
Bärm'y, *a.* Containing barm.
Bärn, *n.* A building for hay and other farm produce.
Bär'na-cle, *n.* A kind of shell-fish; a kind of goose ; (*pl.*) an instrument to put on a horse's nose to confine him ; a pair of spectacles.
Ba-rŏm'e-ter, *n.* [Gr. *baros*, weight, and *metron*, measure.] An instrument to measure the weight of the atmosphere.
Bär'o-mĕt'ric-al, *a.* Relating to a barometer.
Băr'on, *n.* Rank of nobility next to a viscount.
Băr'on-aġe, *n.* Body of barons; estate of a baron.
Băr'on-ess. *n.* A baron's wife.
Băr'on-et, *n.* A dignity next below that of baron.
Băr'on-et-aġe, *n.* Body of baronets.
Băr'on-et-çy, *n.* The rank, state, or title of a baron.
Ba-rō'ni-al, *a.* Belonging to a barony.
Băr'o-ny, *n.* Lordship or fee of a baron. [rometer
Băr'o-seōpe, *n.* A sort of ba-
Ba-rouche' (-rōosh'), *n.* A two-seated four-wheeled open carriage.
Bär'ra-can, *n.* A thick strong stuff like camlet. [soldiers.
Bär'rack, *n.* A building for
Bär'ra-cōōn', *n.* A slave warehouse or inclosure.
Bär'ra-tor, *n.* One who excites lawsuits.
Bär'ra-try, *n.* Encouragement of lawsuits; breach of duty on the part of a ship-captain or of his crew.

BARREL 52 BAYOU

Băr'rel, *n.* A sort of cask; a cylinder; a tube. — *v. t.* (8) To put into a barrel.

Băr'ren, *a.* Not prolific; unfruitful; sterile; dull. — *n.* An unfertile tract of land.

Băr'ren-ness, *n.* Unfruitfulness; sterility.

Băr'ri-cāde', *n.* A hastily made fortification; a bar or obstruction. — *v. t.* To stop up, as a passage; to fortify.

Băr'ri-er, *n.* A limit; defense; a bar; obstruction; boundary. [at law.

Băr'ris-ter, *n.* A counselor

Băr'rōw, *n.* A hand-carriage; a mound; a gelt swine.

Băr'-shŏt, *n.* Two balls joined by a bar.

Băr'ter, *v. t.* To traffic by exchanging articles. — *n.* Traffic by exchange.

Băr'ter-er, *n.* One who barters. [the cartas.

Ba-ry̆'tă, *n.* The heaviest of

Ba-ry̆'tĕs, *n.* Sulphate of baryta.

Băr'y-tōne, *n.* [Gr. *barus*, heavy, and *tonos*, tone.] A male voice partaking of the common bass and tenor.

Bī'sal, *a.* Relating to, or constituting, the base.

Ba-sa̤lt', *n.* A very hard greenish-black mineral.

Ba-sa̤lt'ic, *a.* Pertaining to basalt.

Băs'çi-net, *n.* A light kind of helmet.

Bāse, *n.* Bottom; foundation; pedestal; gravest part in music. — *a.* Low in value, rank, spirit, estimation, &c. — SYN. Mean; vile; worthless. — *v. t.* To found, set, or lay.

Bāse'-bŏrn, *a.* Illegitimate.

Bāse'less, *a.* Without support.

Bāse'ly, *adv.* In a base manner; illegitimately.

Bāse'ment (132), *n.* The lower story of a building.

Bāse'ness, *n.* Quality of being base; meanness; vileness; deepness of sound.

Bāse'vī-ol, *n.* A musical instrument.

Băss'vī-ol,

Ba-shaw', *n.* A title of honor in the Turkish dominions.

Băsh'ful, *a.* Wanting confidence; modest; shy; diffident.

Băsh'ful-ly, *adv.* In a bashful manner; diffidently.

Băsh'ful-ness, *n.* Extreme modesty; diffidence.

Bā'sic, *a.* Relating to a base.

Băs'il, *n.* The slope of a tool; the skin of a sheep tanned. — *v. t.* To grind to an angle.

Ba-sĭl'i-cà, *n.* Any large hall or court of justice; a church, chapel, or cathedral.

Ba-sĭl'i-cŏn, *n.* A kind of salve.

Băs'i-lĭsk, *n.* A cockatrice; a kind of cannon.

Bā'sĭn (bā'sn), *n.* A small vessel; a dock; a pond; any hollow place.

Bā'sis, *n.* (*pl.* Bā'sĕs.) Foundation; support; base.

Băsk (6), *v. i.* To lie in warmth. — *v. t.* To warm with genial heat.

Băs'ket, *n.* A vessel made of twigs, &c., interwoven.

Băss, *n.* A fish; a species of tree.

Băss, *n.* (*Mus.*) The base. — *a.* Grave; low; deep. See *Base*.

Băs'set, or Bas-sĕt', *n.* An old game at cards.

Bas-sōon', *n.* A musical wind instrument.

Băs'tard, *a.* Illegitimate; spurious; born out of wedlock. — *n.* A spurious child.

Băs'tard-y, *n.* State of being a bastard.

Bāste, *v. t.* To beat with a stick; to sew slightly; to drip butter on.

Bas-tīle' (bas-teel' *or* băs'teel), *n.* An old castle used as a prison.

Băs'ti-nāde', *v. t.* To beat

Băs'ti-nā'do, on the soles of the feet with a cudgel. — *n.* A cudgeling, especially on the soles of the feet.

Băs'tion (băst'yun), *n.* A mass of earth standing out from a rampart.

Băt, *n.* A stick; a small bird-like animal.

Bătch, *n.* Bread baked at one time; work done at once; quantity of things taken together.

Bāte, *v. t.* To lessen; to abate.

†**Ba-teau'** (bat-tō'), *n.* (*pl.* Bateaux, bat-tōz'.) A long light boat.

Bāth, *n.* (*pl.* Bāths.) A bathing; a place to bathe in.

Bāthe, *v. t.* To wash in water. — *v. i.* To be or lie in a bath. [scent in style.

Bī'thos, *n.* A ludicrous de-

Băt'let, *n.* A small bat for beating linen.

Bă-tŏn' (-tŏng'), *n.* A staff

Ba-tōon', or truncheon. [fantry.

Bat-tăl'ion, *n.* A body of in-

Băt'tel, *n.* Provisions taken by the Oxford students from the buttery, and also the charges thereon.

Băt'ten (băt'tn), *v. t.* To make fat; to fatten; to form or fasten with battens. — *v. i.* To grow fat. — *n.* A narrow piece of board.

Băt'ter, *v. t.* To beat down. — *n.* A mixture of flour, water, eggs, &c.

Băt'ter-ing-răm, *n.* An engine for beating down walls.

Băt'ter-y, *n.* A raised work for cannons to rest on; a body of cannon taken collectively; apparatus for containing or producing electricity; unlawful beating of another.

Băt'ting, *n.* Cotton or wool in sheets for quilting.

Băt'tle, *n.* A combat; encounter; engagement; a fight. — *v. i.* To contend in fight. [battle.

Băt'tle-ar-rāy', *n.* Order of

Băt'tle-ăx, *n.* A kind of ax

Băt'tle-ăxe, anciently used in battle.

Băt'tle-dōor, *n.* An instrument to strike shuttlecocks with.

Băt'tle-ment, *n.* A notched or indented parapet or wall. Battlement.

Baw'ble, *n.* A gewgaw; trinket; trifle.

Bawd, *n.* A lewd woman; a procuress.

Bawd'i-ness, *n.* Obscenity.

Bawd'y, *a.* Filthy; obscene.

Bawl, *v. t.* To proclaim as a crier. — *v. i.* To cry aloud.

Bāy, *v. i.* To bark as a dog. — *a.* Red inclining to chestnut. — *n.* Inlet of the sea; inclosure in a barn; a tree.

Bāy'bĕr-ry, *n.* Fruit of the bay-tree; a species of laurel; a plant (called also wax-myrtle) and its fruit.

Bāy'o-net, *n.* [First made at *Bayonne*.] A sort of dagger fixed to a gun. — *v. t.* To stab with a bayonet.

Bay'ou (bī'oo), *n.* Outlet of a lake, &c.

ā, ĕ, ī, ō, ū, ȳ, *long*; ă, ĕ, ĭ, ŏ, ŭ, y̆, *short*; cȧre, cär, ȧsk, ạll, whạt; ẽre, veil, tẽrm; pīque, fĩrm;

Bāy′-rŭm, *n.* A spirit obtained by distilling leaves of the bay-tree. [evaporation.
Bāy′-salt, *n.* Salt formed by
Ba-zāar′, } *n.* An Eastern
Ba-zär′, } market-place or exchange; a fair.
Bdel′lium (dĕl′yum), *n.* A gummy resinous exudation from an oriental tree.
Bē, *v. i.* and *auxiliary.* [*imp.* WAS; *p. p.* BEEN.] To exist.
Bĕach, *n.* A sandy or pebbly shore; strand.
Bēa′con (bē′kn), *n.* A signal light to direct seamen.
Bĕad (140), *n.* A little ball strung on thread, used for necklaces.
Bēa′dle, *n.* A crier or messenger of a court; an inferior parish officer.
Bēad′-rōll, *n.* A list of persons to be prayed for.
Bēads′man (143), *n.* One who prays for others.
Bēa′gle, *n.* A small hound.
Bĕak, *n.* The bill of a bird; any thing like a bird's bill.
Bēaked (bēekt), *a.* Having a beak.
Bēak′er, *n.* A drinking-cup.
Bĕam, *n.* A main timber; part of a balance; a ray of light. — *v. i.* To emit rays; to shine.
Bĕam′y, *a.* Shining; radiant.
Bēan, *n.* A leguminous plant and its seed, of many varieties.
Bēar, *v. t.* [*imp.* BORE; *p. p.* BORN.] To bring forth, as young; to produce. — *v. t.* [*imp.* BORE; *p. p.* BORNE.] To carry; to endure; to sustain; to support. — *v. t.* To suffer. —
n. A kind of wild animal; a stock-jobber who is interested in depressing the value of stocks. **Bear.**
Beār′a-ble, *a.* Capable of being borne; tolerable.
Beār′-bāit′ing, *n.* Act of baiting bears with dogs.
Bēard, *n.* Hair on the chin, lips, and sides of the face. — *v. t.* To take or pull by the beard; to oppose to the face.
Bēard′ed, *a.* Having a beard.
Bēard′less, *a.* Without a beard.
Bēar′er, *n.* A carrier.

Beār′-gär′den (-gär′dn), *n.* A place where bears are kept for sport.
Beār′-hĕrd, *n.* A man who tends bears. [mien.
Beār′ing, *n.* Deportment;
Beār′ish, *a.* Like a bear.
Beār′s′-fŏŏt, *n.* A plant; a species of hellebore.
Bēast, *n.* An irrational animal; a brute.
Bēast′li-ness, *n.* Brutality; filthiness. [brutal.
Bēast′ly, *a.* Like a beast;
Bēat, *v. t.* [*imp.* BEAT; *p. p.* BEAT, BEATEN.] To strike with repeated blows; to ontdo; to surpass; to conquer. — *v. i.* To strike; to dash; to throb, as a pulse. — *n.* A stroke; a blow.
Bēat′en, *p. p.* of *Beat.*
Bē′a-tĭf′ie, *a.* Making happy.
Be-ăt′i-fi-eā′tion, *n.* Admission to heavenly honors.
Be-ăt′i-fy, *v. t.* [Lat. *beatus,* happy, and *facere,* to make.] To make or pronounce happy.
Bēat′ing, *n.* Act of striking.
Be-ăt′i-tūde (50), *n.* Blessedness; perfect bliss or felicity.
Beau (bō), *n.* (*pl.* Beaux, bōz.) A man of dress; a lady's attendant; a coxcomb; a fop.
Beau I-dē′al. A mental model of beauty or excellence.
Beau′ish (bō′ish), *a.* Like a beau; gay; foppish; gallant.
†**Beau Monde (bo mōnd).** The fashionable world.
Beaū′te-oŭs, *a.* Beautiful; handsome; fair.
Beaū′te-oŭs-ly, *adv.* In a beauteous manner.
Beaū′te-oŭs-ness, *n.* Handsomeness; beauty.
Beaū′ti-fī′er, *n.* That which makes beautiful.
Beaū′ti-fŭl, *a.* Having the qualities that constitute beauty. — SYN. Handsome; fair; elegant; lovely.
Beaū′ti-fŭl-ly, *adv.* In a beautiful manner.
Beaū′ti-fŭl-ness, *n.* Quality of being beautiful; beauty.
Beaū′ti-fy, *v. t.* To make beautiful. — *v. i.* To grow beautiful. — SYN. To adorn; grace; embellish; deck.
Beaū′ty (bū′tȳ), *n.* Whatever pleases the eye or the mind; assemblage of graces; loveliness; elegance; a lovely woman.
Beaū′ty-spŏt, *n.* A patch put on the face to heighten beauty.

Bēa′ver, *n.* An amphibious quadruped and his fur; a hat; part of a helmet.
Be-cälm′ (be-käm′), *v. t.* To quiet; to calm; to appease. **Beaver.**
Be-cāme′, *imp.* of *Become.*
Be-eause′, *conj.* For the cause or reason that; for; since; as.
Be-chānçe′, *v. i.* To happen; to befall.
Bĕck, *n.* A sign with the hand or head. — *v. i.* To make a sign with the head or hand; to nod. — *v. t.* To intimate a command to by a nod or motion of the hand.
Bĕck′on (bĕk′n), *v. t.* To make a significant sign to. — *v. i.* To make a sign to another.
Be-cloud′, *v. t.* To obscure.
Be-cŏme′ (-kŭm′), *v. t.* [*imp.* BECAME; *p. p.* BECOME.] To fit, or befit; to suit. — *v. i.* To be made; to be changed to. [graceful.
Be-cŏm′ing, *a.* Suitable; fit;
Be-cŏm′ing-ly, *adv.* So as to be becoming; fitly.
Be-crĭp′ple, *v. t.* To lame; to cripple.
Bĕd, *v. t.* To place in bed; to lay in order. — *v. i.* To go to bed.
Be-dăb′ble, *v. t.* To wet. [bed.
Be-dăg′gle, *v. t.* To soil.
Be-dăsh′, *v. t.* To wet by spattering. [to daub.
Be-daub′, *v. t.* To smear;
Be-dăz′zle, *v. t.* To make dim; to dazzle.
Bĕd′-bŭg, *n.* An offensive bug that infests beds.
Bĕd′-chăm′ber, *n.* A chamber for a bed.
Bĕd′-clōthes, *n.* Sheets, blankets, coverlets, &c.
Bĕd′ding, *n.* Materials for a bed. [trim.
Be-dĕck′, *v. t.* To deck; to
Be-dew′ (be-dū′), *v. t.* To moisten with dew.
Bĕd′-fĕl′lōw, *n.* One lying in the same bed.
Bĕd′-hăng′ingṣ, *n.* Curtains of a bed.
Be-dĭm′, *v. t.* To make dim.
Be-dĭz′en (-dĭz′n), or **Be-dīz′en (-dīz′n),** *v. t.* To adorn tawdrily; to deck with cheap finery.
Bĕd′lam, *n.* A mad-house.
Bĕd′lam-īte, *n.* A madman.
Bĕd′mate, *n.* A bed-fellow.

BED–QUILT   54   **BELL–METAL**

Bĕd'-quĭlt, *n.* A quilted covering for a bed.
Be-drăg'gle, *v. t.* To soil.
Be-drĕnch', *v. t.* To soak completely; to drench.
Bĕd'rĭd, *a.* Confined to
Bĕd'rĭd-den, the bed.
Bĕd'room, *n.* A room for a bed. [over.
Be-drŏp', *v. t.* To sprinkle
Bĕd'sĭde, *n.* The side of a bed. [bed.
Bĕd'stĕad, *n.* A frame for a
Bĕd'tīme, *n.* The usual hour of going to bed.
Be-dwärf', *v. t.* To hinder the growth of.
Bee (140), *n.* A four-winged insect of many genera and species; an insect that makes honey.
Bee'-brĕad, *n.* The pollen of flowers collected by bees.
Beech, *n.* A kind of forest-tree.
Beech'en (bēch'n), *a.* Belonging to, or made of, beech.
Beef, *n.* The flesh of an ox or cow; an animal of the ox kind. [In the latter sense it has a plural, **Beeves.**]
Beef'-ĕat'er, *n.* A yeoman of the guard; a kind of South African bird.
Beef'steak, *n.* A slice of beef for broiling.
Bee'-hĭve, *n.* A box or case for holding bees.
Been (bin), *p. p.* of *Be.*
Beer, *n.* A liquor made of malt and hops.
Bees'-wăx, *n.* The wax secreted by bees.
Beet, *n.* A garden vegetable.
Bee'tle, *n.* A mallet; an insect. — *v. i.* To jut out; to hang over.
Beeves, *n. pl.* of *Beef.* Cattle.
Be-făll' (158), *v. t.* [*imp.* BEFELL; *p. p.* BEFALLEN.] To happen to. — *v. i.* To happen; to occur.
Be-fĭt', *v. t.* To become; suit.
Be-fĭt'ting, *a.* Suiting; becoming.
Be-fool', *v. t.* To make a fool of; to impose on.
Be-fōre', *prep.* In front of; prior to; in presence of. — *adv.* Previously; sooner.
Be-fōre'hănd, *adv.* Previously. — *a.* Well provided.
Be-foul', *v. t.* To make foul; to pollute; to foul.
Be-frĭend', *v. t.* To favor; to aid; to treat or serve as a friend. [fringe.
Be-frĭnge', *v. t.* To adorn with

Bĕg, *n.* A Turkish governor of a town.
Bey (bā),
Bĕg, *v. t.* [Probably a modification of *to bag*]. To ask earnestly; to entreat; to solicit. — *v. i.* To live on alms; to ask for alms.
Be-gĕt', *v. t.* [*imp.* BEGAT; *p. p.* BEGOT, BEGOTTEN.] To generate or produce; to procreate. [gets.
Be-gĕt'ter, *n.* One who be-
Bĕg'gar, *n.* One who begs, or who lives by begging. — *v. t.* To bring to want; to reduce to beggary.
Bĕg'gar-lĭ-nĕss, *n.* State of being beggarly; meanness.
Bĕg'gar-ly, *a.* Very poor; mean. — *adv.* Meanly.
Bĕg'gar-y, *n.* Extreme indigence or poverty.
Be-gĭn', *v. t.* [*imp.* BEGAN; *p. p.* BEGUN.] To take rise; to commence; to enter upon something new; to do the first act. [gins.
Be-gĭn'ner, *n.* One who be-
Be-gĭn'ning, *n.* The first cause, state, or part of time; commencement.
Be-gĭrd', *v. t.* [*imp.* BEGIRDED; *p. p.* BEGIRT.] To surround; to gird.
Be-gōne' (19), *interj.* Go away! depart!
Be-gŏt',
Be-gŏt'ten, *p. p.* of *Beget.*
Be-grīme', *v. t.* To soil with dirt; to grime.
Be-grŭdge', *v. t.* To envy the possession of; to grudge.
Be-guīle', *v. t.* To impose upon; to deceive; to amuse.
Be-guīle'ment, *n.* Act of beguiling.
Be-gŭn', *p. p.* of *Begin.*
Be-hălf', *n.* Favor; cause; account; sake; defense.
Be-hāve', *v. i.* or *t.* To carry; to act; to demean; to conduct.
Be-hāv'ior, *n.* Manner of behaving; a course of life. — SYN Conduct; deportment.
Be-hĕad', *v. t.* To cut off the head of.
Be-hĕld', *imp.* of *Behold.*
Bē'he-mŏth, *n.* A large beast described in Job xl.
Be-hĕst', *n.* A command; mandate; injunction.
Be-hĭnd', *prep.* At the back of; on the other side of. — *adv.* At or towards the rear; past. [rears.
Be-hĭnd'hănd, *adv.* In ar-
Be-hōld', *v. t.* [*imp. & p. p.*

BEHELD.] To see; to look at. — *interj.* Lo! see!
Be-hōld'en, *a.* Indebted.
Be-hōld'er, *n.* One who beholds; a spectator.
Be-hoof', *n.* Profit; advantage; interest.
Be-hoōv'a-ble (11), *a.* Useful; fit; expedient.
Be-hoōve', *v. t.* To be necessary to; to be fit or meet for; to become.
Bē'ing, *n.* Existence; any thing that exists.
Be-lā'bor, *v. t.* To thump; to beat soundly.
Be-lāte', *v. t.* To make late; to delay; to retard.
Be-lāt'ed, *a.* Too late; detained; delayed.
Be-lāy', *v. t.* To fasten, as a rope, by winding it round something.
Bĕlch, *v. t.* To eject wind from the stomach. — *v. i.* To eject wind upward. — *n.* Act of belching.
Bĕl'dam, *n.* [Fr. *belle-dame,* fine lady; — in irony.] An ugly old woman; a hag.
Be-lēa'guer, *v. t.* To besiege; to invest. [bells are rung.
Bĕl'fry (141), *n.* A place where
Bē'lĭ-al, *n.* Satan; the Devil.
Be-līe', *v. t.* To speak falsely of; to vilify; to slander.
Be-lĭef', *n.* Credit given to evidence; the thing believed; opinion; creed.
Be-lĭev'a-ble, *a.* Capable or worthy of being believed; credible.
Be-lĭeve', *v. t.* To trust in; to give credit to. — *v. i.* To have faith. [lieves.
Be-lĭev'er, *n.* One who be-
Bĕll (123), *n.* A sounding vessel of metal. — *v. i.* To grow like a bell in shape.
Bĕl'la-dŏn'na, *n.* Deadly nightshade.
Bĕlle (bĕl), *n.* A handsome young lady, much admired.
†**Bĕlles-lĕt'tres** (bel-lĕt'ter), *n. pl.* [Fr.] Polite or elegant literature.
Bĕll'-found'er, *n.* One who casts or founds bells.
Bel-lĭg'er-ent, *a.* [Lat. *bellum,* war, and *gerere,* to carry.] Carrying on war. — *n.* One who wages war; a nation engaged in war.
Bĕll'man (143), *n.* One who rings a bell; a crier of goods.
Bĕll'-mĕt'al (-mĕt'l or -mĕt'al), *n.* A composition of copper, tin, zinc, and antimony.

ā, ĕ, ī, ō, ū, ȳ, *long;* ă, ĕ, ĭ, ŏ, ŭ, ȳ, *short;* cāre, cär, ȧsk, ạll, whạt; ẽre, veil, tẽrm; pïque, fïrm;

Bĕl'lōw, v. i. To roar like a bull. — n. A loud outcry ; a roar.
Bĕl'lows (bĕl'lus), n. sing. & pl. An instrument to blow with. [a bell.
Bĕll'-pŭll, n. A cord to ring
Bĕll'-rĭng'er, n. One who rings a bell.
Bĕll'-wĕth'er, n. A sheep which carries a bell, and leads the flock.
Bĕl'ly, n. The part of the body containing the bowels; abdomen. — v. i. To bulge ; to project ; to swell ; to puT out ; to become protuberant.
Bĕl'ly-āche, n. Pain in the bowels. [horse.
Bĕl'ly-bănd, n. A girth for a
Be-lŏng' (19), v. i. To be the property of ; to pertain ; to adhere.
Be-lŏved', p. p. Greatly loved.
Be-lŏv'ed (-lŭv'ed, 57), a. Dear ; much loved.
Be-lōw', prep Under in time or place ; beneath ; inferior to. — adv. In a lower place: beneath ; on earth ; in hell.
Bĕlt, n. A girdle; sash; band. — v. t. To gird.
Bĕl've-dēre', n. A pavilion on the top of a house.
Be-mīre', v. t. To sink or drag in the mire.
Be-mōan', v. t. To lament ; to bewail. [mock.
Be-mŏck', v. t. To insult ; to
Be-mōurn', v. t. To mourn.
Bĕnch, n. A long seat; a judge's seat ; body of judges ; a court.
Bĕnch'er, n. A senior in the English inns of court.
Bĕnd, v. t. & i. [imp. & p. p. BENDED, BENT.] To crook; to bow ; to submit. — n. A curve or flexure ; a turn.
Bĕnd'a-ble, a. Capable of being bent.
Be-nēath', or Be-nĕath', prep. Lower than ; under ; below. — adv. In a lower place.
Bĕn'e-dĭct,) n. A newly mar-
Bĭn'e-dĭck,) ried man.
Bĕn'e-dĭc'tion, n. [Lat. benedictio, fr. bene, well, and dicere, to speak.] Blessing ; invocation of happiness ; thanks.
Bĕn'e-făc'tion, n. Charitable gift ; donation ; gratuity.
Bĕn'e-făc'tor, n. One who confers a benefit.
Bĕn'e-făc'tress, n. She who confers a benefit.
Bĕn'e-fĭçe, n. A church living.

Bĕn'e-fĭçed (bĕn'e-fīst), a. Possessed of a benefice.
Be-nĕf'i-çençe, n. Active goodness ; bounty ; kindness.
Be-nĕf'i-çent, a. Delighting in good works ; charitable ; kind.
Bĕn'e-fĭ'cial (-fĭsh'al), a. Useful ; advantageous.
Bĕn'e-fĭ'cial-ly, adv. Advantageously ; usefully.
Bĕn'e-fĭ'ci-a-ry (-fĭsh'Y-a-), n. One who holds a benefice ; one benefitted or assisted by another. — a. Holding some office or possession in subordination to another.
Bĕn'e-fĭt, n. Advantage ; profit ; favor conferred. — v. t. To do good to. — v. i. To gain advantage.
Be-nĕv'o-lençe, n. Disposition to do good ; good will ; benignity ; kindness.
Be-nĕv'o-lent, a. Having good will ; kind ; affectionate ; friendly.
Be-nīght' (-nīt'), v. t. To involve in night or darkness.
Be-nīgn' (-nīn'), a. Gracious ; kind ; generous ; benevolent.
Be-nīgn'ly (-nīn'-), adv. Favorably ; graciously.
Be-nīg'nant, a. Gracious ; kind ; favorable.
Be-nīg'ni-ty, n. Graciousness ; favor ; kindness.
Bĕn'i-son, n. A blessing ; a benediction.
Bĕnt, imp. & p. p. of Bend. — n. A curve ; tendency ; inclination ; propensity.
Be-nŭmb' (be-nŭm'), v. t. To deprive of feeling ; to make numb or torpid.
Bĕn-zoin', n. A resinous juice.
Be-prāiṣe', v. t. To praise extravagantly.
Be-quēath', v. t. To give by will. [will.
Be-quēst', n. A legacy left by
Be-rāte', v. t. To scold ; to chide ; to take to task.
Be-rēave', v. t. [imp. & p. p. BEREAVED, BEREFT.] To make destitute ; to deprive ; to take away from.
Be-rēave'ment, n. Deprivation ; loss. [reav.-
Be-rĕft', imp. & p. p. of Be-
Bĕr'ga-mŏt, n. A pear ; a citron ; a perfume.
Be-rhȳme' (-rīm'), v. t. To mention in rhyme.
Bĕr'lin, or Ber-lĭn', n. A kind of four-wheeled carriage.
Bĕr'ry (161), n. Any small fruit containing seeds.

Bĕrth (12), n. [From the root of bear.] A ship's station at anchor ; a place in a ship to sleep in ; official situation.
Bĕr'yl, n. A greenish mineral or gem.
Be-sēech', v. t. [imp. & p. p. BESOUGHT.] To entreat ; to pray ; to beg ; to implore.
Be-seem', v. t. To become ; to befit.
Be-seem'ly, a. Fit ; decent.
Be-sĕt', v. t. [imp. & p. p. BESET.] To set on, in, or round ; to besiege ; to waylay ; to perplex ; to harass.
Be-sĕt'ting, a. Habitually attending or harassing.
Be-shrew' (-shrȳ'), v. t. To wish a curse to ; to execrate.
Be-sīde', prep. At the side of ; out of ; over and above. [In the last sense, written also besides.]
Be-sīdes', adv. Over and above. — prep. Over and above ; in addition to.
Be-sĭĕġe', v. t. To lay siege to ; to hem in ; to beset.
Be-sĭĕġ'er, n. One who besieges.
Be-slŏb'ber, v. t. To smear with spittle running from the mouth. [soil ; to smear over.
Be-smēar', v. t. To daub ; to
Be-smŭt', v. t. To blacken with smut ; to slander.
Bĕ'som, n. A brush of twigs.
Be-sŏt', v. t. To make sottish ; to stupefy ; to infatuate.
Be-sŏught' (be-sawt'), imp. & p. p. of Beseech.
Be-spăn'ġle, v. t. To set or adorn with spangles.
Be-spăt'ter, v. t. To soil by spattering.
Be-spēak', v. t. [imp. BE-SPOKE ; p. p. BESPOKEN.] To speak for beforehand ; to foretell ; to betoken ; to address. [over.
Be-sprĕad', v. t. To spread
Be-sprĭnk'le, v. t. To scatter or sprinkle over.
Bĕst, a., superl. of Good. Most good ; most advanced or complete. — adv., superl. of Well. In the highest degree. — n. Utmost. [stains ; to spot.
Be-stāin', v. t. To mark with
Bĕs'tial (bĕst'yal), a. [From Lat. bestia, a beast.] Belonging to a beast ; brutal ; carnal ; sensual ; filthy.
Bes-tial'i-ty (best-yăl'-), n. Qualities of a beast.
Be-stĭck', v. t. To stick over, as with sharp points.

sŏn, ôr, dǫ, wǫlf, tōō, tōŏk ; ûrn, rụe, pụll ; ç, ġ, soft ; c, ġ, hard ; aṣ ; eẋist ; ŋ as ng ; this.

Be-stir', v. t. To cause to move quick; to hasten.
Be-stow', v. t. To stow; to make use of; to lay out or up; to give; to confer.
Be-stow'al, } n. Act of
Be-stow'ment, } bestowing.
Be-strew' (-strṳ' or -strō'), v. t. To scatter over; to sprinkle.
Be-stride', v. t. [imp. BE-STRID or BESTRODE; p. p. BESTRID, BESTRIDDEN.] To sit or stand with the legs extended across; to stride over.
Be-stud', v. t. To adorn with studs or bosses.
Bet, n. A wager; stake.—v. t. [imp. & p. p. BETTED.] To lay a wager.
Be-take', v. t. [imp. BETOOK; p. p. BETAKEN.] To have recourse; to apply.
Be'tel (bē'tl), n. A species of pepper growing in the East Indies.
Be-think', v. t. [imp. BE-THOUGHT.] To reflect; to recollect. — v. i. To consider.
Be-tide', v. t. To befall; to happen to.—v. i. To happen; to occur; to come to pass.
Be-time', } adv. In good
Be-times', } time; seasonably; early.
Be-tō'ken, v. t. To signify; to show by signs.
Bet'o-ny, n. A kind of plant.
Be-took', imp. of Betake.
Be-tray', v. t. To give up or disclose treacherously; to indicate.
Be-tray'al, } n. Act of
Be-tray'ment, } betraying; breach of trust.
Be-tray'er, n. One who betrays; a traitor.
Be-troth', v. t. To pledge marriage to.
Be-troth'al, n. Contract of marriage.
Bet'ter, a., compar. of Good. More good: superior. —adv., compar. of Well. In a higher degree; more; rather. —v. t. To make better. —SYN. To improve; mend; advance.
Bet'ter-ment, n. Improvement.
Bet'ters. n. pl. Superiors.
Bet'tor, n. One who bets.
Bet'ty, n. A burglar's instrument to break open doors.
Be-tween', } prep. In the mid-
Be-twixt' } dle of; from

one to another of; shared by two or both of.
Bev'el, n. Slant of a surface; a kind of square used by masons, &c. — v.
t. To cut or form a bevel.—v. i. — a. Slanting.
Bev'er-age, n. Liquor for drinking.
Bev'y, n. A flock of birds; a company.
Be-wail', v. t. To lament; to grieve for.
Be-ware', v. i. To be cautious.
Be-wil'der, v. t. To puzzle; to perplex; to confuse.
Be-witch', v. t. To charm; to fascinate; to enchant.
Be-witch'ing, a. Having power to charm; fascinating.
Bey (bā), n. A Turkish governor.
Be-yond', prep. On the further side of. — adv. At a distance. [of a stag.
Be-zant'ler, n. Second antler
Bez'el, n. The part of a ring in which the stone is set.
Bi'as, n. Weight on one side; partiality; propensity. — v. t. (130) To incline to one side.
Bi-ax'al, } Having two axes.
Bi-ax'i-al, }
Bib, n. A cloth worn by children under the chin.
Bib'ber, n. A drinker; a tippler.
Bi'ble, n. The book that contains the sacred Scriptures.
Bib'li-cal, a. Relating to the Bible.
Bib'li-og'ra-pher, n. One versed in bibliography.
Bib'li-o-graph'ic, } a. Per-
Bib'li-o-graph'ic-al, } taining to a description of books.
Bib'li-og'ra-phy, n. [Gr. biblion, a book, and graphein, to describe.] A history or account of books.
Bib'li-o-ma'ni-a, n. A rage for possessing rare and curious books.
Bib'li-o-ma'ni-ac, n. One who has a rage for books.
Bib'li-op'o-list, } A book-
Bib'li-o-pole, } seller.
Bib'u-lous, a. Apt to imbibe; porous: spongy.
Biçe, n. A blue or green paint.
Bi-çeph'a-lous, a. Having two heads.
Bi-çip'i-tal, } a. Having two
Bi-çip'i-tous, } heads or origins.

Bick'er, v. i. To contend petulantly about trifles.
Bick'er-ing, n. Petulant contention about trifles.
Bi'córn, } a. Having two
Bi-cór'noûs, } horns.
Bi-cór'po-ral, a. Having two bodies.
Bid, v. t. [pret. BID, BADE; p. p. BID, BIDDEN.] To offer; to command; to order. — n. An offer of a price.
Bid'den (bid'dn), p. p. of Bid.
Bid'der, n. One who bids, or makes an offer.
Bid'ding, n. An invitation; command; offer of price.
Bide, v. t. To dwell. — v. i. To endure; to wait for. [teeth.
Di-den'tal, a. Having two
Bi-dét', n. A small horse.
Bi-en'ni-al, a. Happening every two years; continuing for two years.
Bier, n. A frame of wood to bear the dead to the grave.
Beest'ings, n. pl. First milk of a cow after calving.
Bi-fa'ri-oûs, a. Twofold; in two rows. [twice a year.
Bif'er-oûs, a. Bearing fruit
Bif'fid, n. Opening with a cleft. [flowers.
Bi-flō'roûs, a. Having two
Bi'fōld, a. Twofold; double.
Bi'form, a. Having two forms.
Bi-fur'cáte, } a. Having
Bi-fur'cā-ted, } two forks or branches.
Bi'fur-cā'tion, n. A forking into two branches.
Big, a. [From W. baich, burden.] Large; great; huge; swollen; pregnant.
Big'a-mist, n. One who has two wives or two husbands at the same time.
Big'a-my, n. The crime or the state of having two wives or two husbands at once.
Big'gin, n. A child's cap or hood; a small wooden vessel.
Bight (bīt), n. A bend in a sea-coast; a bend or coil of a rope.
Big'ness, n. Size; bulk.
Big'ot, n. One unreasonably devoted to a party or creed.
Big'ot-ed (130), a. Full of bigotry; illiberal.
Big'ot-ry, n. Excessive prejudice; blind zeal.
†Bi-jou' (be-zhū'), n. (pl. Bi-joux',-be-zhū'z.) A jewel.
Bi-lā'bi-ate, a. Having two lips. [sides.
Bi-lāt'er-al, a. Having two
Bil'ber-ry, n. A shrub of the

whortleberry kind, and its fruit.
Bil'bo, n. [From *Bilboa*, in Spain.] (*pl.* Bil'boes, 140.) A rapier; a sword. (*pl.*) A kind of stocks for the feet.
Bile, n. A yellowish bitter fluid secreted by the liver.
Bilge, n. The protuberant part of a cask; broadest part of a ship's bottom. — *v. i.* To leak from fracture in the bilge.
Bilge'-wa'ter, n. Offensive water in the bottom of a ship's hold.
Bil'ia-ry, a. Belonging to, or partaking of, the bile.
Bi-lin'gual, a. Having or speaking two languages.
Bil'ious (bĭl'yus), a. Pertaining to bile.
Bi-lit'er-al, a. Consisting of two letters. [deceive.
Bilk, *v. t.* To defraud; to
Bill, n. Beak of a bird; an account, as of goods sold and delivered; a note; a draft of a law or act. — *v. t.* or *i.* To caress; to fondle.
Bil'let, n. A small note or letter; a stick of wood. — *v. t.* To quarter, as soldiers in private houses.
†Billet-doux (bĭl'le-dōō'), n. A love-letter.
Bill'iards, *n. pl.* A game played on a kind of table with balls and sticks. [guage; ribaldry.
Bill'ings-gāte, n. Foul lan-
Bill'ion (bĭl'yun), n. In *Eng.* a million of millions; in *Amer.* a thousand millions.
Bĭl'lōw, n. A large wave.
Bĭl'lōw-y, a. Swelling like a wave.
Bi-lŏc'u-lar, a. Divided into two cells. [hands.
Bi-mā'nous, a. Having two
Bi-mĕn'sal, a. Occuring once in two months.
Bĭn, n. A repository for any commodity, as grain.
Bī'na-ry, a. Composed of two.
Bī'nate, a. Being in couples.
Bīnd, *v. t.* or *i.* [*imp.* & *p. p.* BOUND.] To tie; to confine; to restrain; to oblige by kindness: to confirm; to form a border round; to make costive. — *v. i.* To become contracted; to be obligatory.
Bīnd'er, n. One who binds books. [ing books.
Bīnd'er-y, n. Place for bind-
Bīnd'ing, n. A bandage; cover of a book.

57

Bĭn'na-cle, n. The compass-box of a ship.
Bĭn'o-cle, n. A telescope with two tubes joining.
Bi-nŏc'u-lar, a. Having two eyes.
Bi-nō'mi-al, n. Having two names. [biography.
Bī-ŏg'ra-pher, n. A writer of
Bī/o-grăph'ic-al, a. Pertaining to the history of a person's life.
Bi-ŏg'ra-phy, n. [Gr. *bios*, life, and *graphein*, to write] A history of one's life and character. [life.
Bī-ŏl'o-gy, n. The science of
Bī-pā'rous, or Bĭp'a-rous, a. Bringing forth two at a birth.
Bi-pär'tīte, or Bĭp'ar-tīte, a. Capable of being divided into two parts.
Bi'pär-ti'tion (-tĭsh'un), n. Division into two parts.
Bī'ped, n. An animal having only two feet, as man.
Bi-pĕ'dal, a. Having two feet.
Bi-pĕn'nate, a. Having two wings. [petals.
Bi-pĕt'al-ous, a. Having two
Bi-quăd'rate, n. The fourth power; square of a square.
Bi'quad-răt'ic, a. Relating to the fourth power of a quantity. [rays.
Bi-rā'di-ate, a. Having two
Birch (16), n. A tree of several species.
Birch'en, a. Made of birch.
Bird, n. A feathered, flying animal. [keep birds in.
Bird'-cāge, n. A cage to
Bird'-eÿe, } *a.* Seen as if by
Bird's-eÿe, } a flying bird above.
Bird'-līme, n. A glutinous substance to catch birds.
Birth (16), n. The act of coming into life; lineage; origin; extraction.
Birth'dây, n. Day, or anniversary of the day, of one's birth. [one is born.
Birth'-plăçe, n. Place where
Bĭrth'-right (-rīt), n. The right or privilege to which one is born.
Bĭs'cuit (-kĭt), n. A kind of small baked cake.
Bi-sĕct', *v. t.* To divide into two parts, usually equal parts.
Bi-sĕc'tion, n. A division into two equal parts.
Bi-sĕg'ment, n. One of the parts of any thing bisected.

BLAB

Bĭsh'op, n. The head of a diocese.
Bĭsh'op-rīc (127), n. Jurisdiction of a bishop; a diocese.
Bĭg'muth, n. A reddish-white metal.
Bī'son (or bī'sn), n. A North-American quadruped, popularly called *Buffalo*.

Bison.

Bis-sĕx'tīle, n. Leap-year.
Bĭs'ter, } *n.* A brown paint
Bĭs'tre, } made of soot.
Bĭs'tou-ry, n. A surgical instrument for making incisions.
Bī-sŭl'cous, a. Cloven-footed.
Bĭt, n. The iron mouth-piece of a bridle; a morsel; a boring tool. — *v. t.* To put a bit in the mouth of.
Bĭtch, n. A she-dog.
Bīte, *v. t.* [*imp.* BIT; *p. p.* BITTEN.] To seize or crush with the teeth; to cheat; to trick. — n. Act of biting; a wound made by the teeth; a cheat; a trick.
Bīt'er, n. One that bites.
Bīt'ing (133), a. Sharp; severe; sarcastic; caustic.
Bĭt'ten (bĭt'tn), *p. p.* of *Bite*.
Bĭt'ter, a. [From *bite*.] Having a peculiar, acrid, biting taste; sharp; severe; afflictive. [somewhat
Bĭt'ter-ĭsh, a. Somewhat
Bĭt'tern, n. A wading-bird allied to the heron.
Bĭt'ter-ness, n. State or quality of being bitter; a bitter taste. [uous drink.
Bĭt'ters, *n. pl.* A bitter spirit-
Bi-tū'men, n. An inflammable substance of a strong smell. [bitumen.
Bi-tū'mi-nous, a. Containing
Bī'vălve, n. A shell having two valves.
Bī'vălve, } *a.* [Lat. *bi*,
Bī-vălv'u-lar, } *bis*, twice, and *valva*, valve.] Having two valves.
Bĭv'i-ous, or Bī'vi-ous, a. Having or leading two ways.
Bĭv'ou-ăc (bĭv'wak), *v. i.* To be on watch all night, as an army. — n. A watching by night, as of a whole army.
†Bi-zärre', a. [Fr.] Odd; fantastic; strange.
Blăb, *v. t.* or *i.* To tell a se-

sŏn, ŏr, dọ, wọlf, tọo, tọok; ûrn, rụe, pụll; ç, ġ, *soft*; c, ġ, *hard*; aṣ; eχist; ụ *as* ng; this.

cret; to tattle. — *n.* One who blabs; a tell-tale.

Black, *a.* Destitute of light; very dark; cloudy; dismal. — *n.* A negro; the darkest of colors. — *v. t.* To make black; to blacken.

Black'a-mōor, *n.* A negro.

Black'-ärt, *n.* Magic.

Black'ball, *n.* A composition for blackening shoes; a ball of black color used as a negative in voting. — *v. t.* To reject by black ballots.

Black'ber-ry, *n.* The berry of the bramble.

Black'bird, *n.* A kind of singing bird of a black color.

Black'bōard, *n.* A board painted black used for writing on with chalk.

Black'-cat'tle, *n. pl.* Oxen, cows, &c., of any color.

Black'en (blăk'n), *v. t.* To make black; to defame. — *v. i.* To grow black.

Black'guard (blăg'gard), *n.* [Orig. the guard of the Devil.] A person who uses foul language.

Black'ing, *n.* A preparation for making boots, shoes, &c., black. [black.

Black'ish, *a.* Somewhat

Black'-lēad, *n.* A mineral; plumbago.

Black'-lĕg, *n.* A notorious gambler and cheat; a sharper.

Black'-lĕt'ter, *n.* The old English letter or character. See TYPE.

Black'mōor, *n.* A black man.

Black'ness, *n.* Quality of being black, in a literal or figurative sense; a black color.

Black'smith, *n.* A smith who works in iron.

Black'thŏrn, *n.* A spiny plant used for hedges.

Blăd'der, *n.* A vessel in the body containing some liquid, as the urine.

Blāde, *n.* A spire of grass; the cutting part of an instrument; the flat part of an oar; a gay or dashing fellow.

Blāde'bōne, *n.* The bone of the shoulder.

Blād'ed, *a.* Having blades.

Blāin, *n.* A blister; blotch.

Blām'a-ble (133), *a.* Deserving blame. — SYN. Culpable; faulty; censurable.

Blām'a-ble-ness, *n.* State of being blamable.

Blām'a-bly, *adv.* In a manner deserving blame; culpably.

Blāme, *v. t.* To censure; to charge with a fault. — *n.* Expression of disapprobation; imputation of a fault; fault.

Blāme'ful, *a.* Faulty: censurable. [blame.

Blāme'less, *a.* Without

Blāme'wor-thy (-wâr'thȳ), *a.* Deserving blame; censurable.

Blánch, *v. t.* or *i.* To whiten; to peel; to skin.

Blanc-mange' (blo-mŏnj'), *n.* A preparation of isinglass, milk, sugar, &c., boiled.

Blănd, *a.* Courteous; mild; soft; gentle.

Blan-dĭl'o-quençe, *n.* Fair, mild, flattering speech.

Blănd'ish, *v. t.* [From Lat. *blandus,* mild.] To smooth; to soften; to caress; to flatter.

Blănd'ish-ment, *n.* Soothing words; artful caresses.

Blănk, *a.* White; pale; unwritten; without rhyme. — *n.* Any void space; a ticket drawn of no value.

Blănk'et, *n.* A woolen covering for a bed. [low.

Blāre, *v. i.* To roar; to bellow.

Blär'ney, *n.* Smooth, deceitful talk; flattery.

Blas-phēme', *v. t.* To speak impiously of, as of God. — *v. i.* To utter blasphemy.

Blas-phĕm'er, *n.* One who blasphemes. [ing blasphemy.

Blăs'phe-moŭs, *a.* Containing

Blăs'phe-moŭs-ly, *adv.* In a blasphemous manner

Blăs'phe-my, *n.* Language uttered impiously against God or sacred things.

Blāst, *n.* A destructive wind; a forcible stream of air; blight; explosion of powder; one smelting of ore. — *v. t.* To cause to wither; to split with powder; to injure.

Blā'tant, *a.* Bellowing, as a calf.

Blāze, *v. i.* To shine or burn with flame. — *v. t.* To make public far and wide. — *n.* A flame; a stream of light.

Blā'zon (blā'zn), *v. t.* To display with ostentation. — *n.* The art of heraldry; show.

Blā'zon-ry, *n.* The art of describing coats of arms.

Blēach, *v. t.* or *i.* To whiten.

Blēach'er-y, *n.* A place for bleaching.

Blēak, *a.* Open; desolate and exposed; cold; cheerless.

Blēak'ness, *n.* Quality of being bleak.

Blēar, *a.* Dim or sore with rheum. — *v. t.* To make the eyes sore or watery.

Blēar'-eyed (-ĭd), *a.* Having eyes dim with rheum.

Blēat, *v. i.* To cry like a sheep.

Blēat, } *n.* The cry of a **Blēat'ing,** } sheep or lamb.

Blēed, *v. i.* [*imp. & p. p.* BLED.] To lose blood. — *v. t.* To let blood.

Blĕm'ish, *v. t.* To disfigure; to mark with deformity; to tarnish; to defame. — *n.* Mark of deformity; disgrace; taint. [linch.

Blĕnch, *v. t.* To shrink; to

Blĕnd, *v. t.* To confound in a mass; to mingle together.

Blĕss, *v. t.* [*imp. & p. p.* BLESSED (57) *or* BLEST.] To make happy; to wish happiness to; to praise; to extol.

Blĕss'ed, *a.* Happy; heavenly.

Blĕss'ed-ness, *n.* Happiness.

Blĕss'ing, *n.* Divine favor; benediction.

Blĕst, *imp. & p. p.* of *Bless.*

Blew (blū), *imp.* of *Blow.*

Blīght (blīt), *n.* A disease; mildew; decay. — *v. t.* To affect with blight; to blast.

Blīnd, *a.* Destitute of sight; dark; obscure. — *v. t.* To prevent from seeing; to darken. — *n.* Any thing that intercepts the sight; something to mislead.

Blīnd'fōld, *a.* Having the eyes covered. — *v. t.* To cover the eyes of.

Blīnd'-man's-bŭff', *n.* A kind of game.

Blīnd'ly, *adv.* Without sight; without judgment or examination.

Blīnd'ness, *n.* Want of sight; ignorance.

Blīnd'-sīde, *n.* The side most assailable; foible; weakness.

Blĭnk (79), *v. i.* To wink; to see darkly. — *v. t.* To avoid; to evade. — *n.* Glimpse; glance; a dazzling whiteness.

Blĭnk'ard, *n.* One with bad eyes.

Blĭnk'er, *n.* One who blinks; a blind for horses.

Blĭss, *n.* The highest happiness; blessedness; felicity.

Blĭss'ful (139), *a.* Very happy; filled with ecstatic joy; blessed.

Blĭs'ter, *n.* A thin watery bladder on the skin. — *v. t.* To raise blisters upon. — *v. i.* To rise in blisters.

Blithe, *a.* Gay; merry; joyous.
Blithe′ful, } *a.* Gay; joyous; merry.
Blithe′some, }
Bloat, *v. t.* To cause to swell. —*v. i.* To puff up; to grow turgid.
Bloat′ed, *a.* Puffed; swelled.
Block, *n.* A piece of wood, stone, &c.; a pulley; an obstacle or obstruction. — *v. t.* To shut or stop up; to hinder.
Block-ade′, *n.* The shutting up of a place by troops or ships. — *v. t.* To surround with a force; to shut up.
Block′head, *n.* A person of dull intellect.
Block′-house, *n.* A sort of wooden fort.
Block′ish, *a.* Deficient in understanding; stupid; dull.
Blom′a-ry (blōom′a-rỹ), *n.* The first forge for iron.
Blonde, *n.* A person with fair complexion, light hair, and light blue eyes.
Blood (blŭd), *n.* The red fluid which circulates in animals; kindred; lineage; honorable birth; race; life; a rake.
Blood′-guilt′i-ness, *n.* Guilt of shedding blood unlawfully.
Blood′-heat, *n.* Heat of the same degree as the blood.
Blood′hound, *n.* A ferocious kind of dog.
Blood′i-ly, *adv.* In a bloody manner.
Blood′less, *a.* Without blood.
Blood′shed, *n.* Slaughter.
Blood′shot, *a.* Red and inflamed with blood.
Blood′-stained, *a.* Stained with blood.
Blood′-suck′er, *n.* A leech; a cruel man. [blood.
Blood′-thirst′y, *a.* Eager for
Blood′-ves′sel, *n.* An artery or vein.
Blood′y, *a.* Stained with blood; murderous. — *v. t.* To stain with blood.
Bloom, *n.* Blossom; flower; the flush on the cheek; a mass of crude iron. — *v. i.* To yield blossoms; to flourish.
Bloom′ing, *a.* Thriving with youth, health, and beauty.

Bloom′y, *a.* Full of bloom; flowery.
Blos′som, *n.* The flower of a plant. — *v. i.* To put forth blossoms.
Blot (129), *v. t.* To stain; to spot; to efface. — *n.* Spot; disgrace.
Blotch, *n.* An inflamed spot on the skin. — *v. t.* To mark with spots.
Blot′ter, *n.* One who blots; a waste-book.
Blouse, } *n.* A light, loose
Blowse, } outer garment.
Blow, *n.* A stroke; sudden or severe calamity; egg of a fly; a gale. — *v. i.* [*imp.* BLEW; *p. p.* BLOWN.] To make a current of air; to pant; to puff; to breathe; to blossom. — *v. t.* To drive by a current of air; to deposit, as flies their eggs; to put out of breath; to sound, as a wind instrument.
Blow′er, *n.* A contrivance for increasing a current of air.
Blow′-pipe, *n.* A tube by which a current of air is forced through flame upon any substance.
Blowze, *n.* A ruddy woman.
Blow′zy, *a.* Ruddy; fat and ruddy-faced; high colored.
Blub′ber, *n.* The fat of whales. — *v. i.* To weep so as to swell the cheeks.
Blud′geon, *n.* A short, thick club.
Blue, *a.* Of a color called blue. — *n.* One of the seven primary colors. — *v. t.* To dye, stain, or make blue.
Blue′-bot′tle, *n.* A plant with blue flowers; a fly with a big blue belly.
Blue′-dev′i!s, *n. pl.* Lowness of spirits. [ing blue.
Blue′ness, *n.* Quality of being
Blues, *n. pl.* Lowness of spirits. [lady.
Blue′-stock′ing, *n.* A literary
Bluff, *a.* Roughly frank; blustering; steep; bold. — *n.* A steep bank overhanging the sea or a river.
Bluff′ness, *n.* Quality of being bluff. [degree.
Blu′ish (133), *a.* Blue in a small
Blun′der, *v. i.* [Allied to *blend.*] To mistake grossly. —*n.* A gross mistake. — SYN. Error; mistake; bull.
Blun′der-buss, *n.* A short gun with large bore.
Blun′der-er, } *n.* A stupid
Blun′der-head, } person.

Blunt, *a.* Dull on the edge or point; rough; rude; abrupt. —*v. t.* To dull; to depress; to weaken. [ner.
Blunt′ly, *adv.* In a blunt man-
Blunt′ness, *n.* Want of edge or point; dullness; abruptness.
Blur, *n.* A blot; spot; stain. —*v. t.* (129) To obscure without quite effacing; to stain; to spot.
Blurt, *v. t.* To utter inadvertently.
Blush, *v. i.* To redden in the face. — *n.* A red color in the cheeks caused by shame or confusion.
Blush′ing, *n.* Act of turning red. — *a.* Reddish; modest.
Blus′ter (130), *v. i.* [Allied to *blast*] To roar; to boast; to bully. — *n.* A roar; tumult; boast; swagger.
Blus′ter-er, *n.* A bully.
Blus′ter-ing, *n.* Tumult; noise; boasting. — *a.* Noisy; boastful; windy.
Bo′à (149), *n.* The largest kind of serpent, — often called *Boa constrictor*; a tippet.
Boar, *n.* A male swine.
Board, *n.* A piece of timber sawed thin and broad; a table; food; a council; deck of a ship. — *v. t.* To lay with boards; to enter by force, as a ship; to furnish food regularly for pay. — *v. i.* To receive food regularly for pay.
Board′er, *n.* One who pays for board taken at another's table; one who enters a ship by force.
Board′ing-school, *n.* A school where the pupils board with the teacher.
Boast, *v. i.* or *t.* To talk ostentatiously; to vaunt; to brag. — *n.* A vaunting speech; cause of vaunting.
Boast′er, *n.* One who boasts.
Boast′ful, *a.* Given to boasting; vainglorious.
Boat (18), *n.* A small open vessel. — *v. t.* To convey or transport in a boat.
Boat′a-ble, *a.* Navigable with boats.
Boat′-hook, *n.* An iron hook with a point on the back, fixed to a long pole, to pull or push a boat.
Boat′man (143), *n.* One who manages a boat.
Boat′swain (*colloq.* bō′sn), *n.* An officer in a ship, who has

sŭn, ôr, dọ, wọlf, tọo, tŏŏk; "rn, rye, pụll; ç, ġ, *soft*; ç, ġ, *hard*; aẓ; eẋist; ṇ *as* ng; this.

charge of the boats, rigging, &c.

Bŏb, *n.* Any thing that plays loosely, as at the end of a string. — *v. t.* or *i.* To move in a short, jerking manner; to fish for eels.

Bŏb′bĭn, *n.* A small pin on which thread is wound for making lace.

Bŏb′bĭn-ĕt, *n.* A kind of lace.

Bŏb′tāil, *n.* A tail cut short.

Bŏck′ĭng, *n.* A kind of baize.

Bōde, *v. t.* To presage; to foreshow. — *v. i.* To be an omen.

Bŏd′ĭçe, or **Bŏd′dĭçe,** *n.* A sort of stays: a corset.

Bŏd′ĭed (bŏd′ĭd), *a.* Having a body.

Bŏd′ĭ-less, *a.* Without a body.

Bŏd′ĭ-ly (135), *a.* Relating to the body. — *adv.* Corporeally; completely.

Bŏd′ĭng, *n.* An omen.

Bŏd′kĭn, *n.* An instrument for making holes ; a dagger.

Bŏd′y, *n.* The whole trunk of an animal; person ; main part; bulk ; mass; system ; a corporation; consistency ; thickness. — *v. t.* To give a body or form to.

Bŏd′y-guārd, *n.* A guard of the person ; a life-guard.

Bŏg, *n.* A fen or morass.

Bŏg′gle, *v. i.* & *t.* To hesitate from fear of difficulties.

Bŏg′gler, *n.* One who hesitates.

Bŏg′gy, *a.* Marshy; swampy.

Bŏg′-ōre, *n.* Iron ore found in boggy or swampy land.

Bō-hēa′, *n.* A coarse kind of black tea.

Boil, *n.* A sore swelling. — *v. i.* To bubble through heat. — *v. t.* To cause to boil.

Boil′er, *n.* A vessel for boiling, or generating steam.

Boil′er-y, *n.* A place for boiling.

Bois′ter-oŭs, *a.* Violent ; noisy ; stormy.

Bois′ter-oŭs-ly, *adv.* In a boisterous manner.

Bōld, *a.* Having or requiring courage; markedly conspicuous. — SYN. Courageous ; brave ; valiant ; daring ; prominent.

Bōld′-fāçed (-fāst), *a.* Impudent ; shameless. [ner.

Bōld′ly, *adv.* In a bold man-

Bōld′ness, *n.* Courage; confidence ; impudence.

Bōle, *n.* Stem of a tree ; a kind of fine clay.

Bōll, *n.* A pod ; a seed-vessel.

— *v. i.* To form into a round pod.

Bŏl′ster (18), *n.* A long pillow. — *v. t.* To pad ; to support ; to prop ; to uphold.

Bōlt (18), *n.* Bar for fastening; an arrow ; lightning ; a piece of canvas of 38 yards. — *v. t.* To fasten : to sift. — *v. i.* To leave suddenly ; to swallow hastily.

Bōlt′er, *n.* A sieve to separate flour from bran.

Bō′lus, *n.* A large pill.

Bŏmb (bŭm), *n.* [Gr. *bombus*, a deep, hollow sound.] An iron shell to be filled with powder and discharged from a mortar. **Bomb.**

Bŏm-bärd′, *v. t.* To attack with bombs.

Bŏm′bard-iēr′, *n.* One who serves a mortar.

Bŏm-bärd′ment, *n.* An attack with bombs.

Bŏm′ba-gīne′, } *n.* A slight **Bŏm′ba-zīne′,** } twilled stuff.

Bŏm′băst (bŭm′băst), *n.* High sounding language ; fustian.

Bŏm′băst, } *a.* Consisting **Bŏm-băst′ĭc,** } of swelling words; inflated ; pompous.

Bŏm′ba-zĕtte′, *n.* A thin woolen stuff.

Bŏmb′-kĕtch } (bŭm′-), *n.* A **Bŏmb′-vĕs′sel** } ship to carry bombs.

Bŏn′bon (or bŏng′bŏng), *n.* A sugar-plum ; confectionery.

Bŏnd, *n.* Any thing that binds; chord ; chain : union ; an obligation in writing. — *v. t.* To secure by bond. — *a.* In a servile state; captive ; bound.

Bŏnd′age, *n.* Slavery ; captivity ; imprisonment ; involuntary servitude. [slave.

Bŏnd′māid, *n.* A woman

Bŏnd′man, *n.* A man slave.

Bŏnd′-sĕrv′ant, *n.* A slave.

Bŏnds′man (143), *n.* One bound as surety for another.

Bŏnd′wom-an (143), *n.* A woman slave.

Bōne (18), *n.* The solid frame of an animal, or a piece of this frame. — *v. t.* To take out bones from.

Bōne′-sĕt′ter, *n.* A man who sets broken bones.

Bŏn′fīre, *n.* A triumphal fire.

Bŏn-mŏt′ (bŏng-mō′), *n.* A witty speech ; a jest.

Bŏn′net, *n.* A covering for the head. [ry ; gay.

Bŏn′ny, *a.* Handsome ; mer-

Bŏn′ny-elăb′ber, *n.* Thick part of milk that has turned sour.

Bō′nus, *n.* A premium, as on a loan or other privilege.

Bō′ny, *a.* Full of bones ; strong. [bird.

Bōō′by (141), *n.* A dunce ; a

Bōōdh′ĭṣm (bōōd′izm), *n.* A system of religion in Asia.

Bōŏk, *n.* A volume ; a work ; or a definite part of a work. — *v. t.* To enter in a book.

Bōŏk′-bīnd′er, *n.* One who binds books. [books.

Bōŏk′-cāse (106), *n.* A case for

Bōŏk′ish, *a.* Much given to books or study.

Bōŏk′-keep′er (106), *n.* A keeper of account-books.

Bōŏk′ish-ness, *n.* Fondness for reading or study.

Bōŏk′-keep′ing, *n.* The keeping of accounts.

Bōŏk′-sĕl′er, *n.* One who sells books.

Bōŏk′worm (-wûrm), *n.* A worm or mite that eats holes in books ; a close student.

Bōōm, *n.* A spar to extend the bottom of a sail; a bar across a river or harbor ; a hollow roar or cry. — *v. i.* To rush and roar; to cry as the bittern.

Bōōn, *a.* [Lat. *bonus*, good.] Gay ; merry ; kind. — *n.* A gift ; present ; grant ; favor.

Bōōr, *n.* A clown ; a countryman.

Bōōr′ish, *a.* Clownish ; rustic.

Bōōr′ish-ness, *n.* Clownishness ; rusticity.

Bōōṣe, *v. i.* To drink to excess.

Bōōst, *v. t.* To push up ; to lift.

Bōō′sy, *a.* Tipsy ; merry with liquor.

Bōōt, *v. t.* To profit ; to put on boots ; to furnish with boots — *n.* Profit ; a covering for the leg and foot ; part of a coach. — *To boot*, in addition.

Bōōt-ee′, *n.* A short boot.

Bōōth, *n.* A temporary shelter of slight construction.

Bōōt′-jack, *n.* An instrument for pulling off boots.

Bōōt′less, *a.* Unprofitable ; useless ; vain.

Bōōt′-tree, *n.* A sort of last to shape a boot on. [spoil.

Bōōt′y, *n.* Pillage ; plunder ;

Bō′rax (186), *n.* A compound of

BORDER 61 BRACKET

Boracic acid and soda, used as a styptic.
Bôr'der, *n.* An edge; boundary. — *v. t.* To adorn with a border. — *v. i.* To make a border; to be near or contiguous.
Bôr'der-er, *n.* One who dwells near a border.
Bôre, *v. t.* To make a hole in; to pierce; to weary. — *n.* A hole made by boring; a tiresome person.
Bôre, *imp.* of *Bear.* [erly.
Bô're-al, *a.* Northern; north-
Bô're-as, *n.* The north wind.
Bôre'-côle, *n.* A species of cabbage. [forth.
Bôrn. *p. p.* of *Bear.* Brought
Bôrne, *p. p.* of *Bear.* Carried.
Bôr'ough (bŭr'ō), *n.* A corporation town.
Bôr'row, *v. t.* To take the use of for a time. [rows.
Bôr'row-er, *n.* One who borrows.
Bo'som (bŏŏz'um), *n.* The breast; heart; any receptacle. — *v. t.* To conceal; to inclose.
Bŏss, *n.* A stud; knob.
Bŏssed (bŏst), *a.* Ornamented with bosses.
Bŏss'y, *a.* Containing bosses.
Bo-tăn'ic, } *a.* Relating to
Bo-tăn'ic-al, } plants.
Bŏt'a-nist, *n.* A person skilled in plants. [plants.
Bŏt'a-nize, *v. i.* To study
Bŏt'a-ny, *n.* [Gr. *botanē*, plant.] That branch of natural history that treats of plants.
Bŏtch, *n.* Swelling; pustule; work ill-finished. — *v. t.* To mend clumsily.
Bŏtch'er, *n.* One who mends old clothes. [botches.
Bŏtch'y, *a.* Covered with
Bŏth (18), *n.* The one and the other; the two. [Used also as a *pron.* and a *conj.*]
Bŏth'er, *v. t.* To perplex; to confuse.
Bŏt'ry-old, } *a.* Having the
Bŏt'ry-oid'al, } form of a bunch of grapes.
Bŏts, *n. pl.* Small worms in the intestines of horses.
Bŏt'tle, *n.* A narrow mouthed vessel for liquor. — *v. t.* To put in bottles.
Bŏt'tom, *n.* The lowest part; the ground under water; foundation; a valley; dregs; a ship. — *v. t.* To found or build upon.
Bŏt'tom-less, *a.* Without a bottom; unfathomable.

Bŏt'tom-ry, *n.* The act of borrowing money on a ship.
Bou'doir (bōō'dwôr), *n.* A small private apartment.
Bough (bou), *n.* A branch.
Bou-giê' (bōō-zhā'), *n.* A wax candle; a surgical instrument.
Bought (bawt), *imp.* & *p. p.* of *Buy.* Purchased.
Boul'der, *n.* See *Bowlder.*
Bounçe, *v. i.* To leap; to spring. — *n.* A leap; sudden noise; a boast.
Boun'çer, *n.* A boaster; a lie.
Boun'çing, *a.* Stout; plump and healthy.
Bound, *v. t.* To limit; to restrain; to inclose. — *v. i.* To spring; to jump. — *a.* Destined; going to. — *n.* A barrier; limit; leap.
Bound'a-ry, *n.* A limit; mark; barrier.
Bound'en, *a.* Required; necessary.
Bound'less, *a.* Without bound; infinite.
Boun'te-oûs, *a.* Liberal; kind; bountiful.
Boun'te-oûs-ly, *adv.* Liberally; generously.
Boun'te-oûs-ness, *n.* Liberality; munificence.
Boun'ti-fŭl (135, 139), *a.* Liberal; generous. [ously.
Boun'ti-fŭl-ly, *adv.* Generously.
Boun'ti-fŭl-ness, *n.* Quality of being bountiful.
Boun'ty, *n.* [Lat. *bonitas*, fr. *bonus*, good.] Liberality in giving; generosity; munificence; a premium.
Bou-quet' (bōō-kā'), *n.* A bunch of flowers; a nosegay.
Boûr-ǵeois' (bur-jois'), *n.* A kind of printing type.

☞ Bourgeois Type.

Boûrn, *n.* A bound; limit.
Boûrse, *n.* A French Exchange.
Bout, *n.* A turn; trial; essay.
Bō'vine, *a.* Relating to cattle of the ox kind.
Bow (bou), *v. t. & i.* To bend down. — *n.* An act of reverence or respect; the rounding part of a ship's side forward.
Bōw, *n.* An instrument to shoot arrows; a fiddle-stick; any thing curved.
Bow'el, *v. t.* To take out the bowels of; to eviscerate.
Bow'els, *n. pl.* The intestines; entrails.
Bow'er, *n.* An arbor; an anchor at the bow.

Bow'er-y, *a.* Full of bowers; shady.
Bōw'ie-knife (bō'e-nif), *n.* A long knife or dagger.
Bôwl. *n.* A deep vessel; a round ball of wood. — *v. t.* To roll along as a bowl — *v. i.* To play at bowls.
Bōw'-lĕgged, *a.* Having crooked legs.
Bôwl'der, *n.* A roundish mass of rock. [bowls.
Bôwl'er, *n.* One who plays at
Bôwl'ine, *n.* A rope to hold a sail to the wind.
Bôwl'ing-ăl'ley, *n.* A place to play at bowls.
Bôwl'ing-green, *n.* A green for bowlers.
Bōw'man (143), *n.* An archer.
Bow'man (bou'man), *n.* Foremost rower.
Bōw'sprit, *n.* A spar projecting from a ship's head.
Bōw'string, *n.* A string for a bow; a Turkish punishment.
Bōw'-win'dōw, *n.* A projecting window.
Bŏx, *n.* A tree; a wooden case; a blow on the ear; a plant; a driver's seat; an iron cylinder for an axle-tree to run in. — *v. t.* To put in a box; to strike. — *v. i.* To fight with the fist. [box.
Bŏx'en (bŏks'n), *a.* Made of
Bŏx'er, *n.* One who fights with the fists; a pugilist.
Boy, *n.* A male child; a lad.
Boy'hŏod, *n.* State of a boy.
Boy'ish, *a.* Pertaining to or like, a boy.
Boy'ish-ly, *adv.* In a boyish manner.
Boy'ish-ness, } *n.* The man-
Boy'ism, } ners of a boy; boyhood; puerility.
Brăb'ble, *v. i.* To clamor.
Brăçe, *n.* That which holds or binds; a bandage; a strap; a piece of timber; a pair; a curved connecting line used in printing. [See *Braggart*, below.] — *v. t.* To bind; to tie; to tighten; to furnish with braces.
Brăçe'let, *n.* An ornament for the wrist.
Brā'çer, *n.* One who braces.
Brăch'i-al, or Brā'chi-al, *a.* Belonging to the arm.
Bra-chŷg'ra-phy, *n.* Shorthand writing.
Brăck'et, *n.* [Old Fr. *braquet*, from Lat. *brachium*, arm.] A small support of wood; (*pl.*) hooks, thus [ ], for inclosing words.

sŏn, ôr, dọ, wọlf, tōō, tŏŏk; ûrn, rụe, pụll; ç, ġ, *soft*; c, g, *hard*; a̤; ex̌ist; ŋ *as* ng; *this.*

BRACKISH 62 BREVET

Brack'ish, *a.* Saltish; salt.
Bract, *n.* A small leaf or set of leaves.
Brad, *n.* A slender nail without a head.
Brag (129), *v. t.* To boast; to swagger; to vaunt. — *n.* A boast; a game at cards.
Brag'ga-do'ci-o (-sbl-o), *n.* A vain boaster. [ness.
Brag'gard-ism, *n.* Boastful-
Brag'gart,) *n.* A boaster; a
Brag'ger,) vain fellow.
Brag'gart, *a.* Roastful.
Brah'min, *n.* A Hindoo priest.
Braid (130), *v. t.* To weave or plait, as three or more strands to form one. — *n.* Something braided; a sort of lace.
Brain, *n.* The soft substance within the skull which is the seat of sensation and intellect; the understanding; the fancy. — *v. t.* To beat out the brains of.
Brain'less, *a.* Destitute of thought; thoughtless; foolish.
Brain'-pan, *n.* The skull.
Brake, old *imp.* of *Break.* — *n.* An instrument for dressing flax; a contrivance for stopping wheels; a fern.
Brake'man (143), *n.* One who manages the brake on railway carriages.
Bram'ble, *n.* A prickly shrub.
Bra'min. See *Brahmin.*
Bran, *n.* The outer coats of grain separated from the flour; husk.
Branch, *n.* A limb; a bough; a shoot; offspring; division. — *v. i.* or *t.* To divide into branches; to ramify.
Branch'let, *n.* A little branch.
Branch'y, *a.* Full of branches.
Brand, *v. t.* [A.-S., from *brinnan,* to burn.] To burn with a hot iron; to stigmatize. — *n.* A burnt or burning piece of wood; a thunderbolt; an iron to burn the figure of letters; the mark burnt; a stigma; a sword.
Bran'dish, *v. t.* To wave; to flourish, as a weapon. — *n.* A flourish.
Bran'dish-er, *n.* One who brandishes. [worm.
Brand'ling, *n.* A kind of
Brand'-new, *a.* Perfectly new.
Bran'dy, *n.* A spirit distilled from wine, cider, or fruit.
Bran'gle (brang'gl), *n.* A brawl. — *v. i.* To wrangle.
Bra'zier (bra'zhur), *n.* One

who works in brass; a pan for holding coals.
Brass, *n.* A yellow alloy of copper and zinc; impudence.
Brass'y, *a.* Made of brass; like brass; impudent.
Brat, *n.* A child; — in contempt.
Bra-va'do, *n.* An arrogant threat; a boasting fellow.
Brave, *a.* Fearless of danger.
— SYN. Courageous; gallant; valiant; bold; intrepid.
— *n.* -An Indian warrior. —
v. t. To encounter with firmness; to defy.
Brave'ly, *adv.* Gallantly; generously. [ism.
Brav'er-y, *n.* Courage; hero-
Bra'vo, *n.* A daring villain.
Bra'vo, *interj.* Well done!
Brawl, *v. i.* To make a great noise; to quarrel noisily. —
n. A quarrel; squabble.
Brawl'er, *n.* A wrangler; a noisy fellow.
Brawn, *n.* A boar's flesh; full, strong, muscles.
Brawn'y, *a.* Having large, strong muscles; muscular.
Bray, *v. t.* To beat in a mortar. — *v. i.* To make a harsh noise like an ass. — *n.* The cry of an ass.
Bray'ing, *n.* The cry of an ass; clamor; noise.
Braze, *v. t.* To cover or solder with brass.
Bra'zen (bra'zn), *a.* Made of brass; bold; impudent. — *v. i.* To be impudent.
Bra'zen-fåced (bra'zn-fast),*a.* Impudent; bold.
Bra'zen-ness (106), *n.* A brazen quality; brassiness.
Bra'zier (bra'zhur), *n.* See *Brasier.*
Breach, *n.* A break or gap; infraction; violation; quarrel.
Breach'y, *a.* Apt to break fences; unruly.
Bread, *n.* Food made of flour or meal; support of life.
Bread'-corn, *n.* Grain of which bread is made.
Bread'-stuff, *n.* That of which bread is made.
Breadth, *n.* Width; measure from side to side.
Break, *v. t.* [*imp.* BROKE; *p. p.* BROKE, BROKEN.] To part or open by force; to rend; to crush; to tame; to make bankrupt; to remove from office. — *v. i.* To part in two; to burst; to become a bankrupt; to dawn. — *n.*

An opening; breach; pause; failure.
Break'age (42), *n.* Allowance for things broken.
Break'er, *n.* One who breaks; a rock on which waves break; the waves so broken.
Break'fast, *n.* The first meal in the day. — *v. i.* To eat breakfast.
Break'neck, *n.* A steep or precipitous place.
Break'wa-ter, *n.* A mole or wall to break the force of the waves.
Bream, *v. t.* To cleanse, as c. ship's bottom. — *n.* A fish.
Breast, *n.* Upper foreparf of the body; seat of the affections; the heart. — *v. t.* To meet in front.
Breast'-bone, *n.* Bone of the breast.
Breast'-knot, (-nŏt), *n.* A knot of ribbons worn on the breast.
Breast'pin, *n.* A pin to wear on the breast. [the breast.
Breast'-plate, *n.* Armor for
Breast'work (-wŭrk), *n.* A low parapet for defense.
Breath, *n.* Air respired; life; breeze.
Breath'a-ble, *a.* Capable of being breathed; respirable.
Breathe, *v. i.* To respire; to live; to utter softly. — *v. t.* To exhale.
Breath'ing, *n.* Respiration; aspiration; vent.
Breath'less, *a.* Out of breath; exhausted; dead.
Bred, *imp.* & *p. p.* of *Breed.*
Breech, *n.* The lower part of the body; part of a fire-arm behind the bottom of the bore. — *v. t.* To put into breeches.
Breech'es (brĭch'ez), *n.* A lower garment worn by men, covering the hips and thighs.
Breech'ing (brĭch'ing), *n.* The hinder part of a harness.
Breed, *v. t.* [*imp.* & *p. p.* BRED.] To give birth to; to generate; to hatch; to bring up; to educate — *v. i.* To be with young. — *n.* Offspring; progeny; race.
Breed'er, *n.* One that breeds.
Breed'ing, *n* Bringing up; education; nurture; manners.
Breeze, *n.* A gentle wind
Breez'y, *a.* Fanned with gentle breezes. [*Brother.*
Breth'ren (145), *n. pl.* of
Bre-vĕt', *n.* A commission

ā, ē, ī, ō, ū, ȳ, *long* ; ă, ĕ, ĭ, ŏ, ŭ, ў, *short* ; cāre, cär, àsk, ạll, whạt ; ẽre, veil, tẽrm ; pïque, fïrm ;

BREVIARY 63 BROKEN-WINDED

which entitles an officer to rank above his pay.

Brē'vi-ā-ry, *n.* The prayer-book of the Roman Catholic church. [pend.

Brē'vi-āte, *n.* A short compendium.

Brē'vi-a-tūre, *n.* An abbreviation. [ing type.

Bre-viēr', *n.* A small printing Brevier Type.

Brĕv'i-ty, *n.* Conciseness.

Brew (brṉ), *v. i.* To make beer; to be in a state of preparation. — *v. t.* To mingle; to contrive. [brews.

Brew'er (brṉ'-), *n.* One who brews.

Brew'er-y (brṉ'-), *n.* A house for brewing. [brewery.

Brew'-house (brṉ'-), *n.* A brewery.

Brew'is (brṉ'-), *n.* Bread soaked in gravy or in water and butter.

Bribe, *n.* A gift to corrupt the conduct. — *v. t.* To corrupt by gifts.

Brīb'er, *n.* One who bribes.

Brīb'er-y, *n.* The giving or receiving of bribes.

Brick, *n.* [Armoric *prick*, clayey.] A mass of burnt clay. — *v. t.* To lay with bricks.

Brick'bāt, *n.* A broken piece of brick.

Brick'-kiln (-kĭl), *n.* A kiln for burning brick. [mason.

Brick'-lāy'er, *n.* A bricklayer.

Brick'-māk'er, *n.* One who makes brick.

Brīd'al (133), *a.* Belonging to marriage. — *n.* A wedding.

Brīde, *n.* A woman newly married, or about to be married.

Brīde'-cāke, *n.* Cake distributed at a wedding.

Brīde'grōōm, *n.* A man newly married, or about to be married.

Brīde'māid, *n.* A woman who attends the bride.

Brīde'man, *n.* A man who attends the bride and bridegroom. [correction.

Brīde'well, *n.* A house of Bridge, *n.* A structure to pass over water on; a support. — *v. t.* To form a bridge over.

Brī'dle, *n.* An instrument to restrain or govern a horse. — *v. t.* To put on a bridle; to restrain. — *v. i.* To hold up the head.

Brī-dōōn', *n.* A light snaffle distinct from that of the principal bit.

Brief, *a.* Short; concise. — *n.*

An epitome, or short writing; an abstract.

Brief'ness, *n.* Shortness; conciseness.

Brief'ly, *adv.* In few words.

Brī'er, *n.* A prickly shrub; a bramble.

Brī'er-y, *a.* Full of briers.

Brĭg, *n.* A vessel with two masts square rigged.

Brĭ-gāde', *n.* A division of troops. — *v. t.* To form into brigades.

Brĭg'a-diēr', *n.* An officer commanding a brigade.

Brĭg'and, *n.* One of a band of robbers; a freebooter.

Brĭg'an-tīne, *n.* A kind of small brig.

Brĭght (brīt), *n.* Shining; clear; promising.

Brĭght'en (brīt'n), *v. t.* or *i.* To make or become bright.

Brĭght'ly (brīt'-), *adv.* With luster; splendidly.

Brĭght'ness (brīt'-), *n.* Luster; splendor; acuteness.

Brĭll'ian-çy, *n.* Sparkling luster or brightness.

Brĭll'iant, *a.* Shining; sparkling. — *n.* A diamond cut into angles.

Brim, *n.* The edge; upper edge; side; bank. — *v. i.* To be filled to the brim.

Brim'ful, *a.* Full to the brim.

Brim'mer, *n.* A bowl filled to the top. [the brim.

Brim'ming (129), *a.* Full to

Brim'stōne, *n.* A mineral; sulphur.

Brĭn'ded, } *a.* Streaked;
Brĭn'dled, } spotted.

Brīne, *n.* Water impregnated with salt; the ocean.

Brīne'-pān, } *n.* A pit of salt
Brīne'-pit, } water for evaporation.

Bring, *v. t.* [*imp.* & *p. p.* BROUGHT.] To convey or carry to; to fetch from.

Brĭn'y, *a.* Consisting of, or resembling, brine.

Brĭnk (79), *n.* The edge of a steep place. [active; lively.

Brisk, *a.* Quick; full of life;

Brisk'et, *n.* That part of the breast of an animal that lies next to the ribs. [ner.

Brisk'ly, *adv.* In a brisk manner.

Brisk'ness, *n.* Quality of being brisk; activeness.

Brĭs'tle (brĭs'l), *n.* A stiff, coarse hair, as of swine. — *v. i.* To raise the bristles.

Brĭs'tly (brĭs'ly), *adv.* Set thick with bristles.

Brĭ-tăn'nĭ-à, *n.* A metallic compound, consisting chiefly of block tin, with antimony, and some bismuth and copper. [Britain.

Brĭt'ish, *a.* Pertaining to

Brĭt'on, *n.* A native of Britain.

Brĭt'tle, *a.* Apt to break; fragile.

Brĭt'tle-ness, *n.* Aptness to break; fragility.

Brōach, *n.* A spit. — *v. t.* To tap; to let out.

Brōach'er, *n.* One who broaches; a spit.

Broad (brawd), *a.* Extended from side to side; wide; coarse; indelicate. — SYN. Ample; comprehensive; large.

Broad'-ăx, } *n.* An ax for
Broad'ăxe, } hewing timber.

Broad'cāst, *n.* A scattering of seed with the hand. — *a.* Dispersed with the hand, as seed; widely spread.

Broad'clōth, *n.* A fine woolen cloth.

Broad'en, *v. t.* or *i.* To make or grow broad.

Broad'sīde, *n.* A discharge of all the guns on one side of a ship.

Broad'swōrd (-sōrd), *n.* A broad-bladed sword.

Bro-cāde', *n.* [It. *broccare*, to figure, to stitch.] Silk stuff variegated with gold and silver, or enriched with flowers.

Bro-cād'ed, *a.* Worked, or dressed, in brocade.

Brō'cage, *n.* Trade of a broker; brokerage.

Brŏck, *n.* A badger; a brocket.

Brŏc'co-li (140), *n.* A species of cabbage. [years old.

Brŏck'et, *n.* A red deer, two

Brō'gan, or **Bro-găn'**, *n.* A thick shoe.

Brōgue, *n.* A corrupt dialect or pronunciation.

Broid'er, *v. t.* To embroider.

Broil, *n.* A tumult; quarrel. — *v. t.* To dress over coals. — *v. i.* To be in a heat.

Broil'er, *n.* One who broils.

Brōke (18), *imp.* of *Break*.

Brō'ken (brō'kn), *p. p.* or *a.* of *Break*.

Brō'ken-heärt'ed, *a.* Having the spirits crushed.

Brō'ken-wīnd'ed, *a.* Having short breath.

sōn, ōr, dọ, wọlf, tōō, tŏŏk; ûrn, rṉe, pṵll; ç, ġ, *soft*; e, ġ, *hard*; aṣ; eẋist; ọ *as* ug; *this*.

Brō'ker, n. An agent who transacts business on commission.
Brō'ker-age, n. Business or commission of a broker.
Brŏn'chi-al, a. Relating to the throat. [fection.
Brŏn-chī'tis, n. A throat affection.
Brŏn-chŏt'o-my, n. An incision into the windpipe.
Brŏnze. n. A compound of copper and tin.—v. t. To color or harden like bronze.
Brōoch, n. A jewel; a bosompin.
Brōod, n. Offspring; progeny.—v. i. To sit on eggs; to cover chickens; to muse.
Brōok. n. A natural stream less than a river.—v. t. To bear; to endure; to submit to.
Brōok'let, n. A small brook.
Brōom, n. A shrub; an instrument to sweep with; a besom.
Brōom'stick, n. The staff or handle of a broom.
Brōom'y, a. Full of broom; like or containing broom.
Brŏth, n. Liquor in which flesh has been boiled. [fame.
Brŏth'el, n. A house of illBrŏth'er (brŭth'er, 90), n. A male born of the same parents; an associate; a companion.
Brŏth'er-hōod, n. State of being a brother; fraternity.
Brŏth'er-ly, a. Like a brother.
Brought (brawt), imp. & p. p. of Bring.
Brow, n. The forehead; the hairy ridge over the eye; the edge.
Brow'bēat, v. t. To beat down by sternness or arrogance.
Brow'bēat'ing, n. Act of beating down or endeavoring to intimidate.
Brown, a. [The root is A.-S. brúnan, Eng. burn.] Dusky; inclining to red.—n. A dusky reddish color.—v. t. To make brown.—v. i. To become brown.
Brown'ie, n. A kind of imaginary good-natured spirit.
Brown'ish, a. Inclined to brown.
Brown'-stŭd'y, a. Dull thoughtfulness; reverie.
Browse (brouz), v. t. To feed on the shoots of shrubs.
Browse (brouz), n. The twigs of shrubs.
Bru'in, n. A bear.

Bruise, v. t. To hurt with blows.—n. A contusion.
Bruiṣ'er, n. A boxer.
Bruit, n. Report; rumor.—v. t. To report. [ter.
Bru'mal, a. Belonging to winBru-nette', n. A woman of a dark or brown complexion.
Brŭnt, n. A shock; attack; onset; violence.
Brŭsh, n. A hairy instrument; a pencil; brisk attack; a thicket; branches of trees lopped off.—v. t. To rub or sweep with a brush.—v. i. To move in haste.
Brŭsh'-wŏŏd, n. Underwood.
Brŭsh'y, a. Like a brush; shaggy. [crackle; to bully.
Brŭs'tle (brŭs'l), v. i. To Bru'tal (133), a. Savage; cruel.
Bru-tăl'i-ty, n. Savageness; cruelty; insensibility to pity.
Bru'tal-ize, v. t. To make brutal.—v. i. To become brutal.
Bru'tal-ly, adv. In a brutal manner; cruelly.
Brute, n. An irrational animal.—a. Senseless; savage.
Bru'ti-fy, v. t. To make brutish or unfeeling.
Bru'tish, a. Bestial; savage.
Bru'tish-ness, n. Quality of being brutish. [ity.
Bru'tism, n. Extreme stupidBry'o-ny, n. A certain wild climbing plant. [liquor.
Bŭb, n. Strong beer or malt
Bŭb'ble, n. A small bladder of water; a false show; empty project.—v. i. To rise in bubbles; to run with a gurgling sound.—v. t. To cheat; to impose on.
Bŭb'bler. n. One who cheats.
Bŭb'bly. a. Full of bubbles; like bubbles.
Bŭc'ca-neer', n. A piratical adventurer; a freebooter.
Bŭck, n. Male of rabbits, deer, &c.; a dandy; lye.—v. t. To steep clothes in lye.
Bŭck'-băs'ket, n. A basket in which clothes are carried to the wash.
Bŭck'et, n. A vessel to draw or carry water in.
Bŭck'ish, a. Pertaining to a gay fellow; foppish.
Bŭck'le (bŭk'l), n. An instrument for fastening straps.—v. t. To fasten with a buckle; to apply.—v. i. To join in battle.
Bŭck'ler. n. A kind of shield.
Bŭck'ram, n. A coarse linen cloth stiffened with glue.

Bŭck'skin, n. The leather from a buck.
Bŭck'thōrn, n. A plant bearing a black berry.
Bŭck'whēat, n. A plant, the seed of which is used as a grain.
Bu-cŏl'ic, a. [Gr. boukolos, herdsman.] Relating to shepherds; pastoral.—n. A pastoral poem.
Bŭd, n. First shoot of a plant.—v. i. To put forth buds.—v. t. To inoculate, as a tree.
Bŭd'dle. v. t. To wash, as ores.
Bŭde'-light (-lit), n. An intense white light produced by burning purified coal-gas in a peculiar kind of lamp.
Bŭdge, v. i. To stir; to go; to move.—a. Stiff; rigid; pompous; surly.
Bŭdg'et, n. A bag; pouch; stock; store; a statement respecting finances.
Bŭff, n. A leather dressed with oil; a color between light pink and light yellow.
Bŭf'fa-lo, n. (pl. Bŭf'fa-lōes. 140.) A kind of wild ox.
Bŭf'fet (130), v. t. Buffalo. To box; to beat; to strike with the fist.—n. A blow with the hand; a cuff; a kind of cupboard or closet.
Bŭf'fo, n. The comic actor in an opera.
Buf-foon', n. A clown; a mountebank.
Buf-foon'er-y, n. Low jests.
Bŭg. n. A generic term for various insects. [ject.
Bŭg'bēar, n. A frightful obBŭg'gy, a. Full of, or having, bugs.—n. A light four-wheeled carriage.
Bū'gle,
Bū'gle-hōrn, } n. A military instrument of music.
Bū'gle, n. An elongated glass Bugle. bead.
Bū'gloss. n. A plant used in dyeing.
Bŭhl (būl), n. Metallic figures inlaid in dark wood or tortoise-shell.
Bŭhr'stōne (bŭr-), n. A species of quartz, used for millstones.

BUILD 65 BURST

Build (bĭld), *v. t.* [*imp. & p. p.* BUILDED, BUILT.] To raise a structure; to construct; to erect. — *v. i.* To rest or depend for support.
Build′er, *n.* One who builds.
Build′ing, *n.* An edifice; fabric.
Built, *imp. & p. p.* of *Build.*
Bŭlb, *n.* A round root, as that of the onion or tulip.
Bul-bā′ceoŭs, *a.* Having bulbs; bulbous.
Bŭlb′oŭs, *a.* Having round roots or heads; protuberant.
Bŭlge, *n.* Protuberant part of a cask; a protuberance. — *v. i.* To swell in the middle.
Bŭlk, *n.* Size; substance in general; quantity; main part.
Bŭlk′-hĕad, *n.* A partition in a ship, to form separate apartments.
Bŭlk′i-ness, *n.* Largeness.
Bŭlk′y, *a.* Of great size; big.
Bull, *n.* The male of cattle; edict of the pope; a blunder.
Bŭll′a-ry, *n.* A collection of papal bulls.
Bull′-bāit′ing, *n.* Practice of exciting bulls with dogs.
Bull′-dŏg, *n.* A kind of large fierce dog.
Bull′et, *n.* A ball for a gun.
Bull-dog.
Bŭl′le-tĭn, *n.* Official report or notice.
Bull′-fight (-fīt), *n.* A fight with a bull.
Bull′-finch, *n.* A singing bird.
Bull′-frŏg, *n.* A large species of frog. [gold.
Bull′ion, *n.* Uncoined silver or
Bull′ock, *n.* A young bull; an ox.
Bull′s′-eȳe (-ī), *n.* A small window of rounded or projecting glass.
Bull′y, *n.* A blustering, quarrelsome fellow. — *v. i.* To bluster. — *v. t.* To threaten with noisy menaces.
Bull′rush, *n.* A rush growing in water
Bŭl′wark, *n.* A fortification; shelter; sides of a ship above the upper deck.
Bŭm-bāi′liff, *n.* [A corruption of *bound-bailiff.*] An under bailiff.
Bŭm′ble-bee, *n.* A kind of large bee.

Bŭmp, *n.* A swelling; a blow.
— *v. i.* To make a loud noise. — *v. t.* To thump; to strike. [the brim.
Bŭm′per, *n.* A glass filled to
Bŭmp′kin, *n.* An awkward person: a clown; a rustic.
Bŭn } (125), *n.* A small cake,
Bŭnn } or sweet bread.
Bŭnch, *n.* A cluster; a hard lump; a protuberance. — *v. i.* To grow in clusters. — *v. t.* To tie in bunches.
Bŭnch′y, *a.* Full of bunches; like a bunch.
Bŭn′dle, *n.* A number of things bound together. — *v. t.* To tie together.
Bŭng, *n.* A stopper for a barrel. — *v. t.* To stop with a bung.
Bŭn′ga-lŏw, *n.* In India, a house of a single floor.
Bŭng′-hōle, *n.* A hole in a barrel.
Bŭn′gle, *v. i.* To do clumsily.
Bŭn′gler, *n.* A clumsy workman.
Bŭn′gling, *a.* Very clumsy.
Bŭn′gling-ly, *adv.* Clumsily.
Bŭn′ion (bŭn′yun), *n.* An excrescence on the toe. [a bed.
Bŭnk, *n.* A case of boards for
Bŭnn, *n.* See *Bun.*
Bŭnt′ing, *n.* A thin woolen cloth; a bird of different species.
Buoy (bwoȳ or bwȯy), *n.* A piece of wood or cork floating on the water, to indicate shoals, rocks, &c., or to bear a cable. — *v. t.* To keep afloat; to sustain.
Buoy.
Buoy′an-çy (bwōȯy′- or bwŏy′-), *n.* The quality of floating; specific lightness. — SYN. Animation; elasticity; vivacity.
Buoy′ant (bwooȳ- or bwŏy′-), *a.* Floating; light.
Bŭr } (125), *n.* The prickly
Bŭrr } head of a plant.
Bŭr′den (bŭr′dn), *n.* [From the root of *bear.*] That which is borne; a load; chorus of a song; refrain. — *v. t.* To load; to oppress.
Bŭr′den-sŏme, *a.* Grievous to be borne. — SYN. Heavy; ponderous; oppressive.
Bŭr′dŏck, *n.* A wild plant that bears burs.
Bū′reau (bū′rō), *n.* (*pl.* Bū′-reaus.) A chest of drawers for papers or clothes; office.

Bŭrg, *n.* A borough.
Bŭr′gess, *n.* A freeman of a city.
Bŭrg′grave, *n.* A German noble.
Bŭrgh′er (bŭrg′er), *n.* A freeman of a borough.
Bŭr′glar, *n.* One who breaks into a house by night.
Bur-glā′ri-oŭs, *a.* Consisting in burglary.
Bŭr′gla-ry, *n.* The crime of house-breaking by night, with intent to steal.
Bŭrg′o-mȧs′ter, *n.* A city magistrate.
Bŭr′gun-dy, *n.* Wine made in Burgundy.
Bū′ri-al (bĕr′ĭ-al), *n.* Act of burying; a funeral.
Bū′rin, *n.* A graving tool.
Bŭrl, *v. t.* To pick knots, &c., from, in fulling cloth.
Bur-lĕsque′ (-lĕsk′), *a.* Tending to excite laughter; ludicrous. — *n.* A ludicrous representation. — *v. t.* To make ludicrous; to turn to ridicule.
Bŭr′ly, *a.* Great in size; boisterous.
Bŭrn, *v. t.* [*imp. & p. p.* BURNED, BURNT.] To consume by fire. — *v. i.* To scorch; to be inflamed; to be on fire. — *n.* A hurt caused by fire.
Bŭrn′er, *n.* One who sets on fire; appendage to a lamp or gas-fixture. [plant.
Bŭr′net, *n.* A certain garden
Bŭrn′ing, *n.* Combustion; heat. — *a.* Flaming; vehement; ardent.
Bŭrn′ing-glȧss, *n.* A convex lens for converging the sun's rays to a focus.
Bŭr′nish, *v. t.* To polish; to brighten. — *n.* A gloss.
Bŭr′nish-er, *n.* One who, or that which, burnishes.
Bŭrnt, *imp. & p. p.* of *Burn.*
Bŭrnt′-ŏf′fer-ing, *n.* Something offered and burnt on an altar as a sacrifice.
Bŭrr, *n.* See *Bur.*
Bŭr′rōw, *n.* A lodge in the earth for rabbits, &c. — *v. i.* To lodge in a hole in the earth.
Bŭr′sar, *n.* The treasurer of a college; a charity student.
Bŭr′sa-ry, *n.* (Gr. *bursa,* a skin, a purse.) Treasury of a college or monastery.
Bŭrse, *n.* A mercantile exchange.
Bŭrst, *v. i.* [*imp. & p. p.* BURST.] To break or fly

---

sŏn, ôr, dọ, wọlf, tŏō, tŏŏk; ûrn, rụe, pụll; ç, ġ, *soft;* c, ġ, *hard;* ạṣ; ęxĭst; ŋ *as* ng; this.

open. — *n.* A sudden rent or disruption.
Bûr'then. See *Burden*.
Bur'y (bĕr'y̆), *v. t.* To inter in a grave; to cover with earth; to conceal; to hide.
Bush, *n.* A shrub; a bough. — *v. t.* To furnish with a bush or with bushes.
Bush'el, *n.* A dry measure of eight gallons, or four pecks.
Bush'i-ness, *n.* State of being bushy.
Bush'y, *a.* Full of bushes; thick, as hair.
Bus'i-ly (bĭz'ĭ-ly̆), *adv.* With constant occupation.
Bus'i-ness (bĭz'nes), *n.* Employment; trade; occupation; concern.
Busk, *n.* A piece of steel or whalebone worn in corsets.
Bŭsk'in, *n.* A half boot, anciently worn on the stage.
Bŭs'kined, *a.* Wearing buskins.
Bŭs'ket, *n.* A small bush; a collection of shrubs.
Bŭsk'ined, *a.* Wearing buskins. [kiss.
Bŭss, *n.* A kiss. — *v. t.* To
Bŭst, *n.* A statue of the head and shoulders.
Bŭs'tard, *n.* A bird of the ostrich family.
Bŭs'tle (bŭs'l), *v. i.* To be busy or active. — *n.* A tumult; hurry; commotion.
Bŭs'tler (bŭs'ler), *n.* An active, stirring person.
Bus'y (bĭz'y̆), *a.* Employed with earnestness; officious. — *v. t.* To employ; to occupy.
Bus'y-bŏd'y (bĭz'y̆-), *n.* A meddling, officious person.
Bŭt, *prep.* Except; unless. — *conj.* More; further. — *n.* End; limit; bound. — *v. t.* To be bounded; to touch with the end.
Butch'er, *n.* One who kills animals to sell. — *v. t.* To slay inhumanly.
Butch'er-ly, *n.* Barbarous; cruel; bloody.

Butch'er-y, *n.* The business of a butcher; slaughter of cattle for market; cruel murder; carnage.
Bŭt'-ĕnd, *n.* The thicker end of a thing.
Bŭt'ler, *n.* A servant who has the care of liquors.
Bŭt'ler-shĭp, *n.* The office of a butler.
Bŭt'ment, *n.* A buttress of an arch.
Bŭtt, *n.* The larger end of a thing; a mark to shoot at; a large cask; a kind of hinge; a push or thrust with the head; thickest part of tanned ox-hides; end; limit; one who is ridiculed. — *v. t.* To strike with the head; to be bounded; to abut.
Bŭt'ter, *n.* An oily substance obtained from cream by churning. — *v. t.* To cover or spread with butter.
Bŭt'ter-cŭp, *n.* A plant with bright yellow flowers; crowfoot.
Bŭt'ter-flȳ, *n.* [Named from the color of the yellow species.] A genus of insects.
Bŭt'ter-milk, *n.* The milk which remains after the butter is separated.
Bŭt'ter-nŭt, *n.* A tree and its oily fruit.
Bŭt'ter-print, *n.* A stamp for butter.
Bŭt'ter-tōoth, *n.* A broad fore tooth.
Bŭt'ter-y, *n.* A room where provisions are kept; pantry. — *a.* Resembling butter; having the qualities or appearance of butter.
Bŭt'tock, *n.* Protuberant part of the body behind; rump.
Bŭt'ton (bŭt'tn), *n.* A knob or catch for fastening clothes; a piece of wood or metal made to turn so as to fasten doors, &c. — *v. t.* To fasten with a button or with buttons.
Bŭt'ton-hōle, *n.* A hole for a button.

Bŭt'tress, *n.* A projecting support to the outside of a wall. — *v. t.* To support by a buttress; to prop.
Bū'ty-rā'ceoŭs, *a.* Having the qualities of butter; like butter.
Bŭx'om, *a.* Lively; brisk; jolly; frolicsome.
Bŭx'om-ly, *adv.* Briskly; gayly.
Bŭx'om-ness, *n.* Quality of being buxom; briskness; gayety.
Buȳ (bī), *v. t.* [*imp. & p. p.* BOUGHT (bawt).] To acquire by paying a price for; to purchase.
Buȳ'er, *n.* A purchaser.
Bŭzz (125), *n.* A humming sound, as of bees. — *v. i.* To make a low humming sound, like bees. — *v. t.* To whisper; to spread by whispers.
Bŭz'zard, *n.* A species of hawk.
Bŭzz'er, *n.* One who buzzes; a whisperer.
Bȳ, *prep.* Near; close to; from one to the other side of; with; through means of; in presence. — *By and by,* presently; pretty soon; before long.
Bȳ'-ĕnd, *n.* Private interest.
Bȳ'-gōne, *a.* Past; gone by.
Bȳ'-law, *n.* A private law or regulation.
Bȳ'-păth, *n.* A private path.
Bȳre, *n.* A cow-house.
Bȳ'-stănd'er, *n.* A looker on; a spectator.
Bȳ'-street, *n.* A private street.
Bȳ'-wāy, *n.* A private or secluded way.
Bȳ'-word (-wûrd), *n.* A common saying; a proverb.
By-zăn'tĭne, or **Bȳz'an-tīne,** *a.* Pertaining to Byzantium

Buttress.

C.

CAB, *n.* A kind of covered carriage.
Ca-bāl', *n.* A number of persons united to effect some private purpose; a junto; intrigue. — *v. i.* (129) To intrigue privately; to plot.
Căb'a-lă, *n.* Jewish secret traditions; any secret science; mystery.
Căb'a-list, *n.* One skilled in Jewish traditions.

CABALISTIC 67 CALORIMETER

Cab'a-list'ic, a. Pertaining to the mysteries of Jewish traditions; secret; occult.

Ca-bal'ler, n. One who plots.

Cab'bage, v. i. To steal pieces of, in cutting clothes. — n. A garden plant.

Cab'in, n. An apartment in a ship; a hut. — v. i. To live in a cabin. — v. t. To confine in a cabin.

Cab'i-net, n. A set of drawers; a closet to a private room; a council of state.

Cab'i-net-māk'er, n. A maker of fine furniture of wood.

Ca'ble, n. A large strong rope or chain to hold a vessel at anchor. [a ship.

Ca-boose', n. A cook room of

Cab'ri-o-let (-lā), n. A one-horse pleasure carriage, with two seats and a calash top.

Ca-cā'o, n. The chocolate tree.

Cache (kāsh), n. A place for hiding and preserving provisions.

Ca-chec'tic, a. Having an ill habit of body. [body.

Ca-chex'y, n. Ill habit of

Cach'in-nā'tion, n. Loud or immoderate laughter.

Cāck'le, v. i. To make the noise of a hen; to giggle; to prattle. — n. The noise of a hen or goose.

Ca-eōph'o-ny, n. A disagreeable sound of words.

Cāc'tus, n. A genus of prickly tropical plants.

Ca-dāv'er-ous, a. Like a dead body; pale; ghastly.

Căd'dy, n. A small box for tea.

Cāde, a. Bred by hand; tame; gentle; soft. — n. A barrel or cask.

Cā'dence, n. A fall of the voice in reading or speaking; modulation.

Ca-dĕt', n. A volunteer in the army; a military pupil.

Cā'di (140), n. A Turkish judge.

Çæ-sū'rà, or **Çæ-sū'rà,** n. A pause or division in a verse.

Cāg, n. A little barrel or cask; a keg.

Cāge, n. An inclosure for confining birds or other animals. — v. t. To shut up in a cage.

Cāirn, n. A pile of stones.

Cāis'son, n. A chest containing ammunition; a wooden box for laying the foundations of a bridge.

Cāi'tiff, n. [From Lat. captivus, captive.] A base fellow; a villain. — a. Base; servile.

Ca-jōle', v. t. To deceive by flattery; to wheedle.

Ca-jōl'er, n. One who cajoles.

Ca-jōl'er-y, n. A wheedling; flattery.

Cāke, n. A kind of bread, sweet and delicate. — v. i. To form into a hard mass.

Căl'a-bāsh, n. A large gourd.

Căl'a-mān'co, n. A woolen stuff.

Ca-lăm'i-tous, a. Distressing; disastrous.

Ca-lăm'i-ty, n. A condition producing great distress. — SYN. Disaster; mishap; misfortune.

Căl'a-mus, n. A kind of reed.

Ca-lāsb', n. A cover for the head; a kind of carriage.

Cal-cā're-ous, a. Having the properties of lime.

Căl'çe-ā'ted, a. Wearing shoes.

Căl'çi-nāte, v. t. To calcine.

Căl'çi-nā'tion, n. The operation of calcining.

Cal-çīne', or **Căl'çine,** v. t. To reduce to a powder by heat. — v. i. To be changed into powder by the action of heat.

Căl'eu-la-ble, a. Capable of being calculated.

Căl'eu-lāte, v. t. To compute; to reckon. — v. i. To make a computation.

Căl'eu-lā'tion, n. Computation; estimate.

Căl'eu-lā'tive, a. Pertaining to calculation.

Căl'eu-lā'tor, n. One who computes; a reckoner.

Căl'eu-lous, a. Like stone; affected with the stone.

Căl'eu-lŭs, n. (pl. †Căl'eu-lī, 147). The stone in the bladder; a method of computation.

Căl'dron, n. A large kettle.

Căl'e-fā'çient, a. Making warm; heating.

Căl'e-făe'tion, n. Act of heating or state of being heated.

Căl'e-făe'tive, } a. Making
Căl'e-făe'to-ry, } warm or hot.

Căl'e-fȳ, v. t. To make warm or hot. — v. i. To grow warm or hot.

Căl'en-dar, n. An almanac; a register. — v. t. To enter or write in a calendar.

Căl'en-der, v. t. To make glossy and smooth by pressing between rollers. — n. A hot press.

Căl'ends, n. pl. First day of each month among the Romans.

Căl'en-tūre, n. An ardent fever with delirium.

Cālf (käf), n. (pl. Cālves, kävz), n. The young of a cow; a stupid fellow; thick part of the leg.

Căl'i-ber, } n. Bore of a gun;
Căl'i-bre, } mental capacity.

Căl'i-co, n. (pl. Căl'i-coes, 140). A stuff made of cotton.

Căl'i-duet, n. A pipe to convey heat.

Ca-līd'i-ty, n. Burning heat.

Căl'i-perṣ, n. pl. Compasses with curved legs for measuring the diameters of round bodies.

Cā'liph, n. Title of the successors of Mohammed.

Căl'iph-ate, n. The office of a caliph.

Căl'is-thĕn'ies, n. pl. Healthful and graceful bodily exercises.

Cālk (kawk), v. t. To stop the seams of, as of a ship; to arm with sharp points, as the shoes of a horse. — n. A sharp point on an animal's shoe. [calks.

Cālk'er (kawk'er), n. One who

Căll, v. t. To name; to invite; to summon. — v. i. To cry out; to make a visit. — n. An address; a demand; a summons; a short visit.

Căl'li-grăph'ic, a. Pertaining to fine writing.

Cal-lig'ra-phy, n. Beautiful penmanship.

Căll'ing, n. Employment; vocation; occupation.

Cal-lōs'i-ty, } n. Any horny
Căl'lus, } hardness of the skin. [unfeeling.

Căl'lous, a. Hard; indurated;

Căl'low, a. Unfledged; naked.

Cālm (käm), a. Still; quiet; undisturbed. — n. Serenity. — v. t. To quiet; to still.

Cālm'ly (käm'-), adv. In a calm manner: quietly.

Cālm'ness (käm'ness), n. Serenity; stillness; quiet.

Căl'o-měl, n. A preparation of mercury.

Ca-lōr'ic, n. The principle or matter of heat. [heat.

Căl'o-rif'ic, a. Producing

Căl'o-rim'e-ter, n. An apparatus for measuring the amount of heat contained in bodies.

sŏn, ôr, dǫ, wǫlf, tōō, tŏŏk; ûrn, rṳe, pṳll; ç, ġ, soft; e, ḡ, hard; aṣ; exist; n as ng; this.

CALOTYPE 68 CANONIST

Cǎl′o-tȳpe, *n.* A method of taking photographic pictures on prepared paper.

Cǎl′trop, *n.* A military instrument with four iron points so arranged that one of them always projects upwards;—used for impeding the advance of cavalry.

Cǎl′u-mět, *n.* [Lat. *calamus*, reed.] Indian pipe of peace.

Ca-lŭm′ni-āte, *v. t.* To accuse falsely; to slander.

Ca-lŭm′ni-ā′tion, *n.* False accusation of crime; slander.

Ca-lŭm′ni-ā′tor, *n.* A false accuser; a slanderer.

Ca-lŭm′ni-oŭs, *a.* Defamatory; abusive; slanderous.

Cǎl′um-ny, *n.* False and malicious accusation.— SYN. Slander; defamation; libel; abuse. [birth to a calf.

Cǎlve (käv), *v. i.* To give

Cǎl′vin-ĭsm, *n.* The doctrines of Calvin.

Cǎl′vin-ĭst, *n.* One who adheres to Calvinism.

Cǎl′vin-ĭst′ic, *a.* Relating to Calvin, or to Calvinism.

Cǎlx, *n.* (*Eng. pl.* **Cǎlx′es**, *Lat. pl.* †**Cǎl′cēs**.) Earthy residuum of a calcined mineral.

Cā′lyx, *n.* (*pl.* **Cā′lyx-es**.) [Gr. *kalux*, from *kalupto*, to cover.] The outer covering of a flower. Calyx.

Cǎm, *n.* The projection on a wheel or axle to produce reciprocating motion.

Cǎm′bist, *n.* One skilled in the science of banking.

Cǎm′bric, *n.* A fine linen or cotton.

Cǎme, *imp.* of **Come**.

Cǎm′el, *n.* A large ruminant quadruped of Asia and Africa; a contrivance for lifting ships over bars.

Ca-měl′o-pard, or **Cǎm′el-o-pärd′**, *n.* The giraffe; an African animal remarkable for its long neck.

Cǎm′e-o (140), *n.* A precious stone sculptured in relief.

†**Cǎm′e-rä Ob-scū′rä**. An optical apparatus in which the images of external objects are thrown in an inverted form upon a white surface within a darkened chamber or box.

Cǎm′i-sāde′, *n.* An attack made in the dark.

Cǎm′let, *n.* A stuff of wool or hair and silk.

Cǎmp, *n.* A place where troops lodge, or tents, huts, &c., are erected.— *v. i.* To pitch tents; to encamp.

Cam-pāign′ (-pān′), *n.* The time an army keeps the field. — *v. i.* To serve in a campaign.

Cam-pǎn′i-fôrm, *a.* In the shape of a bell.

Cǎm′pa-nŏl′o-gy, *n.* Art of ringing bells.

Cam-pǎn′u-late, *a.* Bell-shaped.

Cam-pěs′tral, *a.* Pertaining to, or growing in, a field.

Cǎm′phēne, *n.* Oil or spirit of turpentine.

Cǎm′phor, *n.* A kind of solidified sap from the East Indies.

Cǎm′phor-ate, } *a.* Impregnated with camphor.

Cǎm′phor-ā′ted, }

Cam-phŏr′ic. *a.* Pertaining to, or containing, camphor.

Cǎn, *v. i.* (*imp.* COULD.) To be able.— *n.* A metallic cup or vessel for liquors.

Ca-nǎl′, *n.* An artificial watercourse; a pipe; a duct.

Ca-nā′ry, *n.* A kind of wine; a species of singing-bird.

Cǎn′cel (130), *v. t.* To blot out; to efface; to obliterate.

Cǎn′cel-lā′ted, *a.* Marked by cross lines.

Cǎn′cel-lā′tion, *n.* Act of cancelling, or crossing out; obliteration.

Cǎn′cer, *n.* The Crab, a sign in the zodiac; a virulent ulcer.

Cǎn′cer-āte, *v. i.* To become cancerous.

Cǎn′cer-oŭs, *a.* Consisting of, or relating to, a cancer.

Cǎn′de-lā′brum, *n.*(*pl.* †**Cǎn′de-lā′brä** or **Cǎn′de-lā′brums**.) A candlestick with branches.

Cǎn′dent, *a.* Glowing with heat. [nous.

Cǎn′did, *a.* Frank; ingenuous.

Cǎn′di-date, *n.* One who sues, or is proposed, for an office. [frankly.

Cǎn′did-ly, *adv.* Fairly;

Cǎn′did-ness, *n.* Openness of mind; frankness.

Cǎn′dle, *n.* A light made of tallow, wax, &c.

Cǎn′dle-light (-lit), *n.* Light of a candle.

Cǎn′dle-mas, *n.* The feast of the purification of the Virgin Mary, February 2.

Cǎn′dle-stĭck, *n.* An instrument for holding a candle.

Cǎn′dor, *n.* Fairness; frankness; openness; sincerity.

Cǎn′dy, *v. t.* To conserve with sugar.— *v. i.* To be changed into sugar.— *n.* A preparation of sugar.

Cāne, *n.* A reed; the sugar plant; a walking-stick. — *v. t.* To beat with a cane.

Cāne′brāke, *n.* A thicket of canes.

Ca-nīne′, *a.* Pertaining to, or having the properties of, a dog.

Cǎn′is-ter, *n.* A kind of tin box for tea or coffee, &c.

Cǎn′ker, *n.* A disease in animals and plants; a kind of ulcer. — *v. i.* To become corrupt. — *v. t.* To corrode or corrupt; to infect.

Cǎn′kered, *p. a.* Corroded.

Cǎn′ker-oŭs, *a.* Corroding, like a canker.

Cǎn′ker-worm (-wûrm), *n.* A worm that destroys certain plants and fruit.

Cǎn′nel-cōal, *n.* [A corruption of *candle*-coal.] A hard black coal, which burns readily with a bright flame.

Cǎn′ni-bal, *n.* A man-eater.

Cǎn′ni-bal-ĭsm, *n.* The eating of human flesh by man.

Cǎn′non, *n.* A great gun for throwing balls and the like, by means of gunpowder. Cannon.

Cǎn′non-āde′, *n.* Hostile attack with cannon.— *v. t.* To attack with cannon.

Cǎn′non-bǎll, *n.* A ball to be thrown from cannon.

Cǎn′non-cer′, } *n.* One who

Cǎn′non-ier′, } manages a cannon.

Cǎn′non-shŏt, *n.* A cannon ball. [unable.

Cǎn′not (*cǎn* and *nǒt*.) To

Ca-nōe′ (ka-nōō′), *n.* A boat made of a tree.

Cǎn′on, *n.* A rule: the Scriptures; an ecclesiastical dignitary.

Cǎn′on-ess, *n.* A woman who enjoys a prebend.

Ca-nŏn′ic-al, *a.* According to canons; ecclesiastical.

Ca-nŏn′ic-als, *n. pl.* The prescribed dress of the clergy.

Ca-nŏn′ic-ate, *n.* Office of a canon. [canon law.

Cǎn′on-ĭst, *n.* One versed in

CANONISTIC 69 CARBINE

Can'on-ist'ic, *a.* Relating to canon law.
Can'on-i-za'tion, *n.* An enrolling among saints.
Can'on-ize, *v. t.* To enroll in the catalogue of saints.
Can'on-ry, *n.* A benefice
Can'on-ship, } In a cathedral or collegiate church, which has a prebend annexed to it.
Can'o-py, *n.* A covering over the head. —*v. t.* To cover with a canopy. [lodious.
Ca-no'rous, *a.* Musical; melodious.
Cant, *v. t.* To give a sudden turn to. —*v. i.* [Lat. *cantare*, to chant.] To speak in a whining voice; to play the hypocrite. —*n.* A sudden turn; a whining or sing-song tone; slang; secret language of gypsies, &c. [muskmelon.
Can'ta-loupe, *n.* A species of Can-ta'ta or Can-tä'tà (140), *n.* A poem set to music.
Can-teen', *n.* A tin vessel for liquors, &c.
Can'ter, *v. i.* To move in a moderate gallop. —*n.* A moderate gallop.
Can-thär'i-dēs, *n. pl.* [Lat.] Beetles used for blistering; Spanish flies.
Can'ti-cle, *n.* A song. —*Canticles*, the Song of Solomon.
Can'to, *n.* (*pl.* Can'tos, 140). A division of a poem.
Can'ton, *n.* Division of a country. —*v. t.* To divide into districts; to allot separate quarters to, as troops.
Can'ton-ize, *v. t.* To divide into cantons.
Can'ton-ment, *n.* A district occupied by soldiers. [tian.
Can-toon', *n.* A kind of fustian.
Can'vas, *n.* A coarse cloth for sails, tents, &c.; sails in general.
Can'vass, *v. t.* To examine; to discuss; to solicit. —*v. i.* To solicit votes. —*n.* Close inspection; examination; solicitation.
Ca'ny, *a.* Abounding with, or resembling, canes.
Căn'zo-net', *n.* A short song.
Caou'tchouc (kōō'chook), *n.* India-rubber, or gum elastic.
Căp, *n.* A cover for the head; top. —*v. t.* To cover the head or top.
Ca'pa-bil'i-ty, *n.* Capacity; qualification; ability.
Ca'pa-ble, *a.* Having capacity or ability. —*Syn.* Able; competent; fitted; efficient.

Ca'pa-ble-ness, *n.* Capacity.
Ca'pa-bly, *adv.* With capability.
Ca-pa'cious, *a.* Having capacity; wide; large.
Ca-pa'cious-ness, *n.* Quality of being capacious.
Ca-pac'i-tāte, *v. t.* To make capable; to fit.
Ca-păc'i-ty, *n.* The power of receiving and containing; ability; character; qualification. [to foot.
Căp'-a-piē', *adv.* From head
Ca-păr'i-son, *n.* Trappings for a horse. —*v. t.* To dress pompously; to adorn.
Cāpe, *n.* A head-land; neck-piece of a garment:
Cā'per, *n.* A kind of flower-bud used for pickling; a leap. —*v. i.* To skip; to leap; to dance; to frisk.
Cā'pi-as, *n.* A writ commanding the officer to arrest the person named in it.
Căp'il-lā'ceous, *a.* Hairy.
Ca-pil'la-ment, *n.* A filament or fine, hair-like fiber.
Căp'il-la-ry, *a.* Resembling a hair. —*n.* A fine vessel or canal.
Căp'i-tal, *n.* Upper part of a column; chief city or town; stock in trade; principal sum; a large letter. —*a.* Relating to the head; principal; chief; deserving death.
Căp'i-tal-ist, *n.* A man of large property.
Căp'i-tal-ly, *adv.* In a capital manner; finely.
Căp'i-lā'tion, *n.* Numeration by heads; a poll-tax.
Căp'i-tol, *n.* A temple in Rome; a government house.
Ca-pit'u-lar, *n.* A statute; the member of a chapter.
Ca-pit'u-lāte, *v. i.* To surrender on conditions.
Ca-pit'u-lā'tion, *n.* A surrender on terms, or conditionally. [capitulates.
Ca-pit'u-lā'tor, *n.* One who
Ca-poch', *n.* A monk's hood.
Cā'pon (kā'pn), *n.* A cock emasculated, to improve his flesh for the table.
Căp'-pā'per, *n.* A kind of coarse brown paper.
Ca-prīce', *n.* Sudden or unreasonable change of mind or humor. —*Syn.* Whim; freak; fancy; vagary.
Ca-pri'cious (-prish'us), *a.* Whimsical; fanciful; freakish.
Căp'ri-cörn, *n.* The tenth sign in the zodiac, into which the sun enters about the 21st of September.
Cap-sīze', *v. t.* To overturn.
Căp'stan, *n.* A machine in ships for raising great weights.
Căp'su-lar, } *a.*
Căp'su-la-ry, } Hollow like a capsule. [Capstan.
Căp'sūle, *n.* The seed-vessel of a plant.
Căp'tain, *n.* The commander of a company, a ship, &c.; a warrior.
Căp'tain-cy, } *n.* Commis-
Căp'tain-ship, } sion or office of a captain.
Căp'tain-ry, *n.* Captainship.
Căp'tion, *n.* A certificate appended to a legal instrument.
Căp'tious, *a.* Apt to cavil; petulant; peevish.
Căp'tious-ly, *adv.* In a captious manner.
Căp'tious-ness, *n.* Disposition to cavil or find fault.
Căp'ti-vāte, *v. t.* To please exceedingly; to fascinate; to charm. [captivating.
Căp'ti-vā'tion, *n.* Act of
Căp'tive, *n.* One taken in war. —*a.* Made prisoner.
Cap-tiv'i-ty, *n.* Subjection; bondage; thralldom.
Căp'tor, *n.* One who takes a prisoner or a prize.
Căp'tūre, *n.* Seizure of a prize. —*v. t.* To take, as a prize in war.
Căp'u-chïn' (-sheen'), *n.* A monk of the order of St. Francis; a cloak and hood worn by women.
Cär, *n.* A cart; a railway carriage; a chariot of war.
Cär'a-bīne, *n.* See *Carbine*.
Cär'a-cōle, *n.* An oblique movement of a horse. —*v. i.* To move in a curacole.
Cär'at, *n.* A weight of four grains, used in weighing gems; a twenty-fourth part (used to express the fineness of gold).
Cär'a-van, *n.* A body of traveling pilgrims, traders, or showmen.
Cär'a-vän'sa-ry, *n.* A house or inn for travelers in Asia.
Cär'a-vēl, *n.* A light, round, old-fashioned ship.
Cär'a-wāy, *n.* An aromatic plant, and its seed.
Cär'bīne, *n.* A short gun borne by light horsemen.

Car'bi-nier', *n.* A man who carries a carbine.
Car'bon. *n.* [Lat. *carbo*, coal.] Pure charcoal.
Car'bon-a'ceous, *a.* Relating to, or containing, carbon.
Car'bon-ate, *n.* A salt formed by the union of carbonic acid with a base.
C. r-bon'ic, *a.* Pertaining to, or containing, carbon.
Car'boy, *n.* A globular bottle protected by basket-work.
Car'bun-cle (-bunk-kl, 79), *n.* An inflammatory tumor; a beautiful red gem.
Car-bunc'u-lar, *a.* Like, or pertaining to, a carbuncle.
Car'cass, *n.* A dead body of an animal; decaying remains of an animal.
Card, *n.* A piece of pasteboard prepared for various uses; a written note; a paper containing an address; a large comb for wool; (*pl.*) a game. — *v. t.* To comb, as wool. [wool.
Card'er, *n.* One who cards
Car'di-ac, } *a.* [Gr. *kardia*,
Car-di'ac-al, } heart.] Pertaining to the heart.
Car'di-nal, *a.* Principal; chief. — *n.* A high dignitary of the Roman Catholic church; a woman's short cloak.
Car-doon', *n.* A plant resembling the artichoke.
Card'-ta'ble, *n.* A small table with one leaf for playing cards.
Care (3), *n.* Uneasiness of mind; solicitude; caution management. — *v. i.* To be anxious; to heed.
Ca-reen', *v. t.* To heave on one side, as a ship. — *v. i.* To incline to one side, as a ship.
Ca-reer', *n.* A course; race.
Care'ful (139), *a.* Anxious; watchful; saving.
Care'ful-ly, *adv.* With care — *v. t.* To run or move rapidly. [caution.
Care'ful-ness, *n.* Great care;
Care'less, *a.* Heedless; unconcerned; having no care.
Care'less-ly, *adv.* Without care.
Care'less-ness, *n.* Negligence; heedlessness.
Ca-ress', *v. t.* To embrace; to fondle. — *n.* Act of endearment.
Ca'ret, *n.* [Lat., there is wanting.] A mark [ʌ], noting omission in any writing.
Car'go, *n.* A ship's freight or lading.

Car'i-ea-ture' (50), *n.* A representation exaggerated to deformity; a ludicrous likeness. — *v. t.* To represent ludicrously. [caricatures.
Car'i-ca-tur'ist. *n.* One who
Ca'ri-eg, *n.* Ulceration of a bone. [ship's keel.
Car'i-na'ted, *a.* Shaped like a
Car'i-ole, *n.* A light carriage.
Ca'ri-os'i-ty, *n.* Ulceration of a bone. [ed; defective.
Ca'ri-ous, *a.* Decayed; ulcerated.
Carl, *n.* A rude, rustic man.
Car'man (143), *n.* One who drives a cart. [friar.
Car'mel-ite, *n.* A mendicant
Car'mine, *n.* A bright red pigment or color.
Car'nage, *n.* Destruction of lives; slaughter; massacre.
Car'nal, *a.* Fleshly; sensual.
Car'nal-ist, *n.* One given to lust. [sires.
Car-nal'i-ty, *n.* Fleshly desires.
Car-na'tion, *n.* Flesh color; a beautiful flower.
Car-nel'ian, *n.* A precious stone of a clear deep red, or a reddish white color.
Car'ne-ous, *a.* Consisting of, or like, flesh.
Car'ni-fy, *v. i.* To form or become flesh.
Car'ni-val, *n.* [It. *carnivale*, farewell to meat.] A Catholic festival celebrated for a number of days before Lent.
Car-niv'o-rous, *a.* Feeding on flesh. [crescence.
Car-nos'i-ty, *n.* A fleshy excrescence.
Car'ol, *n.* A song of joy; a hymn. — *v. i.* (139) To warble; to sing. — *v. t.* To praise in song.
Ca-rot'id, *n.* One of the two chief arteries of the neck.
Ca-rous'al, *n.* A drunken revel.
Ca-rouse', *v. i.* To drink freely and in a jovial manner. — *n.* A jovial drinking match.
Ca-rous'er, *n.* One who carouses.
Carp, *n.* A fresh-water fish. — *v. i.* To find fault; to cavil.
Car'pen-ter, *n.* A builder of houses or ships. [ing.
Car'pen try, *n.* Art of building.
Car'pet, *n.* A covering for a floor. — *v. t.* To cover with a carpet.
Car'pet-ing, *n.* Carpets in general; cloth or materials for carpets.
Car-pol'o-gy, *n.* That branch of botany which treats of seeds and fruits.

Car'ri-a-ble, *a.* Capable of being carried.
Car'riage (kăr'rij), *n.* A vehicle; conveyance; behavior; conduct.
Car'ri-er, *n.* One who carries.
Car'ri-on, *n.* Putrid flesh.
Car'ron-ade', *n.* A kind of short cannon.
Car'rot, *n.* A common garden vegetable.
Car'ry, *v. t.* To bear; to convey; to effect; to behave.
Car'ry-all, *n.* A light four-wheeled vehicle.
Cart, *n.* A carriage with two wheels for heavy commodities. — *v. t.* To convey in a cart.
Cart'age, *n.* Act of, or charge for, carting.
Car-tel', *n.* Agreement in relation to exchange of prisoners; a challenge. [cart.
Cart'er, *n.* One who drives a
Car'ti-lage (45), *n.* Gristle.
Car'ti-lag'i-nous, *a.* Pertaining to, or like, cartilage; gristly.
Car-tog'ra-phy, *n.* The art of preparing charts or maps.
Car-toon', *n.* A drawing or design on large, strong paper.
Car'touch' (-tōōch'), *n.* A case for musket-balls, &c.
Car'tridge, *n.* A paper case for a charge of powder.
Car'tridge-box, *n.* A box for cartridges.
Cart'wright (-rit), *n.* A maker or mender of carts.
Car'un-cle (79), *n.* A small fleshy excrescence.
Carve, *v. t.* To cut artistically, as wood, stone, &c.; to cut into small pieces, as meat.
Carv'er, *n.* One who carves; a sculptor; a large knife.
†**Ca'ry-at'i-des,** *n. pl.* [Lat.] Figures of women, serving to support entablatures
Cas'ca-bel, *n.* That part of a cannon in the rear of the base-ring.
Cas-cade', *n.* A waterfall.
Case, *n.* A covering; a box; state; variation of nouns, &c. ; a cause or suit in court. — *v. t.* To put in a case.
Case'härd'en (-härd'n), *v. t.* To make hard on the outside, as iron. [knife.
Case'-knife (-nif), *n.* A table
Case'mate. *n.* A bomb-proof chamber for cannon.
Case'ment, *n.* The glazed

ā, ē, ī, ō, ū, y, *long;* ă, ĕ, ĭ, ŏ, ŭ, y̆, *short;* câre, cär, àsk, ạll, whạt; ēre, veil, tērm; p'que, firm;

CASEOUS 71 CATERWAUL

frame of a window, opening on hinges.
Ca'se-ous, a. Pertaining to, or like, cheese.
Ca'gern, n. A lodge for soldiers in garrison towns; barracks.
Case'-shot, n. Bullets inclosed in cases.
Case'-worm (-wûrm), n. A grub that makes itself a case.
Cash, n. Money; coin; bank-notes. — v. t. To convert into money.
Cash'-book, n. A book in which accounts of money are kept.
Cash-ier', n. One who has the charge of money in a bank, &c. — v. t. To dismiss from office. [of shawl.
Cash'mere, n. A rich kind
Cas'ing, n. A covering; a case. [barrel.
Cask, n. A small vessel like a
Cask'et, n. A small chest for jewels.
Casque, n. A helmet.
Cas-sa'tion, n. Act of repealing; a making void.
Cas'sia (kăsh'ă), n. A cheap kind of cinnamon.
Cas'si-mere, n. A kind of thin twilled woolen cloth.
Cas-si'no, n. A game at cards.
Cas'sock, n. A close kind of frock-coat for clergymen.
Cas'so-wa-ry, n. A large bird resembling the ostrich.
Cast (5), v. t. [imp. & p. p. CAST.] To throw; to fling; to found or form; to calculate. — n. A throw; motion; mold; turn; appearance; shape.
Cas'ta-net, n. [Lat. castanea, a chestnut.] A rattling instrument used in dancing.
Cast'a-way, n. One abandoned to destruction.
Caste, n. A fixed class in society.
Cas'tel-lan, n. A governor or keeper of a castle.
Cas'tel-la'ted, a. Turreted like a castle.
Cast'er, n. One who casts; a small wheel; a cruet or phial; a stand for cruets.
Cas'ti-gate, v. t. To chastise.
Cas'ti-ga'tion, n. Correction; chastisement; punishment.
Cast'ing, n. Act of one who casts; any thing shaped in a mold.
Cast'ing-net, n. A net that is cast and drawn.
Cast'ing-vote, n. A vote

that decides when the others are equally divided.
Cas'tle (kăs'l), n. A fortified house; a fortress. — v. t. (chess.) To protect with a castle; — said of the king.
Cas'tle-build'er (kăs'l-), n. One who builds castles in the air; a visionary.
Cas'tled (kăs'ld), a. Furnished with castles.
Cas'tor, n. A beaver; a hat.
Cas'tor-oil, n. A cathartic vegetable oil.
Cas'tra-me-ta'tion, n. Art or act of encamping.
Cas'trate, v. t. To geld; to unman; to emasculate.
Cas-tra'tion, n. The act of gelding; emasculation.
Cas'trel, n. A kind of hawk.
Cas'u-al (kăzh'ŭ-al, 104), a. Happening without design. — SYN. Accidental; incidental; occasional.
Cas'u-al-ly (kăzh'ŭ-al-), adv. By chance; accidentally.
Cas'u-al-ty (kăzh'ŭ-), n. An accident; an accidental injury; chance.
Cas'u-ist, n. One who resolves cases of conscience.
Cas'u-ist'ic, } a. Relating
Cas'u-ist'ic-al, } to cases of conscience.
Cas'u-ist-ry, n. The science or practice of a casuist.
Cat, n. A domestic animal; a kind of ship; a tackle; a whip.
Cat'a-clysm, n. An extensive overflow; a deluge.
Cat'a-comb (-kōm), n. [Gr. kata, downward, and kumbē, a cavity.] A cave or subterranean place for the burial of the dead.
Cat'a-cous'tics, n. sing. Science of echoes, or reflected sounds.
Cat'a-lep'sy, n. Sudden suppression of sensation.
Cat'a-logue, n. A list; register of names. — v. t. To make a list of.
Ca-tăl'pă, n. A large tree with white, showy flowers.
Cat'a-mount, n. A wild cat.
Cat'a-phŏn'ics, n. sing. The doctrine of reflected sounds.
Cat'a-plăsm, n. A poultice.
Cat'a-ract, n. A large waterfall; disorder in the eye.
Ca-tărrh' (ka-tär'), n. A cold in the head.
Ca-tărrh'al, } a. Pertaining
Ca-tărrh'ous, } to a catarrh.
Ca-tăs'tro-phe, n. Final event; calamity; disaster.

Cat'-call, n. A squeaking instrument used in theaters to condemn plays or actors.
Catch, v. t. [imp. & p. p. CATCHED, CAUGHT.] To seize; to take; to receive; to find; to overtake. — n. Act of seizing; that which seizes; a snatch; a song.
Catch'a-ble, a. Capable of being caught.
Catch'er, n. One who catches.
Catch'ing, a. Infectious; contagious.
Catch'pen-ny, n. Something worthless, meant to gain money.
Catch'up, } n. A sauce prepared from tomatoes or walnuts, &c.
Cat'sup, }
Catch'word (-wûrd), n. First word of a page inserted at the bottom of the preceding page.
Cat'e-chet'ic, } a. Consist-
Cat'e-chet'ic-al, } ing of, or pertaining to, question and answer.
Cat'e-chise (153), v. t. To teach by questions and answers; to question; to interrogate.
Cat'e-chis'er, n. One who catechises; a catechist.
Cat'e-chism, n. A form of instruction by means of questions and answers.
Cat'e-chist, n. One who catechises; a catechiser.
Cat'e-chu, n. An astringent vegetable extract.
Cat'e-chu'men (-kū'men), n. One learning the rudiments of Christianity.
Cat'e-gor'ic-al, a. Absolute; positive; express.
Cat'e-gor'ic-al-ly, adv. Absolutely; directly; expressly.
Cat'e-go-ry (107), n. One of the highest classes to which the objects of knowledge or thought can be reduced; predicament; state; condition.
Cat'e-nā'ri-an (41), a. Re-
Cat'e-na-ry } lating to, or like, a chain. [by links.
Cat'e-nāte, v. t. To connect
Cat'e-nā'tion, n. Connection by links; regular connection.
Cā'ter, v. i. To provide food.
Cā'ter-er, n. One who provides food; a purveyor.
Cā'ter-ess, n. A female purveyor or caterer.
Cat'er-pil'lar, n. A worm; the larve or worm state of insects. [a cat.
Cat'er-waul, v. i. To cry, as

CATES 72 CELTIC

Cates, *n. pl.* Delicious food; viands. [fresh-water fish.
Cat'-fish, *n.* An American
Cat'gut, *n.* Intestines dried and twisted for strings.
Ca-thar'tic, *a.* Purgative; laxative. — *n.* A purgative medicine.
Ca-the'dral, *n.* The principal church in a diocese.
Cath'e-ter, *n.* An instrument to draw urine from the bladder.
Cath'o-lic (120), *a.* Universal; liberal; pertaining to all Christians; pertaining to the Church of Rome. — *n.* A member of the Church of Rome.
Ca-thol'i-cism, *n.* Liberality; adherence to the Roman Catholic church. [cism.
Cath-o-lic'i-ty, *n.* Catholi-
Ca-thol'i-cize, *v. i.* To become a Catholic. [medicine.
Ca-thol'i-con, *n.* A universal
Cat'kin, *n.* [Diminutive of *cat*, from its resemblance to a cat's tail.] A species of inflorescence.
Cat'ling, *n.* A double-edged dismembering knife. Catkin.
Cat'nip, *n.* A well-known aromatic plant.
Cat'-o'-nine'-tails, *n.* A whip with nine lashes.
Cat'-pipe, *n.* A cat-call.
Cat's'-paw, *n.* The tool of another; a dupe.
Cat'tle (kăt'tl), *n. pl.* Domestic quadrupeds collectively, especially those of the bovine genus.
Cau'cus, *n.* [Orig. an association of *caulkers*.] A preparatory meeting for political purposes. [tail.
Cau'dal, *a.* Pertaining to the
Cau'dle, *n.* A mixture of wine and other ingredients.
Caught (kawt), *imp.* and *p. p.* of *Catch*.
Caul, *n.* A net for the head; a membrane covering the intestines. [of cabbage.
Cau'li-flow'er, *n.* A species
Caus'a-ble, *a.* Capable of being caused.
Caus'al, *a.* Relating to, or implying, causes.
Cau-sal'i-ty, *n.* The agency of a cause. [causing.
Cau-sa'tion, *n.* The act of
Caus'a-tive, *a.* Expressing a cause; causing.

Cause, *n.* That which produces an effect; reason; a suit in law; side of a question. — *v. t.* To make; to effect; to exist.
Cause'less, *a.* Without cause, or a just cause.
Cause'less-ly, *adv.* Without cause, or a good cause.
Caus'er, *n.* One who causes.
Cause'way, } *n.* A raised
Caus'ey, } way over wet ground.
Caus'tic, *a.* Corrosive; burning. — *n.* A burning or corrosive application.
Caus-tic'i-ty, *n.* The quality of being caustic. [iron.
Cau'ter, *n.* A hot, searing
Cau'ter-ism, *n.* Application of cautery. [cauterizing.
Cau-ter-i-zā'tion, *n.* Act of
Cau'ter-ize, *v. t.* To burn or sear with a hot iron, &c.
Cau'ter-y, *n.* A searing with a hot iron or caustic medicines.
Cau'tion, *n.* Prudence; care; admonition; injunction; warning. — *v. t.* To advise against; to admonish.
Cau'tion-a-ry, *a.* Containing caution; given as a pledge.
Cau'tious, *a.* Prudent; watchful against danger; wary.
Cau'tious-ly, *adv.* Warily; prudently. [on horseback.
Cav'al-cāde', *n.* A procession
Cav'a-liēr', *n.* An armed horseman; a knight. — *a.* Brave; haughty; disdainful.
Cav'a-liēr'ly, *adv.* Haughtily.
Cav'al-ry, *n.* Mounted troops.
Cāve, *n.* A den; a cavern; a hollow place in the earth. — *v. t.* To make hollow. — *v. i.* To fall in.
†**Cā've-ăt,** *n.* [Lat., let him beware.] A notice to some officer not to do a certain act until the one who gives the notice is heard in opposition; a description of an invention lodged in the patent office before the patent right is taken out.
Cav'ern, *n.* A cave; a den.
Cav'erned, *a.* Full of caverns.
Cav'ern-ous, *a.* Hollow; full of caverns.
Ca-viāre' (-veer'), } *n.* The
Cav'i-är, } roes of certain fish salted.
Cav'il (130), *v. i.* To find fault; to raise captious and frivolous objections. — *n.* Captious objection.
Cav'il-er, } *n.* One who raises
Cav'il-ler, } captious objections.

Cav'i-ty, *n.* A hollow place hollowness.
Caw, *v. i.* To cry, as a rook, crow, or raven. — *n.* Cry of a rook, raven, or crow.
Cay-enne', *n.* A pungent pepper.
Ca-zique' (-zeek'), *n.* An Indian chief or king.
Cēase, *v. i.* To stop; to leave off. — SYN. To desist; forbear; fail.
Cēase'less, *a.* Never ceasing; incessant. [santly.
Cēase'less-ly, *adv.* Incessantly.
Cē'dar, *n.* An evergreen tree.
Cēde, *v. t.* To yield; to give up; to resign.
Ce-dil'lā, *n.* A mark under the letter *c* (thus, ç), giving it the sound of *s*. [cedar.
Cē'drine, *a.* Belonging to
Cēil, *v. t.* To line the roof of.
Cēil'ing, *n.* [Lat. *cælum*, heaven, vault, arch.] Covering of the inner roof.
Cĕl'an-dīne, *n.* A plant of the poppy family.
Cĕl'a-tūre, *n.* The art of engraving; the thing engraved.
Cĕl'e-brāte, *v. t.* To praise; to extol; to solemnize; to commemorate.
Cĕl'e-brāt'ed, *a.* Distinguished; famous.
Cĕl'e-brā'tion, *n.* Honor or distinction bestowed; commemoration. [celebrates.
Cĕl'e-brā'tor, *n.* One who
Ce-lĕb'ri-ty, *n.* Honorable fame or distinction; renown; a distinguished person.
Ce-lĕr'i-ty, *n.* Swiftness; velocity; rapidity; speed.
Cĕl'er-y, *n.* A plant cultivated for the table.
Ce-lĕs'tial (-lĕst'yal), *a.* Heavenly. — *n.* An inhabitant of heaven. [monk.
Cĕl'es-tine, *n.* A kind of
Cĕ'li-ăc, *a.* Pertaining to the belly.
Cĕl'i-ba-cy, *n.* Unmarried state; single life.
Cĕll (123), *n.* A small room; a small, closed cavity; minute vesicle. [building.
Cĕl'lar, *n.* A room under a
Cĕl'lar-age, *n.* Cellars in general; space for cellars.
Cel'lu-lar, *a.* Consisting of, or containing, cells.
Cĕl'si-tūde, *n.* Height.
Cĕlt, *n.* One of ancient race, from whom the Welsh, Irish, &c., are descended.
Cĕlt'ic, *a.* Pertaining to the Celts.

CEMENT 73 CHAGRIN

Çĕm'ent, or Çe-ment', n. An adhesive substance which unites two bodies.

Çe-mĕnt', v. t. To join closely. — v. i. To unite; to cohere.

Çĕm'en-tā'tion, n. The act of uniting by cement.

Çĕm'e-tĕr'y, n. A place where the dead are buried.

Çĕn'o-bīte, n. A monk dwelling in a convent or community.

Çĕn'o-bīt'ic-al, a. Living in community.

Çĕn'o-tăph, n. A monument to one buried elsewhere.

Çĕns'er, n. An incense-pan.

Çĕn'sor, n. A Roman magistrate; one who examines manuscripts for the press; a harsh critic.

Çen-sō'ri-al, a. Belonging to a censor.

Çen-sō'ri-oŭs (86), a. Severe; prone to find fault.

Çen-sō'ri-oŭs-ly, adv. In a censorious manner.

Çen-sō'ri-oŭs-ness, n. Quality of being censorious.

Çĕn'sor-ship, n. Office of a censor.

Çĕn'su-al (sĕn'shụ-al), a. Relating to the census.

Çĕn'sur-a-ble (sĕn'shụr-), a. Deserving of censure.

Çĕn'sure (sĕn'shụr), n. Blame. — v. t. To blame; to find fault with; to condemn.

Çĕn'sus, n. An official enumeration of inhabitants.

Çĕnt, n. [Lat. centum, a hundred.] A copper, nickel, or bronze coin of the United States.

Çĕnt'age, n. Rate by the hundred; percentage.

Çĕn'taur, n. A fabulous monster, half man, half horse.

Çĕn'te-na-ry, a. Pertaining to a hundred. — n. A hundred things collectively; a century.

Çen-tĕn'ni-al, a. Happening once in a hundred years.

Çĕn'ter } (151), n. The middle
Çĕn'tre } point. — v. t. To place on the middle point. — v. i. To meet in the middle.

Çĕn'ter-bĭt, } n. An instru-
Çĕn'tre-bĭt, } ment for boring holes.

Çen-tĕs'i-mal, a. Hundredth; by the hundred.

Çĕn'ti-grāde, a. Having a hundred degrees.

Çĕn'ti-pĕd, n. An insect with a great many feet.

Çĕn'to, n. A piece made up of passages from different authors.

Çĕn'tral, a. Relating to the center; in or near the center.

Çĕn'tral-ly, adv. In a central manner; in the center.

Çen-trăl'i-ty, n. The state of being central.

Çĕn'tral-i-zā'tion, n. Act of centralizing.

Çĕn'tral-īze, v. t. To bring to a center.

Çĕn'tric, } a. Placed in the
Çĕn'tric-al, } center; central.

Çĕn'tric-al-ly, adv. In a central position.

Çen-triç'i-ty, n. State of being centric.

Çen-trĭf'u-gal, a. Tending from the center.

Çen-trĭp'e-tal, a. Tending to the center.

Çen-tŭm'vir, n. (Lat. pl. Çen-tŭm'vi-rī.) A judge in ancient Rome who decided common causes among the people.

Çen-tŭm'vi-ral, a. Pertaining to a centumvir, or to the centumviri.

Çĕn'tu-ple, a. A hundred fold.

Çen-tū'ri-al, a. Pertaining to a century.

Çen-tū'ri-on, n. A Roman military officer placed over one hundred men.

Çĕnt'u-ry, n. A hundred years.

Çe-phăl'ic, a. Relating to the head. — n. A medicine for headache, or other disease of the head.

Çē'rate, n. An ointment made of wax, oil, &c. [wax.

Çē'rāt-ed, a. Covered with

Çēre, v. t. To wax, or cover with wax.

Çē're-al (86), a. Pertaining to edible grain, as wheat, rye, &c. — n. Any edible grain.

Çĕr'e-bel, n. Lower part of the brain.

Çĕr'e-bĕl'lum, n. The hinder and lower division of the brain.

Çĕr'e-bral, a. Pertaining to the cerebrum or brain.

Çĕr'e-brum, n. The superior and larger division of the brain.

Çēre'cloth, n. A waxed cloth.

Çĕr'e-mō'ni-al, a. Relating to rites; ritual. — n. Outward form or rite.

Çĕr'e-mō'ni-oŭs, a. Full of ceremony; formal; exact.

Çĕr'e-mo-ny, n. Outward rite; forms of civility.

Çe-rŏg'ra-phy, n. Art of engraving on wax.

Çĕr'tain (39), a. Sure; regular; one or some.

Çĕr'tain-ly, adv. Without doubt or question.

Çĕr'tain-ty, n. Full assurance; established fact; truth. [in writing.

Çĕr-tĭf'i-cate, n. A testimony

Çĕr'ti-fi-cā'tion, n. Act of certifying. [tifies.

Çĕr'ti-fī'er, n. One who cer-

Çĕr'ti-fȳ, v. t. To give certain notice; to testify to in writing.

Çĕr'ti-tūde, n. Freedom from doubt; certainty

Çe-rū'le-an, } a. Sky-colored;
Çe-rū'le-oŭs, } blue.

Çe-rū'men, n. The wax secreted by the ear.

Çē'ruse, n. White lead; native carbonate of lead. [neck.

Çĕr'vic-al, a. Relating to the

Çẽr'vīne, a. Pertaining to deer.

Çĕss, v. t. To assess; to rate. — n. A tax, or rate.

Çes-sā'tion, n. Stop; pause; rest; respite.

Çĕs'sion (sĕsh'un), n. A giving up; a yielding; surrender.

Çe-sū'rā (140), n. A pause in verse. [cesura.

Çe-sū'ral, a. Relating to a

Çe-tā'cean, n. An animal of the whale kind. [kind.

Çe-tā'ceoŭs, a. Of the whale

Çĕt'ic, a. Pertaining to the whale.

Çe-tŏl'o-ġy, n. The natural history of cetaceous animals.

Chāfe, v. t. & i. To fret by rubbing; to gall; to irritate. — n. Irritation.

Chāf'er, n. One who chafes; an insect.

Chāf'er-y, n. A forge for hammering iron into bars.

Chăff (5, 123), n. Husks of grain; refuse. — v. t. To make fun of.

Chăf'fer, v. t. or i. To bargain.

Chăf'fer-er, n. One who treats about buying.

Chăf'finch, n. A singing bird; a kind of finch.

Chăff'y, a. Full of chaff; resembling chaff.

Chā'fing-dish, n. A dish for holding hot coals, &c.

Cha-green' (sha-green'), n. A rough-grained leather.

Cha-grin', n. Ill-humor; vexation. — v. t. To vex; to mortify.

Chain, n. A line of links; a continued series. — v. t. To fasten with a chain; to enslave.
Chain'-pump, n. A pump used in ships, &c.
Chain'-shot, n. pl. Shot connected by a chain or bar.
Chair (3), n. A movable seat with a back, for one person; a presiding officer; a kind of carriage; a sedan.
Chair'man (143), n. A presiding officer.
Chaise, n. A two-wheeled covered carriage.
Chal-ced'o-ny, or **Chal'ce-do-ny,** n. A variety of quartz of a whitish color.
Chal-cog'ra-phy, n. Engraving on brass or copper.
Chal'dron, n. A measure of 36 bushels of coal.
Chal'ice, n. A kind of cup; a communion cup.
Chalk (chawk), n. A white calcareous earth. — v. t. To rub or mark with chalk.
Chalk'y (chawk'y), a. Containing, consisting of, or resembling, chalk.
Chal'lenge, v. t. To call to fight; to claim as due; to object to. — n. A summons to a contest; demand; exception to a juror.
Chal'lenge-a-ble, a. Capable of being challenged.
Chal'len-ger, n. One who challenges.
Cha-lyb'e-ate, a. Impregnated with some salt of iron. — n. Any water or medicine into which iron enters.
Cham'ber, n. An upper room; a hollow place; a kind of court. — v. i. To lodge; to be wanton.
Cham'ber-er, n. One who intrigues or indulges in wantonness.
Cham'ber-lain, n. An overseer of the chambers; one of the high officers of a royal court.
Cham'ber-maid, n. A female who has the charge of bedchambers.
Cha-me'le-on, n. [Gr. chamaileōn, literally groundlion.] A species of lizard, whose color is changeable.

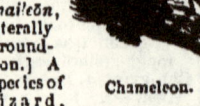
Chameleon.

Cham'fer, v. t. To cut a groove in; to bevel. — n. A small gutter; a groove.
Cham'ois (sham'my or sha-moy'), n. A kind of antelope.
Cham'o-mile, n. A bitter plant. Chamois.
Champ, v. t. or i. To chew; to bite.
Cham-pagne' (sham-pān'), n. A brisk, sparkling wine.
Cham-paign' (sham-pān'), a. Open; flat; level. — n. An open, flat country.
Cham'pi-on, n. A combatant for another, or for a cause.
Chance, n. An unforeseen occurrence. — SYN. Accident; hazard; opportunity. — v. i. to happen; to come unexpectedly. — a. Accidental; fortuitous.
Chan'cel, n. Part of a church where the altar stands.
Chan'cel-lor (129), n. An officer of state; judge of a court of chancery or equity.
Chan'cel-lor-ship, n. Office of a chancellor. [equity.
Chan'cer-y, n. A court of
Chan'cr ous, a. Ulcerous.
Chan'de-lier', n. A frame or support for lights.
Chan'dler, n. One who deals in candles, or in certain other commodities.
Chan'dler-y, n. Articles sold by a chandler.
Change, v. t. or i. To alter; to exchange. — n. Alteration; small money.
Change'a-ble, a. Subject to change; fickle; mutable.
Change'a-ble-ness, n.
Change'a-bil'i-ty, Fickleness; mutability; inconstancy.
Change'ful, a. Full of change.
Change'less, a. Constant; invariable.
Change'ling, n. A fickle person; an idiot; a child left in place of another, as by fairies.
Chan'nel, n. [A different spelling of canal.] Course of a stream; a furrow; a groove. — v. t. (130) To cut into channels; to groove.
Chant, v. t. or i. To sing; to recite to musical tones without musical measure. — n. Song; melody; musical recitation.

Chant'er, n. One who chants.
Chant'i-cleer, n. The male of domestic fowls; a cock.
Chant'ress, n. A female singer.
Chant'ry, n. A chapel to sing mass in for the souls of the founder.
Cha'os (kā'os), n. Confused mass of matter; confusion.
Cha-ot'ic (ka-ot'ik, 41), a. Resembling chaos; confused.
Chap (chăp or chŏp), n. A crack in flesh. — v. t. or i. To open; to crack; to split. — n. A boy; a buyer.
†**Chap'ar-ral',** n. [Sp.] A thicket of low evergreen oaks.
†**Chapeau** (shăp'o), n. (pl. Chapeaus, shăp'ōz.) A hat.
Chap'el, n. A place of worship, especially in England, one used by dissenters.
Chap'el-ry, n. The bound or jurisdiction of a chapel.
Chap'er-on (shăp'er-ōn), v. t. To attend and protect in public. — n. A lady's attendant and protector.
Chap'i-ter, n. The upper part of a column or pillar.
Chap'lain (89), n. A clergyman of the army or navy, or of a legislative body, a public institution, or a family.
Chap'lain-cy, { n. Office of
Chap'lain-ship, } a chaplain.
Chap'let, n. A garland or wreath; a string of beads for counting prayers.
Chap'man (143), n. A dealer.
Chaps (chŏps), n. pl. The mouth or jaws.
Chap'ter, n. [From Lat. caput, head.] A division of a book; an organized branch of some body.
Char, v. t. To reduce to coal.
Char, or **Chare,** n. See Chore.
Char'ac-ter, n. A mark or letter; peculiar or distinctive quality; a person; reputation.
Char'ac-ter-is'tic, a. Constituting or indicating character. — n. That which marks the character.
Char'ac-ter-ist'ic-al-ly, adv. In a manner to distinguish character.
Char'ac-ter-ize, v. t. To distinguish or express the peculiar qualities of.
Cha-rāde', n. A kind of riddle in which each syllable of a word, as well as the whole word, expresses an enigma.
Char'coal, n. Coal from wood.

CHARGE 75 CHICK-PEA

Chärge, v. t. To impose; to enjoin; to accuse; to impute; to load. — v. i. To make an onset. — n. Care; command; commission; expense; onset.

Chärge'a-ble, a. Expensive; ascribable; imputable.

†**Chargé d'affaires (shär-zhā′ daf'lär′),** n. [Fr.] An inferior diplomatic representative at a foreign court.

†**Chargéship (shär-zhā′ship),** n. Office of a chargé d'affaires.

Chär'ger, n. A large dish; a war-horse. [gaily.

Chär'i-ly, adv. Warily; fru-

Chär'i-ot, n. A carriage of pleasure or state.

Chär'i-ot-eer′, n. Driver of a chariot.

Chär'i-ta-ble, a. Full of love and good will; liberal; kind.

Chär'i-ty, n. Love; liberality; alms; candor. [quack.

Chärl'a-tan (shärl′-), n. A

Chärl'a-tan-ry, n. Quackery.

Chärm, n. [Lat. *carmen*, song, incautation.] Magic power; spell; enchantment. — v. t. To delight; to delude; to subdue. — v. i. To act as a charm. [charms.

Chärm'er, n. One who

Chärm'ing, a. Enchanting; highly delightful.

Chär'nel-house, n. A place under a church for bones of the dead. [coasts, &c.

Chärt, n. A delineation of

Chär'ter, n. A deed or conveyance; a patent; a grant. — v. t. To establish by charter; to let or hire, as a vessel.

Chärt'ism, n. Principles of the Chartists.

Chärt'ist, n. An English political reformer.

Chär'y, a. Careful; cautious.

Chāse, v. t. To hunt; to pursue. — n. Pursuit; a printer's frame; a wide groove.

Chās'er, n. A pursuer.

Chăsm (kăzm), n. A cleft; gap; opening.

Chāste, a. Undefiled; pure.

Chāste′ly, adv. In a chaste manner; with purity.

Chās′ten (chās′n), v. t. To correct by punishment.

Chās′ten-er (chās′n-), n. One who chastens.

Chās′ten-ing, n. Correction.

Chas-tīse′, v. t. To correct by punishing.

Chās′tīse-ment, n. Corrective punishment. [tise.

Chas-tīs′er, n. One who chas-

Chăs′ti-ty, n. Purity of

Chāste′ness, body or words.

Chăt (129), v. i. To talk familiarly. — n. Idle or familiar talk.

†**Chât-eau′ (shat-ō′),** n. A castle or country-seat.

Chât′el-la-ny, n. Jurisdiction of a governor of a castle.

Chăt′tel (chăt′tl), n. Any movable property.

Chăt′ter, v. i. To talk idly; to jabber. — n. A prating; noise of birds.

Chăt′ter-bŏx, n. One who talks incessantly. [ters.

Chăt′ter-er, n. One who chat-

Chăt′ty, a. Talkative.

Chēap, a. Of low price; common; of little value.

Chēap′en, v. t. To attempt to buy; to chaffer for.

Chēap′en-er, n. One who cheapens.

Chēap′ly, adv. At a low rate.

Chēap′ness, n. Lowness of price.

Chēat, n. A trick; a deceiver. — v. t. To defraud; to impose on in a bargain.

Chēat′er, n. One who cheats.

Chĕck, v. t. To curb or restrain; to mark off, as in a list. — n. Restraint; a curb; an order for money.

Chĕck′er, v. t. To variegate with little squares or with cross lines; to diversify.

Chĕck′er-bōard, n. A board for playing checkers on.

Chĕck′ers, n. pl. A game on a checkered board.

Chĕck′māte, n. [Per. *shah mât*, the king is dead.] A movement in chess that ends the game. — v. t. To defeat, by checkmating; to defeat completely.

Chēek, n. The side of the face.

Chēer, n. State of gayety or mirth; entertainment; acclamation. — v. t. To cause to rejoice; to enliven; to encourage; to salute by cheers.

Chēer′ful, a. Lively; gay; sprightly; animated.

Chēer′ful-ness, n. Gayety; alacrity; good spirits.

Chēer′less, a. Comfortless; sad; gloomy. [animated.

Chēer′y, a. Gay; sprightly;

Chēese, n. The curd of milk congulated and pressed.

Chēese′-cāke, n. A cake made of soft curds, sugar, and butter.

Chēese′-mŏn′ger, n. One who deals in, or sells, cheese.

Chēese′-prĕss, n. A machine for pressing curds.

Chēeg′y, a. Like cheese.

Chĕm′ic-al, a. Pertaining to chemistry.

Che-mīse′ (she-mēez′), n. An under garment of a woman.

Chĕm′ist, n. One versed in chemistry.

Chĕm′is-try, n. The science which treats of the composition and changes of substances.

Chĕr′ish, v. t. To treat with tenderness; to nourish.

Chĕr′ish-er, n. One who cherishes.

Chĕr′ry, n. A small stone fruit, or the tree that bears it. — a. Red like a cherry.

Chĕr′so-nēse, n. A peninsula.

Chĕrt, n. A kind of quartz; hornstone.

Chĕr′ub (147), n. A celestial spirit; an angel.

Che-ru′bic:n. Angelic.

†**Chĕr′u-bim,** n. Hebrew plural of *Cherub*.

Chĕss, n. A certain game of skill played by two persons on a checkered board.

Chĕss′-bōard, n. A board used in the game of chess.

Chĕss′-man (25), n. One of the pieces used in the game of chess. [thorax.

Chĕst, n. A large box; the

Chĕst′nut, n. [From *Kastana*, a city of Pontus.] A tree and and its nut. — a. Reddish brown.

Chĕv′a-liēr′ (shĕv′-), n. [Fr., from *cheval*, horse.] A knight; horseman; cavalier.

†**Chevaux-de-frise (shĕv′o-de-freez),** n. pl. [Fr., lit., Friesland horses.] A piece of timber armed with spikes, used for defense in war.

Chĕv′er-īl, n. Soft kid-leather.

Chĕv′ron, n. A distinguishing mark on the sleeve of a non-commissioned military officer's coat.

Chew (chōō), v. t. To grind with the teeth; to masticate.

Chī-bouque′ (chī-bōōk′), n. A Turkish pipe.

Chī-cāne′ (shī-), } n. Shift;

Chī-cān′er-y, } stratagem; trickery; mean artifice.

Chick, } n. The young of

Chick′en, } fowls.

Chick′en-heärt′ed, a. Cowardly; timid.

Chick′en-pŏx, n. A contagious eruptive disease.

Chick′-pēa, n. A species of pea.

sŏn, ôr, dọ, wọlf, tōō, tŏŏk; ûrn, rṳle, pṳll; ç, ġ, *soft*; c, ḡ, *hard*; aṣ; eẋist; ŋ as ng; this.

Chick'weed, n. A kind of weed.
Chide, v. t. [imp. CHID; p. p. CHID, CHIDDEN.] To scold; to reprove; to rebuke.
Chief, a. Highest in office; principal. — n. A leader; commander; head of a clan or tribe.
Chief'ly, adv. Principally: especially. [or leader.
Chief'tain (30), n. A captain
Chil'blain (17), n. An itching swelling or sore caused by cold. [daughter.
Child (144), n. A son or
Child'-bear'ing, n. Act of producing children.
Child'bed, n. The state of travail or childbirth.
Child'birth, n. Travail; labor.
Child'hood, n. State of a child; time of being a child.
Child'ish, a. Like a child; simple; trifling; puerile.
Child'ish-ly, adv. In the manner of a child.
Child'ish-ness, n. State or qualities of a child.
Child'less, a. Having no child.
Child'-like, a. Like or becoming a child; dutiful.
Chil'dren, n.; pl. of Child.
Chill (123), n. Cold; inducing a shivering. — n. Moderate cold. — v. t. To make cold; to discourage; to depress.
Chill'i-ness, } n. Coldness.
Chill'ness,
Chill'y, a. Somewhat cold.
Chime, n. A set of bells arranged to ring in a tune; the sound thus produced; edge of a cask. — v. i. To sound in harmony.
Chim'er, n. One who chimes.
Chi-me'ra (140), n. A vain, idle fancy. [fanciful.
Chi-mer'i-cal, a. Imaginary;
Chim'ney (141), n. A flue or passage for smoke. [face.
Chin, n. Lower end of the
Chi'na (140), n. A fine kind of earthenware; porcelain.
Chine'a-pin, n. A tree otherwise called the dwarf chestnut.
Chin-chil'la, n. A small animal remarkable for its soft gray fur. [ing-cough.
Chin'-cough (-kof), n. Hooping
Chine, n. Backbone; part of a barrel or cask in which the head is fixed.
Chink, n. Gap; opening; aperture; crack. — v. i. To crack; to jingle. — v. t. To cause to jingle.

Chink'y, a. Having chinks.
Chintz (chints, 105), n. Cotton cloth printed with colors.
Chip, n. A piece cut off; a fragment. — v. t. To cut into small pieces. — v. i. To break off in small pieces.
Chi'ro-graph, n. A writing requiring a counterpart.
Chi-rog'ra-pher, n. A writer.
Chi-rog'ra-phy, n. One's own hand-writing; penmanship.
Chi-rol'o-gy, n. Art of conversing with the hands.
Chi'ro-man'cy, n. Divination by inspecting the hand.
Chi-rop'o-dist, n. One who extracts corns from feet.
Chirp (16), v. i. To make the noise of small birds. — n. A short, sharp note, as of a small bird.
Chirp'ing, n. The cheerful noise of birds. [chirping.
Chir'rup, v. t. To animate by
Chis'el, n. A tool for paring, hewing, or gouging. — v. t. (130) To cut with a chisel.
Chit, n. A shoot; small child.
Chit'chat, n. Familiar talk.
Chiv'al-ric, a. Chivalrous.
Chiv'al-rous (shiv'-), a. Pertaining to chivalry; gallant.
Chiv'al-ry (shiv'al-ry), n. [Fr. chevalerie, from chevalier, knight.] Knight errantry; valor.
Chives, n. pl. Slender threads in the blossoms of plants.
Chlo'rate, n. A compound of chloric acid with a salifiable base.
Chlo'ride, n. A compound of chlorine with another element. [ish colored gas.
Chlo'rine, n. A heavy green-
Chlo'ro-form, n. A volatile liquid, consisting of carbon, hydrogen, and chlorine, used to produce insensibility.
Chock, n. A kind of wedge.
Chock'-full, a. Completely full.
Choc'o-late, n. A paste made from the cacao-nut, or a beverage made from the paste.
Choice, n. Act or power of choosing; a thing chosen. — a. Select; precious.
Choir (kwir), n. Part of a church; body of singers.
Choke (18), v. t. To stop the windpipe; to suffocate. — v. i. To have the windpipe stopped.
Choke'-damp, n. A noxious vapor in wells, mines, &c.
Choke'-full, a. Full to choking; quite full.

Choke'-pear, n. A kind of pear, very astringent.
Chok'y, a. Tending to choke.
Chol'er, n. Bile; gall; anger.
Chol'er-a, n. A malignant disease characterized by vomiting and purging.
Chol'er-a-mor'bus, n. A milder form of cholera.
Chol'er-ic (120), a. Passionate.
Choose, v. t. [imp. CHOSE; p. p. CHOSEN, CHOSE.] To make choice of. — SYN. To prefer; elect; select. — v. i. To make a selection.
Choos'er, n. One who chooses.
Chop (129), v. t. To cut; to mince; to barter. — v. i. To change, as the wind: to wrangle. — n. A small piece of meat. [house.
Chop'-house, n. A dining-
Chop'ping, a. Large; plump.
Chops, n. pl. The jaws.
Chop'stick, n. A small stick used by the Chinese to convey food to the mouth.
Cho'ral (kō'ral), a. Belonging to a choir.
Chord, n. String of a musical instrument: harmonious combination of musical tones simultaneously performed; a line AC, AB, chords, uniting the extremities of an arc. [Chord.
Chore, n. A small job of work.
Cho'rist, n. A chorister.
Chor'is-ter, n. A leader of a choir; a chorist.
Cho-rog'ra-pher, n. One who describes a region.
Cho'ro-graph'ic-al, a. Pertaining to chorography.
Cho-rog'ra-phy, n. [Gr. choros, place, and graphein, to describe.] Description of a particular region.
Cho'rus (140), n. A company of singers; part of a song in which all join.
Chose, imp. & p. p. of Choose.
Cho'sen (chō'zn), p. p. of Choose.
Chough (chŭf), n. A bird of the crow family.
Chouse (chowss), v. t. To cheat; to trick. — n. A simpleton; a trick or imposition.
Chow'der, n. Fish, biscuit, &c., stewed together.
Chrism, n. Consecrated oil, used in baptism, ordination, &c.

CHRISMATORY 77 CIRCUMCISION

Chris'ma-to-ry, *n.* A vessel for the chrism.
Christ, *n.* The Anointed; the Messiah; the Savior.
Chris'ten (kris'n), *v. t.* To baptize and name.
Chris'ten-dom (kris'n-), *n.* Portions of the world inhabited by Christians.
Chris'ten-ing, *n.* Baptism.
Christ'ian (krist'yan), *n.* A disciple of Christ; one born in a Christian land. — *a.* Pertaining to Christ. — *Christian name*, the first name, or that given in baptism.
Christ-ian'i-ty, *n.* The religion taught by Christ.
Christ'ian-ize, *v. t.* To convert to Christianity.
Christ'ian-ly, *a.* In a Christian manner.
Christ'less, *a.* Having no faith in Christ.
Christ'mas (kris'mas), *n.* The feast of Christ's nativity, 25th of December.
Christ'mas-box (kris'-), *n.* A box for Christmas presents.
Chro-mat'ic, *a.* Relating to colors and to a scale in music which proceeds by semitones.
Chro-mat'ics, *n. sing.* The science of colors.
Chrome, } *n.* A hard,
Chrō'mi-um, } brittle metal of a grayish-white color.
Chrŏn'ic, } *a.* [Gr. *chroni-*
Chrŏn'ic-al, } *kos*, fr. *chronos*, time.] Of long duration.
Chrŏn'i-cle (krŏn'i-kl), *n.* A register of events. — *v. t.* To record in history.
Chro-nŏl'o-ger, } *n.* One who
Chro-nŏl'o-gist, } studies or explains chronology.
Chrŏn'o-lŏġ'ic, } *a.* Per-
Chrŏn'o-lŏġ'ic-al, } taining to chronology.
Chro-nŏl'o-ġy, *n.* The science of measuring time, and which assigns to events their proper dates.
Chro-nŏm'e-ter, *n.* A very exact time-piece.
Chrȳs'a-lĭs, *n.* The form of a butterfly before it reaches the winged state.
Chrys-ăn'the-mum, *n.* A genus of plants. [mineral.
Chrȳs'o-līte. *n.* A greenish
Chrȳs'o-prāṣe, *n.* A kind of grayish or greenish quartz.
Chŭb, *n.* A fresh-water fish.
Chŭb'bed, } *a.* Big-headed;
Chŭb'by, } stupid; short and thick.

Chŭck, *v.* To make a noise as a hen; to strike gently; to thrust. — *n.* The noise of a hen; a gentle blow.
Chŭck'-fär'thing, *n.* A play in which a farthing is chucked into a hole.
Chŭck'le, *v. i.* To laugh inwardly. — *v. t.* To call, as a hen.
Chŭff, *n.* A coarse surly fellow.
Chŭff'y, *a.* Blunt; clownish; surly.
Chŭm, *n.* A room-mate.
Chŭnk, *n.* A short, thick piece of wood.
Chûrch (140), *n.* [Gr. *kuriakē*, Lord's house, from *kurios*, lord.] A place of worship; a body of Christians. — *v. t.* To perform the giving of thanks in church after childbirth.
Chûrch'man (143), *n.* An Episcopalian; a clergyman.
Chûrch'-war'den (-wôr'dn), *n.* An officer of the church.
Chûrch'-yärd, *n.* A graveyard near a church.
Chûrl, *n.* A rustic; a rough, surly fellow; a niggard.
Chûrl'ish, *a.* Surly; rude.
Chûrl'ish-ness, *n.* Rudeness of manners; moroseness.
Chûrn, *n.* A vessel in which butter is made. — *v. t.* To agitate, as cream, for making butter.
Chûrn'ing, *n.* The making of butter by means of a churn.
Chȳle, *n.* A milky fluid derived from chyme.
Chȳl'i-făc'tion, *n.* Act or process by which chyle is formed.
Chȳme, *n.* Pulp formed from food digested in the stomach.
Çĭc'a-trĭçe, } *n.* A scar; a
Çĭ-cā'trĭx, } mark.
Çĭc'a-trĭ-zā'tion, *n.* The process of healing a wound.
Çĭc'a-trīze, *v. i. or t.* To heal by forming a skin over a wound.
†**Cicerone** (chĕ/che-rō'nā or sĭs'e-rō'ne), *n.* [It., fr. *Cicero*, the eloquent Roman orator.] One who shows strangers the curiosities of a place; a guide.
Çī'der, *n.* Juice of apples, usually fermented.
Çī-gär', *n.* A small roll of tobacco for smoking.
Çĭl'i-a-ry, *a.* Belonging to the eyelids.
Çĭ-lĭ'cioŭs (-lĭsh'us), *a.* Made of hair; hairy.

Çĭm'e-ter, *n.* A short sword with a recurvated point.
Çin-chō'nȧ, *n.* A kind of medicinal bark; Peruvian bark.
Çĭnc̨t'ūre (50), *n.* A belt; a girdle; inclosure.
Çĭn'der, *n.* A small coal; an ember; a scale thrown off in forging metal.
Çĭn'e-rĭ'tioŭs, } *a.* Of the col-
Çĭn-ē're-oŭs, } or of ashes.
Çĭn'na-bär, *n.* Red sulphuret of mercury; vermilion.
Çĭn'na-mon, *n.* The inner bark of a species of laurel.
Çĭnque (sĭŋk), *n.* The number five; — *used in games*.
Çĭnque'foil, *n.* A five-leaved rosette in architecture.
Çī'on, *n.* A shoot or twig of a tree for grafting.
Çī'pher, *n.* [Ar. *sifrun*, empty.] The figure 0; initial letters of a name inwoven; a secret writing. — *v. i.* To use figures in arithmetical operations.
Çī'pher-ing, *n.* Art of performing sums in arithmetic.
Çĭr'cle (16), *n.* A curve every point of which is equally distant from the center; circult; compass; Circle. an orb; surrounding company; a province. — *v. t.* or *i.* To move round or circularly.
Çĭr'clet, *n.* A little circle.
Çĭr'cuit (sĭr'kĭt), *n.* A circularspace; a judicial district; a regular journeying, as of a judge. — *v. t.* To move or make to go round.
Çĭr-cū'i-toŭs, *a.* Roundabout; not direct.
Çĭr'eu-lar, *a.* Round; like a circle; ending in itself.
Çĭr'cu-lăr'i-ty, *n.* State of being circular.
Çĭr'cu-lar-ly, *adv.* In the form of a circle.
Çĭr'cu-lāte, *v. i.* To move or pass round — *v. t.* To cause to pass round.
Çĭr'cu-lā'tion, *n.* Act of circulating; a passing round; currency. [ing.
Çĭr'cu-la-to-ry, *a.* Circulat-
Çĭr'cum-ăm'bi-ent, *a.* Surrounding.
Çĭr'cum-ăm'bu-lāte, *v. t.* To walk round about.
Çĭr'cum-çīṣe, *v. t.* To deprive of the foreskin.
Çĭr'cum-çĭṣ'ion (-sĭzh'un), *n.* Act of circumcising.

sŏn, ôr, d₂, wọlf, tōō, tŏŏk; ûrn, rye, pụll; ç, ġ, *soft*; c, ḡ, *hard*; ǣ; eẋist; ṇ *as* ṇġ; this.

CIRCUMFERENCE 78 CLASH

Cir-cŭm'fer-ençe, n. The line that bounds the circle.
Çir'eum-flex, n. An accent (marked thus ˆ or thus ˜).
Çir-cŭm'flu-ençe, n. Flowing round.
Çir-cŭm'flu-ent, } a. Flowing
Çir-cŭm'flu-oŭs, } round.
Çir'eum-fo-rā'ne-oŭs, a. Going about or abroad.
Çir'eum-fūṣe', v. t. To pour or spread round.
Çir'eum-fū'ġion, n. Act of pouring round.
Çir'eum-jā'çent, a. Lying around; bordering.
Çir'eum-lo-cū'tion, n. The use of indirect expressions.
Çir'eum-lŏe'u-to-ry, a. Consisting in circumlocution.
Çir'eum-năv'i-gāte, v. t. To sail round.
Çir'eum-năv'i-gā'tion, n. A sailing round.
Çir'eum-năv'i-gā'tor, n. One who sails around.
Çir'eum-pō'lar, a. About one of the poles of the earth.
Çir'eum-rō'ta-ry, a. Revolving; turning round.
Çir'eum-seribe', v. t. To inclose; to limit; to confine.
Çir'eum-serip'tion, n. Limitation; bound; confinement.
Çir'eum-speet, a. Guarded; prudent; wary; watchful.
Çir'eum-spĕe'tion, n. Watchfulness; prudence.
Çir'eum-spĕet'ive, a. Cautious; wary; circumspect.
Çir'eum-spĕet-ly, adv. Warily; watchfully.
Çir'eum-stançe (107), n. Something pertaining to a fact, but not essential thereto; (pl.) state as to property. — SYN. Fact; event; incident. — v. t. To place relatively or in a particular situation.
Çir'eum-stăn'tial, a. Particular; minute; abounding with circumstances.
Çir'eum-stăn'tial-ly, adv. In every circumstance or particular.
Çir'eum-stăn'tials, n. pl. Things incident, but not essential.
Çir'eum-val-lā'tion, n. A fortification round a place.
Çir'eum-vĕnt', v. t. To deceive; to impose upon.
Çir'eum-vĕn'tion, n. Deception; imposture; fraud.
Çir'eum-vŏlve', v. t. or i. To roll round; to revolve.

Çir'eum-vo-lū'tion, n. Act of rolling round.
Çir'eus (40), n. A place for games or feats of horsemanship.
Çis-ăl'pine, a. On this side of the Alps; south of the Alps.
Çis'at-lăn'tie, a. On this side of the Atlantic.
Çis'tern, n. A large vessel for water, &c.; a reservoir; tank. [tempt.
Çit, n. A citizen; — in con-
Çit'a-del, n. A fortress in or near a city.
Çi-tā'tion, n. A summons; notice; quotation.
Çi'ta-to-ry, a. Citing; calling.
Çite, v. t. To summon; to quote.
Çith'ern, n. A sort of guitar.
Çit'i-zen, n. An inhabitant of a city; a freeman.
Çit'i-zen-ship, n. State of being a citizen. [ons.
Çit'rie, a. Belonging to lem-
Çit'rine, a. Like a citron or lemon. [on.
Çit'ron, n. A species of lem-
Çit'y (141), n. [Lat. civitas, fr. civis, citizen.] An incorporated town; a large town.
Çives, n. pl. A kind of garlic.
Çiv'et, n. A quadruped, and a perfume produced by it.
Çiv'ie, a. Relating to civil life.
Çiv'il, a. Pertaining to a city or state, or to society; political; courteous.
Çi-vil'ian, n. One versed in civil law; one in a civil capacity.
Çi-vil'i-ty, n. Politeness; courtesy; an act of courtesy.
Çiv'il-i-zā'tion, n. Act of civilizing.
Çiv'il-īze (133), v. t. To reclaim from barbarism. [lite.
Çiv'il-īzed, a. Polished; po-
Çiv'il-īz'er, n. One who civilizes. [ner.
Çiv'il-ly, adv. In a civil man-
Çlăck, v. i. To make a sudden sharp noise, as by striking. — n. A sudden sharp noise.
Çlăck'er, n. One who, or that which, clacks.
Çlăd, p. p. of Clothe.
Çlaim, v. t. To demand as due; to require. — n. A demand as of right; a title to any thing; that to which one has a right.
Çlaim'a-ble, a. Capable of being demanded.
Çlaim'ant, n. One who claims.
Çlair-voy'ançe, n. Discernment, through mesmeric in-

fluence, of things not present to the senses.
Çlair-voy'ant, a. Discerning objects not present to the senses.
Çlam, n. [Another form of clamp.] A bivalve shell-fish
Çla'mant, a. Crying earnestly.
Çlăm'ber, v. i. To climb with difficulty, or with hands and feet.
Çlăm'mi-ness, n. Stickiness.
Çlăm'my, a. Viscous; sticky; glutinous; slimy.
Çlăm'or, n. Noise of voices; outcry; vociferation. — v. i. To be vociferous.
Çlăm'or-oŭs, a. Noisy with the tongue; loud; vociferous.
Çlăm'or-oŭs-ly, adv. With loud noise or words.
Çlămp, n. A piece of iron or timber for fastening things together. — v. t. To unite or strengthen by a clamp.
Çlăn, n. A family; race; tribe; sect.
Çlan-dĕs'tine, a. Concealed; secret; private.
Çlan-dĕs'tine-ly, adv. In a secret manner.
Çlăng, v. i. To make a sharp, shrill sound. — n. A sharp ringing sound. [sound.
Çlăng'or, n. A loud, harsh
Çlănk (79), n. A loud ringing sound, as of a chain. — v. t. To make such a sound.
Çlăn'nish, a. Closely united, like a clan; disposed to unite.
Çlăn'ship, n. A state of union, as in a clan.
Çlăp (129), v. t. To strike together. — n. A striking of hands; a sudden explosion.
Çlăp'board (klăb'urd), n. A narrow kind of board for covering houses.
Çlăp'per, n. One who, or that which, claps. [and scratch.
Çlăp'per-claw, v. t. To fight
Çlăp'-trăp, n. A trick or device to gain applause.
Çlâre'-ob-seŭre', n. Light and shade in painting.
Çlăr'et, n. A French wine of a reddish color.
Çlăr'i-fi-eā'tion, n. Act of making clear or fining.
Çlăr'i-fȳ, v. t. To make clear; to purify. — v. i. To grow clear or fine.
Çlăr'i-nĕt', } n. A wind in-
Çlăr'i-o-nĕt', } strument of music.
Çlăr'i-on, n. A wind instrument of the reed kind.
Çlash, v. t. To strike noisily

ā, ē, ī, ō, ū, ȳ, long; ă, ĕ, ĭ, ŏ, ŭ, ў, short; cāre, cär, ȧsk, ạll, whạt; ēre, veil, tĕrm; pīque, fïrm;

CLASHING 79 CLODPOLE

Clash'ing, *a.* Contrary; interfering. — *n.* Opposition; collision.

Clasp (5), *n.* A hook; a close embrace. — *v. t.* To embrace; to hold fast; to inclose.

Clasp'er (124), *n.* One who, or that which, clasps.

Clasp'-knife (-nīf), *n.* A knife, the blade of which shuts into the handle.

Class (124), *n.* A group; a rank; order, division, or set of persons or things. — *v. t.* To arrange in a class.

Clas'sic, *n.* An author of the first rank; one learned in such authors.

Clas'sie, } *a.* Pertaining
Clas'sic-al, } to authors of acknowledged excellence; chaste; refined.

Clas'si-fi-ca'tion, *n.* Act of arranging, or state of being arranged, in classes.

Clas'si-fy, *v. t.* To form into a class or classes.

Clat'ter, *n.* A rattling noise. — *v. i.* To make rattling sounds.

Clat'ter-ing, *n.* Clatter; rattle; confusion of sounds.

Clause, *n.* Part of a sentence.

Claus'tral, *a.* Relating to a cloister.

Cla'vat-ed, *a.* Club-shaped.

Clav'i-cle, *n.* The collar-bone.

Claw, *n.* A sharp, hooked nail, as of a beast or bird. — *v. t.* To tear with claws.

Clay, *n.* A kind of soft, tenacious earth. — *v. t.* To manure, or to purify, with clay.

Clay'ey, *a.* Consisting of clay; like clay.

Clean, *a.* Free from dirt; pure; innocent. — *v. t.* To free from dirt; to purify. — *adv.* Fully; entirely.

Clean'li-ness (135), *n.* Neatness; purity.

Clean'ly (klěn'lỹ) *a.* Free from dirt; neat.

Clean'ly, *adv.* Nicely.

Clean'ness (103), *n.* State of being clean. [cleansed.

Cleans'a-ble, *a.* Capable of

Cleanse, *v. t.* To make clean; to purify.

Cleans'er, *n.* One who, or that which, cleanses or purifies.

Clear, *a.* Free from mixture; pure; transparent; audible;

obvious; indisputable. — *n.* Full extent. — *v. t.* To free from impurities; to acquit; to pass over; to obtain beyond expenses. — *v. i.* To become fair; to become free; to have permission to sail. *adv.* Plainly; completely.

Clear'age, *n.* Removal of any thing.

Clear'ance, *n.* Act of clearing; a permit to sail.

Clear'er, *n.* One who clears.

Clear'ing, *n.* A justification; defense; a tract of land cleared of wood.

Clear'ly, *adv.* Brightly; plainly; evidently.

Clear'ness, *n.* State or quality of being clear.

Clear'-sight'ed (-sīt'ed), *a.* Having acuteness of sight.

Clear'-starch, *v. t.* To stiffen uniformly with starch.

Cleat, *n.* A narrow strip for fastening. [of cleaving.

Cleav'age, *n.* Act or quality

Cleave, *v. i.* [*imp.* CLEAVED; *p. p.* CLEFT, CLOVEN, CLEAVED.] To stick; to hold; to adhere. — *v. t.* To split; to divide. [strument.

Cleav'er, *n.* A butcher's instrument.

Clef (123), *n.* (*Mus.*) A character to show the key.

Cleft, *p. p.* or *p. a.* Split; divided. — *n.* A crack; a split.

Clem'a-tis, *n.* A climbing plant.

Clem'en-cy, *n.* A disposition to treat with lenity. — SYN. Mildness; tenderness; lenity; kindness.

Clem'ent, *n.* Mild; kind; merciful; lenient.

Cler'gy (12), *n.* The ministers of the gospel.

Cler'gy-man (143), *n.* A minister of the gospel.

Cler'ic-al, *a.* Pertaining to the clergy.

Clerk (*in Eng.* klärk), *n.* A parish officer; a scribe; an accountant; an assistant in a shop or store. [clerk.

Clerk'ship, *n.* Office of a

Clev'er, *a.* Dexterous; expert; adroit; agreeable.

Clev'is, } *n.* A bent iron on
Clev'y, } the end of a cart-tongue.

Clew, *n.* A ball of thread; a guide; corner of a sail. — *v. t.* To truss up to the yard, as a sail.

Click, *v. i.* [From the sound.] To make a small sharp noise; to tick. — *n.* A sharp noise.

Cli'ent, *n.* Employer of an attorney.

Cliff (123), *n.* A steep rock; a precipice.

Cliff'y, *a.* Having cliffs; broken; craggy.

Cli-măc'ter-ic, or **Clim'ac-tèr'ic**, *n.* A critical period of human life. — *a.* Relating to such a period.

Cli'mate, *n.* A region or tract of country; condition of a place as to temperature, &c.

Cli-mat'ic, *a.* Relating to climate.

Cli'ma-tŏl'o-gy, *n.* Science of climates, or a treatise on climates.

Cli'max, *n.* [Gr. *klimax*, a ladder.] Gradation of ascent in a sentence.

Climb (klīm), *v. i.* or *t.* To mount by the hands and feet.

Climb'er (klĭm'-), *n.* One who climbs.

Clime, *n.* A climate; region.

Clinch, *v. t.* To gripe; to hold fast. — *n.* Fast hold.

Clinch'er, *n.* One who, or that which, clinches.

Cling, *v. i.* [*imp.* & *p. p.* CLUNG.] To adhere; to hang to or upon. [hesive.

Cling'y, *a.* Apt to cling; adhesive.

Clin'ic, } *a.* Pertaining to
Clin'ic-al, } a sick bed.

Clin'ic, *n.* One confined to the bed by sickness.

Clink, *v. i.* or *t.* To make or to cause to make a slightly ringing sound.

Clink'er, *n.* Vitrified matter or slag which collects in furnaces.

Clip (129), *v. t.* To cut off; to cut short; to curtail.

Clip'per, *n.* One who clips; a vessel built for fast sailing.

Clip'ping, *n.* That which is clipped off.

Cloak (18), *v. t.* To cover with a cloak; to conceal; to hide. — *n.* A loose outer garment.

Clock, *n.* An instrument for measuring time; a time-piece.

Clock'-mak'er, *n.* One who makes clocks.

Clock'-work (-wûrk), *n.* Well-adjusted machinery like that of a clock.

Clod, *n.* A lump of earth. — *v. i.* To harden into a lump.

Clod'dy, *a.* Containing clods; gross.

Clod'hop-per, *n.* A rustic; a clown. [head.

Clod'pòle, *n.* A dolt; a block-

Cloff, n. See *Clough*.
Clog, v. t. To obstruct; to encumber; to hinder in motion. — n. Obstruction; a kind of heavy shoe, often of wood.
Clog′gy, a. Apt to clog; thick; heavy.
Clois′ter, n. [From Lat. *claudere*, to shut up.] A nunnery or monastery. — v. t. To immure in a cloister.
Cloke, n. See *Cloak*.
Close, v. t. To stop; to shut; to conclude. — v. i. To unite; to terminate. — n. Conclusion; end; a small inclosed field.
Close, a. Shut fast; private; solid; niggardly; sly. — *adv*. In a close manner or state.
Close′-bod′ied, a. Fitting the body exactly.
Close′-fist′ed, a. Covetous.
Close′ly (132), *adv*. In a close manner; very near.
Close′ness, n. State of being close; compactness; tightness.
Close′-stool, n. A stool made to hold a chamber-vessel.
Clos′et, n. A small private apartment. — v. t. To shut up in privacy.
Clos′ing, n. End; conclusion. — a. Concluding.
Clos′ure (klō′zhụr), n. A closing; termination; inclosure.
Clot, n. A concretion; coagulation. — v. t. or i. (129) To form clots; to concrete.
Cloth (19), n. (*pl*. **Cloths**.) Stuff or material formed by weaving.
Clothe, v. t. [*imp*. & *p. p*. CLAD, CLOTHED.] To furnish with garments; to dress; to invest.
Clothes (klōthz or klōz), n. *pl*. Dress; garments.
Cloth′ier (-yer), n. One who makes, sells, or fulls cloth.
Cloth′ing, n. Garments.
Clot′ty, a. Full of clots.
Cloud, n. Collection of vapor in the air. — v. t. To darken with clouds; to obscure. — v. i. To grow cloudy.
Cloud′-capt, a. Topped with clouds.
Cloud′i-ly, *adv*. With clouds; darkly; obscurely.
Cloud′i-ness, n. State of being cloudy.
Cloud′less, a. Free from clouds.
Cloud′y, a. Covered with clouds; obscure.

Clough (klŭf), n. An allowance made in weighing.
Clough (klŭf), n. A narrow valley.
Clout, n. A patch; a cloth for some mean use; a small nail. — v. t. To patch; to mend.
Clove, n. [Lat. *clavus*, a nail, from the resemblance.] A very pungent spice. — v., *imp*. from *Cleave*.
Clo′ven (klō′vn). *p. p*. or *p. a*. of *Cleave*. Cleft; split.
Clo′ven-foot′ed, **Clo′ven-hoofed** (-hŭŭft), } a. Having the foot in two parts.
Clo′ver, n. A genus of three-leaved plants.
Clown, n. A rustic; an ill-bred man; a buffoon.
Clown′ish, a. Coarse; rustic; clumsy; ill-bred. [glut.
Cloy, v. t. To fill to satiety; to
Club, n. A heavy stick; an association. — v. i. To join in common expense, or for a common end.
Club′-foot′ed, a. Having deformed feet.
Club′-law, n. Government by violence.
Cluck, v. i. To call, as a hen.
Clue, n. See *Clew*.
Clump, n. A cluster, as of trees.
Clum′sy, a. Awkward; uncouth; ill-made.
Clung, *imp*. & *p. p*. of *Cling*.
Clus′ter, n. A bunch; a collection. — v. i. or i. To unite in a bunch. [ters.
Clus′ter-y, a. Growing in clusters.
Clutch, n. A gripe; grasp; claw; (*pl*.) hands; rapacity. — v. t. To hold fast; to gripe; to clinch.
Clut′ter, n. A noise; confusion; disorder. — v. t. To crowd together in disorder.
Clys′ter, n. An injection.
Coach (18), n. A four-wheeled carriage for pleasure or traveling. — v. t. To convey in a coach.
Coach′-box, n. The seat on which the driver of a coach sits.
Coach′man (143), n. One who drives a coach. [force.
Co-ăc′tion, n. Compulsion;
Co-ăct′ive, a. Acting together; serving to compel.
Co-ăd′ju-tant. a. Mutually assisting; helping.
Co′ad-jū′tor, n. An assistant.
Co′ad-jū′trix, n. A female assistant.
Co-ā′gent, n. An assistant.

Co-ăg′u-la-ble, a. Capable of coagulating.
Co-ăg′u-lāte, v. t. or i. To change into a curd-like state; to curdle.
Co-ăg′u-lā′tion, n. Process of curdling.
Co-ăg′u-la-tive, a. Having power to coagulate.
Co-ăg′u-lā′tor, n. That which causes coagulation.
Co-ăg′u-lum, n. A coagulated mass, as curd; runnet.
Coal, n. Wood charred; a black combustible fossil.
Coal′er-y, n. A place where coal is dug; a colliery.
Co′a-lesçe′ (-lĕs′), v. i. To grow together; to unite.
Co′a-les′çence, n. The act of uniting; union.
Co′a-lĕs′çent, a. Growing together; uniting.
Co′a-li′tion (-lĭsh′ụn), n. Union of persons, parties, or states; combination.
Coal′-mine, } n. A mine or **Coal′-pit**, } pit where coal is dug. [like coal.
Coal′y, a. Containing coal.
Co′ap-tā′tion, n. Mutual adjustment of parts.
Coarse, a. Large; gross; rude; rough; not refined.
Coarse′ly, *adv*. Without fineness or refinement.
Coarse′ness, n. Quality of being coarse; grossness.
Coast, n. Land next the sea; seashore. — v. i. To sail along the shore.
Coast′er, n. A person or vessel that sails near the coast.
Coat, n. A man's upper garment; fur or hair of a beast; an external covering. — v. t. To cover with a coat.
Coat′-card, n. A card bearing the king, queen, or knave.
Coat′ing, n. A covering; cloth for coats.
Coax, v. t. To wheedle; to persuade by flattery.
Coax′er, n. One who coaxes.
Cob, n. Spike of maize; pony.
Co′balt, n. A brittle reddish-gray mineral.
Cŏb′ble, n. A roundish stone. — v. t. [Lat. *copulare*, to couple, join.] To mend coarsely or clumsily, as shoes.
Cŏb′bler, n. A mender of shoes.
Cŏb′nut, n. A large nut; a game.
Cŏb′web, n. A spider's web.
Coc-çif′er-oŭs, n. Bearing or producing berries.

ā, ē, ī, ō, ū, ȳ, *long*; ă, ĕ, ĭ, ŏ, ŭ, ў, *short*; cāre, cär, ȧsk, ạll, whạt; ẽre, veil, tẽrm; pïque, fïrm;

COCHINEAL 81 COHERENCY

Cŏch'i-nēal, *n.* An insect used to dye scarlet.
Cŏch'le-a-ry,) *a.* Being in
Cŏch'le-ā'ted,) the form of a screw; spiral.
Cŏck, *n.* The male of birds. — *v. t.* To set erect.
Cock-āde', *n.* A knot of ribbon worn on the hat.
Cŏck'a-tōō', *n.* A bird of the parrot kind.
Cŏck'a-trĭçe, *n.* A fabulous serpent, thought to be hatched from a cock's egg.
Cŏck'-bōat, *n.* A ship's small boat.
Cŏck'-erōw'ing, *n.* Early morning.
Cŏck'er, *v. t.* To fondle; to caress; to indulge; to pamper.
Cŏck'er-el, *n.* A young cock.
Cŏck'et, *n.* A ticket from the custom-house.
Cŏck'-fīght (-fīt), *n.* Battle between game-cocks.
Cŏck'-hōrse, *n.* A child's rocking-horse.
Cŏck'le (kŏk'l), *n.* A weed; darnel: a shell-fish. — *v. t.* To wrinkle.
Cŏck'-lŏft(10), *n.* A room over the garret; a lumber-room.
Cŏck'ney (141), *n.* A native of London; — in contempt.
Cŏck'pit, *n.* An area where cocks fight; a room in a ship under the gun-deck.
Cŏck'rōach, *n.* A troublesome insect; a kind of beetle.
Cŏck's'cŏmb (-kŏm), *n.* Crest of a cock; a plant.
Cŏck'swain (*or* kŏk'sn), *n.* An officer who has the care of a boat and boat's crew.
Cō'cōa (kō'kō), *n.* A kind of palm-tree bearing the cocoa-nut; the chocolate tree, and a decoction of the nut or the paste.
Cō'cōa-nŭt, *n.* The nut of a kind of palm-tree.   Cocoa.
Co-cōōn' (140), *n.* A ball spun by the silk-worm.
Cŏc'tion, *n.* Act of boiling.
Cŏd, *n.* A kind of sea-fish; a husk or envelope; a pod; a bag.   [of laws.
Cōde, *n.* A system or digest

Cŏd'ger, *n.* A covetous or clownish fellow.   [will.
Cŏd'i-çil, *n.* Supplement to a
Co'di-fi-cā'tion, *n.* Act of reducing laws to a system.
Cŏd'i-fỹ, *v. t.* To reduce to a code or digest, as laws.
Cŏd'dle, *v. t.* To parboil; to treat tenderly.
Cŏd'ling, *n.* A kind of apple.
Cō'ef-fĭ'cien-çy (-fĭsh'en-), *n.* Joint operation.
Cō'ef-fĭ'cient (-fĭsh'ent), *a.* Co-operating. — *n.* That which co-operates.
Cœ'li-ăc,) *a.* Pertaining to
Çē'li-ăc,) the belly or intestines.
Co-ē'qual, *a.* Equal with another. — *n.* One who is equal to another.
Cō'e-qual'i-ty (-kwŏl'-), *n.* Equality with another.
Co-ērçe' (12), *v. t.* To restrain by force. — SYN. To check; constrain; compel.
Co-ēr'çi-ble, *a.* Capable of being coerced.   [pulsion.
Co-ēr'cion, *n.* Restraint; compulsion.
Co-ēr'çive, *a.* Restraining by force; compulsory.
Cō'es-sĕn'tial, *a.* Partaking of the same essence.
Cō'e-tā'ne-oŭs, *a.* Of the same time or age.   [nal.
Cō'e-tēr'nal, *a.* Equally eternal.
Cō'e-tēr'ni-ty, *n.* Equal existence or eternity.
Co-ē'val, *a.* Of the same age. — *n.* One of the same age.
Cō'-ex-ĭst', *v. i.* To exist together.
Cō'-ex-ĭst'ençe, *n.* Existence at the same time.
Cō'-ex-ĭst'ent, *a.* Existing at the same time.
Cō'-ex-tĕnd', *v. t.* To extend through the same space.
Cō'-ex-tĕn'sion, *n.* Equal extension.   [extensive.
Cō'-ex-tĕn'sĭve, *a.* Equally
Cŏf'fee, *n.* The berry of a tropical tree, or a beverage made from it.
Cŏf'fee-house, *n.* A house of entertainment.   Coffee.
Cŏf'fee-mĭll, *n.* A small mill for grinding coffee.
Cŏf'fee-pŏt, *n.* A pot in which coffee is boiled.
Cŏf'fer, *n.* A chest, especially one for money.

Cŏf'fer-dăm, *n.* A tight box placed at the bottom of a river for erecting a pier, the water being pumped out of the box so as to leave the bottom dry.
Cŏf'fĭn, *n.* [Gr. *kophinus,* basket.] A box for a dead human body. — *v. t.* To put in a coffin.
Cŏg, *n.* The tooth of a wheel. — *v. t.* To furnish with cogs; to deceive; to wheedle.
Cō'gen-çy, *n.* Power; urgency; strength; force.
Cō'gent, *a.* Having great force. — SYN. Powerful; urgent; forcible; convincing.
Cō'gent-ly, *adv.* Forcibly.
Cŏg'i-ta-ble, *a.* Capable of being thought on.
Cŏg'i-tāte, *v. i.* To reflect; to meditate.
Cŏg'i-tā'tion, *n.* Deep thought; meditation.
Cŏg'i-ta-tĭve, *a.* Able to think; given to thought.
Cŏg'nāte, *a.* Born together; allied by blood or birth; related; one of a number of related things.
Cog-nā'tion, *n.* Kindred; relation by common descent.
Cŏgn'iac) (kŏn'yak), *n.* The
Cŏgn'ac) best kind of brandy.
Cog-nĭ'tion (-nĭsh'un), *n.* Act of knowing; knowledge; an object known.
Cŏg'ni-za-ble (*or* kŏn'i-za-bl), *a.* Liable to be tried or examined.
Cŏg'ni-zançe (*or* kŏn'i-zanss), *n.* Knowledge; notice; judicial notice.
Cŏg'ni-zant (*or* kŏn'ĭ-zant), *a.* Having cognizance or knowledge.
Cog-nō'men, *n.* A surname; the family name.
Cog-nŏm'i-nal, *a.* Pertaining to a surname.
Cog-nŏs'çi-ble, *a.* Capable of being known.
Cŏg'-wheel, *n.* A wheel with cogs, or teeth.
Co-hăb'it, *v. i.* To live as man and wife.
Cō'hab-it-ā'tion, *n.* A living together as man and wife.
Cō-hêir' (-âr'), *n.* A joint heir.
Co-hêir'ess (-âr'-), *n.* A joint heiress.
Co-hēre', *v. i.* To stick together; to be united; to agree.
Co-hēr'ence,) *n.* A sticking
Co-hēr'en-çy,) together; consistency.

són, ôr, dọ, wọlf, tōō, tŏŏk; ũrn, rụe, pụll; ç, ġ, *soft;* c, ḡ, *hard;* aᶻ; eẋist; ṇ *as* ng; *this.*
4*

Co-hēr'ent, a. Sticking together; consistent.
Co-hē'sion, n. A sticking together; state of union.
Co-hē'sive, n. Sticking together; adhesive.
Co'hŏrt, n. A body of soldiers; anciently about 500 or 600 soldiers.
Coif, n. A head-dress — v. i. To cover with a coif.
Coif'fūre, n. A head-dress.
Coil, v. i. To wind into a ring. — n. Circular form as of a rope or serpent.
Coin, n. Metal stamped for money. — v. t. To stamp metal; to make or forge.
Coin'age, n. Act of coining; money coined; invention.
Cȳ'in-çīde', v. i. [Lat. con, with, in, in, and cadere, to fall.] To agree; to concur; to be consistent.
Co-ĭn'çi-dençe, n. Agreement. [or agreeing together.
Co-ĭn'çi-dent, a. Occurring
Cȳ'in-di-çā'tion, n. A concurrent sign.
Coin'er, n. One who coins money; an inventor.
Co-ĭ'tion (-ĭsh'un), n. Sexual intercourse; copulation.
Cōke, n. Mineral coal charred.
Cŏl'an-der (kŭl'-), n. A kind of strainer.
Cōld, a. Not warm; frigid; chill; reserved. — n. Sensation produced by want of heat; cause of such sensation; a form of disease; catarrh.
Cōld'ly, adv. In a cold manner; without warmth.
Cōld'ness, n. Quality of being cold; want of heat; reserve.
Cōle'wort (-wŭrt), n. A cabbage cut young.
Cŏl'ic, n. A pain in the bowels. [colic.
Cŏl'ick-y, a. Pertaining to
Col-lăpse', v. t. To fall together. — n. A sudden falling together.
Col-lăpsed'(-lăpst'), a. Fallen together; closed.
Col-lăp'sion, n. State of shrinking up.
Cŏl'lar, n. [Lat. collum, neck.] Something worn around the neck: a ring. — v. t. To put a collar on; to seize by the collar.
Col-lāte', v. t. To compare; to examine; to gather and place in order, as printed sheets for binding.

Col-lăt'er-al, a. Being on the side; indirect.
Col-lăt'er-al-ly, adv. In a collateral manner or relation.
Col-lā'tion, n. A repast; gift; act of comparing.
Col-lā'tor, n. One who collates. [in office.
Cŏl'lēague, n. An associate
Col-lĕct', v. t. or i. To gather; to bring or get together.
Cŏl'lect, n. A short prayer.
Col-lĕct'ed, a. Cool; composed; calm; tranquil.
Col-lĕct'ed-ness, n. A collected or self-possessed state of mind.
Col-lĕct'i-ble, a. Capable of being collected.
Col-lĕc'tion, n. Act of collecting; that which is collected. — SYN. Assemblage; contribution; gathering.
Col-lĕct'ĭve, a. Formed by gathering; inferring; comprehending many.
Col-lĕct'ĭve-ly, adv. In a body. [receiver of taxes, &c.
Col-lĕct'or, n. A gatherer; a
Col-lĕct'or-ship, n. Office of a collector of customs or taxes.
Cŏl'lēge (44), n. An assembly or society; a seminary of learning; a learned body.
Col-lē'gi-al, a. Pertaining
Col-lē'gi-ate, to a college.
Col-lē'gi-an, n. A member of a college.
Cŏl'let, n. The part of a ring in which a stone is set. [er.
Col-līde', v. t. To dash together.
Cŏl'lier (kŏl'yer), n. A digger of, or dealer in, coals; a coal-ship.
Cŏl'lier-y, n. A coal mine.
Cŏl'li-mā'tion, n. Act of aiming at a mark.
Col-liq'ue-făc'tion (-we-), n. melting together.
Col-lĭş'ion (-lĭzh'un), n. A striking together; a clash.
Cŏl'lo-cāte, v. t. To set or place.
Cŏl'lo-cā'tion, n. Act of placing; arrangement.
Cŏl'lop, n. A cut or slice, as of meat.
Col-lō'qui-al, a. Pertaining to, or used in, conversation.
Col-lō'qui-al-ĭşm, n. An expression used only in conversation. [a dialogue.
Cŏl'lo-quist, n. A speaker in
Cŏl'lo-quy (141), n. [Lat. con, with, and loqui, to speak.] A mutual conversation between two; a dialogue.

Col-lūde', v. i. To conspire in a fraud.
Col-lū'şion, n. A secret agreement to defraud.
Col-lū'sĭve, n. Deceitful; fraudulently concerted.
Col-lū'sĭve-ly, adv. By means of collusion.
Col-lū'so-ry, a. Characterized by collusion.
Co-logne' (-lōn'), n. A perfumed alcoholic liquid, used in the toilet.
Cō'lon, n. The largest of the large intestines; a mark of punctuation (formed thus :).
Colonel (kŭr'nel), n. The commander of a regiment.
Colonel-cy (kŭr'nel-), n.
Colonel-ship, Office or rank of a colonel.
Co-lō'ni-al, a. Belonging to a colony or colonies.
Cŏl'o-nĭst, n. A member or inhabitant of a colony.
Cŏl'o-ni-zā'tion, n. The settling of a colony.
Cŏl'o-nīze, v. t. To plant or settle with inhabitants.
Cŏl'on-nāde', n. A row or range of columns.
Cŏl'o-ny, n. A body of people who remove and settle in a distant country, continuing subject to the parent state; the country colonized.
Cŏl'o-phon, n. An inscription on the last page of a book.
Cŏl'or (kŭl'ur, 155), n. A property of light; paint; pretense; (pl.) a banner; flag; ensign. — v. t. To dye; to stain; to make plausible. — v. i. To blush.
Cŏl'or-a-ble, a. Designed to cover or conceal; plausible; specious. [or.
Cŏl'or-ĭf'ic, a. Producing color.
Cŏl'or-ĭst, n. A painter who excels in giving color to his designs.
Cŏl'or-less, a. Without color.
Co-lŏs'sal, a. Like a colossus; huge in size; gigantic
Co-lŏs'sus, n. (Lat. pl. Co-lŏs'sī: Eng. pl. Co-lŏs'sus-es). A statue of gigantic size.
Cōlt (18), n. A young horse.
Cōlt'er (18), n. The sharp
Cōul'ter fore-iron of a plow.
Cōlt'ish, a. Like a colt.
Cōlt's'-fōot, n. A plant.
Cŏl'u-brĭne, a. Relating to serpents; cunning.
Cŏl'um-ba-ry, n. A pigeon-house.

COLUMBINE 83 COMMITTAL

Col'um-bine, *n.* A genus of plants.

Col'umn (kŏl'um), *n.* A cylindrical pillar; a perpendicular set of lines in a book; a body of troops.

Co-lum'nar, *a.* Having the form of a column.

Co-lure', *n.* One of two great circles intersecting the solstitial or equinoctial points.

Co'ma, *n.* Hairiness of a comet; lethargy; morbid sleepiness. [thargic.

Co'ma-tōse', *a.* Drowsy; lethargic.

Comb (kōm, 18), *n.* An instrument for dressing the hair, or wool, &c.; crest of a cock; substance in which bees lodge honey. — *v. t.* To dress with a comb.

Com'bat, *n.* [Lat. *con*, with, and *batuere*, to strike.] A battle; fight; contest. — *v. t.* To fight with; to oppose. — *v. i.* To struggle or contend.

Com'bat-ant, *n.* A fighter; a champion. [combat.

Com'bat-ive, *a.* Disposed to **Com'bat-ive-ness**, *n.* (*Phrenology*.) Disposition to contend.

Comb'er (kōm'-), *n.* One who combs; a long, curling wave.

Com-bīn'a-ble, *a.* Capable of being combined.

Com'bi-nā'tion, *n.* Union or association. — SYN. Coalition; conjunction; conspiracy.

Com-bīne', *v. t.* or *i.* To unite; to join; to agree.

Com-bŭs'ti-bīl'i-ty, }
Com-bŭs'ti-ble-ness, } *n.*
Quality of being combustible, or of burning.

Com-bŭs'ti-ble, *a.* Capable of burning; apt to burn. — *n.* A substance that will burn.

Com-bŭs'tion (-bŭst'yun), *n.* A burning; conflagration.

Come (kŭm), *v. i.* [*imp.* CAME; *p. p.* COME.] To move toward; to approach; to draw near. [comedies.

Co-mē'di-an, *n.* An actor of

Com'e-dy, *n.* A humorous dramatic piece. [ty.

Come'li-ness, *n.* Grace; beauty.

Come'ly, *a.* Handsome; graceful; becoming.

Com'et, *n.* [Gr. *komētēs*, lit., long-haired.] A member of the solar system with a train of luminous matter and a very eccentric orbit.

Com'et-a-ry, } *a.* Relating to
Co-met'ic, } comets.

Com'fit, *n.* A dry sweetmeat.

Com'fort (kŭm'-), *v. t.* To cheer under affliction or depression. — *n.* A relief from pain; consolation.

Com'fort-a-ble, *a.* Affording or enjoying ease.

Com'fort-a-bly, *adv.* In a manner to give comfort.

Com'fort-er, *n.* One who comforts; the Holy Spirit.

Com'fort-less, *a.* Being without comfort.

Com'frey, *n.* A medicinal plant.

Com'ic, *a.* Relating to comedy; droll; amusing.

Com'ic-al, *a.* Diverting; droll.

Com'ing (133), *a.* Future. — *n.* Approach; arrival.

Com'i-ty, *n.* Courtesy of intercourse; civility.

Com'ma (141), *n.* A point [,] used in writing and printing.

Com-mănd' (5), *v. t.* To order; to direct; to govern. — *v. t.* To have supreme authority. — *n.* Order; injunction; body of troops under a particular officer.

Com'man-dănt', *n.* A commanding officer.

Com-mănd'er, *n.* One who directs; a leader; chief officer of an army, or of any division of it; in the navy, an officer next above a lieutenant.

Com-mănd'er-y, } *n.* A man-
Com-mănd'ry, } or belonging to an order of knights.

Com-mănd'ing, *a.* Fitted to impress or control.

Com-mănd'ment, *n.* Command; order; injunction; a precept of the moral law.

Com-měm'o-ra-ble, *a.* Worthy to be remembered.

Com-měm'o-rāte, *v. t.* To celebrate by a solemn act.

Com-měm'o-rā'tion, *n.* A solemn public celebration.

Com-měm'o-ra-tive, *a.* Tending or designed to preserve in remembrance.

Com-mĕnce', *v. t.* To begin; to enter upon. — *v. i.* To take rise.

Com-mĕnce'ment, *n.* Beginning; day of taking degrees in an American college.

Com-mĕnd', *v. t.* To praise; to recommend.

Com-mĕnd'a-ble, *a.* Worthy of praise; laudable.

Com'men-dā'tion, *n.* Praise; approbation.

Com-mĕnd'a-to-ry (107), *a.* Serving to command.

Com-měn'su-ra-bĭl'i-ty, }
Com-měn'su-ra-ble-ness, } *n.* Capacity of having a common measure.

Com-měn'su-ra-ble, *a.* Having a common measure.

Com-měn'su-rate, *a.* Of equal measure; proportional.

Com-měn'su-rā'tion, *n.* Reduction to a common measure.

Com'ment, *v. i.* To explain by means of remarks. — *n.* Note or remarks for explanation.

Com'men-ta-ry, *n.* Comment; exposition; annotation; a book of comments.

Com'men-tā'tor, *n.* One who comments.

Com'merçe, *n.* [Lat. *con*, with, and *merx*, *mercis*, merchandise.] Interchange of commodities; personal intercourse. — SYN. Trade; traffic; dealing.

Com-mĕr'cial, *a.* Relating to commerce or trade.

Com'mi-nā'tion, *n.* A threat; denunciation.

Com-mĭn'a-to-ry, *n.* Threatening; denunciatory.

Com-mĭn'gle (-ming'gl), *v. t.* To mix together; to blend.

Com'mi-nūte, *v. t.* To break into small parts; to pulverize.

Com'mi-nū'tion, *n.* Act of breaking into small parts.

Com-mĭs'er-āte, *v. t.* To pity.

Com-mĭs'er-ā'tion, *n.* Compassion; sympathy.

Com'mis-sa-ry, *n.* A commissioner; an army officer having charge of a special department.

Com-mĭs'sion (-mĭsh'un), *n.* Performance; perpetration; a trust; compensation to an agent or factor. — *v. t.* To give a commission to; to authorize; to empower.

Com-mĭs'sion-er(-mĭsh'un-), *n.* One empowered to act.

Com-mĭs'sūre (-mĭsh'yur), *n.* A joint; a seam or closure.

Com-mĭt', *v. t.* To intrust; to imprison; to pledge; to do; to perpetrate.

Com-mĭt'ment, *n.* Act of committing.

Com-mĭt'tal, *n.* Act of committing; a pledge, actual or implied.

---
sŏn, ôr, dǫ, wǫlf, tōō, tŏŏk; ûrn, rṳe, pṳll; ç, ġ, *soft*; c, g, *hard*; a̱ẕ; exist; ṇ *as* ng; this

COMMITTEE   84   **COMPILE**

Com-mĭt'tee, *n.* Persons especially appointed to manage any business.

Com-mĭx', *v. t.* or *i.* [Lat. *con,* with, and *miscere,* to mix.] To unite in one mass; to mix.

Com-mĭx'tion (-mĭkst'yun), *n.* A blending; mixture.

Com-mĭxt'ūre, *n.* Act of mixing; a mingled mass.

Com-mōde', *n.* An article of furniture.

Com-mō'di-oŭs, *a.* Affording ease and convenience.

Com-mŏd'i-ty, *n.* Interest; advantage; any article of merchandise.

Com-mō'di-oŭs-ly, *adv.* In a commodious manner.

Com-mō'di-oŭs-ness, *n.* Adaptation to its purpose; convenience; fitness.

Cŏm'mo-dōre, *n.* The commander of a squadron.

Cŏm'mon, *a.* Belonging to many; general; public; usual; vulgar; of no rank. — *n.* An open public ground. — *v. i.* To use together; to diet together.

Cŏm'mon-age, *n.* A right of pasturing on a common.

Cŏm'mon-al-ty, *n.* The common people. [ble.

Cŏm'mon-er, *n.* One not noble.

Cŏm'mon-ly, *adv.* Usually; generally; ordinarily.

Cŏm'mon-ness (103), *n.* State of being common; frequent occurrence.

Cŏm'mon-plăçe, *n.* General head or title; a memorandum; a trite remark. — *a.* Common; trite.

Cŏm'mons, *n. pl.* Common people; lower house of parliament; food at a common table.

Cŏm'mon-wēal', *n.* Public government; whole body of people.

Cŏm'mon-wēalth', *n.* A state; a body politic.

Com-mō'tion, *n.* Disturbance; tumult; agitation.

Com-mūn'al, *a.* Pertaining to a commune.

Cŏm'mūne, *n.* A small territorial district in France; — *v. i.* To converse; to confer.

Com-mū'ni-ca-ble, *a.* Capable of being communicated.

Com-mū'ni-cant, *n.* A partaker of the Lord's supper.

Com-mū'ni-cāte, *v. t.* [From Lat. *communis,* common.] To impart. — *v. i.* To share;

to have intercourse, or the means of passing.

Com-mū'ni-eā'tion, *n.* Act of communicating; correspondence; connecting passage.

Com-mū'ni-ea-tĭve, *a.* Ready to communicate; unreserved.

Com-mū'ni-ca-tĭve-ness, *n.* Freedom from reserve.

Com-mūn'ion (-yun), *n.* Intercourse; fellowship; a partaking of the Lord's supper.

Com-mū'ni-ty, *n.* Common possession; the public; society at large.

Com-mū'ta-bĭl'i-ty, *n.* Quality of being commutable.

Com-mūt'a-ble, *a.* Capable of being commuted, or changed one for another.

Cŏm'mu-tā'tion, *n.* Exchange; substitution.

Com-mū'ta-tĭve, *a.* Relating to exchange.

Com-mūte', *v. t.* To exchange; to substitute.

Com-pāct', *v. t.* To thrust or press together; to league with. — *a.* Firm; dense; condensed.

Cŏm'pact, *n.* An agreement between parties; covenant.

Com-păn'ion, *n.* An associate; comrade; mate; partner.

Com-păn'ion-a-ble, *a.* Sociable; agreeable.

Com-păn'ion-ship, *n.* Fellowship; association.

Cŏm'pa-ny (kŭm'-, 41), *n.* Fellowship; persons assembled or acting together; band; crew; firm.

Cŏm'pa-ra-ble, *a.* Worthy to be compared.

Com-păr'a-tĭve, *a.* Estimated by comparison; not positive.

Com-păr'a-tĭve-ly, *adv.* By way of comparison.

Com-pāre', *v. t.* [Lat. *con,* with, together, and *par,* like, equal.] To examine the mutual relations of; to liken; to inflict, as an adjective, according to the degrees of comparison. — *v. i.* To be like. — *n.* Comparison.

Com-păr'i-son, *n.* Act of comparing; comparative estimate; simile.

Com-pärt', *v. t.* To divide.

Cŏm'pär-tĭ'tion (-tĭsh'un), *n.* Act of dividing; part divided.

Com-pärt'ment, *n.* One of the separate parts into which a thing is divided.

Cŏm'pass, *v. t.* To surround; to obtain; to plot. — *n.* A

circumference; boundary; magnetic instrument; (*pl.*) an instrument to describe circles.

Com-păs'sion, *n.* [Lat. *con,* with, and *pati, passus,* to suffer.] A suffering with another; pity; mercy; sympathy.

Com-păs'sion-ate (42), *a.* Inclined to pity; merciful.

Com-păs'sion-āte, *v. t.* To pity; to sympathize with; to commiserate.

Com-păt'i-bĭl'i-ty, *n.* Consistency; agreement.

Com-păt'i-ble, *a.* Consistent; agreeable; fit.

Com-păt'i-bly, *adv.* Consistently.

Com-pā'tri-ot, *n.* A fellow-patriot, or one of the same country.

Com-peer', *n.* An equal; colleague; companion.

Com-pĕl' (129), *v. t.* To drive by force. — SYN. To necessitate; constrain; oblige.

Com-pĕl'la-ble, *a.* Capable of being compelled.

Cŏm'pel-lā'tion, *n.* Style of address or salutation.

Cŏm'pend, } *n.* Abridgment; summary; epitome.
Com-pĕnd'i-um,

Com-pĕnd'i-oŭs, *a.* Short; concise; brief; summary.

Cŏm'pen-sāte, or **Com-pĕn'sāte,** *v. t.* To make amends.

Cŏm'pen-sā'tion, *n.* Recompense; amends; remuneration.

Com-pĕn'sa-tĭve, } *a.* Making amends; affording compensation.
Com-pĕn'sa-to-ry,

Com-pēte', *v. i.* [Lat. *con,* with, together, and *petere,* to seek.] To strive for a like end; to rival.

Cŏm'pe-tence, } *n.* Sufficiency; legal capacity or right; adequacy.
Cŏm'pe-ten-çy,

Cŏm'pe-tent, *a.* Adequate to some end or duty; having legal capacity. — SYN. Sufficient; fitted; qualified.

Cŏm'pe-tĭ'tion (-tĭsh'un), *n.* Rivalry; strife for superiority; emulation.

Com-pĕt'i-tor, *n.* One who competes; a rival.

Com-pĕt'i-tĭve, *a.* Pertaining to competition; emulous.

Cŏm'pi-lā'tion, *n.* A selection from various authors.

Com-pīle', *v. t.* To compose

ā, ē, ī, ō, ū, ȳ, *long*; ă, ĕ, ĭ, ŏ, ŭ, ў, *short*; cāre, cär, ăsk, ạll, whạt; ẽre, veil, tẽrm; pïque, fïrm;

COMPILEMENT 85 CONCATENATION

out of materials got from other works.
Com-pile'ment (132), n. Act of compiling; compilation.
Com-pil'er, n. One who compiles.
Com-plā'çence,) n. Pleas-
Com-plā'çen-çy,) ure; satisfaction of mind; civility.
Com-plā'çent, a. Gratified; displaying satisfaction.
Com-plāin', v. i. To murmur; to lament; to make a charge.
Com-plāin'ant, n. One who complains; a plaintiff.
Com-plāin'er, n. One who complains.
Com-plāint', n. A murmuring; lamentation; accusation; disease.
Com'plai-sançe', n. Civility; courtesy; urbanity; politeness. [courteous.
Com'plai-sānt', a. Polite;
Com'ple-ment, n. That which completes something else; the full number.
Com'ple-ment'al, a. Filling up; completing.
Com-plēte', a. Finished; entire; perfect. — v. t. To fulfill; to accomplish.
Com-plēte'ly, adv. Perfectly.
Com-plēte'ness (132), n. State of being complete.
Com-plē'tion, n. Act of finishing; accomplishment; perfect state.
Com'plex, a. Of many parts; intricate; complicated. — n. Assemblage; collection.
Com-plex'ion (-plĕk'shun), n. The color of the face or skin; connection of parts; general appearance.
Com-plex'ion-al, a. Pertaining to complexion.
Com-plex'i-ty, n. A complex state; intricacy.
Com'plex-ly, adv. In a complex manner.
Com-plī'a-ble, a. Capable of complying or yielding.
Com-plī'ançe (135), n. A yielding; assent.
Com-plī'ant, a. Yielding; submitting; obliging.
Com'pli-ea-çy, n. State of being complex.
Com'pli-eāte (42), v. t. [Lat. con, with, together, and plicare, to fold, twist.] To make complex or intricate. — SYN. To entangle; infold; involve; perplex.
Com'pli-eate, a. Involved; intricate; complex.
Com'pli-eā'tion, n. A mixture of many things; intricacy.
Com'pli-ment, n. Act or expression of civility; praise.
— v. t. To flatter or gratify by bestowing praise upon.
Com'pli-ment'al,) a. Ex-
Com'pli-ment'a-ry,) pressive of praise or civility.
Com'plot, n. A conspiracy; plot. [gether; to conspire.
Com-plŏt', v. t. To plot to-
Com-plȳ', v. i. To yield; to assent.
Com-pō'nent, a. Helping to form. — n. An elementary or constituent part.
Com-pōrt', v. i. To agree; to suit. — v. i. To behave; to conduct.
Com-pōrt'a-ble, a. Consistent.
Com-pōṣe', v. t. To put together; to write as an author; to allay; to quiet.
Com-pōṣed', a. Calm; tranquil; quiet.
Com-pōṣ'ed-ly, adv. In a composed manner.
Com-pōṣ'er, n. One who composes; author of music.
Com-pŏṣ'ite, a. Made up of parts; compounded.
Com'po-ṣi'tion (-zĭsh'un), n. Mixture; combination; arrangement or setting of type; a written work.
Com-pŏṣ'i-tor, n. One who sets type. [manure.
Com'pŏst, n. A mixture for
Com-pōṣ'ūre, n. A composed state of mind; calmness; form.
Com'po-tā'tion, n. Act of drinking together.
Com'pound, a. Formed of two or more ingredients. — n. A mixture of ingredients.
Com-pound', v. t. [Lat. con, with, together, and ponere, to set, place.] To mix in one mass; to combine or unite; to adjust. — v. i. To come to terms of agreement.
Com-pound'er, n. One who compounds.
Com'pre-hĕnd', v. t. To contain; to comprise; to include; to understand.
Com'pre-hĕn'si-ble, a. Capable of being understood; intelligible.
Com'pre-hĕn'sion, n. Act of comprehending; a comprising; capacity.
Com'pre-hĕn'sive, a. Including much in small space. — SYN. Large; full; capacious.
Com'pre-hĕn'sive-ly, adv.

With great extent of inclusion.
Com'pre-hĕn'sive-ness, n. Quality of being comprehensive.
Com-press', v. t. To press together; to squeeze close.
Com'press, n. A soft pad used by surgeons.
Com-press'i-bil'i-ty, n. Quality of being compressible.
Com-press'i-ble, a. Capable of being compressed.
Com-pres'sion, n. Act of pressing together.
Com-press'ive, a. Having power to compress.
Com-press'ūre (-prĕsh'ṵr), n. Pressure. [prising.
Com-prī'ṣal, n. Act of com-
Com-prīṣe', v. t. To contain; to include; to embrace.
Com'pro-mīṣe, n. Amicable agreement in which mutual concessions are made. — v. t. To settle by mutual agreement; to put to hazard. — v. i. To make an agreement.
Com'pro-mĭt', v. t. To promise; to pledge; to compromise.
Comp-trŏl'ler (kon-trōl'-), n. A public officer who examines and certifies accounts.
Com-pŭl'ṣa-to-ry, a. Compelling; constraining.
Com-pŭl'sion, n. Act of compelling; force applied.
Com-pŭl'sive,) a. Compel-
Com-pŭl'so-ry,) ling; constraining; forcing.
Com-pŭl'sive-ly, adv. By compulsion; by force.
Com-pŭne'tion, n. Remorse.
Com-pŭne'tious, a. Attended with compunction or pain for offenses.
Com-pūt'a-ble, a. Capable of being computed.
Com'pu-tā'tion, n. Act of reckoning; estimate.
Com-pūte', v. t. To calculate; to reckon. [putes.
Com-pūt'er, n. One who com-
Com'pu-tist, or Com-pūt'ist, n. A reckoner.
Com'rade, n. An associate; a mate; a companion.
Cŏn, v. t. To revolve in thought; to study over.
Con-căm'er-āte, v. t. To arch over; to vault.
Con-căm'er-ā'tion, n. An arch or vault.
Con-eăt'e-nāte, v. t. To link together; to unite in a series.
Con-eăt'e-nā'tion, n. A series of links, or of things dependent on each other.

Con'cave, a. Hollow and curved. — n. A hollow; an arch or vault.
Con-cav'i-ty, n. Hollowness of a rounded body.
Con-ca'vo-con'cave, a. Concave on both sides.
Con-ca'vo-con'vex. a. Concave on one side and convex on the other.
Con-ca'vous, a. Concave; hollow.
Con-ceal' (130), v. t. To keep in secret. — SYN. To hide; disguise; secrete.
Con-ceal'a-ble, a. Capable of being hid or kept secret.
Con-ceal'ment, n. Act of hiding; a hiding place.
Con-cede', v. t. To grant; to admit as true or proper.
Con-ceit', n. Fancy; vanity; pride of opinion. — v. t. To fancy; to imagine.
Con-ceit'ed, a. Vain; proud.
Con-ceiv'a-ble, a. Capable of being conceived.
Con-ceiv'a-bly, adv. In a conceivable manner.
Con-ceive', v. t. To form in the mind; to imagine. — v. i. To become with child.
Con-cen'ter,) v. i. or t. To
Con-cen'tre,) come or bring to a point.
Con'cen-trate, or **Con-cen'trate** (114), v. t. To bring to a common center, or to a closer union.
Con-cen-tra'tion, n. Act of concentrating.
Con-cen'tra-tive-ness, n. Faculty of concentrating the intellectual force.
Con-cen'tric,) a. Having
Con-cen'tric-al,) a common center.
Con'cen-tric'i-ty, n. State of being concentric.
Con-cep'tion, n. Act of conceiving; idea; notion; thought. [conceiving.
Con-cep'tive, a. Capable of
Con-cern' (12), v. t. To affect; to belong to; to interest. — n. An affair; anxiety; solicitude; business; care.
Con-cern'ing, p. pr. Pertaining to. [concern.
Con-cern'ment, n. Business;
Con-cert', v. t. [Lat. con, with, together, and certare, to strive.] To contrive together; to plan.
Con'cert, n. Agreement; plan; a musical entertainment.
Con-ces'sion (-sĕsh'un), n.

Act of conceding; thing conceded; grant; boon.
Con-ces'sive, a. Implying concession.
Conch (kŏnk, 79), n. A marine shell. [curve.
Conch'oid, n. A geometrical
Conch-oid'al, a. Resembling a marine shell.
Con-chŏl'o-gist, n. One versed in conchology.
Con-chŏl'o-gy, n. [Gr. kongchē, a shell, and logos, discourse.] The science of shells.
Con-cĭl'i-āte, v. t. To gain by favor; to win over. — SYN. To propitiate; to engage.
Con-cĭl'i-ā'tion, n. Act of conciliating.
Con-cĭl'i-ā'tor, n. One who conciliates.
Con-cĭl'i-a-to-ry, a. Tending to conciliate; pacific.
Con-cĭn'ni-ty, n. Fitness; suitableness; neatness.
Con-cīse', a. Brief; short; terse; comprehensive.
Con-cīse'ly, adv. In few words.
Con-cīse'ness, n. Brevity in speaking or writing.
Con-cĭs'ion (-sĭzh'un), n. A cutting off; circumcision.
Con'clave, n. An assembly of cardinals; a private meeting.
Con-clūde', v. t. To bring to an end; to finish. — v. i. To come to an end; to infer.
Con-clūd'er, n. One who concludes.
Con-clū'sion, n. End: close; inference; determination.
Con-clū'sive, a. Decisive; final; closing debate.
Con-clū'sive-ly, adv. Decisively.
Con-clū'sive-ness, n. Quality of being conclusive.
Con-cŏct', v. t. To digest; to ripen; to mature; to contrive.
Con-cŏc'tion, n. Act of concocting; digestion.
Con-cŏct'ive, a. Tending to digest or mature.
Con-cŏm'i-tance,) n. A
Con-cŏm'i-tan-cy,) being together; accompaniment.
Con-cŏm'i-tant, a. Accompanying. — n. A companion; accompaniment.
Con'cord (79), n. Union; agreement; consonance; harmony.
Con-cŏrd'ance, n. A minute verbal index to a book; agreement; consonance.

Con-cŏrd'ant, a. Agreeing; suitable; harmonious.
Con'cŏurse, n. An assembly; a crowd; a multitude.
Con-crĕs'çence, n. A growing by spontaneous union, or by coalescence.
Con-crĕs'çive, a. Growing together; uniting.
Con-crēte', v. t. or i. To unite in a mass.
Con'crēte, a. Formed by concretion; not abstract. — n. A compound; a mixed mass.
Con-crē'tion, n. Act of concreting; a mass or lump.
Con-crē'tive, a. Causing to concrete.
Con-cū'bi-nage, n. Cohabitation of a man and woman not married.
Con'cu-bīne, n. A kept mistress.
Con-cū'pis-çence, n. Lust.
Con-cū'pis-çent, a. Lustful.
Con-cŭr' (129), v. i. [Lat. con, with, together, and currere, to run.] To tend to one point; to unite in action or opinion. — SYN. To agree; coincide; combine; join.
Con-cŭr'rence, n. Union; conjunction; agreement.
Con-cŭr'rent, a. Acting together or in conjunction.
Con-cŭs'sion (-kŭsh'un), n. A shaking; a sudden jar.
Con-cŭs'sive, a. Able to shake.
Con-dĕmn' (-dĕm'), v. t. To pronounce to be wrong; to doom; to sentence.
Con-dem-nā'tion, n. Act of condemning: sentence.
Con-dĕm'na-ble, a. Worthy of condemnation; blameworthy.
Con-dĕm'na-to-ry, a. Expressing or implying condemnation.
Con-dĕm'ner, n. One who condemns.
Con-dĕn'sa-ble, a. Capable of being condensed.
Con-dĕn'sāte, v. t. or i. To condense.
Con-den-sā'tion, n. Act of condensing.
Con-dĕnse', v. t. or i. To make or become more dense.
Con-dĕns'er, n. He who, or that which, condenses.
Con'de-sçĕnd', v. i. To waive a privilege of rank; to behave with courtesy to inferiors.
Con'de-sçĕnd'ing, a. Yielding to inferiors; obliging.

ā, ē, ī, ō, ū, y, long; ă, ĕ, ĭ, ŏ, ŭ, y̆, short; câre, cär, ȧsk, ạll, whạt; ēre, vẽil, tẽrm; pīque, fĭrm;

CONDESCENSION 87 CONFRONT

€ŏn′de-sçĕn′sion, n. Act of condescending; affability.

€on-dīgn′ (-dīn′), a. Deserved; suitable; merited.

€on-dīgn′ly (-dīu′-), adv. According to merit.

€ŏn′di-ment, n. A reasoning.

€ŏn′dis-çī′ple, n. A fellow-disciple; a school-mate.

€on-dī′tion (-dĭsh′un), n. State; quality; term or article of agreement. — v. To make terms; to stipulate.

€on-dī′tion-al } (-dĭsh′-
€on-dī′tion-a-ry } un-), a. Implying terms.

€on-dī′tion-al-ly (-dĭsh′un-), adv. With certain limitations.

€on-dī′tioned (-dĭsh′und), a. Having terms, qualities or properties.

€on-dōle′, v. i. [Lat. con, with, and dolere, to grieve.] To grieve; to express sorrow.

€on-dō′lĕnçe, n. Expression of grief or sympathy.

€on-dōl′er, n. One who condoles.

€ŏn′dor (39, 140), n. A large bird of the vulture kind.

€on-dūçe′, v. i. To tend; to contribute.

€on-dū′çi-ble, } a. Having a
€on-dū′çive, } tendency to conduce.

€ŏn′duct, n. Behavior; deportment; guidance; escort.

€on-dŭct′, v. t. To lead; to guide; to control; to manage. —v. i. To behave.

€on-dŭct′or, n. A leader; director; manager.

€on-dŭc′tress, n. A woman who conducts.

€ŏn′duit (kŏn′dit or kŭn′dit), n. A water-pipe; a canal; a duct.

€on-dū′pli-eate, a. Doubled together.

€ōne, n. A solid body tapering to a point from a circular base; fruit of various evergreen trees.

€on-făb′u-lāte, v. t. To talk together.

€on-făb′u-lā′tion, n. Familiar talk.

€ŏn′fect, } n. A sweet-
€on-fĕc′tion, } meat.

€on-fĕc′tion-er, n. One who makes or sells confectionery.

€on-fĕc′tion-er-y, n. Sweetmeats in general; a place where sweetmeats are sold.

€on-fĕd′er-a-çy, n. A league; coalition; conspiracy.

€on-fĕd′er-ate (142), a. United in a league. — n. Member of a confederacy; ally.

€on-fĕd′er-āte, v. t. or i. [Lat. con, with, together, and fœdus, fœderis, a league.] To unite in alliance.

€on-fĕd′er-ā′tion, n. Alliance; league.

€on-fĕd′er-a-tĭve, a. Constituting a federal compact.

€on-fēr′, v. t. To bestow; to grant; to award. — v. i. To discourse seriously; to consult.

€ŏn′fer-ençe, n. Serious conversation; a meeting for consultation.

€on-fĕss′, v. To own; to acknowledge; to avow; to grant; to hear confession.

€on-fĕss′ed-ly, adv. Avowedly.

€on-fĕs′sion (-fĕsh′un), n. Acknowledgment; act of confessing, especially to a priest; thing confessed.

€on-fĕs′sion-al, n. A place where confession is made.

€on-fĕss′or, n. One who confesses or hears confessions.

€ŏn′fi-dănt, n. m. } A bo-
€ŏn′fi-dănte′, n. fem. } som friend.

€on-fīde′, v. i. To put faith; to trust; to rely. — v. t. To intrust.

€ŏn′fi-dençe, n. Firm belief; trust; boldness; self-reliance.

€ŏn′fi-dent, a. Having great confidence or boldness.

€ŏn′fi-dĕn′tial, a. Trusty; private.

€ŏn′fi-dĕn′tial-ly, adv. In confidence.

€ŏn′fi-dent-ly, adv. With confidence.

€on-fĭg′u-rā′tion, n. External form or figure.

€on-fĭg′ūre, v. t. To dispose in a certain form or figure.

€on-fīn′a-ble, a. Capable of being confined or limited.

€on-fīne, n. A limit; border.

€on-fīne′, v. t. To restrain; to limit; to shut up.

€ŏn′fīne, or €on-fīne′, v. i. To border.

€on-fīne′ment, n. Restraint; imprisonment; child-bed.

€on-fĭrm′ (16), v. t. To make certain; to admit to the full privileges of the church. — SYN. To strengthen; verify; assure.

€on-fīrm′a-ble, a. Capable of being confirmed.

€ŏn′fir-mā′tion, n. Act of confirming or establishing; proof; rite of admitting a baptized person to the privileges of the church.

€on-fĭrm′a-tĭve, } a. Tend-
€on-fĭrm′a-to-ry, } ing to confirm. [confirms.

€on-fĭrm′er, n. One who

€on-fĭs′ca-ble, a. Liable to be confiscated.

€ŏn′fis-eate, or €on-fĭs′eate, a. Forfeited to the public use.

€ŏn′fĭs-eāte, or €on-fĭs′eāte (114), v. t. To forfeit to the public treasury.

€ŏn′fis-eā′tion, n. The act of forfeiting or confiscating.

€ŏn′fis-eā′tor, n. One who confiscates.

€on-fĭs′ea-to-ry, a. Consigning to, or promoting, confiscation.

€ŏn′fla-grā′tion, n. A great fire, or burning of buildings.

€on-flĭct′, v. t. [Lat. con, with, together, and fligere, to strike.] To strive; to contend; to fight. [gle.

€ŏn′flĭct, n. A contest; strug-

€on-flū-ençe, n. A flowing together; a concourse.

€ŏn′flu-ent, a. Running together — n. A stream flowing into a larger one.

€ŏn′flux. n. A junction of currents.

€on-fōrm′. v. t. To make like. — v. i. To comply; to yield.

€on-fōrm′a-ble, a. Suitable; agreeable.

€on-fōrm′a-bly, adv. Suitably; agreeably.

€ŏn′for-mā′tion, n. Act of conforming; disposition of parts; structure.

€on-fōrm′ist, n. One who complies with the worship of the church of England.

€on-fōrm′i-ty, n. Compliance; likeness; resemblance; agreement.

€on-found′, v. t. [Lat. con, with, together, and fundere, to pour.] To mix; to mingle; to perplex.

€on-found′ed, p. p. Blended; mixed. — p. a. Enormous.

€ŏn′fra-tĕr′ni-ty, n. A religious brotherhood.

€on-frī-eā′tion, n. Act of rubbing together; friction.

€on frönt′ (-frŭnt′), v. t. To face; to set face to face; to oppose.

sŏn, ôr, dọ, wọlf, tōō, took; ûrn, rụe, pụll; ç, ġ, soft; c, ġ, hard; aṣ; exist; ŋ as ng; this.

Con-fron-ta'tion, *n.* Act of confronting.
Con-fūṣe', *v. t.* To confound; to perplex; to abash.
Con-fūṣ'ed-ly, *adv.* In confusion.
Con-fū'ṣion, *n.* Disorder; tumult; ruin; indistinctness.
Con-fūt'a-ble, *a.* Capable of being confuted.
Con'fu-tā'tion, *n.* Act of disproving; refutation.
Con-fūte', *v. t.* To disprove; to prove to be false. [futes.
Con-fūt'er, *n.* One who confutes.
Con'gē, *n.* A bow; reverence; farewell. — *v. i.* To take leave; to bow or courtesy.
Con-gēal', *v. t.* or *i.* To freeze; to thicken; to stiffen.
Con-gēal'a-ble, *a.* Capable of being congealed.
Con-gēal'ment, *n.* Act of congealing; mass congealed.
†**Congé d'élire** (kŏn'jā dḗ-lēer'), *n.* The king's permission to a dean and chapter to choose a bishop.
Con'ge-lā'tion, *n.* Process of congealing; thing congealed.
Con'ge-ner, *n.* A thing of the same nature or origin.
Con'ge-nĕr'ic, *a.* Of the same kind.
Con-gē'ni-al, *a.* Of the same nature or disposition; agreeable.
Con-gē'ni-ăl'i-ty, *n.* Natural affinity; suitableness. [kind.
Con-gĕn'i-tal, *a.* Of the same birth; dating from birth.
Cŏn'ger, *n.* A large kind of eel.
Con-gē'ri-ēṣ, *n.* Mass or collection of bodies. [amass.
Con-gēst', *v. t.* To heap up; to
Con-gĕs'tion (-jĕst'yun), *n.* An unnatural collection of blood in the body.
Con-gĕst'ive, *a.* Indicating an accumulation of blood in some part of the body. [ball.
Con-glō'bate, *a.* Formed into a
Cŏn'glo-bā'tion, *n.* Act of forming into a ball.
Con-glō'bate, } *v. i.* To
Con-glōbe', } gather into
Con-glōb'u-late, } a globule or ball.
Con-glŏm'er-āte, *v. t.* To gather into a round mass.
Con-glŏm'er-ate (42), *a.* Gathered together in a mass.
Con-glŏm'er-ā'tion, *n.* A gathering into a round mass.
Con-glū'ti-nant, *a.* Gluing together; uniting.
Con-glū'ti-nāte, *v. t.* To glue together. — *v. i.* To coalesce.

Con-glū'ti-nate, *a.* Glued together.
Con-glū'ti-nā'tion, *n.* A gluing together; union.
Con-glū'ti-na-tive, *a.* Able or tending to cause union.
Cŏn'go, *n.* A kind of black tea.
Con-grăt'u-lant, *a.* Rejoicing in participation.
Con-grăt'u-lāte, *v. t.* To wish joy to. — SYN. To felicitate.
Con-grăt'u-lā'tion, *n.* Act of congratulating; felicitation.
Con-grăt'u-lā'tor, *n.* One who offers congratulation.
Con-grăt'u-la-to-ry, *a.* Expressing joy or pleasure.
Cŏn'gre-gāte, *v. t.* or *i.* [Lat. *con*, with, together, and *grex, gregis*, flock, herd.] To assemble; to meet; to gather.
Cŏn'gre-gā'tion (79), *n.* An assembly, especially a religious assembly.
Cŏn'gre-gā'tion-al, *a.* Relating to a congregation; public.
Cŏn'gre-gā'tion-al-iṣm, *n.* Government of itself by each local church.
Cŏn'gre-gā'tion-al-ist, *n.* An adherent to the congregational mode of church government.
Cŏn'gress (140), *n.* A meeting; the legislature of the United States.
Con-grĕs'sion-al (-grĕsh'un-), *a.* Pertaining to congress.
Con-grĕss'ive, *a.* Encountering; meeting.
Cŏn'gru-ence, *n.* Agreement; suitableness.
Cŏn'gru-ent, *a.* Agreeing; correspondent.
Con-grū'i-ty, *n.* Consistency; correspondence; harmony.
Cŏn'gru-oŭs (kŏng'gru-us), *a.* Being suitable; fit; meet.
Cŏn'ic, } *a.* Pertaining to,
Cŏn'ic-al, } or like, a cone.
Cŏn'ic-al-ly, *adv.* In the form of a cone.
Cŏn'ics, *n. sing.* The science which treats of the properties of the cone.
Co-nĭf'er-oŭs, *a.* Bearing cones, as the pine.
Con-jĕct'ur-al, *a.* Depending on conjecture.
Con-jĕct'ūre, *n.* Opinion based on imperfect knowledge; surmise; guess. — *v. t.* [Lat. *con*, with, together, and *jacere, jectus*, to throw.] To guess; to suspect; to surmise.

Con-join', *v.* To connect; to unite; to join.
Con-joint', *a.* United; connected; associated.
Con-joint'ly, *adv.* With united efforts; together.
Cŏn'ju-gal, *a.* Relating to marriage; matrimonial.
Cŏn'ju-gāte, *v. t.* To inflect as verbs.
Cŏn'ju-gā'tion, *n.* The inflection of verbs.
Con-jūnct', *a.* Joint; concurrent; united.
Con-jūnc'tion, *n.* Union; connection; a connecting word.
Con-jūnct'ive, *a.* Serving to unite; connecting.
Con-jūnct'ive-ly, *adv.* In conjunction, or union.
Con-jūnct'ūre, *n.* Union; connection; combination; critical time; crisis.
Cŏn'ju-rā'tion, *n.* Solemn treaty; enchantment.
Cŏn'jure (kŭn'jur), *v. t.* To charm; to enchant. — *v. i.* To practice magical arts.
Con-jūre', *v. t.* To call on or summon solemnly.
Cŏn'jur-er (kŭn'jur-), *n.* An enchanter.
Cŏn'nāte, *a.* Born at the same time; united in origin.
Con-năt'u-ral, *a.* Connected by nature. [ural union.
Con-năt'u-răl'i-ty, *n.* Nat-
Con-nĕct', *v. t.* [Lat. *con*, with, together, and *nectere*, to bind.] To knit together; to unite; to join.
Con-nĕc'tion, *n.* Act of joining; a relation by blood or marriage. — SYN. Union; coherence; junction; intercourse.
Con-nĕct'ive, *a.* Serving to connect. — *n.* Any thing that connects: especially a word that connects sentences.
Con-nĕx'ion. See *Connection*.
Con-nīv'ançe, *n.* Act of conniving; a giving secret assistance or sympathy.
Con-nīve', *v. i.* To wink at; to fail, by intention, to see.
Con-nīv'er, *n.* One who connives.
Cŏn'nois-seûr' (kŏn'nis-sûr'), *n.* A critical judge or master of any art.
Cō'noid, *n.* A figure resembling a cone.
Con-nū'bi-al, *a.* Pertaining to marriage; matrimonial.

Conoid.

CONQUER 89 CONSPIRACY

Con'quer (kŏnk'er, 79), v. t. or i. To overcome; to subdue.

Con-quer-a-ble, a. Capable of being conquered.

Con'quer-or, n. One who conquers; a victor.

Con'quest (kŏnk'west), n. Act of conquering; thing conquered. — SYN. Victory; triumph; subjection.

Con'san-guin'e-ous, a. Being of the same blood.

Con'san-guin'i-ty, n. Relation by blood or birth.

Con'science (02), n. Internal or self-knowledge, or sense of right and wrong; truth.

Con'sci-en'tious (-shĭ-ĕn'-shus), a. Regulated by conscience.

Con'sci-en'tious-ly (kŏn'-shi-), adv. In accordance with the doctrines of conscience.

Con'sci-en'tious-ness, n. A scrupulous regard to conscience.

Con'scion-a-ble, a. Reasonable.

Con'scious (kŭn'shus), a. Having the power of knowing one's own thoughts; pertaining to self-knowledge.

Con'scious-ly, adv. With inward persuasion; knowingly.

Con'scious-ness, n. Perception of what passes in one's own mind.

Con'script, n. An enrolled soldier. — a. Written; enrolled; registered.

Con-scrip'tion, n. Act of enrolling or registering.

Con'se-crate, v. t. To dedicate; to declare to be sacred.

Con'se-crate (42), a. Devoted; hallowed; sacred.

Con'se-cra'tion, n. The act of dedicating to sacred uses.

Con'se-cra'tor, n. One who consecrates. [in order.

Con-sec'u-tive, a. Following

Con-sec'u-tive-ly, adv. In succession.

Con-sent', n. [Lat. con, with, together, and sentire, to feel, think.] Agreement; correspondence; accord. — v. i. To agree in opinion; to give assent.

Con'sen-ta'ne-ous, a. Accordant; agreeable; consistent.

Con'sen-ta'ne-ous-ness, n. Mutual agreement. [sents.

Con-sent'er, n. One who consents.

Con-sen'tient (-sĕn'shent), a. Agreeing in opinion.

Con'se-quence, n. That which follows; effect; inference.

Con'se-quent, a. Following, as a result. — n. That which results from a cause.

Con'se-quen'tial, a. Conceited; important; pompous.

Con'se-quen'tial-ly, adv. By consequence; pompously.

Con'se-quent-ly, adv. By consequence; therefore.

Con-serv'ant, a. Having the power of preserving.

Con'ser-va'tion, n. Preservation from loss or injury.

Con-serv'a-tism, n. Opposition to change; desire to preserve what is established.

Con-serv'a-tive, a. Tending or desiring to preserve things as they are. — n. One opposed to radical changes.

Con'ser-va'tor, or **Con'ser-va'tor**, n. A preserver.

Con-serv'a-to-ry, a. Tending to preserve. — n. A greenhouse for keeping exotic or tender plants.

Con'serve, n. A sweetmeat; preserved fruit.

Con-serve', v. t. To preserve; to save; to prepare with sugar, &c. [conserves.

Con-serv'er, n. One who

Con-sid'er, v. To think with care; to study; to ponder.

Con-sid'er-a-ble, a. Worthy of regard; moderately large.

Con-sid'er-a-bly, adv. In a considerable degree.

Con-sid'er-ate (42), a. Given to reflection. — SYN. Thoughtful; prudent; discreet.

Con-sid'er-ate-ly, adv. With serious thought.

Con-sid'er-ate-ness, n. Quality of exercising consideration.

Con-sid'er-a'tion, n. Act of considering; serious thought; prudence; motive; reason; compensation. [considers.

Con-sid'er-er, n. One who

Con-sid'er-ing, p. pr. Regarding; having regard to.

Con-sign' (-sīn'), v. t. To give in a formal manner; to intrust; to assign.

Con'sign-ee' (kŏn'sīn-ee'), n. One to whom a thing is consigned for sale.

Con-sign'er (-sīn'-),) n.

Con'sign-or' (-sīn-ŏr'),) One who commits to another in trust, usually for sale.

Con-sign'ment (-sīn'ment), n. Act of consigning; goods consigned.

Con-sist', v. i. To be made up of; to subsist; to agree.

Con-sist'ençe,) n. Fixed

Con-sist'en-çy,) state; agreement; congruity; degree of density.

Con-sist'ent, a. Agreeing; accordant; compatible.

Con-sist'ent-ly, adv. In a consistent manner.

Con'sis-to'ri-al, a. Relating to a consistory.

Con-sist'o-ry (107, 141), n. A spiritual court; any solemn assembly. [associate.

Con-so'ci-ate (-sō'shi-), n. An

Con-sō'ci-āte, v. t. or i. To unite in a body.

Con-sō'ci-a'tion (-sō'shĭ-ā'-shun), n. A union of neighboring churches.

Con-sol'a-ble, a. Admitting consolation.

Con'so-la'tion, n. Alleviation; solace; comfort.

Con-sōl'a-to-ry, a. Tending to give consolation; comforting.

Con-sōle', v. i. To comfort; to cheer under sorrow.

Con'sōle, n. A bracket to support a cornice, &c. [soles.

Con-sōl'er. n. One who consoles.

Con-sōl'i-dāte, v. t. or i. [Lat. con, with, together, and solidus, solid.] To make or grow solid or firm.

Con-sōl'i-dā'tion, n. Act of making hard or firm; combination of several actions into one.

Con'sols, or **Con-sōls'**, n. pl. An English funded government security.

Con'so-nançe, n. Agreement of sounds; concord; accord; consistency.

Con'so-nant, a. Agreeable; consistent; accordant. — n. A sound less open than a vowel; a letter representing such sound.

Con'so-nant-ly, adv. Consistently; agreeably.

Con'sort, n. A husband or wife; companion; partner.

Con-sŏrt', v. i. To keep company; to associate. — v. t. To unite or join.

Con-spic'u-ous, a. Obvious to the sight; plain; manifest; evident.

Con-spic'u-ous-ly, adv. Evidently; plainly.

Con-spic'u-ous-ness,) n.

Con-spi-cū'i-ty,) Openness to view; clearness.

Con-spir'a-çy, n. A plot;

---

sŏn, ôr, do, wolf, too, took, ûrn, rue, pull; ç, ġ, soft; c, ġ, hard; aş; exist; ŋ as ng; this.

cŏm-bĭn-a'tion for an evil purpose.
Con-spĭr'a-tor, *n.* A plotter of evil; a conspirer.
Con-spĭre', *v. i.* To unite for an evil purpose; to plot.
Con-spĭr'er, *n.* A plotter.
Con'sta-ble (kŭn'sta-bl), *n.* An officer of the peace.
Con-stăb'u-la-ry, *a.* Pertaining to constables.— *n.* Whole body of constables.
Con'stan-cy, *n.* Stability; firmness of mind; steadiness.
Con'stant, *a.* [Lat. *constans,* standing firm, from *con,* with, together, and *stare,* to stand.] Firm; unchanging; faithful in affection; persevering.
Con'stant-ly, *adv.* Invariably.
Con'stel-la'tion, *n.* A cluster of fixed stars.
Con'ster-na'tion, *n.* Terror that confounds.
Con'sti-pāte, *v. t.* To make costive. [ness.
Con'sti-pā'tion, *n.* Costiveness.
Con-stĭt'u-en-cy, *n.* Body of constituents.
Con-stĭt'u-ent, *a.* Composing; component; essential. — *n.* A person who establishes or appoints; an element.
Con'sti-tūte, *v. t.* To establish; to make; to appoint.
Con'sti-tūt'er, *n.* One who constitutes.
Con'sti-tū'tion (27), *n.* Act of constituting; frame of body, mind, or government.
Con'sti-tū'tion-al, *a.* Pertaining to, or consistent with, the constitution.
Con'sti-tū'tion-ăl'i-ty, *n.* Consistency with the constitution.
Con'sti-tū'tion-al-ist, *n.* An adherent to a constitution.
Con'sti-tū'tion-al-ly, *adv.* In consistency with the constitution. [ing.
Con'sti-tū'tive, *a.* Establish-
Con-strāin', *v. t.* To impel with overpowering force. — SYN. To compel; force; drive; urge.
Con-strāin'a-ble, *a.* Capable of being constrained.
Con-strāin'er, *n.* One who constrains.
Con-strāint', *n.* Irresistible force or its effect; compulsion.
Con-strĭct', *v. t.* To bind; to contract; to cause to shrink
Con-strĭc'tion, *n.* Contraction; compression. [tract.
Con-strĭnge', *v. t.* To con-

Con-strĭn'gent, *a.* Binding; contracting.
Con-strŭct', *v. t.* [Lat. *con,* with, together, and *struere, structum,* to pile up.] To build; to compose; to form; to devise. [constructs.
Con-strŭct'er, *n.* One who
Con-strŭc'tion, *n.* Act or form of constructing; thing constructed; structure; fabrication; edifice; interpretation.
Con-strŭc'tion-ist, *n.* One who construes a writing or public instrument.
Con-strŭct'ive, *a.* By construction; deduced; inferred.
Con-strŭc'tive-ly, *adv.* By way of construction or interpretation.
Con'strue, *v. t.* To translate, interpret, or explain.
Con'stu-prā'tion, *n.* Act of ravishing.
Con'sub-stăn'tial, *a.* Having the same substance.
Con'sub-stăn'ti-āte (-stăn-shĭ-), *v. t.* To unite in one common substance or nature.
Con'sub-stăn'ti-ā'tion (-shĭ-ā'shun), *n.* Actual presence of the body of Christ with the sacramental elements.'
Con'sue-tū'di-nal, *a.* Customary; usual.
Con'sul, *n.* [Lat. from *consulere,* to consult, deliberate.] The chief magistrate in ancient Rome; a commercial agent of a government, in a foreign country.
Con'su-lar, *a.* Pertaining to a consul.
Con'su-late,) *n.* Office or
Con'sul-ship,) residence of a consul.
Con-sŭlt', *v. i* To ask advice of. — *v. t.* To take advice.
Con'sul-tā'tion, *n.* Act of consulting; deliberation.
Con-sŭlt'er, *n.* One who consults.
Con-sŭm'a-ble (133), *a.* Capable of being consumed.
Con-sūme', *v. t.* To waste slowly; to destroy; to spend. — *v. i.* To waste away.
Con-sūm'er, *n.* One who consumes.
Con'sum-māte, or **Con-sŭm'māte** (114), *v. t.* To complete; to perfect.
Con-sŭm'mate, *a.* Accomplished; complete; perfect.
Con'sum-mā'tion, *n.* Completion; termination; perfection.
Con-sŭmp'tion, *n.* Act of

consuming; a wasting disease of the lungs.
Con-sŭmp'tive, *a.* Inclined to consumption.
Con-sŭmp'tive-ness, *n.* Tendency to consumption.
Con'tact, *n.* Touch; close union.
Con-tā'gion (-jun), *n.* Communication of disease by contact; infection.
Con-tā'gioŭs (-jus), *a.* Having the quality of infecting.
Con-tā'gioŭs-ness, *n.* Quality of being contagious.
Con-tāin', *v. t.* To hold; to comprise; to embrace. — *v. i.* To live chastely.
Con-tāin'a-ble, *a.* Capable of being contained.
Con-tăm'i-nāte, *v. t.* To defile; to corrupt; to pollute.
Con-tăm'i-nate, *a.* Polluted; tainted.
Con-tăm'i-nā'tion, *n.* Pollution; defilement; taint.
Con-tĕmn' (kon-tĕm'), *v. t.* To despise; to scorn.
Con-tĕm'ner, *n.* One who contemns; a scorner.
Con-tĕm'per,) *v. t.* To
Con-tĕm'per-ate,) temper; to moderate; to reduce by mixture. [perament.
Con-tĕm'per-a-ment, *n.* Temperament.
Con'tem-plāte, or **Con-tĕm'plāte** (114), *v. t.* or *i.* To meditate; to consider; to study; to design.
Con'tem-plā'tion, *n.* Meditation; study, as opposed to action. [to thought.
Con-tĕm'pla-tive, *a.* Given
Con-tĕm'pla-tive-ly, *adv.* With contemplation.
Con'tem-plā'tor, *n.* One engaged in deep thought.
Con-tĕm'po-ra-ry,)
Con-tĕm'po-ra'ne-oŭs,) *a.* [Lat. *con,* with, together, and *tempus, temporis,* time.] Living or being at the same time.
Con-tĕm'po-ra-ry, *n.* One living at the same time with another.
Con-tĕmpt', *n.* Act of despising; disdain; scorn; disobedience of the orders of a court or legislature.
Con-tĕmpt'i-ble, *a.* Deserving contempt; mean; vile.
Con-tĕmpt'i-ble-ness, *n.* State of being contemptible.
Con-tĕmpt'i-bly, *adv.* Meanly.
Con-tĕmpt'u-oŭs, *a.* Manifesting contempt; scornful.
Con-tĕmpt'u-oŭs-ly, *adv.* In a scornful manner.

CONTEND 91 CONTUMACIOUSLY

Con-tĕnd', *v. i.* To strive; to struggle.
Con-tĕnd'er, *n.* A combatant.
Con-tĕnt', *a.* Satisfied; quiet. — *n.* Satisfaction of mind. — *v. t.* To satisfy; to please; to gratify.
Con-tĕnt'ed, *a.* Satisfied; pleased; content.
Con-tĕnt'ed-ly, *adv.* In a contented manner.
Con-tĕnt'ed-ness, *n.* State of being content.
Con-tĕn'tion, *n.* Strife; debate; quarrel.
Con-tĕn'tious, *a.* Given to strife; quarrelsome. [tion.
Con-tĕnt'ment, *n.* Satisfac-
Cŏn'tent, or **Con-tĕnt'**, *n.* That which is contained; (*pl.*) general introductory index.
Con-tĕr'mi-na-ble, *a.* Capable of the same bounds.
Con-tĕr'mi-noŭs, *a.* Bordering; contiguous.
Cŏn'test, *n.* A dispute; struggle; debate.
Con-tĕst', *v. t.* or *i.* To dispute; to strive.
Con-tĕst'a-ble, *a.* Capable of being contested; disputable.
Cŏn'text, *n.* [Lat. *con*, with, together, and *textus*, knit.] Parts of a discourse that precede and follow a sentence quoted.
Con-tĕxt'ūre, *n.* Composition of parts; texture; system.
Cŏn'ti-gū'i-ty, *n.* Contact; nearness.
Con-tĭg'u-oŭs, *a.* Being in actual contact. — SYN. Adjoining; adjacent.
Con-tĭg'u-oŭs-ly, *adv.* In close contact.
Cŏn'ti-nençe, *n.* Forbearance of carnal pleasure.
Cŏn'ti-nent, *a.* Not indulging in sensual pleasure. — *n.* One of the larger divisions of the earth.
Cŏn'ti-nĕnt'al, *a.* Pertaining to a continent.
Cŏn'ti-nent-ly, *adv.* With continence.
Con-tĭn'gençe, } *n.* Casual
Con-tĭn'gen-çy, } event; chance; possibility; accident.
Con-tĭn'gent, *a.* Accidental; possible; liable. — *n.* Chance; a quota; proportion.
Con-tĭn'gent-ly, *adv.* By chance.
Con-tĭn'u-al, *a.* Uninterrupted; incessant.
Con-tĭn'u-al-ly, *adv.* Without intermission.

Con-tĭn'u-ançe (133), *n.* Permanence, as of condition, habits, &c.
Con-tĭn'u-ā'tion, *n.* Continued succession.
Con-tĭn'u-ā'tor, *n.* One who continues.
Con-tĭn'ūe, *v. i.* To remain; to stay; to persevere. — *v. t.* To protract; to persevere in.
Cŏn'ti-nū'i-ty, *n.* Uninterrupted connection.
Con-tĭn'u-oŭs, *a.* Closely united, as it were into one.
Con-tĭn'u-oŭs-ly, *adv.* In continuation.
Con-tŏrt', *v. t.* To twist; to writhe.
Con-tŏr'tion, *n.* A twisting; a wry motion.
Con-tour' (-tōōr'), *n.* The general outline of a figure.
Cŏn'tra-bănd, *a.* Prohibited by law or treaty. — *n.* Illegal trade.
Cŏn'tra-bănd'ist, *n.* A smuggler in time of war.
Cŏn'tract, *n.* An agreement; covenant; bargain.
Con-trăct', *v. t.* To draw together or nearer; to incur; to shorten. — *v. i.* To shrink; to bargain.
Con-trăct'ed, *a.* Narrow; selfish; illiberal; mean.
Con-trăct'i-ble, } *a.* Capable
Con-trăct'ĭle, } of contracting.
Cŏn'trac-tĭl'i-ty, *n.* The quality of contracting or shrinking.
Con-trăc'tion, *n.* A drawing together, or shrinking; a shortening.
Con-trăct'or, *n.* One who contracts or covenants.
Cŏn'tra-dănçe, *n.* A dance with partners opposite.
Cŏn'tra-dĭct', *v. t.* [Lat. *contra*, against, and *dicere*, *dictum*, to say, speak.] To oppose verbally; to gainsay.
Cŏn'tra-dĭc'tion, *n.* A denying; opposition.
Cŏn'tra-dĭc'tioŭs, *a.* Inclined to contradict.
Cŏn'tra-dĭc'to-ry, *a.* Inconsistent; disagreeing.
Cŏn'tra-dis-tĭnc'tion, *n.* Distinction by opposites.
Cŏn'tra-dis-tĭnct'ĭve, *a.* Distinguishing by contrast.
Cŏn'tra-dis-tĭn'guish, *v. t.* To distinguish by opposites.
Con-trăl'to, *n.* The alto or counter-tenor.
Cŏn'tra-rī'e-ty, *n.* Opposition; inconsistency.

Cŏn'tra-ries, *n. pl.* Things of opposite qualities.
Cŏn'tra-ri-ly, *adv.* In a contrary manner; in opposition.
Cŏn'tra-ri-wĭse, *adv.* On the contrary; oppositely.
Cŏn'tra-ry, *a.* In direct opposition; inconsistent.
Cŏn'trăst, *n.* Opposition or difference in things.
Con-trăst', *v. t.* or *i.* To place or stand in opposition.
Cŏn'tra-val-lā'tion, *n.* A trench and parapet formed by besiegers.
Cŏn'tra-vēne', *v. t.* To oppose; to cross; to obstruct.
Cŏn'tra-vĕn'tion, *n.* Opposition; violation; obstruction.
Con-trĭb'ūte, *v. t.* To participate in giving. — *v. i.* To give a part.
Con-trĭ-bū'tion, *n.* Act of contributing; sum given.
Con-trĭb'u-tĭve, *a.* Tending to promote. [contributes.
Con-trĭb'u-tor, *n.* One who
Con-trĭb'u-to-ry, *a.* Advancing the same end.
Cŏn'trīte, *a.* Broken down with grief; humble; penitent.
Con-trī'tion (-trĭsh'un), *n.* Deep sorrow for sin.
Con-trīv'a-ble, *a.* Capable of being contrived.
Con-trīv'ançe, *n.* Scheme; device; thing contrived.
Con-trīve', *v. t.* To invent; to devise; to plan; to project. — *v. i.* To make devices.
Con-trīv'er, *n.* One who contrives; an inventor.
Con-trōl' (129) *n.* Power to govern; command; authority; restraint. — *v. t.* To restrain; to govern.
Con-trōl'la-ble, *a.* Subject to control.
Con-trōl'ler, *n.* One who controls; an officer who checks other officers by a counter register of accounts.
Con-trōl'ler-ship, *n.* The office of controller.
Cŏn'tro-vēr'sial, *a.* Relating to controversy.
Cŏn'tro-vēr'sial-ist, *n.* One engaged in controversy.
Cŏn'tro-ver-sy, *n.* Dispute.
Cŏn'tro-vērt', *v. t.* To dispute; to debate; to contest.
Cŏn'tro-vērt'i-ble, *a.* Capable of being controverted.
Cŏn'tu-mā'cioŭs, *a.* Obstinate; perverse; stubborn.
Cŏn'tu-mā'cioŭs-ly, *adv.* With obstinacy.

sŏn, ŏr, dǫ, wǫlf, tōō, tŏŏk; ûrn, rᵫe, pᵫll; ç, ġ, *soft*; c, ġ, *hard*; aȥ; eẋist; ɴ as ng; this.

CONTUMACY 92 COPARTNER

Còn'tu-ma-çy, *n.* Persistent obstinacy; stubbornness.
Còn'tu-mēl'ioŭs (-mēl'yus), *a.* Reproachful; contemptuous; abusive.
Còn'tu-me-ly, *n.* Contemptuous language; reproach.
Con-tūṣe', *v. t.* To bruise or injure by beating. [the flesh.
Con-tū'ṣion, *n.* A bruise in
Co-nūn'drum, *n.* A riddle turning on a point of resemblance between things very unlike.
Còn'va-lĕs'çençe, *n.* Recovery from sickness.
Còn'va-lĕs'çent, *a.* Recovering health.
Con-vēne', *v. t.* [Lat. *con,* with, together, and *venire,* to come.] To call together. — *v. i.* To assemble; to meet.
Con-vĕn'ience, } *n.* Accom-
Con-vĕn'ien-çy, } modation fitness: commodiousness.
Con-vĕn'ient, *a.* Fit; suitable; adapted. [ably.
Con-vĕn'ient-ly, *adv.* Suit-
Còn'vent, *n.* A body of monks or nuns; a monastery or nunnery.
Con-vĕn'ti-cle, *n.* A meeting; an assembly for worship.
Con-vĕn'tion, *n.* Assembly; arbitrary custom; temporary treaty.
Con-vĕn'tion-al, *a.* Agreed on; stipulated; sanctioned by usage.
Con-vĕn'tion-al-iṣm, *n.* That which is received by tacit agreement.
Con-vĕnt'u-al, *a.* Belonging to a convent; monastic.
Con-vērge', *v. i.* To tend toward one point.
Con-vērġ'ençe, *n.* Tendency to one point.
Con-vērġ'ent, *a.* Tending to one point; converging.
Con-vērs'a-ble, *a.* Sociable.
Con-vērs'a-bly, *adv.* In a conversable manner; sociably.
Còn'ver-sant, *a.* Familiar; well acquainted; having relation.
Còn'ver-sā'tion, *n.* Familiar discourse; behavior.
Còn'ver-sā'tion-al, *a.* Pertaining to conversation.
Con-vērse', *v. i.* To discourse; to talk familiarly.
Còn'verse, *n.* Conversation; a reversed or opposite proposition. — *a.* Directly opposite. [of order.
Còn'verse-ly, *adv.* By change

Con-vēr'sion, *n.* A turning from one state to another; change; transformation.
Còn'vert, *n.* One who has changed his opinions or religion.
Con-vērt', *v. t.* To change to another form or state.
Con-vērt'er, *n.* One who converts.
Con-vērt'i-bĭl'i-ty, *n.* Possibility of being converted.
Con-vērt'i-ble, *a.* Capable of being converted or changed.
Còn'vex, *a.* Roundish on the outside. — *n.* A convex body.
Con-vĕx'i-ty, } *n.* Spherical
Còn'vex-ness, } form on the outside. [vex form.
Còn'vex-ly, *adv.* In a con-
Con-vey', *v. t.* To carry; to bear; to transmit; to transfer.
Con-vey'ançe, *n.* Act of conveying; that which conveys.
Con-vey'an-çer, *n.* One who draws deeds, &c.
Con-vey'an-çing, *n.* The business of a conveyancer.
Con-vey'er, *n.* One who conveys or carries.
Còn'vict, *n.* A person proved guilty of crime; a felon.
Con-vict', *v. t.* To prove to be guilty.
Con-vic'tion, *n.* A proving guilty; state of being convinced; sense of guilt; confutation.
Con-vinçe', *v. t.* To satisfy by evidence. — SYN. To persuade.
Con-vin'çi-ble, *a.* Capable of being convinced.
Con-vĭv'i-al, *a.* Festive; jovial; social; gay.
Con-vĭv'i-ăl'i-ty, *n.* Jovial disposition; festive mirth.
Còn'vo-cāte, *v. t.* To call together; to convoke.
Còn'vo-cā'tion, *n.* A meeting; an ecclesiastical assembly. [gether; to summon.
Con-vōke', *v. t.* To call to-
Còn'vo-lū'ted, *a.* Rolled upon itself.
Còn'vo-lū'tion, *n.* The act of rolling together. [gether.
Con-vŏlve', *v. t.* To roll to-
Con-voy', *v. t.* To accompany for protection; to escort.
Còn'voy, *a.* Attendance for protection.
Con-vŭlse', *v. t.* To affect by violent, irregular motion.
Con-vŭl'sion, *n.* A violent spasm; any violent and irregular motion or agitation.

Con-vŭl'sĭve, *a.* Producing convulsion; spasmodic.
Cō'ny, or **Cŏn'y** (141), *n.* A rabbit. [a dove.
Cōō', *v. i.* To make a noise as
Cŏŏk, *n.* One who prepares food for the table. — *v. t.* To prepare food for the table.
Cŏŏk'er-y, *n.* Act of preparing food for the table.
Cŏŏk'y, *n.* A small, hard, sweetened cake.
Cōōl, *a.* Somewhat cold; lacking warmth; indifferent. — *n.* A moderate state of cold. — *v. t.* To make moderately cold. — *v. i.* To grow cool.
Cōōl'er, *n.* A vessel for cooling; that which cools.
Cōōl'ĭsh (130), *a.* Somewhat cool. [passion.
Cōōl'ly, *adv.* Without heat or
Cōōl'ness, *n.* Moderate cold; indifference.
Cōō'ly, } *n.* An East Indian
Cōō'lie, } or Chinese porter, or transported laborer.
Cōōm *n.* Wheel-grease, or other dirty refuse matter.
Cōōmb (kōōm), *n.* A dry measure of four bushels; a kind of valley on a hill.
Cōōp, *n.* A cage for fowls, &c.; a barrel. — *v. t.* To cage; to shut up. [casks, &c.
Cōōp'er, *n.* A maker of
Cōōp'er-age, *n.* Price for cooper's work; shop or work of a cooper.
Co-ŏp'er-āte, *v. i.* [Lat. *co* or *con*, with, together, and *operare, operatus*, to work.] To work together; to act jointly with others. [labor.
Co-ŏp'er-ā'tion, *n.* Joint
Co-ŏp'er-a-tĭve, *a.* Promoting the same end.
Co-ŏp'er-ā'tor, *n.* One who works with others.
Co-ōr'di-nate (42), *a.* Holding the same rank or degree.
Co-ōr'di-nate-ly, *adv.* With equal rank.
Co-ōr'di-nā'tion, *n.* State of being co-ordinate, or of equal value.
Cōot, *n.* A kind of waterfowl; a foolish fellow.
Co-pāi'bā, } *n.* A medicinal
Co-pāi'vā, } resinous juice.
Cō'pal, *n.* A resinous substance used in making varnishes.
Co-pär'çe-na-ry, } *n.* Joint
Co-pär'çe-ner, } heirship.
Co-pär'çe-ner, *n.* A joint heir. [partner.
Co-pärt'ner, *n.* A joint

ă, ĕ, ī, ō, ū, ȳ, *long;* ă, ĕ, ĭ, ŏ, ŭ, ў, *short;* câre, cär, ȧsk, ąll, whąt; ēre, vēil, tērm; pīque, fĭrm;

Co-part'ner-ship, *n.* A joint concern in business.
Cope, *n.* A priest's cloak; a kind of hood; arch-work. — *v.* To contend; to strive; to oppose with success.
Cop'i-er (135), *n.* One who copies or transcribes.
Cop'ing, *n.* The top or cover of a wall.
Co'pi-ous, *a.* Plentiful; abundant; large in amount.
Co'pi-ous-ly, *adv.* Abundantly; amply. [ply.
Co'pi-ous-ness, *n.* Full supply.
Cop'per, *n.* A familiar reddish metal; a large boiler. — *v. t.* To cover or sheathe with copper.
Cop'per-as, *n.* Sulphate of iron; green vitriol.
Cop'per-plate, *n.* A plate of copper engraved, or an impression from it.
Cop'per-smith, *n.* One who manufactures copper utensils. [resembling, copper.
Cop'per-y, *a.* Containing, or
Cop'pice, } *n.* A wood of
Copse, } small growth.
Cop'u-late, *v. i.* To have sexual intercourse; to embrace; to unite. (ulating.
Cop'u-la'tion, *n.* Act of copulating.
Cop'u-la'tive, *a.* Serving to unite. — *n.* A copulative conjunction.
Cop'y (141), *n.* A transcript; pattern; imitation; manuscript to print from. — *v. t.* To transcribe; to imitate. — *v. i.* To make, as a copy.
Cop'y-book, *n.* A book in which copies are written or printed for learners to imitate.
Cop'y-hold, *n.* A tenure in England by copy of record.
Cop'y-ist (135), *n.* One who copies.
Cop'y-right (-rit), *n.* The sole right of an author to publish a book, &c. — *v. t.* To secure by copyright, as a book.
Co-quet' (ko-kĕt'), *v. t.* To attempt to excite admiration from vanity. — *v. i.* To trifle in love. [love.
Co-quet'ry, *n.* Trifling in
Co-quette' (ko-kĕt', 83), *n.* A vain, jilting girl.
Co-quet'tish (-kĕt'-), *a.* Befitting a coquette.
Cŏr'al, *n.* A calcareous secretion by zoöphytes. [al.
Cŏr'al-line, *a.* Of, or like, coralban.
Cŏr'ban, *n.* An alms-basket; a gift to God; a vow not to

give to another, or to receive from him, a particular object.
Cŏr'bel, *n.*
A short piece of timber, &c., in a wall, Corbel. jutting out in the manner of a shoulder-piece.
Cŏrd, *n.* A line; a measure of wood containing 128 cubic feet. — *v. t.* To tie up; to pile up for measurement.
Cŏrd'age, *n.* Ropes or cords.
Cŏrd'ate, *a.* Heart-shaped.
Cŏrd'de-lier', *n.* A Franciscan friar.
Cŏrd'di-al, or **Cŏrd'ial,** *n.* An exhilarating liquor; any thing that cheers. — *a.* Hearty; sincere.
Cŏr'di-al'i-ty, or **Cord-ial'i-ty,** *n.* Sincerity; warm affection.
Cŏr'di-al-ly, or **Cŏrd'ial-ly,** *adv.* With sincere affection; heartily. [posts or troops.
Cŏr'don, *n.* A line of military
Cŏr'du-roy', *n.* A thick, ribbed cotton stuff.
Cŏrd'wain-er, *n.* A shoemaker. [part.
Cŏre, *n.* The heart or inner
Co-ri-a'ceous, *a.* Consisting of, or like, leather; leathery.
Co-ri-ăn'der, *n.* A plant having strong-scented medicinal seeds.
Co-rin'thi-an, *a.* Pertaining to Corinth, or to a certain order of architecture.
Cŏrk, *n.* A tree, or its bark; a stopper. — *v. t.* To stop with a cork.
Cŏrk'-screw (-skrụ), *n.* A screw to draw corks from bottles.
Cŏrk'y, *a.* Of, or like, cork.
Cŏr'mo-rant, *n.* A voracious sea-bird; a glutton.
Cŏrn, *n.* Grain of any kind; maize; a hard, horny excrescence on the feet. — *v. t.* To sprinkle with salt; to granulate.
Cŏr'ne-a (140), *n.* The horny, transparent membrane in the fore part of the eye.
Cŏr'nel, *n.* A shrub and its fruit. [horn; hard.
Cŏr'ne-ous, *a.* Horny; like
Cŏr'ner, *n.* An angle; a secret or retired place.
Cŏr'ner-stōne, *n.* A stone placed at the corner of a foundation.
Cŏr'ner-wise, *adv.* From

corner to corner; with the corner in front.
Cŏr'net, *n.* [Lat. *cornu,* a horn.] A musical wind-instrument; a cavalry officer who carries the standard.
Cŏr'net-cy, *n.* Office of a cornet.
Cŏr'nice, *n.* Molding at the top of a wall or column.
Cŏr'nu-cō'pi-a (140), *n.* A horn of plenty.
Cŏr'ny'y, *a.* Cornucopia. Hard, like horn.
t'ŏr'ol, | *n.* The **Co-rŏl'la,** } inner part of a flower, composed of petals.
Cŏr'ol-la-ry (41), *n.* An inference derived incidentally: a consequent truth.
Cŏr'o-nal, *n.* A crown; a garland; a chaplet. — *a.* Pertaining to the top of the head.
Cŏr'o-na-ry, *a.* Relating to, or like, a crown. [crowning.
Cŏr'o-nā'tion, *n.* Act of
Cŏr'o-ner, *n.* An officer who inquires into the cause of any sudden death.
Cŏr'o-net, *n.* A crown worn by a nobleman.
Cŏr'po-ral, *n.* An inferior military officer. — *a.* Pertaining to the body.
Cŏr'po-rāl'i-ty, *n.* State of being embodied.
Cŏr'po-ral-ly, *adv.* Bodily.
Cŏr'po-rate, *a.* United in a community or association.
Cŏr'po-rā'tion, *n.* A society acting as an individual.
Cŏr'po-rā'tor, *n.* A member of a corporation.
Cor-pō're-al, *a.* Having a body; bodily: not spiritual.
Cor-pō're-al-ist, *n.* A materialist.
Cor-pō're-al-ly, *adv.* In a bodily form or manner.
Cŏr'po-rē'i-ty, *n.* Bodily substance; materiality.
Cŏrps (kōr), *n.* A body of troops.
Cŏrpse, *n.* A dead body.
Cŏr'pu-lençe, *n.* Fleshiness.
Cŏr'pu-lent, *a.* Very fleshy; bulky.
Cŏr'pus-cle (-pus-sl, 62), *n.* An atom: a minute particle.
Cor-pŭs'cu-lar, *a.* Relating

to, or consisting of, corpuscles.
Cor-rect', v. t. To make right; to reprove or punish. —a. Free from faults; exact; accurate.
Cor-rec'tion, n. Act of correcting; punishment; amendment. [to correct.
Cor-rec'tion-al, a. Intended
Cor-rect'ive, a. Tending to correct. —n. That which has the power of correcting.
Cor-rect'ly, adv. Exactly; justly.
Cor-rect'ness, n. Accuracy; exactness. [corrects.
Cor-rect'or, n. One who
Cor-rel'a-tive, a. Having mutual relation. —n. One who, or that which, stands in a reciprocal relation to some other person or thing.
Cor're-spond', v. i. To suit; to agree; to send and receive letters.
Cor're-spond'ence, n. Agreement; mutual relation or adaptation; interchange of letters.
Cor're-spond'ent, a. Suited; conformable. —n. One who has intercourse by letters.
Cor're-spond'ing, p. a. Suiting; correspondent.
Cor'ri-dor, n. A gallery leading to independent apartments. [being corrected.
Cor'ri-gi-ble, a. Capable of
Cor-ri'val, n. A fellow rival.
Cor-rob'o-rant, a. Strengthening; confirming.
Cor-rob'o-rate, v. t. To confirm; to strengthen.
Cor-rob'o-ra'tion, n. Act of corroborating.
Cor-rob'o-ra-tive, a. Tending to corroborate.
Cor-rode', v. t. To eat away or consume by degrees.
Cor-rod'ent, a. Having the power of corroding.
Cor-rod'i-ble, a. Capable of being corroded. [lug away.
Cor-ro'sion, n. Act of eat-
Cor-ro'sive, a. Eating away gradually. —n. Something that corrodes.
Cor'ru-gate, v. t. To wrinkle; to contract.
Cor'ru-gate, a. Wrinkled.
Cor'ru-ga'tion, n. Contraction into wrinkles.
Cor-rupt', v. To spoil; to decay; to vitiate. —a. Decayed; spoiled; debased.
Cor-rupt'er, n. One who corrupts.

Cor-rupt'i-bil'i-ty, n. Capacity of being corrupted.
Cor-rupt'i-ble, a. Capable of being corrupted.
Cor-rup'tion, n. Putrescence; pollution; putrid matter; depravity of morals.
Cor-rupt'ive, a. Tending to corrupt.
Cor-rupt'ly, adv. With corruption. [being corrupt.
Cor-rupt'ness, n. State of
Cor'sair, n. A pirate or piratical vessel.
Corse, n. A corpse. [Poetical.]
Corse'let, n. A light breastplate. [ladies.
Cor'set, n. A bodice for
Cor'tege (kôr'tāzh), n. A train of attendants.
†Cortes (kôr'tes), n. The legislative assembly of Spain and of Portugal.
Cor'ti-cal, a. Of, or belonging to, bark. [glittering.
Co-rus'cant, a. Flashing;
Cor'us-cate, or Co-rus'cate, v. i. To glitter; to sparkle.
Cor'us-ca'tion, n. A sudden flash of light. [war.
Cor-vette', n. A sloop of
Cor'ymb, n. A species of inflorescence.
Co'sey, a. See Cozy.
Cos-met'ic, a. Promoting beauty. —n. A wash for improving the complexion.
Cos'mic, } a. Pertaining to
Cos'mic-al, } the solar system, or to the universe; rising or setting with the sun.
Cos-mog'o-ny, n. Science of the formation of the world.
Cos-mog'ra-pher, n. One versed in cosmography.
Cos'mo-graph'ic, a. Relating to cosmography.
Cos-mog'ra-phy (117), n. A description of the world.
Cos-mol'o-gist, n. One versed in cosmology.
Cos-mol'o-gy, n. [Gr. kosmos, the world, and logos, a discourse.] Science of the world or universe.
Cos-mop'o-lite, n. A citizen of the world.
Cos'mo-ra'ma, or Cos'mo-ri'ma, n. A kind of optical exhibition.
Cos'set, n. A lamb reared by hand; a pet. —v. t. To fondle.
Cost (19), n. Price paid; charge; expense; loss of any kind. —v. i. [imp. & p. p. COST.] To be had at the price of. [ribs.
Cos'tal, a. Pertaining to the

Cos'tive, a. Constipated.
Cos'tive-ness, n. State of being costive; constipation.
Cost'li-ness (135), n. Expensiveness.
Cost'ly, a. Expensive; dear.
Cos-tume', or Cos'tume, n. Style or mode of dress.
Cot, } n. A small house; hut;
Cote, } a cover for a sore finger; a shed or inclosure.
Cot, } n. A little bed or
Cott, } cradle.
Co-tem'po-ra'ne-ous, } a.
Co-tem'po-ra-ry, } Living at the same time; contemporary. [lives in the same age.
Co-tem'po-ra-ry, n. One who
Co'te-rie' (140), n. A set of people who meet familiarly.
Co-til'ion (-til'yun), } n. A
Co-til'lion, } brisk lively dance and tune.
Cot'tage (42, 140), n. A small house; a hut; a villa.
Cot'ta-ger, n. One living in a cottage.
Cot'ter, n. A cottager.
Cot'ton (kŏt'tn), n. A plant and a downy substance produced by it; cloth made of cotton. —a. Made of cotton.
Cot'ton-y, a. Cotton. Like cotton; soft; downy.
Cot'y-le'don, n. One of the seed-lobes of a plant.
Cot'y-led'o-nous, n. Having a seed-lobe.
Couch, v. i. To lie down; to stoop, as in fear. —v. t. To lay down; to compose to rest; to express; to remove, as a cataract, from the eye. —n. A place for repose.
Couch'ant, a. Squatting.
Cough (kawf, 19, 72), n. Effort of the lungs to throw off phlegm. —v. t. To try to throw off phlegm. —v. t. To expel by a cough.
Could (kŏŏd, 38), imp. of Can.
Coul'ter. See Colter.
Coun'cil, n. An assembly for consultation or advice.
Coun'cil-or, } n A member of
Coun'cil-lor, } a council.
Coun'sel, n. Advice; an adviser; an advocate. —v. t. To give advice; to advise.
Coun'sel-or } (130, n. One
Coun'sel-lor } who gives advice; a lawyer.

COUNT 95 COWARD

Count, *v. t.* To reckon; to number; to esteem. — *v. i.* To number or be counted. — *n.* A tale; a title; part of a declaration.
Coun'te-nance, *n.* The face; air; look; support. — *v. t.* To support; to patronize.
Count'er, *n.* Something used in reckoning; a shop table; a high tenor in music. — *adv.* In opposition.
Coun'ter-âct', *v. t.* To act in opposition to; to hinder.
Coun'ter-âc'tion, *n.* Opposing action; hindrance.
Coun'ter-băl'ançe, *n.* Equal opposing weight.
Coun'ter-băl'ançe, *v. t.* To weigh against.
Coun'ter-chärm, *n.* That which dissolves a charm.
Coun'ter-chĕck, *n.* Check; stop; rebuke.
Coun'ter-cûr'rent, *n.* A current running contrary to the main current.
Coun'ter-feit, *a.* Forged; deceitful. — *n.* A forgery; a cheat; an imposture. — *v. t.* To forge; to imitate.
Coun'ter-feit-er, *n.* A forger.
Coun'ter-mănd, *n.* A contrary order.
Coun'ter-mănd', *v. t.* To revoke, as a command.
Coun'ter-märch, *n.* A marching back; a change of the wings or face of a battalion. [march back.
Coun'ter-märch', *v. i.* To
Coun'ter-märk, *n.* An aftermark on goods or coin.
Coun'ter-märk', *v. t.* To apply a countermark to.
Coun'ter-mīne, *n.* A subterranean gallery excavated to frustrate the use of another.
Coun'ter-mīne', *v. t.* To defeat secretly. [of a bed.
Coun'ter-pāne, *n.* The cover
Coun'ter-pärt, *n.* A corresponding part.
Coun'ter-plĕa, *n.* A replication. [against a plot.
Coun'ter-plŏt, *n.* A plot
Coun'ter-point, *n.* An opposite point; art of composing music in parts.
Coun'ter-poise, *n.* Equal weight in opposition.
Coun'ter-poise', *v. t.* To balance; to equal.
Coun'ter-rĕv'o-lū'tion, *n.* A change to a former state.
Coun'ter-scarp, *n.* Exterior slope of the ditch in fortifications; also, the whole covered way, with its parapet and glacis.
Coun'ter-sīgn' (-sīn'), *v. t.* To sign as secretary opposite to the signature of a superior. [military watchword.
Coun'ter-sīgn (-sīn), *n.* A
Coun'ter-sig'nal, *n.* A corresponding signal.
Coun'ter-tĕn'or, *n.* High tenor in music.
Coun'ter-vāil', *v. t.* To act against equally.
Coun'ter-work' (-wûrk'), *v. i.* To work in opposition.
Count'ess, *n.* The wife of an earl or count.
Count'ing-house, } *n.* A
Count'ing-room, } house or room for the keeping of accounts.
Count'less, *a.* Numberless; innumerable; infinite. [rude.
Coŭn'tri-fied, *a.* Rustic;
Coŭn'try (kŭn'trȳ), *n.* Land around a city; a kingdom or state; native place. — *a.* Belonging to the country; rural; rustic; rude.
Coŭn'try-dănçe, *n.* A contra-dance.
Coŭn'try-man (143), *n.* One of the same country; a rustic.
Coŭn'try-sēat, *n.* Country residence of a city gentleman.
Coun'ty, *n.* A shire; district.
Coŭp'le (kŭp'l, 38), *n.* Two of a kind; a pair; a brace. — *v.* To join; to link; to connect; to embrace.
Coŭp'let (kŭp'let), *n.* Two verses that rhyme; a pair.
Coŭp'ling (kŭp'-), *n.* That which couples or connects.
Cou'pon (kōō'pon *or* kōō'-pong), *n.* An interest certificate.
Coŭr'age (kŭr'ej), *n.* Boldness to encounter danger. — SYN. Bravery; intrepidity; valor; daring.
Coŭr-ā'geoŭs, *a.* Brave; bold; daring; valiant. [ly.
Coŭr-ā'geoŭs-ly, *adv.* Brave-
Coŭ'ri-er (kōō'ri-er), *n.* [Fr., from *courir,* to run.] A messenger sent in haste.
Coŭrse, *n.* A passing or running; place of running; race; career; progress; service of meat. — *v. i. or t.* To hunt; to run.
Coŭrs'er, *n.* A swift horse.
Coŭrt, *n.* Residence of a prince; seat of justice; an inclosed space; addresses; attentions. — *v. t.* To solicit in marriage; to address; to woo.
Coûrt'-cärd, *n.* See *Coat-card.*
Coûrt'e-oŭs (kûrt/e-us), *a.* Polite; civil; complaisant.
Coûrt'e-oŭs-ly, *adv.* Politely.
Coûrt'e-san, *n.* A lewd woman; a prostitute.
Coûrte'sy (kûrt'sȳ), *n.* Act of respect by women. — *v. i.* To make a courtesy.
Coûrt'e-sy (kûrt'e-sȳ), *n.* [From *court.*] Politeness; civility.
Coûrt'-hănd, *n.* The hand, or manner of writing, used in records and judicial proceedings.
Coûrt'ier (kōrt'yer), *n.* One who frequents courts.
Coûrt'li-ness, *n.* Complaisance with dignity.
Coûrt'ly, *a.* Polite; elegant.
Coûrt'-mär'tial (148), *n.* A court to try crimes in military or naval affairs.
Coûrt'-plăs'ter, *n.* Sticking-plaster made of silk.
Coûrt'ship, *n.* Solicitation in marriage.
Coŭs'in (kŭz'n), *n.* The child of an uncle or aunt.
Cōve, *n.* A small creek or bay. — *v. t.* To arch over.
Cŏv'e-nant, *n.* An agreement; contract. — *v. i.* To agree; to stipulate; to contract. [makes a covenant.
Cŏv'e-nant-er, *n.* One who
Cŏv'er (kŭv'er), *v. t.* To spread over; to clothe; to conceal. — *n.* Shelter; concealment; pretense.
Cŏv'er-ing, *n.* Any thing spread over. [cover.
Cŏv'er-let, *n.* An upper bed-
Cŏv'ert (kŭv'-), *a.* Hid; secret; private. — *n.* A shelter; thicket; defense.
Cŏv'ert-ly, *adv.* Secretly; closely; privately.
Cŏv'ert-ūre (50), *n.* The state of a married woman.
Cŏv'et, *v. t.* To desire unlawfully or inordinately.
Cŏv'et-oŭs, *a.* Avaricious; greedy for gain.
Cŏv'et-oŭs-ness, *n.* An eager desire of gain.
Cŏv'ey (141), *n.* A brood or small flock of birds.
Cow, *n.* Female of the bull. — *v. t.* To depress by frightening.
Cow'ard, *n.* One wanting courage; a poltroon; a dastard. — *a.* Timid; base; pusillanimous; dastardly.

sŏn, ôr, do, wolf, too, took; ûrn, rue, pull; ç, ċ, *soft*; e, ġ, *hard*; as; exist; ɳ *as* ng; this.

COWARDICE   96   CREDIT

Cow'ard-Ice, } *n.* Want of
Cow'ard-li-ness, } courage; mean timidity; pusillanimity; poltroonery.
Cow'ard-ly, *a.* Meanly timid. — *adv.* With mean timidity.
Cow'er, *v. i.* To sink or waver through fear.
Cow'-hērd, *n.* One who tends cows.
Cow'hīde, *n.* The hide of a cow, or leather made of it. — *v. t.* To beat with a cowhide.
Cowl, *n.* A monk's hood; a cover for a chimney.
Cow'lick, *n.* A tuft of hair turned wrongly over the forehead. [ense.
Cow'pŏx, *n.* The vaccine disease.
Cow'slip, } *n.* A kind of
Cow'g'-lip, } primrose.
Cŏx'cŏmb (-kōm), *n.* A fop.
Cox-cŏmb'ic-al (-kŏm'-), *a.* Foppish; conceited.
Cŏx'cŏmb-ry (-kŏm-), *n.* The manners of a coxcomb.
Coy, *a.* Shrinking from familiarity. — SYN. Modest; reserved; shy; bashful.
Coy'ly, *adv.* With reserve.
Coy'ness, *n.* Unwillingness to be familiar; shyness.
Cŏz'en (kŭz'n), *v. t.* To cheat.
Cŏz'en-age, *n.* Fraud; deceit; cheating.
Cŏz'en-er (kŭz'n-er), *n.* A cheater; a knave.
Cō'zy, *a.* Snug; comfortable.
Crăb, *n.* A shellfish having ten legs; a kind of wild sour apple.   Crab.
Crăb'bed (57), *a.* Peevish; cross; morose; difficult.
Crăb'bed-ly, *adv.* In a crabbed manner.
Crăb'bed-nĕss, *n.* Peevishness; difficulty.
Crăck, *n.* A sudden sharp noise; a fissure. — *v. t.* or *i.* To break into chinks.
Crăck'-brāined, *a.* Crazed.
Crăck'er, *n.* A hard biscuit; a kind of fire-work.
Crăck'le (krăk'l), *v. i.* To make sharp, sudden noises.
Crăck'ling, *n.* The noise of something that crackles
Crā'dle, *n.* A machine for rocking children; also one for cutting grain. — *v. t.* To lay or rock in a cradle; to cut and lay with a cradle.
Crăft, *n.* Manual art; trade; cunning; small vessels.
Crăft'i-ly, *adv.* With cunning.
Crăft'i-ness (135), *n.* Cunning; artifice; wiliness.
Crăfts'man (143), *n.* A mechanic; an artificer.
Crăft'y, *a.* Cunning; artful.
Crăg, *n.* A rough, steep rock.
Crăg'ged, } *a.* Rugged with
Crăg'gy, } broken rocks.
Crăg'ged-ness, } *n.* Fullness
Crăg'gi-ness, } of crags.
Crāke, *n.* A bird; — so called from its singular cry.
Crăm (139), *v. t.* or *i.* To stuff; to crowd; to fill to satiety.
Crăm'bo, *n.* A game at finding rhymes.
Crămp, *n.* A spasm of the muscles; an iron instrument to hold things together. — *v. t.* To confine; to hinder; to stop.
Crămp'-I'ron (-I'urn), *n.* An iron for holding things together.
Crăm-pōons', *n. pl.* Hooked pieces of iron for hoisting things
Crăn'ber-ry, *n.* A sour, red berry, growing in swamps.
Crāne, *n.* A migratory wading bird; a machine for raising heavy weights; a siphon.   Crane.
Crā'ni-ŏl'o-gy, *n.* A treatise on the cranium or skull.
† **Crā'ni-ŭm** (*pl.* **Crā'ni-ä**, 147), *n.* The skull.
Crănk, *n.* The end of an axis bent; a bend or winding: a verbal conceit. — *a.* Bold; liable to overset.
Crănk'le, *v.* To run in a winding course. — *n.* A bend or turn.
Crăn'nied, *a.* Full of crannies.
Crăn'ny, *n.* Crevice; crack; fissure.
Crāpe, *n.* A loosely woven stuff used in mourning, &c.
Crăsh, *v. i.* To make a noise, as of things falling. — *n.* A loud noise, as of things falling and breaking.
Crăss'a-ment, *n.* The thick part of the blood; clot.
Crăs'si-tūde (50), *n.* Grossness; coarseness; thickness.
Crāte, *n.* A wicker pannier for carthen ware.
Crā'ter, *n.* The mouth of a volcano.
Crāunch (krănch), *v. t.* To crush with the teeth; to chew.
Cra-văt', *n.* A neckcloth.
Crāve, *v. t.* To ask or desire earnestly; to beseech; to long for.
Crā'ven, *a.* Mean and cowardly. — *n.* A coward; a poltroon.
Craw, *n.* The crop of birds.
Craw'fish, or **Cray'fish,** *n.* A shell-fish, resembling the lobster.
Crawl, *v. i.* To creep; to move as a worm.
Cray'on, *n.* A pencil made of chalk; a drawing made with a crayon. — *v. t.* To sketch with a crayon.
Crāze', *v. t.* To impair the intellect; to make crazy.
Crā'zi-ness, *n.* State of being crazy or deranged.
Crā'zy, *a.* Deranged; insane; broken.
Crēak, *v. i.* To make a sharp, grating sound.
Crēak'ing, *n.* A sharp, harsh, continued noise.
Crēam, *n.* The oily part of milk; the best part of a thing. — *v. i.* To yield cream. — *v. t.* To skim; to take off, as cream. [rich.
Crēam'y, *a.* Full of cream;
Crēase, *n.* A mark left by folding. — *v. t.* To mark by folding.
Cre-āte, *v. t.* To bring into existence.
Cre-ā'tion, *n.* The act of creating; thing or things created; the universe.
Cre-ā'tive, *a.* Having power to create.
Cre-ā'tor, *n.* One who gives existence; a maker: God.
Crēat'ūre (50), *n.* A being or thing created; a man; a servile dependent.
Crē'dence, *n.* Belief; faith.
Cre-dĕn'tials, *n. pl.* That which gives credit; testimonials.
Crĕd'i-bĭl'i-ty, *n.* Just claim to belief.
Crĕd'i-ble, *a.* Worthy of credit; trustworthy.
Crĕd'i-bly, *adv.* In a credible manner.
Crĕd'it, *n.* Belief; trust; influence; reputation; esteem; amount due. — *v. t.* To be-

---

ā, ē, ī, ō, ū, y, *long*; ă, ĕ, ĭ, ŏ, ŭ, y, *short*; câre, cär, ȧsk, ạll, whạt; ẽre, vḙil, tẽrm; pïque, fïrm;

CREDITABLE 97 CROSS-EYED

lieve ; to trust ; to confide in ; to give faith to.
Cred'it-a-ble, *a.* Reputable.
Cred'it-a-bly, *adv.* Reputably ; without disgrace.
Cred'it-or, *n.* One to whom a debt is due.
Cre-du'li-ty, *n.* Easiness of belief; readiness to believe.
Cred'u-lous, *a.* Too apt to believe; easily imposed on.
Creed, *n.* [Lat. *credo*, I believe.] Belief; summary of articles of faith.
Creek, *n.* A small inlet, bay, or river.
Creek'y, *a.* Like, or containing, creeks.
Creel, *n.* An osier fishing basket.
Creep, *v. i.* [*imp.* CREPT, CREEPED.] To move as a worm or reptile ; to move slowly ; to crawl ; to fawn.
Creep'er, *n.* One who creeps ; a creeping plant.
Cre-ōle, *n.* Any native of the West Indies or tropical America, except a full-blooded Indian ; in Louisiana, a person of French descent.
Cre'o-sōte, *n.* An oily liquid having the smell of smoke.
Crep'i-tāte, *v. i.* To crackle in burning. [sound.
Crep'i-ta'tion, *n.* A crackling
Crept, *imp.* of *Creep.*
Cre-pus'cu-lar, *a.* Pertaining to, or like, twilight.
Cres'cent, } *a.* Increasing ;
Cres'cive, } growing.
Cres'cent, *n.* The increasing moon ; Turkish standard.
Cress (124), *n.* A plant.
Cres'set, *n.* A light set upon a beacon, or carried on a pole.
Crest, *n.* A plume of feathers ; tuft; comb ; pride.
Crest'ed, *a.* Wearing a crest.
Crest'-fallen (-fawln), *a.* Dejected ; cowed ; spiritless.
Cre-tā'ceous (-shus), *a.* [Lat. *creta*, chalk.] Of the nature of chalk ; chalky.
Crev'ice (140), *n.* A small crack ; a cranny.
Crew (krṳ), *n.* A ship's company.— *imp.* of *Crow.*
Crew'el (krṳ'el), *n.* A ball of yarn ; two-threaded worsted.
Crib, *n.* A manger ; rack ; stall ; a small inclosed bedstead for a child. — *v. t.* To cage or confine ; to pilfer.
Crib'bage, *n.* A game at cards.
Crib'ble, *n.* A corn-sieve.
Crick, *n.* A cramp; spasmodic affection, as of the neck.

Crick'et, *n.* A small insect; a sort of low stool ; a game.
Cried, *imp.* & *p. p.* of *Cry.*
Cri'er (135), *n.* One who cries ; one who makes proclamation.
Crime, *n.* A violation of law ; any outrage or great wrong. — SYN. Sin ; vice ; offense.
Crim'i-nal, *a.* Guilty of a crime. — *n.* A man guilty of a crime.
Crim'i-năl'i-ty, *n.* The quality of being criminal.
Crim'i-nal-ly, *adv.* With guilt.
Crim'i-nāte, *v. t.* To charge with crime ; to accuse.
Crim'i-nā'tion, *n.* Accusation.
Crim'i-na-to-ry, *a.* Relating to, or involving, crimination ; accusing.
Crimp, *a.* Crumbling easily ; brittle. — *v. t.* To catch ; to make crisp ; to form into little ridges.
Crim'ple, *v. t.* To lay in plaits ; to cause to shrink.
Crim'son (krim'zn), *n.* A deep red color. — *a.* Colored as crimson. — *v. t.* To tinge with a deep red. — *v. i.* To blush.
Cringe, *n.* A low bow ; mean servility. — *v. i.* To bow with servility ; to flatter meanly ; to fawn.
Crin'kle (kriŋk'l), *v. i.* To bend in turns or flexures. — *v. t.* To form with short turns. — *n.* One of several folds or flexures; a wrinkle.
Crip'ple, *n.* [From *creep.*] A lame person. — *v. t.* To make lame; to disable.
Cri'sis (147), *n.* A critical time or turn.
Crisp, *v. t.* To wrinkle or curl; to make brittle.
Crisp, } *a.* Brittle ; short ;
Crisp'y, } wrinkled ; curled ; brisk.
Crisp'ing-I'ron (-ī'urn), *n.* A curling-iron.
Crisp'ness, *n.* State of being crisp, curled, or brittle.
Cri-tē'ri-on, *n.* (*pl.* †Cri-tē'ri-ă, 45, 147.) A standard for judging.
Crit'ic, *n.* One skilled in judging ; a fault-finder.
Crit'ic-al, *a.* Relating to criticism ; nice ; captious ; indicating a crisis.
Crit'ic-al-ly, *adv.* In the manner of a critic; exactly.
Crit'i-çīşe (153), *v. t.* To judge and remark upon with exact-

ness. — *v. i.* To act as a critic.
Crit'i-çişm, *n.* Art or act of criticising ; critical examination or remark. [nation.
Cri-tique', *n.* Critical exami-
Crōak, *n.* Cry of a frog. — *v. i.* To utter a rough sound like that of a frog.
Crōak'er, *n.* One who croaks.
Crŏck, *n.* A pot ; black matter from combustion. — *v. t.* To blacken with soot or the coloring matter of cloth.
Crŏck'er-y, *n.* All kinds of coarse earthen ware.
Croc'o-dīle, *n.* An amphibious animal of the lizard kind.
Cro'cus, *n.* A plant and its flower.
Crŏft, *n.* A small inclosed field.
Crōne, *n.* An old woman.
Crō'ny, *n.* An intimate acquaintance ; a familiar friend.
Crŏok, *n.* A bend ; a shepherd's staff. — *v. t.* or *i.* [*imp.* & *p. p.* CROOKED (krŏokt).] To bend ; to turn from a straight line.
Crŏok'ed (57), *p. a.* Bent; curving ; perverse.
Crŏok'ed-ness, *n.* State of being crooked ; perverseness.
Crŏp, *n.* The harvest ; fruits or vegetables gathered ; the stomach of a bird. — *v. t.* To cut off ; to reap.
Cro'şier (kro'zhur), *n.* A bishop's pastoral staff.
Cross (19, 124), *n.* A straight body crossing another ; gibbet; adversity ; trial ; a mixing of breeds or stock. — *a.* Athwart ; peevish ; adverse. — *v. t.* To lay athwart; to cancel ; to obstruct.
Cross'-bär, *n.* A transverse bar.
Cross'-bill, *n.* A defendant's bill in chancery.
Cross'-bōw, *n.* A bow for shooting arrows.
Cross'-breed, *n.* A breed produced from parents of different breeds.
Cross-ex-ăm'ĭne, *v. t.* To examine by the opposite party.
Cross'-ēyed (-id), *a.* Having eyes looking in directions that cross each other.

cŏn, ôr, dọ, wǫlf, tọo, tŏok ; ûrn, rṳe, pṳll ; ç, ģ, *soft* ; ¢, ḡ, *hard*; aẓ ; eẋist ; n as ng ; this.
5

Cross'-grained, *a.* Having the grain or fibers crossed; contrary; vexatious.

Cross'ing, *n.* Place of passing.

Cross'let, *n.* A small cross.

Cross'ly, *adv.* In a cross manner; peevishly.

Cross'ness, *n.* Peevishness.

Cross'-pur'pose (-pûr'pus), *n.* A contrary purpose; inconsistency.

Cross'-ques'tion (-kwĕs'-), *v. t.* To cross-examine.

Cross'-road,) *n.* A way or
Cross'-way,) road that crosses another.

Cross'wise, *adv.* In form of a cross.

Crotch, *n.* The forking of a tree.

Crotch'et, *n.* A note equal to half a minim; a whim; (*pl.*) hooks, [ ], inclosing words in printing; brackets.

Crouch, *v. i.* To stoop low; to bend servilely; to cringe.

Croup (krōōp), *n.* A disease in the throat; buttocks of a quadruped.

Crow, *n.* A black fowl; the cock's voice; an iron lever with a claw at one end. — *v. t.* [*imp.* CREW or CROWED.] To utter the cry of a cock. — *v. i.* To boast; to exult.

Crow'bar, *n.* A heavy iron bar, used as a lever.

Crowd, *n.* A throng; a multitude; a violin. — *v. t.* To press close; to urge; to squeeze. — *v. i.* To press together.

Crow'-foot, *n.* A plant of many species.

Crown, *n.* Top of the head; a royal ornament; royalty; a garden; a coin; completion; accomplishment. — *v. t.* To invest with a crown; to dignify; to complete.

Crown'-glass, *n.* A fine kind of window-glass.

Crown'-im-pē'ri-al, *n.* A kind of lily.

Crow's'-foot, *n.* Wrinkle at the outer corner of the eye.

Cru'cial (krụ'shal), *a.* Transverse; intersecting; severe.

Cru'ci-āte (krụ'shī-), *v. t.* To torture.

Cru'ci-ble, *n.* A chemical vessel.

Cru-cif'er-oŭs, *a.* Bearing a cross.

Crucibles.

Cru'ci-fi-er, *n.* One who crucifies.

Cru'ci-fĭx, *n.* [Lat. *crux, crucis*, cross, and *figere*, to fix.] A cross with an image of Christ on it.

Cru'ci-fĭx'ion, *n.* A nailing to a cross.

Cru'ci-fōrm, *a.* Being in the form of a cross.

Cru'ci-fy, *v. t.* To fasten and put to death on a cross.

Crude, *a.* Being in a raw or rough state. — SYN. Raw; unfinished; unripe; immature.

Crude'ly, *adv.* With rawness.

Crude'ness, *n.* Rawness; immaturity.

Cru'di-ty, *n.* Undigested matter; immaturity.

Cru'el, *a.* Inhuman; void of pity; unfeeling.

Cru'el-ly, *adv.* In a barbarous manner; inhumanly.

Cru'el-ty, *n.* Inhumanity; savage disposition; a barbarous deed.

Cru'et, *n.* A vial for sauces.

Cruise, *v. i.* To rove back and forth on the sea. — *n.* A cruising voyage.

Cruis'er, *n.* A person or a vessel that cruises.

Crumb (krŭm), *n.* A fragment or piece, as of bread. — *v. t.* To break into crumbs or small pieces.

Crum'ble, *v. t.* To break into small pieces. — *v. i.* To fall to decay; to perish. [soft.

Crŭm'my, *a.* Full of crumbs;

Crŭm'pet, *n.* A kind of soft bread-cake.

Crŭm'ple, *v. t.* To draw into wrinkles. — *v. i.* To shrink irregularly.

Crŭp'per (krōōp'er), *n.* A leather to hold a saddle back; buttocks of a horse. — *v. t.* To put a crupper on.

Cru'ral (29), *a.* Pertaining to the leg.

Cru-sāde', *n.* A military expedition to recover the Holy Land; any religious or fanatical expedition.

Cru-sād'er, *n.* One employed in a crusade. [vial.

Cruse, *n.* A small cup or

Cru'set, *n.* A goldsmith's crucible or melting-pot.

Crush, *v. t.* To bruise or break by pressure; to subdue; to ruin. — *n.* A violent collision and compression.

Crŭst, *n.* A hard covering. — *v. t.* To cover with a hard case. — *v. i.* To gather a crust.

Crus-tā'cean, *n.* A shell-fish with a crust-like shell, as the lobster.

Crus-tā'ceoŭs, *a.* Having jointed crust-like shells, as the lobster.

Crŭst'i-ly, *adv.* Peevishly.

Crŭst'i-ness, *n.* Quality of being crusty; moroseness.

Crŭst'y, *a.* Like crust; snappish; peevish; surly.

Crŭtch, *n.* A staff with a cross-piece at the head for cripples. — *v. t.* To support on crutches.

Cry, *v. t.* or *i.* To call; to exclaim; to proclaim; to weep. — *n.* A bawling; outcry; yell; a weeping.

Crypt, *n.* [Gr. *krupte*, from *kruptein*, to hide.] A cell or vault under a church.

Cryp-tŏg'ra-phy, *n.* Art of writing in secret characters.

Cryp-tŏl'o-gy, *n.* Secret or enigmatical language.

Crys'tal, *n.* [Gr. *krustallos*, ice.] A regular solid mineral body; fine glass; a watchglass.

Crys'tal,) *a.* Consisting
Crys'tal-line,) of crystal.

Crys'tal-li-zā'tion, *n.* The process of forming crystals.

Crys'tal-līze (129), *v. t.* or *i.* To form into crystals.

Crys'tal-lŏg'ra-phy, *n.* The science of crystallization.

Cub, *n.* The young of many beasts, especially of the dog.

Cu'ba-ture (50), *n.* The finding the exact cubic contents of a body.

Cūbe (26), *n.* A regular solid body with six equal sides; the third power of a root.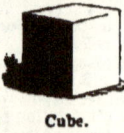

Cube.

Cū'beb, *n.* A small, spicy, tropical berry.

Cū'bic, *a.* Having the form of a cube.

Cū'bi-fōrm, *a.* Being in the form of a cube.

Cū'bit, *n.* The fore arm; measure of a man's arm from the elbow to the wrist.

Cū'bit-al, *a.* Containing, or belonging to, a cubit.

Cŭck'old, *n.* A man whose wife is false to him.

Cŭck'ōō, *n.* A bird; — so called from its note.

Cū'cul-late, or **Cu-cŭl'late,** *a.* Hooded; like a hood.

CUCUMBER 99 CURSIVE

Cū'cum-ber, *n.* A certain garden plant, and its fruit.
Cū'cur-bit, *n.* A chemical vessel like a gourd.
Cŭd, *n.* A portion of food or of tobacco chewed. [saug.
Cŭd'dle, *v. i.* To lie close or
Cŭd'dy, *n.* A small cabin in a lighter or boat.
Cŭd'ĝel (130), *n.* A thick heavy stick. —*v. t.* To beat with a heavy stick.
Cūe (140), *n.* [Fr. *queue*, tail, fr. Lat. *cauda*.] End or tail of a thing; a hint; an intimation; a rod used in playing billiards.
Cŭff (123), *n.* A blow; part of a sleeve. —*v. t.* To strike with the open hand.
Cuī'rǎss' (kwē-rǎs' *or* kwô'rąs), *n.* A breastplate.
Cuī'ras-siēr' (kwō'-), *n.* A soldier armed with a cuirass.
Cū'lī-na-ry, *a.* Belonging to the kitchen or to cookery.
Cŭll (123), *v. t.* To select or pick out. [strainer.
Cŭl'len-der, *n.* A kind of
Cŭl'ler, *n.* One who culls.
Cŭl'ly, *n.* The dupe of a woman. —*v. t.* To cheat; to deceive.
Cŭlm, *n.* The stem of grasses; anthracite coal.
Cŭl'mi-nāte, *v. i.* To reach the highest point.
Cŭl/mi-nā'tion, *n.* Highest point of altitude. [able.
Cŭl'pa-ble, *a.* Faulty; blamable.
Cŭl'pa-bĭl'i-ty, *n.* Blamableness; faultiness; guilt.
Cŭl'pa-bly, *adv.* With blame.
Cŭl'prit, *n.* One who is accused or convicted of crime; a criminal.
Cŭl'ti-va-ble, *a.* Capable of being cultivated.
Cŭl'ti-vāte, *v. t.* To till; to foster; to ameliorate; to raise by tilling.
Cŭl'ti-vā'ted, *p. a.* Improved or raised by culture.
Cŭl'ti-vā'tion, *n.* Improvement by tillage, or by study.
Cŭl'ti-vā'tor, *n.* One who cultivates; an implement for loosening the surface of the ground. Cultivator.
Cŭlt'ūre (50), *n.* Act of cultivating; improvement of mind or manners.—*v. t.* To cultivate.
Cŭl'ver-in, *n.* A long and slender species of ordnance.
Cŭl'vert, *n.* An arched drain.

Cŭm'ber, *v. t.* To clog; to burden; to load; to embarrass.
Cŭm'ber-sŏme, *a.* Burdensome. [clog.
Cŭm'brançe, *n.* Burden;
Cŭm'broŭs, *a.* Troublesome; embarrassing; oppressive; burdensome.
Cŭm'in, *n.* A plant having aromatic seeds.
Cu-mū'lāte, *v. t.* To heap up.
Cū'mu-lā'tion, *n.* Act of heaping together.
Cū'mu-la-tĭve, *a.* Augmenting by addition. [wedge.
Cū'ne-al, *a.* Shaped like a
Cū'ne-āte, } *a.* Wedge-
Cū'ne-āt/ed, } shaped; cuneiform. [shaped.
Cu-nē'i-fôrm, *a.* Wedge
Cŭn'ning, *a.* Artful; crafty; sly; skillful. —*n.* Art; skill; craft; artifice.
Cŭn'ning-ly, *adv.* In a cunning manner; artfully.
Cŭn'ning-ness, *n.* Quality of being cunning; craft.
Cŭp, *n.* A small drinking vessel, or any thing resembling it; (*pl.*) revelry. —*v. t.* To bleed by scarification.
Cŭp'-bear/er, *n.* One who fills and hands the cups at an entertainment.
Cŭp'board (kŭb'urd), *n.* A small closet with shelves for cups, &c.
Cū'pel, *n.* A little cup used in refining metals.
Cū'pel-lā'tion, *n.* Process of refining metals by a cupel.
Cu-pĭd'i-ty, *n.* Inordinate desire, particularly of wealth.
Cū'po-là (140), *n.* [From Lat. *cupa*, a tub, cask.] A dome; an arched roof.
Cŭp'ping, *n.* A mode of bleeding. [copper.
Cŭp'pel, *n.* A little cup used
Cū'pre-oŭs, *a.* Of, or like,
Cūr, *n.* A worthless or degenerate dog; a mean or snappish fellow. [ing cured.
Cūr'a-ble, *a.* Capable of being
Cū'ra-çōa' (-sō'), *n.* A cordial flavored with orange peel and spices.
Cū'ra-çy, *n.* Office of a curate.
Cū'rate, *n.* An assistant to a rector or vicar. [cure.
Cū'ra-tĭve, *a.* Tending to
Cu-rā'tor, *n.* A guardian; a trustee.
Cŭrb, *v. t.* To keep in subjection. — SYN. To check; restrain; bridle; control. — *n.* Part of a bridle; box round a well; restraint.

Cŭrb'-stōne, *n.* A stone placed edgewise against earth or stone work to prevent its giving way.
Cŭrd, *n.* Coagulated part of milk. —*v. t.* To coagulate or thicken.
Cŭr'dle, *v. t.* or *i.* To coagulate; to thicken.
Cŭrd'y, *a.* Like curd; coagulated.
Cūre (84), *n.* Remedy; a healing; care of souls; office of a curate.—*v. t.* To restore to health; to heal; to salt and dry.
Cūre'less, *a.* Incurable.
Cūr'er, *n.* One who cures.
Cŭr'few, *n.* An evening bell
Cū'ri-ŏs'i-ty, *n.* Great inquisitiveness; a rarity; a sight.
Cū'ri-oŭs, *a.* Inquisitive; nice; singular.
Cū'ri-oŭs-ly, *adv.* Inquisitively; neatly; artfully.
Cŭrl, *n.* A ringlet of hair. —*v. t.* or *i.* To form or bend into ringlets.
Cŭr'lew, *n.* An aquatic wading bird.
Cŭrl'i-ness, *n.* State or quality of being curly.
Cŭrl'y, *a.* Having curls.
Cur-mŭd'ĝeon (-jun), *n.* A surly miser; a churl.
Cŭr'rant, *n.* [From *Corinth*, in Greece.] A shrub and its fruit.
Cŭr'ren-çy, *n.* Circulation; money; paper passing for money.
Cŭr'rent, *a.* Circulating; common; generally received; now passing.—*n.* A stream; general course.
Cŭr'rent-ly, *adv.* With general reception; fashionably.
Cŭr'ri-cle, *n.* A chaise or two wheels for two horses.
Cŭr'ri-er, *n.* A dresser of tanned leather.
Cŭr'rish, *a.* Like a cross dog; snappish; quarrelsome.
Cŭr'ry, *v. t.* To dress, as leather; to rub and clean, as horses.
Cŭr'ry-cŏmb (-kōm), *n.* A comb to clean horses.
Cŭrse, *v. t.* To wish evil to; to execrate.— *v. i.* To use oaths. — *n.* A wish of evil; execration; malediction.
Cŭrsed (kŭrst), *p. p.* Execrated.
Cŭrs'ed (57), *a.* Deserving a curse; vexatious; hateful.
Cŭr'sĭve, *a.* Running; flowing; hasty.

sŏn, ôr, dọ, wọlf, tōo, tŏok; ûrn, rṳe, pụll; ç, ġ, *soft*; c, ḡ, *hard*; aş; eẋist; ụ *as* ng; thįs.

Cŭr'so-ri-ly (135), *adv.* In a cursory manner; hastily.
Cŭr'so-ry, *a.* Hasty; hurried; rapid; slight. [crusty.
Cŭrt, *a.* Short; abrupt:
Cur-tāil', *v. t.* To cut short; to abridge; to cut off.
Cŭr'tain, *n.* A hanging cloth for a bed or window. — *v. t.* To incluse or furnish with curtains.
Cŭr'rule, *a.* Belonging to a chariot; — said of a kind of chair placed in a chariot, and in which the Roman magistrates sat when they went to council.
Cŭrv'a-ted, *a.* Curved; bent.
Cur-vā'tion, *n.* Act of curving or bending.
Cŭrv'a-tūre, *n.* A curve.
Cŭrve, *n.* Bending; inflected. — *n.* Any thing bent. — *v. t.* To inflect; to bend.
Cŭr'vet, *n.* A particular leap of a horse. — *v. i.* To make a curvet; to leap and frisk.
Cŭrv'i-lĭn'e-al, } *a.* Having
Cŭrv'i-lĭn-e-ar, } a curve line. [curvature.
Cŭrv'i-ty, *n.* A bent state;
Cŭsh'at, *n.* The ringdove.
Cŭsh'ion (kŏŏsh'un), *n.* A pillow for a seat. — *v. t.* To furnish with cushions.
Cŭsp, *n.* Point of the new moon; projecting point in arches, &c. [point.
Cŭsp'i-dal, *a.* Ending in a
Cŭsp'i-date, } *a.* Ending in a
Cŭsp'i-dā'ted, } point; acute.
Cŭs'tard, *n.* A composition of milk, eggs, sugar, &c.
Cus-tō'di-al, *a.* Relating to custody.
Cus-tō'di-an, *n.* One who has the care of a public building.
Cŭs'to-dy, *n.* A keeping or guarding; imprisonment.
Cŭs'tom, *n.* Habitual practice; usage; way of acting;

(*pl.*) duties on imported or exported goods. [ually.
Cŭs'tom-a-ri-ly, *adv.* Habit-
Cŭs'tom-a-ry, *a.* Conformable to custom; conventional.
Cŭs'tom-er, *n.* An accustomed buyer at a shop.
Cŭs'tom-house, *n.* The place where customs or duties are paid.
Cŭt, *v. t.* or *i.* [*imp. & p. p.* CUT.] To make an incision in; to divide; to hew; to carve; to chop. — *n.* A cleft or gash; a slice; an engraved block, or an impression from it. [the skin.
Cu-tā'ne-oŭs, *n.* Relating to
Cŭ'ti-cle, *n.* Outermost skin of the body; scarf-skin.
Cu-tĭc'u-lar, *a.* Pertaining to the cuticle. [sword.
Cŭt'lass, *n.* A broad curving
Cŭt'ler, *n.* A maker of knives, and the like.
Cŭt'ler-y, *n.* Articles made by cutlers, as knives, scissors, &c. [meat for broiling.
Cŭt'let, *n.* A small piece of
Cŭt'pûrse, *n.* One who cuts purses to steal their contents: a pickpocket.
Cŭt'ter, *n.* One who cuts; a swift sailing vessel.
Cŭt'-thrōat, *n.* A murderer; an assassin.
Cŭt'ting, *a.* Severe; pungent. — *n.* A piece cut off.
Cŭt'tle-fĭsh, *n.* A molluscous animal that fastens itself to other bodies. *Cuttle-fish.*

Cŭt'-wa'ter, *n.* The fore part of a ship's prow.
Cȳ'cle, *n.* A circle or orbit; a round of time.
Cȳc'lic, } *a.* Pertaining to
Cȳ'clic-al, } a cycle.
Cȳ'cloid, *n.* A geometrical curve.
Cȳ'clo-pē'an, } *a.* Pertaining
Cȳ-clōp'ic, } to the Cyclops; vast; massive.
Cȳ'clo-pæ'di-à } (140), *n.* A
Cȳ'clo-pē'di-à } body or circle of sciences; a dictionary of arts and sciences.
Cȳg'net, *n.* A young swan.
Cȳl'in-der, *n.* A long circular body of uniform diameter. *Cylinder.*
Cȳ-lĭn'dri-cal, *a.* Of the nature of a cylinder.
Cȳm'bal, *n.* An instrument of music.
Cȳn'ic, } *a.* Sur-
Cȳn'ic-al, } ly; snarling; satirical.
Cȳn'ic, *n.* A morose man or philosopher.
Cȳn'o-sure, or Cȳ'-no-sure (-shur, 50), *n.* The constellation of the Lesser Bear, containing the north or polar star; hence, a center of attraction. *Cymbals.*
Cȳ'press, *n.* An evergreen tree, anciently used at funerals and to adorn tombs, and hence an emblem of mourning.
Cȳst, *n.* A bag in animal bodies, inclosing matter.
Czär (zär), *n.* [From *Cæsar.*] A king; a chief; a title given to the emperor of Russia.
Cza-rī'nå (za-ree'nä), *n.* A title of the empress of Russia.
Czär'o-witz (zar'o-wĭts), *n.* The title of the eldest son of the Czar of Russia.

D.

DĂB (120), *v. t.* To hit gently with the hand or with something soft or moist. — *n.* A blow with something soft; a small lump of any thing soft; an expert.
Dăb'ble, *v. i.* To play in water. — *v. t.* To wet by little dips or strokes: to meddle.
Dăb'bler, *n.* One who dabbles.
Dăb'ster, *n.* One who is expert; an adviser.
Dāce, *n.* A small river fish.
Dăc'tyl, *n.* A poetical foot of

one long and two short syllables, or one accented and two unaccented syllables.
Dăd, } *n.* A child's term
Dăd'dy, } for father.
Dăf'fo-dĭl, *n.* A plant with yellow flowers.

Daft (5), *a.* Insane; foolish.
Dag, *n.* A loose end, as of a lock of wool.
Dag'ger, *n.* A short sword; a reference mark [†].
Dag'gle, *v. i.* To trail in the dirt; to draggle.
Da-guerre'o-type (-gĕr'o-), *n.* [From *Daguerre*, the discoverer.] A photographic picture on a plate of silvered copper.
Dahl'ia (dāl'yȧ *or* dăl'yȧ), *n.* [From *Dahl*, a Swedish botanist.] A plant bearing beautiful flowers.
Dai'ly (136), *a.* Being or happening every day. — *adv.* Every day; day by day.
Dain'ti-ly (135), *adv.* Nicely; delicately; fastidiously.
Dain'ti-ness, *n.* Quality of being dainty.
Dain'ty, *a.* Nice; fastidious; delicious. — *n.* A nice bit; a delicacy.
Dai'ry (86), *n.* The place where milk is kept, and made into butter or cheese.
Dai'ry-maid, *n.* A woman who attends to a dairy.
Dai'sy, *n.* A well-known plant.
Dale, *n.* A low place between hills; a vale.
Dal'li-ance (135), *n.* Act of fondness; mutual embrace.
Dal'li-er, *n.* One who dallies.
Dal'ly, *v. i.* To delay; to linger; to trifle or sport with; to fondle.
Dam, *n.* The mother of brutes; a bank to confine water. — *v. t.* To confine or shut in by dams, as water.
Dam'age, *n.* Injury; hurt; harm; loss; (*pl.*) compensation for an injury actually sustained. — *v. t.* To injure; to hurt; to impair.
Dam'age-a-ble (133), *a.* Liable to receive damage.
Dam'ask, *n.* [From *Damascus.*] A silk woven with flowers or figures. — *v. t.* To decorate with ornamental figures, as silk, steel, &c. (ask.
Dam'ask-een', *v. t.* To damask.
Dame, *n.* A lady; a matron.
Damn (dăm, 78), *v. t.* To condemn; to sentence to eternal punishment.
Dam'na-ble, *a.* Deserving damnation; odious.
Dam'na-bly, *adv.* So as to incur or deserve damnation.
Dam-na'tion, *n.* Sentence to everlasting punishment.

Dam'na-to-ry, *a.* Tending to condemn; condemnatory.
Damned (damd; *in serious discourse*, dăm'ned), *p. a.* Sentenced to punishment in a future state; hateful; abominable.
Damp, *a.* Moist; humid; watery. — *n.* Moist air; moisture; humidity. — *v. t.* To wet; to moisten; to dispirit.
Damp'er, *n.* One who, or that which, damps; a valve to stop air.
Damp'ish, *a.* Rather damp; moist; humid.
Damp'ness, *n.* Moisture; humidity.
Dam'sel, *n.* A young maiden.
Dam'son (dăm'zn), *n.* A small black plum.
Dance, *v. i.* To move to music with varied motions of the feet. — *v. t.* To cause to dance. — *n.* A stepping or moving to the sound of music.
Dan'cer, *n.* One who dances.
Dan'de-li'on, *n.* A well-known plant with yellow flowers. [low.
Dan'di-prat, *n.* A little fellow.
Dan'dle, *v. t.* To shake on the knee; to fondle.
Dan'dler, *n.* One who dandles.
Dan'druff, *n.* Scurf on the head.
Dan'dy, *n.* A fop; a coxcomb.
Dan'dy-ism, *n.* Manners and character of a dandy.
Dane, *n.* A native of Denmark.
Dan'ger (79), *n.* Exposure to injury; peril; hazard.
Dan'ger-ous, *a.* Full of danger.
Dan'ger-ous-ly, *adv.* With danger or hazard.
Dan'gle, *v. i.* To hang loose and waving; to follow closely.
Dan'gler, *n.* One who hangs about women. [damp.
Dank, *a.* Moist; humid;
Dap'per, *a.* Little and active.
Dap'ple, *a.* Of various colors; spotted. — *v. t.* To variegate with spots.
Dap'pled, *a.* Variegated with spots.
Dare, *v. i.* [*imp. & p. p.* DURST.] To have courage; to venture. — *v. t.* To challenge; to defy; to venture.
Dar'ing, *a.* Having great courage. — SYN. Fearless; intrepid; defiant; brave.
Dar'ing-ly, *adv.* Fearlessly.
Dark, *a.* Wanting light; ob-

scure; opaque. — *n.* Darkness; gloom; obscurity.
Dark'en, *v. t.* To make dark. — *v. i.* To grow dark.
Dark'ish, *a.* Rather dark; dusky.
Dark'ly, *adv.* Obscurely; blindly; with imperfect light.
Dark'ness, *n.* Want of light; gloom; obscurity.
Dark'some, *a.* Void of light; gloomy; dim; obscure.
Dar'ling, *a.* Dearly beloved. — *n.* One much beloved.
Darn, *v. t.* To mend holes in by drawing threads across the rents.
Dar'nel, *n.* A kind of grass, including rye-grass.
Dart, *n.* A pointed missile weapon. — *v. t.* To throw; to hurl; to emit. — *v. i.* To fly, as a dart; to issue suddenly.
Dash, *v. t.* To throw violently. — *v. i.* To rush or strike violently. — *n.* Collision; sudden onset; flourish; parade; slight infusion; a mark [—], used in writing and printing.
Das'tard, *n.* One who meanly shrinks from danger. — SYN. Coward; poltroon.
Das'tard-ly, *a.* Meanly timid.
Da'tȧ, *n. pl.* Propositions given and admitted; premises.
Date, *n.* [Lat. *datus*, given.] The time of an event; the fruit of a palm-tree. — *v. t.* To note the time of.
Date'less, *a.* Having no date. [Date-tree.
Da'tive, *n.* The third of the Greek and Latin cases.
Daub (130), *v. t.* To smear; to paint coarsely. — *n.* A coarse painting.
Daub'er, *n.* One who daubs.
Daub'er-y, *n.* Coarse painting.
Daub'y, *a.* Sticky; ropy; glutinous; viscous.
Daugh'ter (daw'ter) *n.* A female child.
Daugh'ter-ly (daw-), *adv.* Becoming a daughter.
Daunt, *v. t.* To check by fear of danger. — SYN. To intimidate; dishearten; dismay.
Daunt'less, *a.* Fearless; intrepid; bold. [lessly.
Daunt'less-ly, *adv.* Fearlessly.
Daunt'less-ness, *n.* Fearlessness.

són, ôr, dọ, wọlf, tōō, tŏŏk; ûrn, rụe, pụll; ç, ġ, *soft*; ɇ, g̃, *hard*; aẓ; eẓist; ɳ *as* ng; this.

Dau'phin, n. Eldest son of the king of France.

Dăv'it, or Dā'vit, n. Projecting pieces of iron in a ship to suspend a boat from.

Daw'dle, v. t. To waste time by trifling.

Dawn, v. i. To begin to grow light in the morning; to begin to open and give promise. — n. Break of day; beginning; first rise or appearance.

Day, n. Time from sunrise to sunset; the 24 hours from midnight to midnight; victory.

Day'-book, n. A tradesman's journal of accounts.

Day'-break, n. First appearance of day; dawn.

Day'light (-līt), n. Light of day. [pire or arbiter.

Days'man (143), n. An umpire.

Day'-spring, n. The dawn.

Day'-star, n. The morning star. [wilder.

Daze, v. t. To dazzle; to bewilder.

Daz'zle, v. t. To overpower with light or splendor.

Dea'con (dē'kn), n. A subordinate church officer.

Dea'con-ry, } n. The office
Dea'con'ship, } of a deacon.

Dead, a. Destitute of life; lifeless; dull; still. — n. Stillness; gloom; silence; (pl.) those who are dead.

Dead'en (dĕd'n), v. t. To make dead, lifeless, or spiritless.

Dead'-lift, n. A lift with unaided strength.

Dead'-light (-līt), n. A strong shutter for a cabin window, with a glass in the center.

Dead'ly, a. Fatal; mortal; implacable. — adv. Mortally; fatally.

Dead'ness, n. Want of life or spirit; vapidness.

Deaf (or deef), a. Wanting the sense of hearing.

Deaf'en (or dĕf'n), v. t. To make deaf; to stun.

Deaf'-mute (or dĕf'-mūt), n. One both deaf and dumb.

Deaf'ness (or dĕf'-), n. Want of the ability to hear.

Deal, n. A part; quantity; distribution, as of cards; a pine or fir board or plank. — v. t. [imp. & p.p. DEALT.] To distribute; to divide. — v. i. To traffic; to trade.

Deal'er, n. One who deals; a trader.

Dean, n. An ecclesiastical dignitary subordinate to a bishop.

Dean'er-y, n. Office or mansion of a dean.

Dear, a. Beloved; costly; of high value; precious. — n. A person beloved.

Dear'ly, adv. At a high price; with great fondness.

Dear'ness, n. High price; nearness of affection; fondness.

Dearth (12), n. Great scarcity; want; barrenness.

Death, n. Extinction of life; mortality. [person.

Death'-bed, n. Bed of a d.ing

Death'less, a. Immortal; undying.

Death'-war'rant, n. A warrant for an execution.

De-bā'cle, n. A violent rush of waters, having great transporting power.

De-bär' (129), v. t. To hinder; to exclude. [to land.

De-bärk', v. t. To disembark;

De-bāse', v. t. To degrade; to lower; to adulterate; to vitiate. [bases.

De-bās'er, n. One who debases.

De-bāse'ment, n. Act of debasing; degradation.

De-bāt'a-ble, a. Disputable.

De-bāte', v. To dispute; to discuss; to controvert. — n. dispute; public discussion.

De-bāt'er, n. One who debates.

De-bauch', n. Excess in eating and drinking; intemperance. — v. t. To corrupt; to vitiate.

Dĕb'au-chee' (-o-shee'), n. A drunkard; a rake.

De-bauch'er, n. One who debauches.

De-bauch'er-y, n. Intemperance; habitual lewdness.

De-bent'ure (60), n. A custom-house certificate entitling to a drawback; bonds, &c., for money loans.

De-bil'i-tāte, v. t. To weaken; to enfeeble. [weakness.

De-bil'i-ty, n. Feebleness;

Dĕb'it, n. Debt; debtor side of an account-book. — v. t. To charge with debt.

Dĕb'o-nâir', a. Courteous; affable.

De-bouch' (-bōosh'), v. i. To issue or march out of a confined place, as troops.

Dē-bris' (da-bree'), n. Ruins; fragments of rocks piled up.

Debt (dĕt), n. What is due.

Debt'or (dĕt'or), n. One who owes another.

Debut (dā-bū' or dā-bṳ'), n. A first appearance, as of an actor. [ten.

Dĕc'ade, n. The number of Dē-cā'dence, } n. State of
Dē-cā'den-cy, } decay.

Dĕc'a-gŏn, n. A plane figure of ten sides and ten angles.

Dĕc'a-logue (-lŏg), n. The ten commandments.

De-cămp', v. i. To depart from a camp; to march off.

De-cămp'ment, n. Act of decamping or marching off.

Dĕc'a-nal, a. Pertaining to a deanery.

Dec-ăn'gu-lar, n. Having ten angles. [gently.

De-cănt', v. t. To pour off

Dē'can-tā'tion, n. Act of decanting.

De-cănt'er, n. A glass vessel for liquor.

De-căp'i-tāte, v. t. To behead. [beheading.

De-căp'i-tā'tion, n. Act of

De-cāy', n. [Lat. de, from, and cadere, to fall.] Gradual failure of health, strength, soundness, &c.; decline. — v. t. To decline; to fail.

De-cēase', n. Departure from life; death. — v. i. To depart from life; to die.

De-cēased' (-sēest'), a. Departed from life; dead.

De-cĕit', n. Device intended to deceive. — SYN. Duplicity; artifice; fraud.

De-cĕit'ful, a. Full of deceit or guile.

De-cĕit'ful-ly, adv. In a deceitful manner; fraudulently.

De-cĕit'ful-ness, n. Disposition to deceive.

De-cĕiv'a-ble, a. Liable to be deceived.

De-cĕive', v. t. To lead into error; to impose upon; to delude; to beguile.

De-cĕiv'er, n. One who deceives or misleads; an impostor.

De-cĕm'ber, n. The twelfth or last month of the year.

De-cĕm'vir, n. (pl. De-cĕm'-virs, or † De-cĕm'vi-rī). One

of 10 magistrates who had absolute authority in ancient Rome.

De-çĕm′vi-ral, *a.* Relating to the decemvirs.

De-çĕm′vi-rate (42), *n.* Office of decemvirs.

Dē′çen-çy, *n.* Fitness; propriety; modesty.

De-çĕn′na-ry, *n.* A period of ten years.

De-çĕn′ni-al, *a.* Continuing ten years; happening every ten years.

Dē′çent, *a.* Suitable or becoming. — SYN. Proper; seemly; fit.

Dē′çent-ly, *adv.* Fitly; properly; modestly.

De-çĕp′tion, *n.* Act of deceiving; cheat; fraud; deceit.

De-çĕp′tive, *a.* Tending to deceive; deceitful; false.

De-çīd′a-ble (133), *a.* Capable of being decided.

De-çīde′, *v. t.* or *i.* To determine; to finish; to settle to form a definite opinion.

De-çīd′ed, *a.* Determined; resolute; clear.

De-çīd′ed-ly, *adv.* With determination; fixedly.

De-çīd′u-oŭs, *a.* Falling off every season; not perennial.

Dĕç′i-mal, *a.* Proceeding by tens; tenth. — *n.* A fraction or other number expressed in the scale of tens.

Dĕç′i-mal-ly, *adv.* By decimals.

Dĕç′i-māte, *v. t.* To take one in every ten; to destroy every tenth man of.

Dĕç′i-mā′tion, *n.* The taking of every tenth.

De-çī′pher, *v. t.* To explain; to unravel; to unfold.

De-çī′pher-er, *n.* One who deciphers or unravels.

De-çĭs′ion (-sĭzh′un), *n.* Determination; conclusion; firmness.

De-çī′sive, *a.* Final; conclusive. [sively.

De-çī′sive-ly, *adv.* Conclu-

De-çī′so-ry, *a.* Able to decide.

Dĕck, *v. t.* To dress; to array; to adorn; to set off or embellish. — *n.* The floor of a ship.

De-clāim′ (130), *v. i.* To speak an oration; to harangue.

De-clāim′er, *n.* One who declaims.

Dĕc′la-mā′tion, *n.* A set speech or harangue.

De-clăm′a-to-ry, *a.* Being in the style of declamation.

Dĕc′la-rā′tion, *n.* Affirmation; assertion; announcement.

De-clăr′a-tĭve, } *a.* Making
De-clăr′a-to-ry, } declaration or explanation; assertive.

De-clāre′, *v. t.* or *i.* To make known publicly; to proclaim, to affirm; to assert.

De-clĕn′sion, *n.* Act of declining; decay; tendency to fail; variation of nouns.

De-clīn′a-ble, *a.* Capable of being grammatically varied.

Dĕc′li-nā′tion, *n.* Act of declining; descent; angular distance of any object from the celestial equator.

De-clīne′, *v. i.* To bend over; to fall; to decay. — *v. t.* To bend downward; to shun; to refuse; to inflict. — *n.* Tending to a worse state; decay; diminution.

De-clĭv′i-ty, *n.* Inclination downward; gradual descent.

De-eŏct′, *v. t.* To prepare by boiling; to digest.

De-eŏc′tion, *n.* A boiling; preparation made by boiling.

Dē′eol-lā′tion, *n.* Act of beheading.

De-eŏl′or-ā′tion, *n.* Removal or absence of color.

Dē′eom-pōṣ′a-ble, *a.* Capable of being decomposed.

Dē′eom-pōṣe′, *v. t.* To resolve into original elements.

Dē′eom-pŏṣ′īte, *a.* Compounded more than once.

De-eŏm′po-ṣī′tion (-zĭsh′un), *n.* Resolution or separation into constituent parts.

Dē′eom-pound′, *v. t.* To compound a second time. — *a.* Compounded a second time, or repeatedly.

Dĕç′o-rāte, *v. t.* To adorn; to embellish; to ornament.

Dĕç′o-rā′tion, *n.* Act of decorating; embellishment.

Dĕç′o-ra-tĭve, *a.* Fitted to adorn.

De-eō′roŭs, or **Dĕç′o-roŭs,** *a.* Becoming; behaving with decorum; suitable.

De-eō′roŭs-ly, or **Dĕç′o-roŭs-ly,** *adv.* Decently; becomingly.

De-eŏr′ti-eāte, *v. t.* To strip off bark; to peel. [peeling.

De-eŏr′ti-eā′tion, *n.* Act of

De-eō′rum, *n.* Propriety of speech and behavior; decency.

De-eoy′, *v. t.* To allure into a snare or net; to mislead. — *n.* Allurement to mischief; temptation; snare; lure for birds.

De-erēase′, *v. t.* To make less. — *v. i.* To grow or become less. — *n.* A becoming less; decay; diminution.

De-erēe′ (130), *v. t.* To determine; to ordain. — *n.* An edict; order; ordinance.

Dēe′re-ment, *n.* Decrease.

De-erĕp′it, *a.* Infirm; wasted; worn with age.

De-erĕp′i-tāte, *v.* To roast so as to cause crackling.

De-erĕp′i-tā′tion, *n.* The act of roasting with a crackling.

De-erĕp′i-tūde, *n.* Broken state of the body by age.

De-erĕs′çent, *a.* Decreasing.

De-erē′tal, *a.* Of, or pertaining to, a decree. — *n.* A letter of the pope; a book of edicts or decrees.

Dĕe′re-to-ry (107), *a.* Established by decree; official.

De-erī′al (135), *n.* A crying down; a clamorous censure.

De-erī′er, *n.* One who decries.

De-erȳ′, *v. t.* To cry down; to censure as faulty, mean, or worthless.

De-eŭm′bençe, } *n.* Act or
De-eŭm′ben-çy, } posture of lying down.

De-eŭm′bent, *a.* Lying down; prostrate.

Dēe′u-ple, *a.* Tenfold.

De-eū′ri-on, *n.* An officer over ten men.

De-eŭs′sāte, *v. t.* To cross at an acute angle.

Dē′eus-sā′tion, *n.* A crossing at an acute angle. [ing.

De-dēe′o-roŭs, *a.* Uubecoming.

Dĕd′i-eāte (42), *v. t.* To consecrate; to devote; to inscribe.

Dĕd′i-eā′tion, *n.* Consecration; address to a patron or friend, prefixed to book.

Dĕd′i-eā′tor, *n.* One who dedicates or inscribes.

Dĕd′i-ea-to-ry, *a.* Comprising a dedication.

De-dūçe′, *v. t.* [Lat. *de*, from, and *ducere*, to lead.] To draw, as an inference; to infer.

De-dūçe′ment, *n.* That which is deduced; inference.

De-dū′çi-ble, *a.* Capable of being inferred or deduced.

De-dū′çĭve, } *a.* Performing
De-dŭet′ĭve, } the act of deduction.

De-dŭet′, *v. t.* To take away; to subtract.

---

sŏn, ôr, dọ, wọlf, tọō, tŏŏk; ûrn, rụe, pụll; ç, ġ, *soft*; ¢, ḡ, *hard*; aẓ; eẋist; ṇ *as* ng; this.

De-duc'tion, n. An abatement; that which is deducted; an inference.
De-duc'tive-ly, adv. By way of deduction.
Deed, n. That which is done; action; exploit; a sealed writing to convey property.— v. t. To transfer by deed.
Deem, v. t. To think; to judge; to suppose.
Deep, a. [Allied to dip.] Far to the bottom; profound; sagacious; artful; intricate; of low tone; grave. — n. The sea; an abyss.
Deep'en (55), v. t. To make more deep; to darken.— v. i. To grow more deep.
Deep'ly, adv. To a great depth; to a low degree.
Deer, n. An animal hunted for venison.
De-face', v. t. To disfigure; to erase; to destroy; to mar.
De-face'ment (132), n. Injury to the surface; razure.
De-fal'cate, v. t. To lop off.
Def'al-ca'tion, n. That which is cut off; diminution; deficit.
Def'a-ma'tion, n. Slander; calumny; detraction.
De-fam'a-to-ry, a. Slanderous; calumnious.
De-fame', v. t. To slander; to speak evil of. [ders.
De-fam'er, n. One who slanDe-fault', n. Omission; failure; non-appearance in court.— v. t. To recall in court, and record for not appearing.
De-fault'er, n. One guilty of default; a peculator.
De-fea'gance, n. Act of annulling.
De-fea'si-ble, a. Capable of being annulled or abrogated.
De-feat', n. An overthrow; rout.— v. t. To overthrow; to rout; to frustrate.
Def'e-cate, v. t. To purify, as liquors, from foul matter.
Def'e-ca'tion, n. Act of purifying liquors.
De-fect', n. Want or deficiency; imperfection; fault; blemish.
De-fec'tion, n. A falling away; apostasy; revolt.
De-fec'tive, a. Full of defects; imperfect; incomplete; deficient. [fects.
De-fec'tive-ly, adv. With de-

De-fence', n. Protection from injury. See Defense.
De-fend', v. t. or i. [Lat. de, from, and fendere, to guard.] To guard from injury.— SYN. To protect; to vindicate.
De-fend'ant, n. One who makes defense, or opposes a complaint.
De-fend'er, n. One who defends.
De-fense' (149), n. Protection from injury; vindication.
De-fense'less, a. Unarmed.
De-fen'si-ble, a. Capable of being defended.
De-fen'sive, a. Serving to defend. — n. Safeguard; state of defense.
De-fer' (12, 129), v. t. To put off; to delay.— v. i. To wait; to yield out of respect.
Def'er-ence, n. Respect or concession to another.
Def'er-en'tial, a. Expressing deference.
De-fi'ance, n. Act of defying; a challenge to fight.
De-fi'ant, a. Bold; insolent.
De-fi'cien-cy (-fish'en-), n. Defect; want; imperfection.
De-fi'cient (-fish'ent), a. Wanting; imperfect.
Def'i-cit, n. Deficiency.
De-fi'er, n. One who defies.
De-file', or De'file, n. A narrow passage, as between hills.
De-file', v. t. To pollute.— v. i. To go off file by file.
De-file'ment, n. Pollution.
De-fin'a-ble, a. Capable of being defined.
De-fine', v. t. To end; to make the limits of; to explain; to interpret.
Def'i-nite, a. Having precise limits; certain; exact.
Def'i-nite-ly, adv. With certain limitation.
Def'i-nite-ness, n. State or quality of being definite.
Def'i-ni'tion (-nish'un), n. Description of a thing by its properties; explanation of the meaning of a word.
De-fin'i-tive, a. Determinate; final; conclusive. — n. That which ascertains or defines.
De-fin'i-tive-ly, adv. Positively; finally; unconditionally.
De-fla'gra-ble, or Def'la-gra-ble, a. Combustible.
Def'la-grate, v. t. To burn suddenly.
Def'la-gra'tion, n. A rapid and sparkling combustion.

De-fleet', v. i. or t. To turn aside; to deviate.
De-flec'tion (149), n. A turning; deviation.
De-flex'ure, n. Deflection.
Def'lo-ra'tion, n. Act of deflouring. [seduce.
De-flour', v. t. To ravish; to
De-flux'ion, n. A flowing down, as of humors.
De-fo'li-a'tion, n. Fall of the leaf.
De-force', v. t. To keep from the owner unlawfully.
De-force'ment, n. A wrongful withholding, as of lands or tenements.
De-form', v. t. To mar; to disfigure; to make ugly.
De-formed', a. Ugly; disfigured.
De-form'i-ty, n. Want of beauty or symmetry; ugliness; unnatural shape.
De-fraud', v. t. To cheat, esp. to injure by embezzlement.
De-fraud'er, n. One who defrauds; a cheat.
De-fray', v. t. To bear or pay, as expenses.
De-funct', a. Deceased; dead. — n. A dead person.
De-fy', v. t. To dare; to challenge; to set at naught.
De-gen'er-a-cy, n. Decline in good qualities; meanness.
De-gen'er-ate (42), a. Having declined in worth; base.
De-gen'er-āte, v. i. To decline in virtue or good qualities; to deteriorate.
De-gen'er-a'tion, n. A growing worse; deterioration.
Deg'lu-ti'tion (-tish'un), n. Act or power of swallowing.
Deg'ra-da'tion, n. A depriving of rank; degeneracy.
De-grade', v. t. To deprive of rank or title; to lower.
De-grad'ed, p. a. Reduced in rank; lowered.
De-gree' (146), n. A step; extent; grade; rank; the 360th part of a circle.
De-his'cence, n. Act of gaping; the opening of pods, &c.
De-his'cent, a. Opening, as a pod.
De-hort', v. t. To dissuade.
De'hor-ta'tion, n. A dissuasion.
De-hort'a-to-ry, a. Fitted or designed to dissuade.
De'i-fi-ca'tion, n. The act of enrolling among deities.
De-if'ic, a. Making divine or god-like.
De'i-form, a. [Lat. deus, god.

and *forma*, form.] Of a godlike form. [rank of deity.
Dē′i-fȳ, *v. t.* To exalt to the
Deign (dān), *v. i.* To condescend; to vouchsafe.—*v. t.* To grant; to allow.
Dē′ism, *n.* A belief in God accompanied by a denial of revelation.
Dē′ist, *n.* One who believes in a god, but not in revealed religion.
De-ist′ic, *a.* Pertaining
De-ist′ic-al, } to deism.
De-ī′ty, *n.* A divinity; God.
De-jĕct′, *v. t.* To cast down; to dispirit; to discourage.
De-jĕct′ed, *a.* Cast down.
De-jĕct′ed-ly, *adv.* In a dejected manner.
De-jĕct′ed-ness, *a.* Dejection.
De-jĕe′tion, *n.* Depression of spirits; melancholy.
De-lāy′, *v. t.* To put off; to defer; to detain.—*v. i.* To move slowly; to linger.—*n.* Hindrance; detention; a stay or stop.
Dē′le, *v. t.* To erase; to remove, as something which has been put in type.
Dēl′e-ble, *a.* Capable of being effaced.
De-lĕct′a-ble, *a.* Delightful; highly pleasing.
De-lĕc′ta-bly, *adv.* In a delectable manner.
Dē′lec-tā′tion, *n.* Delight.
Dĕl′e-gāte, *v. t.* To send as representative; to depute; to intrust.
Dĕl′e-gate (42, 118), *n.* A deputy; a representative.
Dĕl′e-gā′tion, *n.* A sending away; persons delegated; deputation.
Dĕl′e-tē′ri-oŭs (86), *a.* Destructive; highly injurious.
Dĕlf, *n.* Earthen ware glazed.
De-lib′er-āte, *v.* To weigh in the mind; to reflect or consider.
De-lib′er-ate (42), *a.* Circumspect; well considered. [ly.
De-lib′er-ate-ly, *adv.* Slow-
De-lib′er-ā′tion, *n.* Act of weighing in the mind; slowness. [deliberate.
De-lib′er-a-tīve, *a.* Act of
Dĕl′i-ca-cy, *n.* Refinement of sensibility or taste; something delicate.—SYN. Fineness; nicety; softness; small-ness.
Dĕl′i-cate, *a.* Nice; pleasing to the taste; soft; effeminate.
Dĕl′i-cate-ly, *adv.* With nicety; daintily; tenderly.

De-lī′cioŭs (-lĭsh′us), *a.* Sweet to the palate or other sense; delectable.
De-līght′ (-līt′), *n.* Great joy or pleasure.—*v. t.* To give great pleasure to.—*v. i.* To have or take great pleasure.
De-līght′ed (-līt′-), *a.* Greatly pleased.
De-līght′ful (-līt′-), *a.* Very pleasant; charming; delectable.
De-līght′ful-ly (-līt′-), *adv.* In a manner to delight.
De-līn′e-a-ment, *n.* Representation by delineation.
De-līn′e-āte, *v. t.* To draw the outline of; to sketch.
De-līn′e-ā′tion, *n.* Act of drawing the outline of a thing. [delineates.
De-līn′e-ā′tor, *a.* One who
De-līn′quen-cy (-lĭnk′wen-), *n.* Failure or omission of duty; fault.
De-līn′quent (79), *a.* Failing in duty.—*n.* One who fails to do his duty. [air.
Dĕl′i-quĕsce′, *v. i.* To melt in
Dĕl′i-quĕs′cence, *n.* A melting in the air.
Dĕl′i-quĕs′cent, *a.* Liquefying in the air. [in the air.
De-līq′ui-um, *n.* A melting
De-līr′i-oŭs, *a.* Wandering in mind; light-headed.
De-līr′i-um, *n.* Derangement.
†**De-līr′i-um Trē′mens.** Violent delirium brought on by excessive use of intoxicating drinks.
De-līv′er, *v. t.* [Lat. *de*, from, and *librare*, to set free.] To free; to release; to give or transfer; to utter; to pronounce.
De-līv′er-ance, *n.* Act of freeing; rescue; release.
De-līv′er-er, *n.* One who delivers.
De-līv′er-y, *n.* Release; surrender; style of utterance; childbirth.
Dĕll, *n.* A valley; a hollow.
Dĕl′phin, *a.* Relating to the dauphin of France, or to an edition of the classics, prepared for his use.
Dĕl′tă, *n.* [From its resemblance to the Greek letter Δ, or delta.] The space between the two mouths of a river.
De-lūde′, *v. t.* To deceive; to mislead by arts.
De-lūge′, *n.* A general inundation; a flood.—*v. t.* To overflow; to drown; to overwhelm; to inundate.

De-lū′sion, *n.* Act of deluding, or state of being deluded; deception; cheat.
De-lū′sive, *a.* Tending to delude; deceptive.
Dĕlve, *v. t.* To dig; to penetrate. [politician.
Dĕm′a-gŏgue, *n.* An artful
De-māin′, } *n.* A
De-mēsne′ (-mēn′), } manorhouse and land.
De-mănd′, *v. t.* To claim; to ask.—*n.* A claim by right or authority; a question.
De-mănd′a-ble, *a.* Capable of being demanded. [iff.
De-mănd′ant, *n.* The plaint-
Dē′mar-cā′tion, } *n.* Divi-
Dē′mar-kā′tion, } sion of territory; boundary.
De-mēan′, *v. t.* To behave; to carry one's self.
De-mēan′or, *n.* Manner of behaving; deportment; carriage.
De-mĕnt′ed, *a.* Imbecile in mind; infatuated; mad.
De-mĕr′it, *n.* Ill desert; fault.
De-mĕr′sion, *n.* A plunging in a liquid.
De-mesne′ (-mēn′), *n.* See *Demain*.
Dĕm′i-gŏd, *n.* A deified hero.
Dĕm′i-jŏhn, *n.* A large glass bottle inclosed in a wicker cover.
De-mis′a-ble, *a.* Capable of being demised or leased.
De-mīse′, *n.* Death of a distinguished personage; conveyance or transfer of an estate.—*v. t.* To bequeath by will.
De-mŏc′ra-cy (117), *n.* [Gr. *demos*, the people, and *kratein*, to rule.] Government by the people.
Dĕm′o-crăt, *n.* An adherent to democracy.
Dĕm′o-crăt′ic, *a.* Relating to democracy; republican.
De-mŏl′ish, *v. t.* To throw or pull down; to destroy.
Dĕm′o-lī′tion (-lĭsh′un), *n.* Act of overthrowing; destruction; ruin.
Dē′mon, *n.* An evil spirit.
De-mō′ni-ăc, } *a.* Belong-
Dĕm′o-nī′ac-al, } ing to, or influenced by, demons.
De-mō′ni-ăc, *n.* One possessed by an evil spirit.
Dē′mon-ĭsm, *n.* A belief in demons, or false gods.
Dē′mon-ŏl′a-try, *n.* Worship of demons or evil spirits.

DEMONOLOGY 106 DEPOSIT

De'mon-ŏl'o-gy, *n.* A treatise on evil spirits.
De-mŏn'stra-ble, *a.* Capable of being fully proved.
De-mŏn'stra-bly, *adv.* In a manner to demonstrate.
Dĕm'on-strāte, or **De-mŏn'strāte** (114), *v. t.* To prove fully or to a certainty. — SYN. To evince; manifest.
Dĕm'on-strā'tion, *n.* Proof to a certainty.
De-mŏn'stra-tive, *a.* Tending to demonstrate; conclusive. [demonstrates.
Dĕm'on-strā'tor, *n.* One who
De-mŏr'al-i-zā'tion, *n.* Destruction of morals or discipline.
De-mŏr'al-īze (153), *v. t.* To destroy the morals or discipline of.
De mūl'çent, *a.* Softening.
De-mŭr', *v. i.* To hesitate; to have scruples. — *n.* Hesitation; doubt.
De-mūre', *a.* Affectedly grave or modest.
De-mūre'ly, *adv.* With affected reserve.
De-mūre'ness, *n.* State or quality of being demure.
De-mŭr'rage, *n.* Payment for the detention of a ship.
De-mŭr'rer, *n.* One who demurs; a pause in law.
De-my', *n.* A kind of small paper. [a beast.
Dĕn (13), *n.* A cave; lodge of
De-nā'tion-al-īze (-năsh'un-), *v. t.* To divest of national character or rights.
Dĕn'drīte, *n.* A mineral on which are branching figures like shrubs or trees.
Den-drīt'ic, *a.* Containing branching figures resembling shrubs or trees.
Den-drŏl'o-gy, *n.* [Gr. *dendron,* a tree, and *logos,* discourse.] Natural history of trees.
De-nī'a-ble, *a.* Capable of being denied.
De-nī'al (135), *n.* Refusal; contradiction; negation.
De-nī'er, *n.* A refuser.
Dĕn'i-zā'tion, *n.* Act of making a citizen.
Dĕn'i-zen, *n.* A foreigner made a citizen.
De-nŏm'i-nāte, *v. t.* To give a name to; to call.
De-nŏm'i-nā'tion, *n.* A name; a title; a sect.
De-nŏm'i-na-tive, *a.* Conferring a name or appellation.
De-nŏm'i-nā'tor, *n.* The

lower number in vulgar fractions.
De-nŏt'a-ble, *a.* Capable of being denoted.
Dĕn'o-tā'tion, *n.* The act of denoting.
De-nōte', *v. t.* To indicate; to signify; to mark; to show.
De-nounçe', *v. t.* To accuse publicly; to threaten by some outward sign.
De-nounçe'ment, *n.* Act of proclaiming a threat.
Dĕnse, *a.* Having its parts closely pressed together. — SYN. Close; compact; thick.
Dĕnse'ness, *n.* Compactness.
Dĕn'si-ty, *n.* Compactness; closeness of parts.
Dĕnt, *n.* A small hollow; an indentation. — *v. t.* To make a dent in. [teeth.
Dĕnt'al, *a.* Pertaining to the
Dĕn'tate, *a.* Toothed; sharply notched.
Dĕnt'i-cle, *n.* A point like a small tooth.
Den-tic'u-late, } *a.* Being
Den-tic'u-lā'ted, } notched so as to resemble little teeth.
Den-tic'u-lā'tion, *n.* State of being set with small notches or teeth.
Dĕn'ti-fôrm, *a.* Formed as a tooth.
Dĕn'ti-friçe, *n.* [Lat. *dens,* tooth, and *fricare,* to rub.] Something to cleanse teeth; tooth-powder.
Dĕn'til, *n.* A square block in cornices. [the teeth.
Dĕn'tist, *n.* An operator on
Dĕn'tist-ry, *n.* The business of a dentist.
Den-ti'tion (-tĭsh'un), *n.* The process of cutting the teeth.
Dĕn'toid, *a.* Tooth-shaped.
Dĕn'u-dā'tion, *n.* A making bare, or stripping naked.
De-nūde', *v. t.* To lay bare.
De-nŭn'çi-ā'tion (-shĭ-ā'shun), *n.* Declaration of a threat; the threat declared.
De-nŭn'ci-ā'tor (-nŭn'shī-), *n.* One who threatens.
De-nŭn'ci-a-to-ry (-nŭn'shī-), *a.* Containing a public threat.
De-ny', *v. t.* To contradict; to refuse; to withhold.
De-ŏb'stru-ent, *a.* Removing obstructions; aperient. — *n.* A medicine that removes obstructions.
Dē'o-dănd, *n.* Something forfeited to the state for pious uses. [of duty.
Dē'on-tŏl'o-gy, *n.* Science

De-pärt', *v. i.* To go away; to forsake; to die.
De-pärt'ment, *n.* A distinct part, office, or division.
De-pärt-mĕnt'al, *a.* Pertaining to a department.
De-pärt'ūre (50), *n.* A going away; decease; death.
De-pĕnd', *v. i.* To hang; to rely; to adhere.
De-pĕnd'ençe, } *n.* Reliance;
De-pĕnd'en-çy, } trust; subordination.
De-pĕnd'ent, *a.* Relying; subordinate. — *n.* One subordinate to another.
De-pĭct', *v. t.* To paint; to portray; to describe.
De-pĭct'ūre, *v. t.* To paint.
Dĕp'i-lā'tion, *n.* Act of pulling the hair off.
De-pĭl'a-to-ry, *a.* Taking off the hair.
De-plē'tion, *n.* Blood-letting.
De-plē'to-ry, *a.* Calculated to deplete.
De-plōr'a-ble, *a.* Lamentable; sad. [ably.
De-plōr'a-bly, *adv.* Lament-
De-plōr'a-ble-ness, *n.* State of being deplorable.
De-plōre', *v. t.* To lament; to bewail; to be grieved at.
De-ploy', *v. t.* To display; to open or extend, as a column of troops.
Dĕp'lu-mā'tion, *n.* A stripping off plumes.
De-plūme', *v. t.* To deprive of plumes or feathers.
De-pō'nent, *a.* Having a passive form with an active meaning. — *n.* One who gives written testimony on oath; a deponent verb.
De-pŏp'u-lāte, *v. t.* To deprive of inhabitants.
De-pŏp'u-lā'tion, *n.* Act of depopulating.
De-pŏp'u-lā'tor, *n.* One who depopulates.
De-pōrt', *v. t.* To behave; to carry; to conduct; to transport.
Dē'por-tā'tion, *n.* A carrying away; exile; banishment.
De-pōrt'ment, *n.* Manner of behaving; behavior.
De-pōṣ'a-ble, *a.* Capable of being deposed.
De-pōṣ'al, *n.* Act of deposing.
De-pōṣe', *v. t.* To dethrone. — *v. i.* To testify under oath.
De-pŏṣ'it, *v. t.* To lodge or place; to lay up or aside. — *n.* That which is laid up or aside; any thing intrusted.

ā, ĕ, ī, ō, ū, ȳ, *long*; ă, ĕ, ĭ, ŏ, ŭ, ў, *short*; cáre, cär, åsk, ąll, whąt; ẽre, veil, tẽrm; p'que, fĭrm;

DEPOSITARY 107 DESPAIR

De-pŏṣ'i-ta-ry, n. One with whom something is left in trust.

Dĕp'o-ṣi'tion (-zĭsh'un), n. Act of dethroning or degrading; an affidavit.

De-pŏṣ'i-tor, n. One who deposits.

De-pŏṣ'i-to-ry (107), n. A place where any thing is deposited for sale or keeping.

De-pōt' (de-pō' or dē'po), n. Place of deposit; a magazine; a railway station.

Dĕp'ra-vā'tion, n. Act of making worse. [to vitiate.

De-prāve', v. t. To corrupt;

De-prăv'i-ty, n. Corruption of morals; a vitiated state.

Dĕp're-cāte (118), v. t. [Lat. de, from, and precari, to pray.] To pray for deliverance from; to regret deeply.

Dĕp're-cā'tion, n. Act of deprecating.

Dĕp're-ca-to-ry, a. Serving to deprecate.

De-prē'ci-āte (-prē'shǐ-, 92), v. t. To decline in value.— v. t. To lower the price of; to undervalue.

De-prē'ci-ā'tion (-prē'shǐ-), n. Act of depreciating.

Dĕp're-dāte, v. t. To rob; to plunder; to spoil.

Dĕp're-dā'tion, n. A robbing or plundering.

De-prĕss', v. t. To sink; to humble; to cast down; to deject; to abase.

De-prĕs'sion (-prĕsh'un), n. Dejection; melancholy; low state.

De-prĕs'sīve, a. Tending to depress. [be deprived.

De-prīv'a-ble, a. Liable to

Dĕp'ri-vā'tion, n. Act of depriving; loss; bereavement.

De-prīve', v. t. To take from; to bereave.

Dĕpth, n. Deepness; profundity; a deep place; obscurity.

Dĕp'u-rāte, v. t. To purify.

Dĕp'u-rā'tion, n. A cleansing; purification.

Dĕp'u-tā'tion, n. Act of deputing; persons deputed.

De-pūte', v. t. To appoint as substitute.

Dĕp'u-ty, n. One appointed to act for another; an agent.

De-răç'i-nāte, v. t. To root up; to extirpate.

De-rānge', v. t. To put out of order; to confuse; to make insane; to craze.

De-rānged', a. Delirious; insane.

De-rānge'ment (132), n. State of disorder; insanity; delirium.

Dĕr'e-lĭct, n. A thing abandoned.— a. Abandoned.

Dĕr'e-lĭc'tion, n. An utter forsaking; abandonment.

De-rīde', v. t. To laugh at in scorn.— SYN. To ridicule; mock; taunt.

De-rĭṣ'ion (-rĭzh'un), n. A laughing at in contempt.

De-rī'sīve,) a. Mocking;
De-rī'so-ry,) ridiculing.

De-rīv'a-ble, a. Capable of being derived.

Dĕr'i-vā'tion, n. Deduction from a source; act of tracing origin or descent, as of words.

De-rīv'a-tīve, a. Derived.— n. A word or thing derived.

De-rīve', v. t. To deduce; to draw.

Dĕr'ni-er, a. The last.

Dĕr'o-gāte, v. t. or i. To take away; to detract.

Dĕr'o-gā'tion, n. A detracting; disparagement.

De-rŏg'a-to-ry, a. Detracting.

Dĕr'rick (127), n. A machine for raising heavy weights.

Dĕr'vĭs (140), n. An oriental monk.

Des-cănt', v. i. To sing; to comment at large.

Dĕs'cant, n. A song in parts; a variation of an air; comment.

De-scĕnd', v. t. or i. To go or come down.

De-scĕnd'ant, n. Offspring of an ancestor.

De-scĕnd'ent, a. Falling; sinking.

De-scĕnd'i-ble, a. Admitting descent.

De-scĕn'sion, n. Act of descending.

De-scĕnt', n. Act of descending; progress downward; incursion; lineage; extraction.

De-scrīb'a-ble, a. Capable of being described.

De-scrībe', v. t. To represent by words or other signs.

De-scrī'er, n. One who descries.

De-scrĭp'tion, n. Act of describing; account; class.

De-scrĭp'tīve, a. Containing description.

De-scrȳ', v. t. To discover, of objects at a distance.

Dĕs'e-crāte, v. t. To pervert from a sacred purpose.

Dĕs'e-crā'tion, n. A diverting from a sacred purpose.

De-ṣẽrt' (12), n. Merit; worth; claim to reward.— v. t. To abandon.— v. i. To run away.

Dĕṣ'ert, a. Wild; solitary; unsettled.— n. A wilderness; solitude.

De-ṣẽrt'er, n. One who forsakes his colors, &c. [ing.

De-ṣẽr'tion, n. Act of desert-

De-ṣẽrve' (12), v. t. To merit.

De-ṣẽrved', a. Merited.

De-ṣẽrv'ed-ly, adv. According to desert.

De-ṣẽrv'ing, a. Meritorious; worthy.

Dĕs'ha-bille', n. An undress.

Dĕs'ic-cāte, or De-sĭc'cāte, v. t. or i. To dry up.

Dĕs'ic-cā'tion, n. Act or process of making dry.

De-sĭc'ca-tīve, a. Tending to dry.

De-sĭd'er-āte, v. t. To feel the want of; to desire.

†De-sĭd'e-rā'tum, n. (pl. De-sĭd'e-rā'tà, 147.) A thing desired.

De-sīgn' (-sīn' or -zīn'), v. t. To intend; to plan; to sketch.— n. A purpose; intention; plan; sketch.

Dĕṣ'ig-nāte, v. t. To point out; to indicate; to set apart.

Dĕṣ'ig-nā'tion, n. Act of pointing or marking out.

De-sīgn'ing (-sīn'- or -zīn'-), a. Artful; scheming.

De-sīgn'ed-ly (-sīn'- or zīn'-), adv. With design.

De-sīgn'er (-sīn'- or -zīn'-), n. One who designs.

De-ṣīr'a-ble (86), a. Worthy of desire.

De-ṣīr'a-ble-ness, n. Quality of being desirable.

De-ṣīre', n. A wish to obtain; the thing desired.— v. t. To wish for; to ask.

De-ṣīr'ous (133), a. Full of desire; eager.

De-sĭst', v. i. [Lat. de, from, and sistere, to stop.] To cease; to stop; to forbear.

De-sĭst'ançe, n. Act of desisting; cessation.

Dĕsk (140), n. An inclined table for writing at; a pulpit.

Dĕs'o-lāte, v. t. To lay waste.

Dĕs'o-late (42), a. Laid waste.

Dĕs'o-lā'tion, n. Act of laying waste; state of being desolate; ruin.

De-spāir', n. Utter loss of hope.— v. i. To abandon hope; to be without hope.

---

sŭn, ôr, dọ, wọlf, tōō, tŏŏk; ûrn, rụe, pụll; ç, ġ, soft; ç, ġ, hard; aṣ; exist; ɴ as ng; this.

De-spatch', v. t. & i. See *Dispatch*.
Des'per-a'do (pl. Des'per-a'-does), n. A desperate man; a madman.
Des'per-ate (42), a. Without hope; rash.
Des'per-ate-ly, adv. In a desperate manner.
Des'per-a'tion, n. Hopelessness; despair.
Des'pi-ca-ble, a. Contemptible; vile; mean.
De-spise', v. t. To contemn; to scorn; to disdain.
De-spite', n. Malice; malignity. — prep. In spite of; notwithstanding.
De-spite'ful, a. Full of hate; malicious.
De-spite'ful-ly, adv. In a despiteful manner.
De-spite'ful-ness, n. Malice; malignity; hate.
De-spoil', v. t. To spoil; to rob; to strip. [despoiling.
De-spo'li-a'tion, n. Act of
De-spoil'er, n. A plunderer.
De-spond', v. i. To lose hope; to despair.
De-spond'en-çy, n. Loss of hope; discouragement.
De-spond'ent, a. Despairing.
De-spond'ing-ly, adv. In a desponding manner.
Des'pot, n. An absolute prince; a tyrant.
Des-pot'ic, a. Absolute in power; tyrannical; arbitrary.
Des-pot'ic-al-ly, adv. In a despotical manner.
Des'pot-işm, n. Absolute power; tyranny.
Des'pu-ma'tion, n. Foam; scum; frothiness.
Des'qua-ma'tion, n. A scaling or exfoliation of bone.
Des-sert', n. Service of fruit, &c., at the close of a meal.
Des'ti-na'tion, n. Place to be reached; end.
Des'tine, v. t. To doom; to devote; to appoint.
Des'ti-ny, n. State or condition predetermined; fate.
Des'ti-tute (27), a. Being in utter want; poor.
Des'ti-tu'tion, n. Utter want.
De-stroy' (130), v. t. To demolish; to ruin; to lay waste.
De-stroy'er, n. One who destroys or ruins.
De-strue'ti-ble, a. Liable to destruction.
De-strue'tion, n. Ruin; demolition; overthrow.
De-strue'tive, a. Ruinous.
Des'ue-tude (-we-), n. Disuse.

Des'ul-to-ry, a. Without method; unconnected; loose.
De-tach', v. t. To separate; to disunite; to send off.
De-tach'ment, n. A party sent from the main army, &c.
De'tail, or De-tail' (111), n. A minute account or portion; a particular
De-tail', v. t. To narrate in particulars; to particularize; to appoint for a particular service.
De-tain', v. t. [Lat. *de*, from, and *tenere*, to hold.] To withhold; to restrain from departure.
De-tain'er, n. One who detains.
De-teet', v. t. To bring to light; to discover; to find out.
De-tee'tion, n. Act of detecting; discovery.
De-tee'tive, n. A policeman employed to detect.
De-tent', n. A stop in a clock.
De-ten'tion, n. Act of detaining.
De-ter' (129), v. t. To prevent by fear; to hinder.
De-terġe', v. t. To cleanse.
De-ter'ġent, a. Cleansing; purging.
De-te'ri-o-rate, v. t. or i. To make or become worse.
De-te'ri-o-ra'tion, n. Act of becoming worse.
De-ter'ment, n. That which deters; hindrance.
De-ter'mi-na-ble, a. Capable of being determined.
De-ter'mi-nate, a. Fixed; definite; conclusive.
De-ter'mi-na'tion, n. Termination; resolution taken.
De-ter'mine, v. t. To end; to decide; to resolve.
De-ter'mined, a. Resolute.
De-ter'sion, n. Act of cleansing. [cleanse.
De-ter'sive, a. Able to
De-test', v. t. To hate extremely. — SYN. To abhor, loathe; abominate.
De-test'a-ble, a. Very hateful; abominable.
De-tes'ta-bly, adv. Very hatefully.
Det'es-ta'tion, or De'tes-ta'tion, n. Extreme hatred; abhorrence.
De-throne', v. t. To divest of royalty; to depose.
De-throne'ment, n. Act of dethroning.
Det'i-nūe, n. A writ to recover goods detained.

Det'o-nāte, } v. t. or i. To
Det'o-nīze, } explode.
Det'o-na'tion, n. Explosion; discharge; report.
De-tort', v. t. To twist; to wrest; to turn.
De-tor'tion, n. A perversion or wresting.
De-traet', v. i. [Lat. *de*, from, and *trahere*, *tractum*, to draw.] To depreciate worth. — v. t. To slander.
De-traë'tion, n. Slander; defamation.
De-traet'ive, a. Tending to lessen reputation.
De-traet'or. n. One who detracts or slanders.
De-traet'o-ry, a. Slanderous.
Det'ri-ment, n. Loss; damage; injury; mischief.
Det'ri-ment'al, a. Causing loss.
De-tri'tion (-trish'un), n. A wearing off or away.
De-tri'tus, n. Small portions rubbed off from solid bodies by attrition. [down.
De-trude', v. t. To thrust
De-trun'eāte, v. t. To lop off.
De-tru'sion, n. Act of thrusting down.
Deūçe, n. A card of two spots; the devil.
Dev'as-tāte, or De-vas'tāte, v. t. To lay waste; to ravage.
Dev'as-ta'tion, n. A laying waste; havoc; ravage.
De-vel'op, v. t. To unfold; to uncover; to lay open to view.
De-vel'op-ment, n. An unfolding; disclosure.
De-vest', v. t. or i. To strip.
De'vi-āte, v. i. [Lat. *de*, from, and *viare*, to travel.] To wander; to go astray; to err.
De'vi-a'tion, n. A departure from rule; error; variation.
De-viçe' (140), n. Scheme; contrivance; design; emblem.
Dev'il (dev'l), n. The evil one.
Dev'il-ish, a. Fiendish; diabolical.
Dev'il-try, n. Diabolical or mischievous conduct.
De'vi-oŭs, a. Going or leading astray; erring.
De-viṣ'a-ble, a. Capable of being devised.
De-viṣe', v. t. To contrive; to plan; to invent; to give by will. — v. i. To lay a plan. — n. A will.
Dev'iṣ-ee', n. One to whom a thing is bequeathed.
De-viṣ'er, n. One who devises.

De-vīṣ'or, n. One who bequeaths or wills.
De-void', a. Not possessing; void; empty; destitute.
†**Devoir** (dev-wôr'), n. Duty; act of civility; due respect.
De-vŏlve', v. t. or i. To roll down; to transfer or be transferred.
De-vōte', v. t. To dedicate; to appropriate by vow; to doom.
De-vōt'ed, a. Zealous; attached.
†**De-vōt'ed-ness,** n. Addictedness; state of being devoted.
Dĕv'o-tee', n. One wholly devoted; a bigot.
De-vō'tion, n. Consecration; affection; piety; a devout act.
De-vō'tion-al, a. Pertaining to devotion.
De-vour', v. t. To eat up ravenously; to consume.
De-vout', a. Pious; religious; reverent.
De-vout'ly, adv. Piously.
De-vout'ness, n. Quality of being devout.
Dew (dū. 20), n. Moisture from the atmosphere deposited at night. — v. t. To wet as with dew.
Dew'lap, n. The flesh hanging from an ox's throat.
Dew'y, a. Moist with dew.
Dĕx'ter,) a. Right as opposed
Dĕx'tral,) to left.
Dex-tĕr'i-ty, n. Activity and expertness. — SYN. Adroitness; skill; cleverness; address.
Dĕx'ter-oŭs, a. Expert in manual acts; skillful; adroit.
Dĕx'ter-oŭs-ly, adv. With dexterity or skill.
Dey, n. Formerly, a title of the governor of Algiers.
†**Dī'a-bē'tēṣ,** n. A disease attended by excessive discharge of urine.
Dī'a-bŏl'ic,) a. Devilish;
Dī'a-bŏl'ic-al,) fiendish; wicked.
Dī'a-bŏl'ic-al-ly, adv. In a diabolical manner.
Dī-ăb'o-liṣm, n. Actions of the devil.
Dī-ăc'o-nal, a. Pertaining to a deacon.
Dī'a-cous'tic, a. Pertaining to diacoustics.
Dī'a-cous'tics, n. sing. Science of sounds refracted by passing through different mediums.

Dī'a-crĭt'ic-al, a. Serving to discriminate; distinctive.
Dī'a-dem, n. A kingly crown or fillet.
Dī-ær'e-sĭs,) n.(pl. †**Dī-ær'e-**
Dī-ĕr'e-sĭs,) sēṣ or **Dī-ĕr'- e-sēṣ.**) A mark [¨] over the second of two vowels, to show that they are to be pronounced separately.
†**Dī'ag-nō'sĭs,** n. Determination of a disease by means of distinctive characteristics.
Dī'ag-nŏs'tic, a. Indicating the nature of a disease.
Dī-ăg'o-nal, a. Passing from one angle to another not adjacent. — n. A diagonal line.
Dī-ăg'o-nal-ly, adv. In a diagonal direction.
Dī'a-grăm, n. A mathematical drawing or figure.
Dī'al, n. [From Lat. dies, day.] A plate to show the hour by the sun.
Dī'a-lĕct, n. A local form of speech; language.
Dī'a-lĕc'tic-al, a. Pertaining to a dialect; logical.
Dī'a-lec-tī'cian (-tĭsh'an), n. A logician.
Dī'a-lĕc'tics, n. sing. Logic.
Dī'al-ing, n. Science of making dials.
Dī'al-ĭst, n. One skilled in dialing.
Dī-ăl'o-gĭst, n. A speaker in a dialogue.
Dī-ăl'o-gĭst'ic, a. Relating to, or having the form of, a dialogue.
Dī'a-lŏgue, n. A discourse between two or more.
Dī-ăm'e-ter, n. A right line passing through the center of a circle, dividing it into two equal parts.
Dī'a-mĕt'ric al, a. Diameter. Relating to, or describing, a diameter: direct.
Dī'a-mĕt'ric-al-ly, adv. Directly.
Dī'a-mond (or dī'mund), n. The most precious of gems; a geometrical figure, thus:
Dī'a-pā'ṣon, n. An octave in music; harmony; an organ stop.
Dī'a-per, n. Figured linen; a towel or napkin. — v. t. To

diversify with figures, as cloth.
Dī-ăph'a-noŭs, a. Transparent; clear.
Dī'a-pho-rĕt'ic, a. Increasing perspiration.
Dī'a-phrăgm (-frăm), n. A muscle separating the chest from the bowels; midriff.
Dī'a-rĭst, n. One who keeps a diary.
Dī'ar-rhē'à,) n. Unusual
Dī'ar-rhœ'à,) evacuation of the intestines.
Dī'ar-rhĕt'ic, a. Promoting evacuations; purgative.
Dī'a-ry (141), n. An account of daily transactions; a journal. [the heart.
Dī-ăs'to-le, n. A dilatation of
Dī'a-tŏn'ic, a. Pertaining to the scale of eight tones, the eighth of which is the octave of the first.
Dī'a-trībe, n. A continued discourse; an invective.
Dĭb'ble, n. A tool for planting.
Dĭçe, n. pl. of Die.
Dĭçe'-bŏx, n. A box for dice or shirt-bosom.
Dĭck'y, n. A false shirt-collar
Dĭc'tāte, v. t. To tell to another to write; to deliver to a subordinate, as a command. — n. Order; suggestion; hint.
Dic-tā'tion, n. Act of dictating or prescribing; an order.
Dic-tā'tor, n. One invested with absolute power.
Dic'ta-tō'ri-al, a. Unlimited in power; absolute; imperious.
Dic-tā'tor-ship, n. Office of a dictator.
Dĭc'tion, n. Manner of expression; choice of words.
Dĭc'tion-a-ry, n. A book in which words are explained; a lexicon.
†**Dĭc'tum,** n. (pl. Dĭc'tä, 147.) An authoritative word or assertion.
Dĭd, imp. of Do.
Dī-dăc'tic, a. Fitted or intended to instruct.
Dī-dăc'tics, n. sing. I t or science of teaching.
Die, v. i. To lose life; to expire. — n. (pl. Dĭçe.) A small cube. — n. (pl. Dīeṣ). A stamp.
Dī-ĕr'e-sĭs, n. See Diæresis.
Dī'et, n. [Gr. diaita, manner of living.] Food; an assembly of princes or estates. — v. t. To feed sparingly. — v. i. To eat sparingly.

Dī'e-ta-ry, n. Prescribed allowance of food.
Dī'e-ta-ry,) a. Pertaining to
Dī'e-tět'ic,) diet.
Dī'e-tět'ics, n. sing. The science that relates to food.
Dif'fer, v. i. To be unlike; to be at variance; to disagree. [disagreement.
Dif'fer-ence, n. Unlikeness;
Dif'fer-ent, a. Not the same; unlike; distinct.
Dif'fer-ent-ly, adv. In a different manner; variously.
Dif'fer-en'tial, a. Creating a difference; meant to produce or show difference.
Dif'fi-cult, a. Hard to be done; hard to please.
Dif'fi-cul-ty (107), n. Hardness to be done; impediment; distress.
Dif'fi-dence, n. Want of confidence; doubt; distrust.
Dif'fi-dent, a. Distrustful; bashful. [diffidence.
Dif'fi-dent-ly, adv. With
Dif'form, a. Not uniform; unlike; different.
Dif-fūse', v. t. To pour out; to spread; to disperse.
Dif-fūse', a. Copious; widely spread; not concise.
Dif-fūse'ly, adv. Widely copiously.
Dif-fū'si-bīl'i-ty, n. Quality of being diffusible.
Dif-fū'si-ble, a. Capable of being diffused.
Dif-fū'sion, n. A spreading; dispersion; extension.
Dif-fū'sive, a. Spreading widely; scattered widely.
Dif-fū'sive-ly, adv. Widely; extensively.
Dif-fū'sive-ness, n. Quality of being diffusive.
Dig (129), v. t. or i. [imp. & p. p. DIGGED; DUG.] To turn up with a spade.
Dī'gest, n. A collection or body of laws; an abridgment.
Dī-gěst', v. t. To dissolve in the stomach; to arrange.
Dī-gěst/i-bĭl'i-ty, n. Quality of being digestible.
Dī-gěst'i-ble, a. Capable of being digested.
Dī-gěs'tion, n. The process of digesting. [gestion.
Dī-gěst'ive, a. Causing digestion.
Dĭg'it (140), n. [Lat. digitus, a finger.] Three fourths of an inch; one of the ten figures 0, 1, 2, &c., by which all numbers are expressed; 12th part of the diameter of the sun or moon.

Dĭg'it-al, a. Relating to a digit.
Dĭg'ni-fīed, a. Noble; exalted. [give distinction to.
Dĭg'ni-fy, v. t. To exalt; to
Dĭg'ni-ta-ry, n. A person, especially a clergyman, of rank. [rank; nobleness.
Dĭg'ni-ty, n. Elevation of
Dī'graph, n. Two letters with the sound of one only.
Dī-grěss', v. i. To turn from the main subject; to wander.
Dī-grěs'sion (-grěsh'un), n. A deviation.
Dī-grěss'ive, a. Tending to digress. [mound of earth.
Dīke, n. A ditch; a bank or
Dī-lăp'i-dāte, v. t. To pull down. — v. i. To go to ruin.
Dī-lăp'i-dā'tion, n. Decay; waste; ruin. [being dilated.
Dī-lāt'a-ble, a. Capable of
Dĭl'a-tā'tion, n. Act of dilating; expansion.
Dī-lāte', or Dī-lāte', v. t. or i. To expand; to enlarge; to widen; to expatiate.
Dī-lā'tion, or Dī-lā'tion, n. Act of dilating; expansion.
Dĭl'a-to-ri-ly, adv. Tardily.
Dĭl'a-to-ri-ness, n. Quality of being dilatory.
Dĭl'a-to-ry, a. Late; tardy.
Dī-lěm'ma, or Dī-lěm'mă (140), n. [Gr. di, double, and lēmma, an assumption.] A perplexing state or alternative.
†Dĭl'et-tǎn'te, n. (pl. Dĭl'et-tǎn'tī.) A lover of the fine arts; an amateur.
Dĭl'i-gence, n. Steady application to business.
†Diligence (dĕ/lē/zhŏngss'), n. A French stage-coach.
Dĭl'i-gent, a. Constant in application to business; assiduous.
Dĭl'i-gent-ly, adv. With steady application; assiduously. [le seeds.
Dĭll, n. A plant with aromatic
Dĭl'u-ent, a. Making thin, as liquor. — n. That which dilutes or makes thinner.
Dī-lūte', v. t. To make more thin. — a. Thin; diluted.
Dī-lū'tion, n. Act of diluting; a weak liquid.
Dī-lū'vi-al,) a. Relating to,
Dī-lū'vi-an,) or caused by, a flood.
Dī-lū'vi-um, n. A deposit of earth, &c., caused by a flood.
Dĭm, a. Not clear; obscure; imperfect. In vision. — v. t.

To cloud; to darken; to obscure.
Dīme, n. [Fr., from Lat. decem, ten.] A silver coin of the United States of ten cents' value.
Dī-měn'sion, n. Bulk; size; extent of a body; capacity.
Dī-mĭd'i-āte, a. Divided into two equal parts.
Dī-mĭn'ish, v. t. or i. To make or become less. — SYN. To lessen; decrease; abate.
Dĭm'i-nū'tion, n. A making or growing smaller.
Dī-mĭn'u-tive, a. Little; small. — n. A noun denoting a small or young object of the same kind with that denoted by some other noun.
Dī-mĭn'u-tive-ly, adv. In a diminutive manner.
Dī-mĭn'u-tive-ness, n. Smallness; littleness.
Dĭm'is-so-ry, a. Dismissing to another ecclesiastical jurisdiction. [cotton cloth.
Dĭm'i-ty, n. A kind of ribbed
Dĭm'ly, adv. In a dim or obscure manner.
Dĭm'ness, n. Quality of being dim; dullness; gloom.
Dĭm'ple, n. A little hollow in the cheek or chin. — v. i. To form dimples.
Dĭn, n. Loud noise; clamor. — v. t. To stun with noise.
Dīne, v. i. To eat dinner. — v. t. To give a dinner to.
Dĭng'-dŏng, n. A word used to express the sound of bells.
Dĭn'gi-ness, n. A dusky hue.
Dĭn'gle, n. A hollow between hills; a dale. [foul.
Dĭn'gy, a. Dusky; soiled;
Dĭn'ner, n. The chief meal of the day.
Dĭnt, n. Mark of a blow; power; means. — v. t. To mark by a blow; to indent.
Dī-ŏç'e-san, or Dī'o-çē'san, a. Pertaining to a diocese. — n. A bishop.
Dī'o-çēse, n. The jurisdiction of a bishop.
Dī-ŏp'trĭc, a. Relating to dioptrics.
Dī-ŏp'trĭcs, n. sing. Science which treats of the 1 ws of the refraction of light.
Dī'o-rā'ma, or Dī-o-rä'mă (140), n. A mode of scenic representation, in which a painting is seen from a distance through a large opening.
Dip (129), v. t. To plunge; to immerse. — v. i. To immerse

DIPHTHERIA 111 DISCLOSE

one's self; to thrust in and partake. — *n.* Inclination downward.

Diph-the'ri-å (dif'- *or* dĭp'-), *n.* A very dangerous disease of the throat.

Diph'thong (dif' *or* dĭp'-, 182), *n.* A union of two vowels in one sound or syllable.

Diph'thong-al (dif'- *or* dĭp'-), *a.* Consisting of a diphthong.

Di-plō'må (115, 140), *n.* A writing conferring some privilege, honor, etc.

Di-plō'ma-cy, *n.* Act of conducting negotiations between nations.

Dĭp'lo-måt, } *n.* A diploma-
Dĭp'lo-mate, } tist.

Dĭp'lo-måt'ic, *a.* Pertaining to diplomacy.

Di-plō'ma-tist, *n.* One skilled in diplomacy; a diplomat.

Dĭp'per, *n.* One who dips; a vessel for dipping.

Dire, *a.* Dreadful; dismal.

Di-rĕct', *a.* Straight; right; express. — *v. t.* To aim; to direct; to order; to regulate.

Di-rĕc'tion, *n.* Aim; order; line or point of tendency; superscription of a letter, &c.

Di-rĕct'ive, *a.* Giving direction.

Di-rĕct'ly, *adv.* In a straight line; immediately.

Di-rĕct'ness, *n.* Straightness; tendency to a point.

Di-rĕct'or, *n.* One who directs; a superintendent.

Di-rĕe-tō'ri-al, *a.* Serving for direction.

Di-rĕct'o-ry, *n.* A book of directions; a guide-book; a body of directors. — *a.* Tending to direct. [directs.

Di-rĕct'ress, *n.* A woman who

Dire'ful, *a.* Dreadful; horrible: dire.

Dire'ful-ly, *adv.* Dreadfully.

Dirge (140), *n.* A funeral song.

Dirk, *n.* A kind of dagger. — *v. t.* To stab with a dirk.

Dirt (16), *n.* Earth; any foul matter; mud; mire. — *v. t.* To make dirty.

Dirt'i-ly, *adv.* Filthily; foully.

Dirt'i-ness, *n.* Quality or state of being dirty.

Dirt'y, *a.* Foul with dirt; base. — *v. t.* To make foul with dirt.

Dis'a-bĭl'i-ty, *n.* Want of power or qualifications.

Dis-ā'ble, *v. t.* To deprive of power or competency; to disqualify.

Dis'a-būse, *v. t.* To undeceive.

Dis'ac-cŏm'mo-dāte, *v. t.* To incommode.

Dis'ac-cūs'tom, *v. t.* To render unaccustomed.

Dis'ad-văn'tage, *n.* Loss; unfavorable state; injury to interest.

Dis-ăd'van-tā'geoŭs, *a.* Unfavorable to success; injurious; hurtful.

Dis-ăd'van-tā'geoŭs-ly, *adv.* With disadvantage.

Dis'af-fĕct', *v. t.* To make less friendly.

Dis'af-fĕct'ed, *a.* Filled with discontent and unfriendliness.

Dis'af-fĕc'tion, *n.* Want of affection; dislike; alienation.

Dis'af-firm', *v. t.* To deny; to contradict.

Dis'a-gree', *v. i.* To differ in opinion; to quarrel; not to be the same.

Dis'a-gree'a-ble, *a.* Unpleasant to the mind or senses; offensive.

Dis'a-gree'a-bly, *adv.* Unpleasantly.

Dis'a-gree'ment, *n.* Difference; diversity; discord.

Dis'al-low', *v. t.* To refuse to allow; to disown and reject. — *v. t.* To refuse permission.

Dis'al-low'ançe, *n.* Disapprobation; prohibition.

Dis'an'i-māte, *v. t.* To deprive of life or spirit.

Dis'an-nŭl'. See *Annul.*

Dis'ap-pār'el, *v. t.* To strip of clothes; to disrobe.

Dis'ap-pēar', *v. i.* To vanish from sight; to cease to be.

Dis'ap-pēar'ançe, *n.* Act of disappearing; a vanishing.

Dis'ap-point', *v. t.* To defeat of expectation or hope; to balk.

Dis'ap-point'ment, *n.* Defeat of hopes or expectation.

Dis'ăp-pro-bā'tion, *n.* Disapproval; dislike.

Dis'ăp-prŏv'al (133), *n.* Disapprobation; dislike.

Dis'ap-prŏve', *v. t.* To censure; to refuse to approve.

Dis-ärm', *v. t.* To deprive of arms, or of the means or disposition to harm.

Dis'ar-rānge', *v. t.* To put out of order.

Dis'ar-rānge'ment, *n.* Act of disturbing order; disorder.

Dis'ar-rāy', *v. t.* To throw into disorder; to undress. —

n. Want of order; confusion; undress.

Dis-ās'ter, *n.* Unfortunate event; mishap; calamity.

Dis-ăs'troŭs, *a.* Unlucky; calamitous; afflictive.

Dis'a-vow', *v. t.* To disown; to deny knowledge of.

Dis'a-vow'al, *n.* A denial.

Dis-bănd', *v. t.* To dismiss from military service. — *v. i.* To retire from service.

Dis'be-liĕf', *n.* Want or refusal of belief.

Dis'be-liĕve', *v. t.* To *in* credit; to refuse to credit.

Dis'be-liĕv'er, *n.* An infidel.

Dis-bûr'den (-bûr'dn), *v. t.* To ease of a burden; to unload.

Dis-bûrse', *v. t.* To expend; to pay out; to spend.

Dis-bûrse'mont, *n.* Act of disbursing; sum spent.

Disc. See *Disk.* [cast off.

Dis-eärd', *v. t.* To dismiss; to

Dis-çĕrn' (diz-zẽrn', 62), *v. t.* or *i.* To see; to perceive and recognize; to judge.

Dis-çĕrn'i-ble (diz-zẽrn'-), *a.* Capable of being discerned.

Dis-çĕrn'i-bly (-zẽrn'-), *adv.* In a manner to be discerned.

Dis-çĕrn'ing, *a.* Judicious.

Dis-çĕrn'ment, *n.* Act or power of discerning. — SYN. Penetration; judgment; discrimination; sagacity.

Dis-chärge', *v. t.* To dismiss; to unload; to acquit; to fire. — *v. t.* To throw off a charge or burden. — *n.* An unloading; release; explosion.

Dis-çī'ple (140), *n.* [Lat. *discipulus,* from *discere,* to learn.] A learner; a scholar or follower. [disciple.

Dis-çī'ple-ship, *n.* State of a

Dis'çi-plĭn-a-ble, *a.* Capable of instruction.

Dis'çi-plĭn-ā'ri-an, *n.* One who keeps good discipline. — *a.* Pertaining to discipline.

Dis'çi-plĭn-a-ry, *a.* Related to, or intended for, discipline.

Dis'çi-plĭne, *n.* Education and government; order; regulation; rule. — *v. t.* To instruct and govern; .o regulate.

Dis-çlāim', *v. t.* To disown; to refuse to acknowledge.

Dis-çlāim'er, *n.* One who disclaims; an express denial.

Dis-clōse', *v. t.* To uncover; to lay open; to reveal.

són, ôr, dọ, wọlf, tōō, tŏŏk; ûrn, rụe, pụll; ç, ğ, *soft;* e, ğ, *hard;* aş; exist; ŋ as ng; this

Dis-clōg'ūre, n. Act of disclosing or revealing; that which is disclosed.
Dis'coid, *a.* Having the form of a disk.
Dis-cold'al,
Dis-cŏl'or (-kŭl'ur), v. t. To alter the color of.
Dis-cŏl'or-ā'tion, n. Change of color; stain.
Dis-cŏm'fit, v. t. To cause to flee.— SYN. To rout; defeat; overthrow.
Dis-cŏm'fit-ūre, n. Defeat.
Dis-cŏm'fort, n. Uneasiness; disquiet.— v. t. To disturb the peace of.
Dis'com-mōde', v. t. To incommode; to put to inconvenience.
Dis'com-pōṣe', v. t. To ruffle; to disorder; to disturb the temper of.
Dis'com-pōṣ'ūre, n. Disorder; disturbance.
Dis'con-çẽrt', v. t. To disturb; to throw into disorder; to unsettle the mind of.
Dis'con-nĕct', v. t. To disunite; to separate.
Dis'con-nĕc'tion, n. Separation; want of union.
Dis-cŏn'so-late (42), a. Destitute of comfort or consolation; dejected; melancholy.
Dis'con-tĕnt', n. Uneasiness; dissatisfaction.
Dis'con-tĕnt'ed, a. Dissatisfied; uneasy.
Dis'con-tĕnt'ment, n. Dissatisfaction.
Dis'con-tĭn'u-ançe,
Dis'con-tĭn'u-ā'tion, } n. A ceasing; interruption.
Dis'con-tĭn'ūe, v. t. To put off.— v. i. To leave off; to cease.
Dis-cŏn'ti-nū'i-ty, n. Separation of parts.
Dis'con-tĭn'u-oŭs, a. Not continuous; interrupted.
Dis'cord, n. Disagreement; strife.
Dis-cõrd'ançe, n. Want of harmony; discord.
Dis-cõrd'ant, a. Inconsistent; disagreeing; not harmonious.
Dis-cõrd'ant-ly, adv. In a discordant manner.
Dis'count, n. Deduction of a sum; allowance.
Dis'count, or **Dis-count',** v. t. To allow discount; to lend money upon, deducting the allowance for interest.
Dis-count'a-ble, a. Suitable to be discounted.
Dis-coun'te-nançe, v. t. To discourage.— n. Disfavor; disapprobation.
Dis-coûr'age (-kûr'ej), v. t. To dishearten; to depress.
Dis-coûr'age-ment, n. That which abates courage.
Dis-coûrse', n. Conversation; talk; sermon; treatise. — v. i. To converse; to talk. — v. t. To utter or give forth.
Dis-coûr'te-oŭs (-kûr'te-), a. Uncivil; rude.
Dis-coûr'te-sy, n. Incivility; ill manners; rudeness.
Disc'oŭs, a. Like a disk.
Dis-cŏv'er, v. t. To find out; to disclose; to reveal.
Dis-cŏv'er-a-ble, a. Capable of being discovered.
Dis-cŏv'er-er, n. One who discovers.
Dis-cŏv'er-y, n. A finding out; disclosure.
Dis-crĕd'it, n. Want of credit; reproach.— v. t. To disbelieve; to disgrace.
Dis-crĕd'it-a-ble, a. Injurious to reputation.
Dis-crēet', a. Prudent; cautious; sagacious.
Dis-crēet'ly, adv. Prudently.
Dis-crĕp'an-çy,
Dis-crĕp'ançe, } n. Difference; disagreement; discordance.
Dis-crĕp'ant, a. Different; disagreeing; contrary.
Dis-crēte', a. Distinct; separate; disjoined.
Dis-crē'tion (-krĕsh'un), n. Prudence; sagacity; freedom to act at will.
Dis-crē'tion-al,
Dis-crē'tion-a-ry, } a. Left to discretion; to be governed by judgment only.
Dis-crē'tive, a. Disjunctive; separating.
Dis-crĭm'i-nāte, v. t. To distinguish; to separate.
Dis-crĭm'i-nā'tion, n. Act of discriminating; mark of distinction.
Dis-crĭm'i-na-tive, a. Serving to distinguish.
Dis-cûr'sion, n. Desultory talk.
Dis-cûr'sive, a. Roving; irregular; desultory.
Dis-cûr'sive-ly, adv. In a roving manner.
Dis'cus, n. The ancient quoit; a disk.
Dis-cŭss', v. t. [Lat. dis, apart, and quatere, to shake, strike.] To disperse; to examine by discussion.— SYN. To debate.
Dis-cŭs'sion (-kŭsh'un), n. A

debate; disquisition; disputation.
Dis-cŭss'ive, a. Able or tending to discuss.
Dis-cū'tient, a. Serving to disperse morbid matter.— n. A medicine to disperse morbid matter.
Dis-dāin', n. Haughty contempt; scorn — v. t. To scorn; to despise; to slight; to deem worthless.
Dis-dāin'ful (139), a. Scornful; haughty; contemptuous. [scorn.
Dis-dāin'ful-ly, adv. With
Dis-dāin'ful-ness, n. State of being disdainful.
Dis-ēase', n. Distemper; malady; sickness.— v. t. To affect with sickness.
Dis'em-bärk', v. t. or i. To put or go on shore; to land.
Dis-ĕm'bark-ā'tion, n. Act of disembarking.
Dis'em-bär'rass, v. t. To free from embarrassment.
Dis'em-bŏd'ied, p. a. Divested of body.
Dis'em-bŏd'y, v. t. To divest of a material body.
Dis'em-bōgue', v. To discharge at the mouth, as a stream.
Dis'em-bow'el, v. t. To take out the bowels of; to eviscerate.
Dis'en-ā'ble, v. t. To disable.
Dis'en-chánt', v. t. To free from enchantment.
Dis'en-cŭm'ber, v. t. To free from obstruction.
Dis'en-cŭm'brançe, n. Deliverance from any thing burdensome or troublesome.
Dis'en-gāge', v. t. To free from an engagement or a tie.— SYN. To detach; release; extricate; withdraw.
Dis'en-gāged', a. Vacant; at leisure.
Dis'en-gāge'ment, n. Release from engagement.
Dis'en-rōll', v. t. To erase from a roll or list.
Dis'en-tăn'gle, v. t. To set free from entanglement or perplexity.
Dis'en-tăn'gle-ment, n. Act of disentangling. [throne.
Dis'en-thrōne', v. t. To de-
Dis'en-tŏmb' (-tōōm'), v. t. To take out from a tomb.
Dis'en-trançe', v. t. To awaken from a trance.
Dis'es-teem', n. Want of esteem.— v. t. To dislike.
Dis-fā'vor, n. Want of favor;

ā, ĕ, ī, ō, ū, y̆, *long*; ă, ĕ, ĭ, ŏ, ŭ, ў, *short*; cāre, cär, åsk, ạll, what; ẽre, veil, tẽrm; pique, firm;

DISFIGURATION 113 DISPATCH

dis̟regard. — *v. t.* To discountenance.
Dis-fig'u-ra'tion, *n.* Act of disfiguring.
Dis-fig'ūre, *v. t.* To deform ; to mar ; to deface.
Dis-fig'ūre-ment, *n.* A defacement.
Dis-frän'chīṣe (-chĭz), *v. t.* To deprive of citizenship.
Dis-frän'chīṣe-ment, *n.* A deprivation of the privileges of a free citizen.
Dis-gär'nish, *v. t.* To strip of ornaments.
Dis-gôrģe', *v. t.* To vomit ; to discharge ; to give up.
Dis-grāçe', *n.* State of shame ; disfavor ; dishonor ; ignominy. — *v. t.* To dishonor ; to bring to shame.
Dis-grāçe'ful, *a.* Shameful.
Dis-grāçe'ful-ly, *adv.* In a disgraceful manner.
Dis-grāçe'ful-ness, *n.* Dishonor ; baseness ; ignominy.
●**Dis-guise'** (69, 153), *n.* A dress to conceal ; false appearance. — *v. t.* To conceal ; to hide ; to disfigure.
Dis-gŭst', *n.* Distaste ; dislike ; aversion. — *v. t.* To give dislike to ; to displease.
Dis-gŭst'ful, } *a.* Provoking
Dis-gŭst'ing, } dislike.
Dis-gŭst'ing-ly, *adv.* So as to excite disgust.
Dĭsh (140), *n.* A vessel to serve food in ; food. — *v. t.* To put in dishes.
Dĭs'ha-bĭlle', *n.* Loose dress ; an undress ; deshabille.
Dis-heärt'ĕn, *v. t.* To discourage ; to depress.
Dis-heärt'ĕn-ing, *a.* Tending to discourage.
Dĭ-shĕv'el (130), *v. t.* To suffer to hang negligently, as the hair.
Dĭsh'ing, *a.* Concave ; hollow.
Dĭṣ-hŏn'est (-ŏn'est), *a.* Void of honesty ; marked by fraud ; faithless ; knavish.
Dĭṣ-hŏn'est-ly (-ŏn'est-), *adv.* Knavishly ; with fraud.
Dĭṣ-hŏn'est-y (-ŏn'est-), *n.* Knavery ; want of integrity.
Dĭṣ-hŏn'or (-ŏn'ur, 155), *n.* Want of honor ; whatever injures the reputation ; disgrace. — *v. t.* To bring shame on ; to disgrace ; to refuse payment of.
Dĭṣ-hŏn'or-a-ble (-ŏn'ur-), *a.* Reproachful ; disgraceful ; base ; vile.
Dĭṣ-hŏn'or-a-bly (-ŏn'ur-), *adv.* Disgracefully ; basely.

Dis-ĭn'cli-nā'tion, *n.* Slight dislike or aversion.
Dis-ĭn-clīne', *v. t.* To produce dislike in.
Dĭs'in-fĕct', *v. t.* To purify from infection.
Dĭs'in-fĕc'tion, *n.* A purifying from infection.
Dĭs'in-gĕn'u-oŭs, *a.* Wanting in frankness and honesty. — SYN. Unfair ; illiberal ; deceitful ; artful.
Dĭs'in-gĕn'u-oŭs-ly, *adv.* Unfairly ; deceitfully.
Dĭs'in-gĕn'u-oŭs-ness, *n.* Want of fairness.
Dĭs'in-hĕr'i-son, *n.* Act of disinheriting.
●**Dĭs'in-hĕr'it,** *v. t.* To cut off from inheriting.
Dis-ĭn'te-grāte, *v. t.* To separate into integrant parts.
Dis-ĭn'te-grā'tion, *n.* A separation of integrant parts.
Dĭs'in-tĕr', *v. t.* To take out of a grave.
Dis-ĭn'ter-est-ed, *a.* Free from self-interest ; impartial.
Dis-ĭn'ter-est-ed-ly, *adv.* In a disinterested manner.
Dis-ĭn'ter-est-ed-ness, *n.* Freedom from self-interest.
Dĭs'in-tĕr'ment, *n.* Act of taking out of a grave.
●**Dĭs'in-thrăll',** *v. t.* To set free ; to liberate from bondage.
Dĭs'in-thrăll'ment, *n.* Emancipation.
Dĭs-join', *v. t.* To separate ; to disunite.
Dĭs-joint', *v. t.* To separate the joints of ; to dislocate.
Dĭs-jŭnçt', *a.* Separate ; disjoined.
Dĭs-jŭnç'tion, *n.* Disunion ; separation. [disjoin.
Dĭs-jŭnç'tive, *a.* Tending to
Dĭs-jŭnç'tive-ly, *adv.* In a disjunctive manner.
Dĭsk, *n.* A quoit ; face of the sun, moon, or planet.
Dis-līke', *n.* Positive aversion. — *v. t.* To have an aversion to ; to hate.
●**Dĭs'lo-cāte,** *v. t.* To displace ; to put out of joint.
Dĭs'lo-cā'tion, *n.* Act of displacing ; a joint put out.
Dis-lŏdģe', *v. t.* To drive from a place of rest or a station.
Dis-loy'al, *a.* Not loyal or true to allegiance.
Dis-loy'al-ly, *adv.* Faithlessly.
Dis-loy'al-ty, *n.* Want of fidelity.
Dĭṣ'mal. *a.* [Lat. *dies malus,* evil day.] Dark ; gloomy.

Dĭṣ'mal-ly, *adv.* Gloomily ; darkly.
Dis-măn'tle, *v. t.* To strip of dress, apparatus, equipments, &c. [a mast or of masts.
Dis-măst', *v. t.* To deprive of
Dis-māy', *v. t.* To daunt ; to appall. — *n.* Loss of courage ; fright ; terror.
Dis-mĕm'ber, *v. t.* To divide member from member.
Dis-mĕm'ber-ment, *n.* Separation ; division ; partition.
Dis-mĭss', *v. t.* To send away ; to discharge.
Dis-mĭss'al, *n.* A dismissing.
Dis-mĭs'sion (-mĭsh'un), *n.* A sending away ; discharge ; rejection. [to depart.
Dis-mĭss'ive, *a.* Giving leave
Dis-mount', *v. i.* To alight from a horse, &c. — *v. t.* To throw from a horse.
●**Dĭṣ'o-bē'di-ençe,** *n.* Neglect or refusal to obey.
Dĭṣ'o-bē'di-ent, *a.* Neglecting or refusing to obey.
●**Dĭṣ'o-bey',** *v. t.* To neglect or refuse to obey.
Dĭṣ'o-blīģe', *v. t.* To offend by unkindness or incivility.
Dĭṣ'o-blīģ'ing, *a.* Not disposed to gratify ; unkind.
Dĭṣ'o-blīģ'ing-ly, *adv.* In a disobliging manner.
Dis-ôr'der, *n.* Confusion ; disease. — *v. t.* To throw into confusion ; to discompose ; to make sick. [indisposed.
Dis-ôr'dered, *p. a.* Confused ;
Dis-ôr'der-ly, *a.* Confused ; lawless ; vicious ; irregular.
Dis-ôr'gan-i-zā'tion, *n.* Subversion of order.
Dis-ôr'gan-īze, *v. t.* To throw into utter disorder.
Dĭṣ-ōwn', *v. t.* To refuse to own ; to renounce.
Dis-păr'aġe, *v. t.* To injure by depreciating comparisons.
Dis-păr'aġe-ment (132), *n.* Injurious comparison with something else. — SYN. Detraction ; derogation: decrying. [difference.
Dis-pär'i-ty, *n.* Inequality ;
Dis-pärt', *v. t.* or *i.* To part.
Dis-păs'sion, *n.* Freedom from passion.
Dis-păs'sion-ate, *a.* Free from passion ; cool ; calm.
Dis-păs'sion-ate-ly, *adv.* In a dispassionate manner.
●**Dis-pătch',** *v. t.* To send away ; to execute speedily ; to put out of the way ; to kill. — *n.* Speed ; haste ; message sent.

---

sŭn, ôr,'dọ, wolf, tōō, tōok; ŭrn, rụe, pụll; ç, ġ, *soft*; c, ġ, *hard*; aṣ; eẋist; ŋ *as* ng; this.

Dis-pel' (129), v. t. To drive away; to disperse.
Dis-pen'sa-ble, a. Capable of being dispensed or dispensed with.
Dis-pen'sa-ry, n. A place for dispensing medicines.
Dis-pen-sa'tion, n. Distribution; exemption from a law.
Dis-pen'sa-tive,) a. Having
Dis-pen'sa-to-ry,) power of granting dispensation.
Dis-pen'sa-to-ry (107), n. A book telling how to compound medicines.
Dis-pense', v. t. To deal out.
Dis-pens'er, n. One who dispenses. [ulate.
Dis-peo'ple, v. t. To depopulate.
Dis-perse', v. t. To scatter.
Dis-per'sion, n. Act of scattering, or state of being scattered. [disperse.
Dis-per'sive, a. Tending to
Dis-pir'it, v. t. To discourage; to deject.
Dis-plaçe', v. t. To put out of place; to remove.
Dis-plaçe'ment, n. Act of displacing.
Dis-plant', v. t. To remove, as a plant.
Dis-play', v. t. To spread wide; to open; to exhibit. — n. Exhibition; show.
Dis-pleáse', v. t. To give offense to. — v. i. To disgust.
Dis-pleas'ure (-plezh'ur), n. Slight anger; pain received.
Dis-plode', v. t. or i. To burst with a loud report.
Dis-plo'sion, n. A bursting with noise; detonation.
Dis-port', n. Play: sport; pastime. — v. i. To sport; to play; to wanton. — v. t. To amuse; to divert.
Dis-pos'a-ble, a. Capable of being disposed of.
Dis-pos'al (133), n. Act or power of disposing; management.
Dis-pose', v. t. To place; to incline; to adapt or fit.
Dis-posed', a. Inclined, minded. [poses.
Dis-pos'er, n. One who disposes.
Dis-po-si'tion (-zish'un), n. Order; arrangement; distribution; temper of mind.
Dis-pos-sess' (or -poz-zes'), v. t. To put out of possession.
Dis-pos-ses'sion (-pos-sesh'un or -poz-zesh'un), n. Act of dispossessing.
Dis-praise', n. Censure; blame. — v. t. To blame.

Dis-proof', n. Refutation; confutation.
Dis-pro-pôr'tion, n. Want of proportion or symmetry. — v. t. To make unsuitable.
Dis-pro-pôr'tion-al,) a. Un-
Dis-pro-pôr'tion-ate,) equal; without proportion.
Dis-prove', v. t. To confute.
Dis-pu-ta-ble, a. Capable of being disputed.
Dis-pu-tant, n. One who disputes or argues.
Dis-pu-tā'tion, n. Act of disputing; argumentation.
Dis-pu-tā'tious, a. Given to dispute.
Dis-pūte', v. t. or i. To debate; to quarrel; to contend for. — n. Contest in words.
Dis-pūt'er, n. One who disputes.
Dis-qual'i-fi-ca'tion, n. That which disqualifies.
Dis-qual'i-fȳ, v. t. To make unfit; to disable.
Dis-qui'et, v. t. To make uneasy. — SYN. To disturb; vex; fret. — n. Restlessness; uneasiness.
Dis-qui'e-tūde, n. Uneasiness; anxiety.
Dis'qui-si'tion (-zĭsh'un), n. A formal discussion on any subject; inquiry.
Dis're-gärd', n. Slight; neglect; omission of notice. — v. t. To slight; to disregard.
Dis're-gärd'fụl, a. Negligent.
Dis-rĕl'ish, n. Distaste; dislike. — v. t. To dislike the taste of.
Dis-rĕp'u-ta-ble, a. Not creditable; dishonorable.
Dis're-pūte', n. Loss or want of reputation or esteem.
Dis're-spĕct', n. Want of respect; incivility. [rude.
Dis're-spĕct'fụl, a. Uncivil;
Dis're-spĕct'fụl-lȳ, adv. With disrespect.
Dis-rōbe', v. t. or i. To undress.
Dis-rŭp'tion, n. Act of breaking asunder; breach.
Dis-săt'is-făc'tion, n. Discontent: dislike; displeasure.
Dis-săt'is-fȳ, v. t. To displease.
Dis-sĕct', v. t. To divide and examine minutely.
Dis-sĕct'i-ble, a. Capable of being dissected.
Dis-sĕc'tion, n. Act or art of dissecting; anatomy.
Dis-sĕct'or, n. An anatomist.
Dis-seize', v. t. To dispossess wrongfully.

Dis-sei'zin, n. Unlawful possession. [seizes.
Dis-sei'zor, n. One who dis-
Dis-sĕm'ble, v. t. To conceal; to feign. — v. i. To act the hypocrite. [sembles.
Dis-sĕm'bler, n. One who dis-
Dis-sĕm'i-nāte, v. t. To scatter in various directions, like seed; to sow.
Dis-sĕm'i-nā'tion, n. Act of scattering, as seed; diffusion.
Dis-sĕm'i-nā'tor, n. One who disseminates.
Dis-sĕn'sion, n. Contention; disagreement; strife.
Dis-sĕnt', v. i. To disagree; to differ in opinion. — n. Disagreement.
Dis-sĕnt'er, n. One who dissents, esp. a Protestant who dissents or separates from the church of England.
Dis-sĕn'tient, a. Disagreeing.
Dis'ser-tā'tion, n. A discourse; essay; treatise.
Dis-sĕrve', v. t. To injure.
Dis-sĕrv'içe, n. Injury done.
Dis-sĕrv'içe-a-ble, a. Hurtful.
Dis-sĕv'er, v. t. To part in two; to disunite.
Dis-sĕv'er-ance, n. Act of severing. [ment.
Dis'si-dence, n. Disagreement.
Dis'si-dent, n. A dissenter. — a. Dissenting; disagreeing. [ferent.
Dis-sĭm'i-lar, a. Unlike; different.
Dis-sĭm'i-lăr'i-tȳ,) n. Un-
Dis'si-mĭl'i-tūde,) likeness; difference; want of resemblance.
Dis-sĭm'u-lā'tion, n. Act of dissembling; hypocrisy.
Dis'si-pāte, v. t. To drive asunder; to scatter.
Dis'si-pā'ted, a. Given to pleasure; dissolute; loose.
Dis'si-pā'tion, n. Dispersion; a dissolute course of life.
Dis-sō'cia-ble, a. Not well associated; ill-matched.
Dis-sō'cial, a. Unfriendly to society.
Dis-sō'ci-āte (-sō'shi-, 92), v. t. To disunite; to separate.
Dis-sō'ci-ā'tion (-so-shī-), n. Separation; division.
Dis'so-lu-ble, a. Capable of being dissolved.
Dis'so-lūte, a. Loose in morals or conduct.
Dis'so-lūte-lȳ, adv. In a loose or wanton manner.
Dis'so-lūte-nĕss, n. State of being dissolute; debauchery.

ā, ĕ, ī, ō, ū, ȳ, long; ă, ĕ, ĭ, ŏ, ŭ, ў, short; câre, cär, ăsk, ạll, whạt; ẽre, vẹil, tẽrm; pīque, firm;

DISSOLUTION 115 DIVERSITY

Dis·so·lū′tion, *n.* Act of dissolving; ruin; end; death.
Dis·sōlv′a·ble, *a.* Capable of being dissolved.
Dis·sōlve′, *v. t.* or *i.* To melt; to liquefy; to separate; to terminate; to perish.
Dis·sōlv′ent, *n.* That which dissolves. — *a.* Having power to dissolve.
Dis·sōlv′er, *n.* One who dissolves.
Dis′so·nance, *n.* Discord.
Dis′so·nant, *a.* Discordant; harsh to the ear.
Dis·suāde′ (-swād′, 99), *v. t.* To advise or exhort against.
Dis·suā′sion, *n.* Act of dissuading.
Dis·suā′sive, *a.* Tending to dissuade. — *n.* Argument employed to deter.
Dis′syl·lāb′ic, *a.* Consisting of two syllables only.
Dis·sȳl′la·ble, or **Dis′syl·la·ble**, *n.* [Gr. *dis*, twice, and *sullabē*, syllable.] A word of two syllables.
Dis′taff (140), *n.* A staff from which flax is drawn in spinning.
Dis·tāin′, *v. t.* To stain; to discolor.
Dis′tance, *n.* Space between bodies; remoteness; reserve. — *v. t.* To leave behind, as in a race.
Dis′tant, *a.* Remote in time, place, or connection, &c. — SYN. Separate; far; indistinct; shy; cool; haughty.
Dis′tant·ly, *adv.* At a distance; with reserve.
Dis·tāste′, *n.* Disrelish; disgust; aversion. — *v. t.* To dislike; to loathe.
Dis·tāste′ful, *a.* Nauseous; offensive.
Dis·tĕm′per, *n.* A morbid state of the body; disease; malady; a peculiar preparation of opaque colors, in painting. — *v. t.* To affect with disease; to disturb.
Dis·tĕm′per·a·tūre, *n.* Violent disturbance; slight illness; distemper.
Dis·tĕnd′, *v. t.* To extend in all directions; to swell.
Dis·tĕn′tion, *n.* A stretching.
Dis′tich (dis′tik), *n.* A couplet, or two poetic lines.
Dis·till′ (138), *v. i.* To fall in
Dis·til′ } drops; to drop. — *v.*

t. To let fall in drops; to extract spirit from.
Dis′til·lā′tion, *n.* The act of distilling. [tills.
Dis·till′er, *n.* One who distills.
Dis·till′er·y, *n.* A place for distilling.
Dis·tinct′, *a.* Separate; different; clear; not confused.
Dis·tinc′tion, *n.* Difference.
Dis·tinct′ive, *a.* Marking distinction or difference.
Dis·tinct′ive·ly, *adv.* With distinction; plainly.
Dis·tinct′ly, *adv.* In a distinct manner.
Dis·tinct′ness, *n.* Clearness; precision.
Dis·tin′guish (-ting′gwish), *v. t.* To note the difference between. — *v. i.* To make distinctions.
Dis·tin′guish·a·ble, *a.* Capable of being distinguished.
Dis·tin′guished (-gwisht), *a.* Eminent; celebrated; illustrious.
Dis·tort′, *v. t.* To twist out of shape; to pervert.
Dis·tor′tion, *n.* Act of distorting; grimace; perversion.
Dis·tract′, *v. t.* To perplex; to agitate; to craze.
Dis·tract′ed, *n.* Disordered in intellect; deranged.
Dis·tract′ed·ly, *adv.* Wildly; with confusion.
Dis·trac′tion, *n.* Confusion; state of disordered reason.
Dis·tract′ive, *a.* Causing distraction.
Dis·trāin′, *v. t.* To seize for debt without legal process.
Dis·trāint′, *n.* A seizure for debt, without legal process.
Dis·trĕss′, *n.* Act of distraining; thing seized; extreme pain; state of danger. — *v. t.* To pain; to afflict.
Dis·trĕss′ing, *a.* Afflicting.
Dis·trĭb′u·ta·ble, *a.* Capable of being distributed.
Dis·trĭb′ute, *v. t.* To divide among a number; to allot.
Dis·trĭb′u·ter, *n.* One who distributes.
Dis′tri·bū′tion, *n.* Act of distributing; allotment.
Dis·trĭb′u·tive, *a.* Distributing, or tending to distribute; expressive of distribution.
Dis·trĭb′u·tive·ly, *adv.* By distribution; singly.
Dis′trict, *n.* A circuit; region; tract. — *v. t.* To divide into circuits.
Dis·trust′, *v. t.* To suspect;

to disbelieve. — *n.* Want of confidence; suspicion.
Dis·trust′ful, *a.* Suspicious.
Dis·trust′ful·ly, *adv.* In a distrustful manner.
Dis·tûrb′, *v. t.* To perplex; to disquiet; to agitate.
Dis·tûrb′ance, *n.* Agitation; confusion; tumult.
Dis·tûrb′er, *n.* One who causes disturbance.
Dis·ūn′ion (-yun′yun), *n.* Want of union; separation.
Dis′ū·nīte′, *v. t.* To separate.
Dis′ū′ni·ty, *n.* A state of separation; want of unity.
Dis·ū′sage, *n.* Cessation of use or practice.
Dis·ūse′, *v. t.* To cease to make use of.
Dis·ūse′, *n.* Cessation or neglect of use; desuetude.
Ditch (140), *n.* A trench in the earth. — *v. t.* or *i.* To trench; to make a ditch.
Dĭth′y·răm′bic, *a.* Wild; impetuous. — *n.* A wild enthusiastic poem.
Dĭt′to, *n.* The same thing as before.
Dĭt′ty (141), *n.* A poem to be sung. [urine.
Dī′u·rēt′ic, *a.* Promoting
Dī·ûr′nal (45), *a.* [Lat. *diurnalis*, from *dies*, day.] Constituting a day; daily.
Dī·vǎn′, *n.* A Turkish council of state; a council chamber; a kind of small sofa, or cushioned seat.
Dī·vǎr′i·cāte, *v. i.* To divide into two branches.
Dī·vǎr′i·cā′tion, *n.* A parting or forking; separation.
Dīve, *v. i.* To plunge under water; to go deep.
Dī′ver, *n.* One who dives; a certain bird remarkable for diving.
Dī·vêrge′, *v. i.* To tend different ways from one point.
Dī·vêr′gence, *n.* Departure in different directions from a common point.
Dī·vêr′gent, *a.* Separating from each other.
Dī′vers, *a.* Several; sundry.
Dī′verse, *a.* Varied; different; unlike; various.
Dī′verse·ly, *adv.* Differently.
Dī·vêr′si·fi·cā′tion, *n.* The act of making various.
Dī·vêr′si·fy, *v. t.* To make diverse or various.
Dī·vêr′sion, *n.* A turning aside; sport; amusement.
Dī·vêr′si·ty, *n.* Difference; unlikeness; variety.

---

sŏn, ôr, dọ, wọlf, tōō, tŏŏk; ûrn, rụe, pụll; ç, ġ, *soft*; c, g, *hard*; aṣ; exist; ŋ as ng; this.

Di'verse-ly, *adv.* In different ways or directions.
Di-vert' (12), *v. t.* To turn aside; to gratify; to amuse.
Di-vērt'ing, *a.* Serving to amuse or entertain; pleasing.
Di-vērt'ise-ment, *n.* Diversion.
Di-vĕst', *v. t.* To strip, as of clothes, arms, &c.; to dispossess.
Di-vĕst'ūre, *n.* The act of putting off. [ing divided.
Di-vĭd'a-ble, *a.* Capable of being divided.
Di-vīde', *v. t.* To part or separate, as a whole; to distribute.— *v. i.* To part.
Div'i-dend, *n.* Number to be divided; share divided.
Di-vĭd'er, *n.* One who, or that which, divides; (*pl.*) mathematical compasses.
Div'i-nā'tion, *n.* A foretelling; prediction.
Di-vīne', *a.* Pertaining to God; godlike; heavenly.— *n.* A minister of the Gospel.— *v.* To foretell; to practice divination.
Di-vīne'ly, *adv.* In a godlike manner.
Div'ing-bĕll, *n.* A machine for going under water in.
Di-vĭn'i-ty, *n.* Divine nature; the Deity; theology.
Di-vĭs'i-bĭl'i-ty, *n.* Quality of being divisible.
Di-vĭs'i-ble, *a.* Capable of being divided.
Di-vĭs'ion (-vĭzh'un), *n.* Act of dividing; state of being divided; that which divides; portion separated by dividing; section of an army or fleet commanded by a general officer.
Di-vĭs'ion-al, *a.* Relating to division.
Di-vĭs'or, *n.* A number that divides another.
Di-vŏrçe', *n.* Legal dissolution of marriage.
Di-vŏrçe'ment,
Di-vŏrçe', *v. t.* To separate, as a husband and wife.
Di-vŭlge', *v. t.* To publish; to disclose or make known.
Diz'en or **Dī'zen**, *v. t.* To dress gaudily. [vertigo.
Diz'zi-ness, *n.* Giddiness;
Diz'zy (135), *a.* Affected with vertigo; giddy.
Dọ (dọọ), *v.* [*imp.* DID; *p. p.* DONE.] To act; to perform; to practice; to execute; to succeed; to answer the purpose.
Dŏç'i-ble, *a.* Easily taught.

Dŏç'īle, *a.* Ready to be taught; teachable.
Do-çĭl'i-ty, *n.* Teachableness.
Dŏç'i-măs'tic, *a.* Proving by experiments.
Dŏck, *n.* A place for ships; a certain plant.— *v. t.* To cut short; to place in a dock.
Dŏck'age, *n.* Pay for using a dock.
Dŏck'et, *n.* A label tied to goods; a register of cases in court.— *v. t.* To mark with titles; to enter in a docket.
Dŏck'-yärd, *n.* A yard for naval stores.
Dŏc'tor, *n.* [Lat., from *docere*, to teach.] A title in divinity, law, &c.; a physician.
Dŏc'tor-ate, *n.* The degree of a doctor. [cian
Dŏc'tress, *n.* A female physician.
Dŏc'tri-nal, *a.* Consisting in, or containing, doctrine.— *n.* Something that is part of doctrine.
Dŏc'tri-nal-ly, *adv.* In a doctrinal manner or form.
Dŏc'trine, *n.* What is taught; a gospel truth; tenet.
Dŏc'u-ment, *n.* Written instruction; proof.— *v. t.* To furnish with documents.
Dŏc'u-mĕnt'al, *a.* Consisting
Dŏc'u-mĕnt'a-ry, in written evidence.
Do-dĕc'a-gŏn, *n.* A figure of twelve equal sides.
Do-dĕc'a-hē'dron, *n.* A solid having twelve equal faces.
Dŏdge, *v. i.* To start suddenly aside.— *v. i.* To evade by Dodecahestarting aside. drons.
Dō'do, *n.* (*pl.* **Dō'dŏes**, 140.) A large bird of the island of Mauritius, now extinct.
Dōe (149), *n.* A she-deer; a female of the fallow deer.
Dō'er, *n.* One who performs.
Dŏes (dŭz), *third person singular, indicative present of Do.*
Dŏff (123), *v. t.* [From *do off*.] To put off, as dress; to strip.
Dŏg, *n.* A domestic animal; an andiron; an iron hook.— *v. t.* To follow continually.
Dŏg'-dāys, *n. pl.* Days when the dog-star rises and sets with the sun in July and August.
Dŏge, *n.* Formerly the chief magistrate of Venice and of Genoa.
Dŏg'ged (57), *a.* Sullen; morose; sour.

Dŏg'ged-ly, *adv.* Sullenly; morosely; sourly.
Dŏg'ged-ness, *n.* Sullenness; moroseness; sourness.
Dŏg'ger-el, *n.* A kind of irregular measure in poetry.
Dŏg'gish, *a.* Like a dog; snappish; churlish.
Dŏg'mȧ (140), *n.* [Gr., from *dokein*, to think.] A settled opinion; a maxim; a tenet; a principle.
Dog-măt'ic, *a.* Pertaining
Dog-măt'ic-al, to dogmas; positive; magisterial.
Dog-măt'ic-al-ly, *adv.* In a dogmatical manner.
Dog-măt'ics, *n. sing.* Doctrinal theology.
Dŏg'ma-tĭsm, *n.* Positiveness in opinion; arrogance.
Dŏg'ma-tĭst, *n.* One who dogmatizes.
Dŏg'ma-tīze, *v. i.* To assert positively without proof.
Dŏg'ma-tīz'er, *n.* One who dogmatizes.
Dŏg'-stär, *n.* Sirius, a star of the first magnitude.
Dŏg'-tōoth (143), *n.* A tooth like a dog's.
Dŏg'-trŏt, *n.* A gentle trot.
Doi'ly (141), *n.* A small colored napkin.
Dō'ings, *n. pl.* Things done; actions; deeds.
Doit, *n.* A small piece of money; a trifle.
Dōle, *n.* A thing dealt out; share; part; grief; sorrow.— *v. t.* To deal out in small portions.
Dōle'ful (139), *a.* Expressing or causing grief.— SYN. Mournful; sorrowful; melancholy.
Dōle'ful-ly, *adv.* In a doleful manner.
Dōle'some (-sŭm), *a.* Gloomy; dismal.
Dŏll (123), *n.* A puppet or baby for a child.
Dŏl'lar, *n.* A silver coin of the United States worth 100 cents; a similar coin current in Mexico, Spain, &c.
Dō'lŏr, *n.* Pain; grief; sorrow; distress.
Dŏl'or-ĭf'ic, *a.* Causing pain.
Dŏl'or-oŭs, *a.* Sorrowful; painful; grievous.
Dŏl'or-oŭs-ly, *adv.* In a dolorous manner.
Dō'phin, *n.* A cetaceous fish.
Dŏlt (18), *n.* A stupid fellow.
Dŏlt'ish, *a.* Stupid; dull.
Do-māin', *n.* Extent of territory or sway.— SYN. Em-

pire; dominion; possession; estate.
Dōme (140), *n.* An arched roof or cupola; a house.
Do-mĕs'tic, *a.* [Lat. *domesticus*, fr. *domus*, a house.] Belonging to a mansion or home; tame. — *n.* A houseservant.
Do-mĕs'ti-eāte. *v. t.* To make domestic or tame.
Do-mĕs'ti-cā'tion, *n.* Act of domesticating.
Dŏm'i-çīl, } *n.* A permanent
Dŏm'i-çīle, } dwelling or residence.
Dŏm'i-çīle, } *v. t.* To es-
Dŏm'i-çīl-i-āte, } tablish a fixed residence.
Dom-i-çīl'i-a-ry (*or* -sīl'ya-rȳ), *a.* Pertaining to an abode.
Dŏm'i-nant, *a.* Ruling; prevailing, — *n.* The fifth tone of the scale.
Dŏm'i-nāte, *v. t.* To rule; to govern.
Dŏm'i-nā'tion, *n.* Rule; dominion. [master.
Dŏm'i-nīe, *n.* A school-
Dŏm'i-neer', *v. i.* To rule with insolence.
Do-mĭn'i-cal, *a.* Relating to our Lord.
Do-mĭn'i-can, *n.* One of an order of monks.
Do-mĭn'ion, *n.* Sovereign authority; territory governed.
Dŏm'i-no (140), *n.* A hood or cloak; a game.
Dŏn, *n.* A Spanish title. — *v. t.* [From *do on.*] To put on, as a dress. [give.
Dō'nāte, *v. t.* To bestow; to
Do-nā'tion, *n.* Act of giving; a gift; a present.
Dŏn'a-tive, *n.* A gift; a largess.
Dōne (dŭn), *p. p.* of *Do.*
Do-nee' (121), *n.* One to whom a donation is made.
Dŏn'key (141), *n.* An ass or mule.
Dō'nor, *n.* One who gives.
Dōōm, *v. t.* To sentence; to destine. — *n.* Sentence given; judgment; fate.
Dōōms'dāy, *n.* The day of judgment.
Dōōr, *n.* The gate of a house; entrance; avenue; access.
Dōōr'-keep'er, *n.* A porter; a janitor.
Dŏr'ic, *a.* Relating to an order of Grecian architecture.
Dŏr'man-çy, *n.* State of being dormant. [vate.
Dŏr'mant, *a.* Sleeping; pri-

Dŏr'mer, }
Dŏr'mer-wĭn'dōw, } *n.* An upright window in the roof of a house. *Dormer-window.*
Dŏr'mi-to-ry, *n.* A place to sleep in.
Dŏr'mouse (143), *n.* A small animal resembling the squirrel in its habits. [back.
Dŏr'sal, *a.* Relating to the
Dōse, *n.* [Gr. *dosis,* something given.] As much medicine as is taken at one time. — *v. t.* To give in doses.
Dŏs'sil, *n.* A pledget of lint.
Dŏt, *n.* A point used in writing and printing — *v. t.* To mark with dots.
Dō'tage, *n.* Imbecility of mind from old age. [dower.
Dō'tal, *a.* Pertaining to
Dō'tard, *n.* One whose mind is impaired by age.
Do-tā'tion, *n.* Endowment.
Dōte (130), *v. i.* To be or become silly through age, or from love.
Dŏt'tard, *n.* A decayed tree.
Dŏt'ter-el, *n.* A kind of wading bird.
Doŭb'le (dŭb'l), *a.* [Lat. *duplus,* from *duplex,* twofold] Twofold; in pairs; deceitful. — *v. t.* To make twofold; to fold; to pass round a headland. — *n.* Twice the quantity or number; a shift; a counterpart.
Doŭb'le-dēal'ing (dŭb'l-), *n.* Dealing with duplicity.
Doŭb'le-ness, *n.* State of being double or doubled.
Doŭb'let, *n.* A pair; a waistcoat; (*pl.*) the same number on both dice, &c.
Doŭb-lōōn', *n.* A Spanish coin of about sixteen dollars.
Doŭb'ly, *adv.* In twice the quantity.
Doubt (dout), *v. i.* To be in suspense; to hesitate. — *v. t.* To distrust; to suspect. — *n.* Hesitation; distrust.
Doubt'ful (dout'-), *a.* Uncertain; not confident.
Doubt'ful-ly (dout'-), *adv.* With doubt.
Doubt'ful-ness (dout'-), *n.* State of being doubtful; dubiousness.
Doubt'less (dout'less), *adv.* Without doubt; unquestionably. [gift; bribe.
† **Dou-çeūr'** (dōō-sūr'), *n.* A

Douçhe (dōōsh), *n.* A jet of water thrown on some part of the body.
Dōugh (dō), *n.* Unbaked paste of bread. [fried cake.
Dōugh'nŭt (dō'-), *n.* A small
Dōugh'ty (dow'ty), *a.* Brave; illustrious; noble; strong.
Dōugh'y (dō'ȳ), *a.* Like dough.
Douse, *v. t.* or *i.* To plunge over head into water.
Dŏve, *n.* A domestic pigeon.
Dŏve'-cŏt, } *n.* A place for
Dŏve'-house, } pigeons.
Dŏve'tāil, *n.* A joint in form of a dove's tail spread. — *v. t.* To join by dovetail.] dower.
Dow'a-ble, *a.* Entitled to
Dow'a-ġer, *n.* A widow with a jointure; a widow of rank.
Dow'dy, *n.* An awkward, illdressed woman. — *a.* Awkward; ill-dressed.
Dow'el (130), *v. t.* To fasten together by pins, as boards.
Dow'er, *n.* The portion of a married woman or a widow.
Dow'ered, *a.* Portioned.
Dow'er-less, *a.* Destitute of dower. [linen cloth.
Dow'las, *n.* A kind of coarse
Down, *prep.* Along a descent. — *adv.* Below the horizon; on the ground; below. — *n.* Bank of sand; level, sandy land; soft feathers or tender hair; (*pl.*) a road for shipping.
Down'ēast, *a.* Cast downward.
Down'fall, *n.* A fall; ruin.
Down'hill, *n.* Declivity; slope of a hill; descent. — *a.* Descending; sloping.
Down'right (-rīt), *a.* Open; plain; undisguised. — *adv.* Plainly; frankly.
Down'ward, *a.* Descending. — *adv.* To a lower place.
Down'y, *a.* Like down; soft.
Dox-ŏl'o-ġy, *n.* A short hymn giving praise to God.
Dōze, *v. i.* To slumber; to drowse. — *n.* Imperfect sleep; slumber.
Dŏz'en (dŭz'n), *a.* or *n.* [Fr. *douzaine,* fr. *douze,* twelve.] Twelve.
Dōz'i-ness, *n.* Drowsiness.
Dōz'y, *a.* Drowsy; sleepy.
Drăb, *n.* A strumpet. — *a.* Of a dull brownish-yellow or gray color.
Drăb'ble, *v. t.* or *i.* To draggle.
Drăchm (drăm), } *n.* The
Drăch'ma (drăk'mà), } eighth part of an ounce.

sŭn, ôr, dọ, wọlf, tōō, tŏŏk; ûrn, rṇe, pṳll; ç, ġ, *soft*; ċ, ġ, *hard*; a**ẓ**; eẋist; ṇ *as* ng; *this*.

Draff (123), *n.* Dregs; lees; refuse. [worthless.
Draf'fy, *a.* Dreggy; waste;
Draft, *n.* Act of drawing; order for money; a drawing or sketch; a detachment. — *v. t.* To draw from a military band; to select.
Drag, *v. t.* To pull with force. — *v. i.* To be drawn along on the ground. — *n.* A net; a harrow; a kind of sledge.
Drag'gle, *v.* To draw or be drawn on the ground.
Drag'net, *n.* A net to be drawn along.
Drag'o-man (143), *n.* An interpreter.
Drag'on, *n.* A kind of fabulous winged serpent.
Drag'o-net, *n.* A little dragon.
Drag'on-fly, *n.* An insect with a long, slender body.
Dra-goon', *n.* A kind of cavalry soldier. — *v. t.* To persecute; to force.
Drain, *n.* A channel for water. — *v. t.* or *i.* To draw off gradually; to exhaust.
Drain'a-ble, *a.* Capable of being drained.
Drain'age, *n.* A draining; a system of drains.
Drake, *n.* A male duck.
Dram, *n.* A glass of spirit; eighth of an ounce troy.
Dra'ma, or **Dra'ma** (18), *n.* [Gr. *drama*, fr. *dran*, to act.] A theatrical composition; a tragedy or comedy; a play.
Dra-mat'ic,) *a.* Pertain-
Dra-mat'ic-al,) ing to the drama.
Dram'a-tist, *n.* A dramatic author or writer of plays.
Dram'a-tize, *v. t.* To represent in a drama.
Drank, *imp.* & *p. p.* of *Drink.*
Drape, *v. t.* To cover with drapery. [in cloths.
Dra'per, *n.* One who deals
Dra'per-y, *n.* The dress of a picture or statue. [ive.
Dras'tle, *a.* Powerful; act-
Draught (draft), *n.* Act of drawing; quantity drank at once; delineation; current of air; depth of water; (*pl.*) a game.
Draught'-horse (draft'-), *n.* A horse for drawing.
Draughts'man (143), *n.* One who draws writings or designs.
Draw, *v. t.* or *i.* [*imp.* DREW; *p. p.* DRAWN.] To pull; to allure; to delineate; to sketch. — *n.* Act of drawing: a lot drawn.
Draw'back, *n.* A hindrance; duty refunded on goods; any loss of advantage.
Draw'-bridge, *n.* A bridge to be drawn up or aside.
Draw-ee', *n.* One on whom a bill is drawn.
Draw'er, *n.* One who draws a bill; a sliding box; (*pl.*) an under garment for the legs. [sketch.
Draw'ing, *n.* A delineation;
Draw'ing-room, *n.* A room for company.
Drawl, *v. t.* or *i.* To speak in a slow, lengthened tone. — *n.* A lengthened utterance of the voice.
Drawn, *p. p.* of *Draw.*
Dray, *n.* A low cart on wheels. [in a dray.
Dray'-horse, *n.* A horse used
Dray'man (143), *n.* A man that drives a dray.
Dread, *n.* Great and continuing fear; terror. — *v. t.* To be in great fear. — *a.* Awful; terrible.
Dread'ful, *a.* Inspiring dread. — SYN. Terrible; shocking; frightful.
Dread'ful-ly, *adv.* Terribly.
Dread'less, *a.* Fearless; bold.
Dread'naught (-nawt), *n.* A very thick cloth, or a garment made of it.
Dream, *n.* Thoughts in sleep; vain fancy. — *v. i.* or *t.* [*imp.* & *p. p.* DREAMED, or DREAMT.] To think in sleep; to think idly; to fancy.
Dream'er, *n.* One who dreams; visionary. [*Dream.*
Dreamt, *imp.* & *p. p.* of
Drear,) *a.* Sorrowful; dis-
Drear'y,) mal; gloomy.
Drear'i-ness, *n.* Gloominess.
Dredge, *n.* An oyster-net. — *v. t.* To sprinkle flour on; to gather with a dredge.
Dredg'er, *n.* A man who fishes with a dredge.
Dredg'ing-box, *n.* A box for sprinkling with flour.
Dreg'gy, *a.* Containing dregs.
Dregs, *n. pl.* Lees; refuse.
Drench, *v. t.* To wet thoroughly; to soak; to physic violently. — *n.* A draught; a potion of medicine.
Dress (124), *v. t.* [*imp.* & *p. p.* DRESSED, DREST.] To clothe; to deck; to cook; to cover a wound; to make straight. — *n.* Clothes worn; garments.

Dress'er, *n.* One who dresses; a kitchen table; shelves for dishes.
Dress'ing, *n.* Dress; application to a sore; manure; stuffing; force meat.
Dress'ing-room, *n.* A room for dressing in.
Dress'y, *a.* Showy in dress.
Drib'ble, *v. t.* To slaver; to drivel.
Drib'blet,) *n.* A small part
Drib'let,) or quantity; a petty sum.
Drift, *n.* Pile of snow or sand driven together; design; aim. — *v. i.* or *t.* To float; to form in heaps.
Drill (113), *n.* A tool for boring holes. — *v. t.* To bore, as metal; to train by exercise.
Drill'-plow,) *n.* A plow
Drill'-plough,) for sowing in drills.
Drink, *v. i.* [*imp.* & *p. p.* DRANK,] To swallow liquor. — *v. t.* To swallow; to imbibe. — *n.* Liquor of any kind for drinking.
Drink'a-ble, *a.* Capable of being, or fit to be, drunk.
Drink'er, *n.* One who drinks.
Drip, *v. i.* To fall in drops. — *v. t.* To let fall in drops.
Drip'pings, *n. pl.* Fat falling from roasting meat.
Drive, *v. t.* [*imp.* DROVE; *p. p.* DRIVEN.] To urge or force; to compel; to carry on. — *v. i.* To rush on; to be impelled. — *n.* An excursion in a carriage.
Driv'el (driv'l, 130), *v. i.* To slaver; to dote. — *n.* Slaver; spittle.
Driv'el-er,) *n.* A simpleton;
Driv'el-ler,) a dotard.
Driv'en, *p. p.* of *Drive.*
Driv'er, *n.* One who drives.
Driz'zle, *v. i.* Fine rain or mist. — *v. i.* To fall in small drops or fine rain. [small drops.
Driz'zly, *a.* Shedding very
Droll, *a.* Comical; odd; diverting; queer; strange. — *n.* A jester; a buffoon.
Droll'er-y, *n.* Buffoonery; low sport; idle jokes.
Drom'e-da-ry (drum'-) *n.* [From Gr. *dromas*, running.]

Dromedary.

ā, ē, ī, ō, ū, y, *long*; ă, ĕ, ĭ, ŏ, ŭ, y̆, *short*; câre, ôar, åsk, ạll, whạt; ẽre, veil tẽrm; pïque, fïrm;

DRONE 119 DUODENUM

A camel with one hump on the back.
Drōne, *n.* The male bee; a sluggard; a low humming sound.— *v. i.* To live idly.
Drōop, *v. i.* [Allied to *drop.*] To sink down, as from weakness; to pine; to languish; to be dispirited.
Drŏp, *n.* A globule of moisture; a small quantity; an ear-ring; part of a gallows. — *v. i.* (129) To fall in drops. — *v. t.* To let fall.
Drŏp'si-cal, *a.* Diseased with, or inclined to, dropsy.
Drŏp'sy, *n.* A morbid collection of water in the body.
Drŏss (124), *n.* The scum of metals; refuse.
Drŏss'y, *a.* Full of dross.
Drought, } *n.* Dry weather; **Drouth,** } dryness; thirst.
Drōve, *imp.* of *Drive.* — *n.* A number of cattle driven.
Drōv'er, *n.* One who drives cattle to market.
Drown, *v. t.* To suffocate in water; to overflow, — *v. i.* To be suffocated in water.
Drowse, *v. i.* To grow heavy with sleep; to doze.
Drows'i-ly, *adv.* Sleepily.
Drow'si-ness, *a.* Sleepiness.
Drow'ġy, *a.* Sleepy; heavy.
Drŭb, *n.* A thump; a blow. — *v. t.* To beat soundly.
Drŭb'bing, *n.* A beating.
Drŭdġe, *v. i.* To labor in mean offices; to toil; to slave. — *n.* A slave to work.
Drŭdġ'er-y, *n.* Hard labor; ignoble toil.
Drŭġ, *n.* A substance used in medicine; a thing worthless or of slow sale. — *v. t.* To administer drugs to; to affect with drugs.
Drŭġ'ġet, *n.* A coarse woolen cloth. [drugs.
Drŭġ'ġist, *n.* One who deals in
Dru'id, *n.* An ancient Celtic priest.
Dru-id'ic-al, *a.* Pertaining to the druids. [druids.
Dru'id-iṣm, *n.* Religion of the
Drŭm, *n.* A military instrument; part of the ear.— *v. i.* To beat a drum; to beat. — *v. t.* To expel by beat of drum. [drummer.
Drŭm'-mā'jor, *n.* The chief
Drŭm'mer, *n.* One who beats a drum. [beating drums.
Drŭm'stick, *n.* A stick for
Drŭnk, *a.* Intoxicated; inebriated. [to drunkenness.
Drŭnk'ard, *n.* One addicted

Drŭnk'en (drŭnk'n), *a.* Intoxicated.
Drŭnk'en-ness (103), *n.* Intoxication; inebriation.
Dru-pā'ceoŭs, *a.* Producing drupes.
Drupe, *n.* A fruit without valves, as the plum.
Dry (135), *a.* Having no moisture; thirsty; sarcastic; keen.— *v. t.* or *i.* To make or grow dry. — *Dry goods*, cloths, &c., in distinction from groceries.
Drȳ'ad, *n.* A wood-nymph.
Drȳ'ly, *adv.* Coldly; sarcastically.
Drȳ'ness, *n.* Want of moisture; thirst; drought.
Drȳ'-rŏt, *n.* A decay of timber. [dry.
Drȳ'-shŏd, *a.* Having the feet
Dū'al, *a.* Expressing the number two.
Dū'al-iṣm, *n.* A system founded on a double principle.
Du-äl'i-ty, *n.* State of being two.
Dŭb, *v. t.* To confer a title on.
Dū'bi-oŭs, *a.* Of uncertain issue; not clear or plain. — SYN. Unsettled; doubtful; equivocal. [fully.
Dū'bi-oŭs-ly, *adv.* Doubt-
Dū'bi-oŭs-ness, *n.* Uncertainty. [duke.
Dū'cal, *a.* Pertaining to a
Dūe'at, *n.* A coin struck in the dominions of a duke.
Dŭch'ess, *n.* Wife of a duke; a female sovereign of a dukedom.
Dŭch'y, *n.* Territory of a duke or duchess.
Dŭck, *n.* A water-fowl; a species of canvas.— *v. t.* or *i.* To plunge under water; to stoop or nod.
Dŭck'ing, *n.* Immersion of the head in water.
Dŭck'ling, *n.* A young duck.
Dŭet, *n.* A tube; a canal; a passage.
Dŭe'tile, *a.* Easily led or drawn; extensible.
Duc-til'i-ty, *n.* The quality of being easily extended.
Dŭdġ'eon (dŭj'un), *n.* A small dagger; malice; ill-will; resentment.
Dŭdṣ, *n. pl.* Old clothes.
Due (27), *a.* Owed; owing; proper; seasonable.— *adv.* Directly; exactly.— *n.* A debt; right; claim.
Dū'el, *n.* A fight between two.
Dū'el-ing, } *n.* A fighting in **Dū'el-ling,** } single combat.

Dū'el-ist } (130), *n.* A frequent **Dū'el-list** } fighter in duels.
Du-ĕn'nâ (140), *n.* An old woman or governess.
Du-ĕt', *n.* A musical piece for two performers.
Dŭġ, *n.* A teat, especially of a beast.— *v., imp. & p. p.* of *Dig.*
Duke, *n.* [Lat. *dux*, leader.] A nobleman of the highest rank.
Dūke'dōm, *n.* Estate, title, or rank, of a duke.
Dŭl'çet, *a.* Sweet; harmonious. [sweetening.
Dŭl'çi-fi-cā'tion, *n.* Act of
Dŭl'çi-fȳ, *v. i.* To sweeten.
Dŭl'çi-mer, *n.* A musical instrument played with sticks.
Dŭll, *a.* Stupid; slow; blunt.
* — *v. t.* To blunt; to stupefy. — *v. i.* To become blunt.
Dŭll'ard, *n.* A stupid person.
Dŭll'ness, } *n.* State of being **Dŭl'ness,** } dull; stupidity; bluntness; want of edge.
Dŭl'ly, *adv.* In a dull manner.
Dū'ly, *adv.* Fitly; properly.
Dŭmb (dŭm), *a.* Mute; incapable of speech; silent.
Dŭmb'-bĕll (dŭm'-), *n.* A weight to swing in the hands.
Dŭmb'ness (dŭm'-), *n.* Inability to speak; muteness.
Dŭmb'-shōw(dŭm'-), *n.* Gesture without words.
Dŭmp'ish, *a.* Stupid; moping; dull.
Dŭmp'ling, *n.* A kind of small pudding. [ing state.
Dŭmps, *n. pl.* A dull, mop-
Dŭmp'y, *a.* Short and thick.
Dŭn, *a.* Of a dark color; gloomy; obscure. — *n.* A dark color; a clamorous creditor.— *v. t.* To urge for a debt.
Dŭnçe, *n.* A blockhead; dolt.
Dŭn'-fĭsh, *n.* Codfish cured in a particular manner.
Dŭng, *n.* Excrement of animals; manure. — *v. t.* To manure with dung; to void excrement.
Dŭn'ġeon (dŭn'jun), *n.* A dark, close prison.
Dū'o-dĕç'i-mal, *a.* Proceeding by twelves. — *n. (pl.)* Multiplication in which the denominations proceed by twelves.
Dū'o-dĕç'i-mo (140), *n.* A book having twelve leaves to a sheet.
†**Dū'o-dē'num**, *n.* The first of the small intestines.

---

sŏn, ôr, dọ, wọlf, tȯȯ, tȯȯk; ûrn, rụe, pụll; ç, ġ, *soft;* c, g, *hard;* aṣ; eẋist; ṇ *as* ng; this.

DUPE   120   **EASY**

Dūpe, n. One easily deceived.
— v. t. To impose on; to deceive; to mislead.
Dū'pli-cāte, v. t. To double.
Dū'pli-cate, n. An exact copy. — n. Double; twofold.
Dū'pli-cā'tion, n. Act of doubling; a fold.
Dū'pli-ca-tūre, n. A fold.
Du-plĭç'i-ty, n. [Lat. *duplicitas*, from *duplex*. double.] Doubleness of art or speech.
— SYN. Dissimulation; deceit; guile.
Dū'ra-bĭl'i-ty, n. Power of lasting without perishing.
Dū'ra-ble (86), a. Lasting; permanent.
Dū'ra-bly, adv. So as to last.
Dū'rance, n. Imprisonment.
Du-rā'tion, n. Continuance in time.
Dū'ress, or Du-rĕss', n. Constraint; confinement.
Dūr'ing, prep. Continuing.
Dūrst, imp. of *Dare*.
Dŭsk, a. Slightly dark; darkish. — n. A tending to darkness; twilight.
Dŭsk'y, a. Partially dark.
Dŭst, n. Very fine particles of dry earth; a low condition; the grave. — v. t. To brush dust from; to throw dust on.

Dŭst'er, n. A utensil for dusting; a light overcoat to protect from dust.
Dŭst'i-ness, n. State of being dusty.
Dŭst'y, a. Covered with dust.
Dū'te-oŭs, a. Fulfilling duty; obedient; dutiful.
Dū'ti-a-ble (135), a. Subject to duties.
Dū'ti-ful, a. Obedient to parents and superiors; respectful.
Dū'ti-ful-ly, adv. Obediently.
Dū'ti-ful-ness, n. Obedience; submission.
Dū'ty (19), n. What one is bound to perform; obligation; military service; obedience; tax or customs.
Dwarf, n. A person or plant below the common size. — v. t. To hinder from growing. — a. Below the natural size.
Dwarf'ish, a. Below the usual size; little; low; small.
Dwĕll, v. [imp. DWELLED, DWELT.] To live in n place; to inhabit; to reside; to abide.

Dwĕll'er, n. An inhabitant.
Dwĕll'ing, n. A mansion; habitation; residence
Dwĭn'dle, v. i. To become less; to diminish; to fall away; to lose health.
Dȳe, v. t. To color; to stain.
— n. Coloring liquor; tinge.
Dȳe'ing (11), p. pr. Staining.
— n. Art of coloring cloths.
Dȳ'er, n. One whose trade is to color cloths, &c.
Dȳ'ing (134), p. pr. Expiring.
— p. a. Pertaining to death.
Dȳke, n. See *Dike*.
Dy-năm'ies, n. sing. [Gr. *dunamis*, power.] That branch of mechanics which treats of bodies in motion.
Dȳ'nas-ty, n. A race of sovereigns of the same family, who govern a particular country.
Dȳs'en-tĕr'y, n. A bloody discharge from the bowels, attended with griping pains.
Dys-pĕp'sy, | n. [From Gr.
Dys-pĕp'si-â, | *dus-*, ill, and *peptein*, to digest.] Indigestion, or difficulty of digestion.
Dys-pĕp'tic, a. Afflicted with, pertaining to, or consisting in dyspepsy.

E.

Ēach, a. Every one of a number taken separately.
Ēa'ger, a. [Lat. *acer*, sharp.] Keenly desirous; ardent.
Ēa'ger-ly, adv. With ardor.
Ēa'ger-ness, n. Earnestness.
Ēa'gle (146), n.
A bird of prey; a gold coin worth 10 dollars. Eagle.
Ēa'glet, n. A young eagle.
Ēar, n. The organ or sense of hearing; innate sense of melody; a spike of corn.
— v. t. To shoot into ears.
Ēarl (12), n. A nobleman ranking below a marquis.
Ēarl'dom, n. Dignity or jurisdiction of an earl.
Ēar'less, a. Without ears.
Ēar'li-ness, n. State of being early; seasonableness.
Ēar'ly, a. Being in good time

or season; soon. — adv. Soon; in good time.
Ēarn, v. t. To gain or merit by labor or services.
Ēarn'est, a. Eager; diligent. — n. Seriousness; money advanced as a pledge.
Ēar'nest-ly, adv. Eagerly.
Ēarn'ings, n. pl. The rewards of service.
Ēar'-ring, n. A pendent jewel for the ear.
Ēarth (12), n. Mold or fine particles of the globe; the world; land; country. — v. t. To cover with mold.
Ēarth'en, a. Made of earth or clay. [earth.
Ēarth'ly, a. Pertaining to
Ēarth'quāke, n. A shaking or trembling of the earth.
Ēarth'y, a. Consisting of, or relating to, earth; like earth.
Ēar'-wax, n. A thick matter secreted in the ear.
Ēar'wig, n. An insect.
Ēase, n. Freedom from pain;

rest; facility. — v. t. To relieve from pain; to alleviate.
Ēa'sel (3'zl), n. A painter's frame to rest his canvas on.
Ēase'ment n. Ease; relief.
Ēa'si-ly, adv. With ease; gently.
Ēa'si-ness, n. State of being easy; Easel.
Ēast, n. The quarter where the sun rises. — a. From or toward the rising sun.
Ēast'er, n. The feast of Christ's resurrection.
Ēast'er-ly, a. Pertaining to the east; coming from the east. — adv. Toward the east; the east. [the east.
Ēast'ern, a. Being in or from
Ēast'ward, adv. Toward the east.
Ēa'sy, a. Free from pain or anxiety; not difficult. — SYN.

ā, ē, ī, ō, ū, y, *long*; ă, ĕ, ĭ, ŏ, ŭ, y̆, *short*; cāre, cär, ȧsk, ạll, whạt; ēre, vȩil, tērm; pīque, fĭrm;

EAT 121 EFT

Quiet; tranquil; secure; calm.
Eat, *v. t.* [*imp.* ATE; *p. p.* EAT, EATEN.] To take food; to devour; to consume; to corrode. — *v. i.* To take food; to feed.
Eat'a-ble, *a.* Fit to be eaten. — *n.* Any thing to be eaten.
Eaves, *n. pl.* Edges of a roof.
Eaves'drŏp-per, *n.* An insidious listener.
Ebb (3), *v. i.* To flow back; to decay; to decline. — *n.* Reflux of the tide; decline.
Ebb'-tīde, *n.* Reflux of a tide.
Ĕb'on, *a.* Like ebony; black.
Ĕb'on-y, *n.* A species of hard, heavy wood, generally black.
E-brī'e-ty, *n.* Drunkenness.
E-bŭll'ient, *a.* Boiling; bubbling.
Ĕb'ul-lĭ'tion (-lĭsh'un), *n.* Act of boiling or bubbling.
E-bûr'ne-an, *a.* Made of, or relating to, ivory.
Ec-çĕn'tric, *a.* Deviating
Ec-çĕn'tric-al. Ⳇ from the center; irregular; anomalous; abnormal.
Ec'çen-trĭç'i-ty, *n.* Deviation from the center; irregularity; singularity. [man.
Ec-clē'ṣi-ȧs'tic, *n.* A clergy-
Ec-clē'ṣi-ȧs'tic, Ⳇ *a.* Per-
Ec-clē'ṣi-ȧs'tic-al, taining to the church.
Ĕch'o (140), *n.* A sound reflected or reverberated. — *v. i.* or *t.* - To reverberate or resound.
E-claîr'çisse-ment (or e-klâr'siz-mŏng'), *n.* A clearing up of any thing obscure.
Eclat' (e-klä'), *n.* Striking effect; applause; renown.
Ec-lēc'tic, *a.* Selecting.
Ec-lēc'ti-çĭṣm, *n.* The practice of selecting from different systems.
E-elĭpse', *n.* [Gr. *ekleipsis*, lit. a forsaking.] Obscuration of the light of a heavenly body by the intervention of some other body. — *v. t.* To darken.
E-clĭp'tic, *n.* The apparent path of the sun.
Ec'lōgue, *n.* A pastoral poem.
E'co-nŏm'ic-al, *a.* Saving; frugal; thrifty.
E-cŏn'o-mĭst, *n.* One who is frugal; a good manager.

E-cŏn'o-mīze (153), *v. t.* To use with economy. — *v. i.* To be economical.
E-cŏn'o-my, *n.* Frugal use of money or means; management of any undertaking; system of rules by which any thing is managed.
Ee'sta-sy, *n.* Excessive joy; rapture; enthusiasm.
Ec-stăt'ic, *a.* Transporting; rapturous. [universal.
Ĕc'u-mĕn'ic-al, *a.* General;
Ed'dy (141), *n.* Circular motion of water. — *v. i.* To move as in an eddy.
Edge, *n.* Sharp side; keenness; brink. — *v. t.* To sharpen; to border; to fringe.
Edged (ĕjd), *a.* Sharp; keen.
Edg'ing, *n.* A narrow lace; a border. [strument.
Edge'-tool, *n.* A cutting in-
Edge'wīṣe, *adv.* In the direction of the edge.
Ed'i-ble, *a.* Fit to be eaten.
E'dict, *n.* A law promulgated; a decree; an ordinance.
Ed'i-fi-cā'tion, *n.* A building up; instruction.
Ed'i-fīçe, *n.* A large structure.
Ed'i-fy, *v. t.* To build up or instruct; to improve.
E'dīle, *n.* A Roman magistrate. [lication.
Ed'it, *v. t.* To prepare for pub-
E-dĭ'tion (-dĭsh'un), *n.* Impression of a book; whole number of copies published at once.
Ed'i-tor, *n.* [Lat. *e*, out, and *dare*, to give.] One who edits, or prepares for publication.
Ed'i-tō'ri-al (83), *a.* Pertaining to, or written by, an editor. — *n.* An article in a newspaper written by the editor. [an editor.
Ed'i-tor-ship, *n.* Business of
Ed'u-eāte. *v. t.* [Lat. *e*, out, forth, and *ducere*, to lead.] To bring up. — SYN. To instruct; train; teach; foster; discipline.
Ed'u-eā'tion, *n.* Instruction; tuition; formation of manners.
Ed'u-eā'tion-al, *a.* Pertaining to education. [cates.
Ed'u-eā'tor, *n.* One who edu-
E-dūçe', *v. t.* To draw out; to elicit; to extract.
E-dŭe'tion, *n.* The act of drawing out [like fish:
Eel (140), *n.* A kind of snake-
Ef-fāçe', *v. t.* To scratch or rub out; to erase. [effacing.
Ef-fāçe'ment, *n.* The act of

Ef-fĕet', *n.* That which is done; result; issue; consequence; (*pl.*) goods. — *v. t.* To bring to pass; to accomplish. [being effected.
Ef-fĕet'i-ble, *a.* Capable of
Ef-fĕet'ĭve, *a.* Able for service. — SYN. Efficient; efficacious; active. [fect.
Ef-fĕet'ĭve-ly, *adv.* With ef-
Ef-fĕet'u-al, *a.* Producing effect; efficacious.
Ef-fĕet'u-al-ly, *adv.* With effect. [to pass.
Ef-fĕet'u-āte, *v. t.* To bring
Ef-fĕm'i-na-çy, *n.* Womanish delicacy.
Ef-fĕm'i-nate (42), *a.* Womanish; weak; unmanly.
Ĕf'fer-vĕsçe', *v. i.* To be in a state of natural ebullition; to bubble and hiss.
Ĕf'fer-vĕs'çence, *n.* Commotion; bubbling; ebullition.
Ĕf'fer-vĕs'çent, *a.* Gently boiling or bubbling.
Ef-fēte', *a.* Barren; worn out.
Ef-fi-cā'cious, *a.* Productive of effects.
Ef-fi-cā'cious-ly, *adv.* With the desired effect.
Ef-fi-ea-çy, *n.* Power to produce the desired effect.
Ef-fĭ'cien-çy (-fĭsh'en-), *n.* Power of producing effect.
Ef-fĭ'cient (-fĭsh'ent), *a.* Producing effect. — *n.* An active cause; agent. [a person.
Ef'fi-gy (141), *n.* The image of
Ef'flo-rĕsçe', *v. i.* To form a mealy powder on the surface.
Ef'flo-rĕs'çence, *n.* Act of efflorescing; production of flowers; time of flowering; an eruption.
Ef'flo-rĕs'çent, *a.* Shooting out like flowers.
Ĕf'flu-ençe, *n.* A flowing out; something that flows out.
Ĕf'flu-ent, *a.* Flowing out.
Ef-flū'vi-um, *n.* (*pl.* †Ef-flū'vi-ȧ, 147.) Exhalations from putrefying substances.
Ef'flux, Ⳇ *n.* A flowing
Ef-flŭx'ion, out; effusion.
Ĕf'fort (ĕf'furt), *n.* Exertion of strength; endeavor.
Ef-frŏnt'er-y. *n.* Impudence; excessive assurance.
Ef-fŭl'gençe, *n.* A flood of light; luster; splendor.
Ef-fŭl'gent, *a.* Shining with a flood of light; luminous.
Ef-fūṣe', *v. t.* To pour out, as a fluid; to shed.
Ef-fū'ṣion, *n.* A pouring out.
Ef-fū'ṣive, *a.* Pouring out.
Eft, *n.* A kind of lizard; newt.

Egg (125), *n.* A body formed in the females of birds, and of some other animals, from which their young is produced.

Eg'lan-tine, *n.* The sweetbrier; the honeysuckle.

E'go-tişm, *n.* [Lat. *ego,* I.] Self-commendation; vanity.

E'go-tist, *n.* One always talking of himself.

E'go-tist'ic, *a.* Addicted to egotism; conceited; full of self.
E'go-tist'ic-al,

E'go-tize, *v. i.* To talk or write much of one's self.

E-grē'ġioŭs (-grē'jus), *a.* Remarkable; extraordinary.

E-grē'ġioŭs-ly, *adv.* Enormously; remarkably.

E'gress, *n.* Act of going out.

E-grĕs'sion (e-grĕsh'un), *n.* The act of going out; egress.

E'gret, *n.* The lesser white heron.

E-grĕtte', *n.* Ornaments of feathers, ribbons, &c.

Ei'der, *n.* A kind of duck.

Ei'der-down (i'der-), *n.* Soft feathers of the eider-duck.

Eight (āt), *a.* Twice four.

Eigh'teen (ā'teen), *n.* Ten and eight; twice nine.

Eight'fold (āt-), *a.* Eight times. [the seventh.

Eighth (ātth), *a.* Next after

Eighth'ly (ātth'ly), *adv.* In the eighth place. [ten.

Eigh'ty (ā'ty), *a.* Eight times

Ei'ther (ē'ther *or* i'ther), *a. or pron.* One or the other; one of two; each.

E-jăc'u-lāte, *v. t.* To throw out; to shoot; to dart.

E-jăc'u-lā'tion, *n.* A short exclamation or prayer.

E-jăc'u-la-to-ry (107), *a.* Suddenly darted out.

E-ject', *v. t.* [Lat. *e,* out, and *jacere,* to throw.] To cast out. [expulsion.

E-jĕc'tion, *n.* A casting out;

E-jĕct'ment, *n.* Ejection; a writ to gain possession.

Eke, *v. t.* To increase; to lengthen; to protract. — *adv.* Also; moreover.

E-lăb'o-rāte, *v. t.* To produce with labor.

E-lăb'o-rate (42), *a.* Finished with great care.

E-lăb'o-rate-ly, *adv.* With great care. [orating.

E-lăb'o-rā'tion, *n.* Act of elab-

E-lăpse', *v. i.* To pass away gradually.

E-lăs'tic, *a.* Having elasticity. *n.* A kind of garter.

E-lăs-tiç'i-ty, *n.* The property by which bodies recover a former state after being bent or compressed.

E-lāte', *a.* Flushed with success. — *v. t.* To puff up; to make proud or vain.

E-lā'tion, *n.* Elevation of mind; vanity; pride.

El'bōw (140), *n.* The bend of the arm. — *v. t.* or *i.* To push with the elbow; to jostle.

El'bōw-chāir, *n.* A chair with arms.

Eld'er, *a.* Having lived longer; older. — *n.* An older person; an ecclesiastical officer; a kind of tree.

Eld'er-ly, *a.* Somewhat old.

Eld'est, *a.* Oldest; most aged.

El'e-cam-pāne', *n.* A plant whose root has a pungent taste.

E-lĕct', *v. t.* [Lat. *e,* out, from, and *legere,* to choose.] To choose for office; to prefer. — *a.* Chosen; selected. — *n.* One chosen.

E-lĕc'tion, *n.* Power of choosing; choice; preference.

E-lĕc'tion-cer', *v. t.* To make interest for office.

E-lĕct'ive, *a.* Relating to, or regulated by, choice.

E-lĕct'or, *n.* One who elects or has the right of voting.

E-lĕct'or-al, *a.* Belonging to an elector or to elections.

E-lĕc'trie, *a.* Pertaining
E-lĕc'trie-al, to electricity.

E'lee-tri'cian (-trĭsh'an), *n.* One versed in electricity.

E'lee-trĭç'i-ty, *n.* A subtle natural agent or power; the science which treats of this agent.

E-lĕc'tri-fȳ (135), *v. t.* To communicate electricity to; to excite suddenly.

E-lĕc'trīze, *v. t.* To electrify.

E-lĕc'tro-măg'net-işm, *n.* A form of magnetism produced or affected by electricity.

E-lee-trŏm'e-ter, *n.* An instrument for generating a current of electricity.

E-lĕc'tro-tȳpe, *n.* A fac-simile in metal deposited by an electro-chemical process. — *v. t.* To make a fac-simile of a metal by means of electromagnetism.

E-lĕct'u-a-ry, *n.* A medicinal confection made of powders.

El'ee-mŏṣ'y-na-ry, *a.* Given in, or living on, charity.

El'egançe, *n.* Quality of being elegant; beauty produced by training and art.

El'e-gant, *a.* Pleasing by acquired beauty or grace.

El'e-gant-ly, *adv.* With elegance; richly; gracefully.

E-lē'ġi-ăc, or **El'e-ġī'ac,** *a.* Belonging to, or used in, elegy; plaintive. [egy.

El'e-ġī'ac-al, *a.* Used in el-

El'e-ġist, *n.* A writer of elegies.

El'e-ġy, *n.* A funeral poem.

El'e-ment, *n.* The constituent part of a thing.

El'e-mĕnt'al, *a.* Pertaining to, or produced by, elements.

El'e-mĕnt'a-ry (41), *a.* Primary; rudimentary.

El'e-phant, *n.* The largest of quadrupeds.

El'e-vāte, *v. t.* [Lat., fr. *e,* out, and *levare,* to lift up.] To raise to a higher place. — SYN. To exalt; elate; cheer; excite.

El'e-vā'tion, *n.* Act of raising; a high station.

El'e-vā'tor, *n.* One who, or that which, elevates; a contrivance for lifting grain.

E-lĕv'en, *n.* Ten and one.

Elf, *n.* (*pl.* **Elves,** 142). An imaginary diminutive spirit.

Elf'in, *a.* Pertaining to
Elf'ish, elves.

E-lĭç'it, *v. t.* To draw forth.

El'i-ġi-bil'i-ty, *n.* Fitness to be chosen to office.

El'i-ġi-ble, *a.* Capable of being elected; desirable.

El'i-ġi-bly, *adv.* Suitably; desirably.

E-lĭm'i-nāte, *v. t.* To cause to disappear from an equation; to set aside as unimportant; to leave out of consideration; to deduce; to infer.

E-lĭṣ'ion (-lĭzh'un) *n.* The cutting off of a vowel at the end of a word.

E-lĭx'ir, *n.* A compound tincture or medicine.

Elk, *n.* A species of stag.

Ell (123), *n.* A measure of different lengths. The English ell is forty-five inches.

ELK.

El-lipse', n. An oval figure.
†El-lip'sis, n. (pl. El-lip'sĕṣ.) In grammar, the Ellipse. omission of a word or phrase.
El-lip'tic,) a. Being in
El-lip'tic-al,) the form of an ellipse; oval; having a part omitted.
El'lip-tĭç'i-ty, n. Deviation from the form of a circle or sphere.
Elm, n. A kind of shade-tree.
El'o-cū'tion, n. Pronunciation or delivery of words.
El'o-cū'tion-a-ry, a. Relating to elocution.
El'o-cū'tion-ist, n. One who is versed in elocution.
E-lŏn'gāte (-lŏng'gāte), v. t. To draw out in length.
E-lŏn-gā'tion, n. A lengthening; distance.
E-lōpe', v. i. To run away with a lover. [clandestinely.
E-lōpe'ment, n. A departure
El'o-quençe, v. Beauty, power, and appropriateness of language.
El'o-quent, a. Speaking with eloquence or elegance.
Else, pron. Other; beside.— adv. Otherwise.
Else'whêre, adv. In some other place.
E-lū'çi-dāte, v. t. To explain; to make clear.
E-lū'çi-dā'tion, n. Explanation. [plain or clear.
E-lū'çi-dā'tive, a. Making
E-lū'çi-dā'tor, n. One who elucidates or explains.
E-lūde', v. t. To escape by stratagem.— SYN. To avoid; shun; evade; flee.
E-lūd'i-ble, a. Capable of being eluded. [sion.
E-lū'sion, n. Escape; evasive, a. Tending to elude; eluding. [elude.
E-lū'so-ry, n. Tending to
El'vĭsh, a. Relating to elves; elfish.
E-lyṣ'ian, a. Pertaining to Elysium; blissful.
E-lyṣ'i-um (-lĭzh'I-um), n. In mythology, the abode of the good after death; any delightful place.
Em, n. A square type, used by printers as the unit of measure of the amount of any printed matter.
E-mā'çi-ate (-mā'shI-), v. i. To lose flesh; to pine.
E-mā'çi-ā'tion (-shI-ā'shun), n. Act of becoming lean.

Ĕm'a-nant, a. Emanating; issuing.
Ĕm'a-nāte, v. i. [Lat. e, out, and manare, to flow.] To flow forth; to proceed; to arise.
Ĕm'a-nā'tion, n. Act of flowing forth; that which flows.
Ĕm'a-nā'tive, a. Issuing from another.
E-măn'çi-pāte, v. t. To free from servitude.
E-măn'çi-pā'tion, n. Act of emancipating.— SYN. Liberation; release; freedom.
E-măn'çi-pā'ter, n. One who frees from slavery.
E-mās'eu-lāte, v. t. To deprive of virility; to unman.
Em-bälm' (-bäm'), v. t. To impregnate with aromatics, as a body for preservation.
Em-bănk', v. t. To inclose with a bank. [or bank.
Em-bănk'ment, n. A mound
Em-bär'go (140), n. Prohibition of vessels from sailing.
Em-bärk', v. i. To enter on board; to engage.
Ĕm'bär-kā'tion, n. A going on board.
Em-bär'rass, v. t. To perplex; to confuse.
Em-bär'rass-ing, a. Tending to perplex or confuse.
Em-bär'rass-ment, n. Perplexity; pecuniary distress.
Em-băs'sa-dor, n. A public minister of the first rank.
Ĕm'bas-sy, n. Duty of an embassador; persons sent as embassadors. [battle.
Em-băt'tle, v. t. To form for
Em-bĕd', v. t. To lay us in a bed.
Em-bĕl'lĭsh, v. t. To make beautiful by adornment.
Em-bĕl'lĭsh-ment, n. Act of adorning; decoration.
Ĕm'bers, n. pl. Hot cinders.
Em-bĕz'zle, v. t. To appropriate by breach of trust.
Em-bĕz'zle-ment, n. Unlawful appropriation of what is intrusted to one's care.
Em-bĕz'zler, n. One who embezzles.
Em-blā'zon, v. i. To adorn with figures of heraldry; to deck in glaring colors.
Em-blā'zon-ry, n. Display of figures on shields.
Ĕm'blem, n. A picture or representation imaging forth a truth; a type.
Ĕm'blem-ăt'ic,) a. Comprising
Ĕm'blem-ăt'ic-al,) prising an emblem.

Ĕm'blem-a-tīze,) v. t. To
Ĕm'blem-īze,) represent by means of emblems.
Em-bŏd'y, v. t. To form into a body; to incorporate.
Em-bōld'en, v. t. To give boldness or courage to.
Em-bŏss', v. t. To adorn with protuberances. [work.
Em-bŏss'ment, n. Raised
†Embouchure (ŏng'bōō'-shūr'), n. Mouth of a river, cannon, &c.; mouth-hole of a flute, &c.
Em-bow'el (120), v. t. To take out the bowels of.
Em-bow'er (130), v. t. To place in a bower.
Em-brāçe', v. t. [Fr. en, in, and bras, arm.] To clasp in the arms; to comprise.— v. i. To join in an embrace.— n. A clasp with the arms.
Em-brāçe'ment, n. A clasp; a hug; an embrace.
Em-brā-sūre (-brā'-zhụr), n. An opening in a wall through which cannon are pointed. E, E, Embrasures in a parapet: A, A, A.
Ĕm'bro-ēāte, v. t. To moisten and rub, as a diseased part.
Ĕm'bro-eā'tion, n. A moistening and rubbing with cloth, &c., a diseased part.
Em-broid'er, v. t. To cover with ornamental needlework. [needle-work.
Em-broid'er-y, n. Variegated
Em-broil' (130), v. t. To disturb; to involve.
Em-broil'ment, n. A state of contention.
Ĕm'bry-o (140), n. The first rudiments of an animal or plant.— a. Unfinished.
Ĕm'en-dā'tion, n. Correction; improvement.
Ĕm'en-dā'tor, n. One who corrects or improves. [ing.
E-mĕnd'a-to-ry, a. Amend-
Ĕm'er-ald, n. A precious stone of a bright green color.
E-mẽrge' (12), v. i. To rise out of a fluid; to issue.
E-mẽr'ġen-çy, n. A rising out of a fluid; a sudden occasion; pressing necessity.
E-mẽr'ġent, a. Rising out of a fluid or the like.
†E-mẽr'i-tus, a. [Lat.] Honorably discharged from service.
E-mẽr'sion, n. A rising out of.

Ĕm'er-y, *n.* A mineral used in polishing.
E-mĕt'le, *a.* Producing vomiting. — *n.* A medicine that causes vomiting.
Ĕm'i-grant, *a.* Removing from one country or state to another for residence. — *n.* One who emigrates.
Ĕm'i-grāte, *v. i.* [Lat. *e*, out, forth, and *migrare*, to migrate.] To remove from one country or state to another for residence.
Ĕm'i-grā'tion, *n.* Act of removing to another country.
Ĕm'i-nençe, *n.* A rising ground; loftiness; distinction; a title of cardinals.
Ĕm'i-nent, *a.* Exalted in rank or public estimation. — SYN. Distinguished; conspicuous; celebrated.
Ĕm'i-nent-ly, *adv.* Conspicuously; in a high degree.
Ĕm'is-sa-ry, *n.* A secret agent; a spy.
E-mĭs'sion (-mĭsh'un), *n.* Act of sending out.
E-mĭt' (129), *v. t.* To send out; to put into circulation.
Ĕm'met, *n.* An ant.
E-mŏl'li-āte, *v. t.* To soften.
E-mŏll'ient, *a.* Softening. — *n.* A softening application.
E-mŏl'u-ment, *n.* Profit; advantage; gain in general.
E-mō'tion, *n.* Excitement of the feelings; agitation.
Em-pāle', *v. t.* To inclose with pickets; to fix on a stake and put to death.
Em-pāle'ment, *n.* A fortifying with stakes; an empaling. [a park.
Em-pärk', *v. t.* To inclose in
Ĕm'per-or, *n.* The sovereign of an empire.
Ĕm'pha-sis, *n.* (*pl.* †Ĕm'pha-sēṣ.) Force of voice given to particular words.
Ĕm'pha-sīze (153), *v. t.* To utter with a particular stress of voice.
Em-phăt'ic, | *a.* Forcible;
Em-phăt'ic-al, | strong; uttered with emphasis.
Em-phăt'ic-al-ly, *adv.* With emphasis or force; forcibly.
Ĕm'pīre, *n.* Dominions of an emperor; imperial power.
Em-pĭr'ic, or Ĕm'pir-ic (120), *n.* A quack.
Em-pĭr'ic-al, *a.* Used and applied without science.
Em-pir'i-çişm, *n.* Quackery.
Em-ploy', *v. t.* To use; to exercise. — *n.* Employment.

Em-ploy'er, *n.* One who employs.
Em-ploy'ment, *n.* Business; service; occupation; agency.
Em-pō'ri-um (140), *n.* A place of merchandise; a mart. [ize.
Em-pow'er, *v. t.* To author-
Ĕm'press, *n.* Wife of an emperor; a woman who governs an empire.
Em-prīse', *n.* Enterprise.
Ĕmp'ti-ness (81), *n.* State of being empty; vacuity.
Ĕmp'ty (135), *a.* Void; vacant; not filled. — *v. t.* or *i.* To exhaust; to make or become void.
Ĕmp'ty-ingṣ, *n. pl.* Lees of beer, cider, &c. [purple.
Em-pûr'ple, *v. t.* To dye
Em-pȳr'e-al, *a.* Formed of pure fire or light.
Ĕm'py-rē'an, *n.* The highest heaven, thought by the ancients to be of pure fire. — *a.* Empyreal.
Ĕm'u-lāte, *v. t.* To vie with; to strive to equal; to rival.
Ĕm'u-lā'tion, *n.* Rivalry; competition.
Ĕm'u-lā'tive, *a.* Inclined to contend for superiority.
Ĕm'u-lā'tŏr, *n.* A competitor; a rival.
Ĕm'u-loŭs, *a.* Eager to equal or excel; rivalling. [medicine.
E-mŭl'sion, *n.* A soft liquid
En-ā'ble, *v. t.* To make able.
En-ăct', *v. t.* To establish by law; to pass, as a law.
En-ăct'ment, *n.* The passing of a bill into a law.
En-ăct'or, *n.* One who enacts.
En-ăm'el, *n.* A substance imperfectly vitrified; the smooth hard covering of the teeth. — *v. t.* (130) To cover with enamel.
En-ăm'el-er, | *n.* One who
En-ăm'el-ler, | enamels.
En-ăm'or, *v. t.* To inflame with love; to make fond.
En-eāġe', *v. t.* To confine in a cage; to imprison.
En-camp', *v.* To form, or form into, a camp.
En-camp'ment, *n.* Act of pitching tents or forming a camp; a camp.
En-eaus'tic, *a.* or *n.* Painting in heated or burnt wax; fixing colors by heat.
En-chāin', *v. t.* To fasten with, or hold in, a chain.
En-chănt', *v. t.* To charm; to fascinate; to delight greatly.
En-chănt'ment, *n.* Fascination; irresistible influence.

En-chănt'ress, *n.* A woman who enchants.
En-chāse', *v. t.* To adorn with raised or embossed work.
En-çĭr'cle, *v. t.* To inclose by or in a circle. — SYN. To embrace; encompass; environ; surround.
En-clīt'ic, | *a.* Inclining or
En-clīt'ic-al, | leaning upon.
En-clăsp', *v. t.* To embrace.
En-clōṣe', *v. t.* To inclose. See *Inclose*.
En-cō'mi-ăst, *n.* One who praises another.
En-cō'mi-ăst'ic, *a.* Containing praise; eulogistic.
En-cō'mi-um (140), *n.* Panegyric; praise.
En-cŏm'pass, *v. t.* To shut in; to inclose.
En-cōre' (ŏng-kōr'). A word used to call for a repetition of some performance. — *v. t.* To call for a repetition of.
En-coun'ter, *n.* A sudden meeting; combat; engagement. — *v. t.* To meet face to face; to meet suddenly. — *v. i.* To meet, especially as enemies.
En-coŭr'aġe, *v. t.* To give courage to; to incite.
En-coŭr'aġe-ment, *n.* Incitement; hope; support.
En-coŭr'a-ġing, *a.* Favoring.
En-crōach', *v. i.* To intrude on another's rights.
En-crōach'ment, *n.* Unlawful intrusion; inroad.
En-cŭm'ber, *v. t.* To impede action by a load or burden.
En-cŭm'brançe, *n.* A load; clog; burden on an estate.
En-çȳ'clie-al, *a.* [Gr. *en*, in, and *kuklos*, a circle.] Sent to many persons or places; circular.
En-çȳ'clo-pē'di-ā, | *n.* A
En-çȳ'clo-pæ'di-ā, | work that embodies the whole circle of arts and sciences.
En-çȳst'ed, *a.* Inclosed in a vesicle or bag.
Ĕnd, *n.* Extreme point; ultimate object; close; death. — *v. t.* or *i.* To come or bring to an end; to terminate; to finish; to close.
En-dăn'ġer, *v. t.* To put to hazard. [dear.
En-dēar', *v. t.* To render
En-dēar'ment, *n.* That which excites tender affection.
En-dĕav'or (155), *n.* Effort; attempt. — *v. i.* To try; to strive; to make an effort.

En-dĕm'ic, *a.* Peculiar to a country.
End'ing, *n.* Termination.
En'dive, *n.* A kind of succory, used as a salad.
End'less, *a.* Having no end.
End'less-ly, *adv.* Without end.
En-dôrse', *v. t.* See *Indorse.*
En-dow', *v. t.* To furnish with dower, or with a fund; to enrich.
En-dow'ment, *n.* Act of settling a fund; dower; talents.
En-dūe', *v. t.* To invest; to endow. See *Indue.*
En-dūr'a-ble (133), *a.* Capable of being borne.
En-dūr'ance, *n.* Sufferance.
En-dūre', *v. i.* [Lat. *in*, in, and *durare*, to harden, to persist.] To continue. — *v. t.* To bear or undergo.
End'wīse, *adv.* On one end.
En'e-my (141), *n.* A foe; an adversary.
En'er-ġet'ic, *a.* Operat-
En'er-ġet'ic-al, } ing with vigor. — SYN. Forcible; strong; potent; active; effective; vigorous.
En'er-ġīze, *v. i.* To act with energy. — *v. t.* To employ with energy; to give vigor to.
En'er-ġy, *n.* Internal strength; force of expression. — SYN. Vigor; spirit; resolution.
E-nêr'vāte, *v. t.* To deprive of nerve or strength.
En'er-vā'tion, *n.* Act of weakening.
En-fee'ble, *v. t.* To weaken.
En-fee'ble-ment, *n.* A weakening; enervation.
En-fĕoff' (-fĕf'), *v. t.* To invest with a fee.
En-fĕoff'ment (-fĕf'ment), *n.* The act of enfeoffing.
En'fi-lāde', *n.* A straight line. — *v. t.* To rake with shot through the whole length of.
En-fôrce', *v. t.* To put in force or execution.
En-fôrce'ment (132), *n.* Act of enforcing; compulsion.
En-frăn'chīse (-frăn'chīz), *v. t.* To set free; to admit to political privileges.
En-frăn'chīse-ment, *n.* Act of setting free.
En-gāġe', *v. t.* To bind; to enlist; to encounter in combat. — *v. i.* To enlist; to enter into conflict; to engage.
En-gāġed', *a.* Promised.
En-gā'ged-ness, *n.* Great zeal.

En-gāġe'ment, *n.* Promise; obligation, duty; a battle.
En-gāġ'ing, *a.* Attractive; winning. [produce.
En-ġĕn'der, *v. t.* To beget; to
En'ġīne (ĕn'jĭn), *n.* [Lat. *ingenium*, natural capacity, invention.] A mechanical instrument of complicated parts; a machine.
En'ġin-eer', *n.* One skilled in mathematics and mechanics, and who superintends works for military or civil objects.
En'ġin-eer'ing, *n.* Art or business of an engineer.
En'ġine-ry, *n.* A combination of engines.
En-ġīrd', *v. t.* [*imp.* & *p. p.* ENGIRDED, ENGIRT.] To encompass; to encircle.
Ĕn'ġlish (ĭng'glish), *a.* Pertaining to England. — *n.* The people or the language of England. — *v. t.* To translate into English; to Anglicize.
En-gôrġe', *v.* To swallow or feed greedily.
En-grāve', *v. t.* [*imp.* EN-GRAVED; *p. p.* ENGRAV-EN.] To cut with a chisel or graver. [graves.
En-grāv'er, *n.* One who en-
En-grāv'ing, *n.* Act or art of engraving; that which is engraved.
En-grŏss', *v. t.* To seize or buy the whole of; to absorb; to copy in a large, fair hand.
En-grŏss'er, *n.* A monopolizer; one who writes a large, fair hand.
En-grŏss'ment, *n.* Act of engrossing; exorbitant acquisition.
En-gulf', *v. t.* To throw into, or absorb in, a gulf.
En-hānçe' (ō), *v. t.* To heighten in price; to aggravate; to increase.
En-hānçe'ment, *n.* Increase; aggravation.
E-nig'ma (140), *n.* A riddle.
E'nig-măt'ic, } a. Con-
E'nig-măt'ic-al, } taining a riddle; obscure.
E-nig'ma-tĭst, *n.* A dealer in enigmas or riddles.
En-join', *v. t.* To command; to order; to forbid judicially.
En-joy', *v. t.* To feel or perceive with pleasure; to possess. [being enjoyed.
En-joy'a-ble, *a.* Capable of
En-joy'ment, *n.* Possession with pleasure; fruition.

En-kin'dle, *v. t.* To set on fire; to inflame.
En-lārġe', *v. t.* or *i.* To swell; to increase; to amplify.
En-lārġe'ment, *n.* Increase of bulk; release.
En-līght'en (-līt'en), *v. t.* To illuminate; to instruct.
En-līst', *v. t.* To enter on a list; to enroll. [listing.
En-līst'ment, *n.* Act of enlisting.
En-līv'en (-līv'n), *v. t.* To animate; to cheer.
En-līv'en-er, *n.* One who animates. [ity.
Ĕn'mi-ty, *n.* Hatred; hostil-
En-nō'ble, *v. t.* To make noble; to dignify.
En-nō'ble-ment, *n.* Act of ennobling; dignity.
E-nôr'mi-ty, *n.* Atrociousness; depravity.
E-nôr'mous, *a.* [Lat. *enormis*, out of rule.] Beyond all natural or ordinary limits — SYN. Immense; excessive; atrocious.
E-nôr'mous-ly, *adv.* Beyond measure; atrociously.
E-nough' (e-nŭf'), *a.* Sufficient. — *n.* Sufficiency. — *adv.* Sufficiently.
En-quīre', *v. t.* See *Inquire.*
En-rāġe', *v. t.* To fill with rage; to provoke to fury.
En-răpt'ūre (-răpt'yụr, 50), *v. t.* To throw into rapture.
En-răv'ish, *v. t.* To throw into ecstasy; to enchant.
En-răv'ish-ment, *n.* Rapture; ecstasy.
En-rich', *v. t.* To make rich.
En-rich'ment, *n.* The state of being enriched.
En-rōbe', *v. t.* To attire; to dress. [record.
En-rōll', *v. t.* To register; to
En-rōll'ment, } *n.* A register-
En-rōl'ment, } ing; record.
En-rōōt', *v. t.* To implant
En-săm'ple, *n.* An example.
En-săn'guine (-săng'gwin), *v. t.* To suffuse with blood.
En-scônçe', *v. t.* To shelter.
En-sēal', *v. t.* To fix a seal on.
En-shrīne', *v. t.* To inclose in a chest; to lay up choicely.
Ĕn'si-fôrm, *a.* Sword-shaped.
Ĕn'sīgn (ĕn'sīn), *n.* A standard, or the officer that carries it; a flag; a badge.
En'sīgn-çy (-sĭn-), *n.* Rank or commission of an ensign.
En-slāve', *v. t.* To deprive of liberty; to subject.
En-slāve'ment, *n.* Servitude; slavery. [with a stamp.
En-stămp', *v. t.* To impress

ENSUE 126 EPITAPH

En-sūe', v. i. To follow as a consequence; to succeed.
En-sure' (-shūr'), v. t. See Insure.
En-tăb'la-tūre (50), n. Part of a column over the capital.
En-tāil', n. An estate limited in descent.— v. t. To settle an estate so as to descend to a particular heir.
En-tāil'ment, n. Act of limiting an estate to a particular heir.
En-tăŋ'gle, v. t. To make intricate; to perplex; to involve. [cy; perplexity.
En-tăŋ'gle-ment, n. Intricacy.
En'ter (130), v. t. or i. To go or come in; to embark in; to write down; to penetrate.
En'ter-prīṣe, n. An undertaking; a bold attempt.
En'ter-priṣ'ing, a. Bold or resolute to undertake.
En'ter-tāin', v. t. To treat with hospitality; to amuse
En'ter-tāin'er, n. One who entertains.
En'ter-tāin'ing, a. Adapted to entertain; amusing.
En'ter-tāin'ment, n. Hospitality; amusement.
En-thrōne', v. t. To place on a throne.
En-thrōne'ment (132), n. Act of enthroning.
En-thū'ṣi-ȧṣm, n. Ardent zeal in respect to some object or pursuit; heat of imagination.
En-thū'ṣi-ȧst, n. One whose imagination is heated.
En-thū'ṣi-ȧst'ic, a. Full of enthusiasm.
En-tīçe', v. t. To incite to evil; to allure.
En-tīçe'ment, n. The act or means of alluring.
En-tī'çer, n. One who entices.
En-tīre', a. Forming an unbroken whole. — SYN. Complete; unbroken; full.
En-tīre'ly, adv. Wholly; fully; completely.
En-tīre'ness, } n. Fullness;
En-tīre'ty, } completeness; wholeness.
En-tī'tle, v. t. To give a title or right to; to name.
En'ti-ty, n. Real existence.
En-tŏmb' (-tōōm'), v. t. To deposit in a tomb.
Ĕn'to-mŏl'o-ġist, n. One versed in entomology.
Ĕn'to-mŏl'o-ġy, n. [Gr. entomon, insect, and logos, discourse.] Science or description of insects.

Ĕn'trāilṣ, n. pl. The bowels; intestines.
Ĕn'trançe, n. A going or coming in, or a passage for doing so.
En-trançe', v. t. To put into a trance or into ecstasy.
En-trăp' (129), v. t. To catch in a trap; to ensnare.
En-trēat', v. t. To supplicate; to importune.— v. i. To make petition.
En-trēat'y, n. Urgent prayer or petition. [sage.
Ĕn'try, n. Entrance; passage.
En-twīne', } v. t. To twine
En-twĭst', } or twist round; to wreathe.
E-nū'cle-āte, v. t. To clear from intricacy; to explain.
E-nū'mer-āte, v. t. To number; to reckon up singly.
E-nū'mer-ā'tion, n. A numbering. [ing up.
E-nū'mer-a-tīve, a. Reckoning up.
E-nŭn'ci-āte (-nŭn'shĭ-), v. t. To declare; to utter.
E-nŭn'ci-ā'tion (-uun'shĭ-ā'shuu), n. Utterance of words or syllables.
En-vĕl'op, v. t. To cover by wrapping or folding.— n. A wrapper.
En-vĕl-ōpe, n. A wrapper for letters; a cover.
En-vĕl'op-ment, n. A wrapping or enfolding.
En-vĕn'om, v. t. To poison.
Ĕn'vi-a-ble, a. Capable of exciting envy; desirable.
Ĕn'vi-oŭs, a. Feeling envy; full of envy.
Ĕn'vi-oŭs-ly, adv. With envy.
En-vī'ron, v. t. To surround.
En-vī'ron-ment (86), n. Act of surrounding.
En-vī'rong, or Ĕn'vi-rong, n. pl. Places that lie around a town. [to a foreign court.
Ĕn'voy, n. A public minister
Ĕn'voy-shĭp, n. The office of an envoy.
Ĕn'vy, v. t. To repine at another's good; to grudge.— n. Pain or vexation excited by another's prosperity.
Ē'pact, n. Excess of the solar month beyond the lunar.
E-paule'ment, n. A sidework in fortification, made of earth, often in bags, gabions, &c.
Ĕp'au-lĕt, } n. A knot or
Ĕp'au-lĕtte', } badge worn on the shoulder.
†E-phĕm'e-rä, n. An insect that lives one day only, or that is very short-lived.

E-phĕm'e-ral, a. Lasting one day, or for a very short time; fleeting.
†E-phĕm'e-ris, n. (pl. Ĕph'e-mĕr'i-dēṣ.) An astronomical almanac.
Ĕph'od, n. A linen girdle worn by Jewish priests.
Ĕp'ic, n. Containing heroic narration. — n. An epic or heroic poem.
Ĕp'i-çēne, a. Common to both sexes. [dainty eater.
Ĕp'i-cūre, n. A luxurious and
Ĕp'i-cū're-an, a. Luxurious; sensual. — n. An epicure.
Ĕp'i-cu-riṣm, n. Devotion to luxurious living.
Ĕp'i-dĕm'ic, } a. Common;
Ĕp'i-dĕm'ic-al, } generally prevailing. [disease.
Ĕp'i-dĕm'ic, n. A prevailing
Ĕp'i-dẽr'mis, n. The cuticle, or scarf skin.
Ĕp'i-glŏt'tis, n. A cartilage that prevents food entering the wind-pipe.
Ĕp'i-grăm, n. A short and pointed poem.
Ĕp'i-gram-măt'ic, } (120)
Ĕp'i-gram-măt'ic-al, } a. Like an epigram; pointed; poignant.
Ĕp'i-grăm'ma-tĭst, n. A dealer in epigrams.
Ĕp'i-grȧph, n. An inscription on a building, tomb, &c.
Ĕp'i-lĕp'sy, n. The falling sickness.
Ĕp'i-lĕp'tic, a. Diseased with epilepsy.
Ĕp'i-lōgue (-lŏg), n. A short speech or poem after a play.
E-pĭph'a-ny, n. [Gr. epiphania, appearance.] A church festival held the 12th day after Christmas, commemorating the visit of the wise men to the Savior.
E-pĭs'co-pa-çy, n. Church government by bishops.
E-pĭs'co-pal, a. Pertaining to episcopacy or to bishops.
E-pĭs'co-pā'li-an, a. Pertaining to government by bishops. — n. One who adheres to episcopacy. [opric.
E-pĭs'co-pate (42), n. A bish-
Ĕp'i-sōde, n. An incidental narrative; a digression.
Ĕp'i-sŏd'ic, a. Pertaining to, or consisting of, an episode.
E-pĭs'tle (e-pĭs'l), n. A letter.
E-pĭs'to-la-ry, a. Relating to, or contained in, letters.
E-pĭs'to-līze, v. i. To write letters. [inscription.
Ĕp'i-tȧph, n. A monumental

ā, ē, ī, ō, ū, ȳ, long; ă, ĕ, ĭ, ŏ, ŭ, y̆, short; cāre, cär, ȧsk, ąll, whąt; ēre, vęll, tẽrm; pīque, fĭrm;

EPITHALAMIUM 127 ERYSIPELAS

†Ep′i-tha-lā′mi-um, n. A nuptial song or poem.
Ep′i-thět, · n. An adjective expressing some especial appropriate quality or attribute.
Ep′i-thět′ic, a. Consisting in epithets. [ment.
E-pit′o-me (18), n. An abridg-
E-pit′o-mĭst,) n. One who
E-pit′o-mīz′er,) abridges.
E-pit′o-mīze, v. t. To abridge.
Ep′och, n. A remarkable period or point of time.
Ep′ŏde, n. The third or last part of an ode.
Ep′o-pee′, n. An epic poem.
E′qua-bĭl′i-ty, n. Uniformity.
E′qua-ble, a. Equal and uniform. [formity.
E′qua-bly, adv. With uni-
E′qual, a. Like in amount, degree, or value, &c.; uniform. — n. One of the same age or rank. — v. t. or i. (130) To make or become equal.
E-qual′i-ty, n. State of being equal; uniformity; likeness.
E′qual-i-zā′tion, n. Act of equalizing. [equal.
E′qual-īze (153), v. t. To make
E′qual-ly. adv. In the same degree; impartially.
Ē′qua-nĭm′i-ty, n. Evenness of mind; composure.
E-quăn′gu-lar, a. Consisting of equal angles.
E-quā′tion, n. An expression of the equality of two quantities.
E-quā′tor, n. A great circle midway between the poles, dividing the earth into two hemispheres.
E′qua-tō′ri-al, a. Pertaining to the equator.
E-quĕr′ry,) n. One who has
Ĕq′ue-ry,) the care of the horses of nobles or princes.
◆E-quĕs′tri-an, a. [Lat. equus, a horse, eques, a horseman.] Pertaining to horses or horsemanship. — n. A horseman; a rider.
Ē′qui-ăn′gu-lar, a. Having equal angles.
Ē′qui-dĭs′tant, a. Being at the same distance.
Ē′qui-lăt′er-al, a. Having the sides equal. [poise.
Ē′qui-lī-brā′tion, n. Equi-
Ē′qui-lĭb′ri-ty, n. Equality of weight; equilibrium.
◆Ē′qui-lĭb′ri-ŭm, n. Equality of weight or force; a just poise; equipoise.
Ē′quine, a. Pertaining to horses.

Ē′qui-nŏc′tial, n. The celestial equator; so called because when the sun is on it the days and nights are equal in all parts of the world. — a. Pertaining to the equinox.
Ē′qui-nŏx, n. The time when the days and nights are of equal length in all parts of the world. [to arm.
E-quĭp′ (129), v. t. To dress;
Ĕq′ui-page (ŏk′wi-pej), n. Attendance; retinue, as horses, carriages, &c.; furniture, of an army, a ship, a soldier, &c.
E-quĭp′ment, n. Act of equipping; any apparatus furnished.
Ē′qui-poise, n. Equality of weight or force.
Ē′qui-pŏl′lençe, n. Equality of power or force.
Ē′qui-pŏl′lent, a. Having equal force or power.
Ē′qui-pŏn′der-ançe (99), n. Equality of weight.
Ē′qui-pŏn′der-ant, a. Of the same weight.
Ĕq′ui-ta-ble, a. Giving, or disposed to give, each his due. — SYN. Just; impartial; fair; upright. [ly.
Ĕq′ui-ta-bly, adv. Impartial-
Ĕq′ui-ty (ŏk′wĭ-tỹ), n. Justice; impartiality.
E-quĭv′a-lençe, n. Equality of value or worth.
E-quĭv′a-lent, a. Equal in value, power, or effect. — n. That which is equal in value or worth.
E-quĭv′o-cal, a. Ambiguous; doubtful. [fully.
E-quĭv′o-cal-ly, adv. Doubt-
◆E-quĭv′o-cāte, v. i. To use words of double meaning; to quibble; to prevaricate.
E-quĭv′o-cā′tion, n. Ambiguity of speech.
E-quĭv′o-cā′tor, n. One who equivocates.
Ĕq′ui-vōke,) n. An ambig-
Ĕq′ui-vŏque,) uous term; a quibble.
Ē′rȧ (86, 140), n. A point or period of time from which to compute.
E-răd′i-cāte, v. t. To root out; to extirpate.
E-răd′i-cā′tion, n. Act of rooting out.
E-rās′a-ble, a. Capable of being erased.
E-rāse′, v. t. To blot out; to efface; to rub or scrape out; to obliterate.
E-rā′gion, n. Act of erasing.

E-rāg′ūre (-rā′zhur), n. Act of erasing or rubbing out.
Ēre (âr), adv. Before; sooner than. — prep. Before.
E-rĕct′, a. Upright; perpendicular; bold. — v. t. To set upright; to build; to establish.
E-rĕc′tion, n. A setting upright; act of building.
E-rĕct′ly, adv. In an erect posture. [ing erect.
E-rĕct′ness, n. State of be-
Ēre′lŏng (âr′lŏng, 19), adv. Before a long time.
Ĕr′got, n. A protuberance on a horse's leg; an excrescence on grain; a spur.
Ĕr′mine (12), n. [From Armenia, where it is found.] An animal allied to the weasel; the fur of the animal, taken as an emblem of judicial purity.
E-rōde′, v. t. To eat away.
E-rō′gion, n. An eating; canker.
E-rō′sĭve, a. Corrosive.
Ĕrr (125), v. i. To wander; to mistake.
Ĕr′rand, n. A message; business of one sent. [ing.
Ĕr′rant, a. Wandering; rov-
Ĕr′rant-ry, n. An errant state.
Er-răt′ic, a. Wandering; irregular.
†Er-rā′tum, n. (pl. Er-rā′tä, 25). Error or mistake in printing or writing. [Err.
Ĕrr′ing, p. pr. & p. a. from
Er-rō′ne-oŭs, a. Wrong; false; incorrect.
Er-rō′ne-oŭs-ly, adv. By mistake; incorrectly.
Ĕr′ror, n. A mistake; blunder; offense; sin.
Ĕrst, adv. At first; long ago.
Ĕr′u-bĕs′çence, n. A blushing. [ing.
Ĕr′u-bĕs′çent, a. Red; blush-
Ĕr′ue-tā′tion, n. A belching.
Ĕr′u-dīte, a. Learned.
Ĕr′u-dĭ′tion (-dĭsh′un, 49), n. Knowledge; learning.
◆E-rŭp′tion, n. A breaking forth; pustules on the skin.
E-rŭp′tive, a. Bursting out, attended with eruption.
Ĕr′y-sĭp′e-las, n. [Gr. erusipelas, lit. red skin.] St. Anthony's fire, a kind of fever in which the skin is inflamed.

sôn ôr, do, wolf, too, took; ûrn, rue, pull; ç, ġ, soft; ¢, ġ, hard; aş; exĭst; ŋ as ng; this.

Ér'y-si-pĕl'a-toŭs, a. Resembling erysipelas.
Es'ca-lāde', n. A scaling of walls. — v. t. To mount by ladders.
Es-cal'op, n. A bivalve shell; a regular curving indenture.
Es-cāpe', v. t. To avoid; to shun by flight. — v. i. To hasten away; to flee. — n. Act of avoiding; flight.
Es-cāpe'ment, n. That part of a time-piece which regulates its movements.
Es-chēat', n. A falling of lands to the lord of the fee or to the state for want of heirs. — v. i. To revert to the lord, crown, or state. Escapement.
Es-chew', v. t. To shun or avoid; to forsake.
Es'cort, n. A guard from place to place. [guard.
Es-cort', v. t. To attend and Es'cri-toir' (-twŏr'), n. A writing desk.
Es'cu-lent, a. Good for food.
Es-cŭtch'eon (-kŭtch'un), n. A shield or coat of arms.
Es'o-tĕr'ic, a. Secret.
Es-păl'ier (-yer), n. A frame or trellis for fruit-trees.
Es-pĕ'cial (-pĕsh'al), a. Principal; chief; peculiar.
Es-pĕ'cial-ly, adv. Peculiarly.
Es-pī'al, n. Act of espying.
Es'pi-on-age, n. Practice of employing spies.
Es'pla-nāde', n. An open space before a fortification; a sloping grass-plat.
Es-pous'al, n. Act of espousing; (pl.) betrothal or marriage ceremony.
Es-pouse', v. t. To betroth; to marry; to embrace.
Es-py', v. t. To see; to spy.
Es-quīre', n. A title of magistrates and gentlemen. — v. t. To wait on; to attend.
Es-sāy', v. t. To attempt.
Es'say, n. A trial; attempt; a short, informal treatise.
Es'sāy-ist, or Es-sāy'ist, n. A writer of essays.
És'sence, n. [Lat. essentia, fr. esse, to be.] The nature of a thing; perfume; scent. — v. t. To perfume; to scent.
Es-sĕn'tial, n. Necessary to existence; very important. — n. Constituent principle.
Es-sĕn'tial-ly, adv. Necessarily.

Es-tăb'lish, v. t. To fix; to settle firmly; to found.
Es-tăb'lish-ment, n. Settlement; confirmation; place of residence or business; income.
Es-tāte', n. Condition; property, especially in land; one of the classes of men constituting a state.
Es-teem', v. t. To value; to regard; to think highly of. — n. High value in opinion.
Es-thĕt'ics, n. sing. See Æsthetics.
Es'ti-ma-ble, a. Worthy of esteem; valuable.
Es'ti-māte, v. t. To set a value on. [value set.
Es'ti-māte, n. Calculation;
Es'ti-mā'tion, n. A valuing; esteem; honor; opinion.
Es'ti-mā'tor, n. One who estimates. [summer.
Es'ti-val, n. Pertaining to
Es-tŏp', v. i. To bar; to impede; to stop the progress of.
Es-tŏp'pel, n. A conclusive admission.
Es-trānge', v. t. To keep at a distance; to alienate.
Es-trānge'ment, n. Alienation. [ing or lost.
Es-trāy', n. A beast wandering
Ĕst'u-a-ry, n. An arm of the sea; a frith.
Ĕst'u-āte, v. i. To be agitated; to boil.
Ĕst'u-ā'tion, n. A boiling; agitation of water.
Ĕtch, v. t. To engrave by drawing lines through wax and corroding them with some strong acid.
Ĕtch'ing, n. Impression from etched copper-plate.
E-tĕr'nal (12), a. Having no beginning or end. — n. The Deity; God. [ly.
E-tĕr'nal-ly, adv. Perpetually.
E-tĕr'ni-ty, n. Duration without beginning or end.
E-tĕr'nīze, v. t. To immortalize; to make endless.
Ē'ther, n. A subtle fluid supposed to fill all space; a kind of very volatile fluid.
E-thē're-al, a. Consisting of ether; heavenly.
E-thē're-al-īze, v. t. To convert into ether.
Ĕth'ic,) a. Relating to
Ĕth'ic-al,) morals.
Ĕth'ics, n. sing. The science of moral philosophy.
Ē'thi-ŏp,) n. A native of
Ē'thi-ō'pi-an,) Ethiopia; a negro.

Ĕth'nic,) n. Belonging to
Ĕth'nic-al,) races; heathen; pagan.
Eth-nŏg'ra-phy, n. A description of the different races of men.
Eth-nŏl'o-gy, n. A treatise on the natural races of men.
Ē'ti-o-lāte, v. t. To whiten by excluding the sun's rays.
Ē'ti-o-lā'tion, n. A blanching or being blanched by exclusion of the rays of the sun.
Ĕt'i-quétte' (-kĕt', 107), n. Forms of ceremony.
Ĕt'y-mo-lŏg'ic,) a. Relat-
Ĕt'y-mo-lŏg'ic-al,) ing to etymology.
Ĕt'y-mŏl'o-gĭst, n. One who is versed in etymology.
Ĕt'y-mŏl'o-gy, n. Derivation of words from their originals.
Ĕt'y-mŏn, n. A root or primitive word.
Eū'cha-rĭst, n. The Lord's supper; communion.
Eū'cha-rĭst'ic, a. Pertaining to the eucharist.
Eū'lo-gĭst, n. One who praises or commends.
Eū'lo-gĭs'tic, a. Relating to, or containing, praise; commendatory.
Eū'lo-gīze, v. t. To praise by eulogy; to commend.
Eū-lō'gi-ŭm (140), n. Commendation; praise; laudation.
Eū'lo-gy, n. [Gr. eulogia, lit. a speaking well.] Marked or studied praise. — SYN. Encomium; panegyric; laudation.
Eū'nuch, n. A male human being who has been unmanned.
Eū-pĕp'tic, a. Having good digestion; easy of digestion.
Eū'phe-mĭsm, n. A delicate word or expression used for one that is offensive.
Eū-phŏn'ic,) a. Having
Eū-phŏn'ic-al,) a sound
Eū-phō'ni-oŭs,) agreeable to the ear.
Eū'pho-ny, n. An agreeable sound or combination of sounds.
Eū'phu-ĭsm, n. Affectation of excessive refinement in language.
Eū'ro-pē'an, a. Pertaining to Europe. — n. A native of Europe.
Eū-thăn'a-sy, n. Easy death.
E-văc'u-ant, n. A medicine that evacuates.
E-văc'u-āte, v. t. To make empty; to void; to quit.

E-văc'u-ā'tion, n. Act of evacuating; withdrawal.
E-vāde', v. t. To avoid; to elude; to slip away.
Ev'a-nĕs'çençe, n. A gradual vanishing.
Ev'a-nĕs'çent, a. Vanishing; fleeting; passing away.
E-van-gĕl'ic-al, a. According to, or contained in, the gospel; orthodox.
E-văn'gel-ism, n. Promulgation of the gospel.
E-văn'gel-ist, n. One who preaches or spreads the gospel.
E-văn'gel-īze, v. t. To instruct in the gospel of Christ.
E-văp'o-rāte, v. i. To pass off in vapor; to waste insensibly. — v. t. To convert into vapor.
E-văp'o-rā'tion, n. Conversion of a fluid into vapor.
E-vā'sion, n. Artifice; equivocation; escape.
E-vā'sive, a. Using evasion.
E-vā'sive-ly, adv. With evasion.
Ēve, n. Evening.
Ē'ven (ē'vn), a. Level; smooth; uniform; parallel; fair; not odd. — v. t. To make level or smooth. — adv. Exactly; at the very time; so much as.
Ē'ven-ing (ē'vn-), n. Close of the day; beginning of night.
Ē'ven-ly, adv. Equally; uniformly. [of being even.
Ē'ven-ness, n. State or quality
E-vĕnt', n. That which happens. — SYN. Incident; issue; end; result.
E-vĕnt'ful, a. Full of incidents. [ing.
Ē'ven-tīde, n. Time of evenE-vĕnt'u-al, a. Consequential; final.
E-vĕnt'u-āte, v. i. To issue; to close; to end. [ways.
Ev'er, adv. At any time; alEv'er-glāde, n. A tract of land covered by water and grass.
Ev'er-green, a. Always green. — n. A plant or shrub always green.
Ev'er-lăst'ing, a. Continuing without end; eternal.
Ev'er-mōre', adv. Eternally.
Ev'er-y, a. Each one of a whole. [places.
Ev'er-y-whēre', adv. In all
E-vīct', v. t. To dispossess by judicial process.
E-vĭc'tion, n. Dispossession.
Ev'i-dençe, n. That which proves or shows facts; testimony; witness. — v. t. To show; to prove.
Ev'i-dent, a. Clear; plain.
Ev'i-dent-ly, adv. Clearly.
Ē'vĭl (ē'vl), n. Ill; wicked; bad. — n. Calamity; wickedness.
E-vĭnçe', v. t. To prove; to show in a clear manner.
E-vĭn'çi-ble, a. Capable of being proved.
E-vĭs'çer-āte, v. t. To take out the bowels of.
Ev'i-ta-ble, a. Capable of being avoided. [forth.
Ev'o-cā'tion, n. A calling
E-vōke', v. t. To call forth.
Ev'o-lū'tion, n. Act of unfolding; prescribed or regular movement.
E-vŏlve', v. t. To unfold; to expand; to emit.
Ewe (yū), n. A female sheep.
Ew'er (yū'er), n. [From Lat. aqua, water.] A pitcher with a wide spout. [tate.
Ex-ăç'er-bāte, v. t. To irriEx-ăç'er-bā'tion, n. Increased violence of a disease.
Ex-ăct' (101), a. Minutely correct or regular; punctual. — SYN. Accurate; precise; methodical; careful. — v. t. To demand; to require; to extort.
Ex-ăc'tion, n. Act of extorting; a heavy tax.
Ex-ăct'ly, adv. Accurately; nicely. [uicety.
Ex-ăct'ness, n. Accuracy;
Ex-ăg'ger-āte (101), v. t. To heighten unduly in representation.
Ex-ăg'ger-ā'tion, n. A representation beyond the truth.
Ex-ält', v. t. To lift high; to extol; to magnify.
Ex'al-tā'tion, n. A raising; elevation. [lime.
Ex-ält'ed, a. Dignified; subEx-ăm'i-nā'tion, n. Inquiry; inspection; search.
Ex-ăm'īne, v. t. To inspect; to search into; to question.
Ex-ăm'in-er, n. One who examines; an inspector.
Ex-ăm'ple, n. A pattern; model; specimen.
Ex'an-thĕm'a-tous, a. Efflorescent; eruptive.
Ex'ärch, n. A viceroy.
Ex-ăs'per-āte, v. t. To make very angry; to enrage.
Ex-ăs'per-ā'tion, n. State of being exasperated.
Ex'can-dĕs'çençe, n. A glowing or white heat.

Ex'can-dĕs'çent, a. White with heat. [hollow.
Ex'ca-vāte, v. t. To make
Ex'ca-vā'tion, n. A making hollow; a hollow.
Ex-çeed', v. t. or i. To surpass; to excel.
Ex-çeed'ing, a. Very great
Ex-çeed'ing-ly, adv. To a great degree; very much.
Ex-çĕl' (129), v. To surpass, especially in good qualities; to exceed.
Ex'çĕl-lençe (129), n. Superior goodness; eminence.
Ex'çel-len-çy, n. Excellence; — a title of honor.
Ex'çel-lent, a. Having great value; eminent.
Ex'çel-lent-ly, adv. In an excellent degree.
Ex-çĕpt', v. t. To take or leave out; to exclude. — v. i. To object. — prep. Not including.
Ex-çĕpt'ing, prep. or p. pr. Taking or leaving out; except; save.
Ex-çĕp'tion, n. Exclusion; thing excluded; objection.
Ex-çĕp'tion-a-ble, a. Liable to objections.
Ex-çĕp'tion-al, a. Forming exception. [jects.
Ex-çĕpt'or, n. One who obEx-çĕrpt', n. An extract; a selection.
Ex-çĕss', n. More than enough; surplus; Intemperance.
Ex-çĕss'īve, a. Exceeding just limits; extreme. [ingly.
Ex-çĕss'īve-ly, adv. Exceed
Ex-chānge', v. t. To give for something else. — n. Act of bartering; balance of money; place where merchants meet.
Ex-chānge'a-ble (133), a. Capable of being exchanged.
Ex-chān'ger, n. One who exchanges.
Ex-chĕq'uer (-chĕk'er), n. A court in England that has charge of the public treasury. [excīse.
Ex-çīṣ'a-ble, a. Subject to
Ex-çīṣe', n. A duty on goods. v. t. To lay an excise or duty on.
Ex-çīṣe'man (143), n. One who inspects excised goods.
Ex-çĭṣ'ion (-sĭzh'un), n. Utter destruction.
Ex-çī'ta-bĭl'i-ty, n. Capacity of being easily excited.
Ex-çī'ta-ble. a. Capable of being roused into action.
Ex'çi-tā'tion, n. Act of exciting.

son, ôr, do, wolf, too, tŏŏk; ûrn, rye, pull; ç, ġ, soft; ҫ, g̃, hard; aṣ; exist; n as ng; this.
6*

Ex-cīte', v. t. To stir; to rouse; to stimulate; to call into action.
Ex-cīt'ing, p. a. Producing excitement.
Ex-cīte'ment, n. Act of exciting; agitation.
Ex-claim', v. t. To cry out.
Ex'cla-mā'tion, n. A loud outcry; a mark [!], noting some emotion.
Ex-clăm'a-to-ry, a. Using, or containing, exclamation.
Ex-clūde', v. t. To shut out; to debar; to except.
Ex-clū'sion, n. Act of excluding; rejection.
Ex-clū'sive, a. Shutting out; not including.
Ex-clū'sive-ly, adv. To the exclusion of others.
Ex-clū'sive-ness, n. State of being exclusive. [out.
Ex-cŏg'i-tāte, v. t. To think
Ex-cŏg'i-tā'tion, n. Invention by thought.
Ex'com-mū'ni-cāte, v. t. To exclude from communion.
Ex'com-mū'ni-cā'tion, n. Act of excommunicating.
Ex-cō'ri-āte, v. t. To flay; to strip off the skin of; to gall.
Ex-cō'ri-ā'tion, n. Act of stripping off the skin.
Ex'cre-ment, n. Matter discharged from the body.
Ex'cre-měnt'al, a. Pertaining to excrement.
Ex-crĕs'çence, n. Preternatural growth or protuberance.
Ex-crĕs'çent, a. Growing out unnaturally.
Ex-crēte', v. t. To discharge through the pores.
Ex-crē'tion, n. Separation of animal matters through the pores.
Ex'cre-tive,) a. Tending to
Ex'cre-to-ry,) excrete.
Ex'cre-to-ry, n. A little duct for discharging a fluid.
Ex-crū'ci-āte (-shi-āt), v. t. To torture.
Ex-crū'ci-ā'ting (-shi-), a. Distressing; very painful.
Ex-cŭl'pāte, v. t. To clear from fault or guilt or blame.
Ex'cul-pā'tion, n. Act of clearing from blame; excuse.
Ex-cŭl'pa-to-ry, a. Clearing from blame.
Ex-eŭr'sion, n. [Lat. excursio, lit. a running out.] A ramble; a digression.
Ex-cŭr'sive, a. Wandering; rambling.
Ex-cūṣ'a-ble, a. Capable or worthy of being excused.

Ex-cūṣe' (-kūz'), v. t. To pardon; to judge leniently.
Ex-cūṣe' (-kūs'), n. Apology; that which excuses.
Ex'e-cra-ble, a. Detestable; hateful. [bly.
Ex'e-cra-bly, adv. Detestably.
Ex'e-crāte, v. t. To curse.
Ex'e-crā'tion, n. Imprecation of evil.
Ex-e-cūte, v. t. To carry into effect; to put to death by law; to complete. — SYN. To accomplish; do; perform; effect; fulfill; finish.
Ex'e-cūt'er, n. One who executes.
Ex'e-cū'tion, n. Act of executing; a putting to death as a legal punishment.
Ex'e-cū'tion-er, n. One who puts to death by law.
Ex-ĕc'u-tive, a. Carrying into effect. — n. The person or power that executes the laws.
Ex-ĕc'u-tor, n. One who settles the estate of a testator.
Ex-ĕc'u-tor-ship, n. Office of executor.
Ex-ĕc'u-to-ry, a. Performing official duties. [executor.
Ex-ĕc'u-trix, n. A female
Ex'e-gē'sis, n. Science of interpretation. [ry.
Ex'e-gĕt'ic-al, a. Explanatory.
Ex-ĕm'plar, n. Example to be imitated; copy; pattern.
Ex'em-pla-ri-ly, adv. By way of example.
Ex'em-pla-ry (101), a. Serving as a pattern; worthy of imitation.
Ex-ĕm'pli-fi-cā'tion, n. Illustration by example; a copy. [trate by example.
Ex-ĕm'pli-fȳ, v. t. To illustrate.
Ex-ĕmpt' (81), a. Free. — v. t. To free from. — n. One who is not subject.
Ex-ĕmp'tion, n. Freedom from what others are liable to; immunity.
Ex'o-quā'tur, n. A written recognition of a person as consul.
Ex'er-çīṣe, n. Use: practice: performance; activity; a lesson. — v. t. (153) To use: to employ; to practice; to keep busy. — v. i. To take or use exercise.
Ex-er'ci-tā'tion, n. Practice.
Ex-ĕrgue' (-ērg'), n. A little space on a medal for the date, &c.
Ex-ĕrt', v. t. To use strength or effort; to strive.

Ex-ĕr'tion, n. Act of exerting; effort.
Ex-fō'li-āte, v. i. To scale off.
Ex-fō'li-ā'tion, n. A scaling off.
Ex-hāl'a-ble, a. Capable of being exhaled.
Ex'ha-lā'tion (101), n. Vapor.
Ex-hāle', v. t. To send out, as vapor. — v. i. To emit.
Ex-haust', v. t. To drain to emptiness; to empty.
Ex-haust'i-ble, a. Capable of being exhausted.
Ex-haus'tion, n. Act of exhausting; state of being exhausted. [exhausted.
Ex-haust'less, a. Not to be
Ex-hib'it, v. t. To display; to show publicly. — n. A paper produced in proof of facts.
Ex-hib'it-er, n. One who exhibits.
Ex'hi-bī'tion (-bĭsh'un), n. A setting forth; public show; display.
Ex-hil'a-rāte, v. t. To make cheerful; to enliven.
Ex-hil'a-rā'tion, n. Act of exhilarating.
Ex-hŏrt', v. t. To advise.
Ex'hor-tā'tion, n. Act of advising; counsel.
Ex-hor'ta-to-ry, a. Tending to exhort. [horts.
Ex-hŏrt'er, n. One who exhorts.
Ex'hu-mā'tion, n. A digging up, as from the grave.
Ex-hūme', v. t. To dig up, as from a grave.
Ex'i-gençe,) n. Necessity;
Ex'i-gen-çy,) pressing want.
Ex'i-gent, a. Pressing.
Ex'īle (113), n. Banishment; a person banished. — v. t. To banish; to transport.
Ex-ist', v. i. To be; to live; to have support.
Ex-ist'ençe, n. Being; life.
Ex-ist'ent, a. Having being.
Ex'it, n. A going out; departure; death.
Ex'o-dus, n. Departure, esp. of the Israelites from Egypt; second book in the Bible.
Ex-ŏn'er-āte, v. t. To unload; to free from a charge.
Ex-ŏn'er-ā'tion, n. Act of exonerating.
Ex'o-ra-ble, a. Capable of being moved by entreaty.
Ex-ŏr'bi-tançe,) n. Extrav-
Ex-ŏr'bi-tăn-çy,) agance; enormity.
Ex-ŏr'bi-tant, a. Excessive; unreasonable.
Ex-ŏr'bi-tant-ly, adv. Excessively; enormously.

ā, ĕ, ī, ō, ū, ȳ, long; ă, ĕ, ĭ, ŏ, ŭ, ȳ, short; câre, cär, åsk, ạll, whạt; ēre, vçil, tẽrm; p"que, fĭrm;

EXORCISE 131 EXPRESSIVELY

Ex'or-çīṣe (153), *v. t.* To expel, as evil spirits, by conjuration.

Ex'or-çīṣm, *n.* Act of exorcising.

Ex'or-çīst, *n.* One who casts out evil spirits.

Ex-ôr'dĭ-al, *a.* Introductory.

Ex-ôr'dĭ-um, *n.* Introduction, preface, or preamble.

Ex'o-tēr'ĭc, *a.* External; public.

Ex-ŏt'ĭc, *a.* [Gr. *exotikos*, fr. *exo,* outside.] Foreign; not native. — *n.* A foreign plant.

Ex-pănd', *v. t. or i.* To open; to spread; to dilate.

Ex-pănse, *n.* Wide extent of space or body.

Ex-păn'sĭ-bĭl'ĭ-ty, *n.* Capacity of being expanded.

Ex-păn'sĭ-ble, *a.* Capable of being expanded.

Ex-păn'sĭon, *n.* Act of expanding; dilatation; extent.

Ex-păn'sĭve, *a.* Spreading.

Ex-pā'tĭ-ate (-shĭ-āt), *v. i.* To rove; to wander; to enlarge; to descant. [ish.

Ex-pā'trĭ-āte, *v. t.* To banish.

Ex-pă'trĭ-ā'tĭon, *n.* The quitting of one's country; banishment; exile.

Ex-pēct', *v. t.* To look or wait for; to anticipate.

Ex-pēct'an-çy, *n.* A state of waiting.

Ex-pēct'ant, *a.* Waiting; looking for. — *n.* One who is expecting.

Ex'pec-tā'tĭon, *n.* A waiting for; prospect.

Ex-pĕc'to-rant, *a.* Promoting discharges from the lungs or throat. — *n.* A medicine that promotes such discharges.

Ex-pĕc'to-rāte, *v. t.* To discharge from the lungs or throat.

Ex-pĕc'to-rā'tĭon, *n.* Act of discharging from the lungs or throat.

Ex-pĕc'to-rā'tĭve, *a.* Promoting expectoration.

Ex-pē'dĭ-ençe, } *n.* Fitness;
Ex-pē'dĭ-en-çy, } propriety.

Ex-pē'dĭ-ent, *a.* Fit; proper; advisable. — *n.* Means to an end; shift; device.

Ex-pē'dĭ-ent-ly, *adv.* Fitly; with advantage.

Ex'pe-dīte, *v. t.* To hasten forward; to render easy. — SYN. To dispatch; accelerate; hurry. — *a.* Free of impediment; expeditious.

Ex'pe-dī'tĭon, *n.* Haste; dispatch; a voyage; an enterprise.

Ex'pe-dī'tĭoŭs (-dĭsh'us), *a.* Done with dispatch; quick.

Ex'pe-dī'tĭoŭs-ly (-dĭsh'us-), *adv.* With dispatch.

Ex-pĕl' (129), *v. t.* To drive or force out; to banish; to eject.

Ex-pĕnd', *v. t.* To spend for an object; to lay out.

Ex-pĕn'dĭ-tūre, *n.* Act of spending; sum expended.

Ex-pĕnse' (149), *n.* Cost; charge; money laid out.

Ex-pĕn'sĭve, *a.* Costly; dear.

Ex-pĕn'sĭve-ness, *n.* Costliness.

Ex-pē'rĭ-ençe, *n.* Trial or repeated trial, or the instruction thus gained. — *v. t.* To try; to know by practice.

Ex-pē'rĭ-ençed (-enst), *p. a.* Taught by experience; practiced; versed.

Ex-pēr'ĭ-ment, *n.* Trial; essay; operation for proving some fact or principle. — *v. i.* To make trial; to try.

Ex-pĕr'ĭ-mĕnt'al, *a.* Founded on experiment.

Ex-pĕr'ĭ-mĕnt'al-ly, *adv.* By experiment; by trial.

Ex-pĕr'ĭ-ment-er, *n.* One who makes experiments.

Ex-pĕrt', *a.* Skillful; dexterous. — *n.* One who is skillful.

Ex-pĕrt'ly, *adv.* Dexterously.

Ex'pĭ-a-ble, *a.* Capable of being expiated.

Ex'pĭ-āte, *v. t.* To atone for, as a crime. [satisfaction.

Ex'pĭ-ā'tĭon, *n.* Atonement.

Ex'pĭ-a-to-ry, *a.* Making expiation; atoning.

Ex'pĭ-rā'tĭon, *n.* Act of breathing out; end; close.

Ex-pīre', *v. t.* To breathe out; to exhale. — *v. i.* To die; to decease.

Ex-plāin', *v. t.* To illustrate; to interpret; to make plain. — *v. i.* To give explanations.

Ex-plāin'a-ble, *a.* Capable of being explained.

Ex'pla-nā'tĭon, *n.* Act of making plain; interpretation.

Ex-plăn'a-to-ry, *a.* Serving to explain.

Ex'ple-tĭve, *n.* A word that adds nothing to the sense.

Ex'plĭ-ca-ble, *a.* Capable of being explained.

Ex'plĭ-cāte, *v. t.* To unfold; to explain; to show.

Ex'plĭ-cā'tĭon, *n.* An explanation.

Ex'plĭ-cā'tĭve, } *a.* Serving
Ex'plĭ-cā'to-ry, } to explain.

Ex-plĭç'it, *a.* Clear; plain; express; not obscure.

Ex-plĭç'it-ly, *adv.* Clearly.

Ex-plōde', *v. i.* To burst with a loud report. — *v. t.* To bring into disrepute.

Ex-ploit', *n.* An heroic deed.

Ex'plo-rā'tĭon, *n.* Act of exploring; examination.

Ex-plōr'a-to-ry, *a.* Searching; exploring.

Ex-plōre', *v. t.* To search carefully; to examine.

Ex-plō'ṣĭon, *n.* A sudden bursting with a loud noise; a discharge.

Ex-plō'sĭve, *a.* Driving or bursting with force.

Ex-pō'nent, *n.* Index of a power in algebra; a representative.

Ex-pōrt', *v. t.* To transport from one country to another.

Ex'pōrt, *n.* A commodity sent abroad. [being exported.

Ex-pōrt'a-ble, *a.* Capable of

Ex'pōr-tā'tĭon, *n.* Act of exporting; that which is exported. [ports.

Ex-pōrt'er, *n.* One who exports.

Ex-pōṣe', *v. t.* To lay open or bare; to put in danger.

†**Exposé** (ĕx'pō-zā'), *n.* A formal statement or exposition.

Ex'po-ṣĭ'tĭon (-zĭsh'un), *n.* Explanation; interpretation; an exhibition of arts, &c.

Ex-pŏṣ'ĭ-tor, *n.* An interpreter; expounder. [explain.

Ex-pŏṣ'ĭ-to-ry, *a.* Serving to

Ex-pŏst'u-lāte, *v. i.* To remonstrate earnestly.

Ex-pŏst'u-lā'tĭon, *n.* The act of expostulating; remonstrance.

Ex-pŏst'u-la-to-ry, *a.* Containing expostulation.

Ex-pō'ṣūre (50), *n.* Act of exposing, or state of being exposed.

Ex-pound', *v. t.* To explain.

Ex-pound'er, *n.* One who explains or interprets.

Ex-prĕss', *v. t.* To press out; to utter in language; to make known. — SYN. To denote; declare; indicate; exhibit. — *a.* Plain; direct; explicit. — *n.* A special messenger or conveyance.

Ex-prĕss'ĭ-ble, *a.* Capable of being expressed.

Ex-prĕs'sĭon (-prĕsh'un), *n.* A pressing out; act or mode of speech. [express.

Ex-prĕss'ĭve, *a.* Adapted to

Ex-prĕss'ĭve-ly, *adv.* With force.

---

sŏn, ôr, dọ, wọlf, tōō, tŏŏk; ûrn, rụe, pụll; ç, ġ, *soft*; e, ġ, *hard*; aṣ; eẋıst; ṇ *as* ng; this.

EXPRESSIVENESS — EYESIGHT

Ex-press'ive-ness, n. State or quality of being expressive. [terms.
Ex-press'ly, adv. In direct
Ex'pro-brāte, v. t. To upbraid; to blame; to condemn.
Ex'pro-brā'tion, n. Act of upbraiding; censure.
Ex-pūgn' (-pūn'), v. t. To take by assault.
Ex-pūg'na-ble, or **Ex-pūgn'-a-ble** (-pūn'-), a. Capable of being conquered.
Ex-pūl'sion, n. Act of expelling; state of being expelled.
Ex-pūl'sive, a. Having power to expel. [punging.
Ex-pūnc'tion, n. Act of ex-
Ex-pūnge', v. t. [Lat. expungere, to prick out.] To blot out; to efface.
Ex'pur-gāte, or **Ex-pūr'-gāte,** v. t. To cleanse; to purify; to expunge.
Ex'pur-gā'tion, n. Act of expurgating. [ing.
Ex-pūr'ga-to-ry, a. Purify-
Ex'qui-site, a. Very fine; excellent; keenly felt. — n. A fop.
Ex'qui-site-ly, adv. Nicely.
Ex-scind', v. t. To cut off.
Ex-sic'cant, a. Tending to dry.
Ex'sic-cate, or **Ex-sic'cāte,** v. t. To dry. [ing.
Ex'sic-cā'tion, n. Act of drying.
Ex'tant, a. Now in being; existing.
Ex-tĕm'po-rā'ne-oŭs,) a.
Ex-tĕm'po-ra-ry,) Uttered without previous study; unpremeditated.
†Ex-tĕm'po-re, a. or adv. Without previous study.
Ex-tĕm'po-rīze, v. i. To utter without study.
Ex-tĕnd', v. To stretch out; to spread; to reach.
Ex-tĕn'si-bĭl'i-ty, n. Quality of being extensible.
Ex-tĕn'si-ble, a. Capable of being extended.
Ex-tĕn'sion, n. Act of extending; enlargement.
Ex-tĕn'sive, a. Large; wide; of great extent.
Ex-tĕn'sive-ly, adv. Widely; largely.
Ex-tĕnt', n. Space; compass.
Ex-tĕn'u-āte, v. t. To palliate; to lessen.
Ex-tĕn'u-ā'tion, n. Act of extenuating; palliation.
Ex-tē'ri-or, a. Outward; foreign. — n. Outside; surface.
Ex-tē'ri-or-ly, adv. Outwardly.

Ex-tĕr'min-āte, v. t. To drive away; to root out.
Ex-tĕr'min-ā'tion, n. Destruction; extirpation.
Ex-tĕr'min-ā'tor, n. One who exterminates.
Ex-tĕr'nal, a. Outward.
Ex-tĕr'nal-ly, adv. Outwardly; in show.
Ex-tĕr'nals, n. pl. Outward parts or rites; exterior form.
Ex-tĭn'et, a. Extinguished; ended; dead.
Ex-tĭnc'tion, n. Destruction; suppression.
Ex-tĭn'guish (-tĭng'gwĭsh), v. t. To quench; to put out; to destroy.
Ex-tĭn'guish-a-ble, a. Capable of being extinguished.
Ex-tĭn'guish-er, n. A utensil to put out candles.
Ex-tĭn'guish-ment, n. A putting out or quenching; destruction; abolition.
Ex'tir-pāte, or **Ex-tir'pāte,** v. t. To root out; to destroy.
Ex'tir-pā'tion, n. The act of rooting out. [extirpates.
Ex'tir-pā'tor, n. One who
Ex-tŏl' (130), v. t. To praise greatly. — SYN. To exalt; laud; eulogize; glorify.
Ex-tŏrt', v. t. To exact unlawfully; to wrest.
Ex-tŏr'tion, n. Unlawful exaction. [ive.
Ex-tŏr'tion-ate, a. Oppress-
Ex-tŏr'tion-er, n. One who practices extortion.
Ex'tract, n. A substance drawn from another; a passage from a book or writing.
Ex-trăct', v. t. To draw out; to take. [out; lineage.
Ex-trăc'tion, n. A drawing
Ex-trăct'ive, a. Capable of being extracted.
Ex-trăct'or, n. One who, or that which, extracts.
Ex'tra-dĭ'tion (-dĭsh/un), n. Delivery on the part of one government to another of an accused person.
Ex'tra-ju-dĭ'cial (-dĭsh/al), a. Out of the regular course of law. [not intrinsic.
Ex-trā'ne-oŭs, a. Foreign;
Ex-traŏr'di-na-ri-ly (-trŏr'- or -tra-ŏr'-), adv. Uncommonly.
Ex-traŏr'di-na-ry (-trŏr'- or -tra-ŏr'-), a. Uncommon; unusual; remarkable.
Ex-trăv'a-gançe, n. State of being extravagant; excess; prodigality.

Ex-trăv'a-gant, a. Exceeding due bounds; lavish in expenses. — SYN. Excessive; prodigal; wasteful.
Ex-trăv'a-gant-ly, adv. Lavishly; profusely.
Ex-trăv'a-sāte, v. t. To let out of the proper vessels, as blood.
Ex-trăv'a-sā'tion, n. A letting out of the proper vessels, as blood.
Ex-trême', a. Outermost; utmost; greatest; highest. — n. Utmost limit; extremity. [most degree.
Ex-trême'ly, adv. In the utmost degree.
Ex-trĕm'ist (133), n. A supporter of extreme doctrines or practice.
Ex-trĕm'i-ty, n. Utmost point or degree; necessity.
Ex'tri-ca-ble, a. Capable of being extricated.
Ex'tri-cāte, v. t. To disentangle; to set free.
Ex'tri-cā'tion, n. Act of extricating; disentanglement.
Ex-trĭn'sĭc,) a. Outward;
Ex-trĭn'sĭc-al,) external.
Ex-trūde', v. t. To thrust out.
Ex-trū'sion, n. Act of thrusting out. [ous abundance.
Ex-ū'ber-ançe, n. Superflu-
Ex-ū'ber-ant, a. Luxuriant; superabundant.
Ex-ū'ber-ant-ly, adv. Very abundantly; luxuriantly.
Ex'u-dā'tion, n. The act of sweating out.
Ex-ūde', v. t. To discharge through the pores. — v. i. To flow; to issue forth.
Ex-ūlt', v. i. To rejoice greatly. [triumph.
Ex-ūlt'ant, a. Rejoicing in
Ex'ul-tā'tion, n. Expression of great joy.
Eye (ī), n. The organ of sight; a bud. — v. t. To watch; to observe; to view. [eye.
Eye'ball, n. The ball of the
Eye'brow, n. Hairy arch over the eyes.
Eye'-glăss, n. A glass to assist the sight.
Eye'lash, n. Hair on the edge of the eyelid.
Eye'less (i'less), a. Having no eyes; blind. [or cord.
Eye'let, n. A hole for a lace
Eye'-sĕrv'ant, n. A servant that requires watching.
Eye'-sĕrv'içe, n. Service done only under the employer's eye.
Eye'sight (-sīt), n. Sight of the eye.

ă, ĕ, ĭ, ŏ, ŭ, ў, long; ă, ĕ, ĭ, ŏ, ŭ, ў, short; câre, cär, ăsk, ąll, whąt; ẽre, vẽil, tẽrm; pïque, fïrm;

EYESORE 133 FALSITY

Eye'sore, n. Something offensive to the eye or sight.
Eye'-tooth (143), n. An upper tooth next the grinders, pointing up toward the eye.
Eye'-wa'ter, n. A medicated water or lotion for the eyes.
Eye'-wit'ness, n. One who saw what he testifies; one who sees a thing done.
Eyre, n. A court of itinerant justices.
Ey'ric } (ā'rȳ), n. A place
Ey'ry } where birds of prey build and hatch.

F.

FA'BLE, n. A fictitious story enforcing a useful truth. — v. t. To feign; to lie; to falsify.
Fab'ric, n. A building; an edifice; a structure; a manufactured article, as cloth.
Fab'ri-cāte, v. t. To construct; to manufacture; to devise falsely; to forge.
Fab'ri-cā'tion, n. Act of fabricating or building; construction; invention.
Fab'ri-eā'tor, n. One who constructs or forms.
Fab'u-list, n. One who writes or invents fables.
Fab'u-lous, a. Feigned; invented; unreal; false.
†Fa-çāde' (fa-sād' or fa-säd'), n. [Fr.] A front elevation of a building.
Fāce (140), n. Fore part of the head; visage; front: principal surface; boldness. — v. t. To meet in front; to oppose.
Fāç'et, n. A little face; a small surface. [witty.
Fa-çē'tious, a. Humorous;
Fa-çē'tious-ly, adv. With humor.
Fā'cial (fā'shal), a. Pertaining to the face.
Făç'ile, a. [Lat. facilis, from facere, to do.] Easy to be done, or to yield; pliant; flexible. [easy.
Fa-çĭl'i-tāte, v. t. To make
Fa-çĭl'i-ty, n. Ease; easiness; dexterity; (pl.) means to render easy.
Fāç'ing (133), n. A covering in front. [ness.
Fac-sĭm'i-le, n. Exact likeness.
Făct, n. [Lat. factum, a thing done.] An act; deed; reality; truth; circumstance.
Făc'tion, n. ●●●●● all political party; n ● ●●●●● clique.
Făc'tious, a. ●●●●ven to faction; turbulent; disorderly.
Fac-ti'tious (-tish'us), a. Made by art; artificial.
Făc'tor, n. An agent in trade.

Făc'tor-age, n. Commission allowed to a factor.
Făc'to-ry, n. House of a factor; body of factors; a manufactory.
Fac-tō'tum, n. A servant to do all sorts of work.
Făc'ul-ty, n. Power of the mind; ability; power; talent; officers of a college; members of a profession.
Fāde, v. i. To wither or decay; to lose color or vigor.
Fadge, v. i. To suit; to join closely.
Fæ'çēs. See Feces.
Făg, v. i. To become weary. — v. t. To compel to drudge. — n. A drudge; one obliged to drudge for another.
Făg'-ēnd', n. Untwisted end of a rope; refuse; meaner part.
Făg'ot, n. A bundle of twigs.
Fāil, v. i. To decay; to perish; to decline; to miss; to become insolvent. — v. t. (126) To desert; to disappoint; to omit. — n. Omission.
Fāil'ūre (fāl'yųr), n. Defect; deficiency; fault; act of becoming insolvent.
Fāin, a. Glad. — adv. Gladly.
Fāint, a. Weak; °langaid. — v. i. To swoon; to sink senseless from loss of strength.
Fāint'ish, a. Slightly faint.
Fāint'ly, adv. Feebly; weakly.
Fāint'ness, n. State of being faint; feebleness.
Fāir, a. Free from blemish, perversion, &c.; of a light shade. — SYN. Pure; frank; honest; equitable. — adv. Openly; frankly; civilly; justly. — n. A handsome woman; a stated market. — The Fair, the female sex.
Fāir'ly, adv. Openly; honestly.
Fāir'ness, n. State of being fair; clearness; beauty; candor.
Fāir'y (141), n. A fabled

spirit. — a. Belonging to, or given by, the fairies.
Fāith, n. Belief; object of belief; creed; fidelity; honor; promise given.
Fāith'fụl (139), a. Firm to the truth; loyal; exact; true.
Fāith'fụl-ly, adv. With faith.
Fāith'fụl-ness, n. Firm adherence to truth or trust.
Fāith'less, a. Without faith. — SYN. Treacherous; unbelieving; disloyal; false.
Făl'cāte, } a. Hooked; bent
Făl'cāt-ed, } like a sickle.
Făl'chion (fawl'chun), n. A short crooked sword.
Făl'con (faw'kn), n. A hawk trained for sport.
Făl'con-er (faw'kn-), n. A person who trains hawks for taking wild fowl.
Făl'con-ry (faw'kn-rȳ), n. Art of training hawks; practice of taking game by means of hawks.
Fąll (123), v. i. [imp. FELL; p. p. FALLEN.] To drop; to decline; to happen; to apostatize. — n. Descent; degradation; decrease; cadence; a cascade or cataract; autumn.
Fal-lā'cious, a. Producing mistake; deceitful; delusive.
Făl'la-çy, n. Deceitfulness; deception; sophistry.
Făll'en (fawln, 55), p. p. of Fall. [to err.
Făl'li-bĭl'i-ty, n. Liableness
Făl'li-ble, a. Liable to err.
Făll'ing-sick'ness, n. A disease in which the patient falls down senseless; epilepsy.
Făl'lōw, a. Pale, red, or yellow; plowed but not sown. — n. Land left untilled. — v. t. To plow, harrow, and break, as land, without seeding it.
False, a. Not true; counterfeit; not faithful or honest; hypocritical. [treacherously.
Falseʼly, adv. Erroneously;
False'hŏŏd, } n. Want of truth
Făls'i-ty, } or veracity; a false assertion.

FALSETTO 134 FATUITY

Fal-sĕt'to, *n.* A kind of voice in man above his natural voice.
Fal'si-fi-cā'tion, *n.* Act of falsifying; a falsehood.
Fal'si-fī'er, *n.* One who falsifies.
Fal'si-fȳ, *v. t.* To counterfeit; to prove to be false. — *v. i.* To tell lies.
Fal'si-ty, *n.* Contrariety to truth; falsehood.
Fal'ter (130), *v. i.* To hesitate in speech; to waver.
Fal'ter-ing, *a.* Hesitating.
Fāme, *n.* Reputation; renown; celebrity.
Fāmed. *a.* Celebrated; noted.
Fa-mil'iar (103), *a.* [Lat. *familiaris,* fr. *familia,* family.] Intimate; well-known; knowing intimately; common; affable. — *n.* An intimate acquaintance; a demon.
Fa-mil-iăr'i-ty, *n.* Intimate acquaintance; ease in intercourse. [custom.
Fa-mil'iar-īze, *v. t.* To accustom.
Fa-mil'iar-ly, *adv.* Intimately.
Făm'i-ly (141), *n.* Household; lineage; race; class.
Făm'ine, *n.* Want of sufficient food.
Făm'ish, *v. i.* To die of hunger. — *v. t.* To destroy with hunger; to starve.
Făm'ish-ment, *n.* Extreme hunger. [ed.
Fā'mous, *a.* Renowned; noted.
Fā'mous-ly, *adv.* With great renown.
Făn (140), *n.* An instrument to blow and cool the face; also, one to winnow grain. — *v. t.* (129) To blow with a fan; to winnow. [siast.
Fa-năt'ic, *n.* A wild enthusiast.
Fa-năt'ic, *a.* Wild and enthusiastic in opinions. [fanaticism.
Fa-năt'ic-al,
Fa-năt'ic-al-ly, *adv.* With
Fa-năt'i-çism, *n.* Extravagant notions; religious frenzy. [ined.
Făn'çied. *a.* Conceived; imagined.
Făn'çi-fṳl (135), *a.* Dictated by fancy; whimsical; odd; visionary.
Făn'çy, *n.* Imagination; notion; groundless opinion; preference; taste. — *v. t.* or *i.* To imagine; to conceive; to suppose; to long for. — *a.* Pleasing the fancy; fine.
Fan-dăn'go, *n.* A lively Spanish dance.
Fāne, *n.* A temple; a church.

Fan-făr'on-āde', *n.* A vain boasting; bluster.
Făng, *n.* Tusk of an animal; a long claw; talon.
Fan-tä'si-ȧ (-tä'ze-ȧ), *n.* A fanciful piece of music.
Fan-tăs'tic, *a.* Fanciful;
Fan-tăs'tic-al, whimsical.
Făn'ta-sy, *n.* A fancy; conceit; whimsey.
Fär (85), *a.* Distant; remote. — *adv.* At or to a great distance; very much.
Färçe, *n.* A short, ludicrous play. — *v. t.* To stuff.
Fär'çi-cal, *a.* Belonging to a farce; ludicrous.
Fāre, *v. i.* To be in any state, good, or bad; to be entertained. — *n.* Price of passage; food.
Fāre'well, or Fāre-wĕll', *n.* Wish of welfare at parting; act of taking leave. [adieu.
Fāre-wĕll', *interj.* Good-by;
Fa-rī'nȧ, or Fa-rī'nȧ, *n.* Pollen of flowers; the flour of grain, starch, &c.
Fär'i-nā'ceoŭs, *a.* Consisting of meal or flour; mealy.
Färm, *n.* Land occupied by a farmer. — *v. t.* To lease or rent for a price; to cultivate, as a farm.
Färm'er, *n.* One who cultivates land. [ing land.
Färm'ing, *n.* Practice of tilling.
Fär'o, *n.* A game at cards.
Far-rä'go (115), *n.* A medley.
Făr'ri-er, *n.* [From Lat. *ferrum,* iron.] A horse-shoer; one who cures the diseases of horses. [farrier.
Făr'ri-er-y, *n.* Business of a
Făr'row, *n.* A litter of pigs. — *a.* Not producing a calf in the year. — *v. t.* or *i.* To bring forth, as pigs.
Fär'ther (85), *a.* Being at a greater distance; more remote. — *adv.* Beyond; more remotely. See *Further.*
Fär'thing, *n.* The fourth of a penny. [ticoat.
Fär'thin-gale, *n.* A hoop petticoat.
Făs'çi-cle, *n.* A kind of inflorescence. [bundle.
Fas-çĭc'u-lar, *a.* United in a
Făs'çi-nāte, *v. t.* To charm; to captivate; to enchant.
Făs'çi-nā'tion, *n.* Act or power of charming.
Făsh'ion, *n.* [From Lat. *factis,* a making.] Form; custom; general practice; mode; style. — *v. t.* To form; to mold.
Făsh'ion-a-ble, *a.* Being according to, or observant of, the prevailing mode.
Făsh'ion-a-bly, *adv.* In a fashionable manner.
Fāst, *v. i.* To abstain from food. — *n.* Abstinence from food; time or day for fasting. — *a.* Firmly fixed; steadfast; rapid; swift; dissipated. — *adv.* With speed.
Fāst'-dāy, *n.* A day set apart for fasting and prayer.
Fāst'en (fäs'n), *v. t.* To make firm; to hold together.
Fāst'en-ing, *n.* That which confines or makes fast.
Fas-tĭd'i-oŭs, *a.* Difficult to please; squeamish; nice.
Fas-tĭd'i-oŭs-ly, *adv.* With squeamishness.
Fāst'ness, *n.* State of being fast; a strong fort.
Făt, *n.* An oily, concrete, animal substance. — *a.* Abounding in fat; plump; corpulent; gross; greasy. — *v.* To make or grow fat.
Fā'tal, *a.* Necessary; deadly; destructive; mortal.
Fā'tal-Ĭsm, *n.* The doctrine of fate or inevitable necessity.
Fā'tal-ĭst, *n.* One who holds to fatalism.
Fa-tăl'i-ty, *n.* Invincible necessity; mortality.
Fā'tal-ly, *adv.* Necessarily; mortally.
Fāte, *n.* Inevitable necessity; final lot; (*pl.*) the destinies supposed to preside over men. — SYN. Destiny; fortune; doom; death
Fāt'ed, *a.* Decreed by fate.
Fä'ther, *n.* A male parent; an ancestor; a protector. — *v. t.* To adopt as one's own.
Fä'ther-land, *n.* Native land of one's fathers. [father.
Fä'ther-less, *a.* Having no
Fä'ther-ly, *a.* Like a father; paternal; tender.
Făth'om, *n.* A measure of length of six feet. — *v. t.* To sound the depth of; to penetrate.
Făth'om-less, *a.* Bottomless.
Fa-tigue' (-tēg'), *n.* Great weariness; toil. — *v. t.* To weary to excess; to tire.
Făt'ling, *n.* A fat animal.
Făt'ness, *n.* Fleshiness; unctuous quality.
Făt'ten, *v. t.* To make fat. — *v. i.* To grow fat.
Făt'ty, *a.* Containing, or consisting of, fat; greasy.
Fa-tū'i-ty, *n.* Weakness of mind; mental imbecility.

FATUOUS 135 FENNY

Făt'u-oŭs, *a.* Feeble in mind; foolish; silly; impotent.

Fau'çet, *n.* A contrivance for drawing liquors from a cask, &c.

Fault, *n.* Want; blemish; a defect; offense; failing.

Fault'less, *a.* Free from fault; perfect.

Fault'y, *a.* Guilty of a fault; defective; imperfect.

Faun, *n.* A rural deity.

†Fau'nà. *n.* The entire group of animals belonging to a country.

Fā'vor (155), *n.* Kind regard; support; mildness; a gift. — *v. t.* To countenance.

Fā'vor-a-ble, *a.* Propitious to success; kind; advantageous. [or affection.

Fā'vor-a-bly, *adv.* With favor

Fā'vor-īte, *n.* A particular friend. — *a.* Regarded with favor; esteemed; preferred.

Fā'vor-it-ĭsm, *n.* Disposition to favor a friend; partiality.

Fawn, *n.* A young fallow deer. — *v. i.* To court, or flatter servilely.

Fāy (140), *n.* A fairy; an elf. — *v. i.* To join closely.

Fē'al-ty, *n.* Homage; loyalty.

Fēar, *n.* Apprehension of evil. — *v. t.* or *i.* To stand in awe of; to be afraid; to dread.

Fēar'ful, *a.* Afraid: terrible.

Fēar'ful-ly, *adv.* In a fearful manner; with fear.

Fēar'less, *a.* Free from fear; undaunted; intrepid. [fear.

Fēar'less-ly, *adv.* Without

Fēar'less-ness, *n.* Freedom from fear; courage; boldness; intrepidity.

Fēa'şĭ-bĭl'ĭ-ty, { *n.* Practica-

Fēa'şĭ-ble-ness, } bility.

Fēa'şĭ-ble. *a.* Capable of being performed; practicable.

Fēast. *n.* A sumptuous entertainment; a festival; a holiday. — *v. i.* To eat sumptuously. — *v. t.* To entertain sumptuously.

Fēat, *n.* An extraordinary action; exploit; trick.

Fĕath'er. *n.* A plume: that which forms the covering of birds. — *v. t.* To cover with plumage; to adorn.

Fĕath er-bĕd, *n.* A bed stuffed with feathers.

Fĕath'er-y, *a.* Covered with, or resembling, feathers.

Fēat'ūre, *n.* Form or appearance, especially of the face; lineament.

Fĕb'rĭ-fūġe, *n.* A medicine to cure fever.

Fĕ'brĭlc, or Fĕb'rĭlc, *a.* Pertaining to fever.

Fĕb'ru-a-ry, *n.* The second month of tho year.

Fē'cal, *a.* Containing dregs.

Fē'çĕs, *n. pl.* Excrement; dregs.

Fēç'u-lençe, *n.* Foul matter in liquors; lees; dregs.

Fēç'u-lent, *a.* Foul; full of dregs.

Fēç'und, *a.* Fruitful; fertile; productive. [prolific.

Fēç'un-dāte, *v. t.* To make

Fēç'un-dā'tion, *n.* Act of making fruitful. [ness.

Fe-cŭn'di-ty, *n.* Fruitful-

Fĕd, *imp.* & *p. p.* of *Feed.*

Fĕd'er-al, *a.* [Lat. *fædus,* a league.] Pertaining to a league or contract.

Fĕd'er-ate, *a.* Leagued.

Fĕd'er-ā'tion, *n.* Act of uniting in a league; a confederacy; a league.

Fĕd'er-a-tĭve, *a.* Joining in league.

Fee (140), *n.* A reward; recompense: perpetual right. — *v. t.* To retain by a fee.

Fee'ble, *a.* Wanting in strength or activity. — Syn. Infirm; imbecile; languid.

Fee'ble-ness, *n.* Infirmity.

Fee'bly, *adv.* Weakly; faintly.

Feed, *v. t.* [*imp.* & *p. p.* FED.] To give food to; to supply. — *v. i.* To eat; to take food. — *n.* Food; meat; pasture.

Feed'er, *n.* One that feeds; any medium of supply.

Feel, *v. t.* or *i.* [*imp.* & *p. p.* FELT.] To perceive by the touch; to be affected; to experience. — *n.* Sensation communicated by touching.

Feel'er, *n.* One who, or that which, feels; antenna of an insect.

Feel'ing, *n.* Touch; sensibility; emotion. — *a.* Full of sensibility; tender.

Feel'ing-ly, *adv.* Tenderly.

Fee'-sĭm'ple, *n.* An absolute or unconditional fee.

Feet, *n.; pl.* of *Foot.*

Feign (fān), *v. t.* To pretend; to counterfeit. [pretense.

Feint (fānt), *n.* A false show; a

Fe-lĭç'ĭ-tāte, *v. t.* To make happy; to congratulate.

Fe-lĭç'ĭ-tā'tion, *n.* Kind wish: congratulation.

Fe-lĭç'ĭ-toŭs, *a.* Happy; delightful; very appropriate.

Fe-lĭç'ĭ-ty, *n.* Great happiness. — Syn. Bliss; blissfulness; blessedness. [cats.

Fē'līne, *a.* Pertaining to

Fĕll, *a.* Fierce; savage; cruel. — *v. t.* To prostrate; to strike or cut down; to hem, as a seam. — *n.* Skin: hide of a beast. — *v., imp.* of *Fall.*

Fĕl'lōw, *n.* An associate or equal; a person. — *v. t.* To match; to pair with; to suit.

Fĕl'lōw-crēat'ūre, *n.* One of the same race.

Fĕl'lōw-feel'ing, *n.* A like feeling; sympathy. [heir.

Fĕl'lōw hēir (-âr), *n.* A joint

Fĕl'lōw-ship, *n.* Society; intercourse; companionship; foundation for maintaining a resident scholar.

Fĕl'ly, *n.* Rim of a wheel.

†Fĕ'lo-de-sē', *n.* A suicide.

Fĕl'on, *n.* One guilty of felony; a painful tumor.

Fe-lō'nĭ-oŭs, *a.* Having the quality of felony; villainous.

Fe-lō'nĭ-oŭs-ly, *adv.* In a felonious manner.

Fĕl'o-ny, *n.* A heinous or capital crime.

Fĕlt, *imp.* & *p. p.* of *Feel.* — *n.* Cloth or stuff of wool. — *v. t.* To make compact by fulling.

Fē'māle, *a.* One of the sex that bears young. — *a.* Feminine; not male.

†Fĕme-cŏv'ert, *n.* A married woman. [woman.

†Fĕme-sōle', *n.* An unmarried

Fĕm'ĭ-nīne, *a.* Pertaining to females of the human race; tender; effeminate.

Fĕm'o-ral, *a.* Belonging to the thigh.

Fĕn, *n.* A marsh; bog; morass.

Fençe (140), *n.* [Abbreviated from *defence.*] A wall or other structure to inclose land. — *v. t.* To inclose with a fence. — *v. i.* To practice fencing. [fence.

Fençe'less, *a.* Destitute of a

Fĕn'çer, *n.* One who fences.

Fĕn'çĭ-ble, *n.* A soldier trained for defensive warfare.

Fĕn'çing, *n.* Materials for fences; art of self-defense with the sword; use of the foil.

Fĕnd, *v. t.* To repel: to keep or ward off. — *v. i.* To parry.

Fĕnd'er, *n.* One who, or that which, fends or wards off.

Fĕn'nel, *n.* An aromatic plant.

Fĕn'ny, *a.* Marshy; boggy.

sōn, ôr, dọ, wọlf, tōō, tŏŏk; ûrn, rụe, pụll; ç, ġ, *soft;* c, ḡ, *hard;* aẓ; eẓist; ṇ *as* ng; this.

FEOFF 136 FIGURE

Fĕoff (fĕf), v. t. To invest with the fee of land.
Fĕoff'ment, n. Grant of a fee; gift in fee of land, &c., with delivery of possession.
Fē'ri-al, a. Pertaining to holidays or week-days.
Fē'rīne, a. Wild; savage.
Fĕr'ment, n. Tumult; agitation; that which causes agitation.
Fĕr-mĕnt', v. t. To excite by internal motion. — v. i. To undergo fermentation.
Fŏr'men-tā'tion, n. Act of fermenting: a certain chemical change in animal and vegetable substances.
Fĕr-mĕnt'a-tive, a. Causing fermentation.
Fĕrn, n. A genus of plants.
Fe-rō'cious, a. Savage; wild and cruel; fierce.
Fe-rŏç'i-ty, n. Savage wildness and fierceness; cruelty.
Fĕr're-oŭs, a. Made of, like, or pertaining to, iron.
Fĕr'ret (130), v. t. To drive from a lodge. — n. An animal of the weasel kind.
Fĕr'ri-āge, n. Fare or toll for passing a ferry.
Fĕr-rṳ'gi-noŭs, a. Partaking of, or containing, iron.
Fĕr'rule (fĕr'ril or fĕr'rṳl), n. A ring on the end of a stick.
Fĕr'ry, n. A place for passing a river or lake; a boat. — v. t. To convey over water in a boat. [attends a ferry.
Fĕr'ry-man (143), n. One who
Fĕr'tile, a. Fruitful; productive; prolific; rich.
Fĕr'til-īze, v. t. To enrich, as land. [soil; fruitfulness.
Fer-tĭl'i-ty, n. Richness of
Fĕr'ule (fĕr'il or fĕr'ṳl), n. A flat piece of wood for punishing children. — v. t. To punish with a ferule.
Fĕr'ven-çy, n. Heat of mind; zeal; ardor; fervor.
Fĕr'vent, a. [Lat. *fervens*, boiling.] Warm; ardent.
Fĕr'vent-ly, adv. With fervor; zealously.
Fĕr'vid, a. Warm; vehement.
Fĕr'vid-ly, adv. With glowing warmth. [warmth of mind.
Fĕr'vor, n. Heat; ardor;
Fĕs'cŭe, n. A wire or straw to point out letters.
Fĕs'tal, a. Relating to a feast; joyous; merry.
Fĕs'ter, v. i. To rankle; to grow virulent. — n. A sore that rankles and discharges.
Fĕs'ti-val, a. Pertaining to a

feast; joyous. — n. A feast; a solemn or joyful anniversary.
Fĕs'tive, a. Gay; mirthful; festal. [mirth; gayety.
Fes-tĭv'i-ty, n. Social joy or
Fes-toōn', n. A kind of wreath. — v. t. To adorn with festoons.
Fĕtch, v. t. To go and bring; to bring; to sell for. — n. A stratagem; artifice; trick.
Fête (fāt), n. A festival. — v. t. To feast. [ing.
Fĕt'id, a. Ill-smelling; stinking.
Fĕt'lock, n. Tuft of hair behind the pastern joint of a horse.
Fĕt'ter, n. A chain for the feet; a restraint. — v. t. To chain; to shackle; to bind.
Fē'tus, n. (*pl*. Fē'tus-eṣ.) An animal in the womb or egg.
Feūd, n. Quarrel; broil; a feudal tenure; a fief; a fee.
Feūd'al, a. Held of a lord; pertaining to fiefs or fees.
Feūd'al-ĭṣm, n. The system of feudal tenures.
Fē'ver, n. A disease marked by heat, thirst, and accelerated pulse.
Fē'ver-ish, a. Affected with slight fever; hot; fickle.
Few (fū, 99), a. Not many; small in number.
Few'ness, n. Smallness of number; paucity.
Fī'at, n. A decree; command.
Fib', n. A lie; falsehood. — v. i. To tell what is false.
Fī'ber (151), n. A slender
Fī'bre thread or thread-like substance.
Fī'bril, n. A small fiber.
Fī'broŭs, a. Containing, or consisting of, fibers. [mind.
Fĭck'le, a. Changeable in
Fĭck'le-ness, n. Inconstancy.
Fĭc'tile, a. Moulded into form by art.
Fĭc'tion, n. An invented story; a lie. — SYN. Fabrication; falsehood.
Fĭc-tĭ'tioŭs (-tĭsh'us), a. Feigned; counterfeit.
Fĭc-tĭ'tioŭs-ly (-tĭsh'us-), adv. Falsely.
Fĭd'dle, n. A violin. — v. i. To play on a violin.
Fĭd'dler, n. One who plays on a fiddle.
Fĭ-dĕl'i-ty, n. Faithfulness; loyalty; honesty; integrity.
Fĭdg'et, v. i. To move by fits and starts. — n. Uneasy motion of the body. [easy.
Fĭdg'et-y, a. Restless; un-

Fĭ-dū'cial, } a. Confident;
Fĭ-dū'cia-ry, } held in trust.
Fĭ-dū'cia-ry, n. One who holds in trust: a trustee.
Fīe, *interj*. denoting dislike.
Fĭef, n. An estate held of a superior on condition of military service; a fee; fend.
Fīeld, n. A piece of inclosed land; a battle-ground; compass; extent; space.
Fīeld'-boōk, n. A book used in surveying.
Fīeld'-mär'shal, n. The commander of an army; — a high military title.
Fīeld'-ŏf'fĭ-çer, n. A major, lieutenant-colonel, or colonel. [non.
Fīeld'-plēçe, n. A small can-
Fīend, n. An implacable foe; the devil; an infernal being.
Fīerçe, a. Violent; eager to attack; furious; ferocious.
Fīerçe'ly, adv. Furiously.
Fīerçe'ness, n. Violence; vehemence; rage.
Fī'er-i-ness, n. Great heat.
Fī'e-ry, a. Consisting of, or like, fire; hot; irritable; fierce; passionate.
Fīfe, n. A small musical pipe. — v. i. To play on a fife.
Fīf'er, n. One who plays on a fife.
Fĭf'teen, a. Five and ten.
Fĭfth, a. The ordinal of five; an interval of three tones and a semitone. [place.
Fĭfth'ly, adv. In the fifth
Fĭf'tĭ-eth (135), a. Next after the forty-ninth. [added.
Fĭf'ty, a. Sum of five tens
Fĭg, n. A tree and its fruit.
Fight (fīt), v. i. [*imp*. & *p. p.* FOUGHT.] To contend in battle or in single combat. — v. t. To war against. — n. A battle; a combat.
Fĭght'er (fīt'er), n. One who fights. [tion.
Fĭg'ment, n. Invention; fic-
Fĭg'u-ra-ble, a. Capable of being formed.
Fĭg'u-rate, a. Of a certain determinate form or figure.
Fĭg'u-rā'tion, n. Act of giving figure or determinate form.
Fĭg'u-ra-tive, a. Metaphorical; represented by figure.
Fĭg'u-ra-[tive-ly], adv. By a figure; [metaphorical]ly.
Fĭg'ūre, n. [sh]ape; fashion; image; pattern; a character standing for a number; a type. — v. t. To make an image of; to symbolize. —

FILAMENT 137 FISTULA

Fil'a-ment, *v. i.* To make a distinguished appearance.
Fil'a-ment, *n.* A slender thread; a fiber.
Fil'a-ment'ous, *a.* Consisting of filaments; like a thread.
Fil'a-to-ry, *n.* A machine for spinning threads.
Fil'a-tūre, *n.* The reeling of silk from cocoons.
Fil'bert, *n.* The nut of the cultivated hazel. [fer.
Filch, *v. t.* To steal; to pilfer.
File, *n.* A tool for smoothing wood, iron, &c.; a row; a series; bundle of papers. — *v. t.* To smooth with a file; to place in order, as papers. —*v. i.* To march in file.
Fil'ial (fĭl'yal), *a.* [Lat. *filius*, a son; *filia*, a daughter.] Relating to, or becoming, a child.
Fil'i-ā'tion, *n.* The relation of a son to a parent.
Fil'i-gree, *n.* Ornamental work in gold or silver like threads or grains.
Fil'ings, *n. pl.* Particles rubbed off by a file.
Fill, *v. t.* or *i.* To make become full. — *n.* Fullness.
Fil'let, *n.* A head-band; a joint of meat.— *v. t.* To bind with a fillet. [ing.
Fil'ling, *n.* The woof in weaving.
Fil'li-bŭs'ter, *n.* A lawless military adventurer
Fil'lip, *v. t.* To strike with the nail of the finger forced from the ball of the thumb. — *n.* A jerk of the finger from the thumb.
Fil'ly (141), *n.* A young mare; a wild girl.
Film, *n.* A thin skin or pellicle. —*v. t.* To cover with a thin skin.
Film'y, *a.* Composed of film.
Fil'ter, *n.* A strainer for liquor. —*v. t.* To purify by passing through a strainer.
Filth, *n.* Foul or dirty matter.
Filth'i-ness, *n.* Dirtiness.
Filth'y, *a.* Abounding in filth; foul; dirty; obscene.
Fil'trāte, *v. t.* or *i.* To filter; to percolate. [ing.
Fil-tra'tion, *n.* Act of filtering.
Fim'bri-āte, *v. t.* To fringe.
Fin, *n.* An organ of a fish.
Fin'a-ble, *a.* Deserving a fine.
Fi'nal, *a.* ... ng; conclusive; last.
Fi'nal-ly, *adv.* In conclusion.
†**Fi-nā'le**, *n.* Last part of a piece in music; termination.
Fi-nănçe', *n.* The science of raising and investing money; state income; revenue; (*pl.*) funds in the treasury.
Fi-năn'cial, *a.* Pertaining to finance.
Fin'an-çiēr', *n.* One skilled in, or having the care of, financial matters. [bird.
Finch, *n.* A small singing
Find, *v. t.* [*imp.* & *p. p.* FOUND.] To discover; to gain; to furnish; to establish.
Find'ings, *n. pl.* The tools, &c., which a journeyman provides for himself.
Fine, *a.* [From Lat. *finitus*, finished.] Elegant; showy; gay; handsome; keen; sharp; nice; exquisite. — *n.* Penalty; forfeiture; the end. — *v. t.* To inflict a penalty on; to purify; to refine.
Fine'ly, *adv.* In minute parts; gayly; dexterously.
Fine'ness, *n.* State or quality of being fine. [metals.
Fin'er, *n.* One who purifies
Fin'er-y, *n.* Fine dress; jewels, trinkets, &c.; splendor.
Fi-nesse', *n.* Art; artifice; stratagem. — *v. i.* To use stratagem or artifice.
Fin'ger, *n.* One of the five extremities of the hand. — *v. t.* To handle; to touch; to pilfer. [fastidious.
Fin'i-cal, *a.* Affectedly fine;
†**Fi'nis**, *n.* End; conclusion.
Fin'ish, *v. t.* To bring to an end; to perfect. — *n.* That which finishes; last hard, smooth coat of plaster.
Fin'ish-er, *n.* One who finishes.
Fin'ish-ing, *n.* That which terminates or perfects. [ed.
Fi'nīte, *a.* Bounded; limited.
Finned, *a.* Having fins.
Fin'ny, *a.* Furnished with fins.
Fir, *n.* A tree allied to the pine, or its wood.
Fire, *n.* Heat and light; any thing burning; a conflagration; passion. — *v. t.* To set on fire; to kindle; to discharge. — *v. i.* To take fire.
Fire'-arms, *n. pl.* Guns, pistols, &c. [wood on fire.
Fire'-brănd, *n.* A piece of
Fire'-dămp, *n.* An explosive gas in mines.
Fire'-ĕn'ġine, *n.* An engine to extinguish fires.
Fire'-fly, *n.* A winged, luminous insect.
Fire'lŏck, *n.* A musket.
Fire'man (143), *n.* A man who extinguishes fires, or who tends the fires of a steam-engine.
Fire'-plăçe, *n.* Part of a chimney; hearth.
Fire'-plŭg, *n.* A plug for drawing water at fires.
Fire'prōof, *a.* Incombustible.
Fire'-shĭp, *n.* A ship to set others on fire.
Fire'sīde, *n.* The hearth; home.
Fire'ward, } *n.* An officer
Fire'ward-en, } whose duty is to guard against fires.
Fire'wŏŏd, *n.* Wood for fuel.
Fire'-works (-wûrks), *n. pl.* Preparations of powder for exploding in the air.
Fīr'ing, *n.* Fuel.
Fĭr'kin, *n.* A vessel of eight or nine gallons.
Firm, *a.* Fixed; solid; strong; compact. — *n.* A partnership; a house or its name.
Firm'a-ment, *n.* The region of the air; the sky.
Firm'ly, *adv.* Strongly; steadily; with fixedness.
Firm'ness, *n.* Compactness; solidity; constancy.
First, *a.* Earliest; foremost; chief. — *adv.* Before any thing else. [child.
First'-bŏrn, *n.* The eldest
First'-fruits, *n. pl.* First produce. [est excellence.
First'-rāte, *a.* Of the highest
First'ling, *n.* Offspring of cattle first produced.
Fisc'al, *a.* Pertaining to a public treasury. — *n.* Public revenue; a treasurer.
Fish (140), *n.* An animal living in water, particularly one breathing by gills. — *v. t.* To search, as for fish. — *v. i.* To try to catch fish.
Fish'er-man (143), *n.* One employed in fishing.
Fish'er-y, *n.* The business or place of fishing.
Fish'hŏŏk, *n.* A hook for catching fish.
Fish'ing, *n.* The practice of catching fish.
Fish'-mŏng'ġer (-mŭng'ġer), *n.* A dealer in fish.
Fish'y, *a.* Tasting or smelling like a fish; fish-like. [split.
Fis'sĭle, *a.* Capable of being
Fis'sūre (fish'yụr), *n.* A cleft; a narrow chasm.
Fist, *n.* The hand clinched. — *v. t.* To beat with the fist.
Fist'i-cŭffs, *n. pl.* Blows with the fist. [chronic abscess.
Fist'u-lă, *n.* A deep, narrow,

sŏn, ôr, dọ, wọlf, tōō, tŏŏk; ûrn, rụe, pụll; ç, ġ, *soft*; ¢, ġ, *hard*; a̱ẕ; exist; ŋ *as* ng; this.

FISTULAR 138 FLESHLY

Fist'u-lar, *a.* Hollow, like a pipe or reed.
Fist'u-lous,
Fit, *n.* Attack of spasms, or of disease; a passing humor. — *a.* Suitable; convenient; proper. — *v. t.* (129) To suit; to adapt; to equip; to qualify. — *v. i.* To be becoming.
Fit'ful, *a.* Varied by fits.
Fit'ly, *adv.* Suitably.
Fit'ness, *n.* State of being fit. — SYN. Adaptation; justness; propriety. [priate.
Fit'ting, *p. a.* Fit; appro-
Five, *n.* or *a.* Four and one.
Five'fold, *a.* Taken five times.
Fix, *v. t.* To set firmly; to fasten. — *v. i.* To settle.
Fix-ā'tion, *n.* Act of fixing; firm state; stability.
Fix'ed-ness, *n.* State of being fast.
Fix'i-ty, *n.* Firm coherence of parts; fixedness.
Fixt'ūre (fīkst'yųr), *n.* Fixed furniture or appendage.
Fizz, *v. i.* To make a hissing sound; to bungle. [state.
Fiz'zle,
Flăb'bi-ness, *n.* A flabby
Flăb'by, *a.* Soft; yielding; loose; easily shaking. [ber.
Flăc'cid, *a.* Weak and limber
Flăc-cĭd'i-ty, *n.* Laxness; want of tension.
Flăg, *v. i.* To become weak; to droop. — *v. t.* To lay with flags or flat stones. — *n.* A plant; a flat stone; colors, or an ensign.
Flăg'el-lāte, *v. t.* To scourge.
Flăg'el-lā'tion, *n.* Act of whipping. [flute.
Flăg'eo-let, *n.* A kind of
Flăg'gy, *a.* Weak; flexible.
Fla-gĭ'tioŭs (-jĭsh'us), *a.* Extremely wicked; atrocious.
Flăg'-ŏf'fi-çer, *n.* The commander of a squadron.
Flăg'on (39), *n.* A vessel with a narrow mouth, for liquors.
Flā'gran-çy, *n.* Heinousness; enormity.
Flā'grant, *a.* [Lat. *flagrans*, flaming.] Ardent; enormous; eager; notorious.
Flā'grant-ly, *adv.* Notoriously.
Flăg'-ship, *n.* The ship which bears the commander of a squadron.
Flăg'-stăff (142), *n.* A staff to support a flag.
Flăg'-stōne (18), *n.* A flat stone for a pavement.
Flāil, *n.* An instrument for thrashing grain.
Flāke, *n.* A scale of snow; a scale; a scaffold. — *v. t.* To form into flakes. — *v. i.* To break into flakes.
Flāk'y, *a.* Consisting of flakes.
Flăm, *n.* A pretense; a lie. — *v. t.* To deceive; to gull.
Flăm'beau (flăm'bō), *n.* A lighted torch.
Flāme, *n.* Light emitted from fire; blaze; ardor. — *v. i.* To burn with a blaze.
Flām'ing (133), *a.* Burning with blaze; bright; violent.
Fla-min'go, *n.* A bird of a bright red color, with long legs and a long neck.
Flănge, *n.* A projecting edge or rim, as on a car-wheel.
Flănk (79), *n.* Side of the body, or of an army or fleet, &c. — *v. t.* To attack or turn the flank of; to border on. — *v. i.* To border; to touch.
Flăn'nel, *n.* A soft woolen cloth of loose texture.
Flăp, *n.* A piece of cloth that flaps; noise or motion of a flap. — *v. t.* To move, as wings. — *v. i.* To make a motion, as with wings.
Flăp'jăck, *n.* A griddle-cake.
Flăp'per, *n.* One who, or that which, flaps.
Flāre, *v. i.* To waver; to burn with an unsteady light; to open or spread out. — *n.* A broad, unsteady light.
Flăsh, *n.* A sudden burst of light. — *v. i.* To burst suddenly, as light. [show.
Flăsh'i-ly, *adv.* With empty
Flăsh'y, *a.* Gay; showy; gaudy; insipid.
Flăsk (5), *n.* A narrow-necked bottle; a powder-horn.
Flăsk'et, *n.* A long, shallow basket.
Flăt, *a.* Level; insipid; vapid; positive; in *music*, depressed. — *n.* A level piece of land; a shoal; mark of depression in music. — *v. t.* To make flat. — *v. i.* To become flat. [peremptorily.
Flăt'ly, *adv.* Horizontally;
Flăt'ness, *n.* State of being flat. [come flat.
Flăt'ten, *v.* To make or become
Flăt'ter (130), *v. t.* To praise falsely. [ters.
Flăt'ter-er, *n.* One who flat-
Flăt'ter-y, *n.* Act of flattering; praise, especially false praise; adulation.
Flăt'u-lençe (49), *n.* Wind in the stomach or intestines.
Flăt'u-lent, *a.* Windy; producing wind in the stomach.
Flāunt, *v. i.* To display ostentatiously.
Flā'vor (155), *n.* A peculiar taste or smell; relish; savor. — *v. t.* To give a peculiar taste or smell to. [flavor.
Flā'vor-oŭs, *a.* Pleasing in
Flăw, *n.* A break; sudden gust; defect; fault. — *v. t.* To break; to crack.
Flăw'y, *a.* Full of flaws.
Flăx, *n.* A plant from the fiber of the bark of which linen is made.
Flăx'en,
Flăx'y, *a.* Like, or pertaining to, flax.
Flāy, *v. t.* To strip off the skin of; to skin.
Flēa, *n.* A troublesome insect.
Flēam, *n.* An instrument for opening veins.
Flĕck, *v. t.* To spot; to streak or stripe. [fleck.
Flĕck'er, *v. t.* To spot; to
Flĕc'tion, *n.* Act of bending, or state of being bent.
Flĕd, *imp.* & *p. p.* of *Flee*.
Flĕdge, *v. t.* To furnish with feathers. [bird just fledged.
Flĕdge'ling, *n.* A young
Flee, *v. i.* [*imp.* & *p. p.* FLED.] To run away with rapidity; to try to escape.
Fleeçe, *n.* A coat of wool that covers a sheep. — *v. t.* To deprive of a fleece; to strip by severe exactions.
Fleeç'y, *a.* Covered with wool; like wool; woolly.
Fleer, *v. i.* To grin with scorn; to deride. — *n.* Derision; mockery.
Fleet, *a.* Moving with velocity; quick in motion. — *n.* A number of ships in company; a navy. — *v. i.* To pass swiftly; to flit.
Fleet'ing, *a.* Not durable. — SYN. Transient; transitory.
Fleet'ness, *n.* Swiftness.
Flĕm'ish, *a.* Pertaining to Flanders, or to its inhabitants.
Flĕsh, *n.* The muscular parts of animals; animal nature; carnal state; human family. — *v. t.* To train by feeding with flesh; to glut; to accustom.
Flĕsh'-brŭsh, *n.* A brush to excite action of the skin.
Flĕsh'-cŏl'or (-kŭl'ur), *n.* The color of flesh.
Flĕsh'i-ness, *n.* Corpulence. [sions and appetites.
Flĕsh'li-ness, *n.* Carnal pas-
Flĕsh'ly, *a.* Animal; corporeal; carnal.

ā, ē, ī, ō, ū, ȳ, *long;* ă, ĕ, ĭ, ŏ, ŭ, ў, *short;* câre, cär, ȧsk, ạll, whạt; ẽre, veil, tẽrm; pīque, fĭrm;

FLESHY 139 FLUX

Flesh'y, *a.* Corpulent; fat.
Flew (flū, 27), *imp.* of *Fly*.
Flex, *v. t.* To bend.
Flex'i-bil'i-ty, *n.* Pliancy.
Flex'i-ble, *a.* Capable of being bent; pliant; tractable.
Flex'ile, *a.* Pliable; easily bent.
Flex'ion (flĕk'shun), *n.* Act of bending; a bend; a turn.
†**Flex'or**, *n.* A muscle that produces flexion.
Flex'ure (fleks'yur), *n.* A bending or winding.
Flick'er, *v. i.* To flutter; to flap the wings as a bat.
Flight (flīt), *n.* Act of flying; flock of birds; series, as of stairs.
Flight'i-ness (flīt'-), *n.* Capricious feeling; delirium.
Flight'y (flīt'y), *a.* Wild; fanciful; fleeting.
Flim'si-ness, *n.* Thin, weak texture.
Flim'sy, *a.* Slight and weak in texture; feeble.
Flinch, *v. i.* To draw back; to shrink, from irresolution.
Fling, *v. t.* [*imp.* & *p. p.* FLUNG.] To cast from the hand. — *v. i.* To flounce; to utter harsh language. — *n.* A gibe; a sneer.
Flint, *n.* A hard stone.
Flint'y, *a.* Made of, or resembling, flint; hard.
Flip, *n.* A drink made of beer, spirit, and sugar, heated.
Flip'pan-cy, *n.* Volubility of tongue. [and pert.
Flip'pant, *a.* Voluble; fluent
Flip'pant-ly, *adv.* In a flippant manner.
Flirt (10), *v. t.* To throw with a jerk. — *v. i.* To coquet. — *n.* A sudden jerk; a coquette: a pert girl.
Flir-tā'tion, *n.* Desire of attracting notice; coquetry.
Flit (129), *v. i.* To flutter; to dart along; to remove.
Flitch, *n.* A side of pork cured.
Float, *n.* Something that floats; a raft; a kind of wooden trowel. — *v. t.* or *i.* To swim on the surface.
Flŏc'cu-lence, *n.* Adhesion in small locks.
Flŏc'cu-lent, *a.* Adhering in small locks.
Flock, *n.* A collection of small animals; a crowd; a lock, as of wool. — *v. i.* To gather in a crowd; to assemble.
Floe, *n.* A large mass of floating ice.

Flog, *v. t.* To whip; to lash; to chastise.
Flog'ging, *n.* Chastisement.
Flood (flŭd), *n.* Flow of tide; the sea; inundation. — *v. t.* To overflow; to inundate.
Flood'-gāte, *n.* A gate to stop or let out water.
Floor, *n.* The bottom of a room or of a building; a story; platform. — *v. t.* To cover with a floor; to prostrate; to silence. [floors.
Floor'ing, *n.* Materials for
Flop, *v. t.* To flap.
†**Flo'ra**, *n.* [Lat., from *flos*, flower.] All the vegetable species native in a given locality or period. [ers.
Flo'ral, *a.* Pertaining to flow-
Flo-rĕs'çence, *n.* A bursting into flower; a blossoming.
Flor'et (86), *n.* A small or partial flower.
Flor'id (84), *a.* [Lat. *floridus*, from *flos*, flower.] Flushed with red; flowery; embellished.
Flo-rĭd'i-ty, *n.* Freshness or brightness of color; redness.
Flor'in, *n.* A coin of different values. [vates flowers.
Flo'rist, *n.* One who culti-
Flŏt'agç, *n.* Act of floating; something that floats..
Flo-tĭl'la (140), *n.* A little fleet.
Flŏt'sam, } *n.* Goods found
Flŏt'son, } floating on the sea.
Flounçe, *v. t.* To deck with flounces. — *v. i.* To struggle violently; to flounder. — *n.* A loose trimming on apparel; a sudden jerk or dash.
Floun'der, *v. i.* To flounce; to struggle violently. — *n.* A flat fish allied to the halibut.
Flour, *n.* The fine part of ground grain, esp. wheat. — *v. t.* To sprinkle with flour.
Flour'ish (flŭr'ish), *v. i.* or *t.* To thrive; to embellish; to brandish. — *n.* (140) Decoration; show; parade of words; musical embellishment.
Flout, *v. t.* To treat with contempt. — *v. i.* To sneer. — *n.* A contemptuous fling.
Flōw (flō), *v. i.* To move as a liquid; to rise as the tide; to hang loose and waving; to issue. — *v. t.* To cover with water; to flood. — *n.* A stream; current.
Flow'er (flour), *n.* The blossom of a plant; choicest

part. — *v. i.* To blossom forth; to bloom. — *v. t.* To embellish with figures.
Flow'er-de-lūçe, *n.* A plant of several species; iris.
Flow'er-et, *n.* A small flower.
Flow'er-ing, *n.* Season of blossoming.
Flow'er-y, *a.* Full of flowers; highly ornamented; florid.
Flōw'ing, *a.* Liquid; fluent.
Flōwn, *p. p.* of *Flee* or *Fly*.
Flŭet'u-āte, *v. i.* To waver; to rise and fall, as a wave.
Flŭet'u-ā'tion, *n.* Sudden rise and fall; undulation.
Flūe, *n.* A passage for smoke; soft fur or down.
Flū'en-cy, *n.* Facility of utterance; volubility.
Flū'ent, *a.* Flowing; voluble; copious.
Flū'ent-ly, *adv.* With easy flow of utterance; volubly.
Flū'id (27), *a.* Having parts which easily move, as water or air; liquid. — *n.* A liquid or flowing substance.
Flu-ĭd'i-ty, } *n.* The quality
Flū'id-ness, } of being fluid.
Flūke, *n.* The part of an anchor which fastens in the ground. [ter.
Flūme, *n.* A channel for wa-
Flŭm'mer-y, *n.* A kind of jelly of milk and flour; flattery.
Flŭng, *imp.* & *p. p.* of *Fling*.
Flŭr'ry, *n.* A hasty blast; sudden gust or commotion. — *v. t.* To agitate; to disturb.
Flŭsh, *a.* Fresh; full of vigor; affluent; liberal; level. — *n.* A flow of blood to the face; sudden excitement. — *v. i.* To redden suddenly. — *v. t.* To make red; to start; to cause to flush. [agitate.
Flŭs'ter, *v. t.* To confuse; to
Flūte, *n.* [From Lat. *flatus*, a blowing.] A musical pipe; a furrow in a column. — *v. t.* To play on a flute. — *v. t.* To furrow or channel.
Flūt'ing, *n.* Furrows on a column, &c. [flute.
Flūt'ist, *n.* A performer on tho
Flŭt'ter (130), *v. i.* To move or flap the wings rapidly; to fluctuate. — *v. t.* To agitate. — *n.* Act of fluttering; hurry; confusion.
Flū'vi-al, } *a.* Belonging
Flū'vi-āt'ile, } to a river.
Flŭx, *n.* A flowing; a substance for melting metals; dysentery. — *v. t.* To melt or fuse.

sŏn, ôr, dọ, wọlf, too, tŏŏk; ûrn, rṵe, pṵll; ç, ġ, *soft*; ç, ḡ, *hard*; a<u>z</u>; ęxist; ŋ as ng; this.

Flūx'ĭ-bĭl'ĭ-ty, *n.* Capacity of being fused. [melted.
Flūx'ĭ-ble, *a.* Capable of being
Flūx'ion (flŭk'shun), *n.* A flowing; a method of mathematical analysis.
Fly, *v. i.* [*imp.* FLEW; *p. p.* FLOWN.] To move with the wings; to move rapidly; to shun; to part or burst open. — *n.* (141) A winged insect; part of a machine to regulate the rest; a light carriage.
Flȳ'-blōw, *n.* The egg of a fly. — *v. t.* To lay an egg in or on, as a fly.
Flȳ'-fish, *v. i.* To angle for fish by baiting with flies.
Flȳ'-lēaf, *n.* A blank leaf at the beginning or end of a book.
Flȳ'ing-bridge, *n.* A bridge of pontoons or of boats.
Flȳ'-wheel, *n.* A wheel attached to machinery to equalize its movements.
Fōal, *n.* The young of a mare. — *v. i.* To bring forth a colt.
Fōam, *v. i.* To froth; to be in a rage. — *n.* Froth; rage.
Fōam'y, *a.* Covered with foam or froth; frothy.
Fŏb, *n.* A small watch-pocket. — *v. t.* To trick; to defraud.
Fō'cal, *a.* Belonging to a focus.
Fō'cus, *n.* (*pl.* Fō'cus-es, †Fō'çī, 147.) The point in which rays of light meet, when reflected or refracted; a central point.
Fŏd'der, *n.* Food for cattle. — *v. t.* To feed, as cattle.
Fōe (140), *n.* An enemy; an adversary; an ill-wisher.
Fŏg, *n.* A thick vapor from the earth or water.
Fŏg'gĭ-ness (135), *n.* State of being foggy. [filled with fog.
Fŏg'gy, *a.* Dark with a fog;
Fō'gy, *n.* A stickler for old things; one opposed to progress. [ness; a failing.
Foi'ble, *n.* A moral weakness
Foil, *v. t.* To frustrate; to defeat. — *n.* Defeat; a blunt sword; a thin leaf of metal.
Foist, *v. t.* To insert wrongfully or secretly.
Fōld, *n.* A doubling; a plait; a pen for sheep. — *v. t.* To double over; to confine in a fold. — *v. i.* To double over another. [fold paper.
Fōld'er, *n.* An instrument to
Fō'li-ā'ceoŭs, *a.* Leafy or with scales.
Fō'li-age, *n.* Leaves of trees.

Fō'li-āte, *v. t.* To beat into a thin plate. [plates.
Fō'li-ā'tion, *n.* A beating into
Fō'li-o (fō'li-o or fōl'yo, 140), *n.* A book of two leaves to a sheet; a page.
Fŏlk (fōk, 18), or **Fōlks** (fōks), *n. pl.* People in general.
Fŏl'li-cle, *n.* A simple pod opening down the inner suture.
Fŏl'lōw, *v.* To go or come after; to copy or imitate; to succeed; to result.
Fŏl'lōw-er, *n.* One who follows; a disciple: an adherent.
Fŏl'ly, *n.* Want of sense; absurd action; criminal weakness.
Fo-mĕnt', *v. t.* To apply lotions to; to abet.
Fō'men-tā'tion, *n.* A bathing with warm lotions.
Fŏnd, *a.* Foolish; silly; loving. [caress.
Fŏn'dle, *v. t.* To doat on; to
Fŏnd'ling, *n.* One fondled or caressed much.
Fŏnd'ly, *adv.* Lovingly.
Fŏnd'ness, *n.* Affection; love.
Fŏnt, *n.* A baptismal basin; an assortment of type.
Fōod, *n.* That which supplies nutriment. — SYN. Sustenance; provisions; fare.
Fōol, *n.* One destitute of reason; a buffoon. — *v. t.* To impose on; to cheat.
Fōol'er-y, *n.* Acts of folly.
Fōol'-hard'y, *a.* Madly rash or adventurous.
Fōol'ish, *a.* Silly; indiscreet.
Fōol'ish-ly, *adv.* Weakly; absurdly.
Fōol'ish-ness, *n.* Want of understanding; folly.
Fōols'cap, *n.* [From the original water-mark.] A long folio writing paper.
Fōot (143), *n.* That on which a thing stands; the bottom of the leg; a measure of 12 inches; measure in poetry; infantry. — *v. i.* To dance; to walk. — *v. t.* To kick; to tread; to sum up.
Fōot'-ball, *n.* An inflated ball for kicking about.
Fōot'-boy, *n.* A boy in livery.
Fōot'fall, *n.* A footstep.
Fōot'-hōld, *n.* That which sustains the feet firmly; basis; support; state; settlement.
Fōot'ing, *n.* Ground for the foot; firm position; foundation. [servant.
Fōot'man (143), *n.* A man-

Fōot'pād, *n.* A highwayman.
Fōot'-path (96), *n.* A way for foot-passengers.
Fōot'step, *n.* Mark of a foot; track: mark; way. [feet.
Fōot'stōol, *n.* A stool for the
Fŏp, *n.* A vain, trifling fellow; a coxcomb; a dandy.
Fŏp'per-y, *n.* Foolish vanity in dress or manners.
Fŏp'pish, *a.* Fop-like; vain; gaudy; affected.
Fŏp'pish-ness, *n.* Foppish dress or manners.
Fŏr (122), *prep.* In the place of; because of; during. — *conj.* Because; since.
Fŏr'age, *n.* Food for horses or cattle; provisions. — *v. t.* To go in search of provision for horses; to plunder; to spoil.
Fŏr'as-mŭch', *adv.* or *conj.* Since; seeing.
Fo-rāy', or **Fŏr'āy**, *n.* A pillaging excursion.
For-bāde', *imp.* of Forbid.
For-bēar', *v. i.* or *t.* [*imp.* FORBORE; *p. p.* FORBORNE.] To cease; to abstain; to delay.
For-bēar'ançe, *n.* Long-suffering; abstinence.
For-bĭd', *v. t.* [*imp.* FORBID; *p. p.* FORBIDDEN.] To command not to do; to prohibit.
For-bĭd'ding, *a.* Repulsive.
For-bōrne', *p. p.* from Forbear.
Fŏrçe (85), *n.* Strength: active power; vigor; efficacy; armament; compulsion. — *v. t.* To compel; to urge; to ravish.
Fŏrçe'-mēat, *n.* Spiced meat chopped fine.
Fŏr'çeps, *n. pl.* A pair of surgeon's tongs or pincers.
Fŏr'çi-ble (133), *a.* Manifesting force; violent; mighty.
Fŏr'çi-ble-ness, *n.* Force.
Fŏr'çi-bly, *adv.* With violence; powerfully.
Fŏrd, *n.* A shallow place where water is passed on foot. — *v. t.* To pass by wading. [foot.
Fŏrd'a-ble, *a.* Passable on
Fōre, *a.* Coming or going first — *adv.* Before; in the forepart. [forehand.
Fōre-ärm', *v. t.* To arm beforehand.
Fōre-bōde', *v. t.* To prognosticate; to predict.
Fōre-cāst', *v. t.* or *i.* To plan beforehand; to foresee.
Fōre'cāst, *n.* Contrivance beforehand: foresight.
Fōre'căs-tle (-kăs-l), *n.* The

ā, ē, ī, ō, ū, ȳ, *long*; ă, ĕ, ĭ, ŏ, ŭ, ў, *short*; câre, cür, ȧsk, ạll, whạt; ẽre, veil, tẽrm; pïque, fïrm;

FORECLOSE 141 FORTUITOUSLY

Õrepart of a ship, under deck, where the sailors live.
Fōre-clōṣe', *v. t.* To shut up; to stop; to preclude; to cut off from right of redemption.
Fōrṣ-clōṣ'ūre (-klō'zhụr), *n.* Act of precluding.
Fōre'fā-ther, *n.* An ancestor.
Fōre-fĭn'ḡer, *n.* The finger next to the thumb.
Fōre'frŏnt, *n.* Front; van.
Fōre-gō', *v. t.* [*p. p.* FORE-GONE.] To forbear to possess; to give up. [hand.
Fōre-gŏne', *a.* Formed before-
Fōre'ground, *n.* The front part of a picture.
Fōre'hand-ed, *a.* Early; timely; easy in property.
Fōre'hĕad (fŏr'ed), *n.* Upper part of the face.
Fŏr'eign (fŏr'in), *a.* Belonging to another country; not to the purpose. — SYN. Alien; remote; extrinsic.
Fŏr'eign-er (fŏr'in-), *n.* An alien, or one from another country. [know before.
Fore-know' (-nō'), *v. t.* To
Fore-knowl'edge (-nŏl'ej), *n.* Knowledge of future events.
Fōre'land, *n.* A promontory or cape; a headland.
Fōre'lŏck, *n.* A lock of hair on the forehead.
Fōre'man (143), *n.* Chief man of a jury or in a shop.
Fōre'mŏst, *a.* First in order.
Fōre'nŏŏn, *n.* First half of the day.
Fo-rĕn'sic (127), *a.* Relating to courts of law.
Fōre'cr-dāin', *v. t.* To ordain beforehand.
Fōre-ŏr'di-nā'tion, *n.* Previous ordination or appointment.
Fōre'pärt, *n.* Part before.
Fōre'raṇk, *n.* The first or front rank.
Fōre-rŭn', *v. t.* To precede.
Fōre-rŭn'ner, *n.* One sent before; a precursor.
Fōre-see', *v. t.* [*p. p.* FORE-SEEN.] To see beforehand.
Fōre-shŏrt'en, *v. t.* To represent as seen obliquely.
Fōre-shōw', *v. t.* [*pt p.* FORE-SHOWN.] To indicate beforehand.
Fōre'sīght (-sit), *n.* A seeing beforehand; prescience.
Fōre'skin, *n.* The skin that covers the *glans penis*.
Fŏr'est (84), *n.* An extensive wood.
Fōre-stǎll', *v. t.* To buy, as

goods, before they reach the market; to anticipate.
Fŏr'est-er, *n.* One who guards, or who lives in, a forest.
Fōre'tāste, *n.* Anticipation.—*v. t.* To anticipate.
Fōre-tĕll', *v.* [*imp. & p. p.* FORETOLD.] To predict.
Fōre'thought (-thawt), *n.* Previous thought; provident care. [show.
Fōre-tō'ken, *v. t.* To fore-
Fōre'top, *n.* Hair above the forehead; platform at the head of the foremast.
For-ĕv'er, *adv.* Through endless ages; to eternity.
Fōre-warn', *v. t.* To warn beforehand. [admonition.
Fōre-warn'ing, *n.* Previous
Fŏr'feit (fŏr'fit, 30), *v. t.* To lose by an offense.—*n.* What is lost by an offense.
Fŏr'feit-a-ble, *a.* Subject to forfeiture.
Fŏr'feit-ūre, *n.* Act of forfeiting; thing forfeited.
Fer-gāve', *imp. of Forgive.*
Fŏrḡe, *n.* A place where iron is beaten into form.—*v. t.* To form by hammering; to counterfeit.
Fŏrḡ'er, *n.* One who forges.
Fŏrḡ'er-y, *n.* Act of counterfeiting; thing counterfeited.
For-ḡĕt', *v. t.* [*imp.* FORGOT; *p. p.* FORGOT, FORGOTTEN.] To lose the remembrance of; to neglect.
For-ḡĕt'fụl, *a.* Apt to forget.
For-ḡĕt'fụl-ness, *n.* Aptness to forget; neglect.
For-ḡĭve', *v. t.* [*imp.* FOR-GAVE; *p. p.* FORGIVEN.] To pardon; to excuse.
For-ḡĭve'ness, *n.* Pardon.
For-ḡĭv'ing, *a.* Inclined to forgive; merciful.
For-ḡŏt', *imp. & p. p.* from *Forget*. [*get*.
For-ḡŏt'ten, *p. p.* from *For-*
Fŏrk, *v. i. or t.* To shoot into branches; to divide.—*n.* An instrument with prongs.
Fŏrked (fŏrkt), *a.* Divided into branches or prongs.
Fŏrk'y, *a.* Divided into shoots or branches.
For-lŏrn', *a.* [A.-S. *forloren*, lost.] Forsaken and wretched; helpless.—*Forlorn hope*, a detachment of men to lead in an assault, &c.
Fĕrm (85), *n.* Shape; figure; method; manner; model; order; show.—*v. t.* To give shape to; to model; to plan; to make.

Fŏrm, *n.* A long bench or seat; a class in a school.
Fŏrm'al, *a.* According to form; stiff; ceremonious.
Fŏrm'al-ist, *n.* An observer of forms.
For-măl'i-ty, *n.* Observance of ceremony. [to forms.
Fŏrm'al-ly, *adv.* According
For-mā'tion, *n.* Act of forming; creation; production.
Fŏrm'a-tīve, *a.* Forming or tending to form.—*n.* Part of a word that gives it form and is distinct from the root; a word formed agreeably to some analogy.
Fŏrm'er, *n.* One who forms.
Fŏr'mer, *a.* First of two; preceding; previous. [past.
Fŏr'mer-ly, *adv.* In time
Fŏr'mi-da-ble, *a.* Adapted to excite fear; tremendous.
Fŏr'mi-da-bly, *adv.* In a manner to excite fear.
Fŏrm'less, *a.* Having no regular form. [form.
Fŏrm'u-lă (147), *n.* Prescribed
Fŏrm'u-la-ry, *n.* A book of stated forms.—*a.* Stated.
Fŏr'ni-cā'tion, *n.* Incontinence of unmarried persons.
Fŏr'ni-cā'ter, *n.* One guilty of fornication.
For-sāke', *v. t.* [*imp.* FOR-SOOK; *p. p.* FORSAKEN.] To quit entirely.—SYN. To abandon; renounce.
For-sōōth', *adv.* In truth; verily.
For-sweār', *v.* [*imp.* FOR-SWORE; *p. p.* FORSWORN.] To renounce or deny upon oath; to swear falsely.
Fŏrt, *n.* [Lat. *fortis*, strong.] A fortress; a castle.
Fŏrte, *n.* That in which one excels.
Fŏrth, *adv.* Forward; abroad.
Fŏrth-cŏm'ing (-kŭm'ing), *a.* Ready to appear.
Fŏrth-wĭth' or **Fŏrth-wĭth'**, *adv.* Immediately.
Fŏr'ti-fi-cā'tion, *n.* Military architecture; a work for defense; a fortified place.
Fŏr'ti-fȳ, *v. t.* To erect works for the defense of; to confirm.
Fŏr'ti-tūde (50), *n.* Firmness of mind to endure.—SYN. Resolution; endurance.
Fŏrt'night (-nit), *n.* The space of two weeks.
Fŏr'tress, *n.* A fortified place.
For-tū'i-toŭs, *a.* Accidental.
For-tū'i-toŭs-ly, *adv.* By chance; accidentally.

sǒn, ŏr, dǫ, wǫlf, tōō, tŏŏk; ûru, rụe, pụll; ç, ḡ, *soft*; ç, ḡ, *hard*; aẓ; eẋist; ṇ *as* ṇḡ; th.s.

For-tū'i-ty, n. Any thing occurring by chance.
Fort'u-nate (49), a. Lucky; successful.
Fort'u-nate-ly, adv. Luckily.
Fort'une (fört'yųn), n. The good or ill that befalls man; luck; riches. — r. i. To happen; to befall.
Fort'une-těl'ler, n. One who tells the events of one's life.
Fôr'ty, a. Four times ten.
Fō'rum (140), n. A public place in Rome; a court of justice; tribunal.
Fôr'ward, a. Being before or in front: prompt; bold. — v. t. To advance; to promote. — adv. In front; onward.
Fôr'ward-ness, n. Eagerness; promptness.
Fŏsse, n. A ditch; a moat.
Fŏs'sil, a. Dug from the earth; a petrified plant or animal dug from the earth.
Fŏs'sil-if'er-oŭs, a. Containing fossil remains.
Fŏs'sil-ĭst (130), n. One versed in the knowledge of fossils.
Fŏs'ter, v. t. To nurse; to feed; to cherish.
Fŏs'ter-age, n. Charge of nursing a child.
Fŏs'ter-brŏth'er, n. A male nursed at the same breast.
Fŏs'ter-child, n. A child nursed by another than its parent.
Fŏs'ter-sĭs'ter, n. A female nursed at the same breast.
Fŏs'ter-sŏn. n. One brought up like a son.
Fŏth'er, n. A weight of lead containing 2400 pounds.
Fought (fawt), imp. and p. p. of Fight.
Foul, a. Turbid; impure; defiled; not clear or fair. — r. t. To make foul; to pollute.
Foul'ly, adv. Filthily. [lute.
Foul'ness, n. Filthiness.
Found, imp. & p. p. of Find. — v. t. To lay a basis; to establish; to cast of metal.
Foun-dā'tion, n. Settlement; basis; establishment; bottom; support; endowment.
Found'er, n. One who founds or builds; a caster of wares. — v. i. To fill and sink. — v. t. To make lame.
Foun'der-y, } n. A place for
Found'ry, } casting metals.
Found'ling, n. A deserted or exposed child found.
Fount, } n. A spring;
Fount'ain, } source; jet; head of a river; first cause.

Four, a. Two and two added.
Four'fōld, a. Four times as much. [feet.
Four'fōot-ed, a. Having four
Four'i-er-ĭṣm, n. The scheme of Fourier for the reorganization of society.
Four'score, a. Eighty.
Four'squâre, a. Having four equal sides.
Four'teen, n. Four and ten.
Fourth, a. Next after the third. [place.
Fourth'ly, adv. In the fourth
Fowl, n. [A.-S. fugol, allied to fleogan, to fly.] A winged animal; a bird. — v. i. To catch or kill wild fowl.
Fowl'er, n. A sportsman who catches birds.
Fowl'ing-piēçe, n. A gun for shooting birds.
Fŏx, n. A wild animal remarkable for its cunning. — v. t. To cover the feet of, as boots, with new leather.
Frā'cas (140), n. A noisy quarrel.
Frăc'tion, n. A fragment; part of an integer or whole number.
Frăc'tion-al, a. Pertaining to, or consisting in, fractions.
Frăc'tioŭs, a. Apt to quarrel; cross; fretful; peevish.
Frăct'ûre, n. A breach of a solid; disruption. — v. t. To break or crack, as a bone.
Frăg'ile, a. Easily broken; brittle; weak; frail.
Fra-gĭl'i-ty, n. Brittleness; frailty; weakness.
Frăg'ment, n. A piece broken off; a small portion.
Frăg'ment-a-ry, a. Composed of fragments. [smell.
Frā'grançe, n. Sweetness of
Frā'grant, a. Sweet-smelling; odorous.
Frāil, a. Weak; liable to error; of easy virtue. — n. A basket made of rushes.
Frāil'ty, n. Weakness; infirmity; foible.
Frāme, v. t. To construct; to adjust and put together; to form; to fashion. — n. Fabric; structure; timbers of an edifice; form; humor.
Frāme'-work (-wŭrk), n. The frame.
†Frāne, n. A French coin, value of 18 cents, 6 mills.
Frăn'chĭṣe (frăn'chiz), n. [Fr., from franc, free.] A privi-

lege; immunity. — v. t. To make free.
Frăn'gi-bĭl'i-ty, n. Quality of being frangible. [break.
Frăn'gi-ble, a. Liable to
Frănk (79), a. Free in utter-ing sentiments. — SYN. Open; candid; ingenuous; undisguised. — n. A free letter. — v. t. To exempt from postage.
Frănk-ĭn'çense, or Frănk'-in-çense, n. A fragrant resinous substance. [ly.
Frănk'ly, adv. Freely; openly
Frănk'ness, n. Ingenuousness; openness; candor.
Frăn'tic (127), a. Transported with passion; wild.
Frăn'tic-ly, adv. Wildly; madly.
Fra-tĕr'nal, a. Brotherly.
Fra-tĕr'ni-ty, n. A brotherhood; a society or association.
Frā'ter-nīze, or Fra-tĕr'-nīze, v. i. To associate as brothers.
Frăt'ri-çīd'al, a. Pertaining to fratricide.
Frăt'ri-çīde, n. Murder, or the murderer of a brother.
Fraud, n. Deception; deceit; trick; breach of trust.
Fraud'u-lençe, n. Fraud; deceitfulness.
Fraud'u-lent, a. Deceitful; crafty; trickish. [fraud.
Fraud'u-lent-ly, adv. By
Fraught (frawt), a. Loaded; laden; filled; full.
Frāy, n. A quarrel; a riot. — v. t. To rub; to wear.
Freak, n. A whim; a capricious notion. [odd.
Freak'ish, a. Whimsical;
Frĕck'le (frĕk'l), n. A yellow-ish spot on the skin. — v. To give or acquire freckles.
Frĕck'led (frĕk'ld), a. Full of freckles.
Frĕck'ly, a. Full of freckles.
Free, a. Being at liberty; candid; liberal; easy; licentious. — v. t. To deliver from restraint or bondage.
Free'boot-er, n A robber.
Free'bôrn, a. Born free.
Freed'man (143), n. A man freed from slavery.
Free'dom. n. Exemption from the control of another; liberty; familiarity.
Free'hōld, n. Land held by free tenure. [freehold.
Free'hōld-er. n. Owner of a
Free'ly, adv. At liberty; liberally; in abundance.

ā, ē, ī, ō, ū, ȳ, long; ă, ĕ, ĭ, ŏ, ŭ, ў, short; câre, cär, ȧsk, ạll, whạt; ẽre, vẽil, tẽrm; pīque, fĭrm;

FREEMAN 143 FROST-WORK

Free'man (143), *n.* One who enjoys liberty, or is entitled to the privileges of citizenship. [lug free

Free'ness, *n.* Quality of being free.

Free'-school (-skōōl), *n.* A school open to all.

Free'stōne, *n.* A stone composed of sand, and hence easily cut.

Free'think-er, *n.* One who disbelieves revelation.

Free-will', *n.* Power of acting at pleasure. —*a.* Voluntary; spontaneous.

Freeze, *v. t.* or *i.* [*imp.* FROZE; *p. p.* FROZEN.] To congeal with cold; to die or cause to die by cold

Freight (frāt), *n.* lading, as of a ship; price of transporting. — *v. t.* To load, as a vessel.

Freight'er (frāt'-). *n.* One who receives and forwards freight.

French, *a.* Belonging to France. — *n.* The language of France.

Frěnch'-hōrn, *n.* A wind-instrument of music.

Frěn'zied, *a.* Affected with frenzy. [mind.

Frěn'zy, *n.* Distraction of

Frē'quen-çy, *n.* Occurrence often repeated.

Frē'quent (99), *a.* Often done, or happening; common.

Fre-quēnt', *v. i.* To visit often.

Fre-quěnt'a-tīve, *a.* Denoting frequent repetition.

Fre-quěnt'er, *n.* One who frequents.

Frē'quent-ly, *adv.* Often.

Frěs'co, *n.* A kind of painting on fresh plaster.

Fresh, *a.* New and strong; recently made, or obtained; raw; green; cool; brisk; not salt. — *n.* A freshet.

Frěsh'en (frěsh'n), *v. t.* To make fresh; to revive.

Frěsh'et, *n.* A flood in rivers.

Frěsh-ly, *adv.* In a fresh manner; newly; coolly.

Frěsh'man (143), *n.* One of the youngest class in an American college.

Frěsh'ness, *n.* State of being fresh.

Frět (129), *v. t.* or *i.* To wear away by rubbing; to irritate; to be peevish; to corrode. — *n.* Agitation of liquor; irritation of mind.

Frět'fųl (139), *a.* Disposed to fret. — SYN. Peevish; cross.

Frět'fųl-ly, *adv.* Peevishly.

Frět'fųl-ness, *n.* Peevishness.

Frět'work (-wûrk), *n.* Raised work.

Frī'a-bĭl'ĭ-ty,) *n.* The quality of being easily reduced to powder.
Frī'a-blė-ness,)

Frī'a-blė, *a.* Easily crumbled.

Frī'ar, *n.* [Fr. *frère*, Lat. *frater*, brother.] A member of any religious order; a monk.

Frī'ar-y, *n.* A monastery.

Frĭb'blė, *a.* Frivolous; silly. — *n.* A trifling fellow.

Frĭc'as-see', *n.* Dish of stewed or fried fowls. — *v. t.* To dress in fricassee.

Frīc'tion, *n.* A rubbing; attrition. [week.

Frī'day, *n.* Sixth day of the

Frĭĕnd, *n.* A person attached to another by affection; a Quaker. [friends.

Frĭĕnd'less, *a.* Without

Frĭĕnd'lĭ-ness, *n.* State of being friendly.

Frĭĕnd'ly, *a.* Kind; amicable; favorable.

Frĭĕnd'ship, *n.* Intimacy based on mutual esteem.

Frĭēze, *n.* A coarse woolen cloth, with a nap; part of the entablature of a column.

Frĭg'ate, *n.* A ship of war, carrying from 28 to 50 guns.

Fright (frīt), *n.* Sudden terror; panic. — *v. t.* To disturb with sudden terror.

Fright'en (frīt'n), *v. t.* To affect with sudden terror.

Fright'fųl (frīt'-), *a.* Adapted to excite sudden terror.

Fright'fųl-ly (frīt'-), *adv.* Dreadfully.

Fright'fųl-ness (frīt'-), *n.* The quality of impressing sudden terror.

Frĭg'ĭd, *a.* Cold; dull; insensible; impotent. [ness.

Frĭ-gĭd'ĭ-ty, *n.* Coldness; dullness.

Frĭg'ĭd-ly, *adv.* Coldly; dully; impotently.

Frĭg'o-rĭf'ĭe, *a.* Causing cold.

Frill (123), *n.* An edging or ruffle. — *v. t.* To shiver with cold.

Fringe, *n.* A kind of trimming. — *v. t.* To adorn with fringe.

Frĭp'per-y, *n.* Old clothes; ridiculous finery; useless matter.

Frisk, *v. i.* To leap, dance, skip, or gambol.

Frisk'et, *n.* A frame to confine sheets of paper in printing.

Frisk'ĭ-ness (135), *n.* Liveliness; airiness; gayety.

Frisk'y, *a.* Lively; frolicsome; gay; wanton.

Frit, *n.* Materials of which glass is made after being baked, but before fusion.

Frith, *n.* Narrow arm of a sea.

Frit'ter, *n.* A kind of pancake; a fragment; a bit. — *v. t.* To break into fragments. — To *fritter away,* to diminish gradually.

Frī-vŏl'ĭ-ty,) *n.* Acts or
Frĭv'o-loŭs-ness,) habits of trifling. [ding.

Frĭv'o-loŭs, *a.* Light; trifling.

Friz, or **Frizz,** *v. t.* To curl or crisp.

Frĭz'zle (frĭz'zl), *v. t.* To crisp in short curls. — *n.* A little crisp curl.

Frō, *adv.* From; back.

Frŏck, *n.* An outer garment.

Frŏg, *n.* A well-known amphibious animal.

Frŏl'ĭe (127), *a.* Gay; full of pranks; playful. — *n.* A wild prank; merriment. — *v. i.* (128) To be merry.

Frŏl'ĭe-sŏme, *a.* Full of gayety and mirth.

Frŏm (122), *prep.* Out of; by reason of; by aid of; — noting departure, absence, separation, &c.

Frŏnd, *n.* The leaf peculiar to palms and ferns.

Fron-dĕs'çence, *n.* Time of putting forth leaves.

Frŏnt (frŭnt), *n.* The forepart; forehead; face; impudence. — *v. t.* To stand before; to stand or oppose face to face. — *v. i.* To stand foremost or opposite.

Frŏnt'age, *n.* The front part of an edifice or lot.

Frŏnt'al, *a.* Belonging to the front. — *n.* A pediment over a small door or window.

Frŏnt'ĭer, *n.* Utmost verge of a country. — *a.* Bordering; lying on the exterior part.

Frŏnt'ĭs-pĭeçe, *n.* A picture facing the first page of a book. [impudent.

Frŏnt'less, *a.* Void of shame;

Frŏnt'let (frŭnt'let), *n.* A bandage worn on the forehead.

Frŏst (19), *n.* Frozen dew; severe cold weather. — *v. t.* To cover with frost, or with something like frost.

Frŏst'-work (-wŭrk), *n.* Work resembling hoar frost.

sǒn, ôr, dǫ, wolf, tǎo, tǒok; ûrn, rụe, pụll; ç, ġ, *soft*; e, ġ, *hard*; aẹ; eẋist; ŋ as ng; this.

Fröst'y, *a.* Like frost; freezing; frozen.
Fröth (19), *n.* Foam; empty show of wit.
Fröth'y, *a.* Full of foam; empty; vain.
Frounce, *v. t.* To curl or frizzle, as the hair. — *n.* A wrinkle or curl.
Frou'zy, *a.* Musty; fetid.
Frō'ward, *a.* Perversely disobedient. — SYN. Refractory; wayward; cross.
Frō'ward-lỹ, *adv.* In a froward manner.
Frō'ward-ness, *n.* Perverseness; waywardness.
Frown, *n.* A wrinkled look; a scowl. — *v. i.* To express displeasure by contracting the brow; to scowl. — *v. t.* To rebuke with a look.
Frown'ing-ly, *adv.* With a frown. [*Freeze.*
Frōze, *imp.* and *p. p.* of
Frō'zen, *p. p.* of *Freeze.*
Fruc-tĕs'çence, *n.* The time when fruit ripens. [fruit.
Fruc-tĭf'er-oŭs, *a.* Bearing
Frŭc'ti-fi-cā'tion, *n.* Act of fructifying.
Frŭc'ti-fỹ, *v. t.* [Lat. *fructus*, fruit, and *facere*, to make.] To make fruitful; to fertilize.
Frū'gal (29), *a.* Saving of expenses; economical.
Fru-găl'ĭ-ty, *n.* Prudent economy; thrift. [omy.
Frū'gal-lỹ, *adv.* With economy
Fru-ġif'er-oŭs, *a.* Producing fruit.
Fruit, *n.* Produce of the earth, of trees, or animals; effect or consequence. [eral.
Fruit-age, *n.* Fruit in general.
Fruit'er-er, *n.* One who deals in fruit. [storing fruit.
Fruit'er-y, *n.* A place for
Fruit'ful, *a.* Producing fruit; fertile; prolific.
Fruit'ful-ness, *n.* Productiveness; fertility.
Fru-ĭ'tion (-ĭsh'ŭn), *n.* Enjoyment; realization.
Fruit'less, *a.* Destitute of fruit; unprofitable; useless.
Fruit'less-lỹ, *adv.* Unprofitably.
Fruit'-tree (106), *n.* A tree cultivated for its fruit.
Fru'men-tā'ceoŭs, *a.* Made of, or resembling, grain.
Fru'men-ty, *n.* Food made of wheat boiled in milk.
Frŭsh, *n.* A tender horn in the sole of a horse.
Frŭs'trāte, *v. t.* To disappoint; to defeat; to nullify.

Frus-trā'tion, *n.* Disappointment; defeat.
Frŭs'tum, *n.* (*pl.* †**Frŭs'tā** or **Frŭs'tums**.) Part of a Frustums. solid left after cutting off the top.
Frỹ, *v. t.* To cook with fat in a frying-pan. — *v. i.* To be heated, as meat in a pan over the fire. — *n.* A crowd of small fish.
Frỹ'ing-pān, *n.* A kitchen utensil to fry food in.
Fŭd'dle, *v. t.* To make drunk.
Fŭdġe, *interj.* Expressing contempt or disbelief.
Fū'el (26), *n.* Any substance that feeds fire.
Fu-gā'cioŭs (92), *a.* Fleeing away; volatile.
Fu-găç'i-ty, *n.* Volatility.
Fū'ġi-tive, *a.* Flying; wandering. — *n.* A runaway; a deserter.
Fū'gle-man (143), *n.* One who stands in front of soldiers at drill to show them the movements; a director.
Fūgue (fūg), *n.* A repetition of parts in music.
Fŭl'crum, *n.* (*pl.* †**Fŭl'cra** or **Fŭl'crums**, Fulcrum. 147.) The *A*, lever; *c*, fulprop on crum; *w*, weight. which a lever rests.
Ful-fĭl' (13¹, 139, *v. t.* To
Ful-fĭl' } accomplish; to carry into effect; to complete.
Ful-fĭl'ment, } *n.* Complete
Ful-fĭl'ment, } performance.
Fŭl'ġen-çy, *n.* Brightness.
Fŭl'ġent, *a.* Shining; bright.
Full, *a.* Having all it can contain; complete; ample. — *n.* Complete measure. — *adv.* Fully; quite. — *v. t.* To thicken and scour, as cloth, in a mill. [cloth.
Full'er, *n.* One who fulls
Full'ness] (131), *n.* State of
Fŭl'ness } being full; repletion; plenty.
Ful'lỹ, *adv.* To the full.
Fŭl'mi-nāte, *v. i.* or *t.* To explode; to utter denunciation; to denounce.
Fŭl'mi-nā'tion, *n.* Explosion; detonation; denunciation of censure.
Fŭl'some, *n.* Gross; disgusting; nauseous.

Fŭl'voŭs, *a.* Yellow.
Fŭm'ble, *v. i.* To attempt awkwardly; to grope about.
Fŭm'bler, *n.* One who fumbles; an awkward person.
Fūme (26), *n.* Smoke; vapor; rage. — *v. i.* To smoke; to give off vapor; to rage.
Fū'mi-gāte, *v. t.* To smoke.
Fū'mi-gā'tion, *n.* Diffusion of smoke or vapors in healing or cleansing.
Fūm'y, *a.* Producing fumes.
Fŭn, *n.* [A. S. *fean*, joys.] Sport; merriment.
Fu-năm'bu-list, *n.* A ropedancer. [ployment.
Fŭnc'tion, *n.* Office; employment.
Fŭnc'tion-al (79) *a.* Pertaining to some office.
Fŭnc'tion-a-ry, *n.* One who holds an office; an official.
Fŭnd, *n.* A stock; capital; (*pl.*) money for supplies. — *v. t.* To invest in funds.
Fŭn'da-ment, *n.* The seat.
Fŭn'da-mĕnt'al, *a.* Pertaining to the foundation; essential.
Fŭn'da-mĕnt'al-lỹ, *adv.* Primarily; essentially.
Fū'ner-al, *n.* A burial; procession at a burial. — *a.* Used at the interment of the dead.
Fu-nē're-al, *a.* Suiting a funeral; mournful; gloomy; sad. [crescence.
Fun-gŏs'i-ty, *n.* Fungous excrescence.
Fŭn'goŭs, *a.* Like a mushroom; spongy.
Fŭn'gus, *n.* (*pl.* †**Fŭn'ġī** or **Fŭn'gus-ĕs**, 147.) An order of plants including mushrooms, toadstools, mildew, mold, &c.; proud flesh.
Fū'ni-cle, *n.* A small cord or ligature; a fiber.
Fŭn'nel (130), *n.* Passage for smoke; a tunnel for pouring liquors into bottles.
Fŭn'ny, *a.* Droll; comical.
Fŭr, *n.* Fine, soft hair; skins; a coating, as on the tongue. — *v. t.* To line with fur.
Fŭr'be-lōw, *n.* Fur or fringe round the lower part of a lady's dress. — *v. t.* To adorn with furbelows.
Fŭr'bish, *v. t.* To polish; to scour; to rub up.
Fŭr'cate, *a.* Forked.
Fū'ri-oŭs (86), *a.* Rushing violently; transported with passion. — SYN. Vehement; boisterous; fierce; mad.
Fū'ri-oŭs-lỹ, *adv.* With fury; vehemently; madly.

FURL 145 GALLEY

Furl, v. t. To fold and fasten to a yard, &c.
Fŭr'long, n. [Lit. *furrow long*, i. e. the length of a furrow.] Eighth part of a mile.
Fŭr'lŏugh (fŭr'lō), n. Temporary leave of absence from military service. — v. t. To furnish with a furlough.
Fŭr'năçe, n. A place for melting metals, or for heating water; inclosed fire-place.
Fŭr'nish, v. t. To supply; to provide; to equip.
Fŭr'nish-er, n. One who supplies. [goods.
Fŭr'ni-tūre, n. Movable
Fŭr'ri-er, n. A dealer in furs.
Fŭr'rōw, n. A trench made by a plow; a wrinkle. — v. t. To cut in furrows; to trench; to wrinkle.
Fŭr'ry, a. Covered with fur.
Fŭr'ther, a. More distant; additional. — adv. To or at a greater distance. — v. t. To assist; to promote; to advance. [tion.
Fŭr'ther-ançe, n. Promo-
Fŭr'ther-er, n. A promoter.

Fŭr'ther-mōre, adv. Moreover; besides.
Fŭr'ther-mŏst, } a. Most dis-
Fŭr'thest, } tant.
Fŭr'tĭve, a. Gotten by theft or stealth; secret; sly.
Fū'ry, n. Madness; passion; rage; a raging woman.
Fŭrze, n. A thorny evergreen shrub. [furze.
Fŭrz'y, a. Abounding with
Fŭs'cous, a. Of a brown color.
Fūṣe, v. t. To liquefy by heat. — v. i. To be melted.
Fu-ṣee', n. A firelock.
Fū'ṣi-bĭl'i-ty, n. The quality of being fusible. [melted.
Fū'ṣi-ble, a. Capable of being
Fū'ṣil, n. A light musket.
Fū'ṣi-leer', n. An infantry soldier wearing a bear-skin cap.
Fū'ṣion (fū'zhun), n. The operation of converting a solid into a liquid by heat; union, as of parties.
Fŭss, n. A tumult; a bustle.
Fŭss'y, a. Bustling in small matters.

Fŭs'tian (fŭst'yan), n. A kind of coarse cotton stuff; a swelling style; bombast. — a. Made of fustian.
Fŭs'tĭc (127), n. A West India wood used for dyeing yellow.
Fŭs'ty, a. Moldy; musty.
Fū'tĭle (26), a. Useless; vain; worthless; ineffectual.
Fu-tĭl'i-ty, n. Want of importance or effect.
Fŭt'tock, n. One of the timbers raised over the keel, which form the breadth of the ship. — *Futtock shrouds*, small shrouds over the lower ones.
Fūt'ūre (fŭt'yụr), a. Liable to come or be hereafter. — n. Time to come.
Fu-tū'ri-ty, n. State of being yet to come; future time or event; the future.
Fŭzz (125), v. i. To fly off in small particles. — n. Fine, light particles; loose, volatile matter.
Fŭz'zy, a. Light and loose.
Fȳ, interj. Expressing dislike, contempt, or abhorence.

G.

GĂB, n. The mouth; loquacity. — v. t. To prate.
Găb'ar-dīne, n. A kind of coarse frock.
Găb'ble, v. i. To talk fast or without meaning. — n. Loud or rapid and senseless talk.
Gā'bi-on, n. A wicker cylinder filled with earth, used in hasty defenses.
GȲ'ble, n. Triangular end of a building from the caves to the top.
Găd, n. A wedge; a goad; a spear-point. — v. i. To ramble or rove about idly.
Găd'a-bout, } n. One who
Găd'der, } roves about idly. [stings cattle.
Găd'flȳ, n. An insect which
Gaff (123), n. A light spear; a sort of boom or yard.
Găf'fer, n. An old man; a term of address. [cocks.
Găf'fle, n. A spur for fighting
Găg, v. t. To stop the mouth of. — v. i. To heave with

nausea. — n. Something thrust into the mouth, to hinder speaking.
Gāģe, n. A pledge or pawn; a measure. — v. t. To pledge; to measure, as a cask.
Gāi'ly. See *Gayly*.
Gāin, n. Profit; advantage; benefit. — v. t. To obtain; to reach. — v. i. To advance.
Gāin'ful (139), a. Producing profit; lucrative.
Gāin'less, a. Unprofitable; useless; without gain.
Gāin-sāy', or **Gāin'sāy,** v. t. [imp. & p. p. GAINSAID.] A.-S. *gean*, against, and *say*.] To deny; to oppose; to contradict.
Gāin-sāy'er, or **Gāin'sāy-er,** n. One who gainsays.
Gāir'ish, a. Gaudy; showy.
Gāit, n. Manner of walking.
Gāit'er, n. A covering for the leg or foot.
Gā'lā, n. Show; festivity.
Găl'ăc-tŏm'e-ter, n. An instrument for ascertaining the quality of milk.
Gā'lā-dāy, n. A festival day.

Găl'ax-y, n. The milky way, a splendid assemblage.
Gāle, n. Strong wind; breeze.
Gall (123), n. A bitter yellowish animal fluid; the bile; rancor; an excrescence on the oak. — v. t. To hurt the skin of; to fret; to vex.
Gal-lănt', n. A man attentive to ladies; a lover. — v. t. To wait on, as a lady. — a. Polite and attentive to ladies.
Găl'lant, a. High-spirited; daring in fight; brave.
Găl'lant-ly, adv. Bravely.
Gal-lănt'ly, adv. In the manner of a gallant.
Găl'lant-ry, n. Bravery; nobleness; politeness to ladies; in a bad sense, intrigue.
Găl'le-on, n. A large Spanish ship formerly in use.
Găl'ler-y (141), n. A covered walk; a kind of platform with seats, on brackets for columns; a collection of paintings, or statues, &c.
Găl'ley (141), n. A kind of low, flat-built vessel; cook-room of a ship-of-war; a frame for

---

sọn, ôr, dọ, wọlf, tōō, tȯȯk; ŭrn, rṳe, pṳll; ç, ġ, *soft*; ç, ġ, *hard*; aṣ; eẋist; ŋ as ng; this.

7

GALLEY-SLAVE 146 GAUNTLET

holding type that has been set up. [works in the galleys.
Gal'ley-slāve, n. A slave who
Gal'lic, a. French.
Gal'lic, a. Belonging to gall-nuts. [our.
Gal'li-çişm, n. A French idiom.
Gal'li-gas'kĭnş, n. pl. Large open hose or trousers; leather guards for the legs.
Gal'li-nā'ceoŭs, a. Pertaining to fowls of the barn-door or pheasant kind. [quito.
Gal'li-nĭp'per, n. A large mosquito.
Gal'li-pŏt, n. A small pot, painted and glazed, used by apothecaries.
Gall'-nut, n. An excrescence on the oak, used in dyeing, &c. [quarts.
Găl'lon, n. A measure of four
Gal-lōōn', n. A kind of ribbon of silk, cotton, &c., for binding.
Găl'lŏp (39, 130), v. i. To move by leaps, as a horse.—n. A running by leaps, of a quadruped.
Găl'lows (găl'lus), n. A frame for the execution of criminals.
Ga-lōche' (-lŏsh'), n. An over-shoe. Gallows.
Gal-văn'ic, a. Pertaining to galvanism.
Gal'van-ĭşm, n. [From Galvani, the discoverer.] A species of electricity.
Gal'van-īze, v. t. To affect by galvanism.
Găm'bĭt, n. A mode of opening the game, in chess-playing. [money.
Găm'ble, v. i. To play for
Găm'bler, n. One who gambles.
Cam-boge', or **Gam-bōge'**, n. A reddish-yellow gum-resin.
Găm'bol, n A skipping and leaping.—v. i. (130) To leap and skip in sport. [a horse.
Găm'brel, n. The hind leg of
Gāme, n. Sport; play; scheme; animals hunted.—v. i. To play for money: to sport.—a. Brave; courageous.
Gāme'sŏme, a. Gay; sportive.
Gāme'ster, n. One addicted to gaming.
Găm'mer, n. An old wife;—a term of address.
Găm'mon (39), n. Thigh of a hog smoked; a hoax; humbug.—v. t. To pickle and smoke; to impose upon; to beat, in backgammon, in a certain manner. [in music.
Găm'ut, n. The scale of notes
Găn'der, n. Male of the goose.
Găng, n. A crew; a band.
Găn'gli-on, n. A tumor in the tendinous parts.
Găn'grēne, n. Mortification of living flesh.—v. To mortify.
Găn'gre-noŭs, a. Mortified.
Găngue (gang), n. The mineral substance inclosing a vein of metallic ore.
Găng'wāy, n. A passage.
Găn'net, n. A sea-fowl allied to the pelican.
Gănt'let, n. A kind of military punishment in which the criminal runs between two files of men, receiving a blow from each.
Gāol (jāl), n. A jail. See Jail.
Gāol'er, n. A jailer.
Găp, n. A breach; opening.
Gāpe, v. i. To open the mouth wide involuntarily; to yawn.
Gärb, n. Clothes; dress; appearance.
Gärb'age, n. Offals of animals.
Gär'ble, v. t. To pick out or sift; to mutilate.
Gär'bler, n. One who garbles.
Gär'den (gär'dn, 69), n. A place for the cultivation of plants, fruits, flowers, &c.—v. i. To cultivate a garden. [a garden.
Gär'den-er, n. One who tills
Gär'gĕt, n. A disease in the udders of cows.
Gär'gle, v. t. To wash or rinse, as the throat.—n. A liquid for washing the throat.
Gär'land (18, 140), n. A wreath of flowers.
Gär'lic, n. A plant having a strong smell and taste.
Gär'lick-y, a. Like garlic.
Gär'ment, n. An article of clothing, as a coat or gown.
Gär'ner, n. A store-house for grain; a granary.—v. t. To store in a granary. [gem.
Gär'net, n. A red mineral or
Gär'nish, v. t. To adorn; to decorate.—n. Decoration.
Gär'nish-ee', n. One in whose hands property of another is attached.
Gär'nish-ment, } n. Furni-
Gär'ni-tūre, } ture; ornament; decoration.
Gär'ret, n. Part of a house directly under the roof.
Gär'ret-eer', n. One who lives in a garret.
Gär'ri-son (går'ri-sn), n. A body of troops in a fort.—v. t. To place soldiers in for defense.
Gar-rōte', v. t. To seize by the throat from behind, so as to strangle and rob. [ness.
Gar-ru'li-ty, n. Talkative-
Gär'ru-loŭs, a. Disposed to talk much; loquacious.
Gär'ter, n. A band to hold up a stocking.—v. t. To fasten with a garter.
Gās (by some pron. gäz), n. (pl. Gās'ĕs, 123, 140] An aëriform, elastic fluid.
Gās'con-āde', n. A boasting.—v. i. To boast; to bluster.
Găş'e-oŭs (129), a. Being in the form of gas.
Găsh, n. A deep and long cut.—v. t. To make a long, deep cut in. [gas.
Găs'i-fȳ, v. t. To convert into
Gas'-līght (-līt), n. Light produced by gas.
Gas-ŏm'e-ter, n. A reservoir for collecting gases.
Găsp (6), v. i. To labor for breath; to pant.—v. t. To emit convulsively.—n. A painful catching of the breath.
Găs'trĭc, a. Belonging to the stomach. [loquist.
Gas-trĭl'o-quĭst, n. A ventri-
Gas-trĭl'o-quy, n. Ventriloquism.
Gas-trŏn'o-mer, n. One who likes good living.
Găs'tro-nŏm'ĭc, a. Pertaining to gastronomy.
Gas-trŏn'o-my, n. [Gr. gaster, stomach, and nomos, law.] Art of good living; epicurism.
Gāte, n. Passage-way; a large door or frame-work for closing a passage.
Găth'er, v. To collect.—n. A plait or fold. [gathers.
Găth'er-er, n. One who
Găth'er-ing, n. A collection; an accumulation.
Gaud'i-ly, adv. Showily.
Gau'di-ness, n. Showiness.
Gaud'y (135), a. Showy; ostentatiously fine.
Gāuge (gāj), v. t. To measure the contents of, as of a cask.—n. A measure; a rod for measuring.
Gāug'er (gāj'er), n. One who gauges.
Gaunt (gănt), a. Lean; thin.
Găunt'let, n. A glove with metal plates on the back; a long glove.

ă, ŭ, ī, ŏ, ŭ, y̆, long; ă, ĕ, ĭ, ŏ, ŭ, y̆, short; cāre, cär, ȧsk, ạll, whạt; ēre, veil, tẽrm; pīque, fīrm;

GAUZE 147 GERANIUM

Gauze, *n.* A thin silk or linen.
Gāve, *imp.* of *Give.*
Gāv'el, *n.* A small heap or parcel of grain; mallet of a presiding officer.
Gawk, *n.* A cuckoo; a fool.
Gawk'y, *n.* Foolish; awkward. — *n.* An awkward and overgrown or stupid person.
Gāy, *a.* Cheerful; merry; jovial; fine; showy.
Gāy'o-ty, *n.* Merriment.
Gāy'ly (135), *adv.* Finely; merrily; with mirth.
Gāze, *v. i.* To look intently. — *n.* A fixed or eager look.
Ga-zĕlle', *n.* A beautiful species of antelope.
Ga-zĕtte', *n.* A newspaper. — *v. t.* To announce officially. **Gazelle.**
Găz'et-teer', *n.* A geographical dictionary; a writer for a gazette. [at with scorn.
Gāz'ing-stŏck, *n.* One gazed
Gēar, *n.* Goods; dress; apparatus; harness. — *v. t.* To put gear on.
Gēese, *n.; pl.* of *Goose.*
Ge-lăt'i-nāte, *v. t.* or *i.* To make into, or to become, jelly.
Gĕl'a-tine (30), *n.* An animal substance that forms jelly.
Ge-lăt'i-noŭs, *a.* Of the nature of gelatine.
Gĕld, *v. t.* [*imp.* & *p. p.* GELDED or GELT.] To deprive of an essential part; to castrate. [horse.
Gĕld'ing, *n.* A castrated
Gĕl'id, *a.* Cold, or very cold.
Gĕm, *n.* A bud; a jewel; a precious stone. — *v. t.* (129) To adorn with jewels. — *v. i.* To bud.
†**Gĕm'i-ni,** *n. pl.* The Twins, — a constellation.
Gem-mā'tion, *n.* Form of budding in plants.
Gĕm'me-oŭs, *a.* Of the nature of gems. [gems.
Gĕm'my, *a.* Resembling
Gĕn'der, *n.* Sex, male or female. — *v.* To beget; to engender.
Gĕn'e-a-lŏg'ic-al, *a.* Pertaining to genealogy.
Gĕn'e-ăl'o-ġist, *n.* One skilled in genealogy.
Gĕn'e-ăl'o-gy, *n.* History of descents; lineage; pedigree.

†**Gĕn'er-ā,** *n.; pl.* of *Genus.*
Gĕn'er-al, *a.* Common; public; extensive. — *n.* Commander of an army, or of a division of an army.
Gĕn'er-al-ĭs'si-mo (140), *n.* Commander in chief.
Gĕn'er-ăl'i-ty, *n.* State of being general; the greatest part. [generalizing.
Gĕn'er-al-i-zā'tion, *n.* Act of
Gĕn'er-al-īze, *v. t.* To arrange under general heads.
Gĕn'er-al-ly, *adv.* In general; commonly.
Gĕn'er-al-shĭp, *n.* The skill or conduct of a general.
Gĕn'er-āte, *v. t.* To beget; to produce; to cause.
Gĕn'er-ā'tion, *n.* A race; family; an age. [duce.
Gĕn'er-a-tive, *a.* Able to produce.
Gĕn'er-ā'tor, *n.* One who produces or begets.
Ģe-nĕr'ic, *a.* Comprehending, or pertaining to, a genus.
Ģe-nĕr'ic-al-ly, *adv.* With regard to genus.
Gĕn'er-ŏs'i-ty, *n.* Liberality of soul; magnanimity.
Gĕn'er-oŭs, *a.* Liberal; free.
Gĕn'er-oŭs-ly, *adv.* With liberality; magnanimously.
Gĕn'e-sĭs, *n.* Origin; the first book of Scripture.
Ģĕn'et, *n.* A small horse.
Ģe-nĕt'ic, *a.* Relating to origin or production.
Ģē'ni-al, *a.* Contributing to production; enlivening.
Ģē'ni-al-ly, *adv.* In a genial manner.
Ģē'nĭe, *n.* A fabulous being in Arabian mythology.
Gĕn'i-tĭve, *a.* Noting the second case of Greek and Latin nouns.
Gĕn'i-tor, *n.* A sire; a father.
†**Ģē'nĭ-us,** *n.* (*pl.* Ģē'ni-ī, 147.) A good or an evil spirit.
Gĕn'lus (jēn'yus), *n.* (*pl.* Ģē'nĭus-es.) Nature; special disposition; mental superiority; a man of remarkable mental vigor.
Gens-d'ärmes (zhŏng-därm'), *n. pl.* Armed police in France.
Gen-tēel', *a.* Polished in manners; polite; well-bred.
Gen-tēel'ly, *adv.* With polite manners. [bitter root.
Gĕn'tian, *n.* A plant with a
Ģĕn'tile (54), *n.* Any one not a Jew; a heathen. — *a.* Pertaining to heathen.
Gĕn'til-ĭsm, *n.* Heathenism.

Gĕn'ti-lī'tioŭs (-lĭsh'us), *a.* Peculiar to a nation or people; hereditary.
Gen-tĭl'i-ty, *n.* Politeness.
Gĕn'tle, *a.* Well-born; refined; not wild. — SYN. Tame; mild; meek; quiet.
Gĕn'tle-fōlk (-fōk), } *n. pl.*
Gĕn'tle-fōlks (-fōks), } People of good birth and breeding.
Gĕn'tle-man (143), *n.* A man of good breeding.
Gĕn'tle-man-līke, } *a.* Be-
Gĕn'tle-man-ly, } coming a gentleman; polite; refined.
Gĕn'tle-ness, *n.* Softness of manners; mildness.
Gĕn'tle-wom'an (143), *n.* A lady. [care.
Ģĕn'tly, *adv.* Softly; with
Ģĕn'try, *n.* People of education and good breeding.
Ģĕ'nu-flĕe'tion, or **Ģĕn'u-flĕe'tion,** *n.* [Lat. *genu,* knee, and *flexio,* a bending.] Act of bending the knee, as in worship.
Ģĕn'u-ĭne, *a.* Free from adulteration; real; true; pure.
Gĕn'u-ĭne-ness. *n.* A genuine quality; purity; reality.
Gē'nus (147), *n.* A class embracing many species.
Ģē'o-çĕn'trĭe, *a.* Having the same center as the earth.
Ģe-ŏd'e-sy, *n.* Art of measuring the earth.
Ģe-ŏg'ra-pher, *n.* One skilled in geography.
Ģē'o-grăph'ie, } *a.* Relat-
Ģē'o-grăph'ie-al, } ing to geography.
Ģe-ŏg'ra-phy, *n.* Description of the world and its inhabitants.
Ģē'o-lŏg'ie-al, *a.* Pertaining to geology. [geology.
Ģe-ŏl'o-ġist, *n.* One versed in
Ģe-ŏl'o-gy, *n.* The science that treats of the interior structure of the earth.
Ģe-ŏm'e-ter, *n.* A geometrician.
Ģē'o-mĕt'rie-al, *a* Relating or according to geometry.
Ģē'o-mĕt'rie-al-ly, *adv.* According to geometry.
Ģe-ŏm'e-trī'çian (-trĭsh'an), *n.* One skilled in geometry.
Ģe-ŏm'e-try (117), *n.* The science of quantity and mensuration.
Ģē'o-pŏn'ies, *n. sing.* Art or science of cultivating the earth. [bandry.
Ģēŏr'ġie. *n.* A poem on husbandry.
Ģe-rā'ni-ŭm, *n.* A plant with showy flowers.

són, ôr, do, wolf, too, took; ûrn. rye, pull; ç, ġ, *soft*; ¢, ḡ, *hard*; aẓ; exist; ŋ *as* ng; this.

Germ, n. Seed-bud of a plant; first principle.
Ger'man, a. Related by blood.
Ger-māne', a. Entirely appropriate.
Ger'mi-nal, a. Pertaining to the germ, or seed-bud.
Ger'mi-nāte, v. i. To bud; to sprout; to shoot.
Ger'mi-nā'tion, n. Act of sprouting.
Ger'und, n. A kind of verbal noun in Latin.
Ges-tā'tion, n. Act of carrying young in the womb.
Ges-tĭc'u-lāte, v. i. To use gestures. [making gestures.
Ges-tĭc u-lā'tion, n. Act of
Ges-tĭc'u-lā'tor, n. One who gesticulates.
Gĕst'ūre, n. Action; motion, as of the arms in speaking. — v. i. To make gestures; to gesticulate.
Gĕt, v. t. [imp. GOT; p. p. GOTTEN.] To gain; to obtain; to win; to procreate; to persuade; to learn. — v. i. To gain; to become.
Gew'gaw, n. A showy trifle.
Ghāst'li-ness (gäst'-), n. A death-like look; paleness.
Ghāst'ly (gäst'lỹ), a. [A.-S. gástlíc, ghost-like.] Deathly pale.
Ghĕr'kin (gẽr'kin), n. A small pickled cucumber.
Ghōst (gōst), n. A disembodied spirit; an apparition.
Ghōst'ly, a. Like a ghost; pale; spiritual.
Gī'ant, n. A man of extraordinary stature. — a. Like a giant; unusually large.
Gī'ant-ess, n. A female giant.
Gī'ant-like, } a. Like a giant;
Gī'ant-ly, } gigantic.
†Giaour (jour), n. An infidel, as applied by the Turks to Christians.
Gĭb'ber, v. t. To speak rapidly and inarticulately.
Gĭb'ber-ish, n. Rapid inarticulate speech; nonsense.
Gĭb'bet, n. A kind of gallows; the projecting beam of a crane. — v. t. (130) To hang on a gibbet. Gibbet.
Gib-bŏs'i-ty, n. Convexity; protuberance; roundness.
Gĭb'boŭs (69), a. Convex; swelling; protuberant.
Gībe, v. i. or t. To rail at sneeringly; to taunt; to flout. — n. A sneer; taunt; scoff.

Gĭb'lets, n. pl. Heart, liver, gizzard, &c., of a fowl.
Gĭd'di-ly, adv. With a swimming of the head.
Gĭd'di-ness, n. A swimming of the head; dizziness.
Gĭd'dy, a. Light-headed; reeling; dizzy; wild; volatile; inconstant; unstable.
Gĭft, n. Any thing given; a present; a donation; an offering; faculty; power.
Gĭft'ed, a. Endowed with a faculty; talented.
Gĭg, n. A thing that whirls round; a light kind of chaise.
Gī'gan-tē'an, } a. Like a gi-
Gī-gán'tĭc, } ant; of extraordinary size; huge; enormous; mighty.
Gĭg'gle, n. A laugh with short catches of breath. — v. i. To laugh with short catches of breath; to titter.
Gĭld, v. t. [imp. & p. p. GILDED, GILT.] To overlay with gold; to illuminate; to brighten.
Gĭld'er, n. One who gilds.
Gĭld'ing, n. Art of overlaying with gold. [a plant.
Gĭll (jĭl), n. Fourth of a pint;
Gĭll (123), n. Organ of respiration in fishes.
Gĭl'ly-flow'er, n. A flowering plant.
Gĭlt, a. Overlaid with gold.
Gĭm'bals, n. pl. A combination of rings to suspend a compass, so that it may always keep the same position. [toy. Gimbals.
Gĭm'crăck, n. A device; a
Gĭm'lĕt, n. A small implement for boring.
Gĭmp, n. A kind of edging or trimming for dresses.
Gĭn, n. Spirit distilled from rye and barley, and flavored with juniper berries or hops; a machine; trap; snare. — v. t. To clear of its seed, as cotton, by means of a gin.
Gĭn'ger (79), n. A plant and its spicy root.
Gĭn'ger-brēad, n. A sweet cake flavored with ginger.
Gĭn'ger-ly, adv. Cautiously; daintily.
Gĭng'ham (ŭng'am), n. A kind of cotton cloth, the yarn of which is dyed before it is woven.
Gĭn'seng, n. A plant used in medicine.
Gĭp'sy, n. See Gypsy.

Gĭ-rāffe', n. [Egyptian sorafe, i. e. long-neck.] An African quadruped; the camelopard.
Gĭr'an-dōle, n. A large branched candlestick; a chaudelier.
Gĭrd, n. A twitch; a pang; a gibe. — v. t. [imp. & p. p. GIRDED, GIRT] To bind; to tie round. [floor.
Gĭrd'er, n. Chief timber in a
Gĭrd'le, n. A band round the waist. — v. t. To bind; to cut a ring round in order to kill, as a tree.
Gĭrl (60), n. A young woman.
Gĭrl'hōod, n. The state or time of being a girl.
Gĭrl'ish, a. Like a girl; giddy.
Gĭrl'ish-ness, n. Girlish manners; youthfulness.
Gĭrt, } n. A strap for a sad-
Gĭrth, } dle; a circular bandage; measure round the waist; circumference.
Gĭst, n. Main point; pith.
Give, v. t. or i. [imp. GAVE; p. p. GIVEN.] To bestow; to yield; to grant; to utter.
Gĭv'er, n. One who gives.
Gĭz'zard, n. The muscular stomach of a fowl.
Glā'broŭs, a. Smooth and shining.
Glā'cial, a. Like ice; icy, pertaining to glaciers.
Glā'ci-āte (-shĭ-āt), v i To become ice.
Glā'cier (glā'seer or glăs'ī-er), n. A great mass of ice moving slowly down mountain slopes or valleys.
Glā'cis, or Gla-çïs', n. A sloping bank.
Glăd, a. Affected with pleasure. — SYN. Delighted; gratified. — v. t. To make glad.
Glăd'den, v. t. To make glad.
Glāde, n. An opening through or in a wood.
Glăd'i-ā'tor, n. [Lat., from gladius, a sword.] A swordplayer; a prize-fighter.
Glăd'i-a-tō'ri-al, a. Pertaining to gladiators.
Glăd'ly, adv. With gladness; joyfully.
Glăd'ness, n. State of being glad; joy; pleasure.
Glăd'sŏme, a. Pleased; gay; causing joy.

Giraffe.

ă, ā, ĭ, ō, ū, y, long; ă, ĕ, ĭ, ŏ, ŭ, y, short; cāre, cär, ȧsk, ąll, whạt; ẽre, vęil, tẽrm; p;que, firm;

Glair, *n.* The white of an egg.
Glair'y, *a.* Like glair.
Glançe, *n.* A sudden shoot of light; a cast of the sight.— *v.* To dart; to fly off.
Gland, *n.* A soft, fleshy organ of secretion in animals and plants.
Gland'ers, *n. pl.* A contagious disease of horses.
Glan-dif'er-ous, *a.* Bearing acorns or other nuts.
Gland'i-fôrm, *a.* Resembling a gland or nut.
Gland'u-lar, } *a.* Consisting of glands.
Gland'u-loŭs, }
Gland'ūle, *n.* A small gland.
Glare, *n.* A bright dazzling light; a piercing look.—*v. i.* To dazzle the sight; to look fiercely.
Glār'ing, *a.* Open and bold; clear; notorious.
Glăss, *n.* A transparent substance; a mirror; telescope: (*pl.*) spectacles.—*v. t.* To cover with glass. [like glass.
Glăss'i-ness, *n.* Smoothness,
Glăss'y, *a.* Made of, or like, glass; vitreous. [color.
Glau'coŭs, *a.* Of a sea-green
Glāze, *v. t.* To furnish with glass; to cover with a vitreous or glossy substance.
Glā'zier (glā'zhur), *n.* One who sets window glass.
Glāz'ing, *n.* The vitreous substance on potters' ware; art of setting glass.
Glēam, *n.* A faint shooting forth of light.—*v. i.* To shine with flashes of light.
Glēam'y, *a.* Darting light.
Glēan, *v. t.* To gather after a reaper; to collect with patient and minute labor.
Glēan'er, *n.* One who gleans.
Glēbe, *n.* Turf; soil; land belonging to a parish church.
Glee, *n.* Joy; merriment; a song in three or more parts.
Glee'ful, *a.* Merry; gay.
Gleet, *n.* A flux of thin humor from a sore.
Glĕn, *n.* A narrow valley.
Glĭb, *a.* Smooth; slippery; voluble: fluent. [bly.
Glĭb'ly, *adv.* Smoothly; volu-
Glĭb'ness, *n.* Smoothness; volubility.
Glīde, *v. i.* To flow gently.— *n.* Act of passing smoothly.
Glĭm'mer (130), *v. i.* To shoot feeble or scattered rays.—*n.* A faint light.
Glĭm'mer-ing, *n.* A faint view; a glimpse.

Glĭmpse, *n.* A short, hurried view.
Glĭs'ten (glĭs'n), *v. t.* To sparkle with a mild light.
Glĭt'ter, *v. i.* To shine brightly.—*n.* A sparkling light.
Gloat, *v. i.* To gaze with eagerness or desire.
Glōbe, *n.* A round body; the sphere; the earth.
Glo-bōse', } *a.* Round; globu-
Glō'boŭs, } lar; spherical.
Glo-bos'i-ty, *n.* Roundness; sphericity.
Glŏb'u-lar, *a.* Spherical.
Glŏb'ule, *n.* A small round mass. [uhir.
Glŏb'u-loŭs, *a.* Round; globulous.
Glōm'er-āte, *v. t.* To wind or gather into a ball.
Glŏm'er-ā'tion, *n.* The act of forming into a ball.
Gloom, *n.* Darkness; obscurity; sadness.—*v. i.* To shine obscurely.
Gloom'i-ly, *adv.* Darkly; obscurely; sullenly.
Gloom'i-ness, *n.* State or quality of being gloomy.
Gloom'y, *a.* Dark; dim; melancholy.
Glō'ri-fi-cā'tion, *n.* Act of making glorious.
Glō'ri-fȳ, *v. t.* To make glorious; to extol; to adore.
Glō'ri-oŭs, *a.* Splendid; illustrious; grand; renowned.
Glō'ri-oŭs-ly, *adv.* Illustriously; splendidly.
Glō'ry (86), *n.* Brightness; splendor; honor; renown; felicity of heaven.—*v. i.* To exult; to rejoice; to boast.
Glŏss, *n.* Brightness; specious appearance; comment.—*v.* To make smooth and shining; to explain.
Glos-sā'ri-al, *a.* Containing explanations. [glossary.
Glŏss'a-rĭst, *n.* Author of a
Glŏss'a-ry, *n.* A vocabulary for explaining obsolete or peculiar words.
Glŏss'i-ness, *n.* The luster of a smooth surface; polish.
Glŏss-ŏg'ra-pher, *n.* A writer of glosses.
Gloss-ŏg'ra-phy, *n.* The writing of glossaries or glosses.
Gloss-ŏl'o-gy, *n.* Science of language; philology.
Glŏss'y, *a.* Smooth and shining; bright.
Glŏt'tis, *n.* The narrow opening at the upper part of the windpipe.
Glōve (glŭv), *n.* A cover for

the hand with a separate sheath for each finger.
Glōv'er, *n.* One who makes gloves.
Glōw, *v. i.* To shine with intense heat.—*n.* Intense heat; incandescence; brightness of color.
Glōw'ing, *a.* White with heat; ardent; inflamed.
Glōw'-worm (-wûrm), *n.* An insect that emits light in the night.
Glōze, *n.* Flattery; adulation.— *v. t.* To flatter; to wheedle; to smooth over.
Glūe, *n.* A kind of tenacious cement.—*v. t.* To cement with glue.
Glū'ey, *a.* Glutinous.
Glŭm, *a.* Sullen; grave; moody; morose.
Glūme, *n.* The calyx of certain plants; chaff.
Glŭt, *v. t.* To cloy; to overload.—*n.* More than enough; superabundance.
Glū'ten, *n.* The tough adhesive part of dough.
Glū'tí-nā'tion, *n.* A cementing with glue.
Glū'ti-noŭs, *a.* Viscous; viscid; tenacious.
Glŭt'ton (glŭt'tn), *n.* A voracious eater; an animal, called also wolverine.
Glŭt'ton-oŭs, *a.* Given to excessive eating. [ing.
Glŭt'ton-y, *n.* Excess in eat-
Glȳc'er-īne, *n.* (Gr. *glukeros*, sweet.] A sweetish liquid obtained from fat.
Gnärl (närl), *v. i.* To growl.
Gnärled (närld), *a.* Full of knots.
Gnăsh (năsh), *v.* To strike the teeth together.
Gnăt (năt), *n.* A small blood-sucking fly.
Gnąw (nąw), *v. t.* To bite off; to corrode.
Gneiss (nīs), *n.* A crystalline rock resembling granite.
Gnōme (nōm), *n.* A fabled subterranean being; a dwarf; a goblin.
Gnō'mon (nō'mon), *n.* The style or pin of a dial.
Gno-mŏn'ics (nō-), *n. sing.* Art or science of constructing dials.
Gnŏs'tic (nŏs'-), *n.* One of a sect of early Christian philosophers.—*a.* Relating to the Gnostics.
Gnŏs'ti-çĭsm, *n.* The doctrines taught by the Gnostics.

Gnu (nū, 140), *n.* A kind of antelope found in South Africa.

Gō, *v. i.* [*imp.* WENT; *p. p.* GONE.] To move; to proceed; to walk; to depart.

Gnu.

Goad (18), *n.* A pointed instrument to drive oxen. — *v.* To prick with a goad.

Goal, *n.* A starting-post.

Goat, *n.* A well-known animal allied to the sheep.

Goat'-hērd, *n.* One who tends goats.

Goat'ish, *a.* Like goats; rank.

Gob, *n.* A lump; a mouthful.

Gob'ble, *v. t.* To swallow hastily or in large pieces. — *v. i.* To make a noise as a turkey.

Gob'bler, *n.* A greedy eater; a turkey-cock. [ing vessel.

Gob'let, *n.* A kind of drinking vessel.

Gob'lin, *n.* An evil spirit.

Gō'-by̆, *n.* Evasion; a thrusting away.

Gō'-cärt, *n.* A machine to support children while learning to walk.

God, *n.* A divinity; a deity; the Supreme Being; Jehovah.

God'child, *n.* One for whom a person becomes sponsor.

God'dess, *n.* A female deity.

God'fä-ther, *n.* A male sponsor for a child.

God'hēad, *n.* Divine nature; deity. [irreligious.

God'less, *a.* Ungodly; wicked;

God'like, *a.* Resembling God or a god; divine.

God'li-ness (135), *n.* Real piety; a religious life.

God'ly, *a.* Pious; religious.

God'mŏth-er, *n.* A woman who becomes sponsor for a child in baptism.

God'send, *n.* An unexpected piece of good fortune.

God'sŏn, *n.* A male child for whom another is sponsor.

Gŏg'gle, *v. i.* To roll the eyes.

Gŏg'gles (gŏg'glz), *n. pl.* Glasses to protect the eyes.

Gō'ing, *n.* Act of moving; departure; way of life.

Goi'ter } (151), *n.* A swelling
Goi'tre } of the front part of the neck.

Goi'troŭs, *a.* Affected by the goiter. [metals; money.

Gōld, *n.* One of the precious

Gōld'en, *a.* Made of gold; like gold.

Gōld'finch, *n.* A beautiful yellow singing bird.

Gōld'-lēaf, *n.* Gold beaten into a thin leaf.

Gōld'smith, *n.* One who works in gold.

Gŏlf, *n.* A game played with a ball and club.

Gŏn'do-lȧ (140), *n.* A pleasure-boat used in Venice.

Gondola.

Gŏn'do-liēr', *n.* One who rows a gondola.

Gōne (19), *p. p.* of Go. Departed. [drum.

Gŏng, *n.* A kind of metal

Gō'ni-ŏm'e-ter, *n.* An instrument to measure solid angles, especially those of crystals.

Gō'ni-ŏm'e-try̆, *n.* Art of measuring solid angles.

Good, *a.* Having desirable qualities; virtuous; excellent; valid; sound; suitable; not bad. — *n.* That which possesses desirable qualities; advantage.

Good-by̆', *n.* Farewell; adieu.

Good'li-ness, *n.* Beauty; grace.

Good'ly, *a.* Beautiful; comely.

Good'ness, *n.* Quality of being good; excellence.

Goods, *n. pl.* Movables; household furniture; merchandise.

Good-will', *n.* Benevolence; business facilities.

Goose (143), *n.* A fowl; a tailor's utensil; a simpleton.

Goose'bĕr-ry̆, *n.* A thorny shrub and its fruit.

Gŏr'di-an knŏt. An inextricable difficulty.

Gōre, *n.* Clotted blood; a triangular piece of cloth or land. — *v. t.* To wound with the horns.

Gŏrge, *n.* The throat; a narrow passage between mountains or into a bastion. — *v. t.* To swallow with greediness; to satiate; to glut.

Gŏr'geoŭs (-jus), *a.* Very fine or showy; splendid. [ly.

Gŏr'geoŭs-ly̆, *adv.* Splendid-

Gŏr'get, *n.* Armor to defend the throat.

Gŏr'gon, *n.* A fabled monster that turned beholders to stone.

Go-rĭl'lȧ (140), *n.* A large and ferocious monkey, of the size of a man, found in Western Africa.

Gorilla.

Gŏr'mand, *n.* A glutton.

Gŏr'mand-īze (153), *v. i.* To eat greedily.

Gŏr'mand-īz'er, *n.* A voracious eater.

Gŏrse, *n.* A prickly shrub.

Gō'ry̆, *a.* Stained with gore.

Gŏs'hawk, *n.* A kind of short-winged, slender hawk.

Gŏs'ling, *n.* A young goose.

Gŏs'pel, *n.* [A.-S. *godspell*, fr. *gŏd*, good, and *spell*, tidings.] The history of Jesus Christ; any system of religious truth or doctrine.

Gŏs'sa-mer, *n.* A filmy substance floating in the air

Gŏs'sip, *n.* One who tattles idly; tattle. — *v. i.* To tell idle tales.

Gŏt, *imp.* of Get.

Gŏt'ten (gŏt'tn), *p. p.* of Get.

Gŏth, *n.* A barbarian.

Gŏth'ic, *a.* Pertaining to the Goths, or to a certain style of architecture; rude; barbarous.

Gouge (gowj; in *Eng.* gōōj), *n.* A chisel with a round edge. — *v. t.* To scoop out with, or as with, a gouge.

Gōurd, *n.* A plant and its fruit, which has a hard outer rind.

Gour'mand (gōōr'-), *n.* A ravenous eater; a glutton.

Gout, *n.* A painful disease; inflammation of the joints.

†Goŭt (gōō), *n.* Taste; relish.

Gout'y̆, *a.* Diseased with gout, or subject to it.

Gŏv'ern (gŭv'ern), *v. t.* To rule; to control; to exercise authority; in *grammar*, to require to be in a particular case.

Gŏv'ern-a-ble, *a.* Subject to rule; submissive.

Gŏv'ern-ance, *n.* Management; control; government.

Gŏv'er-nănte', *n.* A governess; an instructress.

Gŏv'ern-ess, *n.* A female who governs or instructs.

Gŏv'ern-ment, *n.* Regulation; control; executive power; an empire or state.

Gŏv'ern-mĕnt'al, *a.* Pertaining to government.

ā, ē, ī, ō, ū, ȳ, *long;* ă, ĕ, ĭ, ŏ, ŭ, y̆, *short;* cāre, cär, ȧsk, ạll, whạt; ẽre, vĕil, tẽrm; pīque, fĭrm;

Gŏv'ern-or, *n.*
A chief magistrate; (*Mach.*) a regulator.

Gown, *n.* A woman's dress; a loose habit or robe.

Gowns'man (143), *n.* A Governor. student; a man of letters.

Grăb, *v. t.* To seize suddenly.

Grāçe, *n.* Favor: divine favor; religious affections; a brief prayer; ease of manner: beauty. — *v. t.* To adorn; to dignify; to favor.

Grāçe'ful (152), *a.* Beautiful with dignity; elegant.

Grāçe'ful-ly, *adv.* With dignity. [being graceful.

Grāçe'ful-ness, *n.* Quality of

Grāçe'less, *a.* Destitute of grace.

Grā'cioŭs, *a.* Favorable; kind: condescending. [ably.

Grā'cioŭs-ly, *adv.* Favor-

Grā'cioŭs-ness, *n.* Kind condescension.

Gra-dā'tion, *n.* Order: series.

Grăd'a-to-ry, *a.* Proceeding step by step.

Grāde, *n.* Degree; rank; rate of ascent or descent. — *v. t.* To reduce to a level or to a regular slope.

Gra'di-ent, *a.* Moving by steps. — *n.* Degree of ascent or descent in a road; a grade.

Grăd'u-al, *a.* Proceeding by degrees; progressive.

Grăd'u-al-ly, *adv.* By degrees.

Grăd'u-āte, *v. i.* [Lat. *gradus*, a step.] To receive an academical degree. — *v. t.* To mark with degrees.

Grăd'u-āte, *n.* One who has received an academical degree.

Grăd'u-ā'tion, *n.* Act of graduating, or state of being graduated.

Grăft (5), *n.* A scion inserted in a stock. — *v. t.* To insert a shoot or scion in.

Grāin, *n.* Corn; a small seed; a minute particle; a very small weight; fibers, as of wood; (*pl.*) remains of malt. — *v. t.* To granulate; to paint in imitation of the grain of wood.

Gra-mĭn'e-oŭs, *a.* Pertaining to grass: grassy.

Grăm'i-niv'o-roŭs, *a.* Feeding on grass.

Grăm'mar, *n.* Art of speaking and writing a language correctly, or a system of rules for doing so.

Gram-mā'ri-an, *n.* One who is versed in grammar.

Gram-măt'i-cal, *a.* According to the rules of grammar.

Gram-măt'i-cal-ly, *adv.* According to grammar.

Grăm'pus, *n.* A fish allied to the whale. [for grain.

Grăn'a-ry, *n.* A store-house

Grănd, *a.* Very great; magnificent; principal.

Grăn'dam, *n.* Grandmother.

Grănd'daugh-ter (-daw'ter), *n.* Daughter of a son or daughter.

Grănd'child, *n.* A son's or daughter's child.

Gran-dee', *n.* A man of rank; a nobleman of high rank.

Grăn'deūr, *n.* Magnificence; state; greatness.

Grănd'fā-ther, *n.* A father's or mother's father.

Gran-dil'o-quençe, *n.* Lofty speaking. [grand jury.

Grănd-ju'ror, *n.* One of a

Grănd-ju'ry, *n.* A jury to decide on indictments.

Grănd'mŏth-er, *n.* A father's or mother's mother.

Grănd'sīre, *n.* A grandfather.

Grănd'sŏn, *n.* The son of a son or daughter.

Grānge, *n.* A barn; a farm with its buildings, &c.

Grăn'īte (54), *n.* A stone composed of quartz, feldspar, and mica. [granite.

Gra-nĭt'ic, *a.* Pertaining to

Gra-nĭv'o-roŭs, *a.* Subsisting on grain or corn.

Grănt, *v. t.* To bestow; to give; to yield; to concede. — *n.* A thing granted; act of granting; a conveyance in writing.

Grănt-ee' (140), *n.* One to whom a grant is made.

Grănt'er, } *n.* One who makes
Grănt'or, } a grant.

Grăn'u-lar, *a.* Consisting of grains. [collect into grains.

Grăn'u-lāte, *v. t.* To form or

Grăn'u-lā'tion, *n.* Act of forming into grains.

Grăn'ule, *n.* A small grain.

Grăn'u-loŭs, *a.* Full of grains.

Grāpe, *n.* The fruit of the vine.

Grāp'er-y, *n.* A building for raising grapes in.

Grāpe'-shŏt, *n.* A cluster of small shot in a bag or case.

Grăph'ic, *a.* [From Gr. *graphein*, to write.] Well delineated.

Grăph'īte, *n.* A form of carbon; black-lead; plumbago.

Grăp'nel, *n.*
A kind of small anchor.

Grăp'ple, *v.*
t. To lay   Grapnel.
fast hold of — *v. i.* To contend closely. — *n.* A seizing; a kind of hook.

Grăsp, *v. t.* To seize and hold. — *n.* Gripe of the hands.

Grăss (5, 123), *n.* Herbage; plants that form the food of cattle. — *v. t.* or *i.* To grow over with grass.

Grăss'hŏp-per, *n.* A well-known insect.

Grăss'y, *a.* Covered with, or resembling, grass.

Grāte, *v. t.* or *i.* To rub hard; to fret; to vex. — *n.* A frame of metal bars.

Grāte'ful, *a.* Having a sense of favors; affording pleasure. — SYN. Thankful; pleasing; agreeable; welcome. [tude.

Grāte'ful-ly, *adv.* With gratitude.

Grāte'ful-ness, *n.* Gratitude.

Grāt'er, *n.* An instrument for grating.

Grăt'i-fi-cā'tion, *n.* Pleasure enjoyed; satisfaction.

Grăt'i-fy, *v. t.* To indulge; to please; to humor.

Grāt'ing, *a.* Fretting; harsh. — *n.* A partition of bars or lattice-work; a harsh sound of rubbing. [freely.

;Grā'tis, *adv.* For nothing;

Grăt'i-tūde (50), *n.* Kind feeling toward a benefactor; thankfulness.

Gra-tū'i-toŭs, *a.* Free; voluntary; given without cause; asserted without proof.

Gra-tū'i-toŭs-ly, *adv.* Freely; without cause or proof.

Gra-tū'i-ty, *n.* A free gift.

Grăt'u-lāte, *v. t.* To salute with declarations of joy.

Grăt'u-lā'tion, *n.* A salutation of joy. [jug joy.

Grăt'u-la-to-ry, *a.* Express-

Grāve, *n.* A pit for the dead. — *a.* Serious; weighty; slow; solemn; not acute. — *v. t.* [*imp.* GRAVED; *p. p.* GRAVED; GRAVEN.] To engrave; to clean, as a ship.

Grăv'el, *n.* Small pebbles; concretions in the kidneys. — *v. t.* (130) To cover with gravel; to puzzle.

Grăv'el-ly, *adv.* Full of gravel.

Grāve'ly, *adv.* Seriously; weightily.

sŏn, ôr, dǫ, wǫlf, tōō, tŏŏk; ûrn, rᵫe, pᵫll; ç, ġ, *soft*; c, ḡ, *hard*; aṣ; eḳist; ṇ *as* ng; *this.*

Gräv′er, n. A tool to engrave with.
Gräve′-stōne, n. A stone set by a grave.
Gräve′-yärd, n. Burial place.
Gräv′id, a. Pregnant.
Gräv′i-tāte, v. i. To tend toward the center.
Gräv′i-tā′tion, n. Tendency to the center.
Gräv′i-ty, n. Seriousness; weight; force which draws toward the center of attraction.
Grā′vy, n. Juice of cooked meat, made into a dressing.
*Grāy, a. Hoary; white with a mixture of black.
Grāy′bēard, n. An old man.
Grāy′ish, a. Somewhat gray.
Grāy′ness, n. Quality or state of being gray.
Grāze, v. [From A.-S. *gräs*, grass.] To eat grass; to rub slightly in passing.
Grā′zier (grā′zhur, 104), n. One who feeds, or deals in, cattle.
Grēase, n. Soft animal fat.
Grēase, or Grēase, v. t. To smear with grease.
Grēa′si-ness, or Grēas′i-ness, n. State of being greasy.
Grēa′sy, or Grēas′y, a. Fat; oily; unctuous.
Grēat, a. Large; big; chief; pregnant; important; distinguished. [gree.
Grēat′ly, adv. In a great degree.
Grēat′ness, n. State or quality of being great. [legs.
Grēaveṣ, n. pl. Armor for the
Grē′cian (grē′shan), a. Pertaining to Greece.
Grē′çiṣm, n. A Greek idiom.
Grēed′i-ly, adv. Ravenously.
Grēed′i-ness (135), n. Ravenousness; ardent desire.
Grēed′y, a. Ravenous; covetous; eager to obtain.
Greek, n. A native of Greece; language of Greece.
Green, a. Of the color of growing plants; fresh; raw; inexperienced; not dry; not ripe. — n. A green color; a grassy plot. — v. t. To make green.
Green′-grō′çer, n. A retailer of fresh vegetables.
Green′hôrn. n. A raw youth.
Green′-house, n. A house to keep plants in.
Green′ish, a. Somewhat green.
Green′ness, n. State of being green.
Green′-rōōm, n. A retiring room for the actors in a theater.
Greeng, n. pl. Leaves and stems of young plants used for food. [turf.
Green′sward, n. A close green
Greet, v. t. To salute; to hail.
Greet′ing, n. A salutation.
Gre-gā′ri-oūs, a. Keeping in flocks; herding together.
Gre-gā′ri-oūs-ly, adv. In a flock. [with gunpowder.
Gre-nāde′, n. A ball filled
Grĕn′a-diēr′, n. A soldier distinguished by his height and by uniform.
Grew (grụ), imp. of Grow.
Grey. See Gray.
Grey′-hound (grā′-), n. A tall, fleet kind of dog.
Grid′dle, n. A shallow pan to bake cakes in; cover of a stove.
Grid′i-ron (-ī′urn), n. A kind of grate to broil meat on.
Grief, n. [From Lat. *gravis*, heavy.] A painful sense of loss; sorrow; sadness.
Griev′ançe, n. That which causes grief.
Grieve, v. i. To mourn; to sorrow; to lament. — v. t. To wound acutely.
Griev′oūs (39), a. Giving pain; painful; afflictive.
Griev′oūs-ly, adv. Painfully.
Grif′fin,) n. A fabled animal, part lion and part eagle.
Grif′fon,)
Grill (123), v. t. To broil.
Grim, a. Fierce; hideous.
Gri-māçe′, n. A distorted or made-up face.
Gri-măl′kin, n. An old cat.
Grime, v. t. To sully deeply. — n. Dirt deeply insinuated.
Grim′ly, adv. In a grim or fierce manner. [visage.
Grim′ness, n. Frightfulness of
Grin (129), v. i. To show the teeth. — n. A showing of the teeth.
Grīnd, v. t. [*imp.* GROUND.] To rub; to reduce to powder; to sharpen by rubbing; to oppress. [a back tooth.
Grīnd′er, n. One who grinds;
Grīnd′stōne, n. A stone to grind edged tools on.
Grip, n. A seizing; a grasping.
Gripe, v. t. To seize; to
clutch. — v. i. To get money by hard bargains. — n. A squeeze; a grasp; oppression; (*pl.*) pain in the bowels.
†Gri-ṣĕtte′ (93), n. A young workwoman in France. [ful.
Griṣ′ly, a. Horrible; fright-
Grist, n. Corn ground, or for grinding, at once.
Gris′tle (gris′l), n. Cartilage.
Grist′ly (gris′lỵ), a. Like gristle; cartilaginous.
Grist′mill, n. A mill for grinding grain.
Grit, n. Coarse part of meal; sand; gravel.
Grit′ti-ness (129, 135), n. Quality of being gritty.
Grit′ty, a. Full of grit; sandy; spirited.
Griz′zle, n. A gray color.
Griz′zly, a. Somewhat gray.
Grōan (130), v. i. To breathe with a deep noise, as in pain. — n. A deep, mournful sound.
Grōan′ing, n. Act of uttering groans; lamentation.
Groat (grawt), n. Fourpence sterling.
Groats, n. pl. Oats or wheat deprived of the hulls.
Grō′çer, n. [Orig. one who sold by the *gross*, or by wholesale.] A dealer in sugar, tea, liquors, spices, &c.
Grō′çer-y, n. A grocer′s shop or store; (*pl.*) goods sold by grocers.
Grŏg, n. Spirit and water.
Grŏg′ram, n. A stuff made of silk and hair.
Groin, n. Part between the belly and the thigh; curve made by two intersecting arches.
Grōōm, n. One who tends horses; an officer of the royal household; a newly married man. — v. t. To feed and tend, as horses.
Grōōve, n. A furrow; a long hollow cut by a tool. — v. t. To cut a furrow or channel in.
Grōpe, v. i. To feel in the dark.
Grŏss (124), a. Great; bulky; corpulent; immodest; indelicate; dense; total. — n. The whole bulk; twelve dozen.
Grŏss′ly, adv. Thickly; coarsely; palpably.
Grŏss′ness, n. Thickness; fatness; indelicacy.

GROT 153 GURGE

Gröt, *n.* (*pl.* **Gröt'tōes.**) A
Gröt'to, } cavern; an ornamental cave.
Gro-těsque' (-těsk'), *a.* Wildly formed; odd; whimsical.
Gro-těsque'ly (-těsk'-), *adv.*
Fantastically.
Ground, *n.* Upper part of
land; soil; foundation; (*pl.*)
lees. — *v. t.* or *i.* To lay;
to found; to run aground. —
imp. & p. p. of *Grind.*
Ground'-floor, *n.* The lower
floor of a building.
Ground'less, *a.* Void of foun-
dation.
Ground'less-ness, *n.* Want
of just cause.
Ground'-nŭt, *n.* A plant and
its fruit, of several kinds.
Ground'-plŏt, *n.* The site of
a building.
Ground'-rĕnt, *n.* Rent for
building-ground.
Ground'-work (-wûrk), *n.*
Foundation; first principle.
Group, *n.* Cluster; crowd;
assemblage. — *v. t.* To form
into a cluster [bird.
Grouse, *n.* A kind of wild
Grōve. *n.* A small wood.
Grŏv'el (59, 130), *v. i.* To
creep on the earth.
Grŏv'el-er, } *n.* One who
Grŏv'el-ler, } creeps.
Grow, *v. t.* or *i.* [*imp.* GREW;
p. p. GROWN] To vegetate;
to increase; to raise.
Growl, *v.* To grumble; to
snarl. — *n.* A cross murmur.
Grōwn, *p. p.* of *Grow.*
Growth, *n.* Increase of size;
progress; vegetation.
Grŭb, *n.* A small worm. — *v.
t.* or *i.* To dig.
Grŭdge, *v. t.* To part with
reluctantly. — *v. i.* To be
covetous or envious. — *n.* A
cherished ground of ill-feel-
ing; spite; ill-will.
Gru'el, *n.* Food made of meal
boiled in water.
Gruff (123), *a.* Stern; surly;
grum; morose.
Grŭff'ly, *adv.* In a gruff manner; with surliness.
Grŭff'ness, *n.* Quality of
being gruff; moroseness.
Grŭm, *a.* Deep in the throat.
Grŭm'ble, *v. i.* To murmur
with discontent; to growl;
to complain unreasonably.
Grume, *n.* Clotted blood.
Grŭm'ly, *adv.* In a grum
manner; morosely.
Grŭnt, *v. i.* To utter a sound
like a hog. — *n.* The sound
made by a hog.

Guā'la-cum (gwā'ya-), *n.* The
resin of lignum-vitæ.
Guā'no (gwä'no), *n.* Manure
of the dung of sea-fowls.
Guăr'an-tee' (137), *v. t.* To
warrant. — *n.* A surety for
performance.
Guăr'an-tôr, *n.* A warrantor.
Guăr'an-ty, *v. t.* To undertake for the performance of,
as of an agreement. — *n.*
One who warrants; an en-
gagement.
Guärd (gärd, 69), *n.* A watch;
defense; a body of men for
protection. — *v. t.* To watch;
to defend.
Guärd'i-an, *n.* One who has
the care of another. — *a.*
Protecting. [a guardian.
Guärd'i-an-ship, *n.* Office of
Guärd'-room, *n.* A room in
which guards assemble or
lodge.
Guā'va, *n.* A tree, and its
fruit, from which a jelly is
made.
Gū'ber-na-tō'ri-al, *a.* Pertaining to a governor.
Gŭd'ġeon (-jun), *n.* A small
fish; a person gulled; a pin
on which a wheel turns.
Guer-ril'lä (ğer-ril'lä, 140), *a.*
An irregular or predatory
mode of warfare.
Guĕss (124), *v. t.* [Allied to
get, to obtain.] To conject-
ure; to suppose. — *n.* A conjecture.
Guĕst. *n.* A visitor. [leading.
Guīd'ançe, *n.* Direction; a
Guīde, *v. t.* To lead; to di-
rect. — *n.* One who shows
the way; a regulator.
Guīde'-pōst. *n.* A post to
point out the way.
Guild, *n.* An association of
workmen, &c.
Guild'er, *n.* A Dutch coin.
Guīle (69), *n.* Cunning; craft.
Guīle'ful, *a.* Deceitful; crafty.
Guīle'less, *a.* Free from guile;
artless; sincere.
Guil'lo-tĭne' (-tēen'), *n.* A
machine for beheading. — *v.
t.* To behead with the guillo-
tine.
Guilt, *n.* Criminality; sin.
Guilt'i-ly, *adv.* With guilt.
Guilt'i-ness, *n.* Criminality.
Guilt'less, *a.* Without guilt.
Guilt'less-ness, *n.* Freedom
from guilt; innocence.
Guilt'y, *a.* Criminal; wicked.
Guĭn'ea (140), *n.* An English
gold coin of the value of 21
shillings sterling. [dress.
Guīse (69), *n.* Manner; garb;

Gui-tär', *n.*
A stringed
instru-
ment of
music;
played
with the
fingers.
Gūles, *n.*
(*Herald-*
ry.) Red.

Guitar.

Gŭlf, *n.* A large bay; an open
sea; au abyss. [or gulfs.
Gŭlf'y, *a.* Full of whirlpools.
Gŭll (123), *v. t.* To cheat; to
trick; to defraud. — *n.* A
sea-fowl; one easily cheated;
a dupe.
Gŭl'let, *n.* Passage for food
in the throat; esophagus.
Gŭl'li-bĭl'i-ty, *n.* Credulity.
Gŭl'ly, *n.* A channel worn by
water. — *v. t.* To wear by
water into a channel.
Gŭlp, *v. t.* To swallow eagerly. — *n.* A swallow, or as
much as is swallowed at
once.
Gŭm, *n.* The fleshy substance
that incloses the teeth; mu-
cilage of vegetables hardened. — *v. t.* To unite or
stiffen with gum.
Gŭm-Är'a-bĭc, *n.* A gum
from the acacia.
Gŭm'-boil, *n.* A boil or small
abscess on the gum.
Gŭm'mi-ness, *n.* Quality or
state of being gummy.
Gŭm'my, *a.* Consisting of,
or like, gum.
Gŭmp, *n.* A dolt; a dunce.
Gŭmp'tion, *n.* Shrewdness,
address; capacity.
Gŭn, *n.* A cannon, musket,
&c. — *v. i.* To practice fowl-
ing.
Gŭn'-bōat, *n.* A small vessel fitted to carry a gun or
two at the bow.
Gŭn'ner, *n.* One who works
a gun; a cannoneer.
Gŭn'ner-y, *n.* The art and
science of firing guns.
Gŭn'ning. *n.* Act of shooting.
Gŭn'pow-der, *n.* An explosive
composition of saltpeter, sulphur, and charcoal mixed,
dried, and granulated.
Gŭn'shŏt, *n.* The reach or
range of a shot. — *a.* Made
by the shot of a gun.
Gŭn'smith, *n.* A gun-maker.
Gŭn'stŏck, *n.* Wood in which
the barrel of a gun is fixed.
Gŭn'wale (gŭn'nel), *n.* Upper
edge of a ship's side.
Gûrġe, *n.* A whirlpool; abyss.

sŏn, ôr, dọ, wọlf, tōō, tŏŏk; ûrn, rụe, pụll; ç, ġ, *soft*; c, ġ, *hard*; aᶻ; ex̣ist; ụ as ng; this.

GURGLE 154 HALLOW

Gûr'gle, v. i. To gush irregularly and noisily, as water from a bottle.
Gŭsh, v. i. To rush out, as a fluid. — n. A sudden and violent issue of a fluid.
Gŭs'set, n. A piece of cloth inserted in a garment to strengthen it.
Gŭst, n. Taste; enjoyment; a sudden blast of wind.
Gŭs'to, n. Relish; taste.
Gŭst'y, a. Subject to gusts, or blasts of wind.
Gŭt, n. The intestinal canal. — v. t. To disembowel; to destroy the interior of.
Gŭt'tà-pĕr'cha, n. A substance exuding from certain trees in Asia and resembling India rubber in some of its properties.
Gŭt'ter, n. [Lat. gutta, a drop.] A passage for water; a small channel. — v. t. To cause to become hollow or channeled.
Gŭt'tur-al, a. Belonging to, or formed in, the throat.
Guy, n. A rope to keep a body steady in hoisting.
Gŭz'zle, v. i. or t. To swallow much or frequently.
Gŭz'zler, n. One who guzzles.
Gym-nā'ṣi-um (-nā/zhi-), n. A place for athletic exercises; a school for higher branches.
Gym'nast, n. One who teaches or practices gymnastic exercises.
Gym-nǎs'tic, a. Relating to athletic exercises for health.
Gym-nǎs'tics, n. sing. Art of performing athletic exercises.
Gȳp'se-oŭs, a. Partaking of the qualities of gypsum.
Gȳp'sum, n. Sulphate of lime; plaster-of-Paris.
Gȳp'sy (141), n. One of a vagabond race scattered over Europe.
Gȳ'ral, a. Whirling; moving round; rotatory.
Gy-rā'tion,) n. A circular motion.
Gȳre,
Gȳ'ra-to-ry, a. Moving in a circle or spirally.
Gȳve, n. A fetter or shackle for the leg. — v. t. To shackle; to fetter.

H.

H Ä, interj. denoting surprise.
†Hā'be-as Côr'pus. [Lat., you may have the body.] A writ to produce the body of a prisoner in court.
Hăb'er-dăsh'er, n. A dealer in small wares.
Hăb'er-dăsh'er-y. n. Goods sold by a haberdasher.
Ha-bĭl'i-ment, n. Dress; clothing; garment.
Hăb'it. n. Ordinary state; temperament of body; fixed custom; dress; a garment. — v. t. To clothe; to equip.
Hăb'it-a-ble, a. Capable of being inhabited.
Hăb'it-ā'tion, n. A place of abode; dwelling; residence.
Ha-bĭt'u-al (49), n. Formed by, or according to, habit. — Syn. Customary; usual.
Ha-bĭt'u-al-ly, adv. With frequent practice; commonly; customarily.
Hă-bĭt'u-āte, v. t. To accustom; to inure.
Hăb'i-tūde, n. Customary mode of living, feeling, or acting.
Hăck, v. t. To cut awkwardly. — v. i. To try to raise phlegm. — n. A horse or coach for hire; a notch; a cut. — a. Hackneyed; mercenary.
Hăck'le, v. t. To comb, as flax or hemp; to hatchel.
Hăck'ney (141), n. A horse or coach for hire. — a. Let for hire; common. — v. t. To use much; to make trite.
Hăck'neyed, a. Let out for hire; much used; trite.
Hăck'ney-cōach, n. A coach for hire.
Hăd, imp. & p. p. of Have.
Hăd'dock, n. A fish much like the cod.
Hăft, n. A handle; the hilt.
Hăg, n. An ugly old woman; a witch.
Hăg'gard, a. Wasted by want or suffering; ugly.
Hăg'gish, a. Like a hag.
Hăg'gle, v. t. To notch or hack. — v. i. To be difficult in making a bargain. [gles.
Hăg'gler, n. One who haggles.
Hā'gi-ŏg'ra-pher, n. A writer of sacred books.
Hā'gi-ŏg'ra-phy, n. Sacred writings. [prise.
Hah, interj. expressing surprise.
Hāil, n. Frozen drops of rain: a wish of health. — v. t. To call; to salute. — v. i. To fall, as icy masses.
Hāil'stōne. n. A small mass of ice falling.
Hāir, n. A small animal filament, or a mass of them.
Hāir'-brēadth, n. A very small distance. — a. Very narrow.
Hāir'-brŭsh. n. A brush to smooth the hair with.
Hāir'-cloth, n. Cloth made of hair. [being hairy.
Hāir'i-ness (135), n. State of Hāir'less, a. Destitute of hair. [of hair.
Hāir'y, a. Full of hair; made
Hạl'berd (bŏl'-), n. A military weapon with an iron head.
Hăl'cy-on (hăl'sĭ-un), n. The kingfisher. — a. Calm; quiet; peaceful; happy.
Hāle, a. Robustly healthy.
Hāle, or Hạle, v. t. To drag; to haul.
Hălf (hăf), n. (pl. Hălves, hăvz, 142.) One of two equal parts. — adv. In part; in equal part. — a. Consisting of half.
Hălf'-blōod (hăf'-), n. A relation by one parent only.
Hălf'-cāste (hăf'-), n. One born of a Hindoo and a European. [duced pay.
Hălf'-pāy (hăf'-), n. Reduced pay.
Hălf'pen-ny (hăp'pen-nȳ), n. Half a penny.
Hălf'-wĭt'ted (hăf'-), a. Weak in intellect; silly; foolish.
Hăl'i-but (hŏl'-), n. A large, flat sea-fish.
Hall (123), n. Entrance of a house; a public room; a stately edifice; college.
Hăl'le-lū'iah } (hal'le-lū'yà),
Hăl'le-lū'jah } n. & interj. Praise ye the Lord.
Hal-lōō'. v. i. or t. To cry out. — interj. An exclamation to excite attention.
Hăl'lōw, v. t. To consecrate; to keep sacred.

ā, ē, ī, ō, ū, ȳ, long; ă, ĕ, ĭ, ŏ, ŭ, ỹ, short; cāre, cär, ȧsk, ąll, whąt; ẽre, veil, tẽrm; pïque, fïrm;

HALLUCINATION 155 HARNESS

Hal-lū'çi-nā'tion, n. A delusion of the imagination.
Hā'lo (140), n. A circle round the sun or moon.
Halt, v. i. or t. To limp; to stop. — a. Lame; crippled. — n. A stop; a limping.
Halt'er, n. A rope or strap to tie a horse; a hangman's rope. — v. t. To put a halter on.
Hälve (häv), v. t. To divide into two equal parts.
Hälveş (hävz), n.; pl. of Half.
Hāl'yard, n. [From hale, or haul, and yard.] A rope or tackle for raising or lowering a sail.
Hăm, n. The hind part of the knee; thigh of a hog.
Hăm'a-drȳ'ad, n. A kind of wood-nymph.
Hāmeş, n. pl. A kind of collar for horses.
Hăm'let, n. A small village.
Hăm'mer, n. An instrument for driving nails. — v. t. (130) To drive with a hammer.
Hăm'-mock (127), n. A hanging bed.

 Hammock.

Hăm'per, n. A kind of covered basket. — v. t. To perplex; to embarrass.
Hăm'string, n. One of the tendons of the ham. — v. t. To cut the tendons of the ham.
Hănd, n. The palm with the fingers; pointer of a clock, watch, or dial; manner of writing. — v. t. To give; to deliver; to lead; to conduct.
Hănd'bĭll, n. A loose printed sheet for public information.
"ănd'bōok, n. A manual of reference.
"ănd'cŭff, n. A manacle to confine the hands. — v. t. To put handcuffs on; to manacle.
Hănd'fụl (130), n. As much as the hand can hold.
Hănd'-găl'lop, n. A gentle gallop. [cupation.
Hănd'i-erăft, n. Manual occupation.
Hănd'i-ly, adv. In a handy manner; dexterously.
Hănd'i-ness, n. Ease or dexterity in performance.
Hănd'i-wŏrk (-wûrk), n. Work done by the hands.
Hănd'ker-chĭef (hăŋk'er-chĭf, 167), n. A cloth used for wiping the face, &c.

Hăn'dle, v. t. To touch; to manage; to treat of. — n. Part by which a thing is held.
Hănd'māid, } n. A waiting-maid.
Hănd'māid-en, }
Hănd'-rāil, n. A rail to hold by, as in a staircase.
Hănd'-saw, n. A small saw.
Hănd'sŏme (hăn'sum), a. Comely; good-looking; appropriate; generous.
Hănd'sŏme-ly (hăn'sum-), adv. In a handsome manner; dexterously.
Hănd'spīke, n. A kind of wooden lever.
Hănd'y, a. Ready; dexterous; convenient; at hand.
Hăng, v. i. [imp. HANGED, HUNG.] To be suspended. — v. t. To put to death on a gallows. ● [sword.
Hăng'er, n. A short broad-
Hăng'er-ŏn, n. A dependent.
Hăng'ĭngş, n. pl. Drapery hung to walls.
Hăng'man (143), n. A public executioner. [tied together.
Hănk, n. Two or more skeins
Hăŋk'er, v. i. To long for.
Hăŋk'er-ing, n. Eager desire.
Hăp, n. That which comes unexpectedly; chance; accident.
Hăp'-hăz'ard, n. Extra hazard; chance; accident.
Hăp'less, a. Unhappy; unfortunate. [chance.
Hăp'ly, adv. Perhaps; by
Hăp'pen, v. i. To come to pass; to occur.
Hăp'pi-ly, adv. Luckily; fortunately.
Hăp'pi-ness, n. State of enjoyment; unstudied grace.
Hăp'py, a. In a state of felicity; fortunate; ready.
Ha-răngue' (-răng'), n. A noisy speech; an oration. — v. To make a noisy speech; to declaim; to address.
Hăr'ass, v. t. To fatigue to excess; to perplex.
Hăr'bĭn-ġer, n. A forerunner.
Hăr'bor (155), n. A haven for ships; a lodging. — v. t. To lodge; to shelter; to entertain. — v. i. To take shelter.
Hărd, adv. Close; nearly. — a. Not soft; not easily penetrated; firm; solid; not easily done; difficult; not prosperous; rigorous; close.
Hărd'en, v. t. or i. To make or grow hard.
Hărd'-heärt'ed, a. Unfeeling; cruel; inhuman.
Hărd'i-hōod, n. Boldness.

Hărd'i-ness, n. Firm intrepidity; robustness.
Hărd'ly, adv. Not easily; with difficulty.
Hărd'ness, n. Quality or state of being hard.
Hărdş, n. pl. Coarse part of flax; tow.
Hărd'shĭp, n. Any thing hard to bear; severe toil.
Hărd'wāre, n. Wares made of iron, &c.
Hărd'y, a. Strong; brave; bold; robust.
Hāre, n. A small, timid animal.
Hāre'bĕll, n. A plant with blue bell-shaped flowers. [a hare's.
Hāre'-brāined, a. Wild; giddy.
Hāre'lĭp, n. A divided lip like a hare's.
Hā'rem, n. Ladies' apartment in a seraglio.
Härk, v. i. To hear; to listen. — interj. Hear!
Här'le-quĭn (-kĭn or -kwĭn), n. A buffoon; a clown.
Här'lot, n. A lewd woman.
Här'lot-ry, n. Prostitution.
Härm, n. Injury; hurt; damage. — v. t. To injure; to hurt; to damage.
Härm'fụl, a. Hurtful; injurious.
Härm'less, a. Innocent; not hurtful; unhurt.
Härm'less-ly, adv. In a harmless manner.
Härm'less-ness, n. Quality of being harmless; innocence.
Har-mŏn'ĭe, } a. Relating
Har-mŏn'ĭe-al, } to harmony; having musical proportion.
Har-mŏn'ĭe-à, n. A kind of musical instrument.
Har-mŏn'ĭes, n. sing. Science of musical sounds.
Har-mō'nĭ-oŭs, a. Agreeing together; accordant; musical. [harmony.
Har-mō'nĭ-oŭs-ly, adv. With
Här'mo-nĭst, n. A musical composer.
Här'mo-nīze, v. t. or i. To make or become harmonious; to agree.
Här'mo-ny, n. [Gr. harmonia, from harmozein, to fit together.] Agreement; concord of musical strains that differ in pitch and quality.
Här'ness, n. Equipments of a horse, &c. — v. t. To put on harness; to equip.

sŏn, ôr, dọ, wọlf, tŏō, tŏŏk; ûrn, rụe, pụll; ç, ġ, soft; c, g, hard; aş; exĭst; ṇ as ng; thĭs.

Harp, n. A stringed instrument of music. — v. i. To play on a harp; to dwell long.

Härp'er,) **Härp'ist,**) n. One who plays on a harp.

Här-pōōn', n. A barbed fishing-spear. — v. t. To strike with a harpoon.

Harp.

Här-pōōn'er, n. One who uses a harpoon.

Härp'si-chôrd, n. A large stringed instrument of music.

Här'py (141), n. A fabulous animal; an extortioner.

Här'ri-er, n. A kind of hunting dog.

Här'rōw, n. An instrument to break or smooth land. — v. t. To break with a harrow; to harass; to disturb.

Här'ry, v. t. To harass.

Härsh, a. Rough to the touch, taste, or feelings.

Härsh'ly, adv. In a harsh manner; roughly.

Härsh'ness, n. Roughness.

Härs'let, n. See *Haslet*.

Härt, n. A stag or male deer.

Härts'hôrn, n. Horn of the hart; carbonate of ammonia.

Ha-rūs'pice, n. A soothsayer.

Här'vest, n. Season for gathering any crop; crop gathered; effects. — v. t. To gather, as a crop, when ripe.

Hăsh, v. t. To mince; to chop. — n. Minced meat.

Hǎs'let, n. Inwards of a hog, used for food.

Hǎsp, n. Clasp for a staple. — v. t. To fasten with a hasp.

Hǎs'sock, n. A mat to kneel on in church.

Hǎst, second person of *Have*.

Hǎste, n. Celerity of motion or action. — SYN. Hurry; speed; dispatch.

Hǎste,) v. t. or i. **Hǎst'en** (hās'n),) To make speed; to hurry; to move fast; to dispatch.

Hǎs'ti-ly, adv. With haste.

Hǎst'i-ness, n. Haste; rashness.

Hǎs'ty, a. Quick in action; passionate: rash; irritable.

Hǎt, n. A cover for the head.

Hǎtch, v. t. To produce from eggs. — n. A brood; one of the openings in a ship's deck.

Hǎtch'el, n. An instrument to clean flax. — v. t. (130) To draw through the teeth of a hatchel, as flax.

Hǎtch'et, n. A small ax.

Hǎtch'wāy, n. An opening in a ship's deck.

Hāte, v. t. To dislike greatly. — n. Great dislike; enmity; detestation.

Hāte'fųl (132, 130), a. Exciting great dislike. [odiously.

Hāte'ful-ly, adv. With hate;

Hā'tred, n. Great dislike or ill-will; hate.

Hǎt'ter, n. A maker of hats.

Haugh'ti-ly (haw'-), adv. With pride and contempt.

Haugh'ti-ness (haw'-), n. Arrogance.

Haugh'ty (haw'ty), a. Proud and overbearing.

Haul (126), v. t. To draw with force. — n. A pull; draught.

Haunch, n. The hip.

Haunt, v. t. or i. To frequent; to visit, as a ghost. — n. A place of frequent resort.

Haut'boy (hō'boy), n. [Fr. *haut bois*, lit. high wood, on account of its high tone.] A wind instrument of music.

Hǎve, v. t. [*imp.* & *p. p.* HAD.] To possess; to hold; to own; to enjoy.

Hā'ven (hā'vn), n. A harbor.

Hǎv'oc (39, 127), n. Waste; devastation. — v. t. To lay waste.

Haw, n. The berry and seed of the hawthorn.

Hawk, n. A bird of prey; the falcon. — v. i. To force up phlegm. — v. t. To cry and sell, as goods; to hunt with hawks.

Hawk'er, n. One who hawks.

Hawk'-eyed (-īd), a. Having acute sight.

Haw'ser, n. A small cable.

Haw'thôrn, n. A shrub much used for hedges.

Hāy, n. Grass dried for fodder.

Hāy'ing, n. Act or time of making hay.

Hāy'-lŏft, n. A scaffold for hay. [hay.

Hāy'-mow, n. A mow for

Hāy'-rĭck, n. A long pile of hay in the open air.

Hāy'-stăck, n. A conical pile of hay in the open air.

Hăz'ard, n. Risk of loss or evil; danger. — v. t. To risk; to expose to danger.

Hăz'ard-oŭs, a. Exposing to danger; perilous.

Hāze, n. A thin mist or fog.

Hā'zel (58), n. A shrub bearing nuts. — a. Like a hazelnut; brown.

Hā'zi-ness (135) n. State of being hazy. [dark.

Hā'zy, a. Foggy; misty;

Hē, pron. of the third person, masculine gender, referring to some male.

Hĕad, n. Upper part of the body; the chief; front; source. — v. t. or i. To lead; to direct; to get in front of; to form a head. [the head.

Hĕad'āche (-āk), n. Pain in

Hĕad'-drĕss (16), n. Covering worn on the head.

Hĕad'i-ness, n. Rashness; obstinacy. [of casks.

Hĕad'ing, n. Material for heads

Hĕad'land, n. A promontory.

Hĕad'less, a. Without a head.

Hĕad'long, a. Rash; precipitate. — adv. Precipitately.

Hĕad'-pĭeçe, n. Armor for the head; a helmet.

Hĕad'-quar'ters, n. pl. or sing. Quarters of a chief commander.

Hĕad'spring, n. Source; origin. [idle.

Hĕad'stall, n. Part of a bridle.

Hĕad'strong, a. Obstinate.

Hĕad'wāy, n. Progress of an advancing ship.

Hĕad'-wind, n. A wind from the direction opposite to a ship's course.

Hĕad'y, a. Willful; rash; hasty; intoxicating.

Hēal, v. t. To cure. — v. i. To become well.

Hēalds, n. pl. Harness for warp-threads in a loom.

Hĕalth, n. Freedom from sickness; sound state.

Hĕalth'ful, a. Free from disease; wholesome; salubrious. [manner.

Hĕalth'i-ly, adv. In a healthy

Hĕalth'i-ness, n. State of being in health. [of health.

Hĕalth'y, a. Being in a state

Hēap, n. A pile; accumulation; mass. — v. t. To pile; to amass; to accumulate.

Hēar, v. t. To perceive by the ear. — v. i. To be told.

Hēard (hẽrd), imp. & p. p. of *Hear*.

Hēar'er, n. One who hears.

Hēar'ing, n. Sense of perceiving sounds; audience.

Hēark'en, v. i. To listen; to lend the ear.

ā, ĕ, ĭ, ō, ū, y, *long*; ă, ĕ, ĭ, ŏ, ŭ, y, *short*; cāre, cär, åsk, ạll, whạt; ōre, veil, tẽrm; p'que, firm;

HEARSE 157 HENCE

Hĕarse, *n.* A carriage to bear the dead.
Hĕar'say, *n.* Report; rumor.
Hĕart, *n.* Organ of the blood's motion; inner part; seat of love; spirit. [sorrow.
Heart'-āche (-āk), *n.* Deep
Heart'-bûrn. *n.* Burning sensation in the stomach.
Heart'-fĕlt. *a.* Sincere; deep.
Hĕărth (4), *n.* Floor of a fireplace.
Hĕart'i-ly, *adv.* From the heart; sincerely.
Heart'i-ness, *n.* Sincerity.
Heart'less, *a.* Void of affection or courage; spiritless.
Heart'less-ness, *n.* Want of affection or courage.
Heart'-sĭck, *a.* Depressed.
Heart'-strings, *n. pl.* A nerve or tendon thought to brace and sustain the heart.
Heart'y, *a.* Exhibiting or promoting strength; strong; sincere; rich.
Hĕat. *n.* Caloric; great warmth; glow. — *v. t.* To make hot. — *v. i.* To grow or become hot.
Hĕath, *n.* A shrub; a place overgrown with shrubs.
Hĕa'then (55), *n.* [Orig. one who lived on the *heath*, or in the country] A pagan; a gentile. — *a.* Gentile; pagan.
Hĕa'then-ish, *a.* Like heathen; idolatrous.
Hĕa'then-ĭsm, *n.* Paganism.
Hĕath'er (hĕth'er), *n.* Heath.
Hĕath'y, *a.* Full of heath.
Hĕave, *v. t.* [*imp. & p. p.* HEAVED, HOVE.] To lift; to raise; to throw; to throw off; to pant. — *v. i.* To try to vomit. — *n.* A rising; swell.
Hĕav'en (55), *n.* Region of the air; expanse of the sky; place of the blessed.
Hĕav'en-ly, *a.* Pertaining to heaven; celestial.
Hĕaves, *n.* A disease of horses marked by difficult breathing.
Hĕav'i-ly, *adv.* With weight.
Hĕav'i-ness, *n.* Weight; depression; affliction.
Hĕav'y, *a.* Weighty; ponderous; grievous; dull; burdensome; clammy.
Hĕb-dŏm'a-dal, *a.* Weekly.
Hĕb'e-tāte, *v. t.* To blunt; to dull. [dullness.
Hĕb'e-tūde, *n.* Bluntness;
Hō'bra-ĭsm, *n.* A Hebrew idiom. [Hebrew.
Hō'bra-ĭst, *n.* One versed in

Hē'brew, *n.* A Jew; the language of the Jews. — *a.* Relating to the Hebrews.
Hĕc'a-tomb (-tōōm), *n.* A sacrifice of a hundred oxen.
Hĕc'tic, *a.* Habitual; constant. — *n.* A fever of irritation and debility.
Hĕc'tor, *n.* A bully; one who teases. — *v. t.* To bully; to tease; to vex.
Hĕdge, *n.* A thicket or fence of shrubs. — *v. t.* To fence with a hedge.
Hĕdge'-hŏg, *n.* A small animal armed with prickles or spines. Hedgehog.
Hĕdge'-rōw, *n.* A row of shrubs planted for a fence.
Heed, *v. t.* To mind; to observe. — *n.* Care; attention; notice. [watchful.
Heed'ful, *a.* Attentive;
Heed'less, *a.* Careless; inattentive; negligent.
Heed'less-ly, *adv.* Carelessly.
Heed'less-ness, *n.* Carelessness.
Heel, *n.* Hind part of the foot. — *v. i.* To lean; to incline. — *v. t.* To add a heel to.
Hĕft, *n.* Weight. — *v. t.* To try the weight of by lifting.
He-gī'ra, or **Hĕg'i-ra**, *n.* [Ar. *hidjrah*, departure.] Flight of Mohammed from Mecca, July 16, 622, from which date the Mohammedans reckon time; any flight.
Hĕif'er, *n.* A young cow.
Height (hīt, 149), *n.* Distance from a point below; an elevated place; elevation in excellence.
Height'en (hīt'n), *v. t.* To raise higher; to advance; to enhance.
Hei'nous (hā'nus), *a.* Characterized by great wickedness; atrocious.
Hei'nous-ly, *adv.* Hatefully.
Hĕir (âr, 10), *n.* He who inherits the property of another. [heir.
Hĕir'ess (âr'-), *n.* A female
Hĕir'-lōom (âr'-), *n.* Any furniture which descends to an heir.
Hĕir'ship (âr'-), *n.* Condition of being an heir.
Hĕld, *imp. & p. p.* of *Hold*.
He-lī'a-cal, *a.* Rising or setting with the sun.

Hē'li-o-çĕn'trĭc, *a.* Relating to the sun's center.
Hē'li-o-trōpe, *n.* A plant with very fragrant flowers.
Hē'lĭx, *n.* (*pl.* †**Hĕl'i-çĕs.**) A spiral line, as of wire in a coil.
Hĕll (123), *n.* The place of the devil and the damned.
Hĕl'le-bōre, *n.* A plant used in medicine.
Hel-lĕn'ic, or **Hel-lē'nie**, *a.* Relating to Greece or the Greeks; Grecian.
Hĕl'len-ĭsm, *n.* A Greek phrase or idiom.
Hĕl'len-ĭst, *n.* One skilled in the Greek language.
Hĕll'ish, *a.* Infernal; wicked.
Hĕlm, *n.* The instrument by which a ship is steered.
Hĕlm'et, *n.* Defensive armor for the head.
Hĕ'lot, or **Hĕl'ot**, *n.* A Spartan slave; any slave.
Hĕlp, *v. i.* To aid; to assist; to prevent. — *v. t.* To lend aid. — *n.* Aid; support; relief. Helmet.
Hĕlp'er, *n.* One who helps.
Hĕlp'ful, *a.* Affording help.
Hĕlp'less, *a.* Destitute of help or of means of relief.
Hĕlp'less-ness, *n.* Want of help or support.
Hĕlp'māte,) *n.* A companion
Hĕlp'meet,) or helper.
Hĕl'ter-skĕl'ter, *adv.* In a hurry and without order.
Hĕlve, *n.* Handle of an ax.
Hĕm, *n.* Border of a garment. — *v. t.* (129) To fold and sew the edge of; to border.
Hĕm'i-sphēre, *n.* Half of a sphere.
Hĕm'i-sphĕr'ic,) *a.* Con-
Hĕm'i-sphĕr'ic-al,) taining half a sphere.
Hĕm'i-stĭch (-stĭk), *n.* Half a poetic verse.
Hĕm'lock (127), *n.* A poisonous plant; an evergreen tree.
Hĕm'or-rhage, *n.* A flowing of blood from a rupture.
Hĕm'or-rhoids, *n.* The piles.
Hĕmp, *n.* A plant whose fibers are used for making rope, cloth, &c.
Hĕmp'en, *a.* Made of hemp.
Hĕn, *n.* The female of birds.
Hĕn'bāne, *n.* A plant poisonous to hens, &c.
Hĕnçe, *adv.* From this place, time or cause.

sŏn, ôr, dọ, wọlf, tōō, tŏŏk; ûrn, rụe, pụll; ç, ġ, *soft*; ȼ, g̱, *hard*; ạs; exĭst; ṇ as ng; thĭs.

Hence-förth', or Hençe'-förth, *adv.* From this time.
Hençe-för'ward, *adv.* From this time forward.
He-pät'ic, *a.* Belonging to the liver. [seven sounds.
Hĕp'ta-chŏrd, *n.* System of
Hĕp'ta-gon, *n.* A figure of seven sides and angles.
Hep-tăg'o-nal, *a.* Having seven sides and angles.
Hĕp'tärch-y, *n.* Government by seven rulers.
Hẽr, *pron.* Objective form of *She.* — *a.* Belonging to a female.
Hẽr'ald, *n.* An officer who regulates coats of arms; a forerunner. — *v. t.* To proclaim; to announce.
He-räl'die, *a.* Pertaining to heralds or heraldry.
Hẽr'ald-ry, *n.* The art or office of a herald; blazonry.
Hẽrb (ẽrb), *n.* A plant with a soft or succulent stalk.
Her-bā'ceoŭs, *a.* Belonging to herbs.
Hẽrb'age (ẽrb'ej *or* hẽrb'ej), *n.* Herbs collectively; grass.
Hẽrb'al, *n.* A book on plants; collection of plants dried. — *a.* Pertaining to herbs.
Hẽrb'al-ĭst, *n.* One skilled in herbs.
Her-bā'ri-um, *n.* (*pl.* Her-bā'ri-ums, or †Her-bā'ri-ȧ, 147.) A collection of dried plants. [herbs.
Her-bĭv'or-oŭs, *a.* Feeding on
Her-cū'le-an, *a.* [From *Hercules*, a Gr. hero famous for his strength.] Very strong, great, or difficult.
Hẽrd, *n.* A collection, as of beasts; a drove. — *v. i. or t.* To associate in herds.
Hẽrd'man, } *n..* An owner
Hẽrds'man, } or keeper of herds. [or state.
Hẽre (85), *adv.* In this place
Hẽre'a-bout', } *adv.* About
Hẽre'a-bouts', } or near this place.
Here-ăft'er, *adv.* In time after the present. — *n.* A future state. [account.
Here-ăt', *adv.* At this; on this
Here-bȳ', *adv.* By this.
Hẽr'e-dit'a-ment, *n.* Hereditary property.
He-rĕd'i-ta-ry, *a.* Descending by inheritance.
Here-ĭn', *adv.* In this.
Here-ŏf' (-ŏf' or ŏv'), *adv.* Of this; from this.
Here-ŏn', } *adv.* On or
Hẽre'up-ŏn', } upon this.

Hẽr'e-si-ärch, or He-rē'si-ärch, *n.* A chief heretic.
Hẽr'c-sy, *n.* A fundamental error in doctrine.
Hẽr'e-tĭc (120), *n.* One who errs in religious faith.
He-rĕt'ic-al, *a.* Containing heresy; not orthodox.
Hẽre-to', } *adv.* To this;
Hẽre'un-to', } unto this.
Hẽre'to-före', *adv.* Formerly.
Hẽre-wĭth', or Hẽre-wĭth', *adv.* With this.
Hẽr'i-ta-ble, *a.* Capable of being inherited.
Hẽr'i-tage, *n.* Inheritance.
Her-mäph'ro-dĭte, *n.* An animal or plant uniting both sexes.
Her-mäph'ro-dĭt'ic. *a.* Partaking of both sexes.
Hẽr'me-neū'tĭcs, *n. sing.* The art or science of interpreting the Scriptures.
Her-mĕt'ic, } *a.* Chemical;
Her-mĕt'ic-al, } perfectly close; air-tight. [ly.
Her-mĕt'ic-al-ly, *adv.* Close-
Hẽr'mĭt, *n.* [Gr. *herēmitēs*, fr. *herēmos*, solitary.] One who lives in solitude.
Hẽr'mit-age, *n.* A hermit's dwelling.
Hẽr'ni-ȧ, *n.* A rupture.
Hē'ro (86). *n.* (*pl.* Hē'rōes, 140.) A brave man; a great person.
He-rō'ic, } *a.* Becoming a
He-rō'ic-al, } hero; bold.
He-rō'ic-al-ly, *adv.* Intrepidly; courageously.
Hẽr'o-ĭne, *n.* A female hero.
Hẽr'o-ĭṣm, *n.* Distinguished bravery; gallantry. [bird.
Hẽr'on, *n.* A large wading
Hẽr'ring, *n.* A small fish.
Hẽrṣ, *pron.* Possessive form of *She.* [person.
Her-sĕlf', *pron.* The female in
Hĕṣ'i-tan-çy, *n.* Uncertainty; doubt.
Hĕṣ'i-tāte, *v. i.* To pause in doubt; to stop in speaking. — SYN. To waver; falter.
Hĕṣ'i-tā'tion, *n.* A pausing; a stammering in speech.
Hĕs'per, *n.* The evening star.
Hes-pē'ri-an, *n.* Western.
Hĕt'e-ro-dŏx, *a.* Contrary to an acknowledged standard, as the Bible; erroneous.
Hĕt'e-ro-dŏx'y, *n.* Heresy.
Hĕt'e-ro-gē'ne-oŭs, *a.* Of a different nature.
Hew, *v. t.* (*imp.* HEWED; *p. p.* HEWED, HEWN.] To cut off chips and pieces of; to chop; to form laboriously.

Hew'er, *n.* One who hews.
Hĕx'a-gon, *n.* A figure with six sides and angles.

Hex-ăg'o-nal (117), *a.* Having six sides and angles. [Hexagon.

Hĕx'a-hē'dron, *n.* A cube.
Hex-ăm'e-ter, *n.* A kind of verse of six metrical feet.
Hex-ăŋ'gu-lar, *a.* Having six angles.
Hey, } *interj.* of exulta-
Hey'dāy, } tion or surprise.
Hī-ā'tus, *n.* A chasm; a gap.
Hī-bẽr'nal, *a.* Pertaining to winter.
Hī'ber-nāte, *v. i.* To pass the winter in seclusion, as some beasts.
Hī'ber-nā'tion, *n.* Act of hibernating. [Ireland.
Hi-bẽr'ni-an, *n.* A native of
Hi-bẽr'ni-çiṣm, *n.* An Irish phrase or idiom.
Hic'cough (hĭk'up), *n.* A spasmodic affection of the stomach. — *v. i.* To have a hiccough.
Hĭck'o-ry, *n.* A walnut tree.
Hid, } *n.* Not seen or
Hĭd'den, } known; concealed.
Hide, *v. t.* or *i.* [*imp.* HID; *p. p.* HID, HIDDEN.] [Icel. *hyda.* to spread *hides* over.] To conceal; to cover; to keep close. — *n.* Skin of a beast.
Hide'-bound, *a.* Having the skin too tight.
Hĭd'e-oŭs, *a.* Shocking to the eye or ear. — SYN. Frightful; horrible; ghastly.
Hĭd'e-oŭs-ly, *adv.* Horribly.
Hĭd'e-oŭs-ness, *n.* Quality of being hideous.
Hīe (134). *v. i.* To hasten.
Hī'e-rärch, *n.* The chief of a sacred order.
Hī'e-rärch'al, } *a.* Per-
Hī'e-rärch'ic-al, } taining to a hierarchy.
Hī'e-rärch'y, *n.* Dominion in sacred things; order of celestial beings.
Hī'e-rät'ic, *a.* Relating to priests; sacerdotal.
Hī'e-ro-glyph. } *n.* A mys-
Hī'e-ro-glyph'ic. } tical symbol in ancient writing.
Hī'e-ro-glyph'ic, } *a.* Ex-
Hī'e-ro-glyph'ic-al, } pressive of meaning by symbols.
Hī'e-rŏg'ra-phy, *n.* Sacred writing.

HI-ĕr'o-phănt, or **HI'e-ro-phănt',** *n.* A chief priest.
Hig'gle, *v. i.* To carry provisions about for sale; to chaffer.
Hig'gler, *n.* One who higgles.
High (hī), *a.* Elevated; lofty; exorbitant; exalted: dear.— *adv.* Aloft; eminently.— *n.* A high place.
High'-bŏrn (hī'-), *a.* Being of noble extraction.
High'-flōwn (hī'-), *a.* Elevated; lofty; proud.
High'land (hī'-), *n.* A mountainous country.
High'land-er (hī'-), *n.* A Scotch mountaineer.
High'-mīnd'ed (hī'-), *a.* Arrogant; magnanimous.
High'ness (hī'-), *n.* Altitude; height; a title of honor.
High'-prĭĕst (hī'-), *n.* The chief priest. [great degree.
High'ly (hī'-), *adv.* In a
Hight (hīt), *n.* See *Height*.
High'-prĕss'ūre (hī'-), *n.* Pressure exceeding about 50 pounds on the square inch.
High'-spĭr'it-ed (hī'-), *a.* Irascible; bold; daring.
High'wāy (hī'-), *n.* A public road.
High'wāy-man (hī'-), *n.* A robber on the public road.
High'-wrŏught (hī'rawt), *a.* Wrought with great skill.
Hī-lăr'i-ty, or **Hi-lăr'i-ty,** *n.* Mirth; gayety.
Hill (123), *n.* An elevation of land. — *v. t.* To draw earth around. [inence.
Hill'ock (127), *n.* A small em-
Hill'y, *a.* Abounding with hills. [sword, &c.
Hĭlt, *n.* The handle of a
Hĭm, *pron.* Objective case of *He*. [form of *He*.
Hĭm-sĕlf', *pron.* Emphatic
Hĭnd, *a.* Backward; back. — *n.* Female of the red deer; a rustic.
Hĭnd'er, *a.* On the rear.
Hĭn'der (130), *v. t.* To impede the progress of; to keep back.—SYN. To stop; interrupt; check; retard.
Hĭn'der-ance, } *n.* Act of de-
Hĭn'drançe, } laying; impediment.
Hĭnd'mōst, } *a.* Behind
Hĭnd'er-mōst, } all others.
Hĭn'doo, } *n.* A native of
Hĭn'du, } Hindostan.
Hĭnge, *n.* [Allied to *hang*.] The joint on which a door turns.— *v. i.* To turn or depend.

Hĭnt, *v. t.* To suggest. — *v. i.* To allude to. — *n.* Slight allusion.
Hĭp, *n.* Joint of the thigh.
Hĭp'po-çĕn'taur, *n.* A fabulous monster, half man and half horse.
Hĭp'po-drōme, *n.* A circus for horse-races, &c.
Hĭp'po-grĭff, *n.* A fabulous winged horse.
Hĭp'po-pŏt'-a-mus, *n.* The river horse; a large African quadruped allied to the hog. Hippopotamus.
Hĭp'-roōf, *n.* A roof with an angle.
Hĭp'shŏt, *a.* Having one hip lower than the other.
Hīre, *v. t.* To engage for pay; to bribe.— *n.* Wages; reward.
Hīre'ling, *n.* A mercenary.— *a.* Serving for wages merely.
Hĭr-sūte', *a.* Shaggy; rough with hair. [case of *He*.
Hĭs (124), *pron.* Possessive
Hĭs'pĭd, *a.* Set with bristles.
Hĭss (124), *v. i.* or *t.* To make, or to condemn by, a sibilant sound. — *n.* A sibilant noise; expression of contempt.
Hĭss'ing, *n.* Sibilant sound; expression of contempt.
Hĭst, *interj.* Hush; be silent.
Hĭs-tō'ri-an, *n.* A writer or compiler of history.
Hĭs-tŏr'ie, } *a.* Pertaining
Hĭs-tŏr'ie-al, } to history; containing history.
Hĭs-tŏr'ie-al-ly, *adv.* In the manner of history.
Hĭs-tō'ri-ŏg'ra-pher, *n.* A writer of history.
Hĭs-tō'ri-ŏg'ra-phy, *n.* The writing of history.
Hĭs'to-ry, *n.* A continuous narrative of events.
Hĭs'tri-ŏn'ie, *a.* Pertaining to the theater; theatrical.
Hĭt, *v. t.* [imp. & p. p. HIT.] To strike; to accord with. — *n.* A striking; a blow; a lucky chance.
Hĭtch, *v. t.* To catch or fasten.— *v. i.* To move by jerks; to fidget. — *n.* A knot; noose; impediment; jerk.
Hĭth'er, *adv.* To this place. — *a.* Nearest to the speaker.
Hĭth'er-mŏst, *a.* Nearest this way; hither.
Hĭth'er-tō', *adv.* To this time or place; as yet; until now.

Hĭth'er-ward, *adv.* This way; hither.
Hīve, *n.* A box for bees to live in.— *v.* To collect into a hive.
Hīves, *n. pl.* The croup.
Hō," } *interj.* Halloo; attend;
Hōa, } — a call to excite attention, or to give notice of approach. [white.
Hŏar, *a.* Gray with age;
Hōard, *v. t.* To collect; to amass. — *n.* A store laid up; a treasure.
Hōar'-frŏst, *n.* Dew frozen.
Hōar'i-ness (135), *n.* State of being hoary.
Hōarse, *a.* Having the voice rough or husky.
Hōarse'ly, *adv.* With a hoarse voice.
Hōarse'ness, *n.* State of being hoarse.
Hōar'y, *a.* Gray; whitish.
Hōax, *n.* Deception for sport. — *v. t.* To deceive for sport.
Hŏb, *n.* Flat part of a grate at the side.
Hŏb'ble, *v. i.* To walk lamely. — *n.* A halting walk.
Hŏb'by, *n.* A nag; a child's horse; a favorite object.
Hŏb'by-hŏrse, *n.* A hobby.
Hŏb'gŏb-lĭn, *n.* Apparition.
Hŏck, *n.* The joint between the knee and fetlock; a Rhenish wine. — *v. t.* To hamstring.
Hō'eus-pō'eus, *n.* A juggler, or juggler's trick. [mortar.
Hŏd, *n.* A bricklayer's tray for
Hŏdge'pŏdge, } *n.* [From Fr.
Hŏtch'pŏtch, } *hocher*, to shake, and *pot*, pot.] A mixed mass; a medley.
Hŏ'di-ĕr'nal, *a.* Of to-day.
Hŏd'man (143), *n.* A man who carries mortar to a mason.
Hōe (140), *n.* A farmer's tool. — *v. t.* (133, 137) To cut, dig, or weed, with a hoe.
Hŏg, *n.* A swine; a greedy fellow.
Hŏg'gish, *a.* Filthy; greedy.
Hŏgs'hĕad, *n.* A measure of 63 gallons; a butt. [romp.
Hoi'den, *n.* A bold girl; a
Hoist, *v. t.* To raise; to lift. — *n.* Act of raising up.
Hoi'ty-toi'ty, *interj.* noting surprise or disapprobation.
Hōld (18), *v. t.* [imp. & p. p. HELD.] To stop; to restrain; to grasp; to receive; to possess; to keep.— *v. i.* To endure; to refrain. — *n.* Catch; support; custody; interior of a ship.

sŭn, ôr, dọ, wọlf, tōō, tŏŏk; ûrn, rye, pyll; ç, ġ, *soft*; c, g, *hard*; a̱; eẋist; ṇ as ng; *this*.

HOLDER   160   **HOROLOGY**

Hōld'er, *n.* One who holds; something by which a thing may be held.

Hōld'fāst, *n.* An iron hook.

Hōle, *n.* A hollow place; a cavity or perforation; cell.

Hŏl'i-dāy, *n.* A festival day.

Hō'li-ness (135), *n.* Perfect rectitude: a title of the pope. — SYN. Purity; piety; sanctity; sacredness.

Hŏl'lōa, *interj.* used in answer to a call.

Hol-lō',

Hŏl'lo, or **Hol-lō'**, *v. i.* To

Hŏl'lā, call out.

Hŏl'land, *n.* A kind of linen.

Hŏl'landṣ, *n.* A kind of gin.

Hŏl'lōw, *n.* Empty; not solid; deceitful; low; deep. — *n.* A low place; a hole. — *v. t.* To make hollow.

Hŏl'lōw-ness, *n.* State of being hollow; insincerity.

Hŏl'ly, *n.* An evergreen tree.

Hŏl'ly-hŏck, *n.* A flowering plant.

Hŏlm (hōm, 18), *n.* The evergreen oak.

Hŏl'o-caust, *n.* A whole-burnt sacrifice.

Hŏl'o-grāph, *n.* A deed or will written wholly by the grantor's or testator's own hand.

Hŏl'ster (18). *n.* A horseman's case for pistols.

Hō'ly, *a.* Perfectly pure; consecrated; pious; godly: sacred. [tival.

Hō'ly-dāy, *n.* A religious festival.

Hŏm'age, *n.* Reverence; worship; respect.

Hōme (18), *n.* One's dwelling-house; one's country. — *a.* Domestic; close; severe; poignant. — *adv.* To the point.

Hōme'-bŏrn, *a.* Native; domestic.

Hōme'-brĕd,

Hōme'li-ness, *n.* Plainness.

Hōme'less, *a.* Having no home.

Hōme'ly (18), *a.* Plain; not handsome; coarse. [home.

Hōmec'-mādē, *a.* Made at

Hō'me-o-păth'ie, *a.* Pertaining to homeopathy.

Hō'me-ŏp'a-thy, *n.* A medical theory founded on the principle that a medicine which will cause will also cure a disease.

Hōme'sĭck, *a.* Sick from being away from home.

Hōme'spun, *a.* Made in the family; coarse; plain; rude.

Hōme'stĕad, *n.* Home or seat of a family. [home.

Hōme'ward, *adv.* Toward

Hŏm'i-çī'dal, *a.* Pertaining to homicide; murderous.

Hŏm'i-çīde, *n.* [Lat. *homicidium*, fr. *homo*, man, and *cædere*, to kill.] The killing of one human being by another. [of preaching.

Hŏm'i-lĕt'ies, *n. sing.* Science

Hŏm'i-ly, *n.* A familiar religious discourse.

Hŏm'i-ny, *n.* Food of maize broken coarse and boiled.

Ho-mo-gē'ne-oŭs, *a.* Being of the same kind throughout.

Hŏm'o-nȳm,

Hŏm'o-nȳme, ing the same sound as another, but different from it in meaning.

Ho-mŏn'y-moŭs, *a.* Equivocal; ambiguous.

Hōne, *n.* A whetstone for sharpening tools on. — *v. t.* To sharpen on a hone.

Hŏn'est (ŏn'est), *a.* Upright in dealing; just; sincere; true.

Hŏn'est-ly (ŏn'est-) *adv.* Uprightly; justly.

Hŏn'est-y (ŏn'est-), *n.* Justice; truth; probity.

Hŏn'ey (hŭn'ȳ, 39), *n.* Sweet juice collected by bees from flowers.

Hŏn'ey-cōmb (-kōm), *n.* Cells of wax for holding honey.

Hŏn'eyĕd (136), *a.* Covered with honey; sweet; flattering.

Hŏn'ey-dew, *n.* A sweet substance found on plants in small drops.

Hŏn'ey-mōōn, *n.* First month after marriage.

Hŏn'ey-sŭck'le, *n.* A sweet-scented flowering plant.

Hŏn'or (ŏn'ur, 155), *n.* Esteem paid to worth; reputation; bravery; dignity; a title. — *v. t.* To esteem; to exalt; to accept and pay.

Hŏn'or-a-ble (ŏn'ur-), *a.* Worthy of honor; actuated by noble motives; illustrious; conferring honor.

Hŏn'or-a-bly (ŏn'ur-), *adv.* With honor; nobly.

Hŏn'or-a-ry (ŏn'ur-), *a.* Conferring honor.

Hōōd, *n.* A covering for the head. — *v. t.* To furnish with a hood; to hide.

Hōōd'wĭnk, *v. t.* To blind; to cover. [beast's foot.

Hōōf, *n.* The horny part of a

Hōōf'bound, *a.* Having dry, contracted hoofs.

Hōōfed (hōōft), *a.* Furnished with hoofs.

Hōōk, *n.* A bent piece of iron.

— *v. t.* To catch or fasten with a hook.

Hōōked (hōōk'ed *or* hōōkt, 57), *n.* Having the form of a hook.

Hōōp, or **Hōōp**, *n.* A band of wood or iron for a cask. — *v. t.* To fasten with hoops.

Hōōp, *v. i.* To cry out; to whoop.

Hōōp'ing-cough (-kawf), *n.* A convulsive cough.

Hōōt, *n.* A shout of contempt. — *v. t.* (130) To shout at in contempt. — *v. i.* To cry, as an owl.

Hŏp (129), *v. i.* To jump on one leg; to skip lightly. — *n.* A leap on one leg; a dance; an aromatic plant.

Hōpe (18), *n.* Desire of good joined with expectation. — *v.* To desire with expectation.

Hōpe'ful (135), *a.* Full of hope; giving hope or promise.

Hōpe'ful-ly, *adv.* With hope.

Hōpe'less, *a.* Destitute of hope. — SYN. Despairing; desponding; forlorn. [hope.

Hōpe'less-ly, *adv.* Without

Hōpe'less-ness, *n.* Destitution of hope: despair.

Hŏp'per, *n.* One who hops; part of a mill.

Hŏp'ple, *v. t.* To tie the feet of loosely together.

Hō'ral, *a.* Relating to

Hō'ra-ry, an hour.

Hŏrde, *n.* A wandering tribe or troop.

Ho-rī'zon (115), *n.* The apparent junction of the earth and sky.

Hŏr'i-zŏn'tal, *a.* Parallel to the horizon; level.

Hŏr'i-zŏn'tal-ly, *adv.* In a horizontal direction.

Hŏrn, *n.* The hard pointed growth on an animal's head; a wind instrument.

Hŏrn'-bŏōk, *n.* A primer; formerly covered with horn to protect it. [horns.

Hŏrned, *a.* Furnished with

Hŏr'net, *n.* [Named from its large antennæ, or *horns*.] A large, strong kind of wasp.

Hŏrn'pīpe, *n.* A tune; a dance. [horn.

Hŏrn'y, *a.* Made of, or like,

Ho-rŏg'ra-phy, *n.* Art of constructing dials.

Hŏr'o-lōge, *n.* A time-piece of any kind.

Hŏr'o-lŏġ'i-e-al, *a.* Relating to horology. [uring time.

Ho-rŏl'o-gy, *n.* Art of meas-

Hŏr′o-seōpe, n. Aspect of planets at the hour of birth.
Hŏr′ri-ble, a. Exciting, or tending to excite, horror; frightful; awful.
Hŏr′ri-bly, adv. Frightfully.
Hŏr′rid, a. Dreadful; hideous; horrible.
Hŏr′rid-ly, adv. Shockingly.
Hor-rĭf′ic, a. Causing horror.
Hŏr′ror, n. A shuddering with fear; terror.
Hôrse. n. A well-known quadruped; cavalry; a wooden frame. [horse.
Hôrse′bȧck, n. Back of a
Hôrse′-chest′nut, n. A kind of shade-tree and its fruit.
Hôrse′-guärds, n. pl. Cavalry for guards. [horses.
Hôrse′-hâir, n. The hair of
Hôrse′-jŏck′ey, n. One who makes a practice of buying and selling horses.
Hôrse′-läugh (-läf), n. A loud, coarse laugh.
Hôrse′-lĭt′ter, n. A carriage borne on poles between horses. [rides on horseback.
Hôrse′man (113), n. One who
Hôrse′man-shĭp, n. Art of riding and training horses.
Hôrse′-plāy, n. Rough, rude play.
Hôrse′-pow′er, n. Power of a horse or its equivalent; 33,000 pounds raised one foot in a minute. [horses.
Hôrse′-race, n. A race by
Hôrse′-rād′ish, n. A vegetable having a very pungent root, used as a condiment.
Hôrse′-shoe (-shōō), n. An iron shoe for a horse.
Hôrse′-thĭēf (142), n. One who steals horses.
Hôrse′whip, n. A whip for driving horses. — v. t. To lash with a horsewhip. [sel.
Hor-tā′tion, n. Advice; counHôr′ta-tive,) a. Giving adHôr′ta-to-ry,) · monition.
Hôr′ti-cŭlt′ur-al, a. Pertaining to horticulture.
Hôr′ti-cŭlt′ūre (-kŭlt′yụr), n. Culture of a garden.
Hôr′ti-cŭlt′ur-ĭst, n. One skilled in gardening.
†Hôr′tus-Sĭc′cus, n. [Lat., a dry garden.] A collection of dried plants.
Ho-sȧn′nȧ, n. Praise to God.
Hōṣe, n. (pl. Hōṣe, 146.) Stockings; covering for the legs; a flexible pipe for conveying water.
Hō′ṣier (hō′zher), n. One who deals in stockings.

Hō′ṣier-y (hō′zher-y), n. Stockings, socks, &c.
Hŏs′pi-ta-ble, a. Kind to strangers or guests. — SYN. Generous; liberal.
Hŏs′pi-ta-bly, adv. In a hospitable manner.
Hŏs′pi-tal, n. A building for the sick or insane.
Hŏs′pi-tăl′i-ty, n. Gratuitous entertainment of strangers and guests.
Hōst, n. One who entertains a stranger; an army; sacrifice of the mass; the consecrated wafer.
Hōs′tage, n. A person given as a pledge for the performance of certain conditions.
Hōst′ess, n. A female host; a landlady.
Hŏs′tĭle (54), a. Unfriendly; opposite. [public foe.
Hos-tĭl′i-ty, n. Enmity of a
Hōst′ler (hŏs′ler or ōs′ler), n. One who has the care of horses. [eager; fiery.
Hŏt (129), a. Having heat;
Hŏt′-bĕd, n. A garden bed covered with glass. [ers.
Ho-tĕl′, n. An inn for travelHŏt′-hĕad′ed, a. Of ardent passions.
Hŏt′-house, n. A house kept warm to shelter plants. [ly.
Hŏt′ly, adv. Violently; keenHŏt′-prĕss, v. t. To press between hot plates, so as to make smooth and glossy.
Hŏt′spur, n. A rash person.
Hough (hŏk), n. The ham. — v. t. To hamstring.
Hound, n. A dog for hunting.
Hour (our), n. Twenty-fourth of a day; a particular time.
Hour′-gläss (our′-), n. A glass to show time by the escape of sand.
Hour′-hănd (our′-), n. The hand of a clock or watch which points to the hour.
Hourĭ′ (hour′ȳ), n. [Ar. hûr. black-eyed (ones).] A nymph of the Mohammedan paradise.
Hour′ly (our′-), a. Done, or happening, every hour; frequent. — adv. Every hour.
House, n. A place of abode; a family; branch of the legislature; a quorum.
House (houz, 88), v. t. To put under shelter; to harbor.
House′-breāk′er, n. One who breaks into a house.
House′-breāk′ing, n. Act of breaking into a house to steal.

House′hōld, n. A family living together. — a. Domestic.
House′hōld-er, n. One who keeps house.
House′keep-er, n. One who occupies a house.
House′keep-ĭng, n. Care of domestic concerns. [plant.
House′leek, n. A succulent
House′less, a. Destitute of a house. [servant.
House′māid, n. A female
House′wīfe (or hŭz′wĭf), n. Mistress of a family; female economist.
House′wīfe-ry (hŭz′wĭf-ry), n. Female management of domestic concerns.
Hous′ĭng. n. A shelter; a saddle-cloth.
Hŏve, imp. of Heave.
Hŏv′el, n. A shed; a cottage.
Hŏv′er, v. i. To flap the wings; to move to and fro near.
How, adv. In what manner; to what extent; for what reason.
How-bē′it, adv. Nevertheless.
How-ĕv′er, adv. Nevertheless; still; though; yet.
How′itz-er (-its-), n. A kind of mortar or cannon for throwing shells.
Howl, v. i. To cry as a dog or wolf. — n. The cry of a dog or wolf.
Howl′et, n. An owl; an owlet.
How′so-ĕv′er, adv. However.
Hoy (140), n. A small coasting vessel.
Hŭb, n. The nave of a wheel.
Hŭb′bub, n. Uproar; tumult.
Hŭck′ster, n. A retailer of small articles.
Hŭd′dle, v. i. or t. To crowd together. — n. A crowd without order; confusion.
Hūe, n. Color; dye; a clamor.
Hŭff (123), n. A swell of anger. — v. t. To bluster. [gant.
Hŭff′ish, a. Insolent; arroHŭff′y, a. Swelled; arrogant.
Hŭg, v. t. To embrace closely; to sail near. — n. A close embrace.
Hūge, n. Bulky; vast.
Hūge′ly, adv. Immensely.
Hū′gue-not (-ẓe-), n. A French Protestant of the 16th cent.
Hŭlk, n. Body of an old ship.
Hŭll (123), n. The outer covering of a nut, or of grain; frame of a ship. — v. t. To strip off the hulls of; to husk; to pierce the hull of.
Hŭm, v. To sing low; to buzz. — n. A low, buzzing sound; deception.

sŭn, ôr, dọ, wǫlf, tōō, tǒǒk; ûrn, rụe, pụll; ç, ġ, soft; c, ḡ, hard; aẕ; eẋist; ŋ as ng; this.

Hū'man, a. Belonging to mankind; not divine.
Hu-māne', a. Benevolent; kind; compassionate. [ness.
Hu-māne'ly, adv. With kindness.
Hū'man-ist, n. One versed in the knowledge of human nature.
Hu-măn'i-ty, n. The nature of man; mankind; kind disposition; (pl.) grammar, rhetoric, poetry, and the ancient languages.
Hū'man-īze, v. t. To render humane. [man race.
Hū'man-kīnd, n. The human-ly, adv. After the manner of men.
Hŭm'ble, a. Low in feelings or condition. — SYN. Lowly; modest; unassuming; meek. — v. t. To make humble; to bring low; to abase.
Hŭm'bly, adv. In a humble manner; without pride.
Hŭm'bug, n. An imposition; a hoax. — v. t. (130) To impose upon; to hoax.
Hŭm'drum, n. A stupid fellow. — a. Dull; stupid.
Hŭ'mer-al, a. Pertaining to the shoulder.
Hū'mĭd. a. Moist; damp.
Hu-mĭd'ĭ-ty, } n. Moisture;
Hū'mĭd-ness, } dampness.
Hu-mĭl'ĭ-āte, v. t. To humble; to mortify; to abase.
Hu-mĭl'ĭ-ā'tion, n. Act of humbling; state of being humbled. [mind.
Hu-mĭl'ĭ-ty, n. Lowliness of
Hŭm'ming-bĭrd, n. A very small bird noted for the swift motion and noise of its wings.
Hū'mor (or yū'mur, 155), n. Moisture; any animal fluid; temper; disposition; a delicate kind of wit; pleasantry. — v. t. To gratify; to indulge by compliance.
Hū'mor-al (or yū'mur-), a. Pertaining to the humors.
Hū'mor-ĭst (or yū'mur-), n. A wag; a droll.
Hū'mor-oŭs (or yū'mur-), a. Exhibiting humor; jocular; waggish; pleasant; playful.
Hū'mor-oŭs-ly (or yū'mur-), adv. With pleasantry.
Hū'mor-sŏme (or yū'mur-), a. Influenced by humor; droll.
Hŭmp, n. A swelling, as of flesh; protuberance.
Hŭmp'băck, n. A person with a crooked back.
Hŭnch, n. A protuberance. — v. t. To push with the elbow; to crook the back.

Hŭn'dred, a. Ten times ten. — n. The sum of ten times ten; territorial division.
Hŭn'dredth, a. Ordinal of a hundred.
Hŭng, imp. & p. p. of Hang.
Hŭn'ger (79), n. Craving appetite. — v. i. To crave food.
Hŭn'gered, a. Hungry.
Hŭn'gri-ly, adv. In a hungry manner.
Hŭn'gry, a. Feeling distress from want of food.
Hŭnks, n. A miser.
Hŭnt, v. t. To chase, as game; to seek for. — v. i. To go in pursuit of game. — n. Chase of game; pursuit; pack of hounds.
Hŭnt'er, n. One who hunts.
Hŭnt'ress, n. A female hunter.
Hŭnts'man (143), n. A man who hunts.
Hŭr'dle, n. A texture of twigs; a crate; a sledge.
Hŭrl, v. t. To throw with violence. — n. Act of throwing with violence. [bustle.
Hŭr'ly-bŭr'ly, n. Tumult;
Hur-rā', } interj. of joy or
Hur-rāh', } triumph.
Hŭr'ri-cāne, n. A violent storm or tempest.
Hŭr'ry, v. t. To hasten. — v. i. To move hastily. — n. Great haste.
Hŭrt, n. Whatever injures or harms. — SYN. Injury; harm; damage. — v. t. [imp. & p. p. HURT.] To wound or bruise; to injure; to harm.
Hŭrt'fŭl, a. Injurious.
Hŭrt'fŭl-ly, adv. Injuriously.
Hŭş'band, n. A man married to a woman. — v. t. To manage frugally. [farmer.
Hŭş'band-man (143), n. A
Hŭş'band-ry, n. Tillage; domestic economy.
Hŭsh, a. Still; silent; calm. — v. t. To silence; to quiet.
Hŭsh'-mŏn'ey (-mŭn'y̌), n. A bribe to secrecy.
Hŭsk, n. Covering of certain fruits. — v. t. To strip the husks from. [harshness.
Hŭsk'i-ness, n. Dryness;
Hŭsk'y, a. Abounding with husks; hoarse; rough in tone; harsh.
Huş'şär' (hŏŏz-zär'), n. A mounted soldier.
Hŭş'şy, n. [Contracted from huswife, housewife.] A worthless woman.
Hŭs'tings, n. pl. A place where the election of a member of parliament is held.

Hŭs'tle (hŭs'sl), v. t. To shake together in confusion.
Huş'wife (hŭz'zĭf or hŭz'wĭf), n. A female housekeeper.
Hŭş'wīfe-ry (hŭz'zĭf-, or hŭz'wĭf-), n. Female management of domestic concerns.
Hŭt, n. A poor cottage or mean abode. — v. t. To furnish with huts.
Hŭtch. n. A chest or box.
Huz-zä', interj. expressing joy or exultation. — n. A shout of joy. — v. i. (137) To shout in joy. [plant.
Hy'a-çinth, n. A flowering
Hy'brĭd or Hyb'rĭd, n. A mongrel.
Hy'brĭd, or Hyb'rĭd, } a. Pro-
Hyb'rĭd-oŭs, } duced by the mixture of two species; mongrel.
Hy'drà (140), n. A fabulous monster with many heads.
Hy'drant, n. A pipe to discharge water from an aqueduct. [hydraulics.
Hy-drăul'ĭc, a. Relating to
Hy-drăul'ĭcs, n. sing. The science which treats of fluids in motion.
†Hy'dro-çĕph'a-lŭs, n. Dropsy of the brain.
Hy'dro-gen, n. An inflammable gas which is one of the elements of water.
Hy-drŏg'ra-pher, n. One versed in hydrography.
Hy'dro-grăph'ĭc, a. Relating to hydrography.
Hy-drŏg'ra-phy, n. Description and representation by charts, of seas, lakes, rivers, &c. [water.
Hy-drŏl'o-gy, n. Science of
Hy-drŏm'e-ter, n. An instrument to determine the specific gravities, and thence the strength of liquids.
Hy-drŏm'e-try, n. Art of measuring the density of fluids. [to hydropathy.
Hy'dro-păth'ĭc, n. Relating
Hy-drŏp'a-thĭst, n. One who practices, or who believes in, hydropathy.
Hy'dro-pa-thy, n. The water-cure; use of water to cure diseases.
Hy'dro-phō'bĭ-à, n. Dread of water; canine madness.
Hy-drŏp'ĭc-al, a. Dropsical.
Hy'dro-stăt'ĭc, } a. Re-
Hy'dro-stăt'ĭc-al, } lating to hydrostatics.
Hy'dro-stăt'ĭcs, n. sing. The science which treats of the properties of fluids at rest.

ā, ă, ī, ō, ū, y̆, long; ă, ĕ, ĭ, ŏ, ŭ, y̆, short; cāre, eär, ăsk, ąll, whąt; ûre, vêil, tērm; pïque, firm;

HYEMAL . 163 IDES

Hy-ē'mal, *a.* Pertaining to winter; wintry.
Hy-ē'na, *n.* (Gr. *huaina*, orig. a sow.) A carnivorous animal of Asia and Africa. Hyena.
Hy'gi-ēne, *n.* Science of the preservation of health.
Hy-gröm'e-ter, *n.* An instrument for measuring the moisture of the atmosphere.
Hy'men, *n.* The god of marriage.
Hy'men-ē'al, } *a.* Pertaining
Hy'men-ē'an, } to marriage.
— *n.* A marriage song; an epithalamium.
Hymn (him), *n.* A song of praise. — *v. t.* (78) To praise in songs.
Hyp, *n.* Melancholy.
Hy-pēr'bo-lā, *n.* A curve formed by a certain section of a cone.
Hy-pēr'bo-le, *n.* Exaggeration. Hyperbola.

Hy'per-bōl'ic-al, *a.* Exaggerating or extenuating.
Hy'per-bō're-an, *a.* Northern.
Hy'per-crit'ic, *n.* A critic exact beyond reason.
Hy'per-crit'ic-al, *a.* Critical beyond use or reason.
Hy'per-crit'i-cism, *n.* Excessive rigor of criticism.
Hy'phen (55), *n.* (Gr. *huphen*, for *huph' hen*, into one.) The mark (-) used to join syllables or the parts of some compound words.
Hyp'o-chŏn'dri-â, *n.* Gloomy depression of spirits.
Hyp'o-chŏn'dri-ăc, *n.* One affected with low spirits.
Hyp'o-chon-dri'ac-al, *a.* Melancholy; dejected.
Hy-pŏc'ri-sy, *n.* Dissimulation; insincerity.
Hyp'o-crite, *n.* A dissembler; a false pretender to virtue or piety.
Hyp'o-crit'ic-al, *a.* Insincere.
Hyp'o-crit'ic-al-ly, *adv.* Insincerely.
Hy'po-stăt'ic } (*or* hĭp'o-),
Hy'po-stăt'ic-al } *a.* Constitutive; elementary; distinctly personal.

Hy-pŏt'e-nūse, or
Hy-pŏt'e-nūse, *n.* Longest side of a right-angled triangle.
Hy-pŏth'e-cāte, or
Hy-pŏth'e-cāte, *a b. Hy-v. t.* To pledge for potenuse. the security of a creditor.
Hy'poth-e-cā'tion, or Hy-pŏth'e-cā'tion, *n.* Act of pledging as security.
Hy-pŏth'e-sis, or Hy-pŏth'-e-sīs (*pl.* Hy-pŏth'e-sēş, hĭ- *or* hī-), *n.* Supposition; proposition assumed.
Hy'po-thĕt'ic-al (*or* hĭp'o-), *a.* Supposed.
Hy'po-thĕt'ic-al-ly (*or* hĭp'-o-), *adv.* Upon supposition.
Hy'son (hī'sn), *n.* [Chinese *hi-tshun*, lit. first crop.] A fragrant species of green tea.
Hys'sop (his'sup *or* hī'zup), *n.* An aromatic plant.
Hys-tĕr'ic, } *a.* Pertaining
Hys-tĕr'ic-al, } to hysteria; convulsive; fitful.
Hys-tĕr'ics, } *n.* A nervous
Hys-tē'ri-â, } affection characterized by alternate laughing and crying.

I.

I *pron.* of the first person, used by a speaker of himself; one's self.
I-ăm'bic, *a.* Relating to, or consisting of, iambuses. — *n.* An iambus.
I-ăm'bus, *n.* A poetic foot consisting of a long and a short, or an accented and an unaccented, syllable.
I'bex (140), *n.* A kind of goat Ibex. found in the mountainous parts of Europe.
I'bis, *n.* A wading bird formerly reverenced in Egypt.
Īçe, *n.* [A.-S. *is,* fr. Goth. *eisan,* to shine.] Water congealed to Ibis.

hardness; concreted sugar. — *v. t.* To cover with ice or concreted sugar.
Içe'bērg, *n.* A mountain of floating ice.
Içe'-crēam, *n.* Cream flavored and frozen.
Içe'-house, *n.* A place for keeping ice.
Ich-neū'-mon, *n.* A small animal in Egypt which destroys eggs. Ichneumon.
Ich-nŏg'ra-phy, *n.* Horizontal section of an object.
I'chŏr (ĭ'kôr), *n.* A thin watery humor. [thin.
I'chor-oŭs, *a.* Like ichor;
Ich'thy-ŏl'o-gĭst, *n.* One versed in ichthyology.
Ich'thy-ŏl'o-gy, *n.* Part of zoölogy which treats of fishes.
I'çi-ele (ĭ'si-kl), *n.* A pendent mass of ice. [being icy.
I'çi-ne-ss (135), *n.* State of
I-cŏn'o-clăst, *n.* A breaker or destroyer of images.

I'con-ŏg'ra-phy, *n.* Description of ancient statues.
Ic-tĕr'ic, } *a.* Affected with
Ic-tĕr'ic-al, } jaundice.
I'çy, *a.* Abounding with, or resembling, ice.
I-dē'â (45, 140), *n.* A mental image; conception; notion; thought.
I-dē'al, *a.* Existing in idea or in fancy. — SYN. Visionary; fanciful; imaginary; unreal. — *n.* The conception of a thing in its most perfect state.
I-dē'al-ĭşm, *n.* The doctrine of ideal existence.
I'de-ăl'i-ty, *n.* A lively imagination united to a love of the beautiful. [tion.
I-dē'al-ly, *adv.* In imagina-
I-dĕn'tic-al, *a.* Precisely the same. [identical manner.
I-dĕn'tic-al-ly, *adv.* In an
I-dĕn'ti-fi-cā'tion, *n.* Act of proving to be the same.
I-dĕn'ti-fy, *v. t.* To prove to be the same.
I-dĕn'ti-ty, *n.* Sameness.
Ides, *n.* The 15th day of

---

sŏn, ôr, dọ, wọlf, tŏŏ, tŏŏk; ûrn, rụle, pụll; ç, ġ, *soft;* c, g, *hard;* aẓ; eẋist; ṇ *as* ng; this.

Id'i-o-cy, *n.* Deficiency of understanding; imbecility.
Id'i-om, *n.* An expression peculiar to a language.
Id'i-om-at'ic, *a.* Peculiar to a language.
Id'i-o-syn'cra-sy, *n.* A peculiarity of bodily or mental constitution.
Id'i-ot, *n.* A natural fool.
Id'i-ot'ic, *a.* Like an idiot.
Id'i-ot-ism, *n.* An idiom; idiocy.
I'dle, *a.* Not occupied; trifling. — *v. t.* To spend idly.
I'dle-ness, *n.* Inaction.
I'dler, *n.* One who idles.
I'dly, *adv.* Sluggishly; vainly; lazily; carelessly.
I'dol, *n.* An image worshiped.
I-dŏl'a-ter, *n.* A worshiper of idols; a pagan.
I-dŏl'a-tress, *n.* A female idolater. [idols.
I-dŏl'a-trize, *v. i.* To worship
I-dŏl'a-troŭs, *a.* Given to, or consisting in, idolatry.
I-dŏl'a-try, *n.* Worship of idols; excessive attachment.
I'dol-īze, *v. t.* To love to excess or adoration.
I'dyl, or **Id'yl**, *n.* A short pastoral poem.
If (123), *v. t.* (but commonly classed among *conjunctions*.) Grant; allow; suppose: admit. [fire.
Ig'ne-oŭs, *a.* Consisting of
†Ig'nis-Făt'u-us, *n.* A kind of meteor seen after dark in marshy places.
Ig-nīte', *v. t.* or *i.* To kindle.
Ig-nīt'i-ble, *a.* Capable of being ignited.
Ig-nī'tion (-nish'un), *n.* Act of kindling or taking fire.
Ig-nō'ble, *a.* Of low birth; not honorable; base: mean.
Ig-nō'bly, *adv.* Meanly; basely; dishonorably.
Ig'no-min'i-oŭs, *a.* Very shameful; dishonorable.
Ig'no-min-y, *n.* Public disgrace; infamy.
Ig'no-rā'mus, *n.* An ignorant person; a blockhead.
Ig'no-rance, *n.* Want of knowledge; illiteracy.
Ig'no-rant, *a.* Wanting knowledge; illiterate.
Ig'no-rant-ly, *adv.* Without knowledge.
Ig-nōre', *v. t.* To declare ignorance of; to refuse to take notice of.

Il'i-ăc', *a.* Pertaining to the lower bowels.
Ill (123), *a.* [Contracted from *evil*.] Bad; sick; indisposed. — *n.* Evil; harm; wickedness; misfortune. — *adv.* Not well; amiss.
Il-lăpse', *n.* Sudden entrance.
Il-lā'tion, *n.* An inference.
Il'la-tive, *a.* Capable of being inferred. [impolite.
Ill'-brĕd, *a.* Not well-bred;
Il-lē'gal, *a.* Contrary to law; unlawful. [ness.
Il'le-găl'i-ty, *n.* Unlawfulness.
Il-lē'gal-ly, *adv.* Unlawfully.
Il-lĕg'i-ble, *a.* Incapable of being read. (be read.
Il-lĕg'i-bly, *adv.* So as not to
Il'le-git'i-ma-cy, *n.* Bastardy; want of genuineness.
Il'le-git'i-mate, *a.* Born out of wedlock; not genuine.
Ill-fā'vored, *a.* Ill-looking; ugly; homely.
Il-lib'er-al, *a.* Not generous; mean; not candid.
Il-lib'er-al-ly, *adv.* Meanly; uncandidly.
Il-lib'er-ăl'i-ty, *n.* Narrowness of mind; parsimony.
Il-lic'it, *a.* Unlawful.
Il-lim'it-a-ble, *a.* Incapable of being bounded or limited.
Il-lit'er-a-cy, *n.* Want of learning; ignorance.
Il-lit'er-ate, *a.* Unlearned.
Ill'-nāt'ure, *n.* Habitual badness of temper. [ish.
Ill'-nāt'ured, *a.* Cross; peevish.
Ill'ness, *n.* Indisposition; sickness; wickedness; evil.
Il-lŏg'ic-al, *a.* Not according to, or violating the rules of, logic.
Ill-stärred', *a.* Fated to be unfortunate. [ceive.
Il-lūde', *v. t.* To mock or deceive.
Il-lūme', *v. t.* To enlighten; to adorn.
Il-lū'mi-nāte, *v. t.* To enlighten; to illustrate.
Il-lū'mi-nā'tion, *n.* Act of enlightening; display of light on festive occasions.
Il-lū'sion (119), *n.* An unreal image; false show; error.
Il-lū'sive, (*a.* Deceiving by
Il-lū'so-ry,) false show.
Il-lŭs'trate, *v. t.* To explain; to make clear; to elucidate.
Il'lus-trā'tion, *n.* Explanation; elucidation. [explain.
Il-lŭs'tra-tive, *a.* Tending to
Il-lŭs'tri-oŭs, *a.* Distinguished for greatness or splendor. — SYN. Eminent; conspicuous; celebrated.

Ill'-wĭll', *n.* Unkind or hostile feeling; enmity; malevolence.
Im'age, *n.* A likeness; statue; idol; idea. — *v. t.* To form a likeness in idea.
Im-ăg'i-na-ble, *a.* Possible to be conceived.
Im'age-ry, *n.* Sensible representation or lively description; figures of speech.
Im-ăg'i-na-ry, *a.* Fancied; existing only in imagination.
Im-ăg'i-nā'tion, *n.* Faculty of forming mental images; conception; idea.
Im-ăg'i-nā'tive, *a.* Gifted with, or pertaining to, imagination; fantastic.
Im-ăg'ine, *v. t.* or *i.* To think; to conceive.
Im-bănk', *v. t.* To inclose or defend with a bank.
Im-bănk'ment, *n.* Act of imbanking. [or body.
Im'be-cīle, *a.* Weak in mind
Im'be-çĭl'i-ty, *n.* Impotency; feebleness of mind or body.
Im-bĕd', *v. t.* To sink or cover, as in a bed. [absorb.
Im-bībe', *v. t.* To drink in; to
Im'bi-bī'tion (-bish'un), *n.* Act of imbibing. [bitter.
Im-bit'ter, *v. t.* To make
Im-bŏs'om, *v. t.* To embrace or hold in the bosom.
Im'bri-cāte,) *a.* Laid one
Im'bri-cā'ted,) over another, as tiles.
Im'bri-cā'tion, *n.* An overlapping like that of tiles.
Im-brown', *v. t.* To make brown. [wet
Im-brue', *v. t.* To steep; to
Im-brūte', *v. t.* or *i.* To degrade or sink to brutality.
Im-būe', *v. t.* To tincture deeply; to cause to imbibe.
Im'i-ta-ble, *a.* Capable or worthy of being imitated.
Im'i-tāte, *v. t.* To follow as a pattern or model; to copy.
Im'i-tā'tion, *n.* Act of imitating; a copy; likeness.
Im'i-tā'tive, *a.* Tending to, or aiming at, likeness.
Im'i-tā'tor, *n.* One who imitates.
Im-măc'u-lāte, *a.* Without blemish; morally spotless.
Im'ma-nent, *a.* Inherent; having permanent existence.
Im'ma-tē'ri-al, *a.* Not consisting of matter; unimportant.
Im'ma-tē'ri-al-ism, *n.* Doctrine of spiritual existence apart from matter.
Im'ma-tē'ri-al-ist, *n.* One who professes immateriality.

IMMATERIALITY 165 IMPERSONAL

Im'ma-tē'ri-ăl'i-ty, *n.* Quality of being distinct from matter.

Im'ma-tūre', *a.* Unripe; unseasonable.

Im'ma-tūre'ly, *adv.* Unseasonably.

Im'ma-tū'ri-ty, *n.* Unripeness; incompleteness.

Im-mĕas'ur-a-ble (-mĕzh'ur-), *a.* Incapable of being measured.

Im-mĕas'ur-a-bly (-mĕzh'ur-), *adv.* Beyond all measure. [a medium; instant.

Im-mē'di-ate, *a.* Without

Im-mē'di-ate-ly, *adv.* Without delay. [be cured.

Im-mĕd'i-ca-ble, *a.* Not to

Im'me-mō'ri-al, *a.* Of an origin which is beyond memory.

Im-mĕnse', *a.* [Lat *immensus*, lit. not measured.] Vast in extent; without known limit. — SYN. Infinite; illimitable; monstrous.

Im-mĕnse'ly, *adv.* Vastly.

Im-mĕn'si-ty, *n.* Unlimited extension; vastness.

Im-mĕrge', *v. t.* To immerse.

Im-mĕrse', *v. t.* To put into a fluid; to engage deeply.

Im-mĕr'sion, *n.* The act of immersing, or state of being immersed.

Im'me-thŏd'ic-al, *a.* Having no method.

Im'mi-grant, *n.* One who immigrates.

Im'mi-grāte, *v. i.* To remove into a country for residence.

Im'mi-grā'tion, *n.* Removal into a country for residence.

Im'mi-nent, *a.* Impending.

Im-mis'ci-ble, *a.* Not capable of being mixed.

Im-mis'sion (-mĭsh'un), *n.* Act of sending in.

Im-mix', *v. t.* To mingle.

Im'mo-bĭl'i-ty, *n.* Resistance to motion; unmoveableness.

Im-mŏd'er-ate, *a.* Excessive.

Im-mŏd'er-ate-ly, *adv.* In an excessive degree.

Im-mŏd'est, *a.* Unchaste; impudent.

Im-mŏd'est-ly, *adv.* Without reserve. [modesty.

Im-mŏd'est-y, *n.* Want of

Im'mo-lāte, *v. t.* To sacrifice.

Im'mo-lā'tion, *n.* Act of sacrificing; a sacrifice.

Im mōr'al, *a.* Evil; wicked.

Im'mo-răl'i-ty, *n.* Any act contrary to the divine law.

Im-mōr'al-ly, *adv.* Viciously.

Im-mōr'tal, *a.* Never dying.

Im'mor-tăl'i-ty, *n.* Immortal existence.

Im-mōr'tal-īze, *v. t.* To make immortal.

Im-mŏv'a-bĭl'i-ty, *n.* Quality of being immovable.

Im-mŏv'a-ble (-mŏŏv'a-bl), *a.* Incapable of being moved.

Im-mŏv'a-bly, *adv.* With firmness. [privilege.

Im-mū'ni-ty, *n.* Peculiar

Im-mūre', *v. t.* To inclose within walls; to imprison.

Im-mū'ta-bĭl'i-ty, *n.* Unchangeableness.

Im-mū'ta-ble, *a.* Incapable of being changed; invariable. [changeably.

Im-mū'ta-bly, *adv.* Un-

Imp. *n.* A young or inferior devil.

Im-păct', *v. t.* To drive close.

Im'păct, *n.* Collision; force communicated.

Im-pâir', *v. t.* To make worse; to injure; to weaken.

Im-pāle', *v. t.* To fix on a stake. [paling.

Im-pāle'ment, *n.* Act of impaling.

Im-păl'pa-bĭl'i-ty, *n.* Quality of being impalpable.

Im-păl'pa-ble, *a.* Incapable of being felt.

Im-păn'el, *v. t.* To form or enroll, as a jury.

Im-pär'i-ty, *n.* Inequality.

Im-pärt', *v. t.* To grant; to bestow on; to make known.

Im-pär'tial, *a.* Free from bias. — SYN. Unprejudiced; just; equitable.

Im-pär'ti-ăl'i-ty (-shi-ăl'- or -shăl'-), *n.* Freedom from bias; justice. [bly.

Im-pär'tial-ly, *adv.* Equitably.

Im-pärt'i-ble, *n.* Capable of being imparted. [passed.

Im-păss'a-ble, *a.* Not to be

Im-păs'si-bĭl'i-ty, *n.* Exemption from suffering or pain. [of passion or pain.

Im-păs'si-ble, *a.* Incapable

Im-păs'sion (-păsh'un), *v. t.* To affect strongly with passion. [powerfully.

Im-păs'sion-āte, *v. t.* To affect

Im-păs'rioned (-păsh'und), *a.* Actuated by passion; animated.

Im-păss'ive, *a.* Exempt from suffering or pain.

Im-păs'sive-ly, *adv.* Without sensibility to pain.

Im-pā'tience, *n.* Uneasiness under suffering; want; delay, &c.; restlessness.

Im-pā'tient (-pā'shent), *a.* Uneasy; not quiet; hasty.

Im-pā'tient-ly, *adv.* With uneasiness.

Im-pēach', *v. t.* To accuse by a public body; to bring into question; to censure.

Im-pēach'a-ble, *a.* Liable to impeachment.

Im-pēach'ment, *n.* Accusation by authority: blame.

Im-pĕc'ca-bĭl'i-ty, *n.* The quality of not being liable to sin. [to sin.

Im-pĕc'ca-ble, *a.* Not liable

Im-pēde', *v. t.* To hinder; to obstruct; to retard. [tion.

Im-pĕd'i-ment, *n.* Obstruc-

Im-pĕl' (129), *v. t.* To urge forward.

Im-pĕl'lent, *n.* A power that drives. — *a.* Urging forward.

Im-pĕnd', *v. i.* To hang over; to menace; to be near.

Im-pĕnd'ençe, } *n.* A hang-

Im-pĕnd'en-cy, } ing over.

Im-pĕnd'ing, *a.* Hanging over; imminent; menacing.

Im-pĕn'e-tra-bĭl'i-ty, *n.* Quality of not being penetrable.

Im-pĕn'e-tra-ble, *a.* Incapable of being penetrated

Im-pĕn'i-tĕnçe, *n.* Obduracy; hardness of heart.

Im-pĕn'i-tent, *a.* Not repenting of sin. [out repentance.

Im-pĕn'i-tent-ly, *adv.* With-

Im-pĕr'a-tive, *a.* Expressive of command. [command.

Im-pĕr'a-tive-ly, *adv.* With

Im-per-çĕpt'i-ble, *a.* Not to be perceived.

Im-per-çĕpt'i-bly, *adv.* So as not to be perceived.

Im-pĕr'fect, *a.* Not perfect; having some defect; defective.

Im'per-fĕc'tion, *n.* Defect; want: blemish; fault.

Im-pĕr'fect-ly, *adv.* Not fully. [perforated.

Im-pĕr'fo-ra-ble, *a.* Not to be

Im-pē'ri-al, *a.* Belonging to an empire or an emperor. — *n.* A tuft of hair on the lower lip.

Im-pē'ri-al-ĭst, *n.* A subject or soldier of an emperor.

Im-pĕr'il, *v. t.* To endanger.

Im-pē'ri-oŭs, *a.* Commanding: haughty; arrogant.

Im-pē'ri-oŭs-ly, *adv.* Insolently.

Im-pē'ri-oŭs-ness, *n.* Quality of being imperious.

Im-pĕr'ish-a-ble, *a.* Not liable to perish.

Im-pĕr'me-a-bĭl'i-ty, *n.* Quality of not being permeable.

Im-pĕr'me-a-ble, *a.* Incapable of being passed through.

Im-pĕr'son-al, *a.* Not varied according to the persons.

---

sŏn, ôr, dọ, wolf, tōō, tŏŏk; ûrn, rye, pụll; ç, ġ, *soft*; ꞓ, g̣, *hard*; a̧ṣ; exist; ụ *as* ng; this.

Im-pĕr'son-ăl'i-ty, n. Want of distinct personality.
Im-pĕr'son-āte, v. t. To personify.
Im-pĕr'son-ā'tion, n. Act of impersonating.
Im-pĕr'ti-nençe, n. Irrelevance; rudeness; incivility.
Im-pĕr'ti-nent, a. Irrelevant; rude; uncivil.
Im-pĕr'ti-nent-ly, adv. Officiously; rudely.
Im'per-tûr'ba-ble, a. Not to be disturbed. [penetrated.
Im-pĕr'vi-oŭs, a. Not to be
Im-pĕt'u-ŏs'i-ty, n. Violence; vehemence.
Im-pĕt'u-oŭs, a. Vehement; passionate; furious. [ously.
Im-pĕt'u-oŭs-ly, adv. Furi-
Im'pe-tus, n. Force of motion; momentum.
Im-pī'e-ty, n. Ungodliness; irreverence. [against.
Im-pinġe', v. t. To dash
Im'pi-oŭs, a. Irreverent toward God; profane.
Im'pi-oŭs-ly, adv. With irreverence: profanely.
Im-plā'ea-bĭl'i-ty, n. Quality or state of being implacable.
Im-plā'ea-ble, a. Not to be appeased. — Syn. Inexorable; unrelenting; irreconcilable; stubborn.
Im-plā'ea-bly, adv. With unappeasable enmity. [iufix.
Im-plănt', v. t. To insert; to
Im'plan-tā'tion, n. Act of implanting. [law.
Im-plēad', v. t. To sue at
Im'ple-ment, n. [Lat. implementum, from implere, to fill up.] A tool or instrument; utensil.
Im'plex, a. Infolded; intricate; complicated.
Im'pli-cāte, v. t. To involve.
Im'pli-cā'tion, n. Act of involving; eutanglement; inference not expressed.
Im-plĭç'it, a. Tacitly implied.
Im-plĭç'it-ly, adv. By inference; unreservedly.
Im-plōre', v. t. To call upon in supplication; to beseech.
Im-plȳ', v. t. To contain by inference; to include virtually; to signify; to mean.
Im-poi'ṣon (-poi'zn), v. t. To poison; to imbitter.
Im-pŏl'i-çy, n. Inexpedience.
Im'po-līte', a. Not having politeness; uncivil; rude.
Im'po-līte'ly, adv. Uncivilly.
Im'po-līte'ness, n. Want of good manners; incivility.

Im-pŏl'i-tic, a. Inexpedient.
Im-pŏn'der-a-ble,) a. Having no sen-ible weight.
Im-pŏn'der-oŭs, } [pores.
Im'po-rŏs'i-ty, n. Want of
Im-pō'roŭs, a. Having no pores; compact.
Im-pŏrt', v. t. To bring in from abroad or from another country; to signify; to mean.
Im'pŏrt, n. Thing imported; signification; moment.
Im-pŏrt'a-ble, a. Capable of being imported.
Im-pŏr'tançe, n. Weight; consequence.
Im-pŏr'tant, a. Weighty; momentous.
Im'pŏr-tā'tion, n. Act of importing; commodities imported.
Im-pŏrt'er, n. One who brings goods from abroad.
Im-pŏrt'u-nate, a. Pressing; urgent.
Im-pŏrt'u-nate-ly, adv. With urgent solicitation.
Im'por-tūne', v. t. To urge.
Im'por-tū'ni-ty, n. Urgency.
Im-pōṣ'a-ble (133), a. Capable of being imposed.
Im-pōṣe', v. t. To put or lay on. — v. i. To deceive.
Im-pōṣ'ing, p. a. Impressive; commanding.
Im'po-ṣĭ'tion (-zĭsh'un), n. Act of laying on; deception.
Im-pŏs'si-bĭl'i-ty, n. That which can not be.
Im-pŏs'si-ble, a. Not to be or to be done.
Im'pŏst, n. Duty on goods; part of a pillar on which the weight of an arch or building rests.
Im-pŏst'hu-māte, v. i. To gather into an abscess.
Im-pŏst'hūme, n. An abscess.
Im-pŏs'tor, n. A deceiver.
Im-pŏst'ūre, n. Deception.
Im'po-tençe,) n. Weak-
Im'po-ten-çy, } ness; imbecility.
Im'po-tent, a. Weak; wanting competent power.
Im'po-tent-ly, adv. Weakly.
Im-pound', v. t. To confine in a pound.
Im-pŏv'er-ĭsh, v. t. To reduce to poverty; to make poor; to exhaust the fertility of.
Im-pŏv'er-ĭsh-ment, n. Reduction to poverty; exhaustion of wealth or strength.
Im-prăc'ti-ea-bĭl'i-ty, n. State or quality of being not practicable.
Im-prăc'ti-ea-ble, a. Inca-

pable of being done; impossible.
Im'pre-eāte, v. t. To invoke, as evil, on any one.
Im'pre-eā'tion, n. Invocation of evil. — Syn. Curse; execration; anathema.
Im'pre-ea-to-ry, a. Of the nature of an imprecation.
Im-prĕġ'na-ble, a. Not to be taken; invincible.
Im-prĕġ'nāte, v. t. To make pregnant; to infuse.
Im'preg-nā'tion, n. The act of impregnating; saturation.
Im'pre-scrĭpt'i-ble, a. Not to be lost, impaired, or alienated; not depending on external authority.
Im-prĕss', v. t. To stamp; to print; to force into service, as seamen.
Im'press, n. Mark; stamp.
Im-prĕss'i-bĭl'i-ty, n. Capacity of being impressible.
Im-prĕss'i-ble, a. Capable of receiving impression.
Im-prĕss'ion (-prĕsh'un), n. Stamp; edition; influence; effect. [effect; susceptible.
Im-prĕss'ive, a. Producing
Im-prĕss'ive-ly, adv. So as to make a deep impression.
Im-prĕss'ment, n. The act of forcing men into service.
Im-prĕss'ūre, n. Mark made by pressure. [place.
Im-prī'mĭs, adv. In the first
Im-prĭnt', v. t. To mark by pressure; to fix deep; to print.
Im'print, n. The publisher's name with date and place of publication.
Im-prĭṣ'on (-prĭz'n), v. t. To put in a prison; to confine.
Im-prĭṣ'on-ment, n. Confinement in a prison.
Im-prŏb'a-bĭl'i-ty, n. Unlikelihood.
Im-prŏb'a-ble, a. Not likely.
Im-prŏb'a-bly, adv. In a manner not likely.
Im-prŏb'i-ty, n. Dishonesty.
Im-prŏmp'tu, adv. Without previous study; off-hand.
Im-prŏp'er, a. Not proper; unfit; unsuitable; unbecoming.
Im-prŏp'er-ly, adv. Unsuitably; not fitly.
Im-prō'pri-ā'tion, n. Act of putting a benefice into the hands of a layman.
Im'pro-prī'e-ty, n. Unfitness; unsuitableness to time, place, or character.
Im-prōv'a-ble, a. Capable of being improved.

IMPROVE 167 INCESSANTLY

Im-prove' (-prōōv'), v. t. To make better; to use to advantage; to cultivate. — v. i. To grow better.

Im-prove'ment (132), n. Progress from good to better; instruction; (pl.) valuable additions. [foresight.

Im-prov'i-dence, n. Want of

Im-prov'i-dent, a. Not making provision; careless.

Im-prov'i-dent-ly, adv. Without forethought.

Im-prov'i-sā'tion, n. Art or act of composing extemporaneously.

Im'pro-vīşe', v. t. or i. To compose extemporaneously.

Im-pru'dençe, n. Want of prudence; rashness.

Im-pru'dent, a. Indiscreet.

Im-pru'dent-ly, adv. Indiscreetly. [rudeness.

Im'pu-dençe, n. Effrontery;

Im'pu-dent, a. [Lat. impudens, from in, not, and pudens, modest.] Wanting modesty; shamelessly bold.

Im'pu-dent-ly, adv. With shameless effrontery; rudely.

Im-pūgn' (-pūn'), v. t. To contradict; to oppose.

Im'pulse, n. Force communicated; influence.

Im-pul'sion, n. Act of impelling; force communicated.

Im-pul'sive, a. Communicating force; acting from impulse.

Im-pū'ni-ty, n. Exemption from punishment or injury.

Im-pūre', a. Not pure; foul; unholy; unchaste; lewd.

Im-pūre'ly, adv. With impurity.

Im-pū'ri-ty, n. Foulness.

Im-pū'ta-ble, a. Capable of being imputed.

Im'pu-tā'tion (121), n. Act of imputing; censure.

Im-pū'ta-tive, a. Capable of being imputed.

Im-pūte', v. t. To charge upon; to attribute.

In, prep. Present; within. — adv. Within some place.

In'a-bil'i-ty, n. Want of power, means, skill, &c.

In'ac-çĕs'si-bil'i-ty, n. Quality of being beyond reach.

In'ac-çĕss'i-ble, a. Not to be reached. [accuracy.

In-ăc'cu-ra-çy, n. Want of

In-ăc'cu-rate, a. Erroneous.

In-ăc'cu-rate-ly, adv. Not correctly; erroneously.

In-ăc'tion, n. Want of action; state of rest; idleness.

In-ăct'īve, a. Unemployed; idle; sluggish; lazy.

In'ac-tiv'i-ty, n. Want of activity; idleness. [ciency.

In-ăd'e-qua-çy, n. Insufficiency.

In-ăd'e-quate, a. Not equal to the purpose.— SYN. Unequal; incompetent; insufficient; defective. [fully.

In-ăd'e-quate-ly, adv. Not

In'ad-mĭs'si-ble, a. Not proper to be admitted.

In'ad-vert'ençe, { n. Negli-

In'ad-vert'en-çy, } gence; oversight.

In'ad-vert'ent, a. Heedless.

In'ad-vert'ent-ly, adv. With negligence. [being alienated.

In-ăl'ien-a-ble, a. Incapable of

In-āne', a. Void; empty.

In-ăn'i-mate, a. Void of life or spirit.

In'a-ni'tion (-nĭsh'un), n. Emptiness; exhaustion from lack of food.

In-ăn'i-ty, n. Emptiness.

In-ăp'pe-tençe, n. Want of appetence or appetite.

In-ăp'pli-ca-bĭl'i-ty, n. Quality of not being applicable.

In-ăp'pli-ca-ble, a. Not suitable to be applied; unfit.

In-ăp'pli-cā'tion, n. Want of application; indolence.

In-ăp'po-şīte, a. Not apposite or appropriate.

In'ap-prē'çi-a-ble (-prē'shǐ-a-), a. Not to be estimated.

In'ap-prō'pri-ate, a. Unbecoming; unsuitable; unfit.

In-ăpt', a. Not fitted.

In-ăpt'i-tūde, n. Unfitness.

In-ärch', v. t. To graft by joining a scion to a stock without separating it from its parent tree.

In'ar-tĭc'u-late, a. Not uttered with articulation.

In'ar-tĭc'u-late-ly, adv. Not with distinct syllables.

In'ar-tĭc'u-late-ness, } n. In-

In'ar-tĭc'u-lā'tion, } distinctness of utterance.

In-är'ti-fĭ'cial (-fĭsh'al), a. Not done by art; artless.

In'as-mŭch', adv. Seeing that; since.

In'at-tĕn'tion, n. Neglect.

In'at-tĕn'tive, a. Heedless.

In'at-tĕn'tive-ly, adv. Heedlessly; carelessly.

In-aud'i-ble, a. Incapable of being heard; making no sound. [to be heard.

In-aud'i-bly, adv. So as not

In-au'gu-ral, a. Relating to inauguration.

In-au'gu-rāte, v. t. To induct into an office; to cause to begin; to consecrate or dedicate.

In-au'gu-rā'tion, n. Act of inducting into office with appropriate ceremonies.

In'au-spĭ'cious (-spĭsh'us), a. Unfortunate; unfavorable.

In'au-spĭ'cious-ly (-spĭsh'-us-), adv. With ill omens.

In'bŏrn, a. Implanted by nature; innate.

In-brēathe', v. t. To infuse by breathing. [nate.

In'bred, a. Bred within; in-

In-cāge', v. t. To confine in a cage, or as in a cage.

In-căl'cu-la-ble, a. Not to be calculated. [heat.

In'can-dĕs'çençe, n. Incipient

In'can-dĕs'çençe, n. A white heat. [with heat.

In'can-dĕs'çent, a. Glowing

In'can-tā'tion, n. A magical charm; enchantment.

In-cā'pa-bĭl'i-ty, n. Incapacity; want of power or of qualifications.

In-cā'pa-ble, a. Wanting power; disqualified. [cious.

In'ca-pā'cious, a. Not capa-

In'ca-păç'i-tāte, v. t. To deprive of power; to disqualify.

In'ca-păç'i-ty, n. Want of capacity.— SYN. Inability; incompetency. [prison.

In-cär'çer-āte, v. t. To im-

In-cär'çer-ā'tion, n. Imprisonment. [flesh.

In-cärn'ate, a. Clothed in

In'cär-nā'tion, n. Act of clothing with flesh. [case.

In-cāse', v. t. To inclose in a

In-eau'tious, a. Unwary; heedless; imprudent.

In-eau'tious-ly, adv. Without caution; heedlessly.

In-çĕn'di-a-rĭşm, n. Crime of house-burning.

In-çĕn'di-a-ry, n. One who maliciously burns a house or foments strife.— a. Relating to the malicious burning of buildings; inflammatory.

In'çense, n. Perfume exhaled by fire.— v. t. To perfume with incense or odors.

In-çĕnse', v. t. To irritate.

In-çĕn'tive, a. Inciting; encouraging.— n. That which encourages; incitement.

In-çĕp'tion, n. A beginning.

In-çĕp'tive, a. Beginning.

In-çĕr'ti-tūde, n. Uncertainty; doubtfulness.

In-çĕs'sant, a. Unceasing.

In-çĕs'sant-ly, adv. Without intermission; continually.

són, ôr, dọ, wolf, tōō, tŏŏk; ûrn, rụe, pụll; ç, ġ, soft; c, g̃, hard; aş; exist; ḷ as ng; this

INCEST 168 INCONVENIENCE

In′cest, n. [Lat. *incestum*, fr. *in*, not, and *castus*, chaste.] Cohabitation of persons within the prohibited degrees of kindred.

In-çest′u-oŭs, a. Consisting in, or guilty of, incest. [foot.

Inch, n. Twelfth part of a

In′cho-ate, a. Begun.

In′çi-dençe, n. The direction in which a ray of light falls on any surface.

In′çi-dent, a. Falling on; casual; liable to happen. — n. That which happens.

In′çi-dĕnt′al, a. Happening occasionally. [ually.

In′çi-dĕnt′al-ly, adv. Cas-

In-çĭn′er-āte, v. t. To burn to ashes.

In-çĭn′er-ā′tion, n. Act of burning to ashes.

In-çĭp′i-en-çy, n. Beginning.

In-çĭp′i-ent, a. Commencing.

In-çīse′, v. t. To cut in; to carve.

In-çĭṣ′ion (-sizh′un), n. A cut; a gash; a wound.

In-çī′sive, a. Cutting.

In-çī′sor, n. A fore-tooth.

In-çī′so-ry, a. Having the quality of cutting. [cut.

In-çĭṣ′ūre (-sizh′ụr), n. A

In-çĭt′ant, n. That which incites; a stimulant; motive.

In′çĭ-tā′tion, n. Incentive.

In-çīte′, v. t. To move or rouse to action.

In-çīte′ment (132), n. That which moves the mind; motive; inciting cause.

In′çĭ-vĭl′i-ty, n. Want of civility; disrespect; rudeness.

In-clĕm′en-çy, n. Severity.

In-clĕm′ent, a. Severe, as applied to weather. — SYN. Rough; stormy; boisterous: cold. [posed.

In-clīn′a-ble (133), a. Dis-

In′cli-nā′tion, n. A leaning; tendency; disposition; slope.

In-clīne′, v. t. or i. To lean; to bend; to feel disposed. — *Inclined plane*, a sloping plane; one of the mechanical powers. Inclined plane.

In-clōse′ (150), v. t. To surround; to shut in: to fence.

In-clōṣ′ūre (-klō′zhụr), n. A place inclosed.

In-clūde′, v. t. To comprehend; to comprise. [ing.

In-clū′ṣion, n. Act of includ-

In-clū′sive, a. Comprehended

in the calculation or statement; inclosing. [include.

In-clū′sive-ly, adv. So as to

In-cŏg′, ¦ adv. [Lat. *in-*

In-cŏg′ni-to, ¦ *cognitus*, unknown.] In disguise; in private.

In-cŏg′ni-to, a. Unknown; in a disguise. — n. One in disguise; state of being in disguise.

In′co-hēr′ençe, ¦ n. Want

In′co-hēr′on-çy, ¦ of connection. [nected.

In′co-hēr′ent, a. Not con-

In′co-hēr′ent-ly, adv. Without connection.

In′com-bŭs′ti-bĭl′i-ty, n. Quality of being incombustible.

In′com-bŭs′ti-ble, a. Not capable of being burned.

In′come (19), n. Rent; revenue; profit from property, &c.

In′com-mĕn′su-rate ¦
In′com-mĕn′su-ra-ble ¦ (-shụ-).a. Not of equal extent.

In′com-mĕn′su-ra-bĭl′i-ty (-mĕn′shụ-), n. Quality or state of a thing when it has no common measure.

In′com-mōde′, v. t. To give inconvenience to; to trouble.

In′com-mō′di-oŭs, a. Inconvenient; unsuitable.

In′com-mū′ni-ca-ble, a. Impossible to be communicated.

In′com-mū′ni-ca-tive, a. Not communicative; unsocial.

In′com-mū′ta-ble, a. Incapable of being commuted.

In-cŏm′pa-ra-ble, a. Admitting no comparison.

In-cŏm′pa-ra-bly, adv. Beyond comparison.

In′com-păt′i-bĭl′i-ty, n. Irreconcilable inconsistency.

In′com-păt′i-ble, a. Irreconcilably inconsistent.

In-cŏm′pe-tençe, ¦ n. Ina-

In-cŏm′pe-ten-çy, ¦ bility; want of means or of legal power; incapability.

In-cŏm′pe-tent, a. Not competent; improper; unfit.

In′com-plēte′, a. Not finished; imperfect; defective.

In′com-plēte′ly, adv. Imperfectly. [finished state.

In′com-plēte′ness, n. An un-

In-cŏm′pre-hĕn′si-bĭl′i-ty, n. Quality or state of being incomprehensible.

In-cŏm′pre-hĕn′si-ble, a. Incapable of being understood.

In-cŏm′pre-hĕn′si-bly, adv. So as not to be intelligible.

In′com-prĕss′i-bĭl′i-ty, n. Quality of resisting compression.

In′com-prĕss′i-ble, a. Incapable of being reduced into a smaller compass.

In′con-çeiv′a-ble. a. Not to be conceived or comprehended.

In′con-çeiv′a-bly, adv. Beyond comprehension.

In′con-clū′sive. a. Not determining a question [polished.

In-cŏn′dite, a. Rude; un-

In-cŏn′gru-ent, a. Inconsistent; unsuitable.

In′con-grū′i-ty, n. Unsuitableness; inconsistency.

In-cŏn′gru-oŭs, a. Not consistent. — SYN. Unfit; inappropriate; unsuitable.

In-cŏn′se-quent, a. Without regular inference.

In-cŏn′se-quĕn′tial, a. Not following; of no importance.

In′con-sĭd′er-a-ble, a. Of small amount or importance; trifling.

In′con-sĭd′er-a-bly, adv. In a small degree. [less.

In′con-sĭd′er-ate, a. Heed-

In′con-sĭd′er-ate-ly, adv. Without thought; heedlessly; rashly.

In′con-sĭd′er-ā′tion, n. Want of consideration.

In′con-sĭst′en-çy, n. Want of agreement; incongruity.

In′con-sĭst′ent, a. Incongruous: unsuitable.

In′con-sĭst′ent-ly, adv. Incongruously.

In′con-sōl′a-ble, a. Not admitting comfort.

In′con-spĭç′u-oŭs, a. Not conspicuous; hardly discernible. [ness.

In-cŏn′stan-çy, n. Fickle-

In-cŏn′stant, a. Subject to change of opinion or purpose; not uniform. — SYN. Incongruous: incompatible; variable; fickle.

In′con-tĕst′a-ble. a. Not to be contested or disputed.

In′con-tĕst′a-bly, adv. Beyond dispute. [ity.

In-cŏn′ti-nençe, n. Unchast-

In-cŏn′ti-nent, a. Unchaste; licentious.

In-cŏn′ti-nent-ly, adv. Without self-control; licentiously; immediately.

In′con-tro-vĕrt′i-ble, a. Not to be controverted or disputed.

In′con-tro-vĕrt′i-bly, adv. Beyond dispute.

In′con-vēn′iençe, n. Want

INCONVENIENT 169 INDICTABLE

of convenience; unfitness; trouble.
In'con-vēn'ient (-vĕn'yent), a. Incommodious; unfit; unsuitable; troublesome.
In'con-vẽrt'i-ble, a. Not convertible into another thing.
In-cōr'po-ral, \ a. Not consisting of matter; not material.
In'cor-pō're-al, /
In'cor-pō're-al-ly, adv. Immaterially.
In-cōr'po-rāte, v. t. or i. To form into a body; to unite.
In-cōr'po-rā'tion, n. Act of incorporating.
In'cor-rĕct', a. Inaccurate; containing faults. [rately.
In'cor-rĕct'ly, adv. Inaccu-
In'cor-rĕct'ness, n. Want of accuracy. [corrected.
In-cŏr'ri-gi-ble, a. Not to be
In-cŏr'ri-gi-ble-ness, n. Quality of being incorrigible.
In-cŏr'ri-gi-bly, adv. Beyond hope of amendment.
In'cor-rŭpt', a. Free from corruption; honest; pure.
In'cor-rŭpt'i-bil'i-ty, n. Quality of being incorruptible. [corrupted.
In'cor-rŭpt'i-ble, a. Not to be
In'cor-rŭp'tion, n. Exemption from decay. [thick.
In-crăs'sāte, v. t. To make
In'eras-sā'tion, n. Act of making thick.
In-crēase', v. i. To grow greater. — v. t. To cause to grow.
In-crēase', or In'crēase (112), n. Augmentation; produce; growth; increment.
In-crĕd'i-bil'i-ty, n. The quality of being incredible.
In-crĕd'i-ble, a. Impossible to be believed. [deserve belief.
In-crĕd'i-bly, adv. So as not to
In'ere-dū'li-ty, n. Indisposition to believe. [lieving.
In-crĕd'u-loŭs, a. Not be-
In'cre-ment, n. Increase.
In-crŭst', v. t. To cover with a crust or hard coat.
In'erus-tā'tion, n. Act of incrusting; a hard coat.
In'cu-bāte, v. i. [Lat. incubare, -batum, fr. in, on, and cubare, to lie.] To sit on, as eggs. [ting on eggs.
In'eu-bā'tion, n. Act of sit-
In'eu-bus, n. The nightmare.
In-cŭl'eāte, v. t. To enforce or urge. [culcating.
In'cul-eā'tion, n. Act of in-
In-cŭl'pa-ble, a. Not blamable; without fault.
In-cŭl'pāte, v. t. To censure; to accuse of crime.

In-cŭm'ben-çy, n. Possession of an office.
In-cŭm'bent, n. One who has a benefice or an office. — a. Imposed as a duty; lying or resting upon.
In-cŭm'branc̦e, n. A burdensome load. [liable to.
In-eŭr' (129), v. t. To become
In-cŭr'a-bĭl'i-ty, n. State of being incurable.
In-eŭr'a-ble (133), a. Incapable of being cured.—n. A patient who is not to be cured.
In-eŭr'a-bly, adv. So as to be incurable. [curiosity.
In-cŭ'ri-oŭs, a. Having no
In-cŭr'sion, n. An inroad; invasion. [crooked.
In-cŭrv'āte, v. t. To make
In-cŭrv'ate, a. Bent or curved inward or upward.
In'eur-vā'tion, n. Act of bending; crookedness.
In-dĕbt'ed (-dĕt'ed), a. Being in debt or under obligation.
In-dĕbt'ed-ness (-dĕt'ed-), n. State of being in debt.
In-dē'çen-çy, n. That which is unbecoming in manner or language; immodesty.
In-dē'çent, a. Offensive to delicacy; immodest.
In-dē'çent-ly, adv. So as to offend delicacy.
In-de-çī'pher-a-ble, a. Impossible to be deciphered.
In'de-çĭs'ion (-sizh'un), n. Want of decision or firmness.
In'de-çī'sive, a. Not decisive.
In-de-clīn'a-ble, a. Not varied in termination.
In'de-eō'roŭs, or In-dĕc'o-roŭs, a. Violating good manners. — SYN. Unbecoming; indecent; coarse; uncivil.
In'de-eō'rum, n. Impropriety of conduct; rudeness; impoliteness. [truth.
In-deed', adv. In fact; in
In'de-fāt'i-ga-ble, a. Not yielding to fatigue.
In'de-fāt'i-ga-bly, adv. Without weariness.
In'de-fēa'şi-ble, a. Not to be defeated or made void.
In-de-fĕct'i-ble, a. Not liable to defect or failure.
In-de-fĕn'sI-ble, a. Not to be defended.
In'de-fīn'a-ble, a. Incapable of being defined.
In-dĕf'i-nĭte, a. Not precise.
In-dĕf'i-nĭte-ly, adv. Without limitation.
In-dĕl'i-ble, a. Not to be blotted out.

In-dĕl'i-bly, adv. So as not to be effaced. [delicacy.
In-dĕl'i-ea-çy, n. Want of
In-dĕl'i-eate, a. Offensive to purity; indecent. [cently.
In-dĕl'i-eate-ly, adv. Inde-
In-dĕm'ni-fi-eā'tion, n. Reimbursement of loss.
In-dĕm'ni-fy, v. t. To secure against loss; to make good.
In-dĕm'ni-ty, n. [Lat. indemnitas, from indemnis, uninjured.] Security against lo.s or penalty.
In-dĕnt', v. t. To notch; to bind to service by contract.— n. A notch in the margin.
In'den-tā'tion, n. A cut; notch in the margin.
In-dĕnt'ūre, n. A mutual agreement in writing. — v. t. To bind by indentures.
In'de-pĕnd'enc̦e, n. Exemption from control.
In'de-pĕnd'ent, n. Not relying on others; not subject to control; Congregational. — n. A Congregationalist.
In'de-pĕnd'ent-ly, adv. Without dependence.
In'de-scrīb'a-ble, a. Impossible to be described.
In'de-strŭc'ti-bĭl'i-ty, n. Incapability of being destroyed.
In'de-strŭc'ti-ble, a. Incapable of being destroyed.
In'de-tẽr'mi-na-ble, a. Incapable of being determined.
In'de-tẽr'mi-nate, a. Indefinite; uncertain.
In'de-tẽr'mi-nate-ly, adv. Without certainty.
In'dex, n. (pl. In'dex-es̨, or In'di-çēs̨, 127.) Something that points; table of contents.
In'dĭà-man (Ĭnd'yȧ- or Ĭu'dĭ-ȧ-), n. A large ship in the India trade.
In'dĭan (Ĭnd'yan or Ĭn'dĭ-an), a. Relating to the Indies, or to the aborigines of America. — n. A native of the Indies; an aboriginal American.
In'dĭà-rŭb'ber (Ĭnd'yȧ- or Ĭn'dĭ-ȧ-), n. Caoutchouc.
In'dĭ-eant, a. Showing.
In'dĭ-eāte, v. t. To show; to be taken; to point out.
In'dĭ-eā'tion, n. Any thing indicative; token. [out.
In-dĭc'a-tive, a. Pointing
In'dĭ-eā'tor, n. He who, or that which, shows.
In-dīct' (in-dīt'), v. t. Te present for judicial trial.
In-dīct'a-ble (-dīt'a-bl), a. Subject to indictment.

sȯu, ôr, dọ, wǫlf, tǀo, took; ȯrn, rṷe, pṳll; ç, ġ, soft; c, ġ, hard; aẓ; eẋist; ṇ as ug; this.

8

In-dict'ment (-dit'-), n. Accusation by a grand jury.
In-dic'tion, n. Declaration; a cycle of fifteen years.
In-dif'fer-ençe, n. Impartiality; unconcernedness; want of affection.
In-dif'fer-ent, a. Of no account; impartial; passable; tolerable. [ably.
In-dif'fer-ent-ly, adv. Toler-
In'di-gençe, n. State of destitution. —SYN. Poverty; want; need. [a country.
In-dig'e-noŭs, a. Native to
In'di-gent, a. Needy; poor.
In'di-gest'i-ble, a. Incapable of being digested.
In'di-gĕs'tion (-jĕst'yun), n. Want of digestive powers.
In-dig'nant, a. Inflamed with anger and contempt.
In'dig-nā'tion, n. Anger mingled with contempt.
In-dig'ni-ty, n. Insult; contemptuous conduct.
In'di-go, n. [From India.] A blue coloring matter.
In'dī-rĕct', a. Not direct; crooked; unfair; dishonest.
In'dī-rĕc'tion, n. Oblique course or means. [ly.
In'dī-rĕct'ly, adv. Not direct-
In'dī-rĕct'ness, n. Obliquity.
In'dis-creet', a. Injudicious.
In'dis-creet'ly, adv. Without prudence. [or separated.
In'dis-crēte', a. Not discrete
In'dis-crē'tion (-krĕsh'ụn), n. Imprudence; folly.
In'dis-crim'i-nate, a. Not making a distinction.
In'dis-crim'i-nate-ly, adv. Without distinction.
In'dis-pĕn'sa-ble, a. Not to be dispensed with; absolutely necessary.
In'dis-pĕn'sa-bly, adv. Necessarily. [cline.
In'dis-pōse', v. t. To disin-
In'dis-pōsed', a. Slightly ill or or disordered; unwell.
In-dis'po-ṣi'tion, (-zĭsh'ụn), n. Disinclination; illness.
In-dis'pu-ta-ble, a. Not to be controverted.
In-dis'pu-ta-bly, adv. Beyond question; undeniably.
In-dis'so-lu-ble, a. Not capable of being dissolved or melted; binding.
In-dis'so-lu-bly, adv. So as not to be dissolved.
In'dis-pōṣed', a. Somewhat ill; disinclined. [obscure.
In'dis-tĭnct', a. Confused;
In'dis-tĭnct'ly, adv. Not clearly; obscurely.

In'dis-tĭnct'ness, n. Want of distinctness or clearness.
In'dis-tĭn'guish-a-ble, a. Not to be distinguished.
In-dīte', v. t. To compose in writing; to dictate.
In-dīte'ment, n. Act of inditing; that which is indited.
In'di-vĭd'u-al, a. Single; numerically one. —n. A single person or thing.
In'di-vĭd'u-al-iṣm, n. Individual existence or essence.
In'di-vĭd'u-ăl'i-ty, n. Separate existence.
In'di-vĭd'u-al-īze, v. t. To select or mark as an individual.
In'di-vĭd'u-al-ly, adv. Singly.
In'di-vĭṣ'i-bĭl'i-ty, n. Quality or state of being indivisible.
In'di-vĭṣ'i-ble, a. Incapable of division.
In-dŏç'ĭle, a. Not teachable; dull; intractable. [intellect.
In'do-çĭl'i-ty, n. Dullness of
In-dŏc'tri-nāte, v. t. To instruct in rudiments or principles.
In-dŏc'tri-nā'tion, n. Instruction in principles.
In'do-lençe, n. Habitual idleness; inaction; sloth.
In'do-lent, a. Habitually idle; slothful; lazy.
In'do-lent-ly, adv. Listlessly.
In-dŏm'i-ta-ble, a. Unconquerable; irrepressible.
In-dōrse', v. t. To write, as one's name, on the back; to assign by indorsement.
In-dōrse'ment, n. A writing of one's name on the back of a note; sanction; approval.
In-dōrs'er, n. One who indorses a note or bill.
In-dōr-sē', n. One to whom a note is indorsed.
In-dū'bi-ta-ble, a. Admitting no doubt; perfectly certain.
In-dū'bi-ta-bly, adv. Certainly. [suasion.
In-dūçe', v. t. To lead by per-
In-dūçe'ment, n. Any thing which induces. [session.
In-dŭct', v. t. To put in pos-
In-dŭct'ĭle, a. Not capable of being drawn into threads.
In-dŭc'tion, n. Introduction; inference or conclusion; a mode of reasoning from particular facts to general principles.
In-dŭct'ĭve, a. Leading to inference. [duction.
In-dŭct'ĭve-ly, adv. By in-
In-dūe', v. t. To invest; to clothe; to furnish; to supply.
In-dŭlġe', v. t. To yield to

the wishes of; to gratify; to humor; to permit to enjoy; to favor.
In-dŭl'gençe, n. Forbearance of restraint. [wishes.
In-dŭl'gent, a. Yielding to
In-dŭl'gent-ly, adv. With indulgence.
In'du-rāte, v. i. or t. To harden. [hardening.
In'du-rā'tion, n. Act of
In-dŭs'tri-al, a. Pertaining to, or consisting in, industry.
In-dŭs'tri-oŭs, a. Habitually diligent. —SYN. Assiduous; active; laborious; careful.
In-dŭs'tri-oŭs-ly, adv. Diligently; assiduously.
In'dus-try, n. Constant diligence; assiduity.
In'dwell-ing, a. Residing within. — n. Residence within. [drunk.
In-ē'bri-āte, v. t. To make
In-ē'bri-ate, n. An habitual drunkard; a sot; a toper.
In-ē'bri-ā'tion,) n. Drunk-
In'e-brī'e-ty,) enness; intoxication.
In-ĕd'it-ed, a. Unpublished.
In-ĕf'fa-ble, a. Not to be expressed; unspeakable.
In-ĕf'fa-bly, adv. Inexpressibly. [to be effaced.
In-ĕf-fāçe'a-ble (133), a. Not
In'ef-fĕct'ĭve, a. Producing no effect; useless.
In'ef-fĕct'u-al, a. Not producing the proper effect.
In'ef-fĕct'u-al-ly, adv. Without effect; in vain.
In-ĕf'fi-cā'çioŭs, a. Not producing the desired effect.
In-ĕf'fi-ca-çy, n. Want of power to produce the desired or proper effect.
In'ef-fĭ'çien-çy (-fĭsh'en-), n. Want of power to produce the effect.
In'ef-fĭ'çient (-fĭsh'ent), a. Not efficient; effecting nothing. [elegance.
In-ĕl'e-gançe, n. Want of
In-ĕl'e-gant, a. Wanting elegance. [out elegance.
In-ĕl'e-gant-ly, adv. With-
In-ĕl'i-ġi-bĭl'i-ty, n. Incapacity of being elected to office.
In-ĕl'i-ġi-ble, a. Not capable of being elected to office; not worthy to be chosen.
In-ĕpt', a. Unfit; unsuitable.
In'e-quăl'i-ty (-kwŏl'-), n. Want of equality; difference.
In-ĕq'ui-ta-ble (-ĕk'wi-), a. Not equitable; not just.
In-ĕrt', a. Sluggish; inactive; slothful; dull.

INERTIA 171 INFORM

In-ẽr'ti-à (-ẽr'shĭ-à), *n.* That property of matter by which it tends when at rest to remain so, and when in motion to continue in motion.
In-ẽrt'ness, *n.* Quality of being inert; sluggishness.
In-ĕs'ti-ma-ble, *a.* Above price; invaluable.
In-ĕs'ti-ma-bly, *adv.* So as not to be estimated.
In-ĕv'i-ta-ble, *a.* Not to be avoided; unavoidable. [ably.
In-ĕv'i-ta-bly, *adv.* Unavoidably.
In'ex-ăct', *a.* Not exact; incorrect.
In'ex-cūs'a-ble, *a.* Not to be excused or justified.
In'ex-cūs'a-bly, *adv.* So as not to be excusable.
In'ex-hăl'a-ble, *a.* Incapable of being exhaled.
In'ex-haust'i-ble, *a.* Not to be exhausted. [existence.
In'ex-ĭst'ençe, *n.* Want of
In'ex-ĭst'ent, *a.* Not existing; not having being.
In-ĕx'o-ra-ble, *a.* Not to be moved by entreaty. — SYN. Inflexible; unyielding; relentless.
In'ex-pē'di-ençe, } *n.* Want
In'ex-pē'di-en-çy, } of fitness.
In'ex-pē'di-ent, *a.* Not fit or suitable. [experience.
In'ex-pē'ri-ençe, *n.* Want of
In'ex-pē'ri-ençed (-enst), *a.* Not having experience; unskilled.
In'ex-pẽrt', *a.* Unskillful.
In-ĕx'pi-a-ble, *a.* Admitting no atonement. [explained.
In-ĕx'pli-ea-ble, *a.* Not to be
In-ĕx'pli-ea-bly, *adv.* So as not to be explained.
In'ex-prĕss'i-ble, *a.* Not to be expressed; unutterable.
In'ex-prĕss'i-bly, *adv.* In an unutterable manner.
In'ex-tĭn'guish-a-ble, *a.* Incapable of being extinguished; unquenchable.
In-ĕx'tri-ea-ble, *a.* Not to be extricated or disentangled.
In-ĕx'tri-ea-bly, *adv.* So as not to be extricable.
In-eye' (in-ī'), *v. t.* To inoculate, as a tree.
In-făl'li-bĭl'i-ty, *n.* The quality of being incapable of error.
In-făl'li-ble, *a.* Incapable of error or mistake.
In-făl'li-bly, *adv.* Certainly.
In'fa-moŭs, *a.* Notoriously bad; detestable. [vilely.
In'fa-moŭs-ly, *adv.* Most

In'fa-my, *n.* Public disgrace.
In'fan-çy, *n.* The first part of life; the beginning.
In'fant, *n.* [Lat. *infans, -fantis,* fr. *in,* not, and *fans,* speaking.] A young child. — *a.* Pertaining to infants.
In-făn'tà, *n.* A princess in Spain and Portugal.
In-fănt'i-çide, *n.* The murderer or the murderer of an infant.
In'fant-ĭle, or **In'fant-īle,** } *a.* Pertaining to infants.
In'fant-īne, or **In'fant-ĭne,** }
In'fant-ry, *n.* Foot-soldiers.
In-făt'u-āte, *v. t.* To make foolish; to besot.
In-făt'u-ā'tion, *n.* Deprivation of reason.
In-fēa'şi-ble, *a.* Impossible to be done. [disease.
In-fĕct', *v. t.* To taint with
In-fĕe'tion, *n.* Morbid matter that communicates disease.
In-fĕe'tioŭs, *a.* Having qualities that may communicate disease. [fection.
In-fĕe'tioŭs-ly, *adv.* By in-
In'fe-eŭnd'i-ty, *n.* Barrenness; unfruitfulness.
In'fe-lĭç'i-toŭs, *a.* Not felicitous; unhappy.
In'fe-lĭç'i-ty, *n.* Unhappiness; unfortunate state.
In-fẽr' (129), *v. t.* To deduce as a fact or consequence.
In-fẽr'a-ble, } *a.* Capable of
In-fẽr'ri-ble, } being inferred.
In'fer-ençe, *n.* Deduction from premises; consequence.
In'fer-ĕn'tial, *a.* Deducible by inferences.
In-fē'ri-or, *a.* Lower in age or place or value; subordinate. — *n.* One who is lower in age or place; a subordinate.
In-fē'ri-ŏr'i-ty, *n.* A lower state or condition.
In-fẽr'nal, *a.* Pertaining to hell; hellish. — *n.* An inhabitant of hell.
In-fẽr'tile, *a.* Unfruitful.
In'fer-tĭl'i-ty, *n.* Unfruitfulness; barrenness. [annoy.
In-fĕst', *v. t.* To disturb; to
In'fi-del, *a.* Not believing the Scriptures; unbelieving. — *n.* One who rejects the Scriptures and Christianity; an unbeliever.
In'fi-dĕl'i-ty, *n.* Disbelief of the inspiration of the Scriptures; unfaithfulness.
In-fĭl'trāte, *v. t.* To enter by the pores.
In'fĭl-trā'tion, *n.* Act of entering a substance by the pores.

In'fi-nīte (46), *a.* Without limits; boundless; immense.
In'fi-nīte-ly, *adv.* Without limit or end.
In-fĭn'i-tĕs'i-mal, *a.* Infinitely divided.
In-fĭn'i-tive, *a.* Expressing action without limitation of person or number.
In-fĭn'i-tūde, *n.* Infinity.
In-fĭn'i-ty, *n.* Unlimited extent or number.
In-fîrm', *a.* Weak; sickly.
In-fîrm'a-ry, *n.* A place to lodge and nurse the sick.
In-fîrm'i-ty, *n.* Weakness; feebleness; failing. [plant.
In-fĭx', *v. t.* To fix deep; to implant.
In-flāme', *v. t.* To set on fire; to provoke; to excite. — *v. i.* To grow hot and painful.
In-flăm'ma-bĭl'i-ty, *n.* Susceptibility of taking fire.
In-flăm'ma-ble, *a.* Easily set on fire.
In'flam-mā'tion, *n.* A setting on fire; a redness and swelling; febrile heat.
In-flăm'ma-to-ry, *a.* Showing inflammation.
In-flāte', *v. t.* To swell with wind; to blow or puff up.
In-flā'tion, *n.* A swelling with wind or vanity.
In-flĕet', *v. t.* To bend; to vary; to modulate.
In-flĕe'tion (149), *n.* Act of bending or turning; variation of ending in words; modulation of voice in speaking.
In-flĕet'ĭve, *a.* Able to bend.
In-flĕx'i-bĭl'i-ty, *n.* Unyielding stiffness; obstinacy.
In-flĕx'i-ble, *a.* Immovably stiff or firm. [ness.
In-flĕx'i-bly, *adv.* With firmness.
In-flĭet', *v. t.* To lay on, as a punishment; to impose.
In-flĭe'tion (149), *n.* The act of inflicting; punishment.
In-flĭet'ĭve, *a.* Tending to inflict.
In'flo-rĕs'çençe, *n.* Mode of flowering.
In'flu-ençe, *n.* Moving or directing power. — *v. t.* To move by moral power; to persuade; to act upon.
In'flu ĕn'tial, *a.* Exerting influence or power.
In'flu-ĕn'zà, *n.* A violent catarrh, often epidemic.
In'flux, *n.* Act of flowing in
In-fōld', *v. t.* To involve; to inwrap; to inclose.
In-fōrm', *v. t.* To tell; to acquaint with; to animate.

---

sŏn, ôr, dọ, wọlf, tōō, tŏŏk; ûrn, ryẹ, pyll; ç, ġ, soft; c, ğ, hard; a͡ş; exĭst; ŋ as ng; this.

— **Syn.** To apprise; teach; instruct. — *v. t.* To give intelligence.
In-fôrm'al, *a.* Wanting form; without ceremony; irregular.
In'for-măl'i-ty, *n.* Want of usual forms.
In-fôrm'al-ly, *adv.* Without the usual forms.
In-fôrm'ant, *n.* One who tells; an informer.
In'for-ma'tion, *n.* Notice given; intelligence; knowledge.
In-fôrm'er, *n.* One who tells.
In-frăc'tion, *n* Breach; violation. [being broken.
In-frăn'gi-ble, *a.* Incapable of
In-fre'quen-cy, *n.* Uncommonness; rarity.
In-fre'quent, *a.* Not usual; uncommon; rare.
In-frĭnĝe', *v. t.* To break, as contracts; to violate.
In-frĭnĝe'ment, *n.* Violation.
In-fū'ri-āte, *v. t.* To enrage.
In-fū'ri-ate, *a.* Like a fury; violently enraged.
In-fūse', *v. t.* [Lat. *infundere,-fusum*; from *in*, in, and *fundere*, to pour.] To pour in; to steep in liquor; to inspire.
In-fū'gi-bĭl'i-ty, *n.* Capacity of being poured in; incapability of fusion.
In-fū'gi-ble, *a.* Capable of being infused; incapable of being made liquid.
In-fū'gion, *n.* Act of pouring in; liquor made by infusion.
In-ĝĕn'er-āte, *v. t.* To produce within. [innate.
In-ĝĕn'er-ate, *a.* Inborn;
In-ĝĕn'ioŭs (-jĕn'yus). *a.* Possessed of genius; skillful.
In-ĝĕn'ioŭs-ly, *adv.* With ingeniousness.
In'ĝe-nū'i-ty, *n.* Ready invention; skill.
In-ĝĕn'u-oŭs, *a.* Free from reserve or dissimulation. — **Syn.** Open: frank; candid.
In-ĝĕn'u-oŭs-ly, *adv.* Candidly. [dor.
In-ĝĕn'u-oŭs-ness, *n.* Candor.
In-glō'ri-oŭs, *a.* Bringing no glory; disgraceful.
In-glō'ri-oŭs-ly, *adv.* Without glory.
In'got (140), *n.* A bar or wedge of metal.
In-grăft', *v. t.* To insert, as a scion in a stock.
In'grāin, or **In-grāin',** *v. t.* To dye before manufacture.

In'grāte, *n.* An ungrateful person.
In-grā'ti-āte (-grā'shi-), *v. t.* To get into favor.
In-grat'i-tūde, *n.* Want of a sense of favors. [neut part.
In-gre'di-ent, *n.* A component.
In'gress, *n.* Entrance.
In-gŭlf', *v. t.* To swallow up in a gulf.
In-hăb'it, *v. t.* To dwell; to live in. — *v. i.* To dwell or abide.
In-hăb'it-a-ble, *a.* Possible to be inhabited. [dence.
In-hăb'it-an-cy, *n.* Legal residence.
In-hăb'it-ant, *n.* A dweller.
In-hăb'it-ā'tion, *n.* Act of residence. [haling.
In'ha-lā'tion. *n.* Act of inhaling.
In-hāle'. *v. t.* To draw into the lungs.
In-hāl'er, *n.* One who inhales; an apparatus for inhaling medicated vapor.
In'har-mō'ni-oŭs, *a.* Unmusical.
In-hēre', *v. i.* To be fixed in.
In-hēr'ençe, } Existence
In-hēr'en-çy, } in something else.
In-hēr'ent, *a.* Existing in something; innate.
In-hēr'ent-ly, *adv.* By inherence. [heritance.
In-hēr'it, *v. t.* To take by inheritance.
In-hēr'it-a-ble, *a.* Incapable of being inherited.
In-hēr'it ançe, *n.* A hereditary estate. [inherits.
In-hēr'it-or, *n.* A man who
In-hē'gion, *n.* State of inhering; inherence. [forbid.
In-hĭb'it, *v. t.* To restrain; to
In'hi-bĭ'tion (-bĭsh/un), *n.* Restraint; prohibition.
In-hŏs'pi-ta-ble, *a.* Not disposed to entertain strangers.
In-hŏs'pi-ta-bly, *adv.* Unkindly to strangers.
In-hŏs'pi-tăl'i-ty, *n.* Want of hospitality. [cruel.
In-hū'man, *a.* Barbarous;
In'hu-măn'i-ty, *n.* Barbarity; cruelty. [rously.
In-hū'man-ly, *adv.* Barbarously.
In'hu-mā'tion, *n.* Act of burying.
In-hūme', } *v. t.* To bury;
In-hū'māte, } to inter.
In-ĭm'i-cal. *a.* Unfriendly.
In-ĭm'i-ta-ble, *a.* Not to be imitated. [imitation.
In-ĭm'i-ta-bly, *adv.* Beyond
In-ĭq'ui-toŭs (-ĭk/wi-), *a.* Characterized by great injustice. — **Syn.** Wicked; nefarious; criminal.

In-ĭq'ui-ty, *n.* Injustice; crime.
In-ĭ'tial (-ĭsh/al), *a.* First. — *n.* The first letter of a name.
In-ĭ'ti-āte (-ĭsh/i-āt), *v. t.* To instruct in rudiments; to introduce.
In-ĭ'ti-ā'tion (-ĭsh/i-), *n.* Instruction in first principles.
In-ĭ'ti-a-tive } (-ĭsh/i-), *a.*
In-ĭ'ti-a-to-ry } Serving to initiate.
In-jĕct', *v. t.* To throw in.
In-jĕc'tion. *n.* Act of throwing in; any thing injected.
In'ju-dĭ'cioŭs (-dĭsh/us), *a.* Not judicious; unwise.
In'ju-dĭ'cioŭs-ly, *adv.* Without judgment. [order.
In-jŭnc'tion, *n.* Command;
In'jure, *v. t.* To hurt; to damage; to harm.
In-jū'ri-oŭs, *a.* Hurtful.
In-jū'ri-oŭs-ly, *adv.* Hurtfully.
In'ju-ry, *n.* Hurt; detriment.
In-jŭs'tiçe, *n.* Want of justice; wrong.
Ĭnk, *n.* A liquor used in writing and printing. — *v. t.* To mark with ink.
Ĭnk'hôrn, *n.* A vessel to hold ink. [inky.
Ĭnk'i-ness, *n.* State of being
Ĭnk'ling, *n.* [Contracted from *inkling*, prou. *in'cli-ning*.] A hint; desire. [ink.
Ĭnk'stand, *n.* A vessel to hold
Ĭnk'y, *n.* Consisting of, or like, ink. [sea.
Ĭn'land, *a.* Remote from the
In-lāy', *v. t.* To diversify with other substances.
Ĭn'lāy, *n.* Pieces of wood, ivory, &c., inlaid.
Ĭn'let, *n.* Passage into a bay.
Ĭn'ly, *adv.* Internally; secretly.
Ĭn'māte, *n.* One who lives in the same house.
Ĭn'mōst, *a.* Deepest within.
Ĭnn (125), *n.* A house of entertainment for travelers.
Ĭn'nāte, or **In-nāte'** (111), *a.* Inborn; natural.
Ĭn'nāte-ly, or **In-nāte'ly,** *adv.* Naturally.
Ĭn'ner, *a.* Interior; further inward.
Ĭn'ner mōst, *a.* Deepest or furthest within.
Ĭn'ning, *n.* The turn for using the bat in cricket.
Ĭnn'keep-er. *n.* A person who keeps an inn or tavern
Ĭn'no-çençe, } *n.* Freedom
Ĭn'no-çen-çy, } from guilt; harmlessness.

INNOCENT 173 INSPECTOR

In'no-çent, *a.* Free from guilt; pure; harmless.
In'no-çent-ly, *adv.* Without guilt; harmlessly.
In-nōçe'u-oŭs, *a.* Harmless.
In'no-vāte, *v. t.* or *i.* To introduce as a novelty.
In'no-vā'tion, *n.* Introduction of novelties.
In'no-vā'tor, *n.* One who innovates.
In-nŏx'ioŭs, *a.* Harmless; innocent.
In'nu-ĕn'do, *n.* (*pl.* **In'nu-ĕn'dōeş,** 140.) A distant hint.
In-nū'mer-a-ble, *a.* Impossible to be numbered.
In-nū'mer-a-bly, *adv.* Beyond number.
In'nu-tri'tioŭs (-trĭsh'us), *a.* Not nourishing.
In-ōç'u-lāte, *v. t.* To insert, as a scion, in a stock; to communicate, as disease, by inserting infectious matter.
In-ōç'u-lā'tion, *n.* Act or practice of inoculating.
In-ōç'u-lā'tor, *n.* One who inoculates. [smell.
In-ō'dor-oŭs, *a.* Destitute of
In'of-fĕn'sĭve, *a.* Giving no offense; harmless.
In'of-fĕn'sĭve-ly, *adv.* Without offense; harmlessly.
In'of-fī'cial (-fĭsh'al), *a.* Not official; in a private capacity.
In'of-fī'cious (-fish'us), *a.* Contrary to duty.
In-ŏp'er-a-tĭve, *a.* Inactive.
In-ŏp'por-tūne', *a.* Not opportune; unseasonable.
In-ŏp'por-tūne'ly, *adv.* Unseasonably. [ate.
In-ŏr'di-nate, *a.* Immoderate
In-ŏr'di-nate-ly, *adv.* Immoderately; excessively.
In'or-găn'ie, *a.* Void of organs; unorganized.
In-ŏs'cu-lāte, *v. t.* To unite, as two vessels, a vein and an artery, at their extremities.
In-ŏs'cu-lā'tion, *n.* Union of two animal vessels by contact of the two extremities.
In'quest, *n.* Judicial inquiry.
In-qui'e-tūde, *n.* A restless state of mind; uneasiness.
In-quīre' (150), *v. t.* To ask about; to seek by asking.
In-quīr'er, *n.* One who inquires.
In-quīr'y (141), *n.* Act of inquiring; a question.
In'qui-sĭ'tion (-zĭsh'un), *n.* Judicial inquiry; a court for punishing heresy.

In'qui-sĭ'tion-al (-zĭsh'un-), *a.* Pertaining to inquiry.
In-quĭs'i-tĭve, *a.* Given to inquiry; curious.
In-quĭs'i-tĭve-ly, *adv.* With curiosity to inquire.
In-quĭs'i-tĭve-ness, *n.* Busy curiosity. [the inquisition.
In-quĭs'i-tor, *n.* A member of
In-quĭs'i-tō'ri-al, *a.* Pertaining to inquisition.
In'rōad, *n.* Sudden invasion; incursion; encroachment.
In'sa-lū'bri-oŭs, *a.* Not salubrious; unhealthy.
In'sa-lū'bri-ty, *n.* Want of salubrity; unwholesomeness.
In-sāne', *a.* Unsound in mind; crazy; deranged.
In-sāne'ly (132), *adv.* Madly; foolishly.
In-sān'i-ty, *n.* Derangement of intellect; craziness.
In-sā'ti-a-ble (-sā'shĭ-), *a.* Not to be satisfied.
In-sā'ti-a-bly (-sā'shĭ-), *adv.* With greediness not to be satisfied.
In-sā'ti-ate (-sā'shĭ-āt), *a.* Not satisfied. [ness.
In'sa-tī'e-ty, *n.* Insatiableness
In-serībe' (54), *v. t.* To write on; to dedicate.
In-serĭp'tion, *n.* That which is written or printed on something; title; address.
In-serū'ta-bĭl'i-ty, { *n.* The
In-serū'ta-ble-ness, } quality of being inscrutable.
In-serū'ta-ble, *a.* Unsearchable; undiscoverable.
In'seet, *n.* [Lat. *insectum*, fr. *insecare*, to cut in.] A small animal with six legs, and breathing through tubes running through the body.
In'see-tĭv'o-roŭs, *a.* Feeding on insects.
In'se-cūre', *a.* Unsafe; not confident of safety.
In'se-cūre'ly, *adv.* Unsafely.
In'se-cū'ri-ty, *n.* Want of safety; danger; hazard.
In-sĕn'sate, *a.* Senseless; stupid; foolish.
In-sĕn'si-bĭl'i-ty, *n.* Want of emotion or affection; dullness.
In-sĕn'si-ble, *a.* Destitute of feeling; imperceptible.
In-sĕn'si-bly, *adv.* Imperceptibly; gradually.
In-sĕn'tient, *a.* Not having perception.
In-sĕp'a-ra-ble, *a.* Impossible to be separated.
In-sĕp'a-ra-bly, *adv.* With indissoluble union.

In-sĕrt', *v. t.* To bring into or among; to introduce.
In-sĕr'tion, *n.* Act of inserting; thing inserted.
In'sīde, *n.* Inner part or place.
In-sĭd'i-oŭs, *a.* Deceitful; sly.
In-sĭd'i-oŭs-ly, *adv.* Deceitfully; slyly.
In'sīght (-sĭt), *n.* Sight of the interior; full knowledge.
†**In-sĭg'ni-à,** *n. pl.* Badges of distinction.
In'sig-nĭf'i-cançe, *n.* Want of meaning; unimportance.
In'sig-nĭf'i-cant, *a.* Void of meaning; without weight of character. — SYN. Unimportant; trivial; immaterial.
In-sin-çēre', *a.* Hypocritical; false. [critically.
In'sin-çēre'ly, *adv.* Hypo-
In'sin-çēr'i-ty, *n.* Deceitfulness; hypocrisy; falseness.
In-sĭn'u-āte, *v. t.* To creep in; to hint; to suggest.
In-sĭn'u-ā'tion, *n.* Act of insinuating; a hint.
In-sĭn'u-ā'tor, *n.* One who insinuates. [vapid.
In-sĭp'id, *a.* Void of taste;
In'si-pĭd'i-ty, *n.* Want of taste; want of life and spirit.
In-sĭp'id-ly, *adv.* Without taste or spirit.
In-sĭst', *v. i.* To be persistent or urgent.
In-snāre', *v. t.* To catch by stratagem; to entrap. [ance.
In'so-brī'e-ty, *n.* Intemper-
In'so-lāte, *v. t.* To expose to the sun's rays.
In'so-lā'tion, *n.* Exposure to the sun's rays.
In'so-lençe, *n.* Haughtiness or pride joined with contempt; audacity.
In'so-lent, *a.* Haughty; insulting; overbearing.
In'so-lent-ly, *adv.* Haughtily.
In'so-lĭd'i-ty, *n.* Want of solidity.
In-sŏl'u-bĭl'i-ty, *n.* The quality of being insoluble.
In-sŏl'u-ble, *a.* Incapable of being dissolved in a fluid.
In-sŏlv'a-ble, *n.* Incapable of being solved or explained.
In-sŏlv'en-çy, *n.* Inability to pay debts in full. [debts.
In-sŏlv'ent, *a.* Unable to pay
In'so-mŭch', *adv.* So that.
In-spĕet', *v. t.* To examine; to superintend; to view.
In-spĕe'tion, *n.* Examination; official view.
In-spĕet'or, *n.* An examiner; a superintendent.

---
sŏn, or dọ, wọlf, tōō, tŏŏk; ûrn, rụe, pụll; ç, ġ, *soft*; e, ġ, *hard*; a$_{\$}$; e$\underline{x}$ist; ŋ *as* ng; **this**.

In-spĕc'tor-ship, n. Office of inspector.
In-spēr'sion, n. The act of sprinkling on something.
In-sphēre', v. t. To place in a sphere. [ing inspired.
In-spīr'a-ble, a. Capable of be-
In'spi-rā'tion, n. Act of drawing in the breath; divine influence on the mind.
In-spī'ra-to-ry, a. Relating to inspiration.
In-spire', v. i. To draw in breath. — v. t. To breathe into; to infuse; to animate or suggest supernaturally.
In-spir'it, v. t. To animate.
In-spis'sāte, v. t. To thicken, as liquids. [thickening.
In'spis-sā'tion, n. Act of
In'sta-bil'i-ty, n. Want of stability; inconstancy.
In-stall', v. t. To invest with office. [installing.
In'stal-lā'tion, n. Act of
In-stall'ment (131), n. Act In stal'ment } of installing; payment of part at particular times.
In'stance, n. Solicitation; example; a case occurring.—v. i. or t. To produce an example.
In'stant, n. [Lat. instans, p. pr. of instare, to stand or press upon.] A moment.— a. Present; urgent.
In'stan-tā'ne-oŭs, a. Done in an instant.
In'stan-tā'ne-oŭs-ly, adv. In an Instant.
In-stăn'ter, adv. Instantly.
In'stant-ly, adv. Immediately. [certain condition.
In-state', v. t. To place in a
In'stau-rā'tion. n. Renewal; renovation; restoration.
In-steā'l', adv. In place of.
In-steep', v. t. To steep.
In'step, n. The upper part of the foot. [ward; to set on.
*n'sti-gāte, v. t. To urge for-
In'sti-gā'tion. n. Incitement, as to evil or wickedness.
In'sti-gā'tor, n. One who incites to evil.
In-still' (138), v. t. To infuse
In-still' } by or as by drops.
In'stil-lā'tion, n. Act of infusing by drops or slowly.
In'stinet, n. Unconscious, involuntary, or unreasoning prompting to action. — a. Moved from within; actuated.
In-stinet'ive, a. Prompted by instinct. [stinct.
In-stinet'ive-ly, adv. By in-
In'sti-tūte (50), v. t. To establish. — n. Established law.

In'sti-tū'tion, n. Act of establishing; system or organization established.
In'sti-tū'tive, a. Tending or intended to institute.
In-strŭct', v. t To teach; to form by precept; to direct.
In-strŭc'tion, n. Act of teaching; direction; command.
In-strŭct'ive, a. Conveying knowledge; serving to instruct.
In-strŭct'ive-ly, adv. In an instructive manner.
In-strŭct'or, n. One who teaches [teacher.
In-strŭct'ress, n. A female
In'stru-ment. n. A tool; machine; a writing; an agent.
In'stru-měnt'al, a. Conducive as a means to some end.
In'stru-ment-ăl'i-ty, n. Agency; subordinate means.
In'stru-měnt'al-ly, adv. By way of instrument.
In'sub-jĕc'tion, n. State of disobedience.
In'sub-ôr'di-nā'tion, n. Disobedience to lawful authority.
In-sŭf'fer-a-ble, a. Not to be borne; unendurable.
In-sŭf'fer-a-bly, adv. To a degree beyond endurance.
In'suf-fi'cien-cy (-fĭsh'en-), n. Want of sufficiency.
In'suf-fi'cient (-fĭsh'ent), a. Inadequate. [water.
In'su-lar, a. Surrounded by
In'su-lāte, v. t. To place in a detached position, like an island; to make an isle.
In'su-lā'ted, a. Separated from other bodies, especially by non-conductors.
In'su-lā'tion, n. Act of insulating; state of being insulated.
In'su-lā'tor, n. One who, or that which, insulates.
In'sult, n. Intended contempt.— SYN. Outrage; insolence; affront; indignity.
In-sŭlt', v. t. To treat with abuse, insolence, or contempt. [gross abuse.
In-sŭlt'ing, a. Containing
In-sŭ'per-a-ble, a. Impossible to be overcome.
In-sŭ'per-a-bly, adv. So as not to be surmounted.
In'sup-pôrt'a-ble, a. Impossible to be endured.
In'sup-pôrt'a-bly, adv. Beyond endurance.
In'sup-press'i-ble, a. Not to be suppressed.
In-sur'a-ble (-shur'-), a. Capable of being insured.

In-sur'ance (-shur'-), n. Security against loss by paying a certain sum.
In-sure' (-shur', 150), v. t. To secure against loss.
In-sur'er (-shur'-), n. One who insures.
In-sûr'gent, a. Exciting sedition; rebellious. — n. One who rises against lawful authority.
In'sur-mount'a-ble, a. Not to be surmounted, or overcome; insuperable.
In'sur-rĕc'tion, n. Open opposition of members to lawful authority.— SYN. Sedition; revolt; rebellion.
In'sur-rĕc'tion-a-ry, a. Relating to insurrection.
In'sus-cĕp'ti-ble, a. Not capable of feeling.
In-tăg'lio (-tăl'yo), n. A precious stone with a figure engraved on it.
In-tăn'gi-ble, a. Not perceptible by touch. [her.
In'te-ger, n. A whole num-
In'te-gral, n. An entire thing. — a. Whole; entire.
In'te-grant, a. Necessary to constitute an entire thing.
In'te-grāte, v. t. To form one whole; to make up.
In-těg'ri-ty, n. Wholeness, uprightness; purity.
In-těg'u ment, n. A natural covering.
In'tel-lect, n. [Lat. intellectus, fr. intelligere, to understand.] Power to judge and comprehend; understanding.
In'tel-lĕc'tion, n. Simple apprehension of ideas.
In'tel-lĕct'ive. a. Pertaining to the intellect.
In'tel-lĕct'u-al, a. Relating to the understanding; mental.
In'tel-lĕct'u-al-ly, adv. By means of the understanding.
In-těl'li-ġence, n. Understanding; information; news.
In-těl'li-ġent, a. Knowing; instructed; skillful.
In-těl'li-ġent-ly, adv. In an intelligent manner.
In-těl'li-ġi-bil'i-ty, n. Quality of being intelligible.
In-těl'li-ġi-ble, a. Capable of being comprehended; plain.
In-těl'li-ġi-bly, adv. So as to be understood; clearly.
In-těm'per-ance, n. Excess; drunkenness; inebriation.
In-těm'per-ate, a. Excessive; ungovernable; inordinate; addicted to the excessive use of spirituous liquors.

In-tĕnd′, v. To purpose.
In-tĕnd′ant, n. An overseer.
In-tĕnse′, a. Strained; close; vehement; extreme.
In-tĕnse′ly, adv. To a high degree; extremely.
In-tĕnse′ness, n. Intensity.
In-tĕn′si-fȳ, v. t. or i. To make or become intense. [gree.
In-tĕn′si-ty, n. Extreme de-
In-tĕn′sĭve, a. Giving force.
In-tĕnt′, a. Fixed closely. — n. Purpose; design; aim.
In-tĕn′tion, n. Design; purpose: aim.
In-tĕn′tion-al, a. Designed.
In-tĕn′tion-al-ly, adv. Purposely. [attention.
In-tĕnt′ly, adv. With close
In-tĕnt′ness, n. Close application of mind.
In-tĕr′ (129), v. t. To bury.
In′ter-áct, n. Performance between acts. [added.
In-tĭr′ca-la-ry, a. Inserted;
In-tĕr′ca-lāte, v. t. To insert between others.
In-tĕr′ca-lā′tion, n. Insertion of a day in a calendar.
In′ter-çēde′, v. i. To interpose; to mediate.
In′ter-çēd′ent, a. Mediating.
In′ter-çĕpt′, v. t. To seize on its passage; to cut off.
In′ter-çĕp′tion, n. Act of intercepting; interruption.
In′ter-çĕs′sion (-sĕsh′un), n. Mediation; interposition.
In′ter-çĕs′sor, n. A mediator.
In′ter-çĕs′so-ry, a. Containing, or relating to, intercession. · [or link together.
In′ter-chāin′, v. t. To chain
In′ter-chānge′, v. t. To change by giving and receiving; to reciprocate.
In′ter-chānge, n. Mutual exchange; barter; exchange.
In′ter-chānge′a-ble, a. Capable of being given and taken mutually.
In′ter-chānge′a-bly, adv. With mutual exchange.
In′ter-co-lŭm′ni-ā′tion, n. Clear space between two columns. [tual communion.
In′ter-com-mūn′ion, n Mu-
In′ter-cŏs′tal, a. Placed or lying between the ribs.
In′ter-cŏurse, n. Mutual dealings; fellowship.
In′ter-cŭr′rençe, n. A passing between.
In′ter-dĭct′, v. t. To forbid.
In′ter-dĭct, n. A prohibition.
In′ter-dĭc′tion, n. Act of prohibiting or forbidding.

In′ter-dĭc′tĭve, } a. Serving
In′ter-dĭct′o-ry, } to prohibit.
In′ter-est, v. t. To concern or relate to; to affect. — n. Concern; share; benefit; premium for the use of money.
In′ter-est-ed, a. Having an interest.
In′ter-est-ing (107), a. Exciting interest; pleasing.
In′ter-fēre′, v. i. To interpose; to clash; to intermeddle; to strike reciprocally.
In′ter-fēr′ençe, n. Interposition; intermeddling.
In′ter-ĭm, n. The mean time.
In-tē′ri-or, a. Internal; being within — n. The inward part; inland part of a country.
In′ter-jā′çent, a. Lying between; intervening.
In′ter-jĕe′tion, n. A word of exclamation.
In′ter-jĕe′tion-al, a. Thrown in between other words, as an interjection.
In′ter-lāçe, v. t. To intermix; to insert.
In′ter-lārd′, v. t. To insert between; to interpose.
In′ter-lēave′, v. t. To insert blank leaves in.
In′ter-līne′, v. t. To wri'e or print between the lines of.
In′ter lĭn′e-ar, a. Written or printed between the lines.
In′ter-lĭn′e-ā′tion, n. A writing or printing between lines.
In′ter-lĭnk′, v. t. To connect by uniting links.
In′ter-lŏe′u-tor, n. One who speaks in dialogue.
In′ter-lŏe′u-to-ry, a. Consisting of dialogue.
In′ter-lōpe, v. t. To forestall; to prevent right; to intrude.
In′ter-lōp′er, n. An intruder.
In′ter-lūde, n. [Lat. inter, between, and ludus, play.] An entertainment between the acts of a play; a piece of instrumental music between the parts of a song or hymn.
In′ter-mār′riage, n. Reciprocal marriage between two families, tribes, &c.
In′ter-mār′ry, v. i. To become connected, as families, by a marriage between two of their members.
In′ter-mĕd′dle, v. i. To meddle in the affairs of others.
In′ter-mĕd′dler, n. An officious person.
In′ter-mē′di-al, } a. Lying
In′ter-mē′di-ate, } between.

In-tĕr′ment, n. Burial.
In-tĕr′mi-na-ble, n. Admitting of no end. — SYN. Boundless; endless; infinite.
In′ter-mĭn′gle, v. t. To mingle or mix together.
In′ter-mĭs′sion (-mĭsh′un), n. Cessation for a time.
In′ter-mĭs′sĭve, a. Coming at times; not continual.
In′ter-mĭt′, v. i. or t. To cease or cause to cease for a time.
In′ter-mĭt′tent, a. Ceasing at intervals. — n. A disease that intermits.
In′ter-mĭx′, v. t. or i. To mix.
In′ter-mĭxt′ūre, n. A mass formed by mixture.
In-tĕr′nal, a. Inward; interior; domestic.
In-tĕr′nal-ly, adv. Inwardly.
In′ter-nā′tion-al (-năsh′un-), a. Existing between nations.
In′ter-nŭn′ci-o (-nŭn′shĭ-o), n. A pope's representative.
In′ter-plēad, v. t. To discuss or try a previous point incidentally happening.
In-tĕr′po-lāte, v. t. To insert, as spurious matter, in a writing; to foist.
In-tĕr′po-lā′tion, n. The act of inserting spurious words in a writing, words inserted.
In-tĕr′po-lāt′or, n. One who interpolates. [posing.
In′ter-pŏs′al, n. Act of inter-
In′ter-pōse′, v. i. To step in between. — v. t. To place between; to interfere; to mediate.
In′ter-po-ṣĭ′tion (-zĭsh′un), n. Act of mediating; intervention.
In-tĕr′pret, v. t. To explain.
In-tĕr′pret-a-ble, a. Capable of being interpreted.
In-tĕr′pret-ā′tion, n. Explanation; exposition; version.
In-tĕr′pret-er, n. One who expounds; an expositor.
In′ter-rĕg′num, n. The time a throne is vacant between the death of a king and the accession of his successor.
In-tĕr′ro-gāte, v. t. To examine by question.
In-tĕr′ro-gā′tion, n. A question; an inquiry: a point [?] denoting a question.
In′ter-rŏg′a-tĭve, a. Denoting a question. — n. A word that indicates a question.
In-tĕr′ro-gā′tor, n. One who asks questions.
In′ter-rŏg′a-to-ry, n. A question. — a. Containing a question.

sŏn, ôr, dǫ, wǫlf, tōō, tŏŏk; ûrn, rṳe, pṳll; ç, ġ, soft; ċ, ġ, hard; aṣ; eẋist; ṇ as ng; this.

In′ter-rŭpt′, v. t. To stop by interfering; to divide.
In′ter-rŭp′tion, n. Interposition; stop; hindrance.
In′ter-sēct′, v. t. To divide; to cross. — v. i. To meet and cross each other.
In′ter-sĕc′tion, n. Act of crossing; point where two lines cut each other.
In′ter-spāçe, n. An intervening space.
In′ter-spērse′, v. t. To scatter among or here and there.
In′ter-spēr′sion, n. Act of scattering here and there.
In′ter-stĕl′lar, a. Being among the stars.
In′ter-stĭçe, or In-tēr′stĭçe, n. An empty space between things closely set.
In′ter-stĭ′tial (-stĭsh′al), a. Containing interstices.
In′ter-tĕxt′ūre, n. State of being interwoven.
In′ter-twīne′, } v. t. To unite
In′ter-twĭst′, } by twining.
In′ter-val (140), n. A space between things; time between events. [between.
In′ter-vēne′, v. i. To come
In′ter-vĕn′tion, n. Act of Intervening; interposition.
In′ter-view, n. A formal meeting; conference.
In′ter-wēave′, v. t. To weave one into another of.
In-tĕs′tate, a. Dying without a will. — n. One who dies without leaving a will.
In-tĕs′ti-nal, a. Pertaining to the bowels.
In-tĕs′tīne, a. [Lat. intestinus, fr. intus, within.] Internal; domestic; not foreign.
In-tĕs′tĭnes, n. pl. Bowels.
In-thrăll′ (133), v. t. To reduce to bondage; to enslave.
In-thrăll′ment } (131), n. Sla-
In-thrăl′ment } very.
In′ti-ma-çy, n. Close familiarity; friendship.
In′ti-māte, v. t. To hint; to suggest; to point out.
In′ti-mate, a. Inmost; near; familiar. — n. A familiar associate or friend. [ly.
In′ti-mate-ly, adv. Familiar-
In′ti-mā′tion, n. A hint; suggestion; notice.
In-tĭm′i-dāte, v. t. To inspire with fear. — Syn. To dispirit; abash; deter.
In-tĭm′i-dā′tion, n. The act of intimidating.
In′to, prep. Noting entrance.
In-tŏl′er-a-ble, a. Not to be borne or endured.

In-tŏl′er-a-bly, adv. Beyond endurance. [toleration.
In-tŏl′er-ançe, n. Want of
In-tŏl′er-ant, a. Unable to bear; illiberal; bigoted.
In′to-nā′tion, n. Manner of utterance; modulation.
In-tōne′, v. t. or i. To read with a musical accentuation and tone.
In-tŏx′i-cāte, v. t. To inebriate; to make drunk.
In-tŏx′i-cā′tion, n. State of drunkenness; inebriation.
In-trăct′a-ble, a. Unmanageable; obstinate; unruly.
In-trăct′a-bĭl′i-ty, n. Obstinacy; indocility.
In-trăn′si-tive, a. Expressing an action or state that does not pass over to an object.
In-trĕnch′, v. t. To fortify with a trench; to encroach.
In-trĕnch′ment, n. A ditch and parapet for defense.
In-trĕp′id, a. Fearless; bold.
In′tre-pĭd′i-ty, n. Undaunted bravery; fearlessness.
In-trĕp′id-ly, adv. Fearlessly.
In′tri-ca-çy, n. Entanglement; perplexed state; complexity; obscurity.
In′tri-cate, a. Entangled or involved; complicated.
In′tri-cate-ly, adv. With entanglement or perplexity.
In-trīgue′ (-trēeg′). n. Stratagem; amour. — v. i. To carry on secret designs.
In-trīgu′er (-trēeg′-), n. One who intrigues.
In-trĭn′sic, a. Internal; true; real; inherent; essential.
In-trĭn′sic-al-ly, adv. Inter-nally; really; essentially.
In′tro-dūçe′, v. t. To bring in; to make known.
In′tro-dŭc′tion, a. Act of introducing; a preface.
In′tro-dŭc′tive, } a. Serving
In′tro-dŭc′to-ry, } to introduce.
In′tro-mĭs′sion (-mĭsh′un), n. Act of sending or conveying in. [let in; to admit.
In′tro-mĭt′, v. t. To send or
In′tro-spĕc′tion, n. A view of the inside.
In′tro-vēr′sion, n. A turning, or being turned, inward.
In′tro-vērt′, v. t. To turn inward.
In-trūde′, v. i. To come unwelcomely. — v. t. To thrust in without invitation.
In-trū′sion, n. Entrance without right or invitation.
In-trū′sive, a. Apt to intrude.

In-trŭst′, v. t. To commit to the care of.
In′tu-ĭ′tion (-ĭsh′un), n. Immediate knowledge, as in perception.
In-tū′i-tive, a. Perceived by the mind immediately.
In-tū′i-tive-ly, adv. By immediate perception.
In′tu-mĕs′çençe, n. A swelling with heat; a tumid state.
In-twīne′, } v. t. To twist to-
In-twĭst′, } gether.
In-ŭn′dāte, v. t. To overflow; to deluge; to flood.
In′un-dā′tion, n. An overflow of water; a flood.
In-ūre′, v. t. or i. To accustom; to serve to the use or benefit of. [urn.
In-ŭrn′, v. t. To put in an
In′u-tĭl′i-ty, n. Uselessness.
In-vāde′, v. t. To enter in a hostile manner; to attack.
In-vād′er, n. One who invades. [void.
In-văl′id, a. Weak; null;
In′va-lid, n. One disabled by wounds or sickness. — a. In ill-health; feeble; infirm.
In-văl′i-dāte, v. t. To make void; to weaken.
In′va-lĭd′i-ty, n. Weakness; want of legal force.
In-văl′u-a-ble, a. Beyond valuation; priceless.
In-vā′ri-a-ble, a. Unchangeable; uniform.
In-vā′ri-a-bly, adv. Without change; uniformly.
In-vā′sion, n. Hostile entrance; infringement.
In-vā′sive, a. Entering with hostile purpose.
In-vĕc′tive, n. A busive; satirical. — n. A harsh or reproachful accusation.
In-vei̇̄gh′ (in-vā′), v. i. To rail against; to reproach.
In-vei̇̄gh′er (in-vā′er), n. One who inveighs.
In-vei̇̄′gle (-vē′gl), v. t. To seduce; to entice; to wheedle; to entrap.
In-vei̇̄′gle-ment, n. Act of inveigling, or state of being inveigled.
In-vĕnt′, v. t. [Lat. invenire, inventum, to come upon; to find.] To discover by study or inquiry; to find out; to contrive; to fabricate; to feign.
In-vĕn′tion, n. Act of finding out: that which is invented.
In-vĕnt′ive, a. Ready at invention; ingenious. [vents.
In-vĕnt′or, n. One who in-

INVENTORY 177 IRREPREHENSIBLE

In'ven-to-ry,'n. A list of articles. — v. t. To make a list of. [trary.
In-vērse', a. Inverted; contrary order or manner.
In-vērse'ly, adv. In a contrary order or manner.
In-vēr'sion, n. A complete change of order or place.
In-vērt', v. t. To turn upside down; to change the order of completely.
In-vērt'ed, a. Reversed.
In-vēst', v. t. To clothe; to besiege; to vest in something else. [into.
In-vēs'ti-gāte, v. t. To search
In-vēs'ti-gā'tion, n. A searching for truth; examination; inquiry. [searches for truth.
In-vēs'ti-gā'tor, n. One who
In-vēst'i-tūre, n. Act or right of giving possession.
In-vēst'ment, n. A vestment; conversion into property less fleeting than money.
In-vēt'er-a-çy, n. Obstinacy confirmed by time. [fixed.
In-vēt'er-ate, a. Old; firmly
In-vēt'er-ate-ly, adv. With obstinate fixedness; violently.
In-vīd'ĭ-oŭs, a. Likely to excite envy. [excite envy.
In-vīd'ĭ-oŭs-ly, adv. So as to
In-vīd'i-oŭs-ness, n. Quality of provoking envy or hatred.
In-vĭg'or-āte, v. t. To strengthen; to give vigor to.
In-vĭg'or-ā'tion, n. Act of invigorating.
In-vĭn'çi-ble, a. Not to be conquered. — SYN. Insuperable; insurmountable.
In-vĭn'çi-bly, adv. Unconquerably.
In-vī'o-la-bĭl'ĭ-ty, n. State or quality of being inviolable.
In-vī'o-la-ble, a. Not to be broken. [breach or failure.
In-vī'o-la-bly, adv. Without
In-vī'o-late, a. Not broken; entire; uninjured.
In-vĭṣ'ĭ-bĭl'ĭ-ty, n. State of being invisible. [seen.
In-vĭṣ'ĭ-ble, a. Not to be
In-vĭṣ'ĭ-bly, adv. So as not to be seen; obscurely.
In'vi-tā'tion, n. Act of inviting; request to attend.
In-vīte', v. t. To request the company of; to allure.
In-vīt'ing, p. a. Attractive.
In-vīt'ing-ly, adv. In a manner to invite or allure.
In'vo-cāte, v. t. To invoke.
In'vo-cā'tion, n. Act of invoking; judicial order.
In'voiçe (140), n. A bill of goods, with the prices annexed. — v. t. To make a list of, with the prices.
In-vōke', v. t. To address in prayer; to implore; to pray to; to supplicate.
In-vŏl'un-ta-ri-ly, adv. Not by choice; against the will.
In-vŏl'un-ta-ry, a. Opposed to, or independent of, the will.
In'vo-lū'tion, n. Action of involving; complication.
In-vŏlve', v. t. To envelop; to infold; to comprise.
In-vŭl'ner-a-bĭl'ĭ-ty, n. State or quality of being invulnerable.
In-vŭl'ner-a-ble, a. Incapable of being wounded.
In-wall', v. t. To inclose with a wall.
In'ward, a. Being within; internal. — adv. Within.
In'ward-ly, adv. In the inner part; internally; secretly.
In'wardṣ, n. pl. Intestines.
In-wēave', v. t. [imp. IN-WOVE; p. p. INWOVE, IN-WOVEN.] To weave together; to intertwine.
In-wrāp' (-răp'), v. t. To involve; to infold.
In-wrēathe' (-rēth'), v. t. To surround as with a wreath.
In-wrought' (in-rawt'), a. Worked in.
Ī-ŏn'ĭc, a. Relating to an order of architecture.
I-ō'tȧ, n. [Name of the smallest letter (ι) of the Gr. alphabet.] A tittle; a jot.
Ĭp'c-căc̣, } n. A drug
Ĭp'e-căc̣'u-ăn'hȧ, } used as an emetic.
I-rǎs'çi-bĭl'ĭ-ty, n. Quality of being easily provoked.
Ī-rǎs'çi-ble, a. Irritable; easily angered or provoked.
Īre (84), n. Anger; wrath.
Īre'ful (139), a. Angry; wroth; furious with anger.
Ĭr'ĭ-dĕṣ'çençe, n. Exhibition of colors like those of the rainbow.
Ĭr'ĭ-dĕṣ'çent, a. Having colors like the rainbow.
Ī'ris (140, 86), n. The rainbow; the colored circle round the pupil of the eye.
Ī'rish, a. Pertaining to Ireland. — n. The native language of the Irish.
Ĭrk, v. t. To weary; to tire.
Ĭrk'ṣome (16), a. Tedious; tiresome. [ness.
Ĭrk'ṣome-ness, n. Tedious-
Ī'ron (ī'urn), n. The most common and useful of the metals. — a. Made of iron; like iron; hard; firm. — v. t. To smooth with a hot iron.
Ī'ron-clăd (ī'urn-), n. A vessel for warfare protected or covered with iron. [irony.
Ī-rŏn'ĭc-al, a. Spoken in
Ī-rŏn'ĭc-al-ly, adv. By way, or by the use, of irony.
Ī'rŏn-mŏn'ġer (ī'urn-), n. A dealer in iron.
Ī'ron-y, n. Speech intended to convey a contrary signification; a species of ridicule.
Ī'ron-y (ī'urn-), a. Made of, or like, iron; hard.
Ir-rā'di-ançe, n. Beams of light; splendor.
Ir-rā'di-āte, v. t. or i. To emit rays; to illuminate.
Ir-rā'di-ā'tion, n. Emission of rays of light; illumination.
Ir-rā'tion-al (-răsh'un-), a. Void of reason; absurd.
Ir-rā'tion-al-ly (-răsh'un-) adv. Absurdly. [reclaimed.
Ir're-clāim'a-ble, a. Not to be
Ir-rĕc'on-çīl'a-ble, a. Impossible to be reconciled.
Ir're-cŏv'er-a-ble, a. Incapable of being recovered. — SYN. Irreparable; irretrievable; incurable.
Ir're-cŏv'er-a-bly, adv. Beyond recovery.
Ir're-deem'a-ble, a. Not to be redeemed. [reduced.
Ir're-dŭç'ĭ-ble, a. Not to be
Ir-rĕf'ra-ga-ble, a. Impossible to be refuted.
Ir-rĕf'u-ta-ble, or Ir're-fūt'-a-ble, a. Incapable of being refuted.
Ir-rĕġ'u-lar, a. Not according to rule; unmethodical.
Ir-rĕġ'u-lăr'ĭ-ty, n. Deviation from rule; anomaly.
Ir-rĕġ'u-lar-ly, adv. Without method, rule, or order.
Ir-rĕl'a-tĭve, a. Having no relation; unconnected.
Ir-rĕl'e-van-çy, n. State of being irrelevant.
Ir-rĕl'e-vant, a. Not applicable or pertinent.
Ir're-lĭġ'ĭon (-lĭj'un), n. Want of religion; impiety.
Ir're-lĭġ'ĭoŭs (-lĭj'us), a. Ungodly; wicked.
Ir're-mē'dĭ-a-ble, a. Admitting of no remedy.
Ir'rĕp'a-ra-ble, a. Impossible to be repaired.
Ir-rĕp'a-ra-bly, adv. So as not to admit of repair.
Ir're-pēal'a-ble, a. Not to be repealed.
Ir-rĕp're-hĕn'sĭ-ble, a. Not to be blamed.

sǫn, ȯr, dǫ, wǫlf, tōō, tǒǒk; ûrn, rụe, pụll; ç, ġ, *soft*; ç, ġ, *hard;* aṣ; eẋist; ṇ as ng; tḥis.

8*

Ir're-prĕss'i-ble, a. Not to be repressed.
Ir're-prōach'a-ble, a. Beyond reproach; blameless.
Ir're-prŏv'a-ble, a. Not to be reproved.
Ir're-sist'i-ble, a. Impossible to be resisted with success.
Ir're-sist'i-bly, adv. So as not to be resisted.
Ir-rĕs'o-lūte, a. Not firm in purpose. — SYN. Wavering; vacillating; unsettled; unsteady; undecided.
Ir-rĕs'o-lute-ly, adv. Without resolution.
Ir-rĕs'o-lū'tion, n. Want of firmness of mind.
Ir're-spĕct'īve, a. Without regard to circumstances.
Ir're-spĕc'tive-ly, adv. Without regard.
Ir-rĕs'pi-ra-ble, a. Unfit for respiration.
Ir're-spŏn'si-ble, a. Not responsible.
Ir're-triĕv'a-ble, a. Incapable of recovery or repair.
Ir're-triĕv'a-bly, adv. Irrecoverably.
Ir-rĕv'er-ençe, n. Want of reverence or veneration.
Ir-rĕv'er-ent, a. Wanting in reverence or veneration.
Ir-rĕv'er-ent-ly, adv. With want of reverence.
Ir're-vẽr'si-ble, a. Not to be reversed or recalled.
Ir're-vẽr'si-bly, adv. So as to preclude reversal or repeal.
Ir-rĕv'o-ca-ble, a. Not to be recalled.
Ir-rĕv'o-ca-bly, adv. So as not to admit of recall.
Ir'ri-gāte, v. t. To wet; to moisten; to water, as land, by means of a stream made to flow over it. [gating.
Ir'ri-gā'tion, n. Act of irrigating.
Ir-rĭg'u-oŭs, a. Watery; wet.
Ir'ri-ta-bĭl'i-ty, n. Capacity of being irritated.
Ir'ri-ta-ble, a. Easily irritated or provoked.
Ir'ri-tant, n. That which excites or irritates.
Ir'ri-tāte, v. t. To excite heat and redness in; to anger.
Ir'ri-tā'tion, n. Act of irritating; exasperation.
Ir'ri-ta-tīve, a. Serving to excite or irritate.
Ir-rŭp'tion, n. Sudden invasion; violent inroad. [upon.
Ir-rŭp'tīve, a. Rushing in or
Is (iz, 123, 124). Third person singular of the substantive verb To be.
I'sin-glass (I'zing-glåss), n. That is ice-glass, fr. icing, ice, and glass.) A kind of gelatine prepared from the air-bladders of the sturgeon; mica.
Is'lam, } n. Religion of
Is'lam-ĭsm,} the Mohammedans.
Is'land (ī'-), } n. Land which
Isle (īl), } is surrounded by water. [land.
Is'let (ī'let), n. A little island.
I-sŏch'ro-noŭs, a. Performed in equal times.
Is'o-lāte, v. t. To place in a detached situation; to place by itself. [isolated.
Is'o-lā'tion, n. State of being
I-sŏs'çe-lĕs, a. Having only two sides that are equal, as triangles.
I'so-thĕrm'al, a. Having equal temperature.
Is'ra-el-īte, n. A descendant of Israel; a Jew.
Is'sụ-a-ble (ĭsh'shụ-), a. Capable of being issued.
Is'sụe (ĭsh'shụ), n. Offspring; final result; a small ulcer kept open. — v. i. To come or send out; to result. — v. t. To put in circulation.
Isth'mus (ĭs'mus or ĭst'mus), n. A neck of land connecting larger portions of land.
It, pron. That thing.
I-tăl'ian, a. Pertaining to Italy. — n. A native of Italy; language of Italy.
I-tăl'ic, a. Relating to Italy or to the letters called Italics.
I-tăl'i-çīze, v. t. To print in Italic letters.
I-tăl'ics, n. pl. Letters inclining as these do.
Itch, n. A cutaneous disease. — v. i. To have irritation in the skin; to long. [lar.
I'tem, n. A separate particular.
It'er-āte, v. t. To repeat.
It'er-ā'tion, n. Act of repeating; repetition.
I-tĭn'er-ant, n. One who travels from place to place. — a. Wandering; traveling; unsettled.
I-tĭn'er-a-ry, n. A book of travels. — a. Traveling; done on a journey.
I-tĭn'er-āte, v. i. To travel.
It-sĕlf', pron. emphatic from it.
I'vo-ry, n. The tusk of an elephant, or any substance closely resembling it. — a. Made of ivory; like ivory.
I'vy, n. A climbing plant.

J.

JĂB'BER, v. i. To talk rapidly and indistinctly. — n. Rapid, indistinct talk.
Jăb'ber-er, n. One who talks fast and indistinctly.
Jā'çinth, n. A pellucid gem.
Jăck, n. A mechanical contrivance of various kinds; an engine; a small flag; male of some animals.
Jăck'al, n. A wild animal of India and Persia, allied to the wolf. [Jackal.
Jăck'a-nāpes, n. A monkey; an ape; a coxcomb.
Jăck'ass, n. Male of the ass; a dolt; a fool.
Jăck'-boots, n. pl. Large boots reaching above the knee.
Jăck'daw, n. A European bird allied to the crows.
Jăck'et, n. A kind of short coat. [Jackdaw.
Jăck'-knife (-nīf), n. A large pocket-knife.
Jăc'o-bĭn, n. A violent revolutionist; a turbulent or factious demagogue.
Jăc'o-bĭn'ic-al, a. Pertaining to secret clubs against government.

American Jack.   English Jack.

Jackdaw.

ā, ē, ī, ō, ū, y, long; ă, ĕ, ĭ, ŏ, ŭ, y̆, short; cāre, cär, ăsk, ạll, whạt; ēre, vẽll, tẽrm; p'que, fĩrm;

Jăc'u-lāte, *v. t.* To throw like a dart; to emit.
Jăc'u-lā'tion, *n.* Act of darting or throwing.
Jăc'u-la-to-ry, *a.* Darting or throwing out suddenly.
Jāde, *n.* A tired horse; a worthless woman; a mineral.
— *v. t.* To wear down by exertion. —SYN. To tire; weary; fatigue; exhaust.
Jăg, *n.* A small load; notch.
— *v. t.* To notch; to indent.
Jăg'ged, *a.* Having notches or teeth. [eveu.
Jăg'gy, *a.* Notched; un-
Jăg'u-är', *n.* A wild animal found from Brazil to Texas, — called also *American tiger*.
Jaguar.
Jāil, *n.* A prison.
Jāil'-bīrd, *n.* A prisoner, or one who has been a prisoner.
Jāil'er, *n.* Keeper of a jail.
Jăl'ap (39), *n.* [From *Jalapa*, in Mexico.] A plant or drug used as a cathartic.
Jăm (140), *n.* A conserve of fruits. — *v. t.* (129) To squeeze closely; to wedge in.
Jămb (jăm), *n.* Side-piece of a chimney or of a door.
Jāne, *n.* A kind of fustian.
Jăn'gle (jăng'gl), *n.* Discordant sound; contention. — *v.* To wrangle; to quarrel.
Jăn'i-tor, *n.* A door-keeper.
Jăn'i-za-ry, *n.* A Turkish soldier of the guards.
Jăn'ty, *a.* Airy; showy.
Jăn'u-a-ry, *n.* First month of the year.
Ja-păn', *n.* A peculiar kind of varnish or varnished work. —
v. t. To varnish with japan.
Jär, *v. t.* To cause to shake.
— *v. i.* To strike together slightly; to interfere. — *n.* A shaking; a clash; a stone or glass vessel.
Jär'gon, *n.* Confused, unintelligible talk; gibberish.
Jăs'mĭne, or **Jăs'mĭne**, *n.* A climbing plant, having fragrant flowers.
Jăs'per, *n.* A mineral.
Jaun'dĭçe, *n.* A disease in which the body becomes yellow.
Jăun'dĭçed (-dĭst), *a.* Affected with jaundice; prejudiced.
Jăunt (jänt), *v. i.* To make an excursion. — *n.* An excursion; a ramble.

Jāve'lin, *n.* A kind of spear.
Javelin.
Jaw, *n.* The bone in which the teeth are fixed; abusive clamor. — *v. i.* To scold.
Jāy, *n.* A reddish-brown bird common in Europe; an American bird of a sky-blue color.
Jĕal'ous, *a.* Suspicious; afraid of rivalship. [ousy.
Jĕal'ous-ly, *adv.* With jeal-
Jĕal'ous-y, *n.* Suspicion; fear of losing some good which another may obtain.
Jeān (jān), *n.* A cotton cloth twilled.
Jeer (130), *n.* A scoff; a taunt; mockery. — *v. i.* To scoff; to deride. [name of God.
Je-hō'vah, *n.* The Hebrew
Je-jūne', *a.* Hungry; barren; void of interest.
Je-jūne'ness, *n.* Barrenness.
Jĕl'ly (141), *n.* Inspissated juice of fruit; a conserve.
Jĕn'ny, *n.* A machine for spinning.
Jĕop'ard, *v. t.* To put in danger; to expose to loss or injury. — SYN. To risk; peril; endanger; hazard.
Jĕop'ard-y, *n.* Danger; peril.
Jĕrk, *v. t.* or *i.* To throw or pull with sudden motion. —
n. A sudden thrust or twitch or spring. [short coat.
Jĕrk'in (55), *n.* A jacket or
Jĕs'sa-mĭne, *n.* A plant; jasmine. [— *n.* A joke.
Jĕst, *v. i.* To make sport.
Jĕs'u-it, *n.* One of a religious order; a crafty person (*an opprobrious use of the word*).
Jĕg'u-ĭt'ĭc-al, *a.* Relating to Jesuits; crafty (*an offensive sense*). [the Jesuits.
Jĕg'u-it-ĭsm, *n.* Principles of
Jĕt, *n.* A black fossil; a sudden rush or spouting, as of water.
— *v. i.* To shoot forward.
Jew (jū *or* jū), *n.* A Hebrew.
Jew'el (jū'el *or* jil'el, 130), *n.* A precious stone; a gem. —
v. t. To dress or adorn with jewels; to fit with a jewel.
Jew'el-er ⎱ (jū'- *or* jil'-), *n.* One
Jew'el-ler ⎰ who deals in jewels.
Jew'el-er-y, ⎱ *n.* Jewels col-
Jew'el-ler-y, ⎰ lectively; gems; jewels.
Jew'el-ry (jū'- *or* jil'-), *n.* Jewels or trinkets in general.
Jew'ess (jū'es *or* jil'es), *n.* A Hebrew woman.
Jew'ish (jū'- *or* jil'-), *a.* Pertaining to the Jews.

Jews'-härp (jūz'- *or* jilz'-), *n.* A musical instrument.
Jib, *n.* Foremost sail of a ship.
Jĭg, *n.* A light dance by two.
Jĭlt, *n.* A woman who trifles with her lover. — *v. t.* To trifle with in love.
Jĭn'gle (jĭng'gl), *v. i.* To cause to sound with a sharp noise.
— *v. i.* To clink; to tinkle.
— *n.* A sharp, clinking sound; a little rattle.
Jŏb, *n.* A piece of work. — *v. t.* or *i.* To do small work; to deal in stocks.
Jŏb'ber, *n.* A dealer in stocks; one who supplies retailers.
Jŏck'ey (141), *n.* One who rides, or who deals in, horses.
— *v. t.* To cheat; to trick.
Jo-cōse', *a.* Given to jesting; jocular; facetious. [antry.
Jo-cōse'ly, *adv.* With pleas-
Jŏc'u-lar, *a.* Jocose; merry.
Jŏc'u-lar-ly, *adv.* Jocosely.
Jŏc'u-lăr'ĭ-ty, *n.* Disposition to jest. [ly.
Jŏc'und, *a.* Merry; gay; live-
Jŏg, *v. t.* or *i.* [Allied to *shock*.] To push with the elbow; to walk slowly. — *n.* A push with the elbow. [ly.
Jŏg'gle, *v. t.* To shake slight-
Join, *v. t.* To couple; to unite; to combine; to close.
Join'er, *n.* A mechanic who does the nicer wood-work of buildings.
Join'er-y, *n.* A joiner's art.
Joint, *n.* Place or part where things are united. — *v. t.* To form into joints; to divide.
— *a.* Shared by two or more.
Joint'ed, *a.* Having joints.
Joint'-heir (-âr), *n.* An heir having a joint interest.
Joint'ly, *adv.* Unitedly.
Joint'-stŏck, *n.* Stock held in company.
Joint'-tĕn'an-çy, *n.* A tenure of office by unity of interest, title, time, and possession.
Joint'-tĕn'ant, *n.* One ,who holds by joint tenancy.
Joint'ūre (joint'yụr), *n.* An estate settled on a wife.
Joist, *n.* A small piece of timber to support a floor.
Jōke, *n.* A jest. — *v. t.* or *i.* To jest; to rally: to banter.
Jōk'er, *n.* One who jokes; a jester. [a fish.
Jōle, *n.* The cheek; head of
Jŏl'li-ty, *n.* Noisy mirth.
Jŏl'ly, *a.* Merry; gay; lively.
Jŏlt (18), *v.* To shake with jerks. — *n.* A sudden shake.

Jŏs'tle (jŏs'l), v. t. To run against and shake.
Jŏt, n. An iota; a tittle. — v. t. To make a note of.
Joûr'nal, n. An account of daily transactions; a diary.
Joûr'nal-ĭsm, n. Profession of editing or writing for journals.
Joûr'nal-ist, n. One who keeps a journal. [journal.
Joûr'nal-īze, v. t. To enter in a
Joûr'ney (141), n. Travel by land; passage; excursion. — v. i. To travel by land.
Joûr'ney-man (143), n. A hired workman.
Joûst, n. A tournament; a mock encounter on horseback.
Jō'vi-al, a. Merry; jolly; gay.
Jōwl. See Jole.
Jōwl'er, or Jowl'er, n. A hunting-dog, or other dog.
Joy (136), n. Gladness; exultation. — v. i. or t. To rejoice; to be or make glad.
Joy'fŭl, a. Full of joy; glad.
Joy'fŭl-ly, adv. With joy.
Joy'fŭl-ness, n. Great joy.
Joy'less, a. Void of joy.
Joy'oŭs, a. Glad; merry; cheerful. [gladness.
Joy'oŭs-ly, adv. With joy or
Joy'oŭs-ness, n. State of being joyous.
Jū'bĭ-lant, a. Uttering songs of triumph.
Jū'bĭ-lee, n. A periodical festivity; season of joy.
Ju-dā'ic, } a. Pertaining
Ju-dā'ic-al, } to the Jews.
Jū'da-ĭsm, n. Religion of the Jews; Jewish tenets and rites.
Jū'da-īze, v. t. To conform to the religious doctrine and rites of the Jews.
Jŭdge, n. One authorized to determine causes in court; one skilled in deciding. — SYN. Umpire; arbitrator; referee. — v. i. To compare facts and distinguish truth; to form an opinion; to pass sentence. — v. t. To hear and decide concerning a cause, a subject, or a party.
Jŭdge'ship, n. Office of a judge.
Jŭdg'ment (132), n. Sentence; opinion; discernment.
Jū'dĭ-ca-to-ry, n. A court of justice. — a. Dispensing justice.
Jū'dĭ-ca-tŭre, n. Power of distributing justice; jurisdiction.
Ju-dī'cial (-dĭsh'al), a. Per-

taining to courts of justice; inflicted as a penalty.
Ju-dī'cial-ly (-dĭsh'al-), adv. In the forms of justice.
Ju-dī'cĭ-a-ry (-dĭsh'ĭ-), a. Pertaining to courts of justice. — n. Courts of justice.
Ju-dī'cious (-dĭsh'us), a. Prudent; acting with judgment.
Ju-dī'cious-ly (-dĭsh'us-), adv. Wisely; prudently.
Jŭg, n. A vessel for liquors, with a protuberant belly.
Jŭg'gle, n. A trick by legerdemain. — v. i. To play tricks by slight of hand.
Jŭg'gler, n. One who juggles.
Jŭg'gler-y, n. Sleight of hand.
Jū'gu-lar, a. Belonging to the throat.
Jūice, n. Sap of vegetables; fluid part of animal substances.
Jūi'cĭ-ness, n. Abundance of juice; succulence.
Jūi'cy, a. Full of juice; succulent.
Jū'jūbe, n. A plant and its sweet pulpy fruit; a paste of gum-arabic sweetened.
Jū'lep, n. A liquor or sirup.
Ju-ly', n. Seventh month of the year.
Jŭm'ble, v. t. To mix confusedly. — n. A confused mixture; a small cake.
Jŭmp, v. i. To spring by raising both feet. — n. A leap with two feet, as by a man.
Jŭnc'tion, n. Act of joining.
Jŭnc'tŭre, n. A joining; critical point of time. [year.
Jūne, n. Sixth month of the
Jŭn'gle (jŭng'gl), n. A thick cluster of small trees.
Jūn'ior (jūn'yur), a. Younger; inferior. — n. One younger or of lower standing. [of being junior.
Jun-iŏr'ĭ-ty (-yŏr'-), n. State
Jū'nĭ-per, n. An evergreen cone-bearing shrub or tree.
Jŭnk, n. A Chinese ship; old ropes; hard, salt beef.

Junk.

Jŭnk'et, n. A private entertainment.
Jūn'to, n. (pl. Jŭn'tŏs.) [Sp., from Lat. junctus, joined.] A cabal; a faction.
Jū'pĭ-ter, n. A heathen deity; the largest of the planets.
Ju-rĭd'ic-al, a. Relating to a judge; used in courts of law.
Ju-rĭd'ic-al-ly, adv. With legal authority or forms.
Jū'ris-cŏn'sult, n. A man learned in the law; a jurist.
Jū'ris-dĭc'tion, n. Legal authority, or the space over which it extends.
Jū'ris-dĭc'tion-al, a. According to legal authority.
Jū'ris-pru'dençe, n. Science of law.
Jū'rist, n. One versed in the law; a civil lawyer.
Jū'ror } (140, 143), n. One
Jū'ry-man } who serves on a jury.
Jū'ry, n. A body of men selected and sworn to investigate matters of fact and decide according to the evidence in court.
Jū'ry-mast, n. A temporary mast.
Jŭst, a. Appropriate or suitable; conformed to truth. — SYN. Exact; accurate; equitable; fair; deserved. — adv. Closely; nicely; exactly; barely. — n. A mock encounter on horseback.
Jŭs'tĭçe (54), n. The giving to every one his due; a civil officer.
Jŭs-tī'cĭ-a-ry (-tĭsh'-), n. One who administers justice.
Jŭs'tĭ-fī'a-ble, a. Capable of being justified; defensible.
Jŭs'tĭ-fī'a-bly, adv. So as to be justified.
Jŭs'tĭ-fĭ-cā'tion, n. Act of justifying; vindication.
Jŭs'tĭ-fĭ-cā'to-ry, a. Tending to justify; vindicatory.
Jŭs'tĭ-fy, v. t. To prove to be just; to absolve from guilt.
Jŭst'ly, adv. Equitably; honestly. [truth.
Jŭst'ness, n. Conformity to
Jŭt, v. i. To shoot out or project.
Jū've-nĕs'çent, a. Becoming young. [ful.
Jū've-nĭle, a. Young; youthful.
Jū've-nĭl'ĭ-ty, n. Youthfulness; the manners or customs of youth.
Jŭx'ta-po-sĭ'tion (-zĭsh'un), n. Nearness in place.

K.

Kāle, *n.* A kind of cabbage.

Ka-lei'do-scōpe, *n.* An optical instrument which exhibits an infinite variety of beautiful colors and forms.

Kăl'mi-à, *n.* [Named for *Peter Kalm.*] An evergreen shrub having showy flowers.

Kăn'ga-rōō', *n.* A singular quadruped found in Australia.

Kangaroo.

Kā'o-lin, *n.* A kind of clay of which porcelain is made.

Kĕdge, *n.* A small anchor.

Keel, *n.* Bottom timber of a ship from stem to stern.

Keel'haul, *v. t.* To haul under the keel as a punishment.

Kĕel'son (kĕl'sun), *n.* A piece of timber laid on the floor timbers of a ship.

Keen, *a.* Eager; sharp; penetrating; piercing; acute.

Keen'ly, *adv.* In a keen manner; sharply; bitterly.

Keen'ness (106), *n.* The quality of being keen.

Keep, *v. t.* [*imp. & p. p.* KEPT.] To preserve; to save; to hold. — *v. i.* To stay; to endure; to dwell — *n.* A stronghold; support.

Keep'er, *n.* One who keeps or preserves; a custodian.

Keep'ing, *n.* Custody; care.

Keep'sāke, *n.* A token of remembrance; a souvenir.

Kĕg, *n.* A small cask.

Kĕlp, *n.* Calcined ashes of sea-weed, used for making glass.

Kĕn, *v. t.* To see; to descry; to know. — *n.* Reach of sight; cognizance.

Kĕn'nel (130), *n.* A cot for dogs; a pack of hounds. — *v. t. or i.* (130) To lodge in a kennel.

Kĕpt, *imp. & p. p.* of *Keep.*

Kĕr'chief, *n.* A cloth to cover the head or neck.

Kĕrn, *n.* A vagabond; part of a type which overhangs the body, as the dot in the letter *i*.

Kĕr'nel, *n.* The substance in the shell of a nut; seed of a pulpy fruit; a grain. — *v. i.* To form into a kernel.

Kĕr'sey, *n.* A woolen cloth.

Kĕr'sey-mēre, *n.* A thin woolen cloth; cassimere.

Kĕtch, *n.* A kind of two-masted vessel.

Kĕt'tle, *n.* A metallic vessel for boiling water, &c.

Kĕt'tle-drŭm, *n.* A kettle-shaped metallic drum covered with parchment.

Kettle-drum.

Key (141), *n.* An instrument to fasten and open locks; a quay; a ledge of rocks near the surface of water; an explanatory index.

Key'stōne, *n.* The top-stone of an arch.

Kick, *n.* Blow with the foot. — *v.* To strike with the foot.

Kid, *n.* A young goat.

Kĭd'nap (130), *v. t.* To steal and secrete, as persons.

Kĭd'nap-er, } *n.* One who
Kĭd'nap-per, } steals a human being.

Kĭd'ney (141), *n.* That part of the viscera which secretes the urine; sort; kind. [rel.

Kĭl'der-kin, *n.* A small barrel.

Kĭll (123), *v. t.* To slay; to destroy; to deprive of life.

Kĭln (kĭl), *n.* A fabric for drying or burning any thing.

Kiln'-dry (kĭl'-), *v. t.* To dry in a kiln.   [petticoat.

Kĭlt, *n.* A Highlander's short

Kĭm'bo, *a.* Bent; crooked.

Kĭn, *n.* Kindred; relation; thing related. — *a.* Of the same nature or kind.

Kīnd (69), *a.* Having, or showing, a humane disposition. — SYN. Benevolent; gracious; mild; indulgent. — *n.* A genus; race; sort.

Kīn'dle, *v. t.* To set on fire. — *v. i.* To ignite; to take fire.

Kīnd'li-ness, *n.* Affectionate disposition; benevolence.

Kīnd'ly, *adv.* With good will. — *a.* Mild; favorable.

Kīnd'ness, *n.* Sympathizing benevolence; goodness; favor.

Kĭn'dred, *n.* People related

to each other; relatives. — *a.* Allied by birth.

Kīne, *n.* Old *pl.* of *Cow.*

Kīne'pŏx, *n.* The vaccine disease.   [foreign.

Kĭng, *n.* A monarch; a sovereign.

King'dŏm, *n.* Territory subject to a king; a region; a division in natural history.

King'fĭsh-er, *n.* A bird living on fresh-water fish.

Kingfisher.

King'ly, *a.* Royal; regal;

King'-pōst, *n.* A beam in the frame of a roof.

King's'-ē'vĭl, *n.* Scrofula.

King'wom-an (143), *n.* A female relation.

Kĭnk, *n.* The twist of a rope spontaneously formed. — *v. t.* or *i.* To twist into a kink.

Kĭns'fŏlk (-fōk), *n.* Relations.

Kĭns'man (143), *n.* A relation.

Kĭp'per, *n.* A salmon in a state of spawning.

Kĭp'-skĭn, *n.* Leather prepared from the skin of young cattle.

Kĭrk, *n.* The church, as in Scotland.

Kĭr'tle, *n.* A short jacket.

Kĭss (124), *n.* A salute with the lips. — *v. t.* To salute with the lips.

Kĭt, *n.* A wooden tub; an outfit, as of tools, &c., or that which contains it; a small violin.   [cooking.

Kĭtch'en (55), *n.* A room for

Kīte, *n.* A rapacious bird of the hawk kind; a toy for flying.

Kite.

Kĭt'ten, *n.* The young of a cat.

Knăb (năb), *v. t.* To seize with the teeth; to lay hold of; to nab.

Knăck (năk), *n.* Dexterity.

Knăg (năg), *n.* A knot in wood; a peg.   [rough.

Knăg'gy (năg'-), *a.* Knotty;

sĕn, ôr, dọ, wọlf, tọō, tọŏk; ûrn, rụe, pỵll; ç, ġ, *soft;* c, g, *hard;* aᶻ; exist; ṇ *as* ng; this

KNAPSACK 182 LAMB

Knăp'sack (năp'-); n. A soldier's sack.
Knär (när), n. A knot in wood.
Knärl (närl),
Knāve (nāv), n. [A.-S. cnafa, a boy, lad, servant, rogue.] A dishonest person; a rascal.
Knāv'er-y (nāv'-), n. Dishonesty; petty villainy.
Knāv'ish (nāv'-), a. Dishonest; rascally; fraudulent.
Knēad (nēed), v. t. To work and mix with the hands.
Knee (nee), n. The joint between the leg and thigh.
Kneel (neel), v. i. [imp. & p. p. KNELT or KNEELED.] To fall on the knees.
Knell (nĕl), n. Sound of a bell, rung at a funeral or death.
Knee'-păn (nee'-), n. The round bone of the knee.
Knew (nū), imp. of Know.
Knĭck'knăck (nĭk'năk), n. A trifle or toy.
Knīfe (nīf, 142), n. An instrument for cutting, usually having a steel blade.

Knīght (nīt), n. A title. — v. t. To dub a knight.
Knīght'-ĕr'rant (nīt'-, 146), n. A roving knight.
Knīght-ĕr'rant-ry (nīt-), n. Practice of wandering in quest of adventures, as a knight-errant.
Knīght'hōōd (nīt'-), n. The dignity of a knight.
Knīght'ly (nīt'-), a. Pertaining to, or becoming, a knight.
Knĭt (nĭt), v. t. [imp. & p. p. KNIT, KNITTED.] To unite as threads by means of needles; to join closely.
Knĭt'ting-nee'dle (nĭt'-), n. A needle used for knitting.
Knŏb (nŏb), n. A knot; a protuberance; a bunch.
Knŏck (nŏk, 127), v. i. or t. To hit; to strike; to dash. — n. A blow; a dashing; a rap.
Knŏck'er (nŏk'er), n. A hammer to rap on a door.
Knōll (nōl), n. A little hill.
Knŏt (nŏt), n. A tie; joint of a plant; bond of union. — v. t. To form knots in.

Knŏt'ted (nŏt'-), a. Full of knots; intricate.
Knŏt'ty
Knout (nowt or nōōt), n. A Russian instrument of punishment; a kind of whip.
Knōw (nō), v. t. [imp. KNEW; p. p. KNOWN.] To understand; to perceive; to recognize.
Knōw'a-ble (nō'-), a. Capable of being known.
Knŏwl'edge (nŏl'ej), n. Clear perception; truth ascertained; information; cognizance; learning. [Know.
Known (nōn), p. p. from
Knŭck'le (nŭk'l), n. A joint of the finger; the knee-joint of a calf. — v. i. To submit in a contest.
Knurl (nŭrl), n. A knot.
Knŭrl'y (nŭrl'-), a. Knotty.
Kō'ran, n. The Mohammedan book of faith.
Ky'an-īze, v. t. [From Kyan, the inventor.] To prevent from rotting, as wood, by the use of corrosive sublimate.

L.

L A (law), interj. Look; behold.
Lā'bel, n. A slip of paper, &c., containing a name or title, fastened to any thing; contents. — v. t. (130) To affix a label to.
Lā'bi-al, a. Pertaining to, or formed by, the lips. — n. A letter uttered with the lips.
Lā'bi-āte, a. Having parts resembling lips.
Lā'bor (155), n. Work; toil; travail. — v. i. or t. (130) To work; to work at; to toil.
Lăb'o-ra-to-ry, n. A place for chemical operations.
Lā'bor-er, n. A workman.
La-bō'ri-oŭs, a. Diligent in work; requiring labor.
La-bō'ri-oŭs-ly, adv. With great toil.
Lăb'y-rĭnth, n. A place full of windings. — SYN. Maze.
Lăc (127), n. A resinous substance.
Lāce (140), n. Work composed of fine threads; a plaited string. — v. t. To fasten or trim with lace. [tear.
Lăç'er-āte, v. t. To rend; to

Lăç'er-ā'tion, n. Act of tearing; a rent.
Lăç'er-ā'tĭve, a. Tending, or having power, to tear. [tears.
Lăch'ry-mal, a. Generating
Lăch'ry-ma-to-ry, n. A vessel for collecting tears in.
Lăck, v. t. or i. To need; to want. — n. Want; need; failure. [edly pensive.
Lăck'a-dāi'sĭc-al, a. Affect-
Lăck'ey (141), n. A footman. — v. t. To attend, as a footman.
La-cŏn'ĭc, a. Brief; pithy; concise. [cisely.
La-cŏn'ĭc-al-ly, adv. Con-
Lā'con-ĭsm, n. A brief,
La-cŏn'i-çĭsm, pithy phrase or expression.
Lăc'quer (lăk'er), n. A kind of varnish. — v. t. To varnish.
Lăc'te-al, a. Pertaining to milk or chyle. — n. One of the vessels of the body that convey chyle.
Lac-tĕs'çent, a. Producing milk or a white juice.
Lac-tĭf'er-oŭs, a. Conveying milk.
Lăd, n. A boy; a young man.

Lăd'der, n. A frame with round steps; gradual rise.
Lāde, v. t. [imp. LADED; p. p. LADED, LADEN.] To load; to throw out with a dipper.
Lād'ing, n. Load; cargo.
Lā'dle, n. A dipper with a handle; a kind of deep spoon.
Lā'dy (141), n. [A. S. hlafdige, lit. bread-keeper.] A mistress; a well-bred woman; a title of respect. [lady.
Lā'dy-shĭp (135), n. Title of a
Lăg (129), v. i. To move slowly; to stay behind. — SYN. To linger; loiter; delay.
La-gōōn', n. A shallow lake.
Lā'ĭc, a. Pertaining to a layman, or to the laity. [Lay.
Lāid (136), imp. & p. p. of
Lāin, p. p. of Lie.
Lāir, n. Couch of a wild beast
Lāird, n. In Scotland, a lord, or a landed proprietor.
Lā'i-ty, n. The people, as distinct from the clergy.
Lāke, n. A body of water surrounded by land; a red color.
Lămb (lăm), n. A young sheep. — v. i. To bring forth lambs.

ā, ē, ī, ō, ū, ў, long; ă, ĕ, ĭ, ŏ, ŭ, ў, short; câre, cär, àsk, ạll, whạt; ēre, veil, tẽrm; pīque, fĭrm;

LAMBENT 183 LATENT

Lăm'bent, *a.* Playing over the surface. (young lamb.
Lămb'kin (lăm'kin), *n.* A
Lăme, *a.* Disabled in a limb; crippled; imperfect. — *v. t.* To make lame; to cripple.
†**La-měl'lă,** *n.* A very thin plate or scale.
Lăm'el-lar, *a.* Formed in thin plates or scales.
Lăme'ly, *adv.* In a lame or crippled manner; imperfectly. [lame.
Lăme'ness, *n.* State of being
La-mĕnt', *v. t.* or *i.* To weep; to mourn; to bewail. [ful.
Lăm'ent-a-ble, *a.* Mournfully; with sorrow.
Lăm'ent-a-bly, *adv.* Mournfully; with sorrow.
Lăm'en-tā'tion, *n.* Expression of sorrow.
†**Lăm'i-nă,** *n. (pl.* **Lăm'i-næ,** 147.) A thin plate or scale lying over another.
Lăm'i-nar, *a.* Consisting of thin plates or scales.
Lăm'i-nā'ted, *a.* Laminar.
Lăm'mas (139), *n.* The first day of August.
Lămp, *n.* A vessel with oil and a wick, for giving light.
Lămp'-blăck, *n.* A fine soot from the smoke of resinous substances.
Lam-pōon', *n.* A personal satire. — *v. t.* To abuse with satire. [an eel.
Lăm'prey (141), *n.* A fish like
Lănce, *n.* A long spear. — *v. t.* To pierce with or as with a lance.
Lăn'çet, *n.* A surgical instrument to let blood.
Lănch, *v. t.* To cast; to dart.
Lănd, *n.* Earth; ground; country; region; soil; an estate. — *v. t.* To put on shore. — *v. i.* To come or go on shore.
Lăn'dau, *n.* A kind of coach with a top to be thrown back.
Lănd'ed, *a.* Having land; consisting in land. [of land.
Lănd'-hōld'er, *n.* An owner
Lănd'ing, *n.* A place to land on; top of a flight of stairs.
Lănd'lā-dy, *n.* Mistress of an inn or lodging-house; a woman who owns houses occupied by tenants.
Lănd'lŏcked (-lŏkt), *p. a.* Inclosed by land.
Lănd'lŏrd, *n.* Lord or owner of land; master of an inn or lodging-house; owner of houses having tenants.
Lănd'märk, *n.* Mark of bounds to land; an elevated object on land serving as a guide to ships at sea.
Lănd'-ŏf'fiçe, *n.* Office for the disposal of public lands.
Lănd'seāpe, *n.* Prospect or picture of a portion of country.
Lănd'-slide, } *n.* A portion of
Lănd'-slip, } land sliding down a mountain.
Lăndş'man (143), *n.* One who lives on the land; a sailor serving for the first time at sea. [traveling
Lāne, *n.* A narrow passage for
Lăn'grage, } *n.* A kind of
Lăn'grel, } shot for tearing sails and rigging.
Lăn'guage, *n.* [Low Lat. *langagium,* from Lat. *lingua,* tongue.] Human speech; tongue; dialect; style or expression of ideas or feelings.
Lăn'guid (lăng'gwĭd, 99), *a.* Weak; faint; feeble.
Lăn'guid-ly, *adv.* Faintly; weakly; feebly.
Lăn'guish, *v. i.* To droop; to become weak or dull.
Lăn'guish-ment, *n.* State of languishing.
Lăn'guor (lăng'gwor), *n.* Faintness; lassitude.
La-nĭf'er-oŭs, *a.* Producing wool. [and slender.
Lănk, *a.* Loose or lax; weak
Lănk'ness, *n.* State of being lank; want of flesh.
Lăn'tern, *n.* A transparent case for a candle. [of rope.
Lăn'yard, *n.* A short piece
Lăp (140), *n.* The loose part of a coat; part of a dress that covers the knees. — *v. t.* (129) To lay over or on; to lick.
Lăp'-dŏg, *n.* A small dog fondled in the lap. [laps over.
La-pĕl', *n.* Part of a coat that
Lăp'i-da-ry, *n.* One who cuts and polishes precious stones. — *a.* Pertaining to the art of cutting stones.
Lăp'i-dĕs'çençe, *n.* A hardening into stone; a stony concretion. [stone.
Lăp'i-dĕs'çent, *a.* Turning to
La-pĭd'i-fȳ, *v. t.* To form into stone. — *v. i.* To become stone or stony.
Lăp'pet, *n.* Part of a garment hanging loose.
Lăpse, *v. i.* To slip; to slide; to fall to another. — *n.* A slip; a fall; a passing.
Lăp'stōne, *n.* A stone on which shoemakers beat leather.
Lăp'wing, *n.* A wading bird.
Lär'board (lär'burd), *n.* Lefthand side of a ship when facing the head. [theft.
Lär'çe-ny, *n.* Theft; petty
Lärch, *n.* A deciduous cone-bearing tree.
Lärd, *n.* The fat of swine. — *v. t.* To stuff or mix with lard.
Lärd'er, *n.* Larch.
A place where meat is kept.
Lärge, *a.* Of great size; bulky; wide; liberal; copious.
Lärge'ly, *adv.* Extensively.
Lärge'ness, *n.* Great size.
Lär'gess, *n.* A gift; a present.
Lärk, *n.* A singing bird; a frolic. [showy flowers.
Lärk'spur, *n.* A plant with
Lär'va (147), *n.* An insect in the caterpillar state.
Lär'um, *n.* An alarm.
Lăr'ynx, *n.* Upper part of the windpipe. [lewd.
Las-çĭv'i-oŭs, *a.* Wanton;
Las-çĭv'i-oŭs-ly, *adv.* In a lascivious manner.
Las-çĭv'i-oŭs-ness, *n.* Wantonness; lustfulness.
Lăsh (140), *n.* Thong of a whip; a cut. — *v. t.* To strike with a lash; to satirize.
Lăss (124), *n.* A young maiden.
Lăs'si-tūde, *n.* Languor of body; weariness.
Lăs'so (140), *n.* A rope with a noose, for catching wild horses, &c.
Lăst, *a.* Latest; hindmost. — *v. i.* To continue; to endure. — *v. t.* Form on or with a last. — *adv.* In the last place. — *n.* A form to shape a shoe on.
Lăst'ing, *a.* Continuing long; durable. — *n.* A durable kind of woolen stuff.
Lăst'ly, *adv.* In the last place; at last.
Lătch (140), *n.* A catch for a door. — *v. t.* To fasten with a latch. [shoe.
Lătch'et, *n.* A fastening for a
Lāte, *a.* Coming after the time; recent, or recently deceased. — *adv.* Far in the day or night; long delayed.
Lāte'ly, *adv.* Not long ago.
Lā'ten-çy, *n.* State of being concealed. [late.
Lāte'ness, *n.* State of being
Lā'tent, *a.* Hidden; secret.

sŏn, ôr, dọ, wọlf, tōō, tŏŏk; ûrn, ryẹ, pụll; ç, ġ, soft; e, ġ, *hard;* aş; ex̧ist; ɳ *as* ng; *this.*

LATERAL — 184 — LEATHER

Lăt'er-al, *a.* Pertaining to, or proceeding from, the side.

Lăt'er-al-ly, *adv.* On one side; by the side.

Lăth, *n.* (*pl.* **Lăths,** 96.) A thin strip of wood to support plaster. — *v. t.* To cover with laths.

Lāthe, *n.* A turner's machine for turning wood, ivory, &c.

Lăth'er, *n.* Froth of soap and water; sweat. — *v. t.* To spread over with lather. — *v. i.* To become foam.

Lĭth'y, *a.* Thin as a lath.

Lăt'in, *a.* Pertaining to the Roman language. — *n.* Language of the ancient Romans.

Lăt'in-ĭṣm, *n.* A Latin idiom.

Lạ-tĭn'i-ty, *n.* Latin style.

Lăt'in-ize, *v. t.* To turn into Latin.

Lăt'ish, *a.* Somewhat late.

Lăt'i-tūdẹ (118), *n.* Distance from the equator; breadth.

Lăt/i-tū'di-nal, *a.* In the direction of latitude.

Lăt/i-tū'di-nā'ri-an, *n.* One who indulges freedom in thinking. — *a.* Unrestrained; lax in religious views.

Lăt/i-tū'di-nā'ri-an-ĭṣm, *n.* Laxity in religious principles or views.

Lā'trant, *a.* Barking.

Lăt'ten (55), *n.* Iron plate covered with tin.

Lăt'ter. *a.* The last of two.

Lăt'ter-ly, *adv.* Of late; lately; recently.

Lăt'tiçẹ, *n.* [Fr. *lattis*, lath-work, from *latte*, lath.] A kind of net-work of cross-bars. — *v. t.* To form with cross-bars.

Lŭd, *n.* Commendation; praise in worship. — *v. t.* To praise; to extol.

Laud'a-ble, *a.* Praiseworthy.

Laud'a-bly, *adv.* So as to deserve praise.

Lau'da-num, *n.* Opium dissolved in spirit or wine.

Laud'a-to-ry, *a.* Containing or bestowing praise.

Laugh (lăf), *v. i.* To manifest mirth by a chuckling of the voice. — *n.* An audible expression of mirth.

Laugh'a-ble (lăf-a-bl), *a.* Capable of exciting laughter.

Laugh'ing-stŏck, *n.* An object of ridicule.

Laugh'ter (lăf'ter), *n.* Convulsive expression of mirth.

Launch (lănch), *v. t.* To cause to slide into water; to dispatch. — *v. i.* To expatiate.

— *n.* The sliding of a ship into water. [woman.

Laun'dress, *n.* A washer-

Laun'dry, *n.* A place where clothes are washed.

Lau're-ate, *a.* Invested with a laurel wreath.

Lau'rel, *n.* The bay-tree; an evergreen shrub.

Lā'vā, or **Lä'vä,** *n.* Melted matter flowing from a volcano.

Lăv'a-to-ry, *n.* A place for washing; a wash or lotion.

Lāve, *v. t.* To wash; to bathe.

Lăv'en-der, *n.* An aromatic plant with grayish-blue flowers. [ing.

Lā'ver, *n.* A vessel for wash-

Lăv'ish, *a.* Expending with wasteful profusion. — SYN. Prodigal; wasteful. — *v. t.* To expend profusely; to squander; to waste.

Lăv'ish-ly, *adv.* With wasteful profusion.

Lăv'ish-ness, *n.* Prodigality.

Law, *n.* Rule of action or motion; statute; decree; edict.

Law'ful (38), *a.* Conformable to law; legal; rightful.

Law'ful-ly, *adv.* Legally.

Law'ful-ness, *n.* Legality.

Law'-ġiv'er, *n.* A legislator.

Law'less, *a.* Not restrained by, or contrary to, law.

Law'less-ly, *adv.* In a lawless manner.

Law'less-ness, *n.* Quality or state of being lawless.

Lawn, *n.* An open, grassy space; a sort of fine linen.

Law'sụit, *n.* A process in law; an action.

Law'yer, *n.* One who is versed in, or who practices, law; an attorney.

Lăx, *a.* Loose; vague; slack.

Lăx'a-tive, *a.* Having the quality of relieving costiveness. — *n.* A medicine that relaxes the bowels. [ness.

Lăx'i-ty, *n.* Slackness; loose-

Lay (133), *v. t.* [*imp.* & *p. p.* LAID.] To put; to wager; to produce eggs. — *n.* A song; a stratum; a row. — *a.* Pertaining to the laity.

Lay'er, *n.* A stratum; a bed; a sprig. [clergyman.

Lay'man (143), *n.* One not a

Lā'zar, *n.* A person with a pestilential disease.

Lăz'a-rĕt'to, *n.* A pest-house for diseased persons.

Lā'zi-ly, *adv.* In a lazy manner; slothfully.

Lā'zi-ness (135), *n.* Habitual inactivity; sloth.

Lā'zy, *a.* Slothful; sluggish.

Lēa, *n.* A meadow; a plain.

Leach, *v. t.* To wash, as ashes, by percolation. — *n.* Wood-ashes washed by percolation of water.

Lēad, *n.* A soft metal. — *v. t.* To cover with lead; to separate, as lines in printing.

Lēad, *v. t.* or *i.* [*imp.* & *p. p.* LED.] To go before; to guide; to pass. — *n.* Guidance; direction.

Lēad'en (lĕd'n), *a.* Consisting of lead; dull.

Lēad'er, *n.* One who leads.

Lēaf (142), *n.* Part of a plant, or something resembling it; part of a book; one side of a double door. — *v. i.* To put forth leaves.

Lēaf'i-ness, *n.* State of being full of leaves. [leaves.

Lēaf'less, *a.* Destitute of

Lēaf'let, *n.* A little leaf.

Lēaf'y, *a.* Full of leaves.

Lēague (lēeg), *n.* Alliance of states; three miles. — SYN. Confederacy; compact, coalition; union. — *v. i.* To unite in a confederacy.

Lēak, *n.* A crack or hole that admits a fluid to pass. — *v. i.* To let a fluid in or out.

Lēak'aġe, *n.* A leaking; allowance for waste by leaking.

Lēak'y, *a.* Letting a fluid in or out; apt to leak.

Lēan, *a.* Wanting flesh or fat; thin; slender. — *n.* Flesh without fat. — *v. i.* To incline; to bend.

Lēan'ness, *n.* Want of flesh.

Lēap, *v. i.* To spring; to bound; to jump. — *n.* A jump; a bound; a skip.

Lēap'-yẽar, *n.* Every fourth year, which has one day more than other years.

Lẽarn, *v.* To gain knowledge or skill. [ing.

Lẽarn'ed (57), *a.* Having learn-

Lẽarn'er, *n.* One who is acquiring knowledge.

Lẽarn'ing, *n.* Knowledge acquired by study; erudition.

Lēase, *n.* A letting for hire. — *v. t.* To let for use by hire.

Lēase'hōld, *n.* A tenure held by lease. — *a.* Held by lease.

Lĕash, *n.* A leather thong; three creatures of any kind; a band.

Lēast, *a.* Smallest. — *adv.* In the smallest degree.

Lĕath'er, *n.* Hide of an an-

LEATHERN 185 LETHAL

Imal dressed and prepared for use.

Leath'ern, *a.* Made of leather.

Leath'er-y, *a.* Like leather.

Leave, *n.* Liberty granted; a parting visit. — SYN. Permission; license.—*v. t.* [*imp. & p. p.* LEFT.] To quit; to forsake; to bequeath.

Leav'en (lěv'n), *n.* A mass of sour dough for making other dough light. — *v. t.* To raise and make light.

Leaves, *n.; pl.* of *Leaf*.

Leav'ings, *n. pl.* Things left.

Lěch'er, *n.* A man given to lewdness and debauchery.

Lěch'er-oŭs, *a.* Lustful.

Lěch'er-y, *n.* Lewdness; free indulgence of lust.

Lěc'tion, *n.* A reading.

Lěct'ūre, *n.* A discourse; a formal reproof.—*v. t.* To read lectures; to reprove. [ures.

Lěct'ūr-er, *n.* One who lect-

Lěd, *imp. & p. p.* of *Lead*.

Lŏdge, *n.* A shelf; a ridge of rocks; a small molding.

Lědg'er, *n.* A chief book of accounts. [wind.

Lee, *n.* Side opposite to the

Leech (40), *n.* A blood-sucking worm; a physician.

Leek, *n.* A plant with edible leaves.

Leer, *n.* An oblique or affected look. — *v. i.* (130) To look obliquely. [of liquor.

Lees, *n. pl.* Dregs; sediment

Lee'-shōre, *n.* The shore toward which the wind blows.

Lee'ward (*colloq.,* lū'ard), *adv.* Toward the lee.— *a.* Relating to the part on the lee.

Lee'wāy, *n.* Movement toward the lee.

Lĕft, *imp. & p. p.* of *Leave*. — *a.* Opposite to the right.

Lĕft'-hănd'ed, *a.* Using the left hand with most skill.

Lĕg, *n.* A limb to support the body or other thing.

Lĕg'a-cy, *n.* A bequest by will.

Lē'gal, *a.* [Lat. *legalis*, from *lex, legis,* law.] According to law; permitted by law.

Le-găl'i-ty, *n.* Lawfulness.

Lē'gal-īze, *v. t.* To make lawful; to authorize. [law.

Lē'gal-ly, *adv.* According to

Lĕg'ate, *n.* An embassador or envoy. [a legacy.

Lĕg'a-tee', *n..* One who has

Le-gā'tion, *n.* An embassy; suite of an embassador.

Lĕg'a-tôr', *n.* One who bequeaths or leaves a legacy.

Lĕg'-bāil, *n.* A clandestine running away; flight.

Lĕ'gend, or Lĕg'end, *n.* A remarkable story; inscription; motto.

Lĕg'end-a-ry, *a.* Traditional; fabulous. [of hand.

Lĕg'er-de-māin', *n.* Sleight

Lĕg'er-līne, *n.* (*Music.*) A line above or under the staff.

Lĕg'gin, } *n.* A covering for
Lĕg'ging, } the leg.

Lĕg'i-bĭl'i-ty, *n.* State or quality of being legible.

Lĕg'i-ble, *a.* Capable of being read. [be read.

Lĕg'i-bly, *adv.* So that it can

Lē'gion, *n.* A body of footsoldiers; a military force; a multitude; a vast number.

Lē'gion-a-ry, *a.* Pertaining to legions. — *n.* One of a legion.

Lĕg'is-lāte, *v. i.* To make laws. [making laws.

Lĕg'is-lā'tion, *n.* Act of

Lĕg'is-lā'tive, *a.* Pertaining to the enactment of laws.

Lĕg'is-lā'tor, *n.* One who makes laws; a lawgiver.

Lĕg'is-lā'tūre, *n.* A body of men having authority to make laws. [ness.

Le-gĭt'i-ma-cy, *n.* Lawful-

Le-gĭt'i-mate, *a.* Lawful; lawfully begotten; genuine.

Le-gĭt'i-māte, *v. t.* To make lawful. [fully.

Le-gĭt'i-mate-ly, *adv.* Law-

Le-gĭt'i-mā'tion, *n.* Act of rendering legitimate.

Le-gĭt'i-mĭst, *n.* One who supports lawful authority or hereditary rights.

Lŏg'ūme, or Le-gūme', *n.* A pod splitting into two valves; (*pl.*) pulse; peas, beans, &c.

Le-gū'mi-noŭs, *a.* Consisting of pulse.

Leis'ūre (lē'zhụr), *n.* Freedom from occupation.— *a.* Deliberate; slow; unoccupied.

Leis'ūre-ly, *adv.* Slowly; deliberately.— *a.* Deliberate; slow.

Lĕm'mȧ, *n.* An auxiliary and previously demonstrated proposition.

Lĕm'on, *n.* An acid fruit and the tree that bears it.

Lĕm'on-āde', *n.* Sugar, water, and lemon-juice mixed.

Lĕnd, *v. t.* [*imp. & p. p.* LENT.] To grant on condition of receiving the thing again or an equivalent.

Lĕngth, *n.* Extent from end to end; extension.

Lĕngth'en (lĕngth'n), *v. t.* To make longer —*v. i.* To grow longer.

Lĕngth'wīse, *adv.* In direction of the length.

Lĕngth'y, *n.* Somewhat long.

Lē'ni-en-cy, *n.* Lenity.

Lē'ni-ent, *a.* Mild; merciful.

Lĕn'i-tĭve, *a.* Assuasive; easing; softening.

Lĕn'i-ty, *n.* Mildness; mercy.

Lĕns, *n.* A glass by which rays of light are changed in direction, and objects are magnified and diminished.

Lĕnt, *imp. & p. p.* of *Lend.* — *n.* [Lenses.
The time of fasting forty days before Easter.

Len-tĭc'u-lar, *a.* Having the form of a lens.

Lĕn'til, *n.* A plant sometimes used as food.

Lē'o-nīne, *a.* Having the qualities of a lion.

Lĕop'ard (lĕp'-), *n.* A spotted wild beast of India and Africa. [Leopard.

Lĕp'er, *n.* One who is infected with leprosy.

Lĕp'o-rīne (*or* -rĭn), *a.* Pertaining to a hare.

Lĕp'ro-sy, *n.* (Gr. *lepros,* scaly.] A cutaneous disease, marked by scaly spots.

Lĕp'roŭs, *a.* Infected with leprosy.

Lē'sion, *n.* A hurt; an injury; a morbid change.

Lĕss, } *a.* Smaller; not so
Lĕss'er, } large.

Lĕss (124), *adv.* In a smaller degree.— *n.* A smaller portion; the younger or inferior.

Les-see', *n.* One to whom a lease is made.

Lĕss'en, *v. i. or t.* To diminish.

Lĕs'son, *n.* A portion of a book to be read or learned; reproof; rebuke. [lease.

Lĕs'sor, *n.* One who grants a

Lĕst, *conj.* That not, for fear that.

Lĕt, *v. t.* [*imp. & p. p.* LET.] To give leave; to permit; to allow; to lease.— *n.* Hindrance; delay; impediment.

Lē'thal, *a.* Mortal; deadly.

sŏn, ôr, dọ, wọlf, tọo, tọok; ûrn, rụe, pụll; ç, ġ, *soft*; c, ġ, *hard*; aᶻ; e̤xist; ŋ *as* ng; this.

Le-thär'gic, a. Unnaturally sleepy; drowsy.
Lĕth'ar-gy, n. Morbid or unnatural drowsiness; dullness.
Lē'the, n. Oblivion; death.
Le-thē'an, a. Inducing sleep or oblivion.
Le-thĭf'er-oŭs, a. Deadly; destructive; mortal.
Lĕt'ter, n. One who leases; a written message; an epistle; a printing type; (pl.) learning; literature. — v. t. To stamp with letters. [type.
Lĕt'ter-press, n. Print from 1 ŝt'tuçe (lĕt'tis), n. A plant used for salad.
Lĕ'vant, a. Eastern; oriental.
Le-vânt', n. The eastern countries along the Mediterranean.
Le-văn'tĭne, or Lĕv'an-tĭne, n. A kind of silk cloth.
Lĕv'ee, n. [Fr. levée, from lever, to rise.] Assembly of people on a morning or evening visit to a great personage; a bank of earth along a river.
Lĕv'el (130), a. Even; flat plain. — v. To make even to aim. — n. A plain; a flat surface; equality.
Lĕv'el-er } (130), n. One who
Lĕv'el-ler } levels.
Lē'ver, or Lĕv'-er, n. One of the mechanical powers. Lever.
Lĕv'i-a-ble, a. Capable of being levied.
Le-vī'a-than, n. A large sea-animal; the whale.
Lĕv'i-gā'tion, n. Reduction to a fine powder.
Lĕv'i-gāte, v. t. To reduce to powder; to polish.
Lē'vĭte, n. One of the tribe of Levi; an attendant on a Hebrew priest.
Le-vĭt'i-cal, a. Pertaining to the Levites.
Lĕv'i-ty, n. Lightness; want of seriousness; vanity; flightiness.
Lĕv'y, v. t. To raise; to collect, as an army. — n. Act of raising money or troops; a small coin worth 12½ cents.
Lewd (lūd), a. Given to the indulgence of lust; licentious; lecherous.
Lewd'ly, adv. Lustfully; licentiously.
Lewd'ness, n. Unlawful indulgence of lust; unchastity; lechery.
Lĕx'ic-al, a. Pertaining to a lexicon or to lexicography.
Lĕx'i-cŏg'ra-pher (117), n. The writer of a dictionary.
Lĕx'i-co-grăph'ic-al, a. Pertaining to lexicography.
Lĕx'i-cŏg'ra-phy, n. The art of composing dictionaries.
Lĕx'i-cŏl'o-gy, n. Science of the derivation and meaning of words.
Lĕx'i-con, n. A dictionary.
Lī'a-bĭl'i-ty, n. A state of being liable; responsibility; tendency.
Lī'a-ble, a. Exposed; responsible; subject.
Lī'ar, n. One who lies.
Lī-bā'tion, n. An offering of wine.
Lī'bel, n. A defamatory writing; a written statement of the cause of a legal action and of the relief sought. — v. t. (130). To defame by writing; to proceed against by filing a libel.
Lī'bel-ant, } n. One who
Lī'bel-lant, } brings a libel.
Lī'bel-er } (130), n. One who
Lī'bel-ler } libels.
Lī'bel-oŭs, } a. Defamatory.
Lī'bel-loŭs, }
Lĭb'er-al, a. Free in giving; generous; bountiful; candid.
Lĭb'er-ăl'i-ty, n. Generosity.
Lĭb'er-al-ĭze, v. t. To free from narrow views.
Lĭb'er-al-ly, adv. Generously.
Lĭb'er-āte, v. t. To set free.
Lĭb'er-ā'tion, n. A setting free; release. [free.
Lĭb'er-ā'tor, n. One who sets
Lĭb'er-tĭne, n. A dissolute man. — a. Licentious.
Lĭb'er-tin-ĭṣm, n. Licentiousness of doctrine or life.
Lĭb'er-ty, n. Freedom; permission; immunity.
Lī-bĭd'ĭ-noŭs, a. Lustful; lewd; licentious.
†Lī'bra, n. The Balance; a sign of the zodiac.
Lī-brā'ri-an, n. One who has charge of a library.
Lī'bra-ry, n. A collection of books; a place for books.
Lī'brāte, v. t. To balance.
Lī-brā'tion, n. Act of balancing. [balance.
Lī'bra-to-ry, a. Moving like a
Līçe. pl. of Louse.
Lī'çense. n. Permission; excess of liberty. — v. t. To permit by legal warrant; to authorize.

Lī-çĕn'tĭ-ate (-shĭ-āt), n. One who has a license to exercise a profession.
Lī-çĕn'tioŭs (-sĕn'shus), a. Loose in morals; dissolute.
Lī-çĕn'tioŭs-ness, n. Contempt of just restraint.
Lī'chen (or lĭch'en, 55), n. A cellular flowerless plant, of a scaly form.
Lĭck (127), v. t. To pass over with the tongue; to lap. — n. A stroke: a blow; a place where beasts lick for salt.
ĭck'er-ĭsh, a. Nice; delicate; dainty; tempting.
Līc'or-īçe, n. A plant and its sweet, medicinal root.
Lĭd, n. A cover.
Līe (lī, 134), n. A false statement uttered to deceive; a falsehood. — v. i. (134) To utter falsehood with intent to deceive. — v. t. [imp. LAY; p. p. LAIN] To rest horizontally; to lean; to remain.
Lĭef, adv. Willingly; gladly.
Liēġe, a. Bound by feudal tenure; sovereign. — n. A vassal; a lord or superior.
Lī'en (lē'en or lī'en), n. A legal claim.
Līĕu (lū), n. Stead; place.
Lieu-tĕn'an-çy (lu- or lef-), n. Office or commission of a lieutenant.
Lieu-tĕn'ant (lu- or lef-), n. [Fr. lieu, place, and tenant, holding.] A deputy; an officer next below a captain.
Lieve, adv. Willingly. See Lief.
Līfe (142), n. Vitality; existence; energy; spirit; animation; conduct; biography.
Līfe'-blŏod (-blŭd), n. Blood necessary to life.
Līfe' bōat, n. A boat rendered buoyant by air-tight chambers, &c. [guard.
Līfe'-guärd, n. A body
Līfe'less, a. Without life, spirit, or energy. — SYN. Dull; inanimate; dead.
Līfe'less-ly, adv. In a lifeless manner.
Lĭft, v. t. To raise; to elevate; to exalt. — n. Act of raising; that which is to be raised.
Lĭg'a-ment, n. Any thing which unites, esp. the bones.
Lĭg'a-mĕnt'oŭs, a. Composing, or of the nature of, a ligament.
Lī-gā'tion, n. Act of binding.
Lĭg'a-tūre, n. A band or bandage; two or more letters united, as fi.

ā, ē, ī, ō, ū, ȳ, long; ă, ĕ, ĭ, ŏ, ŭ, ȳ, short; cāre, cär, ȧsk, all, what; ēre, vêil, tĕrm; pīque, fīrm;

LIGHT 187 LITERAL

Light (lit), *n.* That by which we see; illumination; illustration; a candle, &c.; daytime. — *a.* Bright; clear; nimble; not heavy. — *v. t.* To illuminate; to kindle. — *v. i.* To come by chance; to dismount; to descend; to settle.

Light'en (lit'n), *v. i.* To flash with light; to grow less dark. — *v. t.* To make light; to alleviate.

Light'er (lit'-), *n.* One who lights; a large open boat for unloading vessels.

Light'-head'ed (lit'-), *a.* Delirious; volatile.

Light'-heart'ed (lit'-), *a.* Cheerful; gay.

Light'-horse (lit'-), *n.* Light-armed cavalry.

Light'-house (lit'-), *n.* A tower with a light to direct seamen.

Light'ly (lit'-), *adv.* Nimbly; with levity; easily.

Light'-mind'ed (lit'-), *a.* Volatile; unsteady.

Light'ness (lit'-), *n.* Brightness; want of weight; levity.

Light'ning (lit'-), *n.* A flash of electricity.

Lights (lits), *n. pl.* Lungs.

Light'some (lit'sum), *a.* Luminous; lively; cheering.

Lig'ne-ous, *a.* Wooden; resembling wood. [wood.

Lig'ni-form, *a.* Formed like

†**Lig'num-vi'tæ**, *n.* [Lat., wood of life.] A hard wood, used for wheels, &c.

Like, *a.* Equal; similar; probable. — *n.* That which resembles. — *adv.* In the same manner. — *v. t.* To be moderately pleased with; to approve; to enjoy. — *v. i.* To choose.

Like'li-hood, *n.* Probability.

Like'li-ness, *n.* Probability; qualities that please.

Like'ly, *a.* Probable. — *adv.* Probably.

Lik'en, *v. t.* To compare.

Like'ness, *n.* Resemblance.

Like'wise, *adv.* In like manner; moreover; also.

Lik'ing (133), *n.* Inclination; pleasure; desire.

Li'lac, *n.* A flowering shrub.

Lil'i-a'ceous, *a.* Pertaining to, or like, a lily.

Lil'i-pu'tian, *a.* Diminutive.

Lil'y, *n.* A beautiful flower

Limb (lim), *n.* An extremity of the body; a branch of a tree; an edge. — *v. t.* To dismember.

Lim'ber, *a.* Easily bent; flexible; pliant. — *n.* Forward part of a gun-carriage, to which the horses are attached. [pliancy.

Lim'ber-ness, *n.* Flexibility;

Lim'bo (140), *n.* The borders of hell; a place of restraint.

Lime, *n.* A calcareous earth; a tree; an acid fruit.

Lime'-kiln (-kil), *n.* A kiln for burning lime. [stone.

Lime'stone, *n.* A calcareous

Lim'it, *n.* A bound; border. — *v. t.* To set bounds to; to confine within certain bounds.

Lim'it-a-ble, *a.* Capable of being bounded.

Lim'it-a'tion, *n.* Act of limiting; that which limits; restriction. [infinite.

Lim'it-less, *a.* Without limit;

Limn (lim), *v. t.* To draw or paint. [er.

Lim'ner, *n.* A portrait painter.

Limp, *v. i.* To walk lamely.

Lim'pet, *n.* A small shell-fish.

Lim'pid, *a.* Transparent.

Limp'sy, *a.* Weak; flexible.

Lim'y, *a.* Containing lime.

Linch'-pin, *n.* A pin to keep a wheel on the axle-tree.

Lin'den, *n.* A kind of shade-tree.

Line, *n.* A string or cord; an extended mark; a row or rank; a course; business; a verse; a limit; the equator; the twelfth of an inch. — *v. t.* To cover or put on the inside of.

Lin'e-age, *n.* A race; descent.

Lin'e-al, *a.* Composed of lines; descending in a direct line. [line.

Lin'e-al-ly, *adv.* In a direct

Lin'e-a-ment, *n.* Outline; feature; form.

Lin'e-ar, *a.* Pertaining to, or consisting of, lines.

Lin'en, *a.* Made of flax or hemp. — *n.* Cloth of flax or hemp. [deals in linen.

Lin'en-dra'per, *n.* One who

Ling, *n.* A fish something like the cod.

Lin'ger, *v. i.* To remain long; to delay; to loiter.

Lin'ger-ing, *a.* Slow; tardy.

Lin'go, *n.* Language. [*Vulgar.*]

Lin'gual (ling'gwal), *a.* Pertaining to the tongue.

Lin'guist (ling'gwist), *n.* One skilled in languages.

Lin-guist'ic, *a.* Relating to the affinities of languages.

Lin'i-ment, *n.* A soft ointment. [inner surface.

Lin'ing, *n.* Covering of any

Link (79), *n.* One of the parts of a chain; a kind of torch. — *v. t.* To connect by links.

Lin'net, *n.* A small songbird.

Lin'seed, *n.* Seed of flax.

Lin'sey-wool'sey, *n.* Stuff made of linen and wool mixed.

Lin'stock, *n.* A cannoneer's staff to hold a match.

Lint, *n.* Soft scrapings of linen.

Lin'tel, *n.* Upper horizontal part of a door-frame, &c.

Li'on, *n.* A rapacious quadruped of Asia and Africa; an object of interest or curiosity.

Lion.

Li'on-ess, *n.* A female lion.

Lip, *n.* Border of the mouth; edge of any thing. [melting.

Liq'ue-fac'tion, *n.* Act of

Liq'ue-fi'a-ble, *a.* Capable of being melted.

Liq'ue-fy (-we-), *v. t.* or *i.* To make or become fluid.

Li-ques'cent, *a.* Dissolving.

Liq'uid (lik'wid), *a.* Flowing; fluid. — *n.* A flowing substance. [pay.

Liq'uid-ate, *v. t.* To adjust; to

Liq'uid-a'tion, *n.* Act of liquidating.

Li-quid'i-ty, } *n.* Quality of
Liq'uid-ness, } being liquid.

Liq'uor (lik'ur), *n.* A liquid; strong drink.

Lisp, *v. i.* To sound *s* and *z* as *th*; to speak imperfectly. — *n.* A defective articulation.

List, *v. t.* To enroll for service. — *v. i.* To hearken; to attend. — *n.* A roll; a strip of cloth.

List'el, *n.* A fillet; a little square molding.

List'en (lis'n, 93), *v. i.* To hear watchfully; to attend.

List'en-er (lis'n-), *n.* One who listens.

List'less, *a.* Heedless; careless; indifferent.

List'less-ly, *adv.* Without attention; heedlessly.

List'less-ness, *n.* Indifference to what is passing.

Lit'a-ny, *n.* A solemn form of supplication and prayer.

Lit'er-al, *a.* Word for word.

sŭn, ôr, dṇ, wọlf, tọọ, tọọk; ûrn, rụe, pụll; ç, ģ, *soft*; c, g, *hard*; ᴎ; ex̱ist; ɴ as ng; this.

LITERALLY — LOGICAL

Lit'er-al-ly, *adv.* With strict adherence to words.
Lit'er-a-ry, *a.* Relating to literature.
Lit'er-ate, *a.* Learned.
†Lit'er-ä'ti, *n. pl.* Men of letters; literary men.
Lit'er-a-tūre, *n.* Acquaintance with books; literary productions. — SYN. Learning; erudition.
Lith'arge, *n.* An oxide of lead.
Lithe, *a.* Easy to be bent; pliant; flexible; limber.
Lithe'ness, *n.* Flexibility.
Lith'o-gräph, *n.* [Gr. *lithos*, stone, and *graphein*, to write.] A print from a drawing on stone. — *v. t.* To print from a drawing on stone.
Li-thŏg'ra-pher, *n.* One who practices lithography.
Lith'o-gräph'ic, *a.* Pertaining to lithography.
Li-thŏg'ra-phy, *n.* The art of printing on stone.
Li-thŏl'o-ġy, *n.* The science or natural history of stones.
Li-thŏt'o-mist, *n.* One who cuts for stone in the bladder.
Li-thŏt'o-my, *n.* The operation of cutting for the stone in the bladder.
Lit'i-gant, *n.* One engaged in a lawsuit. — *a.* Contesting in law. [lawsuit.
Lit'i-gāte, *v.* To contest by a
Lit'i-gā'tion, *n.* Contention in law; a law-suit.
Li-tĭġ'ioŭs (-tĭj'us), *a.* Inclined to go to law.
Lit'ter, *v. t.* To bring forth; to strew with scraps. — *n.* A carriage with a bed in it; a brood of pigs; loose matter strewed about.
Lit'tle, *a.* Small; not much; diminutive. — *n.* A small quantity, amount, or space, &c. — *adv.* In a small degree.
Lit'tle-ness, *n.* Smallness; meanness.
Lit'to-ral, *a.* Belonging to a shore, as of the sea.
Li-tūr'ġic-al, *a.* Relating to a liturgy.
Lit'ur-ġy, *n.* A formulary of public prayers; a ritual.
Live (liv), *v. i.* To have life; to pass one's time; to abide; to dwell; to last; to feed.
Live, *a.* Having life; active.
Live'li-hōod, *n.* Means of living; support of life.
Live'li-ness, *n.* Sprightliness.
Live'long, *a.* Long in passing.
Live'ly, *a.* Living; brisk;

active. — *adv.* In a brisk manner.
Liv'er, *n.* One who lives; an organ which secretes bile.
Liv'er-wort (-wûrt), *n.* A plant between the lichens and mosses.
Liv'er-y, *n.* A giving of possession; peculiar dress of servants.
Lives, *n.; pl. of Life.* [&c.
Live'-stŏck, *n.* Cattle; horses,
Liv'id, *a.* Discolored by a bruise; lead-colored.
Liv'id-ness, *n.* A livid color.
Liv'ing, *n.* Subsistence; support; a benefice.
Lix-ĭv'ĭ-al, *a.* Made from
Lix-ĭv'ĭ-oŭs, lye; impregnated with alkaline salts.
Lix-ĭv'ĭ-āte, *v. t.* To impregnate with salts from wood-ashes; to leach.
Lix-ĭv'ĭ-um, *n.* Water impregnated with alkaline salts from wood-ashes.
Liz'ard, *n.* A kind of reptile.
Lŏ, *interj.* Look! see! behold!
Lōach, *n.* A small brook fish, used for food.

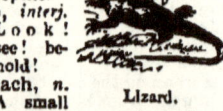
Lizard.

Lōad (18), *n.* That which is carried; weight; pressure; encumbrance. — *v. t.* [imp. LOADED; *p. p.* LOADED, LOADEN.] To burden; to freight; to charge.
Lōad'stär, *n.* The pole-star.
Lōad'stōne, *n.* An ore of iron; a native magnet.
Lōaf (142), *n.* A quantity or mass of bread.
Lōaf'er, *n.* A low idler.
Lōam, *n.* A rich, friable soil.
Lōam'y, *a.* Consisting of, or like, loam.
Lōan, *n.* Act of lending; the thing lent. — *v. t.* To lend.
Lōath. See *Loth.*
Lōathe, *v. t.* To hate; to be disgusted by. [gust.
Lōath'some, *a.* Exciting disgust.
Lōath'some-ness, *n.* Quality of exciting extreme disgust.
Lōaves, *n.; pl. of Loaf.*
Lŏb, *v. t.* To let fall heavily.
Lŏb'by, *n.* An anteroom; a small hall or waiting room.
Lōbe, *n.* A roundish part, as of the lungs, and of the ear.
Lŏb'ster, *n.* A crustaceous fish. [to a place.
Lō'cal, *a.* Pertaining or limited

Lo-căl'i-ty, *n.* Existence in a place; situation; place.
Lō'cal ly, *adv.* With respect to place; in place.
Lō'cāte, *v. t.* To place or set.
Lo-cā'tion, *n.* Act of placing; position; situation.
Lŏch (lŏk), *n.* A lake; a bay or arm of the sea.
Lŏck (140), *n.* Fastening for a door, &c.; part of a gun; tuft of hair; works to confine water in a canal. — *v. t.* To fasten with a lock; to embrace closely.
Lŏck'aġe, *n.* Materials for canal locks; works for locks; toll for passing a lock.
Lŏck'er, *n.* A drawer or close place fastened by a lock.
Lŏck'et, *n.* A catch; a small ornamental picture-case.
Lŏck'-smith, *n.* A maker or mender of locks.
Lō'co-mō'tion, *n.* Act of moving from place to place.
Lō'co-mō'tive, *a.* Having power to change place. — *n.* A steam engine on wheels.
Lō'cust, *n.* A jumping insect, like the grasshopper; a tree.
Lōde, *n.* A metallic or other vein; a cut or reach of water.
Lŏdġe, *n.* A small house; an association. — *v. t. or i.* To rest at night; to place or settle.
Lŏdġ'er, *n.* One who lodges.
Lŏdġ'ing, *n.* A place of rest at night; rooms hired.
Lŏdġ'ment (132), *n.* Act of lodging; position secured by assailants.
Lŏft, *n.* [Allied to *lift.*] An elevated floor or room.
Lŏft'i-ly, *adv.* In a lofty manner or position; highly.
Lŏft'i-ness, *n.* Altitude; haughtiness; pride.
Lŏft'y, *a.* Elevated; high; proud; stately; sublime.
Lŏg, *n.* A bulky piece of wood; an apparatus for measuring the rate of a ship's motion.
Lŏġ'a-rĭth'mic, } *a.* Pertaining
Lŏġ'a-rĭth'mic-al, } taining to logarithms.
Lŏġ'a-rĭthm, *n.* An auxiliary number to abridge mathematical calculations.
Lŏġ'-bōok, *n.* Register of a ship's way.
Lŏġ'ger-hĕad, *n.* A dunce.
Lŏġ'-house, *n.* A house made of logs.
Lŏġ'ic (127), *n.* Science and art of reasoning. [logic.
Lŏġ'ic-al, *a.* According to

ā, ĕ, ī, ō, ū, ȳ, *long*; ă, ĕ, ĭ, ŏ, ŭ, ў, *short*; cāre, cär, åsk, ąll, whąt; ẽre, veil, tẽrm; pįque, fĭrm;

LOGICALLY 189 LUCID

Lŏg'ic-al-ly, *adv.* According to the rules of logic.
Lo-gĭ'cian (-jĭsh'an), *n.* A person versed in logic.
Lŏg'-lĭne, *n.* A line to measure a ship's way.
Lŏg'wŏŏd, *n.* A kind of wood used in dyeing.
Loin, *n.* Part of an animal just above the hip; reins.
Loi'ter, *v. i.* To linger on the way. — SYN. To lag; delay; saunter. [ters.
Loi'ter-er, *n.* One who loiters.
Lŏll (123), *v. i.* To lie at ease. —*v. t.* To thrust out, as the tongue.
Lŏne, *a.* Single; solitary.
Lŏne'li-ness, *n.* Solitude; want of company.
Lŏne'ly, *a.* Solitary; retired.
Lŏne'sŏme, *a.* Secluded from society; wanting company.
Lŏng, *a.* Extended; protracted; tedious. — *adv.* To a great extent. — *v. i.* To desire earnestly.
Lŏng'-bōat, *n.* A ship's largest and strongest boat.
Lŏnge (lŭnj), *n.* A thrust.
Lon-gĕv'i-ty, *n.* Length of life. [ing.
Lŏng'-hēad'ed, *a.* Discerning.
Lŏng'ing, *n.* An earnest desire; eager wish.
Lŏn'gi-tūde, *n.* Distance from east to west; length.
Lŏn'gi-tū'di-nal, *a.* Being in the direction of the length.
Lŏn'gi-tūd'i-nal-ly, *adv.* In the direction of the length.
Lŏng'-līved, *a.* Living or enduring long.
Lŏng'-prĭm'er, *n.* A kind of printing type.

Long-primer Type.

Lŏng-sŭf'fer-ing, *n.* Patience.
Lŏng-wĭnd'ed, *a.* Tedious.
Lōō, *n.* A game at cards.
Lŏŏk, *v. i.* To behold; to appear; to search; to watch; to expect. — *n.* Cast of countenance; appearance; view.
Lŏŏk'ing-glăss, *n.* A glass that reflects images; a mirror.
Lōōm, *n.* A weaver's frame. — *v. i.* To appear above the surface, as a distant object
Lōōn, *n.* A simple fellow; a kind of bird. [string.
Lōōp, *n.* A noose in a rope or
Lōōp'-hōle, *n.* A small opening in a wall; means of escape.
Lōōse, *v. t.* To untie; to re-

lax; to release; to open. — *v. i.* To set sail. — *a.* Unbound; wanton. [wantonly.
Lōōse'ly, *adv.* Negligently;
Lōōs'en (lōōs'n), *v. t.* To make loose; to relax.
Lōōse'ness, *n.* Freedom; flux.
Lŏp, *v. t.* To cut short.
Lo-quā'cioŭs, *a.* Addicted to talking; talkative; garrulous. [ness.
Lo-quăç'i-ty, *n.* Talkativeness.
Lŏrd, *n.* [A.-S. *hláford, láford*, lit. bread-keeper.] A master; husband; ruler; nobleman; God; the Supreme Ruler. — *v. i.* To domineer; to rule despotically.
Lŏrd'li-ness, *n.* Haughtiness.
Lŏrd'ling, *n.* A petty lord.
Lŏrd'ly, *a.* Proud; haughty.
Lŏrd'shĭp, *n.* Dominion of a lord; a title given to a lord.
Lōre, *n.* Learning; knowledge; erudition.
†**Lorgnette** (lorn-yĕt'), *n.* An opera-glass.
Lŏr'i-cāte, *v. t.* To plate over.
Lŏr'i-cā'tion, *n.* Act of plating over.
Lōge (lōōz), *v. t.* [*imp. & p. p.* LOST.] To suffer loss; to miss; to let slip. — *v. i.* Not to win; to incur a forfeit.
Los'er, *n.* One who loses.
Lŏss, *n.* Privation; destruction or ruin; waste.
Lŏst, *imp. & p. p.* of *Lose.*
Lŏt, *n.* Hazard; fortune; state; portion; share; chance; a field. — *v. t.* To allot; to share.
Lōte, *n.* A tree that bears a cherry-like fruit.
Lŏth, *a.* Unwilling; reluctant.
Lō'tion, *n.* A medicinal wash.
Lŏt'ter-y, *n.* A distribution of prizes by lot or chance.
Loud, *a.* Noisy; boisterous; vociferous. [ously.
Loud'ly, *adv.* Noisily; clamorously.
Loud'ness, *n.* Force of sound.
Lŏugh (lŏk), *n.* A lake.
Lounge, *v. i.* To spend time lazily; to loiter; to loll.
Loung'er, *n.* An idle person.
Louse (143), *n.* An insect.
Lous'y, *a.* Infested with lice.
Lout, *n.* An awkward person.
Lŏv'a-ble (133), *a.* Deserving of love; amiable.
Lŏv'age, *n.* An aromatic plant.
Lŏve (lŭv), *v. t.* To regard with affection. — *n.* An affection excited by beauty, or whatever is pleasing. — SYN. Attachment; fondness; yearning.

Lŏve'-fēast, *n.* A religious festival.
Lŏve'-knŏt (lŭv'nŏt), *n.* A knot emblematical of love.
Lŏve'-lĕt'ter, *n.* A letter of courtship.
Lŏve'li-ness, *n.* Qualities that excite love; gentle beauty.
Lŏve'-lŏrn, *a.* Forsaken by one's love. [amiable.
Lŏve'ly, *a.* Worthy of love;
Lŏv'er, *n.* One who loves.
Lŏve'-sick, *a.* Languishing through love.
Lŏve'-sŏng, *n.* A song expressing love. [kindness.
Lŏv'ing, *a.* Expressing love or
Lŏv'ing-kĭnd'ness, *n.* Tender regard; mercy; favor.
Lōw, *a.* [Allied to *lie.*] Deep; not high; humble; poor; cheap; mean. — *adv.* With a low voice; cheaply. — *v. i.* To bellow as an ox.
Lōw'-bŏrn, *a.* Born in low life.
Lōw'-brĕd, *a.* Bred in low condition; vulgar; rude.
Lōw'er (lō'er), *v. t.* or *i.* To let down; to sink.
Low'er (lou'er), *v. i.* To appear dark; to threaten.
Lŏw'er-mōst, *a.* Lowest.
Low'er-y (lou'er-y̆), *a.* Cloudy; threatening rain.
Lōw'land, *n.* Land low and flat; a low, level country.
Lōw'li-ness, *n.* State of being low; humility; meanness.
Lōw'ly, *a.* Humble; meek; mean. — *adv.* Humbly; meekly.
Lōw'ness, *n.* Depression.
Lōw-spĭr'it-ed, *a.* Dejected.
Lōw'-wĭnes, *n. pl.* The first run of the still.
Loy'al, *a.* Faithful to the lawful government, to a lover, or a friend.
Loy'al-ist, *n.* One who adheres to his king or to the government.
Loy'al-ly, *adv.* With fidelity.
Loy'al-ty, *n.* Fidelity.
Lŏz'enge, *n.* A rhomb; a diamond-shaped figure; a small cake of confectionery.
Lŭb'ber, *n.* A heavy, lazy fellow; a gawky.
Lŭb'ber-ly, *a.* Bulky; lazy; awkward. [Lozenge.
Lū'bri-cāte, *v. t.* To make smooth or slippery.
Lu-briç'i-ty, *n.* Smoothness
Lū'bri-coŭs, *a.* Slippery.
Lū'çent, *a.* Shining; bright.
Lū'çid, *a.* Clear; shining; transparent; sane.

sou, ôr, dọ, wọlf, tōō, tŏŏk; ûrn, rụe, pụll; ç, ğ, *soft;* c, ğ, *hard;* ag; eẋist; ṇ *as* ng; this.

Lū'çĭd-ness, n. Brightness; clearness; transparency.
Lū'çĭ-fer, n. [Lat., light-bringing.] The planet Venus when morning star; Satan.
Lŭck (127), n. Chance; accident; fortune; fate.
Lŭck'ĭ-ly, adv. By good chance; fortunately.
Lŭck'less, a. Unfortunate.
Lŭck'y, a. Fortunate; successful; favored by luck.
Lū'cra-tĭve, a. Profitable; gainful. [gain.
Lū'cre (lū'ker, 151), n. Profit;
Lī'cu-brāte, v. i. To study by candle-light or a lamp.
Lū'cu-brā'tion, n. Nocturnal study or composition.
Lū'cu-lent, a. Clear; bright; evident.
Lū'dĭ-croŭs, a. Exciting laughter. — SYN. Laughable; ridiculous.
Lū'dĭ-croŭs-ly, adv. In a ludicrous manner.
Lŭff (123), n. Side of a ship toward the wind. — v. i. To turn the head of a ship toward the wind.
Lŭg, v. t. To carry with labor. — n. A heavy load; a kind of sail. [trunks, &c.
Lŭg'gage, n. A traveler's
Lu-gū'brĭ-oŭs, a. Mournful.
Lūke'warm, a. Moderately warm; indifferent.
Lūke'warm-ness, n. Want of zeal; indifference.
Lŭll (123), v. t. or i. To put to rest; to quiet; to subside.
Lŭll'a-bȳ, n. A song to quiet infants. [ing to lumbago.
Lum-bāg'ĭ-noŭs, a. Pertain-
Lum-bā'go, n. A rheumatic pain in the small of the back.
Lŭm'bar, a. Pertaining to, or near, the loins.
Lŭm'ber, n. Things useless and cumbrous; sawed timber. — v. t. To heap carelessly together.
Lŭm'ber-rōōm, n. A place for useless things.
Lū'mĭ-na-rȳ, n. Any body that gives light.
Lū'mĭ-noŭs, a. Shining; bright; light; clear.
Lŭmp, n. A small, shapeless mass; the whole; the gross. — v. t. To throw into a mass; to take in the gross.
Lŭmp'ish, a. Bulky; inactive; stupid.
Lŭmp'ȳ, a. Full of lumps.
Lū'na-çȳ, n. Mental derangement; madness in general.

Lū'nar, } a. Pertaining to
Lū'na-rȳ, } the moon.
Lū'na-tĭç (120), a. Affected with lunacy. — n. A person whose insanity is supposed to be influenced by the moon.
Lu-nā'tion, n. Revolution of the moon about the earth.
Lŭnch, n. Food taken between breakfast and dinner; an eating-house. — v. i. To take a slight repast between breakfast and dinner.
Lŭnch'eon (-un), n. Food taken between any meals.
Lu-nĕtte', n. A detached bastion.
Lŭng, n. Organ of respiration in air-breathing animals.
Lŭnge, n. A sudden push or thrust. [for firing cannon.
Lŭnt, n. The match cord used
Lū'nu-lar, } a. Shaped like
Lū'nu-late, } a new moon.
Lū'pĭne, n. A plant with showy flowers.
Lŭrch, n. A sudden roll of a ship; deserted condition. — v. i. To roll suddenly to one side, as a ship at sea; to dodge; to play tricks.
Lūre, n. That which allures. — v. t. To entice; to attract; to allure. [mal.
Lū'rĭd (86), a. Gloomy; dis-
Lŭrk, v. i. To lie in wait; to lie close or out of sight.
Lŭrk'ĭng-plāçe, n. A hiding-place.
Lŭs'cĭoŭs (lŭsh'us), a. [A corruption of luxurious.] Sweet or rich, so as to cloy.
Lŭst, n. Longing desire; carnal appetite. — v. i. To desire eagerly or improperly; to have carnal appetite.
Lŭs'ter } (151), n. Brightness;
Lŭs'tre } a kind of lamp.
Lŭst'ful, a. Having irregular or evil desires; inviting to lust.
Lŭst'ĭ-ly, adv. Stoutly; boldly; with vigor.
Lŭst'ĭ-ness, n. Vigor; strength and spirit; energy.
Lŭs'tral, a. Used in, or pertaining to, purification.
Lŭs'trāte, v. t. To purify; to survey.
Lus-trā'tion, n. Purification.
Lŭs'tring, n. A kind of glossy silk cloth.
Lŭs'troŭs, a. Bright; shining; luminous. [years.
Lŭs'trum, n. Space of five
Lŭst'ȳ, a. Able of body; full of vigor; hearty; robust.
Lūte (27), n. A stringed instrument of music; a composition resembling clay. — v. t. To coat with lute.
Lūte'string, n. String of a lute; a plain, stout kind of silk.
Lū'ther-an, a. Pertaining to Luther, the Reformer. — n. A follower of Luther. [window.
Lū'thern, n. A dormer-
Lŭx'āte, v. t. To put out of joint; to dislocate. [joint.
Lux-ā'tion, n. Dislocation of a
Lux-ū'rĭ-ançe (lŭgz-yu'- or luks-yu'-), n. Rank or vigorous growth; exuberance.
Lux-ū'rĭ-ant (lŭgz-yu'- or luks-yu'-), a. Exuberant in growth.
Lux-ū'rĭ-āte (lŭgz-yu'- or luks-yu'-), v. i. To grow exuberantly or to excess; to live luxuriously; to delight exceedingly.
Lux-ū'rĭ-oŭs (lŭgz-yu'- or luks-yu'-), a. Given to luxury; voluptuous.
Lux-ū'rĭ-oŭs-ly (lŭgz- or luks-), adv. Voluptuously; exuberantly.
Lŭx'u-rȳ (lŭk'shu-rȳ, 92), n. Excess in eating, or dress, &c. — SYN. Voluptuousness; effeminacy; sensuality; delicacy.
Ly-çē'um, n. A literary association, or the place where they meet; a seminary.
Lȳe (lī), n. A solution of alkaline salt. [less animal fluid.
Lymph, n. A certain color-
Lym-phăt'ĭc, a. Pertaining to lymph. — n. A vein-like vessel, in vertebrate animals, containing a transparent fluid.
Lynx, n. A wild animal much like a cat.
Lȳre, n. A stringed instrument of music.
Lȳr'ĭc, } a. Per-
Lȳr'ĭc-al, } taining or adapted to a lyre. — n. A song.
Lȳ'rist, n. One who plays on the harp or lyre.

M.

Măb, *n.* Queen of the fairies.
Mac-ăd'am-īze, *v. t.* [From *Mac Adam*, the inventor.] To form or cover, as a road, with small, broken stones.
Măc'a-rō'nĭ, *n.* A food made of paste; a finical fellow; a fop; an exquisite.
Măc'a-rŏn'ĭc, *n.* Relating to, or like, a macaroni; finical.
Măc'ca-boy, *n.* Rose-flavored snuff.
Ma-caw', *n.* A bird allied to the parrots.
Māçe, *n.* A scepter; an ensign of authority; a kind of spice; rod used in playing billiards. **Macaw.**
Măç'er-āte, *v. t.* To make lean; to steep almost to solution.
Măç'er-ā'tion, *n.* Act of making lean, or of steeping till very soft.
Măch'ĭ-nāte, *v. t.* To plan; to plot; to contrive.
Măch'ĭ-nā'tion, *n.* A hostile or treacherous scheme. — SYN. Plot; contrivance; stratagem; intrigue.
Măch'ĭ-nā'tor, *n.* One who contrives or plots.
Ma-chīne' (-shēen', 64), *n.* An engine; a piece of mechanism.
Ma-chīn'er-y, *n.* Works of a machine; machines collectively.
Ma-chīn'ĭst (-shēen'ist), *n.* A constructor of machines.
Măck'er-el, *n.* A sea-fish much used for food. **Mackerel.**
Mā'cro-cŏṣm, or **Măc'ro-cŏṣm,** *n.* The great world; the universe.
Măc'u-lāte, *v. t.* To spot; to stain. [blemish.
Măc'u-lā'tion, *n.* A spot; a
Măd, *a.* Disordered; crazy; enraged; angry. [to a lady.
Măd'am, *n.* A form of address
Măd'cap, *n.* A rash, hotheaded fellow.

Măd'der, *n.* A plant used for dyeing red.
Māde, *imp. & p. p.* of *Make*.
Măd'den, *v. t.* or *i.* To make or become mad.
Ma-dēi'rā (*or* -dī'rā), *n.* A wine made in Madeira.
Măd'house, *n.* A house where crazy persons are confined.
Măd'ly, *adv.* In a mad way.
Măd'man, *n.* An insane man.
Măd'ness, *n.* State of being mad; extreme folly.
Ma-dŏn'nā, *n.* [It., my lady.] The Virgin Mary or her picture. [corals.
Măd're-pore, *n.* A genus of
Măd'rĭ-gal, *n.* An elaborate vocal composition in parts.
Măg'a-zīne' (-zeen'), *n.* A storehouse; a pamphlet periodically published.
Măg'got, *n.* A grub; a worm that produces a fly.
Măg'got-y, *a.* Full of maggots; whimsical. [ophers.
†Mā'ġĭ, *n. pl.* Eastern philos-
Mā'ġĭ-an, *n.* An Eastern philosopher or sage.
Măġ'ĭc (127), *n.* A dealing with spirits; enchantment; sorcery; witchcraft.
Măġ'ĭc, } *a.* Pertaining to,
Măġ'ĭc-al, } or produced by, magic. [skilled in magic.
Ma-ġĭ'cian (-jĭsh'an), *n.* One
Măġ'ĭs-tē'rĭ-al, *a.* Lofty; authoritative; imperious.
Măġ'ĭs-tē'rĭ-al-ly, *adv.* With the air of a master.
Măġ'ĭs-tra-çy, *n.* Office of a magistrate; a body of magistrates.
Măġ'ĭs-trāte, *n.* One invested with power, as a public civil officer.
†Măġ'nā Chär'tā (kär'-), *n.* The great charter of English rights.
Măġ'na-nĭm'ĭ-ty, *n.* Greatness of mind; generosity.
Mag-năn'ĭ-moŭs, *a.* Great in mind; of lofty spirit; noble.
Mag-năn'ĭ-moŭs-ly, *adv.* Nobly; bravely.
Măġ'nāte, *n.* A man of note or distinction.
Măġ'net, *n.* The loadstone, an ore which attracts iron.
Mag-nĕt'ĭc, *a.* Having the properties of the magnet; attractive.

Măġ'net-ĭṣm, *n.* Properties of the magnet; attraction.
Măġ'net-īze, *v. t.* or *i.* To give or receive the properties of the magnet; to influence or be influenced.
Mag-nĭf'ĭc, *a.* Great; noble.
Mag-nĭf'ĭ-çençe, *n.* Grandeur of appearance; splendor.
Mag-nĭf'ĭ-çent, *a.* Splendid; grand; imposing.
Mag-nĭf'ĭ-çent-ly, *adv.* In a magnificent manner.
Măġ'nĭ-fī'er (185), *n.* One who magnifies; a glass that enlarges objects to the sight.
Măġ'nĭ-fȳ, *v. t.* To make great; to extol.
Măġ-nĭl'o-quençe, *n.* Highsounding language; bombast.
Mag-nĭl'o-quent, *a.* Bombastic.
Măġ'nĭ-tūde, *n.* Greatness of size or importance. — SYN. Largeness; bulk.
Mag-nō'lĭ-ā, *n.* A tree having large, fragrant flowers. [crow.
Măġ'pīe, *n.* A bird allied to the
Ma-hŏg'a-ny, *n.* A hard wood of a reddish-brown color, much used for furniture.
Ma-hŏm'e-tan. See *Mohammedan*.
Māid, *n.* A young, unmarried woman; a female servant.
Māid'en, *n.* A young, unmarried woman; a virgin. — *a.* Fresh; pure; virgin.
Māid'en-hâir, *n.* A plant having slender stalks.
Māid'en-ly, *a.* Modest. [girl.
Māid'-sĕr'vant, *n.* A servant-
Māil, *n.* A coat of steel; armor; a bag for conveying letters. — *v. t.* (140). To put in the mail; to post; to arm.
Māil'a-ble, *a.* Proper to be admitted into the mail.
Māil'-cōach, *n.* A coach that conveys a mail.
Māim, *v. t.* To disable; to mutilate. — *n.* Lameness; injury.
Māin, *a.* Chief; principal. — *n.* Strength; chief part; the ocean; continent.
Māin'-lănd, *n.* A continent.
Māin'ly, *adv.* Chiefly; principally; greatly.
Māin'măst, *n.* The chief mast in a vessel. [sail.
Māin'sāil, *n.* The principal
Main-tāin', *v. t.* To keep; to

---

sŏn, ŏr, dọ, wọlf, tōō, tŏŏk; ûrn, rụe, pụll; ç, ġ, *soft*; c, ḡ, *hard*; aṣ; exįst; ụ *as* ng; this.

MAINTENANCE — MANIPLE

preserve; to support with food, &c.; to uphold.

Main'te-nance, n. Sustenance; support.

Maize, n. Indian corn.

Ma-jes'tic, a. Stately; grand; august.

Ma-jes'tic-al-ly, adv. With dignity or grandeur.

Maj'es-ty, n. Exalted dignity; grandeur; title of a king or queen.

Ma'jor-do'mo, n. A steward.

Ma'jor, a. Greater; elder. — n. A military officer above a captain.

Ma-jor'i-ty, n. The greater number; more than half; full age; rank of a major.

Make, v. t. [imp. & p. p. MADE.] To create; to produce; to form; to compel; to cause to be; to gain. — v. i. To tend; to contribute; to increase. — n. Form; structure. [or creates.

Mak'er, n. One who forms

Make'-shift, n. A temporary expedient.

Make'-weight (-wāt), n. Something thrown into a scale to make weight.

Mal'a-chīte, n. A beautiful ore of copper, usually green.

Mal'ad-min'is-trā'tion, n. Bad management of affairs.

Mal'a-dy, n. Sickness; disease; bodily ailment.

Mal'a-pert, a. Bold; saucy.

Mal-ap'ro-pōs' (-pō'), a. Unseasonably; unsuitable.

Ma-la'ri-a, n. Noxious exhalation.

Mal'con-tent', a. Discontented; dissatisfied.

Māle, a. Belonging to the male sex. — n. One of the sex that begets young.

Mal'e-dic'tion, n. A curse.

Mal'e-fac'tor, n. One guilty of a great crime; a felon; a convict.

Ma-lĕv'o-lençe, n. Ill-will.

Ma-lĕv'o-lent, a. [Lat. malevolens, fr. male, ill, and volens, disposed.] Ill-disposed; spiteful.

Mal-fea'sançe, n. Evil doing.

Mal'for-mā'tion, n. Irregular formation or structure.

Mal'içe, n. Extreme enmity; unprovoked spite.

Ma-li'cious (-lĭsh'us), a. Ill-disposed; malignant.

Ma-li'cious-ly (-lĭsh'us-), adv. With malice or evil intention.

Ma-lign' (-līn'), v. t. To traduce; to slander; to vilify. — a. Malicious; malignant.

Ma-lig'nan-çy, n. Malice; malevolence; virulence.

Ma-lig'nant, a. Malicious; dangerous to life.

Ma-līgn'er (-līn'-), n. One who maligns.

Ma-līg'ni-ty, n. Extreme or virulent enmity; malice.

Ma-lign'ly (-līn'-), adv. With extreme ill-will.

Mal'i-son (-zn), n. Malediction; curse.

Mall (123), n. A kind of hammer. — v. t. To beat with something heavy.

Mall (măl), n. A public walk.

Mal'le-a-bĭl'i-ty, n. Susceptibility of extension by beating.

Mal'le-a-ble, a. Capable of being extended by beating.

Mal'let, n. A wooden hammer.

Mal'low, n. A plant.

Malm'gey (mäm'zy̆), n. A sort of sweet grape and wine.

Mal-prăc'tiçe, n. Evil practice; professional misconduct of a physician.

Malt, n. Grain steeped and dried, for use in brewing. — v. i. To become malt.

Malt'ster, n. A malt-maker.

Mal-trēat', v. t. To treat ill.

Mal-trēat'ment, n. Ill-treatment; abuse.

Mal'ver-sā'tion, n. Evil conduct; fraudulent practice.

Mam-mä', n. Mother; — a word used by children.

Mam'mal, n. An animal that suckles its young.

Mam'mi-fer, n. A mammal.

Mam-mĭf'er-oŭs, a. Nourishing young by breasts.

Mam'mĭl-la-ry, a. Belonging to the breasts. [wealth.

Mam'mon, n. Riches;

Mam'moth, n. A huge quadruped, now extinct.

Man (143), n. The human race; an adult male; a husband; a servant. — v. t. To furnish with men.

Man'a-cle, v. t. To shackle the hands of.

Man'a-cles, n. pl. Shackles for the hands; handcuffs.

Man'age, v. t. To conduct; to transact; to husband. — v. i. To direct affairs.

Man'age-a-ble (133), a. Capable of being managed.

Man'age-ment, n. Conduct.

Man'a-ger, n. A conductor; an economist. [writ.

†**Man-dā'mus,** n. A kind of

Măn'da-rĭn', n. A Chinese public officer.

Măn'dāte, n. An official order or command.

Măn'da-to-ry, a. Containing a command. [lower jaw.

Măn'dĭ-ble, n. The jaw or

Măn-dĭb'u-lar, a. Belonging to the jaw. [strumeut.

Măn'drel, n. A turner's instrument.

Măn'du-cā'tion, n. Act of chewing. [neck of a beast.

Māne (140), n. Long hair on the

†**Ma-nēge'** (ma-nāzh'), n. Art of horsemanship; a school for horsemanship.

†**Mā'nĕs,** n. pl. Departed souls.

Ma-nœŭ'ver (151), n. Evolution; stratagem. — v. t. To change position; to manage with address. [stout.

Măn'ful, a. Bold; brave;

Măn'ful-ly, adv. Like a man.

Măn'ga-nēse', n. A very hard and refractory metal.

Mănge, n. The itch on cattle.

Măn'gel-wŭr'zel (58), n. A plant of the beet kind.

Măn'ger, n. An eating-trough for cattle.

Măn'gle, v. t. To cut roughly or coarsely; to mutilate; to smooth, as linen. — n. A calender for smoothing linen.

Măn'go (140), n. A pickled muskmelon.

Măn'grove, n. A tropical tree.

Măn'gy, a. Scabby, as a beast. [in en.

Măn'hood, n. Adult years in

Mā'ni-a, n. Madness.

Mā'ni-āc (107, 127), a. Raving with madness. — n. A madman.

Ma-nī'a-cal, a. Raving; mad.

Măn'i-fest, a. Not concealed, obscure or difficult. — SYN. Clear; plain; obvious; apparent. — v. t. To make known; to show. — n. An invoice of a cargo.

Măn'i-fest-ā'tion, n. Exhibition; display; revelation.

Măn'i-fest-ly, adv. Evidently; clearly.

Măn'i-fĕs'to, n. (pl. Măn'i-fĕs'tōes, 140.) A public declaration.

Măn'i-fōld, a. Many; diverse.

Măn'i-kĭn, n. A dwarf; a model of a man.

Mā'ni-ŏc (127), n. The plant from which tapioca is made.

Măn'i-ple, n. A handful; a small band of soldiers; a scarf worn by Roman Catholic priests.

MANIPULATE — 193 — MARTYROLOGY

Ma-nip'u-late, *v. t.* To treat or labor with the hands.
Ma-nip'u-la'tion, *n.* Manual operation; a working over.
Man-kind', *n.* The human race.
Man'like, *a.* Becoming a man.
Man'li-ness, *n.* Quality of being manly.
Man'ly, *a.* Having the attributes of a man; brave; noble. [tion from many trees.
Man'na, *n.* A sweetish secretion
Man'ner, *n.* Form; way; mode; air or mien; (*pl.*) deportment; behavior.
Man'ner-ism, *n.* Studied uniformity of manner.
Man'ner-ist, *n.* One addicted to mannerism. [well-behaved.
Man'ner-ly, *a.* Civil; decent;
Ma-nœu'vre (ma-nū'ver). See *Maneuver*. [sel.
Man'-of-war', *n.* A war vessel
Man'or, *n.* A lord's estate in lands. [a manor.
Ma-nō'ri-al, *a.* Pertaining to
Manse, *n.* A parsonage-house; a farm.
Man'sion (89), *n.* A large dwelling-house; place of abode.
Man'slaugh-ter (-slaw-), *n.* The killing of a person in passion, without malice.
Man'tel (58), *n.* The piece of timber or stone over the fireplace. [worn by women.
Man'te-let', *n.* A small cloak
Man-til'lā (140), *n.* A light covering to throw over a lady's dress.
Man'tle, *n.* A loose garment or cloak; a cover.—*v. t.* or *i.* To cloak; to suffuse.
Man'tu-à (or măn'tu), *n.* A woman's gown.
Man'tua-māk'er (măn'tu-), *n.* A dress-maker.
Man'u-al, *a.* [Lat. *manualis*, from *manus*, a hand.] Performed by the hand.—*n.* A small book.
Man'u-făc'to-ry, *n.* A place where goods are made.
Man'u-făct'ūre, *n.* Anything made by the hand or by machinery.—*v. t.* To form by the hand or by art into forms convenient for use.
Man'u-făct'ūr-er, *n.* One who manufactures.
Man'u-mis'sion (-mĭsh'un), *n.* Act of freeing slaves.
Man'u-mĭt', *v. t.* To release from slavery; to set free.
Ma-nūre', *v. t.* Anything that fertilizes land.—*v. t.* To apply fertilizing substances to.

Man'u-script, *n.* Any writing done by hand.
Ma'ny (měn'y), *a.* Numerous. —*n.* A great number.
Map, *n.* A delineation of the earth or any part of it.—*v. t.* To draw or delineate.
Ma'ple, *n.* A certain tree.
Mar, 129, *v. t.* To hurt; to impair; to injure the looks of.
Mar'a-nāth'à, or **Mar'a-nā'thā**, *n.* A curse.
Ma-răs'mus, *n.* A wasting of flesh without fever.
Ma-raud', *v. i.* To rove for plunder.
Ma-raud'er, *n.* A plunderer.
Mar'ble, *n.* A kind of calcareous stone, or anything made of it.—*v. t.* To vein or variegate like marble.
March, *n.* The third month of the year; regulated movement of troops; a procession. —*v. i.* To move in military order.—*v. t.* To cause to march, as an army. [flues.
March'es, *n. pl.* Borders; confines
March'ion-ess (mär'shun-), *n.* The wife of a marquis.
Māre, *n.* The female of the horse kind.
Mar'gin, *n.* An edge; border.
Mar'gin-al, *a.* Placed in the margin.
Mar'i-gōld, *n.* A plant having a yellow flower.
Ma-rīne', *a.* Pertaining to the sea.—*n.* A soldier doing duty in a ship; the navy; shipping. [sailor.
Mar'i-ner, *n.* A seaman; a
Mar'i-tal, *a.* Pertaining to a husband.
Mar'i-tīme (46), *a.* Pertaining to the sea; marine; nautical.
Mar'jo-ram, *n.* An aromatic plant.
Mark, *n.* A coin; a token; indication; note.—*v. t.* To draw a mark upon; to write on; to note; to observe.
Mark'et, *n.* A place or time of sale; emporium.—*v. i.* 130. To deal in market.
Mark'et-a-ble, *a.* Fit for market or sale; merchantable.
Mar'ket-man (143), *n.* One who sells provisions at market.
Marks'man (143), *n.* A man skillful in shooting.
Marl, *n.* A species of earth.
Marl-ā'ceoŭs, *a.* Consisting
Marl'y,) in, like, or abounding with, marl.
Mar'lĭne, *n.* A small line of two strands.

Mar'ma-lāde, *n.* A preserve made of quinces, or apples, &c., boiled with sugar.
Mar-mō're-an, *a.* Relating to marble. [small monkey.
Mar'mo-sĕt', *n.* A kind of
Ma-rōon', *n.* A free black on the West India mountains; a kind of claret color.—*v. t.* To put ashore on a desolate isle as a punishment.
Marque (märk), *n.* A license to make reprisal at sea on an enemy. [field-tent.
Mar-quee' (-kē'), *n.* A large
Mar'quet-ry (-ket-), *n.* Inlaid work of shells, &c.
Mar'quis (-kwis), *n.* A title of nobility.
Mar'quis-ate, *n.* Dignity or lordship of a marquis.
Mar'riage (mär'rĭj), *n.* State or condition of being married. —SYN. Matrimony; wedlock.
Mar'riage-a-ble (133), *a.* Of a fit age to be married.
Mar'row, *n.* A soft substance in bones; essence of a thing.
Mar'row-bōne, *n.* A bone containing marrow.
Mar'row-făt, *n.* A large, delicious pea. [row.
Mar'row-y, *a.* Full of marrow
Mar'ry, *v. t.* To be joined in wedlock.—*v. t.* To join in wedlock. [ground.
Marsh (140), *n.* Low, wet
Mar'shal, *n.* Chief military commander; a civil officer; one who directs processions, &c.—*v. t.* (130). To arrange in due order. [marshal.
Mar'shal-ship, *n.* Office of a
Marsh'y, *a.* Wet; boggy.
Mart, *n.* A place of public sale; market; emporium.
Mar'ten 55, *n.* An animal allied to the weasel; a martin.
Mar'tial, *a.* Warlike; bold.
Mar'tin, *n.* A bird of the swallow kind. [ciplinarian.
Mar'ti-nĕt', *n.* A strict dis-
Mar'tin-mas 139, *n.* Festival of Saint Martin, November 11th.
Mar'tin-gal, *n.* A strap to hold down the head of a horse.
Mar'tyr, *n.* One who suffers death for the truth.—*v. t.* To make a martyr of; to torment. [of a martyr.
Mar'tyr-dŏm, *n.* The death
Mar'tyr-ŏl'o-gĭst, *n.* An historian of martyrs.
Mar'tyr-ŏl'o-gy, *n.* History or register of martyrs.

sŏn, ôr, dọ, wọlf, tŏŏ, tŏŏk; ûrn, rụe, pụll; ç, ġ, soft; c, ġ, hard; aṣ; eẋist; ụ as ng; this.
9

MARVEL 194 MAWKISH

Mär'vel (130), v. i. To be struck with surprise; to wonder. — n. A wonder; a prodigy.
Mär'vel-oŭs, a. Wonderful.
Mär'vel-oŭs-ly, adv. In a wonderful manner.
Măs'cu-line, a. Male; like a man; not effeminate.
Măsh, n. A mixture of things; bran and water. — v. t. To bruise into a soft mass; to crush.
Mäsk, n. A cover for the face; disguise. — v. t. To disguise.
Măs'lin, n. Different sorts of grain mixed.
Mā'son (mā'sn), n. An artificer in brick and stone.
Ma-sŏn'ic, a. Pertaining to masonry.
Mā'son-ry, n. Work of a mason; craft of freemasons.
Măs'quer-āde' (-ker-), n. A nocturnal assembly of persons in disguise. — v. i. To assemble in masks.
Măs'quer-ād'er (-ker-), n. A masked person.
Măss (124), n. A lump; an assemblage; bulk; a Roman Catholic service.
Măs'sa-cre (-ker, 151), n. Promiscuous slaughter. — v. t. To kill promiscuously or with cruelty; to slaughter.
Măss'i-ness, } n. Bulk;
Măss'ive-ness, } ponderousness.
Măss'ive, } a. Bulky; heavy;
Măss'y, } ponderous.
Măst, n. An upright pole or timber for sails, &c., in a vessel; nuts; acorns.
Măs'ter, n. A ruler; a superior; a proprietor; a teacher; a chief. — v. t. To conquer; to subdue.
Măs'ter-key, n. A key that opens many locks.
Măs'ter-ly, a. Becoming a master; most excellent.
Măs'ter-piēçe, n. A capital performance.
Măs'ter-y, n. Superiority. — SYN. Rule; dominion; supremacy.
Măs'ti-cāte, v. t. To chew.
Măs'ti-cā'tion, n. Act of chewing.
Măs'tic, n. A resin from a tree.
Măs'tiff, n. A large variety of dog.
Măs'to-don, n. An animal resembling the elephant, now extinct.
Măt, n. A texture of rushes, husks, straw, &c. — v. t. To weave into a mat; to twist together.

Mastodon.

Mătch (140), n. A contest; an equal; marriage; something to take fire. — v. t. To pair; to suit; to marry. — v. i. To correspond; to equal.
Mătch'less, a. Having no equal; peerless; unequaled.
Mătch'lŏck, n. A musket fired by means of a match.
Māte, n. A companion; second officer of a vessel. — v. t. To match; to compete with.
Ma-tē'ri-al, a. Consisting of matter; bodily; of consequence; weighty. — n. The substance of which any thing is made.
Ma-tē'ri-al-ism, n. The doctrine of materialists.
Ma-tē'ri-al-ĭst, n. One who denies the existence of spiritual substances.
Ma-tē'ri-ăl'i-ty, n. Material existence; importance.
Ma-tē'ri-al-ĭze, v. t. or i. To reduce to a state of matter; to occupy with material interests solely.
Ma-tē'ri-al-ly, adv. In a state of matter; essentially.
Ma-tĕr'nal, a. [Lat. maternus, from mater, mother.] Motherly.
Ma-tĕr'ni-ty, n. State, character, or relation of a mother.
Măth'e-măt'ic, } a. Relat-
Măth'e-măt'ic-al, } ing or according to mathematics.
Măth'e-măt'ic-al-ly, adv. By mathematics.
Măth'e-ma-ti'cian (-tĭsh'an), n. One versed in mathematics.
Măth'e-măt'ies, n. sing. The science of quantity or of magnitude and number.
Măt'in, a. Pertaining to the morning. [ship or service.
Măt'ins, n. pl. Morning worMăt'rass, n. A chemical vessel. [mold for castings.
Mā'trĭçe, or Măt'rĭçe, n. A
Măt'ri-çĭd'al, a. Relating to matricide.
Măt'ri-çĭde, n. The murder or murderer of a mother.
Ma-trĭc'u-lāte, v. t. To admit to membership, as in a college.
Ma-trĭc'u-late, n. One entered in a college, &c.
Ma-trĭc'u-lā'tion, n. Act of admitting to membership.
Măt'ri-mō'ni-al, a. Pertaining to marriage; connubial.
Măt'ri-mo-ny, n. Marriage; wedlock; the nuptial state.
Mā'trix, n. The womb; a mold.
Mā'tron, n. An elderly woman; a wife; a nurse in a hospital.
Mā'tron-al, or Mā'tron-al, a. Grave; motherly.
Mā'tron-ly, a. Becoming a wife or matron.
Măt'ter, n. Substance of which bodies are constituted; pus; subject; affair; importance. — v. i. To signify; to be of importance; to form pus.
Măt'ting, n. A texture of rushes, straw, &c.; materials for mats.
Măt'tock (127).
n. A kind of pick-ax.
Măt'tress, n. A bed stuffed with hair, husks, or the like. [ripen; to suppurate.
Ma-tūre', v. t. or i. To
Măt'u-rāte, v. t. or i. To
Măt'u-rā'tion, n. A ripening, as of an abscess.
Ma-tūre', a. Ripe; full-grown; well digested. — v. t. To bring to perfection; to consider well.
Ma-tūre'ly, adv. With ripeness; completely.
Ma-tū'ri-ty, n. A mature state; ripeness.
Maud'lin, a. Fuddled; sickly sentimental.
Mau'ger, } a. In spite of; not-
Mau'gre, } withstanding.
Maul, n. A wooden hammer. — v. t. To beat and bruise.
Maul'stick, n. [A corruption of Ger. maler-stock, lit. painter-stick.] The stick used by painters to keep the hand steady.
Maund'er, or Maund'er, v. i. To mutter; to beg.
Mau'so-lē'um, n. [Lat., fr. the tomb of Mausolus, king of Caria.] A magnificent tomb or monument.
Mā'vis, n. The throstle or song-thrush.
Maw, n. Stomach of a beast.
Mawk'ish, a. Apt to cause satiety and loathing.

Max'il-lar, *a.* Relating to the jaw.
Max'il-la-ry, *a.* Relating to the jaw.
Max'im, *n.* An established principle; axiom; aphorism.
{Max'i-mum, *n.* (*pl.* Max'i-ma). The greatest quantity or value attainable in a given case.
May, *n.* The fifth month of the year.—*v. aux.* [*imp.* MIGHT.] To be possible; to be able; to have license.
May'-day, *n.* The first day of May. [a person.
May'hem, *n.* The maiming of
May'or (*colloq.* mâr), *n.* Chief magistrate of a city or borough.
May'or-al-ty (*colloq.* mâr'al-ty), *n.* Office of a mayor.
May'or-ess (*colloq.* mâr'es), *n.* Wife of a mayor. [color.
Maz'a-rine', *n.* A deep blue
Maz'ard, *n.* A kind of small, black cherry.
Maze (140), *n.* A labyrinth; astonishment.—*v. t.* To bewilder.
Ma'zy, *a.* Intricate; perplexed with turns and windings.
Me, *pron.* Objective case of *I.*
Mead, *n.* A liquor composed of honey and water; a meadow.
Mead'ow (měd'ō), *n.* Low or level grass land.
Mea'ger (151), *a.* Wanting flesh; lean; thin; poor.
Mea'gre, *a.* Wanting flesh; lean; thin; poor.
Mea'ger-ly, *adv.* In a meagre manner.
Mea'gre-ly, *adv.* In a meagre manner.
Mea'ger-ness, *n.* Quality or state of being meager.
Mea'gre-ness, *n.* Quality or state of being meager.
Meal, *n.* Grain ground to powder; food taken at once.
Meal'y, *a.* Resembling meal.
Mean, *a.* Low; base; average. —*n.* A middle point; place, rate, or degree.—*v. t.* [*imp.* & *p. p.* MEANT.] To intend; to design; to have in view; to purpose; to signify.
Means, *n. pl.* Medium; instrument; income.
Me-an'der, *n.* A winding course.—*v. i.* (130). To run in windings.—*v. t.* To make winding or sinuous.
Mean'ing, *n.* Intention; signification. [nity.
Mean'ly, *adv.* Without dignity.
Mean'ness, *n.* Lowness; sordidness; baseness.
Meant, *imp.* & *p. p.* of *Mean.*
Mean'time, *adv.* In the intervening time.
Mean'while, *adv.* In the intervening time.

Mea'sles (mē'zlz), *n.* An eruptive disease. [measles.
Mea'sly, *a.* Infected with
Meas'ur-a-ble (mězh'ur-), *a.* Capable of being measured.
Meas'ur-a-bly (mězh'ur-), *adv.* To a limited extent; moderately.
Meas'ure (mězh'ur), *n.* That which measures; extent; time in music; limit; degree; meter; means to an end.—*v. t.* To ascertain the extent or quantity of.
Meas'ure-less, *a.* Boundless.
Meas'ure-ment, *n.* Act of measuring; dimensions.
Meas'ur-er (mězh'ur-, 133), *n.* One who measures.
Meat, *n.* Flesh for food; food in general.
Me-chān'ic, *n.* An artisan.
Me-chan'ic, *a.* Pertaining to machines; acting by physical power.
Me-chan'ic-al, *a.* Pertaining to machines; acting by physical power.
Me-chan'ic-al-ly, *adv.* By physical force or power like a machine; unthinkingly.
Mech'a-ni'cian (-nĭsh'an), *n.* One skilled in mechanics.
Me-chan'ics, *n. sing.* The science that treats of the laws of motion and force.
Mech'an-ism, *n.* Structure or parts of a machine.
Mech'an-ist, *n.* One skilled in machines.
Med'al, *n.* A piece of metal stamped with a device.
Med'al-ist, (13¹⁴), *n.* A person skilled in medals.
Me-dăl'lion (-yun), *n.* A large medal; a circular tablet on which figures are embossed.
Med'dle, *v. i.* To interfere.
Med'dler, *n.* A busybody.
Med'dle-some, *a.* Apt to meddle; intrusive; officious.
Mē'di-æ'val, *a.* Relating to the Middle Ages.
Mē'di-al, *a.* Noting average.
Mē'di-āte, *v. i.* To interpose.
Mē'di-āte, *a.* Middle; acting as a mean.
Mē'di-ate-ly, *adv.* By a secondary cause.
Mē'di-ā'tion, *n.* Agency between parties; interposition.
Mē'di-ā'tor, *n.* One who mediates; an intercessor;—applied particularly to Christ.
Mē'di-a-tō'ri-al, *a.* Belonging to a mediator or to mediation. [a mediator.
Mē'di-ā'tor-ship, *n.* Office of
Med'i-ca-ble, *a.* Capable of being cured.

Med'ic-al, *a.* Pertaining to medicine, or to the art of healing.
Med'ic-al-ly, *adv.* In a medical manner; medicinally.
Med'i-ca-ment, *n.* A healing application; medicine.
Med'i-cāte, *v. t.* To tincture or impregnate with medicines.
Me-dĭç'i-nal, *a.* Healing; curative; sanatory. [icine.
Me-dĭç'i-nal-ly, *adv.* By medicines.
Med'i-çine, *n.* Any thing that cures; a remedy.
Mē'di-ōc'ri-ty, *n.* Middle state; moderate degree.
Med'i-tāte, *v. t.* or *i.* To think; to muse; to contemplate.
Med'i-tā'tion, *n.* Contemplation; continued thought.
Med'i-ta-tive, *a.* Given to contemplation; thoughtful.
Mē'di-um, *n.* (*pl.* † Mē'di-à or Mē'di-ums, 147) A means or instrument; any thing intervening; a substance passed through.
Med'lar, *n.* A tree and its fruit. [miscellany.
Med'ley, *n.* A mixture; a miscellany.
Mĕd'ul'lar, *a.* Consisting of marrow, or resembling it. [pense.
Mĕd'ul la-ry, *a.* Consisting of marrow, or resembling it. [pense.
Meed, *n.* A reward; recompense.
Meek, *a.* Mild; soft; gentle.
Meek'ly, *adv.* Mildly; softly.
Meek'ness, *n.* Mildness of temper; gentleness.
Meer'schaum (-shawm), *n.* (liter. sea-foam.] A fine white clay, of which pipes are made; a pipe made of this clay.
Meet, *v. t.* or *i.* [*imp.* & *p. p.* MET.] To come together; to join.—*a.* Fit; suitable.
Meet'ing, *n.* An assembly; an interview.
Meet'ing-house, *n.* A place of worship (in England, for dissenters).
Meet'ly, *adv.* Fitly; suitably; duly. [ableness.
Meet'ness, *n.* Fitness; suitableness.
Mē'grim, *n.* A vehement pain in one side of the head; a whim. [choly.
Měl'an-chōl'ic, *a.* Melancholy.
Měl'an-chol-y, *a.* Dejected; gloomy.—*n.* Dejection of spirits; a gloomy state of mind.
Měl'ior-āte (mēl'yor-), *v. t.* To make better. [ment.
Měl'ior-ā'tion, *n.* Improvement.
Mel-lif'lu-ençe, *n.* A sweet, smooth flow.

sŭn, ôr, dọ, wọlf, tŏō, tŏŏk; ûrn, rụe, pụll; ç, ġ, *soft*; c, ġ, *hard*; aş; e̱xist; ŋ *as* ng; this.

Mel-lif′lu-ent, } *a.*
Mel-lif′lu-oŭs (117), } Sweetly flowing.
Měl′lŏw, *a.* Soft with ripeness. — *v. t.* or *i.* To ripen to softness. [ripeness.
Měl′lŏw-ness, *n.* Softness;
Me-lō′di-oŭs, *a.* Musical; agreeable to the ear.
Měl′o-dist, *n.* A composer or singer of melodies. [lodious.
Měl′o-dīze, *v. t.* To make me-
Měl′o-drä/mȧ, } *n.* A sensa-
Měl′o-dräme, } tional play with songs intermixed.
Měl′o-dra-măt′ic, *a.* Done for effect merely.
Měl′o-dy, *n.* An agreeable succession of single tones.
Měl′on, *n.* A plant, and its fruit, which is eaten raw.
Mĕlt, *v. t.* or *i.* To dissolve; to make or become liquid.
Mĭm′ber, *n.* A limb of the body; a clause; a part; one of a society.
Měm′ber-ship, *n.* The state of being a member.
Měm′bra-nā′ceoŭs, *a.* Consisting of membranes.
Měm′brāne, *n.* A thin tissue, or kind of skin.
Měm′bra-noŭs, *a.* Consisting of a membrane.
Me-měn′to, *n.* (*pl.* Me-měn′tōes, 140.) That which reminds; a memorial.
Měm′oir (měm′wor *or* mē′- uwor), *n.* A written account or history; a biography; a record of investigations.
Měm′o-ra-ble, *a.* Worthy of remembrance.
Měm′o-ra-bly, *adv.* In a memorable manner.
Měm′o-răn′dum, *n.* (*pl.*
Měm′o-răn′dums, *or*
†**Měm′o-răn′dȧ,** 147.) A note or record to help the memory.
Me-mō′ri-al, *a.* Preserving remembrance. — *n.* That which preserves remembrance; an address or statement with petition.
Me-mō′ri-al-ĭst, *n.* One who presents a memorial.
Me-mō′ri-al-īze, *v. t.* To present a memorial to.
Měm′o-rīze (153), *v. t.* To cause to be remembered.
Měm′o-ry, *n.* The faculty by ․ which ideas are retained in the mind; recollection; remembrance.
Měn. *pl.* of *Man.*
Měn′ace, *v. t.* To threaten. — *n.* A threat.

Men-ăg′er-ĭe (men-ăzh′-), *n.* A collection of animals.
Měnd, *v. t.* or *i.* To repair; to correct; to improve.
Men-dā′cioŭs, *a.* Given to deception, lying; false.
Men-dăç′i-ty, *n.* A habit of lying; a lie; falsehood.
Měn′di-can-çy, } *n.* State of
Měn′diç′i-ty, } beggary.
Měn′di-cant, *n.* A beggar. — *a.* Begging; poor.
Mē′ni-al, *a.* Low; servile. — *n.* A domestic servant.
Měn′stru-al. *a.* Monthly.
Měn′stru-um, *n.* (*pl.* Měn′- stru-ums, *or* †Měn′stru-ȧ, 147.) A dissolving fluid; a solvent.
Měn′su-ra-bĭl′i-ty (měn′- shṷ-), *n.* Quality of being mensurable. [Measurable.
Měn′su-ra-ble (měn′shṷ-), *a.*
Měn′su-rā′tion, *n.* Act or result of measuring.
Měn′tal, *a.* Belonging to the mind; intellectual.
Měn′tal-ly, *adv.* In mind.
Měn′tion, *n.* Notice; cursory remark. — *v. t.* To express; to name.
Me-phĭt′ic, *a.* Poisonous; noxious: foul; pestilential.
†**Me-phī′tis,** } *n.* Noxious
Měph′i-tĭsm, } exhalations.
Měr′can-tĭle, *a.* Pertaining to merchants or their business; commercial.
Měr′çe-na-ry, *a.* Capable of being hired; greedy of gain. — SYN. Venal; selfish; mean; contracted. — *n.* A hireling. [silks.
Měr′çer, *n.* One who deals in
Měr′çer-y, *n.* Goods of mercers.
Měr′chan-dīse, *n.* Goods for sale; commodities; trade. — *v. t.* To trade; to buy or sell.
Měr′chant, *n.* An exporter or importer of goods; a trader. [sale.
Měr′chant-a-ble, *a.* Fit for
Měr′chant-man (143), *n.* A ship employed in trade
Měr′çi-fṳl, *a.* Full of mercy; compassionate; tender.
Měr′çi-ful-ly, *adv.* With compassion; tenderly.
Měr′çi-less (135), *a.* Hard- hearted: unfeeling.
Mer-cū′ri-al, *a.* Composed of quicksilver; spirited; gay.
Měr′cu-ry, *n.* Quicksilver; one of the planets.
Měr′çy (141). *n.* Tenderness toward an offender; kindness: clemency.
Mēre (84), *a.* Pure; unmixed;

bare. — *n.* A pool or lake; a boundary.
Mēre′ly, *adv.* Simply; only.
Mēr′e-trĭ′cioŭs (-trĭsh′us), *a.* Lewd; false; gaudy.
Mērġe, *v. t.* or *i.* To immerse.
Me-rĭd′i-an, *n.* A great circle which the sun crosses at noon; noon; the highest point. — *a.* Relating to the meridian or to midday.
Me-rĭd′i-on-al, *a.* Pertaining . to the meridian.
Me-rī′no (-rē′no), *n.* A variety of sheep or their wool.
Měr′it, *n.* Desert; worth. — *v. t.* (84, 130). To earn by services; to deserve.
Měr′i-tō′ri-oŭs, *a.* Deserving reward; having merit.
Měr′maid, *n.* (Fr. *mer,* the sea, and *Eng.* maid.) A fabled sea-woman with the tail of a fish instead of legs.
Měr′man (144), *n.* A fabled seaman. [mirth.
Měr′ri-ly (135), *adv.* With
Měr′ri-ment, *n.* Gayety with laughter; noisy sport.
Měr′ry, *a.* Gay; jovial; noisy.
Měr′ry-Ăn′drew, *n.* A buffoon; a zany. [val.
Měr′ry-māk′ing, *n.* A festi-
Měr′ry-thŏught (-thawt), *n.* The forked bone of a fowl's breast.
Měs′en-ter-y, *n.* A membrane that keeps the intestines, &c., in a proper position.
Měsh (140), *n.* A space between threads in a net. — *v. t.* To catch in a net.
Meṣ-mēr′ic, *a.* Pertaining to mesmerism.
Meṣ′mer-ĭṣm, *n.* [From *Mesmer,* who first brought it into notice.] Art of inducing a certain abnormal state of the nervous system.
Meṣ′mer-īze, *v. t.* To bring into a state of mesmeric sleep.
Měss, *n.* A dish of food: persons who eat together. — *v. i.* To join in a mess.
Měs′sage, *n.* Notice sent; official communication.
Měs′sen-ger, *n.* One who bears a message; a harbinger.
Mes-sī′ah, *n.* The Anointed; CHRIST.
Mes-sī′ah-ship, *n.* Office of the Messiah.
Měs′sieurs (měsh′yerz), *n. pl.* Sirs; gentlemen ; — abbreviated *Messrs.,* and used as the plural of *Mr.*

MESSMATE 197 MILDLY

Mĕss'māte, n. One who eats ordinarily at the same table.
Mĕs'suaġe (mĕs'swej), n. A house and adjoining land.
Met, imp. & p. p. of Meet.
Mĕt'al (mĕt'al or mĕt'l, 130), n. A simple, fixed, opaque substance, fusible by heat, as iron, gold, &c.
Me-tăl'lic, a. Relating to, or partaking of, the properties of metals. [ducing metals.
Mĕt'al-lĭf'er-oŭs, a. Pro
Mĕt'al-line (129), a. Like metal. [in metals.
Mĕt'al-list (130), n. One skilled
Mĕt'al lize, v. t. To give its proper metallic properties to.
Mŏt'al-lûr'ġic, a. Relating to metallurgy. [in metallurgy.
Mĕt'al-lûr'ġist, n. One skilled
Mĕt'al-lûr'ġy (129), n. Art of working metals, or of obtaining them from their ores.
Mĕt-a-mŏr'phic, a. Relating to changes which minerals or rocks may have undergone since their deposition.
Mĕt'a-mŏr'phōṣe, v. t. To transform or change the shape of.
† Mĕt'a-mŏr'pho-sĭs, n. (pl. Mĕt'a-mŏr'pho-sēṣ.) A change of form.
Mĕt'a-phor, n. A short similitude; a trope.
Mĕt-a-phŏr'ic-al, a. Containing a metaphor; figurative.
Mĕt-a-phŏr'ic-al-ly, adv. By a figure; not literally.
Mĕt'a-phor-ist, n. One who makes use of metaphor.
Mĕt'a-phraṣe, n. A verbal translation; a repartee.
Mĕt'a-phrăs'tic, a. Literal; rendered word for word.
Mĕt'a-phŷṣ'ic-al, a. Pertaining or according to metaphysics; abstract.
Mĕt'a-phy̆-ṣĭ'cian (-zĭsh'an), n. One versed in metaphysics.
Mĕt'a-phy̆ṣ'ics, n. sing. Science of mental phenomena.
Mēte, v. t. To measure. — n. Measure; limit; boundary.
Me-tĕmp'sy̆-chō'sĭs, n. The passing of the soul after death into some other body; transmigration.
Mē'te-or, n. A luminous body passing in the air.
Mē'te-or'ic, a. Pertaining to, or proceeding from, meteors; influenced by the weather
Mē'te-or-īte, [n. A meteMē'te-ōr'o-līte,] oric stone.
Mē'te-ōr'o-lŏġ'ic-al, a. Pertaining to meteorology.

Mē'te-or-ŏl'o-ġĭst, n. One skilled in meteorology.
Mē'te-or-ŏl'o-ġy, n. The science of the atmosphere and its phenomena.
Mē'ter ((151), n. Rhythm;
Mē'tre) verse; measure.
Me-thĕġ'lin, n. Fermented liquor made of honey and water. [to me; I think.
Me-thĭnks', v. imp. It seems
Mĕth'od, n. Orderly arrangement; way of doing things.
— Syn. Mode; manner.
Me-thŏd'ic,) a. Ranged or
Me-thŏd'ic-al,) proceeding in order; regular; exact.
Me-thŏd'ic-al-ly, adv. In due or methodical order.
Mĕth'od-ĭṣm, n. Doctrines and worship of Methodists.
Mĕth'od-ĭst, n. One of a sect of Christians founded by John Wesley.
Mĕth-od-ĭst'ic, a. Resembling the Methodists, or partaking of their strictness.
Mĕth'od-īze, v. t. To reduce to method; to regulate.
Mĕt'o-nȳm'ic,) a. Used
Mĕt'o-nȳm'ic-al,) by way of metonomy.
Me-tŏn'o-my, or Mĕt'o-nȳm'y, n. A figure of speech in which one word is put for another.
Mē'tre (mē'ter), n. See Meter.
Mĕt'ric-al. a. Pertaining to meter; consisting of verses.
Mĕt'ric-al-ly, adv. In a metrical manner.
Me-trŏp'o-lĭs, n. The mother city or chief city.
Mĕt'ro-pŏl'i-tan, a. Pertaining to the chief city. — n. An archbishop.
Mĕt'tle (mĕt'tl), n. Courage; spirit; ardor.
Mĕt'tle-sŏme, a. Spirited.
Mew, n. A cage or coop. —
v. t. To confine in a cage. —
v. i. To cry as a cat.
Mewl, v. i. To cry as a child.
Mews, n. (pl. Mews'eṣ). An inclosure; a stable.
Mĕz'zo-tĭn'to (mĕd'zo-, or mĕz'zo-), n. A particular kind of engraving on copper.
Mī'aṣm, n. Same as Miasma.
† Mī-ăṣ'mä, n. (pl. Mī-ăṣ'ma-tä.) Noxious effluvia.
Mī-ăṣ'mal,) a. Pertaining
Mī'aṣ-măt'ic,) to, or consisting of, miasm.
Mī'eä, n. A mineral separable into thin, transparent plates.
Mī-cā'ceoŭs, a. Of, or pertaining to, mica.

Mĭçe, n. pl. of Mouse.
Mĭch'ael-mas (-el-, 139), n. The feast of St. Michael, celebrated September 29th.
Mī'cro-cŏṣm, n. A little world; man.
Mī'cro-seōpe, n. (Gr. mikros, small, and skopein, to view.) An optical instrument to magnifying very small objects.
Mī'cro-seōp'ic,) a. Very
Mī'cro-seōp'ic-al,) small; extremely minute.
Mid, a. Middle; intervening.
Mĭd'dāy, n. Noon.
Mĭd'dle, a. Equally distant from the ends; intermediate.
— n. The point equally remote from the extremes.
Mĭd'dling, a. Of a middle rank; of moderate capacity or ordinary.
Mĭdġe, n. A kind of fly.
Mĭd'land, a. Surrounded by the land. [o'clock at night.
Mĭd'night (-nīt), n. Twelve
Mĭd'riff, n. The diaphragm.
Mĭd'ship-man (143), n. A naval cadet or young officer.
Mĭdst, n. The middle.
Mĭd'sŭm-mer, n. The middle of summer.
Mĭd'wāy, n. The middle.
Mĭd'wīfe (142), n. A woman who assists at childbirth.
Mĭd'wife-ry, or Mid'wife-ry, n. Assistance in childbirth; obstetrics.
Mien, n. Look; air; manner.
Mĭff (123), n. Slight resentment.
Mīght (mīt), imp of May. —
n. Power; strength of body; force; ability; capacity.
Mīght'i-ly (mīt'-, 135), adv. Powerfully.
Mīght'i-ness (mīt'-), n. Power; a title of dignity.
Mīght'y (mīt'ȳ), a. Having great strength. — Syn. Powerful; strong; vigorous.
Mīgn'on-ĕtte' (mĭn'yon-ĕt'), n. A fragrant plant and its flower.
Mī'grāte, v. i. To remove to another place or climate.
Mī-grā'tion, n. Act of migrating. [migrate.
Mī'gra-to-ry, a. Disposed to
Mĭlch, a. Giving milk.
Mĭld, a. Gentle; calm; soft; meek; placid; bland.
Mĭl'dew, n. Fungous spots on cloth or paper. — v. t. or i. To taint or be tainted with mildew.
Mĭld'ly, adv. Gently; softly.

sŏn, ôr, dọ, wọlf, tŏŏ, tŏŏk; ûrn, rụe, pụll; ç, ġ, soft; ẹ, ḡ, hard; aṣ; eẋist; n as ng; this.

MILDNESS 198 MIRE

Mild'ness, n. Quality of being mild; gentleness; meekness.
Mile, n. A linear measure of 320 rods, 1760 yards, or 5280 feet. [travel by the mile.
Mile'age (133), n. Fees for
Mil'i-tant, a. Engaged in warfare; fighting.
Mil'i-ta-ry, a. Pertaining to soldiers or to war; martial. — n. Soldiers; an army.
Mil'i-tāte, v. i. To be opposed; to contend.
Mi-li'tiȧ (-lĭsh'ȧ), n. [Lat., fr. *miles*, a soldier.] National enrolled military force.
Milk, n. A white liquor drawn from the female of certain animals; the white juice of certain plants. — v. t. To draw milk from. [milk.
Milk'i-ness, n. Qualities like
Milk'māid, n. A woman employed in a dairy.
Milk'man (143), n. A man who carries milk to market.
Milk'-pāil, n. A pail for milk.
Milk'sŏp, n. A soft, effeminate man. [milk.
Milk'y, a. Made of, or like,
Milk'y-wāy, n. A luminous zone in the heavens supposed to be the blended light of innumerable stars; galaxy.
Mill (123), n. A machine for grinding, &c., or the building that contains it; the tenth of a cent. — v. t. To grind; to stamp, as coin; to full.
Mill'-dăm, n. A dam to keep water for a mill.
Mil'le-nā'ri-an, n. One who believes in the millennium.
Mil'le-na-ry, a. Consisting of a thousand.
Mil-lĕn'ni-al, a. Pertaining to the millennium.
Mil-lĕn'ni-um, n. The thousand years of Christ's expected reign on earth.
Mil'le-pōre, n. A species of coral. [a mill.
Mill'er, n. One who attends
Mil'let, n. A plant and its grain; a kind of grass.
Mil'li-ner, n. One who makes or sells ladies' caps, hats, head-dresses, &c.
Mil'li-ner-y, n. Articles sold by milliners.
Mill'ion (mĭl'yun), n. Ten hundred thousand.
Mill'ion-âire', n. One worth a million or more.
Mill'-rāce, n. A canal to convey water to a mill-wheel.
Mill'-stōne, n. A stone used for grinding grain.

Milt, n. The spleen; soft roe or spermatic part of the male fish. [an actor in it.
Mime, n. A kind of farce or
Mi-mĕt'ic, a. Given to aping.
Mim'ic, n. One who imitates. — v. t. (128). To imitate for sport; to ape.
Mim'ic, } a. Acting the
Mim'ic-al, } mimic; imitative. [ies.
Mim'ick-er, n. One who mimics
Mim'ic-ry, n. Ludicrous imitation for sport.
Mi-nā'cioŭs, a. Full of threats.
Min'a-ret, n. A tall, slender turret on Mohammedan mosques.
Mĭnçe, v. t. or i. To chop into small pieces; to speak or walk with affected nicety.
Mind, n. The intelligent power in man; understanding; soul; purpose; opinion. — v. t. To heed; to regard; to obey. — v. i. To be inclined or disposed. [clined.
Mind'ed, a. Disposed; inclined
Mind'ful (139), a. Regardful; attentive; observant.
Mīne, a. Belonging to me. — n. A pit where minerals are dug; an excavation. — v. t. or i. To dig; to sap. [mines.
Mīn'er, n. One who digs
Mĭn'er-al, n. A substance not organic, existing on or in the earth. — a. Pertaining to, or impregnated with minerals.
Min'er-al-i-zā'tion, n. Process of mineralizing.
Min'er-al-īze, v. t. To combine with a metal in forming an ore. — v. i. To seek minerals.
Min'er-al-ŏg'ic-al, a. Pertaining to mineralogy.
Min'er-ăl'o-gĭst, n. One versed in minerals. [minerals.
Min'er-ăl'o-gy, n. Science of
Min'gle (mĭng'gl), v. t. or i. To mix; to blend.
Min'i-a-tūre (mĭn'i-at-yụr or mĭn'it-yụr), n. A small painted likeness. — a. Being on a small scale.
Min'im, n. A dwarf; a note in music; a small liquid measure; a drop.
†Min'i-mum, n. (pl. Min'i-ma.) The least quantity assignable in a given case.
Min'ion (mĭn'yun, 102), n. A favorite; a small kind of type.
☞ This type is *Minion*.
Min'is-ter (113), n. A servant; an agent; an embassador;

a pastor. — v. t. To give; to communicate; to supply.
Min'is-tē'ri-al, a. Pertaining to a minister; done under authority; sacerdotal.
Min'is-trā'tion, n. Office of a minister; service.
Min'is-try, n. Office; service; agency; ecclesiastical function; ministers of state.
Mĭnk, n. An animal of the weasel kind.
Mĭn'nŏw, n. A very small fresh-water fish.
Mī'nor, a. Less; smaller. — n. A person under the age of twenty-one.
Mi-nŏr'i-ty, n. State of being a minor, or under age; nonage; the smaller number.
Mīn'o-tạur, n. A fabled monster, half man, half bull.
Mĭn'ster, n. Church of a monastery; a cathedral church.
Mĭn'strel, n. A singer and player on an instrument.
Mĭn'strel-sy, n. Music and song conjoined; lyric poetry; a company of minstrels.
Mĭnt, n. A place where money is coined; a plant. — v. t. To coin, as money.
Mĭnt'age, n. That which is coined or stamped; duty for coining.
Mĭn'u-end, n. A number from which another is to be subtracted. [ful dance.
♦Mĭn'u-et, n. A slow, graceful
Mī'nus, a. An algebraic term denoting subtraction.
Mĭn'ute (mĭn'ĭt), n. The sixtieth part of an hour; short note or sketch. — v. t. To set down in short notes or minutes.
Mi-nūte', a. Very small; of little consequence.
Min'ute-bŏŏk (mĭn'ĭt-), n. A book for short notes.
Min'ute-gŭn (mĭn'ĭt-), n. A gun fired every minute.
Mi-nūte'ly, adv. In a minute manner.
Mi-nūte'ness, n. Quality of being minute.
†Mi-nū'ti-æ (-nū'shĭ-ē), n. pl. [Lat.] Minute particulars.
Mĭnx (45, 79), n. A pert, wanton or flippant girl.
Mĭr'a-cle, n. A wonder or wonderful thing; a supernatural event; a prodigy.
Mi-răc'u-loŭs, a. Supernatural; wonderful.
†Mī-rāge' (-räzh'), n. A kind of optical illusion.
Mīre (85), n. Soft, wet earth;

MIRROR 199 MISSIONARY

mud. — *v. t.* To plunge and fix in mud.
Mir'ror (39), *n.* A looking-glass. — *v. t.* To reflect, as in a looking-glass.
Mirth, *n.* Noisy gayety. — SYN. Festivity; glee; fun; hilarity; merriment; jollity.
Mirth'ful, *a.* Merry; gay.
Mirth'less, *a.* Having no mirth or gayety.
Mir'y, *n.* Full of mire.
Mis'ad-vent'ūre, *n.* A mischance; misfortune.
Mis'an-thrōpe, } *n.* [Gr.
Mis-ăn'thro-pist, } *misanthrōpos,* from *misein,* to hate, and *anthrōpos,* a man.] A hater of mankind.
Mis'an-thrŏp'ic, } *a.*
Mis'an-thrŏp'ic-al, } Hating, or having a dislike to, mankind.
Mis-ăn'thro-py, *n.* Hatred or dislike of mankind.
Mis-ăp'pli-cā'tion, *n.* Wrong application. [wrongly.
Mis'ap-plȳ', *v. t.* To apply
Mis-ăp'pre-hěnd', *v. t.* To misunderstand. [mistake.
Mis-ăp'pre-hěn'sion, *n.* A
Mis'be-cōme', *v. t.* To suit ill. [improperly.
Mis'be-hāve', *v. i.* To behave
Mis'be-hāv'ior, *n.* Improper behavior; ill-conduct.
Mis'be-liēve', *v. t.* To believe erroneously.
Mis-căl'cu-lāte, *v. t.* To calculate wrong. [calculation.
Mis-căl'cu-lā'tion, *n.* Wrong
Mis-call', *v. t.* To call by a wrong name.
Mis-căr'riage (-rĭj), *n.* Failure; abortion.
Mis-căr'ry, *v. i.* To fail of success; to have an abortion.
Mis'cel-lā'ne-oŭs, *a.* Mixed; consisting of various kinds.
Mis'cel·la-ny (41), *n.* A collection of writings; a mixture.
Mis-chănçe', *n.* Misfortune.
Mis'chief, *n.* Evil, whether intended or not. — SYN. Damage; harm.
Mis'chiev-oŭs, *a.* Injurious.
Mis'chiev-oŭs-ly, *adv.* Hurtfully. [wrongly.
Mis-chōōse', *v. t.* To choose
Mis'çi-tā'tion, *n.* A wrong citation. [neously.
Mis-çīte', *v. t.* To quote erroneously.
Mis'con-çeīve', *v. t.* To have a wrong notion of.
Mis'con-çĕp'tion, *n.* Wrong conception. [behavior.
Mis-cŏn'duct (116), *n.* Bad

Mis'con-dŭct', *v. t.* or *i.* To conduct amiss; to behave ill.
Mis'con-jĕet'ūre, *n.* A wrong conjecture.
Mis'con-strŭc'tion, *n.* Wrong construction or interpretation. [terpret wrong.
Mis-cŏn'strue, *v. t.* To in-
Mis-count', *v. t.* To mistake in counting. — *n.* A wrong count.
Mis'cre-ant, *n.* A vile wretch.
Mis-dāte', *v. t.* To date erroneously. [fault; offense.
Mis-deed', *n.* An evil action;
Mis-deem', *v. t.* To judge amiss. [have ill.
Mis'de-mēan', *v. i.* To be-
Mis'de-mēan'or, *n.* Ill-behavior; evil conduct; offense.
Mis'di-rĕct', *v. t.* To direct to a wrong person or place.
Mis-dō'ing, *n.* A wrong done.
Mis'em-ploy', *v. t.* To use to a wrong purpose.
Mis'em-ploy'ment, *n.* Improper application.
Mis-ĕn'try, *n.* Wrong entry in a book. [cess; a niggard.
Mī'ser, *n.* One covetous to excess.
Mis'er-a-ble, *a.* Wretched; unhappy; worthless. [ly.
Mis'er-a-bly, *adv.* Wretched-
Mī'ser-ly, *a.* Very covetous.
Mis'er-y, *n.* Wretchedness; distress; calamity.
Mis-fôrt'une, *n.* Calamity.
Mis-gīve', *v. t.* To fill with doubt; to give amiss.
Mis-gīv'ing, *n.* A weakening of confidence; distrust.
Mis-gŏv'ern, *v. t.* To govern amiss. [administration.
Mis-gŏv'ern-ment, *n.* A bad
Mis-guīd'ance, *n.* Wrong direction; guidance into error.
Mis-guīde', *v. t.* To mislead.
Mis-hăp', *n.* Ill chance or accident; misfortune.
Mis'im-prōve', *v. t.* To use to no purpose, or to a bad one; to abuse; to misuse.
Mis'in-fôrm', *v. t.* To give erroneous information to.
Mis-in'for-mā'tion, *n.* Wrong information.
Mis'in-tēr'pret, *v. t.* To explain erroneously.
Mis'in-tēr'pret-ā'tion, *n.* Interpreting erroneously.
Mis-jŭdge', *v. t.* To judge amiss.
Mis-jŭdg'ment, *n.* A wrong or unjust determination.
Mis-lāy', *v. t.* To lay in a wrong place; to lose.
Mis'le (mĭz'l), *v. i.* To rain in in minute drops.

Mis-lēad', *v. t.* To lead into error; to delude.
Mis-lēd', *imp.* of *Mislead.*
Mis-măn'age, *v. t.* or *i.* To manage ill; to behave ill.
Mis-măn'age-ment, *n.* Bad management. [unsuitably.
Mis-mătch', *v. t.* To match
Mis-nāme', *v. t.* To call by a wrong name.
Mis-nō'mer, *n.* A wrong or inapplicable name.
Mī-sŏg'a-mist, *n.* A hater of marriage. [marriage.
Mī-sŏg'a-my, *n.* Hatred of
Mis-plāçe', *v. t.* To put in a wrong place.
Mis-print', *v. t.* To print wrong. — *n.* An error in printing.
Mis-prīs'ion (-prĭzh'un), *n.* Neglect, as of treason, by not revealing it, or by failing to expose it when observed.
Mis'pro-nounçe', *v. t.* To pronounce incorrectly.
Mis'pro-nŭn'ci-ā'tion (-nŭn'shi-), *n.* Improper pronunciation. [quoting wrong.
Mis'quo-tā'tion, *n.* Act of
Mis-quōte', *v. t.* To quote incorrectly. [falsely.
Mis're-çīte', *v. t.* To recite
Mis-rĕck'on, *v. t.* To compute falsely.
Mis're-lāte', *v. t.* To relate erroneously. [relation.
Mis're-lā'tion, *n.* Erroneous
Mis're-pôrt', *v. t.* To report erroneously. — *n.* A false or incorrect report. [resent falsely.
Mis-rĕp're-sĕnt', *v. t.* To rep-
Mis-rĕp're-sĕnt-ā'tion, *n.* False representation or account. [just domination.
Mis-rule', *n.* Confusion; un-
Miss (124), *n.* A young woman; loss; want; mistake; omission. — *v. t.* To err; not to hit. [olic mass-book.
Mis'sal, *n.* The Roman Cath-
Mis-shāpe', *v. t.* [*p. p.* or *p. a.* MISSHAPEN.] To shape ill; to give an ill form to.
Mis'sile, *n.* [Lat. *missilis,* fr. *mittere, missum,* to send, throw.] A weapon to be thrown. — *a.* Capable of being thrown. [lost.
Miss'ing, *n.* Not to be found;
Mis'sion (mĭsh'un), *n.* Act of sending; duty on which one is sent; persons sent. — SYN. Message; commission; delegation; deputation.
Mis'sion-a-ry, *n.* One sent to spread religion. — *a.* Pertaining to missions.

sŏn, ôr, dọ, wọlf, tōō, tŏŏk; ûrn, rụe, pụll; ç, ġ, *soft;* ɔ, ġ, *hard;* a̱ɀ; e̱x̱i̱s̱t̲; ṇ as ng; this.

MISSIVE 200 MOLDING

Mis'sive, *a.* Sent or intended to be sent. — *n.* A message or letter sent. [ueously.
Mis-spell', *v. t.* To spell erroneously.
Mis-spend', *v. t.* [*imp.* & *p. p.* MISSPENT.] To waste or spend ill. [accurately.
Mis-state', *v. t.* To state incorrectly.
Mis-state'ment, *n.* An incorrect statement.
Mist, *n.* Rain in very fine drops. — *v. i.* To rain in very fine drops.
Mis-take', *n.* Unintentional error. — *v. t.* or *i.* To err.
Mis-tāk'en (-tāk'n), *p. p.* or *a.* Misunderstood, — *used of things;* wrong; being in error, — *used of persons.*
Mis'ter, *n.* A title of address, used for *Master;* — commonly abbreviated Mr. [aright.
Mis-time', *v. t.* Not to time
Mist'i-ness, *n.* State of being misty; obscurity.
Mĭs'tle (mĭz'l). See *Misle.*
Mis'tle-tōe } (mĭz'l-to), *n.* A
Mis'le-tōe } plant that grows on trees.
Mis-tŏŏk', *imp.* of *Mistake.*
Mis'trans-lāte', *v. t.* To translate erroneously.
Mis'trans-lā'tion, *n.* Erroneous translation.
Mis'tress, *n.* A woman who governs; a term of address; a female teacher; a sweetheart; a concubine.
Mis-trŭst', *n.* Want of confidence; suspicion; doubt. — *v. t.* To regard with suspicion; to doubt.
Mis-trŭst'ful, *a.* Suspicious.
Mist'y, *a.* Raining in very fine drops; cloudy with mist.
Mis-ŭn'der-stand', *v. t.* To misconceive; to mistake.
Mis-ŭn'der-stand'ing, *n.* Misconception; disagreement; slight quarrel.
Mis-ūṣ'age, *n.* Bad treatment; abuse. [treat ill.
Mis-ūṣe', *v. t.* To abuse; to
Mis-ūṣe', *n.* Bad use.
Mīte, *n.* Something very small; hence, a small insect.
Mī'ter }
Mī'tre } (151), *n.* A bishop's cap or crown.
Mit'i-ga-ble, *a.* Capable of mitigation. [alleviate; to assuage.
Mit'i-gāte, *v. t.* To lessen; to

Mit'i-gā'tion, *n.* Alleviation; relief.
Mĭt'ten (mĭt'tn, 55), *n.* A cover for the hand, without fingers.
Mĭt'ti-mus, *n.* A warrant of commitment to prison.
Mĭx (129), *v. t.* [*imp.* & *p. p.* MIXED.] To unite or blend promiscuously.
Mĭxt'ūre (mĭkst'yụr), *n.* A mingled mass.
Mĭz'zen (mĭz'zn), *n.* Hindmost; nearest the stern.
Mĭz'zle, *v. t.* See *Misle.*
Mne-mŏn'ic (ne-), *a.* Assisting the memory.
Mne-mŏn'ics (ne-), *n. sing.* The art of memory.
Mōan, *v. i.* or *t.* To mourn; to lament audibly. — *n.* Lamentation; audible grief.
Mōat, *n.* A deep ditch round a castle, &c. — *v. t.* To surround with a moat.
Mŏb, *n.* A tumultuous or disorderly crowd. — *v. t.* To attack, as a crowd.
Mo-bĭl'i-ty, *n.* Activity; fickleness; inconstancy.
Mŏc'ca-sin, *n.* A shoe of soft leather, without a sole; a poisonous serpent.
Mŏck (127), *v. t.* To deride; to ridicule; to ape. — *v. i.* To speak deridingly. — *n.* Counterfeit; false. — *n.* Ridicule; derision; sneer.
Mŏck'er-y, *n.* Derision; scorn; ridicule.
Mō'dal, *a.* Relating to the mode or form.
Mo-dăl'i-ty, *n.* Quality of being modal, or in form only.
Mōde, *n.* Form; method; fashion; manner of conjugating a verb.
Mŏd'el (130), *n.* Something designed to be imitated; pattern. — *v. t.* (130). To plan; to shape; to fashion.
Mŏd'el-er, } *n.* One who
Mŏd'el-ler, } models.
Mŏd'er-āte, *v. t.* To allay; to lessen; to repress. — *v. i.* To become less violent.
Mŏd'er-ate, *a.* Not violent or excessive; temperate; sober.
Mŏd'er-ate-ly, *adv.* With little violence.
Mŏd'er-ā'tion, *n.* State of being moderate.
Mŏd'er-ā'tor, *n.* One who presides. [time.
Mŏd'ern, *a.* Of the present
Mŏd'ern-ĭṣm, *n.* A thing of recent date. [modern.
Mŏd'ern-īze, *v. t.* To make

Mŏd'erns, *n. pl.* People of modern times.
Mŏd'est, *a.* Diffident; reserved; virtuous. [dence.
Mŏd'est-ly, *adv.* With diffi-
Mŏd'est-y, *n.* Absence of conceit; diffidence; chastity.
Mŏd'i-cum, *n.* A small portion or quantity.
Mŏd'i-fi-cā'tion, *n.* Act of modifying; modified state.
Mŏd'i-fī'er (15), *n.* He who, or that which, modifies.
Mŏd'i-fȳ, *v. t.* To change the form of; to qualify; to vary.
Mo-dĭl'lion (-dĭl'yun), *n.* A kind of bracket.
Mŏd'ish, *a.* According to the mode; fashionable.
†**Mo-dĭste',** *n.* [Fr.] A female artist in dress.
Mŏd'u-lāte, *v. t.* To vary or inflect as sounds.
Mŏd'u-lā'tion, *n.* Act of modulating; melody.
Mŏd'u-lā'tor, *n.* That which varies sounds.
Mŏd'ule, *n.* A model or representation.
Mo-gŭl', *n.* A person of the Mongolian race. [hair.
Mō'hâir, *n.* A stuff of goat's
Mo-hăm'med-an, *a.* Pertaining to Mohammed. — *n.* A follower of Mohammed.
Mo-hăm'med-ĭṣm, } *n.*
Mo-hăm'med-an-ĭṣm, } The religion or doctrines of Mohammed.
Moi'e-ty (or maw'e-ty), *n.* Half; one of two equal parts.
Moil, *v. i.* or *t.* To work with painful effort; to drudge.
Moist, *a.* Damp; wet in a small degree; humid.
Moist'en (mois'n), *v. t.* To make humid, or moist.
Moist'ness, *n.* Dampness.
Moist'ūre (moist'yụr), *n.* Slight wetness; dampness.
Mō'lar, *a.* Adapted to grind. — *n.* A double tooth.
Mo-lăs'seṣ, *n. sing.* [Fr. *mélasse,* from Lat. *mellaceus,* honey-like.] The sirup which drains from sugar; treacle.
Mōld } (154), *n.* Soft, rich
Mōuld } earth; a natural downy substance; a form, or something to regulate the form. — *v. t.* To shape. — *v. i.* To contract mold.
Mōld'er, } *n.* One who
Mōuld'er, } molds, or gives shape. — *v. i.* To decay; to perish; to turn to dust.
Mōld'ing, } *n.* Any thing
Mōuld'ing, } cast; a pro-

ā, ē, ī, ō, ū, ÿ, *long;* ă, ĕ, ĭ, ŏ, ŭ, ў, *short;* câre, cär, àsk, ạll, whạt; ẽre, vẹil, tẽrm; pīque, fĭrm;

MOLDY 201 MOORINGS

jection beyond a wall, column, &c.

Mōld′y,) *a.* Covered with
Mōuld′y,) mold.

Mōle, *n.* A natural spot on the body; a pier; a mound; a small burrowing animal.

Mo-lēc′u-lar, *a.* Pertaining to, or consisting of, molecules.

Mŏl′e-cule, *n.* A minute or invisible particle. [by a mole.

Mōle′-hĭll, *n.* A hillock raised

Mo-lĕst′, *v. t.* To disturb; to annoy; to disquiet. [ance.

Mŏl′es-tā′tion, *n.* Annoy-

Mŏl′li-ent (*or* mŏl′yent), *a.* Assuaging; soothing.

Mŏl′li-fī′a-ble, *a.* Capable of being softened or assuaged.

Mŏl′li-fi-cā′tion, *n.* A mollifying; mitigation.

Mŏl′li-fī′er, *n.* One who, or that which, mollifies.

Mŏl′li-fȳ, *v. t.* To soften; to assuage; to qualify.

Mōlt) (154, 13), *v. i.* To cast
Mōult) or shed feathers, skin, horns, &c.

Mōlt′en (18), *p. a.* Melted.

Mō′ment, *n.* A minute portion of time; importance; weight. [moment.

Mō′ment-a-ri-ly, *adv.* Every

Mō′ment-a-ry (41), *a.* Done in, or lasting for, a moment only. [ment.

Mō′ment-ly, *adv.* In a mo-

Mo-mĕnt′ous, *a.* Important.

Mo-mĕn′tum, *n.* (*pl.* †Momĕn′tā, or Mo-mĕn′tums, 147). Quantity of motion in a moving body. [life.

Mŏn′a-ehism, *n.* Monastic

Mŏn′ad, *n.* An ultimate atom.

Mo-năd′ic, *a.* Having the nature of a monad.

Mŏn′areh, *n.* (Gr. *monarchos,* fr. *monos,* alone, and *archein,* to rule.] A supreme ruler; an emperor, king, prince, or chief. — SYN. Potentate; sovereign.

Mo-närch′ic,) Relat-
Mo-närch′ie-al,) ing to a monarch. [monarchy.

Mŏn′arch-ĭst, *n.* A friend to

Mŏn′arch-y, *n.* Government vested in one man; a kingdom; an empire.

Mŏn′as-ter-y (*colloq.* mŏn′as-try), *n.* A house of monks.

Mo-năs′tic, *a.* Pertaining to monks; secluded.

Mo-năs′ti-çĭsm, *n.* Monastic life. [ing Sunday.

Mŏn′day, *n.* The day follow-

Mŏn′e-ta-ry, *a.* Relating to money.

Mŏn′ey (41), *n.* Coin for current use in trade, or a substitute for it.

Mŏn′ey-brō′ker, *n.* A broker who deals in money.

Mŏn′eȳed (mŭn′id), *a.* Possessed of money; wealthy; rich; opulent.

Mŏn′eȳ-less, *a.* Destitute of money; penniless.

Mŏn′grel (mŭng′grel), *a.* Of a mixed breed. — *n.* An animal of a mixed breed.

Mo-nĭ′tion (-nĭsh′un), *n.* Warning; instruction.

Mŏn′i-tĭve, *a.* Conveying warning or instruction.

Mŏn′i-tor, *n.* One who warns; a subordinate instructor.

Mŏn′i-tō′ri-al, *a.* Pertaining to a monitor. [ing.

Mŏn′i-to-ry, *a.* Giving warn-

Mŏn′i-tress, *n.* A female monitor. [monastery.

Mŏnk, *n.* One who lives in a

Mŏnk′er-y, *n.* Monastic life or practices.

Mŏnk′ey (141), *n.* An animal like the ape or baboon.

Mŏnk′ish, *a.* Pertaining to monks. [monodies.

Mŏn′o-dĭst, *n.* A writer of

Mŏn′o-dy, *n.* Poetical lament of a single person.

Mo-nŏg′a-mĭst, *n.* One who disallows second marriages.

Mo-nŏg′a-my, *n.* Marriage to one wife only.

Mŏn′o-grăm, *n.* A cipher composed of letters interwoven.

Mŏn′o-grăph, *n.* A written account of a single thing.

Mŏn′o-lĭth, *n.* A column consisting of a single stone.

Mŏn′o-lĭth′ic, *a.* Consisting of a single stone.

Mŏn′o-lōgue, *n.* A speech by one person.

Mŏn′o-mā′ni-à, *n.* Derangement with regard to one subject only.

Mŏn′o-mā′ni-ăc, *n.* A person affected by monomania.

Mŏn′o-pĕt′al-ous, *a.* Having the corolla in one piece.

Mŏn′oph-thŏng (mŏn′of-thŏng, *or* mo-nŏp′thong), *n.* A single uncompounded vowel sound.

Mo-nŏp′o-lĭst,) *n.* One
Mo-nŏp′o-lĭz′er,) who monopolizes.

Mo-nŏp′o-lĭze, *v. t.* To engross the whole of.

Mo-nŏp′o-ly, *n.* Sole right of buying and selling or of trading in some article or at some place.

Mŏn′o-syl-lăb′ic,) *a.* Of
Mŏn′o-syl-lăb′ie-al,) , one syllable only.

Mŏn′o-sȳl′la-ble, *n.* A word of one syllable.

Mŏn′o-thē′ĭsm, *n.* The belief in one God only.

Mŏn′o-tōne, *n.* A single unvaried tone or sound.

Mo-nŏt′o-noŭs, *a.* In the same tone; without variety.

Mo-nŏt′o-noŭs-ly, *adv.* In a monotonous manner.

Mo-nŏt′o-ny, *n.* Uniformity of tone; want of variety.

†**Monsieur** (mo-sĕer′, *or* mōs′-yûr′), *n.* [Fr.] Sir or mister; a Frenchman; in contempt.

Mon-sōon′, *n.* A periodical wind in the Indian ocean.

Mŏn′ster, *n.* Something horrid or unnatural.

Mon-strŏs′i-ty, *n.* State of being monstrous.

Mŏn′stroŭs, *a.* Abnormal; enormous; unnatural; horrible. [monstrous manner.

Mŏn′stroŭs-ly, *adv.* In a

Mŏnth, *n.* One revolution of the moon; twelfth part of the year.

Mŏnth′ly. *a.* Happening every month. — *adv.* Once a month.

Mŏn′u-ment, *n.* [Lat. *monumentum,* fr. *monere,* to remind.] A memorial; a tomb.

Mŏn′u-mĕnt′al. *a.* Pertaining to, or serving as, a monument; memorial.

Mŏod, *n.* Temper of mind; humor; disposition; musical style; form of conjugation of a verb; mode.

Mōod′i-ness, *n.* Quality of being moody.

Mōod′y, *a.* Governed by moods of feeling; ill-humored; peevish; angry; abstracted.

Mōon, *n.* A satellite of this earth, revolving round it; a month.

Mōon′lĭght (-lĭt),) *n.* Light of
Mōon′shĭne,) the moon.

Mōon′-strŭck, *a.* Affected by the moon; lunatic.

Mōor, *n.* A black man; a marsh; heathy land. — *v. t.* To secure, as a vessel, by means of cables and anchors.

Mōor′age, *n.* A place for mooring ships.

Mōor′ings, *n. pl.* Anchors, chains, &c., to hold a ship.

---

sŏn, ôr, do, wolf, too, took; ûrn, rue, pull; ç, ġ, *soft;* ç, ġ, *hard;* aṣ; eẋist; ɳ as ng; this.

9*

Moor'ish, *a.* Marshy; fenny; relating to the Moors.
Moor'land, *n.* Marshy land.
Moose, *n.* An animal of the deer kind.
Moot, *v. t.* To discuss or debate. *a.* Disputable.

Moose.

Moot'-case, *n.* A case admitting of dispute.
Mop, *n.* A cloth, or collection of threads for cleaning floors. — *v. t.* To wipe with a mop.
Mope, *v. i.* To be very dull or spiritless. — *n.* A dull, stupid person.
Mop'ish, *a.* Dull; spiritless.
Mop'pet, *n.* A rag baby; a little girl.
Mop'sey, *n.* A rag baby; a little girl.
Mor'al, *a.* Pertaining to practice or manners in reference to right and wrong; virtuous; just; probable. — *n.* The precept inculcated by a fable; (*pl.*) Conduct; behavior.
Mor'al-ist (13Ô), *n.* One who teaches morality.
Mo-ral'i-ty, *n.* System or practice of moral duties
Mor'al-ize, *v. t.* or *i.* To discourse on moral subjects; to apply to moral purposes.
Mor'al-iz-er, *n.* One who moralizes.
Mor'al-ly, *adv.* In a moral sense; honestly; according to human judgment.
Mor'als, *n. pl.* The practice of the duties of life; ethics.
Mo-rāss', *n.* A tract of wet, soft ground; a marsh; a fen.
Mor'bid, *a.* [Lat. *morbidus*, from *morbus*, disease.] Not sound or healthy. — SYN. Diseased; sickly; sick.
Mor-bif'ic, *a.* Tending to produce disease. [castic.
Mor-dā'cious, *a.* Biting; sarcastic.
Mor-dăç'i-ty, *n.* Quality of biting.
Mor'dant, *n.* Serving to fix colors. — *n.* A substance to fix colors in cloth.
More, *a.* Greater in quantity or number. — *adv.* To a greater degree. — *n.* Greater quantity or amount.
Mo-reen', *n.* A stout kind of woolen stuff.
More-ō'ver (137), *adv.* Furthermore; besides; in addition.

Mo-resque' (mo-rĕsk'), *a.* Done after the manner of the Moors, as paintings.
Mŏr'gan-ăt'ic, *a.* Relating to a marriage between a man of superior and a woman of inferior rank, in which neither the latter nor her children can enjoy the rank or inherit the possessions of her husband.
Morn, *n.* The first part of the day.
Morn'ing, *n.* The first part of the day.
Mo-rŏc'co, *n.* Leather of goat or sheep-skin tanned with sumach.
Mo-rōse', *a.* Of a sour temper. — SYN. Sullen; peevish; surly; austere.
Mo-rōse'ly, *adv.* Sullenly.
Mo-rōse'ness, *n.* Sourness of temper. [face.
Mŏr'phew, *n.* A scurf on the
Mŏr'ris, *n.* A dance; a game.
Mŏr'rōw, *n.* Next day after the present.
Mŏrse, *n.* The walrus or seahorse. [piece.
Mŏr'sel, *n.* A bite; a small
Mŏr'tal, *a.* [Lat. *mortalis*, fr. *mors*, death.] Subject to death; deadly; human. — *n.* A human being.
Mor-tăl'i-ty, *n.* Subjection to death; number of deaths.
Mŏr'tal-ly, *adv.* So as to cause death; fatally.
Mŏr'tar, *n.* A kind of cement for building; a vessel

Mortar.

used for pounding things in; a piece of ordnance for throwing bombs.
Mŏrt'gage (môr'gej, 98), *n.* A pledge of real estate. — *v. t.* To pledge or convey for securing a debt.
Mŏrt'ga-gee' (môr'-), *n.* One to whom a mortgage is given.
Mŏrt'ga-ger (môr'-), *n.* One who executes a mortgage.
Mŏr'ti-fi-cā'tion. *n.* Process of corrupting; humiliation.
Mŏr'ti-fȳ, *v. t.* or *t.* To corrupt: to gangrene; to humble.
Mŏr'tise, *n.* opening or cut to receive a tenon. — *v. t.* To form with a mortise.
Mŏrt'māin, *n.* An inalienable estate.
Mo-sā'ic, *n.* Work variegated by shells and stones of various colors. — *a.* Com-

Mortise.

posed of mosaic; relating to Moses.
Mŏsque (mŏsk), *n.* A Mohammedan house of worship.
Mos-qui'to (-kē'-), *n.* (*pl.* **Mos-qui'tos**, 140). A small blood-sucking insect.
Mŏss (2), *n.* A cellular plant growing on trees, &c. — *v. t.* To cover with moss.
Mŏss'i-ness, *n.* State of being mossy. [moss.
Mŏss'y, *a.* Overgrown with
Mŏst (16), *a.* Greatest in number or quantity. — *n.* The greatest number or quantity. — *adv.* In the greatest degree.
Mŏst'ly, *adv.* For the greatest part; usually. [ticle.
Mōte, *n.* A very small particle.
Mŏth, *n.; pl.* **Mŏths**. A winged insect.
Mŏth'er (mŭth'er), *n.* A female parent; a slimy substance in vinegar.
Mŏth'er-hŏŏd (mŭth'er-), *n.* The state of a mother.
Mŏth'er-less, *a.* Destitute of a mother.
Mŏth'er-ly, *a.* Like a mother; tender; maternal.
Mŏth'er wit, *n.* Native wit.
Mŏth'er-y, *a.* Full of mother; concreted; slimy.
Mō'tion, *n.* Act of changing place; movement; a proposal made. — *v. i.* To make proposals; to move.
Mō'tion-less, *a.* Quiescent.
Mō'tive, *a.* Causing to move. — *n.* That which incites to volition or action. — SYN. Inducement; reason.
Mŏt'ley, *a.* Variegated in color; party-colored.
Mō'tōr, *n.* A moving power.
Mŏt'tled, *a.* Marked with spots of different color.
Mŏt'to (140), *n.* A phrase or sentence prefixed to an essay, poem, &c.; an inscription.
Mould, Mŏul'der, Mŏuld'y, &c. See *Mold, Molder, Moldy*, &c.
Mŏult. See *Molt*.
Mound, *n.* A raised bank; a bulwark; a rampart; a knoll. — *v. t.* To fortify with a mound.
Mount, *n.* A hill; mountain; heap. — *v. i.* To rise; to soar. — *v. t.* To put on any thing that sustains and fits for use; to ascend.
Mount'ain (39), *n.* A mass of earth and rock higher than a hill. — *a.* Pertaining to mountains.

MOUNTAINEER 203 MURIATIC

Mount'ain-eer', *n.* A dweller on a mountain.
Mount'ain-oŭs, *a.* Abounding with mountains; huge.
Mount'e-bănk, *n.* A quack doctor; a boastful pretender.
Mŏurn, *v. i.* or *t.* To grieve; to lament; to sorrow.
Mŏurn'er, *n.* One who grieves or laments. [mentable.
Mŏurn'ful, *a.* Sorrowful; la-
Mŏurn'fŭl-ly, *adv.* So as to bring or express sorrow.
Mŏurn'fŭl-ness, *n.* Sorrow; grief.
Mŏurn'ing, *n.* Act of sorrowing; dress of mourners.
Mouse (145), *n.* A small well-known animal.
Mouṣe, *v. i.* To watch for and catch mice; to be sly.
Mous'er, *n.* A cat that catches mice. [tache.
Mous-tăche', *n.* See *Mus-*
Mouth (96), *n.* The aperture between the lips and the cavity within them; an opening, as of a cavern.
Mouth, *v. t.* or *i.* To utter with a loud, affected voice.
Mouth'ful (139, 148), *n.* As much as the mouth holds at once.
Mouth'-piĕçe, *n.* Part of an instrument for the mouth: one who speaks for another; a spokesman. [being moved.
Mŏv'a-ble (133), *a.* Capable of
Mŏv'a-bleṣ, *n. pl.* Goods, furniture, &c.
Mŏve, *v. t.* To put in motion; to excite to action or compassion; to propose or recommend. — *v. i.* To change place; to act; to make a proposal. — *n.* Act of moving; movement.
Mŏve'ment (132), *n.* Act of moving; change of place; excitement. — SYN. Motion.
Mŏv'er, *n.* One who moves.
Mŏv'ing, *a.* Changing place; pathetic.
Mow (mou), *n.* A pile of hay in a barn. — *v. t.* To heap up in a barn.
Mōw, *v. t.* [*imp.* MOWED; *p. p.* MOWED, MOWN.] To cut down with a scythe.
Mōw'er, *n.* One who mows.
Mōwn, *p. p.* of *Mow.*
Much, *a.* Great in quantity or amount. — *n.* A great quantity. — *adv.* In a great degree.
Mū'çid, *a.* Musty; slimy.
Mū'çi-laġe, *n.* A slimy or viscous mass; an aqueous solution of gum.

Mū'çi-lăġ'i-noŭs, *a.* Slimy; ropy.
Mŭck, *n.* A mass of moist matter; any thing filthy. — *v. t.* To manure with muck.
Mŭck'worm (-wŭrm), *n.* A worm that lives in muck; a miser.
Mū'coŭs, *a.* Slimy; viscous.
Mū'cus, *n.* A slimy or viscous animal fluid.
Mŭd, *n.* Earth wet, soft, and adhesive; mire. — *v. t.* To make foul with mud; to bespatter. [being muddy.
Mŭd'di-ness, *n.* State of
Mŭd'dle, *v. t.* To make muddy or confused.
Mŭd'dy (135), *a.* Foul; dirty; turbid. — *v. t.* To make foul; to soil with mud.
†**Mu-ĕz'zin**, *n.* [Ar.] A Mohammedan crier of the hour of prayer.
Mŭff (123), *n.* A warm fur cover for the hands. [cake.
Mŭf'fin, *n.* A light kind of
Mŭf'fle, *v. t.* To cover close.
Mŭf'fler, *n.* A cover for the face, head, or neck.
†**Mŭf'tĭ** (140), *n.* [Ar.] An official expounder of Mohammedan law in Turkey.
Mŭg, *n.* A kind of cup or vessel to drink from.
Mŭg'gy, *a.* Moist and close.
Mu-lăt'to, *n.* (*pl.* Mu-lăt'tōes, 140.) The child of a black and a white person.
Mŭl'bĕr-ry, *n.* A tree and its berry or fruit.
Mŭlçt, *n.* A pecuniary penalty. — *v. t.* To punish by a fine; to fine.
Mūle (26), *n.* An animal or plant of a mongrel kind; esp. the offspring of an ass and a mare. [mules.
Mū'let-eer', *n.* A driver of
Mŭl'ish, *a.* Like a mule; stubborn; perverse.
Mŭll (123), *v. t.* To spice and sweeten, as wine.
Mŭl'ler, *n.* A stone for grinding pigments. [dow frame.
Mŭll'ion, *n.* A bar in a win-
Mult-ăn'gu-lar, *a.* Having many angles.
Mŭl'tĭ-fā'rĭ-oŭs, *a.* Having great variety. [divisions.
Mŭl'tĭ-fĭd, *a.* Having many
Mŭl'tĭ-fōrm, *a.* Having various forms or shapes.
Mŭl'tĭ-fōrm'ĭ-ty, *n.* Diversity of forms.
Mŭl'tĭ-lăt'er-al, *a.* Having many sides. [many names.
Mŭl'tĭ-nō'mĭ-al, *a.* Having

Mul-tĭp'a-roŭs, *a.* Producing many at a birth.
Mul-tĭp'ar-tīte, *a.* Divided into many parts. [many feet.
Mŭl'tĭ-pĕd, *n.* An insect with
Mŭl'tĭ-ple, *n.* A number exactly divisible by another.
Mŭl'tĭ-plī'a-ble, *a.* Capable of being multiplied.
Mŭl'tĭ-plī-cănd', *n.* A number to be multiplied.
Mŭl'tĭ-plĭ-cā'tion, *n.* Act of multiplying. [variety.
Mŭl'tĭ-plĭç'ĭ-ty, *n.* A great
Mŭl'tĭ-plī'er, *n.* One who, or that which, multiplies.
Mŭl'tĭ-plȳ, *v.* To increase in numbers. [ber.
Mŭl'tĭ-tūde, *n.* A great num-
Mŭl'tĭ-tū'dĭ-noŭs, *a.* Consisting of a great number.
Mŭl'tĭ-vălve, *a.* Having many valves.
Mŭm, *n.* A sort of strong beer. — *a.* Silent.
Mŭm'ble, *v. i.* or *t.* To mutter; to speak indistinctly.
Mŭm'mer, *n.* A masked buffoon.
Mŭm'mer-y, *n.* Sport in masks; buffoonery; foolery.
Mŭm'mĭ-fȳ, *v. t.* To embalm, as a mummy.
Mŭm'my (141), *n.* A dead human body embalmed.
Mŭmp'ish, *a.* Grum; sullen.
Mŭmps, *n.* Inflammation of the parotid gland.
Mŭnch, *v. t.* or *i.* To chew continuously upon.
Mŭn'dāne, *a.* [Lat. *mundinus*, fr. *mundus*, the world.] Belonging to this world.
Mu-nĭç'ĭ-pal, *a.* Belonging to a city or corporation.
Mu-nĭç'ĭ-păl'ĭ-ty, *n.* A municipal district.
Mu-nĭf'ĭ-çençe, *n.* Liberality; generosity.
Mu-nĭf'ĭ-çent, *a.* Giving generously. — SYN. Liberal; beneficent; bountiful.
Mū'nĭ-ment, *n.* A fortification; a record or a title-deed.
Mu-nĭ'tion (-nĭsh'un), *n.* Materials for war; military stores.
Mū'ral, *a.* Pertaining to a wall.
Mŭr'der, *n.* Act of killing a human being with premeditated malice. — *v. t.* To assassinate; to destroy.
Mŭr'der-er, *n.* One who is guilty of murder.
Mŭr'der-ess, *n.* A woman who commits murder.
Mŭr'der-oŭs, *a.* Pertaining to, or guilty of, murder.
Mū'rĭ-ăt'ĭc, *a.* Obtained from,

sŏn, ôr, do, wolf, too, took; ûrn, rue, pull; ç, ġ, *soft;* c, ġ, *hard;* aẓ; exist; ṇ *as* ng; thiṣ.

or having the nature of, seasalt.

Mûrk′y, *a*. Dark; gloomy.

Mûr′mur (85), *v. i*. To mutter; to grumble; to purl. — *n*. A low, continued noise; a half-suppressed complaint.

Mûr′rain, *n*. An infectious disease among cattle.

Mŭs′cle (mŭs′sl, 62), *n*. The fleshy fiber in animals; a certain shell-fish. [sugar.

Mŭs′co-vā′do, *n*. Unrefined

Mŭs′cu-lar, *a*. Relating to the muscles; strong; powerful; brawny. [ing muscular.

Mŭs′eu-lăr′i-ty, *n*. State of be-

Mūse (140), *n*. Deep thought; (*pl*.) the nine goddesses presiding over the arts and sciences. — *v. t.* To think deeply.

Mu-ṣē′um (115), *n*. A repository or cabinet of curiosities.

Mŭsh, *n*. Food of maize meal.

Mŭsh′room, *n*. A fungous plant.

Mū′ṣic (127), *n*. Science of harmonical sounds; melody or harmony. [monious.

Mū′ṣic-al, *a*. Melodious; har-

Mū′ṣic-al-ly, *adv*. In a musical manner. [skilled in music.

Mu-ṣī′cian (-zĭsh′an), *n*. One

Mŭsk, *n*. An animal and a strong-scented substance procured from it. — *v. t.* To perfume with musk.

Mŭs′ket, *n*. A kind of fire-arm.

Mŭs′ket-ry, *n*. Muskets in general or collectively.

Mŭsk′-mĕl′on, *n*. A fragrant species of melon.

Mŭsk′-ŏx, *n*. A kind of ox living in the country about Hudson's Bay.

Musk-ox.

Mŭsk′y, *a*. Having the odor of musk.

Mŭs′lin, *n*. [From *Mossoul*, where it was first manufactured.] A fine cotton cloth.

Mus-quī′to. See *Mosquito*.

Mŭs′sul-man (143 , *n*. A believer in the Koran; a Mohammedan.

Must, *v. i*. To be obliged; to be morally fit. — *v. t.* To grow moldy or sour. — *n*. New wine unfermented.

Mus-tăche′, *n. sing.* } Hair on
Mus-tā′ches, *n. pl.*   } the upper lip.

Mŭs′tard, *n*. A plant, and a condiment prepared from it.

Mŭs′ter, *v. t.* or *i*. To assemble. — *n*. A review of troops; assemblage and display. [forces.

Mŭs′ter-rŏll, *n*. A list of

Mŭs′ti-ness (185), *n*. Moldiness; sourness.

Mŭs′ty, *a*. Affected with mold; spoiled by damp or age; stale.

Mū′ta-bĭl′i-ty, *n*. Changeableness; inconstancy; instability: unsettled state.

Mū′ta-ble, *a*. Subject, or given, to change. — SYN. Changeable; fickle; inconstant; variable.

Mu-tā′tion, *n*. Change or process of changing.

Mūte, *a*. Silent; speechless; dumb. — *n*. One who is silent or speechless; a silent letter. — *v. i.* To molt; to dung, as birds.

Mūte′ly (132), *adv*. Silently.

Mūte′ness, *n*. Silence; dumbness; aversion to speech.

Mū′ti-lāte, *v. t.* To cut off, as a limb; to mangle.

Mū′ti-lā′tion, *n*. Deprivation of an essential part.

Mū′ti-neer′, *n*. One who joins in a mutiny. [orderly.

Mū′ti-noŭs, *a*. Seditious; dis-

Mū′ti-ny, *n*. An insurrection of soldiers or seamen. — *v. i.* To rise against military or naval authority.

Mŭt′ter. *v. i*. or *t*. To speak low and sullenly, or in complaint; to murmur; to grumble.

Mŭt′ton. *n*. Flesh of sheep.

Mūt′u-al, *a*. Reciprocal; acting in return.

Mūt′u-ăl′i-ty, *n*. State of being mutual; reciprocation.

Mūt′u-al-ly, *adv*. Reciprocally.

Mŭz′zle, *v. t*. To fasten the mouth of. — *n*. Mouth and nose of an animal; a fastening for the mouth.

Mȳ, *a*. Belonging to me.

Mȳ′o-py, *n*. Short-sightedness.

Mȳr′i-ad, *n*. The number of 10,000; any large number.

Mȳr′mi-don (mẽr′ul-), *n*. A rough soldier; a ruffian.

Myrrh (mẽr, 34), *n*. An inspissated aromatic sap in drops.

Myr′tle (mẽr′tl, 34), *n*. A shrub of several species.

Mȳ-sĕlf′ *pron*. 1; not another.

Mys-tē′ri-oŭs, *a*. Full of mystery; obscure. [scurely.

Mys-tē′ri-oŭs-ly, *adv*. Ob-

Mȳs′ter-y, *n*. A profound secret; an enigma; a trade or calling.

Mȳs′tic, *n*. One who professes to have direct intercourse with God.

Mȳs′tic,   } *a*. Obscure; se-
Mȳs′tic-al, } cret; hidden; allegorical; emblematical.

Mȳs′tic-al-ly, *adv*. With a secret meaning.

Mȳs′ti-cĭṣm, *n*. Obscurity of doctrine; the doctrines of mystics. [purposely.

Mȳs′ti-fȳ, *v. t*. To perplex

Mȳth, *n*. A religious fable; a fiction.

Mȳth′ic, *a*. Fabulous.

Mȳth′o-lŏǵ′ic-al, *a*. Pertaining to mythology.

Mȳ-thŏl′o-ġĭst, *n*. One versed in mythology.

Mȳ-thŏl′o-ġy (117), *n*. A system of fabulous doctrines respecting heathen deities.

N.

NĂB, *v. t*. To catch suddenly; to seize.

Nā′bŏb, *n*. A viceroy in India; a very rich man.

Nā′cre (nā′ker, 151), *n*. Mother-of-pearl.

Nā′dir, *n*. [Ar. *nadīr*, opposite.] That point of the heavens directly opposite the zenith; hence, the lowest point.

Năg, *n*. A small horse.

Nā′iad (nā′yad). *n*. (*pl*. Nā′iads, or †Nā′iad-ēṣ.) A water nymph.

Nāil, *n*. A claw; a horny substance on the ends of the fingers and toes; an iron pin; two inches and a quarter. — *v. t.* (130). To fasten with a nail or with nails; to fix; to catch.

NAILERY 205 NECKCLOTH

Nail'er-y, *n.* A place where nails are made.
Na'ked (57), *a.* Having no covering; bare; nude; open.
Na'ked-ly, *adv.* Openly; plainly; barrenly.
Na'ked-ness, *n.* Bareness.
Name, *n.* Title; appellation; reputation. — *v. t.* To mention by name; to denominate.
Name'less (182), *a.* Having no name.
Name'ly, *adv.* That is to say.
Name'sake (139), *n.* A person of the same name as another.
Nan-keen', *n.* A yellowish cotton cloth.
Nap, *n.* A short sleep; woolly substance on cloth. — *v. i.* To sleep a short time. [neck.
Nape, *n.* The back part of the
Naph'tha (nap'tha or naf'thä, 82), *n.* A bituminous and inflammable liquid which exudes from the earth.
Nap'kin, *n.* A small towel; a cloth to wipe the mouth and hands on.
Nap'py, *a.* Sleepy; causing sleepiness; heady; downy.
Nar-cis'sus, *n.* A genus of flowering plants.
Nar-cot'ic, *a.* Inducing sleep. — *n.* An opiate.
Nard, *n.* An odorous plant and an unguent made from it; spikenard.
Nar'rate, or Nar-rate', *v. t.* To tell; to relate.
Nar-ra'tion, *n.* Relation; rehearsal; recital; account.
Nar'ra-tive, *n.* A recital of particulars; a story. — *a.* Relating particulars. [rates.
Nar-ra'tor, *n.* One who narNar'row, *a.* Having little width; contracted; close; covetous. — *v.* To make or become less broad; to contract.
Nar'row-ly, *adv.* Closely; nearly; hardly; barely.
Nar'row-ness, *n.* Want of breadth; meanness.
Nar'rows, *n. pl.* A narrow passage; a strait.
Nar'whal.
n. A kind of whale, which is also called *sea-unicorn*. Narwhal.
Na'sal, *a.* Pertaining to the nose. — *n.* A letter whose sound is affected by the nose.
Nas'cent, *n.* Beginning to exist or to grow. [ily.
Nas'ti-ly, *adv.* Filthily; dirtNas'ti-ness, *n.* Quality of being nasty.

Nas'ty, *a.* Dirty; filthy; vile.
Na'tal, *a.* Relating to nativity or birth.
Na'tant, *a.* Floating in a fluid.
Na'tion, *n.* People living under one government; a race; a stock.
Na'tion-al (nāsh'un-), *a.* Pertaining to a nation.
Na'tion-äl'i-ty (nāsh'un-), *n.* Love of one's nation; a nation; a race.
Na'tion-al-ize (nāsh'un-), *v. t.* To make national.
Na'tive, *a.* Born with the being; pertaining to the place of one's birth. — SYN. Natural; natal. — *n.* One born in a place.
Na-tiv'i-ty, *n.* Birth; time, place, or circumstances of birth.
Nat'u-ral, *a.* Pertaining to nature; regular; not revealed; unaffected. — *n.* An idiot; a fool.
Nat'u-ral-ism, *n.* A mere state of nature.
Nat'u-ral-ist, *n.* One versed in natural history or physics.
Nat'u-ral-i-zā'tion, *n.* Admission to native privileges.
Nat'u-ral-Ize (153), *v. t.* To confer the rights of citizenship on. [to nature.
Nat'u-ral-ly, *adv.* According Nat'ūre (50), *n.* Native character; kind; sort; the creation or universe; established or regular course; natural affection.
Naught (nawt), *n.* Nothing. — *a.* Worthless; bad; vile.
Naught'i-ly (nawt'-), *adv.* In a naughty manner.
Naught'i-ness, *n.* Badness; perverseness. [corrupt.
Naught'y (nawt'y), *a.* Bad; Nau'se-a (naw'she-ā, 89), *n.* Sickness at the stomach; loathing; qualm.
Nau'se-āte (naw'she-āt), *v. t.* To affect or to reject with disgust; to loathe.
Nau'seoŭs (-shus, 92), *a.* Loathsome.
Nau'tic-al, *a.* Pertaining to seamen or to navigation.
Nau'ti-lus, *n.* A certain mollusk or its shell.
Nā'val, *a.* [Lat. *navalis*, from *naeis*, a ship.] Consisting of, or belonging to, ships. Nautilus.

Nāve, *n.* Middle part of a church and also of a wheel.
Nā'vel (nāv'vl, 58), *n.* The middle of the abdomen. [ships.
Nāv'i-ga-ble, *a.* Passable for Nāv'i-gāte, *v. i.* or *t.* To pass with ships; to sail.
Nāv'i-gā'tion, *n.* Act or art of navigating; ships in general.
Nāv'i-gā'tor, *n.* One who directs the course of a ship.
Nā'vy, *n.* A fleet of ships, especially of war-ships; officers and seamen of such a fleet.
Nāy, *adv.* No; a word of denying. — *n.* Denial.
Năz'a-rēne', *n.* An inhabitant of Nazareth; an early Christian.
Nĕap, *n.* The pole of a cart. — *a.* Low; as, *neap* tides.
Nĕar, *a.* Not distant; close; intimate; immediate; covetous. — *v.* To approach. — *adv.* Within a little. — *prep.* Close by; not far from. [ly.
Nĕar'ly, *adv.* At hand; closeNĕar'ness, *n.* Closeness.
Nĕar'-sīght'ed (-sīt'-), *a.* Seeing at a small distance only.
Nĕat, *a.* Very clean; nice; pure. [and cows.
Nĕat'-căt'tle, *n. pl.* Oxen Nĕat'ly, *adv.* Cleanly; nicely.
Nĕat'ness, *n.* Cleanliness; niceness; purity.
Nĕb, *n.* A nose; beak of a bird.
†Nĕb'u-là, *n.* (*pl.* Nĕb'u-læ, 147.) A faint misty spot in the sky, composed of innumerable stars.
Nĕb'u-lŏs'i-ty, *n.* State of being nebulous.
Nĕb'u-loŭs, *a.* Resembling a nebula, or a collection of vapors. [needful.
Nĕç'es-sa-rĭes, *n. pl.* Things Nĕç'es-sa-ri-ly, *adv.* From necessity; inevitably.
Nĕç'es-sa-ry, *a.* Such as must be; indispensable; needful.
Ne-çĕs'si-tā'ri-an, *n.* One who maintains the doctrine of philosophical necessity in human volitions and all events.
Ne-çĕs'si-tāte, *v. t.* To make necessary; to compel.
Ne-çĕs'si-toŭs, *a.* Very needy.
Ne-çĕs'si-ty, *n.* That which must be; pressing need; extreme indigence; irresistibo force; inevitable consequence.
Nĕck, *n.* The part between the head and body; a narrow tract of land. [men's necks.
Nĕck'cloth, *n.* A cloth for

NECKERCHIEF 206 NICELY

Neck'er-chief (139), *n.* A kerchief for the neck.
Neck'lace, *n.* A string of beads, &c., for the neck.
Ne-crŏl'o-gist, *n.* One who gives an account of deaths.
Ne-crŏl'o-gy, *n.* A register of the dead or of deaths.
Nĕc'ro-măn'çer, *n.* A sorcerer; a wizard; a conjuror.
Nĕc'ro-măn'çy, *n.* Conjuration; sorcery; witchcraft.
Ne-crŏp'o-lis, *n.* A city of the dead; a cemetery.
Nĕc'tar, *n.* The fabled drink of the gods.
Nec-tā're-an,) *a.* Like nectar; sweet.
Nec-tā're-oŭs,)
Nĕc'tar-ine, *n.* A variety of the peach. [tar.
Nĕc'ta-roŭs, *a.* Sweet as nectar.
Nĕc'ta-ry, *n.* The honey-cup of a flower.
Need, *n.* Occasion for something; urgent want. — SYN. Necessity; exigency; strait. — *v. t.* To want. — *v. i.* To be wanted. [requisite.
Need'ful (139), *a.* Necessary.
Nee'dle (140), *n.* A pointed instrument for sewing; pointer of the mariner's compass.
Need'less, *a.* Unnecessary.
Need'less-ly, *adv.* Without necessity.
Needs, *adv.* Necessarily.
Need'y, *a.* Necessitous; poor.
Nē'er, *adv.* A contraction of *never.* [wicked; iniquitous.
Ne-fā'ri-oŭs, *a.* Abominably
Ne-gā'tion, *n.* Denial.
Nĕg'a-tive, *a.* Implying denial. — *n.* A word indicating denial, as *not.* — *v. t.* To prove the contrary of; to deny; to refuse; to reject.
Nĕg'a-tive-ly, *adv.* With or by denial.
Neg-lĕct', *v. t.* To omit by carelessness; to disregard. — *n.* Omission; slight.
Neg-lĕct'ful, *a.* Heedless; careless.
Nĕg'li-gençe, *n.* Habitual omission of that which ought to be done; heedlessness.
Nĕg'li-gent, *a.* Apt to neglect; heedless; inattentive.
Nĕg'li-gent-ly, *adv.* Heedlessly; carelessly.
Ne-gō'ti-a-ble (-shĭ-a-), *a.* Capable of being negotiated.
Ne-gō'ti-āte, (-shĭ-āt), *v.* To trade; to treat with; to sell; to pass.
Ne-gō'ti-ā'tion (-shĭ-ā'shun, 92), *n.* Act of negotiating; a treaty of business.

Ne-gō'ti-ā'tor (-gō'shĭ-), *n.* One who negotiates.
Nē'gress, *n.* A female negro.
Nē'gro, *n.* (*pl.* Nē'groes. 140.) (Sp., from Lat. *niger,* black.) A black African, or a descendant of one.
Nē'gus, *n.* Wine, water, sugar, and lemon-juice, mixed.
Nĕigh (nā), *v. i.* To whinny, or cry, as a horse. — *n.* Voice of a horse.
Nĕigh'bor (nā'bur), *n.* One who lives near; a country or nation near. — *v. i.* To live near; to adjoin.
Nĕigh'bor-hŏŏd (nā'-), *n.* A place near. — SYN. Vicinity.
Nĕigh'bor-ing (nā'-), *a.* Living or being near.
Nĕigh'bor-ly (nā'-), *a.* Cultivating familiar intercourse; becoming a neighbor.
Nēi'ther (nē'ther or nī'ther; — the former mode is much to be preferred), *pron.* Not either. — *conj.* Nor.
Nē'o-lŏg'ic-al, *a.* Pertaining to new words.
Ne-ŏl'o-gĭsm, *n.* A new word or expression. [to neology.
Ne-ŏl'o-gĭst, *n.* One who holds
Ne-ŏl'o-gy, *n.* Introduction or use of new words or terms; new doctrines.
Nē'o-phyte, *n.* A new convert; a novice.
Nĕph'ew (nĕf'yu; in Eng. nĕv'yu, 82), *n.* Son of a brother or sister.
Ne-phrĭt'ic, *a.* Pertaining to the kidneys. — *n.* A remedy for diseases of the kidneys.
Nĕp'o-tĭsm, *n.* Favoritism to relations.
Nep-tū'ni-an, *a.* Pertaining to Neptune or the ocean.
Nē're-id, *n.* A sea-nymph.
Nĕrve (140), *n.* An organ of sensation and motion in animals; firmness; strength. — *v. t.* To give vigor to.
Nĕrve'less (132), *a.* Without strength.
Nĕrv'ĭne (133), *n.* Good for the nerves. — *n.* A medicine that soothes nervous excitement.
Nĕrv'oŭs, *a.* Relating to the nerves; strong; vigorous; having weak or diseased nerves. [ous manner.
Nĕrv'oŭs-ly, *adv.* In a nervous
Nĕrv'oŭs-ness, *n.* State of being nervous. [nornnee.
Nĕs'cience (nĕsh'ens), *n.* Ignorant.
Nĕst, *n.* A bed for birds or insects; a collection of boxes, &c., one within another.

Nĕst'-ĕgg, *n.* An egg left in the nest, to prevent the hen from forsaking it.
Nĕs'tle (nĕs'l), *v. i.* To lie close; to move restlessly.
Nĕst'ling (nĕs'-), *n.* A bird just hatched.
Nĕt, *n.* An instrument of mesh-work for catching fish and fowls. — *v. t.* (129). To make into net-work; to produce in clear profit. — *a.* Clear of all charges and deductions.
Nĕth'er, *a.* Lower; infernal.
Nĕth'er-mōst, *a.* Lowest.
Nĕt'ting, *n.* A piece of net-work.
Nĕt'tle, *n.* A prickly plant. — *v. t.* To sting; to vex; to annoy; to irritate.
Nĕt'work (-wŭrk), *n.* Work wrought for or like a net.
Neŭ-rāl'gĭ-a, *n.* Acute pain in the nerves. [neuralgia.
Neŭ-rāl'gĭc, *a.* Relating to
Neū'ter, *a.* Of neither party; of neither gender. — *n.* One who takes no part; a working-bee.
Neū'tral, *a.* Not of either party. — *n.* One that takes no part in a contest.
Neu-trăl'i-ty, *n.* State of being neutral; indifference.
Neū'tral-i-zā'tion, *n.* Act of rendering neuter.
Neū'tral-īze, *v. t.* To render neutral; to render inert.
Neū'tral-ly, *adv.* In a neutral manner.
Nĕv'er, *adv.* At no time.
Nĕv'er-the-lĕss', *adv.* Notwithstanding; however; yet.
New (nū), *a.* Fresh; recent; modern; novel. [formed.
New-fān'gled, *a.* Newly
New'ly, *adv.* Freshly; lately.
New'ness, *n.* Freshness; novelty; recent change.
News, *n.* Fresh informatiou.
News'mŏn'ger (-mŭng'ger), *n.* A dealer in news.
News'pā-per, *n.* A paper to circulate news.
Newt (nūt), *n.* A small lizard.
Nĕxt, *a.* Nearest in place, time, or rank. — *adv.* At the time or turn nearest.
Nĭb, *n.* A point, as of a pen; the end of a beak.
Nĭb'ble, *n.* A little bite. — *v. i.* or *t.* To eat slowly.
Nĭb'bler, *n.* One who nibbles.
Nīce, *a.* Pleasing; exact; fine; refined; squeamish.
Nīce'ly, *adv.* Accurately; delicately.

NICETY 207 NONCONFORMITY

Ni'çe-ty, *n.* Accuracy; minuteness; delicacy. [in a wall.
Niche (140), *n.* A small recess
Kick, *n.* A notch; a score for keeping an account; exact point. — *v. t.* To cut in notches; to hit. [metal.
Nick'el, *n.* A grayish-white
Nick'-năcks, *n. pl.* Small wares; trifles.
Nick'năme, *n.* A name in sport or contempt. — *v. t.* To name in contempt or familiarity.
Nic'tāte,) *v. i.* To wink;
Nic'ti-tāte,) to blink.
Nic-tā'tion,) *n.* The act
Nic'ti-tā'tion,) of winking.
Nid'i-fi-cā'tion, *n.* Act of forming nests and hatching and feeding the young.
†**Nī'dus,** *n.* [Lat.] A nest.
Nīçe, *n.* A daughter of a brother or sister.
Nig'gard, *n.* A stingy person.
Nig'gard,) *a.* Sordidly
Nig'gard-ly,) parsimonious; meanly covetous.
Nīgh (ni), *a.* Near; allied closely. — *adv.* Nearly;
closely. — *prep.* Near to.
Nīgh'ness (ni'-), *n.* Nearness.
Night (nit), *n.* Time from sunset to sunrise.
Night'cap (nit'-), *n.* A cap worn in bed. [of day.
Night'-fall (nit'-), *n.* Close
Night'gown (nit'-), *n.* A loose gown worn in bed.
Night'hawk (nit'-), *n.* A bird that hunts its prey toward evening.
Night'in-gale (nit'-, 42), *n.* [A. S. *nihtegale,* fr. *niht,* night, and *galan,* to sing.] A small bird that sings at night. *Nightingale.*
Night'ly (nit'lý), *a.* Done by night. — *adv.* Every night.
Night'māre (nit'-), *n.* Sensation of weight on the breast in sleep.
Night'shāde (nit'-), *n.* A plant with small white flowers.
Night'-walk'er (nit'wawk'-er), *n.* One who walks in his sleep; a prostitute.
Night'watch (nit'-), *n.* A division or period of the night; guard at night.
Nī-hīl'i-ty, *n.* Nothingness.
Nim'ble, *n.* Light and quick in motion; brisk; agile.

Nim'ble-ness, *n.* Briskness.
Nim'bly, *adv.* With agility.
†**Nim'bus,** *n.* Circle of rays round the head; a halo.
Nīne, *a.* Eight and one added.
Nīne'fōld, *a.* Nine times.
Nīne'ping, *n.* A kind of play or game.
Nīne'teen, *a.* Nine and ten.
Nīne'ti-eth, *a.* Ordinal of 90.
Nīne'ty, *a.* N*ine* times ten.
Nin'ny, *n.* A simpleton.
Ninth, *n.* The ordinal of nine.
Nīp, *v. t.* To pinch; to blast, as by frost; to destroy; to bite. —*n.* A pinch; a cutting off; a blast.
Nip'pers, *n. pl.* Small pinchers.
Nip'ple, *n.* A teat. *Nippers.*
Nit, *n.* The egg of an insect.
Nī'ter) (151), *n.* Nitrate of
Nī'tre) potassa, a white chemical salt.
Nit'id, *a.* Shining; gay; fine.
Nī'trate, *n.* A salt formed of nitric acid and a base.
Nī'tric, *a.* Containing niter.
Nī'tro-gen, *n.* A gas, having no taste or smell.
Nī'troŭs, *a.* Pertaining to, or containing, niter. [nits.
Nit'ty, *a.* Abounding with
Nō, *adv.* A word of denial.
—*a.* Not any; none.
No-bīl'i-ty, *n.* Dignity of mind; distinction of family or rank; body of nobles.
Nō'ble, *a.* Dignified from rank, intellect, or character.
— SYN. Exalted; elevated; illustrious; honorable; ingenuous. —*n.* A person of rank; a gold coin. [of rank.
Nō'ble-man (143), *n.* A man
Nō'ble-ness, *n.* Greatness of mind; dignity; worth.
'**No-blĕsse',** or **Nō'blesse,** *n.* Body of nobles.
Nō'bly, *adv.* With dignity; with greatness of soul, splendor, &c.
Nō'bŏd-y, *n.* No person; no one; not anybody.
Noe-tăm'bu-lā'tion, *n.* Walking in sleep. [walks in sleep.
Noc-tăm'bu-list, *n.* One who
Nŏe'turn, *n.* A religious song for worship by night.
'**Noc-tûr'nal,** *a.* Nightly; done or happening at night.
Nŏd, *n.* A quick inclination of the head. — *v. t.* To bow the head with a quick motion.
Nŏd'dle, *n.* The head.
Nŏd'dy, *n.* A simpleton.

Nōde, *n.* A knot; point where the orbit of a planet intersects the ecliptic. [knots.
No-dōse', *a.* Knotty; full of
Nŏd'u-lar, *a.* Pertaining to, or in the form of, a nodule.
Nŏd'ule, *n.* A rounded mass of irregular shape.
Nŏg'gin, *n.* A small mug or wooden cup.
Noiṣe (140), *n.* Sound of any kind; outcry; clamor. — *v. t.* or *t.* To sound loud. [noise.
Noiṣe'less, *a.* Making no
Noi'ṣi-ly, *adv.* With noise.
Noi'ṣi-ness, *n.* State of being noisy.
Noi'ṣŏme, *a.* Offensive; hurtful and disgusting.
Noi'ṣŏme-ly, *adv.* With a fetid smell.
Noi'ṣŏme-ness, *n.* Offensiveness to the smell; unwholesomeness.
Noi'ṣy (noi'zy̆), *a.* Clamorous; boisterous; turbulent.
Nŏm'ad, *n.* One who leads a wandering and pastoral life.
No-măd'ic, *a.* Moving from place to place for pasturage.
Nō'men-clā'tor, *n.* One who gives names to things.
Nō'men-clăt'ūre, *n.* System of names in any art or science.
Nŏm'i-nal, *a.* Existing in name only; not real. [only.
Nŏm'i-nal-ly, *adv.* In name
Nŏm'i-nāte, *v. t.* To name; to propose. [inating.
Nŏm'i-nā'tion, *n.* Act of nominating.
Nŏm'i-na-tīve, *a.* Pertaining to a name. —*n.* Case in which the subject of a verb stands.
Nŏm'i-nā'tor, *n.* One who names or nominates.
Nŏm'i-nee', *n.* One designated by another.
Nŏn'age, *n.* Minority in age.
Nŏn'a-ġe-nā'ri-an, *n.* One who is 90 years old.
Nŏn'-at-tĕnd'ançe, *n.* A failure to attend. [sion.
Nŏnçe, *n.* The present occasion.
†**Nonchalance** (nŏng'shä'-lŏngss'), *n.* [Fr.] Indifference; coolness.
†**Nonchalant** (nŏng'shä'-lŏng'), *a.* [Fr.] Indifferent; careless; cool.
Nŏn'-eon-dŭet'or, *n.* A substance that does not transmit heat or electricity.
Nŏn'-eon-fŏrm'ist, *n.* One who does not conform to an established church.
Nŏn'-eon-fŏrm'i-ty (79), *n.* Want of conformity; refusal to conform.

ȧŭn, ȯr, dọ, wọlf, tọ̄ọ, tọ̆ọk; ûrn, rụ̄le, pụll; ç, ġ, *soft;* e, ġ, *hard;* aṣ; eẋist; ṇ *as* ng; thiṣ

Non'de-script, *a.* Not hitherto described. — *n.* Something not described.

None (nŭn *or* nōn, 18), *a.* & *pron.* No one; not any.

Non-en'ti-ty, *n.* A thing not existing; non-existence.

Nōnes, *n. pl.* In ancient Rome, the 7th of March, May, July, and October, and the 5th of the other months.

None'such, *n.* A thing that has not its equal. [existence.

Non'-ex-ist'ençe, *n.* Want of

Non-jū'ror, *or* **Nŏn'-ju-ror,** One who refuses to swear allegiance.

Non-pa-rĕil' (-rĕl'), *n.* A small kind of type like that here used. [payment.

Non-pāy'ment, *n.* Neglect of

Nŏn'plus, *n.* A puzzle. — *v. t.* To put to a stand; to puzzle; to confound.

Non-rĕṣ'i-dençe, *n.* Absence from an estate or charge.

Non-rĕṣ'i-dent, *a.* Not residing in a particular place. — *n.* One who does not reside on his estate, or with his charge.

Nŏn'-re-ṣist'ançe, *n.* Submission to authority, power, or usurpation, without opposition.

Nŏn'-re-ṣist'ant, *a.* Not resisting power or oppression.

Nŏn'sense, *n.* Words without meaning or importance.

Non-sĕns'ic-al, *a.* Unmeaning; absurd; foolish.

Non-sĕn'sic-al-ly, *adv.* Without meaning.

Nŏn'ṣuit, *n.* The stopping of a suit at law. — *v. t.* To adjudge that a plaintiff drops his suit.

Nōō'dle, *n.* A simpleton.

Nŏŏk, *n.* A corner; a recess.

Nōōn, *n.* Middle of the day; twelve o'clock.

Nōōn'dāy, ⎫ *n.* Mid-day;
Nōōn'tide, ⎭ time of noon.

Nōōn'ing, *n.* Repose at noon.

Nōōse (*or* nōōz), *n.* A running knot.

Nōōṣe (nōōz), *v. t.* To catch in a noose. [nies.

Nŏr, *conj.* A word that denies.

Nŏr'mal, *a.* [Lat. *normalis*, from *norma*, a rule, pattern.] Regular; teaching rudiments or principles.

Nŏrth, *n.* The point opposite the south. — *a.* Being in the north.

Nŏrth-ēast', *n.* The point between the north and east.

Nŏrth-ēast'ern, *a.* Pertaining to the north-east.

Nŏrth'er-ly, *a.* Being toward, or from, the north.

Nŏrth'ern, *a.* Being in or toward or from the north.

Nŏrth'ward, *a.* Being toward the north. — *adv.* In a northern direction.

Nŏrth-wĕst', *n.* The point between the north and west. — *a.* Being in, or proceeding from, the north-west.

Nŏrth-wĕst'ern, *a.* Pertaining to the north-west.

Nōṣe, *n.* Prominent part of the face; organ of smell. — *v. t.* To smell; to lead blindly.

Nōṣe'gāy, *n.* A bunch of flowers. [to nosology.

Nŏs'o-lŏġ'ic-al, *a.* Relating

No-sŏl'o-ġist, *n.* One who is versed in nosology.

No-sŏl'o-ġy. *n.* Classification of diseases. [the nose.

Nŏs'tril, *n.* A passage through

Nŏs'trum, *n.* A medicine, the ingredients of which are not made public.

Nŏt, *adv.* A word that expresses denial or negation.

Nŏt'a-ble, *a.* Remarkable; conspicuous; noted. [trious.

Nŏt'a-ble, *a.* Actively industrious.

Nŏt'a-bly, *adv.* Remarkably; eminently. [ly.

Nŏt'a-bly, *adv.* Industrious-

No-tā'ri-al, *a.* Relating to, or done by, a notary.

Nō'ta-ry (141), *n.* An officer who attests writings.

No-tā'tion, *n.* Act of noting by marks, figures, or characters.

Nŏtch (140), *n.* A cut or nick. — *v. t.* To cut in small hollows.

Nōte, *n.* A mark; a token; a short writing; a character in music; a paper promising payment of a debt. — *v. t.* To set down; to observe closely; to denote. [or memoranda.

Nōte'-bŏŏk, *n.* Book for notes

Nōt'ed, *a.* Well known by reputation or report.

Nŏth'ing (nŭth'ing *or* nōth-ing), *n.* Not any thing. — *adv.* Not at all.

Nŏth'ing-ness (*or* nōth'ing-ness), *n.* Non-existence; non-entity; no value.

Nō'tiçe, *n.* Attention; remark; regard; information. — *v. t.* To observe; to see.

Nō'tiçe-a-ble (133), *a.* Worthy of observation.

Nō'ti-fi-cā'tion, *n.* Act of giving notice; notice given.

Nō'ti-fȳ (135), *v. t.* [Lat. *notificare*, from *notus*, known, and *facere*, to make.] To declare; to make known; to give notice to.

Nō'tion, *n.* Conception; opinion; sentiment; a trifle.

Nō'tion-al, *a.* Existing in idea only; whimsical. — SYN. Imaginary; ideal; fanciful.

Nō'tion-al-ly, *adv.* In conception; not in reality.

Nō'to-rī'e-ty, *n.* Public knowledge or exposure to it.

No-tō'ri-oŭs, *a.* Publicly known; usually, known to disadvantage.

No-tō'ri-oŭs-ly, *adv.* In a notorious manner; openly.

Nŏt'with-stănd'ing, *p. pr.* (commonly called an *adv.* or a *conj.*) Not opposing; nevertheless.

Nought (nawt). See *Naught.*

Noun, *n.* A word which is the name of any thing.

Noŭr'ish, *v. t.* To support with food; to nurture; to feed; to cherish.

Noŭr'ish-ment, *n.* Food; sustenance; nutrition.

Nŏv'el, *a.* New; recent; unusual. — *n.* A fictitious tale.

Nŏv'el-ĭst (130), *n.* A writer of novels. [thing.

Nŏv'el-ty, *n.* Newness; a new

No-vĕm'ber, *n.* Eleventh month of the year.

No-vĕn'ni-al, *a.* Done every ninth year.

Nŏv'içe, *n.* A beginner.

No-vĭ'ti-ate (-vĭsh'ĭ-āt), *n.* State of a novice; a novice.

Now, *adv.* At this time.

Now'a-dāys, *adv.* At the present time. [place or state.

Nō'where, *adv.* Not in any

Nō'wĭṣe, *adv.* By no means.

Nŏx'ioŭs (nŏk'shus, 92), *a.* Hurtful; destructive.

Nŏx'ioŭs-ly (nŏk'shus-), *adv.* Hurtfully; perniciously.

Nŏz'zle, *n.* A nose; snout.

Nū'cle-us, *n.* (*pl.* Nū'cle-us-es, *or* †Nū'cle-ī, 147.) A body about which any thing is collected; body of a comet.

Nude, *a.* Bare; naked; void.

Nū'di-ty, *n.* Nakedness.

Nū'ga-to-ry, *a.* Of no force; trifling; vain; futile. [ore.

Nŭġ'ġet, *n.* A lump of metal or

Nū'ṣançe (27), *n.* That which annoys or is offensive to the public.

Null (123), *a.* Void; of no force.

Nŭl'lĭ-fi-cā'tion, *n.* Act of nullifying.

NULLIFY 209 OBJURGATE

Nŭl'li-fȳ, *v. t.* [Lat. *nullificare*, from *nullus*, none, and *facere*, to make.] To make void; to deprive of legal force.

Nŭl'li-ty, *n.* Want of force; any thing void or invalid.

Nŭmb (nŭm), *a.* Torpid; void of feeling. — *v. t.* To deprive of feeling; to make torpid. — SYN. To deaden; benumb; chill; stupefy.

Nŭm'ber, *n.* A unit or any assemblage of units; measure; poetry; verse; (*pl.*) fourth book of the Pentateuch. — *v. t.* To count; to reckon; to enumerate.

Nŭm'ber-less, *a.* More than can be counted.

Nŭmb'ness (nŭm'ness), *n.* Torpidity; torpor.

Nū'mer-a-ble, *a.* Capable of being numbered.

Nū'mer-al, *a.* Relating to, or expressing, number — *n.* A figure or a letter to express a number.

Nū'mer-a-ry, *a.* Belonging to a certain number.

Nū'mer-ā'tion, *n.* Act or art of numbering.

Nū'mer-ā'tor, *n.* A number that shows how many parts are taken. [number.

Nu-mĕr'ic-al, *a.* Denoting

Nu-mĕr'ic-al-ly, *adv.* With respect to number.

Nū'mer-oŭs, *a.* Being or containing many.

Nū'mis-măt'ic, *a.* Relating to coin or medals.

Nū'mis-măt'ics, *n. sing.* The science of coins and medals.

Nŭm'skull (139), *n.* A blockhead; a dunce; a dolt.

Nŭn, *n.* A woman devoted to a religious life, and living in a cloister.

Nŭn'ci-o (nŭn'shi-o), *n.* An embassador of the pope.

Nun-cū'pa-tīve, or **Nŭn'cu-pā'tīve**, *a.* Verbally pronounced; not written.

Nŭn'ner-y, *n.* A house for nuns; a cloister.

Nŭp'tial (nŭp'shal), *a.* Pertaining to marriage.

Nŭp'tials, *n. pl.* Marriage.

Nŭrse, *n.* One who tends a child or a sick person. — *v. t.* To bring up or tend, as a child; to tend, as a sick person.

Nŭrs'er-y, *n.* A room for young children; a plantation of young trees.

Nŭrs'ling 132), *n.* One who is nursed; an infant.

Nûrt'ûre, *n.* That which nurtures; education. — *v. t.* To feed; to educate; to nourish.

Nŭt, *n.* A fruit consisting of a hard shell and a kernel; a small block for holding a bolt.

Nu-tā'tion, *n.* A vibratory motion of the earth's axis.

Nŭt'-gall, *n.* Excrescence of the oak.

Nŭt'meg, *n.* A kind of aromatic nut used in cookery.

Nū'tri-ment, *n.* That which nourishes. — SYN. Aliment; diet; nourishment; food; education; instruction.

Nu-trī'tion (-trĭsh'un), *n.* Act of nourishing; that which nourishes; food; nutriment.

Nū'tri-mĕnt'al,
Nu-trī'tious (-trĭsh'us), } *a.* Nourishing; nutritive.

Nū'trī-tīve, *a.* Nutritious.

Nŭz'zle, *v. t.* or *i.* To root, as a swine; to nestle.

Nymph, *n.* A goddess; a maiden. [of an insect.

Nymph'a, *n.* The chrysalis

O.

O *interj.* used in calling or in direct address; also, to express pain, grief, surprise, desire, &c.

Ọaf, *n.* A changeling; a dolt.

Ọaf'ish, *a.* Dull; stupid.

Ọak, *n.* A valuable tree.

Ọak'en, *a.* Made of oak.

Ọak'um, *n.* Old ropes pulled to pieces; used for calking the seams of ships, &c.

Ọar, *n.* An instrument to row boats. — *v.* To row or impel by rowing.

tỌ'a-sis, or **O-ā'sis**, *n.* (*pl.* Ọ'a-sēṣ, or O-ā'sēṣ.) A fertile spot in a desert.

Ọat, *n.* A plant and its seed [used chiefly in the plural.]

Ọat'en, *a.* Pertaining to oats.

Ọath (96), *n.* A solemn affirmation with an appeal to God for its truth; a blasphemous use of the name of God or Christ.

Ọāt'mēal, *n.* Meal made of oats.

Ob-dū'ra-çy, or **Ŏb'du-ra-çy**, *n.* State of being obdurate; invincible hardness of heart; stubbornness.

Ŏb'du-rate, or **Ob-dū'rate**, (114), *a.* Inflexibly hardened in feelings, especially against moral influence. — SYN. Callous; hardened; stubborn.

O-bē'di-ençe, *n.* Compliance with what is required.

O-bē'di-ent, *a.* Willing to obey; submissive to restraint or control. — SYN. Dutiful; subservient; compliant; obsequious.

O-bei'sançe (-bā'- or -bā'-), *n.* Act of reverence; a bow.

Ŏb'e-lĭsk, *n.* [Gr. *obeliskos*, dim. of *obelos*, a spit.] A kind of quadrangular pillar or monument; a mark thus, †.

O-bēse', *a.* Excessively fat.

Obelisk.

O-bēse'ness, } *n.* Fatness;
O-bēs'i-tȳ, } corpulence.

O-bey' (133), *v. t.* To comply with the orders of; to yield submission to; to perform.

Ob'fus-cā'tion, *n.* A darkening or confusing. [decease.

Ō'bĭt, or **Ŏb'ĭt**, *n.* Death;

O-bĭt'u-a-ry, *n.* A notice of the death of a person. — *a.* Relating to the death of a person.

Ŏb'jeçt, *n.* That on which the mind is employed; ultimate purpose or design; end; aim; motive. [offer in opposition.

Ob-jĕçt', *v. t.* To present or

Ob-jĕç'tion, *n.* Adverse reason; fault found.

Ob-jĕç'tion-a-ble, *a.* Liable to objections.

Ob-jĕçt'ĭve, *a.* Relating to the object; outward; external.

Ob-jĕçt'ĭve-ly, *adv.* In an objective manner; in the state of an object.

Ob-jĕçt'or, *n.* One who objects.

Ob-jŭr'gate, *v. t.* To chide.

sŏn, ôr, dọ, wọlf, tọ̄o, tọ̆ok; ûrn, rụe, pụ̄ll; ç, ġ, *soft*; c, g, *hard*; aṣ; eẋist; ŋ *as* ng: this.

OBJURGATION   210   **OCTAGONAL**

Ob'jur-ga'tion, *n.* Reproof; chiding.
Ob-jūr'ga-to-ry, *a.* Designed to chide or reprove.
Ob-lāte', *a.*, Flattened or depressed at the poles.
Ob-lā'tion, *n.* An offering.
Ob'li-gāte, *v. t.* To bind by contract or duty.
Ob'li-gā'tion, *n.* The binding force of a vow, law, or duty; a bond.
Ob'li-ga-to-ry, *a.* Imposing an obligation; binding.
O-blīge'. *v. t.* To constrain; to bind by a favor; to gratify.
Ob'li-ġee', *n.* One to whom a bond is executed.
O-blīg'ing, *a.* Disposed to do favors; engaging; kind.
Ob-līque' (-lēēk' *or* -līk'), *a.* Deviating from a right line; not parallel; indirect.
Ob-lique'ly (-lēēk'- *or* -līk'-), *adv.* Not directly.
Ob-liq'ui-ty (-lik'wĭ-), *n.* Deviation from a right line, or from moral rectitude.
Ob-lit'er-āte. *v. t.* To blot out; to erase; to efface.
Ob-lit'er-ā'tion, *n.* Act of blotting out; extinction.
Ob-liv'i-on, *n.* Forgetfulness.
Ob-liv'i-oŭs, *a.* Causing forgetfulness; forgetful.
Ob'long, *a.* Being longer than broad.
Ob'lo-quy, *n.* Calumnious language. — SYN. Slander; calumny; abuse.
Ob-nōx'ioŭs (-nŏk'shŭs), *a.* Offensive; odious; liable; exposed.
Ō'bo-e (140), *n.* A wind instrument sounded through a reed; a hautboy.
Ob-ō'vate, *a.* Ovate with the narrow end downward.
Ob-scēne', *a.* Grossly indelicate and disgusting.
Ob-scēne'ly, *adv.* Impurely; indelicately.
Ob-scēn'i-ty, *n.* Impurity in expression, or in representation. [darkening.
Ob'scu-rā'tion, *n.* Act of
Ob-scūre', *a.* Dark; gloomy; not easily understood; not much known. — *v. t.* To darken; to make less clear or beautiful. [dimly.
Ob-scūre'ly, *adv.* Darkly;
Ob-scūre'ness, | *n.* State of
Ob-scū'ri-ty, | being obscure; darkness; privacy.
Ob'se-crā'tion, *n.* Entreaty.
Ob'se-quies (-kwĭz), *n. pl.* Funeral solemnities.

Ob-sē'qui-oŭs, *a.* Meanly submissive or compliant.
Ob-sē'qui-oŭs-ly, *adv.* With servile compliance.
Ob-sē'qui-oŭs-ness, *n.* Mean compliance; servility.
Ob-sĕrv'a-ble, *a.* Capable or worthy of being observed; remarkable; noticeable.
Ob-sĕrv'a-bly, *adv.* In a manner worthy of note.
Ob-sĕrv'ance, *n.* Attention.
Ob-sĕrv'ant, *a.* Regardful.
Ob'ser-vā'tion, *n.* Act of observing; remark; notice.
Ob-sĕrv'a-to-ry, *n.* A place for astronomical observations.
Ob-sĕrve', *v. t.* To see; to notice; to utter, as a remark.
Ob-sĕrv'er, *n.* One who observes, performs, or fulfils
Ob-sĕs'sion (-sĕsh-un), *n.* Act of besieging.
Ob'so-lĕs'cent, *a.* Going out of use. [of date.
Ob'so-lēte, *a.* Disused; out
Ob'so-lēte-ness, *n.* State of being obsolete; disuse.
Ob'sta-cle, *n.* That which hinders; obstruction.
Ob-stĕt'ric, *a.* Pertaining to midwifery.
Ob-stĕt'rics, *n. sing.* Science of midwifery. [ness.
Ob'sti-na-cy, *n.* Stubbornness.
Ob'sti-nate, *a.* Stubborn; stiff; pertinacious.
Ob'sti-nate-ly, *adv.* Stubbornly; pertinaciously.
Ob'sti-pā'tion, *n.* Costiveness.
Ob-strĕp'er-oŭs, *a.* Clamorous; loud; turbulent.
Ob-strĕp'er-oŭs-ly, *adv.* Clamorously; turbulently.
Ob-strŭct', *v. t.* [Lat. *obstruere, obstructum*, from *ob*, against, in front of, and *struere*, to pile up.] To hinder; to stop; to block up.
Ob-strŭc'tion, *n.* That which obstructs. — SYN. Obstacle.
Ob-strŭct'ive, *a.* Hindering.
Ob-tāin', *v. t.* To gain; to get. — *v. i.* To become prevalent or general.
Ob-tāin'a-ble, *a.* Capable of being obtained.
Ob-tĕst', *v. t.* To call to witness; to beseech.
Ob'tes-tā'tion, *n.* Supplication; entreaty.
Ob-trūde', *v. t.* To thrust in or upon; to urge upon against the will.
Ob-trū'sion, *n.* Act of obtruding. [trude.
Ob-trū'sive, *a.* Disposed to ob-

Ob-tŭnd', *v. t.* To dull; to blunt.
Ob-tūse', *a.* Not acute; dull; obscure. [manner.
Ob-tūse'ly, *adv.* In an obtuse
Ob-tūse'ness (132), *n.* Want of sharpness or readiness; bluntness; dullness of sound.
Ob-tū'sion, *n.* Act of blunting or dulling. [coin.
Ob'verse, *n.* The face of a
Ob-vĕrt'. *v. t.* To turn toward or downward.
Ob'vi-āte, *v. t.* To meet; to prevent; to clear the way of.
Ob'vi-oŭs, *a.* Evident; clear.
Ob'vi-oŭs-ly, *adv.* Evidently.
Oc-cā'sion, *n.* Opportunity; incident; accidental cause; need; exigence. — *v. t.* To cause lucidentally; to produce.
Oc-cā'sion-al, *a.* Occurring at times; produced by accident; casual; incidental.
Oc-cā'sion-al-ly, *adv.* Upon occasion; at times.
Ŏc'ci-dent, *n.* The west.
Ŏc'ci-dĕnt'al, *a.* Western.
Oc-cĭp'i-tal, *a.* Pertaining to the back part of the head.
†Ŏc'ci-pŭt, *n.* The hinder part of the head. [up.
Oc-clū'sion, *n.* A shutting
Oc-cŭlt', *a.* Secret; hidden.
Ŏc'cul-tā'tion, *n.* The hiding of one heavenly body from sight by another.
Ŏc'cu-pan-cy, *n.* A taking or holding possession.
Ŏc'cu-pant, *n.* One who takes or holds possession.
Ŏc'cu-pā'tion, *n.* Act of occupying; business; possession; employment.
Ŏc'cu-pȳ (135), *v. t.* To hold for use; to keep; to employ.
Oc-cŭr', *v. i.* [Lat. *occurrere*, fr. *ob*, against, and *currere*, to run.] To be found here and there; to come to the mind.
Oc-cŭr'rence, *n.* Any single event; an incident.
Ō'cean (ō'shun), *n.* The largest body of water on the earth, or one of the chief divisions of it.
Ō'ce-ăn'ic (-she-, 92), *a.* Pertaining to the ocean.
Ō'cher | (151), *n.* Clay containing iron, used
Ō'chre | as a pigment.
Ŏc'ta-gon, *n.* A figure of eight sides and angles.
Oc-tăg'o-nal, *a.* Containing eight angles and sides. Octagon.

ā, ĕ, ĭ, ō, ū, ȳ, *long*; ă, ĕ, ĭ, ŏ, ŭ, ў, *short*; cāre, cŭr, ăsk, ąll, whąt; ēre, veil, tērm; pīque, fïrm;

OCTAHEDRAL 211 OMEN

Oc'ta-he'dral, *n.* Having eight equal faces.

Oc'ta-he'dron, *n.* A figure of eight equal sides. Octahedron.

Oc-tăn'gu-lar, *a.* Having eight angles.

Oc'tave, *n.* (*Mus.*) The interval between one and eight of the scale.

Oc-tā'vo (140), *n.* A book with eight leaves to a sheet.

Oc-těn'ni-al, *a.* Coming once in eight years.

Oc-tō'ber, *n.* Tenth month of the year.

Oc'to-ge-nā'ri-an, *n.* A person eighty years of age.

Oc-tŏg'e-na-ry, or Oc'to-ge-na-ry, *a.* Of 80 years of age.

Oc'u-lar, *a.* Known by, or relating to, the eye.

Oc'u-list, *n.* One skilled in diseases of the eye.

Odd (125), *a.* Uneven in number; strange; peculiar.

Odd'i-ty, *n.* Singularity; a singular person.

Odd'ly (131), *adv.* Unevenly; strangely; singularly.

Odd'ness, *n.* State or quality of being odd.

Odds, *n. pl.* Inequality; excess; advantage. [song.

Ode, *n.* A short poem; a

O-dē'on, *n.* A kind of theater.

O'di-oŭs, *a.* Very offensive; hateful; detestable.

O'di-oŭs-ly, *adv.* Hatefully.

O'di-um, *n.* Quality of provoking hate. — SYN. Offensiveness; hatred.

O'dor (135), *n.* Scent; smell; perfume.

O'dor-if'er-oŭs, *a.* Fragrant.

O'dor-oŭs, *a.* Sweet of scent; fragrant.

O'er, contraction of *Over*.

Of (ŏv, 68, 123), *prep.* From, or out from; proceeding from; belonging or relating to; concerning.

Off (19), *adv.* Denoting distance. — *prep.* Distant from. — *interj.* Away; begone.

Off'al, *n.* Carrion; putrid meat; refuse.

Of-fĕnce', *n.* See *Offense*.

Of-fĕnd', *v. t.* To displease; to make angry; to shock. — *v. i.* To sin. [fends.

Of-fĕnd'er, *n.* One who offends.

Of fĕnse' (149), *n.* Act of offending; displeasure; anger; injury; fault; sin

Of-fĕn'sive, *a.* Displeasing; obnoxious; used in attack.

Of-fĕn'sive-ly, *adv.* In an offensive manner.

Of'fer (39, 130), *v. t.* or *i.* To present; to propose; to bid; to undertake. — *n.* A proposal; price bid.

Of'fer-ing, *n.* A sacrifice; any thing offered.

Of'fer-to-ry, *n.* An anthem chanted at mass; verses of Scripture read while alms are collecting.

Off'-hănd, *adv.* or *a.* Without study or preparation.

Of'fice (140), *n.* Customary duty; public employment; function; place of business; religious truth.

Of'fi-çer, *n.* One who holds an office. — *v. t.* To furnish with officers.

Of-fi'cial (-fĭsh'al), *a.* Pertaining to, or derived from, office. — *n.* An ecclesiastical judge.

Of-fi'cial-ly (-fĭsh'al-), *adv.* By authority.

Of-fi'ci-āte(-fĭsh'ĭ-āt), *v. i.* To perform the duties of an office.

Of-fĭc'i-nal, or Of-fi-çī'nal, *a.* Approved by a college of medicine.

Of-fi'cioŭs (-fĭsh'us), *a.* Excessively forward in doing kind offices. — SYN. Kind; meddling; busy; impertinent; intermeddling.

Of-fi'cioŭs-ly (-fĭsh'us-), *adv.* In an officious manner.

Of-fi'cioŭs-ness (-fĭsh'us-), *n.* Undue forwardness.

Off'ing, *n.* The sea at a good distance from shore.

Off'scour-ing, *n.* Refuse or rejected matter.

Off'set, *n.* A shoot or sprout; any thing given in exchange or retaliation.

Off-set', or Off'set, *v. t.* To set against another account; to balance.

Off'spring, *n.* A child or children; issue; descendants.

Oft. *adv.* Frequently.

Oft'en (ŏf'n, 65) } *adv.* Frequently.

Oft'en-times, } quently.

many times.

O-gee', *n.* A molding which is both concave and convex.

O'gle (ō'gl). *v. t.* or *i.* [From Lat. *oculus*, the eye.] To view or look with side glances. — *n.* A side glance.

Ogee.

O'gler, *n.* One who ogles.

O'gre (ō'ger, 151), *n.* An imaginary monster, who lived on human beings.

O'gress, *n.* A female ogre.

Oh, *interj.* denoting surprise or pain, &c.

Oil, *n.* An unctuous animal or vegetable substance. — *v. t.* To smear or anoint with oil.

Oil'-clŏth, *n.* A cloth oiled or painted for covering floors, and for other uses.

Oil'-cŏl'or, *n.* A pigment mixed with oil.

Oil'i-ness, *n.* Quality of being oily; unctuousness.

Oil'y, *a.* Like oil; smooth.

Oint, *v. t.* To rub with oil.

Oint'ment, *n.* That which serves to anoint; unguent.

Ōld, *a.* Having existed a long time; aged; ancient.

Ōld'en (ōld'n), *n.* Old; ancient. [old.

Ōld'ness, *a.* State of being

O'le-ăg'i-noŭs, *a.* Oily.

O'le-ăs'ter, *n.* A tree much like the olive.

Ol-făc'to-ry, *a.* Of, or having the sense of, smelling.

Ol-ĭb'a-num, *n.* A gum resin.

Ŏl'i-gärch'al, } *a.* Relating

Ŏl'i-gärch'ic-al, } to oligarch.

Ŏl'i-gärch'y, *n.* Government in the hands of a few.

O'li-o (*or* ŏl'yo), *n.* A dish of stewed meat; a mixture; a medley. [of the olive.

Ŏl'i-vā'ceoŭs, *a.* Of the color

Ŏl'ive, *n.* A tree cultivated in the south of Europe for its fruit, and for the oil it yields; the emblem of peace; a color composed of violet and green.

Olive.

O-lým'pi-ăd, *n.* A period of four years in Grecian history.

O-lým'pic. *a.* Pertaining to Olympia and its games.

Om'ber, } *n.* A game at cards,

Om'bre, } usually played by three persons.

tO-mē'gȧ, *or* O-mĕg'ȧ, *n.* The last Greek letter, as Alpha is the first; the last.

Ŏm'e-let, (*colloq.* ŏm'let), *n.* [Fr. *omelette*, from *œufs mêlés*, mixed eggs.] A fritter of eggs, &c.

O'men, *n.* A prognostic; a sign; a presage; an augury.

---

sŏn, ôr, dǫ, wǫlf, tōō, tŏŏk; ûrn, rẏe, pyll; ç, ġ, *soft*; ç, ġ, *hard*; a̧ṣ; e̱x̱i̱s̱ṯ; ṇ *as* ng; this.

Om'i-nous, a. Containing an omen; Inauspicious.
Om'i-nous-ly, adv. In an ominous manner.
O-mis'sion (-mĭsh'un), n. Neglect or failure to do something; a leaving out.
O-mit', v. t. To leave out; to pass by; to neglect.
Om'ni-bus, n. A large four-wheeled vehicle for conveying passengers.
Om-nif'ic, a. All-creating.
Om'ni-um, n. Average value of the different stocks in which a loan to government is funded.
Om-nip'o-tençe, n. Unlimited or infinite power.
Om-nip'o-tent, a. Having all power. — n. The Almighty.
Om'ni-prĕṣ'ençe, n. Presence in every place.
Om'ni-prĕṣ'ent, a. Present in every place at the same time.
Om-nis'çience (-nĭsh/ens), n. Universal knowledge.
Om-nis'çient (-nĭsh/ent), a. Having infinite or universal knowledge. [ing.
Om-niv'o-rous, a. All-devouring.
On, prep. At the upper part of a thing, and supported by it; at; near; with; toward; for; upon. — adv. Forward; onward. [time; formerly.
Onçe (wŭnss), adv. At one
One (wŭn), a. Single; individual; any.
O-nei'ro-crit'ic, n. Relating to the interpretation of dreams. [ity.
One'ness (wŭn'nes), n. Unity.
On'er-a-ry, a. Fitted for carrying burdens.
On'er-ous, a. Burdensome.
On'ion (ŭn'yun), n. A culinary plant having a bulbous root.
On'ly (18), a. Single. — adv. Singly; barely; simply.
On'set, n. A violent attack; an assault. [tack.
On'slaught (-slawt), n. Attack.
On'to-lŏġ'ic-al, a. Pertaining to the science of being in general.
On-tŏl'o-ġy, n. The science of being in general.
†O'nus, n. [Lat.] The burden.
On'ward, } adv. Forward;
On'wards, } further. — a. Advanced or advancing; improving.
O'nyx, n. A precious stone.
Ooze, n. Soft mud. — v. i. To flow or issue gently. [mud.
Ooz'y, a. Containing soft

O-păç'i-ty, n. Want of transparency. [ent.
O-pā'cous, a. Not transparent.
O'pal, n. A precious stone of changeable colors.
O'pal-ĕs'çençe, n. A milky reflection from the interior of a mineral.
O'pal-ĕs'çent, a. Like opal.
O'pal-ine, a. Pertaining to, or like, opal.
O-pāque' (-pāk'), a. Not transparent; impervious to the light.
O-pāque'ness (-pāk'-), n. Quality of being opaque.
Ope, v. t. To open.
O'pen (ō'pn, 18), v. t. To unclose; to unfold; to enter upon; to begin; to make plain. — a. Not shut up; unclosed; public; candid; plain. [a breach.
O'pen-ing, n. An aperture;
O'pen-ly, adv. Publicly; plainly; frankly.
O'pen-ness, n. Plainness.
Op'e-rā (140), n. A dramatic composition set to music.
Op'er-āte, v. [Lat. operari, operatus, from opus, operis, work.] To exert power of any kind; to act; to put in motion or action; to work.
Op'er-ăt'ic, a. Pertaining or appropriate to the opera.
Op'er-ā'tion, n. Exertion of power; action; agency.
Op'er-a-tive, a. Exerting force; efficient. — n. A laboring person.
Op'er-ā'tor, n. One who operates. [dious.
Op'er-ōse', a. Laborious; tedious.
Oph'i-cleide, n. A large brass wind-instrument.
O-phĭd'i-an, n. An animal of the group of snakes.
O'phi-ŏl'o-ġy, n. The natural history of serpents.
Oph-thăl'mic (of- or op-), a. Relating to the eye.
†Oph-thăl'mi-ă } (of- or op'-,
Oph'thal-my } 82), n. A disease of the eyes.
O'pi-ate, n. A medicine that contains opium; a narcotic. —a. Causing sleep. [pose.
O-pine', v. i. To think; to suppose.
O-pin'ion (119), n. Judgment formed by the mind; notion; sentiment; persuasion.
O-pin'ion-ā'ted, } a. Obsti-
O-pin'ion-a-tive, } nate in adherence to opinions; obstinate.
O'pi um, n. The inspissated juice of the poppy.

O'po-dĕl'doc, n. A saponaceous camphorated liniment.
O-pŏs'sum, n. A marsupial quadruped found in America.
Op-pō'nent, a. Opposing; antagonistic. — n. An opposer; an antagonist.
Op'por-tūne', a. Timely; seasonable. [venient time.
Op'por-tūne'ly, adv. Seasonably.
Op'por-tū'ni-ty, n. Fit or convenient time.
Op-pōṣe', v. t. To resist; to combat; to withstand.
Op-pōṣ'er, n. One who opposes; an opponent.
Op'po-ṣīte, a. Contrary in position; facing; adverse.
Op'po-ṣīte-ly, adv. In a situation to face each other; adversely.
Op'po-ṣĭ'tion (-zĭsh/un), n. Repugnance; resistance; obstacle; an opposite party.
Op po-ṣĭ'tion-ist (-zĭsh/un-), n. One in an opposite party.
Op-press', v. t. To burden with impositions.
Op-prĕs'sion (-prĕsh/un), n. Act of oppressing, or state of being oppressed.
Op-prĕss'ive, a. Burdensome; unjustly severe.
Op-prĕss'ive-ly, adv. In an oppressive or cruel manner.
Op-prĕss'ive-ness, n. Quality of being oppressive.
Op-prĕss'or, n. One who oppresses; a tyrant.
Op-prō'bri-ous, a. Reproachful and contemptuous; made hateful.
Op-prō'bri-ous-ly, adv. Reproachfully; infamously.
Op-prō'bri-um, n. Contemptuous or disdainful reproach.
Op-pŭgn' (-pūn'), v. t. To oppose; to fight against.
Op-pŭgn'er (-pūn/-), n. One who opposes or attacks.
Op'ta-tive, a. Expressing desire or wish.
Op'tic, } a. Pertaining to
Op'tic-al, } the eye or vision, or to optics.
Op-tĭ'cian (-tĭsh'an), n. A person skilled in optics.
Op'tics, n. sing. Science of the the nature and laws of vision.
Op'ti-miṣm, n. The doctrine that every thing in nature is ordered for the best.
Op'ti-mist, n. One who holds that all events are ordered for the best.
Op'tion, n. Right or power of choosing. — SYN. Choice.
Op'tion-al, a. Left to choice.

Op′u-lençe, n. Wealth; riches; affluence.
Op′u-lent, a. Very rich.
Or, conj. A connective that marks an alternative.
Or′a-çle, n. An answer considered infallible; a wise man; (pl.) the revelations of God.
O-răç′u-lar, a. Uttering oracles; authoritative; ambiguous. [oracular manner.
O-răç′u-lar-ly, adv. In an
O′ral, a. Delivered by the mouth. [word of mouth.
O′ral-ly, adv. By
Or′anġe (140), n. A certain tree and its round yellow fruit. — a. Having the color of an orange. _Orange._
Or′an-ġer-y, n. A plantation of orange trees.
O-răng′-ou-tăng′, n. [Malayan _orăng ūtan_, i. e., man of the woods.] A large ape, having a deformed resemblance to man. _Orang-outang._
O-rā′tion, n. A public and elaborate discourse.
Or′a-tor (115), n. An eloquent public speaker; a petitioner.
Or′a-tôr′i-al, a. Pertaining to an orator or to oratory. — SYN. Rhetorical; eloquent; flowery. [rhetorical manner.
Or′a-tôr′iç-al-ly, adv. In a
Or′a-tō′ri-o (140), n. A sacred drama set to music; an oratory.
Or′a-to-ry, n. Art of public speaking; a small chapel. — SYN. Eloquence; elocution.
Ŏrb, n. A round body; a sphere; a globe; an orbit.
Ŏrbed, a. Round; circular; spherical. [cular; spherical.
Or-bĭç′u-lar, a. Round; cir-
Ŏrb′it, n. Path of a planet or comet round its center; cavity of the eye. [orbit.
Ŏr′bit-al, a. Pertaining to an
Ŏr′chard, n. An inclosure or assemblage of fruit trees.
Or′ches-trà, or **Or-chĕs′trà,** n. The part of a theater appropriated for the musicians; the musicians.

Or′ches-tral, a. Relating to an orchestra.
Or′chis (-kis), n. A plant.
Or-dāin′, v. t. To establish; to appoint; to decree; to invest with ministerial or sacerdotal functions.
Or′de-al, n. Trial by fire or by water; severe scrutiny.
Or′der, n. Regular arrangement; command; rule; a rank or class; a written direction to pay money; (pl.) rank of deacon, priest, or bishop. — v. t. To regulate; to bid; to command.
Or′der-li-ness, n. Regularity.
Or′der-ly, a. Regular; not unruly. — adv. Methodically; according to rule. — n. A non-commissioned officer who attends on a superior officer.
Or′di-nal, a. Noting established order. — n. A number noting order; a book of rites.
Or′di-nançe (140), n. Rule established by law; law; rite.
Or′di-na-ri-ly (135), adv. Usually; commonly.
Or′di-na-ry, a. Usual; common; of little merit. — n. An ecclesiastical judge; a public table; place of eating at a fixed hour and rate; establishment for ships laid up.
Or′di-nate, a. Regular; methodical. [daining.
Or′di-nā′tion, n. Act of or-
Ôrd′nançe, n. Heavy artillery; cannon, mortars, &c.
Ôrd′ure, n. Dung; filth.
Ore (84), n. A natural compound of metal and other matter.
Or′gan, n. An instrument of action or motion; a medium of communication; a wind instrument of music.
Or-găn′ic, } a. Containing
Or-găn′ic-al, } organs.
Or-găn′ic-al-ly, adv. In an organic manner; by means of organs. [ure.
Or′gan-ĭṣm, n. Organic struct-
Or′gan-ĭst, n. One who plays on an organ.
Or′gan-i-zā′tion, n. Act of organizing; structure.
Or′gan-īze, v. t. To furnish with organs; to arrange in parts; to form in due order.
Or′gaṣm, n. Immoderate excitement or action.
†**Orgeat** (ôr′zhat or ôr′zhā), n. [Fr.] A liquor extracted from barley and sweet almonds.
Ôr′ġieṣ, n. pl. Frantic revels.

O′ri-el, n. A projecting window.
O′ri-ent, a. Rising as the sun; eastern; bright; shining. — n. The East.
O′ri-ĕnt′al (107), a. Eastern. — n. An inhabitant of the East.
O′ri-ĕnt′al-ĭṣm, n. Any system, doctrine, or form of expression peculiar to inhabitants of the East.
O′ri-ĕn′tal-ĭst, n. One versed in Eastern languages. [ture.
O′ri-fiçe, n. An opening; aper-
Or′i-ġin, n. Beginning; commencement; source.
O-rĭġ′i-nal, a. First; primitive; having new or striking ideas. — n. Origin; first copy; an eccentric person.
O-rĭġ′i-năl′i-ty, n. Quality of being original.
O-rĭġ′i-nal-ly, adv. At first.
O-rĭġ′i-nāte, v. t. To bring into existence. — v. i. To take rise; to begin.
O-rĭġ′i-nā′tion, n. Act of bringing or coming into existence. [originates.
O-rĭġ′i-nā′tor, n. One who
O′ri-ōle, n. A bird allied to the thrushes. [constellation
O-rī′on, n. A large and bright
Or′i-ṣon, n. A prayer.
Or′lop, n. Deck on which cables are stowed in ships.
†**Or′mo-lū′,** n. A kind of brass made to resemble gold.
Or′na-ment, n. Decoration; embellishment. — v. t. To decorate; to embellish; to adorn.
Or′na-mĕnt′al, a. Tending to adorn or embellish.
Or′nate, a. Adorned; decorated; beautiful.
Or′ni-thŏl′o-ġist, n. One skilled in ornithology.
Or′ni-tho-lŏġ′ic-al, a. Pertaining to ornithology.
Or′ni-thŏl′o-ġy, n. [Gr. _ornis, ornithos_, a bird, and _logos_, discourse.] The science which treats of birds.
O-rŏl′o-ġy, n. The science or description of mountains.
Ôr′phan, n. A child having neither father nor mother, or only one of them.
Ôr′phan-aġe, } n. State of an
Ôr′phan-ĭṣm, } orphan.
Or-phē′an, or **Ôr′phe-an,** } a. Pertaining to Orpheus, an
Ôr′phic, } old Greek poet.
Or′re-ry (141), n. An instrument to show the revolutions of the planets, &c.

sọn, ôr, dọ, wolf, tōō, tŏŏk; ûrn rụe, pụll; ç, ġ, soft; c, ġ, hard; a̤; exist; ṇ as ng; this.

Or'tho-dŏx, *a.* Correct in doctrine; sound in the Christian faith; not heretical.

Or'tho-dŏx'y, *n.* Soundness in opinion and doctrine.

Or'tho-ĕp'ic-al, *a.* Pertaining to orthoëpy.

Or'tho-e-pist. *n.* A person well skilled in orthoëpy.

Or'tho-e-py, *n.* Correct pronunciation of words.

Or-thŏg'ra-pher, } *n.* One
Or-thŏg'ra-phist, } versed in orthography.

Or'tho-grăph'ic, } *a.* Per-
Or'tho-grăph'ic-al, } taining to orthography.

Or-thŏg'ra-phy, *n.* The spelling or writing of words with the proper letters.

Or'tive, *a.* Rising; eastern.

Or'to-lan, *n.* A European song-bird.

Os'cil-late, *v. i.* To swing; to vibrate; to sway.

Os'cil-la'tion, *n.* Vibration.

Os'cil-la-to-ry, *a.* Moving as a pendulum; vibratory.

Os'ci-tan-cy, *n.* A yawning.

Os'ci-tant, *a.* Yawning; sleepy. [ing or yawning.

Os'ci-ta'tion, *n.* Act of gaping.

Os'cu-late, *v. t.* To kiss; to touch, as two curves.

Os'cu-la'tion, *n.* Act of kissing; contact of one curve with another.

O'sier (ō'zher). *n.* A species of willow or the twig of the willow.

Os'mōse, *n.* Tendency in fluids to mix; the action produced by this tendency.

Os'prey, *n.* A long-winged eagle living on fish.

Os'se-oŭs (*colloq.* ŏsh'us), *a.* Bony; like bone. [bone.

Os'si-cle (-kl), *n.* A small

Os-sif'ic, *a.* Having power to ossify. [changing to bone.

Os'si-fi-ca'tion, *n.* Process of

Os'si-frage, *n.* The young of the sea-eagle or bald eagle.

Os'si-fy, *v. t.* or *i.* To change into bone. [bones.

Os-siv'o-roŭs, *a.* Feeding on

Os-tĕn'si-ble, *a.* Apparent; manifest.

Os-tĕn'si-bly, *adv.* Plausibly.

Os-tĕn'sive, *a.* Tending to show; exhibiting.

Os'ten-ta'tion, *n.* Ambitious display. — SYN. Pomp; pageantry; parade.

Os'ten-ta'tious, *a.* Affectedly showy; gaudy; pretentious.

Os'ten-ta'tious-ly, *adv.* In an ostentatious manner.

Ŏs'te-ŏl'o-ger, } *n.* A describ-
Ŏs'te-ŏl'o-gist, } er of bones; one versed in osteology

Ŏs'te-ŏl'o-gy, *n.* Part of anatomy that treats of bones.

Ŏs'ti-a-ry, *n.* Mouth of a river; an estuary.

Ŏst'ler, *n.* See *Hostler.*

Ŏs'tra-cĭṣm, *n.* Banishment.

Ŏs'tra-çīze, *v. t.* To banish, to exile; to put under ban.

Ŏs'trich (140), *n.* A large, swift-running bird, with very short wings, and long, soft plumes in place of feathers. It is found in Africa and Arabia.

Ŏth'er (ŭth'er), *z.* Second of two; not the same; different.

Ŏth'er-wīṣe, *adv.* In a different manner.

Ŏt'tar, } *n.* A highly fragrant
Ŏt'to, } oil obtained from the rose.

Ŏt'ter, *n.* A small carnivorous and aquatic quadruped.

Ŏt'to-man (143), *n.* [From the Sultan *Othoman* or *Othman.*] A Turk; a stuffed seat without a back. — *a.* Relating to Turkey. [a ring.

Ŏuch, *n.* The bezel or socket of

Ŏught (awt), *n.* See *Aught.* — *v. imperfect.* Is fit or necessary; should.

Ounce, *n.* Twelfth of a pound troy, and sixteenth of a pound avoirdupois; an animal resembling the leopard.

Our (85), *a.* Pertaining to us.

Ours, *pron.* Of us; belonging to us.

Our-sĕlves', *pron. pl.* We; us; — used emphatically.

Qu'ṣel (ōo'zl, 58), *n.* A bird of the thrush family.

Oust, *v. t.* To eject with force.

Out, *adv.* On the outside; beyond the limits of any inclosed place or given line; abroad; not at home.

Out-băl'ance, *v. t.* To exceed in weight; to outweigh.

Out-bid', *v. t.* To bid more.

Out'bound, *a.* Proceeding to a foreign port.

Out'break, *n.* A breaking forth; eruption.

Out'burst, *n.* A breaking or bursting out.

Out'cǎst, *n.* A person banished.

Out'crop, *n.* The coming out of a stratum to the surface of the ground.

Out'cry, *n.* Clamor; loud cry.

Out-do', *v. t.* [*p. p.* OUTDONE.] To do more than; to surpass; to excel.

Out'er, *a.* Being without.

Out'er-mōst, *a.* On the extreme external part.

Out-fāçe', *v. t.* To bear down with impudence.

Out'fit, *n.* Equipment, as of a ship for a voyage.

Out-gĕn'er-al, *v. t.* To exceed in generalship.

Out-gō', *v. t.* To go beyond; to surpass. — *n.* Outlay; expenditure. [out.

Out'gō-ing, *n.* Act of going

Out-grōw', *v. t.* To surpass in growth.

Out-Hĕr'od, *v. t.* To exceed in cruelty or absurdity.

Out'-house, *n.* A small building near the main house.

Out-lănd'ish, *a.* Foreign; strange; rude; barbarous.

Out-lăst', *v. t.* To last longer than; to exceed in duration.

Out'law, *n.* One excluded from the benefit of the law. — *v. t.* To deprive of the benefit and protection of the law.

Out'law-ry, *n.* Act of depriving of the benefit or protection of the law.

Out'lāy, *n.* Expenditure.

Out'let, *n.* A passage outward.

Out'līne, *v. t.* To sketch; to delineate. — *n.* The exterior line of a figure; a sketch.

Out-līve', *v. t.* To live longer than; to survive.

Out-lŏŏk', *n.* Act of looking out; a watch-tower; prospect; sight.

Out-lȳ'ing, *a.* Being at a distance from the main body or design.

Out-mărch', *v. t.* To march faster than. [in number.

Out-nŭm'ber, *v. t.* To exceed

Out'pŏst, *n.* A station without a camp, or at a distance.

Out-pŏur', *v. t.* To pour out.

Out'rāge, *v. t.* To treat with violence and wrong. — *n.* Violence; gross injury.

Out-rāge'oŭs (153), *a.* Exceeding all bounds of reason or of decency. — SYN. Violent; furious; exorbitant.

Out-rāge'oŭs-ly, *adv.* In an outrageous manner.

Out-reach', *v. t.* To go or extend beyond.

OUTRIDE 215 OVERTURE

Out-rīde′, *v. t.* To ride faster than.
Out′rīd-er, *n.* An attending servant on horseback.
Out′right (-rit), *adv.* Immediately; at once; completely.
Out-rŭn′, *v. t.* To surpass in running; to exceed.
Out-sāil′, *v. t.* To leave behind in sailing.
Out-sĕll′, *v. t.* To exceed in amount of sales.
Out′set, *n.* Beginning; opening; start. [brightness.
Out-shīne′, *v. t.* To excel in
Out′sīde, *n.* The outward part. —*a.* Exterior; external.
Cut′skirt, *n.* Border; suburb.
Out-sprĕad′, *v. t.* To spread open; to extend; to diffuse.
Out-stănd′ing, *a.* Not collected; unpaid. [far.
Cut-strĕtch′, *v. t.* To extend
Out-strĭp′, *v. t.* To outgo; to exceed; to leave behind.
Out-tȧlk′ (-tawk′), *v. t.* To overpower by talking.
Out-vōte′, *v. t.* To exceed in the number of votes.
Out-wȧlk′ (-wawk′), *v. t.* To leave behind in walking.
Out′ward, } *a.* External; exterior; outer.
Out′wards,} —*adv.* Toward the outside.
Out′ward-ly, *adv.* On the outside; externally.
Out-weȧr′, *v. t.* To endure or wear longer than.
Out-wēigh′ (-wā′), *v. t.* To exceed in weight or value.
Cut-wĭt′, *v. t.* To overcome by stratagem.
Out′work (-wŭrk), *n.* Part of a fortress without the principal wall.
Ō′val, *a.* Of the form of an egg; elliptical. —*n.* A body shaped like an egg. Oval.
Ō′va-ry (141), *n.* Place where, or organ by which eggs are formed.
Ō′vate, *a.* Oval, or egg-shaped, with the lower extremity broadest.
O-vā′tion, *n.* [Lat. *ovatio*, from *ovare*, to exult.] An inferior or less formal triumph.
Ŏv′en (ŭv′n), *n.* An arched or other cavity for baking.
Ō′ver, *prep.* Across; above; upon; on the surface. —*adv.* From side to side; more than.
Ō′ver-ăct′, *v. t.* To perform to excess.
Ō′ver-ȧlls, *n.* A kind of long trowsers worn over others.

Ō′ver-ärch′, *v. t.* To cover with an arch. [by awe.
Ō′ver-ȧwe′, *v. t.* To restrain
Ō′ver-băl′ançe, *v. t.* To weigh down; to preponderate.
Ō′ver-beȧr′, *v. t.* To bear down; to repress; to subdue.
Ō′ver-beȧr′ing, *a.* Haughty and dogmatical; insolent.
Ō′ver-bōard, *adv.* Over the side of, or out of, a ship.
Ō′ver-bûr′den, *v. t.* To load to excess.
Ō′ver-cȧst′, *v. t.* To cloud; to obscure. —*a.* Overspread with gloom; sewed over.
Ō′ver-chärge′, *v. t.* To charge to excess. [load or charge.
Ō′ver-chärge, *n.* Excessive
Ō′ver-cloud′, *v. t.* To cover with clouds.
Ō′ver-cōat, *n.* A coat worn over the other clothing.
Ō′ver-cŏme′ (-kŭm′), *v. t.* To get the better of. —SYN. To conquer; to vanquish.
Ō′ver-dō′, *v.* To do too much.
Ō′ver-dōse, *n.* Too great a dose; excess.
Ō′ver-drȧw′, *v. t.* To draw orders upon beyond one's credit.
Ō′ver-flōw′, *v. t.* or *i.* To spread over, as water; to inundate; to flood.
Ō′ver-flōw, *n.* Inundation; deluge; superabundance.
Ō′ver-grōw′, *v. t.* To cover with herbage; to grow beyond the natural size.
Ō′ver-grōwth. *n.* Exuberant or excessive growth. [over.
Ō′ver-häng′, *v. t.* To jut
Ō′ver-haul′, *v. t.* To turn over and examine thoroughly; to overtake.
Ō′ver-hĕad′, *adv.* Above; aloft. [accident.
Ō′ver-heȧr′, *v. t.* To hear by
Ō′ver-hēat′, *v. t.* To heat to excess. [with joy.
Ō′ver-joy′, *v. t.* To transport
Ō′ver-lā′bor, *v. t.* To harass with toil; to jade.
Ō′ver-lănd, *a.* Carried by land
Ō′ver-lāy′, *v. t.* To lay or spread over; to smother.
Ō′ver-lēap′, *v. t.* To leap over; to pass by leaping.
Ō′ver-lōad′, *v. t.* To load too heavily; to fill to excess.
Ō′ver-lōok′, *v. t.* To inspect; to neglect; to excuse.
Ō′ver-līe′, *v. t.* To lie over or upon. [powerful for.
Ō′ver-mătch′, *v. t.* To be too
Ō′ver-mătch, *n.* One superior in power or skill.

Ō′ver-mŭch′, *a.* Too much.— *adv.* In too great a degree.
Ō′ver-nīght′ (-nīt′), *adv.* During the night previous; last night. [to cross; to omit.
Ō′ver-pàss′, *v. t.* To go over;
Ō′ver-pāy′, *v. t.* To pay too much or more than is due.
Ō′ver-per-suāde′, *v. t.* To persuade against inclination.
Ō′ver-plus, *n.* More than is wanted; surplus.
Ō′ver-poișe, *n.* Preponderant weight. —*v. t.* To outweigh.
Ō′ver-pow′er, *v. t.* To vanquish by superior force; to affect too strongly.
Ō′ver-rāte′, *v. t.* To rate too high or beyond the truth.
Ō′ver-rēach′, *v. t.* To deceive; to cheat.
Ō′ver-rule′, *v. t.* To control.
Ō′ver-rŭn′, *v. t.* To spread over; to ravage. —*v. i.* To overflow; to run over.
Ō′ver-see′, *v. t.* To superintend; to supervise.
Ō′ver-seer′, *n.* A supervisor.
Ō′ver-sĕt′, *v. t.* or *i.* To overturn; to subvert.
Ō′ver-shăd′ōw, *v. t.* To throw a shadow over; to shelter.
Ō′ver-shōōt′, *v. t.* To shoot over or beyond.
Ō′ver-shŏt, *a.* Receiving water over a wheel.
Ō′ver-sīght (-sīt′), *n.* A mistake; omission; failure to notice; superintendence.
Ō′ver-sleep′, *v. t.* To sleep beyond. —*v. i.* To sleep too long.
Ō′ver-sprĕad′, *v. t.* To spread or cover over.
Ō′ver-stāte′, *v. t.* To state too strongly; to exaggerate.
Ō′ver-stĕp′, *v. t.* To step beyond. [full.
Ō′ver-stŏck′, *v. t.* To fill too
Ō′ver-strāin′, *v. t.* To strain to excess. [ifest.
Ō′vert, *a.* Open; public; manifest.
Ō′ver-tāke′, *v. t.* [*imp.* OVERTOOK; *p. p.* OVERTAKEN.] To come up with; to catch.
Ō′ver-tȧsk′, *v. t.* To impose too much work on.
Ō′ver-thrōw′, *v. t.* To subvert; to defeat. [defeat.
Ō′ver-thrōw′ (116), *n.* Ruin;
Ō′vert-ly, *adv.* In open view; openly; publicly.
Ō′ver-tŏp′, *v. t.* To rise above, to surpass.
Ō′ver-trāde′, *v. i.* To trade beyond one's means
Ō′vert-ūre, *n.* An offer; a proposal; an introductory piece of music

sŭn, ôr, dọ, wǫlf, tōō, tŏŏk; ûrn, rụe, pụll; ç, ġ, *soft*; ȩ, ġ, *hard*; aş; eẓist; ɴ as ng; this.

O'ver-tûrn', v. t. To throw over or down; to destroy.
O'ver-turn, n. Overthrow; subversion. [excessively.
O'ver-val'ūe, v. t. To value
O'ver-ween'ing, a. Conceited; arrogant; vain.
O'ver-weigh' (-wā'), v. t. To exceed in weight.
O'ver-weight (-wāt). n. Preponderance; greater weight.
O'ver-whelm', v. t. To spread over or crush beneath; to immerse and bear down.
O'ver-work' (-wûrk'), v. t. [p. p. OVERWROUGHT.] To cause to labor too much.
O'vi-fôrm, a. Egg-shaped.
O-vip'a-rous (117), a. Producing eggs, as a hen.
O'void, a. [Lat. ovum, egg, and Gr. eidos, shape.] Having the shape of an egg.
Owe (ō, 137), v. t. To be indebted.

Ōw'ing, p. pr. or a. Due; imputable; ascribable.
Owl, n. A nocturnal bird, of a short, stout form, with downy feathers and large head.
Owl'ing, n. The offense of transporting wool or sheep out of England contrary to law.
Owl'ish, a. Resembling an owl.
Own, a. Noting property or title; belonging exclusively to; peculiar.—v. t. To possess; to confess; to avow.
Own'er, n. The rightful proprietor of any thing.
Own'er-ship, n. Exclusive right of possession.
Ox, n. (pl. Ox'en, 144.) A castrated male of the bovine genus.
Ox-ăl'ic, a. Relating to, or obtained from, sorrel.

Owl.

Ovoid.

Ox'ide (152), n. A compound of oxygen and a base.
Ox'id-āte, } v. t. To convert
Ox'id-īze, } into an oxide.
Ox'id-ā'tion, n. Operation of converting into an oxide.
Ox'y-gen, n. A kind of gas which produces combustion and serves to support life. With hydrogen, it forms water.
Ox'y-gen-āte, } v. t. To cause
Ox'y-gen-īze, } to combine with oxygen.
Ox-ȳġ'e-nous, a. Pertaining to, or obtained from, oxygen.
Ox'y-mĕl, n. A mixture of vinegar and honey.
O'yer, n. A hearing in court, as of a deed, bond, &c.
O'yez (o'yes), interj. Hear; attend;— a term used by criers of courts.
Oys'ter, n. A bivalvular mollusk of which some species are used for food.
O'zōne, n. Oxygen in a condensed form.

P.

PĀÇE, n. A step; gait; measure of five feet.—v. t. To measure by steps or paces.—v. i. To walk.
Pā'çer, n. A horse that paces.
Pa-chā', or Pā'chă, n. See Pasha.
Păch'y-dĕrm, n. A non-ruminant hoofed animal, having a thick skin, as the elephant.
Păch'y-dĕrm'a-tous, a. Relating to a pachyderm.
Pa-çĭf'ic, a. Conciliatory; peaceable; mild; gentle.
Pa-çĭf'i-cā'tion, or Păç'i-fi-çā'tion, n. Act of making peace.
Pa-çĭf'i-cā'tor, or Păç'i-fi-cā'tor, n. A peace-maker.
Pa-çĭf'i-ca-to-ry, a. Tending to peace; conciliatory.
Păç'i-fy, v. t. [Lat. pacificare, from pax, pacis, peace, and facere, to make.] To appease; to allay; to calm; to still; to tranquilize.
Păck, n. A bundle; load; 52 cards assorted; a number of hounds; a set; a crew.—v. t. To make into a bundle; to send off in haste.

Păck'age, n. A bundle; a packet; a parcel; a bale.
Păck'et, n. A small package; a vessel for dispatches, or for passengers.
Păck'-hôrse, n. A horse used for carrying packs or other burdens.
Păck'man (143), n. A peddler.
Păck'-săd'dle, n. A saddle on which packs are borne.
Păck'-thrĕad, n. A thread for binding parcels.
Păct, n. A contract; a bargain; a covenant; a compact.
Păd. n. A small cushion; a robber; an easy-paced horse.—v. t. To stuff, as a saddle, cushion, &c.
Păd'dle, v. t. To propel by an oar or paddle; to play in water.—n. A kind of short oar.
Păd'dock (127), n. A small inclosure.
Păd'lock, n. A lock for a staple.—v. t. To fasten with a padlock.
Păd'ūa-soy' (păd'u-), n. A kind of silk stuff.
Pæ'an, n. A song of triumph or joy.
Pā'gan, n. A heathen; an

idolater.—a. Heathenish; idolatrous.
Pā'gan-ĭsm, n. Heathenism.
Pā'gan-īze (153), v. t. To convert to heathenism.
Pāge (140), n. A boy that waits on some great personage or on a legislative body; one side of a leaf.—v. t. To mark with pages.
Păġ'eant (păj'ant or pā'jant), n. A pompous show.
Păġ'eant-ry păj'ant- or pā'jant-, n. Pompous exhibition.—SYN. Spectacle; show; pomp. [pages.
Păġ'i-nal, a. Consisting of
Pa-gō'da (140), n. [Hindu butkadah, a house of idols.] An East Indian idol, temple, or coin.
Pāid (136), imp. & p. p. of Pay.
Pāil, n. A vessel for water, milk, &c [a pail holds.
Pāi'ful (139), n. As much as
Pāin, n. Distress; suffering; penalty.—v. t. To distress; to afflict. [borious.
Pāin'ful, a. Full of pain; laborious.
Pāin'ful-ly, adv. Laboriously.
Pāin'less, a. Free from pain.
Pāins, n. Care; trouble.

PAINT 217 PANTHEIST

Paint, *v. t.* To cover or represent with colors. — *v. i.* To practice painting; to color the face. — *n.* A coloring substance; pigment.

Paint'er, *n.* One who paints; a rope to fasten a boat.

Paint'ing, *n.* Art of forming figures in colors; a picture.

Pair, *n.* Two things suited or used together; a couple. — *v. i.* To be joined in couples. — *v. t.* To unite in couples.

Pal'ace, *n.* A magnificent house of some great personage. [knight.

Pal'a-din, *n.* An eminent

Pal'an-quin' (-keen'), *n.* An Eastern covered carriage borne on the shoulders.

Pal'a-ta-ble, *a.* Pleasing to the taste.

Pal'a-ta-ble-ness, *n.* Quality of being palatable.

Pal'a-tal, *a.* Pertaining to, or uttered by the aid of, the palate. — *n.* A letter uttered by the aid of the palate.

Pal'ate, *n.* The roof of the mouth; taste; relish.

Pa-la'tial, *a.* Pertaining to a palace; magnificent.

Pa-lat'i-nate, *n.* Province of a palatine.

Pal'a-tine, *n.* One invested with royal privileges. — *a.* Possessing royal privileges.

Pa-la'ver, *n.* Idle talk; flattery. — *v. t.* or *i.* To flatter; to use idle talk.

Pale, *a.* Destitute of color; white of look. — *n.* A narrow pointed board; a stake; a district. — *v. t.* To inclose with pales.

Pale'ness (132), *n.* State of being pale; defect of color.

Pa'le-og'ra-phy, *n.* Science of deciphering ancient documents.

Pa'le-ol'o-gist, *n.* One versed in paleology.

Pa'le-ol'o-gy, *n.* Treatise on antiquities; archæology.

Pa'le-on-tol'o-gy, *n.* The science of fossils.

Pa-les'tric, *a.* Pertaining to the exercise of wrestling.

Pal'ette, *n.* A tablet upon which a painter lays and mixes his pigments. Palette.

Pal'frey, *n.* A small saddle-horse. [work.

Pal'ing, *n.* A kind of fence-

Pal'in-ode, *n.* A song repeated; a recantation.

Pal'i-sade', *n.* A fortification of stakes. — *v. t.* To fortify with pales or posts.

Pall, *n.* A covering for the dead. — *v. i.* or *t.* To make or become vapid; to cloak; to cloy.

Pal-la'di-um, *n.* A statue of Pallas; an effective defense.

Pal'let, *n.* A palette; a lever in a watch or clock; a small, poor bed.

Pal'li-ate, *v. t.* To cover; to excuse or extenuate.

Pal'li-a'tion, *n.* Extenuation.

Pal'li-a-tive, *n.* That which extenuates. — *a.* Mitigating.

Pal'lid, *a.* Pale; wan.

Palm (päm), *n.* A tree; a measure equal to three or four inches; inner part of the hand. — *v. t.* To conceal in the hand; to impose upon.

Pal'ma-ry, *a.* Worthy of the palm; chief; principal.

Pal'ma-ted, *a.* Like the hand with the fingers spread; web-footed.

Palm'er (päm'er), *n.* A pilgrim from the Holy Land, who bore a branch of palm.

Pal-met'to (*pl.* Pal-met'tōs, 140), *n.* A kind of palm-tree.

Pal'mi-pēd, *n.* A bird with webbed feet.

Pal'mis-try, *n.* Art of telling fortunes by examining the palm of the hand.

Palm'y (päm'y), *a.* Flourishing; prosperous.

Pal'pa-bil'i-ty, } *n.* Quality
Pal'pa-ble-ness, } of being palpable.

Pal'pa-ble, *a.* Capable of being felt. [obviously.

Pal'pa-bly, *adv.* Plainly;

Pal'pi-tāte, *v. i.* To throb or beat, as the heart; to flutter.

Pal'pi-tā'tion, *n.* A beating or fluttering, as of the heart.

Pal'sied (pawl'zid), *a.* Having the palsy; paralytic.

Pal'sy, *n.* [Contracted from *paralysis.*] Loss of the power of voluntary muscular motion; paralysis. — *v. t.* To strike with palsy; to paralyze.

Pal'ter, *v. i.* To act insincerely; to trifle.

Pal'tri-ness, *n.* Meanness.

Pal'try, *a.* Mean; pitiful; insignificant. [full.

Pam'per, *v. t.* To feed to the

Pam'phlet, *n.* Sheets stitched but not bound.

Pam'phlet-eer', *n.* One who writes pamphlets.

Pan, *n.* A broad, shallow vessel; part of a gun-lock; hard stratum of earth below the soil. [remedy.

Pan'a-çē'a, *n.* A universal

Pan'cāke, *n.* A thin cake fried in a pan or baked on an iron plate or griddle.

Pan'cre-as, *n.* A soft gland of the body; the sweetbread.

Pan'cre-ăt'ic, *a.* Pertaining to the pancreas.

Pan'dect, *n.* A treatise containing the whole of any science.

Pan'de-mō'ni-um, *n.* The council-hall of evil spirits.

Pan'der, *n.* A pimp; a procurer; one who ministers to the evil passions of another. — *v. i.* To act as agent for the lusts or passions of others.

Pāne, *n.* A square of glass.

Pan'e-gyr'ic, *n.* A laudatory speech; encomium. — *a.* Containing praise or eulogy.

Pan'e-gyr'ist, *n.* A eulogist.

Pan'e-gy-rīze (153), *v. t.* To praise highly; to eulogize.

Pan'el, *n.* A compartment, as of a door; jury roll. — *v. t.* (130). To form with panels; to form, as a list of jurors.

Pang, *n.* Momentary agony.

Pan'ic (127), *n.* Sudden fright without good cause. — *a.* Extreme or sudden and causeless.

Pan'nier (păn'yer), *n.* A wicker-basket to be carried on horses.

Pan'o-ply, *n.* Armor covering the whole body.

Pan'o-rā'mā, or **Păn'o-rā'mä**, *n.* [Gr. *pas, pan*, all, and *horama*, a view.] Complete view; a large or continuous picture.

Pan'o-răm'ic, *a.* Pertaining to, or like, a panorama.

Pan'sy, *n.* A plant and flower; the garden violet.

Pant, *v. i.* To breathe rapidly; to gasp. — *n.* A rapid breathing; a gasp.

Pan'ta-gräph, *n.* See *Pantograph.* [drawers.

Pan'ta-lĕts', *n. pl.* Loose

Pan'ta-loons', *n. pl.* A kind of trowsers.

Pan'the-ism, *n.* The doctrine that the universe is God.

Pan'the-ist, *n.* One who believes in pantheism.

---

sŏn, ôr, dǫ, wǫlf, tōō, tǫǫk; ûrn, rṳe, pṳll; ç, ġ, *soft*; e, ġ, *hard*; aẓ; eẓist; ŋ as ng; thɪs.

10

Păn'the-ĭst'ĭc, *a.* Relating to pantheism.

Pan-the'on, or Păn'the-on, *n.* A temple dedicated to all the deities. [animal.

Păn'ther, *n.* A ferocious feline

Păn'tĭle, *n.* A curved or hollowed tile. [per.

Pan-tŏ'fle (-tōō'fl), *n.* A slipper.

Păn'tŏ-grăph, *n.* An instrument to copy any drawing.

Pan-tŏg'ra-phy, *n.* General description; entire view.

Păn'to-mīme, *n.* A representation in dumb show.

Păn'to-mĭm'ĭc, } *a.* Representing characters and actions by dumb show.
Păn'to-mĭm'ĭc-al, }

Păn'try, *n.* A store-room or closet for provisions.

Păp, *n.* A nipple; soft food.

Pa-pä', *n.* Father; — a word used by children.

Pā'pa-çy, *n.* Office and dignity of the Pope; popedom.

Pā'pal, *a.* Belonging to the Pope; popish.

Pa-păv'er-oŭs, *a.* Like, or pertaining to, the poppy.

Pa-pǎw', *n.* A tree and its sweet edible fruit.

Pā'per, *n.* A substance for writing or printing on.— *v. t.* To cover with paper.

†Papier-maché (păp'yā-mā'shā), *n.* [Fr.] A hard substance made of a pulp from rags or paper.

Pa-pĭl'ĭo-nā'ceoŭs, *a.* Resembling a butterfly.

Păp'ĭl-la-ry, *a.* Pertaining to, or resembling, nipples.

Pā'pĭst, *n.* One who adheres to the Roman Catholic religion and the papal authority.

Pa-pĭst'ĭc, } *a.* Pertaining to popery; popish. [babe.
Pa-pĭst'ĭc-al, }

Păp-poose', *n.* An Indian

Păp'poŭs, *a.* Downy.

Păp'py, *a.* Like pap; succulent; soft.

Pa-py'rus, *n.* An Egyptian plant, and a kind of paper made from it.

Pär, *n.* State of equality; equality of nominal and actual value.

Păr'a-blc, *n.* A moral fable.

Pa-răb'o-lā, *n.* One of the conic sections.

Păr'a-bŏl'ĭc, } *a.* Expressed by parable, or similitude.
Păr'a-bŏl'ĭc-al, }

Păr'a-chute (-shōōt, Parabo-107), *n.* [Fr., from la.

parer, to ward off, and chute, a fall.] A contrivance resembling an umbrella, to prevent rapidity of descent in a balloon.

Păr'a-clēte, *n.* A comforter; an intercessor; the Holy Spirit.

Pa-rāde', *n.* A pompous exhibition; military display.— SYN. Ostentation.— *v. i.* To assemble or go about, as troops.— *v. t.* To display; to show off.

Păr'a-dĭgm (-dĭm), *n.* An example of a word declined or conjugated, &c.

Păr'a-dīse, *n.* The garden of Eden; a place of bliss.

Păr'a-dĭ-sī'ac-al, *a.* Pertaining to, or like, paradise.

Păr'a-dŏx (140), *n.* A tenet seemingly absurd, yet true.

Păr'a-dŏx'ĭc-al, *a.* Having the nature of a paradox.

Păr'a-gō'ġe, *n.* (Gr.) Addition of a letter or syllable to the end of a word.

Păr'a-gŏġ'ĭc, } *a.* Lengthening a word by adding a syllable or letter.
Păr'a-gŏġ'ĭc-al, }

Păr'a-gon, *n.* Pattern of superior excellence.

Păr'a-grăph, *n.* A distinct part of a discourse; the character ¶; a brief notice.

Păr'al-lăc'tĭc, *a.* Pertaining to a parallax.

Păr'al-lăx, *n.* Apparent change of place in a heavenly body as viewed from different points.

Păr'al-lel, *a.* Equally distant in all parts; like; similar.— (130), *n.* A line equally distant from another at all points; resemblance; comparison.— *v. t.* (8) To equal; to compare. [Parallels.

Păr'al-lel-ĭsm, *n.* State of being parallel.

Păr'al-lĕl'o-grăm, *n.* A right-lined figure of four sides, Parallelogram. whose opposite sides are equal and parallel.

Păr'al-lĕl'o-pī'ped, *n.* A regular solid, the faces of which are six parallelograms. Parallelopiped.
Pa-răl'o-ġĭsm, }
Pa-răl'o-ġy, } *n.* False reasoning.

Pa-răl'y-sĭs, *n.* Palsy; loss of voluntary motion.

Păr'a-lyt'ĭc, *a.* Affected with paralysis or palsy.— *n.* One affected with palsy.

Păr'a-lȳze (153), *v. t.* To strike with paralysis or palsy; to destroy action in.

Păr'a-mount, *a.* Chief; superior to all others.

Păr'a-mour (-mōōr), *n.* A kept mistress; a concubine.

Păr'a-nymph, *n.* A bridemanan.

Păr'a-pet, *n.* A wall for defense; a breast-work.

Păr'a-pher-nā'lĭ-ā, *n. pl.* Apparel and ornaments; trappings.

Păr'a-phrāse, *n.* A copious explanation or re-statement.— *v. t.* To explain or interpret amply. [terprets.

Păr'a-phrăst, *n.* One who in-

Păr'a-phrăst'ĭc, *a.* Ample in explanation; not literal.

Păr'a-plē'ġy, *n.* Paralysis of the lower half of the body.

†Păr'a-se-lē'nc, *n.* (*pl.* Păr'a-se-lē'næ.) A luminous circle around the moon.

Păr'a-sīte, *n.* A hanger-on; a plant growing on another.— SYN. Sycophant.

Păr'a-sĭt'ĭc, } *a.* Having the qualities of a parasite.
Păr'a-sĭt'ĭc-al, }

Păr'a-sŏl', *n.* A small umbrella used as a screen from the sun.

Pär'boil, *v. t.* To boil partly.

Pär'çel (*colloq.* pŭr'sl), *n.* [Fr. parcelle, dim. of part, a part.] A small bundle; a portion; a package.— *v. t.* (130) To divide and distribute by portions; to apportion.

Pär'çe-na-ry, *n.* Co-heirship.

Pär'çe-ner, *n.* A joint heir; coparcener.

Pärch, *v.* To burn the surface; to scorch.

Pärch'ment, *n.* Skin of a sheep or goat dressed for writing on.

Pärd, *n.* The leopard; any spotted beast.

Pär'don (pär'dn), *n.* Forgiveness; remission of penalty.— *v. t.* To forgive; to excuse.

Pär'don-a-ble, *a.* Admitting of pardon; excusable.

Pär'don-a-bly, *adv.* So as to admit of pardon.

Pâre, *v. t.* To cut or shave off the surface of; to diminish gradually.

Păr'e-gŏr'ĭc, *n.* A medicine that mitigates pain.

ā, ĕ, ī, ō, ū, ȳ, *long*; ă, ĕ, ĭ, ŏ, ŭ, ў, *short*; câre, cär, Ȧsk, ȧll, whạt; ẽre, vẹil, tẽrm; p˙que, fïrm;

Pâr'ent (3), *n.* A father or mother. [traction.
Pâr'ent-age, *n.* Birth; ex-
Pa-rĕnt'al, *a.* Like a parent; tender; affectionate.
Pa-rĕn'the-sĭs, *n.* (Gr., fr. *parenthenai,* to insert.] A sentence or a part of one included in curved lines, thus ( ); the curved lines themselves.
Păr'en-thĕt'ic, *a.* In-
Păr'en-thĕt'ic-al, cluded in a parenthesis.
Pâr'er, *n.* One who, or that which, pares.
Păr'get (pär'jet), *n.* Plaster for covering walls, &c.— *v. t.* To plaster.
†**Pär-hēl'ion** (-hēl'yun), *n.* (*pl.* **Pär-hēl'ia.**) A mock sun or meteor.
Pā'ri-ah, or **Pā'ri-ah,** *n.* The lowest caste in Hindostan; an outcast.
Pa-rī'e-tal, *a.* Pertaining to a wall or building.
Pâr'ing, *n.* A thin strip cut off.
Păr'ish, *n.* A religious society, or the precinct of one.— *a.* Belonging to a parish.
Pa-rĭsh'ion-er (-rĭsh'un-), *n.* One belonging to a parish.
Păr'i-syl-lăb'ic, *a.* Having the same number of syllables.
Pâr'i-ty, *n.* Equality of number, likeness, quantity, &c.
Pârk, *n.* A piece of inclosed ground kept for game, or for recreation, &c.; a place for artillery.— *v. t.* To inclose in a park.
Pâr'lance, *n.* Talk; form of speech; conversation.
Pâr'ley, *n.* Conference; mutual discourse.— *v. i.* To treat by word of mouth; to discuss orally.
Pär'lia-ment (pär'li-), *n.* The supreme legislative assembly of Great Britain, &c.
Pär'lia-mĕnt'a-ry, *a.* Pertaining to parliament; according to legislative usages.
Pär'lor (155), *n.* A room for receiving company, &c.
Pa-rō'chi-al, *a.* Belonging to a parish.
Păr'o-dĭst, *n.* One who writes a parody.
Păr'o-dy, *n.* A ludicrous adaptation of a poem.— *v. t.* To apply differently; to give a burlesque imitation of.
Pa-rōl', *n.* Word of mouth;
Pa-rōle', a verbal promise.
— *a.* Oral; verbal.

Păr'o-nȳm, *n.* A paronymous word.
Păr'o-nȳme,
Pa-rŏn'y-moŭs, *a.* Sounding alike, but of different meaning and spelling.
Păr'o-quĕt (-kĕt), *n.* A small kind of parrot.
Pa-rŏt'id, *a.* Pertaining to certain glands near the ears.
Păr'ox-ȳsm, *n.* A violent fit of pain.
Par-quet' (-kā' or -kĕt'), *n.* Lower floor of a theater.
Păr'quet-ry (-ket-), *n.* Cabinet work of wood inlaid with figures.
Păr'ri-çī'dal, *a.* Relating to, or committing, parricide.
Păr'ri-çīde, *n.* One who murders his parent.
Păr'rot, *n.* A tropical bird of brilliant plumage.
Păr'ry, *v. t.* To ward off.
Pärse, *v. t.* To analyze and describe grammatically.
Pär'si-mō'ni-oŭs, *a.* Frugal; sparing; penurious.
Pär'si-mō'ni-oŭs-ly, *adv.* Sparingly; frugally.
Pär'si-mo-ny, *n.* Frugality; niggardliness.
Pärs'ley, *n.* A plant used in cookery. [root.
Pärs'nip, *n.* A plant and its
Pär'son (pär'sn), *n.* The clergyman of a parish.
Pär'son-age, *n.* House of the minister of a parish.
Pärt, *n.* A portion; division; share; side.— *v. t.* or *i.* To divide; to share; to separate; to quit.
Par-tāke', *v. t.* To have a part of.
Par-tāk'er, *n.* One who shares.
Par-tĕrre' (par-târ'), *n.* An ornamental plot of ground.
Pär'tial, *a.* Affecting or including a part only; not general; biased.
Pär-ti-ăl'i-ty (-shl-ăl'i-), *n.* Undue bias or fondness.
Pär'tial-ly, *adv.* In part only; with undue bias.
Pärt'i-ble, *a.* Divisible.
Par-tĭç'i-pant, *a.* Sharing; partaking.— *n.* A partaker.
Par-tĭç'i-pāte, *v. t.* To partake; to share.
Par-tĭç'i-pā'tion, *n.* A sharing; distribution.
Par-tĭç'i-pā'tor, *n.* One who partakes with another.
Pär'ti-çĭp'i-al, *a.* Having the nature of, or formed from, a participle.
Pär'ti-çi-ple, *n.* A word par-

taking of the properties of a noun and a verb.
Pär'ti-cle, *n.* A minute portion of matter; an atom.
Par-tĭç'u-lar, *a.* Pertaining to a single person or thing; minute; exact; peculiar. — *n.* A single point or circumstance.
Par-tĭç'u-lăr'i-ty, *n.* Something peculiar; exactness.
Par-tĭç'u-lar-īze (153), *v. t.* To mention in particulars.
Par-tĭç'u-lar-ly, *adv.* Distinctly; singly; especially.
Pär'ti-zăn', *n.* An adherent to a party or faction.— SYN. Follower; disciple.
Par-tī'tion (-tĭsh'un), *n.* Separation; that which separates. — *v. t.* To divide into parts.
Pärt'i-tive, *a.* Distributive.
Pärt'ly, *adv.* In part.
Pärt'ner, *n.* An associate in business; a sharer; companion, as in a dance.
Pärt'ner-ship, *n.* Union or joint interest in business.
Par-tŏŏk', *imp.* of *Partake.*
Pär'tridge (140), *n.* A name given to different birds.
Par-tū'ri-ent, *a.* Giving birth to young.
Par-tu-rī'tion (-rĭsh'un), *n.* Act of giving birth.
Pär'ty (141), *n.* A number of persons united by some tie; a select assembly; one of two litigants.
Pär'ty-çŏl'ored, *a.* Variegated; of various colors.
Pär'ty-wall, *n.* A wall that separates two buildings.
Päs'chal, *a.* Pertaining to the passover.
Pa-shä', or **Pā'shä,** *n.* A Turkish viceroy or governor.
Pa-shä'lic, *a.* Jurisdiction of a pasha.
Păs'quin-āde' (-kwin-), *n.* A satirical writing; a lampoon. — *v. t.* To satirize.
Păss (5, 124), *v. t.* To go beyond; to spend; to omit; to enact.— *v. i.* To go; to move; to circulate; to be current.— *n.* A passage; license to pass; a thrust.
Păss'a-ble, *a.* Capable of being passed; tolerable.
Păss'a-bly, *adv.* Tolerably.
Păs'sage, *n.* Act of passing; journey; way; course; hall; incident; portion of a book; enactment.
Păss'-bŏŏk, *n.* A book in which a trader enters articles bought on credit and then

passes or sends it to the purchaser.

Pas'sen-ger, *n.* A traveler on foot or by some public conveyance.

Pas'si-bil'i-ty, *n.* Capacity of receiving impressions.

Pas'si-ble, *a.* Susceptible of impressions.

†**Pas'sim**, *adv.* Everywhere.

Pass'ing, *n.* Act of going by.

Pass'ing-bell, *n.* A bell that rings at death or interment.

Pas'sion (pash'un, 83), *n.* That which is suffered; any strong emotion. — SYN. Feeling; emotion. [cited.

Pas'sion-ate, *a.* Easily excited.

Pas'sion-ate-ly, *adv.* With passion; ardently.

Pas'sion-flow'er, *n.* A flower and the plant that bears it.

Pas'sion-less, *a.* Not easily excited.

Pas'sion-week (pash'un-), *n.* The week preceding Easter.

Pas'sive, *a.* Receiving impressions; not active; unresisting. [sive manner.

Pas'sive-ly, *adv.* In a passive manner.

Pas'sive-ness, } *n.* Quality
Pas-siv'i-ty, } of being passive.

Pass'o-ver, *n.* A feast of the Jews. See *Exod.* xii.

Pass'port, *n.* A permission to travel; a safe conduct.

Pass'word (-wûrd), *n.* A word to be given before one can pass; a watch-word.

Past, *prep.* Beyond. — *n.* Time that has gone by. — *a.* Elapsed; ended.

Paste (54), *n.* An adhesive mixture, esp. of flour and water; an imitation of precious stones. — *v. t.* To unite or cement with paste.

Paste'board, *n.* A species of thick paper.

Pas'tern, *n.* Part of a horse's leg next to the hoof.

Pas-tille' (-teel'), *n.* A small cone made of perfumed paste for burning.

Pas'time (139), *n.* Diversion; amusement; sport.

Pas'tor, *n.* A shepherd; minister of a church.

Pas'tor-al, *a.* Rural; relating to a pastor. — *n.* A poem describing rural life.

Pas'tor-ate, } *n.* The office
Pas'tor-ship, } of a pastor.

Pas'try, *n.* Pies, tarts, cake, and the like.

Pas'tur-age, *n.* Lands grazed by cattle; grass for cattle.

Past'ure, *n.* Land for grazing. — *v. t.* or *i.* To graze.

Pas'ty, *a.* Like paste or dough. — *n.* A pie made of paste.

Pat, *a.* Fit; exactly suitable. — *n.* A light blow.

Patch (140), *n.* A piece of cloth used in mending; plot. — *v. t.* To put a patch on; to repair clumsily.

Patch'work (-wûrk), *n.* Bits of cloth sewed together; bungling work.

Pate, *n.* The head; skin of a calf's head.

Pat'en (55), *n.* A small plate used at the eucharist.

Pat'ent, or **Pāt'ent**, *n.* A grant of an exclusive right to an invention. — *v. t.* To make a public grant of.

Pat'ent, or **Pāt'ent**, *a.* Open; public; manifest.

Pat'ent-ee', or **Pāt'ent-ee'**, *n.* One to whom a patent is granted.

Pa-ter'nal, *a.* Fatherly; hereditary.

Pa-ter'ni-ty, *n.* Relation of a father to his offspring; fatherhood. [prayer.

Pa'ter-nos'ter, *n.* The Lord's

Path (96), *n.* (*pl.* Paths), *n.* [A.-S. *pädh*, *padh*, Skr. *patha*, fr. *path*, to go.] A way trod by man or beast; course of action or life. — SYN. Road; route; passage; track.

Pa-thet'ic, *a.* Affecting or moving the tender emotions.

Pa-thet'ic-al-ly, *adv.* In a pathetic manner.

Path'less, *a.* Having no path.

Path'o-log'ic, } *a.* Pertaining
Path'o-log'ic-al, } to pathology.

Pa-thol'o-gist, *n.* One who treats of pathology.

Pa-thol'o-gy, *n.* The science of diseases.

Pa'thos, *n.* That which awakens tender emotions.

Path'way, *n.* A path conducting to any point.

Pa'tience, *n.* Power of suffering without complaint; perseverance; resignation.

Pa'tient, *a.* Enduring without complaint. — *n.* A sick person.

Pa'tient-ly, *adv.* Without complaint; with resignation.

Pa'tri-arch, *n.* The head of a family or church.

Pa'tri-arch'al, *a.* Pertaining to a patriarch.

Pa'tri-arch'ate, *n.* Office or jurisdiction of a patriarch.

Pa-tri'cian (-trish'an), *a.* Of noble family. — *n.* A nobleman. [by inheritance.

Pat'ri-mō'ni-al, *a.* Possessed

Pat'ri-mo-ny, *n.* An estate derived by inheritance.

Pā'tri-ot, *n.* One who loves his country. [one's country.

Pā'tri-ŏt'ic, *a.* Having love to

Pā'tri-ŏt-ism, *n.* Love of one's country.

Pa-tris'tic, *a.* Relating to the ancient Christian fathers.

Pa-trōl', *n.* The guard that goes round camp or a garrison at night. — *v. i.* To go round, as a sentry. — *v. t.* To pass round, as a sentry.

Pā'tron, *n.* One who countenances or protects. — SYN. Advocate; benefactor.

Pāt'ron-age (153), *n.* Special countenance or support; aid.

Pāt'ron-al, *a.* Protecting; favoring. [trou.

Pā'tron-ess, *n.* A female patron.

Pāt'ron-ize (153), *v. t.* To act the patron to. — SYN. To support; favor; aid; defend; uphold.

Păt'ro-nym'ic, *n.* A name derived from an ancestor.

Pat'ten, *n.* The base of a column; a kind of wooden shoe standing on an iron ring.

Pat'ter, *v. i.* [A frequentative form of *pat*, to strike gently.] To strike, as drops of rain.

Pat'tern, *n.* A model for imitation. — *v. i.* To copy.

Pat'ty, *n.* A little pie.

Pau'ci-ty, *n.* Smallness of number or quantity.

Paunch, or **Pâunch**, *n.* The belly.

Pau'per, *n.* A poor person; one who receives alms.

Pau'per-ism, *n.* State of being a pauper; indigence.

Pause, *n.* A stop; cessation; suspense. — *v. i.* To stop; to cease; to wait.

Pāve, *v. t.* To lay with stone or brick. [stone or brick.

Pāve'ment, *n.* A floor of

Pāv'er, } *n.* One who lays
Pāv'ier, } stones for a pavement; one who paves.

Pa-vil'ion (-vil'yun), *n.* A tent; a kind of building or turret.

Paw, *n.* The foot of a beast. — *v. i.* or *t.* To scrape or strike with the foot.

Pawl, *n.* A catch, to check the backward revolution of a wheel or windlass, &c.

Pawn, *n.* A pledge deposited. — *v. t.* To leave as security.

PAWNBROKER   221   PENCE

Pawn'bro-ker, *n.* One who lends money on pledge.
Pay (13ǎ), *v. t.* [*imp. & p. p.* PAID.] To discharge, as a debt or duty; to reward; to rub over, as with tar, &c. — *v. i.* To be remunerative. — *n.* Payment; reward.
Pay'a-ble, *a.* Justly due.
Pay'-day, *n.* A day of reckoning.
Pay-ee', *n.* One to whom a note is made payable.
Pay'er, *n.* One who pays.
Pay'-mas'ter, *n.* An officer who makes payment.
Pay'ment, *n.* Act of paying; what is paid, esp. money.
Pēa, *n.* (*pl.* Pēas, Pēase, 145.) A plant and its fruit, used for food.
Pēaçe, *n.* Quiet; repose; freedom from war or disturbance.
Pēaçe'a-ble (133), *a.* Disposed to peace; quiet.
Pēaçe'a-bly, *adv.* Quietly.
Pēaçe'ful (13J), *a.* Quiet in mind; undisturbed; calm.
Pēaçe'ful-ly, *adv.* Quietly.
Pēaçe'ful-ness, *n.* Quality or state of being peaceful.
Pēaçe'-māk'er, *n.* One who makes peace by reconciling parties at variance.
Pēaçe'-ōf'fi-çer, *n.* A civil officer; a constable.
Pēach (140), *n.* A delicious stone-fruit. [fowl.
Pēa'çŏck, *n.* A beautiful
Pēa'hen, *n.* Female of the peacock.
Pēa'-jăck'et, *n.* A thick woolen jacket. [a point.
Pēak, *n.* The top of a hill;
Pēal, *n.* A loud sound or succession of sounds. — *v. i.* To utter loud and solemn sounds. [a pæan.
Pē'an, *n.* A triumphal song;
Peär, *n.* A tree and its fruit.
Pēarl, *n.* A beautiful white substance found in the oyster. — *v. t.* To adorn with pearls.
Pēarl'ash, *n.* Refined potash.
Pēarl'y, *a.* Like pearl.
Pēas'ant, *n.* One who lives by rural labor. [rustics.
Pēas'ant-ry, *n.* Peasants;
Pēase, *n. pl.* Peas collectively.
Pēat (126), *n.* A species of turf, often used for fuel.
Pēat'-mŏss, *n.* A fen producing peat. [stone.
Pĕb'ble, *n.* A small roundish
Pĕb'bly, *a.* Full of pebbles.
Pe-cān', *n.* A tree and its nut.

Pĕç'ca-bĭl'ĭ-ty, *n.* Liability to sin.
Pĕç'ca-ble, *a.* Liable to sin.
Pĕç'ca-dĭl'lo (140), *n.* A slight fault; a petty offense.
Pĕç'cant, *a.* Criminal; faulty.
Pĕck, *n.* Fourth of a bushel. — *v. t.* To strike with the beak or something pointed.
Pĕc'ti-nal, *a.* Like a
Pĕc'ti-nate. comb.
Pĕc'to-ral, *a.* Belonging to the breast. — *n.* A breast-plate; a medicine for the breast.
Pĕç'u-lāte, *v. i.* To steal public moneys intrusted to one.
Pĕç'u-lā'tion, *n.* Act of peculating; embezzlement.
Pĕç'u-lā'tor, *n.* A robber of the public property.
Pe-cūl'iar, *a.* Appropriate; singular; special.
Pe-cūl'iăr'i-ty (-yăr'ǐ-), *n.* Singularity.
Pe-cūl'iar-ly, *adv.* In a peculiar manner; particularly.
Pe-cūn'ia-ry (-kūn'ya-), *a.* Pertaining to, or consisting in, money.
Pĕd'a-gŏġ'ic, *a.* Sniting,
Pĕd'a-gŏġ'ic-al, or pertaining to, a pedagogue.
Pĕd'a-gŏġ-ĭsm, *n.* Business or character of a pedagogue.
Pĕd'a-gŏġue, *n.* [Gr. *paidagōgos,* fr. *pais,* a boy, and *agein,* to lead.] A schoolmaster.
Pē'dal, *a.* Relating to the foot.
Pē'dal, *n.* The foot-key of an organ or piano-forte.
Pĕd'ant, *n.* One who makes a display of learning.
Pe-dănt'ic, *a.* Displaying pedantry. [learning.
Pĕd'ant-ry, *n.* Ostentation of
Pĕd'dle, *v. i.* To travel and retail goods.
Pĕd'dler, *n.* A traveling trader in small wares.
Pĕd'dler-y, *n.* Small wares sold by a peddler.
Pĕd'es-tal, *n.* The base of a column, statue, or the like.
Pe-dĕs'tri-an, *a.* Going or performed on foot. — *n.* One who goes on foot.
Pe-dĕs'tri-an-ĭsm, *n.* Act of walking, and going on foot.
Pĕd'i-gree, *n.* Genealogy; lineage; account of descent.
Pĕd'i-ment, *n.* An ornamental crowning of a door, window, &c. [of infants.
Pē'do-băp'tĭsm, *n.* Baptism
Pē'do-băp'tist, *n.* One who holds to infant baptism.
Pe-dūn'cle (-dŭŋk'l), *n.* Stem

of a flower and of the fruit of a plant. [a peduncle.
Pe-dūn'cu-lar, *a.* Relating to
Peel (13ǐ), *v. t.* To strip of skin or rind; to flay; to plunder. — *v. i.* To come off, as the skin. — *n.* Rind; bark; a large fire shovel.
Peep, *n.* Sly look; first appearance; cry of chickens. — *v. i.* To look slyly; to begin to appear; to cry as a chicken.
Peer, *n.* [From Lat. *par,* equal.] An equal; a nobleman. — *v. i.* To come in sight; to look curiously.
Peer'age (86), *n.* Rank or dignity of a peer; body of peers.
Peer'ess, *n.* Wife of a peer.
Peer'less, *a.* Without an equal; unequaled.
Peev'ish, *a.* Easily vexed. — **SYN.** Cross; testy; irritable; captious; fretful.
Peev'ish-ly, *adv.* In a peevish manner. [ness.
Peev'ish-ness, *n.* Fretful-
Peg, *n.* A small wooden pin. — *v. t.* (129). To fasten with a peg or pin. [*sense.*
Pĕlf, *n.* Money; — *in an odious*
Pĕl'i-can, *n.* A large web-footed water-fowl.
Pe-lisse' (-lees'), *n.* A silk habit for a female.
Pĕll (123), *n.* A skin; a hide.
Pĕl'let, *n.* A little ball.
Pĕl'li-cle, *n.* A thin external skin; film.
Pĕll-mĕll', *adv.* Confusedly.
Pel-lū'çid, *a.* Admitting the passage of light; translucent.
Pĕlt, *n.* A raw or undressed hide. — *v. i.* To strike with pellets or missiles.
Pĕlt'ry, *n.* Furs.
Pĕl'vis, *n.* The open, bony structure at the lower extremity of the body, which supports and contains the intestines, &c.
Pĕm'mi-can, *n.* Meat dried, pounded, and mixed with melted fat and dried fruit.
Pĕn, *n.* Instrument for writing; a writer; a small inclosure for beasts. — *v. t.* To write; to confine.
Pē'nal, *a.* Denouncing or incurring punishment.
Pĕn'al-ty, *n.* Punishment attached to the commission of a crime.
Pĕn'ançe, *n.* Suffering or pain inflicted or self-imposed for sin; punishment.
Pĕnçe, *n.; pl.* of *Penny.*

---

sōu, ôr, do, wolf, tōō, tōŏk; ûrn, rṳe, pṳll; ç, ġ, *soft;* ȩ, ḡ, *hard;* ạs; eẍist; ŋ *as* ng; this

†Penchant (pŏng'shŏng'), *n.* Inclination; decided taste.

Pĕn'çĭl, *n.* A small brush used by painters; an instrument of black lead, colored chalk, or the like, for writing and drawing. — *v. t.* (130) To draw or paint.

Pĕnd'ant, *n.* A hanging appendage; a pennant.

Pĕnd'en-çy, *n.* Suspense; delay of decision.

Pĕnd'ent, *a.* Hanging; suspended; pendulous.

Pĕnd'ing, *a.* Remaining undecided; in suspense.

Pĕnd'u-loŭs, *a.* Swinging.

Pĕnd'u-lum, *n.* A body suspended and vibrating.

Pĕn'e-tra-bĭl'i-ty, *n.* Quality of being penetrable.

Pĕn'e-tra-ble, *a.* Capable of being penetrated.

Pĕn'e-trāte, *v. t.* To pierce; to enter; to feel deeply.

Pĕn'e-trā'tion, *n.* Act of entering; sagacity.

Pĕn'e-trā'tive, } *a.* Discerning; acute.
Pĕn'e-trā'ting, }

Pĕn'guĭn (-gwĭn, 79), *n.* A web-footed marine bird.

Pen-ĭn'su-lá (-sū- *or* -shū-), *n.* [Lat., from *pæne*, almost, and *insula*, an island.] Land nearly surrounded by water.

Penguin.

Pen-ĭn'su-lar (-sū- *or* -shū-). *a.* Having the form of a peninsula.

Pĕn'i-tençe, *n.* Sorrow of heart for sin; contrition.

Pĕn'i-tent, *a.* Suffering sorrow for sin. — *n.* One sorrowful for sin.

Pĕn'i-tĕn'tial, *a.* Pertaining to, or expressing, penitence.

Pĕn'i-tĕn'ti-a-ry, (-shĭ-a-ry), *a.* Relating to penitence. — *n.* A house of correction; prison. (tence.

Pĕn'i-tent-ly, *adv.* With penitence.

Pĕn'knife (pĕn'nīf), *n.* (*pl.* **Pĕn'knīveṣ,** pen'īvz). A knife for pens.

Pĕn'man (143), *n.* One who writes a good hand; an author.

Pĕn'man-ship, *n.* Manner of writing; use of the pen.

Pĕn'nant, } *n.* A small flag or
Pĕn'non, } streamer.

Pĕn'nate, *a.* Winged.

Pĕn'ni-less (135), *a.* Having no money.

Pĕn'ny, *n.* (*pl.* **Pĕn'nies,** **Pĕnçe.** 145. 147.) Twelfth of a shilling, equal to four farthings, or about two cents.

Pĕn'ny-a-līn'er. *n.* One who writes for a public journal at so much a line; hence, a worthless scribbler.

Pĕn'ny-pŏst, *n.* One who carries letters for a small sum.

Pĕn'ny-roy'al, *n.* An aromatic herb.

Pĕn'ny-weight (-wāt), *n.* A troy weight of 24 grains.

Pĕn'ny-wīṣe. *a.* Saving small sums at the risk of losing larger ones.

Pĕn'ny-worth (-wŭrth), *n.* As much as is bought for a penny; a bit.

Pĕn'sĭle, *a.* Hanging.

Pĕn'sion, *n.* [Lat. *pensis.* payment.] A settled yearly allowance by government. — *v. t.* To grant a pension or annual allowance to.

Pĕn'sion-a-ry, *a.* Receiving, or consisting of, a pension.

Pĕn'sion-er, *n.* One who receives a pension; a student who pays for his commons himself.

Pĕn'sĭve, *a.* Thoughtful; sad.

Pĕn'sĭve-ly, *adv.* In a pensive manner. (thoughtfulness.

Pĕn'sĭve-ness, *n.* Melancholy;

Pĕnt'-stŏck, *n.* A place to confine water.

Pĕnt, *imp.* & *p. p.* of *Pen.* Closely confined.

Pĕn'ta-gon, *n.* A figure of five angles and five sides.

Pen-tăg'o-nal. *a.* Having five angles.

Pentagon.

Pĕn'ta-grăph, *n.* An instrument for copying figures in various sizes. [equal sides.

Pĕn'ta-hē'dral, *a.* Having five

Pĕn'ta-hē'dron, *n.* A figure having five equal sides.

Pen-tăm'e-ter, *n.* A poetic verse of five feet.

Pen-tăng'u-lar, *a.* Having five angles.

Pĕn'ta-teŭch, *n.* First five books of the Old Testament.

Pĕn'te-cŏst, *n.* A Jewish festival fifty days after the Passover. [to Pentecost.

Pĕn'te-cŏs'tal, *a.* Pertaining

Pĕnt'-house, *n.* A shed sloping from the main building.

Pē'nŭlt, or **Pe-nŭlt',** *n.* Last syllable but one.

Pe-nŭl'ti-má, } *n.* The last
Pe-nŭl'ti-mate, } syllable but one of a word; penult.

Pe-nŭl'ti-mate, *a.* Of the last syllable but one.

Pe-nŭm'brá, *n.* A partial shade in an eclipse.

Pe-nū'ri-oŭs, *a.* Very parsimonious; niggardly.

Pe-nū'ri-oŭs-ly, *adv.* With parsimony.

Pe-nū'ri-oŭs-ness, *n.* State of being penurious. [gence.

Pĕn'u-ry, *n.* Poverty; indi-

Pē'on, *n.* A debtor held as a slave till he works out his debt.

Pē'on-age, *n.* The servitude of a peon. [flower.

Pē'o-ny, *n.* A plant and its

Pēo'ple (pē'pl), *n.* A nation; persons generally; folks. — *v. t.* To stock with inhabitants; to populate.

Pĕp'per, *n.* A plant and its hot, pungent reed. — *v. t.* To sprinkle with pepper; to pelt.

Pĕp'per-cŏrn, *n.* The berry of the pepper plant.

Pĕp'per-mint, *n.* An aromatic and pungent plant.

Pĕp'per-y, *a.* Hot; pungent; fiery; irritable.

Pĕp'tic, *a.* Relating to, or promoting, digestion.

Pĕr'ad-vĕnt'ūre, *adv.* By chance; perhaps.

Per-ăm'bu-lāte, *v. t.* To walk round or over.

Per-ăm'bu-lā'tion, *n.* A passing or walking over.

Per-ăm'bu-lā'tor, *n.* One who perambulates; an instrument for measuring distances.

Per-çeiv'a-ble (133). *a.* Capable of being perceived.

Per-çeive', *v. t.* To feel; to observe; to discern.

Per-çent'age, *n.* Allowance or duty on a hundred.

Per-çep'ti-bĭl'i-ty, *n.* Quality of being perceptible.

Per-çep'ti-ble, *a.* Capable of being perceived.

Per-çep'ti-bly, *adv.* So as to be perceived.

Per-çep'tion, *n.* Act or power of perceiving. — SYN. Idea; conception; sentiment; sensation; observation.

Per-çep'tĭve, *a.* Able to perceive.

Pẽrch, *n.* A kind of fish; a pole; a roost; a rod. — *v. i.* To light; to roost.

Per-chànçe', *adv.* Perhaps.

ā, ē, ī, ō, ū, ў, *long*; ă, ĕ, ĭ, ŏ, ŭ, ў, *short*; cāre, cär, åsk, ąll, whąt, ẽre, veil, tẽrm; pīque, firm;

PERCIPIENT 223 PERPENDICULAR

Per-çĭp′ĭ-ent, *a.* Having the faculty of perception.
Pẽr′co-lāte, *v. i.* or *t.* To strain through; to filter.
Pẽr′co-lā′tion, *n.* A passing through small interstices; filtration.
Per-cŭs′sion (-kŭsh′un), *n.* Act or effect of striking; vibratory shock; a stroke.
Per-cŭ′tient (-shent),*a.* Striking, or having power to strike
Per-dĭ′tion (-dĭsh′un), *n.* Ruin; loss of the soul.
Per-dū′, *adv.* Lost; in a state of concealment.
Pẽr′e-gri-nā′tion, *n.* A traveling; a wandering
Pẽr′emp to-ri-ly, *adv.* Positively; absolutely.
Pẽr′emp-to-ri-ness, *n.* Positiveness. [absolute.
Pẽr′emp-to-ry, *a.* Positive;
Per-ĕn′ni-al. *a.* Durable; lasting perpetually.
Pẽr′fect, *a.* [Lat. *perfectus*, performed, finished.] Complete; finished; consummate.
Pẽr′fect, or Per-fĕct′ (112), *v. t.* To finish; to complete.
Pẽr′fect-er, or Per-fĕct′er, *n.* One who perfects.
Per-fĕc′ti-bĭl′ĭ-ty, *n.* Quality of being perfectible.
Per-fĕc′ti-ble, *a.* Capable of becoming, or of being made, perfect.
Per-fĕc′tion, *n.* State of being perfect; completeness.
Per-fĕct′ĭve, *a.* Conducive to perfection.
Pẽr′fect-ly, *adv.* Completely.
Per-fĭd′ĭ oŭs, *a.* False to trust: faithless; treacherous.
Per-fĭd′i-oŭs-ly, *adv.* In a perfidious manner.
Per-fĭd′ĭ-oŭs-ness, *n.* Quality of being perfidious.
Pẽr′fi-dy, *n.* Violation of faith. — SYN. Treachery; disloyalty; faithlessness.
Pẽr′fo-rāte, *v. t.* To bore or pierce through.
Pẽr′fo-rā′tor, *n.* Act of boring through; a hole bored.
Pẽr′fo-rā′tor, *n.* An instrument that perforates.
Per-fôrçe′, *adv.* Violently; of necessity.
Per-fôrm′, *v. t.* To do; to execute thoroughly.
Per-fôrm′ançe, *n.* That which is done; composition; work.
Per-fôrm′er, *n.* One who performs, esp. on a musical instrument.
Pẽr′fūme, or Per-fūme′ (112), *n.* A sweet scent; fragrance.

Per-fūme′, *v. t.* To scent.
Per-fūm′er-y, *n.* Perfumes in general.
Per-fūne′to-ry, *a.* Done to get rid of the duty; indifferent; negligent.
Per-hăps′, *adv.* By chance.
Pē′rĭ (140), *n.* A kind of fairy.
†**Pĕr′i-cär′di-um,** *n.* The membrane inclosing the heart.
Pĕr′i-cärp, *n.* The ripened ovary of a plant.

a, b, drupe of peach; *c,* nut; *d,* filbert; *d,* strobile of pine; *e, f,* capsule of poppy; *g,* capsule of Aristolochia. Pericarps.

†**Pĕr′i-crā′ni-um,** *n.* The membrane that immediately invests the skull.
Pĕr′ĭ-gee, *n.* That point in the orbit of the moon which is nearest to the earth.
†**Pĕr′i-hēl′ion** (or-hē′lĭ-un), *n.* The point in a planet's orbit nearest the sun.
Pĕr′ĭl (130), *n.* Danger; risk; hazard. — *v. t.* (130). To hazard.
Pĕr′ĭl-oŭs, *a.* Full of danger.
Pe-rĭm′e-ter, *n.* The outer boundary of a figure.
Pē′ri-od (107), *n.* A circuit; time of a revolution; series of years; epoch; era; age; end; a complete sentence; the point [.], used in writing and printing.
Pē′ri-ŏd′ĭc-al, *a.* Regularly returning. — *n.* A publication issued periodically.
Pē′ri-ŏd′ĭc-al-ly, *adv.* At stated periods.
Pĕr′i-pa-tĕt′ic, *a.* Relating to the philosophy of Aristotle, who gave his instructions while walking.
Pe-rĭph′er-y, *n.* Circumference of a circle.
Pĕr′i-phrāse, *n.* A round-
†**Pe-rĭph′ra-sĭs,** about mode of expression; a circuit of words; circumlocution.

Pĕr′i-phrăs′tic, *n.* Expressing or expressed in many words; circumlocutory.
Pĕr′ip-neū′mo-ny, *n.* Inflammation of the lungs.
Pẽr′ish, *v. i.* To decay; to die; to go to ruin.
Pẽr′ish-a-ble, *a.* Liable to perish; subject to decay.
Pĕr′i-stăl′tie, *a.* Contracting with a worm-like motion.
Pĕr′i-stȳle, *n.* A range of columns round an edifice.
Pĕr′i-wĭg (130), *n.* A small wig. [shell-fish.
Pĕr′i-wĭnk′le, *n.* A small
Pẽr′jure, *v. t.* To make a false oath to.
Pẽr′ju-rer, *n.* One who wilfully takes a false oath.
Pẽr′ju-ry, *n.* The act of wilfully taking a false oath.
Pẽrk, *a.* Lively; pert.
Pẽr′ma-nençe, *n.* Continuance;
Pẽr′ma-nen-cy, duration; fixedness.
Pẽr′ma-nent, *a.* Durable; lasting; without change.
Pẽr′ma-nent-ly, *adv.* With long continuance; durably.
Pẽr′me-a-bĭl′ĭ-ty, *n.* Quality of being permeable.
Pẽr′me-a-ble, *a.* Capable of being passed through.
Pẽr′me-āte, *v. t.* [Lat. *permeare*, *-atum*, from *per*, through, and *meare*, to go.] To pass through the interstices or pores of.
Pẽr′me-ā′tion, *n.* The act of passing through pores.
Per-mĭs′si-ble, *a.* Proper to be permitted; allowable.
Per-mĭs′sion (-mĭsh′un), *n.* Act of permitting; formal consent; leave; liberty.
Per-mĭs′sĭve, *a.* Granting.
Per-mĭt′, *v. t.* To give permission, or leave; to license.
Pẽr′mit, or Per-mĭt′ (112),*n.* A warrant in writing.
Pẽr′mu-tā′tion, *n.* Arrangement of a given number of things in all possible ways.
Per-nĭ′cioŭs (-nĭsh′us), *a.* Injuring or tending to injure. — SYN. Hurtful; noxious; destructive.
Per-nĭ′cioŭs-ly (-nĭsh′us-), *adv.* In a pernicious manner; injuriously.
Pẽr′o-rā′tion, *n.* The closing part of an oration.
Pẽr′pen-dĭc′u-lar, *a.* Upright; meeting at right angles. — *r.* A *ad,* Perpendicular.

sŭn, ôr, do̱, wo̱lf, to̱o̱, to̱o̱k; ûrn, ru̱e, pu̱ll; ç, g̱, *soft*; ȩ, g̱, *hard*; a̱ș; e̱x̱ist, ṋ *as* ng; this.

line or plane at right angles to another.
Pĕr'pen-dĭc'u-lăr'i-ty, n. State of being perpendicular.
Pĕr'pen-dĭc'u-lar-ly, adv. At right angles.
Pĕr'pe-trāte, v. t. To do or commit; to perform.
Pĕr'pe-trā'tion, n. Commission of something wrong.
Pĕr'pe-trā'tor, n. One who perpetrates.
Per-pĕt'u-al, a. Never ceasing; everlasting.
Per-pĕt'u-al-ly, adv. Unceasingly. [perpetual.
Per-pĕt'u-āte, v. t. To make
Per-pĕt'u-ā'tion, n. A rendering perpetual. [ration.
Pĕr'pe-tū'ī-ty, n. Endless duration.
Per-plĕx', v. t. To embarrass; to puzzle. [ing.
Per-plĕx'ing, a. Embarrassing.
Per-plĕx'i-ty, n. State of intricacy; embarrassment.
Pĕr'qui-sīte, n. An extra allowance in money or other things. [made from pears.
Pĕr'ry, n. A kind of cider
Pĕr'se-cūte, v. t. To pursue with malignity; to harass.
Pĕr'se-cū'tion, n. Act of persecuting, or state of being persecuted. [persecutes.
Pĕr'se-cū'tor, n. One who
Pĕr'se-vēr'ançe, n. A persisting in what is undertaken.
Pĕr'se-vēre', v. i. To persist.
Pĕr'se-vēr'ing-ly, adv. With perseverance.
†Persiflage (pĕr'se-flăzh'), n. Frivolous or bantering talk.
Per-sĭm'mon, n. A tree and its fruit, found from New York southward.
Per-sĭst', v. i. To persevere steadily and firmly.
Per-sĭst'ençe, n. Perseverance against opposition; steady pursuit.
Pĕr'son (pĕr'sn), n. A living human being; one; outward appearance.
Pĕr'son-a-ble, a. Having a well-formed body.
Pĕr'son-age, n. A person of distinction.
Pĕr'son-al, a. Belonging to a person; peculiar; movable.
Per'son-ăl'i-ty, n. Direct application to a person.
Pĕr'son-al-ly, adv. In person.
Pĕr'son-al-ty, n. Personal property or estate.
Pĕr'son-āte, v. t. To represent. [representing.
Pĕr'son-ā'tion, n. Act of

Per-sŏn'ĭ-fĭ-cā'tion (107), n. A representation of inanimate things as living beings.
Per-sŏn'ĭ-fȳ, v. t. To regard or treat as a person.
Per-spĕc'tive, a. Relating to vision. — n. Art of representing objects correctly on a plain surface.
Pĕr'spi-cā'cioŭs, a. Quick-sighted; discerning; keen.
Pĕr'spi-eăç'i-ty, n. Acuteness of sight or discernment.
Pĕr'spi-cū'i-ty, n. Clearness.
Per-spĭc'u-oŭs, a. Clear; especially in statement; plain.
Per-spīr'a-ble, a. Capable of being perspired.
Pĕr'spi-rā'tion, n. Excretion through the pores; sweat.
Per-spīre', v. To emit fluid matter through the pores; to sweat.
Per-suād'a-ble, a. Capable of being persuaded.
Per-suāde', v. t. To influence by argument or entreaty.
Per-suā'si-bĭl'i-ty, n. Capability of being persuaded.
Per-suā'si-ble (-swā'-), a. Capable of being persuaded.
Per-suā'sion, n. Act of persuading; creed; belief; opinion; reason.
Per-suā'sive, } a. Tending
Per-suā'so-ry, } to persuade.
Per-suā'sive-ly, adv. In a persuasive manner.
Per-suā'sive-ness, n. Quality of being persuasive.
Pĕrt, a. Smart; brisk; saucy.
Per-tāin' (130), v. i. To belong; to relate to.
Pĕr'ti-nā'cioŭs, a. Holding firmly to any opinion or purpose. — SYN. Firm; constant; stubborn; obstinate.
Pĕr'ti-nā'cioŭs-ly, adv. In a pertinacious manner.
Pĕr'ti-nāç'i-ty, n. Obstinacy in adherence.
Pĕr'ti-nence, } n. Fitness;
Pĕr'ti-nen-çy, } suitableness.
Pĕr'ti-nent, a. Appropriate to the case. — SYN. Relevant; apposite; appropriate; apt.
Pĕr'ti-nent-ly, adv. To the purpose; fitly.
Pĕrt'ly, adv. Smartly; saucily; impertinently.
Pĕrt'ness, n. Quality of being pert; sauciness.
Per-tŭrb', v. t. To disturb the mind of; to agitate.
Pĕr'tur-bā'tion, n. Disturbance of the mind or passions; disquiet. [of hair.
Per'uke, n. An artificial cap

Pe-rṳ'sal, n. Act of perusing.
Pe-rūse', v. t. To read with attention.
Per-vāde', v. t. [Lat. pervadere, fr. per, through, and vadere, to go.] To pass through. [vading.
Per-vā'sion, n. Act of per-
Per-vā'sive, a. Tending, or having power, to pervade.
Per-vērse', a. Obstinate in the wrong; froward.
Per-vērse'ly, adv. In a perverse manner.
Per-vērse'ness (132), n. Quality of being perverse.
Per-vēr'sion, n. A diverting from the proper use.
Per-vēr'si-ty (133), n. State of being perverse.
Per-vēr'sive, a. Tending to pervert or corrupt.
Per-vērt', v. t. To turn from truth or from the right; to corrupt. [penetrated.
Pĕr'vi-oŭs, a. Capable of being
Pĕr'vi-oŭs-ness, n. Quality of being pervious.
Pĕst, n. Plague; pestilence.
Pĕs'ter, v. t. To harass with little vexations; to annoy.
Pĕst'-house, n. A hospital for infectious diseases.
Pes-tĭf'er-oŭs, a. Pestilential; troublesome.
Pĕs'ti-lençe, n. Contagious distemper; plague.
Pĕs'ti-lent, a. Noxious to health, morals, society, &c.
Pĕs'ti-lĕn'tial, a. Containing, or tending to, the plague.
Pĕs'tle (pĕs'l), n. An instrument for pounding and breaking things in a mortar.
Pĕt, n. Fit of peevishness; any creature fondled or indulged. — v. t. (129) [p. p. PETTED.] To treat as a pet; to fondle. [leaf.
Pĕt'al, or Pē'tal, n. A flower-
Pĕt'al-oŭs, a. Having petals.
Pe-tărd', n. A piece of ordnance for blowing up works.
Pĕt'i-ōle, n. Foot-stalk of a leaf. [tle; mean.
Pĕt'it (pĕt'ȳ), a. Small; lit-
Pe-tĭ'tion (-tĭsh'un), n. Request; prayer. — v. t. To supplicate; to solicit.
Pe-tĭ'tion-a-ry (-tĭsh'un-), a. Coming with, or containing, a petition.
Pe-tĭ'tion-er (-tĭsh'un-), n. One who offers a petition.
†Petit-maître (pĕ̇-mā'tr or pĕt'te-mā'tr), n. A dangler about ladies; fop; coxcomb.
Pĕt'rel, n. [A dim. of Peter;

prob. In allusion to Peter's walking on the sea.] A longwinged, web-footed sea-fowl.
Pe-tres'cence, n. A changing into stone. [stone.
Pe-tres'cent, a. Becoming
Pet'ri-fac'tion, n. Conversion into stone.
Pet'ri-fact'ive, a. Having power to change into stony matter; petrific.
Pe-trif'ic, a. Having power to turn to stone.
Pet'ri-fy, v. t. To convert into stone or a stony substance.
— v. i. To become stone.
Pe-tro'le-um, n. An inflammable, bituminous liquid exuding from the earth.
Pet'ti-coat, n. A woman's under garment. [lawyer.
Pet'ti-fog'ger, n. A petty
Pet'ti-fog'ger-y, n. Mean business of a lawyer.
Pet'tish, a. Fretful; peevish
Pet'tish-ly, adv. Peevishly.
Pet'tish-ness, n. Fretfulness.
Pet'ti-toes, n. pl. The toes or feet of a pig.
Pet'ty, a. Small; trifling.
Pet'u-lance, n. Peevishness; fretfulness. [ful; irritable.
Pet'u-lant, a. Peevish; fret-
Pet'u-lant-ly, adv. In a petulant manner.
Pew (pū), n. An inclosed seat in a church. [wing.
Pe'wit, n. A bird; the lap-
Pew'ter, n. A compound of tin and lead.
Pha'c-ton, n. An open four-wheeled carriage.
Phal'anx, n. A compact body of soldiers; any firm combination of men.
Phal'an-ster'y, n. The residence or the common stock of a community of Fourierites; the community itself.
Phan'tasm, n. Mental image of a real or of an imaginary object; an optical illusion.
Phan-tas'ma-go'ri-a, n. Illusive images.
Phan'tom, n. An apparition.
Phar'i-sa'ic, } a. Like the
Phar'i-sa'ic-al, } Pharisees; formal. [in religion.
Phar'i-sa-ism, n. Hypocrisy
Phar'i-see, n. One of a Jewish sect strict in the externals of religion.
Phar'ma-ceu'tic, a. Pertaining to pharmacy.
Phar'ma-ceu'tics, n. sing. Science of preparing medicines.
Phar'ma-co-poe'ia, n. A book describing the preparations of medicines. [of medicines.
Phar'ma-cy, n. Preparation
Pha'ros, n. A light-house.
Phar'ynx (79), n. Cavity above the windpipe, and into which the nose and mouth open.
Phase (130), n. Appearance.
†**Pha'sis.** n. (pl. **Pha'ses.**) An appearance; a phase.
Pheas'ant, n. A gallinaceous bird found wild in Europe.
Phe'nix, n. A fabulous bird, thought to exist single, and to rise again from its own ashes.
Phe-nom'e-nal, a. Relating to a phenomenon, or to phenomena.
Phe-nom'e-non, n. (pl. †**Phenom'e-na.**) An appearance; any thing remarkable.
Phi'al, n. A glass vessel. — v. t. To put or keep in a phial.
Phil'an-throp'ic, } a. Hav-
Phil'an-throp'ic-al, } ing good will to mankind.
Phi-lan'thro-pist, n. A person of general benevolence.
Phi-lan'thro-py, n. The love of mankind at large.
Phil'har-mon'ic, a. Loving harmony or music.
Phi-lip'pic, n. Any invective discourse or declamation.
Phil'o-log'ic-al, a. Pertaining to philology.
Phi-lol'o-ger, } n. One versed
Phi-lol'o-gist, } in philology.
Phi-lol'o-gy, n. The study of language, especially in a philosophical manner.
Phil'o-mel, n. The nightingale.
Phil'o-pe'na, n. A forfeit of one friend to another, arising out of their partaking together of a double-kerneled almond.
Phil'o-pro-gen'i-tive-ness, n. The love of offspring.
Phi-los'o-pher, n. One skilled in philosophy.
Phil'o-soph'ic, } a. Per-
Phil'o-soph'ic-al, } taining or according to philosophy; rational; cool.
Phil'o-soph'ic-al-ly, adv. According to philosophy; calmly; wisely; rationally.
Phi-los'o-phize, v. t. To reason like a philosopher.
Phi-los'o-phy, n. Knowledge of phenomena, as explained by, and resolved into, causes and reasons, powers and laws.
Phil'ter, n. A potion to excite love.
Phiz, n. The face; visage.
Phle-bot'o-mist, n. One who lets blood with a lancet.
Phle-bot'o-my, n. Act or art of opening a vein.
Phlegm (flem), n. Cold animal fluid; mucus; sluggishness; coldness; dullness.
Phleg-mat'ic, a. Abounding with phlegm; cold; dull.
Phlox, n. A flowering plant.
Phoe'nix, n. See *Phenix*.
Pho-net'ic, a. Relating to the representation of sounds by characters.
Pho-net'ics, n. sing. Science of the sounds of the human voice; phonology.
Phon'ic, a. Same as *Phonetic*.
Phon'ics, n. sing. Same as *Phonetics*.
Phon'o-graph'ic, a. Pertaining to, or based upon, phonography.
Pho-nog'ra-phy, n. A representation of sounds, each by its distinctive character.
Pho-nol'o-gy, n. The science of vocal elementary sounds.
Phos'pho-resce', v. i. To exhibit a phosphoric light.
Phos'pho-res'cence, n. A faint light without heat.
Phos'pho-res'cent, a. Shining without heat.
Phos-phor'ic, a. Obtained from phosphorus.
Phos'phor-ous, a. Pertaining to, or obtained from, phosphorus.
Phos'pho-rus, n. [Gr. *phosphoros*, lit. light-bringer.] A combustible substance exhibiting a faint light in the dark.
Pho'to-graph, n. A picture obtained by the action of light on chemically prepared surfaces.
Pho-tog'ra-phy (117), n. Art of producing pictures on chemically prepared paper by the agency of light.
Pho-tom'e-ter, n. An instrument to measure the relative intensities of light.
Phrase, n. A sentence; mode of speech; style; diction.
— v. t. To name or style.
Phra'se-ol'o-gy, n. Manner of expression.
Phre-net'ic, a. Mad; frantic.
Phren'o-log'ic-al, a. Relating to phrenology.
Phre-nol'o-gist, n. One versed in phrenology.
Phre-nol'o-gy, n. Science of the special functions of the parts of the brain.

Phrĕn'ŝy, n. Madness.
Phthis'ic (tiz/ik, 97), n. Habitual difficulty of breathing.
Phthis'ic-al (tiz/-), a. Breathing hard.
Phthi'sis (thi'sis), n. Consumption of the lungs.
Phy-lăc'ter-y, n. A parchment with a passage of Scripture written on it.
Phyŝ'ic (127), n. The art of healing; medicine. — v. t. To evacuate the bowels of.
Phyŝ'ic-al, a. Pertaining to nature; external; corporeal.
Phyŝ'ic-al-ly, adv. According to nature.
Phy-ŝi'cian (-zĭsh'an), n. One who practices physic; a doctor of medicine.
Phyŝ'ics, n. sing. Science of nature or natural objects.
Phyŝ'i-og-nŏm'ic, a. Relating to physiognomy.
Phyŝ'i-ŏg'no-mist, n. One skilled in physiognomy.
Phyŝ'i-ŏg'no-my, n. The art of discerning the character of the mind from the face.
Phyŝ'i-o-lŏg'ic, } a. Pertaining
Phyŝ'i-o-lŏg'ie-al, } to physiology.
Phyŝ'i-ŏl'o-gist (117), n. One who is versed in physiology.
Phyŝ'i-ŏl'o-gy, n. The science of living beings.
Phy-tŏl'o-gy, n. Doctrine of plants; botany.
Pi, n. Type confusedly mixed.
Pi'ăc'u-lar, a. Expiatory.
Pi-ă'nĭst, n. A performer on the piano-forte.
Pi-ă'no-fŏr'te, n. A musical keyed instrument. [walk.
Pi-ăz'za (140), n. A covered
Pi'că, n. A printing type of which there are two sizes, called respectively } **pica** and **small pica**.
Pick, v. t. To choose; to gather; to open. — n. A sharp-pointed tool.
Pick'ăx, } n. An ax that
Pick'axe, } has a point.
Pick'ed (57), a. Pointed; sharp at the end.
Pick'et, n. A sharpened stake; a guard in front of an army. — v. t. To fortify with pickets; to fasten to a picket.
Pick'le (pĭk/l), n. Brine; any thing pickled. — v. t. To preserve in brine.
Pick'pŏck-et, n. One who steals from another's pocket.
Pic'nic, n. A pleasure party

in which each one furnishes refreshment.
Pic-tō'ri-al, a. Pertaining to, or illustrated by, pictures.
Pĭct'ūre, n. A likeness in colors; any kind of drawing. — v. t. To draw or paint a resemblance of; to represent.
Pict'ŭr-ēsque', a. Fitted to form a pleasing picture.
Pĭd'dle, v. i. To deal in trifles; to feed squeamishly.
Pīe, n. Paste baked with something in it, or under it; the magpie.
Pīe'bald, a. Of various colors.
Pĭēçe, n. A part; a patch; a fragment. — v. t. To mend by the addition of a piece; to patch.
Pĭēçe'mēal, a. Single. — adv. In or by pieces or parts; in fragments.
Pīed (pĭd), a. Party-colored.
Pĭer, n. [Fr. pierre, stone.] Support of an arch; a mound; a mole.
Pĭērçe, v. t. To penetrate.
Pĭērç'ing, a. Keen; sharp.
Pĭer'-glăss, n. A glass hanging between windows.
Pĭer'-tā/ble, n. A table standing between windows.
Pī'e-tĭṣm, n. Strict devotion.
Pī'e-ty, n. Veneration with love of God; filial duty.
Pĭg, n. A young swine; mass of metal, as extracted from the ore. — v. i. To bring forth pigs; to lie together like pigs.
Pĭġ'eon (pĭj/un), n. A gallinaceous bird of several species; a dove.
Pĭġ'eon-hōle (pĭj-un-), n. A little division in a case for papers.
Pĭġ'gin, n. A kind of pail.
Pĭġ'ment, n. A colored substance for painting; paint.
Pĭġ'my, n. See Pygmy.
Pīke, n. A lance; a spear; a kind of fresh-water fish.
Pīked, a. Ending in a point.
Pi-lăs'ter, n. A square column.
Pĭl'chard, n. A fish resembling the herring.
Pīle, n. A heap; an edifice; a piece of timber driven into the ground; fiber of Pilaster. wool. — v. t. To heap; to accumulate.
Pīles, n. pl. A disease.
Pĭl'fer, v. t. To steal in a petty way; to filch.

Pĭl'fer-er, n. One who pilfers; one guilty of petty theft.
Pĭl-gär'lĭc, n. One who has lost his hair by disease; a poor forsaken wretch.
Pĭl'grim, n. A traveler to holy places; a wanderer.
Pĭl'grim-age, n. A journey to a place deemed sacred.
Pĭll (129), n. A medicine in form of a small ball.
Pĭl'lage, n. That which is taken by open force. — SYN. Plunder; rapine; spoil. — v. t. To plunder; to strip.
Pĭl'la-ġer, n. One who pillages. [a prop.
Pĭl'lar, n. A column; a pier;
Pĭl'lion, n. A cushion attached to the hinder part of a saddle for riding on.
Pĭl'lo-ry, n. A frame to confine criminals by the head and hands as a punishment.
Pĭl'lōw, n. A cushion as a support for the head. — v. t. To rest on a pillow.
Pĭl'lōw-cāse, n. A cloth cover for a pillow.
Pī'lot (39), n. One who steers a ship; a guide. — v. t. To steer; to guide; to direct.
Pī'lot-age, n. The pay or office of a pilot.
Pi-mĕn'ta, } n. The aromatic
Pi-mĕn'to, } fruit of a certain tree; allspice. [curer.
Pĭmp, n. A pander; a procurer.
Pĭm'per-nel, n. A plant.
Pĭm'ple, n. A small poluted elevation on the skin.
Pĭm'pled, a. Having pimples on the skin.
Pĭn, n. A pointed instrument for fastening clothes, &c. — v. t. (129) To fasten with a pin.
Pĭn'a-fōre, n. A kind of apron; a tire. [ing pins.
Pĭn'-cāse, n. A case for holding
Pĭn'çers, } n. pl. A tool for
Pĭnch'ers, } drawing nails.
Pĭnch, v. t. To squeeze, as with the ends of the fingers. — n. A squeezing or gripe.
Pĭnch'beck, n. A yellow mixture of copper and zinc.
Pĭn'cush-ion, n. A small cushion for pins.
Pīne, n. An evergreen tree or its wood. — v. i. To languish.
Pīne'-ăp'ple, n. A fruit which resembles the cone of a pine-tree.
Pĭn'-feăth'er, n. A Pine-small or short feath-apple. er.

PINFOLD 227 PLAINTIVE

Pin'fold, *n.* A place in which to confine beasts.
Pin'ion (-yun), *n.* A quill; a wing; tooth of a wheel. — *v. t.* To bind the wings or arms of.
Pink, *n.* A flower; a small eye; a reddish color. — *v. t.* To work with eyelet-holes.
Pin'-mon'ey, *n.* A wife's pocket-money. [a boat.
Pin'nace, *n.* A small vessel;
Pin'na-cle, *n.* A turret; summit; a high point.
Pin'nate, *a.* Shaped like a feather; furnished with fins.
Pint, *n.* Half a quart; four gills.
Pin'tle, *n.* A little pin; a long iron bolt. [pines.
Pin'y, *a.* Abounding with
Pi'o-neer', *n.* One who goes before to clear the way; a first settler. [a peony.
Pi'o-ny, *n.* A perennial plant;
Pi'ous, *a.* Religious; godly.
Pi'ous-ly, *adv.* In a pious manner; with piety.
Pip, *v. i.* To chirp. — *n.* The seed of an apple, orange, &c.; a disease of fowls.
Pipe, *n.* A tube, especially one for smoking; a cask; a musical instrument. — *v.* To play on a pipe; to whistle.
Pip'er, *n.* One who plays on a pipe.
Pip'ing, *a.* Simmering; boiling. — *n.* A kind of cord trimming. [boiler.
Pip'kin, *n.* A small earthen
Pip'pin, *n.* A species of apple. [ness; severity.
Piq'uan-cy (-an-), *n.* Sharp-
Piq'uant (pik'ant), *a.* Pricking; pungent; severe; tart.
Pique (peek), *n.* A feeling of resentment. — SYN. Spite; grudge. — *v. t.* To irritate; to nettle; to stimulate.
Pi-quet' (-kĕt'), *n.* A game at cards.
Pi'ra-cy, *n.* Robbery on the seas; literary theft.
Pi'rate, *n.* [Gr. *peiratēs*, from *peirao*, to attempt.] One who robs on the seas; a vessel employed in piracy. — *v. t.* To publish without permission, as books or writings.
Pi-rât'ic-al, *a.* Practicing robbery on the sea.
Pi-rôgue', } *n.* A canoe
Pi-ra'gua, } formed from the trunk of a tree; a kind of narrow ferry-boat.
Pis'ca-ry, *n.* Right of fishing in another man's waters.

Pis'ca-tō'ri-al, } *a.* Relating
Pis'ca-to-ry, } to fishing or fishes. [tempt.
Pish, *interj.* expressive of contempt.
Pis'mire, *n.* The ant.
Pis-tā'chiō, *n.* Nut of a kind of turpentine-tree. [coin.
Pis'ta-reen', *n.* A small silver
Pis'til, *n.* An organ in a flower, inclosing the seed.
Pis'tol, *n.* The smallest of fire-arms. — *v. t.* (39, 130) To shoot with a pistol.
Pis-tôle', *n.* A gold coin of Spain, worth about $3.60.
Pis'ton, *n.* A short solid cylinder fitted to a hollow one within which it moves.
Pit, *n.* A deep hole; the stone of certain fruits; floor part of a theater. — *v. t.* To sink in hollows.
Pit'-a-pāt, *adv.* In a flutter.
Pitch, *n.* A black, sticky substance obtained from tar; point; descent; degree of elevation of the voice, of an instrument, &c. — *v. t.* To smear with pitch; to fix firmly; to toss; to set the tone of. — *v. i.* To rise and fall, as a ship on the waves; to light.
Pitch'er, *n.* A vessel with a spout. [hay, &c.
Pitch'fōrk, *n.* A fork to throw
Pitch'-pipe, *n.* An instrument to give the key-note.
Pitch'y, *a.* Like pitch; smeared with pitch; sticky; black; dismal.
Pit'cōal, *n.* Coal dug from the earth.
Pit'e-oŭs, *a.* Capable of exciting pity; sorrowful.
Pit'e-oŭs-ly, *adv.* In a piteous manner.
Pit'fall, *n.* A pit slightly covered, as a trap.
Pith, *n.* The soft substance in plants; strength or force.
Pith'i-ly, *adv.* With strength or energy.
Pith'i-ness, *n.* State of being pithy. [or strength.
Pith'less, *a.* Wanting pith
Pith'y, *a.* Consisting of pith; energetic; forcible.
Pit'i-a-ble, *a.* Deserving pity.
Pit'i-ful (135), *a.* Compassionate; base; mean; paltry.
Pit'i-ful-ly, *adv.* In a pitiful manner; contemptibly.
Pit'i-less, *a.* Void of pity.
Pit'man (14?), *n.* One who works in a pit.
Pit'saw, *n.* A large saw to be used by two men.

Pit'tance, *n.* A small allowance; a mere trifle.
Pi-tū'i-toŭs, } *a.* Consisting
Pi-tū'i-ta-ry, } of mucus.
Pit'y, *n.* Sympathy for another's distresses. — SYN. Sympathy; compassion. — *v. t.* To have sympathy for.
Piv'ot, *n.* A pin on which any thing turns.
Plā'ca-bĭl'i-ty, *n.* Willingness to forgive. [give.
Plā'ca-ble, *a.* Willing to forgive.
Pla-cärd', *n.* A printed paper posted in a public place. — *v. t.* To notify publicly.
Plā'cāte, *v. t.* To appease or pacify.
Plāçe, *n.* A portion of space; locality; rank; office; room; residence. — *v. t.* To fix; to establish; to locate; to settle.
Plāçe'man (143), *n.* One holding an office under government.
†**Pla-çer'** (pla-thēr'; *by Mexicans and Californians* pla-sēr'), *n.* A gravelly place where gold is found.
Plăç'id, *a.* [Lat. *placidus*, fr. *placere*, to please.] Pleased; contented; calm; quiet; mild.
Pla-çĭd'i-ty, } *n.* Calmness;
Plăç'id-ness, } mildness; unruffled state.
Plăç'id-ly, *adv.* In a placid manner; calmly; mildly.
Plā'gia-rĭṣm, *n.* Literary theft; piracy.
Plā'gia-rĭst, } *n.* One who pur-
Plā'gia-ry, } loins the writings of another.
Plā'gia-rīze, *v. i.* To be guilty of literary theft.
Plāgue, *n.* A contagious disease; vexation. — *v. t.* To trouble; to vex.
Plāgu'i-ly, *adv.* Vexatiously.
Plāgu'y (plāg'y), *a.* Vexatious.
Plāiçe, *n.* A fish allied to the flounder.
Plāid, *n.* A variegated stuff.
Plāin, *a.* Flat; level; frank; clear; evident; homely. — *n.* A level ground.
Plāin'ly, *adv.* In a plain manner; sincerely; bluntly; clearly.
Plāin'ness, *n.* State of being plain; flatness; clearness; want of ornament.
Plāint, *n.* A complaint; cry of distress; lamentation.
Plāint'iff, *n.* One who commences a lawsuit.
Plāint'ive (54), *a.* Mournful.

són, ôr, dọ, wọlf, tọo, tọok; ûrn, rụe, pụll; ç, ġ, *soft*; c, g, *hard*; aẓ; eẋist; ŋ *as* ng; this.

Plait, n. A fold, as of cloth.
— v. t. To fold; to braid.
Plan, n. Any thing devised; a scheme; model. — v. t. (129) To scheme; to contrive in thought; to devise.
Planch, v. t. To plauk.
Planch'et, n. A flat piece of metal or coin.
Plane, n. A level surface; a joiner's tool. — v. t. To smooth with a plane.
Plan'et. n. [Gr. planētēs, lit. a wanderer.] A celestial body revolving about another.
Plan'et-a'ri-um, n. An astronomical machine for exhibiting the motions of the planets.
Plan'et-a-ry, a. Pertaining to, or consisting of, planets.
Plane'-tree, n. An oriental tree; also, a North American tree, often called buttonwood. [smooth.
Plan'ish, v. t. To make
Plan'i-sphēre, n. A sphere projected on a plane, as a map.
Plank, n. A piece of sawed timber thicker than a board. — v. t. To cover with planks.
Pla'no-con'cave, a. Flat on one side, concave on the other.
Pla'no-con'vex, a. Flat on one side, convex on the other.
Plant, n. An organic body without sensation or voluntary motion; any vegetable production; an herb; a tree. — v. t. To set in the earth; to settle.
Plant'ain, n. A West India tree and its fruit; an herb.
Plan-tā'tion, n. A place planted with trees; a colony; a large cultivated estate.
Plant'er, n. The owner of a plantation. [embryo.
Plant'l-cle, n. A plant in
Plan'ti-grāde, n. An animal that walks on the sole of the foot, as the bear.
Plash, n. A puddle of water. — v. t. To dash, as water; to splash; to cut and interweave, as branches.
Plash'y, a. Watery; abounding with puddles.
Plasm, n. A mold for metals.
Plas'ter, n. A composition of lime, sand, and water; an adhesive salve. — v. t. (130) To cover with plaster. [tern.
Plas'ter-er, n. One who plas-
Plas'ter-ing, n. A covering of plaster; plaster-work.
Plas'tic, a. Giving form; capa-

ble of being formed, molded, or modeled. [ing plastic.
Plas-tic'i-ty, n. Quality of be-
Plat, v. t. To interweave. — n. A level piece of ground.
Plāte, n. A flat piece of metal; wrought silver; a shallow vessel; a casting from type. — v. t. To coat with metal.
Plāt'ed, p. a. Overlaid with some other metal, esp. silver.
Pla-teau' (pla-tō', 140), n. A flat, broad, and elevated area of land.
Plāte'fyl (148), n. Enough to fill a plate.
Plāte'-glass, n.. A fine glass for mirrors and windows.
Plāt'en (55), n. The flat part of a printing-press.
Plat'fŏrm, n. Floor of boards or planks; a terrace; a declaration of principles.
Plat'i-nà, or Pla-ti'nà, }
Plat'i-num, or Pla-ti'num, } n. A very heavy metal resembling silver.
Plat'i-tūde, n. Insipidity; a weak or empty remark.
Pla-tŏn'ic, a. Relating to Plato; intellectually refined.
Plā'to-nism, n. The philosophy of Plato. [Plato.
Plā'to-nist, n. A follower of
Pla-toon', n. Half of a company of soldiers. [dish.
Plat'ter, n. A broad shallow
Plau'dit, n. Expression of applause; praise bestowed.
Plau-si-bil'i-ty, n. Speciousness; appearance of right.
Plau'si-ble, a. Superficially pleasing; apparently right. — SYN. Specious. [show.
Plau'si-bly, adv. With fair
Plāy, v. i. To sport; to contend in a game; to act. — v. t. To put in action; to perform. — n. (135) Sport; recreation; game; a drama.
Plāy'-bill, n. Advertisement of a play.
Plāy'er, n. One who plays.
Plāy'fēl-lōw, n. A companion in play. [of, play; sportive.
Plāy'fyl, a. Given to, or full
Plāy'fyl-ly, adv. Sportively.
Plāy'fyl-ness, n. Sportiveness.
Plāy'-house, n. A theater.
Plāy'māte, n. A play-fellow.
Plāy'thing, n. A toy.
Plēa (140), n. What is advanced in support of a cause; an excuse.
Plēad, v. i. To urge; to supplicate earnestly; to argue.
Plēad'er, n. One who pleads.

Plēad'ing, n. Allegation.
Plēas'ant, a. Giving pleasure; pleasing; gratifying; delightful; gay.
Plēas'ant-ly, adv. In a pleasant manner; gayly.
Plēas'ant-ness, n. Agreeableness; gayety.
Plēas'ant-ry, n. Cheerfulness; sprightly talk; liveliness; gayety; merriment.
Plēase, v. t. To give pleasure; to make glad. — v. i. To choose; to like.
Plēas'ing, a. Giving pleasure.
Plēas'ur-a-ble, a. Giving pleasure; pleasing.
Plēas'ure (plĕzh'ur), n. Gratification; delight. — v. t. To afford gratification to.
Ple-bē'ian (-bē'yan), a. [Lat. plebeius, fr. plebs, the common people.] Vulgar; common. — n. One of the common people.
Plĕdġe, n. A pawn; a deposit given as a security. — v. t. To give as security; to pawn; to drink to the health of. [flint.
Plĕdġ'et. n. A small tent of
†Plē'ia-dēs (-ya-), } n. pl. A
Plē'iads (-yadz), } cluster of seven stars in the constellation Taurus.
Plē'na-ry, a. Full; complete.
Ple-nip'o-tençe, n. Fullness of power. [of full power.
Ple-nip'o-tent, a. Possessed
Plĕn'i-po-tĕn'ti-a-ry (-shi-a-), n. One having full power to transact any business; an envoy. — a. Having full power.
Plĕn'i-tūde, n. Fullness.
Plĕn'te-ous. a. Abundant.
Plĕn'te-ous-ly, adv. In abundance; copiously.
Plĕn'te-ous-ness, n. Abundance; copious supply.
Plĕn'ti-ful, a. Affording ample supply; copious.
Plĕn'ti-ful-ly, adv. In great abundance; copiously.
Plĕn'ti-ful-ness, n. Abundance; copiousness.
Plĕn'ty, n. Adequate supply; abundance. — a. Abundant.
Plē'o-nasm, n. Redundancy of words.
Plē'o-nas'tic, a. Partaking of pleonasm; redundant.
Plĕth'o-rà, n. Fullness or excess of blood; repletion; over fullness of any kind.
Ple-thŏr'ic, or Plĕth'o-rīc (120), a. Having a full habit of body; evincing plethora.
†Pleu'rà, n. Membrane that

PLEURISY 229 POINTED

covers the inside of the thorax, and invests the lungs.
Pleu'ri-sy, *n*. Inflammation of the pleura. [pleurisy.
Pleu-rit'ic, *a*. Diseased with
†**Pleu'ro-pneu-mō'ni-à** (-nū-), *n*. Inflammatory disease of the pleura and lungs.
Plĕx'i-fôrm, *a*. Like network; complicated.
Plī'a-bil'ī-ty, *n*. The quality of yielding; flexibleness.
Plī'a-ble, *a*. Easily yielding to pressure; flexible.
Plī'an-cy, *n*. Easiness to be bent; flexibility. [bent.
Plī'ant, *a*. Flexible; easily
Plī'ers, *n. pl.* An instrument to bend small things.
Plīght (plīt), *v. t.* To pledge, as the hand, faith, or honor. —*n*. Pledge: security; gage; condition; state; case.
Plīnth, *n*. The square member at the base of a column.
Plŏd, *v. i.* To travel steadily and laboriously; to toil; to drudge. [laborious person.
Plŏd'der, *n*. A dull, heavy,
Plŏt, *n*. A stratagem; a conspiracy; a scheme; a plat. —*v. t.* To plan; to project.
Plŏt'ter. *n*. One who plots; a schemer. [quatic bird.
Plŏv'er (plŭv'er), *n*. An a-
Plow,) *n*. An instrument
Plough,) to turn and break the soil.—*v. t.* To trench and turn up, as the ground.
Plow'a-ble,) *a*. Arable; admitting of
Plough'a-ble,) being plowed.
Plow'er,) *n*. One who
Plough'er,) ploughs land; a plowman; a cultivator.
Plow'man) (143), *n*. One
Plough'man) who plows, or holds a plow.
Plow'shâre,) *n*. The iron
Plough'shâre,) of a plow.
Plŭck, *v. t.* To pull with sudden force; to snatch.— *n*. The heart, liver, and lights of an animal; spirit; courage; perseverance.
Plŭg, *n*. Stopper of a hole in a vessel or cask.— *v. t.* To stop with a plug.
Plŭm, *n*. A tree and its fruit; £100,000. [of a bird.
Plū'mage (133), *n*. Feathers
Plŭmb (plŭm), *n*. [Lat. *plumbum*, lead.] A leaden weight on a line.— *a*. Perpendicular.— *v. t.* To adjust by a plumb line.
Plum-bā'go, *n*. A mineral consisting of carbon; black lead.

Plŭmb'er (plŭm'er), *n*. One who works in lead.
Plŭmb'er-y plŭm'-), *n*. Work done by a plumber.
Plŭmb'-line plŭm'-', *n*. A line perpendicular to the horizon; a plummet.
Plŭm'-câke, *n*. Cake containing raisins, &c.
Plūme, *n*. A feather; token of honor; pride. — *v. t.* To adjust the feathers of; to pride; to value.
Plū'mi-pĕd, *n*. A bird that has feathers on its feet.
Plŭm'met, *n*. [Fr. *plumbet*, fr. *plumb*, lead.] A long piece of lead attached to a line, used for sounding the depth of water, &c.
Plŭmp, *a*. Fat; sleek; full; round. —*v. t.* To fatten; to swell; to fall heavily. —*adv*. At once, or with a sudden fall.
Plŭmp'er, *n*. Something to dilate the cheeks; an unqualified lie.
Plŭmp'ly, *adv*. Fully; without reserve.
Plŭmp'ness, *n*. Fatness; fullness of skin; distention.
Plŭm'-pud'ding, *n*. A pudding with raisins or currants in it. [plumes.
Plū'my, *a*. Adorned with
Plŭn'der, *v. t.* To take by pillage or open force. —SYN. To pillage; sack; rifle. — *n*. Spoil taken by open force.
Plŭn'der-er, *n*. A pillager.
Plŭnge, *v. t.* To put suddenly into water; to immerse in a fluid. — *v. i.* To dive. — *n*. Act of plunging.
Plū'ral, *a*. Consisting of, or expressing, more than one.
Plū'ral-ĭst, *n*. A clergyman who holds several benefices.
Plu-răl'ĭ-ty, *n*. A number greater than any other, but less than half the aggregate.
Plū'ral-ly, *adv*. In a sense that implies more than one.
Plŭs, this sign +, noting addition.
Plŭsh, *n*. A shaggy cloth.
Plu-tō'ni-an,) *n*. One who
Plū'to-nist,) holds that the world was formed by the action of fire.
Plu-tŏn'ic, *a*. Relating to the system of the Plutonists; igneous.
Plū'vi-al, *a*. Rainy; wet.
Plū'vi-ăm'e-ter, *n*. A raingauge.
Plȳ, *v. t.* or *i*. [*imp*. & *p. p.* PLIED.] To work at closely.

Pneu-măt'ic (nu-), *a*. Consisting of air; moved by air.
Pneu-măt'ics (uu-), *n. sing.* Science that treats of the mechanical properties of air and other elastic fluids.
Pneū'ma-tŏl'o-gy (nū'-), *n*. The doctrine of, or a treatise on, spiritual existences.
Pneu-mō'ni-à (nu-), *n*. Inflammation of the lungs.
Pneu-mŏn'ic (nu-), *a*. Pertaining to the lungs.
†**Pneū'mo-nī'tis (nū'-)**, *n*. Inflammation of the lungs.
Pōach, *v. t.* To boil slightly; to steal, as game. —*v. i.* To steal or pocket game.
Pōach'er, *n*. One who poaches; a stealer of game.
Pōach'y, *a*. Soft; wet; marshy.
Pŏck (127), *n*. A pustule on the skin in small pox. &c.
Pŏck'et, *n*. A small bag or pouch. —*v. t.* To put in the pocket; to steal.
Pŏck'et-bŏŏk, *n*. A book to be carried in the pocket.
Pŏck'y, *a*. Full of pocks or pustules.
Pŏd, *n*. Capsule; seed-case. —*v. i.* To grow, as pods.
Pō'em, *n*. A composition in verse. [ems.
Pō'e-sy, *n*. Art of writing po-
Pō'et, *n*. One who writes poetry; a bard.
Pō'et-ăs'ter, *n*. A pitiful versifier; a rhymester. [poet.
Pō'et-ess (108), *n*. A female
Po-ĕt'ic,) *a*. Written in
Po-ĕt'ic-al,) verse; pertaining to poetry.
Po-ĕt'ic-al-ly, *adv*. In a poetical manner.
Pō'et Lau're-ate. A poet whose office is to compose poems for the birthdays of a prince, or other special occasion.
Pō'et-ry, *n*. Imaginative, and usually metrical, composition; verse.
Poign'an-cy (poin'-), *n*. Sharpness; point; asperity.
Poign'ant (poin'-), *a*. Sharp; satirical; severe; painful.
Poign'ant-ly (poin'-), *adv*. With keen point; sharply.
Point, *n*. A sharp end; a stop; a cape; object; end; aim. — *v. t.* To sharpen; to aim; to divide by stops. — *v. i.* To direct the finger toward an object; to aim.
Point'-blank. *adv*. Directly.
Point'ed, *a*. Keen; satirical.

sŏn, ôr, dǫ, wǫlf, tōō, tŏŏk; ûrn, rụe, pụll; ç, ġ, *soft*; c, ḡ, *hard*; aṣ; eẋist; ŋ *as* ng; this.

Point'ed-ly, *adv.* With point.
Point'er, *n.* An index; a variety of dog.
Point'less, *a.* Having no point.
Poise, *n.* Weight; balance. — *v. t.* To balance for weighing.
Poi'son (poi'zn), *n.* Any thing infectious or malignant. — SYN. Venom. — *v. t.* To infect with poison. [sons.
Poi'son-er, *n.* One who poisons.
Poi'son-ous, *a.* Having the qualities of poison.
Poke, *n.* A pocket; a sack; a push; a machine to check unruly beasts from leaping fences. — *v. t.* To put a poke on; to thrust against.
Pok'er, *n.* An iron bar for stirring a fire.
Po'lar, *a.* Pertaining to the poles. [the pole.
Po-lär'i-ty, *n.* Tendency to
Po'lar-i-zā'tion, *n.* Act of polarizing; polarity.
Po'lar-ize, *v. t.* To communicate polarity to.
Po'lar-y, *a.* Tending to a pole.
Pōle (18), *n.* Extremity of an axis; the sky; a long, slender piece of wood; a rod or perch. — *v. t.* To furnish with poles; to convey on poles; to push with poles.
Pōle'-ax, } *n.* A hatchet fixed
Pōle'-axe, } on a pole.
Pōle'cat, *n.* An ill-smelling animal allied to the weasel.
Po-lem'ic, *n.* A disputant.
Po-lem'ic, } *a.* Controver-
Po-lem'ic-al, } sial.
Po-lem'ics, *n. sing.* Controversy, especially on religious subjects.
Pōle'-stär, *n.* A star vertical to the pole of the earth.
Po-liçe' (-leess'), *n.* Civil officers of a city organized to preserve good order, and enforce the laws.
Pol'i-çy, *n.* Art or system of government; prudence; contract of insurance.
Pol'ish, *v. t.* To make smooth; to refine in manners. — *n.* Artificial gloss; elegance of manners.
Po-lite', *a.* Polished; refined.
Po-lite'ly (132), *adv.* Genteelly; with courtesy.
Po-lite'ness, *n.* Good breeding; courtesy.
Pol'i-tie (120, *a.* Wise; prudent. [politics; public.
Po-lit'ic-al, *a.* Relating to
Po-lit'ic-al-ly, *adv.* With reference to a state or to politics.

Pol'i-ti'cian (-tish'an), *n.* One versed in politics.
Pol'i-ties, *n. sing.* The science of government.
Pol'i-ty, *n.* Civil constitution; form of government.
Pol'kà (18), *n.* [Bohemian *pulka,* half, from the half-step prevalent in it.] A kind of dance.
Poll, *n.* The head; a register of persons; election. — *v. t.* To lop the tops of, as trees; to clip; to register, as the names of voters.
Pol'lard, *n.* A tree lopped; bran and meal mixed.
Pol'len, *n.* The fecundating dust of plants.
Pol'lock, *n.* A fish of the cod kind; the whiting.
Poll'-tax, *n.* A tax levied by the poll or head.
Pol-lute', *v. t.* To make foul or unclean. — SYN. To defile; coutaminate; dishonor; corrupt.
Pol-lū'tion, *n.* Defilement.
Pol-troon', *n.* An arrant coward; a dastard.
Pol-troon'er-y, *n.* Cowardice.
Pol'y-an'thus, *n.* An ornamental plant.
Pol'y-är'çhy, *n.* A government by many persons.
Po-lyg'a-mist, *n.* One who advocates polygamy.
Po-lyg'a-my, *n.* Plurality of wives at the same time.
Pol'y-glot, *n.* A book containing many languages. — *a.* Pertaining to, or containing, several languages.
Pol'y-gōn, *n.* A figure of many angles and sides.

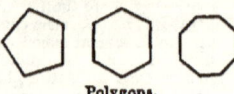

Polygons.

Po-lyg'o-nal, *a.* Having many angles.
Pol'y-graph, *n.* An instrument to multiply copies of a writing with expedition.
Pol'y-graph'ic, } *a.* Per-
Pol'y-graph'ic-al, } taining to polygraphy; done with a polygraph.
Po-lyg'ra-phy, *n.* The art of writing in various ciphers.
Pol'y-hē'dron, *n.* A body having many sides.
Pol'y-nō'mi-al, *a.* Containing many terms.
Pol'yp, *n.* An aquatic animal of the radiate kind.

Pol'y-pous, *a.* Having the nature of the polypus.
Pol'y-pus, *n.* Something that has many feet or roots; a fleshy tumor.
Pol'y-scōpe, *n.* A glass that makes a single object appear as many.
Pol'y-syl-lab'ic, } *a.* Hav-
Pol'y-syl-lab'ic-al, } ing many syllables.
Pol'y-syl'la-ble, *n.* A word of more syllables than three.
Pol'y-tĕch'nic (-tĕk'nik), *a.* Comprehending many arts.
Pol'y-thē'ism, *n.* The doctrine of a plurality of gods.
Pol'y-thē'ist, *n.* One who believes in a plurality of gods.
Pol'y-the-ist'ic, *a.* Pertaining to polytheism.
Pom'açe, *n.* Substance of apples crushed. [ment.
Po-māde', *n.* Perfumed oint-
Po-mā'tum, *n.* An unguent for the hair. [its fruit.
Pōme-grăn'ate, *n.* A tree and
Po-mif'er-ous, *a.* Apple-bearing; fruit-bearing.
Pom'mel (pŭm'-, *n.* A knob or ball; a protuberance on a saddle. — *v. t.* (130) To beat; to thump.
Pom-mēl'ion (-meel'yun), *n.* The knob of a cannon.
Po-mŏl'o-ġist, *n.* One interested in pomology.
Po-mŏl'o-ġy, *n.* Art or science of raising fruit. [rade.
Pŏmp, *n.* Ostentation; pa-
Pŏmp'i-on, *n.* A pumpkin.
Pom-pŏs'i-ty, *n.* Ostentation, exterior show; parade.
Pŏmp'ous, *a.* Showy with grandeur; ostentatious.
Pŏmp'ous-ly, *adv.* With parade or display. [ing water.
Pŏnd, *n.* A body of fresh stand-
Pŏn'der, *v. t.* To think upon deliberately. — SYN. To consider; muse; weigh.
Pŏn'der-a-ble, *a.* Capable of being weighed.
Pŏn'der-ŏs'i-ty, *n.* Weight; gravity; heaviness. [ay.
Pŏn-der'ous, *a.* Heavy; mas-
Pŏn-gee', *n.* An inferior kind of India silk.
Pŏn'iard (-yard), *n.* A small dagger. — *v. t.* To stab.
Pŏn'tiff, *n.* A high-priest; the pope.
Pon-tif'ic } (131), *a.* Be-
Pon-tif'ic-al } longing to a high priest, or to the Pope.
Pon-tif'ic-al, *n.* A book of rites and forms; (*pl.*) the full dress of a pontiff or bishop.

Pon-tif'ic-ate (131), *n.* Office or reign of a pontiff.
Pon-toon'. *n.* A boat used by armies for making bridges.
Pō'ny .141 , *n.* A small horse; a nag.
Pŏŏ'dle, *n.* A lap-dog.
Pool, *n.* A small pond; the stakes played for in card-playing.
Poop, *n.* A deck raised above the after-part of the spar-deck.
Poor (84', *a.* Needy; indigent; necessitous; lean; meagre; mean; unfertile.
Poor'ly, *a.* Somewhat ill. — *adv.* Without wealth; with poor success; meanly; without spirit.
Poor'ness, *n.* Poverty; want.
Pŏp, *n.* A small, smart, quick sound. — *v. i.* or *t.* To dart suddenly; to offer suddenly.
Pōpe, *n.* The head of the Roman Catholic church.
Pōpe'dŏm, *n.* The dignity or jurisdiction of the pope.
Pŏp'er-y, *n.* The Roman Catholic religion.
Pŏp'gŭn, *n.* A child's air-gun for shooting pellets.
Pŏp'in-jāy, *n.* A parrot, or a mark in the shape of one for shooting at; a fop.
Pŏp'lar, *n.* A genus of trees.
Pŏp'lin, *n.* A stuff of silk or worsted of many varieties.
Pŏp'ish, *a.* Relating to the pope; papal.
Pŏp'py (141 , *n.* A soporific plant. [people.
Pŏp'u-laçe, *n.* The common
Pŏp'u-lar, *a.* Pertaining to, or pleasing to, the people; prevailing; familiar. [vor.
Pŏp'u-lăr'i-ty, *n.* Public fa-
Pŏp'u-lar-īze, *v. t.* To make common or popular. [vor.
Pŏp'u-lar-ly, *adv.* With fa-
Pŏp'u-lāte, *v. t.* To furnish with inhabitants; to people.
Pŏp'u-lā'tion, *n.* The whole people, as of a country.
Pŏp'u-loŭs, *a.* Full of people.
Pŏp'u-loŭs-ness, *n.* The state of being populous.
Pŏr'çe-laīn, *n.* A fine translucent species of earthen ware
Pŏrch 140 , *n.* An entrance to a building; a portico. [swine.
Pŏr'çĭne, *a.* Pertaining to
Pŏr'cu-pĭne, *n.* [Lat. *porcus*, swine, and *spina*, thorn.] A quadruped armed with spines or prickles.
Pōre, *n.* An orifice in the skin. — *v. i.* To look steadily.

Pōr'ĭ-ness (135), *n.* State of being full of pores.
Pŏrk, *n.* The flesh of swine.
Pŏrk'er, *n.* A young hog.
Po-rōs'i-ty, *n.* The quality of having pores.
Pō'roŭs, *a.* Having pores.
Pŏr'phy-rit'ĭc, *a.* Pertaining to, or like, porphyry.
Pŏr'phy-ry, *n.* A hard mottled kind of stone.
Pŏr'poise (-pus), *n.* A fish of the whale kind.
Pŏr'ridge, *n.* A mixture of meal or flour and water boiled; vegetables boiled in water, with or without meat.
Pŏr'rin-ġer, *n.* A small metal vessel for warming liquids in.
Pŏrt, *n.* A harbor; a gate; carriage or mien; a wine; the larboard or left side of a vessel. — *v. t.* To carry to the port or larboard side.
Pŏrt'a-bīl'ĭ-ty, *n.* Quality of being portable.
Pŏrt'a-ble, *a.* Capable of being carried.
Pŏrt'age, *n.* Price of carriage; a carrying place.
Pŏrt'al, *n.* An imposing gate or entrance.
Pŏrt-cŭl'lis, *n.* A frame-work of crossed timbers for obstructing a passage.
Pŏrte, *n.* The Ottoman court.
Pŏrte'-mŏn-naĭe' mun-nā'), *n.* [Fr.] A small pocket-book or wallet for carrying money.
Por-tĕnd', *v. t.* To foretoken.
Por-tĕnt', *n.* An omen of ill.
Por-tĕnt'oŭs, *a.* Foreshadowing ill; ominous.
Pŏr'ter, *n.* A door-keeper; a carrier; a kind of strong beer, or malt liquor.
Pŏr'ter-age, *n.* Money paid for carriage by a porter.
Pŏrt-fō'li-o (-fōl'yo *or* -fō'li-o), *n.* (*pl.* **Pŏrt-fō'li-ŏs,** -fōl'yŏz *or* -fō'li-ōz, 140). A portable case for loose papers.
Pŏrt'-hōle, *n.* An opening in a ship's side for cannon.
Pŏrt'ti-co, *n.* (*pl.* **Pŏr'ti-cōs,** 140.) A covered space with columns at the entrance of a building.
Pŏr'tion, *v. t.* To divide; to allot; to endow. — *n.* Part assigned; allotment; share of an estate; a wife's fortune.
Pŏrt'lĭ-ness, *n.* Dignity of mien; largeness of person.
Pŏrt'ly, *a.* Large and full; of noble appearance.
Pŏrt-măn'teau (-măn'to), *n.* [Fr., from *porter*, to carry,

and *manteau*, a cloak.] A bag to carry clothes in.
Pŏr'traĭt, *n.* A picture **Pŏr'traĭt-ūre,** of a person drawn from life.
Pŏr-trāy', *v. t.* To paint the likeness of; to describe.
Pŏr-trāy'al, *n.* The act or art of portraying. [ter.
Pŏr'tress, *n.* A female por-
Pōşe, *v. t.* To puzzle.
Pōş'er, *n.* One who poses; that which puzzles.
Po-şĭ'tion (-zĭsh'un), *n.* Situation; station; posture; principle laid down.
Pŏş'i-tĭve (46, *a.* Certain; real; absolute; confident.
Pŏş'i-tĭve-ly, *adv.* Absolutely; really; confidently.
Pŏş'i-tĭve-ness, *n.* State or quality of being positive.
†**Pōş'se Cŏm'i-tā'tus.** [Lat.] Citizens who may be summoned to assist an officer in suppressing a riot, &c.
Pos-sĕss' (pos-sĕs' *or* poz-zĕs'), *v. t.* To have or hold as one's own; to own.
Pos-sĕs'sion (-sĕsh'un *or* -zĕsh'un), *n.* The state of owning: the thing owned.
Pos-sĕss'ĭve (-sĕs'sĭv *or* -zĕs'-sĭv), *a.* Denoting possession.
Pos-sĕss'or (-sĕs'sor *or* -zĕs'-sor), *n.* One who possesses; one who holds or occupies.
Pos-sĕss'o-ry (pos-sĕs'- *or* poz-zĕs'-), *a.* Relating to a possessor, or to a thing possessed; having possession.
Pŏs'set, *n.* Milk curdled with wine or other liquor.
Pŏs'sĭ-bĭl'i-ty, *n.* The power of being or doing; that which is possible.
Pŏs'sĭ-ble, *a.* Capable of being or of being done.
Pŏs'sĭ-bly, *adv.* By any power really existing.
Pŏst, *n.* A messenger; an express; office; place; a piece of timber; a kind of letter paper. — *v. t.* To station; to put in the mail. — *v. i.* To carry to a ledger.
Pōst'age, *n.* Money paid for conveyance of letters.
Pōst'al, *a.* Belonging to the post-office or mail service.
Pōst'-boy, *n.* A boy that rides as post; a courier.
Pōst'-chāise, *n.* A traveling carriage.
Pōst'-dāte, *v. t.* To date after the true time.
Pōst'-dĭ-lū'vi-an, *a.* Being after the deluge.

sŏn, ôr, dǫ, wǫlf, tǒo, tǒok; ûrn, rye, pyll; ç, ġ, *soft*; ¢, ḡ, *hard*; a̱; eẋiṣt; ŋ *as* ng; this.

Pos-tē'ri-or, *a.* Later in time or order; subsequent.
Pos-tē'ri-orṣ, *n. pl.* The hinder parts of an animal.
Pos-tēr'i-ty, *n.* Descendants.
Pōst'ern, *n.* A small back gate, or private entrance
Pōst'fix, *n.* A letter or syllable added. [end.
Pōst-fix', *n.* To annex at the
Pōst'-hāste, *adv.* As fast as possible; at full speed.
Pōst'hu-moŭs, *a.* Born, published, or continuing, after one's decease. [one's decease.
Pōst'hu-moŭs-ly, *adv.* After
Pōs-til'ion (-yun), *n.* [Written also *postillion.*] One who rides and guides a horse in a coach or post-chaise.
Pōst'man (143), *n.* A letter-carrier.
Pōst'märk, *n.* Stamp of the post-office on a letter, &c.
Pōst'mȧs-ter, *n.* One who superintends a post-office.
Pōst'me-rid'i-an, *a.* Belonging to the afternoon.
Pōst-mōr'tem, *a.* [Lat.] After death.
Pōst'-nōte, *n.* A bank-note payable at some future specified day.
Pōst'-ŏf'fiçe, *n.* A place where mail letters are received and delivered.
Pōst'pāid, *a.* Having the postage paid in advance.
Pōst-pōne', *v. t.* [Lat. *postponere,* from *post,* after, and *ponere,* to place.] To put off; to delay; to defer. [ting off.
Pōst-pōne'ment, *n.* A put-
Pōst'script, *n.* Something added to a writing.
Pōst'-town (106), *n.* A town having a post-office.
Pōst'u-late, *n.* Any thing assumed without proof. — *v. t.* To take for granted.
Pōst'u-lā'tion, *n.* An assumption without proof.
Pōst'ūre, *n.* Attitude; position; situation.
Pō'ṣy (141), *n.* A motto on a ring; a nosegay.
Pŏt, *n.* A large deep vessel for various uses. — *v. t.* To preserve in pots.
Pō'tȧ-ble, *a.* Fit to be drunk.
Pŏt'ash, *n.* An alkaline salt from the ashes of plants.
Po-tā'tion, *n.* A drinking; an excessive draught.
Po-tā'to (140), *n.* A well-known esculent root.
Pō'ten-çy, *n.* Relative power, strength, or efficacy.

Pō'tent, *a.* Having great power or authority. — SYN. Mighty; puissant; forcible; powerful; strong; efficient.
Pō'tent-āte, *n.* A monarch.
Po-těn'tial, *a.* Existing in possibility, not in act.
Po-těn'ti-ăl'I-ty (-těn'shi-), *n.* Possibility. [bility.
Po-těn'tial-ly, *adv.* In possi-
Pō'tent-ly, *adv.* Powerfully.
Pŏt'-hăng'er, *n.* A hook to hang pots on over the fire.
Pŏth'er, *n.* Confusion; bustle.
Pŏt'-hŏŏk, *n.* A hook to hang pots on over a fire; a character resembling such hook.
Pŏt'-house, *n.* An ale-house.
Pō'tion, *n.* A draught; a liquid medicine.
Pŏt'-lŭck, *n.* A chance or picked-up dinner.
Pŏt'sherd, *n.* A piece of a broken pot.
Pŏt'tage, *n.* Meat and vegetables boiled together till soft; a thick soup.
Pŏt'ter, *n.* One who makes earthen vessels.
Pŏt'ter-y, *n.* Wares of a potter, or place where they are made.
Pŏt'tle, *n.* A measure of two quarts; a small basket for holding fruit.
Pŏt'-văl'iant (-yant), *a.* Made courageous by liquor.
Pouch, *n.* A small bag; a pocket; a purse. — *v. t.* To pocket; to save.
Pou-chŏng' (pŏŏ-shŏng'), *n.* A kind of black tea.
Pou-drĕtte', *n.* A kind of manure. [in poultry.
Pōul'ter-er, *n.* One who trades
Pōul'tiçe (140), *n.* A soothing application for sores. — *v. t.* To apply a poultice to.
Pōul'try (18), *n.* Domestic fowls.
Pouncę, *n.* The claw of a bird of prey; a fine kind of powder. — *v. t.* To sprinkle with pounce; to fall and seize.
Pound, *n.* Weight of 16 ounces avoirdupois, or 12 of troy; a pinfold; 20 shillings. — *v. t.* To beat; to pulverize; to confine in a pen.
Pound'age, *n.* A duty rated on the pound.
Pound'er, *n.* One who, or that which, pounds; a thing denominated from a certain number of pounds.
Pour, *v. t.* To throw out in a continuous stream. — *v. i.* To issue; to flow.

Pout, *n.* A sullen look; a fish. — *v. i.* To push out the lips in sullenness.
Pŏv'er-ty, *n.* [Lat *paupertas,* fr. *pauper,* poor.] Want of riches; indigence; penury.
Pow'der, *n.* A fine dust; composition for firing guns, &c. — *v. t.* To sprinkle with powder; to reduce to dust.
Pow'der-y. *a.* Easy crumbling; friable; dusty.
Pow'er, *n.* Faculty of doing; force; ability; strength; influence: a state; a sovereign; legal authority.
Pow'er-fŭl, *a.* Having power; strong. [great force.
Pow'er-ful-ly, *adv.* With
Pow'er-less, *a.* Without power; weak; impotent.
Pow'er-lōom, *n.* A loom worked by some mechanical power.
Pow'-wow, *n.* An Indian conjurer, or conjuration for the cure of diseases; a noisy assembly.
Pŏx, *n.* An eruptive disease.
Prăc'ti-ca-bĭl'i-ty, *n.* Quality or state of being practicable; feasibility.
Prăc'ti-ca-ble, *a.* Capable of being done. — SYN. Possible.
Prăc'ti-ca-bly, *adv.* So that it may be done.
Prăc'ti-cal, *a.* Relating to practice; capable of being turned to use.
Prăc'ti-cal-ly, *adv.* By use.
Prăc'tiçe, *n.* Customary use; habit; performance. — *v. t.* (149) To do frequently or habitually; to use.
Prac-ti'tion-er (-tish'un-), *n.* One engaged in the practice of a profession.
Prag-măt'ic, } *a.* Very forward in acting; officious; meddlesome; impertinent.
Prag-măt'ic-al, }
Prāi'rie, *n.* [Fr., from Lat. *pratum,* a meadow.] An extensive tract of level grass land destitute of trees.
Prāiṣe, *n.* Commendation; object or ground of praise. — *v. t.* To commend; to extol; to applaud.
Prāiṣe'wor-thy (-wŭr-), *a.* Commendable; laudable.
Prançe, *v. i.* To spring; to leap; to bound.
Prănk, *v. t.* To adorn; to decorate. — *n.* A frolic; a trick.
Prāte, *v. i.* To talk much and foolishly. — *n.* Idle talk; unmeaning loquacity.

PRATIQUE 233 PREDOMINANCY

†Prăt′ique (prăt′eek), *n.* A license to trade after performing quarantine.

Prăt′tle, *n.* Childish or idle talk. — *v. i.* To talk much and idly; to chatter.

Prăt′tler, *n.* One who prattles. [ceous fish.

Prawn, *n.* A small crusta-

†Prăx′is, *n.* Examples to teach practice.

Pray, *v. t.* or *i.* To ask with earnestness; to supplicate.

Prāy′er (3), *n.* One who prays.

Prāyer (prâr), *n.* A petition; a supplication.

Prāyer′-book (prâr′-), *n.* A book containing forms of prayers.

Prāyer′ful (prâr′-), *a.* Given to prayer. [prayer.

Prāyer′ful-ly, *adv.* With

Prāyer′less (prâr′-), *a.* Habitually neglecting prayer.

Prēach, *v. i.* or *t.* To discourse publicly on a religious subject. [preaches.

Prēach′er, *n.* One who

Prēach′ing, *n.* Act of one who preaches.

Prē′ad-mŏn′ish, *v. t.* To admonish previously.

Prē′am-ble, *n.* An introductory writing; something previous; a kind of preface.

Prĕb′end, *n.* A stipend in a cathedral church.

Prĕb′end-al, *a.* Belonging to a prebend.

Prĕb′end-a-ry, *n.* The stipendiary of a cathedral.

Pre-cā′ri-oŭs, *a.* Held by a doubtful tenure. — SYN. Uncertain; unsettled; doubtful; dubious.

Pre-cā′ri-oŭs-ly, *adv.* Uncertainly; doubtfully.

Prēc′a-to-ry, *a.* Suppliant; beseeching. [tion or care.

Pre-cau′tion, *n.* Previous cau-

Pre-cau′tion-a-ry, *a.* With a view to prevent mischief.

Pre-cēde′, *v. t.* To go before.

Pre-cēd′ence, } *n.* A going

Pre-cēd′en-cy, } before; priority of time; superior rank or influence.

Pre-cēd′ent, *a.* Going before; anterior; antecedent.

Prĕc′e-dent, *n.* Something previously done or said that serves as an example.

Prĕc′e-dent-ed, *a.* Authorized by example.

Pre-cēd′ent-ly, *adv.* At a former time; beforehand.

Pre-cēd′ing, *p. a.* Going before; precedent.

Pre-çĕn′tor, *n.* Leader of a cathedral choir.

Prē′çept, *n.* A commandment; order; rule; direction; instruction. [cepts.

Pre-çĕpt′ĭve, *a.* Giving pre-

Pre-çĕpt′or, *n.* A teacher.

Pre-çĕp′to-ry, *a.* Giving precepts. — *n.* A subordinate religious house of the Knights Templars. [teacher.

Pre-çĕp′tress, *n.* A female

Pre-çĕs′sion (-sĕsh′un), *n.* A going before; a slow backward motion, as the equinoctial points.

Prē′çinçt, *n.* An outward limit; a territorial district.

Prē′cioŭs (prĕsh′us), *a.* Of great price or value; costly.

Prē′cioŭs-ly (prĕsh′us-), *adv.* In a precious or costly way; in great esteem.

Prĕç′i-pĭçe, *n.* A steep descent of land or rock.

Pre-çĭp′i-tançe, } *n.* Great

Pre-çĭp′i-tan-çy, } or rash haste; headlong hurry.

Pre-çĭp′i-tant, *a.* Rushing hastily or headlong. [ly.

Pre-çĭp′i-tant-ly, *adv.* Hasti-

Pre-çĭp′i-tāte, *v. t.* To throw headlong; to hasten rashly; to cast to the bottom.

Pre-çĭp′i-tāte, *a.* Very hasty; headlong; rash. — *n.* A substance in solution chemically separated from its solvent, and thrown to the bottom of the vessel.

Pre-çĭp′i-tāte-ly, *adv.* In a precipitate manner.

Pre-çĭp′i-tā′tion, *n.* Rash haste; headlong hurry.

Pre-çĭp′i-toŭs, *a.* Very steep; headlong; rash.

Pre-çĭp′i-toŭs-ly, *adv.* Descending rapidly.

Pre-çīse′, *a.* Exact; over-nice; strict; stiff. [ly.

Pre-çīse′ly (132), *adv.* Exact-

Pre-çīse′ness, *n.* Exactness

Pre-çĭş′ian, *n.* One rigidly exact in observing rules.

Pre-çĭş′ion (-sĭzh′un), *n.* Exactness; accuracy.

Pre-clūde′, *v. t.* To prevent from entering; to hinder.

Pre-clū′sion, *n.* Act of preventing or shutting out.

Pre-clū′sĭve, *a.* Preventing.

Pre-cō′cioŭs, *a.* Ripe prematurely; too forward.

Pre-cō′cioŭs-ness, *n.* Premature ripeness or development.

Pre-cŏç′i-ty, *n.* Premature growth and ripeness.

Prē′cog-nī′tion (-nĭsh′un), *n.* Previous knowledge.

Pre′con-çēive′, *v. t.* To conceive beforehand.

Pre′con-çĕp′tion, *n.* Previous conception or opinion.

Prē′con-çĕrt′, *v. t.* To concert or plan beforehand.

Prē′con-çĕrt′ed, *a.* Previously concerted or planned.

Pre-cŏn′tract, *n.* A contract previous to another.

Pre-cûr′sor, *n.* One who, or that which, precedes an event. — SYN. Forerunner; harbinger; omen; sign.

Pre-cûr′sor-y, *a.* Preceding as the harbinger.

Pre-dā′ceoŭs (-shus), *a.* Living by plunder.

Prēd′a-to-ry, *a.* Plundering.

Prĕd′e-çĕs′sor, *n.* One who has gone before; an ancestor.

Pre-dĕs′ti-nā′ri-an, *n.* One who believes in predestination. — *a.* Pertaining to predestination.

Pre-dĕs′ti-nāte, } *v. t.* To

Pre-dĕs′tine, } foreordain.

Pre-dĕs′ti-nā′tion, *n.* The purpose of God from eternity respecting all events.

Pre-de-tĕr′mi-nate, *a.* Determined beforehand.

Pre-de-tĕr′min-ā′tion, *n.* Previous determination.

Pre′de-tĕr′mine, *v. t.* To determine beforehand.

Prē′dĭ-al, *a.* Relating to, or consisting of, land or farms.

Prĕd′i-ca-bĭl′i-ty, *n.* The quality of being predicable.

Prĕd′i-ca-ble, *a.* Capable of being affirmed of or attributed to.

Pre-dĭc′a-ment, *n.* Class; state; particular condition.

Prĕd′i-cate, *n.* That which is affirmed or denied.

Prĕd′i-cāte, *v. t.* To affirm; to assert to belong to something.

Prĕd′i-cā′tion, *n.* An affirmation concerning any thing.

Prĕd′i-ca-to-ry, *a.* Affirmative; positive.

Pre-dict′, *v. t.* To foretell.

Pre-dic′tion, *n.* A prophecy.

Pre-dict′ive, *a.* Foretelling.

Prē′di-lĕc′tion, *n.* A previous liking; partiality.

Prē′dis-pōşe′, *v. t.* To incline or adapt previously.

Prē′dis′po-şi′tion (-zĭsh′un), *n.* Previous propensity.

Pre-dŏm′i-nançe, } *n.* As-

Pre-dŏm′i-nan-çy, } cendency; superiority.

---

sōn, ôr, dọ, wọlf, tōō, tŏŏk; ûrn, rụe, pụll; ç, ġ, *soft*; c, ġ, *hard*; aş; ex̱ist; ŋ *as* ng; this.

Pre-dŏm′i-nant, *a.* Prevalent over others; predominating.
Pre-dŏm′i-nant-ly, *adv.* With superior strength or influence.
Pre-dŏm′i-nāte, *v. i.* To be superior; to have controlling influence; to rule; to prevail.
Pre-ĕm′i-nençe, *n.* Superiority to others in place or rank. [others.
Prē-ĕm′i-nent, *a.* Surpassing
Prē-ĕm′i-nent-ly, *adv.* In a preeminent degree.
Pre-ĕmp′tion, *n.* Act or right of buying something, as land, before others.
Preen, *n.* A forked instrument used by clothiers. — *v. t.* To clean and adjust the feathers of, as birds.
Prē′-en-gāge′, *v. t.* To engage beforehand.
Prē′-en-gāge′ment, *n.* A prior engagement or obligation; previous attachment.
Prē′-es-tăb′lish, *v. t.* To establish beforehand.
Prē′-ex-ĭst′, *v. i.* To exist beforehand. [existence.
Prē′-ex-ĭst′ençe, *n.* Previous
Prē′-ex-ĭst′ent, } *a.* Existing
Prē′-ex-ĭst′ing, } in time previous.
Prĕf′açe (42), *n.* An introductory speech or writing. — *v. t.* To introduce by preliminary remarks.
Prĕf′a-to-ry, *a.* Introductory.
Prē′fect, *n.* A governor or chief officer; a commander.
Prē′fect-ūre, *n.* Office or jurisdiction of a prefect.
Pre-fēr′ (12, 129, 130), *v. t.* To esteem above others; to choose; to offer; to exalt.
Prĕf′er-a-ble, *a.* Worthy of preference. [ence.
Prĕf′er-a-bly, *adv.* In preference
Prĕf′er-ençe, *n.* Estimation or choice above another.
Pre-fēr′ment, *n.* Advancement to a higher office or honor.
Pre-fĭg′u-rā′tion, *n.* Previous representation by similitude.
Pre-fĭg′u-ra-tive, *a.* Showing by previous types or signs.
Pre-fĭg′ūre, *v. t.* To show by a figure beforehand.
Pre-fĭg′ūre-ment, *n.* Prefiguration. [fore.
Pre-fĭx′, *v. t.* To place before.
Prē′fix, *n.* A letter, syllable, or word prefixed.
Prĕg′nan-cy, *n.* State of being with young; fertility.

Prĕg′nant, *a.* Being with young; fertile; teeming.
Prĕg′nant-ly, *adv.* In a pregnant manner; fruitfully.
Pre-hĕn′sīle, } *a.* Grasping;
Pre-hĕn′so-ry, } adapted to grasp or seize.
Pre-hĕn′sion, *n.* A seizing, as with the hand.
Pre-jūdge′, *v. t.* To judge before hearing.
Pre-jŭdg′ment, *n.* Act of prejudging.
Pre-jū′di-cate, *v. t.* To determine beforehand; to prejudge.
Pre-jū′di-cā′tion, *n.* Act of judging without due examination.
Prĕj′u-dĭçe, *n.* Prejudgment; unreasonable prepossession; bias; injury. — *v. t.* To bias unduly.
Prĕj′u-di′cial (-dĭsh′al), *a.* Likely to injure; hurtful.
Prĕl′a-çy, } *n.* Office of a
Prĕl′a-tism, } prelate; government by prelates.
Prĕl′ate, *n.* A high dignitary of the church.
Pre-lăt′ic, } *a.* Pertaining
Pre-lăt′ic-al, } to prelates or the prelacy.
Prĕl′a-tist, *n.* One who supports prelacy.
Pre-lĕc′tion, *n.* A public lecture or discourse.
Prē-lī-bā′tion, *n.* A foretaste.
Pre-lĭm′i-na-ry, *a.* Preceding. — SYN. Introductory; previous; preparatory. — *n.* A first step; introduction.
Prē′lūde, or **Prĕl′ude**, *n.* Previous air in music; an introductory performance.
Pre-lūde′, *v. t.* or *i.* To preface; to serve as an introduction; to play an introduction.
Pre-lū′sive, } *a.* Serving to
Pre-lū′so-ry, } introduce.
Prē′ma-tūre′, *a.* [Lat. *præmaturus*, fr. *præ*, before, and *maturus*, ripe.] Ripe too soon; too hasty; too early.
Prē′ma-tūre′ly, *adv.* Before the proper time.
Prē′ma-tūre′ness, } *n.* Qual-
Prē′ma-tūr′i-ty, } ity of being premature.
Pre-mĕd′i-tāte, *v. t.* or *i.* To meditate beforehand.
Pre-mĕd′i-tā′ted, *a.* Conceived, designed, or contrived beforehand.
Pre-mĕd′i-tā′tion, *n.* Previous deliberation; forethought.
Prē′mi-er (or **prĕm′yer**), *n.*

First minister of state. — *a.* First; chief; principal.
Pre-mīse′ (153), *v.* To lay down premises.
Prĕm′ĭs-es, *n. pl.* Propositions admitted; a building and its adjuncts.
Prē′mi-um, *n.* Reward; advance: something given or offered for the loan of money; money paid for insurance.
Pre-mŏn′ish, *v. t.* To forewarn; to admonish beforehand.
Prē′mo-nī′tion (-nĭsh′un), *n.* Previous warning, notice, or information.
Pre-mŏn′i-to-ry, *a.* Giving previous notice.
Prē-ŏc′cu-pan-cy, *n.* Previous possession.
Prē-ŏc′cu-pā′tion, *n.* Prior occupation.
Prē-ŏc′cu-pȳ, *v. t.* To take possession of before another.
Prē′or-dāin′, *v. t.* To ordain or appoint beforehand.
Prē-ŏr′di-nā′tion, *n.* Act of foreordaining.
Prĕp′a-rā′tion, *n.* Act of preparing, or making ready; preparatory act.
Pre-păr′a-tive, } *a.* Adapted
Pre-păr′a-to-ry, } or tending to prepare.
Pre-păr′a-tive, *n.* That which prepares or is done to prepare; preparation.
Pre-pāre′, *v. t.* To make fit or ready; to qualify.
Prē-pāy′, *v. t.* To pay in advance, as postage.
Pre-pĕnse′, *a.* Premeditated.
Pre-pŏn′der-ançe, *n.* Superiority of weight or power.
Pre-pŏn′der-ant, *a.* Superior in weight or influence.
Pre-pŏn′der-āte, *v. t.* or *i.* To outweigh.
Pre-pŏn′der-ā′tion, *n.* Act of outweighing.
Prĕp′o-sĭ′tion (-zĭsh′un), *n.* A particle governing a noun or pronoun, and showing its relation to some other word.
Prĕp′o-sĭ′tion-al (-zĭsh′un-), *a.* Relating to prepositions.
Pre-pŏṣ′i-tive, *a.* Put before.
Prē′pos-sĕss′ (-pos-sĕs′ or -poz-zĕs′), *v. t.* To preoccupy; to bias; to prejudice.
Prē′pos-sĕss′ing (-pos-sĕs′- or -poz-zĕs′-), *a.* Adapted to invite favor.
Prē′pos-sĕs′sion (-sĕsh′un or -zĕsh′un), *n.* Prior possession; preconceived opinion.
Pre-pŏs′ter-oŭs, *a.* Absurd.

Pre-pŏs'ter-oŭs-ly, *adv.* Absurdly; foolishly.

Prē-rĕq'uĭ'ṣīte (-rĕk'wĭ-), *a.* Previously required or necessary. — *n.* Something previously necessary.

Pre-rŏg'a-tive, *n.* An exclusive or peculiar privilege.

Prĕ'ṣage, or Prĕs'age, *n.* A prognostic; a token.

Pre-ṣāge', *v. t.* To foreshow; to foretoken; to forebode.

Prĕṣ'by-ter, *n.* An elder; a priest.

Prĕṣ'by-tē'ri-an, *a.* Pertaining to, or consisting of, presbyters. — *n.* One who belongs to the Presbyterian church.

Prĕṣ'by-tē'ri-an-ĭṣm, *n.* Principles and government of Presbyterians.

Prĕṣ'by-ter-y, *n.* A body of pastors and ruling elders.

Prē'sci-ençe (prē'shĭ-enss), *n.* Foreknowledge.

Prē'sci-ent (prē'shĭ-ent), *a.* Foreknowing.

Pre-scrībe', *v. t.* or *i.* To direct; to dictate; to lay down rules.

Prē'script, *n.* An official or authoritative direction.

Pre-scrĭp'tion, *n.* Medical direction of remedies; claim from long use or possession.

Pre-scrĭp'tīve, *a.* Arising from prescription.

Prĕṣ'ençe, *n.* A being present; neighborhood; mien.

Prĕṣ'ent, *a.* In company; being now or here; immediate. — *n.* Something presented; the present time.

Pre-ṣĕnt', *v. t.* To give; to bestow; to exhibit; to view; to prefer; to indict.

Pre-ṣĕnt'a-ble, *a.* Admitting of being present.

Prĕṣ'en-tā'tion, *n.* Act of presenting; exhibition.

Pre-ṣĕn'ti-ment. *n.* Previous notion or apprehension.

Prĕṣ'ent-ly, *adv.* Shortly; soon; immediately.

Pre-ṣĕnt'ment, *n.* A presenting; representation; accusation by a grand jury.

Pre-ṣĕrv'a-ble, *a.* Capable of being preserved.

Prĕṣ'er-vā'tion, *n.* Act of preserving; safety; security.

Pre-ṣĕrv'a-tīve, | *a.* Having
Pre-ṣĕrv'a-to-ry, | power to preserve. — *n.* That which preserves.

Pre-ṣĕrve', *v. t.* To keep safe from injury or destruc-

tion; to save; to secure; to defend. — *n.* Fruit preserved; a place to keep game or fish in.

Pre-ṣĕrv'er, *n.* One who, or that which, preserves.

Pre-ṣīde', *v. i.* To exercise superintendence or control.

Prĕṣ'i-den-çy, *n.* Office or jurisdiction of president.

Prĕṣ'i-dent, *n.* One at the head of a society, college, or republic.

Prĕṣ'i-dĕn'tial, *a.* Pertaining to a president.

Prĕss (124, *v. t.* To squeeze; to crowd; to urge.— *v. i.* To encroach; to urge vehemently. — *n.* A machine for pressing; a machine for printing; art of printing and publishing; publications collectively; urgency; a crowd; a throng.

Prĕss'-bĕd, *n.* A bed that may be turned up and inclosed in a closet.

Prĕṣṣ'-găng, *n.* A crew that impresses men as seamen.

Prĕss'ing, *a.* Urgent.

Prĕss'-man (123, 143), *n.* The man who impresses the sheets in printing.

Prĕss'ure (presh'ur', *n.* Act of pressing; affliction; weight; force; urgency.

Prĕs'tīge, *n.* Influence coming from past success, character, or deeds. [denly.

Prĕs'to, *adv.* Quickly; suddenly.

Pre-ṣūm'a-ble, *a.* Such as may be presumed.

Pre-ṣūme', *v. i.* [Lat. *præsumere*, fr. *præ*, before, and *sumere*, to take.] To suppose; to venture without leave.

Pre-ṣŭmp'tion, *n.* Opinion; strong probability; excess of confidence.

Pre-ṣŭmp'tīve, *a.* Partaking of presumption.

Pre-ṣŭmpt'u-oŭs, *a.* Rashly bold; unduly confident.

Prē'sup-pōṣ'al, *n.* Previous supposition.

Prē'sup-pōṣe', *v. t.* To suppose as previous; to take for granted.

Pre-tĕnçe', *n.* See *Pretense*.

Pre-tĕnd', *v. t.* To hold out an appearance of; to simulate; to feign; to claim. — *v. i.* To use pretense.

Pre-tĕnd'ed, *p. a.* Having a false appearance or claim.

Pre-tĕnd'er, *n.* One who pretends or lays claim.

Pre-tĕnse' (149), *n.* A simu-

lated claim or assumption; a pretext; assumption.

Pre-tĕn'sion, *n.* Claim, true or false; pretense.

Pre-tĕn'tioŭs, *a.* Making great pretensions.

Prē'ter-im-pĕr'fect, *a.* Not absolutely or distinctly past.

Prĕt'er-it, or Prē'ter-it, *a.* (*Gram.*) Past or perfectly past. [Written also *preterite.*]

Prē'ter-ī'tion (-ĭsh'un), *n.* Act of passing or going past.

Prē'ter-mĭs'sion (-mĭsh'un), *n.* The act of omitting.

Prē'ter-mĭt', *v. t.* To pass by; to omit; to disregard.

Prē'ter-năt'u-ral, *a.* Beyond, or different from, what is natural; aside from nature.

Prē'ter-pĕr'fect, *a.* Expressing action or being absolutely past; perfect.

Prē'ter-plu-pĕr'fect, *a.* Expressing action or being at or before another past event or time; pluperfect.

Pre-tĕxt', or Prē'text (111), *n.* A pretense; an excuse.

Prē'tor, *n.* A civil officer among the ancient Romans.

Pre-tō'ri-an, *a.* Belonging to a pretor or judge.

Prĕt'ti-ly (prĭt'ti- or prĕt'tĭ-), *adv.* Neatly; pleasingly.

Prĕt'ty (prĭt'tỹ or prĕt'tỹ), *a.* Neat; handsome. — *adv.* In some degree; tolerably.

Pre-vāil', *v. i.* To be prevalent; to be generally received. [predominant.

Pre-vāil'ing, *a.* Prevalent;

Prĕv'a-lençe, *n.* Most general reception; predominance.

Prĕv'a-lent, *a.* Predominant; powerful.

Pre-văr'i-cāte, *v. i.* To avoid giving a direct answer. — SYN. To evade; equivocate; quibble. [quibbling.

Pre-văr'i-cā'tion, *n.* Act of

Pre-văr'i-cā'tor, *n.* One who quibbles; a shuffler.

Pre-vēn'i-ent, *a.* Going before; preceding; preventive.

Pre-vĕnt', *v. i.* To hinder; to stop; to anticipate.

Pre-vĕn'tion, *n.* Hindrance.

Pre-vĕnt'īve, *a.* Tending to hinder or prevent. — *n.* Something that prevents.

Prē'vi-oŭs, *a.* [Lat. *prævius*, going before, fr. *præ*, before, and *via*, the way.] Going before in time; prior; antecedent.

Prē'vi-oŭs-ly, *adv.* Antecedently; beforehand.

---

sŏn, ôr, dọ, wọlf, tōō, tŏŏk; ûrn, rụe, pụll; ç, ġ, *soft*; c, ḡ, *hard*; aṣ; exist; ŋ *as* ng; this.

Pre-vis'ion (-vĭzh'un), *n.* Foresight; foreknowledge.

Prey (prā), *n.* Spoil; booty; plunder. — *v. i.* To take food by violence; to collect spoil; to plunder.

Price, *n.* Equivalent paid for any thing; value; reward.

Price'-cŭr'rent, *n.* A published list of the prevailing prices of merchandise, &c.

Price'less, *a.* Invaluable; inestimable.

Prick, *v. t.* To pierce; to spur. — *v. i.* To become acid. — *n.* A puncture; a sharp point.

Prick'er, *n.* One who, or that which, pricks.

Prick'le (prĭk'l), *n.* A sharp pointed projection.

Prick'li-ness, *n.* Fullness of prickles.

Prick'ly, *a.* Full of prickles.

Pride, *n.* Inordinate self-esteem; generous elation of heart; dignity; that of which one is proud. — *v. t.* To indulge in self-esteem.

Priest, *n.* A clergyman; an ecclesiastic.

Priest'craft, *n.* Religious fraud or imposition.

Priest'ess, *n.* A female priest.

Priest'hood, *n.* Office of a priest; the order of priests.

Priest'li-ness, *n.* Appearance and manners of a priest.

Priest'ly, *a.* Pertaining to, or like, a priest; sacerdotal.

Prig, *n.* A conceited fellow. — *v. t.* To steal.

Prig'gish (129), *a.* Conceited; pert; affected.

Prim, *a.* Formal; precise; affectedly nice. — *v. t.* To deck with great nicety.

Pri'ma-cy, *n.* Office or dignity of an archbishop.

†**Pri'ma-Dŏn'na**, *n.* [It.] The first female singer in an opera.

Prim'age, *n.* A charge imposed in addition to the freight. [naut.]

Pri'ma-ri-ly (135), *adv.* Originally.

Pri'ma-ry, *a.* Original; first in time, meaning, or rank.

Pri'mate, *n.* Chief ecclesiastic; an archbishop.

Prime, *a.* First; original; chief; early. — *n.* The dawn; spring; the best part; youth; full health. — *v. t.* To put powder in the pan of, as of a gun; to lay the first color in painting.

Prim'er, *n.* A small first book for children; a kind of type of which there are two species, one called **Long-primer**, and the other called **Great-primer.**

Pri-me'val (45), *a.* [Lat. *primævus*, fr. *primus*, first, and *ævum*, age.] Belonging to the earliest ages; primitive.

Prim'ing, *n.* Powder in the pan of a gun; first color laid on in painting.

Prim'i-tive, *a.* First; original. — *n.* A primitive word.

Prim'ness, *n.* Affected niceness or formality.

Pri'mo-gē'ni-al, *a.* First born or made.

Pri'mo-gĕn'i-tor, *n.* The first father or forefather.

Pri'mo-gĕn'i-tūre, *n.* Seniority by birth; exclusive right of inheritance belonging to the eldest son or daughter. [der] original.

Pri-mor'di-al, *a.* First in order.

Prim'rōse, *n.* An early flowering plant.

Prince (140), *n.* A king's son; a sovereign; a ruler.

Prince'dom, *n.* The dignity or domain of a prince; sovereignty.

Prince'li-ness, *n.* State or manner of a prince.

Prince'ly, *a.* Of or relating to a prince; grand.

Prin'cess, *n.* The consort of a prince; a king's daughter.

Prin'ci-pal, *a.* Chief; capital. — *n.* A chief man; a head; a sum of money at interest.

Prin'ci-păl'i-ty, *n.* A prince's domain; sovereignty.

Prin'ci-pal-ly, *adv.* Chiefly; above all.

Prin'ci-ple, *n.* A settled or right rule of conduct; fundamental truth; tenet; an original element.

Prink, *v. t.* To dress for show.

Print, *v. t.* To mark by impression. — *n.* A mark made by pressure; impressions of type; cloth stamped with figures.

Print'er, *n.* One who prints.

Print'ing, *n.* The art or practice of a printer.

Pri'or, *a.* Former; antecedent. — *n.* The superior of a monastery.

Pri'or-ess, *n.* The lady superior of a convent.

Pri-ŏr'i-ty, *n.* State of being first in time or rank, &c.

Pri'or-y, *n.* A religious house, a convent.

Prĭsm, *n.* A solid, whose bases are similar, equal, parallel, plane figures, and whose sides are parallelograms.

Pris-măt'ic, *a.* Pertaining to, or formed by, prisms. [Prism.]

Pris'on (prĭz'n), *v. t.* To shut up; to confine. — *n.* A jail.

Prĭs'on-er, *n.* One under arrest; a captive. [nal.]

Pris'tine, *a.* Ancient; original.

Prĭth'ee, *adv.* I pray thee.

Pri'va-cy, *n.* Retirement; secrecy; a place of retreat.

Pri'vate, *a.* Secret; peculiar to one's self; alone. — *n.* A common soldier.

Pri'va-teer', *n.* A private ship of war commissioned to take prizes. — *v. i.* To cruise in a privateer.

Pri'vate-ly, *adv.* In a private or secret manner.

Pri-va'tion, *n.* Act of depriving; absence; loss.

Priv'a-tive, *a.* Causing privation. — *n.* A prefix to a word, giving it a negative signification. [shrub.]

Priv'et, *n.* An ornamental

Priv'i-lĕge, *v. t.* To invest with peculiar rights — *n.* Peculiar advantage or right. — SYN. Prerogative. [vately.

Priv'i-ly, *adv.* Secretly; privately.

Priv'i-ty, *n.* Private knowledge and concurrence.

Priv'y, *a.* Privately knowing and consenting; private. — *n.* A partaker; a necessary house.

Prize, *n.* [Fr. *prise*, fr. *prendre*, to take, *pris*, taken.] A reward; something taken from an enemy. — *v. t.* To value; to esteem.

Pro and Con. [Lat. *pro* and *contra.*] For and against.

Prŏb'a-bĭl'i-ty, *n.* Appearance of truth; likelihood.

Prŏb'a-ble, *a.* Likely to be, or to be true. [hood.

Prŏb'a-bly, *adv.* In likelihood.

Prō'bate, *n.* Proof of a will; a court for the trial of wills.

Pro-bā'tion, *n.* A proof; trial.

Pro-bā'tion-al, *a.* Serving for probation or trial.

Pro-bā'tion-a-ry, *a.*

Pro-bā'tion-er, n. One undergoing probation: a novice.
Prō'ba-to-ry, a. Serving for trial or proof.
Prōbe, n. A surgeon's instrument. — v. t. To try with a probe; to search thoroughly.
Prŏb'i-ty, n. Uniform uprightness; integrity. [solved.
Prŏb'lem, n. A question to be
Prŏb'lem-ăt'ic, } a. Questionable; uncertain.
Prŏb'lem-ăt'ic-al, }
†Pro-bŏs'çis, n. [Gr. probos-kis, fr. pro, before, and boskein, to feed.] The snout or trunk of an elephant, &c.
Pro-çēd'ūre, n. Act or manner of proceeding; process.
Pro-çeed', v. i. To go forward.
Pro-çeed'ing, n. A transaction; operation. [sue; rents.
Prō'çeeds (112), n. pl. Issues.
Prŏç'ess (prŏs'es), n. A proceeding; progress; order.
Pro-çĕs'sion, n. A train of persons.
Pro-çĕs'sion-al, a. Pertaining to, or consisting in, procession.
Pro-claim', v. t. To pronounce publicly and solemnly; to publish; to promulgate.
Prŏc'la-mā'tion, n. A publication by authority.
Pro-cliv'i-ty, n. Habitual or natural inclination.
Pro-cŏn'sul, n. A governor of a province.
Pro-cŏn'su-lar, a. Pertaining to a proconsul. [a proconsul.
Pro-cŏn'su-late, n. Office of
Pro-crăs'ti-nāte, v. t. or i. To put off from day to day.
Pro-crăs'ti-nā'tion, n. Delay; dilatoriness.
Pro-crăs'ti-nā'tor, n. One who puts any thing off to a future time: a dilatory person.
Prō'ere-āte, v. t. To generate.
Prō'ere-ā'tion, n. Production of young; generation.
Prō'ere-ā'tive, a. Having the power to beget; generative.
Prō'ere-ā'tor, n. One who begets; a sire.
Pro-crŭs'te-an, a. Relating to, or like, Procrustes, a fabulous highwayman, who is said to have placed his captives on a couch, and stretched out or cut off their legs to adapt them to its length.
Proc'tor, n. An officer in admiralty and ecclesiastical causes; an officer of a university.
Proc-tō'ri-al, a. Pertaining to a proctor.
Pro-eŭm'bent, a. Lying down or on the face.
Pro-eŭr'a-ble, a. Obtainable.
Prŏc'u-rā'tion, n. Act of procuring; procurement.
Prŏc'u-rā'tor, n. One who manages another's affairs.
Pro-cūre', v. t. To obtain; to gain; to cause; to acquire.
Pro-cūre'ment (132), n. Act of procuring or obtaining.
Prŏd'i-gal, a. Lavish; wasteful. — n. A spendthrift.
Prŏd'i-găl'i-ty, n. Wasteful expenditure; excessive liberality. — Syn. Extravagance; profusion; waste.
Prŏd'i-gal-ly, adv. Lavishly.
Pro-dĭg'ious (-dĭj'us), a. Very great; astonishing; enormous in size, quantity, &c.
Pro-dĭg'ious-ly (-dĭj'us-), adv. Astonishingly; enormously; wonderfully.
Prŏd'i-gy (141), n. Any surprising thing; a wonder.
Pro-dūçe', v. t. To bring forth; to bear; to yield; to exhibit.
Prŏd'uçe, n. That which is produced or yielded; grain.
Pro-dū'çer, n. One who produces. [being produced.
Pro-dū'çi-ble, a. Capable of
Prŏd'uet, n. A thing produced; effect; result; sum.
Pro-dŭe'tile, a. Capable of being extended.
Pro-dŭe'tion, n. Act of producing; fruit; product.
Pro-dŭet'ive, a. Causing to exist; fertile; efficient.
Pro-dŭet'ive-ness, n. The quality of producing.
Prō'em, n. A preface; introduction; prelude.
Pro-ē'mi-al, a. Introductory.
Prŏf'a-nā'tion, n. A violation of sacred things.
Pro-fāne', a. [Lat. profanus, fr. pro, before, without, and fanum, temple.] Irreverent to God, and to sacred things; impious. — v. t. To violate; to put to a wrong use; to pollute. [ly.
Pro-fāne'ly, adv. Irreverent-
Pro-fāne'ness, } n. Impiety;
Pro-făn'i-ty, } irreverence for sacred things.
Pro-fĕss', v. t. To declare openly; to avow. [al.
Pro-fĕss'ed-ly, adv. By avowal
Pro-fĕs'sion (-fĕsh'un), n. Open declaration; avowal; vocation; occupation.
Pro-fĕs'sion-al, a. Belonging to a profession.
Pro-fĕs'sion-al-ly, adv. By profession.
Pro-fĕss'or, n. One who makes any profession; a public teacher in literature or science. [ing to a professor.
Prō'fes-sō'ri-al, a. Pertain-
Pro-fĕss'or-ship, n. Office of a professor.
Prŏf'fer (130), v. t. To propose for acceptance. — n. An offer made; attempt.
Pro-fi'cien-çy (-fĭsh'en-), n. Progress made; advance.
Pro-fi'cient (-fĭsh'ent), n. One who has made progress or advance; an expert; an adept.
Prō'file (or prō'feel), n. Outline; side face. — v. t. To draw a side view of.
Prŏf'it (121), n. Gain; advantage: use; benefit. — v. (130) To benefit; to improve; to be of advantage.
Prŏf'it-a-ble, a. Yielding advantage; lucrative; useful.
Prŏf'it-a-ble-ness, n. Quality of being profitable.
Prŏf'it-a-bly, adv. With advantage; advantageously.
Prŏf'it-less, a. Void of profit.
Prŏf'li-ga-çy, n. A profligate or very vicious life.
Prŏf'li-gate, a. Lost to virtue. — n. An abandoned or shamefully vicious man.
Pro-found', a. Deep; thorough; low; learned. — n. The sea or ocean; an abyss.
Pro-found'ly, adv. Deeply.
Pro-found'ness, } n. Depth
Pro-fŭnd'i-ty, } of place, or of knowledge.
Pro-fūse', a. Liberal to excess; exuberant. — Syn. Lavish; prodigal.
Pro-fūse'ly, adv. Prodigally.
Pro-fūse'ness, n. Prodigality; great abundance.
Pro-fū'sion, n. Great abundance; lavish supply; extravagance: prodigality.
Prŏg, n. Mean or inferior food; victuals. — v. i. To go about begging; to steal.
Pro-gĕn'i-tor, n. An ancestor; a forefather.
Prŏg-ē'ny, n. Offspring; race.
†Prog-nō'sis, n. The art or act of foretelling the course of a disease by its symptoms.
Prog-nŏs'tic, a. Foreboding —n. A sign; token.

Prog-nŏs'ti-āte, *v. t.* To foreshow or foretell.
Prog-nŏs'ti-cā'tion, *n.* The act of foretelling.
Prog-nŏs'ti-cā'tor, *n.* One who foretells.
Prŏ'gram, *n.* An outline
Prŏ'gramme, of some public performance.
Prŏg'ress. *n.* A course onward; advance.
Pro-grĕss'. *v. i.* To advance; to proceed; to go on.
Pro-grĕs'sion, *n.* Advance.
Pro-grĕs'sion-al, *a.* Advancing. [ward; advancing.
Pro-grĕss'ive, *a.* Going on-
Pro-grĕss'ive-ly, *adv.* With progress.
Pro-grĕss'ive-ness, *n.* State of being progressive.
Pro-hĭb'it. *v. t.* To forbid.
Prō'hi-bĭ'tion (-bĭsh'un), *n.* Act of forbidding.
Pro-hĭb'it-ĭve, *a.* Contain-
Pro-hĭb'it-o-ry, ing, or implying, prohibition.
Pro-jĕct', *v. i.* [Lat. *projicere, jectum,* fr. *pro, forward,* and *jacere,* to throw.] To jut out; to be prominent. — *v. t.* To scheme; to devise; to draw.
Prŏj'ect, *n.* A plan, scheme.
Pro-jĕct'ĭle, *a.* Impelling forward. — *n.* A body projected or impelled forward through the air.
Pro-jĕc'tion, *n.* Act of projecting; plan; delineation.
Pro-jĕct'or, *n.* One who projects or plans. [out.
Pro-jĕct'ūre, *n.* A jutting
Prō'late, *a.* Elongated in the direction of a line joining the poles.
Prŏl'i-çīde, *n.* The crime of destroying one's offspring.
Pro-lĭf'ic, *a.* Generative; fruitful; productive.
Pro-lĭx' (111), *a.* Long; tediously minute.
Pro-lĭx'i-ty, *n.* Great.
Pro-lĭx'ness, length; tediousness.
Prŏl'o-cū'tor, or **Pro-lŏc'u-tor,** *n.* One who speaks for another; a spokesman.
Prō'lŏgue (prō'lŏg), *n.* Introduction to a play.
Pro-lŏng', *v. t.* To lengthen.
Prō'lon-gā'tion, *n.* Act of lengthening in time or space; delay.
Prŏm'e-nāde', or **Prŏm'e-näde',** *n.* A walk. — *v. i.* To walk for amusement or exercise.

Pro-mē'the-an, *a.* Relating to Prometheus, who is fabled to have formed men of clay, whom he animated by means of fire which he stole from heaven. [ing prominent.
Prŏm'i-nence, *n.* State of be-
Prŏm'i-nent, *a.* Conspicuous; eminent. [nently.
Prŏm'i-nent-ly, *adv.* Emi-
Pro-mĭs'cu-oŭs, *a.* Mixed; indiscriminate; confused.
Pro-mĭs'cu-oŭs-ly, *adv.* Without distinction.
Prŏm'ĭse, *n.* A declaration which binds the one who makes it; ground of hope. — *v. t.* To engage by declaration; to give hopes.
Prŏm'is-ee', *n.* One to whom a promise is made.
Prŏm'is-er, *n.* One who
Prŏm'is-or, promises.
Prŏm'is-so-ry, *a.* Containing a promise.
Prŏm'on-to-ry, *n.* A headland; high land jutting out into the sea.
Pro-mōte', *v. t.* To forward; to advance; to raise; to elevate.
Pro-mōt'er, *n.* An encourager. [ment.
Pro-mō'tion, *n.* Advance-
Pro-mō'tive, *a.* Tending to promote, advance, or aid.
Prŏmpt, *a.* Ready; expeditious; quick. — *v. t.* To incite to action; to dictate.
Prŏmpt'er, *n.* One who reminds a speaker.
Prŏmpt'i-tūde, *n.* Readi-
Prŏmpt'ness, ness; expedition; alacrity.
Prŏmpt'ly, *adv.* With readiness; immediately.
Pro-mŭl'gāte, *v. t.* To make
Pro-mŭlge', known by open declaration.
Prŏ'mul-gā'tion, *n.* A notice; open publication.
Prŏ'mul-gā'tor, *n.* One who publishes or makes known.
Prōne, *a.* Flat on the face; bending downward; sloping; inclined; disposed.
Prōne'ness, *n.* A bending down; inclination [fork.
Prŏng, *n.* The branch of a
Pro-nŏm'i-nal, *a.* Belonging to a pronoun. [for a noun.
Prō'noun, *n.* A word used
Pro-noūnçe', *v. t.* To speak; to utter rhetorically.
Pro-noūnçed' (-nounst'), *a.* Strongly marked; decided.
Pro-noūnçe'a-ble, *a.* Capable of being pronounced.

Pro-nŭn'çi-a-mĕn'to, *n.* A proclamation or manifesto.
Pro-nŭn'ci-ā'tion (-shǐ-ā'-shun), *n.* Act or mode of utterance.
Prōof, *n.* Testimony; full evidence; trial; test; demonstration; a proof-sheet. — *a.* Impenetrable.
Prōof'-sheet, *n.* An impression from type, an engraved plate, &c., for correction.
Prŏp, *n.* That on which a body rests; support. — *v. t.* To support; to uphold.
Prŏp'a-ga-ble, *a.* Capable of being propagated.
Prŏp'a-gän'dà, *n.* A Roman Catholic missionary society in Rome.
Prŏp'a-gän'dĭsm, *n.* Art or practice of propagating tenets.
Prŏp'a-gän'dist, *n.* A person who propagates opinions.
Prŏp'a-gāte (118), *v. t.* To generate; to increase; to promote. [sion; increase.
Prŏp'a-gā'tion, *n.* Exten-
Prŏp'a-gā'tor, *n.* One who propagates. [urge forward.
Pro-pĕl' (129), *v. t.* To drive or
Pro-pĕl'ler, *n.* One who, or that which, propels; a steamboat propelled by a screw, or the screw itself. [prone.
Pro-pĕnse', *a.* Inclined;
Pro-pĕn'sion, *n.* Inclina-
Pro-pĕn'si-ty, tion; bent of mind; tendency; bias; proclivity.
Prŏp'er, *a.* One's own; natural; fit; just; correct; denoting a particular person or place.
Prŏp'er-ly, *adv.* In a proper manner; fitly; suitably.
Prŏp'er-ty, *n.* Inherent or peculiar quality; ownership; thing possessed; an estate; goods. [tion.
Prŏph'e-çȳ (141), *n.* Predic-
Prŏph'e-sī'er, *n.* One who prophesies.
Prŏph'e-sȳ, *v. t.* or *i.* To foretell, as events. — SYN. To predict; foreshow.
Prŏph'et (121), *n.* One who prophesies. [prophet.
Prŏph'et-ess, *n.* A female
Pro-phĕt'ic, Unfold-
Pro-phĕt'ic-al, ing future events; relating to prophecy.
Pro-phĕt'ic-al-ly, *adv.* In a prophetical manner.
Prŏph'y-lăc'tĭc, *a.* Defending from disease; preventive.
Pro-pĭn'qui-ty, *n.* Nearness in place, time, or relation.

ā, ē, ī, ō, ū, ȳ, *long*; ă, ĕ, ĭ, ŏ, ŭ, ў, *short*; cāre, cär, àsk, all, whạt; ēre, veil, tẽrm; pïque, fĭrm;

PROPITIABLE 230 PROTRUSIVE

Pro-pi'ti-a-ble (-pĭsh'ĭ-), *a.* Capable of being propitiated.

Pro-pi'ti-āte (-pĭsh'ĭ-āt), *v. t.* To appease and make favorable; to conciliate.

Pro-pi'ti-ā'tion (-pĭsh-ĭ-ā'- shŭn), *n.* Act of appeasing.

Pro-pi'ti-ā'tor (-pĭsh'ĭ-), *n.* One who propitiates.

Pro-pi'ti-a-to-ry (-pĭsh'ĭ-a-), *a.* Having the power to make propitious; expiatory. — *n.* The mercy-seat.

Pro-pi'tious (-pĭsh'ŭs), *a.* Highly favorable to success. — SYN. Auspicious; kind.

Pro-pi'tious-ly (-pĭsh'ŭs-), *adv.* Favorably; auspiciously; kindly.

Prō'po-lĭs, *n.* A substance used by bees to stop crevices in their hives, &c.

Pro-pō'nent, *n.* One who makes a proposal.

Pro-pōr'tion, *n.* Comparative relation; equal share; equality of ratios. — *v. t.* To adjust in a suitable proportion, as one part to another.

Pro-pōr'tion-a-ble, *a.* Capable of being proportioned.

Pro-pōr'tion-a-bly, *adv.* According to proportion.

Pro-pōr'tion-al, } *a.* Having
Pro-pōr'tion-ate, } a due proportion, or comparative relation.

Pro-pōr'tion-al-ly, *adv.* In due proportion.

Pro-pōr'tion-āte, *v. t.* To make proportional.

Pro-pōr'tion-ate-ly, *adv.* In a proportionate degree.

Pro-pōṣ'al, *n.* Offer; proffer; proposition.

Pro-pōṣe', *v. t.* To offer for consideration; to purpose.

Prŏp'o-ṣĭ'tion (-zĭsh'ŭn), *n.* A thing proposed; offer of terms.

Pro-pound', *v. t.* To propose: to offer for consideration.

Pro-pri'e-ta-r/, *n.* An owner. — *a.* Belonging to an owner.

Pro-pri'e-tor, *n.* A possessor in his own right; an owner.

Pro-pri'e-tor-ship, *n.* State of being proprietor.

Pro-pri'e-ty, *n.* Fitness; justness; decorum.

Pro-pŭl'sion, *n.* Act of propelling, or driving forward.

Prō'ro-gā'tion, *n.* Continuance of Parliament from one session to another.

Pro-rōgue', *v. t.* To continue from session to session.

Pro-ġā'ic, *a.* Consisting in,

or like, prose; commonplace; prosy.

†**Pro-scē'ni-um**, *n.* Front part of the stage of a theater; part before the drop-scene.

Pro-scrībe', *v. t.* To denounce and condemn; to outlaw; to interdict.

Pro-scrĭp'tion, *n.* A dooming to death, exile, or outlawry.

Pro-scrĭp'tive, *a.* Relating to, or consisting in, proscription.

Prōṣe, *n.* Language not in verse. — *v. i.* To-talk in a dull, tedious manner.

Prōṣ'e-cūte, *v. t.* [Lat. *prosequi*, *-secutus*, from *pro*, forward, and *sequi*, to follow.] To pursue as a claim or an investigation; to sue at law.

Prōṣ'e-cū'tion, *n.* Act of prosecuting. [prosecutes.

Prōṣ'e-cū'tor, *n.* One who

Prōṣ'e-lȳte, *n.* A new convert. — *v. t.* To convert.

Prōṣ'e-lȳt'ĭṣm, *n.* Zeal to make converts.

Prōṣ'er, *a.* A writer of prose; a tedious writer or speaker.

Pro-sō'di-al, } *a.* Pertaining,
Pro-sōd'ic-al, } or according, to prosody.

Pro-sō'di-an, } *n.* One skilled
Prŏṣ'o-dĭst, } in prosody.

Prōṣ'o-dy, *n.* The part of grammar which treats of accent and versification.

Prōs'pect, *n.* A view; object of view; reason to hope.

Pro-spĕc'tion, *n.* Act of looking forward.

Pro-spĕct'ive, *a.* Looking forward; regarding the future; coming.

Pro-spect'ive-ly, *adv.* With reference to the future.

Pro-spĕc'tus, *n.* Plan of a proposed literary work.

Prōs'per, *v. i.* To be successful. — SYN. To succeed; thrive; flourish. — *v. t.* To render successful; to favor.

Prŏs-pĕr'i-ty, *n.* Good fortune; success.

Prōs'per-oŭs, *a.* Successful.

Prōs'per-oŭs-ly, *adv.* Successfully; fortunately.

Prōs'ti-tūte, *v. t.* To offer to a lewd or bad use. — *a.* Devoted to base or lewd purposes. — *n.* A woman given to indiscriminate lewdness.

Prōs'tĭ-tū'tion, *n.* Act of prostituting; common lewdness

Prōs'trāte, *a.* Lying at length.

Prōs'trāte, *v. t.* To throw down; to lay flat.

Pros-trā'tion, *n.* Act of prostrating; total dejection or depression. [unins in front.

Prō'stȳle, *n.* A range of columns.

Prōs'ȳ, *a.* Dull and tedious.

†**Prŏt'a-sĭs**, *n.* Subordinate member of a conditional sentence.

Prō'te-an, *a.* Relating to Proteus, a sea-god who had the faculty of assuming different shapes; hence, readily changing the form or appearance.

Pro-tĕct', *v. t.* [Lat. *protegere*, *-tectum*, fr. *pro*, before, and *tegere*, to cover.] To shield from danger; to save harmless; to defend.

Pro-tĕc'tion, *n.* Defense from injury or danger.

Pro-tĕct'ive, *a.* Defensive.

Pro-tĕct'or, *n.* One who defends from injury.

Pro-tĕct'or-ate, *n.* Government by a protector. [tector.

Pro-tĕct'ress, *n.* A female protector.

Protégé (pro/tā'zhā'), *n.* One under the care and protection of another.

Pro-tĕst', *v. i.* To affirm solemnly. — *v. t.* To declare against; to disown.

Prō'test (112), *n.* A formal declaration of dissent.

Prŏt'est-ant, *n.* One who protests against the doctrines and practices of the Church of Rome. — *a.* Relating to Protestants or to Protestantism. [ligion of Protestants.

Prŏt'est-ant-ĭṣm, *n.* The religion of Protestants.

Prŏt'es-tā'tion, *n.* A solemn declaration.

Pro-thŏn'o-ta-ry, *n.* The chief clerk of a court.

Prō'to-cōl, *n.* An original copy or rough draught of a treaty, &c.

Prō'to-mär'tyr, *n.* The first martyr, Stephen.

Prō'to-plăst, *n.* The thing first formed; an original.

Prō'to-tȳpe, *n.* An original model; exemplar.

Pro-trăct', *v. t.* To lengthen in time; to prolong.

Pro-trăc'tion, *n.* Act of protracting; a lengthening out.

Pro-trăct'ive, *a.* Delaying.

Pro-trūde' *v. t.* [Lat. *protrudere*, fr. *pro*, forward, forth, and *trudere*, to thrust.] To thrust out. — *v. i.* To shoot forward.

Pro-trū'sion (-trụ/zhụn), *n.* Act of thrusting out.

Pro-trū'sive, *a.* Thrusting or impelling outward.

sọn, ôr, dọ, wọlf, tụo, tụok; ûrn, rụe, pụll; ç, ġ, *soft*; c, ġ, *hard*; aṣ; eẋist; ŋ *as* ng; this.

Pro-tū′ber-ançe, n. A prominence; a swelling.
Pro-tū′ber-ant, a. Prominent, swelling out.
Pro-tū′ber-āte, v. i. To become prominent; to swell or bulge out. [jection.
Pro-tū′ber-ā′tion, n. A pro-
Proud, a. Having inordinate self-esteem; conceited; arrogant; haughty; fungous, as proud flesh.
Proud′ly, adv. Haughtily.
Prov′a-ble (133), a. Capable of being proved.
Prove, v. t. To try; to test; to ascertain by experiment; to verify; to demonstrate; to experience. — v. i. To make trial; to be found by trial.
Prŏv′en-der, n. Dry food for cattle and horses.
Prŏv′erb, n. A short sentence often repeated, expressing an important truth; a wise saying; an adage; a maxim.
Pro-vĕrb′i-al, a. Pertaining to a proverb; universally acknowledged or spoken of.
Pro-vĕrb′i-al-ly, adv. By or as a proverb.
Pro-vīde′, v. t. To procure beforehand; to prepare.
Prŏv′i-dençe, n. Foresight; the care of God over his creatures. [forehand.
Prŏv′i-dent, a. Preparing be-
Prŏv′i-dĕn′tial, a. Relating to, or effected by, divine providence.
Prŏv′i-dĕn′tial-ly, adv. By means of providence.
Prŏv′i-dent-ly, adv. With prudent foresight. [vides.
Pro-vīd′er, n. One who pro-
Prŏv′inçe (140), n. A distant portion of an empire or state; a region of country; district; office; business.
Pro-vin′çial, n. An inhabitant of a province. — a. Belonging to a province; unpolished.
Pro-vin′çial-ism, n. Peculiarity of speech in a province.
Pro-vī′sion (-vĭzh′un), n. Preparation; something provided; food; previous stipulation. — v. t. To supply with stores.
Pro-vī′sion-al } (-vĭzh′un),
Pro-vī′sion-a-ry } a. Prepared for the occasion; temporary.
Pro-vī′sion-al-ly (-vĭzh′un-), adv. Temporarily.
Pro-vī′so, n. (pl. Pro-vī′sōs,

18.) A conditional stipulation.
Pro-vī′ṣo-ry, a. Conditional; temporary. [of anger.
Prŏv′o-cā′tion, n. A cause
Pro-vŏc′a-tive, a. Serving to provoke or excite. — n. Any thing that tends to provoke; a stimulant.
Pro-vōke′, v. t. To excite; to offend; to incense.
Prŏv′ŏst (prŏv′ust, 39), n. A chief officer, or magistrate.
Prŏv′ost-mär′shal (usually pron. pro-vo′-), n. A military officer who arrests deserters, &c.
Prow, n. Forepart of a ship.
Prow′ess, n. Bravery; valor.
Prowl, v. i. To rove for prey — n. A roving for prey.
Prowl′er, n. One who prowls.
Prŏx′i-mate, n. Next immediately preceding or following. — SYN. Nearest; immediate; direct.
Prŏx′i-mate-ly, adv. By immediate relation; immediately. [nearness.
Prox-im′i-ty, n. Immediate
†Prŏx′i-mo, n. The next, or the coming month.
Prŏx′y (141), n. Agency of a substitute; a substitute.
Prude, n. A woman of affected modesty or reserve.
Pru′dençe, n. Practical wisdom; caution; discretion.
Pru′dent, a. Practically wise.
Pru-dĕn′tial, a. Proceeding from, or guided by, prudence.
Pru′dent-ly, adv. Discreetly.
Pru′der-y, n. Affected modesty or reserve. [coy.
Pru′dish (133), a. Affectedly
Prune, n. A dried plum. — v. t. To cut or lop off branches from; to trim.
Pru-nĕl′la, } n. [Prob. from
Pru-nĕl′lo, } the color, resembling that of prunes.] A kind of lasting, or smooth woolen stuff.
Pru′ri-ençe, n. Itching or longing desire.
Pru′ri-ent, a. Uneasy with desire; itching.
Prus′sian (prŭsh′an, or prōō′shan), a. Relating to Prussia.
Prŭs′sic, or Prŭs′sic, a. Pertaining to Prussian blue; applied to an acid which is a deadly poison.
Prȳ, v. i. To examine or inspect closely. — v. t. To lift with a lever.

Psalm (säm), n. A sacred song or hymn. [psalms.
Psalm′ist, n. A writer of
Psalm′o-dĭst (sälm′- or säm′-), n. One who sings psalms.
Psalm′o-dy (sälm′- or säm′-), n. Art or practice of singing psalms or hymns.
Psạl′ter (sawl′ter), n. The book of Psalms.
Psạl′ter-y (sawl′ter-), n. An ancient instrument of music.
Pshạw (shaw), interj. expressing contempt.
Psȳ′cho-lŏg′ic } (sī-), a.
Psȳ′cho-lŏg′ic-al } Pertaining to the soul or to the science of the soul.
Psȳ-chŏl′o-ġy (sī-), n. The doctrine of, or a treatise on, the soul.
Ptŏl′e-mā′ic (tŏl-), a. Pertaining to Ptolemy, an ancient astronomer.
Pty′a-lĭṣm (tī-), n. Salivation. [sexes.
Pū′ber-ty, n. Ripe age in the
Pu-bĕs′çençe, n. A state of puberty; soft, short hairs.
Pu-bĕs′çent, a. Arriving at puberty; covered with soft, short hairs.
Pŭb′lic (127), a. Pertaining to a nation or to the community; common; open; general. — n. The body of the people.
Pŭb′li-can, n. Keeper of an inn or public house; a collector of taxes or tribute.
Pŭb′li-cā′tion, n. Act of publishing; thing published.
Pŭb′li-çĭst, n. A writer on the laws of nations.
Pub-lĭç′i-ty, n. State of being public; notoriety.
Pŭb′lic-ly, adv. Openly.
Pŭb′lish, v. t. To make known or public; to put forth; to advertise. [lishes.
Pŭb′lish-er, n. One who pub-
Pŭb′lish-ment, n. Public notice of an intended marriage. [ter, or plant-louse.
Pūçe-ron, n. The vine-fret-
Pŭck′er, v. t. To gather into small folds or wrinkles. — n. A small fold or wrinkle.
Pŭd′ding, n. A kind of food variously compounded.
Pŭd′dle, n. A small pool of muddy water. — v. t. To make muddy; to render impervious to water; to deprive of carbon, as iron.
Pū′er-īle, a. [Lat. puerilis, fr. puer, a boy.] Childish; boyish.
Pū′er-ĭl′i-ty, n. Childishness.

Pu-ĕr'per-al, *a.* Pertaining to childbirth.
Pŭff (123), *n.* A slight blast of wind; a kind of light pastry; exaggerated commendation. — *v. t.* or *i.* To swell with wind; to pant; to praise extravagantly.
Pŭff'-ball, *n.* A fungus or mushroom full of dust.
Pŭff'y, *a.* Inflated; swollen; bombastic. [dog.
Pŭg, *n.* A monkey; a little
Pŭgh (pŏŏ), *interj.* expressing contempt.
Pū'ġil-ĭsm, *n.* A fighting with the fist; boxing.
Pū'ġil-ĭst, *n.* A boxer.
Pū'ġil-ĭst'ic, *a.* Pertaining to fighting with the fist.
Pug-nā'cious, *a.* Inclined to fight; quarrelsome.
Pug-năç'i-ty, *n.* Disposition to fight.
Pūis'ne (pū'ne), *a.* Small; younger; inferior in rank.
Pū'is-sançe, *n.* Power; strength; might.
Pū'is-sant, *a.* Powerful; strong; mighty. [vomit.
Pūke, *v. i.* To vomit. — *n.* A
Pūle, *v. i.* To cry and whine like a child.
Pull, *v. t.* To pluck; to draw. — *n.* Act of pulling.
Pŭl'let, *n.* A young hen.
Pŭl'ley (141), *n.* [From *pull.*] A small wheel turning in a block, with a groove for a running cord. **Pulleys.**
Pŭl'mo-na-ry, } *a.* Pertain-
Pul-mŏn'ic, } ing to, or affecting, the lungs.
Pŭlp, *n.* The soft, juicy part of fruit; any softness; marrow. — *v. t.* To deprive of pulp.
Pŭl'pit, *n.* An elevated station or desk for a preacher.
Pŭlp'oŭs, } *a.* Of, or like,
Pŭlp'y, } pulp; soft.
Pŭl'sāte, *v. i.* To throb, as an artery; to beat.
Pŭl'sa-tile, *a.* Capable of being struck or beaten.
Pul-sā'tion, *n.* A throb.
Pŭl'sa-tĭve, } *a.* Beating like
Pŭl'sa-to-ry, } a pulse.
Pūlse, *n.* A beating of arteries; peas, beans, &c.
Pŭl'ver-a-ble, *a.* Capable of being pulverized, or reduced to fine powder.

Pŭl'ver-ĭ-zā'tion, *n.* A reducing to powder.
Pŭl'ver-īze, *v. t.* To reduce to powder; to comminute.
Pul-vĕr'u-lent, *a.* Consisting of, or like, fine powder.
Pūm'ĭçe, *n.* A porous substance ejected from volcanoes.
Pu-mĭ'cious (-mĭsh'us), *a.* Consisting of pumice.
Pŭmp, *n.* An engine for raising water; a low shoe with a thin sole. — *v.* To raise with a pump; to draw out.
Pŭmp'kin (81), *n.* A well-known plant and its fruit.
Pŭn, *n.* A word or expression with two meanings; a quibble. — *v. i.* (129) To play upon words.
Pŭnch, *n.* A tool for making holes; a kind of liquor; a buffoon; a blow. — *v. t.* To thrust; to perforate.
Pŭnch'eon (-un), *n.* A tool for piercing, stamping, or the like; a cask holding 84 or 120 gallons.
Pŭn'chi-nĕl'lo, *n.* A buffoon; a character in a puppet-show.
Punc-til'io (140), *n.* A nice point.
Punc-til'ious, *a.* Exact in ceremony or bargain; nice.
Pŭnc'to, *n.* A nice point of form or ceremony; a punctilio; the point in fencing.
Pŭnct'u-al, *a.* Prompt; exact to the time appointed; strict; nice.
Pŭnct'u-ăl'i-ty, *n.* Scrupulous exactness in time.
Pŭnct'u-al-ly, *adv.* Exactly.
Pŭnct'u-āte, *v. t.* To mark with written points.
Pŭnct'u-ā'tion, *n.* Act or art of dividing sentences by means of points.
Pŭnct'ūre, *n.* A small point or a hole made by pricking. — *v. t.* To prick with a pointed instrument. [min.
Pŭn'dit, *n.* A learned Brahming, *n.* A kind of sleigh rudely made.
Pŭn'ġen-çy, *n.* Sharpness; keenness.
Pŭn'ġent, *a.* [Lat. *pungens,* pricking.] Sharp; acrid.
Pŭn'ġent-ly, *adv.* In a pungent manner.
Pū'nic, *a.* Pertaining to Carthage; faithless; perfidious.
Pŭn'ish, *v. t.* To inflict pain on for an offense. — SYN. To correct; scourge; chasten; castigate.

Pŭn'ish-a-ble, *a.* Worthy to be punished. [ishes.
Pŭn'ish-er, *n.* One who punishes.
Pŭn'ish-ment, *n.* Any penalty inflicted or suffered as the reward of a crime.
Pū'ni-tĭve, } *a.* Inflicting
Pū'ni-to-ry, } punishment.
Pŭnk, *n.* Substance used for tinder; a strumpet.
Pŭn'ster, *n.* One who puns.
Pŭnt, *n.* A flat-bottomed boat, used for various purposes.
Pū'ny (26), *a.* Little and weak.
Pŭp, *n.* A young dog; a whelp. — *v. i.* To bring forth puppies.
†**Pū'pa,** *n.* (*pl.* Pū'pæ.) A chrysalis.
Pū'pil, *n.* A scholar; apple of the eye.
Pū'pil-aġe (130), *n.* The state of a pupil or scholar.
Pū'pil-la-ry, *a.* Pertaining to a pupil or ward.
Pŭp'pet, *n.* A small image moved by wires; a doll.
Pŭp'py (141), *n.* A young dog.
Pŭp'py-ĭṣm, *n.* Cringing meanness; coxcombry.
Pŭr (125), *v. i.* To murmur as a cat. — *n.* A murmuring sound made by cats.
Pŭr'blīnd, *a.* Near-sighted.
Pŭr'chas-a-ble, *a.* Capable of being purchased.
Pŭr'chase, *v. t.* To buy; to procure; to obtain; to acquire. — *n.* A buying; thing bought; power of a lever. [buys.
Pŭr'cha-ser, *n.* One who
Pūre, *a.* Clear; unpolluted; real; genuine; chaste.
Pūre'ly (132), *adv.* In a pure manner; merely. [pure.
Pūre'ness, *n.* State of being
Pur-gā'tion, *n.* Act of cleansing or cleaning from a crime.
Pŭr'ga-tĭve, *a.* Cleansing; cathartic. — *n.* A cathartic medicine. [to purgatory.
Pŭr'ga-tō'ri-al, *a.* Pertaining
Pŭr'ga-to-ry, *n.* A place in which some suppose the souls of the dead are purified by punishment.
Pŭrġe, *v. t.* [Lat. *purgare,* contracted fr. *purum agere,* to make clean.] To cleanse; to purify; to clear from guilt. — *n.* A cathartic medicine.
Pū'ri-fi-cā'tion, *n.* Act of purifying; a cleansing.
Pū'ri-fī'er, *n.* One who, or that which, purifies.
Pū'ri-fȳ, *v. t.* or *i.* To make

sŏn, ôr, dọ, wọlf, tŏŏ, tŏŏk; ûrn, rụe, pụll; ç, ġ, *soft;* c, ġ, *hard;* aṣ; eḳist; ụ *as* ng; this.
11

PURISM 242 PYX

or grow pure or clean; to cleanse; to refine.

Pū'rism, *n.* Nicety, especially in the use of words.

Pū'rist, *n.* One nice in the choice of words.

Pū'ri-tan, *n.* A dissenter from the church of England in the 16th and 17th centuries.

Pū'ri-tăn'ic, } *a.* Pertain-
Pū'ri-tăn'ic-al, } ing to the Puritans and their doctrines; rigid.

Pū'ri-tăn'ic-al-ly, *adv.* In a puritanical manner.

Pū'ri-tan-ĭsm, *n.* The notions or practice of Puritans.

Pū'ri-ty (133), *n.* State of being pure; cleanness; clearness; chastity.

Pûrl, *v. i.* To flow with a gentle noise. — *n.* A gentle murmur of a stream; a border; malt liquor spiced.

Pûr'lieu, *n.* Environs.

Pûr'lin, *n.* A timber to support rafters. [pilfer.

Pur-loin', *v. t.* To steal; to

Pur-loin'er, *n.* One who steals.

Pûr'ple, *a.* Red tinged with blue. — *n.* A color composed of red and blue; a robe; (*pl.*) spots of a livid color on the skin. — *v. t.* To color with purple. [ple.

Pûr'plish, *a.* Somewhat purple

Pûr'pōrt, *n.* That which is meant; meaning; tendency. — *v. t.* To intend; to signify.

Pûr'pose (pûr'pus), *n.* Object to be accomplished. — SYN. Intention; aim; view; end. — *v. t.* To intend; to design; to resolve.

Pûr'pose-ly (pûr'pus-), *adv.* Intentionally; with design.

Pûrr. (125) See *Pur*.

Pûrse, *n.* A small money-bag. — *v. t.* To put in a purse; to contract.

Pûrse'-pride, *n.* Pride of money. [wealth.

Pûrse'-proud, *a.* Proud of

Pûrs'er, *n.* The paymaster of a ship.

Pur-sū'a-ble, *a.* Capable of being, or fit to be, pursued.

Pur-sū'ance, *n.* A following; prosecution; consequence.

Pur-sū'ant, *a.* Done in consequence; conformable.

Pur-sūe', *v. t.* To follow; to chase. — *v. i.* To proceed, in argument or discourse.

Pur-sū'er, *n.* One who pursues, chases, or follows.

Pur-sūit', *n.* Act of following; chase; course of business.

Pûr'sui-vant (-swĭ-), *n.* A state messenger.

Pûrs'y, *a.* Fat and short-breathed.

Pū'ru-lençe, *n.* Generation of pus; matter.

Pū'ru-lent, *a.* Consisting of, or pertaining to, pus.

Pur-vey' (-vā'), *v. t.* To furnish or provide. — *v. i.* To buy provisions; to cater.

Pur-vey'ançe, *n.* Procurement of provisions.

Pur-vey'or, *n.* One who provides; a caterer.

Pûr'view, *n.* The body of a statute; limit; scope; extent; sphere.

Pŭs, *n.* The matter or yellowish-white, creamy liquid of a sore or ulcer.

Push, *v. t.* To urge or impel. — *n.* An urging; a thrust.

Pū'sil-la-nĭm'i-ty, *n.* Weakness of mind; cowardice; poltroonery.

Pū'sil-lăn'i-moŭs, *a.* [Lat *pusillaninis,* from *pusillus,* very little, and *animus,* mind.] Destitute of courage. — SYN. Cowardly; dastardly.

Puss, *n.* A cat; a hare.

Pŭst'u-late, *v. i.* To form into pustules.

Pŭst'ule, *n.* A small pimple containing pus. [tules.

Pŭst'u-loŭs, *a.* Having pus-

Pŭt, *v. t.* [*imp. & p. p.* PUT.] To lay in a place; to apply; to propose. — *v. i.* To go or move; to steer; to direct.

Pū'ta-tive, *a.* Supposed.

Pŭt'log, *n.* A short piece of timber supporting the floor of a scaffold.

Pŭt'-ŏff, *n.* A shift for evasion or delay; a subterfuge.

Pū'tre-făc'tion, *n.* Process of decaying or rotting.

Pū'tre-făc'tive, *a.* Pertaining to, or tending to promote, putrefaction; making rotten.

Pū'tre-fȳ, *v. t.* or *i.* To dissolve or rot, as organized matter. [rotting.

Pu-trĕs'çence, *n.* State of

Pu-trĕs'çent, *a.* Becoming putrid or rotten, as organized bodies.

Pu-trĕs'çi-ble, *a.* Liable to become putrid. [ten.

Pū'trid, *a.* Decomposed; rot-

Pu-trĭd'i-ty, } *n.* State of
Pū'trĭd-ness, } being putrid.

Pŭt'ty, *n.* A kind of paste or cement of whiting and linseed oil.

Pŭz'zle, *n.* Perplexity; a toy which perplexes. — *v. t.* To perplex, as the mind; to nonplus.

Pyg-mē'an, *a.* Dwarfish.

Pyg'my (141), *n.* A dwarf. — *a.* Small; diminutive.

Pyr'a-mid, *n.* A solid, having a rectilinear base, and its sides triangles having a common vertex. Pyramids.

Py-răm'id-al, } *a.* Having
Pyr'a-mid'ic-al, } the form of a pyramid.

Pyre, *n.* A funeral pile.

Pyr'i-fôrm, *a.* Having the form of a pear.

†**Py-rī'tēs,** *n.* A combination of sulphur with iron, copper, cobalt, or nickel.

Pyr'o-lĭg'ne-oŭs, } *a.* Pro-
Pyr'o-lĭg'nic, } duced by the distillation of wood.

Py-rŏl'o-ġy, *n.* Science of heat; a treatise on heat, latent and sensible. [by fire.

Pyr'o-măn'çy, *n.* Divination

Py-rŏm'e-ter, *n.* An instrument for measuring degrees of heat above those indicated by a mercurial thermometer.

Pyr'o-tĕch'nic, *a.* Relating to fire-works, or to the art of forming them.

Pyr'o-tĕch'nics, } *n.* Art of
Pyr'o-tĕch'ny, } making fire-works, as rockets, &c.

Pyr'o-tĕch'nist, *n.* One skilled in pyrotechuy; a manufacturer of fire-works.

Pyr'rhic (pĭr'rĭk), *n.* A metrical foot of two short syllables; an ancient military dance.

Pyr'rho-nĭsm, *n.* Universal doubt or skepticism.

Pyth'a-gō're-an, or **Py-thăġ'o-rē'an,** *a.* Pertaining to Pythagoras, an ancient philosopher, or to the doctrines he taught.

Pyth'i-an, *a.* Relating to the Pythoness, or to certain games celebrated at Delphi.

Pyth'o-ness, *n.* A priestess who gave oracular answers at Delphi, in Greece.

Pyx(140), *n.* Among *Roman Catholics,* the box in which the consecrated host is kept; a box used at the English mint for certain sample coins taken for a trial of the weight and fineness of metal.

Q.

Quăck (5), v. i. To cry like a duck; to boast. — n. A pretender to medical skill. [quack.

Quăck′er-y, n. Practice of a

Quăd′ră-gĕs′ĭ-mȧ, n. Forty days of fast before Easter; Lent.

Quăd′ră-gĕs′ĭ-mal, a. Belonging to, or used in, Lent.

Quăd′ran-gle, n. A plane figure of 4 angles and 4 sides. Quadrangle.

Quăd-răn′gu-lar, a. Having four angles.

Quăd′rant (kwŏd′-), n. [Lat. *quadrans*, a fourth part, from *quatuor*, four.] Quarter of a circle; arc of 90°; an instrument for taking altitudes. [to a quadrant.

Quăd-răntʹal, a. Pertaining

Quăd′rat (kwŏd′-), n. A low piece of metal to make a blank space on the paper in printing.

Quăd′rate, a. Square; suited. — n. A square.

Quăd′rāte, v. t. To square; to fit; to suit. [a square.

Quăd-răt′ic. a. Pertaining to

Quăd′ra-tūre, n. A square; the finding of a square having the same area as a given curvilinear figure.

Quăd-rĕn′ni-al, a. Happening once in four years.

Quăd′ri-lăt′er-al, a. Having four sides and hence four angles. — n. Quadrilateral. A plane figure having four sides.

Qua-drĭlleʹ (kwa-drĭlʹ or ka-drĭlʹ), n. A kind of dance; a game at cards.

Quăd-rĭlʹlion, n. A million involved to the fourth power; in America, a thousand trillions

Quăd-rĭpʹar-tīte, a. Consisting of four parts.

Quădʹri-sȳlʹla-ble, n. A word of four syllables.

Quăd′ri-vălve, n. One of a set of four leaves serving for a door.

Quăd-roon′, n. The offspring of a mulatto and a white person.

Quăd-ruʹma-noŭs, a. Having four feet that take the place of hands.

Quăd′ru-pĕd, n. An animal having four feet.

Quăd′ru-ple, a. Fourfold. — v. t. To increase fourfold.

Quăd-ruʹpli-cate, a. Fourfold. [make fourfold.

Quăd-ruʹpli-cāte, v. t. To

Quăd-ruʹpli-cāʹtion, n. A making fourfold.

Quăff (123), v. t. To drink largely or copiously of.

Quăgʹgy, a. Soft, wet, and yielding to the feet.

Quăgʹmire, n. Soft, wet land that shakes under the feet.

Quaʹhaug (kwawʹhog), n. A species of clam.

Quāil (99), n. A gallinaceous bird; in the United States, the ruffed grouse. — v. t. or i. To become quelled; to shrink; to cower.

Quāint, a. Artificially elegant; odd and antique. — SYN. Strange; whimsical; fanciful; singular; queer.

Quāintʹly, adv. Ingeniously; fancifully; oddly.

Quāintʹness, n. State of being quaint; oddness.

Quāke, v. i. To shake. — n. A shake; a tremulous agitation; a shudder.

Quākʹer, n. One of the society of Friends.

Quākʹer-ĭsm, n. System of the Quakers.

Qualʹi-fī′a-ble (135), a. Capable of being abated or modified; abatable.

Qualʹi-fi-cāʹtion, n. That which qualifies; legal requisite; endowment; accomplishment; restriction; modification.

Qualʹi-fīʹer, n. One who, or that which, qualifies.

Qualʹi-fȳ, v. t. [Lat. *qualificare*, fr. *qualis*, such, and *facere*, to make.] To fit; to prepare; to modify; to limit; to abate; to restrict.

Qualʹi-ty, n. Nature; character; distinguishing property; attribute; high rank.

Quālm (kwäm), n. Sudden illness; nausea; a throe; scruple of conscience.

Quālmʹish (kwämʹ-), a. Affected with sickness at the stomach.

Quănʹda-ry, or **Quăn-dāʹry**, n. State of difficulty or perplexity; uncertainty.

Quănʹti-ty, n. Quality of being measurable; a certain (often a large) extent, sum, or portion. — SYN. Weight; bulk; measure; amount.

Quănʹtum (kwŏnʹtum), n. A quantity; amount.

Quărʹan-tīne (-teen), n. Prohibition of intercourse with the shore, to which an infected ship is subjected.

Quărʹrel (kwŏrʹrel, 130), n. A breach of friendship; an angry contest. — v. i. To dispute; to find fault.

Quărʹrel-sŏme, a. Inclined to quarrel; contentious.

Quărʹry.(kwŏrʹrȳ), n. A mine where stones are cut for building or other purposes; game. — v. t. To dig or take from a quarry.

Quărt. n. Fourth of a gallon.

Quărʹtan, a. Designating a fourth. — n. An ague occurring every fourth day.

Quărʹter, n. A fourth part of any thing; 8 bushels; 3 months; a region; mercy shown to an enemy; (pl.) A station occupied by troops; lodgings. — v. t. To divide into four parts; to lodge, as soldiers.

Quărʹter-dāy, n. The day that completes the term of three months; a day on which rent becomes due.

Quărʹter-dĕck, n. Deck of a ship from the mainmast to the stern.

Quărʹter-ly, a. Happening every three months. — adv. Once in the quarter of a year. — n. A work published four times a year.

Quărʹter-măsʹter, n. An officer who regulates the quarters, provisions, &c., of an army.

Quărʹtern, n. Fourth part of

sŏn, ôr, dọ, wọlf, tọ̄ọ, tọ̆ọk; ûrn, ruẹ, pụll; ç, ġ, soft; c, g̱, hard; aṣ; exist; ṇ as ng; this.

QUARTERSTAFF 244 QUIZZICAL

a plot ; a loaf weighing about four pounds.
Quar'ter-staff, *n.* A stout staff once used as a weapon of defense.
Quar-tette', } *n.* A musical
Quar-tet', } composition in four parts, or the four persons who perform them.
Quar'tile, *n.* An aspect of the planets when they are distant from each other 90°.
Quar'to, *n.* (*pl.* **Quar'tos**, 141.) [Lat., fr. *quartus*, the fourth.] A book in which each sheet is folded into four leaves. — *a.* Having four leaves to a sheet.
Quartz (kwôrts), *n.* Pure silex.
Quash (kwŏsh), *v. t.* To crush ; to subdue ; to annul.
Quas-sā'tion, *n.* A shaking.
Quas'si-a (kwŏsh'i-a or kwăsh'i-à), *n.* A bitter medicinal wood. [of four.
Qua-ter'na-ry, *a.* Consisting
Qua-ter'ni-on, *n.* The number four ; a set of four persons or things.
Qua'ver (129), *v. i.* To shake the voice. — *n.* A shake of the voice ; an eighth note.
Quay (kē), *n.* A mole or bank by the water ; a wharf.
Quay'age (kē'ej), *n.* Money paid for the use of a quay.
Queach'y, *a.* Shaking, as a bog. [slut.
Quean, *n.* A low woman ; a
Quea'sy, *a.* Squeamish ; sick.
Queen, *n.* The consort of a king ; a female sovereign.
Queen'-dow'a-ger, *n.* The widow of a king.
Queer, *a.* Odd ; strange ; singular ; quaint. [ly.
Queer'ly, *adv.* Oddly ; quaint-
Queer'ness, *n.* Oddity ; singularity ; quaintness.
Quell (123), *v. t.* [Allied to *kill*.] To crush ; to subdue ; to put down ; to allay ; to appease.
Quench, *v. t.* To extinguish ; to repress ; to allay.
Quench'a-ble, *a.* Admitting of being quenched.
Quer'cit-ron, *n.* Dyer's oak and the bark.
Que'rist, *n.* One who inquires.
Quern, *n.* A hand-mill for grinding grain.
Quer'u-lous, *a.* Habitually complaining.
Quer'u-lous-ness, *n.* Disposition to complain.
Que'ry (93, 141), *n.* A question ; inquiry. — *v. t.* To ask questions about.

Quest, *n.* Act of seeking ; search ; request.
Ques'tion (kwĕst'yun), *n.* Act of asking ; inquiry ; doubt. — *v. t.* To ask ; to interrogate : to doubt.
Ques'tion-a-ble, *a.* Doubtful ; uncertain ; suspicious.
Ques'tion-er, *n.* One who asks questions ; an inquirer.
Ques'tion-less, *a.* Doubtless.
Quib'ble, *n.* An evasion of the truth ; a cavil ; a pun ; a low concert. — *v. t.* To evade the point ; to pun.
Quib'bler, *n.* One who quibbles ; a punster.
Quick, *a.* Moving or acting with celerity ; living. — SYN. Swift ; speedy. — *adv.* Soon ; hastily. — *n.* Any sensible part ; living flesh.
Quick'en (kwĭk'n), *v. t.* To make alive ; to vivify ; to make quick or rapid.
Quick'lime, *n.* Lime unslacked. [time.
Quick'ly, *adv.* In a short
Quick'ness, *n.* Speed ; haste.
Quick'-sand, *n.* A mass of loose or moving sand mixed with water.
Quick'set, *n.* A living shrub, set to grow, as for a hedge. — *a.* Made of quickset.
Quick'sil-ver, *n.* Mercury.
Quid, *n.* A piece of tobacco for chewing ; a cud. [ty.
Quid'di-ty, *n.* A trifling nice-
Quid'dle, *v. i.* To waste time in trifling employments.
Quid'nunc, *n.* One curious to know every thing that passes ; a gossip.
Qui-es'cence, *n.* Rest ; repose ; silence. [lent.
Qui-es'cent, *a.* At rest ; si-
Qui'et, *a.* Free from motion or disturbance. — SYN. Still ; calm ; unmolested ; tranquil. — *n.* Rest ; tranquillity. — *v. t.* To stop motion in ; to calm ; to lull.
Qui'et-ism, *n.* Peace of mind.
Qui'et-ist, *n.* One of a sect who maintained that religion consists in repose of the mind, employed in contemplating God.
Qui'et-ly, *adv.* Calmly.
Qui'et-ness, *n.* State of being quiet. [tranquillity.
Qui-e-tūde (118), *n.* Rest ;
Qui-ē'tus, *n.* Final discharge ; repose ; death.
Quill, *n.* A large, strong feather ; spine of a porcupine ; a piece of reed. — *v. t.*

To plait or form with ridges, like quills.
Quilt, *n.* A padded cover for a bed. — *v. t.* To stitch together with some warm substance between.
Qui'na-ry, *a.* Consisting of five ; arranged by fives.
Quince, *n.* [From *Cydonia* in Crete.] A small tree and its fruit.
Qui'nine, or **Qui-nīne'**, *n.* An alkaloid obtained from cinchona.
†**Quin'qua-gĕs'i-mà**, *n.* A Sunday about 50 days before Easter. [fire angles.
Quin-quăn'gu-lar, *a.* Having
Quin-quen'ni-al, *a.* Occurring once in five years.
Quin'sy, *n.* Inflammation of the tonsils or throat.
Quint, *n.* A sequence of five, at cards.
Quint'al, *n.* A weight of 100 or 112 pounds.
Quin'tan, *n.* A fever, the paroxysms of which return every fifth day.
Quin-tes'sence, *n.* Fifth or highest essence ; best or essential part.
Quin-tet', } *n.* A musical
Quin-tette' } composition for five voices or instruments.
Quin'tu-ple, *a.* Fivefold. — *v. t.* To make fivefold.
Quip, *n.* A sarcastic taunt. — *v. t.* or *i.* (129) To taunt.
Quire, *n.* 24 sheets of paper.
Quirk, *n.* A sudden turn ; an artful evasion ; a retort.
Quit (129), *v. t.* To leave ; to forsake. — *a.* Clear ; released ; free ; absolved.
Quit'claim, *n.* Relinquishment of a claim ; a deed of release. — *v. t.* To release or relinquish a claim to by deed.
Quite, *adv.* Entirely : wholly ; completely ; considerably.
Quit'rent, *n.* A rent by which a tenant is discharged from all other service.
Quit'tance, *n.* Discharge from a debt ; repayment.
Quiv'er, *n.* A case for arrows. — *v. t.* To shake ; to tremble ; to shiver.
Quix-ot'ic, *a.* Romantic to extravagance.
Quix'ot-ism, *n.* Romantic and absurd notions.
Quiz (125, 129), *n.* A riddle ; a puzzle ; an odd fellow. — *v. t.* To puzzle ; to make sport of by deceiving ; to peer at.
Quiz'zic-al, *a.* Comical.

ă, ĕ, ĭ, ŏ, ŭ, y̆, *long* ; ă, ĕ, ĭ, ŏ, ŭ, y̆, *short* ; cāre, cär, ásk, all, what ; ēre, veil, tẽrm ; pīque, firm ;

Quoin (kwoin *or* koin), *n.* A corner; a wedge.
Quoit, *n.* A horse-shoe, flat stone, or the like, for pitching at a fixed object. — *v. i.* To play at quoits.
Quon'dam, *a.* Former.
Quo'rum, *n.* A bench of justices; a sufficient number for transacting business.

Quo'tà, *n.* A share; proportional part.
Quo'ta-ble, *a.* Capable of being quoted.
Quo-ta'tion, *n.* A passage cited.
Quōte, *v. t.* To cite or adduce, as the words of another.
Quōth (kwōth *or* kwăth), *v. i.* To say; to speak; — used only in the first and third persons in the past tense.
Quo-tid'i-an, *a.* Occurring daily. — *n.* A fever recurring daily.
Quō'tient (kwō'shent), *n.* [Lat. *quoties*, how many times.] The number resulting from the division of one number by another.

R.

Răb'bet, *v. t.* To cut or pare down, as the edge of a board, for lapping. — *n.* A groove in the side of a board.
Răb'bī (*or* -bĭ, 149), *n.* [Heb. *rabi*, my master.] A Jewish teacher or doctor of the law.
Răb'bin, *n.* Same as *Rabbi*.
Rab-bin'ic, } *a.* Pertaining
Rab-bin'ic-al, } to rabbins.
Răb'bit, *n.* A small burrowing animal resembling the hare, but smaller.
Răb'ble, *n.* A tumultuous crowd; a mob. [mad.
Răb'id, *a.* Furious; raging;
Răb'id-ness, *n.* State of being rabid; madness.
Rac-cōōn', *n.* A wild animal of North America, allied to the bear.
Rāçe (140), *n.* A running in competition; a course; a breed; a family; a peculiar flavor. — *v. i.* To run or contend in running.
Rāçe'-hôrse, } *n.* A horse
Rāç'er, } kept for running in contest.
Ra-çēme', *n.* A cluster of flowers arranged along a stem.
Rā'çi-ness (135), *n.* The quality of being racy.
Răck (127), *n.* An engine of torture; extreme pain; a framework on which things are laid; thin, flying clouds. — *v. i.* To torture; to strain; to draw off from the lees. — *v. i.* To move or travel with a quick amble.
Răck'er, *n.* One who torments; a horse that racks, or ambles.

Răck'et, *n.* A clattering noise; a frame used for catching or striking a ball; a snow-shoe.
Răck'-rĕnt, *n.* An annual rent raised to the utmost.
Rā'çy, *a.* Tasting of the soil; flavorous; fresh; distinctive; peculiar and piquant.
Rā'di-al, *a.* Pertaining to a radius; pertaining to one of the bones of the fore-arm.
Rā'di-ance, *n.* Sparkling brightness; brilliancy.
Rā'di-ant, *a.* Emitting rays; shining; sparkling.
Rā'di-āte, *v. i. or t.* To emit rays; to enlighten. [rays.
Rā-di-ā'tion, *n.* Emission of
Rā'di-ā'tor, *n.* A body from which rays of light or heat emanate.
Răd'i-cal, *a.* Original; implanted by nature; fundamental. — *n.* Root of a word; an element; a thorough-going reformer.
Răd'i-cal-ism, *n.* Doctrine or spirit of a radical.
Răd'i-cal-ly, *adv.* Originally; fundamentally.
Răd-i-cā'tion, *n.* The process of taking root.
Răd'i-cle (-kl), *n.* The part of a seed which becomes a root.
Răd'ish, *n.* A plant and its pungent, edible root.
Rā'di-us, *n.* (*pl.* **Rā'di-ī**.) Half of the diameter of a circle.
†**Rā'dix**, *n.* (*pl.* **Răd'ī-çēs**.) A root, or primitive word. *Radius.*
Răff (123), *n.* Sweepings; refuse.
Răf'fle, *v. i.* To cast dice or draw lots for a prize. — *n.* A kind of lottery. [boards.
Răft, *n.* A float of timber or

Răft'er, *n.* One of the roof-timbers of a building.
Răg, *n.* A torn piece of cloth; (*pl.*) worn-out garments.
Răg'a-mŭf'fin, *n.* A paltry fellow; a mean wretch.
Rāge, *n.* Violent anger; fury; wrath. — *v. t.* To be in a fury; to fume.
Răg'ged (57), *a.* Torn into tatters; dressed in tatters.
Răg'ged-ness, *n.* State of being ragged.
Rāg'ing (133), *a.* Furious; violent. [of rags.
Răg'man (143), *n.* A collector
Ra-gout' (ra-gōō'), *n.* A highly seasoned dish.
Rāid, *n.* [A.-S. *rád*, a riding.] A hostile incursion, esp. of mounted men.
Rāil, *n.* A bar of wood or iron; a bird. — *v. t.* (130) To inclose with rails. — *v. i.* To utter reproach; to scoff.
Rāil'ing, *n.* Insulting language; a series of rails.
Rāil'ler-y (răl'ler-ỹ), *n.* Banter; good-humored pleasantry or slight satire.
Rāil'rōad, } *n.* A road laid
Rāil'wāy, } with iron rails.
Rāi'ment, *n.* Clothing in general; garments.
Rāin, *n.* Moisture falling from the clouds in drops. — *v. i.* To fall in drops from the clouds, as water.
Rāin'bōw, *n.* A many-colored arch formed by the refraction and reflection of the sun's rays in drops of rain; the iris.
Rāin'-gauge, *n.* An instrument for measuring the quantity of rain that falls in a given time.
Rāin'y, *a.* Attended or abounding with rain.
Rāise, *v. t.* To lift; to erect; to excite; to levy.

sŏn, ôr, dọ, wolf, tōō, tŏŏk; ûrn, rᵫe, pᵫll; ç, ġ, *soft*; c, g̃, *hard*; aş; eẋist; ɳ *as* ng; this

RAISIN 246 RATIO

Rāi'sin (rā'zn), *n.* A dried grape.

Rā'jah, or **Rä'jah**, *n.* In India, a native prince.

Rāke, *n.* A garden or farming tool; a libertine.—*v. t.* To collect with a rake; to sweep with cannon.

Rāk'ish, *a.* Lewd; debauched.

Ral'ly, *n.* Act of collecting disordered troops; banter.—*v. t.* (135) To attack with raillery; to banter; to reunite.—*v. i.* To come back to order.

Rām, *n.* A male sheep; a mechanical contrivance.—*v. t.* To drive or thrust with violence.

Rām'ble, *n.* A wandering about; an irregular excursion.—*v. i.* To rove hither and thither.—SYN. To roam; range; wander; stroll.

Rām'bler, *n.* One who rambles.

Rām'bling, *a.* Wandering.

Rām'i-fi-cā'tion, *n.* A branching; a subdivision.

Rām'i-fȳ, *v. t.* or *i.* [Lat. *ramus*, a branch, and *facere*, to make.] To separate into branches, as the stem of a plant; to branch.

Rām'mer, *n.* An instrument for ramming or driving.

Rā-mōse', *a.* Consisting or
Rā'moŭs, } full of branches; branchy.

Rāmp, *v. i.* To leap; to frisk.—*n.* A leap; a spring.

Rāmp'an-çy, *n.* Exuberance; extravagance.

Rāmp'ant, *a.* Exuberant; unrestrained; wanton; rearing.

Rām'pärt, *n.* A wall or mound round a place for defense.

Rām'rŏd, *n.* A rod used in loading a gun.

Rān, *imp.* of *Run*.

†**Ran-che'ro** (-chā'ro), *n.* A Mexican peasant employed on a rancho; a herdsman.

Rān'cho, } *n.* A rude hut for
Ranch, } herdsmen; a large farming establishment, or an establishment for rearing cattle and horses.

Rān'çid, *a.* Having a strong, sour smell; musty.

Ran-çid'i-ty, } *n.* A strong,
Rān'çid-ness, } sour smell; mustiness.

Rān'çor (155), *n.* Malignity; inveterate enmity.

Rān'çor-oŭs, *a.* Very spiteful; malignant; malevolent.

Rān'dom, *n.* Course without

definite direction.— *a.* Left to chance; done at hazard.

Răng, *old imp.* of *Ring*.

Rānge, *n.* A row or rank; excursion; extent; a cooking apparatus.— *v. t.* To place in order.— *v. i.* To rove at large; to be placed in order.

Rănk, *a.* Strong-scented; high-tasted; luxuriant.— *n.* A line of men; row; class; order; degree; dignity.— *v. t.* To place in a line; to dispose methodically.— *v. i.* To be ranged or set; to have a certain grade or dignity.

Rănk'le, *v. i.* To become inflamed or violent; to fester.

Rănk'ly, *adv.* With exuberant growth.

Rănk'ness, *n.* A strong scent; luxuriance; rancidity.

Răn'săck (127), *v. t.* To search thoroughly; to pillage.

Răn'sŏm, *n.* The price paid to redeem a person or goods from an enemy.— *v. t.* To redeem from captivity, punishment, or forfeit, by a price.

Rănt, *n.* Boisterous, empty declamation.— *v. i.* To rave.

Rănt'er, *n.* A boisterous declaimer; a noisy talker.

Răp, *n.* A quick, smart blow.— *v. i.* or *t.* (129) To strike with a quick, sharp blow; to snatch away; to transport.

Ra-pā'çioŭs, *a.* Inclined to plunder; greedy; ravenous.

Ra-pā'çioŭs-ly, *adv.* Ravenously; by rapine.

Ra-păç'i-ty, *n.* Disposition to plunder; exorbitaut covetousness; ravenousness.

Rāpe, *n.* A seizing by violence; carnal knowledge by force; a plant of the cabbage tribe.

Răp'id, *a.* Swift; quick.

Ra-pĭd'i-ty, *n.* Swiftness of motion; velocity; haste.

Răp'id-ly, *adv.* Swiftly; with quick motion.

Răp'idș, *n. pl.* Sudden descent of a stream without actual water fall.

Rā'pi-er, *n.* A light sword with a very narrow blade.

Răp'ĭne, *n.* Act of plundering; spoliation; pillage.

Rap-pee', *n.* A kind of snuff.

Răp'per, *n.* One who raps; knocker of a door.

Răpt, *a.* Transported in ecstasy; ravished.

Răpt'ūre, *n.* Extreme joy; ecstasy; bliss.

Răpt'ūr-oŭs, *a.* Causing rapture; ecstatic; blissful.

Râre, *a.* Thin; scattered; nearly raw; underdone.

Râr'e-făç'tion, *n.* Act or process of rarefying; expansion of bodies.

Râr'e-fī'a-ble, *a.* Capable of being rarefied.

Râr'e-fȳ (118), *v. t.* or *i.* To make or become thin or rare.

Râre'ly, *adv.* Seldom; not often; finely; nicely.

Râre'ness, } *n.* State of being
Râr'i-ty, } rare; uncommonness; thinness.

Râre'rīpe, *a.* Early ripe.— *n.* An early fruit.

Răs'cal, *n.* A dishonest man; a rogue.— *a.* Mean; low; dishonest. [low, mean wretch.

Ras-căl'ion (-kăl'yun), *n.* A

Ras-căl'i-ty, *n.* Mean dishonesty; base fraud; villainy.

Răs'cal-ly, *a.* Like a rascal; dishonest; trickish.

Rāșe, *v. t.* To erase.

Răsh, *a.* Excessively hasty or incautious.— SYN. Adventurous; foolhardy; headlong.

Răsh'er, *n.* A thin slice of bacon. [thought; hastily.

Răsh'ly, *adv.* Without fore-

Răsh'ness, *n.* Inconsiderate haste; heedlessness; temerity.

Răsp, *n.* A kind of coarse file; a grater.— *v. t.* To rub or grate with a rasp.

Răsp'ber-ry (răz'-), *n.* A kind of berry, and the shrub that bears it.

Rāș'ūre rŭzh'ŭr), *n.* Erasure.

Răt, *n.* A well-known animal that infests houses and ships.

Răt'a-ble (133), *a.* Liable to be taxed or rated.

Răt'a-fī'a, *n.* A fine spirituous liquor, flavored with fruit.

Ra-tăn', *n.* See *Rattan*.

Rătch, *n.* A ratchet.

Rătch'et, *n.* A bar that falls into the teeth of a wheel or rack; a pawl.

Rătch'et-wheel, *n.* A toothed wheel with a lever and ratchet for moving it forward.

Rāte, *n.* A price; proportion; degree; value; tax.— *v. t.* To value; to tax; to scold.— *v. i.* To have rank.

Rāth'er, *adv.* More willingly.

Răt'i-fi-cā'tion, *n.* Act of ratifying; a sanctioning.

Răt'i-fȳ 135, *v. t.* [Lat. *ratus*, firm, and *facere*, to make.] To sanction; to settle; to confirm.

Rā'ti-o rā'shĭ-o *or* rā'sho', *n.* Proportion; rate.

ā, ē, ī, ō, ū, ȳ, *long*; ă, ĕ, ĭ, ŏ, ŭ, ў, *short*; cāre, cär, åsk, all, what; ẽre, veil, tẽrm; pīque, fîrm;

Rā'ti-ŏç'ĭ-nā'tion (răsh'ĭ-ŏs'-ĭ-, n. Act of reasoning.
Rā'tion (or răsh'un), n. Allowance of provisions.
Rā'tion-al (răsh'un-al), n. Endowed with reason ; agreeable to reason.
Rā'tion-ā'le (răsh'un-), n. Detail of reasons.
Rā'tion-al-ist (răsh'un-), n. One who is guided solely by reason, especially in matters of religion.
Rā'tion-ăl'i-ty (răsh'un-), n. Quality of being reasonable.
Rā'tion-al-ly (răsh'un-), adv. Reasonably.
Ra-tōōn', n. A sprout from the root of sugar-cane which has been cut.
Răts'bāne, n. Poison for rats.
Rat-tăn', n. Stem of a cane or plant growing in India.
Rat-teen', n. A thick woolen stuff quilted. [a party.
Răt'ting, n. Act of deserting
Răt'tle, v. i. or t. To make a rapid succession of sharp sounds ; to clatter. — n. A rapid succession of sharp sounds ; a toy ; (pl.) the croup.
Răt'tle-snake, n. A poisonous serpent.
Rau'çi-ty, n. Harshness of sound ; hoarseness.
Răv'age, v. t. To lay waste. — SYN. To devastate ; waste ; sack ; spoil ; ruin. — n. Waste ; spoil ; ruin ; plunder.
Răv'a-ger, n. A plunderer.
Rāve, v. i. To be delirious ; to talk wildly. — n. Upper side-piece of timber of a cart.
Răv'el 58, 130), v. t. or i. To disentangle ; to take apart ; to entangle ; to involve.
Răve'lin (răv'lĭu), n. A detached work in fortification.
Rā'ven (-vn), n. A bird of a black color, allied to the crow, but larger.   Ravelin.
Răv'en (răv'n), v. i. To devour greedily. — n. Prey ; plunder ; rapine ; pillage.
Răv'en-oŭs, a. Voracious.
Răv'en-oŭs-ly, adv. With raging hunger ; voraciously.
Ra-vīne' (-vēēn'), n. A long, deep hollow between hills.
Rāv'ing, a. Furious.
Răv'ish, v. t. To carry away by force ; to transport with delight ; to know carnally by force. [ishes.
Răv'ish-er, n. One who ravishes.
Răv'ish-ment, n. Act of ravishing ; rapture ; ecstasy.
Raw, a. Not cooked ; crude ; unripe ; unmanufactured ; cold and damp ; chilly ; bare of skin ; sore.
Raw'bōned, a. Having little flesh on the bones.
Raw'hĕad, n. A specter.
Raw'ly, adv. Unskillfully ; without experience.
Raw'ness, n. State of being raw. — SYN. Unskillfulness ; crudeness ; chilliness.
Ray (140), n. A line or beam of light ; a fish. — v. t. To shoot forth. [dark.
Rāy'less, a. Without a ray ;
Rāze, v. t. To lay level with the ground ; to demolish.
Ra-zee', n. A ship of war cut down to an inferior rate. — v. t. (137) To reduce in size, as a vessel. [shaving.
Rā'zor, n. An instrument for
Răz'ūre, n. See Rasure.
Rēach, v. t. To extend to ; to arrive at. — v. i. To be extended. — n. Extent ; stretch ; expanse ; limit ; power ; effort to vomit.
Rē-ăct', v. i. To act or do over again.
Rē-ăc'tion, n. Counteraction ; action in opposition.
Rē-ăct'ĭve, a. Having
Rē-ăc'tion-a-ry, power to react ; tending to reaction.
Rēad, v. t. or i. [imp. & p. p. READ (rĕd).] To peruse ; to know fully ; to learn.
Rēad'a-ble, a. Fit to be read ; worth reading ; legible.
Rēad'er, n. One who reads.
Rēad'ĭ-ly, adv. Quickly ; with facility ; promptly.
Rēad'ĭ-ness, n. Willingness ; promptitude ; alacrity.
Rēad'ing, n. Perusal ; public recital ; interpretation of a passage ; variation in the text of an author.
Rē'ad-mis'sion (-mĭsh'un), n. Act of readmitting.
Rē'ad-mĭt' (129), v. t. To admit a second time or again.
Rēad'y, a. Prepared ; willing ; prompt ; near ; easy ; on the point or brink. [again.
Rē-af-firm', v. t. To affirm
Rē'al, a. [Low Lat. realis, fr. res, a thing.] Having positive existence ; relating to things fixed or permanent. — SYN. Actual ; true ; genuine.
Re-ăl'ĭ-ty, n. Certainty ; that which is real ; truth ; fact.
Rē'al-ĭ-zā'tion, n. Act of realizing, or making real.
Rē'al-īze, v. t. To bring into being or act ; to cause to seem real ; to make real ; to understand by experience. — v. i. To raise money.
Rē'al-ly, adv. In fact ; truly.
Rēalm, n. A royal jurisdiction ; province ; domain.
Rē'al-ty, n. Immobility ; fixed nature of property.
Rēam, n. A bundle of twenty quires of paper.
Rē-ăn'ĭ-māte, v. t. To restore to life ; to revive. [again.
Rē'an-nĕx', v. t. To annex
Rē̄ap (130), v. t. or i. To cut grain with a sickle ; to obtain ; to get ; to receive.
Rēap'er, n. One who reaps.
Rē'ap-pēar', v. i. To appear a second time or again.
Rē'ap-pēar'ançe, n. A second appearance. [again.
Rē'ap-point', v. t. To appoint
Rē'ap-point'ment, n. A second or new appointment.
Rēar, n. The part behind. — a. Hindmost. — v. t. To raise ; to bring up. — v. i. To rise up on the hind legs.
Rēar'-ăd'mĭ-ral, n. An officer next in rank after a vice-admiral.
Rēar'-guard, n. The body that marches in the rear.
Rēar'ward, n. The rear-guard ; latter part ; end.
Rē'as-çĕnd', v. i. To ascend or mount again.
Rēa'son (rē'zn), n. The faculty of judging, or its due exercise ; motive ; argument ; ground ; end ; cause. — v. i. or t. To argue rationally ; to debate.
Rēa'son-a-ble, a. Governed by reason ; rational ; just.
Rēa'son-a-ble-ness, n. Agreeableness to reason.
Rēa'son-a-bly, adv. Agreeably to reason ; moderately.
Rēa'son-er, n. One who reasons or argues.
Rēa'son-ing, n. Act of using the faculty of reason
Rē'as-sĕm'ble, v. To assemble again. [affirm again.
Rē'as-sĕrt', v. t. To assert or
Rē'as-sūme', v. t. To assume again ; to resume.
Rē'as-sŭr'ançe (-shụ̄r'-), n. Assurance or confirmation repeated.
Rē'as-sūre' (-shụ̄r'), v. t. To

REBATE 248 RECOMMITTAL

assure again; to free from fear. [duction.
Re-bāte', n. Abatement; de-
Re-bāte'ment, n. Abatement; deduction.
Rē'bec (127), n. A musical instrument formerly in use.
Rĕb'el, n. One who opposes lawful authority. — a. Acting in revolt; rebellious.
Re-bĕl' (129), v. i. To rise in opposition to lawful authority; to revolt.
Re-bĕll'ion (-yun), n. Open opposition to lawful authority.
Re-bĕll'ious, a. Engaged in rebellion.
Re-bound', v. i. To spring or start back. — n. Act of springing or flying back.
Re-bŭff' (138), n. A sudden check. — v. t. To check suddenly; to repel.
Rē-build', v. t. To build anew.
Re-būke', v. t. To chide; to reprove. — n. Reproof.
Rē'bus (140), n. [Lat., by things.] A kind of pictorial riddle. [pose by argument.
Re-bŭt', v. t. To repel; to op-
Re-bŭt'ter, n. Answer of a defendant to a plaintiff's surrejoinder.
Re-cāll', v. t. To call or take back; to revoke. — n. A calling back; revocation.
Re-cănt', v. t. To retract, as an opinion or declaration.
Rē'ean-tā'tion, n. Act of recanting; retraction.
Rē'ca-pĭt'u-lāte, v. t. To repeat in a summary way. — SYN. To reiterate; recite; rehearse.
Rē'ca-pĭt'u-lā'tion, n. A summary; a recapitulating.
Rē'ca-pĭt'u-la-to-ry, a. Repeating again.
Rē-căp'tion, n. A reprisal.
Rē-căpt'ūre, n. Act of retaking; a prize retaken. — v. t. To retake, as a prize.
Rē-căst', v. t. [imp. & p. p. RECAST.] To cast, mold, or compute a second time.
Re-cēde' v. i. or t. To draw back; to retreat; to desist.
Re-çēipt' (-sēet'), n. Reception; a writing to show that something has been received. — v. t. To give a written acknowledgment for something received.
Re-çēiv'a-ble (133), a. Capable of being received.
Re-çēive', v. t. To take, as something that is offered.
Re-çēiv'er, n. One who receives; a kind of chemical vessel.
Rē'çen-çy, n. State of being recent; newness; freshness.
Re-çēn'sion. n. Examination; editorial review of a text; an edited version.
Rē'çent, n. New; late; fresh.
Rē'çent-ly, adv. Newly; lately. [freshness; lateness.
Rē'çent-ness, n. Newness;
Re-çĕp'ta-cle (108), n. A place to receive things in.
Rĕç'ep-tāc'u-lar, a. Relating to a receptacle, or growing on it.
Re-çĕp'ti-ble, a. Admitting reception; receivable.
Re-çĕp'tion, n. Act of receiving; admission; an informal or general entertainment.
Re-çĕp'tive, a. Having the quality of receiving.
Re-çĕss', n. A withdrawing; privacy; retreat; intermission or suspension; a niche or alcove. [of ceding back.
Re-çĕs'sion (-sĕsh'un), n. Act
†Recherché (rŭ-shâr'shā'), a. Sought out with care; nice.
Rĕç'i-pe, n. A prescription, esp. a medical prescription.
Re-çĭp'i-ent, n. One who receives; a receiver.
Re-çĭp'ro-cal, a. Mutually interchangeable; acting in return; given and received.
Re-çĭp'ro-cal-ly, adv. So that each affects and is affected by the other.
Re-çĭp'ro-cāte (118), v. t. or i. To act by turns; to alternate.
Re-çĭp'ro-cā'tion, n. A giving and receiving in return.
Rĕç'i-prŏç'i-ty, n. Reciprocal obligations, advantages, or rights.
Re-çĭş'ion (-sĭzh'un), n. The act of cutting off.
Re-çīt'al (133), n. Repetition of words of another, or of a writing. — SYN. Rehearsal; recitation; account.
Rĕç'i-tā'tion, n. Rehearsal; repetition; a public reading.
Rĕç'i-ta-tīve', n. A kind of musical recitation.
Re-çīte', v. t. or i. To tell over; to repeat; to rehearse.
Rĕck, v. i. To take heed; to care; to regard.
Rĕck'less, a. Careless of consequences; heedless.
Rĕck'less-ness. n. Heedlessness; carelessness.
Rĕck'on (rĕk'n), v. t. or i. To number; to compute; to esteem.
Rĕck'on-er, n. One who computes.
Rĕck'on-ing, n. Computation; bill of expenses.
Re-clāim', v. t. [Lat. reclamare, fr. re, again, back, and clamare, to call.] To recover, to reform; to restore to use, as submerged land.
Re-clāim'a-ble, a. Capable of being reclaimed. [reclaims.
Re-clāim'ant, n. One who
Rēç'la-mā'tion, n. Recovery; demand of something to be restored. [clining.
Rēç'li-nā'tion, n. Act of re-
Ro-clīne', v. t. or i. To lean back; to rest; to repose.
Re-clūse', a. Living in retirement; solitary. — n. One who lives in retirement from society. [tirement.
Re-elū'şion, n. State of re-
Re-elū'şive, a. Affording retirement or seclusion.
Rēç'og-nī'tion (-nĭsh'un), n. Act of recognizing; acknowledgment; avowal.
Rēç'og-nĭz'a-ble, or Re-cŏg'ni-za-ble, a. Capable of being recognized or acknowledged.
Re-cŏg'ni-zănçe, n. Bond of record; an obligation.
Rĕç'og-nīze, v. t. To know again; to acknowledge.
Re-cŏg'ni-gŏr' (or -kŏn'-), n. One who enters into a recognizance.
Re-coil', v. i. To start or fall back. — n. A movement backward; resilience.
Rē-coin', v. t. To coin again.
Rē-coin'age, n. A coining again; that which is recoined. [or bring to mind.
Rĕç'ol-lĕct', v. t. To recall
Rē'ol-lĕct', v. t. To collect again.
Rĕç'ol-lĕc'tion, n. A recalling to remembrance.
Rē'com-mĕnçe, v. t. To commence or begin anew.
Rĕç'om-mĕnd', v. t. To commend to the favorable notice of another; to praise; to advise.
Rĕç'om-mend-ā'tion, n. Act of praising; that which commends to favor; commendation; act of advising.
Rĕç'om-mĕnd'a-to-ry, a. Serving to recommend.
Rē'com-mĭt', v. t. To commit anew.
Rē'com-mĭt'ment,) n. A
Rē'com-mĭt'tal, } second or renewed commitment.

ā, ē, ī, ō, ū, ȳ, long; ă, ĕ, ĭ, ŏ, ŭ, ў, short; câre, cär, ȧsk, ạll, whạt; ẽre, vẽil, tẽrm; p:que, fĭrm;

RECOMPENSE 249 REDUNDANT

Rĕc'om-pĕnse, *n.* Reward; compensation; pay.—*v. t.* To repay; to reward.

Rē'com-pōṣe', *v. t.* To compose anew; to settle anew.

Rĕc'on-çĭl'a-ble, *a.* Capable of being reconciled; adjusted, or made to agree.

Rĕc'on-çīle', *v. t.* To conciliate anew; to make consistent; to adjust; to settle.

Rĕc'on-çīle'ment, *n.* Act of reconciling, or state of being reconciled; reconciliation.

Rĕc'on-çĭl'i-ā'tion, *n.* Renewal of friendship.

Rĕc'on-dīte, *a.* Secret; hidden; abstruse; profound.

Rē'con-dŭct', *v. t.* To conduct back.

Re-cŏn'nais-sănçe, } *n.* Examination of a tract of country, usually for warlike purposes.
Re-cŏn'nois-sănçe, }

Rē'con-noi'ter, } *v. t.* To survey; to view; to examine.
Rē'con-noi'tre, }

Re-cŏn'quer (-kŏŋk'er), *v. t.* To conquer again; to recover; to regain.

Rē'con-sĭd'er, *v. t.* To consider again; to review.

Rē'con-sĭd'er-ā'tion, *n.* Renewed consideration.

Rē'con-vey', *v. t.* To convey back. [enroll.

Re-cŏrd', *v. t.* To register; to

Rĕc'ord, *n.* Register; authentic memorial.

Re-cŏrd'er, *n.* One who records or keeps records.

Re-coũnt', *v. t.* To relate in detail; to rehearse.

Re-coũrse', *n.* Application, as for help.

Re-cŏv'er (-kŭv'er), *v. t.* To regain; to win back.—*v. i.* To regain health.

Re-cŏv'er-a-ble, *a.* Capable of being recovered.

Re-cŏv'er-y, *n.* Act of recovering; restoration.

Rĕc're-ant, *a.* Apostate; false; cowardly.—*n.* An apostate; a coward.

Rĕc're-āte, *v. t.* To refresh after labor; to amuse.

Rē'cre-āte', *v. t.* To create or form anew.

Rĕc're-ā'tion, *n.* Amusement; relief from toil.

Rĕc're-ā'tĭve, *a.* Tending to refresh after labor.

Rĕc're-ment, *n.* Refuse; dross; scoria.

Rĕc're-mĕnt'al } (-tĭsh'-

Rĕc're-men-tĭ'tioŭs } us), *a.* Drossy; refuse; superfluous.

Re-crĭm'i-nāte, *v. t.* To accuse in return.

Re-crĭm'i-nā'tion, *n.* Return of one accusation with another; a counter-accusation.

Re-crĭm'i-nā'tĭve, } *a.* Re-
Re-crĭm'i-nā'to-ry, } torting accusation.

Rē-crŏss', *v. t.* To cross again.

Re-cruit', *v. i.* To gain new supplies of any thing wasted.—*v. t.* To supply deficiency in, as of troops.—*n.* A newly-enlisted soldier.

Rĕct'ăn-gle, *n.* A right angled parallelogram. Rectangle.

Rect-ăn'gu-lar, *a.* Having right angles.

Rĕc'ti-fi-cā'tion, *n.* Act of correcting; process of refining.

Rĕc'ti-fī'er, *n.* One who, or that which, rectifies.

Rĕc'ti-fȳ (135), *v. t.* [Lat. *rectus*, right, and *facere*, to make.] To correct; to refine by repeated distillation.

Rĕc'ti-lĭn'e-al, } *a.* Consisting
Rĕc'ti-lĭn'e-ar, } of right lines.

Rĕc'ti-tūde, *n.* Uprightness.

Rĕc'tor, *n.* A minister of a parish; ruler or governor.

Rĕc'tor-ship, *n.* The rank or office of a rector.

Rĕc'tor-y, *n.* The mansion of a rector; a parish church.

Rĕc'tum, *n.* The terminal part of the large intestines.

Re-cŭm'ben-çy, *n.* A lying down; repose.

Re-cŭm'bent, *a.* Reclining; leaning. [health.

Re-cū'per-āte, *v.* To recover

Re-cū'per-a-tĭve, *a.* Pertaining to, or tending to, recovery.

Re-cũr' (120), *v. i.* To resort; to return again or repeatedly; to come back.

Re-cũr'rençe, *n.* A recurring; return; resort.

Re-cũr'rent, *a.* Running back.

Re-cũrv'ate, *a.* Bent backward or outward.

Re-cū'san-çy, *n.* Non-conformity.

Re-cū'sant, *a.* Refusing to conform.—*n.* One who refuses to conform to the established church.

Rĕd, *a.* Of a bright color; like blood.—*n.* Color of blood, or a tint resembling it.

Re-dăn', *n.* A kind of rampart or fortification.

Rĕd'den, *v. t.* or *i.* To make or grow red; to blush.

Rĕd'dish, *a.* Somewhat red.

Red-dĭ'tion (-dĭsh'un), *n.* Restitution; surrender.

Re-deem', *v. t.* To purchase back; to ransom; to rescue.

Re-deem'a-ble, *a.* Capable of being redeemed.

Re-deem'er, *n.* One who ransoms; *specifically*, the Savior.

Re-dĕmp'tion (81), *n.* Act of redeeming; repurchase; ransom; rescue; deliverance.

Re-dĕmp'tion-er, *n.* One who redeems himself.

Re-dĕmp'to-ry, *a.* Serving or tending to redeem.

Rĕd'-gŭm, *n.* An eruption of red pimples in children.

Rĕd'-hŏt, *a.* Heated to redness.

Re-din'te-grā'tion, *n.* Restoration to wholeness or entireness. [new.

Re-din'te-grāte, *v. t.* To make

Rĕd'ness, *n.* The quality of being red; red color.

Rĕd'o-lençe, *n.* Sweet scent.

Rĕd'o-lent, *a.* Diffusing a sweet scent; odorous.

Re-doũb'le (-dŭb'l), *v. t.* To increase by doubling.

Re-doubt' (-dowt'), *n.* An outwork within another outwork in fortifications.

Re-doubt'a-ble (-dowt'-), *a.* Formidable; valiant.

Re-dound', *v. i.* To conduce; to result; to contribute.

Re-drĕss', *v. t.* To set right; to deliver from wrongs; to make amends for; to remedy.—*n.* Deliverance from wrong or injury.

Re-drĕss'ĭve, *a.* Affording redress. [red-hot.

Rĕd'-shŏrt, *a.* Brittle when

Rĕd'tŏp, *n.* A kind of grass.

Re-dūçe', *v. t.* [Lat. *reducere*, fr. *re*, again, back, and *ducere*, to lead.] To convert; to lower; to subdue; to change without alteration of value. [being reduced.

Re-dū'çi-ble, *a.* Capable of

Re-dŭc'tion, *n.* Act of reducing; the changing of numbers from one denomination to another without altering their value.

Re-dŭc'tĭve, *a.* Tending, or having power, to reduce.

Re-dŭn'dançe, } *n.* Superflu-
Re-dŭn'dan-çy, } ous quantity; excess.

Re-dŭn'dant, *a.* Superabundant; exuberant.

---

sŏn, ôr, dọ, wọlf, tōo, tŏŏk; ûrn, rụe, pụll; ç, ġ, *soft*; ¢, g, *hard*; aṣ; eχist;.ŋ *as* ng; this.
11 *

Re-dŭn'dant-ly, *adv.* Superfluously; superabundantly.
Re-dū'pli-câte, *v. t.* To redouble; to multiply; to repeat the first letter or letters of. [redoubling.
Re-dū'pli-câ'tion, *n.* Act of
Rē-ĕch'o, *v. t. or i.* To echo back again. — *n.* (140) Echo of an echo; a repeated echo.
Reed, *n.* A hollow jointed stalk; a musical pipe.
Reed'y, *a.* Full of reeds.
Reef, *v. t.* To draw in and fold up, as sails. — *n.* Folded portion of a sail; a chain of rocks lying at or near the surface of water.
Reek, *n.* Steam; vapor; smoke. — *v. i.* To send forth steam or vapor. [foul.
Reek'y, *a.* Smoky; dark;
Reel, *n.* A frame to wind yarn or thread on; a dance. — *v. i. or t.* To wind on a reel; to stagger.
Rē-e-lĕct', *v. t.* To elect again. [repeated election.
Rē-e-lĕc'tion, *n.* A second or
Rē-ĕl'i-gi-ble, *a.* Capable of being re-elected.
Rē'-em-bärk', *v. t. or i.* To embark again. [anew.
Rē'-en-ăct', *v. t.* To enact
Rē'-en-ăct'ment, *n.* The renewal of a law.
Rē'-en-fôrçe', *v. t.* To strengthen with new force.
Rē'-en-fôrçe'ment, *n.* Additional supply, particularly of troops and ships.
Rē'-en-gāge', *v. t.* To engage or covenant a second time.
Rē'-en-list', *v. t. or i.* To enlist again. [again.
Rē-ĕn'ter, *v. t.* To enter
Rē-ĕn'trançe, *n.* Act of entering again. [tablish again.
Rē'-es-tăb'lish, *v. t.* To es-
Rē'-es-tăb'lish-ment, *n.* Act of establishing again.
Reeve, *v. t.* To pass the end of, as of a rope, through a block, or thimble, &c.
Rē'-ex-ăm'i-nā'tion, *n.* A repeated examination.
Rē'-ex-ăm'ine, *v. t.* To examine again or anew.
Rē'-ex-pôrt', *v. t.* To export again, as something imported. [a simple repast.
Re-fĕc'tion, *n.* Refreshment;
Re-fĕc'tive, *a.* Refreshing.
Re-fĕc'to-ry, *n.* A hall or room for refreshment.
Re-fẽr' (129), *v. t. or i.* To send back; to direct attention; to have recourse.

Rĕf'er-a-ble, *a.* Capable of being referred; assignable.
Rĕf'er-ee' (140), *n.* One to whom something is referred.
Rĕf'er-ençe, *n.* Act of referring; respect; relation.
Rĕf'er-ĕn'tial, *a.* Containing a reference.
Re-fẽr'ri-ble, *a.* Capable of being referred; referable.
Re-fīne', *v. t. or i.* To clear from impurities; to polish; to purify; to grow pure.
Re-fīned', *a.* Freed from extraneous matter. — SYN. Purified; polished; polite.
Re-fīne'ment, *n.* Act of refining; polish of manners.
Re-fīn'er, *n.* One who, or that which, refines.
Re-fīn'er-y, *n.* A place and apparatus for refining.
Re-fĭt', *v. t. or i.* To repair.
Re-flĕct', *v. t. or i.* [Lat. *reflectere*, fr. *re*, again, back, and *flectere*, to bend.] To bend or throw back; to consider attentively; to cast reproach.
Re-flĕc'tion (140), *n.* Act of reflecting; attentive consideration; censure; that which is produced by reflecting.
Re-flĕct'ive, *a.* Throwing back images; musing.
Re-flĕct'or, *n.* That which reflects; a polished surface.
Rē'flex, *a.* Directed backward; retroactive.
Re-flĕx'ive, *a.* Bending or bent backward. [back.
Rĕf'lu-ençe, *n.* A flowing
Rĕf'lu-ent, *a.* Flowing back; ebbing. [water; ebb.
Rē'flux, *n.* A flowing back of
Re-fôrm', *v. t.* To correct; to amend. — *n.* Amendment; reformation.
Rē-fôrm', *v. t.* To form anew.
Rĕf'or-mā'tion, *n.* Act of reforming; amendment.
Rē'for-mā'tion, *n.* Act of forming anew.
Re-fôrm'a-tive, *a.* Tending
Re-fôrm'a-to-ry, *a.* to produce reformation.
Re-fôrm'er, *n.* One who promotes reform.
Re-frăct', *v. t.* To break the direct course of.
Re-frăc'tion, *n.* Deviation from a direct course.
Re-frăct'ive, *a.* Having power to refract.
Re-frăc'to-ri-ness, *n.* Obstinacy.
Re-frăc'to-ry, *a.* Perverse; obstinate; contumacious.

Rĕf'ra-ga-ble, *a.* Capable of being refuted; refutable.
Re-frāin', *v. t. or i.* To abstain; to forbear. — *n.* Burden of a song.
Re-frăn'gi-bil'i-ty, *n.* Capability of being refracted.
Re-frăn'gi-ble, *a.* Capable of being refracted.
Re-frĕsh', *v. t.* To revive; to cool; to relieve. [cooling.
Re-frĕsh'ing, *a.* Reviving;
Re-frĕsh'ment, *n.* Act of refreshing; that which refreshes; relief; rest; food.
Re-frĭg'er-ant, *a.* Cooling.
Re-frĭg'er-āte, *v. t.* To cool.
Re-frĭg'er-ā'tion, *n.* A cooling; abatement of heat.
Re-frĭg'er-ā'tor, *n.* A box for keeping things cool by means of ice.
Re-frĭg'er-a-to-ry, *n.* A vessel for cooling. — *a.* Cooling; mitigating heat.
Rĕf'uge, *n.* A shelter from danger; asylum; sanctuary; expedient to secure protection or defense.
Rĕf'u-gee (140), *n.* One who flees for safety to a foreign power or country.
Re-fŭl'gençe, *n.* A flood
Re-fŭl'gen-çy, of light.
Re-fŭl'gent, *a.* Casting a bright light; splendid; radiant; brilliant.
Re-fŭnd', *v. t.* To pay back. — SYN. To repay; restore.
Re-fū'sal, *n.* Act of refusing; denial; rejection; right of choice; option.
Re-fūse', *v. t.* To deny; to reject. — *v. i.* To decline to accept something offered.
Rĕf'use, *n.* Worthless remains. — *a.* Rejected; worthless; of no value.
Re-fūt'a-ble, *a.* Capable of being refuted.
Rĕf'u-tā'tion, *n.* Act of refuting.
Re-fūte', *v. t.* To prove false.
Re-gāin', *v. t.* To obtain again; to recover.
Rē'gal, *a.* Royal; kingly.
Re-gāle', *v. t.* To refresh; to entertain delightfully. — *n.* A magnificent repast.
Re-gā'li-a, *n. pl.* Ensigns of royalty, as the crown, scepter, &c.; insignia.
Re-găl'i-ty, *n.* Royalty.
Rē'gal-ly, *adv.* As befits a sovereign; royally.
Re-gärd', *v. t.* To observe; to heed; to esteem. — *n.* Attention; esteem; eminence.

REGARDFUL 251 RELIANCE

Re-gärd'ful, *a.* Taking notice; attentive; heedful.
Re-gärd'less, *a.* Heedless; careless; indifferent.
Re-gät'tä, *n.* A rowing match; a boat-race. [a regent.
Rē'gen-çy, *n.* Government by
Re-gĕn'er-a-çy, *n.* State of being regenerated.
Re-gĕn'er-āte, *v. t.* To produce anew; to renew as to the spiritual nature.
Re-gĕn'er-ate, *a.* Born anew; spiritually renewed.
Re-gĕn'er-ā'tion, *n.* The new birth; reproduction.
Re-gĕn'er-a-tive, *a.* Pertaining to regeneration.
Rē'gent, *n.* One who governs in the place of a king; a ruler. — *a.* Ruling.
Rĕg'ï-çīde, *n.* The killer or the killing of a king.
†**Régime** (rā-zheem'), *n.* Mode of rule or management; administration.
Rĕg'i-men, *n.* A rule of diet; (*Gram.*) government.
Rĕg'i-ment, *n.* A body of troops under a colonel.
Rĕg'i-mĕnt'al, *a.* Belonging to a regiment.
Rĕg'i-mĕnt'als, *n. pl.* The uniform of a regiment.
Rē'gion (rē'jun), *n.* A tract of land; a country.
Rĕg'is-ter, *n.* A catalogue; list; record; keeper of a record; a sliding plate in a stove, &c. — *v. t.* To record; to enroll.
Rĕg'is-trar, *n.* An officer who keeps public records.
Rĕg'is-trā'tion, *n.* Act of registering; enrollment.
Rĕg'is-try, *n.* A registering; record; place of keeping records.
Rĕg'let, *n.* A thin strip of wood used to separate lines in printing.
Rĕg'nant, *a.* Reigning; ruling.
Rē-grănt', *v. t.* To grant back.
Re-grāte', *v. t.* To forestall.
Rē'gress, *n.* Return; power of returning.
Re-grĕs'sion (-grĕsh'un), *n.* Act of passing back; return.
Re-grĕss'ive, *a.* Passing back; returning.
Re-grĕt', *n.* Pain of mind at something causing unhappiness; sorrow for the past. — SYN. Remorse; repentance. — *v. t.* To feel sorrow for; to lament the loss of.
Re-grĕt'ful, *a.* Full of regret.
Rĕg'u-lar, *a.* Agreeable to rule; stated; orderly; normal. — *n.* A soldier of a permanent or standing army.
Rĕg'u-lăr'i-ty, *n.* Certain order; method; uniformity.
Rĕg'u-lar-ly, *adv.* Statedly.
Rĕg'u-lāte, *v. t.* [Lat. *regulare, -latum*, from *regula*, a rule.] To adjust by rule, method, or established mode; to methodize.
Rĕg'u-lā'tion, *n.* Act of regulating; prescribed rule.
Rĕg'u-lā'tor, *n.* He who, or that which, regulates.
Re-gûr'gi-tā'tion, *n.* Act of flowing back by the orifice of entrance. [or pour back.
Re-gûr'gi-tāte, *v. t.* To throw
Rē'ha-bĭl'ï-tāte, *v. t.* To restore to a forfeited right or rank; to reinstate.
Rē'ha-bĭl'ï-tā'tion, *n.* Restoration to former rights.
Re-hēar', *v. t.* To hear or try again.
Re-hēar'ing, *n.* A second hearing or trial.
Re-hēars'al, *n.* Recital; preparatory repetition.
Re-hēarse', *v. t.* To narrate; to recite before exhibition.
Rēi'gle (rē'gl), *n.* A cut or channel for a guide.
Reign (rān), *n.* Royal authority or government; prevalence; controlling influence. — *v. i.* To rule as a monarch.
Rē'im-būrse', *v. t.* To repay.
Rē'im-būrse'ment, *n.* A refunding; repayment.
Rēin (rān), *n.* The guiding strap of a bridle; restraint. — *v. t.* To guide or govern by a bridle; to restrain.
Rein'deer (rān'-), *n.* An animal of the deer kind.
Reins, *n. pl.* The kidneys; the lower part of the back.

Reindeer.

Rē'in-stall', *v. t.* To install again; to seat anew.
Rē'in-stāte', *v. t.* To replace in possession.
Rē'in-stāte'ment, *n.* A placing in a former state.
Rē'in-sūre' (-shụr'), *v. t.* To insure by other underwriters.
Rē'in-vĕst', *v. t.* To invest anew.
Rē-is'sue (-ĭsh'shụ), *v. t.* To issue a second time.
Rē-ĭt'er-āte, *v. t.* To repeat; to do again. [tion.
Rē-ĭt'er-ā'tion, *n.* Repetition.
Re-jĕct', *v. t.* To cast off; to discard; to refuse. [ing.
Re-jĕc'tion, *n.* Act of rejecting.
Re-joiçe', *v. i.* or *t.* To be or make very glad; to gladden.
Re-joiç'ing, *n.* Expression of joy; exultation.
Re-join', *v. t.* or *i.* To join again; to answer to a reply.
Re-join'der, *n.* An answer, esp. an answer to a reply.
Re-jū've-nāte, *v. t.* To render young again.
Re-jū've-nĕs'çençe, *n.* A being young again.
Rē-kin'dle, *v. t.* To kindle again; to rouse anew.
Rē-lănd', *v. t.* To land again.
Re-lăpse', *v. i.* To fall back; to return to a former and worse state. — *n.* A falling back.
Re-lāte', *v. t.* To tell; to recite. — *v. i.* To pertain.
Re-lā'tion, *n.* Act of relating; narrative of facts; any connection established; kindred.
Re-lā'tion-al, *a.* Having relation. [being related.
Re-lā'tion-ship, *n.* State of
Rĕl'a-tive, *a.* Having relation; respecting. — *n.* One connected by blood or affinity; that which relates to something else.
Rĕl'a-tive-ly (132), *adv.* With relation to something else.
Re-lăx', *v. t.* or *i.* To slacken; to remit in severity.
Rē'lax-ā'tion, *n.* A slackening; relief from laborious or painful duties.
Re-lāy', *n.* Horses at certain stations to relieve others. — *v. t.* To lay again.
Re-lēase', *v. t.* To free from restraint or obligation; to let go, as a legal claim. — *n.* Liberation or discharge from restraint of any kind; a quitclaim. [to remand.
Rĕl'e-gāte, *v. t.* To consign;
Rĕl'e-gā'tion, *n.* Removal; exile. [mild or tender.
Re-lĕnt', *v. i.* To become more
Re-lĕnt'less, *a.* Unmoved by pity; insensible to distress.
Rĕl'e-vançe, } *n.* State of
Rĕl'e-van-çy, } being relevant; pertinence.
Rĕl'e-vant, *a.* Pertinent; applicable.
Re-lī'a-ble, *a.* Suitable or fit to be relied on or trusted.
Re-lī'ançe, *n.* Trust; dependence; confidence.

són, ôr, dọ, wọlf, tōo, tŏok; ûrn, rụe, pụll; ç, ğ, *soft*; ç, ġ, *hard*; aẓ; eẋist; n as ng; this.

RELIC 252 RENOUNCE

Rěl'ic (127), *n.* Remains; a dead body; a memorial.

Rěl'ict, *n.* A widow.

Re-lief', *n.* Aid; alleviation; prominence of a figure, as in sculpture. [being relieved.

Re-liev'a-ble, *a.* Capable of

Re-lieve', *v. t.* To ease; to help; to succor; to aid; to release from a post by substituting others.

Re-lie'vo, *n.* Prominence or projection of figures in sculpture or painting.

Re-lig'ion (-lĭj'un), *n.* A system of faith and worship; pious practice; piety.

Re-lig'ion-ist (-lĭj'un-), *n.* A bigot or devotee.

Re-lig'ious (-lĭj'us), *a.* Pious; godly; devotional; pertaining to religion.

Re-lig'ious-ly (-lĭj'us-), *adv.* Piously; sacredly; exactly.

Re-lin'quish (-lĭŋk'wish), *v. t.* To withdraw from; to give up; to resign; to renounce; to abandon; to quit.

Re-lin'quish-ment, *n.* Act of relinquishing.

Rěl'i-qua-ry, *n.* A small chest, box, or casket, in which relics are kept.

Rěl'ish, *n.* A pleasing taste; flavor. — *v. t.* To give flavor to. — *v. i.* To have a pleasant flavor. [being relished.

Rěl'ish-a-ble, *a.* Worthy of

Re-lŭc'tance, *n.* Unwillingness; aversion; repugnance.

Re-lŭc'tant, *a.* Averse; unwilling; loth; disinclined; granted unwillingly.

Re-lŭc'tant-ly, *adv.* With unwillingness.

Re-lūme', } *v. t.* To rekin-
Re-lū'mine, } die; to light again. [side; to defend.

Re-ly', *v. i.* To rest or con-

Re-māin', *v. i.* [Lat. *remanere*, fr. *re*, again, back, and *manere*, to stay.] To continue; to be left. [left.

Re-māin'der, *n.* Any thing

Re-māins', *n. pl.* What is left; relics; a corpse.

Re-mănd', *v. t.* To send or call back; to recommit.

Re-märk', *n.* An observation; notice; mention; comment. — *v. t.* To observe; to note; to express in words.

Re-märk'a-ble, *a.* Worthy of note; wonderful.

Re-märk'a-bly, *adv.* In an unusual manner; uncommonly. [again.

Re-mar'ry, *v. t.* To marry

Re-mē'di-a-ble, *a.* Capable of remedy; curable.

Re-mē'di-al, *a.* Affording, or designed to afford, a remedy.

Re-mĕd'i-less, or **Rĕm'i-di-less**, *a.* Admitting no cure; without remedy.

Rĕm'e-dy (141), *n.* That which is adapted to cure, or which counteracts an evil. — *v. t.* To cure; to restore to soundness, health, &c.; to repair.

Re-mĕm'ber, *v. t.* To have or keep in mind; to call to mind; to recollect.

Re-mĕm'brançe, *n.* Retention in mind; recollection.

Re-mĕm'bran-çer, *n.* One who, or that which, reminds; a memento.

Re-mĭnd', *v. t.* To put in mind or remembrance.

Rĕm'i-nĭs'çençe, *n.* Recollection; remembered incidents.

Re-mīse', *v. t.* To grant back.

Re-mĭss', *a.* Slack in performance of duty; negligent.

Re-mĭs'si-ble, *a.* Capable of being remitted.

Re-mĭs'sion (-mĭsh'un), *n.* Pardon; discharge from what is due; diminution of intensity.

Re-mĭss'ly, *adv.* Negligently.

Re-mĭss'ness, *n.* Negligence.

Re-mĭt', *v. t.* To send, as money; to give up; to resign. — *v. i.* To abate in force or violence; to relax.

Re-mĭt'tal, *n.* A giving back or up; surrender.

Re-mĭt'tançe, *n.* Act of transmitting money in payment; sum transmitted.

Re-mĭt'tent, *a.* Temporarily ceasing or abating.

Rĕm'nant, *n.* What is left; residue; remainder; rest. — *a.* Remaining. [anew.

Re-mŏd'el, *v. t.* To model

Re-mōld', } *v. t.* To mold or
Re-mōuld', } shape anew.

Re-mŏn'strançe, *n.* Expostulation; earnest advice.

Re-mŏn'strant, *n.* One who remonstrates.

Re-mŏn'strāte, *v. i.* To urge reasons against. — SYN. To expostulate.

Re-mŏrse', *n.* Pain of conscience proceeding from a sense of guilt.

Re-mŏrse'ful, *a.* Full of a sense of guilt.

Re-mŏrse'less, *a.* Unpitying; pitiless; cruel.

Re-mōte', *a.* Distant in place or time; foreign.

Re-mōte'ly, *adv.* At a distance in time or place, &c.

Re-mōte'ness (132), *n.* State of being remote; distance.

Re-mount', *v. i.* or *t.* To mount again; to reascend.

Re-mov'a-ble, *a.* Admitting of being removed.

Re-mov'al, *n.* Act of removing from a place.

Re-move', *v.* To change place; to move. — *n.* Change of place; interval; distance.

Re-mū'ner-āte, *v. t.* To recompense; to repay; to reward. [recompense.

Re-mū'ner-ā'tion, *n.* Reward.

Re-mū'ner-ā'tive, *a.* Affording reward. [kidneys.

Rē'nal, *a.* Pertaining to the

Rĕn'ard, *n.* A fox.

Re-nās'çençe, } *n.* State of
Re-nās'çen-çy, } being produced again.

Re-nās'çent, *a.* Growing again; reproduced.

Ren-coun'ter, *n.* A sudden or casual combat; clash. — *v. t.* or *i.* To meet; to clash.

Rĕnd, *v. t.* [*imp. & p. p.* RENT.] To split; to tear asunder; to break; to lacerate; to rupture.

Rĕn'der (130), *v. t.* To return; to give up; to translate; to boil down and clarify.

Rĕn'der-ing, *n.* Act of returning; a version.

Rĕn'dez-vous (rĕn'de-vōō), *n.* [Fr. *rendez vous*, render yourselves; repair to a place.] A place of meeting; a meeting appointed. — *v. i.* or *t.* To assemble, as troops.

Ren-dĭ'tion (-dĭsh'un), *n.* Act of giving up; surrender.

Rĕn'e-gāde, } *n.* One faith-
Rĕn'e-gā'do, } less to principle; an apostate: a deserter.

Re-new', *v. t.* To make new or as good as new; to repeat; to furnish again.

Re-new'a-ble, *a.* Capable of being renewed.

Re-new'al, *n.* Act of renewing; that which is renewed.

Re-new'ed-ly, *adv.* Anew.

Re-new'er, *n.* One who renews.

Rĕn'i-fôrm, *a.* Having the shape of a kidney.

Re-nĭt'ençe, *n.* Resistance; reluctance. [ure.

Re-nī'tent, *a.* Resisting press-

Rĕn'net, *n.* Inner membrane of a calf's stomach, used to coagulate milk.

Re-nounçe', *v. t.* To disown; to cast off formally.

ā, ĕ, ī, ō, ū, ȳ, *long*; ă, ĕ, ĭ, ŏ, ŭ, ў, *short*; câre, cär, àsk, ąll, whąt; ẽre, vẽil, tẽrm; pīque, fïrm;

RENOUNCEMENT 253 REPRODUCTION

Re-nounce′ment, n. Act of renouncing; renunciation.
Ren′o-vāte, v. t. To renew.
Ren′o-vā′tion, n. Renewal.
Re-nown′, n. Fame; celebrity; exalted reputation.
Re-nowned′, a. Famous; celebrated; distinguished.
Rent, imp. of Rend. Torn asunder. — n. A fissure or laceration; money paid for lease of property. — v. t. To lease, as lands, &c. — v. i. To be leased.
Rent′a-ble, a. Admitting of being rented. [rents.
Rent′al, n. An account of
Rent′-roll, n. A list of rents.
Re-nūn′ci-ā′tion (-shī-ā-shun), n. Act of renouncing; renouncement. [ize anew.
Re-ôr′gan-ize, v. t. To organ-
Re-ôr′gan-i-zā′tion, n. Organization anew.
Re-pāid′ (135), imp. of Repay.
Re-pâir′, v. t. To restore; to mend; to refit. — v. i. To go; to resort. — n. Reparation; supply of loss.
Rep′a-ra-ble, a. Capable of being repaired.
Rep′a-rā′tion, n. Restitution; amends; compensation.
Re-pâr′a-tīve, a. Amending defects.
Rep′ar-tee′ (140), n. A smart reply; a retort.
Re-pāss′, v. To pass again.
Re-pāst′, n. A meal; food.
Re-pāy′, v. t. To pay back.
Re-pāy′ment, n. Act of repaying; thing repaid.
Re-pēal′, v. t. To make void. — SYN. To revoke; annul; abrogate. — n. Abrogation.
Re-pēal′a-bīl′i-ty, n. State of being repealable.
Re-pēal′a-ble, a. Capable of being repealed.
Re-pēal′er, n. One who repeals, or desires repeal.
Re-pēat′, v. t. To do again; to reiterate. — n. Repetition; that which is, or is to be, repeated.
Re-pēat′ed-ly, adv. With repetition; frequently.
Re-pēat′er, n. One who repeats; a watch that strikes the hours. [resist.
Re-pel′, v. t. To drive back; to
Re-pel′len-çy, n. Quality that repels. [repel.
Re-pel′lent, a. Tending to
Re′pent, a. Creeping, as a reptile or plant.
Re-pent′, v. i. To feel sorrow for something done.

Re-pent′ançe, n. Sorrow for sins; penitence; coutrition.
Re-pent′ant, a. Sorrowful for sin; penitent; contrite.
Re-pēo′ple, v. t. To supply anew with inhabitants.
Re′per-cūss′, v. t. To beat back.
Re′per-cūs′sion (-kŭsh′un), n. Act of driving back; rebound; reverberation.
Re′per-cūs′sive, a. Beating back; reverberating.
Rep′er-to-ry, n. A book of records; a magazine.
Rep′e-tēnd′, n. That part of a repeating decimal which recurs continually.
Rep′e-tī′tion (-tĭsh′un), n. Act of repeating; iteration.
Rep′e-tī′tioŭs (-tĭsh′us), a. Containing repetition.
Re-pīne′, v. i. To indulge in envy or complaint; to complain; to murmur.
Re-plāçe′, v. t. To put again in its place; to substitute.
Re-plāçe′ment, n. Act of replacing, or state of being replaced. [again.
Re-plānt′, v. t. To plant
Re-plēn′ish, v. t. To fill again; to supply; to stock.
Re-plēte′, a. Full to excess; completely filled. [fullness.
Re-plē′tion, n. Superabundant
Re-plēv′i-a-ble,) a. Capable of
Re-plēv′i-ṣa-ble,) being replevied.
Re-plēv′in, n. A writ to recover goods distrained.
Re-plēv′y, v. t. To set at liberty on security; to bail.
Rep′li-cant, n. One who replies.
Rep′li-cā′tion, n. A plaintiff's reply to a defendant's plea.
Re-plȳ′, v. i. To answer; to respond; to rejoin. — n. Return in words.
Re-pôrt′, v. t. To bring back as an answer; to relate; to tell. — v. i. To circulate publicly. — n. Account returned; rumor; loud sound, as of a gun. [ports.
Re-pôrt′er, n. One who re-
Re-pōṣ′al, n. Act of reposing.
Re-pōṣe′, v. i. To rest; to sleep; to lie quiet. — v. t. To lay at rest; to place in confidence.
Re-pōṣ′it, v. t. To lodge or lay up for safety.
Rē-pōṣ′i-to-ry, n. A place where things are stored.
Rē′pos-sēss′ (-pos-sĕs′ or -poz-zĕs′), v. t. To possess again.

Rē′pos-sēs′sion (-pos-sĕsh′un or -poz-zĕsh′un), n. Act or state of possessing again.
Rep′re-hĕnd′, v. t. To blame.
Rep′re-hĕn′si-ble, a. Deserving of censure; censurable; blameworthy.
Rep′re-hĕn′si-bly, adv. Culpably.
Rep′re-hĕn′sion, n. Reproof; censure; open blame.
Rep′re-hĕn′sive,) a. Con-
Rep′re-hĕn′so-ry,) taining reproof or censure.
Rep′re-sĕnt′, v. t. To show; to exhibit; to delineate; to supply the place of; to personate.
Rep′re-ṣen-tā′tion, n. Act of representing; thing represented; likeness; description; statement; exhibition; appearance for another; a body of representatives.
Rep′re-ṣĕnt′a-tīve, a. Fitted to represent; exhibiting likeness. — n. One acting for another; a deputy.
Re-prĕss′, v. t. To put down; to subdue; to crush.
Re-prĕs′sion (-prĕsh′un), n. Act of repressing. [press.
Re-prĕss′ive, a. Tending to re-
Re-priēve′, v. t. To respite for a time. — n. Suspension of the execution of a sentence; respite.
Rep′ri-mănd, n. Reproof for a fault. — v. t. To chide; to reprove; to rebuke.
Rē-print′, v. t. To print a new edition of, especially in another country. [sion.
Rē′print, n. A new impres-
Re-prī′ṣal, n. Seizure by way of retaliation.
Re-prōach′, v. t. To accuse; to blame; to upbraid. — n. Censure in opprobrious terms; invective.
Re-prōach′a-ble, a. Deserving reproach. [probrious.
Re-prōach′fụl (139), a. Op-
Re-prōach′fụl-ly, adv. With contempt; scurrilously.
Rep′ro-bāte, a. Lost to virtue; base; depraved. — n. One abandoned to sin.
Rep′ro-bāte, v. t. To disapprove with detestation; to condemn.
Rep′ro-bā′tion, n. Act of reprobating; condemnation.
Rē′pro-dūçe′, v. t. To produce anew.
Rē′pro-dūç′tion, n. Act or process of producing anew; thing reproduced.

REPRODUCTIVE — RESORT

Re'pro-dŭc'tive, *a.* Pertaining to reproduction.

Re-proof', *n.* Censure expressed; rebuke.

Re-prov'a-ble, *a.* Worthy of reproof; culpable.

Re-prov'al (133), *n.* Reproof.

Re-prove', *v. t.* To censure to the face. — SYN. To rebuke; reprimand; blame; chide; reprehend.

Re-prov'er, *n.* One who reproves or blames.

Rĕp'tĭle, *a.* Creeping; grovelling; low; vulgar. — *n.* A creeping animal.

Re-pŭb'lic (127), *n.* [Lat. *res publica*, fr. *res*, a thing, and *publicus*, public.] A state governed by representatives elected by the citizens.

Re-pŭb'lic-an, *a.* Pertaining to, or consistent with, a republic. — *n.* One who favors or prefers a republic.

Re-pŭb'lic-an-ĭṣm, *n.* System of republican government; attachment to republican principles.

Rē-pŭb'li-cā'tion, *n.* A new publication; a reprint.

Re-pŭb'lish, *v. t.* To publish anew, or in another country.

Re-pū'di-āte, *v. t.* To divorce; to reject; to disclaim.

Re-pū'di-ā'tion, *n.* Act of disclaiming; divorce.

Re-pū'di-ā'tor, *n.* One who repudiates.

Re-pŭg'nance,) *n.* Unwillingness;
Re-pŭg'nan-cy,) inconsistency; reluctance.

Re-pŭg'nant, *a.* Unwilling; inconsistent; averse.

Re-pŭlse', *n.* A check in advancing; refusal. — *v. t.* To repel; to drive off.

Re-pŭl'sion, *n.* Act of repelling or driving back.

Re-pŭl'sive, *a.* Forbidding; cold; reserved.

Re-pŭl'sive-ness, *n.* Quality of being repulsive. [back.

Rē-pŭr'chase, *v. t.* To buy

Rĕp'u-ta-ble, *a.* Of good repute; respectable.

Rĕp'u-ta-bly, *adv.* With credit; respectably.

Rĕp'u-tā'tion, *n.* General estimation; good name; credit; honor derived from public esteem.

Re-pūte', *v. t.* To hold in estimation; to think. — *n.* Reputation; estimation.

Re-pūt'ed, *a.* Reckoned.

Re-quĕst', *n.* Expression of desire; a petition; state of being desired. — *v. t.* To solicit; to ask.

Rē'qui-em, *n.* A hymn or mass sung for the dead.

Re-quir'a-ble, *a.* Capable of being required.

Re-quire', *v. t.* To make necessary; to need; to demand; to ask as a right.

Re-quire'ment (132), *n.* Demand; thing required.

Rĕq'ui-ṣīte (rĕk'wĭ-zit), *a.* Required; necessary. — *n.* That which is necessary.

Rĕq'ui-ṣī'tion (rĕk'wĭ-zĭsh'un), *n.* Act of requiring; claim made; demand.

Re-quĭt'al, *n.* Recompense.

Re-quīte', *v. t.* To recompense; to retaliate; to return an equivalent.

Re-scĭnd', *v. t.* To repeal; to abrogate; to revoke.

Re-scĭṣ'ṣion (-sĭzh'un), *n.* Act of rescinding; abrogation.

Rē'script, *n.* Edict or decree of an emperor.

Rĕs'cūe, *v. t.* To deliver from danger or confinement; to set free. — *n.* Deliverance from arrest or danger.

Re-ṣēarch', *n.* Diligent inquiry; investigation.

Rē-ṣēat', *v. t.* To seat again.

Rē-ṣēiz'ūre (-sē'zhụr), *n.* Act of seizing again.

Re-sĕll', *v. t.* To sell again.

Re-ṣĕm'blance, *n.* Likeness.

Re-ṣĕm'ble, *v. t.* To be like.

Re-ṣĕnt', *v. t.* To be angry at; to express anger at.

Re-ṣĕnt'fụl (139), *a.* Apt to resent; easily provoked.

Re-ṣĕnt'ment, *n.* Sense of injury; displeasure.

Rĕṣ'er-vā'tion, *n.* Act of reserving; something reserved; a proviso.

Re-ṣẽrve', *v. t.* To keep in store; to retain. — *n.* That which is reserved; restraint in manner or words.

Re-ṣẽrved', *a.* Not frank; cautious; restrained; cold.

Re-ṣẽrv'ed-ly, *adv.* With reserve; coldly.

Rĕṣ'er-voir' (rĕz'er-vwôr'), *n.* A large cistern or basin.

Rē-ṣĕt', *v. t.* To set again, as a jewel or plant.

Rē-ṣĕt'tle, *v. t.* To settle or install again.

Rē-ṣĕt'tle-ment, *n.* Act of settling again.

Rē-shĭp', *v. t.* To ship again, as what has been imported.

Rē-shĭp'ment, *n.* Act of reshipping; re-exportation.

Re-ṣīde', *v. i.* To dwell; to live; to have one's abode.

Rĕṣ'i-dence, *n.* A place of abode; dwelling.

Rĕṣ'i-dent, *a.* Dwelling; living. — *n.* One who dwells.

Rĕṣ'i-dĕn'ti-a-ry (-shĭ-), *a.* Having residence; residing.

Re-ṣĭd'u-al, *a.* Remaining after a part is taken.

Re-ṣĭd'u-a-ry, *a.* Entitled or pertaining to the residue or remainder.

Rĕṣ'i-dūe, *n.* What is left after any process of separation or purification; remainder; rest.

Re-ṣĭd'u-um, *n.* That which remains; residue.

Re-ṣīgn' (-zīn'), *v. t.* To give up in a formal manner.

Rĕṣ'ig-nā'tion, *n.* Act of resigning; quiet submission.

Re-ṣīgned' (-zīnd'), *p. a.* Submissive; yielding.

Re-sĭl'i-ence, *n.* A recoil.

Re-sĭl'i-ent, *a.* Leaping back; rebounding.

Rĕṣ'in, *n.* An inflammable substance from the pine, &c.

Rĕṣ'in-oŭs, *a.* Containing, or like, resin.

Re-ṣĭst', *v. t.* [Lat. *resistere,* fr. *re*, again, back, and *sistere*, to stand.] To act in opposition to. — SYN. To withstand; oppose.

Re-ṣĭst'ance, *n.* Act of resisting; opposition.

Re-ṣĭst'i-ble, *a.* Capable of being resisted or of resisting.

Re-ṣĭst'less, *a.* Not to be withstood; irresistible.

Rĕṣ'o-lu-ble, *a.* Admitting of being resolved or melted.

Rĕṣ'o-lūte, *a.* Firm to one's purpose; determined; firm.

Rĕṣ'o-lūte-ly, *adv.* With steadiness and courage.

Rĕṣ'o-lū'tion, *n.* Act of resolving; firmness of purpose; formal declaration.

Re-ṣŏlv'a-ble, *a.* Capable of being resolved.

Re-ṣŏlve', *v. t.* To separate into component parts; to analyze. — *v. i.* To determine. — *n.* Fixed purpose.

Re-ṣŏlv'ent, *n.* That which causes solution.

Rĕṣ'o-nance, *n.* A reverberation of sound or sounds.

Rĕṣ'o-nant, *a.* Echoing; resounding.

Re-ṣôrt', *v. i.* To have recourse; to repair; to go. — *n.* Concourse of people; assembly; place of habitual meeting; a haunt.

ā, ĕ, ī, ō, ū, ӯ, *long*; ă, ĕ, ĭ, ŏ, ŭ, ў, *short*; câre, cär, ȧsk, ạll, whạt; ẽre, veil, tẽrm; pīque, fĭrm;

Re-gound', v. t. or i. To sound back; to echo; to reverberate; to celebrate.

Re-source', n. Means of supply; resort; expedient.

Re-spect'. v. t. To regard with esteem; to honor; to relate to. — n. Regard for worth; relation; reference.

Re-spect-a-bil'i-ty, n. Quality of deserving respect.

Re-spect'a-ble, a. Worthy of respect; deserving regard.

Re-spect'a-bly, adv. So as to merit respect.

Re-spect'ed, a. Held in high estimation.

Re-spect'er, n. One who respects. [spect.

Re-spect'ful, a. Full of respect'ful-ly, adv. With due respect.

Re-spect'ive, a. Having relation to; particular.

Re-spect'ive-ly, adv. As relating to each.

Re-spir'a-ble, a. Capable of being, or fit to be, breathed.

Res-pi-ra'tion, n. Act of breathing.

Res'pi-ra'tor, n. A contrivance covering the mouth for warming the air before it reaches the lungs.

Res-pir'a-to-ry, a. Serving for respiration. [breathe.

Re-spire', v. i. or t. To

Res'pite, n. Delay; suspension of punishment; reprieve. — v. t. To suspend the execution of; to delay.

Re-splen'dence, n. Brilliant luster; splendor.

Re-splen'dent, a. Bright; splendid; shining.

Re-splen'dent-ly, adv. With great brightness.

Re-spond', v. i. To answer; to reply; to rejoin. — n. A short anthem.

Re-spond'ent, n. One who responds; an answerer in an action at law. — a. Answering; accordant. [ply.

Re-sponse', n. Answer; reply.

Re-spon'si-bil'i-ty, n. Liability.

Re-spon'si-ble-ness, ability to answer or pay.

Re-spon'si-ble, a. Liable to account. — SYN. Accountable; answerable.

Re-spon'sive, a. Answering.

Re-spon'so-ry, a. Containing or making answer. — n. An answer.

Rest, n. Quiet; peace; repose; sleep; ease; a pause; a support; that which is left. — v. i. To be quiet; to sleep; to lean or rely. — v. t. To lay or place. [lug-house.

Res'tau-rant (-to-), n. An eating-house.

Res-tau'ra-teûr' (-to'-), n. Keeper of an eating-house.

Rest'iff, } a. Unwilling to go,
Rest'ive, } or only running back; stubborn.

Res'ti-tu'tion, n. Act of restoring; indemnification.

Rest'ive-ness, n. Obstinate reluctance to move.

Rest'less, a. Void of rest; unsettled; unquiet; uneasy.

Rest'less-ly, adv. Unquietly.

Rest'less-ness, n. Uneasiness; agitation.

Re-stor'a-ble, a. Admitting of being restored. [recovery.

Res'to-ra'tion, n. Renewal;

Re-stor'a-tive, a. Tending to restore. — n. That which restores.

Re-store', v. t. To give back; to replace; to revive; to heal.

Re-stor'er, n. One who, or that which, restores.

Re-strain', v. t. To check; to repress; to hold back.

Re-straint', n. That which restrains; a hindering; check; restriction.

Re-strict', v. t. To limit; to restrain; to confine.

Re-stric'tion, n. Limitation.

Re-strict'ive, a. Restraining.

Re-strin'gent, a. Astringent.

Re-sult', v. i. To proceed or spring as a consequence. — n. Conclusion to which any course leads; effect.

Re-sult'ant, n. A force which is the joint effect of two or more forces. — a. Resulting.

Re-sume', v. t. [Lat. resumere, fr. re, again, back, and sumere, to take.] To take back; to begin again after interruption.

†Résumé (rā'zṳ-mā'), n. A summing up; summary.

Re-gump'tion, n. Act of resuming, or taking again.

Res'ur-rec'tion, n. A rising again; revival from the grave; the future state.

Re'sur-vey', v. t. To survey again.

Re-sus'çi-tāte, v. t. To revive; to bring to life again.

Re-sus'çi-tā'tion, n. Act of resuscitating; restoration.

Re-tail' (111), v. t. To sell in small quantities.

Rē'tāil (112), n. Sale in small quantities.

Re-tāil'er, or Rē'tāil-er, n. One who sells at retail, or in small quantities.

Re-tāin', v. t. To keep in possession or in pay.

Re-tāin'er, n. One who retains; a dependent; a fee to engage counsel.

Rē-tāke', v. t. To take again.

Re-tǎl'i-āte, v. i. To return like for like.

Re-tǎl'i-ā'tion, n. Return of like for like; reprisal.

Re-tǎl'i-a-tive, } a. Giving
Re-tǎl'i-a-to-ry, } like for like; involving retaliation.

Re-tärd', v. t. To diminish the speed of; to delay; to hinder; to impede.

Re-tar-dā'tion, } n. Act of
Re-tärd'ment, } retarding; that which retards.

Retch, v. i. To make an effort to vomit. [ing.

Re-tĕn'tion, n. Act of retaining.

Re-tĕn'tive, a. Having power to retain.

Re-tĕn'tive-ness, n. Power of retaining.

Re-tic'u-lar, } a. Having the
Ret'i-fôrm, } form of a net.

Re-tic'u-late, } a. Made of,
Re-tic'u-lāt'ed, } or resembling, net-work.

Re-tic'u-lā'tion, n. Net-work.

Ret'i-cūle, n. [Lat. reticulum, fr. rete, a net.] A little bag of net-work.

Ret'i-nà, n. (pl. †Ret'i-næ.) Internal nervous tissue of the eye, which receives the impression resulting in the sense of vision.

Ret'i-nūe, n. A suite or train of attendants.

Re-tīre', v. t. or i. To retreat; to withdraw; to fall back.

Re-tīred', a. Withdrawn.

Re-tīre'ment (132), n. Act of living in seclusion; privacy.

Re-tīr'ing, a. Reserved; not forward.

Re-tôrt', n. Censure returned; repartee; a chemical vessel. — v. t. To throw back; to return; to make a sharp reply.

Rē-touch', v. t. To improve by new touches.

Re-trāçe', v. t. To trace back.

Re-trāct', v. t. To take back; to recall. — v. i. To take back what has been said.

Re-tract'i-ble, } a. Capable
Re-tract'ile, } of being retracted, or drawn back.

Re-trac'tion, n. Act of retracting; recantation. [ing.

Re-tract'ive, a. Withdraw-

Re-treat', n. A retiring; a

RETRENCH 256 REVOLVENCY

place of privacy. — *v. i.* To withdraw; to go back.

Re-trench', *v. t.* To lessen; to curtail, as expenses.

Re-trench'ment, *n.* Act of retrenching; reduction.

Rĕt'ri-bū'tion, *n.* Reward or punishment; repayment; requital.

Re-trĭb'u-tĭve, *a.* Reward-
Re-trĭb'u-to-ry, ing or punishing.

Re-trĭev'a-ble, *a.* Capable of being retrieved.

Re-trieve', *v. t.* To recover; to regain; to repair.

Rĕ'tro-ăc'tion (*or* rĕt'ro-), *n.* Action in return.

Rĕ'tro-ăct'ĭve, or **Rĕt'ro-ăct'ĭve,** *a.* Affecting what is past.

Rĕ'tro-cēde (*or* rĕt'ro-), *v. t.* To cede or grant back. — *v. i.* To go back.

Rĕ'tro-cĕs'sion (*or* rĕt'ro-sĕsh'un), *n.* Act of going back or of ceding back.

Rĕt'ro-grāde (*or* rē'tro-), *a.* Going backward. — *v. i.* To go backward.

Rĕ'tro-grĕs'sion (*or* rĕt'ro-grĕsh'un), *n.* Act of going backward.

Rĕ'tro-grĕss'ĭve, or **Rĕt'ro-grĕss'ĭve,** *a.* Going backward; declining.

Rĕ'tro-spĕct, *n.* A looking back on things past.

Rĕ'tro-spĕc'tion (*or* rĕt'ro-), *n.* A looking back; review.

Rĕ'tro-spĕct'ĭve (*or* rĕt'ro-), *a.* Looking back.

Rē'tro-vĕrt', or **Rĕt'ro-vĕrt,** *v. t.* To turn back.

Re-tūrn' (130), *v. i.* To come or go back. — *v. t.* To send or give back; to repay. — *n.* A going or giving back; relapse; profit of business; restitution.

Re-tūrn'a-ble, *a.* Capable of being returned.

Rē-ūn'ion (-yụn'yun), *n.* Act of reuniting; a second union; a meeting of associates.

Rē'u-nīte', *v. t.* or *i.* To unite again, as things disjoined.

Re-vēal', *v. t.* To make known. — SYN. To divulge; disclose. [veals.

Re-vēal'er, *n.* One who reveals.

Re-veil'le (re-vāl'ye), *n.* The morning beat of drum.

Rĕv'el (130), *v. i.* To feast riotously; to carouse. — *n.* A riotous feast; a carousal.

Rĕv'e-lā'tion, *n.* Act of revealing, or disclosing; divine communication.

Rĕv'el-er, *n.* One who revels.

Rĕv'el-ry, *n.* Act of reveling; riotous feast; a carouse.

Re-vēnge', *n.* Malicious return of injury; disposition to revenge. — *v. t.* To inflict pain or injury upon for injury received.

Re-vēnge'ful, *a.* Disposed to revenge; vindictive.

Re-vēnge'ful-ly, *adv.* By way of revenge; vindictively.

Rĕv'e-nūe (140), *n.* Income of a state or prince.

Re-vĕr'ber-ant, *a.* Resounding.

Re-vĕr'ber-āte, *v. t.* or *i.* To resound; to echo.

Re-vĕr'ber-ā'tion, *n.* Act of reverberating.

Re-vĕr'ber-a-to-ry, *a.* Beating or driving back.

Re-vēre', *v. t.* To regard with fear and respect; to reverence.

Rĕv'er-ençe, *n.* Veneration; very great respect; a low bow or courtesy. — *v. t.* To regard with reverence.

Rĕv'er-end, *a.* Deserving reverence; a title of clergymen.

Rĕv'er-ent, *a.* Express-
Rĕv'er-ĕn'tial, ing reverence; submissive.

Rĕv'er-ĕn'tial-ly, *adv.* In a
Rĕv'er-ent-ly, reverent manner; with reverence.

Rĕv'er-ĭē' (107), *n.* Loose
Rĕv'er-y, and irregular but absorbing train of thought. [opposite.

Re-vēr'sal, *n.* Change to the

Re-vērse', *v. t.* To change from one position to the opposite; to make void. — SYN. To invert; overturn; subvert; repeal. — *n.* Opposite side; change; adversity; vicissitude. — *a.* Turned backward. [other hand.

Re-vērse'ly, *adv.* On the

Re-vēr'si-ble, *a.* Capable of being reversed.

Re-vēr'sion (89), *n.* Return of an estate to the grantor or his heirs; succession.

Re-vēr'sion-a-ry, *a.* Pertaining to, or involving, a reversion; to be enjoyed in succession.

Re-vēr'sion-er, *n.* One entitled to a reversion.

Re-vērt', *v. i.* To return; to fall back.

Re-vĕst', *v. t.* To clothe again; to vest again with possession or office. — *v. i.* To return to a former owner.

Re-view' (-vū'), *v. t.* To consider again; to inspect; to examine; to survey. — *n.* Careful examination; revision; criticism; inspection of troops; a periodical publication containing criticisms on books, &c.

Re-view'er, *n.* One who reviews; an inspector.

Re-vīle', *v. t.* To treat with abusive language; to vilify.

Re-vīl'er, *n.* One who reviles or vilifies.

Re-vī'sal (133), *n.* Act
Re-vĭs'ion (-vĭzh'un), of revising or reviewing.

Re-vīse' (153), *v. t.* To examine with care for correction; to review. — *n.* A second proof-sheet.

Re-vīs'er, *n.* One who revises.

Re-vĭs'it, *v. t.* To visit again.

Re-vī'so-ry, *a.* Having power to revise; relating to revision.

Re-vī'val (133), *n.* Act of reviving; return to life; a religious awakening.

Re-vī'val-ist, *n.* One who promotes revivals.

Re-vīve', *v. t.* To restore or bring to life; to renew; to reanimate. — *v. i.* To recover life and vigor.

Re-vĭv'i-fi-cā'tion, *n.* Act of returning to life; resuscitation.

Re-vĭv'i-fȳ, *v. t.* To recall to life. [being recalled.

Rĕv'o-ca-ble, *a.* Capable of

Rĕv'o-cā'tion, *n.* Act of revoking or recalling; repeal.

Re-vōke', *v. t.* To recall or repeal; to reverse.

Re-vōlt', or **Re-vŏlt'** (18), *v. i.* To renounce allegiance; to be shocked. — *n.* Renunciation of allegiance; desertion; rebellion. [feelings.

Re-vōlt'ing, *n.* Shocking to the

Rĕv'o-lū'tion, *n.* Motion round a center; rotation; a great change in the government of a country.

Rĕv'o-lū'tion-a-ry, *a.* Pertaining to, or producing, great change.

Rĕv'o-lū'tion-ĭst, *n.* One who favors a revolution.

Rĕv'o-lū'tion-īze, *v. t.* To effect a complete change in, as to government or principles.

Re-vŏlve', *v. t.* To roll or turn round. — *v. t.* To move round; to turn in the mind; to consider.

Re-vŏlv'en-çy, *n.* Act or state of revolving; revolution.

Re-volv'er, *n.* A fire-arm with several barrels revolving on an axis.

Re-vul'sion, *n.* A turning back; marked repugnance or hostility.

Re-vul'sive, *a.* Having the power of revulsion.

Re-ward', *v. t.* To recompense; to repay. — *n.* Recompense; requital; pay.

Re-ward'er, *n.* One who rewards or recompenses.

Re-write' (-rit'), *v. t.* To write a second time or again.

Rey'nard, or Reyn'ard, *n.* A fox.

Rhap-sod'ic-al (rap-), *a.* Consisting in rhapsody; wild; unconnected.

Rhap'so-dist (răp'-), *n.* One who sings, recites, or composes rhapsodies.

Rhap'so-dy (răp'-, 141), *n.* A wild, rambling writing or discourse.

Rhen'ish (-rĕn'-), *a.* Pertaining to the river Rhine.

Rhet'o-ric (rĕt'-, 120), *n.* The art of speaking or writing with elegance, propriety, and force.

Rhe-tor'ic-al (re-), *a.* Pertaining to, or involving, rhetoric; oratorical.

Rhe-tor'ic-al-ly (re-), *adv.* In a rhetorical manner.

Rhet'o-ri'cian (rĕt'o-rish'an), *n.* One who teaches or is versed in the rules and principles of rhetoric; an orator.

Rheum (rum), *n.* A thin watery fluid secreted by the mucous glands, &c.

Rheu-măt'ic (ru-), *a.* Pertaining to, or affected with, rheumatism.

Rheu'ma-tism (ru'-), *n.* A painful inflammatory disease of the joints and muscles of the human body.

Rheum'y (rum'-), *a.* Full of rheum.

Rhi-nŏç'er-os (ri-), *n.* [Gr. *rhinokeros*, fr. *ris, rinos*, nose, and *keras*, a horn.] An African quadruped having one or two strong horns on the nose. It is allied to the elephant and the hippopotamus.

Rhinoceros.

Rhomb (romb, 50), *n.* A figure of Rhom'bus,

four equal sides; but unequal angles.

Rhom'bic (rŏm'-), *a.* Having the figure of a rhomb.

Rhomb.

Rhom'boid (rŏm'-), *a.* An oblique-angled parallelogram like a
Rhomboid.
rhomb, but having only the opposite sides equal.

Rhu'barb (ru'-), *n.* A plant, and a cathartic medicine obtained from it.

Rhyme (rim), *n.* Correspondence of sounds; verses. — *v. i.* To accord in sounds. — *v. t.* To turn into rhyme.

Rhym'er | (rim'-), *n.* One
Rhym'ist | who makes rhymes; a versifier.

Rhythm (rithm *or* rithm), *n.* Regular succession of motions, sounds, &c., as in music and dancing.

Rib, *n.* One of the curved bones of the chest; a curved strengthening piece of timber in a ship; a prominent line or rising. — *v. t.* To furnish with ribs.

Rib'ald, *n.* A low, vulgar fellow. — *a.* Low; base; mean.

Rib'ald-ry, *n.* Low, vulgar language. [ribs.

Ribbed, *a.* Furnished with

Rib'bon, *n.* A fillet of silk.

Rice, *n.* A plant and its esculent seed or grain.

Rich, *a.* Opulent; wealthy; affluent; valuable; fertile; fruitful.

Rich'es, *n. pl.* Wealth; opulence; affluence.

Rich'ly, *adv.*
Rice.
Abundantly; plenteously.

Rich'ness, *n.* Wealth; opulence; affluence; fertility; abundance.

Rick, *n.* A long, covered pile of hay or grain in the field or open air.

Rick'ets, *n. pl.* A disease of children. [rickets.

Rick'et-y, *a.* Affected with

Ric'o-chet (rik'o-sha' *or* rik'o-shět'), *n.* The firing of guns so as to cause balls to

rebound from one point to another.

Rid, *v. t.* [*imp. & p. p.* RID.] To set free; to clear; to deliver. [away.

Rid'dance, *n.* A clearing

Rid'dle, *n.* A coarse sieve or sifter; an enigma. — *v. t.* or *i.* To clear from chaff with a riddle; to perforate with many balls; to solve; to speak ambiguously.

Ride, *v. i.* [*imp.* RODE; *p. p.* RID, RIDDEN.] To be carried on horseback, or in a vehicle. — *n.* An excursion on horseback, or in a vehicle.

Rid'er, *n.* One who rides; an additional clause to a bill.

Ridge (140), *n.* Top of the back; a long elevation of land. — *v. t.* To form into ridges. [ridges.

Ridg'y, *a.* Having a ridge or

Rid'i-cule (50), *n.* Laughter with contempt. — *v. t.* To laugh at, or expose to laughter. [ridicule; absurd.

Ri-dic'u-lous, *a.* Deserving

Ri-dic'u-lous-ly, *adv.* In a ridiculous manner.

Rife, *a.* Prevalent; abounding. [use.

Riff'raff, *n.* Sweepings; refuse.

Ri'fle, *n.* A gun with grooved barrel. — *v. t.* To rob; to plunder; to pillage; to groove.

Ri'fle-man (143), *n.* One armed with a rifle.

Ri'fler, *n.* One who rifles; a robber; a plunderer.

Rift, *n.* A cleft; a fissure. — *v. t.* To split.

Rig, *v. t.* To fit with rigging; to dress; to clothe.

Rig'ger, *n.* One who fits a ship with rigging.

Rig'ging, *n.* The ropes of a ship; dress; tackle.

Right (rit), *a.* Straight; just; true; correct; proper; opposite to left. — *n.* That which is right or correct; justice; just claim; property; privilege; side opposed to left. — *adv.* In a straight line; according to rule; properly; justly; very. — *v. t.* To set upright; to do justice to. — *v. i.* To take proper position.

Right'-An'gled (rit'-), *n.* Having an angle of ninety degrees.

Right'eous (ri'chus), *a.* [From Old Eng. *rightwise.*] According with, or performing, that which is right; just; upright; religious; virtuous.

RIGHTEOUSLY 258 ROLL

Right'eous-ly (rī'chus-), *adv.* Justly; uprightly; honestly; religiously.

Right'eous-ness (rī'chus-), *n.* Justice; uprightness; rectitude; virtue; holiness.

Right'ful (rīt'-), *a.* Having a right; just; equitable.

Right'ful-ly (rīt'-), *adv.* According to right; equitably.

Right'-hand'ed (rīt'-), *a.* Using the right hand more easily than the left.

Right'ly (rīt'-), *adv.* With right; properly; justly.

Right'ness (rīt'-), *n.* Straightness; rectitude.

Rig'id, *a.* Difficult to bend; stiff; strict; exact; severe.

Ri-gid'i-ty, } *n.* Stiffness, **Rig'id-ness**, } strictness.

Rig'id-ly, *adv.* Inflexibly; exactly; severely.

Rig'ma-role, *n.* Foolish talk; nonsense.

Rig'or (155), *n.* Strictness; severity; a shivering.

Rig'or-ous, *a.* Strict; severe.

Rig'or-ous-ly, *adv.* Strictly.

Rill (123), *n.* A small brook.

Rim, *n.* A border; edge; margin. —*v. t.* To put a rim on.

Rime, *n.* Hoarfrost; a chink.

Ri-mose', } *a.* Full of chinks. **Ri'mous**, }

Rim'ple, *n.* A wrinkle; a fold.

Rind, *n.* Skin, bark, or outer coat; husk.

Rin'der-pest, *n.* A contagious distemper affecting neat cattle and sheep.

Ring, *n.* A circular line or thing; a hoop; a metallic sound; a chime. —*v. t.* [*imp.* & *p. p.* RUNG.] To cause to sound; to put a ring on. —*v. i.* To sound.

Ring'-bolt, *n.* A bolt with an eye at its head and a ring through the eye.

Ring'dove, *n.* A kind of pigeon; the cushat.

Ring'lead-er, *n.* The leader of a lawless association or band.

Ring'let, *n.* A curl of hair.

Ring'worm (-wŭrm), *n.* An eruption of the skin forming rings. [pond.

Rink, *n.* An inclosed skating

Rinse, *v. t.* To cleanse by agitating in water after washing; to wash lightly.

Ri'ot, *n.* Uproar; tumult. —*v. i.* To make an uproar; to revel. [a riot.

Ri'ot-er, *n.* One who joins in

Ri'ot-ous, *a.* Disposed to riot.

Rip, *v. t.* To cut or tear asunder, especially at a seam. —*n.* A rent made by ripping.

Ripe, *a.* Perfect in growth; mature; complete; finished.

Ripe'ly, *adv.* Maturely.

Rip'en (rīp'n), *v. t.* To mature; to prepare. —*v. i.* To grow ripe. [fection.

Ripe'ness, *n.* Maturity; perfection.

Rip'ple, *v. i.* or *t.* To fret on the surface. —*n.* Agitation of the surface of water.

Rise, *v. i.* [*imp.* ROSE; *p. p.* RISEN.] To get up; to attain greater height; to increase; to grow; to ascend.

Rise, *n.* Act of rising; ascent; increase; beginning; origin.

Ris'en (rĭz'n), *p. p.* Ascended.

Ris'i-bil'i-ty, *n.* Inclination to laughter.

Ris'i-ble, *a.* Capable of exciting laughter.

Ris'ing, *n.* Act of getting up; ascent; insurrection.

Risk, *n.* Hazard; danger; peril. —*v. t.* To expose to danger; to hazard.

Rite, *n.* A ceremonial observance; religious usage.

†**Ri'tor-nel'lo**, *n.* [It.] A short symphony to an air.

Rit'u-al, *n.* A book of rites. —*a.* According to rites.

Rit'u-al-ism, *n.* System of rites. [a ritual.

Rit'u-al-ist, *n.* One devoted to

Ri'val (130), *n.* One in pursuit of the same object as another. — SYN. Competitor; antagonist; emulator. —*a.* Standing in competition. —*v. t.* (§) To emulate; to strive to equal or excel.

Ri'val-ry, *n.* Strife for equality or superiority; competition; emulation.

Rive, *v. t.* [*imp.* RIVED; *p. p.* RIVEN.] To split; to cleave.

Riv'en (rĭv'n), *p. p.* of *Rive*.

Riv'er, *n.* A large stream.

Riv'et, *n.* A pin clinched. —*v. t.* To fasten with rivets; to clinch.

Riv'u-let, *n.* A small stream.

Rix'-dŏl'lar, *n.* A European silver coin varying in value from 60c. to $1.08.

Roach, *n.* A fresh-water fish.

Road (18), *n.* [A.-S. *rád*, fr. *rídan*, to ride.] A public way for traveling; a place for ships to ride at anchor.

Road'stead, *n.* A place where ships can anchor. [ble.

Roam, *v. i.* To rove; to ramble.

Roam'er, *n.* One who roams.

Roan, *a.* Of a dark color with white or gray spots. —*n.* A roan color; a horse of a roan color; a kind of leather used in bookbinding.

Roar, *v. i.* To make a loud, continued noise. —*n.* A loud, continuous noise; clamor.

Roast, *v. t.* To cook by exposure to heat, as before a fire. —*n.* That which is roasted. —*a.* Roasted.

Roast'er, *n.* One who roasts; a pig for roasting.

Rob, *v. t.* To take forcibly, or without the owner's consent. — SYN. To plunder; steal.

Rob'ber (129), *n.* One who robs.

Rob'ber-y, *n.* A taking of property without consent.

Robe, *n.* A long gown. —*v. t.* To invest with a robe.

Rob'in, *n.* A European songbird; also, an American songbird.

Ro-bust', *a.* Strong; healthy.

Ro-bust'ness, *n.* Great and hearty strength.

Roch'et, *n.* A linen habit worn by priests; a surplice.

Rock (127), *n.* A large mass of stone.—*v. t.* or *i.* To move from side to side; to still.

Rock'er, *n.* One who, or that which, rocks; an implement capable of a rocking motion.

Rock'et, *n.* A projectile firework. [rocks.

Rock'i-ness, *n.* Abundance of

Rock'-salt, *n.* Salt in rocklike masses or large crystals.

Rock'y, *a.* Full of rocks; hard.

Rod, *n.* A twig; a slender piece of wood or metal of some length; a pole or perch; 16½ feet.

Rode (18), *imp.* & *p. p.* of *Ride*.

Ro'dent, *a.* Gnawing. —*n.* An animal that gnaws.

Rod'o-mont, *n.* A vain boaster. —*a.* Boasting vainly.

Rod'o-mont-āde', *n.* Empty bluster; vain boasting.

Roe (140), *n.* Female of the hart; eggs of a fish.

Roe'buck, *n.* Male of the roe.

Ro-gā'tion, *n.* Supplication; litany. [person; a knave.

Rogue (18, 140), *n.* A dishonest

Rogu'er-y, *n.* Knavery; dishonest tricks; mischievousness. [waggish.

Rogu'ish (133), *a.* Knavish;

Rogu'ish-ness (rōg'-), *n.* Knavery; mischievousness.

Roil, *v. t.* To make turbid by stirring; to excite.

Roll (123), *v. t.* or *i.* To turn

ā, ē, ī, ō, ū, ȳ, *long*; ă, ĕ, ĭ, ŏ, ŭ, ў, *short*; câre, eär, ȧsk, ạll, whạt; ēre, vẽil, tẽrm; pīque, fĩrm;

ROLLER   259   ROUGH-HEW

in a circle; to revolve; to flatten by a roller; to wrap up. — *n.* A thing rolled up; a small loaf of bread; a list of names. [which, rolls.
Röll'er, *n.* One who, or that
Röll'ing-pin, *n.* A cylinder of wood.
Rō'man, *a.* Pertaining to Rome. — *n.* A native of Rome.
Ro-mănçe', *n.* A fictitious and wonderful tale; a sort of novel. — *v. i.* To tell marvelous tales. [mances.
Ro-măn'çer, *n.* One who romances.
Rō'man-ism, *n.* Tenets of the Roman Catholic church.
Rō'man-ist, *n.* A Roman Catholic. [ful.
Ro-măn'tic, *a.* Wild; fanci-
Ro-măn'tic-al-ly, *adv.* In a romantic manner.
Ro-măn'ti-çişm, *n.* State of being romantic. [Rome.
Rŏm'ish, *a.* Belonging to
Rŏmp, *n.* A rude girl; rude, boisterous play. — *v. i.* To play rudely. [play.
Rŏmp'ish, *a.* Given to rude
Rŏmp'ish-ness, *n.* Quality of being rompish.
Ron-deau' (ron-dō'), *n.* A musical composition, in which the first strain is repeated at the end of each of the other strains.
Rōod, *n.* The fourth of an acre; a crucifix; a representation of the Trinity.
Roof (126), *n.* Cover of a building, or something similar. — *v. t.* To cover with a roof.

Shed Roof.   Hip Roof.

Gable Roof.   Ogee Roof.

M Roof.   Curb Roof.

Mansard Roof.   Conical Roof.

Rōof'less, *a.* Having no roof.
Rŏŏk, *v. t.* or *i.* To cheat; to rob. — *n.* A bird like a crow; a cheat.
Rŏŏk'er-y, *n.* A collection of rooks' nests; a pile of dilapidated buildings.
Rōom, *n.* Space; extent; place; an apartment; stead. — *v. i.* To lodge.
Rōom'i-ness, *n.* Spaciousness.
Rōom'y, *a.* Having ample room. — SYN. Spacious; capacious; large.
Rōost, *n.* A place on which birds or fowls rest; a perch. — *v. i.* To rest, as a bird.
Rōost'er, *n.* Male of the domestic fowl; a cock.
Rōot, *n.* The part of a plant which shoots into the earth; the original; first cause. — *v. i.* To become fixed in the earth, as a root; to take root. — *v. t.* To plant deeply; to dig up; to destroy; to eradicate.
Rōot'let, *n.* A little roof.
Rōpe, *n.* A large, stout cord. — *v. i.* To draw out in a slender string.
Rōpe'-dăn'çer, *n.* One who dances on a rope extended in the air. [ropes.
Rōpe'-măk'er, *n.* A maker of
Rōpe'-walk (-wawk), *n.* A long building where ropes are made.
Rōpe'-yärn, *n.* Threads to be twisted into ropes.
Rōp'i-ness (135), *n.* Stringiness; viscosity.
Rōp'y, *a.* Stringy; viscous.
Rŏq'ue-laur (rŏk'e-lōr), *n.* A kind of surtout.
Rō'ral, *a.* Pertaining to dew.
Rō'ga-ry, *n.* A bed of roses; a string of beads for counting prayers.
Rōṣe, *n.* A plant and flower of many species. — *v., imp.* of *Rise.*
Rō'ṣe-ate, *a.* Full of roses; resembling a rose; blooming.
Rōṣe'-bŭg, *n.* A kind of small beetle that feeds on roses, and on the blossoms of various other plants.
Rōṣe'ma-ry, *n.* A fragrant and aromatic plant.
Ro-ṣĕtte', *n.* An ornament made of ribbons in the form of a rose.
Rōṣe'wa'ter, *n.* Water tinctured with roses by distillation.
Rōṣe'-wŏŏd, *n.* A kind of wood used in cabinet-work. It is

obtained from several different kinds of trees.
Rŏṣ'in, *n.* Resin left after distilling turpentine.
Rō'ṣi-ness, *n.* State of being rosy. [in.
Rŏṣ'in-y, *a.* Partaking of ros-
Rŏss, *n.* The external rough bark of a tree.
Rŏs'ter, *n.* A list or register of military officers.
Rŏs'tral, *a.* Resembling, or pertaining to, a beak.
Rŏs'trum, *n.* Beak of a ship; a platform for speakers.
Rō'ṣy, *a.* Like a rose; red as a rose; blooming.
Rŏt, *v.* To putrefy; to decay. — *n.* Putrefaction; decay; a fatal distemper in sheep.
Rō'ta-ry,   ) *a.* Turning like
Rō'ta-tive,   } a wheel on its
Rō'ta-to-ry,) axis.
Rō'tāte, *a.* Wheel-shaped. — *v. i.* To revolve round an axis, as a wheel.
Ro-tā'tion, *n.* A turning round on an axis, as a wheel; regular succession.
Rōte, *n.* Repetition of words by memory.
Rŏt'ten (rŏt'tn), *a.* Putrid; decayed; unsound.
Rŏt'ten-ness, *n.* A putrid state; putrefaction.
Rŏt'ten-stōne, *n.* A soft stone for polishing metallic substances.
Ro-tŭnd', *a.* Round; circular; spherical; complete.
Ro-tŭn'dȧ } (140), *n.* A build-
Ro-tŭn'dō } ing circular within and without.
Ro-tŭnd'i-ty,) *n.* Round-
Ro-tŭnd'ness, } ness; sphericity.
†**Roué** (rōō/ā'), *n.* [Fr.] A dissipated man; a debauchee.
Rouge (rōōzh), *n.* A red cosmetic. — *v. t.* To paint or tinge with rouge.
Rough (rŭf), *a.* Having an uneven surface; coarse; harsh; rude; uncivil; loud and hoarse; stormy; tempestuous.
Rough'-cȧst (rŭf'kȧst), *v. t.* To cover or plaster with a mixture of lime and shells or pebbles. — *n.* A rude model; plaster mixed with shells or pebbles.
Rough' draw (rŭf'-), *v. t.* To draw coarsely.
Rough'en (rŭf'n), *v.* To make or become rough.
Rough'-hew (rŭf'hū), *v. t.* To hew roughly or coarsely.

---
sŏn, ôr, dọ, wọlf, tōō, tŏŏk; ûrn, rụe, pụll; ç, ğ, *soft*; c, g, *hard*; aş; ęxist; ŋ *as* ng; this.

Rough'ly (rŭf'-), *adv.* Ruggedly; coarsely; harshly.
Rough'ness (rŭf'-), *n.* Ruggedness.
Rough'-shod (rŭf'-), *a.* Having shoes armed with points; calked.
Rou-lette' (rōō-lĕt'), *n.* A game of chance. [ing press.
Rounce, *n.* Handle of a print-
Round, *a.* Spherical; circular; full; approximate. — *n.* A circle; action in a recurring series; a regular course; a volley. — *v.* To make or become round. — *prep.* About; on all sides of. — *adv.* On every side; circularly.
Round'a-bout', *a.* Indirect; circumlocutory.
Round'e-lāy, *n.* A kind of song or poem of very artificial structure.
Round'-hēad, *n.* A Puritan.
Round'-house, *n.* A cabin in the after part of the quarterdeck.
Round'ing, *n.* Somewhat
Round'ish, } round.
Round'ly, *adv.* In a round form; openly; boldly.
Round'ness, *n.* Quality of being round; sphericity; rotundity; openness.
Round'-rōō'in, *n.* A petition or other writing with the names of the signers written in a circle around it.
Rouse, *v. t.* To wake from rest; to start; to excite.
Rout, *n.* Defeat, or confusion from defeat; a multitude; a fashionable assembly. — *v. t.* To put to flight.
Route (rōōt *or* rowt), *n.* A course or way.
Rou-tīne' (rōō-teen'), *n.* Round or course of business.
Rōve, *v. i.* [Orig. to *rob,* and hence to range, to wander.] To ramble; to wander; to roam; to stroll. — *v. t.* To draw through an eye or aperture.
Rōv'er, *n.* One who roves; a wanderer; a pirate.
Row (rou), *n.* A riot.
Rōw (rō), *n.* A line of persons or things; a rank. — *v. t.* To impel with oars.
Row'el (rou'el), *n.* The little wheel of a spur, armed with sharp points; a seton. — *v. t.* (130) To insert a rowel in.
Row'en (rou'en, 55), *n.* Second growth of grass.
Rōw'er, *n.* One who rows.
Roy'al, *a.* Regal; kingly. —

n. A large kind of paper; a sail.
Roy'al-ist, *n.* An adherent to kingly government.
Roy'al-ly, *adv.* In a kingly manner.
Roy'al-ty, *n.* Office, state, or character of a king; a percentage paid to the owner of an article or a right by one who hires the use of it.
Rŭb (129), *v. t.* To wipe; to scour. — *v. i.* To move along with pressure. — *n.* Friction; difficulty.
Rŭb'ber, *n.* One who, or that which, rubs; a decisive game or games.
Rŭb'bish, *n.* Waste matter; ruins; fragments.
Ru-bēs'cent, *n.* Becoming red.
Ru'bi-cŭnd, *a.* Inclining to redness.
Ru'bied, *a.* Red as a ruby.
Ru'ble, *n.* A silver and a gold coin of Russia.
Ru'brie, } *a.* Red; placed
Ru'bric-al, } in rubrics.
Ru'brie, *n.* Directions in a prayer-book as to the order of services.
Ru'brie-āte, *v. t.* To distinguish with red; to arrange as in a rubric.
Ru'by (141), *n.* A gem of a red color. — *a.* Of a red color.
Rŭck, *v. t.* To draw into wrinkles or folds.
Ruc-tā'tion, *n.* A belching of wind from the stomach.
Rŭd'der, *n.* The instrument by which a ship is steered.
Rŭd'di-ness, *n.* Redness.
Rŭd'dy, *a.* Of a lively red color; red; florid.
Rude (20), *a.* Uncivilized; rough; coarse; harsh.
Rude'ly, *adv.* Roughly; harshly; coarsely.
Rude'ness, *n.* Condition of being rude; unevenness; incivility; coarseness; inelegance.
Ru'di-ment, *n.* First principle; element; first part of education.
Ru'di-mĕnt'al, *a.* Pertaining to elements; elementary.
Rue, *n.* A very bitter plant.
— *v. t.* To lament; to regret; to be sorry for.
Rue'ful (130), *a.* Sorrowful; mournful.
Rŭff (123), *n.* [From Old Eng. *ruff,* equiv. to rough.] A plaited cloth round the neck; ruffle; a bird; a fish.
Rŭf'fian (rŭf'yan *or* rŭf'fi-an),

n. A boisterous, brutal fellow; a cut-throat. — *a.* Brutal; savage; vile.
Rŭf'fian-ism (rŭf'yan- *or* rŭf'fi-an-), *n.* Act or conduct of a ruffian.
Rŭf'fle, *v. t.* To wrinkle; to plait; to discompose; to vex; to disturb. — *n.* A plaited article of dress; disturbance; roll of a drum. [ish red.
Ru'fous, *a.* Reddish; brown-
Rŭg, *n.* A coarse, nappy, woolen cloth; a mat.
Rŭg'ged (57), *a.* Rough; uneven; harsh; crabbed; shaggy; robust. [ged manner.
Rŭg'ged-ly, *adv.* In a rug-
Rŭg'ged-ness, *n.* Roughness; unevenness of surface; harshness.
Ru-gōse', *a.* Full of wrinkles.
Ru'in, *n.* Overthrow; destruction; remains of buildings, &c. — *v. t.* To destroy utterly; to demolish.
Ru'in-oŭs, *a.* Destructive; fatal; composed of ruins.
Ru'in-oŭs-ly, *adv.* In a ruinous manner. [rule.
Rul'a-ble, *a.* Conformable to
Rule, *n.* That by which any thing is regulated; government; authority; an instrument for drawing lines, or for measuring. — *v. t.* To govern; to mark with lines. — *v. i.* To have power or command; to decide.
Rul'er, *n.* One who rules; a governor; an instrument for drawing lines.
Rŭm, *n.* A spirituous liquor distilled from molasses.
Rŭm'ble, *v. i.* To make a low, heavy, continued noise, like thunder.
Rŭm'bling, *n.* A low, heavy, continuous sound.
Ru'mi-nant, *a.* Chewing the cud. — *n.* An animal that chews the cud.
Ru'mi-nāte, *v. i.* To chew the cud; to meditate; to muse.
Ru'mi-nā'tion, *n.* Act of ruminating; meditation.
Rŭm'mage, *v. t.* A close search. — *v. t.* To search or examine thoroughly.
Ru'mor (29, 155), *n.* A flying or popular report or story. — *v. t.* To report.
Rŭmp, *n.* End of the back bone and parts adjacent; buttocks.
Rŭm'ple, *v. t.* To wrinkle; to make uneven. — *n.* A wrinkle; an irregular fold.

ā, ē, ī, ō, ū, ȳ, *long*; ă, ĕ, ĭ, ŏ, ŭ, ў, *short*; câre, cär, àsk, ąll, whąt; ēre, vęil, tẽrm; pīque, fĩrm;

Rŭn, v. i. or t. [imp. RAN or RUN; p. p. RUN.] To move with rapidity; to flow; to melt; to form in a mold; to smuggle. — n. Flow; course; way; small stream; result; unusual demands on a bank.
Rŭn'a-gāte, | n. A fugitive;
Rŭn'a-wāy, } deserter; renegade. [der.
Rŭn'dle, n. Round of a ladder.
Rŭng, imp. & p. p. of Ring.
Rŭn'let, n. A small stream.
Rŭn'ner, n. One who runs; a messenger; a part on which a sled slides.
Rŭn'net, n. See Rennet.
Rŭnt, n. A stunted animal.
Ru-pee' (140), n. An East Indian coin; the silver rupee is 46 cents, and the gold 7 dollars.
Rŭpt'ūre, n. A breach; a burst; hernia. — v. t. To break; to burst.
Ru'ral, a. [Lat. ruralis, from rus, ruris, country.] Belonging to the country; rustic.
Ruse, n. Artifice; stratagem.

Rŭsh (140), n. A violent motion or course; a plant. — v. i. To pass or move with vehemence or rapidity.
Rŭsh'-līght (-līt), n. A candle with a wick made of a rush.
Rŭsh'y, a. Abounding with rushes.
Rŭsk, n. A species of cake
Rŭss, or Ryss, a. Pertaining to Russia. — n. The language of the Russians.
Rŭs'set, a. Of a reddish-brown color.
Rŭs'set, | n. An apple of
Rŭs'set-ing, | a russet color.
Rŭs'sian (rŭsh'an or rŭ'shan), a. Pertaining to Russia. — n. A native, or the language, of Russia.
Rŭst, n. A crust or coating which forms on metals. — v. i. To gather rust. — v. t. To make rusty.
Rŭs'tic (127), a. Rural; rude; inelegant; simple. — n. An inhabitant of the country.
Rŭs'tic-āte (118), v. To re-

side in, or banish to, the country.
Rŭs'ti-cā'tion, n. Residence in, or banishment to, the country.
Rus-tiç'i-ty, n. Rustic manners; rudeness; simplicity.
Rŭst'i-ly, adv. In a rusty state or manner.
Rŭst'i-ness, n. State or quality of being rusty.
Rŭs'tle (rŭs'l), v. i. To make a quick succession of small sounds, like the rubbing of silk cloth or dry leaves.
Rŭst'y, a. Covered with rust.
Rŭt, n. Track worn by a wheel. — v. i. To seek copulation. [turnip.
Ru'tà-bā'gà, n. A variety of
Rŭth, n. Pity; tenderness.
Rŭth'less, a. Cruel; pitiless.
Rŭth'less-ly, adv. Without pity; cruelly.
Rŭt'ty, a. Full of ruts; lustful; salacious.
Rye (ri). n. A kind of grain.
Rȳ'ot, n. A peasant in the East Indies.

S.

SĂB'A-ŌTH, or Sa-bā'oth, n. Armies; hosts.
Săb'ba-tā'ri-an, a. Pertaining to the Sabbath. — n. A strict observer of the Sabbath; one who regards the seventh day as holy.
Săb'bath, n. [Heb. shabbāth, fr. shabāth, to rest from labor.] The day of religious rest; Sunday.
Sab-băt'ic, | a. Pertaining
Sab-băt'ic-al, } to the Sabbath.
Sā'ber }
Sā'bre }
(151), n.   Saber.
A sword
with a broad and heavy blade, thick at the back, and a little curved toward the point.
Sā'bi-an, n. A worshiper of the sun, moon, and stars.
Sā'ble, n. An animal of the weasel kind, and its fur. — a. Dark; black.
Săc (127), n. A little bag or receptacle for some animal or vegetable fluid.
Săc'cha-rĭf'er-oŭs, a. Producing sugar.

Săc'cha-rīne, a. Pertaining to, or having the qualities of, sugar.
Săc'cha-roid, | a. Having
Săc'cha-roid'al, } a texture like that of loaf sugar.
Săç'er-dō'tal, a. Priestly.
Săch'el, n. See Satchel.
Sā'chem, n. An Indian chief.
Săck (127), n. A bag; pillage of a town; a loose upper garment; a sweet wine. — v. t. To pillage; to plunder.
Săck'but, n. A brass wind instrument of music. [sacks.
Săck'clŏth, n. Cloth for
Săck'ing, n. Cloth of which sacks are made; canvas fastened to a bedstead for supporting the bed.
Săc'ra-ment, n. A solemn religious ordinance, specifically, the Lord's Supper.
Săc'ra-mĕnt'al, a. Pertaining to a sacrament.
Sā'ered, a. Pertaining to God or religion. — SYN. Holy; divine; consecrated.
Sā'ered-ly, adv. Religiously.
Sā'ered-ness, n. State or quality of being sacred.

Săc'ri-fīce (-fīz, 62), v. t. To offer to God in worship; to destroy; to give up with loss. — n. An offering to God; any loss incurred.
Săc'ri-fī'cial (-fĭsh'al), a. Pertaining to sacrifice.
Săc'ri-lege, n. A violation of sacred things.
Săc'ri-lē'ġioŭs, a. Violating sacred things; involving sacrilege; profane; impious.
Săc'ri-lē'ġioŭs-ly, adv. Impiously; profanely.
Săc'ris-tan, n. A sexton.
Săc'ris-ty, n. A vestry room.
Săd, a. Sorrowful; gloomy; cheerless; grave.
Săd'den (săd'dn), v. To make or become sad.
Săd'dle, n. [A.-S. sadul, sadl, from the root of Eng. sit.] A seat for the back of a horse. — v. t. To put a saddle on. [saddles.
Săd'dler, n. One who makes
Săd'dler-y, n. Materials for saddles and harnesses.
Săd'dle-tree, n. Frame of a saddle.
Săd'du-çee, n. One of a Jew-

sŏn, ôr, dọ, wǫlf, tōō, tŏŏk; ûrn, rye, pull; ç, ġ, soft; c, ġ, hard; aṣ; exist; ŋ as ng; this.

SAD-IRON   262   SAMPHIRE

ish sect which denied the resurrection. [Iron.
Sǎd'-ī'ron (-ī'urn), n. A flat
Sǎd'ly, adv. In a sad manner; sorrowfully; gloomily. [sad.
Sǎd'ness, n. State of being
Sāfe, a. Free from danger; secure. — n. A place to secure provisions, money, &c.
Sāfe'-cŏn'duct, n. A convoy or guard; a pass or warrant of security.
Sāfe'guärd, n. A thing that protects; a defense; a passport; a safe-conduct.
Sāfe'ly, adv. Securely.
Sāfe'ty (132), n. Freedom from danger or loss; security.
Sāfe'ty-vălve, n. A valve by which a steam-boiler is preserved from bursting.
Sǎf'fron, n. A plant bearing a yellow flower. — a. Like saffron.
Săg, v. i. To swag: to incline.
Sa-gā'cious, a. Of keen penetration and judgment; acute: sage; wise.
Sa-gā'cious-ly, adv. With sagacity; sagely.
Sa-găç'i-ty, n. Quick discernment; penetration.
Săg'a-mōre, n. An Indian chief; a sachem.
Sāge, a. Wise; sagacious; discreet. — n. A wise man; a certain plant or herb.
Sāge'ly, adv. Wisely; acutely.
Săg'it-tal, a. Pertaining to an arrow.
†Săg'it-tā'ri-us, n. The archer; one of the twelve signs of the zodiac.
Sā'go, n. Granulated starch from a species of palm.
Said (sěd, 133), imp. & p. p. of Say.
Sāil, n. A ship's canvas; a ship of any kind; an excursion on the water. — v. i. or t. To be conveyed on the water, with or without sails; to fly through; to manage, as a vessel.
Sāil'-clŏth, n. Canvas used for making sails.
Sāil'-lŏft, n. A loft or room where sails are made.
Sāi'lor, n. A seaman.
Sāil'-yärd, n. A yard or spar on which sails are extended.
Sāint, n. One eminent for piety; a holy person. — v. t. To make a saint of; to canonize.
Sāint'ed, a. Holy; sacred.
Sāint'-like, } a. Resembling
Sāint'ly, } a saint.

Sāke, n. Final cause; purpose; end; reason.
Săl, n. Salt.
Săl'a-ble (135), a. Fit for sale; finding a ready sale.
Săl'a-ble-ness, n. State of being salable.
Sa-lā'cious, a. Lustful; lewd.
Săl'ad, n. Food of raw herbs dressed with condiments.
Săl'a-măn'der, n. A small reptile allied to the lizard and the frog, formerly thought to be able to live in fire.
Săl'a-ried, a. Having a salary.
Săl'a-ry (141), n. A stated allowance for services.
Sāle, n. Act of selling; market; demand.
Săl'e-rā'tus, n. A bi-carbonate of potash, used in cookery.
Sāles'man (143), n. One employed to sell goods.
Săl'ic, a. Designating a law which excludes females from the throne.
Sā'li-ent, a. Shooting out or up; heuce, prominent. [salt.
Sa-līf'er-oŭs, a. Producing
Săl'i-fī'a-ble (135), a. Capable of becoming a salt.
Săl'i-fȳ, v. t. To form into a salt, as a base, by combining an acid with it.
Sa-līne', or Sā'līne, a. Salt; consisting of, or containing, salt. — n. A salt spring.
Sa-lī'va, n. The fluid secreted in the mouth; spittle.
Sa-lī'val, } a. Secreting sa-
Săl'i-va-ry, } liva, as the glands.
Săl'i-vāte, v. t. To excite an unusual discharge of saliva in, as by the use of mercury.
Săl'i-vā'tion, n. Act of causing continued unnatural flow of saliva.
Săl'lōw, a. Of a pale, sickly, yellow color. — n. A tree or shrub of the willow kind.
Săl'lōw-ness, n. Paleness tinged with a dark yellow.
Săl'ly, n. [From Lat. salire, to leap.] A sudden eruption; wild gayety. — v. i. To leap or rush out, as from a fortress.
Săl'ly-pōrt, n. A gate through which troops sally.
Săl'ma-gŭn'di, n. Chopped meat and pickled herring, seasoned with oil, vinegar, &c.; a medley.
Săl'mon (săm'un), n. A large fish, of a yellowish red color.
Sa-lōōn', n. A spacious and elegant apartment.

Săl'si-fȳ, n. A garden plant.
Salt (7), n. A substance used for seasoning food; an old sailor; a combination of an acid with a base; wit; a salt-cellar. — v. t. To sprinkle or season with salt.
Sǎlt'a-to-ry, a. Leaping or dancing, or used therein.
Salt'-çĕl'lar, n. A small dish for salt at table.
Salt'ern, n. A salt-work.
Sǎlt'ish, a. Somewhat salt.
Sǎlt'ness, n. Taste of salt.
Sǎlt-pē'ter, } n. A mineral
Sǎlt-pē'tre, } salt composed of nitric acid and potash.
Sǎlt'rheum (-rȳm), n. An affection of the skin.
Sa-lū'bri-oŭs, a. Healthful.
Sa-lū'bri-ty, n. Healthfulness; wholesomeness.
Săl'u-ta-ry, a. Promoting health or safety.
Săl'u-tā'tion, n. Act of greeting another. — SYN. Greeting; salute; address.
Sa-lū'ta-tō'ri-an, n. A student who pronounces the salutatory oration at Commencement.
Sa-lū'ta-to-ry, a. Containing salutations or a welcome.
Sa-lūte', v. t. To greet; to hail; to kiss; to honor. — n. Act of saluting; a kiss; discharge of cannon.
Săl'va-bĭl'i-ty, n. Quality of being salvable.
Săl'va-ble, a. Capable of being saved.
Săl'vage, n. Reward for saving a ship or its cargo.
Sal-vā'tion, n. Act of saving; preservation; preservation from eternal misery.
Sǎlve (säv), n. A substance for covering wounds or sores.
Săl'yer, n. A plate or waiter to present something on.
Săl'vo, n. (pl. Săl'vȯṣ, 140), An exception; military or naval salute; a volley.
Săl'vör, n. One who saves a ship or goods at sea.
Săm'bo, n. Offspring of a black person and a mulatto.
Sāme, n. Identical; not different or other; similar.
Sāme'ness, n. Identity; near resemblance; similarity; correspondence.
Sā'mi-el, n. A destructive wind from the desert, in Arabia; the simoom.
Sămp, n. Maize broken coarse, and boiled with milk.
Săm'phīre (or săm'fur), n.

ā, ĕ, I, ō, ū, ȳ, long; ă, ĕ, ĭ, ŏ, ŭ, ȳ, short; câre, cär, ȧsk, ạll, whạt; ēre, vẹil, tẽrm; p:que, firm ı

SAMPLE 263 SATISFY

A plant growing by the seashore, and used as a pickle.
Sam'ple, *n.* A specimen.
Sam'pler, *n.* A collection of needle-work; patterns.
San'a-ble, *a.* Capable of being healed; curable.
San'a-tive, *a.* Adapted to cure; healing.
San'a-to-ry, *a.* Act of sanctifying.
Sanc'ti-fi-ca'tion, *n.* Act of sanctifying.
Sanc'ti-fi'er, *n.* One who sanctifies; the Holy Spirit.
Sanc'ti-fỹ (118, 135), *v. t.* To make sacred or holy; to secure from violation.
Sanc'ti-mō'ni-oŭs, *a.* Appearing holy; saintly.
Sanc'ti-mo-ny, *n.* Hypocritical devoutness.
Sanc'tion, *n.* That which confirms; solemn ratification.— *v. t.* To ratify; to give sanction or authority to.
Sanc'ti-tūde, *n.* Holiness;
Sanc'ti-ty, *n.* purity; religious binding force.
Sanct'u-a-ry, *n.* A sacred place; house of worship; place of refuge.
Sanc'tum, *n.* A place of retreat for privacy.
Sand, *n.* Fine particles of stony matter; (*pl.*) sandy tracts of land.— *v. t.* To sprinkle with sand.
San'dal, *n.* A kind of shoe or slipper.
San'dal-wŏod, *n.* A yellow, fragrant Eastern wood, and the tree producing it. Sandals.
Sand'i-ness, *n.* State of being sandy or of a sandy color.
Sand'stōne, *n.* A rock made of sand more or less firmly united.
Sand'wich, *n.* Pieces of bread and butter with a slice of meat between them.— *v. t.* To make into a sandwich, or into something like one; to interlard.
San'dy, *a.* Full of sand; being of the color of sand.
Sāne, *a.* Sound in mind; not deranged; whole; healthy.
Sang, *imp.* of *Sing*.
Sang'ga-ree', *n.* Sweetened and spiced wine and water.
†**Sang-froid** (sŏng'frwȧ'), *n.* Cool blood; indifference.
San-guif'er-oŭs, *a.* Conveying blood. [duction of blood.
Sąn'gui-fi-cā'tion, *n.* Pro-

Sąn'gui-fỹ, *v. t.* To produce blood.
Sąn'gui-na-ry, *a.* Bloody; eager to shed blood; cruel.
Sąn'guine (sȧng'gwĭn), *a.* Red, like blood; full of blood; confident; full of hope. [fidence of success.
Sąn'guine-ly, *adv.* With confidence.
San-guin'e-oŭs, *a.* Abounding with blood.
San'he-drim, *n.* The supreme council of the Jews.
†**Sā'ni-ēs**, *n.* A thin, watery fluid from a wound.
Sā'ni-oŭs, *a.* Pertaining to, or emitting, sanies. [health.
Săn'i-ta-ry, *a.* Pertaining to
Săn'i-ty, *n.* [Lat. *sanitas*, fr. *sanus*, sound.] Soundness of
Sănk, *imp.* of *Sink*. [mind.
Săn'scrĭt, *n.* The ancient
Săn'skrĭt, language of Hindostan.
Săp, *n.* Vital juice of plants; a military mine.— *v. t.* To undermine; to subvert by digging.
Săp'id, *a.* Well tasted; having a relish; savory. [ness.
Sa-pĭd'i-ty, *n.* Taste; savoriness.
Sā'pi-ençe, *n.* Wisdom.
Sā'pi-ent, *a.* Wise; sagacious.
Săp'less, *a.* Having no sap; dry; withered.
Săp'ling, *n.* A young tree.
Săp-o-nā'çeoŭs, *a.* Having the qualities of soap; soapy.
Sa-pŏnʻi-fỹ, *v. t.* To convert into soap. [vor; relish.
Sā'por, *n.* Taste; savor; flavor.
Săp'o-rĭf'ic, *a.* Giving flavor.
Săp'per, *n.* One who saps; a kind of miner.
Săp'phie(săffĭk), *a.* Pertaining to Sappho, a Grecian poetess, or to a kind of verse said to have been invented by her.
Săp'phīre (săf'īr or săf'ur), *n.* A precious blue stone.
Săp'py, *a.* Full of sap; juicy.
Săp'sa-go, *n.* Swiss cheese.
Săr'a-bănd, *n.* A grave Spanish dance.
Săr'a-çĕn'ic, *a.* Relating to the Saracens. [a taunt.
Săr'casm, *n.* Bitter reproach;
Sar-căs'tic, *a.* Bitterly
Sar-căs'tic-al, satirical; scornfully severe.
Sar-căs'tic-al-ly, *adv.* In a sarcastic manner.
Sär'çe'net, *n.* A fine, thin silk, used for linings, &c.
Sar-cŏph'a-goŭs, *a.* Flesh-eating. [coffin.
Sar-cŏph'a-gus, *n.* A stone

Sär'dĭne, *n.* [So called from the island of *Sardinia*.] A fish of the herring family.
Sär'di-us, *n.* A precious stone; a carnelian.
Sar-dŏn'ic, *a.* Forced, heartless, or bitter;— said of a laugh or smile.
Sär'do-nyx, *n.* A precious stone of a reddish yellow color, allied to the onyx.
Sär'sa-pa-rĭl'la, *n.* A species of medicinal plant.
Săsh (140), *n.* An ornamental belt or band; a window-frame.
Săs'sa-frăs, *n.* A certain tree that has an aromatic bark.
Săt, *imp.* of *Sit*.
Sā'tan, *n.* The great adversary of man; the devil.
Sa-tăn'ic, *a.* Having the
Sa-tăn'ic-al, qualities of Satan; very wicked; devilish.
Sā'tan-ĭșm, *n.* A diabolical spirit or act.
Sătch'el, *n.* A little sack or bag for books and papers.
Sāte, *v. t.* To satisfy; to glut; to satiate; to surfeit.
Săt'el-līte, *n.* A small planet revolving round a larger; an obsequious attendant.
Sā'ti-āte (sā'shi-āt), *v. t.* To fill or gratify to the utmost;
— SYN. To satisfy; content, sate; glut.
Sā'ti-ate, *a.* Filled to satiety
Sa-tī'e-ty, *n.* [Lat. *satietas*, fr. *sat, satis*, enough.] Fullness beyond desire or pleasure.
Săt'in, *n.* A glossy silk.
Săt'in-ĕt', *n.* A woolen cloth.
Săt'īre (*in Eng.* săt'ur), *n.* A discourse or poem containing severe censure; trenchant wit.
Sa-tĭr'ic, *a.* Censorious;
Sa-tĭr'ic-al, sarcastic; severe in language.
Sa-tĭr'ic-al-ly, *adv.* In a satirical manner. [satire.
Săt'ir-ĭst, *n.* One who writes
Săt'ir-īze (153), *v. t.* To make the object of satire.
Săt'is-făc'tion, *n.* Content; gratification of desire; that which satisfies.
Săt'is-făc'to-ri-ly, *adv.* So as to give content.
Săt'is-făc'to-ry, *a.* Giving content; making amends.
Săt'is-fī'er (135), *n.* One who gives satisfaction.
Săt'is-fỹ, *v. t.* To content; to discharge, as a debt, &c.; to give assurance to.

ạn, ȯr, dọ, wọlf, tōō, tŏŏk; ŭrn, rụe, pụ̈ll; ç, ġ, *soft*; ȼ, g̈, *hard*; aẓ; eẋist; ɳ *as* ng; this

Să'trap, or Săt'rap, n. Governor of a province in ancient Persia.

Săt'u-ra-ble, a. Capable of being saturated.

Săt'u rāte, v. t. To cause to become completely soaked.

Săt'u-rā'tion, n. State of being saturated.

Săt'ur-day, n. The last day of the week.

Săt'urn, n. A remote planet.

†Săt'ur-nā'li-a, n. pl. Festival of Saturn; unrestrained license and merriment.

Săt'ur-nā'li-an, a. Riotously merry; dissolute.

Sa-tûr'ni-an, a. Relating to Saturn, or to his reign; golden; happy.

Săt'ur-nĭne, a. Grave; heavy; gloomy; dull; phlegmatic.

Să'tyr, n. A fabulous sylvan deity, half man, half goat.

Sauçe, n. Something eaten with food to improve its relish. — v. t. To apply sauce to; to be impudent or saucy to.

Sauçe'bŏx, n. A saucy fellow.

Sau'çer, n. A vessel or dish for holding a tea-cup.

Sau'çi-ly, adv. Impudently.

Sau'çy, a. Pert; impudent.

Sauer'krout (sour'krout), n. Cabbage preserved in brine, and allowed to ferment.

Säun'ter (sän'ter), v. t. To wander about idly.

Säun'ter-er, n. One who saunters, or wanders about.

Sau'ri-an, n. A reptile of the lizard kind.

Sau'sage, n. A roll of minced and highly seasoned meat stuffed into a skin.

Săv'a-ble (133), a. Capable of being saved.

Săv'age, a. Uncivilized; barbarous; cruel. — n. An uncivilized person; one who delights in cruelty. [ly.

Săv'age-ly, adv. Barbarously.

Săv'age-ness, n. Barbarousness; cruelty; wildness.

Săv'age-ry, n. Barbarity.

Sa-văn'nà (140), n. An open meadow or plain.

†Savant (sȧ'vŏng'), n. [Fr.] A man of learning.

Sāve, v. t. To preserve; to rescue; to spare; to except. — v. i. To avoid expense.

Sāv'ing, a. Frugal; economical. — n. That which is saved. — prep. With the exception of.

Sāv'ior } (155), n. One who
Sāv'iour } preserves; our Lord Jesus Christ; the Redeemer.

Sā'vor (155), n. Taste; relish; odor; smell; scent. — v. i. To have a taste or smell.

Sā'vor-i-ness, n. A pleasing taste or smell. [vor.

Sā'vor-less, a. Wanting savor.

Sā'vor-y, a. Pleasing to the taste or smell. — n. An aromatic culinary plant.

Sa-voy', n. A kind of cabbage.

Saw, n. An instrument to cut boards, &c.; a saying; a proverb. — v. t. or i. [imp. SAWED; p. p. SAWED, SAWN.] To cut or divide with a saw.

Saw'dust, n. Dust or particles made by sawing.

Saw'-pĭt, n. A pit for a man to stand in when sawing timber placed over it.

Saw'yer. n. One whose occupation is to saw wood, &c.

Săx'i-frage, n. A hardy plant growing on or among rocks.

Săx'on (or săks'n), a. Pertaining to the Saxons. — n. The language of the Saxons.

Sāy (136), v. t. [imp. & p. p. SAID.] To speak; to utter; to tell; to affirm; to recite; to report. — n. A speech; something said.

Sāy'ing, n. An expression; sentence uttered; a maxim.

Scăb, n. Incrustation over a sore or wound.

Scăb'bard, n. Case or sheath of a sword.

Scăb'bed, a. Covered with scabs; paltry; vile.

Scăb'by, a. Full of scabs.

Scā'bi-oŭs, a. Consisting of scabs; scabby.

Sea'brous, a. Having short, hard points; rough; rugged.

Scăf'fold, n. A staging for workmen, or for the execution of a criminal.

Scăf'fold-ing, n. Frame or structure for temporary support.

Scagl-iō'là (skal-yō'-). n. A species of stucco made to imitate marble. [scaled.

Scāl'a-ble, a. Capable of being

Sea-lāde', n. Assault with ladders on a besieged place.

Scȧld, v. t. [Lat. excaldare, from ex and caldus, calidus, warm, hot.] To burn by a hot liquid or steam. — n. A burning with hot liquor or steam; scurf on the head.

Scȧld. n. An old Norse bard or poet.

Scȧld'-hĕad, n. An eruptive disorder of the hairy scalp.

Scāle, n. Dish of a balance; one of the membranous or bony pieces forming the covering of a fish; gradation; gamut. — v. t. To strip of scales: to mount by, or as if by, a ladder. — v. i. To clear off scales; to take off in thin layers.

Sca-lēne', a. Having three sides and angles unequal.

Scā'li-ness, n. State or quality of being scaly.

Scăll'ion, n. A plant allied to the onion; a scullion.

Scăl'lop (skŏl'-), n. A marine shell-fish; a curved indentation on the edge of any thing. — v. t. To cut the edge of into segments of circles.

Scălp, n. Skin of the top of the head. — v. t. To take off the scalp of. [knife.

Scălp'el, n. A surgeon's

Scāl'y, a. Abounding with scales; rough.

Scăm'ble, v. t. To stir quick.

Scăm'mo-ny, n. A plant and an inspissated sap obtained from it.

Scămp. n. A knavish fellow.

Scămp'er, v. i. To run with speed or hurry.

Scăn (129), v. t. To examine closely; to measure by counting the poetic feet.

Scăn'dal, n. Imputed disgrace; defamatory speech or report; calumny.

Scăn'dal-ize, v. t. To offend; to defame; to reproach.

Scăn'dal-oŭs, a. Disgraceful to reputation; defamatory.

Scăn'dal-oŭs-ly, adv. Disgracefully; shamefully.

Scăn'ning, n. Act of resolving a verse into its component feet.

Scăn'sion, n. Act of scanning verse. [climbing.

Scan-sō'ri-al, a. Adapted to

Scănt, v. t. To limit; to straiten; to make scanty. — a. Scarcely sufficient. — adv. Not quite.

Scănt'i-ly, } adv. Not fully
Scănt'ly, } or sufficiently.

Scănt'i-ness, } n. Want of
Scănt'ness, } sufficiency.

Scănt'ling, n. A narrow piece of timber.

Scănt'y, a. Hardly sufficient; sparing; niggardly; scant.

Scāpe, n. A peduncle rising from the ground and bearing the fructification in its apex.

Scape'-goat (139), *n.* One who suffers for the misdeeds of others.
Scape'-grace, *n.* A graceless hair-brained fellow.
†**Scap'u-là,** *n.* (*pl.* **Scap'u-læ.**) The shoulder-blade.
Scap'u-lar, *a.* Belonging to the shoulder or scapula.
Scap'u-la-ry, *n.* Part of an ecclesiastical habit.
Scar, *n.* Mark of a wound. — *v. t.* To mark with a scar.
Scarce, *a.* Uncommon; rare; not abundant. [difficulty.
Scarce'ly, *adv* Hardly; with
Scar'ci-ty, *n.* Deficiency; want; lack; dearth.
Scare, *v. t.* To terrify suddenly; to frighten; to affright.
Scare'crow, *n.* A thing set up to frighten birds.
Scarf (140), *n.* A loose covering of cloth; part cut away from a timber to make it form a joint with another. — *v. t.* To throw on loosely; to cut a scarf on, as for a joint on timber.
Scarf'-skin, *n.* Outer thin skin; cuticle.
Scar'i-fi-ca'tion, *n.* A slight incision in the skin.
Scar'i-fi-ca'tor, *n.* An instrument for scarifying.
Scar'i-fi'er, *n.* One who, or that which, scarifies.
Scar'i-fy, *v. t.* To scratch and cut, as the skin.
Scir'la-ti'nà, *n.* Scarlet fever.
Scar-lat'i-noùs, *a.* Pertaining to the scarlet fever.
Scar'let, *n.* An orange-red color. — *a.* Of an orange-red color.
Scar'let Fē'ver. A contagious disorder characterized by a scarlet rash.
Scarp, *n.* Interior slope of a ditch nearest the parapet.
Scath, ⎱ *v. t.* To do harm to;
Scathe, ⎰ to injure; to damage; to destroy.
Scath'less, *a.* Without harm.
Scat'ter, *v. t.* [A.-S. *scateran,* allied to *sceddan,* to shed.] To spread thinly; to disperse; to dissipate; to strew about.
Scav'en-ger, *n.* One employed to clean streets.
Scēne, *n.* A stage; subordinate part of a play; a series of actions; a curtain; exhibition; place of exhibition.
Scēn'er-y, *n.* Painted representation of the scenes in a play; appearance of places; landscape.

Scēn'ic, or **Scē'nic,** ⎱ *a.* Dra-
Scēn'ic-al (scū-), ⎰ matic; theatrical.
Scen'o-graph'ic, ⎱ *a.*
Scen'o-graph'ic-al, ⎰ Drawn in perspective.
Sce-nog'ra-phy, *n.* Representation in perspective.
Scent, *n.* Odor; smell; sense of smell. — *v. t.* To smell; to perfume. [smell.
Scent'less, *a.* Having no
Scep'ter, ⎱ *n.* Ensign of roy-
Scep'tre, ⎰ alty.
Scep'tered, ⎱ *a.* Invested with
Scep'tred, ⎰ royal authority.
Scep'tic, *n.* See *Skeptic.*
Sched'ule (skĕd'yṳl), *n.* An inventory of property, debts, &c. — SYN. List; catalogue.
Schēme (skēm), *n.* A plan; project; contrivance. — *v. t.* To plan; to contrive.
Schēm'er, ⎱ *n.* A projector;
Schēm'ist, ⎰ a contriver.
Schĭsm (sĭzm), *n.* Division for separation, esp. in a church.
Schis-mat'ic (siz-mat'ik, 120), *n.* One guilty of schism.
Schis-mat'ic ⎱ (sĭz-), *a.*
Schis-mat'ic-al ⎰ Pertaining to, or partaking of, schism.
Schŏl'ar (skŏl'ar), *n.* A learner; a learned person; a pupil; a disciple.
Schŏl'ar-like, ⎱ *a.* Like, or
Schŏl'ar-ly, ⎰ becoming, a scholar.
Schŏl'ar-shĭp, *n.* Learning; erudition; a foundation for the support of a student.
Scho-lás'tic, *a.* Pertaining to a school, or to the schoolmen of the middle ages.
Scho-lás'ti-cism, *n.* The method or subtilties of the schools. [tor.
Schŏ'li-ast, *n.* A commentator.
Schŏ'li-um, *n.* (Lat. *pl.* **Schŏ'li-à** ; *Eng. pl.* **Schŏ'li-ums.**) An explanatory observation.
School (skōōl), *n.* A place of discipline and instruction; pupils assembled for instruction; a sect; a system of doctrines. — *v. t.* To instruct; to tutor; to discipline.
School'-fĕl'low, *n.* One bred at the same school and time with another.
School'-house, *n.* A house for a school. [school.
School'ing, *n.* Instruction in
School'man (143), *n.* One versed in scholastic divinity.
School'-más'ter, *n.* A male teacher of a school.

Schōōn'er, *n.* A small, sharp-built vessel, usually with two masts.
Sci-ág'ra-phy, *n.* Art of delineating shadows as they fall naturally. [hip.
Schooner.
Sci-ăt'ic, *a.* Affecting the
Sci-ăt'ic-à, *n.* Rheumatism in the hip.
Sci'ence, *n.* [Lat. *scientia,* fr. *scire,* to know.] Knowledge; collection of general principles; philosophical knowledge.
Sci'en-tif'ic, ⎱ *a.* Being ac-
Sci'en-tif'ic-al, ⎰ cording to, or versed in, science.
Sci'en-tif'ic-al-ly, *adv.* According to the principles of science.
Scin'til-lant, *a.* Emitting sparks; sparkling.
Scin'til-lā'tion, *n.* Act of sparkling or twinkling.
Scin'til-lāte, *v. t.* To emit sparks; to sparkle; to twinkle. [knowledge.
Sci'o-lĭsm, *n.* Superficial
Sci'o-list, *n.* A superficial scholar; a smatterer.
Sci'on, *n.* Shoot of a plant cut for ingrafting; a descendant.
Sci-ŏp'tic, ⎱ *a.* Pertaining to
Sci-ŏp'tric, ⎰ an optical arrangement for forming images in a darkened room.
Scir-rhōs'i-ty (skĭr-rŏs'-), *n.* A morbid induration, as of a gland. [durated.
Scĭr'rhoŭs (skĭr'rus), *a.* In-
Scĭr'rhus (skĭr'rus), *n.* A hard tumor in the flesh.
Scĭs'sel, *n.* Clippings of metals.
Scĭs'sĭle, *a.* Capable of being cut.
Scĭs'sion (sĭzh'un), *n.* A dividing by means of a sharp instrument.
Scĭs'sors (sĭz'zurz), *n. pl.* A small cutting instrument.
Scĭs'sure (sĭzh'ur), *n.* A longitudinal cut.
Scle-rŏt'ic, *a.* Hard or firm, as the outer coat of the eye.
Scoff (123), *v. i.* or *t.* To treat with scorn; to mock; to jeer; to deride. — *n.* Expression of scorn; mockery; derision.
Scŏff'er, *n.* One who scoffs.
Scōld, *v. i.* or *t.* To find fault; to chide. — *n.* One who scolds; a shrew.
Scōld'ing, *n.* Act of chiding.
Sconce, *n.* A fixed hanging or

projecting candlestick; the skull; sense.

Scōop, *n.* A large ladle; a sweep. — *v. t.* To lade out; to cut into a hollow.

Scōpe, *n.* Sweep or range of the eye or mind; that at which one aims; free course. — SYN. Space; room; intention; tendency; drift.

Scor-bū'tic, *a.* Relating to, or diseased with, scurvy.

Scŏrch, *v. t.* To burn on the surface.

Scōre, *n.* A notch; a tallymark; twenty; a reckoning; account. — *v. t.* To notch; to cut; to mark; to charge.

Seō'ri-à, *n.* Dross; recrement; slag.

Seō'ri-ā'ceoŭs (-shus), *a.* Relating to scoria; like dross.

Seō'ri-fi-eā'tion, *n.* Act of reducing to dross. [scoria.

Seō'ri-fȳ, *v. t.* To reduce to

Scŏrn, *n.* Extreme and passionate contempt; subject of such contempt. — *v. t.* To hold in extreme contempt.

Scŏrn'er, *n.* One who scorns.

Scŏrn'ful (139), *a.* Full of scorn; disdainful; contemptuous.

Scŏrn'ful-ly, *adv.* With scorn.

Scŏr'pi-on, *n.* A reptile; sign in the zodiac.

Scŏt, *n.* A native of Scotland; a tax or fine; a bill or reckoning.

Scorpion.

Scŏtch, *a.* Pertaining to Scotland. — *v. t.* To stop, as a wheel, from rolling back; to cut slightly.

Scŏtch'-cŏl'lops, *n. pl.* Veal cut into small pieces.

Scŏt'-free, *a.* Excused from payment. [the Scots.

Scŏt'ti-çĭşm, *n.* An idiom of

Scŏt'tish, *a.* Pertaining to Scotland or to the Scots.

Scoun'drel, *n.* [Corrupted fr. Ger. *schandkerl,* fr. *schande,* infamy, and *kerl,* fellow.] A mean, worthless fellow; a rascal.

Scoun'drel-ĭşm, *n.* Conduct of a scoundrel.

Scour, *v. t.* To clean by rubbing hard; to pass over swiftly.

Scourge (skūrj), *n.* A whip; a lash; punishment. — *v. t.* To whip severely; to lash.

Scoûrġ'er, *n.* One who scourges or punishes.

Scout, *n.* One sent to discover the movements and condition of an enemy; a spy. — *v. i.* To act as a scout. — *v. t.* To sneer at. [boat.

Seow, *n.* A large flat-bottomed

Seowl, *v. i.* To wrinkle the brows in displeasure. — *n.* A wrinkling of the brows in frowning.

Scrăb'ble, *v. t.* or *i.* To scrape rudely; to scramble; to scrawl; to scribble.

Scrăg, *n.* Something lean and thin; a neck-piece of meat.

Scrăg'ġed, } *a.* Broken; lean

Scrăg'ġy, } and rough

Scrăg'ġi-ness, *n.* Ruggedness of surface; leanness.

Scrăm'ble, *v. i.* To clamber with hands and knees. — *n.* Act of scrambling or climbing. [scrambles.

Scrăm'bler, *n.* One who

Scrăp, *n.* A little piece; a fragment; a crumb; a bit.

Scrăp'-bŏŏk, *n.* A blank book for extracts.

Scrāpe, *v. t.* To rub off the surface of with a rough tool. — *v. i.* To make an awkward bow. — *n.* Act of scraping; a low and awkward bow; a disagreeable predicament.

Scrāp'er, *n.* An instrument for scraping and cleaning.

Scrătch, *v. t.* or *i.* To rub and tear the surface of. — *n.* A slight wound; a sort of wig; (*pl.*) dry scabs between a horse's heel and pastern joint.

Scrawl, *v. t.* or *i.* To write or mark awkwardly. — *n.* Hasty, bad writing.

Scraw'ny, *a.* Meagre; wasted.

Screak, *v. n.* To creak, as a door or wheel. — *n.* A creaking.

Scream, *v. i.* To utter a sudden, shrill cry. — *n.* A shrill outcry; a screech.

Screech, *v. i.* To shriek; to scream. — *n.* A harsh, shrill cry; a scream.

Screed, *n.* A wooden rule for running moldings.

Screen, *v. t.* To conceal; to shelter; to defend; to pass through a screen. — *n.* Something that shelters, or shuts off view, &c.; a partition; a long, coarse sieve.

Screw (skru), *n.* A cylinder, or a cylindrical perforation, grooved spirally, used for various purposes. — *v. t.* To press or fasten with a screw; to squeeze; to distort.

Scrib'ble, *v. i.* or *t.* To write without care. — *n.* Careless writing. Screw.

Scrib'bler, *n.* A petty writer.

Scrībe, *n.* A writer; notary; clerk; a Jewish doctor or teacher of the law.

Scrimp, *v. t.* To contract; to shorten; to scant.

Scrip, *n.* A bag; a certificate of stock, &c.

Scrĭpt, *n.* Type in the form of written letters.

Script Type.

Scrĭpt'ūr-al, *a.* Contained in, or according to, the Scriptures.

Scrĭpt'ūre, *n.* The Old and New Testaments; the Bible; any writing.

Scrīve'ner, *n.* One who draws contracts or other writings.

Scrŏf'u-là, *n.* A disease affecting the lymphatic glands, especially those of the neck.

Scrŏf'u-loŭs, *a.* Diseased with scrofula. [rolled up.

Scrōll (123), *n.* A writing

Scrŭb, *n.* A worn brush; a mean drudge. — *v. t.* or *i.* To rub hard with something coarse.

Scrŭb'by, *a.* Small and mean; stunted in growth.

Scrū'ple, *n.* A doubt; hesitation; a weight of 20 grains. — *v. t.* or *i.* To doubt; to hesitate.

Scrū'pu-lŏs'i-ty, *n.* Quality of being scrupulous.

Scrū'pu-loŭs, *a.* Hesitating or doubtful; careful; cautious; conscientious.

Scrū'pu-loŭs-ly, *adv.* With doubt or nicety.

Scrū'ti-nīze, *v. t.* To examine or search closely.

Scrū'ti-nīz'er, *n.* One who searches closely.

Scrū'ti-ny, *n.* Close search.

Scru-toire' (skru-twôr'), *n.* A case of drawers for papers.

Scŭd, *v. i.* To be driven with haste. — *n.* A low thin cloud driven by the wind.

Scŭf'fle, *n.* A confused quarrel or contest. — *v. i.* To strive with close grapple.

Scŭf'fler, *n.* One who scuffles.

Scŭll, *n.* A short oar; a boat. — *v. t.* To impel, as a boat,

SCULLER 267 SECOND-SIGHT

by turning an oar at the stern.
Scŭll'er, n. One who sculls; a boat rowed by one man with two sculls.
Scŭll'er-y, n. A place for keeping kitchen utensils, and doing dirty work.
Scŭll'ion, n. A menial servant in the kitchen; a kind of imperfect onion. [ures.
Scŭlpt'or, n. One who sculpt-
Scŭlpt'ūre, n. Art of carving stone or wood into images; carved work. — v. t. To carve; to cut; to engrave.
Scŭm, n. Froth or impurities on the surface of liquor. — v. t. To take the scum from; to skim.
Scŭp'per, n. A hole or channel cut through the side of a ship to discharge water from the deck. [a broad head.
Scŭp'per-nāil, n. A nail with
Scŭrf, n. A dry scab or mealy crust. [being scurfy.
Scŭrf'i-ness (135), n. State of
Scŭrf'y, a. Having scurf.
Scŭr'rīle, } a. Grossly op-
Scŭr'ril-oŭs, } probious or abusive; low; mean.
Scur-rīl'i-ty, n. Low, vulgar, abusive language.
Scŭr'ril-oŭs-ly, adv. With low abuse. [basely.
Scŭr'vi-ly, adv. Meanly;
Scŭr'vi-ness, n. Vileness; meanness; baseness.
Scŭr'vy, n. A disease. — a. Scurfy; low; mean; vile.
Scŭtch'eon (skŭch'un), n. An ornamental bit of brass plate, perforated with a key-hole.
Scŭ'ti-fôrm, a. Having the form of a shield.
Scŭt'tle, n. A metal pail for coals; a hatchway; opening in the roof of a house furnished with a lid. — v. i. or t. To sluk by cutting a hole in the bottom.
Scȳm'e-tar, n. See Cimeter.
Scȳthe (sīth), n. An instrument for mowing grass.
Sēa (139, 140), n. A large body of salt water, less than an ocean; the ocean; a high wave. [ocean.
Sēa'-bôrn, a. Born on the
Sēa'-bōard, n. The sea-shore.
Sēa'-breeze, n. A current of air from the sea.
Sēa'-cōast, n. Shore of the sea and land adjacent.
Sēa'-cow, n. The walrus.
Sēa'-ĕl'e-phant, n. A kind of seal.

Sēa'-fâr'er, n. A mariner; a seaman; a sailor.
Sēa'-fâr'ing, a. Following the business of a seaman.
Sēa'-fīght (-fīt), n. A naval engagement.
Sēa'-green, a. Having the color of sea-water.
Sēa'-hôrse, n. The walrus; also, the hippopotamus.
Sēal, n. A marine animal; a stamp with a device on it; wax impressed with a seal. — v. t. (130) To fix a seal to; to fasten with a seal; to ratify; to confirm.
Sēal'ing-wăx, n. A substance for sealing letters.
Sēam, n. [A.-S. seám, from seowian, to sew.] The joining of two edges of cloth; any line of junction; a mineral vein between thicker ones. — v. t. To make a seam on or of; to mark with something like a seam.
Sēa'man (143), n. A sailor.
Sēa'man-ship, n. Skill in navigating.
Sēam'less, a. Having no seam.
Sēa'-märk, n. A beacon; a light-house.
Sēa'-mew, n. A gull.
Sēam'stress, n. A woman whose occupation is sewing.
Sēa'-pīe, n. A dish of paste and meat.
Sēa'-pôrt, n. A port or harbor on the sea-coast.
Sēar, v. t. To burn the surface of; to cauterize; to make callous. — a. Dry; withered.
Sēarch, v. t. To seek for; to look for; to inquire after. — v. i. To seek; to hunt. — n. A seeking; quest.
Sēarch'a-ble, a. Capable of being searched.
Sēarch'er, n. One who searches; a seeker; an inquirer.
Sēarch'ing, a. Trying; close.
Sēar'ed-ne s, n. State of being seared or hardened.
Sēa'-rōom, n. Ample distance from land; open sea.
Sēa'-shĕll, n. A marine shell.
Sēa'-shôre, n. The coast of the sea or ocean.
Sēa'-sick, a. Affected with nausea at sea from the motion of the vessel. [sea.
Sēa'-sīde, n. Land near the

Sēa'son (sē'zn), n. A fit time; a brief period; a division of the year. — v. t. To render palatable; to spice; to dry, as timber.
Sēa'son-a-ble, a. Occurring in due season or in good time; opportune; timely.
Sēa'son-a-bly, adv. In due time; sufficiently early.
Sēa'son-ing, n. That which seasons; act of drying.
Sēat, n. A chair; bench; place of sitting; mansion; abode. — v. t. To place on a seat.
Sēa'ward, a. Directed toward the sea. — adv. In the direction of the sea.
Sēa'-weed, n. One of a class of marine plants.
Sēa'-wor'thi-ness (-wûr'thĭ-), n. Quality of being sea-worthy; fitness for a voyage.
Sēa'-wor'thy (-wûr'thȳ), a. Able to encounter the violence of the sea.
Se-bā'ceoŭs, a. Fat; like fat; yielding fatty secretions.
Sē'cant, n. A line that cuts another. — a. Cutting.
Se-cēde', v. i. To withdraw; to separate.
Se-cēd'er, n. One who secedes.
Se-cĕs'sion (-sĕsh'un), n. Act of seceding or withdrawing.
Sĕck'el (sĕk'l), n. A small, delicious variety of pear.
Se-clūde', v. t. [Lat. secludere, fr. se, aside, and claudere, to shut.] To shut up in retirement; to withdraw.
Se-clū'sion, n. Act of withdrawing; retirement; separation; withdrawal.
Sĕc'ond, a. Next to the first; inferior. — n. The next to the first; 60th part of a minute; attendant in a duel. — v. t. To support; to aid.
Sĕc'ond-a-ri-ly, adv. In a secondary manner or degree.
Sĕc'ond-a-ry, a. Subordinate; inferior; less.
Sĕc'ond-hănd, a. Not new; previously owned by another.
Sĕc'ond-ly, adv. In the second place.
Sĕc'ond-rāte, a. Of the second size, rank, quality, or value. [of flour.
Sĕc'ondṣ, n. pl. A coarse kind
Sĕc'ond-sīght (-sīt), n. Power of seeing things future or distant.

sôn, ôr, dọ, wọlf, tǒo, tǒok; ûrn, rụe, pụll; ç, ġ, soft; e, ġ, hard; aṣ; exist; ŋ as ng; this.

Sē'cre-çy, n. Privacy; concealment; fidelity to a secret.
Sē'eret, a. Concealed; secluded; hidden; unseen; private. — n. Something unknown or hidden; privacy.
Sēe're-ta-ry, n. One who writes for others; head of a particular department of government; a piece of furniture for writing at.
Sēe're-ta-ry-ship (135), n. Office of a secretary.
Se-erēte', v. t. To remove from observation. — SYN. To hide; conceal.
Se-erē'tion, n. A separation of juices; matter secreted.
Sē'eret-ly, adv. In a secret manner. [secretion.
Sē'ere-to-ry, a. Performing
Sēet, n. A religious denomination or school.
See-tā'ri-an, a. Pertaining to a sect or to sects. — n. One of a sect. [tion to a sect.
See-tā'ri-an-ism, n. Devo-
Sēe'ta-rist, ⎫ n. A follower of
Sēet'a-ry, ⎭ a sect.
Sĕc'tile, a. Capable of being cut, especially of being cut smoothly.
Sēe'tion, n. A cutting off; division; portion; distinct part. [section.
Sēe'tion-al, a. Pertaining to a
Sĕet'or, n. Part of a circle between two radii and the included arc; a mathematical instrument.
Sēe'u-lar, a. Worldly; not spiritual. — n. A layman.
Sēe'u-lār'i-ty, ⎫ n. A world-
Sēe'u-lar-ness, ⎭ ly disposition.
Sēe'u-lar-īze, v. t. To convert to a secular use.
Se-eūr'a-ble, a. Capable of being secured.
Se-eūre', a. Free from fear or danger; safe. — v. t. To make safe. [to be safe.
Se-eūre'ly (132), adv. So as
Se-eūr'i-ty (133), n. Freedom from danger; safety; pledge.
Se-dăn', n. A portable covered vehicle for a single person.
Se-dāte', a. Calm; undisturbed; quiet. [posure.
Se-dāte'ly, adv. With composure.
Se-dāte'ness, n. Calmness; serenity.
Sĕd'a-tive, a. Allaying irritability and irritation. — n. A

remedy that allays irritability and irritation.
Sĕd'en-ta-ri-ness, n. State of being sedentary.
Sĕd'en-ta-ry, a. Accustomed to sit much; requiring much sitting.
Sĕdge, n. A coarse grass.
Sĕdg'y, a. Pertaining to, or overgrown with, sedge.
Sĕd'i-ment, n. [Lat. sedimentum, fr. sedere, to sit, to settle.] That which settles at the bottom; lees.
Sĕd'i-mĕnt'a-ry, a. Pertaining to, or consisting of, sediment; feculent.
Se-dī'tion (-dĭsh'un), n. Tumult; insurrection.
Se-dī'tioŭs (-dĭsh'us), a. Engaged in sedition.
Se-dūçe', v t. To lead astray by evil arts; to corrupt.
Se-dūçe'ment, n. Act of seducing; seduction.
Se-dū'çer, n. One who seduces or corrupts.
Se-dū'çi-ble, a. Capable of being seduced.
Se-dūe'tion, n. Leading astray from virtue.
Se-dūe'tive, a. Enticing to evil; tending to seduce.
Se-dūe'tive-ly, adv. By seduction. [gence.
Se-dū'li-ty, n. Great diligence.
Sĕd'u-loŭs, a. Very diligent.
Sĕd'u-loŭs-ly, adv. With application; assiduously.
See, n. The seat of episcopal power; a diocese. — v. t. [imp. SAW; p. p. SEEN.] To perceive by the eye; to behold; to discover. — v. i. To have the sense of sight.
Seed, n. That which produces animals or plants; reproductive principle; first cause; original; offspring; race. — v. t. To sow with seed.
Seed'-bŭd, n. The germ of fruit in embryo.
Seed'-cāke, n. A sweet cake, containing aromatic seeds.
Seed'ling, n. A plant springing from a seed.
Seeds'man (143), n. One who deals in seeds.
Seed'-tīme, n. The season for sowing. [taining seed.
Seed'vĕs'sel, n. A vessel containing seed.
Seed'y, a. Abounding with seeds; shabbily clothed.
Seek, v. t. [imp. & p. p. SOUGHT.] To look for; to endeavor to find.
Seek'er, n. One who seeks or searches; an inquirer.

Seem, v. i. To appear; to have a show or semblance.
Seem'ing, n. Appearance; show; semblance. — a. Apparent; specious.
Seem'ing-ly, adv. In appearance; apparently.
Seem'ly, a. Becoming; decent; decorous; fit.
Seen, p. p. of See. Perceived.
Seer, n. One who foresees events; a prophet.
Sçe'saw, n. A reciprocating motion up and down. — v. i. To move up and down by turns.
Seethe, v. t. [imp. SEETHED or SOD; p. p. SEETHED or SODDEN.] To boil; to decoct.
Sĕg'ment, n. A part cut off from a figure by a line or plane.
Sĕg're-gāte, v. t. To separate; to set a c b, Segment of apart. a circle.
Sĕg're-gā'tion, n. Separation from others.
Sēign-eū'ri-al (seen-ū'rī-al), a. Vested with large powers; manorial.
Sēign'ior (seen'yur), n. A lord.
Sēign'ior-age (seen'yur-), n. A royal right; profit or percentage.
Sēign'ior-y (seen'yur-), n. A lordship; a manor.
Sēine, n. A large fishing-net.
Sēiz'a-ble, a. Capable of being seized; liable to seizure.
Sēize, v. t. To take suddenly; to snatch; to grasp.
Sēi'zin, n. Possession of an estate in freehold; thing possessed.
Sēiz'ūre, n. Act of seizing; the thing seized. [often.
Sĕl'dom, adv. Rarely; not
Se-lĕet', v. t. To choose from a number; to cull. — a. Taken from a number; well chosen. [ing; choice.
Se-lĕe'tion, n. Act of selecting.
Se-lĕet'man (143), n. A town officer chosen to manage the concerns of the town.
Sĕl'e-nŏg'ra-phy, n. A description of the surface of the moon.
Sĕlf (142), pron. or a. A person as a distinct individual.
Sĕlf'-con-çĕit', n. High opinion of one's powers or endowments; vanity.
Sĕlf'-de-nī'al, n. Denial of personal gratification.

ā, ē, ī, ō, ū, y, long; ă, ĕ, ĭ, ŏ, ŭ, y̆, short; câre, cär, àsk, ąll, whąt; ẽre, veil, tẽrm; pīque, fīrm;

SELF-ESTEEM   269   SEPARATE

Sĕlf'-es-teem', n. Good opinion of one's self; complacency.

Sĕlf'-ĕv'i-dent, a. Needing no proof; evident without proof or reasoning.

Sĕlf'-ex-ĭst'ent, a. Existing of or by himself; solely.

Sĕlf'-ĭn'ter-est, n. Private interest or advantage.

Sĕlf'ish, a. Regarding one's own interest solely or chiefly.

Sĕlf'ish-ly, adv. With undue self-love.

Sĕlf'ish-ness, n. Regard to one's own interest solely or chiefly.

Sĕlf-lŏve', n. Love of self.

Sĕlf'sāme, a. Exactly the same; identical.

Sĕlf'-suf-fĭ'cient (-fĭsh'ent), a. Having full confidence in one's self; full of self-conceit. [obstinacy.

Sĕlf-wĭll', n. One's own will;

Sĕll (123), v. t. [imp. & p. p. SOLD.] To transfer to another for an equivalent.—v. i. To be sold.

Sĕll'er, n. One who sells.

Sĕl'vage,) n. Edge of cloth
Sĕl'vedge,) woven so as to prevent raveling.

Sĕlves, pl. of Self.

Săm'blance, n. Seeming; show; likeness. [yearly.

Sĕm'i-ăn'nu-al, a. Half

Sĕm'i-brēve, n. A whole note; the longest note now in general use.

Sĕm'i-çĭr'cle (-sĭr'kl), n. Half of a circle.

Sŭm'i-çĭr'eu-lar, a. Having the form of half a circle. Semicircle.

Sĕm'i-cō'lon, n. A point (marked thus, ;), used in writing and printing.

Sĕm'i-dĭ-ăm'e-ter, n. Half a diameter.

Sĕm'i-lū'nar, a. In form like a half moon.

Sĕm'i-nal, a. Pertaining to seed; original; radical.

Sĕm'i-năl'i-ty, n. The nature of seed.

Sĕm'i-na-ry, n. A place of education; a college; academy; school.—a. Pertaining to seed; seminal.

Sĕm'i-nāte, v. t. To sow; to spread; to propagate.

Sĕm'i-nā'tion, n. Act of sowing; dispersion of seeds.

Sĕm'i-quā'ver, n. A note of half the duration of the quaver.

Sĕm'i-tōne, n. Half a tone.

Sĕm'i-vō'cal, a. Having an imperfect sound; half vocal.

Sĕm'i-vow'el, n. A sound intermediate between a vowel and consonant, or the sign representing such a sound, as w and y. [ing.

Sĕm'pi-tĕr'nal, a. Everlast-

Sĕm'pi-tĕr'ni-ty, n. Endless future duration.

Sĕmp'stress, n. See Seamstress.

Sĕn'a-ry, a. Containing six.

Sŏn'ate, n. [Lat. senatus, fr. senex, old, an old man.] A council of senators; the upper branch of a legislature.

Sĕn'a-tor, n. A member of a senate.

Sĕn'a-tō'ri-al, a. Pertaining to, or becoming, a senator; entitled to elect a senator.

Sĕn'a-tor-ship, n. The office or dignity of a senator.

Sĕnd, v. t. [imp. & p. p. SENT.] To cause to go; to dispatch; to transmit; to throw.

Se-nĕs'cençe, n. A growing old; decay by time.

Sĕn'es-chal (sĕu'e-shal), n. A steward; a head bailiff.

Sē'nīle, a. Belonging to old age; doting.

Se-nĭl'i-ty, n. State of being senile; old age; dotage.

Sēn'ior (sēn'yur), n. One older than another, either in age or office; an aged person.—a. Older in age or office.

Sĕn-ĭor'i-ty, n. Priority in age or office.

Sĕn'nȧ, n. A plant the leaves of which are used as a cathartic. [week.

Sĕn'night (sĕn'nit), n. A

Sen-sā'tion, n. Perception by the senses; state of excited interest.

Sen-sā'tion-al, a. Attended by, or fitted to excite, great interest.

Sĕnse, n. Faculty by which external objects are perceived; sensation; discernment; opinion; meaning.

Sĕnse'less, a. Wanting sense; foolish; stupid.

Sĕnse'less-ly, adv. In a senseless manner; foolishly.

Sĕnse'less-ness, n. Folly; stupidity.

Sĕn'si-bĭl'i-ty, n. Capability of sensation; acuteness of perception.

Sĕn'si-ble, a. Capable of perception; perceptible by the senses.—SYN. Intelligent; wise; reasonable; convinced; judicious.

Sĕn'si-bly, adv. Perceptibly; with good sense.

Sĕn'si-tīve, a. Having sense or feeling; affecting the senses; depending on sensation. [nice sensibility.

Sĕn'si-tīve-ly, adv. With

Sĕn'si-tīve-ness, n. State of being sensitive.

†Sen-sō'ri-um,) n. The whole
Sĕn'so-ry,) nervous system so far as it is susceptible of sensations.

Sĕn'su-al (sĕn'shụ-), 89', a. Affecting the senses; carnal; voluptuous.

Sĕn'su-al-ĭsm (-shụ-), n. A state of subjection to sensual feelings or appetites.

Sĕn'su-al-ĭst (-shụ-), n. One devoted to sensuality.

Sĕn'su-ăl'i-ty (-shụ-), n. Free indulgence in carnal or sensual pleasures. [al manner.

Sĕn'su-al-ly, adv. In a sensu-

Sĕnt, imp. & p. p. of Send.

Sĕn'tençe, n. A judgment pronounced; doom; a short saying; a maxim; a period in writing.—v. t. To pass judgment on; to doom; to condemn.

Sen-tĕn'tial, a. Comprising, or pertaining to, sentences.

Sen-tĕn'tioŭs, a. Short and pithy.

Sen-tĕn'tioŭs-ly, adv. In a sententious manner.

Sĕn'tient, a. Having the faculty of sensation and perception.

Sĕn'ti-ment, n. A thought prompted by feeling; sensibility; opinion; a toast.

Sĕn'ti-mĕnt'al, a. Abounding with sentiment; affectedly tender.

Sĕn'ti-mĕnt'al-ist, n. One who affects fine feelings.

Sĕn'ti-men-tăl'i-ty, n. Affectation of sensibility.

Sĕn'ti-nel,) n. A soldier on
Sĕn'try,) guard; a watch.

Sĕn'try-bŏx, n. A box to shelter a sentinel.

Sĕp'a-ra-ble, a. Capable of being separated. [separates.

Sĕp'a-rā'tor, n. One who

Sĕp'a-rāte, v. t. or i. To disunite; to divide; to disjoin; to withdraw.

Sĕp'a-rate, a. Divided; disconnected; distinct; single.

---

sûn, ôr, dọ, wọlf, tōō, tŏŏk; ûrn, rụe, pụll; ç, ġ, soft; ċ, ġ, hard; ạṣ; eẓist; ṇ as ng; this.

SEPARATELY 270 SEVENTH

Sep'a-rate-ly, *adv.* Singly; distinctly; apart.

Sep'a-ra'tion, *n.* Act of separating; a disjunction; disunion; divorce. [a seceder.

Sep'a-ra'tist, *n.* A dissenter;

Se'poy, *n.* A native of India in the military service of Europeans.

Sept, *n.* A clan, race, or family; — in Ireland.

Sept-an'gu-lar, *a.* Having seven angles.

Sep-tem'ber, *n.* The ninth month of the year. [seven.

Sep'ten-a-ry, *a.* Consisting of

Sep-ten'ni-al, *a.* Returning or happening every seventh year, lasting seven years.

†**Sep-ten'tri-on,** *n.* The north.

Sep'tic, } *a.* Tending to

Sep'tic-al, } produce putrefaction.

Sep'tu-a-ge-na'ri-an, *n.* A person seventy years old.

Sep'tu-ag'e-na-ry, *a.* Consisting of seventy; 70 years old.

Sep'tu-a-ges'i-ma, *n.* The third Sunday before Lent.

Sep'tu-a-ges'i-mal, *a.* Consisting of seventy.

Sep'tu-a-gint, *n.* A Greek version of the Old Testament.

Sep'tu-ple, *a.* Seven times as much.

Sep'ul-cher } (151), *n.* A

Sep'ul-chre } grave; a tomb.

Se-pul'chral, *a.* Relating to burial; deep; grave; hollow.

Sep'ul-tūre, *n.* The act of burying a human being.

Se-quā'cious, *a.* Following; attendant.

Se'quel, *n.* [Lat. *sequela*, fr. *sequi*, to follow.] A succeeding part; consequence; event.

Se'quençe, *n.* Order of following; succession; series.

Se'quent, *a.* Following.

Se-qués'ter, } *v. t.* To seize

Se-qués'trāte, } and hold for a time; to set apart.

Seq'ues-tra'tion, *n.* Act of sequestering, or state of being sequestered.

Seq'ues-tra'tor, *n.* One who sequesters, or has the keeping of sequestered property.

Se'quin, *n.* A gold coin of Italy, and also of Turkey.

Se-răg'lio (se-răl'yo), *n.* Palace of the Turkish sultan; a harem. [the highest order.

Ser'aph (147), *n.* An angel of

Se-răph'ic, *a.* Angelic; pure.

Ser'a-phim, *n.; pl.* of *Seraph*.

Ser'a-phine, *n.* A kind of reed-organ.

Ser'e-nāde', *n.* Music performed at night in the open air in compliment to some one. — *v. t.* To entertain with a serenade.

Se-rēne', *a.* Calm; quiet; peaceful; an epithet forming part of some titles of honor.

Se-rēne'ly, *adv.* Calmly; quietly; clearly.

Se-rēn'i-ty, *n.* State of being serene; calmness; clearness.

Serf (140), *n.* A slave employed in husbandry.

Serge, *n.* A thin woolen stuff.

Ser'geant (sär'jent *or* sēr'jent), *n.* A non-commissioned military officer; a lawyer of high rank.

Se'ri-al, *a.* Pertaining to, or consisting of, a series. — *n.* A tale, or other writing, issued in a series of numbers.

Se'ries (*or* sē'ri-ēz), *n.* Order; succession; course.

Se'ri-oūs, *a.* Sober; grave; earnest; weighty.

Se'ri-oūs-ly, *adv.* Gravely; solemnly; in earnest.

Se'ri-oūs-ness, *n.* Gravity; solemnity; importance; earnest attention.

Ser'mon, *n.* A discourse grounded on a text of Scripture.

Ser'mon-īze, *v. i.* To write or preach a sermon.

Ser'mon-īz'er, *n.* One who writes sermons.

Se-rōon', *n.* A package of skins for drugs, &c.

Se-rōs'i-ty, *n.* The thin, watery part of blood.

Se'roūs, *a.* Consisting of serum; thin; watery.

Ser'pent, *n.* A creeping animal; a snake; a firework.

Ser'pent-īne, *a.* Winding, as a serpent; sinuous.

Ser'rate, *a.* Notched on the edge, like a saw.

Ser'ried, *a.* Compact; being in close array.

Se-rōs'i-ty, *n.* A thin, watery liquid, forming the chief constituent of most animal fluids. [the blood.

†**Se'rum,** *n.* The thin part of

Serv'ant, *n.* One who serves, or labors for, another.

Serve, *v. t.* To work for; to obey; to contribute to; to treat. — *v. i.* To perform duties; to suit; to be of use.

Serv'içe, *n.* Duty of a servant; military duty; office; worship; benefit; use; set of vessels used at table.

Serv'içe-a-ble (108), *a.* Doing service; beneficial.

Serv'içe-a-ble-ness, *n.* State or quality of being serviceable.

Serv'īle, *a.* Slavish; cringing.

Serv'īle-ly, *adv.* In a servile manner; slavishly.

Ser-vīl'i-ty, *n.* Mean submissiveness; obsequiousness.

Serv'i-tor, *n.* A servant; an attendant; an undergraduate at Oxford, partly supported by the college funds.

Serv'i-tūde, *n.* Slavery; thraldom; dependence.

Sés'sile, *a.* Attached without any sensible projecting support.

Sés'sion (sĕsh'un), *n.* A meeting or sitting of a public body.

Sess'-pōōl, *n.* A hollow in the earth to receive the sediment from drains.

Ses'terçe, *n.* A Roman coin worth about four cents.

Set, *v. t.* [*imp.* & *p. p.* SET.] To place; to put; to fix; to regulate. — *v. i.* To descend below the horizon. — *n.* A number of things suited to each other; an assortment. — *p. a.* Fixed; firm; regular; prescribed.

Se-tā'ceoūs, *a.* Bristly; hairy.

Sĕt'-ŏff, *n.* An account set against another; counterbalance; offset.

Sē'ton, *n.* A twist of thread, or a few horse-hairs, to keep a wound open.

Se-tōse', } *a.* Set with bris-

Sē'toūs, } tles; bristly.

Set-tee' (140), *n.* A long seat with a back.

Sĕt'ter, *n.* A sporting dog of the hound kind.

Sĕt'tle, *n.* A long bench with a back. — *v. t.* To fix; to establish; to determine. — *v. i.* To subside; to sink.

Sĕt'tle-ment, *n.* Act of settling; adjustment; a place settled; a colony; jointure.

Sĕt'tler, *n.* One who settles; a colonist.

Sĕt'tlings, *n. pl.* Lees; dregs; sediment.

Sĕt'-to, *n.* A conflict.

Sĕv'en, *a.* Six and one.

Sĕv'en-fōld, *a.* Repeated seven times. [week.

Sĕv'en-night (sĕn'nīt), *n.* A

Sĕv'enth, *a.* Next after the sixth; ordinal of seven. — *n.* One part in seven; a musical interval.

ā, ē, ī, ō, ū, ȳ, *long*; ă, ĕ, ĭ, ŏ, ŭ, ў, *short*; cåre, cär, åsk, ạll, whạt; ẽre, vẽil, tẽrm; pïque, fïrm;

Sĕv'enth-ly, *adv.* In the seventh place. [en.
Sŏv'en-teen, *n.* Ten and seven
Sĕv'en-ti-eth, *a.* The ordinal of seventy.
Sĕv'en-ty, *a.* Seven times ten.
Sĕv'er, *v. t.* To part violently; to disjoin; to separate.
Sĕv'er-al, *a.* Separate; more than two, but not many; divers; sundry.
Sĕv'er-al-ly, *adv.* Separately.
Sĕv'er-al-ty, *n.* A state of separation. [partition.
Sĕv'er-ance, *n.* Separation;
Se-vēre', *a.* Very strict; stern; cruel; painful; extreme.
Se-vēre'ly, *adv.* With severity.
Se-vēr'i-ty, *n.* State of being severe; harshness; rigor; austerity; strictness.
Sew (sō), *v. t.* To unite with needle and thread. [sews.
Sew'er (sō'er), *n.* One who
Sew'er (sū'er), *n.* A passage under ground for water.
Sew'er-age (sū'-), *n.* System of sewers in a town; materials discharged by sewers.
Sĕx, *n.* Distinction of male and female; womankind.
Sĕx'a-ge-nā'ri-an, *n.* A person of sixty years of age.
Sex-ăg'e-na-ry, or Sĕx'a-ge-na-ry, *a.* Pertaining to the number sixty; proceeding by sixties.
Sĕx'a-gĕs'i-ma, *n.* The second Sunday before Lent.
Sĕx'a-gĕs'i-mal, *a.* Sixtieth.
Sex-ăn'gu-lar, *a.* Having six angles.
Sex-ĕn'ni-al, *a.* Happening once in, or lasting, six years.
Sĕx'fid, *a.* Divided into six parts.
Sĕx'tant, *n.* The sixth part of a circle; an instrument for measuring angular distances.
Sĕx'tile, *n.* Aspect of planets sixty degrees apart.
Sĕx'ton, *n.* An under officer of a church, who takes care of the building, attends upon the clergyman, digs graves, &c.
Sĕx'tu-ple, *a.* Six times as much; having six parts.
Sĕx'u-al (sĕk'shy-), *a.* Pertaining to, or distinguishing, sex.
Sĕx'u-ăl'i-ty, *n.* State of being distinguished by sex.
Shăb, *v. i.* To play mean tricks; to act shabbily.
Shăb'bi-ly, *adv.* In a mean manner; raggedly.

Shăb'bi-ness, *n.* Quality of being shabby; meanness.
Shăb'by, *a.* Worn; ragged; mean; paltry; despicable.
Shăck, *n.* Grain left after harvest; fallen acorns; a shiftless fellow.
Shăck'le (shăk'l), *v. t.* To fetter; to chain; to bind.
Shăck'les (shăk'lz), *n. pl.* Fetters or handcuffs.
Shăd, *n. sing. & pl.* A kind of fish much prized for food.
Shăd'dock (127), *n.* A tree and its fruit, which is a species of orange.
Shāde, *n.* Interception of light; obscurity; a screen; a spirit; degree of cold or of darkness; (*pl.*) place of the dead. — *v. t.* To cover or screen from light; to obscure.
Shā'di-ness, *n.* State of being shady.
Shăd'ōw, *n.* A figure formed by the interception of light; a mystical representation; a type; phantom. — *v. t.* To cloud; to darken; to represent faintly.
Shăd'ōw-y, *a.* Full of shade.
Shā'dy, *a.* Sheltered from the glare of light or heat.
Shăft, *n.* An arrow; straight cylindrical part of any thing, as of a column; passage into a mine; thill of a carriage; a long axis in machinery.
Shăg, *n.* Rough, woolly hair; cloth with a long, coarse nap. — *a.* Hairy; rough. — *v. t.* To make hairy or rough.
Shăg'ged, *a.* Hairy; rough,
Shăg'gy, with long wool or hair. [being shaggy.
Shăg'gi-ness, *n.* State of
Sha-green', *n.* A kind of leather prepared from the skins of horses, mules, &c.
Shäh, *n.* A Persian king.
Shāke, *v. t.* [*imp.* SHOOK; *p. p.* SHAKEN.] To agitate; to cause to tremble or to doubt; to trill. — *v. i.* To be agitated; to quake. — *n.* Vibratory motion.
Shăk'er, *n.* One who shakes; one of a religious sect.
Shāle, *n.* A kind of fine-grained slaty rock.
Shăll. An auxiliary verb, used in forming the future tense; as, *I shall go.*
Shal-lōōn', *n.* A kind of worsted stuff.
Shăl'lop, *n.* A kind of large boat with two masts.
Shăl'lōv, *a.* Not deep; shoal;

simple; superficial; silly. — *n.* A place where the water is not deep.
Shăl'lōw-ness, *n.* Want of depth; emptiness; silliness.
Shălt. *Second person of Shall.*
Shăm, *n.* False pretense; imposture. — *a.* False; counterfeit; pretended. — *v. t.* To pretend; to deceive; to imitate; to counterfeit.
Shăm'ble, *v. i.* To walk awkwardly and unsteadily, as if the knees were weak; to shuffle.
Shăm'bles, *n. pl.* A place where butchers kill or sell meat.
Shăm'bling, *n.* A shuffling gait. — *a.* Shuffling along.
Shāme, *n.* Sense or cause of disgrace; reproach; ignominy. — *v. t.* To make ashamed.
Shāme'fāçed (-fāst), *a.* Bashful; diffident; modest.
Shāme'ful, *a.* Disgraceful; scandalous; ignominious.
Shāme'ful-ly, *adv.* Disgracefully; ignominiously.
Shāme'less, *a.* Destitute of shame; impudent.
Shāme'less-ly, *adv.* Without shame. [dence.
Shāme'less-ness, *n.* Impu-
Shăm'my, *n.* See *Chamois.*
Sham-pōō', *v. t.* To rub and Çham-pōō', press the limbs of after warm bathing; to wash thoroughly the head of.
Shăm'rock, *n.* White clover.
Shănk, *n.* The bone of the leg; lower joint of the leg; long part of a tool.
Shăn'ty, *n.* A rude hut.
Shāpe, *v. t.* [*imp.* SHAPED; *p. p.* SHAPED or SHAPEN.] To form; to mold; to give form or figure to; to fashion; to adjust. — *n.* External form or figure; make; appearance.
Shāpe'less, *a.* Wanting regularity of form.
Shāpe'less-ness, *n.* State of being shapeless.
Shāpe'ly, *a.* Well-formed; symmetrical.
Shärd, *n.* A fragment of an earthen vessel; a shell.
Shāre, *n.* A part; a portion; a plow-iron. — *v. t.* To apportion; to divide; to partake with others. — *v. i.* To have part.
Shāre'-hōld'er, *n.* One who holds a share in a joint fund or property.

Shār'er, *n.* One who shares.

Shark, *n.* A voracious sea-fish.

— *v. i.* To play the petty thief; to cheat; to trick; to swindle.

Shārp, *a.* [A.-S. *scearp,* from the root of *shear.*] Having a thin edge or a fine point; keen; acute; sour; acid. — *v. t.* To make sharp; to sharpen. — *v. i.* To grow sharp.

Shārp'en, *v. t.* or *i.* To make or grow sharp. [ler.

Shārp'er, *n.* A cheat; a swindler.

Shārp'ly, *adv.* In a sharp manner; keenly; acutely; severely; violently.

Shārp'ness, *n.* Keenness of edge or point; acuteness.

Shārp'-sĕt, *a.* Very hungry.

Shăt'ter, *v. t.* To break in pieces; to disorder. — *v. i.* To be broken into fragments. — *n. pl.* Broken pieces; fragments.

Shāve, *v. t.* [*imp.* SHAVED; *p. p.* SHAVED, SHAVEN.] To cut or pare off; to defraud. — *n.* To use a razor; to cut closely; to cheat.

Shāve'ling, *n.* A man shaved; a monk.

Shāv'er, *n.* One who shaves; a sharp dealer; a boy.

Shāv'ing, *n.* A thin slice pared off.

Shawl, *n.* A cloth to cover the neck and shoulders.

Shawm, *n.* A wind instrument of music formerly in use.

Shē, *pron. fem.,* standing for the name of a female.

Shēaf (142), *n.* A bundle of stalks of grain; any bundle.

Shēar, *v. t.* [*imp.* SHEARED; *p. p.* SHEARED or SHORN.] To cut or clip from the surface; to reap.

Shēar'er, *n.* One who shears.

Shēars, *n. pl.* A cutting instrument with two blades; an apparatus for raising heavy weights. [bard.

Shēath, *n.* A case; a scabbard.

Shēathe, *v. t.* To put into a sheath or case; to cover or line. [ship's bottom.

Shēath'ing, *n.* Covering of a

Shēath'y, *a.* Forming a sheath. [ley.

Shēave, *n.* A wheel in a pulley.

Shĕd, *n.* A slight building; an out-building. — *v. t.* [*imp.*

& *p. p.* SHED.] To emit; to spill; to cast off; to scatter.

Shĕd'der, *n.* One who sheds.

Shoen, *n.* Brightness; splendor.

Sheen'y, *a.* Bright; shining.

Sheep (146), *n. sing.* and *pl.* An animal that furnishes wool. [sheep.

Sheep'-cōt, *n.* A pen for

Sheep'-fōld, *n.* A fold or inclosure for sheep.

Sheep'ish, *a.* Like a sheep; timorous; bashful; modest.

Sheep'ish-ly, *adv.* Bashfully.

Sheep'ish-ness, *n.* Bashfulness; diffidence.

Sheep's'-eye, *n.* A sly, diffident, loving look.

Sheer, *a.* Clear; unmingled; simple; perpendicular. — *v. i.* To deviate from a course. — *n.* Longitudinal curve or bend of a ship's deck; (*pl.*) an engine to raise heavy weights.

Sheet, *n.* A cloth for a bed; a broad piece of paper; a sail; an expanse, as of water. — *v. t.* To fold up in, or cover as with, a sheet.

Sheet'-ăn'chor, *n.* The largest anchor; last refuge.

Sheet'ing, *n.* Cloth for sheets.

Shĕik, *n.* A chief; — among the Arabians and Moors.

Shĕk'el (58), *n.* A Jewish coin, worth about 62½ cents.

Shĕl'drake, *n.* A species of duck.

Shĕlf, *n.* (*pl.* **Shĕlves,** 142.) A board supported in some way and designed to lay things on; a bank or rock under water.

Shĕll, *n.* A hard covering; a bomb. — *v. t.* or *i.* To remove or cast the shell; to take out of the shell.

Shĕll'-fish, *n.* An aquatic animal covered with a shell.

Shĕl'ter, *n.* A protection; retreat; covert. — *v. t.* To cover; to protect; to shield.

Shĕl'ter-less, *a.* Without shelter or protection.

Shĕlve, *v. i.* To slope. — *v. t.* To furnish with shelves; to put on a shelf.

Shĕlv'y, *a.* Abounding with rocks or sand-banks.

Shĕp'herd, *n.* A man who tends sheep.

Shĕp'herd-ess, *n.* A woman who has the care of sheep.

Shĕr'bet, *n.* A beverage of water, lemon-juice, and sugar.

Shĕr'iff, *n.* Chief officer of a shire or county.

Shĕr'ry, *n.* A Spanish wine.

Shew (shō). See *Show.*

Shewn (shōn), *p. p.* of *Shew.*

Shĭb'bo-leth, *n.* Watchword or test-word of a party.

Shield, *n.* {A.-S. *scild, scyld,* from Icel. *skyla,* to cover, defend.] Armor for defense; a buckler; protection. — *v. t.* To protect; to defend.

Shĭft, *v. t.* or *i.* To transfer; to change; to move; to find some expedient. — *n.* Evasion; artifice; expedient; a woman's under-garment.

Shĭft'less, *a.* Lacking in expedients; without capacity.

Shĭl'ling, *n.* A silver coin; sum of twelve pence.

Shĭn, *n.* Fore part of the leg, between the ankle and knee.

Shīne, *v. i.* [*imp.* & *p. p.* SHINED or SHONE.] To emit rays of light; to be conspicuous. — *n.* Fair weather; brightness; splendor; fancy.

Shĭn'gle, *n.* A thin board; loose water-worn pebbles; (*pl.*) a disease; a kind of tetter. — *v. t.* To cover with shingles; to cut, as hair, so that one portion overlaps another.

Shīn'ing, *a.* Bright in a high degree. — SYN. Brilliant; sparkling; radiant; resplendent; effulgent.

Shīn'y, *a.* Bright; luminous.

Ship, *n.* Any large sea-going vessel, esp. one that is square-rigged and has three masts. — *v. t.* To put on board a vessel of any kind.

Ship'bōard, *adv.* On board of a ship.

Ship'-mās'ter, *n.* A master or captain of a ship.

Ship'ment, *n.* Act of shipping; that which is shipped.

Ship'ping, *n.* Ships in general; vessels collectively.

Ship'-shāpe, *adv.* In a seaman-like manner; hence, properly; according to usage; well put.

Ship'wreck (-rĕk), *n.* Destruction of a ship at sea. — *v. t.* To destroy, as a ship at sea, by running on shore, &c.

Ship'wright (-rīt), *n.* A builder of ships.

Shire, or **Shīre,** *n.* In *England*, a county.

SHIRK 273 SHUCK

Shirk, *v. t.* To get off from; to slink away from.
Shirt, *n.* A man's under-garment. —*v. t.* To cover with a shirt.
Shive, *n.* A slice; a fragment.
Shiv'er, *n.* A little piece. —*v. t.* or *i.* To break into small pieces; to shatter; to cause to shake in the wind.
Shiv'er-ing, *n.* A trembling or shaking. [trembling.
Shiv'er-y, *a.* Easily broken;
Shōal, *n.* A crowd, as of fishes; a sand-bank or bar. —*a.* Shallow. —*v. i.* To become more shallow.
Shōal'y, *a.* Full of shoals.
Shŏck, *n.* [Allied to *shake*.] A sudden shake; concussion; a blow; offense; a pile of sheaves. —*v. t.* To strike with surprise, disgust, or terror.
Shŏck'ing, *a.* Striking as with horror; extremely offensive or disgusting.
Shŏck'ing-ly, *adv.* In a manner to shock.
Shŏd, *imp. & p. p.* of *Shoe.*
Shŏe (133, 143), *n.* A covering or protection for the foot. —*v. t.* (133) [*imp. & p. p.* SHOD.] To put shoes on.
Shoe'-black, \
Shoe'-boy, / *n.* One who cleans shoes.
Shoe'māk-er (shoō'-), *n.* One who makes shoes.
Shoe'string, *n.* A string to fasten a shoe to the foot.
Shōne, or **Shŏne,** *imp.* of *Shine.*
Shŏŏk, *imp. & p. p.* of *Shake.* —*n.* A bundle of staves, or of boards for a box.
Shoot, *v. t.* or *i.* [*imp. & p. p.* SHOT.] To dart; to jut; to sprout; to thrust; to discharge, as a gun. —*n.* A sprout or young branch.
Shoot'er, *n.* One who, or that which, shoots; a gunner; a fire-arm.
Shŏp, *n.* A building for work or for trade. —*v. i.* To visit shops for goods.
Shŏp'-keep'er, *n.* A trader who sells in a shop.
Shŏp'-lift'er, *n.* One who steals from a shop.
Shŏp'-lift'ing, *n.* Larceny committed in a shop.
Shŏp'ping, *n.* Act of visiting shops to purchase goods.
Shōre, *n.* Const; land adjacent to water; a prop; a support. —*v. t.* To support by props.

Shōrn, *p. p.* of *Shear.*
Shŏrt, *a.* Not long; brief; scanty; deficient; brittle.
Shŏrt'en, *v. t.* To make short or shorter.
Shŏrt'en-ing, *n.* The act of contracting; something to make pastry short or friable.
Shŏrt'-hānd, *n.* Abbreviated writing; stenography.
Shŏrt'-līved, *a.* Being of short continuance.
Shŏrt'ly, *adv.* Quickly; briefly; concisely; soon.
Shŏrt'ness, *n.* Quality of being short; brevity; conciseness; succinctness.
Shŏrts, *n. pl.* Coarse part of meal; small clothes.
Shŏrt'-sīght'ed (-sīt'-), *a.* Unable to see far.
Shŏt, *imp. & p. p.* of *Shoot.* —*n.* Act of shooting; a small missile weapon; a reckoning or charge. [hog.
Shōte, *n.* A small or young
Shŏt'ten (shŏt'tn), *a.* Having cast the spawn; sprained.
Shŏugh (shŏk), *n.* A kind of shaggy dog.
Should (shŏŏd), *imp.* of *Shall*, denoting intention or duty.
Shŏul'der, *n.* The joint that connects the arm with the body. —*v. t.* To take on the shoulder; to push or thrust rudely.
Shŏul'der-blāde, *n.* The broad bone of the shoulder.
Shout, *v. i.* To utter a loud and sudden outcry. —*n.* A loud and sudden outcry.
Shŏve, *v. t.* or *i.* To push; to urge. —*n.* A push.
Shŏv'el (shŭv'l, 58), *n.* A utensil for throwing earth, &c.— *v. t.* (130) To throw with a shovel.
Shōw, *v.* [*imp.* SHOWED; *p. p.* SHOWED, SHOWN.] To exhibit; to display; to prove; to direct; to appear. —*n.* Exhibition; sight.
Show'-brēad, \
Shew'-brēad, / *n.* Unleavened bread placed before the Lord in the Jewish sanctuary.
Show'er, *n.* One who shows.
Show'er, *n.* A temporary fall of rain. —*v. t.* or *i.* To rain in showers; to wet, as with rain.
Show'er-y, *a.* Raining in showers; rainy.
Show'i-ly (13), *adv.* In a showy manner.
Show'i-ness, *n.* Quality or state of being showy.

Shōwn, *p. p.* of *Show.*
Show'y, *a.* Making a show; gaudy; fine; ostentatious.
Shrĕd, *v. t.* [*imp. & p. p.* SHRED.] To cut into small pieces, especially long and narrow pieces. —*n.* A long narrow piece cut or torn off a fragment.
Shrew (shrṳ), *n.* An ill-tempered, brawling woman.
Shrewd (shrṳd), *a.* Sagacious; astute.
Shrewd'ly, *adv.* Sagaciously.
Shrewd'ness, *n.* Sagacity.
Shrew'ish (shrṳ'-), *a.* Like a shrew; petulant.
Shrĭēk, *v. i.* To utter a loud, shrill cry. —*n.* A loud, shrill cry; a scream.
Shrīke, *n.* A rapacious European bird. [sound.
Shrĭll, *a.* Sharp; piercing, as
Shrĭll'y, *adv.* Acutely.
Shrĭll'ness, *n.* Acuteness of sound. [fish.
Shrĭmp, *n.* A long-tailed shell-
Shrīne, *n.* A case or box, especially for sacred relics.
Shrĭṅk, *v. i.* or *t.* [*imp. & p. p.* SHRUNK.] To contract; to become or make less.
Shrĭṅk'age, *n.* Act or measure of shrinking.
Shrīve, *v. t.* To receive the confession of, as a priest; to confess.
Shrĭv'el (58, 130), *v. t.* or *i.* To contract into wrinkles.
Shroud, *n.* A cover; a winding sheet; (*pl.*) a set of ropes reaching from the mast-head to the side of a vessel. —*v. t.* To cover; to shelter; to dress for the grave. Shrouds.
Shrōve'-tīde, *n.* Confession-time; Tuesday before Lent.
Shrŭb, *n.* A low, dwarf tree; a liquor of acid, sugar, and a little spirit.
Shrŭb'ber-y, *n.* A collection or plantation of shrubs.
Shrŭb'by, *a.* Full of shrubs; like a shrub.
Shrŭg, *v. t.* [Allied to *shrink*.] To draw up, as the shoulders. —*n.* A drawing up the shoulders. [*Shrink*.
Shrŭṅk, *imp. & p. p.* of
Shŭck, *n.* A shell or covering; a husk or pod.

---

sŏn, ôr, dọ, wọlf, tṳ̄ṅ, tŏŏk; ûrn, rᵭe, pṳll; ç, ġ, *soft*; e, g, *hard*; a₂; exist; ṳ as ng; this
12 *

Shud'der, *n.* A trembling, as with horror. — *v. i.* To quake; to quiver; to tremble.

Shuf'fle, *v. t.* To change the relative position of, as of cards. — *v. i.* To prevaricate; to evade; to shift. — *n.* Act of shuffling; a change of place in cards; a trick.

Shuf'fler, *n.* One who shuffles.

Shuf'fling, *n.* Evasion; trickery; irregular gait.

Shun, *v. t.* To avoid; to get out of the way of.

Shunt, *n.* A turn-off to a side rail; a switch. — *v. t.* To turn off to one side; to switch off.

Shut, *v. t.* or *i.* [*imp.* & *p. p.* SHUT.] To close; to prohibit; to bar.

Shut'ter, *n.* One who, or that which, shuts; a close cover.

Shut'tle, *n.* A weaver's instrument to shoot the threads of the woof between those of the warp.

Shut'tle-cŏck, *n.* An instrument used with a battledoor in play.

Shȳ, *a.* Shunning society or approach; reserved. — SYN. Coy; timid.

Shȳ'ly (135), *adv.* In a shy or timid manner; bashfully.

Shȳ'ness (135), *n.* Reserve; coyness; bashfulness.

Sib'i-lant, *a.* Hissing. — *n.* A letter uttered with a hissing sound.

Sib'i-lā'tion, *n.* A hissing sound.

Sib'yl, *n.* An ancient pagan prophetess; a gypsy.

Sib'yl-līne, *a.* Pertaining to, or resembling, a sibyl.

Sic'ci-ty, *n.* Dryness; aridity.

Sice (sīz, 62), *n.* Six in dice.

Sick (127), *a.* Afflicted with disease; ill; ailing; indisposed; disgusted.

Sick'en (sik'n), *v. t.* or *i.* To make or become sick.

Sick'ish, *a.* Exciting disgust.

Sick'le, *n.* A reaping-hook.

Sick'li-ness, *n.* State of being sickly; unhealthiness.

Sick'ly, *a.* Somewhat sick; unhealthy; infirm.

Sick'ness, *n.* A morbid state of the body; disease.

Side, *n.* The broad part of a thing; part of the body about the ribs; margin; edge; party; interest. — *a.* Lateral; indirect. — *v. i.* To lean to one party.

Sīde'bōard, *n.* A kind of table on one side of a room, to hold dinner utensils, &c.

Sīde'lŏng, *a.* Lateral; oblique; not directly in front. — *adv.* Laterally; obliquely.

Sīd'er-al,) *a.* Pertaining to
Sī-dē're-al.) stars; starry.

Sīd'er-ŏg'ra-phy, *n.* Art of engraving on steel.

Sīde'-săd'dle, *n.* A woman's saddle. [one side.

Sīde'wīse, *adv.* On or toward

Sī'dle, *v. i.* To go side foremost.

Siēge, *n.* Act of besetting a fortified place.

Sī'e-nīte, *n.* See *Syenite.*

Sī-ĕs'tå, *n.* A short sleep at noon or after dinner.

Sieve, *n.* A small utensil used for sifting.

Sift, *v. t.* To separate by means of a sieve.

Sift'er, *n.* One who, or that which, sifts.

Sīgh (sī), *v. i.* To emit breath audibly; to lament. — *n.* A deep breathing.

Sīght (sīt), *n.* [From the root of *see.*] Sense, act, or object of seeing; a show.

Sīght'less (sīt'-), *a.* Wanting sight.

Sīght'li-ness (sīt'-), *n.* Comeliness; conspicuousness.

Sīght'ly (sīt'-), *a.* Pleasing to the eye; conspicuous.

Sīgn (sīn), *n.* A token; mark; signal; symbol; proof; wonder; constellation. — *v. t.* To subscribe one's name to; to mark.

Sīg'nal, *n.* A sign to give notice; a token. — *a.* Eminent; remarkable.

Sīg'nal-īze, *v. t.* To make distinguished; to make a signal in regard to.

Sīg'nal-ly, *adv.* Remarkably.

Sīg'na-tūre, *n.* A name or mark signed or impressed; a sign at the bottom of certain pages of a book as a direction to the binder.

Sīgn'er (sīn'er), *n.* One who subscribes his name.

Sīg'net, *n.* A seal, especially a private royal seal.

Sig-nif'i-cance,) *n.* Impor-
Sig-nif'i-can-cy,) tance; meaning; import; weight.

Sig-nif'i-cant, *a.* Expressive of some fact or meaning; important; weighty.

Sig-nif'i-cant-ly, *adv.* In a significant manner.

Sig'ni-fi-cā'tion, *n.* Meaning expressed by words or signs.

Sig-nif'i-ca-tīve, *a.* Having or expressing meaning.

Sig'ni-fȳ, *v. t.* To make known. — *v. i.* To express meaning with force; to matter.

Sīgn'-măn'u-al (sīn'-), *n.* One's own name written by himself.

Sīgn'-pŏst (sīn'-), *n.* A post on which a sign hangs.

Sī'lence, *n.* Stillness; secrecy; quiet; muteness. — *v. t.* To still; to appease.

Sī'lent (39), *a.* Still; mute; quiet.

Sī'lent-ly, *adv.* Without speech or noise; mutely.

Sī'lex,) *n.* Silicic acid, or
Sil'i-cå,) the substance of pure quartz.

Sil'hou-ĕtte' (-oo-), *n.* A profile likeness in black.

Si-lic'ic, *a.* Pertaining to flint or quartz.

Si-li'cious (-lish'us), *a.* Pertaining to silex; flinty.

Sil'i-quå, *n.* A pod with seeds fixed to both sutures.

Sil'i-quoŭs, *a.* Bearing or resembling a siliqua.

Silk, *n.* The fine, soft thread produced by the silk-worm, or cloth made of the thread; any thing resembling silk.

Silk'en, *a.* Made of silk; like silk; soft; silky.

Silk'i-ness, *n.* State or quality of being silky.

Silk'-worm (-wŭrm), *n.* A caterpillar or larve that produces silk.

Silk'y, *a.* Pertaining to, consisting of, or resembling, silk; soft; silken.

Sill (123), *n.* Foundation timber of a house or window, &c.

Sil'la-bŭb, *n.* A liquor of wine or cider and milk.

Sil'li-ness, *n.* Want of sense.

Sil'ly, *a.* Weak in intellect, and self-satisfied. — SYN. Simple; stupid; foolish.

Silt, *n.* Mud deposited from running or standing water.

Sil'ver, *n.* A precious metal of a white color. — *a.* Made of, or like, silver. — *v. t.* To cover with silver.

Sil'ver-smith, *n.* One who works in silver.

Sil'ver-y, *a.* Resembling silver. [bling.

Sim'i-lar, *a.* Like; resem-

Sim'i-lăr'i-ty, *n.* Resemblance; likeness. [manner.

Sim'i-lar-ly, *adv.* In a like

SIMILE 275 SKATE

Sim'i-le, *n.* Similitude.
Si-mil'i-tūde, *n.* Comparison.
Sim'mer, *v. i.* To boil gently.
Sim'o-nī'a̤e-al, *a.* Guilty of, or consisting in, simony.
Sim'o-ny, *n.* [From *Simon Magus*. See Acts viii.] The crime of buying or selling church preferment.
Sī-moom', *n.* A hot suffocating wind in Arabia, Syria, and the adjacent countries.
Sim'per, *v. i.* To smile in a silly or affected manner. — *n.* An affected or silly smile.
Sim'ple, *a.* Plain; artless; single; unmingled; silly. — *n.* Something not mixed; a medicinal plant.
Sim'ple-ton (sǐm'pl-, 132), *n.* A silly or foolish person.
Sim-plīç'i-ty, *n.* State or quality of being simple; plainness; artlessness; singleness; weakness of intellect.
Sim'pli-fi-eā'tion, *n.* Act of making simple.
Sim'pli-fy, *v. t.* To make simple, plain, or easy.
Sim'ply, *adv.* Without art; plainly; merely; only.
Sim'u-lāte, *v. t.* To counterfeit.
Sim'u-lā'tion, *n.* Hypocrisy.
Sī'mul-tā'ne-oŭs, *a.* Being or happening at the same time with something else.
Sī'mul-tā'ne-oŭs-ly, *adv.* At the same time.
Sin, *n.* A violation of divine law, or rule of duty. — *v. i.* To depart knowingly from a known rule of duty.
Sin'a-pĭṣm, *n.* A poultice of pulverized mustard-seed.
Sinçe, *prep.* After. — *adv.* Before this or now; ago. — *conj.* From the time that; because; considering.
Sin-çēre', *a.* True; honest; undissembling; unfeigned.
Sin-çēre'ly, *adv.* Truly; honestly; unfeignedly.
Sin-çēr'i-ty, *n.* Freedom from disguise; honesty.
Sīne, *n.* A perpendicular line from one end of an arc to the diameter drawn through the other end. Sine.
Sī'ne-cūre, *n.* Office or position with pay, but not requiring active labor.
Sī'ne-cūr'ist, *n.* One who has a sinecure.
Sĭn'ew (sĭn'yṋ), *n.* A tendon;

muscle; strength. — *v. t.* To unite as with sinews.
Sin'ew-y, *a.* Strong; muscular; tendinous; brawny.
Sin'ful, *a.* Guilty of, or marked by, sin; unholy; wicked.
Sin'ful-ly, *adv.* With sin.
Sin'ful-ness, *n.* State of being sinful; iniquity; wickedness; unrighteousness.
Sing, *v. t.* or *i.* [*imp.* SANG, SUNG; *p. p.* SUNG.] To utter musical or melodious sounds; to recite in verse.
Sinġe, *v. t.* (133) To burn the external part of; to scorch. — *n.* A slight burn or scorching. [singing.
Sing'er, *n.* One skilled in
Sing'ing, *n.* Act of uttering musical notes.
Sin'gle (sĭng'gl), *a.* Individual; separate; alone; unmarried; sincere. — *v. t.* To select; to separate.
Sin'gle-ness, *n.* State of being single; sincerity; simplicity.
Sin'gly, *adv.* Individually; separately; only.
Sing'-sŏng, *n.* A drawling, monotonous tone.
Sin'gu-lar, *a.* Single; alone; not plural; particular; remarkable; rare; odd.
Sin'gu-lăr'i-ty, *n.* Peculiarity; oddity.
Sin'gu-lar-ly, *adv.* Peculiarly; strangely; oddly.
Sin'is-ter, *a.* Left; bad; unfair; unlucky.
Sin'is-trôr'sal, *a.* Rising from left to right, as a spiral line, or helix.
Sin'u-troŭs, *a.* Being on, or inclined to, the left side; wrong; perverse.
Sink, *v. i.* [*imp.* SUNK, SANK; *p. p.* SUNK.] To settle; to fall; to subside; to decline; to bring low. — *v. i.* To immerse; to depress; to degrade; to become lower. — *n.* A drain to carry off filth, or a box with such a drain attached.
Sink'ing-fŭnd, *n.* A fund to reduce a public debt.
Sin'less, *a.* Free from sin.
Sin'ner, *n.* A transgressor.
Sin'-ŏf'fer-ing, *n.* A sacrifice for sin.
Sin'u-āte, *v. i.* To wind and turn. [and out.
Sin'u-ā'tion, *n.* A winding in
Sin'u-ŏs'i-ty, *n.* Quality of winding in and out.
Sin'u-oŭs, *a.* Winding in and out; serpentine.

Sĭp, *n.* A slight taste, as of liquor. — *v. t.* or *t.* To drink a little.
Sī'phon, *n.* A bent tube for transferring liquor from one vessel to another.
Sĭr, *n.* A title of address to a man; title of a knight or baronet.
Sĭre, *n.* Father; title of a king; male parent of a beast. — *v. t.* To generate; to beget.
Sī'ren, *n.* A mermaid noted for singing. — *a.* Bewitching; enchanting.
Sĭr'loin, *n.* The loin of beef.
Sĭ-rŏc'co, *n.* A noxious southeast wind in Italy.
Sĭr'rah, *n.* A term of reproach or contempt; — addressed to men.
Sĭr'up, *n.* Vegetable juice boiled with sugar. [bird.
Sĭs'kin, *n.* A certain singing-
Sĭs'ter, *n.* A female born of the same parents or belonging to the same association.
Sĭs'ter-hŏŏd, *n.* A society of sisters. [ter.
Sĭs'ter-ly, *a.* Becoming a sis-
Sĭt, *v. i.* [*imp.* & *p. p.* SAT.] To rest on the haunches; to perch; to brood. [position.
Sīte, *n.* A situation; local
Sĭt'ting, *n.* A session.
Sĭt'u-āte, } *a.* Being in any
Sĭt'u-ā'ted, } condition.
Sĭt'u-ā'tion, *n.* Relative position, location, or condition; state; site.
Sĭx, *a.* Five and one
Sĭx'fōld, *a.* Taken six times.
Sĭx'pençe, *n.* Half a shilling.
Sĭx'teen, *a.* Ten and six.
Sĭx'teenth, *a.* The ordinal of sixteen.
Sĭxth, *a.* Next after the fifth; being one of six equal parts of any thing. [place.
Sĭxth'ly, *adv.* In the sixth
Sĭx'ti-eth, *a.* Ordinal of sixty.
Sĭx'ty, *n.* & *a.* Six times ten; three-score.
Sīz'a-ble (133), *a.* Being of a reasonable or suitable bulk.
Sī'zar, *n.* A student of the rank below a pensioner. [*Cambridge, Eng.*]
Sīze, *n.* Bulk; dimensions; quantity; a glutinous substance. — *v. t.* To adjust or arrange according to size; to cover or prepare with size.
Sīz'y, *a.* Glutinous; viscous.
Skāte, *n.* A frame for the feet, with an iron runner for sliding on ice. — *v. i.* To slide with skates.

sŭn, ôr, dọ, wọlf, tōō, tŏŏk; ûrn, rṵe, pṵll; ç, ġ, *soft;* c, g, *hard;* aẓ; eẋist; ṋ *as* ng; *this.*

Skein, *n.* A knot or number of knots of threads.

Skel'e-ton, *n.* The bones of an animal retained in their natural position, without the flesh; general structure.

Skep'tic, *n.* One who doubts, especially of revelation.

Skep'tic-al, *a.* Doubting.

Skep'ti-cism, *n.* Doubt, esp. as to the fact of revealed religion; uncertainty; universal doubt.

Sketch, *n.* An outline; a rough draught. — *v. t.* To trace by drawing outlines of.

Sketch'y, *a.* Like a sketch; incomplete.

Skew'er (skū'-), *n.* A pointed rod to fasten meat. — *v. t.* To fasten with skewers.

Skid, *n.* A short piece of timber; a slider. [boat.

Skiff (123), *n.* A small, light

Skill (131), *n.* Familiar knowledge united to readiness of performance. — SYN Dexterity; adroitness.

Skilled, *a.* Having familiar knowledge.

Skillet, *n.* A small kind of boiler.

Skill'ful, *a.* Qualified with
Skil'ful, *}* skill; experienced.
Skill'ful-ly, *} adv.* With
Skil'ful-ly, *}* knowledge and dexterity.

Skim, *v. t.* or *i.* To take off scum or cream; to touch slightly. [take off scum.

Skim'mer, *n.* A utensil to

Skim'-milk, *n.* Milk from which the cream has been skimmed, or taken.

Skin, *n.* Covering of the flesh; hide; rind. — *v. t.* To deprive of the skin; to flay. — *v. i.* To form a skin over.

Skin'-flint, *n.* A miser; a niggard.

Skin'ny, *a.* Consisting of skin or of skin only.

Skip, *v. i.* To leap lightly. — *v. t.* To pass over or by. — *n.* A leap; a bound.

Skip'per, *n.* Master of a small trading vessel.

Skir'mish, *n.* A slight fight in war. — *v. i.* To fight slightly or in small parties.

Skirt, *n.* A border; the loose lower part of a coat, of a woman's dress, or of some other garment. — *v. i.* To lie on the border. — *v. t.* To border.

Skit'tish, *a.* Shy; timorous; easily frightened.

Skit'tish-ness, *n.* Timidity; shyness; fickleness.

Skit'tles, *n. pl.* Nine-pins.

Ski'ver, *n.* Split sheepskin tanned with sumac.

Skulk, *v. i.* To lurk; to hide.

Skulk'er, *n.* One who skulks.

Skull, *n.* The bony case that incloses the brain.

Skull'-cap, *n.* A close fitting cap.

Skunk, *n.* A fetid animal of North America.

Sky (69, 141), *n.* The aërial region; the heavens.

Sky'-light (-līt), *n.* A window in a roof or deck.

Sky'-rock'et, *n.* A species of fireworks.

Sky'-sail, *n.* A sail next above the royal.

Slab, *n.* A thin piece of any thing, esp. of stone; outside piece of a sawed log.

Slab'ber (*colloq.* slŏb'ber), *v. i.* To slaver; to drivel.

Slack (127), *a.* Lax; loose; relaxed; remiss; slow; tardy. — *n.* Small, broken coal; part of a rope having no strain on it. — *v. t.* or *i.* To loosen; to relax.

Slack'en (slăk'n), *v. t.* or *i.* To make or become slack; to relax; to be remiss or backward; to flag. [missly.

Slack'ly, *adv.* Loosely; re-

Slack'ness, *n.* State of being slack; remissness.

Slag, *n.* Dross of metal; vitrified cinders.

Slain (136), *p. p.* of *Slay.*

Slake, *v. t.* To quench, as thirst; to extinguish; to mix with water, and reduce to powder, as lime.

Slam, *v. t.* To shut with force and noise. — *n.* A violent shutting or striking.

Slan'der, *v. t.* To injure by false reports. — SYN. To defame; vilify; calumniate. — *n.* False report maliciously uttered; defamation. [ders.

Slan'der-er, *n.* One who slan-

Slan'der-ous, *a.* Defamatory; calumnious.

Slang, *n.* Low, vulgar, unauthorized language.

Slant, *v. t.* or *i.* To slope; to lie or turn obliquely.

Slant'ing, *a.* Sloping; inclining; oblique.

Slap, *v. t.* To strike with open hand. — *n.* A blow with the open hand, or with something flat and broad.

Slash, *v. t.* To cut in long cuts.

— *v. n.* To strike violently and at random with an edged instrument. — *n.* A long incision.

Slat, *n.* A narrow strip of board used for various purposes.

Slate, *n.* A kind of dark stone or a thin flat piece of it used for covering buildings or for writing on. — *v. t.* To cover with slate.

Slat'er, *n.* One whose business is to slate buildings.

Slat'tern, *n.* A woman negligent of her dress or house.

Slat'tern-ly, *a.* Negligent of dress and neatness; sluttish.

Slat'y, *a.* Consisting of, or like, slate.

Slaugh'ter (slaw'ter), *n.* Destruction of life; massacre; carnage; butchery. — *v. t.* To kill; to slay; to butcher.

Slaugh'ter-er (slaw'-), *n.* One who slaughters or slays; a butcher.

Slaugh'ter-house (slaw'-), *n.* Place for butchering cattle.

Slaugh'ter-ous (slaw'-), *a.* Murderous; destructive.

Slave, *n.* [From the *Slavonians* (Low Lat. *Slavi*), who were frequently made slaves by the Germans.] A person held in bondage; a drudge. — *v. i.* To drudge; to toil.

Slav'er, *n.* A slave-ship.

Slav'er, *n.* Spittle driveling from the mouth. — *v. i.* To emit spittle. — *v. t.* To smear with spittle issuing from the mouth.

Slav'er-y, *n.* State of a slave; bondage; thralldom. [slaves.

Slave'-trade, *n.* Traffic in

Slav'ish, *a.* Servile; mean; base. [meanly; basely.

Slav'ish-ly, *adv.* Servilely

Slay (136), *v. t.* [*imp.* SLEW; *p. p.* SLAIN.] To put to death. — SYN. To kill; destroy; slaughter; butcher.

Slay'er, *n.* One who kills.

Sleave, *n.* Silk or thread untwisted. — *v. t.* To separate, as threads.

Slea'zy, *a.* Thin; flimsy.

Sled, *n.* A carriage on runners for carrying heavy burdens on the snow; a light seat on runners for sliding on snow. — *v. t.* To convey on a sled.

Sled'ding, *n.* Act of transporting on a sled; snow enough for sleds.

ā, ē, ī, ō, ū, ȳ, *long*; ă, ĕ, ĭ, ŏ, ŭ, ў, *short*; câre, cär, ȧsk, ąll, whąt; ēre, vẹil, tērm; p'ique, fīrm;

SLEDGE 277 SLY-BOOTS

Slědge, *n.* A large hammer; a sled; a sleigh.
Sleek, *a.* Smooth, soft, and glossy. — *v. t.* To make smooth, soft, and glossy.
Sleek'ness, *n.* Smoothness and glossiness of surface.
Sleep, *n.* Slumber; repose; rest. — *v. i.* [*imp.* & *p. p.* SLEPT] To rest with the voluntary exercise of the powers of body and mind suspended.
Sleep'er, *n.* One who sleeps; a timber for the support of a rail or some superstructure.
Sleep'i-ly, *adv.* In a sleepy manner.
Sleep'i-ness, *n.* Drowsiness.
Sleep'less, *a.* Having no sleep; wakeful; excited.
Sleep'less-ness, *n.* Want of sleep. [drowsy.
Sleep'y, *a.* Disposed to sleep;
Sleet, *n.* Rain and snow or hail falling together.
Sleeve, *n.* Part of a garment covering the arm.
Sleigh (slā), *n.* A vehicle for travelling on snow.
Sleigh'ing (slā/-), *n.* Act of riding in a sleigh; state of snow with respect to riding in a sleigh.
Sleight (slīt), *n.* An artful trick; dexterity.
Slen'der, *a.* Thin and comparatively long; weak; slight; small; spare.
Slen'der-ness, *n.* Smallness of diameter; slightness.
Slěpt, *imp.* & *p. p.* of *Sleep.*
Slew (slū), *imp.* of *Slay.*
Sley, *v. t.* To part and arrange in a reed, as threads.
Slīçe, *n.* A thin piece cut off. — *v. t.* To cut off a thin, broad piece from.
Slīde, *v. i.* or *t.* [*imp.* SLID, *p. p.* SLID, SLIDDEN.] To move along the surface; to slip. — *n.* A smooth, easy passage on something.
Slight (slīt), *a.* Unimportant; weak; trifling; slender. — *n.* Neglect. — *v. t.* To treat with neglect; to disregard.
Slight'ly (slīt/-), *adv.* Superficially; in a small degree.
Slight'ness (slīt/-), *n.* Want of force or strength.
Sli'ly. See *Slyly.* [slight.
Slim, *a.* Slender; weak;
Slīme, *n.* Soft, moist, adhesive earth.
Slim'i-ness, *n.* State of being slimy. [glutinous.
Slīm'y, *a.* Viscous; clammy;

Sling, *n.* A weapon for throwing stones; a throw; a kind of bandage. — *v. t.* [*imp.* & *p. p.* SLUNG.] To hurl by a sling; to cast.
Slink, *v. i.* or *t.* [*imp.* & *p. p.* SLUNK.] To steal or sneak away; to miscarry.
Slip, *v. i.* or *t.* To slide involuntarily; to glide; to escape. — *n.* A sliding; a mistake; a twig; a narrow piece; a strip; a long narrow pew.
Slip'-knŏt (-nŏt), *n.* A knot that slips along the line on which it is made.
Slip'per, *n.* A kind of light shoe worn in undress.
Slip'per-i-ness, *n.* State or quality of being slippery.
Slip'per-y, *a.* Smooth; glib; apt to slip away; unstable.
Slip'shŏd, *a.* Wearing shoes down at the heels; careless.
Slit, *n.* A long cut or rent. — *v. t.* [*imp.* SLIT; *p. p.* SLIT, SLITTED.] To divide lengthwise; to rend or cut.
Slit'ting-mill, *n.* A mill where iron bars are slit into nail-rods, &c.
Sliv'er, or Slī'ver, *v. t.* To divide into thin pieces. — *n.* A long slice cut or torn off.
Slŏb'ber, *v. n.* See *Slabber.*
Slōe (149), *n.* Fruit of the black thorn; a wild plum.
Sloŏp, *n.* A kind of vessel having one mast only, and the mainsail extended by a boom.
Slŏp, *n.* Water carelessly spilled; (*pl.*) dirty water; ready-made clothes. — *v. t.* To cause to overflow; to spill.
Slōpe, *a.* Inclining; slanting. — *n.* Direction downward; a declivity or acclivity. — *v. t.* or *i.* To form with a slope; to be inclined.
Slŏp'py, *a.* Wet and dirty.
Slŏt, *n.* A slit or aperture in a plate of metal.
Slŏth, or Slōth (18), *n.* Sluggishness; laziness; a slow-moving animal of South America, living in trees.
Slŏth'ful, or Slōth'ful, *a.* Lazy; sluggish; indolent.
Slouch, *n.* A hanging down. — *v.* To hang down; to depress; to have a clownish look or manner.

Slough (slou), *n.* A miry place.
Slough (slŭf), *n.* Cast skin of a serpent; part that separates from a sore. — *v. i.* To separate and come off.
Slŏv'en (or slŭv'n-, 55), *n.* A man habitually careless of dress and neatness.
Slŏv'en-li-ness (or slŭv'n-), *n.* Habitual want of cleanliness.
Slŏv'en-ly (or slŭv'n-), *a.* Negligent of dress or neatness; loose; disorderly.
Slōw, *a.* Not fast or quick; not prompt. — SYN. Tardy; dilatory; inactive; deliberate. [dily.
Slōw'ly, *adv.* Not quick; tar-
Slōw'ness, *n.* Quality of being slow; deliberation.
Slŭdge, *n.* Soft mud; slush.
Slūe, *v. t.* To turn about a fixed point.
Slŭg, *n.* [Allied to *slack.*] A drone; a slow or lazy fellow; a kind of snail; an oval or cylindrical piece of metal for the charge of a gun.
Slŭg'gard, *n.* A person habitually lazy; a drone.
Slŭg'gish, *a.* Habitually lazy; slothful. [gish manner.
Slŭg'gish-ly, *adv.* In a slug-
Slŭg'gish-ness, *n.* State or quality of being sluggish.
Slūice, *n.* A stream of water issuing through a floodgate; a floodgate.
Slŭm'ber, *v. i.* To sleep lightly; to doze. — *n.* Light sleep; repose.
Slŭm'ber-oŭs, *a.* Causing **Slŭm'ber-y,** *a.* or inviting slumber.
Slŭmp, *v. i.* To sink through or in, as when walking on ice or snow.
Slŭng, *imp.* & *p. p.* of *Sling.*
Slŭng'-shŏt, *n.* A metal ball, with a string attached, used for striking.
Slŭnk, *imp.* & *p. p.* of *Slink.*
Slŭr, *v. t.* To soil; to sully; to pass lightly; to perform in a smooth, gliding manner. — *n.* Stain; slight disgrace or reproach; innuendo; a mark [⌣ or ⌢] connecting notes to be sung to the same syllable.
Slŭt, *n.* An untidy woman; a slattern; a female dog.
Slŭt'tish, *a.* Negligent of dress or neatness; dirty; slatternly.
Slŭt'tish-ness, *n.* State or quality of being sluttish.
Slȳ (135), *a.* Artful; cunning; crafty.
Slȳ'-boŏts, *n.* A sly person.

Sly'ly (135), *adv.* With art; cunningly; craftily.
Sly'ness, *n.* Quality of being sly; cunning; crafty.
Smack, *v. i.* To kiss loudly; to crack, as a whip; to taste. — *n.* A loud kiss; taste; a small coasting or fishing vessel.
Small, *a.* Little; slender; weak. — *n.* The slender or narrow part of any thing.
Small'-arms, *n. pl.* Muskets, rifles, or pistols.
Small'-beer, *n.* A kind of weak beer. [ness.
Small'ness (131), *n.* Little-
Small'-pox, *n.* A contagious and eruptive disease. [fine.
Smalt, *n.* Blue glass ground
Smart, *a.* Quick; active; brisk; sharp. — *n.* Quick, pungent, lively pain. — *v. i.* To have a keen pain.
Smart'ly, *adv.* Briskly; sharply; wittily.
Smart'ness, *n.* Quality of being smart.
Smash, *v. t.* To dash to pieces. — *n.* A breaking to pieces.
Smat'ter, *v. i.* To talk superficially or ignorantly.
Smat'ter-er, *n.* One who has only a superficial knowledge.
Smat'ter-ing, *n.* Slight, superficial knowledge.
Smear, *v. t.* To daub; to soil.
Smell, *v. t.* or *i.* [*imp. & p. p.* SMELLED, or SMELT.] To perceive by the nose; to affect the nose. — *n.* Odor; scent; sense by which odors are perceived.
Smelt, *v. t.* To melt, as ore. — *n.* [From *smell*, in allusion to its peculiar odor.] A small kind of fish. — r., *imp. & p. p.* of *Smell*.
Smelt'er, *n.* One who smelts.
Smerk, *v. & n.* See *Smirk*.
Smile, *v. i.* To look as when pleased or joyous. — *n.* A peculiar contraction of the face expressive of pleasure or kindness, or of slight contempt, &c. [Joyous.
Smil'ing, *a.* Appearing gay or
Smil'ing-ly, *adv.* With a smile.
Smirch, *v. t.* To cloud; to dirt; to soil.
Smirk, *v. i.* To look affectedly soft or kind. — *n.* An affectedly soft or kind look; a simper.
Smite, *v. t.* [*imp.* SMOTE; *p. p.* SMIT, SMITTEN.] To strike; to kill; to blast; to afflict. — *v. i.* To strike; to collide. [metals.
Smith, *n.* One who works in
Smith'er-y, *n.* The work or workshop of a smith.
Smit'ten (smit'tn), *p. p.* of *Smite*.
Smock, *n.* A shift; a chemise.
Smoke (18), *n.* Exhalation from burning substances. — *v. i.* To emit smoke. — *v. t.* To hang in smoke; to use in smoking, as a pipe or cigar.
Smok'er, *n.* A person who smokes.
Smoke'-jack, *n.* A wheel in a chimney, turned by ascending air.
Smok'y, *a.* Emitting smoke like smoke; apt to smoke; obscure.
Smol'der, } *v. i.* To waste
Smoul'der, } away by slow combustion.
Smooth, *a.* Even on the surface; soft; bland; not rough. — *v. t.* To make even or easy; to calm.
Smooth'ly, *adv.* Evenly; calmly; blandly.
Smooth'ness, *n.* Evenness of surface; mildness of address; gentleness.
Smote, *imp.* of *Smite*.
Smoth'er, *v. t.* To stifle or suffocate. — *v. i.* To be stifled. — *n.* A smoke; thick dust.
Smug'gle, *v. t.* To import or export without paying duties; to convey privately.
Smug'gler, *n.* One who smuggles.
Smut, *n.* Soot; foul matter, or a spot made by it; a kind of fungus; mildew. — *v. t.* To murk with smut; to soil. — *v. i.* To contract smut.
Smutch, *v. t.* To blacken with smoke. [ily.
Smut'ti-ly, *adv.* Dirtily; filth-
Smut'ti-ness, *n.* Soil from smoke; obscenity.
Smut'ty, *a.* Soiled; obscene.
Snack, *n.* A share; equal part or portion; a slight, hasty repast.
Snaf'fle, *n.* A bridle consisting of a slender bit without branches.
Snag, *n.* A short rough branch; a tooth standing out; trunk of a large tree firmly fixed at one end to the bottom of a river.
Snag'ged, } *a.* Full of snags
Snag'gy, } or sharp points.
Snail, *n.* A small reptile which moves very slowly; a sluggard.
Snake, *n.* A serpent, especially one of the oviparous kind.
Snake'root, *n.* One of several very different plants.
Snap (129), *v.* To break short; to seize suddenly with the teeth; to crack. — *n.* Act of breaking suddenly; a sudden bite; a small catch or fastening; a crisp kind of cake.
Snap'-drag'on, *n.* A plant; a kind of game.
Snap'pish, *a.* Apt to snap; peevish; petulant.
Snap'pish-ly, *adv.* In a snappish manner; peevishly.
Snare, *n.* Any thing which entraps; a noose. — *v. t.* To ensnare; to entangle.
Snarl, *v. t.* To entangle; to complicate. — *v. i.* To growl, as a dog. — *n.* Entanglement; an intricate complication; an embarassing difficulty.
Snarl'er, *n.* One who snarls.
Snatch, *v. t.* To seize hastily. — *n.* A hasty catch or seizing; a small piece or quantity.
Snath, *n.* Handle of a scythe.
Sneak (133), *v. i.* To creep slyly; to behave meanly; to hide. — *n.* A mean, sneaking fellow.
Sneak'ing, *a.* Mean; servile; covetous; niggardly.
Sneer, *v. i.* To show contempt by laughing or by a look. — *n.* A scornful or contemptuous look or expression.
Sneer'er, *n.* One who sneers.
Sneer'ing-ly, *adv.* With a look of contempt or scorn.
Sneeze, *v. i.* To eject air suddenly and involuntarily through the nose. — *n.* A violent ejection of air through the nose.
Sniff (123), *v. t.* or *i.* To draw air audibly up the nose.
Snick'er, } *v. i.* To laugh with
Snig'ger, } catches of voice.
Snip, *v. t.* To cut off; to nip; to clip. — *n.* A single cut with scissors.
Snipe, *n.* A bird having a long, straight, slender bill.
Sniv'el (sniv'l, 58, 139), *n.* Mucus running from the nose. — *v. i.* (130) To run at the nose; to cry, as children.
Snob, *n.* A vulgar person who apes gentility; an upstart.
Snob'bish, *a.* Relating to, or like, a snob.
Snooze, *v. i.* To doze; to

SNORE 279 SOLEMNITY

drowse. —*n.* A short sleep; a nap; slumber.
Snōre, *v. i.* To breathe with a rough, hoarse noise in sleep. —*n.* A breathing with a loud noise in sleep.
Snōr'ing, *n.* A loud, hoarse breathing in sleep.
Snôrt, *v. i.* To force air through the nose with a noise. [nose.
Snŏt, *n.* Mucus from or in the
Snout, *n.* The long nose of a beast; end of a pipe or tube.
Snow, *n.* Frozen vapor which falls in flakes. —*v. i.* To fall in flakes.
Snōw'-ball, *n.* A round mass or lump of snow.
Snōw'-bĕr'ry, *n.* A garden shrub with small white berries.
Snōw'-drĭft, *n.* Bank of snow.
Snōw'-drŏp, *n.* A bulbous plant bearing white flowers.
Snōw'-shoe, *n.* A light frame for the foot, to enable a person to walk on snow.
Snōw'y, *a.* Full of snow; white as snow; pure.
Snŭb, *v. t.* To check or rebuke tartly or sarcastically; to slight. —*n.* A reprimand; a check; a rebuke.
Snŭff (123), *n.* Burnt wick of a candle; powdered tobacco. —*v. t.* To crop, as the burnt end of the wick of a candle; to inhale; to smell. —*v. i.* To draw air forcibly into the nose.
Snŭff'-bŏx, *n.* A small box for snuff, to be carried about the person.
Snŭff'ers (131), *n. pl.* An instrument to snuff candles.
Snŭf'fle, *v. i.* To speak or breathe hard through the nose.
Snŭf'fles, *n. pl.* Obstruction of the nose by mucus.
Snŭg, *a.* Lying close; private; compact, convenient, and comfortable. —*v. i.* To lie close; to snuggle.
Snŭg'gle, *v. i.* To lie close for convenience or warmth.
Snŭg'ly, *adv.* Closely; safely.
Snŭg'ness, *n.* State of being snug.
Sō, *adv.* Thus; in like manner or degree; very.
Sōak, *v. t.* or *i.* To steep or be steeped; to drench.
Sōap (18, *n.* A compound of oil or fat and an alkali or oxide, used in washing. —*v. t.* To rub with soap.

Sōap'-boil'er, *n.* One who makes soap.
Sōap'stone, *n.* A soft mineral feeling soapy to the touch.
Sōap'-sŭds, *n.* Water impregnated with soap.
Sōap'y, *a.* Covered with, or like, soap; soft and smooth.
Sōar, *v. i.* [It. *sorare,* from Lat. *ex* and *aura,* the air.] To mount on the wing; to fly aloft. —*n.* A towering flight.
Sŏb, *v. i.* To sigh convulsively. —*n.* A convulsive sigh; a sorrowful cry.
Sō'ber, *a.* Serious; grave; temperate; not intoxicated. —*v. t.* To make sober.
Sō'ber-ly, *adv.* Seriously; gravely; temperately.
Sō'ber-ness, *n.* State of being sober; sobriety.
So-brī'e-ty, *n.* Habitual temperance; gravity; seriousness; calmness.
†**Sō'brī-quet' (sō'bre-kā'),** *n.* A nickname.
Sō'cia-bĭl'i-ty (-sha-), *n.* Disposition for society or conversation.
Sō'cia-ble (-sha-), *a.* Ready to converse; familiar; friendly; companionable.
Sō'cia-ble-ness (sō'sha-bl-), *n.* Inclination to company and conversation.
Sō'cia-bly (-sha-), *adv.* Conversably; familiarly.
Sō'cial (sō'shal), *a.* Pertaining to, or fond of, society; companionable.
Sō'cial-ĭsm, *n.* Doctrine that a community of interests is the best form of society.
Sō'cial-ly, *adv.* In a social manner.
So-cī'e-ty (118), *n.* Union of persons in one interest; fellowship; companionship; an association; company.
So-çĭn'i-an, *n.* A follower of Socinus, who denied the Trinity, the deity of Christ, the vicarious atonement, &c.
So-çĭn'i-an-ĭsm, *n.* Tenets of the Socinians.
Sŏck, *n.* A shoe for a comic actor; a short stocking.
Sŏck'et, *n.* An opening into which any thing is fitted.
Sŏd, *n.* Earth filled with roots of grass. — SYN. Turf; clod; sward. —*v. t.* To cover with sods; to turf.
Sō'dȧ, *n.* An alkali, forming the basis of common salt.
So-dăl'i-ty, *n.* Fellowship.
Sō'dȧ-wạ'ter, *n.* Simple wa-

ter highly charged with carbonic acid.
Sŏd'den, *p. p.* of *Seethe.*
Sŏd'dy, *a.* Consisting of sod.
Sŏd'er, *v. t.* To unite with a metallic cement; to solder. —*n.* Metallic cement.
Sō'fä (18, 20), *n.* A long, stuffed, ornamental seat.
Sŏf'fit, *n.* A ceiling.
Sŏft, *a.* Easily yielding to pressure; gentle; tender; delicate; weak; not hard.
Sŏft'en (sŏf'n), *v. t.* or *i.* To make or become soft.
Sŏft'en-er (sŏf'n-), *n.* One who, or that which, softens.
Sŏft'ly, *adv.* Tenderly; gently; silently.
Sŏft'ness, *n.* Quality of being soft; tenderness; mildness.
Sŏg'gy, *a.* Soaked with water.
Soĭl, *v. t.* To daub; to stain; to make dirty. —*n.* Upper stratum of earth; mold; compost; manure; country.
†**Soirée (swạ-rā'),** *n.* [Fr.] An evening party.
Sō'journ, *v. i.* To dwell for a time. —*n.* Temporary abode.
Sō'journ-er, *n.* A temporary resident, as a traveler.
Sŏl (123), *n.* A note in music.
Sŏl'açe, *v. t.* To give comfort to. — SYN. To comfort; cheer; assuage; relieve. —*n.* Comfort in grief.
Sō'lar, *a.* Pertaining to, or proceeding from, the sun.
Sŏld, *imp.* & *p. p.* of *Sell.*
Sŏl'der, *v. t.* To unite with a fusible metallic cement. —*n.* A fusible metallic composition for uniting the surfaces of metals.
Sōl'dier (sōl'jer, 74), *n.* One who is engaged in military service, either as an officer or a private; a warrior.
Sōl'dier-ly (sōl'jer-), *a.* Like a good soldier; warlike; martial; brave.
Sōl'dier-y (sōl'jer-), *n.* A body of soldiers.
Sōle, *n.* Bottom of the foot or of a shoe or boot. —*v. t.* To furnish with soles. —*a.* Single; alone; solitary.
Sŏl'e-çĭṣm, *n.* Impropriety in language; any absurdity.
Sŏl'e-çĭs'tic, *a.* Pertaining to, or involving, a solecism.
Sōle'ly, *adv.* Singly; only.
Sŏl'emn (sŏl'em), *a.* Religiously grave; marked with solemnity; awful; grave; formal.
So-lĕm'ni-ty, *n.* Religious

sŏn, ôr, dọ, wọlf, tōō, tŏŏk; ûrn, rụe, pụll; ç, ğ, *soft;* ȩ ḡ, *hard;* aṣ; eẋist; ŋ *as* ng; *this.*

ceremony; a rite; gravity; seriousness.

Sŏl'em-ni-zā'tion, *n.* Act of solemnizing; celebration.

Sŏl'em-nīze, *v. t.* To celebrate in due form.

Sŏl'emn-ly (sŏl'em-), *adv.* With solemnity, or religious reverence; gravely.

Sŏl-fä', *v. i.* To sing the notes of the gamut.

So-liç'it, *v. t.* To ask with earnestness. — SYN. To entreat; supplicate; importune; implore.

So-liç'it-ā'tion, *n.* Entreaty.

So-liç'it-or, *n.* An advocate; an attorney. [careful.

So-liç'it-oŭs, *a.* Anxious;

So-liç'it-oŭs-ly, *adv.* With solicitude or anxiety.

So-liç'i-tūde, *n.* Anxiety; carefulness; concern.

Sŏl'id, *a.* [Lat. *solidus*, from *solum*, the bottom.] Hard; firm; compact; sound. — *n.* A substance having a fixed form.

Sŏl'i-där'i-ty, *n.* Entire union of interests and responsibilities; fellowship.

So-lĭd'i-fỹ, *v. t.* To make solid or compact.

So-lĭd'i-ty, *n.* Firmness; hardness; density.

Sŏl'id-ly, *adv.* Compactly; firmly; densely.

Sŏl'i-fĭd'i-an, *n.* One who maintains that faith alone is sufficient for justification.

So-lĭl'o-quīze, *v. i.* To utter a soliloquy.

So-lĭl'o-quy (117), *n.* A talking to one's self.

Sŏl'i-tāire', *n.* A game which one person can play alone.

Sŏl'i-ta-ri-ly, *adv.* In solitude.

Sŏl'i-ta-ri-ness (135), *n.* Lack of company; loneliness.

Sŏl'i-ta-ry, *a.* Lonely; retired; single; sole. — *n.* A hermit; a recluse.

Sŏl'i-tūde, *n.* Loneliness; seclusion; a lonely place.

Sō'lo, *n.* (*pl.* **Sō'lŏs.**) A tune or air performed by one person.

Sŏl'stĭçe, *n.* A point in the ecliptic at which the sun is furthest from the equator.

Sol-stĭ'tial (-stĭsh'al), *a.* Belonging to, or happening at, a solstice. [being soluble.

Sŏl'u-bĭl'i-ty, *n.* Quality of

Sŏl'u-ble, *a.* Capable of being dissolved in a fluid.

So-lū'tion, *n.* Process of dissolving in a fluid; mixture resulting from it; explanation. [solve.

Sŏl'u-tīve, *a.* Tending to dis-

Sŏlv'a-bĭl'i-ty, *n.* Ability to pay all just debts.

Sŏlv'a-ble (133), *a.* Capable of being solved.

Sŏlve, *v. t.* To explain; to unfold; to clear up.

Sŏlv'en-çy, *n.* Ability to pay all debts or just claims.

Sŏl'vend, *n.* A substance to be dissolved.

Sŏlv'ent, *a.* Able to pay debts; dissolving. — *n.* A fluid which dissolves any substance.

Sŏlv'er, *n.* One who solves.

Sŏm'ber, } *a.* Dull; dusky;
Sŏm'bre, } dark; gloomy.

Sŏm'broŭs, *a.* Dark; gloomy.

Sŏme (sŭm), *a.* More or less; indicating a quantity or person unknown; certain.

Some'bŏd-y (139), *n.* A person unknown or indeterminate; some person; one.

Sŏm'er-set (sŭm'-), *n.* A leap in which one turns heels over head. [or another.

Some'how, *adv.* In one way

Some'thing, *n.* A thing indeterminate; a part.

Some'tīmes, *adv.* Now and then; occasionally.

Some'what (sŭm'hwŏt), *adv.* In some degree or quantity.

Some'where, *adv.* In one place or another.

Som-năm'bu-lĭsm, *n.* Act or practice of walking in sleep.

Som-năm'bu-lĭst, *n.* One who walks in sleep.

Som-nĭf'er-oŭs (117), } *a.*
Som-nĭf'ic, } Causing, or tending to cause, sleep. [talking in sleep.

Som-nĭl'o-quençe, *n.* Act of

Som-nĭl'o-quĭst, *n.* One who talks in sleep. [in sleep.

Som-nĭl'o-quy, *n.* A talking

Sŏm'no-lençe, *n.* Sleepiness.

Sŏm'no-lent, *a.* Inclined to sleep; sleepy.

Sŏn (sŭn), *n.* [A.-S. *sunee*, Skr. *sunee*, from *sû*, to beget.] A male child or descendant.

†So-nä'tä, *n.* [It.] A tune for one or two instruments.

Sŏng, *n.* A short poem to be sung. — SYN. A lay; carol; ditty; hymn; lyric; ballad.

Sŏng'ster, *n.* A singer; a bird that sings. [singer.

Sŏng'stress, *n.* A female

Sŏn'net, *n.* A poem of fourteen lines, having the rhymes adjusted according to certain rules.

Sŏn'net-eer', *n.* A composer of sonnets or small poems.

So-nō'roŭs, *a.* Giving sound when struck; loud; resounding; high-sounding.

So-nō'roŭs-ly, *adv.* In a sonorous manner.

So-nō'roŭs-ness, *n.* Quality of being sonorous.

Sŏn'ship, *n.* State or character of a son; filiation.

Sōon, *adv.* In a little time; shortly; before long.

Sŏot (or sōot), *n.* A black substance formed by combustion. — *v. t.* To black with soot.

Sōoth, *n.* Truth; reality.

Soothe, *v. t.* To calm; to allay; to quiet.

Sōoth'sāy, *v. t.* To foretell; to predict. [a prophet.

Sōoth'sāy-er, *n.* A predicter;

Sŏot'i-ness, *n.* Quality of being sooty.

Sŏot'y (or sōot'y), *a.* Pertaining to, covered with, or resembling, soot.

Sŏp, *n.* Food dipped in any liquid. — *v. t.* To steep or dip in liquor.

Sŏph'ĭsm, *n.* A specious but fallacious argument; a fallacy.

Sŏph'ĭst, *n.* A captious or fallacious reasoner.

Sŏph'ĭst-er, *n.* A sophist; a student advanced, in England beyond the first, and in America beyond the second, year of his residence.

So-phĭst'ic-al, *a.* Subtilely fallacious; not sound.

So-phĭst'ic-al-ly, *adv.* In a sophistical manner.

So-phĭst'ic-āte, *v. t.* To pervert; to adulterate; to corrupt. [soning.

Sŏph'ist-ry, *n.* Fallacious rea-

Sŏph'o-mōre, *n.* A student in college in his second year.

Sŏph'o-mŏr'ic, } *a.* Inflat-
Sŏph'o-mŏr'ic-al, } ed in style or manner.

Sŏp'o-rĭf'er-oŭs, } *a.* Causing
Sŏp'o-rĭf'ic, } sleep.

Sŏp'o-rĭf'ic, *n.* A medicine that puts to sleep.

†So-prä'no, *n.* [It.] The treble.

Sŏr'çer-er, *n.* A magician; an enchanter; a conjurer.

Sŏr'çer-ess, *n.* An enchantress. [sorcery.

Sŏr'çer-oŭs, *a.* Pertaining to

Sŏr'çer-y, *n.* Enchantment; witchcraft; magic.

Sôr'did, a. Covetous; base; mean; filthy.
Sôr'did-ly, adv. With covetousness; meanly; basely.
Sôre, n. Flesh tender and painful; a wound; an ulcer.
— a. Tender to the touch; painful.
Sôre, or Sôre′ly, adv. With pain; grievously; greatly.
Sôre′ness, n. Tenderness.
So-rör′l-çide, n. The murder, or murderer, of a sister.
Sôr′rel, a. Of a yellowish or reddish brown color. — n. A plant having a sour juice.
Sôr′ri-ly, adv. Meanly; poorly; despicably.
Sôr′row, n. [A.-S. sorg, sorh, allied to sore.] Pain produced by a sense of loss; regret. — SYN. Grief; sadness; unhappiness. — v. i. To be sorry; to mourn; to grieve; to be sad. [sad.
Sôr′row-fyl, a. Mournful;
Sôr′row-fyl-ly, adv. In a sorrowful manner.
Sôr′row-fyl-ness, n. State of being sorrowful; grief.
Sôr′ry, a. Grieved for something lost or past; poor; mean; vile; worthless.
Sôrt, n. A species; kind; manner; class. — v. t. To dispose in classes. — v. i. To agree; to associate; to suit.
Sôrt′a-ble, a. Capable of being sorted.
Sôrt′i-lēġe, n. Divination by drawing lots.
Sŏt, n. An habitual drunkard.
Sŏt′tish, a. Dull or stupid with drink; drunken.
Sŏt′tish-ness, n. Dullness; drunken stupidity.
†Sou (sōō), n. (pl. Sous, sōō.) (Fr.) The 20th of a franc.
Sou-çhŏng′ (sōō-hŏng′), n. A kind of black tea.
Soŭgh (sŭf), n. A hollow murmur or roaring.
Sought (sawt), imp. of Seek.
Soul, n. The spiritual and immortal part of man; life; intellectual principle; a human being.
Soul′less (106), a. Without a soul; mean; spiritless.
Sound, n. Noise; a narrow sea; air-bladder of a fish.
— a. Whole; unhurt. — v. i. To make a noise; to try the depth of water. — v. t. To cause to make a noise; to try the depth of.
Sound′ingṣ, n. pl. A part of the sea or other water in which the bottom can be reached.
Sound′ly, adv. Healthily; heartily; stoutly; justly; profoundly.
Sound′ness, n. State of being sound; entireness; health; solidity.
Soup (sōōp), n. A decoction of flesh, vegetables, &c.
Sour, a. Acid; tart; crabbed. — v. i. To become acid.
Sôurçe, n. A spring; fountain; origin; first cause.
Sour′ish, a. Somewhat sour.
Sour′ly, adv. With acidity.
Sour′ness, n. Acidity; tartness; austerity.
Souse, n. Pickle made of the ears and feet of swine; a plunge. — v. t. To steep in souse; to plunge; to immerse; to dip; to duck.
South, n. Point opposite the north. — a. Lying in a southern direction. — adv. Toward the south. — v. t. To move toward the south; to cross a north and south line.
South-cast′, n. A point between south and east.
South′er-ly (sŭth′er-), a. Being at, or coming from, the south.
South′ern (sŭth′ern), a. Pertaining to the south.
South′ing, n. Course or distance south; time when the moon passes the meridian.
South′ron (sŭth′-), n. An inhabitant of the south.
South′ward (or sŭth′ard), adv. Toward the south.
South-wèst′, n. A point between south and west. — a. Being at the south-west.
†Souvenir (sōōv′neer′), n. [Fr.] A remembrancer; a keepsake.
Sŏv′er-eign (sŏv′er-in or sŭv′er-in), a. Supreme to power; chief. — n. A supreme ruler; monarch; king; emperor.
Sŏv′er-eign-ty (sŏv′er-in- or sŭv′er-in-), n. Exercise of supreme power.
Sow (sou), n. A female swine.
Sōw (sō), v. t. [imp. SOWED; p. p. SOWED, SOWN.] To scatter as seed for growth; to plant; to spread.
Sōw′er, n. One who sows.
Sōwn. p. p. of Sow. Seat-ured. [fish.
Soy, n. A kind of sauce for
Spä, n. A spring of mineral water.
Spāçe, n. [Lat. spatium, fr. spatiari, to walk about.] Room; extension; distance; interval.
Spā′cious, a. Large in extent. — SYN. Ample; capacious; roomy.
Spā′cious-ly, adv. Widely; extensively.
Spāde, n. An instrument for digging; (pl.) a suit of cards.
Spăn, n. A hand's breadth, with the fingers extended or encompassing the object; 9 inches. — v. t. (129) To measure with the fingers extended.
Spăn′gle, n. A small plate or boss of metal. — v. t. To set with spangles. [Spain.
Spăn′iard, n. A native of
Spăn′iel (spăn′yel), n. A variety of sporting dog.
Spăn′ish, a. Pertaining to Spain. — n. The language of Spain.
Spănk, v. t. To strike with the open hand; to slap.
Spănk′er, n. A small coin; after-sail of a ship or bark.
Spär, n. A mineral; a long round beam, as a yard or boom. — v. i. To fight, as a pugilist. [of a vessel.
Spär′-dĕck, n. Upper deck
Spāre, a. Scanty; parsimonious; lean; thin. — v. t. To use frugally; to do without; to forbear to punish.
Spāre′ness, n. State of being spare.
Spāre′-rib, n. Ribs of pork with little flesh on them.
Spär′ing, a. Scarce; scanty; saving; chary.
Spär′ing-ly, adv. In a sparing manner.
Spärk, n. A particle of fire; a gay man; a lover; a gallant. [showy.
Spärk′ish, a. Lively; gay;
Spärk′le, n. A small spark, or particle of fire. — v. i. To emit sparks.
Spär′row, n. One of several species of small birds.
Spär′ry, a. Resembling spar.
Spärse, a. Thinly scattered or dispersed.
Spärse′ly, adv. Thinly.
Spär′tan, a. Pertaining to Sparta; brave; hardy.
Spaṣm (105), n. [Gr. spasmos, from spaein, span, to draw, convulse.] Involuntary contraction of muscles; cramp.
Spaṣ-mŏd′ic, a. Relating to, or consisting in, spasm; convulsive.

SPATTER 282 SPILL

Spăt'ter, *v. t.* To sprinkle with a liquid, or with mud.
Spăt'u-lă, *n.* An apothecary's broad knife for plasters, &c.
Spăv'in, *n.* A tumor on or near one of the joints of a horse's leg.
Spawn, *n.* Eggs of frogs and fishes. — *v. i.* or *t.* To deposit, as spawn.
Spawn'er, *n.* A female fish.
Spāy, *v. t.* To cut out the ovaries of, as of a female beast.
Spēak, *v.* [*imp.* SPOKE (*obs.* SPAKE); *p. p.* SPOKE, SPOKEN.] To utter words; to talk; to discourse.
Spēak'a-ble, *a.* Capable of being uttered; able to speak.
Spēak'er, *n.* One who speaks; the presiding officer in a deliberative assembly.
Spēar, *n.* A long, pointed weapon of war. — *v. t.* To pierce with a spear.
Spēar'man (143), *n.* One armed with a spear.
Spēar'mint, *n.* A plant.
Spē'cial (spŏsh'al, 92), *a.* Peculiar; appropriate; specific; particular.
Spē'cial-ly (spĕsh'al-), *adv.* Particularly; specifically.
Spē'cial-ty (spĕsh'al-), *n.* A special contract, or the evidence of a debt under seal; a special object of attention.
Spē'cie (spē'shy), *n.* Coined or hard money.
Spē'cies (spē'shēz; *colloq.* spē'shiz), *n.* Sort; kind; a class subordinate to a genus.
Spe-cĭf'ic, *a.* Distinguishing one from another; comprehended under a kind; peculiar. — *n.* An infallible remedy.
Spe-cĭf'ic-al-ly, *adv.* Definitely; particularly.
Spĕç'i-fi-cā'tion, *n.* Act of specifying, or designating particulars; particular mention: thing specified; a written and detailed statement.
Spĕç'i-fȳ, *v. t.* To mention, as a particular thing.
Spĕç'i-men, *n.* A sample; a pattern; a model.
Spē'cious (spē'shus), *a.* Apparently right; appearing well at first sight; plausible.
Spē'cious-ly, *adv.* With fair appearance. [ternal show.
Spē'cious-ness, *n.* Fair ex-
Spĕck, *n.* A stain; a small discolored place. — *v. t.* To spot; to stain.

Spĕck'le, *n.* A small speck. — *v. t.* To mark with small specks, or spots.
Spĕck'led, *a.* Variegated with small spots.
Spēe'ta-cle, *n.* A show; sight; exhibition; (*pl.*) glasses to assist the sight.
Spēe'ta-cled, *a.* Wearing spectacles.
Spec-tāe'u-lar, *a.* Pertaining to shows. [n beholder.
Spec-tā'tor, *n.* A looker on;
Spec-tā'tress, } *n.* A female
Spec-tā'trix, } spectator or beholder.
Spĕe'ter } (151), *n.* An appa-
Spĕe'tre } rition; a ghost.
Spĕe'tral, *a.* Pertaining to a specter; ghostly.
Spĕe'trum, *n.* Rays of light separated by a prism or by other means.
Spĕe'u-lar, *a.* Like a mirror.
Spĕe'u-lāte, *v. i.* To meditate; to buy in expectation of a rise in price.
Spĕe'u-lā'tion, *n.* Act of speculating; mental view; a buying in expectation of an advance in price.
Spĕe'u-la-tive, *a.* Given to speculation; theoretical.
Spĕe'u-la-tive-ly, *adv.* In a speculative manner.
Spĕe'u-lā'tor, *n.* One who speculates.
Spĕe'u-lum, *n.* A glass that reflects images; a mirror.
Spĕd, *imp.* & *p. p.* of *Speed.*
Speech, *n.* Power of speaking; that which is spoken; language; utterance; discourse.
Speech'less, *a.* Not speaking or not able to speak; dumb; mute; silent.
Speech'less-ness, *n.* State of being speechless.
Speed, *v. i.* [*imp.* & *p. p.* SPED.] To make haste; to hasten; to fare. — *n.* Haste; dispatch; celerity.
Speed'i-ly, *adv.* Quickly; hastily; soon. [swift.
Speed'y, *a.* Quick; hasty;
Spĕll (123), *n.* A charm; a turn at work; a short time. — *v. t.* or *i.* [*imp.* & *p. p.* SPELLED, SPELT.] To name or write in order the proper letters of a word; to take a turn at work.
Spĕll'er, *n.* One who spells; a spelling-book.
Spĕlt, *n.* A species of grain.
Spĕl'ter, *n.* Zinc.
Spĕn'çer, *n.* A kind of short over-jacket.

Spĕnd, *v. t.* [*imp.* & *p. p.* SPENT.] To consume; to waste; to exhaust; to wear away; to expend.
Spĕnd'thrift, *n.* A prodigal.
Spĕrm, *n.* Animal seed; spermaceti; spawn of fishes.
Spĕr'ma-çē'ti, *n.* A hard, fatty matter, obtained from the head of whales.
Sperm-ăt'ic, *a.* Pertaining to, or consisting of, semen.
Spew, *v. t.* or *i.* To vomit; to eject. [a wedge.
Sphe-noid'al, *a.* Resembling
Sphēre, *n.* A globe; orb; circuit; province. — *v. t.* To place in a sphere.
Sphĕr'ic, } *a.* Having the
Sphĕr'ic-al, } form of a sphere; globular; round.
Sphĕr'ic-al-ly, *adv.* In the form of a sphere.
Sphĕr'ic-al-ness, } *n.* Ro-
Sphe-riç'i-ty, } tundity.
Sphĕr'ics, *n. sing.* Doctrine of the sphere; spherical geometry and trigonometry.
Sphē'roid, *n.* A body nearly spherical.
Sphe-roid'al, *a.* Formed like a spheroid.
Sphĕr'ule (sfĕr'ŏŏl), *n.* A little sphere or ball.
Sphĭnx (140), *n.* A fabulous monster usually represented with the winged body of a lion and the face and breast of a young woman.
Spīçe, *n.* An aromatic vegetable substance; a small quantity. — *v. t.* To season with spice.
Spī'çer-y, *n.* Spices in general.
Spīe'u-lar, *a.* Having sharp points; resembling a dart.
Spī'çy (185), *a.* Pertaining to, or full of, spice; like spice; pungent; aromatic.
Spī'der, *n.* An animal, resembling an insect, that spins webs for catching its prey.
Spĭg'ot, *n.* A pin or peg to stop a hole in a cask.
Spīke, *n.* An ear of corn or something resembling it; a large nail. — *v. t.* To fasten with a spike.
Spīke'let, *n.* A little spike.
Spīke'nard (spīk'-), *n.* An aromatic plant and an oil obtained from it.
Spīk'y, *a.* Having a sharp point or points.
Spīle, *n.* A small peg or wooden pin to stop a hole.
Spĭll, *v. t.* [*imp.* & *p. p.* SPILLED, SPILT.] To shed

or suffer to be shed. — *v. i.* To be lost by shedding.

Spin, *v. t.* or *i.* [*imp.* & *p. p.* SPUN.] To draw out and twist into threads; to protract; to twirl; to whirl.

Spin'ach } (spĭn'ej), *n.* A **Spin'age** } garden plant.

Spī'nal, *a.* Belonging to the spine or backbone.

Spin'dle, *n.* A pin to form thread on in spinning, or something like this. — *v. i.* To become thin or tall.

Spine, *n.* The backbone; a thorn; a sharp process.

Spī'nel, or **Spī-něl',** *n.,* A mineral of great hardness.

Spin'et, or **Spī-nět',** *n.* A musical instrument now superseded by the piano-forte.

Spin'ning-wheel, *n.* A machine for spinning yarn or thread, in which a wheel drives a single spindle.

Spī-nŏs'ĭ-ty, *n.* State of being spiny or thorny.

Spī'noŭs, } *a.* Full of spines; **Spī'ny,** } thorny.

Spin'ster, *n.* A woman who spins; an unmarried or single woman.

Spīr'a-cle (*or* spī'ra-kl), *n.* A minute breathing-hole in certain animal and vegetable bodies. [screw.

Spī'ral, *a.* Winding like a

Spī'ral-ly, *adv.* In a spiral form.

Spīre, *n.* A winding like a screw; a twist; a steeple; a shoot. — *v. i.* To shoot up pyramidically; to sprout.

Spĭr'it (84), *n.* Breath; life; immaterial and immortal part of man; soul; a ghost; excitement; vigor; distilled liquor. — *v. t.* To animate; to excite; to kidnap.

Spĭr'it-ed, *a.* Full of spirit or life; animated; bold.

Spĭr'it-less, *a.* Without spirit.

Spĭr'it-oŭs, *a.* Refined; ardent; like spirit.

Spĭr'it-u-al, *a.* Pertaining to the spirit; incorporeal; mental; holy; ecclesiastical.

Spĭr'it-u-al-ĭsm, *n.* Doctrine that all which exists is spirit; a belief in the frequent communication of intelligence from the world of spirits.

Spĭr'it-u-al-ĭst, *n.* One who believes in spiritualism.

Spĭr'it-u-ăl'ĭ-ty, *n.* State of being spiritual; immateriality; spiritual nature; holy affections; pure devotion.

Spĭr'it-u-al-īze (153), *v. t.* To make spiritual.

Spĭr'it-u-al-ly, *adv.* Divinely.

Spĭr'it-u-oŭs, *a.* Consisting of refined spirit; ardent.

Spĭrt, *v.* & *n.* See *Spurt.*

Spī'ry, *a.* Of a spiral form, or of the form of a pyramid.

Spĭs'sĭ-tūde, *n.* Thickness of soft substances.

Spĭt, *n.* An iron prong to roast meat on; a point of land running into the sea; saliva; spittle. — *v. t.* To put on a spit; to pierce. — *v. t.* or *i.* [*imp.* & *p. p.* SPIT.] To eject spittle.

Spīte, *n.* Rancorous ill-will. — SYN. Malice; malignity; malevolence. — *v. t.* To be angry at; to thwart; to injure maliciously.

Spīte'ful, *a.* Malicious; malignant. [ice.

Spīte'ful-ly, *adv.* With malice.

Spīte'ful-ness, *n.* State of being spiteful; malice.

Spĭt'tle, *n.* Moisture of the mouth; saliva. [in.

Spĭt-tōōn', *n.* A vessel to spit

Splăsh, *v. t.* To dash with water or mud. — *n.* Water or mud thrown on any thing.

Splăsh'y, *a.* Full of mud and water.

Splāy'-fōōt'ed, *a.* Having the sole flattened; having the foot turned outward.

Spleen, *n.* The milt; a glandular organ to the left of the stomach; ill-humor; melancholy.

Spleen'y, *a.* Angry; peevish.

Splĕn'dent, *a.* Shining; radiant; bright.

Splĕn'dĭd, *a.* [Lat. *splendĭdus,* from *splendere,* to shine.] Bright; showy; magnificent.

Splĕn'dĭd-ly, *adv.* With great show; magnificently.

Splĕn'dor, *n.* Great brightness; magnificence; pomp.

Splĕn'e-tic (120), *a.* Full of spleen.

Splīçe, *v. t.* To unite by interweaving, as two ends of a rope. — *n.* Union of ropes by interweaving.

Splĭnt, } *n.* A thin piece of **Splĭnt'er** } wood used to protect a broken bone.

Splĭnt, *v. t.* To confine with splints, as a broken limb.

Splĭnt'er, *v. t.* To split into long, thin pieces; to secure by splints.

Splĭnt'er-y, *a.* Like, or consisting of, splinters.

Splĭt, *v. t.* [*imp.* & *p. p.* SPLIT.] To divide lengthwise; to cleave; to rive. — *v. t.* To part asunder.

Splŭt'ter, *n.* Bustle; stir

Spoil (130), *v. t.* To rob; to strip by violence; to ruin. — *v. i.* To decay. — *n.* Plunder; booty; pillage.

Spoil'er, *n.* One who spoils.

Spōke (18), *imp.* of *Speak.* — *n.* Ray or bar of a wheel; round of a ladder.

Spō'ken (spō'kn, 18), *p. p.* of *Speak.*

Spōkes'man (143), *n.* One who speaks for others.

Spō'lĭ-āte, *v. t.* or *i.* To plunder or practice plunder.

Spō'lĭ-ā'tion, *n.* Act of plundering. [a spondee.

Spon-dā'ic, *a.* Pertaining to

Spŏn'dee (140), *n.* A poetic foot of two long syllables.

Spŏnge (spŭnj), *n.* A porous marine substance, used for various purposes in the arts; dough that is raised but not kneaded. — *v. t.* To wipe out with a sponge; to imbibe. — *v. i.* To live by mean arts, or by hanging on.

Spŏng'er (spŭnj'er), *n.* One who sponges; a parasite.

Spŏng'ĭ-ness, *n.* Quality of being spongy.

Spŏng'y, *a.* Porous; soft and full of cavities.

Spŏn'sal, *a.* Relating to marriage, or to a spouse.

Spŏn'sion, *n.* Act of becoming surety for another.

Spŏn'sor, *n.* A surety; a godfather or godmother.

Spŏn'ta-nē'ĭ-ty, *n.* Quality of acting freely without restraint; voluntary action.

Spon-tā'ne-oŭs, *a.* [Lat. *spontaneus,* from *sponte,* of free will.] Voluntary; willing; not compelled.

Spon-tā'ne-oŭs-ly, *adv.* Of free will; voluntarily.

Spon-tōōn', *n.* A kind of half pike.

Spool, *n.* A kind of hollow cylinder to wind thread on. — *v. t.* To wind on spools.

Spoon, *n.* A small utensil used in eating liquids.

Spoon'bĭll, *n.* A wading bird, so named from the shape of its bill.

Spoon'ful (148), *n.* As much as a spoon can hold.

Spoon'-meat, *n.* Food eaten with a spoon. [and there.

Spo-răd'ic, *a.* Occurring here

---

sŏn, ôr, dọ, wọlf, tōō, tŏŏk; ûrn, rụe, pụll; ç, ġ, *soft;* e, ġ, *hard;* aṣ; eẋist; ṇ *as* ng; this.

SPORT 284 SQUAT

Sport, *n.* Play; mirth; frolic; diversion; mock. —*v. i.* To play; to make merry.
Sport'ful, *a.* Merry; frolicsome; mirthful.
Sport'ive, *a.* Merry; gay; playful; frolicsome. [ness.
Sport'ive-ness, *n.* Playful-
Sports'man (143), *n.* One fond of field sports.
Spot, *n.* A stain; a blemish; any particular place. —*v. t.* To mark; to stain; to tarnish; to disgrace.
Spot'less, *a.* Free from spots; pure; blameless. [spots.
Spot'ted, *a.* Marked with
Spous'al, *a.* Matrimonial. — *n.* Marriage; nuptials.
Spouse, *n.* A husband or wife.
Spout, *n.* A projecting mouth of a vessel; a pipe. —*v. t.* or *i.* To throw or issue out of a narrow orifice.
Sprain, *n.* Excessive straining of the muscles or ligaments of a joint. —*v. t.* To overstrain, as a joint.
Sprang, *imp.* of *Spring.*
Sprat, *n.* A small fish allied to the herring.
Sprawl, *v. i.* To lie struggling with the limbs stretched out.
Spray, *n.* A small shoot; a twig; water driven in small drops by the wind.
Spread, *v. i.* or *t.* [*imp. & p. p.* SPREAD.] To extend; to expand; to diffuse. —*n.* Extent; expansion.
Spree, *n.* A merry frolic; a drinking frolic; a carousal.
Sprig, *n.* A small shoot or branch; twig. —*v. t.* To work with sprigs.
Spright (sprīt), *n.* A spirit; an apparition.
Spright'ful (sprīt'fụl), } *a.*
Spright'ful-ness (sprīt'-),
 Gay; brisk; lively; vigorous.
Spright'ful-ly (sprīt'-), *adv.* Briskly; gayly; with life.
Spright'li-ness (sprīt'-), *n.* Briskness; liveliness; gayety; vivacity.
Spright'less (sprīt'-), *a.* Destitute of life; dull.
Spright'ly (sprīt'lỹ), *a.* Brisk; lively; active; vigorous; vivacious.
Spring, *v. i.* [*imp.* SPRANG, SPRUNG; *p. p.* SPRUNG.] To leap; to bound; to issue with force; to arise; to start; to begin. —*v. t.* To fire, as a mine; to crack, as a mast. —*n.* A leap; elastic force; season of the year when plants begin to grow; a fountain; a source.

Springe (sprĭnj, 133), *n.* A snare. —*v. t.* To ensnare.
Spring'-halt, } *n.* A lameness
String'-halt, } in which a horse suddenly twitches up his legs.
Spring'i-ness, *n.* Elasticity.
Spring'-tide, *n.* A high tide at the new and full moon.
Spring'y, *a.* Containing springs; elastic; spongy.
Sprink'le, *v. t.* or *i.* To scatter or fall in small drops or particles.
Sprink'ling, *n.* Act of scattering in small particles or drops.
Sprit, *n.* A pole placed diagonally to extend a sail.
Sprite, *n.* A spirit; a ghost.
Sprit'sail, *n.* A sail extended by a sprit.
Sprout, *v. i.* To shoot, as a plant; to germinate; to bud. —*n.* Shoot of a plant.
Spruce, *a.* Neat, without elegance. —*n.* A cone-bearing evergreen tree. —*v.* To dress with affected neatness.
Spruce'ly, *adv.* With affected neatness. [trimness.
Spruce'ness, *n.* Neatness;
Sprung, *imp. & p. p.* of *Spring.*
Spry (135), *a.* Nimble; brisk.
Spud, *n.* An implement for destroying weeds. [scum.
Spume, *n.* Froth; foam;
Spum'ous, } *a.* Consisting of
Spum'y, } froth or scum; foamy.
Spun, *imp.* of *Spin.*
Spunge, *n.* See *Sponge.*
Spunk, *n.* Dry rotten wood; an inflammable temper; resolute spirit.
Spur, *n.* An instrument with sharp points, worn on the heel as a goad by horsemen; incitement. —*v. t.* To prick; to incite; to goad.
Spur'-gall, *n.* A place excoriated by a spur.
Spurge, *n.* A plant having an acrid, milky juice.
Spu'ri-ous, *a.* Not genuine; false; illegitimate; counterfeit.
Spu'ri-ous-ly, *adv.* Falsely.
Spu'ri-ous-ness, *n.* State of being spurious; falseness.
Spurn, *v. t.* To kick; to reject with disdain.
Spurred, *a.* Wearing or having spurs. [spurs.
Spur'ri-er, *n.* One who makes
Spurt, *v. t.* To throw out in a stream. —*n.* A small, quick stream; a jet.
Sput'ter (139), *v. i.* [From the root of *spout* and *spit.*] To throw spittle; to talk indistinctly. [ters.
Sput'ter-er, *n.* One who sputters.
Spy, *n.* One who constantly watches the conduct of others. —*v. t.* To discover; to inspect secretly. [scope.
Spy'-glass, *n.* A small telescope.
Squab, *a.* Unfeathered; short and stout. —*n.* A young pigeon; a person of a short, fat figure.
Squab'ble, *v. i.* To wrangle; to scuffle. —*n.* A wrangle.
Squad (skwŏd), *n.* A company or small party for drill or service.
Squad'ron, *n.* Part of a fleet; a body of cavalry troops.
Squal'id (skwŏl'ĭd), *a.* Dirty through neglect; foul; filthy.
Squa-lid'i-ty, } *n.* Foulness;
Squal'id-ness, } filthiness.
Squall, *n.* A sudden and violent gust of wind; a loud scream. —*v. i.* To scream violently, as a child.
Squall'y (131), *a.* Subject to squalls. [ness.
†**Squa'lor**, *n.* [Lat.] Filthi-
Squa'mous, *a.* Covered with, or consisting of, scales.
Squan'der (skwŏn'der), *v. t.* To spend lavishly; to waste.
Square, *a.* Having four equal sides and four right angles; true; just; fair. —*n.* A figure of four equal sides and equal angles; an open space in a town; an area of four sides, with houses on each; a carpenter's instrument — *v. t.* To make square or equal; to multiply by itself. —*v. i.* To accord exactly; to suit; to agree.
Square'ness, *n.* State of being square.
Square'-rigged, *a.* Having the chief sails extended by yards, suspended by the middle.
Squash (skwŏsh), *n.* A plant. —*v. t.* To beat or press into pulp; to crush.
Squat (skwŏt), *v. i.* To sit upon the hams and heels. — *n.* Posture of sitting on the hams. —*a.* Cowering; short and thick.

ā,ē,ī,ō,ū,ȳ, *long*; ă,ĕ,ĭ,ŏ,ŭ,ў, *short*; câre, cär, ȧsk, ạll, whạt; ēre, vẹil, tērm; pīque, fĭrm;

SQUATTER 285 STANZA

Squat'ter, *n.* One who squats: one who settles on new land without title.
Squaw, *n.* An Indian woman.
Squeak, *v. i.* To utter a short, sharp, shrill sound. — *n.* A short, shrill sound.
Squeal, *v. i.* To cry with a shrill sound. — *n.* A shrill, sharp, prolonged cry.
Squeam'ish. *a.* Nice; fastidious; dainty.
Squeam'ish-ly, *adv.* In a fastidious manner.
Squeam'ish-ness, *n.* Fastidiousness; daintiness.
Squeeze, *v. t.* or *i.* To press close; to crowd. — *n.* Close compression; pressure.
Squib, *n.* A kind of firework; a petty lampoon; a sarcasm.
Squill (123), *n.* A plant with a root having emetic properties; a kind of shell-fish; an insect.
Squint, *v. i.* To look or see obliquely; a want of coincidence of the axes of the eye.
Squint'-eyed, *a.* Having eyes that squint; oblique; indirect.
Squire, *n.* Same as *Esquire.* — *v. t.* To wait on; to attend as a squire or a gallant.
Squirm, *v. i.* [Allied to Skr. *krimi,* a worm.] To twist and struggle; to climb by embracing and scrambling.
Squir'rel (skwĭr'rel or skwŭr'rel), *n.* A small active animal with a bushy tail.
Squirt, *v. t.* To eject from a pipe or in a stream. — *n.* A pipe for ejecting liquids.
Stab, *v. t.* To pierce with a pointed weapon. — *n.* A wound with a pointed weapon. [steadiness; constancy.
Sta-bil'i-ty, *n.* Firmness;
Sta'ble, *a.* Fixed; durable; steady. — *n.* A house for beasts. — *v. t.* To house or keep in a stable. [oral.
Sta'bling, *n.* Stables in general.
Sta'bly, *adv.* Fixedly; firmly.
†Stac-ca'to, *a.* [It.] (*Mus.*) Distinct; — a direction to perform the notes of a passage in a short, distinct, and pointed manner.
Stack (127), *n.* A large pile of hay, grain, wood, &c.; a number of chimneys standing together. — *v. t.* To pile in stacks.
Stad'dle, *n.* A support for a stack of hay, &c.; a small tree of any kind.

†Sta'di-um, *n.* (*pl.* Sta'di-a). A Greek measure of length, equal to 606 feet and 9 inches.
Staff (5, 123, 142), *n.* A stick for support; the five lines and spaces on which music is written; a stanza; certain officers attached to an army.
Stag, *n.* Male of the red-deer; a hart; a young castrated bull.
Stage, *n.* A raised floor or platform; the theater; place of rest; a degree of advance.
Stage'-coach, *n.* A public traveling carriage.
Stage'-play, *n.* A theatrical entertainment; a drama.
Stage'-play'er, *n.* An actor of plays on the stage.
Stag'ger, *v. i.* To reel in walking; to vacillate.
Stag'nan-cy, *n.* State of being stagnant, or without motion or flow.
Stag'nant, *a.* Not flowing; motionless; still; dull.
Stag'nate, *v. i.* To become stagnant; to cease to flow.
Stag-na'tion, *n.* Absence of motion; dullness.
Staid (130), *imp. & p. p.* of *Stay.* — *a.* Steady; grave; sober. [ity of being staid.
Staid'ness, *n.* State or quality
Stain, *v. t.* To discolor; to color; to dye; to tarnish; to disgrace. — *n.* A blot; spot; taint; disgrace. [spotless.
Stain'less, *a.* Free from stains;
Stair, *n.* A step for ascending.
Stair'-case, *n.* Framework of a flight of stairs.
Stake, *n.* A sharpened stick of wood; martyrdom; wager; pledge. — *v. t.* To defend with stakes; to wager; to pledge.
Stal'ac-tit'ic, *a.* Resembling an icicle; pertaining to stalactite.
Sta-lac'tite, *n.* A mineral in form of an icicle.
Sta-lag'mite, *n.* A deposit of calcareous matter on the floor of a cavern.
Stal'ag-mit'ic, *a.* Having the form of stalagmites.
Stale, *a.* Vapid and tasteless from age; worn out. — *n.* A decoy; a long handle; urine, especially that of beasts. — *v. t.* To make vapid. — *v. i.* To discharge urine. [stale.
Stale'ness, *n.* State of being
Stalk (stawk), *n.* Stem of a plant; a proud step. — *v. i.* To walk with a proud step;

to strut; to walk behind a cover
Stalk'y, *a.* Resembling a stalk.
Stall, *n.* A stand for a beast; a bench. — *v. t.* To keep in a stall; to invest.
Stall'-feed, *v. t.* To feed and fatten in a stable.
Stall'-fed, *a.* Fattened in a stable, or on dry fodder.
Stall'ion (stăl'yun), *n.* A horse for raising stock.
Stal'wart, *a.* Brave; bold; strong; powerful.
Sta'men, *n.* (*pl.* Sta'mens, †Stăm'i-na, 147). Foundation; support; male organ of a flower.
Stăm'i-nal, } *a.*
Sta-mĭn'e-oŭs, } Pertaining to, or consisting in, stamens or stamina. [men.
Stăm'mer, *v. i.* To pronounce with hesitation or imperfectly.
Stamp, *v. t.* To strike downward with the foot; to impress with some mark; to coin money. — *n.* An instrument for making an impression; mark impressed; a print; character; make; authority; an official device required by law to be affixed to certain papers.
Stam-pēde', *n.* [From *stamp.*] A sudden fright and running away of cattle, horses, &c.
Stanch, *v. i.* To stop, as flowing blood. — *v. t.* To stop the flowing of, as blood. — *a.* Firm; sound; strong; constant and zealous.
Stăn'chion (stăn'shun), *n.* A prop or support; a small post used for a support.
Stand, *v. i.* or *t.* [*imp. & p. p.* STOOD.] To be on the feet; to stop; to remain; to persist; to be steady or firm; to endure. — *n.* A stop; halt; station; a small table.
Stănd'ard, *n.* An ensign; a banner; criterion; test; a standing tree. — *a.* Having a fixed or permanent value.
Stănd'ing, *n.* Continuance; rank; reputation.
Stănd'ish (139), *n.* A case for holding pens and ink.
Stăn'na-ry, *n.* A tin-mine.
Stăn'nic, *a.* Relating to, or obtained from, tin.
Stăn'za (140), *n.* A number of lines or verses combined together in poetry.

sôu, ôr, dọ, wọlf, tōō, tŏŏk; ûrn, rụe, pụll; ç, ġ, *soft*; c, g, *hard*; a̤; ėxı̆st; ŋ as ng; this.

STAPLE 286 STELLIFEROUS

Sta'ple, n. A loop of iron; a mart for goods; the pile or thread of wool, cotton, &c.; principal production. — a. Chief; principal.

Star, n. A luminous body in the heavens; the mark *, used in printing; a distinguished performer. — v. t. To set or adorn with stars.

Star'board, n. Right-hand side of a ship or boat to one looking forward.

Starch, n. A granular substance used for stiffening cloth. — a. Stiff; precise. — v. t. To stiffen with starch.

Starched (stärcht), a. Stiff; precise; formal.

Starch'y, a. Stiff; precise.

Stare, v. i. To look with fixed eyes wide open. — n. An eager, fixed look.

Star'er, n. An eager gazer.

Star'fish, n. A marine animal in the form of a five-rayed star.

Star'-gaz'er, n. An astronomer; — in contempt.

Stark, a. Stiff; strong; mere; downright. — adv. Wholly; entirely. [visible.

Star'less, a. Having no stars

Star'light (-lit), a. Light from the stars. — a. Lighted by stars. [pean bird.

Star'ling, n. A small European

Star'ry, a. Consisting of, adorned with, or resembling, stars; stellar.

Stirt, v. i. or t. [Old Eng. stirte, sterte, allied to the root of stir.] To move suddenly; to commence; to alarm; to arouse. — n. A sudden motion; act of commencing.

Star'tle, v. t. To alarm suddenly. — v. i. To shrink; to move suddenly. [prising.

Start'ling, a. Suddenly surprising.

Starv-ā'tion, n. Act of starving, or state of being starved.

Starve, v. i. To perish with hunger or with cold. — v. t. To kill with hunger or cold.

Starve'ling, n. One who, or that which, is made lean or thin through want of nutriment. — a. Pining with want.

State, n. Condition; pomp; a community of a particular character; a body politic; civil power. — v. t. To express in words.

Stāt'ed, a. Settled; regular; established; fixed.

Stāt'ed-ly, adv. At appointed or regular times.

State'li-ness, n. Loftiness of mien or manner; grandeur.

State'ly, a. August; majestic; dignified; grand.

State'ment, n. Account of particulars; a recital.

State'-room, n. An apartment for lodging in a vessel.

States'man (143), n. One who is skilled in the art of government.

States'man-ship, n. Qualifications or employments of a statesman.

Stat'ic, | a. Pertaining to

Stat'ic-al, | bodies at rest; acting by mere weight.

Stat'ics, n. sing. Science which treats of bodies at rest, or in equilibrium.

Stā'tion, n. A fixed place; situation; position; post assigned; office; rank; a railroad stopping-place. — v. t. To fix in a certain place; to place; to set.

Stā'tion-al, a. Of, or pertaining to, a station.

Stā'tion-a-ry, a. Fixed in a place; stable; settled.

Stā'tion-er, n. One who sells paper, pens, ink, &c.

Stā'tion-er-y, n. Articles sold by a stationer, as paper, pens, ink, &c.

Stā'tist, n. A statesman.

Sta-tist'ic, | a. Pertaining

Sta-tist'ic-al, | to statistics.

Stat'is-ti'cian (-tish'an), n. A person familiar with statistics.

Sta-tist'ics, n. sing. & pl. A collection of facts, or the science of collecting facts, respecting the civil condition of a people.

Stat'u-a-ry, n. Art of carving statues or images; a carver; a sculptor; statues considered collectively.

Stat'ūe, n. An image carved from some solid substance.

Stat'ūre, n. The natural height of an animal.

Stat'u-ta-ble, a. Made by, or conformable to, statute.

Stat'ute, n. A law enacted by a legislature. [statute.

Stat'u-to-ry, a. Established by

Staunch, v. & a. See STANCH.

Stāve, n. A thin, narrow piece of wood for casks; a stanza. — v. t. [imp. & p. p. STOVE or STAVED.] To break or burst; to push or drive; to delay forcibly.

Stay, v. i. [imp. STAID or STAYED, 136.] To continue in a place; to wait; to tarry.

— v. t. To support; to prop up — n. Continuance; a prop; any support; (pl.) a bodice; a corset.

Stāy'-lāçe, n. Lace for stays.

Stead, n. Place; room; turn.

Stead'fāst, a. Firm; constant;

Stead'fast-ness, n. Firmness of mind or conduct; constancy. [or constancy.

Stead'i-ly, adv. With firmness

Stead'i-ness, n. Constancy.

Stead'y, a. Firm; constant, uniform; to pass or withdraw secretly. — v. t. To hold or keep firm; to support.

Steak, n. A slice of meat, broiled or cut for broiling.

Steal, v. t. or i. [imp. STOLE; p. p. STOLE, STOLEN.] To take goods privately and unlawfully; to pass or withdraw secretly. — SYN. To filch; pilfer; purloin.

Stealth, n. Act of stealing; secret act. [secret: sly.

Stealth'y, a. Done by stealth

Steam, n. The vapor of boiling water; any exhalation. — v. i. To rise in vapor. — v. t. To expose to steam.

Steam'boat, | n. A vessel pro-

Steam'er, | pelled through the water by steam.

Steam'-en'gine, n. An engine worked by steam.

Ste'a-tīte, n. A kind of soft rock; soapstone.

Steed, n. A spirited horse.

Steel, n. Iron combined with a small portion of carbon; a sword. — v. t. To overlay, point, or edge with steel; to harden.

Steel'yard (colloq. stil'yard), n. A kind of balance for weighing.

Steep, a. Greatly inclined; precipitous. — n. A precipitous place. — v. t. To soak in a liquid.

Stee'ple, n. Spire of a church; a pointed belfry.

Steep'ness, n. State of being steep; precipitous declivity.

Steer, n. A young ox. — v. t. or i. To direct; to govern; to guide or be guided.

Steer'age, n. Act of steering; an apartment in the forepart of a ship between decks.

Steers'man (143), n. One who steers a ship.

Stel'lar, a. Relating to stars.

Stel'late, | a. Like a star;

Stel'lāt-ed, | radiated.

Stel-lif'er-oŭs, a. Abounding with stars.

ā, ă, I, ō, ū, y, long; ă, ĕ, I, ŏ, ŭ, y, short; câre, cär, ȧsk, ąll, whąt; ēre, vȩil, tẽrm; pīque, fĩrm;

Stel′li-fôrm, *a.* Like a star; radiated.
Stem, *n.* Main body of a tree or plant; stalk; stock of a family; prow of a ship. — *v. t.* To oppose, as a current.
Stench, *n.* An offensive smell.
Sten′cil, *n.* An open-work pattern over which colors are passed by a brush. — *v. t.* (130.) To paint or color with stencils.
Sten′o-gräph′ic, *a.* Expressing in short-hand.
Ste-nŏg′ra-pher (117), *n.* One who writes in short-hand.
Ste-nŏg′ra-phy, *n.* [Gr. *stenos,* narrow, close, and *graphein,* to write.] The art of writing in short-hand.
Sten-tō′ri-an, *a.* Very loud; able to utter a loud sound.
Step, *v. i.* To move with the feet. — *v. t.* To set; to fix; to erect, as a mast. — *n.* One motion of the foot forward; a pace; a stair; gait; degree.
Step′-child, *n.* A child by marriage only.
Step′-fā′ther, *n.* A father by marriage only.
Step′-mŏth′er, *n.* A mother by marriage only.
Steppe (140), *n.* A vast uncultivated plain in Asia and eastern Europe.
Step′ping-stōne, *n.* A stone to raise the foot above mud or water, in walking; means of advancement. [riage.
Step′-sŏn, *n.* A son by marriage.
Stŏr′co-rā′ceoŭs, *a.* Pertaining to, or partaking of, dung.
Stē′re-o-gräph′ic, *a.* Delineated on a plane.
Stē′re-ŏg′ra-phy, *n.* Art of delineating the forms of solid bodies on a plane.
Stē′re-ŏm′e-try, *n.* Art of measuring solid bodies.
Stē′re-o-scōpe, *n.* An optical instrument to give to pictures the appearance of solid forms, as seen in nature.
Stē′re-o-scōp′ic, *a.* Pertaining or adapted to the stereoscope, or seen through it.
Stē′re-o-tȳpe, *n.* A plate of type-metal resembling the surface of a page of type. — *v. t.* To make stereotype plates for. [makes stereotypes.
Stē′re-o-tȳp′er, *n.* One who
Stĕr′ile. *a.* Barren; unfruitful.
Ste-rĭl′i-ty, *n.* Quality or state of being barren. — SYN. Barrenness; unfruitfulness.
Stĕr′ling, *a.* Of the standard weight; — said of English money; genuine.
Stĕrn, *n.* Hinder part of a ship. — *a.* Severe in look; harsh; rigid; austere.
Stĕrn′-chāse, *n.* A chase in which one vessel follows in the wake of another.
Stĕrn′ly, *adv.* Harshly; severely; austerely.
Stĕrn′ness, *n.* Harshness.
†**Stĕr′num,** *n.* [Lat.] The breast-bone. [sneezing.
Stĕr′nu-tā′tion, *n.* Act of
Ster-nū′ta-to-ry, *n.* A substance provoking sneezing.
Stĕr′to-roŭs, *a.* Breathing heavily or hoarsely; snoring.
Stĕth′o-scōpe, *n.* An instrument used to distinguish and judge of sounds in the human chest.
Stē′ve-dōre, *n.* One whose business is to load or unload vessels in port.
Stew (stū), *v. t.* or *i.* To seethe; to boil slowly. — *n.* Meat stewed; a brothel; a state of worry; confusion.
Stew′ard, *n.* A man who manages the affairs of another; a waiter on board a vessel. [steward.
Stew′ard-ship, *n.* Office of a
Stĭb′i-al, *a.* Like, or having the qualities of, antimony.
Stick (127), *n.* A piece of wood; a staff. — *v. t.* [*imp.* & *p. p.* STUCK.] To stab; to pierce; to fix; to set; to stop. — *v. i.* To adhere; to stop.
Stick′i-ness, *n.* Quality of adhering; adhesiveness.
Stick′le, *v. i.* To contend.
Stick′ler, *n.* One who stickles; obstinate contender.
Stick′y, *a.* Adhesive; glutinous; tenacious.
Stiff (131), *a.* Unbending; rigid; inflexible; stubborn.
Stiff′en (stif′n), *v. t.* To make stiff. — *v. i.* To grow stiff.
Stiff′ly, *adv.* Rigidly; stubbornly; obstinately.
Stiff′ness (131), *n.* Want of pliability; formality.
Stiff′-nĕcked (-někt, 139), *a.* Stubborn; obstinate.
Stī′fle (stī′fl), *v. t.* To suffocate; to choke; to suppress. — *n.* Joint of a horse, corresponding to the knee in man.
Stig′ma. *n.* (*pl.* **Stig′mas** or †**Stig′ma-tā,** 147.) Any mark of infamy; a brand; in *botany,* the top of the pistil.
Stig′ma-tīze, *v. t.* To mark with infamy.
Stile, *n.* A set of steps for passing a fence or wall.
Sti-lĕt′to, *n.* (*pl.* **Sti-lĕt′tōs,** 140.) A small dagger; an instrument to make eyelet holes.
Still, *v. t.* To silence; to calm; to quiet. — *a.* Silent; calm; quiet; motionless. — *adv.* To this time; nevertheless; notwithstanding. — *n.* A vessel for distillation.
Stĭll′-bŏrn, *a.* Born lifeless; dead at birth.
Still′-life, *n.* The class of paintings that represent fruits, flowers, dead game, &c.
Still′ness, *n.* Calmness; quiet; silence.
Still′ly, *adv.* Calmly; quietly.
Still′y, *a.* Still; quiet.
Stilt, *n.* A piece of wood with a rest for the foot to raise it above the ground in walking; a long-legged bird.
Stĭm′u-lant, *a.* Tending to excite action. — *n.* A stimulating medicine.
Stĭm′u-lāte, *v. t.* To excite; to rouse; to animate.
Stĭm′u-lā′tion, *n.* Act of stimulating or exciting.
Stĭm′u-lā′tive, *a.* Tending to excite; stimulating.
Stĭm′u-lā′tor, *n.* One who stimulates.
Stĭm′u-lus, *n.* Something that rouses either to mental action or to vital energy.
Sting, *v. t.* [*imp.* & *p. p.* STUNG.] To pierce or pain acutely. — *n.* A sharp-pointed weapon with which some animals are armed; act of stinging; any thing that gives acute pain.
Stĭn′gi-ly, *adv.* With mean covetousness.
Stĭn′gi-ness, *n.* Mean covetousness; extreme avarice.
Stĭn′gy, *a.* Meanly covetous.
Stĭnk, *n.* An offensive smell. — *v. i.* To emit an offensive smell.
Stint, *n.* A limit; restraint; task. — *v. t.* To limit; to bound; to confine; to restrain.
Stīpe, *n.* Base of a frond; stalk of a pistil; stem of a fungus or mushroom.
Stī′pend, *n.* Settled pay; wages; salary.
Stī-pĕnd′i-a-ry, *a.* Receiving a stipend. — *n.* One who receives a stipend.

Stip′ple, v. t. To engrave by means of dots.
Stip′u-lar, a. Formed of, or growing on, stipules.
Stip′ule, n. A leaf-like appendage at the base of petioles or leaves.
Stip′u-late, v. i. To covenant; to bargain; to contract.
Stip′u-lā′tion, n. An agreement; condition; covenant.
Stip′u-lā′tor, n. One who stipulates or covenants.
Stir, v. t. or i. To move; to incite; to agitate; to prompt. — n. Agitation; tumult; bustle.
Stir′rup (stĭr′rup or stir′rup), n. A kind of ring for a horseman's foot.
Stitch, v. t. To take stitches in; to join. — n. A single pass of a needle; a loop or turn of thread in sewing or knitting; sharp pain. [shop.
Stĭth′y, n. An anvil; a smith's
S:ive, v. t. [Allied to stew, stow, stuff.] To make sultry and close.
Stī′ver, n. A copper coin worth about two cents.
Stōat, n. The ermine; — so called in summer.
Stŏck, n. Body of a plant; stem; progenitor of a family; race; lineage; a handle; a post; a cravat; a fund; shares in the funds; money invested in business; a store; cattle. — v. t. To furnish or store.
Stock-āde′, n. A line of stakes for a barrier. — v. t. To fortify with stakes. Stockade.
Stŏck′-brō′ker, n. One who deals in stocks.
Stŏck′-fish, n. Cod dried in the sun, and not salted.
Stŏck′hōld-er, n. A proprietor of public funds, or of funds in a bank, &c.
Stŏck′ing, n. A covering for the foot and leg.
Stŏck′-jŏb′ber, n. One who speculates in stocks.
Stŏck′-jŏb′bing, n. Speculation in public stocks.
Stŏcks, n. pl. Public funds; frame on which a vessel rests in building; a frame Stocks.

to confine the legs of criminals.
Stŏck′-still, a. Motionless.
Stŏck′y, a. Thick and stout.
Stō′ic (127), n. One who affects insensibility to pleasure and pain; an apathetic person.
Stō′ic, } a. Unfeeling; in-
Stō′ic-al, } different to pleasure or pain.
Stō′ic-al-ly, adv. Without apparent feeling.
Stō′i-çişm, n. Indifference to pleasure and pain; insensibility.
Stōle, n. A long, loose vestment. — v., imp. of Steal.
Stōlen (stoln), p. p. of Steal.
Stŏl′id, a. Hopelessly dull; stupid; foolish.
Sto-lĭd′i-ty, n. Dullness of intellect; stupidity.
Stŏm′ach (stŭm′ak), n. The principal organ of digestion; appetite; inclination. — v. t. To brook or endure.
Stŏm′a-cher (-cher), n. An ornament or support for the breast, worn by women.
Sto-măch′ic, a. Strengthening the stomach. — n. A medicine to strengthen the stomach.
Stōne (18), n. A mass of mineral matter; a concretion in the kidneys; a weight of 14 pounds; nut of certain kinds of fruit. — v. t. To pelt or kill with stones; to free from stones.
Stōne′-cŭt′ter, n. One who cuts or hews stones.
Stōne′-fruit, n. Fruit that contains a stone; a drupe.
Stōne′-still, a. Motionless as a stone. [of potter's ware.
Stōne′-wāre, n. A species
Stōn′i-ness (135), n. Quality or state of being stony; abundance of stones.
Stōn′y, a. Made of stones; full of stones; resembling stone; hard.
Stŏŏd, imp. of Stand.
Stŏŏk, n. A collection of sheaves set up in the field.
Stōŏl, n. A seat without a back, intended for one person; a discharge from the bowels.
Stōŏp, v. i. To bend forward; to condescend; to yield. — n. Act of stooping; a porch.
Stŏp (129), v. t. To check the motion of; to hinder; to close, as an aperture; to obstruct; to suppress. — v. i.

To cease to go forward. — n. Cessation of motion; pause; a point in writing.
Stŏp′-cŏck, n. A contrivance for letting out or stopping a fluid.
Stŏp′page, n. Act of stopping; state of being stopped; obstruction.
Stŏp′per, } n. That which is
Stŏp′ple, } used to close a hole in a bottle or other vessel.
Stŏr′age (133), n. Act of putting in store; price of storing
Stō′rāx, n. A fragrant resin.
Stōre, n. A large quantity; stock; a warehouse. — v. t. To furnish; to put away for preservation.
Stōre′-house, n. A repository or warehouse; a magazine.
Stō′ried (stō′rid). a. Related in story; having stories; having a history.
Stŏrk, n. A large wading bird allied to the heron.
Stŏrm, n. [From the root of stir.] A violent disturbance of the atmosphere; a tempest; commotion; assault. — v. t. To attack by open force; to assault.
Stŏrm′y, a. Agitated with furious winds; boisterous; tempestuous.
Stō′ry (18, 141), n. History; a narrative; a tale; floor or stage of a building. — v. t. To tell; to relate.
Stoup, n. A basin for holy water at the entrance of a Catholic church.
Stout, a. Strong; brave, large; fleshy. [ily.
Stout′ly, adv. Strongly; lust-
Stout′ness, n. Quality of being stout; boldness.
Stōve, n. An apparatus for warming a room or house. — v, imp. of Stave.
Stōw, v. t. To lay up; to fill, by packing closely.
Stōw′age. n. Act of stowing; room for stowing.
†Strā′bişm, } n. The act or
Stra-biş′mus, } habit of looking asquint.
Străd′dle, v. i. or t. To walk, sit, or stand, with the legs wide apart.
Străg′gle, v. i. To wander aside; to rove. [gles.
Străg′gler, n. One who strag-
Strāight (strāt), a. Not crooked; direct: upright. — adv. Directly; immediately.
Strāight′en (strāt′n), v. t. or i. To make or become straight.

Straight'för-ward (strȧt′-), *a.* Proceeding in a straight course; upright.

Straight'ly (strāt′-), *adv.* In a direct line.

Straight'ness (strāt′-), *n.* Directness; rectitude.

Straight'way (strāt′-), *adv.* Immediately; without delay.

Strain, *v. t.* To stretch; to sprain; to filter. — *v. i.* To make violent efforts. — *n.* A sprain; force; song.

Strain'er, *n.* An instrument for filtering any liquid.

Strait, *a.* [From Lat. *strictus*, drawn together, close, tight.] Narrow; close; difficult. — *n.* A narrow pass; distress; difficulty.

Strait'en, *v. t.* To make narrow; to contract; to distress.

Strait'-jăck'et, *n.* An apparatus to confine maniacs.

Strait'laçed (-lāst), *a.* Bound tightly with stays; strict in manners or morals.

Strait'ness, *n.* Narrowness.

Strāke, *n.* Iron band of a wheel; range of planks from stem to stern of a vessel.

Stra-min′e-oŭs, *a.* Consisting of straw.

Strănd, *n.* Shore or beach; one of the twists or parts of which a rope is composed. — *v. i.* or *t.* To run aground; to break one of the strands of.

Strănge, *a.* Foreign; unknown; wonderful; unusual; singular; odd.

Strănge′ly (132), *adv.* In a strange manner.

Strănge′ness, *n.* State of being strange; oddness; singularity.

Strān′ger (79), *n.* A foreigner; one unknown; a guest.

Străn′gle, *v. t.* or *i.* To choke; to suffocate.

Străn′gles, *n. pl.* Swellings in a horse's throat.

Străn′gu-lā′tion, *n.* Act of strangling; suffocation.

Străn′gu-ry, *n.* Painful difficulty in discharging urine.

Străp, *n.* A long strip of leather; a thong; a strop. — *v. t.* To beat or fasten with a strap.

Străp′ping, *a.* Large; lusty.

†**Străp′ta,** *n. pl.* Beds; layers.

Străt′a-gem, *n.* An artifice, particularly in war; a trick.

Străt′e-gĭst, *n.* One skilled in military movements.

Străt′e-gy, *n.* That branch of military science which consists in conducting great military movements; generalship.

Străt′i-fi-cā′tion, *n.* Arrangement in strata.

Străt′i-fȳ, *v. t.* To form into strata or layers.

Strā′tum, *n.* (*pl.* **Strā′tă,** 147.) A layer, as of earth.

Straw, *n.* [From the root of *strew*.] A stalk or stem of grain; mass of stalks.

Straw′bĕr-ry, *n.* A plant and its fruit. [like, straw.

Straw′y, *a.* Pertaining to, or

Strāy, *v. i.* To wander; to rove; to ramble. — *n.* A beast that wanders at large.

Streak, *n.* A line of color; a stripe; a strake. — *v. t.* To stripe.

Streaked (streekt or streek′ed), *p. p.* or *a.* Striped.

Streak′y, *a.* Having streaks; streaked; striped.

Stream, *n.* A current of water or other fluid. — *v. i.* or *t.* To flow; to issue in a current. [ensign.

Stream′er, *n.* A flag; an

Stream′let, *n.* A small stream; a rivulet; a rill.

Stream′y, *a.* Having streams; flowing with a current or stream. [a city or town.

Street, *n.* A way or road in

Strength, *n.* Quality of being strong; power; force; vigor.

Strength′en, *v. t.* or *i.* To make or grow strong.

Strength′en-er, *n.* One who, or that which, strengthens.

Strĕn′u-oŭs, *a.* Eagerly pressing or urgent; active.

Strĕn′u-oŭs-ly, *adv.* With eager zeal; actively; vigorously.

Strĕss (124), *n.* Pressure; importance; force; urgency.

Strĕtch, *v. t.* To extend; to draw out; to strain. — *v. i.* To be extended. — *n.* Extension; reach; effort.

Strĕtch′er, *n.* One that stretches; a piece of timber; a litter.

Strew (strṳ or strō), *v. t.* To scatter; to cover by scattering. [uncld.

Strī′ā-ted, *a.* Streaked; chau-

Strĭck′en (strĭk′n), *p. p.* & *p. a.* Struck; smitten; advanced; worn out.

Strĭck′le, *n.* An instrument to strike grain to a level with the measure.

Strĭct, *a.* Exact; severe; close; rigid; rigorous.

Strĭct′ly, *adv.* Rigorously.

Strĭct′ness, *n.* Severity; rigor; closeness.

Strĭct′ūre, *n.* Censure; criticism; a morbid contraction of any passage of the body.

Stride, *n.* A long step. — *v. i.* To walk with long steps.

Strĭfe, *n.* Contention; struggle; rivalship.

Strīke, *v. t.* (*imp.* STRUCK; *p. p.* STRUCK, STRICKEN.] To give a blow to; to hit; to beat; to impress; to lower; to surrender. — *v. i.* To make a quick blow; to quit work so as to compel an increase of wages.

Strīk′ing, *a.* Impressive; surprising; forcible.

String, *n.* A slender cord; a line of things; a series. — *v. t.* [*imp.* & *p. p.* STRUNG.] To furnish with strings.

Stringed, *a.* Having strings.

Strĭn′gent, *a.* Binding closely; urgent; making severe requirements.

String′halt, *n.* A twitching of a horse's hinder leg.

String′y, *a.* Consisting of, or resembling, strings; fibrous; filamentous; ropy; viscous.

Strĭp, *v. t.* To make naked; to deprive of a covering; to peel; to divest. — *n.* A narrow piece, comparatively long.

Strīpe, *n.* A line of a different color; a lash. — *v. t.* To form with stripes.

Strī′ped, *a.* Having stripes of different colors.

Strĭp′ling, *n.* A youth; a lad.

Strīve, *v. i.* [*imp.* STROVE; *p. p.* STRIVEN.] To make efforts; to struggle in opposition; to contend; to vie.

Strōke, *n.* A blow; a knock; a dash; a touch; masterly effort. — *v. t.* To rub gently.

Strōll, *v. i.* To wander on foot; to rove; to ramble. — *n.* A ramble; excursion.

Strōll′er (131), *n.* One who strolls; a rover; a vagrant.

Strŏng, *a.* Having great power; not easily broken. — SYN. Vigorous; powerful; robust; cogent.

Strŏng′ly, *adv.* Powerfully.

Strŏng′hōld, *n.* A fortress; a fortified place.

Strŏp, *n.* An instrument for sharpening razors on.

Strō′phe, *n.* The former of two stanzas, in ancient lyric poetry.

---

sŏn, ôr, dọ, wọlf, tọō, tọōk; ŭrn, rụe, pụll; ç, ģ, *soft*; ē, ġ, *hard*; aș; eẓist; ụ *as* ng; thiṡ
13

Stróve, *imp.* of *Strive.*
Ström (strō), *v. t.* [*imp.* STROWED: *p. p.* STROWED or STROWN.] See *Strew.*
Struck, *imp. & p. p.* of *Strike.*
Struct'ūr-al, *a.* Pertaining to structure.
Struct'ūre, *n.* [Lat. *structura,* fr. *struere,* to join together.] Form; make; construction; frame; an edifice; fabric.
Strŭg'gle, *v. i.* To strive; to labor hard; to endeavor. — *n.* Vigorous effort; great labor; agony.
Strū'moŭs, *a.* Having swellings in the glands; scrofulous.
Strŭm'pet, *n.* A prostitute.
Strŭng, *imp. & p. p.* of *String.*
Strŭt, *n.* An affected walk. — *v. i.* To walk with an affectation of dignity.
Strych'nīne, *n.* A very poisonous narcotic.
Stŭb, *n.* Stump of a small tree. — *v. t.* To grub up by the roots; to extirpate.
Stŭb'bed (57), *a.* Short and thick.
Stŭb'ble, *n.* Stumps of rye, wheat, oats, &c., left in the ground.
Stŭb'born, *a.* Inflexible in opinion; unreasonably obstinate; obdurate.
Stŭb'born-ly, *adv.* Obstinately; inflexibly. [cy.
Stŭb'born-ness, *n.* Obstinacy.
Stŭb'by, *a.* Short and thick.
Stŭc'co, *n.* A kind of fine plaster. — *v. t.* To overlay with stucco.
Stŭck, *imp. & p. p.* of *Stick.*
Stŭd, *n.* A small timber for a support; a set of breeding horses and mares; a stallion; a kind of button; a nail. — *v. t.* To set with studs.
Stū'dent, *n.* One who studies; a scholar.
Stŭd'ied, *a.* Premeditated.
Stū'di-o, *n.* (*pl.* Stū'di-ōs, 18.) Work-shop of a sculptor.
Stū'di-oŭs, *a.* Given to study.
Stū'di-oŭs-ly, *adv.* With close application; carefully.
Stū'di-oŭs-ness, *n.* Quality of being studious.
Stŭd'y, *n.* Application to books, or to any subject; object of attentive consideration; a room for study. — *v.* (135) To apply the mind to books or learning.
Stŭff (123), *n.* Material; cloth; furniture; worthless matter; nonsense. — *v. t.* To fill to excess, or by crowding; to crowd; to cram.
Stŭff'ing, *n.* That which is used for filling.
Stŭl'ti-fȳ, *v. t.* [Lat. *stultus,* foolish, and *facere,* to make.] To make a fool of.
Stŭm, *n.* Wine revived by new fermentation. — *v. t.* To revive, as wine, by new fermentation.
Stŭm'ble, *v. i.* To trip in walking. — *n.* A trip; a misstep; a blunder.
Stŭm'bler, *n.* One who stumbles.
Stŭm'bling-blŏck, *n.* That which causes one to stumble.
Stŭmp, *n.* Part of a tree left after the trunk is cut down; part of a limb remaining.
Stŭmp'y, *a.* Full of stumps; short and thick.
Stŭn, *v. t.* To make senseless by a blow or fall; to overpower the hearing of.
Stŭng, *imp. & p. p.* of *Sting.*
Stŭnk, *imp. & p. p.* of *Stink.*
Stŭnt, *v. t.* To hinder the growth of.
Stū'pe-făc'tion, *n.* Insensibility; torpor; stupidity.
Stū'pe-făc'tive, *a.* Causing insensibility.
Stū'pe-fȳ, *v. t.* To deprive of sensibility; to make stupid.
Stu-pĕn'doŭs, *a.* Amazingly great; wonderful.
Stu-pĕn'doŭs-ly, *adv.* So as to excite astonishment.
Stū'pid, *a.* Wanting understanding or sensibility; very dull; sluggish; senseless.
Stu-pĭd'i-ty, *n.* Extreme dullness of perception or understanding.
Stū'pid-ly, *adv.* With extreme dullness.
Stū'pid-ness, *n.* Stupidity.
Stū'por, *n.* Suppression of sense; numbness; intellectual or moral insensibility.
Stŭr'di-ly, *adv.* In a sturdy manner; stoutly; hardily.
Stŭr'di-ness, *n.* Quality of being hardy; stoutness.
Stŭr'dy, *a.* Stout; hardy; strong; robust.
Stŭr'geon (stŭr'jun), *n.* A fish of large size.
Stŭt'ter (139), *v. i.* To hesitate in speaking; to stammer. — *n.* A hesitancy in speech.
Stŭt'ter-er, *n.* A stammerer.
Stȳ, *n.* A pen for swine; inflamed tumor on the eyelid.
Stȳg'i-an (stĭj'i-an), *a.* Hellish; infernal; dark; black.
Stȳ'lar, *a.* Belonging to the style of a dial.
Stȳle, *n.* Manner of writing or speaking; title; pin of a dial; an engraver's tool; part of a pistil. — *r. t.* To call; to name; to denominate.
Stȳl'ish (1 3), *a.* Fashionable in form or manner; *b,* Style. showy.
Stȳp'tic, *a.* Serving to stop hemorrhage or bleeding.
Sū'a-ble, *a.* Capable of being sued.
Suā'sion (swā'zhun), *n.* Act of persuading; persuasion.
Suā'sive, *a.* Able or tend-
Suā'so-ry, ing to persuade.
Suāv'i-ty, *n.* Sweetness; pleasantness; agreeableness.
Sub-ăç'id, *a.* Moderately acid.
Sub-ăc'rid, *a.* Moderately acrid.
Sub-ăl'tern, *a.* Inferior; subordinate. — *n.* An inferior officer.
Sub-ā'que-oŭs, *a.* Being under the surface of water.
Sub-ăs'tral, *a.* Under the stars.
Sŭb'di-vīde', *v. t.* To divide again, or what has already been divided.
Sŭb'di-vi'sion (-vĭzh'un), *n.* A part of a division.
Sub-dū'a-ble, *a.* Capable of being subdued.
Sub-dŭçe', To with-
Sub-dŭct', draw; to subtract. [ducting.
Sub-dŭc'tion, *n.* Act of subducting.
Sub-dūe' (137), *v. t.* To conquer; to overcome; to vanquish; to overpower. [cork.
Su-bĕr'ic, *a.* Pertaining to
Sŭb'i-tā'ne-oŭs, *a.* Sudden.
Sub-jā'çent, *a.* Lying under.
Sŭb'ject, *a.* Being under authority; liable; exposed. — *n.* One who lives under the power of another; a matter in discussion; theme; topic.
Sub-jĕct', *v. t.* To bring or put under; to subdue; to cause to undergo; to expose.
Sub-jĕc'tion, *n.* A being under control.
Sub-jĕc'tive, *a.* Relating to the subject; pertaining to one's own consciousness.
Sub-join', *v. t.* To add at the end; to append.
Sŭb'ju-gāte, *v. t.* To reduce to slavery; to subdue.

Sŭb'ju-gā'tion, n. Act of subduing; subjection.
Sub-jŭnc'tion, n. The act of subjoining.
Sub-jŭnct'ive, a. Added; subjoined; expressing condition, hypothesis, or contingency.
Sub-lā'tion, n. Act of taking away.
Sŭb-lĕt', v. t. To lease, as a lessee, to another person.
Sub-lĭm'a-ble, a. Capable of being sublimed.
Sŭb'li-māte,) v. t. To evaporate, as a
Sub-līme',) solid substance, by heat, and then condense by cold; to heighten; to elevate.
Sŭb'li-māte, n. Product of sublimation.
Sŭb'li-mā'tion, n. Act of sublimating.
Sub-līme', a. Lofty in place or style; elevated; grand; magnificent. — n. A lofty style; sublimity.
Sub-līme'ly (132), adv. In a sublime or lofty manner.
Sub-līm'i-ty, n. State of being sublime; loftiness of style.
Sub-lĭn'gual (-lĭng'gwal), a. Situated under the tongue.
Sŭb'lu-na-ry, a. Being under the moon; earthly; terrestrial; mundane.
Sŭb'ma-rīne' (-reen'), a. Being under the sea.
Sub-mērge',) v. t. To put
Sub-mērse',) under water.
Sub-mērsed' (-mērst'), a. Being or growing under water.
Sub-mēr'sion, n. The act of plunging under water.
Sub-mĭs'sion (-mĭsh'un), n. Act of yielding to power or authority; resignation.
Sub-mĭs'sive, a. Inclined or ready to submit; humble.
Sub-mĭs'sive-ly, adv. With submission; humbly.
Sub-mĭs'sive-ness, n. Submissive disposition; humbleness; obedience.
Sub-mĭt' (129), v. t. or i. [Lat. submittere, from sub, under, and mittere, to send.] To yield to the power, will, or opinion of another. — SYN. To surrender; bend; acquiesce; comply.
Sub-mŭl'ti-ple, n. A number contained in another an exact number of times.
Sub-nās'cent, a. Growing underneath.
Sub-ôr'di-na-cy, n. State of being subordinate.
Sub-ôr'di-nate, a. Inferior in order or rank; subject. — n. An inferior.
Sub-ôr'di-nāte, v. t. To make subordinate or inferior.
Sub-ôr'di-nā'tion, n. Act of subordinating; subjection.
Sub-ôrn', v. t. To procure to take a false oath.
Sŭb'or-nā'tion, n. Act or crime of suborning.
Sub-pē'nā,) n. A writ com-
Sub-pœ'nā,) manding the attendance of a witness. — v. t. To summon by subpœna.
Sub-scrībe', v. t. To write underneath; to sign; to attest.
Sub-scrīb'er, n. One who subscribes.
Sub-scrĭp'tion, n. The signing of a name; amount subscribed; attestation.
Sŭb'se-quençe, n. State of being subsequent, or of coming after something.
Sŭb'se-quent, a. Following in time or order of place.
Sŭb'se-quent-ly, adv. Later; afterward.
Sub-sērve', v. t. To serve in subordination; to promote.
Sub-sērv'i-ençe,) n. Use or
Sub-sērv'i-en-çy,) operation that promotes some purpose.
Sub-sērv'i-ent, a. Fitted to subserve; subordinate.
Sub-sērv'i-ent-ly, adv. In a way to aid.
Sub-sīde', v. i. To sink or fall to the bottom.
Sub-sĭd'ençe, n. Act of subsiding, or gradually sinking
Sub-sĭd'i-a-ry, a. Serving to help; auxiliary.
Sŭb'si-dīze (152), v. t. To pay a subsidy to.
Sŭb'si-dy, n. Aid in money.
Sub-sĭst', v. i. To have existence; to be supported. — v. t. To maintain.
Sub-sĭst'ençe, n. Real being; means of support; provisions, or means of procuring them.
Sub-sĭst'ent, a. Having being; existing; inhering.
Sŭb'soil, n. Soil under the surface soil.
Sub-spē'cies (-spē'shĕz), n. A division of a species.
Sŭb'stançe, n. Substratum; essential part; nature; body; matter; estate; property.
Sub-stăn'tial, a. Real; solid.
Sub-stăn'tial-ly, adv. Really; truly; essentially.
Sub-stăn'tials, n. pl. Material or essential parts.
Sub-stăn'ti-āte (-stăn'shi-āt), v. t. To prove; to verify; to make good.
Sŭb'stan-tīve, n. A noun; name of a thing. — a. Betokening or expressing existence; real; enduring.
Sŭb'stan-tīve-ly, adv. In substance; essentially as a substantive or noun.
Sŭb'sti-tūte, n. One person or thing put in place of another. — v. t. To put in the place of another. — SYN. To exchange; interchange.
Sŭb'sti-tū'tion, n. Act of substituting: thing substituted.
Sub-strā'tum, n. (pl. †Sŭb-strā'tā). A stratum or layer under something; subsoil; substance.
Sub-strŭc'tion, n. An understructing; foundation.
Sub-tĕnd', v. t. To extend under or be opposite to.
Sub-tĕnse', n. The cord which subtends an arc.
Sŭb'ter-fūge, n. An evasion or artifice.
Sŭb'ter-rā'ne-an,) a. Being
Sŭb'ter-rā'ne-ous,) under the surface of the earth.
Sŭb'tīle, a. Fine; thin; rare.
Sŭb'tīle-ly, adv. In a subtile manner. [being subtile.
Sŭb'tīle-ness, n. Quality of
Sŭb'til-i-zā'tion, n. Act of making subtile; refinement.
Sŭb'til-īze, v. t. To make thin or fine; to refine.
Sŭb'til-ty, n. Quality of being subtile; fineness.
Sŭbt'le (sŭt'l), a. Sly; artful.
Sŭbt'le-ty (sŭt'l-). n. Cunning; craftiness; shrewdness. [fully.
Sŭbt'ly (sŭt'lȳ), adv. Artfully.
Sub-trăct', v. t. To withdraw or take from the rest; to deduct. [subtracts.
Sub-trăct'or, n. One who
Sub-trăc'tion, n. The taking of a lesser sum from a greater; deduction; withdrawal.
Sub-trăct'ive, a. Tending, on having power, to subtract; having the negative sign.
Sŭb'tra-hĕnd', n. A sum or number to be subtracted from another.
Sub-ûrb'an, a. Pertaining to, or being in, the suburbs.
Sŭb'urbs, n. pl. Region on the confines of a city.
Sŭb'va-rī'e-ty, n. A subordinate variety.
Sub-vēr'sion, n. Total overthrow; ruin. [ruin.
Sub-vēr'sive, a. Tending to

Sub-vĕrt', *v. t.* [Lat. *subvertere,* from *sub,* under, and *vertere,* to turn.] To overthrow; to destroy; to ruin.

Sub-vĕrt'er, *n.* One who subverts.

Sŭc'çe-dā'ne-oŭs, *a.* Supplying the place of something else.

†**Sŭc'çe-dā'ne-um,** *n.* [Lat.] A substitute.

Suc-çeed', *v. i.* or *t.* To follow in order; to come after; to be prosperous. [suc.

Suc-çĕss', *n.* Prosperous issue.

Suc-çĕss'ful, *a.* Prosperous.

Suc-çĕss'ful-ly, *adv.* Prosperously; favorably.

Suc-çĕs'sion (-sĕsh'un), *n.* Act of succeeding, a series of persons or things, order of events; lineage.

Suc-çĕs'sive, *a.* Following in order. [ular order.

Suc-çĕs'sive-ly, *adv.* In reg-

Suc-çĕs'sor, *n.* One who succeeds another.

Suc-çĭnct', *a.* Compressed into a narrow compass. — SYN. Short; concise; brief; compendious; summary.

Suc-çĭnct'ly, *adv.* Briefly.

Suc-çĭnct'ness, *n.* Brevity; conciseness.

Sŭc'cor (130), *v. t.* To relieve in distress; to aid; to assist; to help. — *n.* Assistance in distress; aid; relief.

Sŭc'co-tăsh, *n.* Boiled maize and beans mixed together.

Sŭc'cu-lençe, *n.* Juiciness.

Sŭc'cu-lent, *a.* Juicy.

Suc-cŭmb' (-kŭmb', 59, 128), *v. i.* To yield; to submit; to sink unresistingly.

Suc-cŭs'sion (-kŭsh'un), *n.* Act of shaking; a jolt.

Sŭch, *a.* Of the like kind; like; the same that (with *as*).

Sŭck, *v. t.* To draw in with the mouth; to imbibe. — *v. i.* To draw, as milk from the breast.

Sŭck'er, *n.* One who sucks; a shoot; a fish.

Sŭck'le (sŭk'l), *v. t.* To nurse at the breast.

Sŭck'ling, *n.* A child nursed at the breast.

Sŭc'tion, *n.* Act of sucking.

Suc-tō'ri-al, *a.* Adapted for, or living by, sucking.

Sū'da-to-ry, *n.* A sweating or vapor bath.

Sŭd'den (55), *a.* Coming without previous notice; abrupt; hasty; rapid. [ly.

Sŭd'den-ly, *adv.* Unexpected-

Sŭd'den-ness, *n.* A coming or happening unexpectedly.

Sū'dor-ĭf'ĭc, *a.* Causing sweat; producing perspiration. — *n.* A medicine that produces sweat.

Sŭds, *n. sing.* Water impregnated with soap. [law.

Sūe (137), *v. t.* To prosecute in

Sū'et, *n.* Hard fat about the kidneys and loins.

Sū'et-y, *a.* Consisting of, or resembling, suet.

Sŭf'fer, *v. t.* To bear with pain; to undergo; to permit. — *v. i.* To endure pain.

Sŭf'fer-a-ble, *a.* Capable of being suffered or endured.

Sŭf'fer-ançe, *n.* Pain endured; permission; endurance. [fers.

Sŭf'fer-er, *n.* One who suf-

Sŭf'fer-ing, *n.* Pain endured; distress or loss incurred.

Sŭf-fīçe' (suf-fīz', 62), *v. t.* To satisfy; to content. — *v. i.* To be enough.

Suf-fī'çien-çy (-fĭsh'en-), *n.* A full supply; competence; adequacy; ability.

Suf-fī'çient (-fĭsh'ent), *a.* Adequate to wants; enough.

Suf-fī'çient-ly (-fĭsh'ent-), *adv.* So as to satisfy, or to answer the purpose; enough.

Sŭf'fix, *n.* A letter or a syllable added to the end of a word.

Suf-fix', *v. t.* To add to the end of a word, as a letter or a syllable.

Sŭf'fo-cāte, *v. t.* To choke by excluding air; to stifle; to smother.

Sŭf'fo-cā'tion, *n.* The act of suffocating or smothering; condition of being suffocated.

Sŭf'fo-cā'tive, *a.* Tending to suffocate or choke.

Sŭf'fra-gan, *n.* A bishop, considered as an assistant to his metropolitan; an assistant bishop. — *a.* Assisting.

Sŭf'frage, *n.* A vote; a voice.

Suf-fū'mi-gāte, *v. t.* To apply fumes or smoke to the parts of.

Suf-fū'mi-gā'tion, *n.* Operation of smoking any thing.

Suf-fūse', *v. t.* To overspread.

Suf-fū'sion, *n.* Act of suffusing.

Sŭg'ar (shŭg'ar, 27), *n.* A sweet crystalline substance obtained from the sugar-cane, maple, beet, &c. — *v. t.* To sweeten with sugar.

Sŭg'ar-cāne (shŭg'ar-), *n.* A plant whose juice produces sugar.

Sŭg'ar-lōaf (shŭg'ar-), *n.* A cone or mass of refined sugar.

Sŭg'ar-plŭm (shŭg'ar-), *n.* A kind of candy in the form of a ball. [sacchurine.

Sŭg'ar-y (shŭg'ar-), *a.* Sweet;

Sug-gĕst' (or sud-jĕst'), *v. t.* To hint; to intimate.

Sug-gĕs'tion (sug-jĕst'yun or sud-jĕst'yun), *n.* Hint; intimation; insinuation.

Sug-gĕst'ive (sug- or sud-), *a.* Containing a suggestion, or hint. [of suicide.

Sū'ĭ-çī'dal, *a.* Of the nature

Sū'ĭ-çīde, *n.* [Low Lat. *suicidium,* from Lat. *sui,* of one's self, and *cædere,* to kill.] Self-murder; a self-murderer; a felo-de-se.

Sūit (27), *n.* A set of things used together; retinue; petition; courtship; legal process; prosecution. — *v. t.* or *i.* To fit or be fitted; to adapt; to accord.

Sūit'a-ble, *a.* Fit; proper; meet; apt.

Sūit'a-ble-ness, *n.* Fitness.

Sūit'a-bly, *adv.* Fitly; properly; appropriately.

Sūite (sweet), *n.* A retinue of a train; a set; a series.

Sūit'or, *n.* One who sues; a petitioner; a wooer.

Sŭl'cāt-ed, *a.* Furrowed; grooved. [rosely.

Sŭlk'ĭ-ly, *adv.* Sullenly; mo-

Sŭlk'ĭ-ness (135), *n.* Sullenness; moroseness.

Sŭlk'y, *a.* Sullen; morose. — *n.* A light carriage for one person.

Sŭl'len, *a.* Ill-natured; cross and silent; morose.

Sŭl'len-ly, *adv.* Gloomily; morosely.

Sŭl'len-ness, *n.* State or quality of being sullen.

Sŭl'ly, *v. t.* or *i.* To soil; to spot; to tarnish; to stain.

Sŭl'phate, *n.* A salt composed of sulphuric acid and a base.

Sŭl'phur, *n.* An inflammable yellow mineral; brimstone.

SULPHURATE 293 SUPERNATANT

Sŭl′phu-rāte, *v. t.* To combine with sulphur.

Sul-phū′re-oŭs, *a.* Having the qualities of sulphur.
Sŭl′phur-oŭs,

Sŭl′phu-ret, *n.* A combination of sulphur with another element.

Sul-phū′ric, *a.* Pertaining to, or obtained from, sulphur.

Sŭl′phur-y, *a.* Partaking of, or resembling, sulphur.

Sŭl′tan, *n.* Turkish emperor.

Sul-tā′na, or **Sul-tä′nä,** *n.*

Sŭl′ta-ness, The wife of a Sultan.

Sŭl′tri-ness, *n.* The state of being sultry.

Sŭl′try, *a.* Hot, close, stagnant, and oppressive, as air.

Sŭm, *n.* The whole amount; a quantity; a problem in arithmetic. — *v. t.* To collect into a total; to compute.

Sụ̄′mac (shōō′mak), *n.* A shrub used in medicine, dyeing, &c.
Sụ̄′mach

Sŭm′ma-ri-ly, *adv.* Briefly.

Sŭm′ma-ry, *a.* Brief; short; concise. — *n.* An abridged account; an abstract.

Sum-mā′tion, *n.* Act of summing; an aggregate.

Sŭm′mer, *n.* Warmest season of the year. — *v. t.* or *i.* To pass or cause to pass the summer.

Sŭm′mer-set, *n.* A leap heels over head.

Sŭm′mit, *n.* Highest point; top.

Sŭm′mon, *v. t.* To call by authority; to convoke; to bid; to cite; to notify.

Sŭm′mon-er, *n.* One who summons.

Sŭm′mons, *n. sing.* A call or command to appear at a certain place and time.

Sŭmp′ter, *n.* A pack-horse.

Sŭmpt′u-a-ry, *a.* Regulating expenses of living.

Sŭmpt′u-oŭs (81), *a.* Characterized by expense and magnificence. — SYN. Costly; magnificent; princely.

Sŭmpt′u-oŭs-ly, *adv.* In a sumptuous manner.

Sŭn, *n.* The luminary that enlightens and warms the earth and other planets; sunshine. — *v. t.* To expose to the sun. [sun.

Sŭn′-bēam, *n.* A ray of the

Sŭn′bŭrnt, *a.* Burnt or scorched by the sun.

Sŭn′day, *n.* First day of the week; Christian Sabbath.

Sŭn′der, *v. t.* To separate; to disunite; to sever.

Sŭn′-dī′al, *n.* An instrument to show the time by means of the shadow of a style on a plate.

Sŭn′drĭes, *n. pl.* Many different or small things.

Sŭn′dry, *a.* More than one or two. — SYN. Divers; several.

Sŭn′flow-er, *n.* A plant with large yellow flowers.

Sŭng, *imp. & p. p.* of *Sing.*

Sŭnk, *imp. & p. p.* of *Sink.*

Sŭnk′en, *p. a.* from *Sink.*

Sŭn′less, *a.* Destitute of the sun or its rays. [the sun.

Sŭn′līght (-līt), *n.* Light of

Sŭn′ny, *a.* Exposed to, or resembling, the sun; bright.

Sŭn′rīse, *n.* First appearance of the sun in the morning.
Sŭn′rĭṣ-ing,

Sŭn′set, *n.* Disappearance of the sun at night. [suu.
Sŭn′set-ting,

Sŭn′shīne, *n.* Light of the

Sŭn′shīn-y, *a.* Bright with the sun's rays.

Sŭn′-strōke, *n.* Sudden prostration of the bodily powers occasioned by exposure to excessive heat of the sun.

Sŭp, *v. i.* or *t.* To eat supper. — *n.* A small draught.

Sū′per-a-ble, *a.* Capable of being overcome.

Sū′per-a-bound′, *v. i.* To be very abundant.

Sū′per-a-bŭnd′ançe, *n.* More than is sufficient; excessive abundance; exubernce.

Sū′per-a-bŭnd′ant (107), *a.* More than is sufficient.

Sū′per-a-bŭn′dant-ly, *adv.* More than sufficient.

Sū′per-ădd′, *v. t.* To add over and above.

Sū′per-an-gĕl′ic, *a.* Superior in nature or rank to the angels.

Sū′per-ăn′nu-āte, *v. t.* To impair or disqualify by old age and infirmity.

Sū′per-ăn′nu-ā′ted, *a.* Disqualified by old age.

Su-pĕrb′, *a.* [Lat. *superbus*, from *super*, above, over.] Grand; magnificent; elegant; splendid.

Su-pĕrb′ly, *adv.* Grandly.

Sū′per-cär′go, *n.* One who has the care of a cargo, and manages the sale of it.

Sū′per-çĭl′i-oŭs, *a.* Haughty; dictatorial; overbearing.

Sū′per-çĭl′i-oŭs-ly, *adv.* Haughtily; dogmatically.

Sū′per-çĭl′i-oŭs-ness, *n.* An overbearing manner.

Sū′per-ĕm′i-nençe, *n.* Eminence superior to what is common.

Sū′per-ĕm′i-nent, *a.* Eminent in a superior degree.

Sū′per-ĕr′o-gā′tion, *n.* A doing more than duty or necessity requires.

Sū′per-e-rŏg′a-to-ry, *a.* Exceeding the calls of duty.

Sū′per-ĕx′çel-lençe, *n.* Superior excellence. [cellent

Sū′per-ĕx′çel-lent, *a.* Very ex-

Sū′per-fī′cial (-fĭsh/al), *a.* Being on the surface; shallow; not deep or profound.

Sū′per-fī′cial-ly (-fĭsh′al-), *adv.* On the surface only.

Sū′per-fī′çĭēṣ (-fĭsh′ēz), *n.* Surface; exterior part or face of a thing.

Sū′per-fīne′, *a.* Very fine.

Sū′per-flū′i-ty, *n.* Something beyond what is needed; redundancy.

Su-pĕr′flu-oŭs (117), *a.* More than is wanted; useless.

Su-pĕr′flu-oŭs-ly, *adv.* In a superfluous manner.

Sū′per-hū′man, *a.* Above or beyond what is human.

Sū′per-im-pōṣe′, *v. t.* To impose or lay on something else.

Sū′per-in-cŭm′bent, *a.* Lying on something else.

Sū′per-in-dūçe′, *v. t.* To bring in or upon as an addition to something.

Sū′per-in-tĕnd′ (107), *v. t.* To have the charge and oversight of; to oversee.

Sū′per-in-tĕnd′ençe, *n.* Act of overseeing.

Sū′per-in-tĕnd′ent, *n.* A manager; an overseer. — *a.* Directing; overseeing.

Su-pē′ri-or, *a.* Higher; greater; more exalted; preferable. — *n.* One higher or more excellent; a chief.

Su-pē′ri-ŏr′i-ty, *n.* State of being superior; pre-eminence; predominance.

Su-pĕr′la-tive, *a.* Expressing the highest degree; most excellent; supreme.

Su-pĕr′la-tive-ly, *adv.* In a superlative manner.

Su-pĕr′la-tive-ness, *n.* State or quality of being superlative.

Su-pĕr′nal, *a.* Relating to things above; celestial.

Sū′per-nā′tant, *a.* Swimming or floating on the surface.

sŭn, ŏr, dọ, wọlf, tōō, tŏŏk; ûrn, rụe, pụll; ç, ġ, *soft*; ȼ, ḡ, *hard*; aṣ; exist; ŋ *as* ng; this.

Sū'per-năt'u-ral, a. Exceeding the powers or laws of nature.
Sū'per-năt'u-ral-ly, adv. Beyond the laws of nature.
Sū'per-nū'mer-a-ry, a. Exceeding the number necessary. — n. A person or thing beyond the number stated, or beyond what is necessary or usual.
Sū'per-roy'al, a. Denoting the largest regular size of printing paper.
Sū'per-scrībe', v. t. To write on the outside of; to address.
Sū'per-scrip'tion, n. A writing or engraving on the outside or above something else.
Sū'per-sēde', v. t. To take the place of. — SYN. To overrule; succeed; displace.
Sū'per-sti'tion (-stĭsh'un), n. Excessive exactness or rigor in religion; belief in omens and prognostics.
Sū'per-sti'tious (-stĭsh'us), a. Addicted to, or proceeding from, superstition.
Sū'per-sti'tious-ly (-stĭsh'us-), adv. In a superstitious manner.
Sū'per-strā'tum, n. A stratum or layer above another.
Sū'per-strŭe'tion,) n. Any
Sū'per-strŭet'ūre,) thing built on a foundation or basis.
Sū'per-vēne', v. i. To come upon as something extraneous; to take place; to happen.
Sū'per-vēn'i-ent, a. Added; additional; extraneous.
Sū'per-vī'gal,) n.
Sū'per-vis'ion ('-vĭzh'un)) Inspection; an overseeing; superintendence.
Sū'per-vīse' (153, 155), v. t. To oversee, for direction; to superintend; to inspect.
Sū'per-vī'sor, n. An overseer.
Sū'pi-nā'tion, n. A lying with the face upward.
Sū'pīne, n. A verbal noun.
Su-pīne', a. Lying on the back; indolent; careless.
Su-pīne'ly, adv. Carelessly; heedlessly; indolently.
Su-pīne'ness, n. State of being supine.
Sŭp'per, n. The evening meal.
Sŭp'per-less, a. Being without supper.
Sup-plānt', v. t. To remove or displace by stratagem.
Sup-plănt'er, n. One who supplants.

Sŭp'ple, a. Pliant; flexible; yielding; soft. — v. t. To make soft and pliant. [tion.
Sŭp'ple-ment, n. An addition.
Sŭp'ple-mĕnt'al,) a.
Sŭp'ple-mĕnt'a-ry,) Added to supply what is wanted.
Sŭp'ple-ness, n. Pliancy; flexibility; facility.
Sŭp'pli-ant, a. Entreating.
Sŭp'pli-ant,) n. A humble
Sŭp'pli-cant,) petitioner.
Sŭp'pli-cāte, v. t. To entreat for; to beseech. — v. i. To offer supplication.
Sŭp'pli-cā'tion, n. Humble petition; entreaty.
Sŭp'pli-ca-to-ry, a. Containing supplication.
Sup-plī'er (135), n. One who supplies.
Sup-plȳ', v. t. To fill up; to furnish; to provide. — n. Sufficiency for wants; (pl.) things supplied.
Sup-pōrt', v. n. A prop; maintenance. — v. t. To prop; to sustain; to uphold; to favor; to maintain.
Sup-pōrt'a-ble, a. Capable of being supported.
Sup-pōrt'er, n. One who, or that which, supports.
Sup-pōg'a-ble (153), a. Capable of being supposed.
Sup-pōg'al, n. Supposition.
Sup-pōge', v. t. To admit without proof; to assume to be true; to imply; to think; to imagine.
Sŭp'po-si'tion (-zĭsh'un), n. Something supposed; an hypothesis.
Sup-pōg'i-ti'tious (-tĭsh'us), a. Not genuine; counterfeit; illegitimate.
Sup-prĕss', v. t. To overpower and crush; to conceal.
Sup-prĕs'sion (-prĕsh'un), n. Act of suppressing.
Sup-prĕss'or, n. One who suppresses.
Sŭp'pu-rāte, v. i. or t. To generate pus or matter.
Sŭp'pu-rā'tion, n. Act or process of suppurating; pus.
Sŭp'pu-rā'tive, a. Promoting suppuration; tending to suppurate. [the world.
Sū'pra-mŭn'dāne, a. Above
Su-prĕm'a-çy, n. Highest power or authority.
Su-prēme', a. Highest; greatest; most powerful; chief. — n. The highest and greatest Being: God.
Su-prēme'ly, adv. In the highest degree.

Sur-çēase', v. i. To be at an end. — n. End; cessation.
Sur-chärge', v. t. To overcharge; to overload. — n. Excessive charge or load.
Sûr'çin-gle, n. A girth passing over a saddle or blanket.
Sûr'cle, n. A little shoot.
Sûrd, n. A quantity whose root can not be exactly expressed in numbers. — a. Incapable of being expressed exactly by an integral number or by a vulgar fraction; whispered; without tone.
Sure (shụr, 27), a. Certainly knowing; not liable to fail. — SYN. Certain; stable; firm; confident; secure. [ly.
Sure'ly (shụr'-), adv. Certainly.
Sure'ness (shụr'-), n. State of being sure.
Sure'ty (shụr'-), n. Certainty; security against loss; a bondsman; a bail.
Sure'ty-ship (135), n. State of being surety for another.
Sûrf, n. Continued swell of the sea upon the shore.
Sûr'face, n. The outside; superficies.
Sûr'feit (30), n. Fullness occasioned by excessive eating and drinking. — v. t. or i. To feed to excess.
Sûrge, n. A large wave or billow. — v. i. To swell; to rise high and roll, as waves.
Sûr'geon (-jun), n. One who practices surgery.
Sûr'geon-çy, n. Office of surgeon in the navy or army.
Sûr'ger-y, n. Art of healing external injuries of the body by manual operations.
Sûr'gic-al, a. Pertaining to surgery.
Sûr'li-ness, n. Crabbedness.
Sûr'loin, n. A loin of beef, or the upper part of it. [sour.
Sûr'ly, a. Morose; crabbed;
Sur-mīse' (153, 155), v. t. To imagine; to conjecture. — n. Suspicion; conjecture.
Sur-mount', v. t. [Fr. surmonter, fr. sur, over, and monter, to mount.] To overcome; to surpass; to exceed.
Sur-mount'a-ble, a. Capable of being surmounted.
Sûr'nāme, n. A name added to the baptismal name; a family name.
Sur-nāme', v. t. To call by a family name.
Sur-pāss', v. t. To go beyond; to exceed; to excel; to outdo.

SURPASSABLE 295 SWATH

Sur-pàss'a-ble, *a.* Capable of being surpassed.
Sur-pàss'ing, *p. pr.* or *a.* Exceeding others; excellent in an eminent degree.
Sûr'plîçe, *n.* A white garment worn by clergymen.
Sûr'plus, } *n.* Excess beyond what is necessary; overplus.
Sûr'plus-age, }
Sur-prĭṣ'al, *n.* Act of surprising; state of surprise.
Sur-prĭṣe' (153), *n.* A moderate degree of wonder suddenly excited.— *v. t.* (153; To come or fall upon unexpectedly; to excite wonder in.
Sur-prĭṣ'ing, *a.* Exciting surprise; wonderful.
Sûr're-bŭt'ter, *n.* A reply to a defendant's rebutter.
Sur-rĕn'der, *v. t.* To yield; to deliver up.— *n.* Act of yielding or giving up to another.
Sûr'rep-tĭ'tioŭs (-tĭsh'us), *a.* Done by stealth or fraud.
Sûr'rep-tĭ'tioŭs-ly (-tĭsh'us-), *adv.* By stealth; fraudulently.
Sûr'ro-gāte, *n.* A deputy; a delegate; one who presides over the probate of wills, and the settlement of estates.
Sur-round', *v. t.* To inclose on all sides; to encompass.
Sur-ṣōl'id, *n.* Fifth power of a number.
Sur-tout' (-tōōt'), *n.* [Fr *surtout,* fr. *sur,* over, and *tout* all.] A close-fitting overcoat.
†Surveillance (sur-vāl'youngs'), *n.* [Fr.] Watch; inspection.
Sur-vey' (133), *v. t.* To view attentively; to measure and delineate, as land.
Sûr'vey (112), *n.* A general or a particular view; examination; mensuration; a plan or draft.
Sur-vey'ing, *n.* Act or art of measuring land, and delineating it on paper.
Sur-vey'or, *n.* One who measures land; an inspector of goods, highways, &c.
Sur-vey'or-ship, *n.* Office of a surveyor.
Sur-vī'val, *n.* A living longer than another.
Sur-vīve', *v. t.* To live longer than; to outlive.
Sur-vīv'or, *n.* One who outlives another.
Sur-vīv'or-ship, *n.* State of a survivor.
Sus-çĕp'ti-bĭl'i-ty, *n.* Quality of receiving impressions; sensibility.
Sus-çĕp'ti-ble, } *a.* Capable of receiving impressions.
Sus-çĕp'tive, }
Sus-çĭp'i-en-çy, *n.* Reception; admission.
Sus-çĭp'i-ent, *a.* Receiving admitting.— *n.* One who admits.
Sus-pĕct', *v. t.* To imagine to exist; to mistrust; to doubt; to have suspicion of.
Sus-pĕnd', *v. t.* To attach to something above; to cause to cease for a time. — SYN. To hang; intermit; interrupt; delay; hinder.
Sus-pĕnd'er, *n.* One who suspends: (*pl.*) braces.
Sus-pĕnṣe', *n.* State of uncertainty; cessation for a time; indecision; doubt.
Sus-pĕn'ṣion, *n.* Act of suspending; temporary or conditional interruption or delay. [suspend.
Sus-pĕn'so-ry, *a.* Serving to
Sus-pī'çion (-pĭsh'un), *n.* Mistrust; doubt; jealousy.
Sus-pī'çioŭs (-pĭsh'us), *a.* Apt or inclined to suspect; liable to suspicion.
Sus-pī'çioŭs-ly (-pĭsh'us-), *adv.* So as to excite suspicion.
Sus-pī'çioŭs-ness (-pĭsh'us-), *n.* Quality of being suspicious. [hole; a rent.
Sus-pīr'al, *n.* A breathing
Sŭs'pi-rā'tion, *n.* Act of sighing; a sigh.
Sus-pīre', *v. t.* To sigh.
Sus-tāin', *v. t.* To bear; to support; to uphold; to endure; to maintain.
Sus-tāin'a-ble, *a.* Capable of being sustained. [tains.
Sus-tāin'er, *n.* One who sustains.
Sŭs'te-nançe, *n.* Food that sustains; support; maintenance; provisions.
Sŭs'ten-tā'tion, *n.* Support.
Su-sur-rā'tion, *n.* A whispering.
Sŭt'ler, *n.* One who follows an army and sells provisions and liquors to the troops.
Sut-tee' (140), *n.* A Hindoo widow who immolates herself on the funeral pile of her husband; the immolation itself.
Sut-tee'iṣm, *n.* Self-immolation of widows in Hindostan.
Sūt'ūre, *n.* A seam; joint of the bones of the skull.
Swạb (swŏb), *n.* [From the root of *sweep.*] A mop for cleaning floors, &c.; a sponge for cleaning the mouth.— *v. t.* To wipe with a mop or swab.
Swạd'dle (swŏd'dl), *v. t.* To swathe. — *n.* Clothes bound tight around the body.
Swạd'dling-bănd, } *n.* A band
Swạd'dling-clŏth, } or cloth wrapped round an infant.
Swăg'ger, *v. i.* To boast; to brag; to bluster.— *n.* Insolence of manner.
Swăg, *v. i.* To sink down by its weight.
Swăg'ger-er, *n.* One who swaggers, or blusters.
Swăg'gy, *a.* Hanging down by its own weight.
Swāin, *n.* A rustic; a country gallant or lover.
Swāle, *n.* A tract of low land. — *v. t.* To melt and run down, as a candle.
Swạl'lōw, *n.* A small migratory bird; the throat.— *v. t.* To take into the stomach; to absorb; to engross; to ingulf; to consume.
Swăm, *imp.* of *Swim.*
Swamp (swŏmp), *n.* Low, wet, spongy ground; a marsh; a fen; a bog.— *v. t.* To overset, sink, or cause to become filled, as a boat, in water.
Swamp'y, *a.* Low, wet and spongy, as land.
Swan, *n.* A bird like the goose, but handsomer and more graceful.
Swạp (swŏp), *v.* Swan.
t. To exchange; to barter. — *n.* An exchange; barter.
Sward, *n.* Grassy surface of land; compact turf.
Swarm, *n.* A multitude, esp. of bees; a crowd.— *v. i.* To leave a hive in a body, as bees; to becrowd; to abound.
Swarth'i-ly, *adv.* With a tawny hue; duskily.
Swạr'thi-ness, *n.* State or quality of being swarthy.
Swarth'y, *a.* Of a dark hue.
Swash, *n.* Impulse of water flowing with violence; a narrow channel of water within a sandbank, or between that and the shore.
Swath, *n.* A line of grass, &c., cut down in mowing; whole sweep of a scythe.

sôn, ôr, do, wolf, too, took; ûrn, rue, pull; ç, ġ, *soft*; ҫ, ġ, *hard*; aṣ; exist; ŋ *as* ng; this.

SWATHE 296 SYLLABLE

Swāthe, *n.* A band or fillet; a bandage. — *v. t.* To bind with bands or bandages.

Swāy (135), *v. t. or i.* To wield; to govern; to move or wave. — *n.* Rule; command; power; influence.

Swēal, *v. i.* To melt; to swale.

Swēar, *v. i.* [*imp.* SWORE; *p. p.* SWORN.] To affirm with a solemn appeal to God for the truth of what is affirmed; to use profane language. — *v. t.* To utter solemnly, as an oath; to cause to take an oath.

Swear'er, *n.* One who swears.

Swear'ing, *n.* Act of one who swears; profanity.

Swēat, *n.* The moisture which issues through the pores of an animal; perspiration. — *v. i. or t.* To excrete, or to cause to excrete, moisture from the skin; to perspire.

Sweat'i-ness, *n.* State of being sweaty.

Sweat'y, *a.* Moist with sweat; covered with sweat.

Sweep, *v. t.* [*imp. & p. p.* SWEPT.] To clean with a broom or brush; to pass along. — *v. i.* To pass with swiftness and violence. — *n.* Act of sweeping; compass; range; a large oar; one who sweeps.

Sweep'ings, *n. pl.* Things collected in sweeping; refuse.

Sweep'stakes, *n. pl.* The whole money won at a race; one who wins all.

Sweet, *a.* Grateful to the taste, or to any sense; not sour; fresh; soft and gentle. — *n.* That which is sweet.

Sweet'-brĕad, *n.* The pancreas of an animal.

Sweet'brī-ar, *n.* A fragrant shrub of the rose kind.

Sweet'en, *v. t. or i.* To make or become sweet.

Sweet'en-ing, *n.* Something which sweetens.

Sweet'-fĕrn, *n.* A small aromatic North American shrub.

Sweet'hĕart, *n.* A lover; a mistress.

Sweet'ing, *n.* A sweet apple.

Sweet'ish, *a.* Rather sweet.

Sweet'ly, *adv.* With sweetness; gratefully; agreeably.

Sweet'mĕat, *n.* Fruit preserved with sugar.

Sweet'ness, *n.* Gratefulness to the taste or other sense.

Swĕll, *v. t.* To dilate or extend; to increase the size of.

— *v. i.* To be inflated; to grow larger. — *n.* Extension of bulk. [a tumor.

Swĕll'ing, *n.* Protuberance;

Swĕl'ter, *v. t. or i.* To oppress or to be overcome and faint with heat.

Swĕl'try, *a.* Sultry.

Swĕpt, *imp. & p. p.* of *Sweep.*

Swĕrve, *v. i.* To deviate; to wander.

Swift, *a.* Moving with celerity. — SYN. Rapid; speedy; ready; fleet; quick; nimble. — *n.* A small bird resembling the swallow; a species of lizard.

Swift'ly, *adv.* Rapidly; with celerity or velocity.

Swift'ness, *n.* Rapidity; celerity; speed.

Swig, *v. i. or t.* To drink in large draughts. [greedily.

Swill, *v. t.* To drink largely and — *n.* Wash for swine.

Swĭm, *v. i.* [*imp.* SWAM; *p. p.* SWUM.] To float or move in water; to glide along; to be dizzy.

Swim'mer, *n.* One who swims.

Swim'ming, *n.* Act of one who swims; dizziness.

Swim'ming-ly, *adv.* Without obstruction; very successfully; prosperously.

Swin'dle, *v. t.* To cheat or defraud grossly, or with deliberate artifice.

Swin'dler, *n.* A cheat; a sharper; a rogue. [hogs.

Swīne, *n. sing.* and *pl.* A hog;

Swīne'-hĕrd, *n.* A keeper of swine.

Swing, *v. i. or t.* [*imp. & p. p.* SWUNG.] To move to and fro, as a body suspended; to vibrate. — *n.* A waving motion; apparatus for swinging; tree course.

Swinge (58, 133), *v. t.* To beat soundly; to punish.

Swing'er, *n.* One who swings.

Swing'ing, *a.* Huge.

Swin'gle, *v. t.* To clean, as flax, by beating. — *n.* An instrument of wood like a knife, for cleaning flax.

Swīn'ish (133), *a.* Like swine; gross; bestial; sensual.

Swīpe, *n.* The movable beam by which the water in a well is raised.

Swiss, *n. sing. & pl.* A native of Switzerland; the people of Switzerland.

Switch, *n.* A flexible twig; a movable rail or pair of rails. — *v. t.* To beat; to flog.

Swĭv'el (swĭv'l, 58), *n.* A ring, link, or staple, turning on a pin or neck; a small gun that may be turned on a pivot. — *v. t. or i.* To turn on a movable pin.

Swōllen (swōln, 18), *p. p.* of **Swōln** } *Swell.*

Swoon, *v. i.* To faint. — *n.* A fainting fit.

Swoon'ing, *n.* Act of fainting; a fainting fit.

Swoop, *v. t. or i.* [Allied to *sweep.*] To fall on and seize with a sweeping motion. — *n.* A pouncing on and seizing, as of a bird of prey.

Swŏp, *n. & v.* See *Swap.*

Sword (sōrd), *n.* A military weapon for cutting or thrusting.

Sword'-fĭsh (sōrd'-), *n.* A large fish, having the upper jaw elongated into a sword-shaped process. It is allied to the mackerel.

Sword fish.

Swōre, *imp.* of *Swear.*

Swōrn, *p. p. or p. a.* from *Swear.*

Swŭm, *imp. & p. p.* of *Swim.*

Swŭng, *imp. & p. p.* of *Swing.*

Sўb'a-rīte, *n.* A person devoted to luxury and pleasure.

Sўc'a-mōre, *n.* A large tree allied to the common fig; in England, a large maple; in America, the plane-tree, or buttonwood.

Sycamore.

Sўc'o-phan-cy, *n.* Mean or obsequious flattery; servility.

Sўc'o-phant, *n.* An obsequious flatterer of princes and great men; a base parasite.

Sўc'o-phănt'ic, *a.* Servilely flattering; parasitic.

Sў'e-nīte, *n.* A crystalline rock closely resembling granite. [to syllables.

Syl-lăb'ic (127), *a.* Relating

Syl-lăb'i-cā'tion, *n.* The formation of syllables.

Sўl'la-ble, *n.* A letter or com-

SYLLABUB 297 TABERNACLE

bination of letters uttered together, or by one impulse of the voice.

Syl'la-bub, *n.* A drink made of wine and milk.

Syl'la-bus, *n.* A compendium containing the heads of a discourse, &c.; an abstract.

Syl'lo-gism, *n.* A regular argument consisting of three propositions.

Syl'lo-gist'ic, *a.* Relating to, or consisting of, a syllogism.

Syl'lo-gize, *v. t.* To reason by syllogisms.

Sylph, *n.* A kind of fairy inhabiting the air.

Syl'van, *n.* A fabled deity of the wood; a faun. — *a.* Forest-like; woody; rural; rustic. [sign, or representation.

Sym'bol, *n.* A type, emblem,

Sym-bol'ic, *a.* Express-

Sym-bol'ic-al, ing by means of symbols or signs.

Sym-bol'ic-al-ly, *adv.* By signs; typically.

Sym'bol-ize (31), *v. t.* or *i.* To have resemblance; to represent by a symbol.

Sym-met'ric-al, *a.* Proportional in its parts.

Sym-met'ric-al-ly, *adv.* With due proportions.

Sym'me-try, *n.* Adaptation of parts to each other or to the whole; due proportion of parts.

Sym'pa-thet'ic, *a.* Having, or produced by, sympathy.

Sym'pa-thet'ic-al-ly, *adv.* With or by sympathy.

Sym'pa-thize, *v. i.* To feel for another. [sympathizes.

Sym'pa-thiz'er, *n.* One who

Sym'pa-thy, *n.* [Gr. *sympatheia*, from *sun*, with, and *pathos*, suffering.] Fellow-feeling; commiseration; pity.

Sym-pho'ni-ous, *a.* Agreeing in sound; harmonious.

Sym'pho-ny, *n.* Harmony of sounds; an elaborate musical composition for instruments.

Symp'tom, *n.* A sign or in-

dication, as of disease; token; mark; note.

Symp'tom-at'ic, *a.* Indicating the existence of something else.

†Syn-ær'e-sis, } *n.* Contrac-

Syn-er'e-sis, } tion of a word by drawing two vowels together into one syllable.

Syn'a-gogue (-gŏg), *n.* A Jewish assembly or place of worship.

Syn'chro-nal, } *a.* Hap-

Syn-chron'ic-al, } pening at

Syn'chro-nous, } the same time; simultaneous.

Syn'chro-nism, *n.* Concurrence of two or more events in time.

Syn'chro-nize, *v. i.* To agree in time; to be simultaneous.

Syn'co-pāte, *v. t.* To contract by syncope.

Syn'co-pā'tion, *n.* Contraction of a word by taking a letter or letters from the middle.

Syn'co-pe, *n.* Retrenchment of one or more letters from the middle of a word; a fainting fit; a swoon.

Syn'dic, *n.* A magistrate invested with different powers in different places.

Syn-ĕc 'do-che, *n.* A figure of rhetoric by which the whole is put for a part, or a part for the whole.

Syn'od, *n.* An ecclesiastical council; a convention.

Syn-ŏd'ic, } *a.* Done by, or

Syn-ŏd'ic-al, } pertaining to, a synod.

Syn'o-nym, } *n.* A word

Syn'o-nyme, } which has the same or very nearly the same meaning as another word.

Syn-ŏn'y-mist, *n.* One who treats of synonyms.

Syn-ŏn'y-mīze, *v. t.* To express in different words of the same meaning.

Syn-ŏn'y-moŭs, *a.* [Gr. *sunōnumos*, from *sun*, with, together, and *onoma*, *onuma*, name.] Having the same

meaning; pertaining to, or containing, synonyms.

Syn-ŏn'y-moŭs-ly, *adv.* In the same sense.

Syn-ŏn'y-my, *n.* Quality of expressing the same meaning in different words.

Syn-ŏp'sis, *n.* (*pl.* † Syn-ŏp'sēs). A general view; an abstract; an epitome.

Syn-ŏp'tic, } *a.* Affording a

Syn-ŏp'tic-al, } general view.

Syn-tăc'tic, } *a.* Pertain-

Syn-tăc'tic-al, } ing to syntax.

Syn'tax, *n.* The arrangement or construction of words in sentences.

Syn'the-sis, *n.* Composition, or the putting of two or more things together.

Syn-thĕt'ic, } *a.* Pertain-

Syn-thĕt'ic-al, } ing to, or consisting in, synthesis.

Syn-thĕt'ic-al-ly, *adv.* By synthesis; by composition.

Syph'i-lis, *n.* An infectious venereal disease.

Syr'i-ăc, *a.* Pertaining to Syria, or its language. — *n.* The language of Syria.

Sy-rĭn'gă, *n.* The lilac; also, the mock orange.

Syr'inge, *n.* A kind of pipe for injecting liquids. — *v. t.* To inject or cleanse by means of a syringe.

Sys'tem, *n.* Connected assemblage of parts or things; a whole connected scheme; regular order or method.

Sys'tem-ăt'ic, } *a.* Pertain-

Sys'tem-ăt'ic-al, } ing, or proceeding according, to system; methodical; connected.

Sys'tem-ăt'ic-al-ly, *adv.* In a systematic manner.

Sys'tem-a-tīze, *v. t.* To reduce to system or regular method; to methodize.

Sys'tem-a-tīz'er, *n.* One who systematizes, or reduces things to a system.

Sys'to-le, *n.* The shortening of a syllable; contraction of the heart and arteries.

T.

TĂB, *n.* A border of lace on the inner front edge of a bonnet.

Tăb'ard, *n.* A sort of tunic

or mantle formerly worn over the armor.

Tăb'by, *a.* Wavy; watered; brindled. — *n.* A wavy or

watered silk; a brindled variety of cat.

Tăb'er-na-cle, *n.* A tent; a temporary habitation; a temporary and portable temple of the Jews; place for keeping some holy or precious thing. — *v. i.* To reside for a time.

Tăb'id, *a.* Wasted by disease.

Tăb'la-tūre, *n.* A painting on a wall and ceiling; a picture in general.

Tā'ble (140), *n.* An article of furniture with a flat surface; a board; fare; a synopsis or schedule. — *v. t.* To lay on the table; to postpone; to form into a table.

Tăb'leau (tăb'lō), *n.* (*pl.* **Tăb'leaux,** -lōz, 147.) A picture-like representation of some scene by means of persons grouped together; a still pantomime.

Tā'ble-lănd (106), *n.* Elevated flat land; a plateau.

Tăb'let, *n.* A little table; a flat surface for writing on; a memorandum-book.

Ta-bōō', *n.* A religious interdict; a prohibition. — *v. t.* To forbid approach to or use of; to hold sacred.

Tā'bor, *n.* A small drum.

Tăb'o-ret, } *n.* A small, shallow low drum; a **Tăb'ret,** } small tabor.

Tăb'u-lar, *a.* Having the form of, or relating to, a table.

Tăb'u-lāte, *v. t.* To reduce to tables or synopses; to make flat.

Tăc'a-ma-hăc, *n.* A North American tree.

Tăç'it, *a.* Silent; implied.

Tăç'it-ly, *adv.* Without words; by implication.

Tăç'i-turn, *a.* Habitually silent; reserved; reticent.

Tăç'i-tûr'ni-ty, *n.* Habitual silence; reserve; reticence.

Tăck (127), *n.* A sort of small nail; a rope to confine the lower corner of a sail; course of a ship as to the position of her sails. — *v. t.* To fasten slightly. — *v. i.* To change the course of a ship by means of her sails.

Tăck'le (tăk'l), *n.* A machine for raising heavy weights; rigging and apparatus of a ship. — *v. t.* To harness; to seize. [ship; harness.

Tăck'ling, *n.* Rigging of a

Tăct, *n.* Nice perception or skill. [tactics.

Tăc'tic-al, *a.* Pertaining to

Tac-ti'cian (-tĭsh'an), *n.* One versed in tactics.

Tăc'tics, *n. sing.* Science and art of disposing military or naval forces in order for battle. [touched.

Tăc'tile, *a.* Capable of being

Tăd'pōle, *n.* The young of a frog in its first state.

Tăff'rail, *n.* Upper part of a ship's stern.

Tăf'fe-tā, } *n.* A fine glossy **Tăf'fe-ty,** } silk stuff.

Tăg. *n.* A metallic point at the end of a string; a label tied on. — *v. t.* To fit with a point or points; to touch.

Tāil (126), *n.* [A.-S. *tægel,* *tægl,* from Goth. *tagl,* hair.] Appendage of an animal behind; back, lower, or inferior part.

Tāi'lor, *n.* One who makes men's clothes.

Tāi'lor-ĕss, *n.* A woman who makes men's or boys' clothes.

Tāint, *v. t.* To infect; to contaminate; to corrupt. — *n.* Infection; corruption.

Tāke, *v. t.* [*imp.* TOOK; *p. p.* TAKEN.] To receive; to seize; to catch; to hold; to assume; to convey. — *v. i.* To have the natural effect; to gain reception; to go.

Tāk'ing, *a.* Alluring; attracting.

Tāle (127), *n.* A soft greenish or grayish mineral of a soapy feel.

Tāle, *n.* A story; a narrative; a number or enumeration.

Tāle'-beār'er, *n.* An officious informer; a tell-tale.

Tăl'ent, *n.* An ancient weight and coin; intellectual ability; faculty.

Tăl'ent-ed, *a.* Possessing talents or abilities.

Tāles'man, *n.* A person called to make up a deficiency in the number of jurors.

Tăl'is-man (143), *n.* A magical character; a charm.

Tăl'is-măn'ic, *a.* Affording magical protection.

Tălk (tawk), *n.* Familiar conversation; rumor. — *v. i.* To converse familiarly; to speak, as in familiar discourse.

Tălk'a-tĭve (tawk'-), *a.* Given to much talking. — SYN. Loquacious; garrulous.

Tălk'a-tĭve-nĕss (tawk'-), *n.* Quality or state of being talkative. [talks.

Tălk'er (tawk'-), *n.* One who

Tāll (123), *a.* High in stature; lofty. [ness.

Tāll'ness, *n.* Height; loftiness.

Tăl'lōw, *n.* Hard fat of an animal, especially of the sheep and the ox. — *v. t.* To smear with tallow.

Tăl'lōw-chăn'dler, *n.* One who makes tallow candles.

Tăl'ly, *n.* A notched stick for keeping accounts; a match; a mate. — *v. t.* or *i.* To agree; to correspond; to fit.

Tăl'ly-man (143), *n.* One who keeps tally.

Tăl'mud, *n.* A book of Hebrew laws and traditions.

Tal-mŭd'ic, *a.* Relating to, or contained in, the Talmud.

Tăl'mud-ist, *n.* One versed in the Talmud.

Tăl'on, *n.* The claw of a bird of prey; a kind of molding; an ogee. [of being tamed.

Tām'a-ble (133), *a.* Capable

Tăm'a-rĭnd, *n.* A tropical tree and its acid fruit.

Tăm'a-risk, *n.* A tree or shrub of several species.

Tăm'bour, *n.* A small, flat drum; a circular frame for embroidery; a kind of embroidery.

Tăm'bour-ĭne' (tăm'boor-ēen'), *n.* A shallow drum with only one skin.

Tāme, *a.* Accustomed to man; gentle; mild. — *v. t.* To reclaim from wildness; to subdue; to conquer.

Tambourine.

Tāme'ly, *adv.* With mean submission; servileness.

Tāme'ness (134), *n.* Gentleness; want of spirit. [stuff.

Tăm'my, *n.* A glazed woolen

Tămp, *v. t.* To fill up, as a hole in blasting.

Tăm'per (130), *v. i.* To meddle; to try little experiments.

Tăm'pi-on, } *n.* Stopper of a **Tŏm'pi-on,** } gun or cannon.

Tăn (129), *v. t.* To convert into leather; to make brown. — *v. i.* To become brown. — *n.* Bark prepared for tanning; a yellowish-brown color, like that of tan.

Tăn'dem, *adv.* One behind another; — said of horses.

Tăng, *n.* A strong taste; relish; a kind of sea-weed.

Tăn'gent, *n.* *ac.* tangent; [Lat. *tangens,* *a'l*, radius; *bc,* touching.] A are.

ă, ĕ, ĭ, ŏ, ŭ, ȳ, *long;* ă, ĕ, ĭ, ŏ, ŭ, y̆, *short;* cāre, cär, ȧsk, ąll, whąt; ēre, vĕil, tẽrm; p'que, fĭrm;

right line which merely touches a curve.

Tăn'gi-bĭl'ĭ-ty, *n.* Quality of being tangible.

Tăn'gĭ-ble, *a.* Perceptible by the touch; palpable; readily apprehensible.

Tăn'gle, *v. t.* or *i.* To unite together confusedly; to insnare. — *n.* An intricate knot. [cistern.

Tănk, *n.* A large basin or

Tănk'ard, *n.* A large vessel for liquors, or a drinking-vessel, with a lid.

Tăn'ner, *n.* One whose occupation is to tan hides.

Tăn'ner-y, *n.* House and apparatus for tanning.

Tăn'nin (152), *n.* The astringent principle of the bark of the oak and other trees.

Tăn'sy, *n.* A very bitter plant, used in medicine and cookery.

Tăn'ta-lĭsm, *n.* A teasing with vain hopes.

Tăn'ta-lize (153), *v. t.* To tease with false hopes.

Tăn'ta-mount', *a.* Equivalent in value or signification.

Tan-tiv'y, or **Tăn'tiv-y,** *adv.* Swiftly; — a hunting term.

Tăn'-yärd, *n.* A yard where tanning is carried on.

Tăp, *v. t.* To touch or strike lightly; to pierce, so as to let out a fluid; to put a new sole or heel on. — *n.* A gentle blow; a spile or pipe for drawing liquor; a bar.

Tāpe, *n.* A narrow piece of woven fabric.

Tā'per, *n.* A small wax candle. — *a.* Decreasing regularly toward the point. — *v. t.* or *i.* To decrease gradually toward one end.

Tăp'es-tried, *a.* Adorned with tapestry.

Tăp'es-try, *n.* A kind of woven hangings of wool and silk, often embroidered.

Tāpe'-worm (-wŭrm), *n.* A broad, flat, many-jointed worm, bred in the intestines.

Tăp'ĭ-ō'cȧ, *n.* A starch obtained from the roots of a Brazilian plant.

Tăp'-house, *n.* A house where liquors are retailed.

Tăp'-rōot, *n.* The chief root.

Tăp'ster, *n.* One who draws liquors.

Tär, *n.* A resinous substance obtained from pine trees; a sailor. [See *Tarpaulin*.] — *v. t.* To smear with tar.

Ta-răn'tu-lȧ, *n.* A species of spider.

Tär'di-ly, *adv.* With a slow pace.

Tär'di-ness, (13), *n.* Slowness of motion; lateness.

Tär'dy, *a.* Moving with a slow pace or motion; dilatory; late.

Tāre, *n.* A troublesome weed; allowance in weight for the cask or bag in which a commodity is contained.

Tär'ġet, *n.* A small shield; a mark to shoot at.

Tär'ġet-eer', *n.* One armed with a target.

Tăr'iff, *n.* [Arab. *ta'rif*,] information, explanation, definition.] A table of duties or customs on imports.

Tär'la-tan, *n.* A kind of thin, transparent muslin.

Tärn, *n.* A small lake among the mountains.

Tär'nĭsh, *v. t.* To sully; to lose brightness.

Tar-pau'lĭn, *n.* Canvas tarred; a waterproof hat worn by sailors; a sailor.

Tăr'ry, *v. t.* To stay; to remain; to continue; to delay; to abide.

Tär'ry, *a.* Covered with, or like, tar.

Tärt, *a.* Acid; sharp; severe. — *n.* A kind of small open pie. [en cloth.

Tär'tan, *n.* A checkered wool-

Tär'tar, *n.* An acid salt deposited from wine; concretion on the teeth.

Tar-tā're-an, *a.* Pertaining to Tartarus; hellish.

Tar-tā're-oŭs, } *a.* Consisting

Tär'tar-oŭs, } of, or like, tartar.

Tar-tăr'ĭc, *a.* Pertaining to, or obtained from, tartar.

Tär'tar-īze, *v. t.* To impregnate with tartar.

Tär'ta-rus, *n.* In Greek and Roman mythology, the infernal regions.

Tärt'ĭsh, *a.* Somewhat tart.

Tärt'ly, *adv.* Sharply; sourly; acrimoniously.

Tärt'ness, *n.* Sharpness; acidity; acrimony.

Tär'-wa'ter, *n.* A cold infusion of tar.

Tȧsk, *n.* Business imposed; burdensome employment. — *v. t.* To impose a task on; to oppress with burdens.

Tȧsk'-mȧs'ter, *n.* One who imposes tasks.

Tăs'sel, *n.* A kind of pendant ornament ending in a fringe. — *v. t.* (130) To adorn with tassels. [ing tasted.

Tȧst'a-ble, *a.* Capable of be-

Tāste, *v. t.* To perceive by the palate; to eat a little of; to experience; to relish. — *n.* Act or sense of tasting; intellectual relish or discernment; style; a kind of narrow ribbon.

Tāste'ful, *a.* Having a high relish; exhibiting good taste.

Tāste'ful-ly, *adv.* With good taste.

Tāste'less, *a.* Having no taste; insipid.

Tāste'less-ness, *n.* Quality of being tasteless.

Tāst'er, *n.* One who tastes.

Tāst'ĭ-ly, *adv.* With good taste.

Tāst'y, *a.* Having good taste; according to taste; elegant.

Tăt'ter, *v. t.* To rend into rags. — *n.* A piece torn and hanging; a rag.

Tăt'ter-de-măl'ion (-măl'yun), *n.* A shabby fellow.

Tăt'tle, *v. i.* To tell tales or secrets. — *n.* Idle, trifling talk or chat; prate.

Tăt'tler, *n.* An idle talker.

Tat-too', *n.* A beat of drum at night, to call to quarters; figures stained on the skin. — *v. t.* (137) To stain indelibly, as the skin, by pricking in dye-stuffs.

Taught (tawt), *imp. & p. p.* of *Teach.* — *a.* See *Taut.*

Taunt (tänt), *v. t.* To insult with reproachful words. — SYN. To deride; mock; revile; insult; upbraid. — *n.* A gibe; scoff.

†**Tau'rus,** *n.* The Bull, a sign in the zodiac.

Taut, *a.* Tight; stretched.

Tau-tŏġ', *n.* A fish found on the coast of New England.

Tau'to-lŏġ'ic-al, *a.* Repeating the same meaning.

Tau-tŏl'o-ġist, *n.* One who uses tautology.

Tau-tŏl'o-ġy, *n.* Repetition of the same meaning in different words.

Tăv'ern, *n.* A public house kept for the entertainment and accommodation of travelers and other guests.

Tăv'ern-keep'er, } *n.* One

Tăv'ern-er, } who keeps a tavern.

Taw, v. t. To dress and prepare in white leather.

Taw'dri-ly, adv. With excess of finery.

Taw'dri-ness, n. State of being tawdry; excessive fluery.

Taw'dry, a. Gaudy in dress; showy without taste.

Taw'ny, a. [Fr. tanné, tanned.] Of a dull yellowish brown color, like tan.

Tax, n. A rate assessed on a person for some public use; task exacted. — v. t. To subject to pay a tax; to accuse; to charge. [taxed.

Tax'a-ble, a. Liable to be

Tax-a'tion, n. Act of imposing taxes; impost.

Tax'i-der'my, n. Art of preparing the skins of animals, so as to represent their natural appearance.

Tea, n. A plant, or a decoction of its dried leaves.

Teach, v. t. [imp & p. p. TAUGHT.] To instruct; to inculcate; to show; to tell.

Teach'a-ble, a. Capable of being taught; docile.

Teach'a-ble-ness, n. Aptness to learn; docility. [tutor.

Teach'er, n. An instructor; a

Tea'-cup, n. A small cup to drink tea from.

Teak, n. An East India tree, and its timber.

Tea'-ket'tle, n. A kettle to boil water in for making tea.

Teal, n. A web-footed waterfowl.

Team, n. Two or more horses or oxen harnessed together.

Team'ster, n. One who drives a team. [tea is made.

Tea'-pot, n. A vessel in which

Tear, n. A drop of water or brine from the eyes.

Tear, v. t. or i. (imp. TORE; p. p. TORN.] To pull asunder; to rend; to lacerate.

Tear'er, n. One who tears.

Tear'ful, a. Shedding tears; weeping. [tears.

Tear'less, a. Shedding no

Tease, v. t. To comb or card; to harass; to vex.

Tea'sel (tē'zl, 55), n. A burr, or other thing used for raising a nap on woolen cloth.

Teas'er, n. One who teases.

Tea'-spoon, n. A small spoon, used in drinking tea, &c.

Teat, n. The nipple; a dug.

Tech'i-ness, n. Peevishness; touchiness.

Tech'nic-al, a. Relating to any art, science, or business.

Tech'nic-al-ly, adv. In a technical manner.

Tech'ni-cal'i-ty, n. Quality of being technical; that which is technical.

Tech'nics, n. sing. Such branches of learning as respect the arts.

Tech'no-lōg'ic-al, a. Of, or pertaining to, technology.

Tech-nŏl'o-gĭst, n. One who treats of the terms of art.

Tech-nŏl'o-gy, n. A treatise on the arts.

Tech'y, a. Peevish; fretful.

Tec-tōn'ic, a. Pertaining to building or construction.

Ted'der, n. A tether.

†**Te Dē'um**. [Lat.] An ancient Christian hymn of thanksgiving.

Tē'di-oŭs (or tēd'yŭs), a. Tiresome, from continuance or slowness. — SYN. Wearisome; irksome; fatiguing; sluggish. [ous manner.

Tē'di-oŭs-ly, adv. In a tedi-

Tē'di-um, n. Irksomeness; wearisomeness.

Teem, v. i. To bring forth, as an animal; to be prolific. — v. t. To bring forth; to produce.

Teens, n. pl. Years between twelve and twenty.

Tee'ter, v. i. To ride on the end of a balanced board.

Teeth (143), n.; pl. of Tooth.

Teeth, v. i. To breed teeth.

Tee-tō'tal, a. Entire; total.

Tee-tō'tal-ĭşm, n. Principle of strict temperance.

Tee-tō'tum, n. A kind of top.

Tĕg'u-lar, a. Pertaining to, or resembling, tiles.

Tĕg'u-ment, n. A covering.

Tĕl'e-gram, n. A telegraphic message or dispatch.

Tĕl'e-graph, n. [Gr. tēle, afar, far off, and graphein, to write.] An apparatus for communicating information rapidly between distant places by signals.

Tĕl'e-graph'ic, a. Pertaining to a telegraph.

Te-lĕg'ra-phy, n. Science or art of constructing telegraphs, or of communicating by means of them.

Tĕl'e-scōpe, n. An optical instrument for viewing distant objects.

Tĕl'e-scŏp'ic,) a. Pertaining to a telescope.

Tĕll, v. t. [imp. & p. p. TOLD.] To count; to number; to relate; to inform. — v. i. To produce a marked effect.

Tĕll'er, n. One who tells; an officer of a bank who counts over money received, and pays it out on checks.

Tĕll'-tāle, n. An officious informer. — a. Telling tales.

Te-mĕr'i-ty, n. Rash boldness; foolhardiness.

Tĕm'per, n. Constitution of mind; due mixture; proneness to anger; state of a metal as to hardness. — v. t. (13)) To mix in due proportion; to qualify; to soften; to bring to a proper degree of hardness.

Tĕm'per-a-ment, n. Internal constitution; peculiar physical and mental character.

Tĕm'per-ance, n. Moderate indulgence of the appetites; abstemiousness.

Tĕm'per-ate, a. Moderate; abstemious; sober.

Tĕm'per-ate-ly, adv. With moderation; without excess.

Tĕm'per-a-tūre (50), n. State with regard to heat or cold.

Tĕm'pest, n. A violent storm; commotion; tumult.

Tem-pĕst'u-oŭs, a. Stormy; violent; turbulent.

Tem-pĕst'u-oŭs-ly, adv. With great violence; turbulently; violently.

Tĕm'plar, n. A student of law. [Eng.]

Tĕm'ple, n. An edifice erected to some deity; a church; flat part of the head between the forehead and ear.

Tĕm'plet, n. A piece of timber used in building.

Tĕm'po-ral, a. Pertaining to a temple; pertaining to this life; secular; not spiritual.

Tĕm'po-răl'i-ty, n. Revenues of an ecclesiastic, derived from lands, tithes, &c.

Tĕm'po-ral-ly, adv. With regard to this life.

Tĕm'po-ra-ri-ly (135), adv. For a time only.

Tĕm'po-ra-ry, a. Continuing for a time only; transitory.

Tĕm'po-rīze (153), v. i. To comply with the time or occasion.

Tĕm'po-rīz'er, n. One who temporizes; a time-server.

Tĕmpt (81), v. t. To entice to what is wrong; to lead into evil; to venture on. — SYN. To allure; seduce; solicit.

Temp-tā'tion, n. Act of tempting; state of being

TEMPTER 301 TESSELATE

tempted ; that which tempts ; trial.

Tempt'er, *n.* One who tempts, or entices to evil.

Tĕn, *a.* Twice five ; nine and one ; a decade. [held.

Tĕn'a-ble, *a.* Capable of being

Te-nā'cious, *a.* Holding fast; retentive ; adhesive ; stubborn.

Te-nā'cious-ly, *adv.* Firmly ; adhesively.

Te-năç'i-ty, *n.* The quality of being tenacious.

Tĕn'an-çy, *n.* A holding or temporary possession of what belongs to another.

Tĕn'ant, *n.* One who holds lands or tenements of another. — *v. t.* To hold or possess as a tenant.

Tĕn'ant-a-ble, *a.* Fit to be rented. [tenants.

Tĕn'ant-less, *a.* Having no

Tĕn'ant-ry, *n.* A body of tenants.

Tĕnd, *v. t.* To watch ; to guard ; to move in a certain direction ; to aim at ; to wait on. — *v. i.* To move ; to aim ; to incline ; to conduce.

Tĕnd'en-çy, *n.* Drift ; direction ; inclination ; course.

Tĕnd'er, *n.* A small vessel that attends a larger ; an offer. — *v. t.* To offer.

Tĕn'der, *a.* Easily impressed or injured ; easily moved to pity, forgiveness, or favor. — SYN. Delicate ; soft ; mild ; humane.

Tĕn'der-ly, *adv.* Gently ; kindly ; softly ; mildly.

Tĕn'der-loin, *n.* A tender part of flesh in the hind quarter of beef.

Tĕn'der-ness, *n.* Quality of being tender ; softness ; delicacy ; kindness ; soreness.

Tĕn'di-nous, *a.* Full of tendons ; sinewy.

Tĕn'don, *n.* A hard insensible cord by which a muscle is attached to a bone.

Tĕn'dril, *n.* A spiral shoot or clasper of a vine.

Tĕn'e-ment, *n.* A house or part of a house for the use of one family ; an apartment ; any permanent property that can be held.

Tĕn'et, *n.* Opinion ; principle ; dogma ; doctrine.

Tĕn'fŏld, *a.* Ten times as many or much.

Tĕn'nis, *n.* A play with racket and ball.

Tĕn'on, *n.* That part of a piece of wood which is cut to enter a mortise.

Tĕn'or (155), *n.* General course ; purport ; higher kind of male voice.

Tĕnse, *a.* [Lat. *tendere, tensus,* to stretch.] Strained tight.
— *n.* Form or variation of a verb to express time.

Tĕnse'ness, *n.* State of being tense ; stiffness.

Tĕn'sion (92), *n.* Act or degree of stretching ; stiffness ; elastic power.

Tĕnt, *n.* A pavilion or portable lodge or canvas ; a roll of lint or linen for surgical use. — *v. t.* To lodge in a tent ; to cover with tents ; to probe.

Tĕn'ta-cle, *n.* An organ of certain insects for feeling or motion.

Tĕn'ta-tive, *a.* Experimental.

Tĕnt'ed, *a.* Covered or furnished with tents.

Tĕn'ter, *n.* A frame with hooks for stretching cloth. —
v. t. To stretch on hooks.

Tĕnth, *a.* The ordinal of ten.
— *n.* One part in ten ; a tithe.

Tĕnth'ly, *adv.* In the tenth place.

Te-nū'i-ty, *n.* Thinness ; slenderness ; subtilty.

Tĕn'u-oŭs, *a.* Thin ; slender ; small ; rare ; subtile.'

Tĕn'ūre, *n.* Act, right, or manner, of holding.

Tĕp'e-făc'tion, *n.* Act of warming. [erately warm.

Tĕp'e-fy, *v. t.* To make moderately warm.

Tĕp'id, *a.* Moderately warm.

Tĕp'id-ness, *n.* Moderate warmth ; lukewarmness.

†**Tĕr'a-phim,** *n. pl.* Household deities. [tine tree.

Tĕr'e-binth, *n.* The turpentine

Te-rēte', *a.* Cylindrical and slightly tapering.

Tĕr'ġi-ver-sā'tion (tĕr/ji-), *n.* A shifting ; subterfuge ; fickleness.

Tĕrm, *n.* A boundary ; limited time ; word ; condition ; time of session. — *v. t.* To call ; to name. [lence.

Tĕr'ma-gan-çy, *n.* Turbulence.

Tĕr'ma-gant, *n.* A brawling, turbulent woman. — *a.* Quarrelsome ; shrewish.

Tĕr'mi-na-ble, *a.* Capable of being bounded or ended.

Tĕr'mi-nal, *a.* Ending ; growing at, or forming, the end.

Tĕr'mi-nāte, *v. t.* To set the limit to ; to put an end to. —
SYN. To limit ; complete ;

fluish ; bound. — *v. i.* To end ; to close.

Tĕr'mi-nā'tion, *n.* Limit ; bound ; end ; result.

Tĕr'mi-nā'tion-al, *a.* Relating to, or forming, a termination.

Tĕr'mi-nŏl'o-ġy, *n.* A treatise on terms ; terms used ; nomenclature.

Tĕr'mi-nus, *n.* (*pl.* †**Tĕr'mi-nī,** 147). A boundary ; a boundary-stone ; either end of a railroad. [aut.

Tĕr'mīte (140), *n.* The white

Tĕr'na-ry, *a.* Proceeding by threes. — *n.* Three.

Tĕr'raçe (18), *n.* A raised bank of earth ; a row of houses on a raised site ; a flat roof.

†**Tĕr'ra Çŏt'ta.** [It.] A kind of pottery made from fine clay.

Tĕr'ra-pĭn, *n.* A large kind of turtle or tortoise.

Ter-rā'que-oŭs, *a.* Composed of land and water.

Ter-rēne', *a.* Relating to the earth.

Ter-rĕs'tri-al, *a.* Belonging to the earth ; earthly ; sublunary.

Tĕr'ri-ble, *a.* Fitted to excite terror. — SYN. Fearful ; frightful ; formidable ; awful ; shocking.

Tĕr'ri-bly, *adv.* Frightfully.

Tĕr'ri-er, *n.* A dog that pursues game into holes.

Ter-rif'ic, *a.* Adapted to excite terror ; dreadful.

Tĕr'ri-fy, *v. t.* To frighten.

Tĕr'ri-tō'ri-al, *a.* Pertaining to territory.

Tĕr'ri-to-ry (107), *n.* Extent of land within any jurisdiction ; a tract of land at a distance from the parent country ; a district of country not organized as a State.

Tĕr'ror, *n.* Great fear ; dread.

Tĕr'ror-ĭsm, *n.* A state impressing terror.

Tĕrse, *a.* Elegantly concise.

Tĕrse'ly, *adv.* Neatly and concisely.

Tĕrse'ness, *n.* Smoothness and compactness.

Tĕr'ti-an (tĕr'shan), *a.* Happening every third day. — *n.* A disease whose paroxysms return every third day.

Tĕr'ti-a-ry (tĕr'shi-a-ry), *a.* Third ; of the third formation, rank, or order.

Tĕs'sel-āte, *v. t.* To form into, or lay with, checkered work.

sŏn, ôr, dọ, wǫlf, tōo, tŏŏk ; ûrn, rụe, pụll ; ç, ġ, *soft* ; ç, ġ, *hard* ; aẓ ; eẋist ; ṇ *as* ng ; tḥis.

Tes′sel-a′tion, *n.* Mosaic work, or the making of it.
Test, *n.* A cupel to try metals: critical examination or trial; standard. — *v. t.* To try by a fixed standard; to put to proof.
Tes-ta′cean, *n.* A shell-fish, especially mollusks.
Tes-ta′ceous, *a.* Having a hard, continuous shell, as the oyster or clam.
Test′a-ment, *n.* A will; one of the two general divisions of the Scriptures.
Test′a-ment′a-ry, *a.* Relating to, or bequeathed by, a will or testament.
Test′ate. *a.* Having made and left a will.
Tes-ta′tor, *n.* One who leaves a will.
Tes-ta′trix, *n.* A female testator.
Tes′ter, *n.* Top covering of a bed ; a flat canopy.
Tes′ti-cle, *n.* A gland that secretes seminal fluid.
Tes′ti-fi′er, *n.* One who testifies or bears witness.
Tes′ti-fỹ, *v. i.* [Lat. *testificare*, from *testis*, a witness, and *facere*, to make.] To give testimony ; to bear witness. — *v. t.* To affirm or declare solemnly.
Tes′ti-ly, *adv.* Peevishly.
Tes′ti-mō′ni-al, *n.* A certificate of good character or conduct.
Tes′ti-mo-ny, *n.* Affirmation in proof of some fact. — SYN. Evidence; proof.
Tes′ti-ness, *n.* Peevishness.
Tes′tū′di-nal, } *a.* Relating to,
Tes′tū-din′e-ous, } or resembling, the tortoise.
Tes′ty, *a.* Peevish; fretful.
Tet′a-nus, *n.* The locked-jaw.
Tête-a-tête (tāt-ă-tāt′), *n.* [Fr.] Lit., head to head; hence, private conversation; a form of sofa for two persons.
Teth′er, *v. t.* To confine with a rope, as a horse. — *n.* A rope or chain to confine a beast in a field.
Tet′ra-gon, *n.* A figure with four angles; a quadrangle. Tetragons.
Te-trăg′o-nal, *a.* Having four sides and angles.

Tet′ra-hē′dron, *n.* A solid figure inclosed by four equal triangles.
Te-trăm′e-ter, Tetrahedrons. *n.* A verse consisting of four measures.
Tē′trärch, *n.* A Roman governor of the fourth part of a province.
Te-trärch′ate, } *n.* Office or
Tĕt′rarch-y, } jurisdiction of a tetrarch.
Te-trăs′tich, *n.* A poem of four verses.
Tĕt′ra-stȳle, *n.* A building with four columns in front.
Tĕt′ra-sȳl′la-ble, *n.* A word of four syllables.
Tĕt′ter, *n.* A cutaneous disease, causing a troublesome itching.
Teu-tōn′ic, *a.* Relating to the Teutons, or ancient Germans.
Tew′el, *n.* An iron pipe in forges to receive the pipe of the bellows.
Tĕxt, *n.* A passage of Scripture selected as the subject of discourse ; composition on which a note is written.
Tĕxt′-bŏŏk, *n.* A manual of instruction ; a school-book.
Tĕxt′-hănd, *n.* A large kind of writing. [by weaving.
Tĕx′tĭle, *a.* Woven ; formed
Tĕxt′u-al, *a.* Pertaining to, or contained in, the text.
Tĕxt′u-al-ĭst, } *n.* One versed
Tĕxt′u-a-rĭst, } in Scripture.
Tĕxt′u-a-ry, }
Tĕxt′ūre, *n.* Manner of weaving; fabric formed by weaving.
Thăn, *conj.* A particle expressing comparison.
Thāne, *n.* An Anglo-Saxon baron or dignitary.
Thănk, *v. t.* To express gratitude to for a favor.
Thănk′fŭl (139), *a.* Full of gratitude.
Thănk′fŭl-ly, *adv.* In a thankful manner; gratefully. [tude.
Thănk′fŭl-ness, *n.* Gratitude.
Thănk′less, *a.* Unthankful; ungrateful. [tude.
Thănk′less-ness, *n.* Ingratitude.
Thănks, *n. pl.* Expression of gratitude.
Thănks′gĭv-ing, *n.* Act of giving thanks ; a day for publicly expressing gratitude to God.
Thănk′-wor′thy (-wûr′thy),

a. Deserving thanks ; meritorious.
Thăt (122), *pron.* referring to something before mentioned or understood, or to something more remote ; the other; the former; who; which. — *conj.* introducing a cause or consequence.
Thătch, *n.* Straw for covering a roof. — *v. t.* .To cover with straw, reeds, or the like.
Thau′ma-tûr′gy, *n.* Act of performing something wonderful.
Thaw, *v. i.* or *t.* To melt as ice or snow. — *n.* The melting of ice or snow.
The (122), *definite article*, or *definitive a.* denoting a particular person or thing.
Thē′a-ter } (151), *n.* A play-
Thē′a-tre } house ; a place for dramatic exhibitions, &c. ; region of operations of an army ; a place of action or exhibition.
The-ăt′rĭc, } *a.* Pertaining
The-ăt′rĭc-al, } to, or suiting, a theater.
The-ăt′rĭc-al-ly, *adv.* In the manner of actors on the stage.
Thee, *pron.,* objective case singular of *Thou*.
Thĕft, *n.* A felonious taking of property ; act of stealing ; thing stolen. [ing to them.
Thēir (thâr), *a. pron.* Belonging.
Thēirs, *a. pron.* Of them.
Thē′ĭsm, *n.* [Gr. *Theos*, God.] Belief in a personal God.
Thē′ĭst, *n.* One who believes in a personal God.
The-ĭst′ic, } *a.* Pertaining
The-ĭst′ic-al, } to theism.
Thĕm, *pron.,* objective case of *They*.
Thēme, *n.* Subject or topic ; essay ; a radical verb.
Them-sĕlves′, *pron. ; pl.* of *Himself, Herself*, or *Itself*.
Thĕn, *adv.* At that time ; afterward ; therefore. — *conj.* In that case. [or time.
Thĕnce, *adv.* From that place
Thĕnce′fôrth, } *adv.*
Thĕnce-fôr′ward, } From that time onward.
The-ŏc′ra-cy (117), *n.* A government immediately directed by God.
Thē′o-crăt′ic-al, *a.* Pertaining to theocracy.
The-ŏd′o-līte, *n.* An instrument used in surveying.
Thē′o-lō′gĭ-an, } *n.* One
The-ŏl′o-ġĭst, } versed in theology ; a divine.

The′o-lŏġ′ic, *a.* Pertain-
The′o-lŏġ′ic-al, ing to
theology.
The-ŏl′o-ġīze, *v. t.* or *i.* To
render theological.
The-ŏl′o-ġy, *n.* The science
of God and divine things.
The-ŏr′bo, *n.* A musical instrument like a large lute.
The′o-rem, *n.* A statement
of a principle to be demonstrated.
The′o-rĕt′ic, *a.* Pertain-
The′o-rĕt′ic-al, ing to, or
depending on, theory; speculative; not practical.
The′o-rĕt′ic-al-ly, *adv.* In
theory. [theorizing.
The′o-rĭst, *n.* One given to
The′o-rīze, *v. i.* To form theo-
ries; to speculate.
The′o-ry (141), *n.* Speculation; scheme; science as distinct from art.
The-ŏs′o-phy, *n.* A direct as
distinguished from a revealed
knowledge of God.
Thĕr′a-peū′tic, *a.* Pertaining to the healing art; curative. [place.
Thĕre (thâr, 10), *adv.* In that
Thĕre′a-bout′, *adv.* Near
that place or number.
Thĕre-ăft′er, *adv.* After that.
Thĕre-ăt′, *adv.* At that place;
on that account.
Thĕre-by′, *adv.* By that; for
that cause.
There′fōre (thĕr′fōr or thâr′-
fọr), *adv.* For this or that
reason; consequently.
There-frŏm′, *adv.* From this
or that. [this.
Thĕre-ĭn′, *adv.* In that or
Thĕre′ĭn-tọ′, *adv.* Into that,
or that place.
Thĕrc-ŏf′ (-ŏff′ or -ŏv′), *adv.*
Of that or this. [this.
Thĕre-ŏn′, *adv.* On that or
Thĕre-tọ′, *adv.* To that
Thĕre′un-tọ′, or this.
Thĕre-ŭn′dẽr, *adv.* Under
that or this.
Thĕre′up-ŏn′, *adv.* Upon
that or this.
Thĕre-wĭth′ (-wĭth′ or -wĭth′),
adv. With that or this.
Thĕre′wĭth-ạl′, *adv.* Over
and above that.
Thŏr′mal, *a.* Warm; tepid.
Ther-mŏm′e-ter, *n.* [Gr.
thermē, heat, and *metron*,
measure.] An instrument for
measuring temperature.
Thŭr′mo-mĕt′ric-al, *a.* Per-
taining to a thermometer.
†**The-sạu′rus,** *n.* A treasury;
a storehouse of information.

Thĕşe, *pron.*; *pl.* of *This.*
†**Thē′sis,** *n.* (*pl.* Thē′sēs, 147),
A theme; an essay.
The′ur-ġy, *n.* Art of doing
supernatural things; magic.
They, *pron.*; *pl.* of *He, She,*
or *It.*
Thick, *a.* Not thin; dense;
close; gross. — *adv.* Close-
ly; in quick succession. — *n.*
The thickest part.
Thick′en (thĭk′n), *v. t.* or *i.*
To make or become thick.
Thick′et, *n.* A collection of
trees or shrubs closely set.
Thick′ish, *a.* Rather thick.
Thick′ly, *adv.* Closely;
densely; deeply.
Thick′ness, *n.* The state of
being thick; denseness.
Thick′-sĕt, *a.* Close planted;
having a short, thick body.
Thĭĕf (142), *n.* One who steals.
Thiēve, *v. i.* To steal or
practice theft; to pilfer.
Thiēv′er-y, *n.* The practice
of stealing; theft.
Thiēv′ish, *a.* Given to theft.
Thiēv′ish-ly, *adv.* By theft.
Thigh (thī), *n.* Part of the
leg above the knee.
Thĭlls, *n. pl.* Shafts of a
wagon or other carriage.
Thĭm′ble, *n.* A metal cap for
the finger in sewing.
Thĭn, *a.* Not thick; lean; slender; slight. — *v. t.* To make
thin or thinner; to dilute;
to attenuate; to rarefy.
Thīne, *a.* Belonging to thee.
Thing, *n.* An inanimate object; whatever exists; event
or action.
Think, *v. i.* or *t.* [*imp. & p.
p.* THOUGHT.] To have
ideas; to reflect; to meditate; to imagine; to judge.
Think′er, *n.* One who thinks.
Think′ing, *n.* Imagination;
judgment. — *a.* Having the
faculty of thought.
Thĭn′ly, *adv.* In a thin or
scattered manner.
Thĭn′ness, *n.* State of being
thin; slenderness; tenuity.
Third, *a.* Next after the second. — *n.* A third part; an
interval of three tones in
music; (*pl.*) the third part
of an estate, to which a widow
is entitled by law. [place.
Third′ly, *adv.* In the third
Thirst, *n.* Desire of drink;
eager desire; longing. — *v. i.*
To feel a want of drink; to
long. [ing thirsty.
Thirst′i-ness, *n.* State of be-
Thirst′y, *a.* Suffering from

the want of drink; dry;
parched; very desirous.
Thir′teen, *a.* Ten and three.
Thir′teenth, *a.* Ordinal of
thirteen; third after tenth.
Thir′ti-eth, *a.* Next after the
29th; being one of 30 equal
parts of a thing.
Thir′ty, *a.* Thrice ten.
Thĭs, *pron.* (*pl.* Thĕṣe.) Denoting something present or
near in place or time.
Thĭs′tle (thĭs′l), *n.* A prickly
plant of several genera.
Thĭth′er, *adv.* To that place,
point, or result
Thĭth′er-ward, *adv.* Toward
that place.
Thōle, *n.* A pin in the gun-
wale of a boat, to keep the
oar in place.
Thŏng, *n.* A strap of leather
for fastening any thing.
Tho-răç′ic, *a.* Pertaining to
the thorax, or chest. [chest.
†**Thō′răx,** *n.* Cavity of the
Thŏrn, *n.* A prickly tree or
shrub; a spine; a prickle.
Thŏrn′y, *a.* Full of thorns;
sharp; perplexing.
Thŏr′ough (thŭr′ō), *a.* Pass-
ing through; complete.
Thŏr′ough-fāre (thŭr′o-), *n.*
A passage quite through.
Thŏr′ough-ly (thŭr′o-), *adv.*
Completely.
Thŏr′ough-pāçed (thŭr′o-
pāst), *a.* Perfect in what is
undertaken; complete.
Thŏr′ough-wort (thŭr′o-
wûrt), *n.* A medicinal plant;
boneset.
Thōṣe, *pron.*; *pl.* of *That.*
Thou, *pron.* denoting the per-
son addressed.
Though (thō), *adv. & conj.*
Granting; admitting; allow-
ing; however.
Thought (thạwt), *imp. & p. p.*
of *Think.* — *n.* That which
the mind thinks; idea; con-
ception; reflection; notion.
Thought′fụl (thạwt′-), *a.*
Given to thought; contem-
plative; meditative.
Thought′fụl-ly (thạwt′-), *adv.*
With contemplation.
Thought′fụl-ness (thạwt′-), *n.*
State or quality of being
thoughtful.
Thought′less (thạwt′-), *a.* Un-
thinking; heedless; careless.
Thought′less-ly (thạwt′-),
adv. Without thought;
heedlessly; stupidly.
Thought′less-ness (thạwt′-),
n. Want of thought; heedlessness.

THOUSAND   304   TIER

Thou'sand, *a.* or *n.* Ten hundred. [thousand.
Thou'sandth, *a.* Ordinal of
Thrall'dom (131), *n.* Slavery; boudage;
Thrá/děm servitude.
Thrash, *v. t.* To beat out grain from; to beat soundly.
Thrash'er, *n.* One who thrashes grain; a large species of shark.
Thread, *n.* A small twist of silk, cotton, flax, &c.; a filament. — *v. t.* To put a thread in; to pass through.
Thread'bare, *a.* Worn out; common; trite; stale.
Threat, *n.* Denunciation of ill; menace.
Threat'en (thret'n), *v. t.* To alarm with the promise or prospect of evil; to menace.
Threat'en-ing, *a.* Indicating a threat or some danger; imminent; impending.
Three, *a.* or *n.* Two and one.
Three'fōld, *a.* Thrice repeated; consisting of three.
Three'pence (thrip'ens), *n.* A coin worth three pounies.
Three'pen-ny (thrip'en-nў), *a.* Worth three pence only; poor; mean. [ty; sixty.
Three'scōre, *a.* Thrice twenty.
Thresh, *v. t.* To thrash.
Thresh'ōld, *n.* The door sill; entrance; gate.
Threw (thrụ), *imp.* of *Throw.*
Thrice, *adv.* Three times.
Thrid, *v. t.* To slide or pass through; to thread.
Thrift, *n.* Wise management; economy; prosperity.
Thrift'i-ly, *adv.* With wise or successful economy.
Thrift'i-ness, *n.* Frugality; good husbandry.
Thrift'less, *a.* Extravagant; prodigal; profuse.
Thrift'y, *a.* Thriving by industry. — SYN. Frugal; careful; economical.
Thrill, *v. t.* To pierce. — *v. i.* To feel a sharp tiugling sensation. — *n.* A warbling; a shivering or sharp tiugling sensation.
Thrive, *v. i.* [*imp.* THRIVED; *p. p.* THRIVED, THRIVEN.] To prosper by industry; to flourish.
Thriv'ing (133), *a.* Flourishing; prosperous.
Throat (18), *n.* Fore part of the neck; something resembling the fore part of the neck.
Throb, *v. i.* To beat forcibly,

as the heart or pulse; to palpitate. — *n.* A strong pulsation. [guish; agony.
Throe, *n.* Extreme pain; anguish.
Thrōne, *n.* A royal seat; a chair of state; seat of a bishop. — *v. t.* To place on a throne.
Throng, *n.* [A.-S., fr. *thringan,* to press.] A crowd of people; a multitude. — *v. i.* or *t.* To crowd together.
Throt'tle, *n.* The windpipe. — *v. i.* or *t.* To choke.
Through (thrōō), *prep.* From end to end of; by means of. — *adv.* From one end or side to the other; to the end; to the ultimate purpose.
Through-out' (thrōō-out'), *prep.* Quite through. — *adv.* In every part.
Throve, *old imp.* of *Thrive.*
Throw, *v. t.* [*imp.* THREW; *p. p.* THROWN.] To fling; to cast; to toss; to hurl; to send; to turn; to twist. — *n.* A cast; a fall.
Throw'ster, *n.* One who throws or twists silk.
Thrum, *n.* End of a weaver's thread; coarse yarn. — *v. t.* To insert tufts in. — *v. i.* To play coarsely or rudely on an instrument.
Thrush, *n.* A singing bird; ulcers in the mouth.
Thrust, *v. t.* [*imp.* & *p. p.* THRUST.] To push or drive with force; to urge; to stab. — *n.* A violent push.
Thŭg, *n.* One of a religious association of robbers and assassins in India.
Thŭmb (thŭm), *n.* The short thick finger. — *v. t.* To handle awkwardly; to soil or wear with the thumb or the fingers.
Thŭmp, *v. t.* or *i.* To strike or beat with something thick or heavy. — *n.* A heavy, dull blow.
Thŭn'der, *n.* The sound which follows lightning. — *v. i.* To discharge electrical fluid with noise. [lightning.
Thŭn'der-bōlt, *n.* A shaft of
Thŭn'der-clăp, *n.* Sudden report of an explosion of electricity.
Thŭn'der-shōw'er, *n.* A shower accompanied with thunder. [ished; amazed.
Thŭn'der-strŭck, *a.* Astonished.
Thŭrs'day, *n.* The fifth day of the week. [this manner.
Thŭs (123, 124), *adv.* So; in

Thwăck, *v. t.* To beat; to bang. — *n.* A heavy blow; a thump.
Thwart, *v. t.* To cross; to oppose. — *a.* Being across.
Thỹ, *a.* Belonging to thee.
Thyme (tĭm, 97), *n.* A fragrant plant.
Thy-sĕlf', *pron.* An emphasized form of *Thou.*
Tī-ā'rä (140), *n.* A head-dress or diadem; the pope's triple crown.
Tĭb'i-al, *a.* Relating to the large bone of the leg.
Tick, *n.* Credit; an insect; a slight noise; a case for feathers. — *v. i.* To run upon credit; to make a small noise, as a watch.
Tick'en, *n.* Cloth for bedticks.
Tick'ing,
Tick'et, *n.* A piece of paper entitling to some right or privilege. — *v. t.* To mark or distinguish by a ticket.
Tick'le, *v. t.* To excite a peculiar thrilling sensation by the touch; to please. — *v. i.* To feel, or to excite, a thrilling sensation by the touch.
Tick'lish, *a.* Easily tickled; liable to totter and fall at the slightest touch.
Tīd'al, *a.* Relating to tides.
Tĭd'bĭt, *n.* A delicate piece of any thing eatable; a dainty.
Tīde, *n.* The ebb or flow of the waters of the ocean. — *v. t.* To drive with the tide or stream.
Tīdes'man (143), *n.* An officer who watches the landing of goods, to secure the payment of duties.
Tī'di-ly, *adv.* With neatness and simplicity.
Tī'di-ness (135), *n.* Neatness and simplicity.
Tī'dings, *n. pl.* News; intelligence; information.
Tī'dy, *a.* Neat and simple. — *n.* A pinafore; a cover for the back of a chair, &c.
Tie (134), *v. t.* To bind; to fasten. — *n.* A knot; an obligation; bond; restraint; equality, as of votes.
Tĭer, *n.* One of two or more rows, one above another.

Tiara.

ā, ē, ī, ō, ū, ў, *long;* ă, ĕ, ĭ, ŏ, ŭ, ў, *short;* câre, cär, ăsk, ạll, whạt; ẽre, veil, tẽrm; pïque, fïrm;

TIERCE 805 TITULAR

Tiẽrçe (*or* **tẽrss**), *n.* A cask or measure holding forty-two wine gallons.

Tiff, *n.* A small draught of liquor; a fit of anger.

Tif′fa-ny, *n.* A kind of very thin silk.

Ti′ger, *n.* An Asiatic beast of prey.

Tight (tit), *a.* [O. Eng. *tight*, tied, p. p. of *tie,* to bind.] Compact; close; tense; parsimonious; intoxicated.

Tight′en (tīt′n), *v. t.* To make tight or more tight.

Tight′ly (-tĭt′-), *adv.* Closely; compactly.

Tight′ness (tĭt′-), *n.* Quality of being tight; compactness.

Ti′gress, *n.* A female tiger.

Tike, *n.* A clown; a dog.

Til′bu-ry, *n.* A kind of gig without a top.

Tile, *n.* A thin piece of baked clay for covering buildings, for floors, &c.; a hat. — *v. t.* To cover with tiles.

Till, *n.* A money box in a shop. — *prep.* Up to the time of; until. — *v. t.* To plow and dress, as land; to cultivate.

Till′a-ble, *a.* Capable of being tilled.

Till′age, *n.* Culture of land.

Till′er, *n.* Handle of a rudder; a husbandman; sprout from a root or stump. — *v. i.* To put forth sprouts from the root or stump.

Tilt, *n.* A tent or awning; a thrust; a military exercise; a large hammer; inclination forward. — *v. t.* To incline; to thrust, as a lance; to hammer or forge. — *v. i.* To thrust with a lance; to fight; to lean or fall.

Tilt′-hăm′mer, *n.* A heavy hammer in iron works.

Tim′ber, *n.* Wood for building, for tools, furniture, &c.; a beam. — *v. t.* To furnish with timber.

Tim′brel, *n.* A kind of drum.

Time, *n.* A particular part of duration; season; age; period; the present life; repetition; measure of sound. — *v. t.* To adapt to the occasion; to mark the time of.

Time′-keep′er, *n.* A clock or watch; a time-piece.

Time′less, *a.* Untimely; unseasonable.

Time′ly, *a.* In good time; seasonable. — *adv.* Early; in good time.

Time′-piẽçe, *n.* A clock or watch; a time-keeper.

Time′-sẽrv′er, *n.* One who complies with the times; a temporizer; a trimmer.

Time′-sẽrv′ing, *a.* Obsequiously complying with prevailing opinions; temporizing.

Time′-wōrn, *a.* Worn by long use.

Tim′id, *a.* Wanting courage. — SYN. Fearful; timorous; cowardly; pusillanimous.

Ti-mĭd′i-ty, } *n.* Want of
Tim′id-ness, } courage.

Tim′id-ly, *adv.* In a timid manner; without courage.

Tim′o-roŭs, *a.* Fearful; timid.

Tim′o-roŭs-ly, *adv.* With fear.

Tin, *n.* A soft white metal; a thin plate of iron covered with tin; (*colloq.*) cash. — *v. t.* To cover with tin.

Tĭne′al, *n.* Crude borax.

Tĭnçt′ūre, *n.* Spirituous solution of a substance; tinge or shade of color; slight taste superadded. — *v. t.* To tinge; to imbue.

Tin′der, *n.* Something very inflammable, for kindling fire from a spark. [der.

Tin′der-bŏx, *n.* A box for tinder.

Tine, *n.* A tooth or prong.

Tin′-foil, *n.* Tin reduced to a thin leaf.

Ting, *v. i.* To sound, as a bell; to tinkle.

Tinge (133), *n.* A color; dye; tincture; slight taste. — *v. t.* To color; to dye; to stain; to imbue.

Tin′gle (ting′gl), *v. i.* To feel a sharp thrilling or pricking sensation.

Tink′er, *n.* One who mends vessels of metal. — *v.* To mend, as metal wares.

Tink′le, *v. i.* To make small, quick, sharp sounds, as by striking on metal.

Tink′ling, *n.* A small, quick, sharp metallic sound.

Tin′man, } *n.* One who deals
Tin′ner, } in tin. [tin.

Tin′ny, *a.* Relating to, or like,

Tin′sel (130), *n.* [Fr. *étincelle*, a spark, from Lat. *scintilla*.] A shining material, more gay than valuable. — *a.* Gaudy; showy to excess. — *v. t.* (130) To adorn with tinsel.

Tint. *n.* A slight coloring. — *v. t.* To give a slight coloring to; to tinge.

Ti′ny, *a.* Very small; minute.

Tip, *n.* The end; the point. — *v. t.* To form a point upon; to lower one end of, as of a cart. [for the neck.

Tip′pet, *n.* A covering of fur

Tip′ple, *v. i.* To drink strong liquors habitually.

Tip′pler, *n.* An habitual drinker of strong liquors.

Tip′stăff, *n.* A constable.

Tip′sy, *a.* Partially intoxicated; half drunk.

Tip′tŏe, *n.* The tip or end of the toe.

Ti-rāde′, *n.* A strain or flight of violent invective or declamation.

Tīre, *n.* A row or rank; a band of iron for a wheel. — *v. t.* or *i.* To weary or become weary.

Tīred, *a.* Fatigued; weary.

Tīre′sŏme, *a.* Tedious; fatiguing; wearisome. [ness.

Tīre′sŏme-ness, *n.* Tediousness.

Tĭs′sue (tĭsh′shụ), *n.* Cloth interwoven with gold or silver; union or texture of anatomical elements; a connected series. [mouse.

Tit, *n.* A small horse; a titmouse.

Tĭt′bĭt, *n.* See *Tidbit.*

Tīth′a-ble, *a.* Subject to the payment of tithes.

Tīthe, *n.* Tenth of any thing. — *v. t.* To tax to the amount of a tenth.

Tīth′ing-măn (143), *n.* A parish officer; a kind of constable.

Tĭt′il-lāte, *v. t.* To tickle.

Tĭt′il-lā′tion, *n.* Act of tickling; any slight pleasure.

Tī′tle, *n.* An inscription; right; appellation of honor. — *v. t.* To name; to call; to entitle. [ble.

Tī′tled, *a.* Having a title; noble.

Tī′tle-pāge, *n.* The page of a book which contains its title.

Tĭt′mouse 143), *n.* A small perching bird.

Tĭt′ter, *v. i.* To laugh with the tongue against the upper teeth, or with restraint.

Tĭt′ter, } *n.* A restrained
Tĭt′ter-ing, } laugh.

Tĭt′tle, *n.* A minute part; a point; a dot; a jot.

Tĭt′tle-tăt′tle, *n.* Idle, trifling talk; an idle talker.

Tĭt′u-lar, *a.* Existing in name only; nominal. — *n.* One invested with a title.

---

a͝n, ôr, dọ, wọlf, tụ̄o, tŏŏk; ûrn, rụe, pụll; ç, ġ, *soft;* c, ḡ, *hard;* a̤; e̤xist; ṇ *as* ng; this.

Tit'u-lar-ly, *adv.* Nominally.
Tit'u-la-ry, *a.* Pertaining to, or consisting in, a title; nominal.
To, *prep.* Indicating approach and arrival, or motion, course, or tendency.
Toad (18), *n.* A small well-known reptile.
Toad'stool, *n.* A fungous plant; a mushroom.
Toast, *v. t.* To dry and scorch at the fire; to drink to the health or in honor of. — *n.* Bread dried and scorched; a name or sentiment, &c., honored by drinking.
To-băc'co, *n.* A plant used for smoking and chewing.
To-băc'co-nist, *n.* A dealer in, or a manufacturer of, tobacco.
Tŏc'sin, *n.* [Fr., from O. Fr. *toquer*, to touch, strike, and *sein*, a bell.] An alarm-bell.
Tŏd, *n.* Twenty-eight pounds.
To-dāy', *n.* This present day. — *adv.* On this day.
Tŏd'dle, *v. i.* To walk with short steps, as a child.
Tŏd'dy, *n.* A mixture of spirit and water sweetened.
Toe (133, 140), *n.* One of the extremities of the foot. — *v. t.* (133) To touch with the toes.
To-gĕth'er, *adv.* In the same place or time; in company.
Tŏg'gle-joint, *n.* An elbow or knee joint.
Toil, *v. i.* To work hard. — *n.* (126) Hard labor; a net or snare.
Toi'let, *n.* A dressing-table; dress; attire.
Toil'some, *a.* Laborious; wearisome.
Toil'some-ness, *n.* Laboriousness.
To-kāy', *n.* Wine made at Tokay, in Hungary.
Tō'ken (tō'kn), *n.* Something intended to represent another thing. — SYN. Sign; note; symbol; badge.
Tōld, *imp. & p. p.* of *Tell.*
Tōle, *v. t.* To allure by bait.
Tŏl'er-a-ble, *a.* Capable of being endured; passable.
Tŏl'er-a-bly, *adv.* Moderately well; passably.
Tŏl'er-ance, *n.* Act of enduring; toleration.
Tŏl'er-ant, *a.* Inclined to tolerate; indulgent.
Tŏl'er-āte, *v. t.* To allow by not hindering; to suffer.
Tŏl'er-ā'tion, *n.* Act of tolerating; sufferance.

Tōll (123), *n.* A tax for some liberty or privilege; a miller's portion of grain for grinding; sound of a bell rung slowly. — *v. i.* or *t.* To ring with slow and uniform strokes.
Tōll'-brĭdge, *n.* A bridge where toll is paid for passing.
Tōll'-gāte, *n.* A gate where toll is paid. [takes toll.
Tōll'-găth'er-er, *n.* One who
Tōll'-house, *n.* A house where toll is taken.
Tŏm'a-hăwk, *n.* An Indian war-hatchet. — *v. t.* To cut or kill with a tomahawk.
To-mā'to, or To-mä'to (*pl.* To-ma'toes, -mā'- or -mä'-, 140), *n.* A garden-plant and its fruit.
Tomb (tōōm), *n.* A grave; a vault for the dead.
Tŏm'boy, *n.* A romping girl.
Tomb'stŏne (tōōm'stōn), *n.* A stone at a grave. [ume.
Tōme, *n.* A ponderous vol-
To-mŏr'rŏw, *n.* Day after the present. — *adv.* On the day after this.
Tŏm'tit, *n.* The titmouse.
Tŏn, *n.* Prevailing fashion.
Tŏn (tŭn), *n.* Weight of 2000 gross, or 2240 pounds; 40 cubic feet.
Tōne, *n.* Sound or character of a sound; inflection; whine; strength; vigor; spirit. — *v. t.* To utter with a kind of whine; to tune.
Tŏngs, *n. pl.* Instrument to handle fire or heated metals, and for other purposes.
Tŏngue (tŭng), *n.* The organ of taste and speech, or something resembling it; a language; speech.
Tŏngue'-tied, *a.* Unable to speak freely.
Tŏn'ic, *a.* Increasing strength; relating to tones or sounds. — *n.* A medicine that increases the strength.
To-night' (-nīt'), *n.* This very night. — *adv.* On this very night.
Tŏn'nage (tŭn'ej), *n.* Amount of tons carried in a vessel; duty by the ton.
Tŏn'sil, *n.* One of two glands in the throat.
Tŏn'sure (-shyr), *n.* Act of shaving the crown of the head; state of being shorn.
Ton-tīne' (-teen'), *n.* An annuity or survivorship.
Tōō, *adv.* Over; more than enough; also.
Tōōk, *imp.* of *Take.*

Tool, *n.* An instrument of manual operation; a hireling.
Tōōt, *v. i.* To make a peculiar sound.
Tōōth (143), *n.* A small bone attached to the jaw for chewing; a tine or prong. — *v. t.* To indent; to furnish with teeth. [the teeth.
Tōōth'āche (-āk), *n.* A pain in
Tōōth'-ĕdge, *n.* Sensation excited by grating sounds, and by the touch of keen acids.
Tōōth'less, *a.* Wanting teeth.
Tōōth'-pĭck, *n.* An instrument for cleaning the teeth.
Tōōth'sŏme, *a.* Pleasing to the taste; palatable.
Tŏp, *n.* The highest part; platform round the head of the lower mast; a toy. — *v. i.* or *t.* To tip; to cap; to rise above or aloft; to excel.
To'pärch, *n.* The principal man in a place.
Tō'păz, *n.* A precious stone of a yellowish color.
Tōpe, *v. i.* To drink to excess.
Tō'per, *n.* One who drinks to excess; a drunkard; a sot.
Tŏ'phet, *n.* Hell.
Tŏp'ic, *n.* Subject of discourse; a matter treated of.
Tŏp'ic-al, *a.* Pertaining to a place; limited; local.
Tŏp'ic-al-ly, *adv.* In a topical manner.
Tŏp'-knŏt (-nŏt), *n.* An ornamental bow worn by women on the head.
Tŏp'măst, *n.* The mast next above the lower mast.
Tŏp'mŏst, *a.* Uppermost; highest. [on topography.
To-pŏg'ra-pher, *n.* A writer
Tŏp'o-grăph'ic, *a.* De-
Tŏp'o-grăph'ic-al, scriptive of a place.
To-pŏg'ra-phy, *n.* Minute delineation and description of any place or region.
Tŏp'ping, *a.* Rising above; surpassing; proud.
Tŏp'ple, *v. i.* To fall or pitch forward; to tumble down.
Tŏp'sy-tûr'vy, *a.* With the head downward; upside down.
Tōrch, *n.* A light made of some combustible substance; a flambeau.

TORCH-LIGHT 307 TRADE

Tôrch'-light (-lĭt), n. Light of a torch, or of torches.
Tōre, imp. of *Tear*.
Tôr'ment, n. Extreme pain.
Tor-mĕnt', v. t. To put to extreme pain, or anguish.
Tor-mĕnt'er, } n. One who
Tor-mĕnt'or, } torments.
Tôrn, p. p. of *Tear*.
Tor-nā'do, n. A violent gust of wind; a hurricane.
Tor-pē'do, n. A fish having electric power; an engine for blowing up ships; a small explosive firework.
Tôr'pid, a. Having lost motion or the power of feeling. — SYN. Numb; dull; sluggish; inactive.
Tor-pĭd'i-ty, } n. Numbness;
Tôr'pid-ness, } insensibility; dullness; sluggishness; inactivity.
Tôr'por, n. Numbness; dullness; sluggishness.
Tôr're-fāc'tion, n. The act of roasting or scorching.
Tôr're-fȳ, v. t. To parch; to roast; to scorch.
Tôr'rent, n. A violent stream
Tôr'rid, a. Burning; violently hot; parched.
Tôr'sion, n. Act of twisting; force with which a thing untwists.
Tôrt, n. Wrong; injury done.
Tôr'tious (tôr'shus), a. Done by wrong; injurious.
Tôr'toise (tôr'tis, 35), n. [From Lat. *tor- t u s*, twisted, crooked,— from its crooked feet.] A reptile inclosed in a hard, scaly case. Tortoise.
Tôrt'u-oŭs, a. Twisted; wreathed; winding; deceitful.
Tôrt'ūre, n. Extreme pain; anguish of body or mind; torment. — v. t. To inflict extreme pain upon; to torment.
Tō'ry, n. An advocate for royal power; a conservative.
Tō'ry-ĭṣm, n. The principles of Tories.
Tŏss, v. t. To throw with the hand; to throw upward, or with a jerk. — v. i. To roll and tumble; to writhe. — n. Act of tossing.
Tō'tal, a. Whole; complete; entire. — n. The whole sum or amount.
To-tăl'i-ty, n. The whole sum, quantity, or amount.

Tō'tal-ly, adv. Wholly; completely; entirely.
Tōte, v. t. To carry or bear. [*Southern States*.]
Tŏt'ter, v. i. To shake so as to threaten to fall; to vacillate.
Tŏt'tle, v. i. To toddle.
Toŭch, v. t. To come in contact with; to reach to; to feel; to affect; to treat slightly. — n. Contact; sense of feeling; feature.
Toŭch'i-ness, n. Peevishness.
Toŭch'ing, a. Adapted to affect the feelings.
Toŭch'ing-ly, adv. Pathetically.
Toŭch'-me-nŏt', n. A plant.
Toŭch'-stōne, n. A stone used to ascertain the purity of gold or silver by the streak it leaves on it; any criterion or test.
Toŭch'-wŏŏd, n. Decayed wood that easily takes fire.
Toŭch'y, a. Peevish; irritable; irascible.
Toŭgh (tŭf), a. Flexible but not brittle; firm; strong; stiff; severe; violent.
Toŭgh'en (tŭf'n), v. t. To make tough. — v. i. To grow tough or tougher.
Toŭgh'ly (tŭf'-), adv. In a tough manner.
Toŭgh'ness (tŭf'-), n. Flexibility with firmness of cohesion; tenacity.
Tou-pee', n. A small wig.
Toûr (tōōr), n. A journey in a circuit; turn of duty. — SYN. Circuit; excursion; jaunt; journey
Toûr'ist (tōōr'ist), n. One who makes a tour.
Toûr'na-ment (tûr'-), n. A mock-fight or martial sport on horseback.
Toûr'ni-quet (-kĕt), n. A surgical bandage which is tightened by a screw.
Toŭse, v. t. To pull and haul.
Tōw, n. Coarse and broken part of flax or hemp. — v. t. To draw through the water by a rope.
Tōw'age, n. Act of towing; price for towing.
Tō'ward (tō'ard), } prep. In
Tō'wards (tō'ardz), } the direction of; with respect to; near by.
Tō'ward, a. Ready to do or learn; apt; docile; teachable; tractable.
Tō'ward-ly, a. Ready to learn or to do; tractable.
Tow'el, n. A cloth for wiping

the hands, and for other purposes.
Tow'er, n. A high edifice; a citadel. — v. i. To be lofty; to soar aloft.
Tow'er-ing, a. Very high; elevated; soaring.
Tōw'-līne, } n. A rope used
Tōw'-rōpe, } for towing a ship, &c.
Town, n. A large collection of houses; the inhabitants.
Town'ship, n. Territory or district of a town.
Towns'man (143), n. One of the same town.
Town'-talk (-tawk), n. Common talk of a place.
Tŏx'i-cŏl'o-ġy, n. The science which treats of poisons.
Toy, n. A plaything; a trifle; folly; sport. — v. t. To dally amorously; to trifle.
Toy'ish, a. Given to dallying.
Toy'man (143), n. One who deals in toys.
Toy'-shŏp, n. A shop where toys are sold.
Trāçe, n. A footprint; a track; a vestige; mark; token; (pl.) the straps of a harness for drawing. — v. t. To delineate by marks; to follow by footprints or some other mark.
Trāçe'a-ble (133), a. Capable of being traced.
Trā'çer-y, n. Ornamental work in architecture.
†Trā'che-à, n. The windpipe.
Trăck (127), n. A footstep; mark left by something passing; path; road, as of a railway. — v. t. To follow by traces.
Trăck'less, a. Having no track; untrodden.
Trăct, n. Region of indefinite extent; a short treatise, esp. one on practical religion.
Trăct'a-ble, a. Easily managed; docile.
Trăct'a-bĭl'i-ty, } n. State
Trăct'a-ble-ness, } or quality of being manageable.
Trăct'a-bly, adv. With ready compliance.
Trăc'tate, n. A treatise.
Trăct'īle, a. Capable of being drawn out in length; ductile.
Trac-tĭl'i-ty, n. Capacity of being drawn out in length.
Trăc'tion, n. Act of drawing.
Trăc'tive, a. Serving to draw; attracting.
Trāde, n. Commerce; traffic; business; calling; occupation; men of the same occu-

sŏn, ôr, dǫ, wǫlf, tōō, tŏŏk; ûrn, rṳe, pṳll; ç, ġ, soft; c, g, hard; aş; exist; ṉ as ng; this.

pation.— *v. i.* To buy or sell; to traffic; to deal. [trade.
Trād'er, *n.* One engaged in
Trādes'man (143), *n.* A shop-keeper.
Trāde'-wind, *n.* A periodical wind in or near the torrid zone.
Tra di'tion (-dĭsh'un), *n.* Delivery; oral account transmitted from father to son.
Tra-di'tion-al (-dĭsh'un-), **Tra-di'tion-a-ry** *a.* Delivered or communicated by tradition.
Tra-di'tion-al-ly (-dĭsh'un-), *adv.* By tradition.
Tra-dūce', *v. t.* To defame; to slander; to vilify; to calumniate.
Tra-dū'cer, *n.* One who traduces; a calumniator.
Tra-dūc'tion, *n.* Derivation; transportation.
Tra-dūc'tive, *a.* Capable of being deduced.
Trāf'fic (128), *n.* Dealing for purposes of any kind.— SYN. Commerce; trade; barter. — *v. i.* (128) To buy and sell; to barter; to trade.
Trāf'fick-er (128), *n.* A trader.
Tra-gē'di-an, *n.* An actor or a writer of tragedies.
Trăg'e-dy, *n.* A dramatic poem representing some action having a fatal issue; a fatal and mournful event.
Trăg'ic, *a.* Relating to tragedy; fatal; **Trăg'ic-al,** calamitous; mournful.
Trăg'ic-al-ly, *adv.* With a fatal event; mournfully.
Trăg'i-cŏm'e-dy, *n.* A composition partaking of the nature both of tragedy and comedy.
Trăg'i-cŏm'ic, *a.* Partaking **Trăg'i-cŏm'ic-al,** of a mixture of grave and comic scenes.
Trāil, *v. t. or i.* To draw along the ground. — *n.* Scent left on the ground; a track; any thing drawn along.
Trāin, *v. t.* To draw along; to trail; to allure; to exercise; to discipline; to educate, or bring up. — *n.* Something drawn along; trail; tail; retinue; procession; line, as of cars; series; process. [being trained.
Trāin'a-ble, *a.* Capable of
Trāin'-bănds, *n. pl.* Militia.
Trāin'-bēar'er, *n.* One who holds up a train.
Trāin'-oil, *n.* Oil obtained from the blubber or fat of whales by boiling.
Trāipse, *v. i.* To walk sluttishly or carelessly.
Trāit, *n.* A stroke; a marked feature or peculiarity.
Trāi'tor, *n.* One who violates his allegiance or his trust; one guilty of treason.
Trāi'tor-oŭs, *a.* Treacherous; guilty of treason; faithless; disloyal. [tor.
Trāi'tress, *n.* A female traitor
Tra-jĕct', *v. t.* To throw or cast through.
Tra-jĕc'tion, *n.* A throwing or casting through or across.
Tra-jĕct'o-ry, *n.* A curve which a moving body describes in space.
Trăl'a-tĭ'tioŭs (-tĭsh'us), *a.* Metaphorical; figurative.
Trăm, *n.* A coal-wagon, or one of the rails on which it runs.
Trăm'mel, *n.* A shackle; a hook.— *v. t.* (130) To catch; to shackle; to confine; to hamper.
Tra-mŏn'tane, or **Trăm'on-tăne,** *a.* Lying or being beyond the mountain; foreign; barbarous.
Trămp, *v. t. or i.* To tread; to travel. — *n.* A foot-traveler; a tramper.
Trămp'er, *n.* One who tramps; a vagrant. [foot.
Trăm'ple, *v. t.* To tread under
Trănce, *n.* [From Lat *transitus*, a passage, fr. *transire*, to pass over.] A state of insensibility; catalepsy; ecstasy.
Trăn'quil (trănk'wil), *a.* Quiet; calm; peaceful; undisturbed.
Trăn'quil-īze, (129), *v. t.* To **Trăn'quil-lize,** quiet; to render calm; to allay.
Tran-quil'li-ty (129), *n.* Quietness; a calm state.
Trăn'quil-ly, *adv.* Peacefully; quietly; calmly.
Trans-ăct', *v. t.* To do; to perform: to conduct.
Trans-ăc'tion, *n.* Performance: management; act or affair. [transacts.
Trans-ăct'or, *n.* One who
Trans-ăl'pine, *a.* Being beyond the Alps in regard to Rome.
Trăns'at-lăn'tic, *a.* Being beyond, or on the other side of, the Atlantic.
Tran-scĕnd', *v. t.* To go beyond; to surpass; to exceed; to outdo; to excel.
Tran-scĕnd'ençe, *n.* State **Tran-scĕnd'en-çy,** of being transcendent; supereminent.
Tran-scĕnd'ent. *a.* Surpassing; pre-eminent.
Tran-scĕnd-ĕnt'al, *a.* Supereminent: surpassing others; vague and illusive.
Tran-scĕnd'ent-ly, *adv.* Supereminently; most excellently.
Tran-scrībe', *v. t.* To copy; to write over again, or in the same words.
Tran-scrīb'er, *n.* One who transcribes or copies.
Trăn'script, *n.* A copy from an original.
Tran-scrĭp'tion, *n.* Act of transcribing, or copying.
Trăn'sept, *n.* Part of a church at right angles to the body.
Trans-fẽr', *v. t.* To convey from one place or person to another; to sell; to alienate.
Trăns'fer, *n.* Conveyance to another; removal.
Trans-fẽr'a-ble, *a.* Capable of being transferred.
Trăns'fer-ençe, *n.* Act of **Trăns-fẽr'rençe,** transferring; transfer.
Trans-fẽr'rer, *n.* One who transfers.
Trans-fẽr'ri-ble, *a.* Capable of being transferred.
Trans-fĭg'u-rā'tion, *n.* A change of form or appearance.
Trans-fĭg'ūre, *v. t.* To change the outward form or appearance of. [through.
Trans-fĭx', *v. t.* To pierce
Trans-fôrm', *v. t.* To change the form or appearance of; to metamorphose.
Trăns'for-mā'tion, *n.* Metamorphosis; change of form.
Trans-fūse', *v. t.* To pour out of one into another.
Trans-fū'sion, *n.* Act of pouring from one vessel into another.
Trans-grĕss', *v. t.* To overpass, as a rule; to break; to violate. — *v. i.* To sin.
Trans-grĕs'sion (-grĕsh'un), *n.* Violation of a law: sin.
Trans-grĕss'ive, *a.* Disposed to transgress.
Trans-grĕss'or, *n.* One who transgresses, or breaks a law; a sinner.
Trăn'sient (-shent), *a.* Passing; hasty; not permanent or stationary.

Trăn'sient-ly, *adv.* For a short time.

Trăn'sient-ness, *n.* State of being transient.

Trăn'sit, *n.* A passing, as of goods through a country, or as a planet over the sun's disk; a line of passage.

Tran-sĭ'tion (-sĭzh'un *or* -zĭsh'un, 104), *n.* Passage from one place or state to another; change.

Tran-sĭ'tion-al (-sĭzh'un- *or* -zĭsh'un-), *a.* Involving, or denoting, transition.

Trăn'si-tive, *a.* Expressing action passing from an agent to an object.

Trăn'si-to-ry, *a.* Continuing but a short time; fleeting; transient.

Trans-lāt'a-ble, *a.* Capable of being translated.

Trans-lāte', *v. t.* To remove from one place to another; to render into another language; to interpret; to explain in other words.

Trans-lā'tion. *n.* Act of translating; that which is translated; a version.

Trans-lā'tor, *n.* One who translates.

Trans-lū'çent, *a.* Transmitting rays of light, but not transparent.

Trăns'ma-rine', *a.* Lying beyond the sea.

Trăns'mi-grant, *a.* Migratory.

Trăns'mi-grāte, *v. i.* To pass from one country or body to another; to migrate.

Trăns'mi-grā'tion, *n.* A passing from one country or body to another.

Trans-mĭs'si-ble, *a.* Capable of being transmitted.

Trans-mĭs'sion (-mĭsh'un), *n.* Act of transmitting; state of being transmitted.

Trans-mĭs'sive, *a.* Capable of being transmitted.

Trans-mĭt', *v. t.* [Lat. *transmittere*, fr. *trans*, across, over, and *mittere*, to send] To send from one person or place to another. [sion.

Trans-mĭt'tal, *n.* Transmission.

Trans-mū'ta-ble, *a.* Capable of being transmuted.

Trăns'mu-tā'tion, *n.* Change into another substance, nature, or form.

Trans-mūte', *v. t.* To change into another substance, nature, or form; to transform.

Trăn'som, *n.* A cross-beam; a lintel.

Trans-pâr'en-çy, *n.* Quality of being transparent.

Trans-pâr'ent, *a.* Transmitting rays of light, so that bodies can be distinctly seen; clear; pellucid. [rent.

Tran-spĭç'u-oŭs, *a.* Transparent.

Trans-pĭërçe', *v. t.* To pierce through.

Trăn'spi-rā'tion. *n.* Act of passing through pores.

Tran-spire', *v. t.* or *i.* To emit in vapor; to become publicly known.

Trans-plănt', *v. t.* To remove and plant in another place.

Trăns'plan-tā'tion, *n.* Act of planting in another place.

Trans-plănt'er, *n.* One who transplants.

Trăns'pŏrt, *n.* A ship for transportation; passion; ecstasy; rapture.

Trans-pŏrt', *v. t.* To convey; to remove ; to carry into banishment; to ravish with pleasure.

Trans-pŏrt'a-ble, *a.* Capable of being transported.

Trăns'pŏr-tā'tion, *n.* Act of transporting; banishment.

Trans-pŏṣ'al, *n.* Act of transposing.

Trans-pōṣe', *v. t.* To put each in place of the other.

Trăns'po-ṣĭ'tion (-zĭsh'un), *n.* Mutual change of places.

Trans-shĭp', *v. t.* To transfer from one ship or conveyance to another.

Trăn'sub-stăn'ti-āte (-stăn'-shi-), *v. t.* To change into another substance.

Trăn'sub-stăn'ti-ā'tion (-shĭ-ā'-), *n.* A supposed change of the bread and wine, in the eucharist, into the real body and blood of Christ.

Tran-sūde', *v. t.* To pass out through the pores, as sweat.

Trans-vêr'sal, *a.* Running or lying across.

Trăns'verse, *n.* The longer axis of an ellipse.

Trans-vêrse', *a.* Lying in a cross direction.

Trans-vêrse'ly, *adv.* In a cross direction.

Trăp, *n.* A contrivance for catching animals; a snare; a heavy igneous rock. — *v. t.* or *i.* To catch in a trap; to insnare.

Tra-păn', *v. t.* To trap; to insnare. — *n.* A snare.

Trăp'-dōor, *n.* A door in a floor or roof.

Tra-pē'zi-um, *n.* A plane figure contained under four right lines, of which no two are parallel to each other. Trapezium.

Trăp'e-zoid, *n.* A plane, four-sided figure, having two of the opposite sides parallel to each other. Trapezoid.

Trăp'pings, *n. pl.* Ornaments; horse furniture.

Trăsh, *n.* Any waste or worthless matter.

Trăsh'y, *a.* Waste; worthless.

Trăv'ail, *v. i.* To toil; to suffer the pains of childbirth. — *n.* Toil; labor in childbirth.

Trăv'el (130), *v. i.* To make a journey or voyage; to go. — *n.* A journey or voyage.

Trăv'el-er | (130), *n.* One who
Trăv'el-ler | travels.

Trăv'ers-a-ble, *a.* Capable of being traversed.

Trăv'erse. *a.* Lying across. — *v. t.* To cross; to wander over; to thwart; to deny. — *n.* A barrier or obstruction; a denial.

Trăv'es-ty, *n.* A parody. — *v. t.* To translate so as to turn to ridicule; to parody.

Trāy, *n.* A waiter or salver; a small trough.

Trēach'er-oŭs, *a.* Faithless; false; perfidious.

Trēach'er-oŭs-ly, *adv.* Faithlessly.

Trēach'er-y, *n.* Violation of allegiance or faith : perfidy.

Trēa'cle, *n.* A thick sirup produced in refining sugar; molasses.

Trēad, *v. i.* [*imp.* TROD; *p. p.* TROD, TRODDEN.] To step; to set the foot; to walk. — *v. t.* To step or walk on; to trample. — *n.* Manner of stepping.

Trēad'le, | *n.* The part of a
Trēd'dle, | loom, &c., which is moved by the foot.

Trēad'-mill, *n.* A mill worked by persons treading on a wide horizontal wheel.

Trēa'ṣon, *n.* Violation of allegiance : disloyalty.

Trēa'ṣon-a-ble, *a.* Partaking of treason; traitorous.

Trēaṣ'ūre (trĕzh'ụr), *n.* Wealth accumulated; great abundance; that which is

highly valued. — v. t. To lay up; to hoard.

Treas′ur-er (trĕzh′yr-), n. An officer who has charge of a treasury or of treasure.

Treas′ur-y (trĕzh′yr-), n. A place where public money is kept; financial department of a government.

Treat, v. t. or i. [Fr. traiter, from Lat. tractare, to handle, treat.] To handle; to use; to manage; to negotiate; to entertain. — n. Entertainment given.

Trea′tise (140), n. A written discourse; a dissertation.

Treat′ment, n. Manner of treating; usage; management.

Trea′ty (141), n. A formal agreement between two or more independent states or sovereigns. — SYN. Negotiation; compact.

Treb′le, a. Threefold; triple; acute. — v. t. or i. To make or become threefold. — n. Highest part in music; soprano.

Treb′ly, adv. In a threefold number or quantity.

Tree (140), n. The largest of the vegetable kind; a perennial plant consisting of a trunk, roots, and branches.

Tree′nail (commonly pron. trŭn′nel). n. A long wooden pin to fasten the planks of a ship.

Tre′foil, n. A three-leaved plant of many species; an architectural ornament of three cusps in a circle. [port trees, &c.

Trefoils.

Trel′lage, n. Railwork to support

Trel′lis, n. A frame of crossbarred work, or lattice-work, used for various purposes.

Trem′ble, v. i. To shake or quake; to quiver; to shudder; to quaver

Tre-men′dous, a. Terrible; awful; frightful; dreadful.

Tre-men′dous-ly, adv. In a manner to awaken terror.

Tre′mor, or **Trem′or,** n. An involuntary trembling.

Trem′u-lous, a. Slightly trembling; shaking; quivering.

Trem′u-lous-ness, n. State of being tremulous.

Trench, v. t. To cut or dig, as a ditch. — v. i. To encroach. — n. A ditch; a fosse.

Trench′ant, a. Cutting; sharp; severe; unsparing.

Trench′er, n. One who digs a trench; a wooden plate.

Trench′er-man (143), n. A great eater; a gormandizer.

Trend, v. i. To run; to tend. — n. Inclination; bend; direction.

Tre-pan′, n. A cylindrical saw for perforating the skull. — v. t. To cut with a trepan, as the skull.

Tre-phine′, or **Tre-phīne′,** n. A circular or cylindrical saw for trepanning.

Trep′i-dā′tion, n. A trembling; a state of terror.

Tres′pass, v. i. To intrude; to transgress; to offend. — n. Violation of another's rights; voluntary transgression.

Tres′pass-er, n. One who trespasses; a sinner.

Tress, n. A braid, knot, or curl of hair; a ringlet.

Tres′tle (trĕs′l), n. A frame to support any thing.

Tret, n. An allowance for waste, after tare is deducted.

Trev′et, n. A three-legged stool. [or dice.

Trey, n. The three at cards

Trī′a-ble, a. Capable of being tried.

Trī′ad, n. A union of three; three things united.

Trī′al, n. Act of trying; examination; experiment; test.

Trī′an-gle, n. A figure of three angles and three sides.

Triangles.

Trī-an′gu-lar, a. Having three angles.

Tribe, n. 1, equilateral triangle; 2, isosceles triangle; 3, right-angled triangle; 4, obtuse-angled triangle; 5, scalene triangle. 1, 2, and 3, are also acute-angled triangles. A family or race; a class or division.

Trib′let, n. A tool for making rings; a steel cylinder, used in making tubes. [fliction.

Trib-u-lā′tion, n. A great af-

Tri-bū′nal, n. A court of justice. [tribunes.

Trib′u-na-ry, a. Pertaining to

Trib′ūne, n An ancient Roman magistrate; a kind of pulpit for a speaker.

Trib-u-nī′tial (-nĭsh′al), a.

Relating to, or suiting a tribune.

Trib′u-ta-ry, a. Subject to tribute; paying tribute; contributing. — n. One who pays tribute.

Trib′ūte, n. A periodical tax paid as an acknowledgment of submission.

Trice, n A very short time; an instant.

Trick, n. An artifice for the purpose of deception; a particular habit or manner. — SYN. Stratagem; wile; imposture; cheat; fraud; juggle. — v. t. To cheat; to deceive; to decorate.

Trick′er-y, n. Artifice; knavery; a dressing up.

Trick′ish. a. Knavishly artful

Trick′ish-ness, n. State of being trickish

Trick′le, v. i. To flow in small, slow drops. [cheat.

Trick′ster, n. A deceiver; a

Trī′col-ored, a. Composed of three colors.

Trī-cŭs′pid, a. Having three cusps, or points.

Trī′dent, n. [Lat. tridens, from tri, three, and dens, tooth.] A scepter or spear with three prongs.

Trī-dĕnt′ate, a. Having three prongs.

Trī-en′ni-al, a. Happening every third year; lasting three years. [Trident.

Trī-en′ni-al-ly, adv. Once in three years.

Trī′er, n. One who tries.

Trī′fid, a. Divided into three parts.

Trī′fle, n. A thing of little value or importance. — v. i. To act or talk with levity.

Trī′fler, n. One who trifles.

Trī′fling, a. Of little value or importance; trivial. — n Employment in things of no importance.

Trī′fling-ly, adv. Without importance; with levity.

Trī-fō′li-ate, a. Having three leaves. [form or shape.

Trī′fŏrm, a. Having a triple

Trig (7). v. t. To stop or fasten, as a wheel.

Trig′ger, n. Catch of a wheel, gun, or pistol.

Trī′glyph. n. An ornament in the frieze of Doric columns.

Trig′o-nal, a. Triangular.

Trig′o-no-mĕt′ric-al, a. Pertaining to trigonometry

TRIGONOMETRY 311 TROUBLESOME

Trig′o-nŏm′e-try, *n.* Art of measuring triangles.
Tri′graph, *n.* Three letters used to express one sound.
Tri-hē′dral, *a.* Having three equal sides or faces.
Tri-hē′dron, *n.* A figure having three equal sides.
Tri-lăt′er-al, *a.* Having three sides. [three letters.
Tri-lit′er-al, *a.* Consisting of
Trill (1), *n.* A shake or quaver of the voice in singing. — *v. t.* To quaver or shake. — *v. i.* To flow in drops; to quaver.
Trill′ion (tril′yun), *n.* In England, a million raised to the third power; in America, a thousand billions.
Trim, *a.* Nice; neat; compact; tight. — *v. t.* or *i.* To make trim; to dress; to prune; to balance, as a vessel. — *v. i.* To fluctuate intentionally between parties. — *n.* Dress; condition; state.
Trim′mer, *n.* One who trims; a time-server.
Trim′ming, *n.* Ornamental appendages, as of a garment.
Trim′ness, *n.* Neatness; snugness.
Tri′nal, *a.* Threefold.
Trine, *a.* Three fold. — *n.* Distance of 120 degrees between planets.
Trin′i-tā′ri-an, *a.* Pertaining to the Trinity. — *n.* One who believes in the Trinity.
Trin′i-ty, *n.* [Lat. *trinitas*, from *trini*, three each.] The union of three persons (Father, Son, and Holy Spirit) in one Godhead.
Trink′et, *n.* A small ornament, as a jewel or ring.
Tri-nō′mi-al, *n.* A quantity consisting of three terms.
Tri′o, or Tri′o (149), *n.* A piece of music for three performers; three together.
Trip, *v. i.* To step lightly and quickly; to stumble; to err. — *v. t.* To cause to trip; to supplant. — *n.* Short voyage; excursion; stumble; error.
Trip′ar-tīte, or Tri-pärt′īte, *a.* Divided into three parts.
Tripe, *n.* The large stomach of the ox, cow, &c., prepared for food. [feet.
Trip′e-dal, *a.* Having three
Tri-pĕr′son-al, *a.* Consisting of three persons.
Tri-pĕr′son-ăl′i-ty, *n.* Existence of three persons in one Godhead.

Tri-pĕt′al-oŭs, *a.* Having three petals.
Trip′-hăm′mer, *n.* A heavy hammer moved by projecting teeth on a revolving shaft.
Triph′thong (trif′- or trip′-, 82), *n.* A union of three vowels in a syllable, as *ieu* in *adieu*.
Triph-thŏn′gal (trif- or trip-), *a.* Pertaining to, or consisting of, a triphthong.
Trip′le (trip′l), *a.* Treble; threefold. — *v. t.* To make threefold; to treble.
Trip′let, *n.* Three verses that rhyme; three of a kind; in *music*, three notes executed in the time of two.
Trip′li-cate, *a.* Threefold.
Trip′li-cā′tion, *n.* Act of making threefold.
Tri-plĭç′i-ty, *n.* State of being threefold. [feet.
Tri′pod, *n.* A stool with three
Trip′ping, *a.* Quick; nimble.
Trip′ping-ly, *adv.* Nimbly.
Tri′reme, *n.* A galley with three ranks of oars on a side.
Tri-sĕct′, *v. t.* To cut into three equal parts.
Tri-sĕc′tion, *n.* A division into three equal parts.
Tris′yl-lăb′ic, *a.* Consisting of three syllables.
Tri-sȳl′la-ble, *n.* A word composed of three syllables.
Trīte, *a.* Worn out; stale; hackneyed; common.
Trīte′ly, *adv.* In a trite or hackneyed manner.
Trīte′ness, *n.* State of being trite. [three Gods.
Tri′the-ĭsm, *n.* A belief in
Tri′the-ĭst, *n.* One who believes in three Gods.
Tri′the-ĭst′ic, *a.* Pertaining to tritheism.
Trĭt′u-ra-ble, *a.* Capable of being triturated, or ground to a fine powder.
Trĭt′u-rāte, *v. t.* To reduce to a fine powder by pounding or grinding; to grind; to pound. [urating.
Trĭt′u-rā′tion, *n.* Act of trit-
Tri′umph, *n.* Pomp or joy for victory or success; victory. — *v. t.* To rejoice at success; to obtain victory; to prevail.
Tri-ŭmph′al, *a.* Celebrating victory.
Tri-ŭmph′ant, *a.* With triumph.
Tri-ŭmph′ant-ly, *adv.*
Tri-ŭm′vir, *n.* One of three men united in office.
Tri-ŭm′vi-ral, *a.* Relating to a triumvirate.

Tri-ŭm′vi-rate, *n.* Government by three men.
Tri′ūne, *a.* Being three in one.
Tri-ū′ni-ty, *n.* State of being triune. [stool or table.
Triv′et, *n.* A three-legged
Triv′i-al, *a.* Trifling; light; worthless; inconsiderable.
Trō′car, *n.* An instrument to tap dropsical persons.
Tro-chā′ic, } *a.* Relating
Tro-chā′ic-al, } to, or consisting of, trochees.
Trō′chee, *n.* A medicine in a circular cake, to be dissolved in the mouth.
Trō′chee, *n.* A poetic foot of two syllables, the first long and the second short, or the first accented and the second unaccented.
Trŏd, *imp. & p. p.* of *Tread*.
Trŏd′den, *p. p.* of *Tread*.
Trŏg′lo-dyte, *n.* A dweller in a subterraneous cave.
Trōll, *v. t.* To roll; to turn; to utter volubly; to entice. — *v. i.* To fish by drawing the bait through the water.
Trōl′lop, *n.* A slattern.
Trom-bōne′, *n.* A deep-toned brass instrument of the trumpet kind.
Trŏmp, *n.* A blowing machine used in furnaces.
Troōp, *n.* A company, especially of soldiers; an army. — *v. i.* To march in a body.
Troōp′er, *n.* A horse-soldier.
Trōpe, *n.* Use of a word in a figurative sense. [trophies.
Trō′phied, *a.* Adorned with
Trō′phy (141), *n.* A memorial of victory in battle.
Trŏp′ic, *n.* The line that bounds the sun's greatest declination from the equator, north or south.
Trŏp′ic-al, *a.* Pertaining to, or being within, the tropics; figurative; metaphorical.
Trŏp′ic-al-ly, *adv.* In a tropical manner.
Trŏt, *v. i.* To move in a trot. — *n.* A peculiar pace of a horse, faster than a walk.
Trŏth, *n.* [An old form of *truth*.] Truth; veracity; faith; fidelity.
Trŏt′ter, *n.* A beast that trots; foot, as of a sheep.
Troūb′le, *v. t.* To disturb; to annoy. — *n.* Disturbance; annoyance.
Troūb′le-some, *a.* Giving trouble. — SYN. Harassing; annoying; wearisome; vexatious.

---

*s*ō*n, ȯr, dọ, wọlf, tọ̄o, tọ̄ok; ûrn, rụe, pụll; ç, ċ, *soft*; c, ġ, *hard*; aṣ; ex̧ist; ṉ as ng; th is

Troŭb'loŭs, *a.* Full of disorder.

Trŏugh (trawf, 19), *n.* A long hollow vessel or receptacle.

Trounçe, *v. t.* To beat or punish severely.

Trou'sers, | *n. pl.* Loose pantaloons.
Trow'sers, |

Trous-seau' (trōō-sō′), *n.* The outfit or lighter equipments of a bride.

Trout (146), *n.* A fresh-water fish of the salmon kind, esteemed most delicate food.

Trō'ver, *n.* An action for goods found and not delivered to the owner on demand.

Trŏw, *v. i.* To suppose or think; to believe.

Trow'el, *n.* A tool for laying bricks and stones in mortar.

Trŏy'-weight (-wāt), *n.* A weight of 12 oz. to the pound, for weighing gold, silver, &c.

Tru'ant, *a.* Idle; wandering from school. — *n.* An idler; a boy who absents himself from school without leave.

Truçe, *n.* A temporary cessation of hostilities for negotiation; brief quiet.

Trŭck, *v. t.* or *i.* To barter. — *n.* Exchange of goods; barter; a low cart; a small solid wheel. [tering.

Trŭck'age, *n.* Practice of bar-

Trŭck'le, *n.* A small wheel. — *v. i.* To yield obsequiously.

Trŭck'le-bĕd, *n.* A low bed that runs on little wheels.

Trŭck'man (143), *n.* One who conveys goods on a truck.

Tru'cu-lençe, *n.* Savage ferocity or cruelty.

Tru'cu-lent, *a.* Fierce; cruel; of savage aspect.

Trŭdge, *v. i.* [Allied to *tread*.] To go on foot; to jog along heavily.

Truē, *a.* Conformable to fact or a pattern; exact; right; genuine; real; faithful; honest. [sincere.

True'-heärt'ed, *a.* Honest;

Trŭf'fle (trŭf'fl), *n.* A kind of subterraneous mushroom.

Tru'ism (133), *n.* An undoubted or self-evident truth.

Trŭll, *n.* A low, lewd woman.

Tru'ly (132), *adv.* Certainly; really; exactly.

Trŭmp, *n.* A winning card; a trumpet. — *v. t.* or *i.* To win with a trump; to devise; to fabricate.

Trŭmp'er-y, *n.* Empty talk; trifles; rubbish.

Trŭmp'et, *n.* A wind-instrument of music. — *v. t.* To publish, by sound of trumpet; to proclaim.

Trŭmp'et-ĕr, *n.* One who sounds a trumpet. [to lop.

Trŭn'cāte, *v. t.* To cut off;

Trŭn'cā-ted, *a.* Cut or lopped off short. [cutlug.

Trun-cā'tion, *n.* Act of trun-

Trŭn'cheon (trŭn'shun), *n.* A short staff; a club.

Trŭn'dle, *v. i.* To roll as on little wheels, or as a hoop. — *n.* A little wheel.

Trŭn'dle-bĕd, *n.* A low bed moved on little wheels.

Trŭnk, *n.* Stem or body of a tree; body of an animal; main body of a thing; the proboscis of an elephant; a box or chest for containing clothes, &c.

Trŭn'nion (trŭn'yun), *n.* A knob on each side of a cannon, to support it.

Trŭss (123, 124), *n.* A bundle, as of hay; a bandage or apparatus for ruptures. — *v. t.* To pack or bind close; to skewer.

Trŭst, *n.* Confidence; faith; credit given. — *v. t.* To rely on; to believe; to sell on credit to. — *v. t.* To be confident; to confide.

Trust-ee' (140), *n.* One to whom property is legally committed in trust.

Trŭst'i-ly, *adv.* In a trusty manner; faithfully; honestly.

Trŭst'i-ness, *n.* Fidelity; honesty; integrity.

Trŭst'y, *a.* Worthy of trust.

Truth, *n.* Conformity to reality or fact; exactness; fidelity; faithfulness; veracity; honesty; an established principle.

Truth'fŭl, *a.* Full of truth; veracious; trustworthy.

Trȳ, *v. t.* or *i.* To attempt; to endeavor; to test.

Trȳst, *n.* An appointed meeting, or a place for such a meeting.

Tŭb, *n.* An open wooden vessel, used for various purposes.

Tūbe, *n.* A long hollow cylinder; a pipe. [stem or root.

Tū'ber, *n.* A fleshy rounded

Tū'ber-cle, *n.* A small mass of diseased matter, as in the lungs.

Tu-bĕr'cu-lar, | *a.* Full of
Tu-bĕr'eu-loŭs, | tubercles.

Tūbe'rōse, or **Tū'ber-ōṣe,** *n.* A flowering plant with a tuberous root.

Tū'ber-oŭs, *a.* Full of knobs or tubers.

Tū'bu-lar, *a.* Resembling, or consisting of, a pipe.

Tū'būle, *n.* A small tube.

Tū'bu-loŭs, *a.* Hollow, like a tube or pipe.

Tŭck, *n.* A horizontal fold in a dress. — *v. t.* To thrust in or together; to fold under.

Tŭck'er, *n.* A small thin piece of the dress for covering the breast. [day of the week.

Tūes'day (tūz'dy), *n.* Third

Tŭff (123), *n.* A soft, friable, volcanic sand-rock.

Tŭft, *n.* A bunch of grass, hair, &c. — *v. t.* To adorn with tufts.

Tŭft'ed, *a.* Growing in tufts.

Tŭft'y, *a.* Abounding with, or growing in, tufts.

Tŭg, *v. i.* To pull with great effort. — *n.* A pulling with great effort; trace of a harness; a steam tow-boat.

Tu-ī'tion (-ĭsh'un), *n.* Guardianship; instruction; price of instruction.

Tu-ī'tion-a-ry (-ĭsh'un-), *a.* Relating to tuition.

Tū'lip, *n.* A plant and flower.

Tŭm'ble, *v. i.* To roll about or down. — *v. t.* To turn over or throw about carelessly; to disturb; to rumple. — *n.* A tumbling or rolling over; a fall.

Tŭm'bler, *n.* One who, or that which, tumbles; a kind of drinking glass.

Tŭm'brel, *n.* A ducking stool; a cart; a military wagon; a kind of basket.

Tū'me-făc'tion, *n.* A swelling; a tumor.

Tū'me-fȳ, *v.* To swell.

Tū'mid, *a.* Swelled; distended; pompous.

Tū'mid-ness, | *n.* State or
Tu-mĭd'i-ty, | quality of being tumid.

Tū'mor (155), *n.* [Lat., from *tumere*, to swell.] A morbid swelling.

Tū'mu-lar, | *a.* Consisting
Tū'mu-loŭs, | in a heap.

Tū'mult, *n.* Wild commotion; uproar. [ly.

Tu-mŭlt'u-a-ry, *a.* Disorder-

Tu-mŭlt'u-oŭs, *a.* Full of tumult; conducted with tumult. — SYN. Disorderly; turbulent; noisy; lawless.

†Tū'mu-lus, *n.* (*pl.* **Tū'mu-lī.**) [Lat.] An artificial hillock, esp. one raised over an ancient grave.

Tŭn, *n.* A large cask; a measure for liquids of four hogsheads. See *Ton*. — *v. t.* To put in a cask.

Tŭn'a-ble, *a.* Capable of being put in tune.

Tūne (27), *n.* A series of musical notes; order; harmony. — *v. t.* To put in a proper musical or other state.

Tūne'ful, *a.* Harmonious.

Tū'nic, *n.* A Roman and Eastern under-garment, worn by both sexes; a membrane; an integument.

Tū'ni-cle, *n.* A natural covering; a long ecclesiastical robe.

Tŭn'nage, *n.* See *Tonnage*.

Tŭn'nel (139), *n.* A pipe for pouring liquors into vessels; a funnel; an artificial underground passage for railroads, &c. — *v. t.* (139) To form, like, or into, a tunnel.

Tŭr'ban, *n.* A kind of Eastern head-dress.

Tŭr'bid, *a.* Muddy; not clear.

Tŭr'bid-ness, *n.* Muddiness.

Tŭr'bi-nate, } *a.* Shaped
Tŭr'bi-nā-ted, } like a top; spiral; twisted.

Tŭr'bine, *n.* A horizontal water-wheel, variously constructed.

Tŭr'bot, *n.* A kind of flat fish.

Tŭr'bu-lence, } *n.* Tumult;
Tŭr'bu-len-çy, } confusion.

Tŭr'bu-lent, *a.* Tumultuous; riotous; disorderly.

Tu-reen', *n.* A large, deep vessel for holding soup.

Tŭrf, *n. pl.* **Tŭrfs**, 140.) A stratum of earth filled with roots; sod; sward; peat. — *v. t.* To cover with turf.

Tŭrf'y, *a.* Full of, or covered with, turf; like turf.

Tur-gĕs'çenge, *n.* State of becoming turgid.

Tŭr'gid, *a.* Distended; swelled: tumid; bombastic.

Tur-gĭd'i-ty, } *n.* A turgid
Tŭr'gid-ness, } or swelled state; bombast.

Tŭr'key (141), *n.* A large fowl, a native of America.

Tur-kois' (-koiz' or -keez'), *n.* A bluish-green gem. See *Turquoise*.

Tŭr'mer-ic (120, 127), *n.* An East Indian plant used for dyeing.

Tŭr'moil, *n.* Harassing labor; trouble; disturbance; commotion.

Tŭrn, *v. t.* or *i.* To move or go round; to revolve; to alter; to change; to make or become acid. — *n.* Act of moving or going round; change; purpose.

Tûrn'coat, *n.* One who changes sides or principles; a renegade; a deserter.

Tûrn'er, *n.* One who turns; esp. one who forms articles with a lathe.

Tûrn'er-y, *n.* Art of shaping solid articles by a lathe; wares formed by a turner.

Tûrn'ing, *n.* A winding; flexure; deviation.

Tûr'nip, *n.* A plant and its esculent root.

Tûrn'kēy (141), *n.* One who keeps the keys of a prison.

Tûrn'pīke, *n.* A toll-gate; a road on which are turnpikes. — *v. t.* To form in the manner of a turnpike; to round up in the centre.

Tûrn'sōle, *n.* A heliotrope.

Tûrn'stīle, *n.* A kind of turnpike in a footpath.

Tûr'pen-tīne, *n.* A resinous juice from various trees.

Tûr'pi-tūde, *n.* Baseness.

Tur-quoise' (-koiz' or -keez', 35), *n.* A bluish-green mineral, used in jewelry.

Tûr'ret, *n.* A small tower.

Tûr'ret-ed, *a.* Furnished with turrets; formed like a tower.

Tûr'tle, *n.* A species of wild dove; a sea-tortoise.

Tûr'tle-dōve, *n.* Turtle. A dove or pigeon.

Tŭs'can, *a.* Relating to Tuscany, or to a certain order of architecture.

Tŭsk, *n.* A long, pointed tooth of certain rapacious, carnivorous, or fighting animals.

Tŭs'sle (tŭs'l), *n.* A scuffle.

Tū'te-lage, *n.* Guardianship; protection; care.

Tū'te-lar, } *a.* Guarding;
Tū'te-la-ry, } protecting.

Tū'tor, *n.* [Lat., fr. *tueri*, to watch, defend.] An instructor or teacher. — *v. t.* To instruct; to discipline.

Tū'tor-age, *n.* Instruction; guardianship.

Tū'tor-ess, *n.* A female tutor.

Twad'dle, *v. i.* To prate.

Twāin, *a.* & *n.* Two.

Twăng, *v. i.* or *t.* To sound, or cause to sound, with a quick, sharp noise. — *n.* A sharp, quick sound.

Twăt'tle (twŏt'tl), *v. i.* To prate; to talk much and idly; to twaddle.

Twĕak, *v. t.* To twitch. — *n.* A sharp pinch or jerk.

Twēe'dle, *v. t.* To handle lightly; to coax; to allure.

Tweeds, *n. pl.* Cotton or woolen goods of light fabric.

Twee'zers, *n. pl.* Small nippers for plucking out hairs, and for other purposes.

Twĕlfth, *a.* Ordinal of twelve.

Twĕlve, *a.* Two and ten.

Twĕlve'mŏnth, *n.* A year.

Twĕlve'-pĕnçe, *n.* A shilling sterling, being about 24 cents. [twenty.

Twĕn'ti-eth, *a.* Ordinal of

Twĕn'ty, *a.* Twice ten; a score.

Twīçe, *adv.* Two times; doubly. [second time.

Twī'fāl-lōw, *v. t.* To plow a

Twĭg, *n.* A small shoot or branch of a tree or shrub.

Twī'light (-līt), *n.* Faint light seen after sunset and before sunrise.

Twĭll, *v. t.* To weave so as to make diagonal ridges in.

Twĭn, *n.* One of two produced at a birth.

Twīne, *v. t.* and *i.* [A.-S. *twīnan*, fr. *twī*, two.] To twist; to wrap closely round; to wind. — *n.* Strong twisted thread; a twist.

Twĭnge, *v. i.* To feel a short sharp pain. — *n.* A quick, darting pain.

Twĭnk'le, *v. i.* To blink: to wink; to sparkle; to flash at short intervals. — *n.* A wink; time of a wink.

Twĭnk'ling, *n.* A wink; a sparkling; an instant.

Twîrl, *v. t.* or *i.* To move or whirl round rapidly. — *n.* A rapid whirling or turning.

Twĭst, *v. t.* To wind, as one thread round another; to convolve. — *n.* A contortion; a thread or cord made by twisting.

Twĭt, *v. t.* To reproach; to taunt; to upbraid.

Twĭtch, *v. t.* To pull suddenly. — *n.* A pull with a jerk.

Twĭt'ter (129), *v. i.* To make a small, intermitted noise, as a swallow. — *n.* A small tremulous noise.

Twọ (tōō), *a.* One and one.

Twọ'-ĕdged (tōō'-), *a.* Having an edge on both sides.

Twọ'fōld (tōō'-), *a.* Two of the kind: double.

Twọ'-hănd'ed (tōō'-), *a.*

sọu ôr, dọ, wọlf, tōō, tŏŏk; ûrn, rụe, pụll; ç, ġ, *soft* ; ȼ, g̱, *hard* ; aṣ ; exist; ņ *as* ng; this.

Twopence Having two hands; used with both hands.

Two'pence (tŭb'penss), *n.* A small English coin, equivalent to two pennies.

Tym'bal, *n.* A kettle-drum.

Tym'pan, *n.* A frame for holding sheets of paper for printing. [car.

Tym'pa-num, *n.* Drum of the

Type, *n.* [Gr. *tupos*, from *tuptein*, to beat, strike.] A mark; an emblem; a figure; a sign; a symbol; a letter or other character for printing from.

☞ The types which compose an ordinary book-font consist of Roman CAPITALS, SMALL CAPITALS, and lower-case letters, and *Italic CAPITALS* and *lower-case* letters. Besides the ordinary Roman and *Italic*, the most important varieties of face are

Old English, or Black Letter,

German Text,

Full-face, Antique,

Script,

Old Style, **GOTHIC**.

Ty'phoid, *a.* Resembling typhus fever. — *n.* A fever resembling typhus.

Ty-phōōn', *n.* A violent tornado in the Chinese seas.

Ty'phus, *n.* A fever characterized by great prostration and cerebral disturbance.

Typ'ic, *a.* Emblematical,
Typ'ic-al, figurative.

Typ'ic-al-ly, *adv.* In a typical or figurative manner.

Typ'i-fȳ, *v. t.* To represent by a type or emblem.

Ty-pŏg'ra-pher (tī- or tĭ-), *n.* A printer.

Typ'o-grăph'ic-al, *or* **Ty'po-grăph'ic-al**, *a.* Relating to type or to printing.

Typ'o-grăph'ic-al-ly, *or* **Ty'po-grăph'ic-al-ly**, *adv.* By means of type.

Ty-pŏg'ra-phy (tī- or tĭ-, 117), *n.* Art of printing.

Ty'ran-ness, *n.* A female tyrant.

Ty-răn'nic, *a.* Imperious; despotic; arbitrary; cruel.

Ty-răn'nic-al-ly, *adv.* In the manner of a tyrant.

Ty-răn'ni-çīde, *n.* The killing, or the killer, of a tyrant.

Tyr'an-nīze, *v. t.* To act as a tyrant.

Tyr'an-noŭs, *a.* Cruel; arbitrary; despotic; unjustly severe; tyrannical.

Tyr'an-ny, *n.* Arbitrary exercise of power; despotism.

Ty'rant, *n.* An arbitrary ruler; a cruel master; an oppressor.

Ty'ro, *n.* (*pl.* Ty'rōṣ). A beginner; a novice.

Tzär (zär), *n.* See *Czar*.

U.

U (yōō). The fifth vowel in English. It has a close affinity to the consonant *v*, and these two letters were formerly confounded in writing and printing.

U-biq'ui-ta-ry (bĭk'wĭ-), *a.* Existing everywhere.

U-bĭq'ui-ty, *n.* [Lat. *ubique*, everywhere.] Existence everywhere.

Ŭd'der, *n.* The bag with the teats of a cow, &c.

Ŭg'li-ness (135), *n.* Deformity; moral depravity; ill-nature.

Ŭg'ly, *a.* Not handsome; deformed; ill-natured.

Ŭl'çer, *n.* A sore that discharges pus.

Ŭl'çer-āte, *v. i.* To become ulcerous; to turn to an ulcer.

Ŭl'çer-ā'tion, *n.* Act of ulcerating.

Ŭl'çer-oŭs, *a.* Afflicted with ulcers; discharging purulent or other matters.

Ŭl'lage, *n.* What a cask wants of being full.

Ul-tē'ri-or, *a.* Lying beyond; further; more remote.

Ŭl'ti-mate (42), *a.* Final; concluding; furthest.

Ŭl'ti-mate-ly, *adv.* Finally; at last; in the end.

Ŭl'ti-mā'tum, *n.* Final proposition; last offer.

Ŭl'trȧ, *a.* Radical; extreme.

Ŭl'tra-ma-rīne' (-ma-reen'), *n.* A beautiful blue pigment.

Ŭl'tra-mŏn'tane, *a.* Being beyond the mountains or the Alps.

Ŭl'tra-mŭn'dane, *a.* Being beyond the world.

Ŭm'bel, *n.* A collection of small flowers in a head.

Ŭm'bel-late, *a.* Bearing umbels; relating to, or having the form of, an umbel. [Umbel.

Ŭm'bel-lĭf'er-oŭs, *a.* Bearing umbels.

Ŭm'ber, *n.* [From *Umbria*, in Italy, where it is said to have been first obtained.] A brownish ore of iron, used as a pigment.

Um-bĭl'ic-al, *a.* Pertaining to the navel.

Ŭm'bleṣ, *n.* Entrails of a deer.

Ŭm'brage, *n.* A shade; resentment; offense; affront.

Ŭm-brā'ġeoŭs, *a.* Shady.

Um-brĕl'lȧ (140), *n.* A portable screen from the sun or rain.

Ŭm'pi-rage, *n.* The decision of an umpire; arbitrament; authority of an umpire.

Ŭm'pīre, *n.* A third person to whose sole decision a controversy or question between parties is referred.

Ŭn. A negative prefix, which may be attached at will to almost any English adjective or participle used adjectively, while it is also attached to less numerous classes of nouns and verbs. As the former class of words is unlimited in extent, and such compounds may be formed by any writer or speaker from almost all the adjectives and participles in the language, very many of them will be omitted from this Dictionary, more especially such as are negations of the simple word, and are readily explained by prefixing a *not* to the latter; also, derivatives of these words in *ly* and *ness*. A pretty full list of these words is subjoined.

Un is prefixed to adjectives, or to words used adjectively; as (1.) To adjectives, to denote the absence of the quality designated by the adjective: as, *unaccordant, unaided, unambitious, unanxious, unappreciable, unartificial, unattainable, unauthorized, unbearable, unbrotherly, uncandid, uncanonical, uncheerful, unclassical, uncommercial, uncongenial, uncordial, uncourtly, undeniable, undemocratic, underout, undistinguishable, unendurable, un-English, unenviable, unessential, uneventful, unfamiliar, unfeminine, unfraternal, ungenial, ungenteel, ungentle, ungrammatical, unimportant, uninhabitable, unjustifiable, unkingly, unmaidenly, unmanageable, unmeet, unmelodious, unmotherly, unmusical, unobservant, unpardonable, unpatriotic, unphilanthropic, unphilosophic, unpoetic, unpronounceable, unquenchable, unrational, unremunerative, unromantic, unscholarly, unscientific, unselfish, unserviceable, unsubstantial, unsuspicious, unthankful, untidy, unvocal, unwarlike, unwatchful, unweary, unwelcome, unwomanly, unworldly*, and the like. (2.) To past passive participles, to indicate the absence of the condition or state expressed by the participle: as, *unabated, unabridged, unaccented, unadorned, unadulterated, unaided, unaltered, unanswered, unappreciated, unarmed, unasked, unassisted, unattempted, unattended, unbaptized, unbiased, unbleached, unbought, uncalled, unchanged, unchecked, uncircumcised, unclouded, uncompounded, unconfined, uncongealed, unconquered, unconstrained, uncultivated, undecided, undefeated, undefiled, undeserved, undesigned, undigested, undiminished, undimmed, undisguised, undisputed, undisturbed, uneducated, unemployed, unenlightened, unexhausted, unexplained, unexplored, unfathomed, unfermented, unforeseen, unfulfilled, unfurnished, unguarded, unguessed, unharmed, unheeded, unhelped, unhonoured, unimpeached, unenclosed, uninhabited, uninspired, unleavened, unloved, unmarried, unmasked, unmatched, unmingled, unmitigated, unmixed, unmoored, unnerved, unnoticed, unobserved, unobstructed, unornamented, unperceived, unpolished, unpracticed, unpremeditated, unprepared, unprotected, unprovoked, unpunished, unread, unreconciled, unrefined, unrelated, unrepresented, unresisted, unrewarded, unsatisfied, unsearched, unsettled, unshaved, unsheltered, unshod, unshorn, unskilled, unsolicited, unsought, unstinted, unstudied, unsullied, unsur*passed, unsuspected, untasted, untaught, unterrified, untried, untutored, unvaried, unwarranted, unwedded, unwept*, and the like. (3.) To present participles which come from intransitive verbs, or are themselves employed as adjectives, to mark the absence of the activity, disposition, or condition implied by the participle; as, *unaccommodating, unaspiring, unblenching, uncalculating, unchanging, uncomplaining, unconsuming, unconvincing, undeserving, undiminishing, undiscerning, undoubting, unedifying, unenrying, unfading, unfaltering, unflinching, ungrudging, unheeding, uninteresting, uninviting, unloving, unmoving, unobserving, unoffending, unpitying, unpleasing, unquestioning, unrepining, unresisting, unresting, unsearching, unseeing, unshrinking, unsuspecting, unsympathizing, unvarying, unwavering*, and the like.

Un-ā'ble, *a.* Not having ability or power; impotent.

Un'ac-çept'a-ble. *a.* Not acceptable; disagreeable.

Un'ac-count'a-ble, *a.* Not to be accounted for; inexplicable. [quainted.

Un'ac-quāint'ed, *a.* Not acquainted.

Un'ad-vīs'a-ble, *a.* Not advisable; inexpedient.

Un'af-fēct'ed, *a.* Not affected or moved; not artificial; simple; natural. [pure.

Un'al-loyed', *a.* Not alloyed;

Un-al'ter-a-ble, *a.* Not to be altered; changeless.

Un-al'ter-a-bly, *adv.* Unchangeably.

Un-ā'mi-a-ble, *a.* Not amiable: repelling affection; ill-natured.

U'na-nim'i-ty, *n.* Agreement in opinion or determination.

U-nān'i-mŏŭs, *a.* Being of one mind; harmonious; formed with the agreement of all.

U-nān'i-mŏŭs-ly, *adv.* With entire agreement.

Un-ān'swer-a-ble (-ǎn'ser-a-bl), *a.* Not answerable; not to be refuted.

Un-āpt', *a.* Not apt or ready; dull; stupid.

Un'as-sūm'ing, *a.* Not assuming; humble; modest.

Un'a-vāil'ing, *a.* Of no avail; ineffectual; useless.

Un'a-void'a-ble, *a.* Not to be shunned; necessary; inevitable.

Un'a-void'a-bly, *adv.* Inevitably; necessarily.

Un'a-wāre', *a.* Without thought; inattentive; giving no heed.

Un'a-wāres', *adv.* Suddenly; unexpectedly.

Un-bär', *v. t.* To remove a bar from; to unfasten; to open.

Un'be-cŏm'ing, *a.* Not becoming; improper; unsuitable; indecorous.

Un'be-lief', *n.* Incredulity; skepticism; infidelity.

Un'be-liev'er, *n.* An infidel; a skeptic.

Un'be-liev'ing, *a.* Incredulous; skeptical; infidel.

Un-bĕnd', *v. t.* To relax or slacken. — *v. i.* To become relaxed.

Un-bĕnd'ing, *a.* Unyielding; inflexible; firm; rigid.

Un-bī'as (130), *v. t.* To free from bias or prejudice.

Un-bīnd', *v. t.* To untie; to unfasten; to loose.

Un-blĕm'ished (-blĕm'isht), *a.* Free from blemish; pure; spotless.

Un-blĕst', *a.* Not blessed; unhappy; wretched.

Un-bōlt', *v. t.* To remove a bolt from; to unfasten.

Un-bōrn', *a.* Not born; still to appear; future.

Un-bǒṣ'gm (bŏz'um), *v. t.* To disclose freely; to reveal.

Un-boūnd'ed, *a.* Having no bounds or limits; infinite; unrestrained.

Un-brī'dle, *v. t.* To free from, or as from, the bridle.

Un-brō'ken (-brō'kn), *a.* Entire; whole.

Un-bŭck'le, *v. t.* To loose from buckles; to unfasten.

Un-bŭr'ied (-bĕr'id, 155), *a.* Not buried; disinterred.

Un-bŭr'den, *v. t.* To rid of a burden; to throw off, as a burden; to unload; to relieve.

Un-bŭt'ton (-bŭt'tn), *v. t.* To loose the buttons of.

Un-çēas'ing, *a.* Not ceasing; continual; perpetual.

Un-çĕr'e-mō'ni-oŭs, *a.* Not ceremonious; informal; familiar.

Un-çĕr'tain, *a.* Not certain; precarious; insecure; doubtful; dubious.

Un-çĕr'tain-ly, *adv.* Not certainly; doubtfully.

Un-çĕr'tain-ty, *n.* Want of certainty; doubtfulness.

Un-chāin', *v. t.* To free from chains; confinement, or thraldom.

Un-chānge'a-ble, *a.* Not subject to change; immutable.

UNCHANGEABLY 316 UNDERSHOT

Un-change'a-bly, *adv.* Without change; immutably.
Un-char'i-ta-ble, *a.* Having no charity; severe in judging; harsh; censorious.
Un-char'i-ta-ble-ness, *n.* Want of charity.
Un-char'i-ta-bly, *adv.* With want of charity; harshly.
Un-chaste', *a.* Not chaste; lewd; impure.
Un-chris'tian (-krĭst'yan), *a.* Contrary to Christianity; unbecoming a Christian.
Un-church', *v. t.* To expel from a church.
Un'cial (ŭn'shal), *a.* Relating to ancient letters of a large size. — *n.* An uncial letter.
Un-civ'il, *a.* Not civil; impolite; uncourteous ♦ rude; boorish; unmannerly.
Un-çiv'il-ĭzed, *a.* Not civilized or reclaimed from savage life; rude; barbarous; savage.
Un-çiv'il-ly, *adv.* Rudely.
Un-clasp', *v. t.* To loose the clasp of.
Un'cle (ŭnk'l, 137), *n.* A father's or a mother's brother.
Un-clean', *a.* Not clean; foul; dirty; filthy; impure; sinful; wicked.
Un-clean'ness, *n.* State or quality of being unclean; filthiness; impurity; sinfulness.
Un-clōse', *v. t.* To open.
Un-coil', *v. t.* To unwind and open.
Un-come'ly, *a.* Not comely; homely; disagreeable.
Un-com'fort-a-ble, *a.* Affording no comfort; giving uneasiness.
Un-com'fort-a-bly, *adv.* Without comfort or cheerfulness.
Un-com'mon, *a.* Not common; infrequent; rare; unusual; remarkable.
Un-com'mon-ly, *adv.* Unusually.
Un-com'mon-ness, *n.* Rareness of occurrence; infrequency.
Un-com'pro-mĭṣ'ing, *a.* Not agreeing to terms; inflexible; firm.
Un'con-çêrn', *n.* Want of concern; indifference.
Un'con-çêrn'ed-ly, *adv.* Without concern.
Un'con-di'tion-al (-dĭsh'un-), *a.* Not limited by conditions; absolute.

Un-con'quer-a-ble (-kŏnk'er-a-bl), *a.* Not to be conquered. — SYN. Invincible; insuperable
Un-con'scion-a-ble (-kŏn'shun-), *a.* Unreasonable; inordinate; enormous.
Un-con'scion-a-bly, *adv.* In an unconscionable manner; unreasonably.
Un-con'scious (-kŏn'shus), *a.* Not having consciousness; not made the object of consciousness; imperceptible.
Un-con'scious-ly, *adv.* Without consciousness.
Un-con'scious-ness, *n.* Want of consciousness or perception.
Un-con'sti-tū'tion-al, *a.* Not constitutional; contrary to the constitution.
Un-con'sti-tū'tion-ăl'i-ty, *n.* Quality of being unauthorized by, or opposed to, the constitution.
Un-con'sti-tū'tion-al-ly, *adv.* In an unconstitutional manner.
Un'con-trŏl'la-ble, *a.* Not to be controlled; ungovernable.
Un'con-trŏl'la-bly, *adv.* Beyond control.
Un'con-vêrt'ed, *a.* Not converted or regenerated; sinful; impenitent. [cork from.
Un-cŏrk', *v. t.* To draw the
Un-coûrt'e-oŭs (-kûrt'e-us), *a.* Uncivil; rude; impolite.
Un-couth' (-kooth'), *a.* Unfamiliar; unusual; not rendered pleasing by familiarity. — SYN. Odd; strange; awkward. [ness.
Un-couth'ness, *n.* Awkwardness.
Un-cŏv'er (-kŭv'er), *v. t.* To take the cover from; to open. — *v. i.* To bare the head.
Unç'tion, *n.* Act of anointing; unguent; ointment.
Unçt'u-oŭs (ŭnkt'yụ-us), *a.* Oily; fat; greasy.
Un-cûrb', *v. t.* To free from a curb.
Un-cûrl', *v. t.* To straighten out, as any thing that has been curled.
Un-dāt'ed, *a.* Having no date.
Un-daunt'ed, *a.* Fearless; bold; brave; intrepid.
Un-dĕç'a-gŏn, *n.* A figure of eleven angles and eleven sides.
Un'de-çeive', *v. t.* To free from deception.
Un'de-nī'a-ble, *a.* Impossible to be denied; palpably true; obvious.

Un'de-nī'a-bly, *adv.* Indisputably.
Un'der, *prep.* Lower than; beneath; below. — *a.* Lower in rank; subordinate; inferior. — *adv.* In a lower condition; in subjection.
Un'der-ā'ġent, *n.* A subordinate agent.
Un'der-bid', *v. t.* To bid or offer less than. [breeding.
Un'der-brĕd, *a.* Of inferior
Un'der-brŭsh, *n.* Small trees and shrubs in a wood or forest.
Un'der-cûr'rent, *n.* A current below the surface.
Un'der-do', *v.* To do less than is requisite or desirable.
Un'der-gō', *v. t.* To bear; to endure; to suffer; to sustain; to pass through.
Un'der-grăd'u-ate, *n.* A student in a college who has not taken his degree.
Un'der-ground, *a.* Being below the surface of the ground; subterranean.
Un'der-grŏwth, *n.* Shrubs which grow under trees.
Un'der-hănd, *a.* Clandestine; secret; covert; sly. — *adv.* By secret means; by fraud.
Un'der-hănd'ed, *a.* Clandestine. [or beneath.
Un'der-lāy', *v. t.* To lay under
Un'der-lĕt', *v. t.* To let or lease under a lease.
Un'der-līe', *v. t.* To lie under; to be the basis of.
Un'der-līne', *v. t.* To mark a line beneath, as words.
Un'der-ling, *n.* An inferior.
Un'der-mīne', *v. t.* To excavate the earth beneath; to ruin or injure in an underhand way.
Un'der-mōst, *a.* Lowest in place, rank, or state.
Un'der-nēath' (*or* -nēeth'), *adv.* or *prep.* Under; beneath.
Un'der-pĭn', *v. t.* To lay stones under, as under the sills of a building.
Un'der-pĭn'ning, *n.* The stones on which a building rests.
Un'der-rāte', *v. t.* To rate below the value.
Un'der-scōre', *v. t.* To draw a line or mark under.
Un'der-sĕll', *v. t.* To sell cheaper than another.
Un'der-sĭgn' (-sīn'), *v. t.* To write one's name at the foot or end of.
Un'der-shŏt', *a.* Moved by

ā, ĕ, ī, ō, ū, ȳ, *long*; ă, ĕ, ĭ, ŏ, ŭ, ў, *short*; câre, cär, ăsk, ạll, whạt; ẽre, vẽil, tẽrm; pĭque, fîrm;

water passing beneath ;— said of a water-wheel.

Un'der-stånd', *v. t. [imp. & p. p.* UNDERSTOOD.] To comprehend; to know; to have information; to suppose to mean.

Un'der-stånd'ing (130), *n.* Knowledge; interpretation; the intellectual powers; intellect; judgment; sense.

Un'der-stånd'ing-ly, *adv.* With knowledge.

Un'der-stood', *imp. & p. p. of Understand.*

Un'der-stråp'per, *n.* An inferior agent; a subaltern.

Un'der-tåke', *v. t. [imp.* UNDERTOOK; *p. p.* UNDERTAKEN.] To take in hand: to attempt; to engage in.

Un'der-tåk'er, *n.* One who undertakes; one who takes the management of funerals.

Un'der-tåk'ing, *n.* An enterprise ; any business.

Un'der-took', *imp. of Undertake.*

Un'der-tōne, *n.* A low tone.

Un'der-tōw, *n.* A current of water below having a different direction from that on the surface.

Un'der-vål'ūe, *v. t.* To rate below the worth. *[dergo.*

Un'der-wěnt', *imp. of Un-*

Un'der-wŏŏd, *n.* Small trees growing under larger ones.

Un'der-work' (-wûrk'), *v. t.* To do like work at a less price than.

Un'der-wrīte' (-rīt'), *v. i.* To write under something else ; to insure.

Un'der-wrīt'er (-rīt'-), *n.* An insurer.

Un'de-sign'ing (-sīn'- or -zīn'-), *a.* Artless ; sincere.

Un-dē'vi-ā'ting, *a.* Not deviating ; steady ; regular.

Un-dī-vīd'ed, *a.* Not divided ; whole ; entire.

Un-dọ', *v. t. [imp.* UNDID ; *p. p.* UNDONE.] To reverse what has been done; to take to pieces; to unfasten ; to ruin.

Un-dọ'er, *n.* One who undoes.

Un-dọ'ing, *n.* Reversal ; ruin.

Un-dône' (-dǔn'), *p. p.* Unfastened ; ruined ; not done ; unfinished.

Un-doubt'ed (-dout'ed), *a.* Not doubted ; indubitable ; indisputable.

Un-doubt'ed-ly (-dout'-), *adv.* Without question ; indisputably.

Un-dress', *v. t.* To divest of clothes ; to strip ; to disrobe , to deprive of ornaments.

Un'dress, *n.* A loose, negligent dress.

Un-dūe', *a.* Not due; not yet owing ; excessive ; immoderate.

Un'du-lāte, *v. t.* or *i.* To move backward and forward, or up and down, as a wave ; to vibrate.

Un'du-lā'ted, *a.* Waved ; wavy ; undulatory.

Un'du-lā'tion, *n.* A waving motion or vibration.

Un'du-la-to-ry, *a.* Moving like waves ; vibratory.

Un-dū'ly, *adv.* In an undue manner ; improperly ; excessively.

Un-dȳ'ing, *a.* Not dying; not subject to death ; immortal.

Un-ēarth', *v. t.* To draw from the earth ; to remove the earth from ; to uncover ; to bring to light.

Un-ēarth'ly, *a.* Not terrestrial ; supernatural.

Un-ēa'şi-ly, *adv.* With uneasiness. *[perturbation.*

Un-ēa'şi-ness, *n.* Disquiet ;

Un-ēa'şy, *a.* Not easy ; restless ; disturbed.

Un-ěnd'ing, *a.* Not ending ; everlasting ; eternal.

Un-ē'qual, *a.* Not equal, or even ; inferior ; inadequate ; disproportioned ; partial ; unjust ; unfair.

Un-ē'qual-ly, *adv.* In different degrees ; unfairly.

Un'e-quĭv'o-cal, *a.* Not equivocal ; clear ; evident.

Un'e-quĭv'o-cal-ly, *adv.* Clearly ; evidently.

Un-ěrr'ing, *n.* Committing no mistake ; certain.

Un-ē'ven (-ē'vn), *a.* Not even ; not level or uniform ; rough ; irregular.

Un-ē'ven-ness, *n.* Inequality of surface ; want of uniformity.

Un'ex-ăm'pled, *a.* Having no example ; without precedent.

Un'ex-çěp'tion-a-ble, *a.* Not liable to objection ; faultless ; good.

Un'ex-çěp'tion-a-bly, *adv.* So as to be liable to no objection.

Un'ex-pěct'ed, *a.* Not expected ; sudden ; coming without warning.

Un'ex-pěct'ed-ly, *adv.* Suddenly.

Un-fāil'ing, *a.* Not failing ; not liable to fail ; abiding.

Un-fâir', *a.* Not fair ; disingenuous ; dishonest.

Un-fâir'ly, *adv.* In an unfair manner ; dishonestly.

Un-fâir'ness, *n.* Want of fairness or honesty.

Un-fāith'fụl, *a.* Not faithful ; negligent of duty ; treacherous ; perfidious.

Un-fāith'fụl-ly, *adv.* In violation of promises, vows, or duty.

Un-fāith'fụl-ness, *n.* Breach of faith ; infidelity.

Un-făsh'ion-a-ble, *a.* Not according to the fashion.

Un-fåst'en (-fås'n), *v. t.* To loose ; to unbind ; to untie.

Un-făth'om-a-ble, *a.* Not to be fathomed; profound.

Un-fā'vor-a-ble, *a.* Not favorable ; adverse ; contrary.

Un-fā'vor-a-bly, *adv.* Adversely.

Un-feel'ing, *a.* Void of feeling or sensibility ; insensible ; cruel ; hard-hearted.

Un-feel'ing-ly, *adv.* With insensibility.

Un-feigned' (-fānd'), *a.* Not feigned ; real ; sincere.

Un-feign'ed-ly (-fān'-), *adv.* Without hypocrisy.

Un-fĭl'ial (-yal), *a.* Not becoming a son or daughter.

Un-fĭn'ished (-fĭn'isht), *a.* Not finished ; incomplete ; imperfect.

Un-fĭt', *v. t.* To disable ; to disqualify. — *a.* Not fit or qualified. — SYN. Improper ; unqualified ; incompetent.

Un-fĭx', *v. t.* To loosen ; to unsettle.

Un-fōld', *v. t.* To expand ; to spread out; to disclose ; to reveal.

Un'for-gĭv'ing, *a.* Not disposed to forgive; implacable ; inexorable.

Un-fôrt'u-nate, *a.* Not fortunate ; not successful.

Un-fôrt'u-nate-ly, *adv.* Without success.

Un-found'ed, *a.* Having no foundation ; baseless ; vain.

Un-frē'quent, *a.* Not frequent; not happening often.

Un-frē'quent-ly, *adv.* Rarely.

Un-friend'ly, *a.* Not friendly ; unfavorable ; hostile.

Un-fruit'fụl, *a.* Not fruitful ; barren ; sterile.

Un-fûrl', *v. t.* To unfold ; to open or spread ; to expand.

Un-fûr'nish, *v. t.* To strip of furniture ; to leave naked or bare.

---

sōn, ôr, dọ, wọlf, tōō, tŏŏk; ûrn, rụe, pụll; ç, ġ, *soft;* ȼ, ġ, *hard;* aẓ ; eẋist; ŋ *as* ng; this.

Un-gáin'ly, *a.* Not expert or dexterous; clumsy; awkward; uncouth.
Un-gĕn'er-oŭs, *a.* Not generous; illiberal; unkind; mean; dishonorable.
Un-gŏd'li-ness, *n.* Impiety.
Un-gŏd'ly, *a.* Irreligious; wicked; impious; sinful.
Un-gŏv'ern-a-ble, *a.* Not to be governed or restrained; wild; licentious.
Un-gŏv'ern-a-bly, *adv.* So as not to be restrained.
Un-grāce'ful, *a.* Wanting grace; inelegant; awkward; clumsy; uncouth.
Un-grāce'ful-ly, *adv.* Awkwardly. [wardness.
Un-grāce'ful-ness, *n.* Awk-
Un-grā'cioŭs, *a.* Not gracious; showing no kindness of heart; unpleasing.
Un-grā'cioŭs-ly, *adv.* In an ungracious manner.
Un-grāte'ful, *a.* Not grateful; unthankful; disagreeable. [ingratitude.
Un-grāte'ful-ly, *adv.* With
Un-grāte'ful-ness, *n.* Quality of being ungrateful.
Ŭn'guent (ŭng'gwent), *n.* An ointment.
Un-hăl'lōwed, *a.* Profane; unholy; impure; wicked.
Un-hand'i-ly, *adv.* Awkwardly; inconveniently.
Un-hănd'i-ness, *n.* Awkwardness; inconvenience.
Un-hănd'sŏme (-hăn'sum), *a.* Not handsome; illiberal; unfair; impolite.
Un-hănd'sŏme-ly (-hăn'sum-), *adv.* Ungracefully; illiberally; unfairly.
Un-hănd'y, *a.* Not handy; awkward; inexpert.
Un-hăp'pi-ly, *adv.* Unfortunately; miserably.
Un-hăp'pi-ness, *n.* Calamity; misfortune; infelicity.
Un-hăp'py, *a.* Not happy or fortunate; rather miserable; evil; calamitous.
Un-här'ness, *v. t.* To strip of harness; to divest of armor.
Un-hĕalth'i-ness, *n.* Quality or state of being unhealthy.
Un-hĕalth'y, *a.* Wanting health; unsound; sickly; insalubrious.
Un-hēard' (-hĕrd'), *a.* Not heard; unknown; obscure.
Un-hinge', *v. t.* To take from the hinges; to displace; to unfix by violence.
Un-hitch', *v. t.* To loose from being hitched; to unfasten.

Un-hō'li-ness, *n.* Want of holiness; impiety; sinfulness; wickedness.
Un-hō'ly, *a.* Not holy; profane; wicked; impious.
Un-hŏŏk', *v. t.* To loose from a hook.
Un-hŏŏp' or **Un-hŏŏp'**, *v. t.* To strip of hoops.
Un-hŏrse', *v. t.* To throw from a horse or saddle.
Un-hŭrt', *a.* Not hurt; safe and sound; whole.
Ū'ni-cŏrn, *n.* A fabulous animal with one horn.

Unicorn.

Ū'ni-fi-cā'tion, *n.* Act of so uniting with another as to make one being.
Ū'ni-flō'roŭs, *a.* Bearing only one flower.
Ū'ni-fôrm, *a.* Having always the same form. — SYN. Equal; even; alike; undeviating. — *n.* A dress of the same kind worn by persons who belong to the same regiment, &c.
Ū ni-fôrm'i-ty, *n.* Resemblance to itself at all times; consistency; sameness.
Ū'ni-fôrm-ly, *adv.* In a uniform manner; without variation.
Ū'ni-lăt'er-al, *a.* Having one side.
Ū ni-lĭt'er-al, *a.* Consisting of one letter only.
Ŭn'im-pēach-a-ble, *a.* Not to be impeached; free from stain or fault; blameless.
Ŭn'in-tĕl'li-gi-bĭl'i-ty, } *n.*
Ŭn'in-tĕl'li-gi-ble-ness, } Quality of being unintelligible.
Ŭn'in-tĕl'li-gi-ble, *a.* Not intelligible; not to be understood; obscure.
Ŭn'in-tĕl'li-gi-bly, *adv.* So as not to be understood.
Un-in'ter-est-ed, *a.* Having no interest or property in; not having the mind interested or engaged.
Ŭn'ion (yun'yun), *n.* [Lat. *unio*, from *unus*, one.] Act of uniting: junction: coalition; confederation: harmony; concord; upper inner corner of a flag.
Ŭn'ion-ist, *n.* A lover of union.

U-nip'a-roŭs, *a.* Producing one at a birth.
Ū-nique' (yu-nēek'), *a.* Single in kind or excellence; without a like or equal.
Ū'ni-son, *n.* Agreement: concord; union; accordance or coincidence of sounds.
U-nis'o-nance, *n.* Accordance of sounds.
U-nis'o-nant, } *a.* Being in
U-nis'o-noŭs, } unison; sounded together.
Ū'nit, *n.* One; a single person or thing; the least whole number.
Ū'ni-tā'ri-an, *n.* One who denies the Trinity, believing that God exists only in one person. — *a.* Pertaining to Unitarians.
Ū'ni-tā'ri-an-ĭṣm, *n.* The doctrines of Unitarians.
U-nīte', *v. t.* To join or put together; to form a whole. — *v. i.* To become one; to act in concert.
U-nīt'ed-ly, *adv.* With union, or joint efforts.
U-nī'ty, *n.* State of being one; oneness; concord; any definite quantity or aggregate taken as one.
Ū'ni-vălve, } *a.* Having
Ū'ni-vălv'u-lar, } one valve only, as a shell.
Ū'ni-vălve, *n.* A shell having one valve only.
Ū'ni-vẽr'sal, *a.* Extending to all; whole: total.
Ū'ni-vẽr'sal-ĭṣm, *n.* Belief that all men will be saved.
Ū'ni-vẽr'sal-ĭst, *n.* An adherent to Universalism.
Ū'ni-ver-săl'i-ty, *n.* State or quality of being universal; unlimited extension.
Ū'ni-vẽr'sal-ly, *adv.* Without exception; throughout the whole.
Ū'ni-verse, *n.* The whole system of created things.
Ū'ni-vẽr'si-ty, *n.* An institution where all the sciences and arts are taught.
U-nĭv'o-cal, *a.* Having one meaning only.
Un-jŭst', *a.* Contrary or opposed to justice; wrongful; inequitable.
Un-jŭst'ly, *adv.* Wrongfully.
Un-kĭnd', *a.* Not kind; wanting in kindness; cruel; harsh.
Un-kĭnd'ly, *adv.* With unkindness; cruelly. — *a.* Unnatural; unfavorable; malignant.

UNKINDNESS 319 UNRIPE

Un-kind'ness, *n.* Want of kindness or affection.
Un-knit' (-nĭt'), *v. t.* To separate, as threads that are knit; to open.
Un-know'ing-ly (-nō'ing-), *adv.* Ignorantly.
Un-lāçe', *v. t.* To unfasten; to loose the dress of.
Un-lāde', *v. t.* To unload; to discharge.
Un-law'fy̆l, *a.* Not lawful; contrary to law; illegal.
Un-law'ful-ly, *adv.* In violation of law; illegally.
Un-law'ful-ness, *n.* Illegality; contrariety to law.
Un-lẽarn', *v. t.* To forget, as what has been learned.
Un-lẽarn'ed, *a.* Ignorant; illiterate.
Un-lĕss', *conj.* Except; if not.
Un-lĕt'tered, *a.* Illiterate.
Un-līke', *a.* Not like; dissimilar; diverse.
Un-līke'li-hŏŏd, *n.* Improbability. [improbable.
Un-līke'ly, *a.* Not likely;
Un-līke'ness, *n.* Want of resemblance; dissimilitude.
Un-lĭm'it-ed, *a.* Not limited; boundless; undefined; indefinite; not restrained.
Un-lĭnk', *v. t.* To separate, as links; to disconnect.
Un-lōad', *v. t.* To relieve of a load; to disburden.
Un-lŏck', *v. t.* To unfasten, as what is locked; to explain; to open.
Un-lŏve'li-ness, *n.* Want of loveliness.
Un-lŏve'ly, *a.* Not amiable; disagreeable; repellant.
Un-lŭck'i-ly, *adv.* In an unlucky manner.
Un-lŭck'y, *a.* Not lucky; unfortunate; unhappy.
Un-māke', *v. t.* To destroy the form and qualities of.
Un-mân', *v. t.* To deprive of virility or strength; to dishearten.
Un-mân'ly, *a.* Unsuitable to a man; effeminate; ignoble; base. [rude.
Un-mân'nered, *a.* Uncivil;
Un-mân'ner-li-ness, *n.* Rudeness of behavior.
Un-mân'ner-ly, *a.* Ill-bred; uncivil; rude in behavior; impolite.
Un-māsk', *v. t.* To remove a mask or disguise from.
Un-mēan'ing, *a.* Having no meaning or expression.
Un-mẽr'çi-fy̆l, *a.* Having no mercy; cruel; inhuman.

Un-mẽr'çi-fy̆l-ly, *adv.* Without mercy; cruelly.
Un-mōōr', *v. t.* To cause to ride with a single anchor, after having been moored by two or more cables.
Un-năt'u-ral (106), *a.* Contrary to the laws of nature, or to natural feelings.
Un-năt'u-ral-ly, *adv.* In an unnatural manner.
Un-nĕç'es-sa-ri-ly, *adv.* Without necessity; needlessly.
Un-nĕç'es-sa-ry, *a.* Not necessary; useless; needless.
Un-nẽigh'bor-ly (-nā'bur-), *a.* Not becoming a neighbor; unfriendly; unkind.
Un-nẽrve', *v. t.* To deprive of nerve or strength; to enfeeble; to weaken.
Un-nŭm'bered, *a.* Not numbered, or not possible to be numbered; countless.
Ŭn'ob-trụ'sĭve, *a.* Not obtrusive or forward; modest.
Ŭn-ŏs'ten-tā'tioŭs, *a.* Not ostentatious; not making a showy display; modest.
Un-păck', *v. t.* To open, as things packed.
Un-păl'a-ta-ble, *a.* Not palatable; disagreeable; disgusting.
Un-pär'al-leled, *a.* Having no parallel or equal; matchless; peerless.
Un-pär'lĭa-mĕnt'a-ry, *a.* Contrary to the usages of Parliament or the rules of legislative bodies.
Un-pĭn', *v. t.* To unfasten or undo, as what is pinned.
Un-plĕas'ant, *a.* Not pleasant; displeasing; disagreeable.
Un-plĕas'ant-ly, *adv.* Disagreeably.
Un-plĕas'ant-ness, *n.* State or quality of being unpleasant.
Un-pŏp'u-lar, *a.* Not enjoying public favor; disliked by the people; disposing to public disfavor.
Un-pŏp'u-lăr'i-ty, *n.* State of being unpopular.
Un-prĕç'e-dent-ed, *a.* Having no precedent; novel; new.
Un-prĕj'u-dĭced (-prĕj'ụ-dĭst), *a.* Free from prejudice or bias; impartial.
Ŭn'pre-tĕnd'ing, *a.* Not making pretensions; modest.
Un-prĭn'çi-pled, *a.* Devoid of moral principle; destitute of virtue; profligate.

Ŭn'pro-dŭc'tĭve, *a.* Not fruitful; barren; sterile.
Un-prŏf'it-a-ble, *a.* Producing no profit; serving no purpose; useless.
Un-prŏf'it-a-bly, *adv.* Without profit or gain.
Un-prŏf'it-a-ble-ness, *n.* Quality of being unprofitable. [promise of good.
Un-prŏm'is-ing, *a.* Giving no
Ŭn'pro-pĭ'tioŭs (-pĭsh'ŭs), *a.* Not favorable; dark; discouraging; adverse.
Un-quăl'i-fied, *a.* Not qualified; not fit; absolute; decided.
Un-quĕs'tion-a-ble (-kwĕst'yŭn-), *a.* Not to be questioned or doubted; indubitable; certain.
Un-quĕs'tion-a-bly (-kwĕst'yun-), *adv.* Beyond all doubt; indubitably. [less.
Un-qui'et, *a.* Uneasy; rest-
Un-qui'et-ly, *adv.* In an unquiet manner or state.
Un-răv'el (-răv'l, 130), *v. t.* To disentangle or disengage; to separate; to solve.
Un-rē'al, *a.* Not real; having appearance only.
Un-rēa'son-a-ble (-rē'zn-), *a.* Exceeding the bounds of reason; immoderate; exorbitant; inordinate.
Un-rēa'son-a-ble-ness, *n.* State or quality of being unreasonable.
Un-rēa'son-a-bly, *adv.* Excessively; immoderately.
Ŭn're-gĕn'er-ate, *a.* Not regenerate; remaining at enmity with God.
Un're-lĕnt'ing, *a.* Feeling no pity; hard; cruel.
Un're-mĭt'ting, *a.* Not abating; incessant; continued; persevering.
Ŭn're-sẽrve', *n.* Absence of reserve; perfect frankness.
Ŭn're-sẽrved', *a.* Open; frank; free; ingenuous.
Ŭn're-sẽrv'ed-ly, *adv.* Without reservation; frankly.
Un-rĕst', *n.* Want of rest or repose; unquietness.
Un-rĭg', *v. t.* To strip of rigging.
Un-rīght'eoŭs (-rī'ehus), *a.* Not righteous; unjust; wicked; evil.
Un-rīght'eoŭs-ly (-rī'chus-), *adv.* Wickedly.
Un-rīght'eoŭs-ness (-rī'chus-), *n.* Wickedness.
Un-rīpe', *a.* Not ripe; immature.

sŏn, ôr, dọ, wọlf, tōō, tŏŏk; ûrn, rụe, pụll; ç, ġ, *soft;* c, g, *hard;* aṣ; exist; ŋ as ng; this.

UNRIVALED 320 UNWEARIED

Un-ri'valed, } a. Having no
Un-ri'valled, } rival; peerless; matchless.

Un-riv'et, v. t. To loose the rivets of; to unfasten.

Un-rōbe', v. t. To undress.

Un-rōll', v. t. To open, as what is rolled; to display.

Un-rōōf', v. t. To strip off the roof or covering of.

Un-rōōt', v. t. To extirpate; to eradicate.

Un-rŭf'fled, a. Not ruffled; calm; tranquill; quiet.

Un-rŭ'ly, a. Ungovernable; turbulent; refractory.

Un-sād'dle, v. t. To take a saddle from; to unhorse.

Un-sāfe', a. Not safe; not free from danger; dangerous; perilous.

Un-sāl'a-ble (133), a. Not having a quick sale.

Un-săt'is-făe'to-ri-ly, adv. In an unsatisfactory manner.

Un-săt'is-făe'to-ry, a. Not affording satisfaction.

Un-sā'vor-y, a. Not savory; having a bad taste; insipid.

Un-sāy', v. t. [imp. & p. p. UNSAID.] To recall, as what has been said.

Un-screw' (-skrụ'), v. t. To loose from screws; to withdraw, as a screw.

Un̄-scru'pu-lous, a. Having no scruples; unprincipled.

Un-sēal', v. t. To open, as what is sealed.

Un-sēarch'a-ble, a. Not to be searched into; inscrutable; mysterious.

Un-sēa'son-a-ble (-sĭ'zn-), a. Not seasonable; ill-timed; untimely; unfit.

Un-sēat', v. t. To throw from a seat.

Un-seem'li-ness, n. State or quality of being unseemly.

Un-seem'ly, a. Not seemly; unbecoming; indecent; improper. — adv. Indecently.

Un-seen', a. Not seen; invisible. [disturb.

Un-sĕt'tle, v. t. To unfix; to

Un-shăek'le, v. t. To loose from shackles; to set free.

Un-shāk'en, a. Not shaken; firm; stable.

Un-shēathe', v. t. To draw from the sheath or scabbard.

Un-ship', v. t. To take out of a ship.

Un-sight'ly (-sīt'lỹ), a. Not sightly; deformed; ugly.

Un-skil'ful, } a. Wanting skill
Un-skil'ful, } or dexterity; awkward; clumsy.

Un-skill'ful-ly, } adv. With-
Un-skil'ful-ly, } out skill; clumsily.

Un-skill'ful-ness, } n. Want
Un-skil'ful-ness, } of skill or dexterity; clumsiness.

Un-sō'cia-ble (-sō'sha-bl), a. Not sociable; averse to society.

Un-sō'cia-bly (-sō'sha-), adv. In an unsociable manner.

Un̄'so-phĭs'tĭ-cā'ted, a. Not adulterated; pure; simple; honest.

Un-sound', a. Not sound; defective; infirm; deceptive; sophistical.

Un-sound'ness, n. Defectiveness; infirmity.

Un-spăr'ing, a. Not sparing; liberal; profuse.

Un-spēak'a-ble, a. Not to be uttered or expressed; ineffable; unutterable.

Un-spēak'a-bly, adv. Inexpressibly; unutterably.

Un-spŏt'ted, a. Not spotted; spotless; pure; immaculate.

Un-stā'ble, a. Not stable or steady. — SYN. Inconstant; irresolute; wavering; mutable; changeful.

Un-stēad'ĭ-ly, adv. In an unsteady manner.

Un-stēad'ĭ-ness, n. Quality of being unsteady; inconstancy; irresolution.

Un-stēad'y, a. Not steady; mutable; variable; changeable.

Un-stŏp', v. t. To take a stopple or any obstruction from; to open.

Un-string', v. t. To deprive of strings; to relax; to loosen; to take from a string.

Un-strŭng', a. Relaxed; loosened.

Un'sue-çĕss'ful, a. Not successful; meeting with failure; unhappy.

Un'sue-çĕss'ful-ly, adv. With ill success.

Un-sūit'a-ble, a. Not suitable; unfit; improper.

Un-sūit'a-bly, adv. In an unsuitable manner; incongruously.

Un-sŭng', a. Not recited in song.

Un-swāthe', v. t. To relieve from a bandage.

Un-tām'a-ble, a. Not to be tamed or subdued.

Un-think'ing, a. Thoughtless; inconsiderate.

Un-thrift'y, a. Prodigal; not thriving; profuse; lavish.

Un-tīe', v. t. To loosen, as a knot; to unbind.

Un-tĭl' (133), prep. Till; as far as. — conj. Up to the time that; till.

Un-tīme'ly, a. Not timely; premature; unseasonable.

Un-tīr'ing, a. Not tiring; enduring; patient; indefatigable.

Un'to, prep. To.

Un-tōld', a. Not told; not related; not counted or numbered.

Un-tō'ward, a. Froward; refractory; awkward; cross; inconvenient. [ly.

Un-tō'ward-ly, adv. Perversely.

Un-tō'ward-ness, n. Frowardness; perversity; awkwardness.

Un-trăet'a-ble, a. Ungovernable; stubborn; intractable.

Un-trăet'a-ble-ness, n. Quality of being untractable.

Un-trăv'eled, } a. Not trod-
Un-trăv'elled, } den by passengers; not traveled; never having seen foreign countries.

Un-trūe', a. Not true; false; contrary to fact; disloyal.

Un-trū'ly, adv. Falsely.

Un-trŭss', v. t. To loose from a truss; to let out.

Un-truth', n. Falsehood; treachery; a lie.

Un-truth'ful, a. Wanting in veracity; false.

Un-twīne', v. t. To untwist.

Un-twĭst', v. t. To separate and open, as twisted threads; to disentangle.

Un-ūsed', a. Not used; not accustomed.

Un-ū'su-al (-yụ'zhụ-), a. Not usual; uncommon; rare; infrequent.

Un-ŭt'ter-a-ble, a. Not to be uttered; inexpressible.

Un-vär'nished (-vär'nisht), a. Not varnished; plain; truthful.

Un-veil', v. t. To remove a veil from; to uncover.

Un-wā'ri-ly, adv. Heedlessly.

Un-wā'ri-ness, n. Want of caution; heedlessness.

Un-war'rant-a-ble (un-wŏr'rant-), a. Not warrantable; illegal; improper.

Un-war'rant-a-bly, adv. Without warrant or authority; improperly.

Un-wā'ry, a. Not vigilant or cautious; precipitate.

Un-wēa'ried, a. Not wearied; persistent; indefatigable.

ā, ē, ī, ō, ū, ȳ, long; ă, ĕ, ĭ, ŏ, ŭ, ў, short; câre, cär, ȧsk, ạll, whạt; ẽre, veil, tẽrm; pique, firm;

Un-weave', v. t. To undo, as what has been woven.
Un-well', a. Not well; indisposed; ill; ailing.
Un-whōle'sŏme (-hōl'sum), a. Not wholesome; insalubrious.
Un-wield'i-ness, n. Quality or state of being unwieldy.
Un-wield'y, a. Unmanageable; bulky; ponderous.
Un-will'ing, n. Not willing; loath; disinclined; reluctant.
Un-will'ing-ly, adv. With reluctance.
Un-will'ing-ness, n. Reluctance; disinclination.
Un-wind', v. t. [imp. & p. p. UNWOUND.] To wind off; to untwist; to disentangle.
Un-wīse', a. Not wise; injudicious; indiscreet.
Un-wīse'ly, adv. Not wisely; imprudently.
Un-wit'ting-ly, adv. Without knowledge; ignorantly.
Un-wŏnt'ed, a. Unaccustomed; uncommon; infrequent; rare.
Un-wŏnt'ed-ness, n. Uncommonness; rarity.
Un-wor'thi-ly (-wûr'thĭ-), adv. Not according to desert.
Un-wor'thi-ness (-wûr'thĭ-), n. Want of worth.
Un-wor'thy (-wûr'thy̆), a. Not worthy; wanting merit; worthless; discreditable.
Un-wrăp' (-răp'), v. t. To open, as what is wrapped.
Un-wrēathe' (-rēeth'), v. t. To untwist, as any thing wreathed.
Un-writ'ten (-rĭt'tn), a. Not written; oral; blank.
Un-yield'ing, a. Not yielding; stubborn; obstinate.
Un-yōke', v. t. To loose from a yoke.
Ŭp, adv. Aloft; on high; above; from a lower to a higher position; in a higher place or position; completely.
— prep. From a lower to a higher place on or along; at the top of.
Up-bēar', v. t. To bear up; to raise or hold aloft.
Up-brāid', v. t. To charge with something wrong; to reprove severely. — SYN. To reproach; blame; censure.
Up-brāid'er, n. One who upbraids, or reproaches.
Ŭp'căst, a. Thrown upward.
— n. A throw or cast of bowls.

Up-hēav'al, n. A heaving up from beneath.
Up-hēave', v. t. To heave or lift up from beneath.
Ŭp'hill, a. Ascending; difficult; laborious.
Up-hōld', v. t. [imp. & p. p. UPHELD.] To elevate; to support; to maintain; to countenance. [holds.
Up-hōld'er, n. One who upholster-er (18), n. One who furnishes houses.
Up-hōl'ster-y (18), n. Furniture supplied by upholsterers.
Ŭp'lănd, n. High land, as opposed to meadows. — a. Higher in situation.
Up-lĭft', v. t. To raise aloft.
Up-ŏn', prep. On; — in all the senses of that word.
Ŭp'per, a. Further up; higher in place; superior.
Ŭp'per-hănd', n. Ascendency; superiority.
Ŭp'per-mōst, a. Highest in place, rank, or power.
Up-rāīse', v. t. To raise; to lift up; to exalt.
Ŭp'rīght, or Up-rīght' (-rīt), a. Erect; perpendicular; just; honest. — n. Something standing erect or perpendicular.
Ŭp'rīght-ly or Up-rīght'ly (-rīt-), adv. In an upright manner; honestly
Ŭp'rīght-ness' or Up-rīght'ness (-rīt/-), n. Erectness; honesty; integrity.
Up-rīse', v. i. [imp. UPROSE; p. p. UPRISEN.] To rise up; to get up; to ascend; to mount upward.
Up-rōar, n. Great noise and disturbance; tumult.
Up-rōot', v. t. To root up; to tear up by the roots; to eradicate.
Up-rouse', v. t. To rouse from sleep; to wake. [overset.
Up-sĕt', v. t. To overturn; to
Ŭp'shot, n. Final issue; conclusion; end.
Ŭp'sīde, n. The upper side.
Up-sprĭng', v. i. To spring up.
Ŭp'stärt, n. One suddenly raised to wealth or power.
Ŭp'ward, a. Directed to a higher place.
Ŭp'ward,) adv. Toward a
Ŭp'wards,) higher place; above; more than; in the upper parts.
U-rā'nĭ-um, n. A metal.
Ū'ran-ŏg'ra-phy,) n. A de-
Ū'ran-ŏl'o-gy,) scription

of the heavens and heavenly bodies.
Ū'ra-nus, n. One of the planets. [city.
Ŭr'ban. a. Pertaining to a
Ur-bāne', a. [Lat. urbanus, fr. urbs, a city.] Polite; courteous; of polished manners.
Ur-băn'ĭ-ty, n. Politeness; courtesy.
Ûr'chĭn, n. A child; a hedgehog.
U-rē'ter, n. A tube conveying the urine from the kidney to the bladder.
Ûrge, v. t. To press; to impel; to incite; to solicit; to importune.
Ûr'ġen-cy, n. Pressure of necessity; importunity.
Ûr'ġent, a. Pressing; earnest; importunate.
Ûr'ġent-ly, adv. With earnestness or importunity.
Ū'rī-nal, n. A vessel for urine.
Ū'rĭ-na-ry, a. Relating to, or resembling, urine.
Ū'rĭne, n. A fluid secreted by the kidneys.
Ûrn, n. A vessel of various forms; a kind of vase.
Ûr'sīne, a. Relating to, or like, a bear.
Ŭs (123, 124), pron. Objective case of We.
Ūs'aġe (133), n. Mode of using; treatment; custom; long-continued practice.
Ūs'ance, n. Time allowed for the payment of a bill of exchange.
Ūse (yūss, 88), n. Act of employing; employment; necessity; utility; practice; custom; interest.
Ūse (yūz), v. t. To employ; to handle; to treat; to consume; to render familiar. — v. i. To be accustomed.
Ūse'ful, a. Serviceable; proﬁtable; beneﬁcial; helpful.
Ūse'ful-ly. adv. With use or proﬁt.
Ūse'ful-ness, n. Quality of being useful; utility.
Ūse'less. a. Having no use; answering no purpose; vain; fruitless; ineffectual.
Ūse'less-ly, adv. Without use or proﬁt.
Ūse'less-ness, n. Unﬁtness for proﬁtable use; unserviceableness.
Ūs'er, n. One who uses.
Ŭsh'er, n. An ofﬁcer to introduce strangers, or to walk before a person of rank; an under teacher. — v. t. (130)

sŏn, ôr, dọ, wọlf, tōō, tŏŏk; ûrn, rụe, pụll; ç, ġ, soft; c, ġ, hard; aṣ; eẋist; n as ng; this.
14

To introduce; as a forerunner or harbinger.
Us'que-baugh (-baw), n. A kind of whisky; a compound distilled spirit.
Us'tion (ŭst'yun), n. Act of burning, or state of being burnt.
U'su-al (yu'zhu-), a. Customary; common; ordinary.
U'su-al-ly, adv. Customarily; commonly.
U'su-cap'tion, n. Acquisition of a right to property by having sole possession of it for a certain prescribed term of years.
U'su-frŭct (yu'zhu-), n. Right of using another's property without impairing the substance.
U'su-frŭct'u-a-ry, n. One who has the use and profits of property. — a. Relating to, or being in the nature of, a usufruct.
U'su-rer (yu'zhu-), n. One who practices usury.
U-sū'ri-oŭs (yu-zū'-), a. Practicing usury.

U-sū'ri-oŭs-ly (yu-zū'-), adv. In a usurious manner.
U-sŭrp', v. t. To seize and hold possession of wrougfully or by force.
U'sur-pā'tion, n. Illegal seizure or possession.
U-sŭrp'er, n. One who usurps.
U'su-ry (yu'zhu-), n. Exorbitant or illegal interest for the use of money.
U-těn'sil (108), n. An instrument; a household implement or vessel.
U'ter-ĭne, a. Born of the same mother, but by a different father.
U-til'i-tā'ri-an, a. Consisting in, or pertaining to, utility. — n. One who considers utility as the sole standard of virtue.
U-til'i-tā'ri-an-ĭsm, n. Doctrine or system of general utility.
U-til'i-ty, n. Production of good; profit; usefulness.
Ŭt'mŏst, a. Extreme; last; greatest. — n. The most that can be.

U-tō'pi-an, a. Ideal; fanciful; chimerical.
U'tri-cle, n. A little bag, bladder, or cell.
U-trĭc'u-lar, a. Containing little bladders.
Ŭt'ter, a. Outward; extreme; absolute; entire. — v. t. To speak; to pronounce; to put in circulation.
Ŭt'ter-a-ble, a. Capable of being uttered or expressed.
Ŭt'ter-ance, n. Act or manner of uttering; circulation; pronunciation. [fully.
Ŭt'ter-ly, adv. Completely;
Ŭt'ter-mŏst, a. Furthest; most remote; extreme. — n. Greatest degree.
U've-oŭs, a. Like a grape.
Ux-ō'ri-oŭs, a. [Lat. uxorius, from uxor, a wife.] Submissively or excessively fond of a wife.
Ux-ō'ri-oŭs-ly, adv. With fond or servile submission to a wife.
Ux-ō'ri-oŭs-ness, n. Excessive and foolish fondness for a wife.

V.

V (ve), the twenty-second letter of the alphabet, is only another form of the character U, the two letters having formerly been used indiscriminately, the one for the other. See U.
Vā'can-cy, n. Emptiness; leisure; vacuity; an unoccupied office.
Vā'cant, a. Empty; void; unoccupied; abandoned.
Vā'cāte, v. t. To leave empty; to annul or make void.
Va-cā'tion, n. Intermission of study or business; recess.
Văc'ci-nāte, v. t. To inoculate with cow-pox by means of virus taken (usually indirectly) from cows.
Văc'çi-nā'tion, n. Inoculation with cow-pox.
Văc'çi-nā'tor, n. One who vaccinates.
Văc'çīne, a. Pertaining to, or derived from, cows, or from vaccination.
Văc'il-lan-cy, n. Vacillation.
Văç'il-lāte, v. i. To waver; to reel; to fluctuate.

Văç'il-lā'ting. a. Inclined to fluctuate; inconstant.
Văç'il-lā'tion, n. Act of vacillating; a wavering; unsteadiness; inconstancy.
Va-cū'i-ty, n. Emptiness; void; vacuum.
Văc'u-um, n. Empty space.
Vā'de-mē'cum, n. [Lat., go with me.] A book or other thing that a person carries with him as a constant companion.
Văg'a-bŏnd, n. A vagrant. — a. Wandering idly or without any settled habitation.
Văg'a-bŏnd-ry, n. Condition of a vagabond.
Va-gā'ry (141), n. A wild freak; a whim.
Văg'i-nal, a. Pertaining to a sheath or canal.
Vā'gran-cy, n. A wandering without a settled home.
Vā'grant, a. Wandering; unsettled. — n. An idle wanderer; a strolling beggar; a tramp.
Vāgue, a. Unsettled; indefinite; loose.

Vāgue'ly, adv. In a vague manner.
Vāil, n. A covering to conceal; a veil. — v. t. To hide from sight; to cover.
Vāin, a. Fruitless; ineffectual; having a high opinion of one's self, or of what belongs to one; conceited.
Vāin-glō'ri-oŭs, a. Boastful.
Vāin-glō'ry, n. Empty pride.
Vāin'ly, adv. Without effect; with empty pride.
Vāl'ançe, n. Drapery round a bedstead. [valley.
Vāle, n. A low ground; a
Văl'e-dĭc'tion, n. A bidding farewell; an adieu.
Văl'e-dĭc-tō'ri-an, n. One who pronounces a valedictory oration.
Văl'e-dĭc'to-ry, a. Bidding farewell. — n. A farewell address.
Văl'en-tīne, n. A sweetheart chosen, or a letter sent to a sweetheart, on St. Valentine's day, the 14th of February. [in medicine.
Va-lē'ri-an, n. A plant used

VALET 323 VAUNT

Văl′et (*or* văl′ā), *n.* A body-servant; a personal attendant.

Văl′e-tū′di-nā′ri-an, *a.* Sickly; weakly; infirm. — *n.* A person in a weak state of health.

Văl′e-tū′di-na-ry, *a.* Infirm; sickly; weakly; seeking to recover health.

Văl′iant, *a.* Intrepid in danger; performed with valor. — SYN. Stout; bold; brave; courageous; heroic.

Văl′iant-ly, *adv.* In a valiant manner.

Văl′id, *a.* [Lat. *validus,* from *valere,* to be stroug.] Firm; good in law.

Va-līd′i-ty, *n.* Legal force; strength; cogency; justness.

Văl′id-ly, *adv.* In a valid manner; with legal force.

Vā-līse′, *n.* A travelling case; a portmanteau.

Val-lā′tion, *n.* A rampart; an intreuchment.

Văl′ley (141), *n.* A low place between hills; a vale.

Văl′or (155), *n.* Courage; bravery; prowess; intrepidity; gallantry.

Văl′or-oŭs, *a.* Valiant; gallant; brave. [precious.

Văl′u-a-ble, *a.* Having value;

Văl′u-ā′tion, *n.* Act of fixing the value; appraisement; value set.

Văl′ūe, *n.* Worth; price; rate; importance. — *v. t.* To estimate the worth of; to rate; to appraise; to esteem; to prize.

Vălv′ate, *a.* Having, resembling, or serving as a valve.

Vălve, *n.* A folding door; a lid or cover opening only one way.

Vălv′et, *n.* A little valve.

Vălv′u-lar, *a.* Having, or relating to, valves.

Vămp, *n.* Upper leather of a shoe. — *v. t.* To put new upper leather on; to mend.

Văm′pīre, *n.* A species of bat; a fabled demon said to suck human blood.

Văn, *n.* Front of an army; a kind of wagon; a fan

Văn′dal, *n.* A man of uncommon ferocity; an ignorant barbarian.

Van-dăl′ic, *a.* Relating to, or resembling, the Vandals; ferocious; barbarous.

Văn′dal-ism, *n.* Ferocious cruelty; barbarism; hostility to the arts and literature.

Văn-dyke′, *n.* A kind of neckerchief with points.

Vāne, *n.* A plate to show the direction of the wind; a weathercock.

Văn′guard, *n.* Troops in front; first line of an army.

Va-nĭl′la, *n.* A tropical plant, and an oil and a perfume extracted from it.

Văn′ish, *v. t.* To disappear; to pass away; to become invisible; to be lost to view.

Văn′i-ty, *n.* Empty pride; ostentation; conceit; idle pleasure.

Văn′quish (văŋk′wish), *v. t.* To conquer; to subdue.

Văn′quish-a-ble, *a.* Capable of being vanquished.

Văn′quish-er, *n.* One who conquers; a victor.

Văn′tage, *n.* Superiority.

Văn′tage-ground, *n.* Superiority of place or state.

Văp′id, *a.* Spiritless; flat; insipid; dull.

Va-pĭd′i-ty,) *n.* The state

Văp′id-ness,) of having lost life or spirit; flatness.

Vā′por (155), *n.* A fluid rendered aëriform by heat; steam; (*pl.*) A disease of debility; hypochondriacal affections; spleen. — *v. i.* To emit vapor; to brag; to boast.

Văp′or-a-ble, *a.* Capable of being converted into vapor.

Văp′or-āte, *v. t.* To evaporate.

Văp′o-rā′tion,*n.* Act of converting into vapor.

Vā′por-bāth, *n.* A bath of vapor or steam.

Vā′por-īze, *v. t.* To convert into vapor.

Vā′por-y, *a.* Full of vapors; splenetic; peevish.

Vā′ri-a-bĭl′i-ty, *n.* Quality of being variable.

Vā′ri-a-ble, *a.* Changeable; mutable; inconstant.

Vā′ri-a-ble-ness, *n.* Aptness to change; inconstancy.

Vā′ri-a-bly, *adv.* Changeably; inconstantly.

Vā′ri-ance, *n.* Disagreement; difference; dissension.

Vā′ri-ā′tion, *n.* A change; deviation; difference; alteration.

Vār′i-cōse, *a.* Preternaturally enlarged, as a vein.

Vā′ri-e-gāte, *v. t.* To diversify; to vary.

Vā′ri-e-gā′tion, *n.* Diversity of colors.

Va-rī′e-ty, *n.* Change; difference; diversity; that which is various; a varied assortment; a form subordinate to a species. [cut shapes.

Vā′ri-fôrm, *a.* Having different; 'ri-o-loid, or Văr′i-o-loid', *n.* A disease resembling the small-pox. [the small-pox.

Va-rī′o-loŭs, *a.* Pertaining to

Vā′ri-oŭs, *a.* Different; diverse; manifold. [ways.

Vā′ri-oŭs-ly, *adv.* In different

Vär′let, *n.* A servant or footman; a scoundrel; a rascal.

Vär′let-ry, *n.* The rabble.

Vär′nish, *n.* A viscid, glossy liquid. — *v. t.* To lay varnish on; to give a fair coloring to.

Vā′ry (135), *v. t.* To alter; to differ; to diversify. — *v. i.* To be altered in any manner; to be different; to deviate; to depart; to disagree.

Văs′cu-lar, *a.* Relating to, or consisting of, vessels.

Vāse (*in England,* väz *or* väz), *n.* An ornamental urn-shaped vessel, used for various purposes.

Văs′sal, *n.* A dependant; a bondman; a slave.

Văs′sal-age, *n.* Slavery; bondage; thralldom.

Văst, *a.* Being of great extent; immense; numerous; enormous.

Vas-tā′tion, *n.* A laying waste; devastation. [ly.

Văst′ly, *adv.* Greatly; huge-

Văst′ness, *n.* Immense extent; magnitude, or importance; immensity.

Văst′y, *a.* Immense; vast.

Văt, *n.* A large cistern.

Văt′i-cīde, *n.* The murder, or murderer, of a prophet.

Va-tĭç′i-nal, *a.* Containing prophecy or predictions.

Va-tĭç′i-nāte, *v. i.* To prophesy; to foretell. [cy.

Va-tĭç′i-nā′tion. *n.* Prophe-

†**Vaudeville** (vōd′vĭl), *n.* [Fr., from *Vau-de-vire,* a village in Normandy.] A lively kind of song; a theatrical piece intermingled with flight or satirical songs.

Vault, *n.* A continued arch, or an arched roof or ceiling; a cell; a cellar; a leap or bound. — *v. t.* To arch; to cover, with, or shape to, a vault. — *v. i.* To leap.

Vault′ed, *a.* Arched; concave.

Vaunt (vänt), *v. i.* To boast; to brag. — *n.* Vain boast.

Veal, n. Flesh of a calf dressed for the table.
Ve-dette' (ve-dĕt'), n. A sentinel on horseback.
Veer, v. t. or i. To turn; to turn aside; to change.
Veg'e-ta-ble, n. A plant, especially an edible plant; an organic body, destitute of sense and voluntary motion. — a. Of the nature of plants. [plants
Veg'e-tāte, v. i. To grow, as
Veg'e-tā'tion, n. Growth of plants; plants in general.
Veg'e-tā'tive, a. Growing, plants.
Ve'he-mençe, n. Violent activity or force; ardor.
Ve'he-ment, a. Acting with force. — SYN. Furious; earnest; ardent; eager.
Ve'he-ment-ly, adv. Violently; furiously. [riage.
Ve'hi-cle, n. Any kind of carriage.
Ve-hic'u-lar, a. Pertaining to a vehicle.
Veil, n. A thin cover for the face; a disguise. — v. t. To throw a veil over; to conceal.
Vein, n. A vessel which receives the blood from the arteries, and returns it to the heart; a current; a mineral seam or layer; tendency or turn of mind. — v. t. To form or mark with veins.
Veined, | a. Full of veins;
Vein'y, | variegated.
Vel'li-cāte, v. t. To twitch.
Vel'lum, n. A fine kind of parchment.
Ve-lŏç'i-pēde, n. A kind of light vehicle for, and propelled by, a single person.
Ve-lŏç'i-ty, n. Swiftness; rapidity; celerity; speed.
Vel'vet, n. A rich silk stuff, or stuff of silk and cotton, with a thick nap. — a. Like velvet; soft; smooth.
Vel'vet-een', n. A kind of velvet made partly of cotton.
Vel'vet-y, a. Soft; like velvet, smooth; delicate.
Vē'nal, a. Mercenary; sordid; pertaining to a vein, or to veins.
Ve-nǎl'i-ty, n. Mercenariness. [hunting.
Ven'a-ry, a. Relating to
Vend, v. t. To sell; to offer for sale.
Ven-dee', n. One to whom a thing is sold.
Vĕnd'er, | n. One who sells.
Vend'or, |
Vend'i-ble, a. Capable of being sold; fit to be sold; salable.
Vend'i-ble-ness, n. State or quality of being vendible.
Ven-di'tion (-dĭsh'un), n. Act of selling; sale.
Ven-dūe', n. Public sale to the highest bidder; auction.
Ve-neer', v. t. [From Fr. *fournir*, to furnish.] To overlay with thin pieces of wood.
— n. Thin slices of a valuable wood for overlaying some inferior material.
Vĕn'er-a-ble, a. Worthy of veneration or reverence.
Ven'er-a-bly, adv. In a venerable manner.
Ven'er-a-ble-ness, n. State or quality of being venerable.
Ven'er-āte, v. t. To regard with respect and reverence.
Ven'er-ā'tion, n. Highest degree of respect and reverence. [crates.
Ven'er-ā'tor, n. One who venerates.
Ve-nē're-al, a. Relating to sexual intercourse.
Ven'e-sĕc'tion, n. Act of opening a vein to let blood.
Venge'ance, n. Infliction of pain in return for an injury; revenge.
Venge'ful, a. Vindictive; revengeful. [cusable.
Vē'ni-al, a. Pardonable; excusable.
Ven'i-son (vĕn'i-zn or vĕn'zn), n. The flesh of deer, hares, &c. [malice; spite.
Ven'om (30), n. Poison;
Ven'om-ous, a. Poisonous; noxious to animal life; malignant.
Ven'om-ous-ly, adv. Poisonously; spitefully; malignantly.
Ve'nous, a. Contained in, or relating to, the veins.
Vĕnt, n. A passage for a fluid; aperture; utterance. — v. t. To let out; to emit; to utter; to report.
Vent'-hōle, n. A small hole for air; a vent.
Ven'ti-dūct, n. A passage for air.
Ven'ti-lāte, v. t. To fan; to expose to air; to make public.
Ven'ti-lā'tion, n. Act of ventilating.
Ven'ti-lā'tor, n. One who ventilates; a contrivance to exhaust foul or introduce pure air. [belly.
Ven'tral, a. Belonging to the
Ven'tri-cle, n. A cavity in an animal body, as of the brain, larynx, or heart.
Ven-tril'o-quĭşm, n. Art of speaking so that the voice seems to come from a distance.
Ven-tril'o-quĭst, n. One who practices ventriloquism.
Ven-tril'o-quous, a. Pertaining to ventriloquism.
Ven-tril'o-quy, n. Ventriloquism.
Vĕnt'ūre, v. t. To expose to hazard. — v. i. To have courage to do or undertake something; to run a risk. — SYN. To dare; hazard; risk. — n. A risking; hazard; chance; contingency; stake.
Vĕnt'ūre-sŏme, | a. Inclined
Vĕnt'ūr-oŭs, | to venture; bold; daring; adventurous.
Vĕn'ūe, n. A neighborhood, or near place.
Vē'nus, n. Goddess of female beauty and love; a planet.
Ve-rā'çioŭs, a. Observant of truth; truthful.
Ve-rǎç'i-ty, n. Observance of truth; truthfulness.
Ve-rǎn'dā (140), n. A kind of open portico.
Vĕrb, n. A word which affirms something of some person or thing.
Vĕrb'al (39), a. Spoken; oral; relating to words; relating to verbs; literal.
Verb'al-ly, adv. By word of mouth; orally.
†**Ver-bā'tim**, adv. [Lat.] Word for word; in the same words.
Vĕr'bi-age, n. Wordiness; verbosity; redundancy of words.
Ver-bōse', a. Abounding in words; prolix; wordy.
Ver-bōse'ness, | n. The use
Ver-bŏs'i-ty, | of too many words; prolixity.
Vĕr'dan-çy, n. Greenness; rawness; inexperience.
Vĕr'dant, a. Green; fresh; raw; unpracticed; easily overreached.
Verd-an-tĭque' (-teek'-), n. A green incrustation on brass or copper; a mottled green marble.
Vĕr'dict, n. The decision of a jury in a case submitted to them; opinion pronounced; judgment.
Vĕr'di-grĭs, n. [A corruption of New Lat. *viride æris*, green of brass.] Green rust of copper.
Vĕrd'ūre (vĕrd'yur, 50), n.

VERGE — 325 — VIATIC

Greenness; freshness of vegetation.
Verge (12), *n.* A kind of rod or mace; border; brink; edge. — *v. i.* To approach the limits; to incline; to tend.
Verg'er, *n.* A mace-bearer.
Ver'i-fi'a-ble (135), *a.* Capable of being verified.
Ver'i-fi-ca'tion, *n.* Act of verifying; confirmation.
Ver'i-fy, *v. t.* To prove to be true; to confirm; to authenticate. [ly.
Ver'i-ly, *adv.* Truly; certainly.
Ver'i-sim'i-lar, *a.* Having the appearance of truth; probable.
Ver'i-si-mil'i-tude, *n.* Resemblance to truth; probability; likelihood.
Ver'i-ta-ble, *a.* Agreeable to fact; true; actual; real.
Ver'i-ta-bly, *adv.* Really; truly; actually. [ality.
Ver'i-ty (141), *n.* Truth; reality.
Ver'juice, *n.* Sour juice expressed from wild apples, green grapes, &c.
Ver'mi-cel'li (-chel'li *or* -sel'li), *n.* A paste made into a slender, worm-like form.
Ver-mic'u-lar, *a.* Like a worm.
Ver-mic'u-late, *v. t.* To inlay so as to give the appearance of the tracks of worms.
Ver-mic'u-la'tion, *n.* Motion like that of a worm, or something resembling such motion. [or grub.
Ver'mi-cule, *n.* A little worm
Ver'mi-form, *a.* Having the shape of a worm.
Ver'mi-fuge, *n.* [Lat. *vermis*, a worm, and *fugere*, to flee.] A medicine to expel worms.
Ver-mil'ion (-mil'yun, 119), *n.* A bright red pigment or color; cochineal.
Ver'min, *n.* All sorts of small noxious animals.
Ver'min-ous, *a.* Infested, or caused, by vermin.
Ver-mip'a-rous (117), *a.* Producing worms. [on worms.
Ver-miv'o-rous, *a.* Feeding
Ver-nac'u-lar, *a.* Native; belonging to the country of one's birth.
Ver'nal, *a.* Belonging to, or appearing in, the spring.
Ver'sa-tile, *a.* Turning with ease from one thing to another; variable.
Ver'sa-til'i-ty, *n.* Quality of being versatile.

Verse (140), *n.* A single line of poetry; metrical language; a short division of a prose composition.
Versed (verst), *a.* Well skilled; practiced; acquainted; conversant.
Ver'si-fi-ca'tion, *n.* The art of composing verses.
Ver'si-fi'er, *n.* One who turns prose into verse.
Ver'si-fy, *v. t.* To describe in verse; to turn into verse. — *v. i.* To make verses.
Ver'sion, *n.* A translation.
Vert, *n.* Everything that bears a green leaf.
†**Ver'te-bra,** *n.* (*pl.* **Ver'te-bræ,** 147.) One of the joints of the spine or backbone.
Ver'te-bral, *a.* Relating to the vertebræ, or joints of the spine.
Ver'te-brate, *a.* Having a back-bone. — *n.* An animal having a back-bone.
Ver'te-bre (-ber), *n.* A vertebra; a joint of the spine.
Ver'tex, *n.* (*pl.* **Ver'tex-es** or †**Ver'ti-ces,** 147.) The crown or top; summit.
Ver'ti-cal, *a.* Being in the zenith; perpendicular; upright; plumb.
Ver'ti-cal-ly, *adv.* In a vertical manner.
Ver-tic'i-ty, *n.* Power of turning; rotation.
Ver-tig'i-nous, *a.* Affected with vertigo; giddy; dizzy.
Ver'ti-go, *n.* A swimming of the head; dizziness.
Ver'vain, *n.* A plant.
Ver'y, *a.* True; real; actual. — *adv.* In or to a great degree; eminently.
Ves'i-cant, *n.* A blistering application.
Ves'i-cate, *v. t.* To blister.
Ves'i-ca'tion, *n.* Act of raising blisters.
Ves'i-ca-to-ry, *a.* Having a power to blister. — *n.* A blistering application.
Ves'i-cle, *n.* A little air-bladder.
Ve-sic'u-lar, *a.* Pertaining to, or consisting of, vesicles.
Ves'per, *n.* The evening star; evening; Venus; (*pl.*) evening song or service.
Ves'per-tine, *a.* Relating to, or being in, the evening.
Ves'sel, *n.* A hollow dish of any kind; a cask; a tube; any structure intended for navigation, as a ship, brig, boat, &c.

Vest, *n.* Any garment; a waistcoat. — *v. t.* To clothe; to put in possession. — *v. i.* To come or descend.
Ves'tal, *a.* Pertaining to Vesta, a virgin goddess of the Romans; pure; chaste. — *n.* A virgin consecrated to Vesta.
Vest'ed, *a.* Fixed; not contingent, as rights.
Ves'ti-būle, *n.* An antechamber between the hall and the outer doors; a kind of porch. [a trace.
Ves'tige (140), *n.* A footstep;
Vest'ment, *n.* A garment.
Ves'try, *n.* A room for sacerdotal vestments in a church; a lecture-room or chapel; a parochial assembly; a parochial committee.
Vest'ure, *n.* A garment; articles worn. — SYN. Apparel; dress; clothing.
Vetch, *n.* A leguminous plant.
Vet'er-an, *a.* Long exercised in any thing, especially in war. — *n.* An old soldier; one long exercised.
Vet'er-i-nā'ri-an, *n.* One skilled in diseases of cattle.
Vet'er-i-na-ry, *a.* Pertaining to the art of healing the diseases of domestic animals.
Ve'to (140), *n.* (*pl.* **Ve'tōes.**) [Lat., I forbid.] An authoritative prohibition; power to negative a bill. — *v. t.* To forbid the enactment of.
Vex, *v. t.* To tease; to provoke; to irritate.
Vex-a'tion, *n.* Act of irritating, or state of being irritated; trouble; annoyance.
Vex-a'tious, *a.* Provoking; troublesome. [vex.
Vex-a'tious-ly, *adv.* So as to
Vex-a'tious-ness, *n.* Quality of being vexatious.
Vi'a-ble, *a.* Capable of living, as a child prematurely born.
Vi'a-duct, *n.* A structure for carrying a railroad across a valley or river.
Vi'al, *n.* A small bottle. — *v. t.* (130) To put into a vial, or into vials.
Vi'ands, *n. pl.* Articles of food; victuals. [journey.
Vi-at'ic, *a.* Relating to a

són, ôr, dọ, wọlf, tòo, tòòk; firm, rụe, pụll; ç, ġ, *soft*; c, g, *hard*; aṣ; eḳist; ṇ *as* ng; this.

VIATICUM 326 VIOLENT

†Vi-ăt'i-cum, n. [Lat.] Provisions for a journey; the communion given to dying persons.
Vī'brāte, v. t. or i. To move to and fro; to oscillate.
Vī-brā'tion, n. Act of vibrating; oscillation.
Vī'bra-to-ry, a. Consisting in vibration or oscillation; causing vibration.
Vĭc'ar, n. Incumbent of an appropriated benefice.
Vĭc'ar-age, n. Benefice or residence of a vicar.
Vī-cā'ri-al, a. Of, or belonging to, a vicar.
Vī-cā'ri-āte, a. Having delegated power, as a vicar. — n. Office or oversight of a vicar.
Vī-cā'ri-oŭs, a. Acting in place of another; deputed; delegated; substituted.
Vĭçe, n. A blemish; fault; immoral conduct or habit; a smith's instrument.
†Vī'çe, prep. [Lat.] In the place of; instead of.
Vĭçe'-ăd'mi-ral, n. An officer next in rank to an admiral.
Vĭçe-cŏn'sul, n. One acting for the consul.
Vĭçe-gē'rent, n. An officer acting in place of another; a lieutenant.
Vĭçe-prĕṣ'i-dent, n. An officer next in rank to a president. [a viceroy.
Vĭçe-rō'gal, a. Pertaining to
Vĭçe'roy, n. A governor ruling as the substitute of a king.
Vĭçe-roy'al-ty, n. Office or jurisdiction of a viceroy.
Vĭç'i-nage, n. Neighborhood.
Vĭç'i-nal, a. Near; bordering.
Vĭ-çĭn'i-ty, n. Neighborhood.
Vĭ'cioŭs (vĭsh'us), a. Immoral; depraved; corrupt; wicked; unruly.
Vĭ'cious-ly (vĭsh'us-), adv. Wickedly; corruptly.
Vĭ-çĭs'si-tūde, n. Regular change; alternation; mutation; mutual succession.
Vĭc'tim, n. A living being sacrificed; something destroyed; a dupe.
Vĭc'tim-īze, v. t. To make a victim or dupe of.
Vĭc'tor, n. A conqueror.
Vĭc-tō'ri-oŭs, a. Superior in contest. — SYN. Conquering; triumphant; successful. [victorious manner.
Vĭc-tō'ri-oŭs-ly, adv. In a
Vĭc'to-ry, n. Conquest; triumph; success.

Vĭct'ual (vĭt'l, 130), v. t. To supply with provisions.
Vĭct'ual-er (vĭt'l-er), n. One who supplies provisions.
Vĭct'uals (vĭt'lz), n. pl. Food prepared for the table.
†Vī-dĕl'i-çet, adv. [Lat.] To wit; namely; — abbreviated viz.
Vīe (134), v. i. To strive for superiority; to attempt to surpass or to equal; to contend.
View (vū), v. t. To see; to behold; to survey. — n. Sight; survey; inspection; prospect; opinion. [views.
View'er (vū'-), n. One who
View'less (vū'-), a. Invisible.
Vĭġ'il, n. Watch; nocturnal devotion; eve before a feast; a fast on the day preceding a holiday.
Vĭġ'i-lançe, n. Forbearance of sleep; watchfulness.
Vĭġ'i-lant, a. Watchful; circumspect; attentive.
Vĭġ'i-lant-ly, adv. Watchfully; attentively.
Vĭgnette (vĭn-yĕt' or vĭn'yet), n. A wood-cut or engraving, in a book, not inclosed within a definite border.
Vĭġ'or (155), n. Energy; force of body or strength of mind; strength.
Vĭġ'or-oŭs, a. Full of, or exhibiting, active force. — SYN. Strong; powerful; forcible; agile. [vigor or force.
Vĭġ'or-oŭs-ly, adv. With
Vīle, a. Contemptibly mean or low; base; sordid; morally impure.
Vīle'ly, adv. Basely; meanly; shamefully.
Vīle'ness, n. Baseness; meanness; moral impurity.
Vĭl'i-fī'er, n. One who vilifies; a traducer. [traduce.
Vĭl'i-fȳ, v. t. To defame; to
Vĭl'la (140), n. A country residence, usually of a rich person; a country-seat.
Vĭl'lage (42), n. A small inhabited place. [village.
Vĭl'la-ger, n. Inhabitant of a
Vĭl'lain, n. A feudal tenant of the lowest class; a vile, wicked person; a scoundrel.
Vĭl'lain-oŭs (149), a. Wicked;
Vĭl'lan-oŭs } base; extremely depraved.
Vĭl'lain-y } (149), n. Extreme
Vĭl'la-ny } depravity or wickedness.
Vĭl'lan-age, n. Feudal servitude or tenure of lands.

Vĭl-lōse', } a. Nappy; downy;
Vĭl'loŭs, } shaggy; velvety.
Vĭm'i-nal, } a. Made of, or
Vī-mĭn'e-oŭs, } producing, twigs.
Vī-nā'ceoŭs (-nā'shus), a. Belonging to wine or grapes.
Vĭn'çi-ble, a. Capable of being overcome. [vintage.
Vĭn-dĕ'mi-al, a. Belonging to
Vĭn'di-cāte, v. t. To defend with success; to justify; to maintain; to support.
Vĭn'di-cā'tion, n. Justification; defense; support.
Vĭn'di-cā'tive, } a. Tending
Vĭn'di-ca-to-ry, } to vindicate. [vindicates.
Vĭn'di-cā'tor, n. One who
Vĭn-dĭc'tĭve, a. Revengeful.
Vĭn-dĭc'tĭve-ly, adv. Revengefully; by way of revenge.
Vĭn-dĭc'tĭve-ness, n. Revengeful temper.
Vīne, n. A climbing plant producing grapes; hence, any climbing or trailing plant.
Vĭn'e-gar, n. [Fr. vinaigre, from vin, wine, and aigre, sour.] An acid liquor obtained from wine, cider, &c., by fermentation.
Vīn'er-y, n. A structure for rearing vines.
Vīne'yard (vĭn'yard), n. A plantation of grape-vines.
Vī'noŭs, a. Having the qualities of, or pertaining to, wine.
Vĭnt'age, n. Produce, in grapes or in wine, of vines; time of grape-gathering.
Vĭnt'a-ger, n. One who gathers the vintage.
Vĭnt'ner, n. A dealer in wines.
Vĭnt'ry, n. A place where wine is sold.
Vī'ny, a. Pertaining to vines.
Vī'ol, n. A stringed musical instrument.
Vī'o-là, n. An instrument of the violin kind, a fifth lower in compass than the violin.
Vī'o-la-ble, a. Capable of being violated. [in color.
Vī'o-lā'ceoŭs, a. Like violets
Vī'o-lāte, v. t. To abuse; to infringe; to do violence to; to ravish.
Vī'o-lā'tion, n. Act of violating; transgression; infringement; rape. [lates.
Vī'o-lā'tor, n. One who violates. [lates.
Vī'o-lençe, n. Highly excited action; unjust force; rape.
Vī'o-lent, a. Excited by strong passion; outrageous; furious; extreme.

ā, ä, ī, ō, ū, ȳ, long; ă, ĕ, ĭ, ŏ, ŭ, ў, short; cāre, cär, ȧsk, ạll, whạt; ẽre, vẹil, tẽrm; p͞ique, fĩrm;

VIOLENTLY 827 VOCATIVE

Vī'o-lent-ly, *adv.* With force; vehemently.
Vī'o-let, *n.* A plant and its flower; a dark, reddish-blue color.
Vī'o-lin', *n.* A stringed instrument of music; a fiddle.
Vī'o-lin'ist, *n.* A player on the viol.
Vī'o-lon-cĕl'lo (-chĕl'lo, or -sĕl'lo), *n.* A bass-viol of four strings.
Vī'per, *n.* A kind of poisonous serpent.
Vī'per-īne, *a.* Pertaining to vipers.
Vī'per-oŭs, *a.* Having the qualities of a viper.
Vī-rā'go (*pl.* VĪ-rā'gōes, 18), *n.* A bold, masculine woman; a termagant.
Vir'ġin (16), *n.* A maid; a maiden. — *a.* Chaste; maidenly; modest; pure; undefiled; new; fresh.
Vir'ġin-al, *a.* Belonging to a virgin: maidenly.
Vir-ġin'i-ty, *n.* State of a virgin; maidenhood.
†**Vir'go**, *n.* The Virgin, a sign in the zodiac.
Vī-rid'i-ty, *n.* Greenness.
Vīr'īle, or **Vīr'īle**, *a.* Belonging to males.
Vi-rīl'i-ty (vī- or vĭ-), *n.* Manhood; power of procreation.
Vir-tu', *n.* A love of the fine arts; a taste for curiosities.
Vīrt'u-al, *a.* Being in essence or effect; not in fact.
Vīrt'u-al-ly, *adv.* In efficacy or effect only.
Vīr'tūe (140), *n.* [Lat. *virtus*, strength, courage, virtue, fr. *vir*, a man.] Strength; efficacy; moral excellence.
Vīr'tu-ō'so, *n.* (*pl.* Vĭr'tu-ō'sōs or †Vīr'tu-ō'sī, 140, 147). One skilled in the fine arts, in curiosities, &c.
Vīrt'u-oŭs, *a.* Morally good; righteous: chaste; pure.
Vīrt'u-oŭs-ly, *adv.* In a virtuous manner.
Vir'u-lence, *n.* Poisonousness; malignity.
Vir'u-lent, *a.* Very poisonous; malignant; bitter.
Vir'u-lent-ly, *adv.* In a virulent manner.
Vī'rus, *n.* Contagious matter from ulcers, &c.; poison.
Vĭs'age, *n.* The face; countenance; look; features.
†**Vĭs'çer-a**, *n. pl.* The bowels.
Vĭs'çer-al, *a.* Pertaining to the viscera.
Vĭs'çid, *a.* Glutinous; sticky.

Vĭs-çĭd'i-ty, } *n.* Glutinousness; stickiness;
Vĭs-cōs'i-ty, } tenacity.
Vĭs'count (vī'kount), *n.* A nobleman next in rank below an earl.
Vĭs'count-ess (vī'kount-), *n.* A viscount's wife.
Vĭs'coŭs, *a.* Glutinous; adhesive; sticky.
Vĭs'coŭs-ness, *n.* Viscosity.
Vīse, *n.* An instrument for griping and holding things.
Vĭġ'i-bĭl'i-ty, *n.* The state or quality of being visible.
Vĭġ'i-ble, *a.* Perceivable by the eye; perceptible.
Vĭġ'i-ble-ness, *n.* Visibility.
Vĭġ'i-bly, *adv.* Perceptibly; plainly; clearly.
Vĭs'ion (vĭzh'un), *n.* Faculty or sense of sight; apparition; phantom.
Vĭs'ion-a-ry (vĭzh'un-), *a.* Given to reverie; imaginary; having no foundation. — *n.* One who forms wild or impracticable schemes.
Vĭs'it (130), *v. t.* To go or come to see; to examine. — *n.* Act of going or coming to see; examination.
Vĭs'it-a-ble, *a.* In a state to receive visits.
Vĭs'it-ant, *n.* One who visits.
Vĭs'it-ā'tion, *n.* Act of visiting; access for examination; special dispensation; retributive calamity.
Vĭs'it-or, *n.* One who visits.
Vĭs'it-ō'ri-al, *a.* Belonging to a judicial visitor or superintendent.
Vĭs'or, or **Vī'sor**, *n.* A mask; disguise; forepiece of a cap.
Vĭs'tā (140), *n.* A prospect or view through an avenue; the avenue itself.
Vĭs'u-al (vĭzh'yu-), *a.* Belonging to the sight; used in vision.
Vī'tal, *a.* Pertaining, contributing, or necessary, to life; very important. — SYN. Essential; necessary; immediate; absolute.
Vī-tăl'i-ty, *n.* Quality of being vital; principle of life; animation; tenacity of life.
Vī'tal-ly, *adv.* In a manner affecting life; essentially.
Vī'tals, *n. pl.* Parts of animal bodies essential to life, or to a sound state.
Vī'ti-āte (vĭsh'ī-āt), *v. t.* To make vicious or faulty; to injure; to invalidate.
Vĭ'ti-ā'tion (vĭsh-ĭ-), *n.* Depravation; corruption; invalidation.
Vĭt're-oŭs, *a.* Pertaining to, or resembling, glass.
Vĭt'ri-fāc'tion, *n.* Act of converting into glass by heat.
Vĭt'ri-fī'a-ble, *a.* Capable of being vitrified.
Vĭt'ri-fȳ, *v. t.* or *i.* To convert into, or become, glass.
Vĭt'ri-ol, *n.* A soluble sulphate of any metal.
Vĭt'ri-ŏl'ic, *a.* Pertaining to, or obtained from, vitriol.
Vī-tū'per-āte, *v. t.* To overwhelm with abuse.
Vī-tū'per-ā'tion, *n.* Severe censure; abuse.
Vī-tū'per-a-tive, *a.* Containing severe censure; abusive.
Vī-vā'cioŭs, *a.* Lively; brisk; sprightly; animated.
Vī-văç'i-ty, *n.* Liveliness; sprightliness; animation.
Vīv'id, *a.* Lively; bright; active; spirited; sprightly.
Vīv'id-ly, *adv.* With life and spirit; in glowing colors.
Vīv'id-ness, *n.* Quality of being vivid; life; liveliness.
Vī-vīf'ie, *n.* Giving life.
Vī-vīf'i-cāte, *v. t.* To give life to; to animate; to vivify.
Vīv'i-fī-cā'tion, *n.* Act of vivifying. [to.
Vīv'i-fȳ, *v. t.* To impart life
Vī-vip'a-roŭs (117), *a.* Producing young alive.
Vīx'en, *n.* A cross, ill-tempered woman; a scold.
Vīx'en-ly, *a.* Having the qualities of a vixen.
Vĭz'ard, *n.* A mask.
Vĭz'ier (vĭz'jer or vĭ-zeer'), *n.* A high executive officer in Turkey, &c.
Vō'ca-ble, *n.* A word; term.
Vo-căb'u-la-ry, *n.* A list of words arranged alphabetically and explained; sum of words used.
Vō'cal, *a.* Having a voice; spoken with voice or tone; vocal.
Vo-căl'ic, *a.* Consisting of the voice, or of vowel sounds.
Vō'cal-ĭst, *n.* A singer, or vocal musician.
Vo-căl'i-ty, *n.* Quality of being vocal. [make vocal.
Vō'cal-īze (153), *v. t.* To
Vo-cā'tion, *n.* [Lat. *vocatio*, from *vocare*, to call.] Act of calling; occupation; employment; calling; business.
Vŏc'a-tive, *n.* Fifth case of Latin nouns, used in direct address.

són, ôr, dọ, wọlf, tōō, tōŏk; ûrn, rụe, pụll; ç, ġ, *soft*; ᴄ, ġ, *hard*; aẓ; eẋist; ŋ *as* ng; this.

VOCIFERATE 328 VULTURINE

Vo-çif'er-āte, *v. i.* To cry out with vehemence.
Vo-çif'er-ā'tion, *n.* Loud or violent outcry; clamor.
Vo-çif'er-oŭs, *a.* Clamorous.
Vōgue (vōg), *n.* Temporary fashion or mode.
Voiçe, *n.* Sound uttered by the mouth; a vote; suffrage.
Voiçe'less, *a.* Having no voice.
Void, *a.* Vacant; empty; destitute; null; having no legal force; unsubstantial. — *n.* An empty space; a vacuum. — *v. t.* To quit; to eject; to evacuate; to annul.
Void'a-ble, *a.* Capable of being made void.
Void'ançe, *n.* Act of voiding; ejection.
Void'er, *n.* One who voids; a tray for removing dishes.
Void'ness, *n.* Emptiness; want of binding force.
Vŏl'a-tĭle, *a.* Evaporating quickly; lively; gay; fickle.
Vŏl'a-tĭl'i-ty, *n.* Disposition to fly off in vapor; levity.
Vŏl'a-til-īze, *v. t.* To cause to exhale or evaporate.
Vol-eăn'ic, *a.* Pertaining to, or produced by, a volcano.
Vol-eā'no, *n.* (*pl.* Vol-eā'-nōeṣ, 140). A mountain emitting fire, lava, &c.
Vo-li'tion (-lish'un), *n.* The act or power of willing.
Vŏl'ley (141), *n.* A discharge of many small arms at once. — *v. t.* or *i.* To discharge or be discharged in a volley, or as if in a volley.
Vol-tā'ic, *a.* Relating to Volta, or to electricity developed by chemical action.
Vŏl'ta-ĭsm, *n.* Galvanism.
Vŏl'u-bĭl'i-ty, *n.* Great fluency of speech.
Vŏl'u-ble, *a.* Apt to roll; exceedingly fluent.
Vŏl'u-bly, *adv.* In a rolling or very fluent manner.
Vŏl'ume (vŏl'yụm), *n.* A book; dimensions; compass.
Vo-lū'mi-noŭs, *a.* Consisting of many volumes; copious.
Vo-lū'mi-noŭs-ly, *a.* In many volumes; copiously.
Vŏl'un-ta-ri-ly, *adv.* Of one's own free will; spontaneously.
Vŏl'un-ta-ry, *a.* [Lat. *voluntarius*, from *voluntas*, will,

choice.] Proceeding from choice; willing; free. — *n.* An air played at will or extemporaneously.
Vŏl'un-teer', *n.* One who enters into any service of his own free will. — *v.* To offer or engage voluntarily. — *a.* Entering into service of free will.
Vo-lŭpt'u-a-ry, *n.* One given to luxury; a sensualist
Vo-lŭpt'u-oŭs, *a.* Luxurious; sensual. [uriously.
Vo-lŭpt'u-oŭs-ly, *adv.* Luxuriously.
Vo-lūte', *n.* A kind of spiral scroll, used in the Ionic, Corinthian, and Composite capitals.
Vŏm'it, *v. t.* or *i.* To throw up from the stomach; to spew; to puke. — *n.* An emetic.
Vo-mi'tion (-mish'un), *n.* Act or power of vomiting.
Vŏm'i-tive, *a.* Causing to vomit; emetic.
Vŏm'it-o-ry, *a.* Procuring vomiting; emetic. — *n.* An emetic; a principal door of a large public building.
Vo-rā'cioŭs, *a.* Greedy to eat or devour; ravenous.
Vo-rā'cioŭs-ly, *adv.* Greedily.
Vo-rā'cioŭs-ness, *n.* Greediness of appetite.
Vo-răç'i-ty (114), *n.* Greediness of appetite.
Vŏr'tex, *n.* (*p'.* Vŏr'tex-eṣ, or †Vŏr'tĭ-çeṣ, 147.) A whirlpool; a whirlwind.
Vẽr'ti-cal, *a.* Having a whirling motion.
Vō'ta-reṣṣ, *n.* A female votary.
Vō'ta-ry (141), *n.* One devoted or consecrated by vow to any service or pursuit. — *a.* Devoted; promised; consecrated by vow.
Vōte, *n.* Expression of choice in elections; suffrage; ballot. — *v.* To express one's choice by the voice or by a written ticket; to choose or determine by means of votes.

Vōt'er, *n.* One who votes, or who has a right to vote.
Vō'tive, *a.* Given by vow.
Vouch, *v. t.* To call to witness; to warrant; to support; to establish. — *v. i.* To bear witness.
Vouch'er, *n.* One who vouches; a book or paper that confirms the truth of accounts.
Vouch-sāfe', *v. t.* To condescend to grant. — *v. i.* To deign; to condescend.
Vow, *n.* A solemn promise to God or to some deity. — *v. t.* or *i.* To consecrate by a solemn promise; to devote; to assert solemnly.
Vow'el, *n.* A vocal sound made through an open position of the mouth organs, as *a*, *e*, *o*. — *a.* Pertaining to a vowel; vocal.
Voy'age (*colloq.* voij), *n.* A journey by water. — *v. i.* To travel by water.
Voy'a-ger (*colloq.* voij'er), *n.* One who journeys by water.
Vŭl'ean-īte, *n.* A hard black compound of India rubber and sulphur.
Vŭl'ean-īze, *v. t.* To impart certain properties to, as India-rubber, by causing it to combine with sulphur.
Vŭl'gar, *a.* Pertaining to common people; being in general use; offensively mean or low. — SYN. Common; ordinary; mean; unrefined. — *n.* The common people; the populace.
Vŭl'gar-ĭṣm, *n.* A vulgar phrase or expression.
Vul-găr'i-t̯, *n.* Clownishness; rudeness.
Vŭl'gar-ly, *adv.* Commonly; coarsely; rudely.
Vŭl'gate, *n.* An ancient Latin version of the Bible.
Vŭl'ner-a-ble, *a.* Capable of being wounded. [ing wounds.
Vŭl'ner-a-ry, *a.* Useful in healing wounds.
Vŭl'pĭne, *a.* [Lat. *vulpinus*, fr. *vulpes*, a fox.] Pertaining to, or resembling, the fox; cunning; crafty.
Vŭlt'ūre (140), *n.* A large bird of prey, found only on the Eastern continent.
Vŭlt'ŭr-ine, *a.* Pertaining to, or like, the vulture.

ē, ā, ī, ō, ū, ȳ, *long*; ă, ĕ, ĭ, ŏ, ŭ, ў, *short*; cāre, eär, ȧsk, ạll, whạt; ẽre, vẹil, tẽrm; pīque, fĭrm;

W.

Wab'ble (wŏb'bl), *v. i.* To move staggeringly from side to side. — *n.* A hobbling, unequal motion, as of a wheel.

Wad, *n.* A small mass of paper, tow, &c., to stop the charge of a gun or any aperture. — *v. t.* To form into a wad.

Wad'ded, *a.* Formed into a wad; quilted.

Wad'ding, *n.* A wad, or the materials for wads; a soft stuff used in quilting.

Wad'dle, *v. i.* To walk like a duck or a fat person.

Wade, *v. i.* or *t.* To walk through any yielding substance, as water or snow, &c.

Wa'fer, *n.* A thin kind of cake or bread, esp. that used by the Roman Catholics in the Eucharist; a thin leaf of paste for sealing letters, &c. — *v. t.* To seal with a wafer.

Waf'fle, *n.* A thin, soft kind of cake.

Waft, *v. t.* To bear through a fluid or buoyant medium.

Wag, *n.* A merry, droll fellow. — *v. t.* or *i.* To move one way and the other; to move; to stir.

Wage, *v. t.* To pledge; to stake; to hazard; to bet.

Wa'ger, *n.* Something hazarded; a bet. — *v. t.* To offer to bet.

Wa'ges, *n. pl.* Hire; reward of services.

Wag'ger-y, *n.* Pleasantry; drollery; sportive trick.

Wag'gish, *a.* Roguish; droll.

Wag'gish-ly, *adv.* In sport.

Wag'gish-ness, *n.* Quality of being waggish. [wag.

Wag'gle, *v. t.* To waddle; to

Wag'on, *n.* A vehicle on four wheels, especially one for carrying freight.

Wag'on-er, *n.* One who conducts a wagon.

Waif (126'), *n.* Goods found, but not claimed.

Wail, *v.* To weep; to lament with outcry.

Wain, *n.* A wagon.

Wain'scot, *n.* A wooden lining of rooms, made in panels. — *v. t.* To line with boards in panel.

Waist, *n.* Part of the body just below the ribs; middle part of a ship.

Waist'band, *n.* The band or upper part of trowsers, &c.

Waist'coat, *n.* A garment worn under the coat.

Wait, *v. i.* To stay in expectation; to attend.

Wait'er, *n.* One who waits; an attendant; a salver or tray.

Wait'ing-maid, *n.* A female servant who attends a lady.

Waive, *v. t.* To relinquish voluntarily; to give up claim to; to forego.

Wake, *v. i.* To cease to sleep. — *n.* A watch; the sitting up of persons with a dead body; track of a vessel in water.

Wake'ful (130), *a.* Unable to sleep; vigilant.

Wake'ful-ness, *n.* Inability to sleep; want of sleep.

Wak'en, *v. i.* or *t.* To rouse from sleep; to awake.

Wale, *n.* A ridge or streak; one of the long planks of a ship's side. — *v. t.* To mark with wales, or stripes.

Walk (wawk), *v. i.* To move on foot; to go by steps. — *n.* A gait; a step; a path.

Walk'er (wawk'er), *n.* One who walks.

Wall (123), *n.* An inclosing fence of brick or stone; side of a room; a defense. — *v. t.* To inclose with a wall.

Wal'let, *n.* A bag or knapsack; a pocket-book.

Wall'-eye, *n.* A whitish or very light gray eye.

Wall'-eyed, *a.* Having a wall-eye.

Wal'lop (130), *v. i.* To boil. — *v. t.* To beat soundly.

Wal'low, *v. i.* To roll one's self about, as on mire. — *n.* A rolling, or rolling gait.

Wal'nut, *n.* A tree and its fruit.

Wal'rus, *n.* [D. *walrus*, fr. *wal*, in *walvisch*, a whale, and *ros*, a horse.]

Walrus.

An aquatic animal resembling the seal.

Waltz (wǎlts), *n.* A dance by two persons in circular figures; a tune for the dance. — *v. i.* To dance a waltz.

Wam'pum, *n.* Shells or strings of shells used as current money by the North American Indians.

Wan (wŏn), *a.* Having a pale and sickly hue.

Wand (wŏnd), *n.* A long staff or rod.

Wan'der, *v. i.* To rove; to ramble; to be delirious.

Wan'der-er, *n.* One who wanders; a rover; a rambler.

Wane, *v. i.* To decrease; to decline; to fail. — *n.* Decrease; decline; failure.

Wan'ness (wŏn'ness), *n.* A dead, pale, sickly color.

Want, *n.* Need; necessity; destitution; poverty; thing of which the loss is felt. — *v. i.* or *t.* To be deficient or destitute of; to desire.

Wan'ton (wŏn'tun), *a.* Sportive; loose; licentious. — *v. i.* (130) To revel; to frolic; to be lascivious; to act lewdly. — *n.* A lewd person.

Wan'ton-ly, *adv.* In a wanton manner; gayly; loosely; lasciviously.

Wan'ton-ness, *n.* Levity; lasciviousness; recklessness.

War, *n.* A contest between states, carried on by force. — *v. i.* To carry on war; to contend.

War'ble, *v. i.* To quaver or modulate the voice. — *v. t.* To trill; to carol. — *n.* A quavering of the voice.

War'bler, *n.* One who warbles; a singing-bird.

War'-cry, *n.* A cry or signal used in war.

Ward, *n.* A watch; guard; custody; protection or protector; part of a lock; a person under a guardian; division of a city or of a hospital. — *v. t.* or *i.* To watch; to guard.

Ward'en, *n.* A keeper; a guardian.

Ward'er, *n.* A keeper; a guard.

Ward'robe, *n.* A portable

closet for clothes; wearing apparel.

Ward'-room, *n.* A room in ships in which officers mess.

Ward'ship, *n.* Office of a ward; guardianship.

Wāre, *v. t.* [*imp.* WORE.] To wear; to veer.

Wāres, *n. pl.* Goods; merchandise; commodities.

Wāre'house, *n.* A storehouse for goods. — *v. t.* To deposit in a warehouse.

War'fāre, *n.* Military service; hostilities; contest.

Wā'ri-ly (135), *adv.* Cautiously; with circumspection.

Wā'ri-ness, *n.* Cautiousness; circumspection.

War'like, *a.* Relating or adapted to war; martial.

Warm, *a.* Having moderate heat; zealous; keen. — *v. t.* or *i.* To heat moderately; to become, or cause to become, animated.

Warm'ing-pan, *n.* A covered pan for warming a bed with heated coals.

Warm'ly, *adv.* In a warm manner; with warmth.

Warmth, *n.* Moderate heat; ardor; enthusiasm; zeal.

Warn, *v. t.* To caution; to admonish; to notify.

Warn'ing, *n.* Caution; admonition; previous notice.

War'-ŏf'fĭce, *n.* An office for conducting military affairs.

Warp, *n.* Threads that run lengthwise in a loom; a rope used in towing. — *v. i.* or *t.* To turn or twist out of shape; to deviate; to pervert; to tow with a warp or line attached to buoys, anchors, or the like.

War'rant, *n.* A commission; authority; precept; guaranty; voucher. — *v. t.* To authorize or justify; to assure.

War'rant-a-ble, *a.* Justifiable; defensible.

War'rant-a-bly, *adv.* Justifiably.

War'ran-tee', *n.* One to whom land, or other thing, is warranted.

War'ran-ty, *n.* A covenant of security; a guarantee. — *v. t.* To warrant.

War'ren, *n.* A place for rabbits, fowls, or fish, &c.

War'rior (war'yur), *n.* A military man; a soldier.

Wart, *n.* A small hard excrescence on the skin.

Wart'y, *a.* Having warts; like warts.

War'-whŏop (-hōōp), *n.* A shout uttered by Indians in war.

War'-wŏrn, *a.* Worn with war; battered by military service.

Wā'ry, *a.* Cautious of danger; prudent; circumspect.

Was (123, 124), *past tense* of the substantive verb *To be*.

Wash, *v. t.* To cleanse by water; to wet; to lave; to remove by the action of water. — *n.* Ablution; alluvial matter; a cosmetic; refuse matter from a kitchen; a coating of metal.

Wash'-ball, *n.* A ball of soap.

Wash'-bōard, *n.* A board next the floor; a board on which clothes are rubbed in washing.

Wash'er, *n.* One who washes; a ring of metal or leather, to relieve friction, or to secure tightness of joints, &c.

Wash'er-wŏm'an (143), *n.* A woman who washes clothes.

Wash'ing, *n.* Act of one who washes; clothes washed, especially at one time.

Wash'y, *a.* Watery; weak; thin; diluted. [*severely.*

Wasp, *n.* An insect that stings

Wasp'ish, *a.* Peevish; petulant; like a wasp.

Wasp'ish-ly, *adv.* Peevishly.

Wasp'ish-ness, *n.* Irritability.

Was'sail, *n.* [A.-S. *weshāl*, be in health.] A drinking to one's health; a liquor made of apples, sugar, and ale; a drunken bout.

Wast, *imp.* of *To be*, in the 2d person sing., indicative.

Wāste, *v. t.* To spend; to dissipate; to lavish; to squander. — *v. t.* To dwindle; to be consumed. — *a.* Desolate; valueless; wild. — *n.* Act of wasting; worthless remnant; loss; desolate ground.

Wāste'ful, *a.* Destructive; lavish; extravagant.

Wāste'ful-ly, *adv.* Lavishly.

Wāste'ful-ness, *n.* Lavishness; prodigality.

Watch, *n.* Guard; vigil; one who watches, or those who watch; a pocket time-piece; time of guarding. — *v. i.* To be awake; to keep guard; to wait. — *v. t.* To observe closely; to have in keeping.

Watch'er, *n.* One who watches.

Watch'ful (139), *a.* Careful to observe; guarding with caution. — SYN. Vigilant; cautious; attentive; observant; circumspect; wary.

Watch'ful-ly, *adv.* With care.

Watch'ful-ness, *n.* Vigilance; heedfulness.

Watch'-house, *n.* A house in which a watch or guard is placed.

Watch'man (143), *n.* A sentinel; a night-guard.

Watch'-tow'er, *n.* Tower for a watch or sentinel.

Watch'-wŏrd (-wûrd), *n.* A sentinel's pass-word; a countersign.

Wa'ter, *n.* The most common of all fluids; urine; a body of water; luster of a diamond. — *v. t.* or *i.* To irrigate; to cause or allow to drink; to shed water.

Wa'ter-cŏl'ors, *n. pl.* Colors diluted and mixed with gum-water.

Wa'ter-cōurse, *n.* A channel or canal for water.

Wa'ter-cress, *n.* A small plant, used as a salad.

Wa'ter-fall, *n.* A cascade; a cataract; a kind of female head-gear of hair.

Wa'ter-fowl, *n.* A bird that frequents the water.

Wa'ter-i-ness, *n.* Quality or state of being watery.

Wa'ter-ish, *a.* Like water; thin; moist; wet.

Wa'ter-lĕv'el, *n.* The level formed by the surface of still water.

Wa'ter-man (143), *n.* A boatman.

Wa'ter-mārk, *n.* A device wrought into paper during the process of manufacture.

Wa'ter-mĕl'on, *n.* A plant, and its pulpy fruit.

Wa'ter-mĭll, *n.* A mill turned by water. [hold water.

Wa'ter-pŏt, *n.* A vessel to

Wa'ter-prōōf, *a.* Not admitting water.

Wa'ter-rŏt, *v. t.* To rot by steeping in water, as flax.

Wa'ter-shed, *n.* A range of high land between two river-basins, and discharging its waters into them from opposite directions.

Wa'ter-spout, *n.* A whirling column of water at sea.

Wa'ter-tight (-tīt), *a.* So tight as to retain or not to admit water.

ā, ē, ī, ō, ū, ȳ, *long*; ă, ĕ, ĭ, ŏ, ŭ, ў, *short*; cāre, cär, ȧsk, ạll, whạt; ēre, veil, tērm; pīque, firm;

WATER-WHEEL 331 WEEN

Wa'ter-wheel, *n.* Any wheel for propelling machinery, &c., made to revolve by the action of water; — called an *overshot-wheel*, when the water is applied at the top; an *undershot-wheel*, when at the bottom; a *breast-wheel*, Water-wheels. when at an intermediate point; a *turbine* or horizontal wheel, when at the interior, passing out at the circumference.

Wa'ter-y, *a.* Aqueous; thin; tasteless; wet; washy.

Wat'tle, *n.* A twig; a hurdle; fleshy excrescence under the throat of a cock, &c. — *v. t.* To interweave, as twigs; to plat; to form of platted twigs.

Waul, *v. i.* To cry as a cat.

Wave, *n.* A moving ridge or swell of water; a billow. — *v. i.* or *t.* To move one way and the other, like a wave; to relinquish; to waive.

Wave'less, *a.* Free from waves; calm; smooth.

Wave'-of'fer-ing, *n.* An offering in the Jewish services made by waving the object toward the four cardinal points.

Wa'ver, *v. i.* To fluctuate; to vacillate; to be unsteady or undecided.

Wa'vy, *a.* Rising or swelling in waves; undulating.

Wax (3), *n.* A tenacious substance formed by bees. — *v. i.* [*imp.* WAXED; *p. p.* WAXED, or WAXEN.] To grow; to increase; to become. — *v. t.* To rub or smear with wax. [sembling, wax.

Wax'en, *a.* Made of, or resembling wax.

Wax'-work (-wûrk), *n.* A figure or figures formed of wax. [yielding.

Wax'y, *a.* Like wax: soft;

Way, *n.* [A.-S. *weg,* from *wegan,* to move.] A road; passage; room; course; means; method; mode.

Way'-bill, *n.* A list of passengers or of baggage.

Way'far-er, *n.* A traveler.

Way'far-ing, *a.* Traveling.

Way'lay, *v. t.* [*imp.* & *p. p.* WAYLAID.] To lie in wait for, especially to seize, rob, or slay. [waylays.

Way'lay-er, *n.* One who

Way'ward, *a.* Froward; perverse; willful.

Way'ward-ly, *adv.* Perversely; willfully.

Way'ward-ness, *n.* State or quality of being wayward.

We, *pron.* ; *pl.* of I.

Weak (126), *a.* Feeble; infirm; frail; soft; low; spiritless; inconclusive.

Weak'en, *v. t.* To make weak; to enfeeble; to debilitate; to enervate.

Weak'ly, *adv.* In a weak or feeble manner. — *a.* Infirm.

Weak'ness, *n.* Feebleness; infirmity; debility.

Weal, *n.* Happiness; prosperity; a sound, healthy, prosperous state. [opulence.

Wealth, *n.* Affluence; riches;

Wealth'i-ly, *adv.* Richly.

Wealth'i-ness, *n.* State of being wealthy. [affluent.

Wealth'y, *a.* Rich; opulent;

Wean, *v. t.* To accustom to a deprivation of the breast; to withdraw from any habit or desire.

Wean'ling, *n.* A child or animal newly weaned.

Weap'on, *n.* An instrument of offense or defense.

Wear, *v. t.* or *i.* [*imp.* WORE; *p. p.* WORN.] To carry or have on; to waste by friction or by use; to consume; to turn round, as a ship, with the stern toward the wind.— *n.* Act of wearing; a thing worn.

Wear, *n.* A dam in a river; a fence or net of twigs in the stream.

Wea'ri-ness, *n.* The state of being weary; fatigue.

Wea'ri-some, *a.* Tiresome; fatiguing; tedious.

Wea'ri-some-ly, *adv.* In a wearisome manner.

Wea'ri-some-ness, *n.* Tiresomeness; tediousness.

Wea'ry (86), *a.* Tired; fatigued. — *v. t.* To tire; to fatigue.

Wea'sand, *n.* The windpipe.

Wea'sel (we'zl, 58), *n.* A certain small quadruped, very slender and agile.

Weath'er, *n.* [A.-S. *weder,* allied to Skr. *vâ,* to blow.] State of the atmosphere. — *v. t.* To sail to the windward of; to endure.

Weath'er-cock, *n.* A vane; a vacillating person.

Weath'er-gage, *n.* Position of a ship to the windward of another; position of advantage.

Weath'er-glass, *n.* A contrivance to foreshow changes of weather; a barometer.

Weath'er-wise, *a.* Skillful in foretelling the weather.

Weave, *v. t.* [*imp.* WOVE; *p. p.* WOVE, WOVEN.] To unite, as threads, so as to form cloth: — *v. i.* To work with a loom.

Weav'er, *n.* One who weaves.

Wea'zen, *a.* Thin; sharp; pinched.

Web, *n.* Any thing woven; a film; a membrane.

Webbed (129), *a.* Having the toes united by a membrane.

Web'bing, *n.* A strong narrow fabric of hemp used for various purposes.

Web'-foot'ed, *a.* Having webbed feet.

Wed, *v. t.* To marry; to unite closely or strongly.

Wed'ding, *n.* Nuptial ceremony; marriage.

Wedge, *n.* A piece of metal or of wood sloping to an edge, used for splitting. — *v. t.* To fasten by means of wedges. Wedge.

Wed'lock (127), *n.* Married state.

Wednes'day (wĕnz'dy̆, 67), *n.* The fourth day of the week.

Wee, *a.* Small; little.

Weed, *n.* A useless or troublesome plant; (*pl.*) mourning apparel. — *v. t.* To free from noxious plants; to root out.

Weed'y, *a.* Full of weeds.

Week, *n.* Space or period of seven days.

Week'-day, *n.* Any day except Sunday.

Week'ly, *a.* Happening or done every week. — *adv.* Once a week. — *n.* A publication issued once every week.

Ween, *v. i.* To think; to fancy.

---

sŏn, ôr, dọ, wọlf, tōō, tŏŏk; ûrn, rṳle, pṳll; ç, ġ, *soft*; c, ḡ, *hard*; a̤; exist; ṉ as ng; this.

WEEP 332 WHET

Weep, *v. i.* or *t.* [*imp.* & *p. p.* WEPT.] To shed tears; to bewail; to lament; to bemoan; to drip.

Wee'vil (wē'vl), *n.* A small insect that injures grain.

Weft, *n.* The woof of cloth.

Weigh (wā, 137), *v. t.* To ascertain the weight of; to ponder. — *v. i.* To have weight. [weighs.

Weigh'er (wā'er), *n.* One who

Weight (wāt), *n.* Heaviness; gravity; importance; something for ascertaining the weight of other bodies. — *v. t.* To load with a weight or weights.

Weight'i-ly (wāt'-), *adv.* With weight; heavily.

Weight'i-ness (wāt'-), *n.* Quality of being weighty.

Weight'less (wāt'-), *a.* Light; imponderable; unimportant; trivial. [important.

Weight'y (wāt'-), *a.* Heavy;

Weird, *a.* Skilled in witchcraft; supernatural; unearthly; wild.

Wel'come (139), *n.* Kind reception or salutation. — *a.* Received with gladness; grateful; pleasing. — *v. t.* To salute or entertain kindly.

Weld, *v. t.* To hammer or press into union, as heated metals.

Wel'fare (139), *n.* Health; happiness; prosperity; success. [heavens.

Wel'kin, *n* The sky; the

Well, *n.* [A.-S., from *weallan,* to boil.] A spring; a deep circular pit for water. — *v. i.* To flow forth; to spring; to issue. — *a.* Not sick; being in health, good state, or favor. — *adv.* Not amiss; rightly; properly.

Well'-be'ing, *n.* Welfare; prosperity; weal.

Well'-bred (139), *a.* Educated to polished manners; refined; cultivated.

Well'-nigh (-nī), *adv.* Very nearly; almost.

Well'-spent, *a.* Virtuously employed or passed.

Well'-sweep, *n.* A long pole balanced on a high post, used for raising a bucket in a well.

Well'-wish'er, *n.* One who wishes another well; a friend.

Welsh, *a.* Pertaining to Wales. — *n.* The inhabitants or the language of Wales.

Welt, *n.* A border; an edging. — *v. t.* To sew a welt on.

Wel'ter (130), *v. i.* To roll, as in mire; to wallow.

Wen, *n.* A fleshy tumor or excrescence.

Wench, *n.* A young woman; a strumpet; a negress.

Went, *imp.* of *Go.*

Wept, *imp.* & *p. p.* of *Weep.*

Were (wūr), *imp. indic. pl.* & *imp. subj. sing.* & *pl.* of *Be.*

Wert. Second person singular of *Were.*

West, *n.* Region where the sun sets, or opposite to the east. — *adv.* At or toward the westward. — *a.* Situated toward, or relating to, the west; coming from the west.

West'er-ly, *a.* Being toward, or in, or from, the west.

West'ern, *a.* Being in, or moving toward, the west.

West'ward, *adv.* Toward
West'ward-ly, the west.

Wet, *a.* Full of moisture; very damp; rainy. — *n.* Water; wetness; moisture; humidity. — *v. t.* [*imp.* & *p. p.* WET.] To fill or moisten with a liquid.

Weth'er, *n.* A castrated ram.

Wet'ness, *n.* State of being wet; moisture; humidity.

Whale (hwāl), *n.* The largest of marine animals.

Whale'bone, *n.* A firm elastic substance from the upper jaw of the whale.

Whale'man (143), *n.* A man employed in the whale-fishery.

Wharf (hwąrf, 142), *n.* A mole, pier, or quay, for landing goods at. [wharf.

Wharf'age, *n.* Fee for using a

Wharf'in-ger, *n.* Superintendent or proprietor of a wharf.

What (hwŏt), *pron.* That which; partly; — as an exclamation, how remarkable; how great. It is also used interrogatively. [or that.

What-ev'er, *pron.* Being this

What'not, *n.* A piece of furniture, with shelves for books, ornaments, &c.

What'so-ev'er, *pron.* Whatever.

Wheat, *n.* A species of fine grain or bread corn.

Wheat'en, *a.* Made of wheat.

Whee'dle. *v. t.* To entice by soft words; to coax; to flatter; to cajole.

Wheel (125), *n.* [A.-S. *hweel,* allied to Goth. *ralrjan,* to roll.] A circular frame turning on an axis; a turn or revolution. — *v. t.* To cause to move on wheels. — *v. i.* To turn; to revolve.

Wheel'bar-row, *n.* A sort of hand-cart with one wheel.

Wheel'-wright (-rīt), *n.* A maker of wheels. [hard.

Wheeze, *v. i.* To breathe

Whelk, *n.* A wrinkle; a pustule; a streak or wale; a mollusk having a one-valved spiral shell.

Whelm, *v. t.* To immerse; to bury.

Whelp, *n.* A puppy; a cub. — *v. i.* To bring forth cubs or puppies.

When, *adv.* At what time; while; whereas.

Whence, *adv.* From what or which place; by what means.

Whence'so-ev'er, *adv.* From whatever place.

When-ev'er, *adv.* At
When'so-ev'er, whatever time.

Where, *adv.* At or in what place; at which place; whither.

Where'a-bout,' *adv.* Near
Where'a-bouts', what or which place; concerning which. [in fact.

Where-as', *adv.* Since; when

Where-at', *adv.* At what.

Where-by', *adv.* By which; by what.

Where'fore (140), *adv.* For which reason; for what reason; why. [what.

Where-in', *adv.* In which or

Where'in-tọ', *adv.* Into which or what.

Where-of' (-ŏf' or -ŏv'), *adv.* Of which or what.

Where-ọn', *adv.* On
Where'up-ọn', which or what.

Where'so-ev'er, *adv.* In what place soever; wherever.

Where-tọ', *adv.* To
Where'un-tọ', which; to what end.

Where'up-ọn', *adv.* Upon or in consequence of which.

Wher-ev'er (139), *adv.* At whatever place.

Where-with' (-with' or -with'), *adv.*
Where'with-ạl',
With which; with what.

Wher'ry, *n.* [Allied to *ferry.*] A light shallow boat, built long and narrow for fast rowing or sailing.

Whet (129), *v. t.* To sharpen by friction; to stimulate; to

provoke.—*n.* A sharpening by friction; a stimulant.
Wheth'er, *pron.* Which of the two.—*conj.* Used to introduce the first of two or more alternative clauses. It corresponds to *or*.
Whet'stone, *n.* A stone for sharpening edged tools.
Whey, *n.* The thin watery part of milk.
Which, *pron.* used interrogatively and relatively, both as a substantive and an adjective; relating to things.
Which-ev'er, } *pron.*
Which'so-ev'er, } Whether one or the other. [of air.
Whiff (123), *n.* A quick puff
Whif'fle, *v. i.* To waver; to be unsteady or fickle. [flies.
Whif'fler, *n.* One who whiffles.
Whif'fle-tree, *n.* The bar to which the traces of a carriage are fastened.
Whig (125), *n.* One of a certain political party.—*a.* Pertaining to whigs.
Whig'gish (127), *a.* Inclined to whiggery; pertaining to whigs or to their principles.
Whig'gism, } *n.* The principles of whigs.
Whig'ger-y, }
While, *n.* Time; space of time.—*adv.* During the time that; as long as; in which case.—*v. t.* To spend or pass, as time. [old.
Whi'lom, *adv.* Formerly; of
Whilst, *adv.* While.
Whim, } *n.* A freak of
Whim'sey, } fancy; a caprice, or capricious notion.
Whim'per, *v. i.* To cry with a low, whining, and broken voice; to complain in a shrill tone.
Whim'si-cal, *a.* Full of whims; curious; odd; fantastic; freakish; capricious.
Whim'si-cal'i-ty, } *n.* State
Whim'si-cal-ness, } or quality of being whimsical.
Whim'si-cal-ly, *adv.* In a whimsical manner.
Whin, *n.* Gorse; furze; also, a leguminous plant with yellow flowers.
Whine, *v. i.* To lament or complain in a plaintive tone.—*n.* A nasal, puerile tone of complaint.
Whin'ny, *v. i.* [From the root of *whine*.] To make a certain shrill noise, as a horse; to neigh.
Whip, *n.* An instrument for driving teams or for correction; a coachman.—*v. t.* To strike with a whip; to lash; to flog; to beat; to jerk.
Whip'per-in, *n.* One who keeps hounds from wandering. [who whips.
Whip'ping, *n.* Act of one
Whip'ple-tree, *n.* A bar to fasten the tugs or traces of a carriage to.
Whip'-poor-will, *n.* An American bird, so called from its note.
Whip'saw, *n.* A saw for dividing timber lengthwise.
Whip'ster, *n.* A nimble little fellow. [a whip.
Whip'-stock, *n.* The handle of
Whir, *v. i.* To whirl round with noise.—*n.* A buzzing or whizzing sound of any thing in rapid revolution.
Whirl, *v.* To turn rapidly.—*n.* A rapid rotation.
Whirl'i-gig, *n.* A child's toy spun like a top.
Whirl'pool, *n.* An eddy; a vortex of water.
Whirl'wind, *n.* A violent wind moving circularly.
Whisk, *n.* A small brush; a rapid, sweeping motion.—*v. t.* To brush with a whisk; to move rapidly.
Whisk'er, *n.* Hair growing on the sides of the face.
Whis'ky, } *n.* A spirit dis-
Whis'key, } tilled from barley, wheat, rye, or maize.
Whis'per, *v.* To speak or address in a low voice.—*n.* A soft, sibilant voice; utterance without sonant breath.
Whist, *n.* A certain game at cards.—*a.* Silent; mute.
Whis'tle (hwǐs'l), *v. i.* To make a kind of sharp, musical sound with the breath forced through the lips; to sound shrilly.—*n.* A shrill sound made by the breath, &c.: a pipe that makes a shrill sound. [who whistles.
Whis'tler (hwǐs'ler), *n.* One
Whit, *n.* A bit; a jot; a tittle.
White, *a.* Of the color of snow; pale; pure; clean.—*n.* A white color; any thing white, as part of the eye and part of an egg.
White, } *v. t.* or *i.* To
Whit'en, } make or become white; to bleach; to blanch.
White'ness, *n.* State or quality of being white.
White'-swell'ing. *n.* A lingering inflammation of the knee-joint.
White'wash, *n.* A composition of lime and water for whitening walls, &c.—*v. t.* To cover with whitewash; to give a fair external appearance to. [daisy.
White'-weed, *n.* A kind of
Whith'er, *adv.* To what or which place, point, or degree.
Whith'er-so-ev'er, *adv.* To whatever place.
Whit'ing, *n.* Ground chalk; a sea-fish allied to the cod.
Whit'ish, *a.* Moderately white; somewhat white.
Whit'leath-er, *n.* Leather dressed with alum, salt, &c., very pliable and tough.
Whit'low, *n.* A suppurating tumor on the finger or toe.
Whit'sun-day, } *n.* The sev-
Whit'sun-tide, } enth Sunday after Easter; a feast of commemoration of the descent of the Holy Spirit on the day of Pentecost.
Whit'tle, *v. t.* To pare or cut off the surface of with a knife.—*n.* A knife.
Whiz, *n.* A humming or hissing sound.—*v. t.* (129) To make a humming or hissing sound.
Wno (hōō), *pron.* Which or what person or persons.
Who-ev'er (hōō-), *pron.* Any person whatever.
Whole (hōl, 18), *a.* All; entire; complete; sound.—*n.* The entire thing; totality.
Whole'sale (hōl'-). *n.* Sale by the piece or quantity.—*a.* Pertaining to trade by the piece or quantity.
Whole'some (hōl'sum, 18), *a.* Favorable to health; salutary; useful.
Whole'some-ness (hōl'-), *n.* Salubrity; quality of contributing to health.
Whōl'ly (hōl'y, 18, 132), *adv.* Totally; entirely.
Whom (hōōm), *pron.* Objective case of *Who*.
Whom'so-ev'er (hōōm'-), *pron.* Objective of *Whoever*.
Whoop (hōōp), *n.* A shout.—*v. i.* To shout; to hoot.
Whoop'ing-cough (hōōp'ing-kŏf), *n.* A violent, convulsive cough; hooping-cough.
Whore (hōr), *n.* A prostitute.
Whor'tle-ber'ry (hwûr'tl-), *n.* A plant and its small edible berry. [sive case of *Who*.
Whose (hōōz), *pron.* Posses-
Whose'so-ev'er, *pron.* Possessive of *Whosoever*.

Who'so, *pron.* Same as *Whosoever.*
Who'so-ev'er (hōō'-), *a.* Any person whatever.
Whŭr, *n.* A humming sound; whir. — *v. i.* To make a rough, humming sound.
Why (140), *adv.* For what reason; for which reason; reason or cause for which.
Wick (127). *n.* The cotton cord of a candle or lamp.
Wick'ed (57), *a.* Evil; vicious; sinful; unrighteous; iniquitous. (manner.
Wick'ed-ly, *adv.* In a wicked
Wick'ed-ness. *n.* Vice; crime; sin; guilt; iniquity.
Wick'er, *n.* A small twig. — *a.* Made of small twigs.
Wick'et, *n.* A small gate.
Wide, *a.* Having great extent each way or between the sides; not narrow. — SYN. Broad; extensive; remote; distant. — *adv.* At a distance; far.
Wide'ly (132), *adv.* To a wide degree; extensively.
Wid'en, *v. t.* or *i.* To make or grow wide or wider.
Wide'ness, *n.* Quality of being wide; breadth; width.
Wid'geon (wid'jun), *n.* A water-fowl of the duck kind.
Wid'ōw, *n.* [A.-S. *widuwe*; Skr. *vidhavā*, fr. *vi*, without, and *dhava*, husband.] A woman who has lost her husband. — *v. t.* To deprive of a husband; to bereave.
Wid'ōw-er, *n.* A man whose wife is dead.
Wid'ōw-hōōd, *n.* Condition of a widow.
Width, *n.* Extent from side to side; breadth.
Wield, *v. t.* To control; to manage; to handle; to sway; to employ; to use.
Wield'y, *a.* Manageable.
Wife (142). *n.* The lawful consort of a man.
Wig, *n.* An artificial covering of hair for the head.
Wĭght (wit), *n.* A person; a being; a man or woman.
Wig'wam, *n.* An Indian cabin or hut.
Wild, *a.* Fierce; not tame; growing without culture; desert; rude; savage; licentious; fanciful. — *n.* A wilderness.
Wild'cat, *n.* A feline animal, very strong and fierce.
Wil'der, *v. t.* To cause to lose the way; to bewilder.

Wil'der-ness, *n.* A wild, uncultivated tract.
Wild'fire, *n.* An inflammable composition, very hard to quench when on fire.
Wild'ly, *adv.* In a wild manner. (wild.
Wild'ness, *n.* State of being
Wile, *n.* A trick; insidious artifice; stratagem; fraud.
Wi'li-ness, *n.* State of being wily; cunning; craft.
Will, *n.* The faculty of choosing; choice; inclination; command; testament. — *v. t.* To determine by an act of choice; to dispose of by testament. — *auxiliary verb.* [*imp.* WOULD], used to denote futurity.
Will'ful ((131). *a.* Stubborn;
Wil'ful) obstinate; ungovernable.
Will'ful-ly,) *adv.* Stubborn-
Wil-ful-ly,) ly; obstinately.
Will'ful-ness) (131), *n.* Stub-
Wil'ful-ness) bornness.
Will'ing, *a.* Free to do; ready.
Will'ing-ly, *adv.* By free will or one's own choice.
Will'ing-ness, *n.* Free choice; readiness.
Wil'low, *n.* A kind of tree.
Wil'low-y, *a.* Abounding with willows; like a willow.
Wilt, *v. i.* To begin to wither; to droop. [artful; sly.
Wi'ly, *a.* Cunning; crafty;
Wim'ble, *n.* An instrument to bore holes with.
Win, *v. t.* [*imp. & p. p.* WON.] To gain; to get; to allure.
Wince, *v. i.* To shrink; to start back; to flounce.
Winch, *n.* A kind of lever; a crank-handle.
Wind, *n.* A current of air; breath; flatulence. — *v. t.* To ventilate; to follow by the scent.
Wind, *v. t.* [*imp. & p. p.* WOUND.] To turn; to twist; to coil; to encircle; to sound by blowing
Wind'age, *n.* Difference between the diameter of the bore of a gun and that of the ball.
Wind'bound, *a.* Detained by contrary winds
Wind'-egg, *n.* An addle egg.
Wind'er, *n.* One who winds; a reel.
Wind'fall, *n.* Fruit blown off; any unexpected benefit.
Wind'-flow'er, *n.* The anemone; — formerly thought to open only when the wind was blowing.

Wind'-gall, *n.* A soft tumor on a horse's fetlock.
Wind'-gŭn, *n.* A gun discharged by air.
Wind'i-ness, *n.* State of being windy.
Wind'ing-sheet, *n.* A shroud to wrap the dead in.
Wind'- lass, *n.* A machine for raising weights.

Windlass.

Wind'-mĭll, *n.* A mill turned by the wind.
Win'dōw, *n.* [Icel. *vindauga*, window, lit. wind-eye.] An opening in the wall of a building to admit light.
Wind'pipe, *n.* Passage for the breath to and from the lungs; the trachea.
Wind'rōw, *n.* A line of hay.
Wind'ward, *a.* Lying toward the point from which the wind blows. — *n.* The point from which the wind blows. — *adv.* Toward the wind.
Wind'y, *a.* Stormy; tempestuous; flatulent; empty.
Wine, *n.* Fermented juice of grapes and of other fruits.
Wine'-bib'ber, *n.* One who drinks much wine.
Wine'-glass, *n.* A small glass from which wine is drank.
Wing, *n.* Limb of a bird or of an insect; flight; a side building; right or left division of an army; one of the extremities of a fleet. — *v. t.* To furnish with wings; to transport by flight; to wound on the wing.
Wink, *v. i.* To shut and open the eyelids quickly; to connive. — *n.* A quick closing and opening of the eyelids; a hint given by shutting the eye with a significant cast.
Win'ner, *n.* One who wins.
Win'ning, *a.* Attractive.
Win'nōw, *v. t.* To separate, as chaff, by means of wind.
Win'ter, *n.* The cold season of the year. — *v. i.* (139) To pass the winter. — *v. t.* To feed in winter.
Win'ter-green, *n.* A small evergreen plant having bright red berries.
Win'ter-kill, *v. t.* To kill by the cold of winter.
Win'ter-y,) *a.* Suitable to, or
Win'try,) like, winter.

Win′y, *a.* Having the taste or qualities of wine.
Wipe, *v. t.* To clean or remove by rubbing; to rub off. — *n.* A rub; a stroke.
Wip′er, *n.* One who wipes; something used for wiping.
Wire, *n.* An even thread of metal. [into wire.
Wire′-draw, *v. t.* To draw
Wire′-draw′er, *n.* One who forms wire by drawing.
Wire′-pull′er, *n.* One who pulls the wires of a puppet; hence, an intriguer.
Wir′y (83), *a.* Made of, or like wire; tough; sinewy.
Wis, *v. t.* [*imp.* WIST.] To know: to think; to suppose.
Wis′dom (132), *n.* Knowledge, and the capacity to make due use of it; prudence; sagacity.
Wise, *a.* Having wisdom. — SYN. Sage; sagacious; judicious; prudent; grave. — *n.* A manner or way.
Wise′a-cre, *n.* A shallow pretender to great wisdom.
Wise′ly, *adv.* Judiciously; prudently; with wisdom.
Wish, *v. t. or i.* To desire or long for; to frame or express a desire about. — *n.* A desire; thing desired.
Wish′ful, *a.* Feeling or showing desire; eager.
Wisp, *n.* A small bundle of straw or hay.
Wist, *imp.* & *p. p.* of *Wis.*
Wist′ful, *a.* Eagerly attentive; wishful.
Wist′ful-ly, *adv.* Desiringly.
Wit, *n.* Faculty of associating ideas, or ideas associated, in an unusual and felicitous manner; mind; sense; a man of genius, fancy, or humor. — *v. t.* To know; to be known.
Witch, *n.* A woman who practices sorcery. — *v. t.* To charm. [witches.
Witch′craft, *n.* Practices of
Witch′-elm, *n.* A kind of elm.
Witch′er-y, *n.* Witchcraft; sorcery; enchantment.
With, *prep.* By, denoting cause, nearness, means, or instrument, &c.
With-al′ (130), *adv.* With; likewise; at the same time.
With-draw′, *v. t.* To take back or away. — *v. i.* To retire; to retreat. [drawing.
With-draw′al, *n.* Act of withdrawing.
Withe (with), *n.* A willow twig, or band made of twigs.

With′er, *v. i. or t.* [Orig. to dry by the *weather,* or air.] To fade; to dry up; to decay.
With′ers, *n. pl.* The ridge between the shoulder-bones of a horse, at the bottom of the neck.
With-hold′, *v. t.* [*imp.* & *p. p.* WITHHELD.] To hold or keep back; to restrain.
With-in′, *prep.* In the inner part of. — *adv.* Inwardly.
With-out′, *prep.* Out of; beyond; independently of. — *adv.* On the outside. — *conj.* Unless; except.
With-stand′, *v. t.* [*imp.* WITHSTOOD.] To oppose; to resist.
With′y, *a.* Made of, or like, withes; flexible. — *n.* A withe. [understanding.
Wit′less, *a.* Wanting wit or
Wit′ling, *n.* A pretender to wit; one who has little wit or smartness.
Wit′ness, *n.* Testimony; evidence; one personally present; one who testifies or gives evidence. — *v. t.* To see; to bear testimony to; to attest. — *v. i.* To give evidence.
Wit′ti-cism, *n.* A phrase affectedly witty; a conceit.
Wit′ti-ly, *adv.* With wit.
Wit′ting-ly, *adv.* Knowingly; by design.
Wit′ty (129), *a.* Full of wit; smart; humorous; droll; facetious; satirical.
Wive, *v. t. or i.* To marry; — said of a man.
Wives, *n.; pl.* of *Wife.*
Wiz′ard, *n.* A magician; a conjurer; a sorcerer. — *a.* Enchanting; charming; haunted by wizards.
Wiz′en, *a.* Thin; dried up.
Woad, *n.* A plant, the leaves of which furnish a blue coloring matter.
Woe (149), *n.* A heavy calamity; sorrow; grief.
Woe′-be-gone′ (15), *a.* Overwhelmed with woe.
Woe′ful } (139), *a.* Very sorrowful; full of distress. — SYN. Calamitous; afflictive; miserable.
Woe′ful-ly, } *adv.* Sorrowfully; wretchedly; miserably.
Woe′ful-ness, } *n.* Quality or state of being woful.
Wolf (wulf, 142), *n.* A carnivorous animal.

Wolf′ish, *a.* Like a wolf; rapacious; destructive. [plant.
Wolf′s′-bāne, *n.* A poisonous
Wom′an (143), *n.* An adult female of the human race.
Wom′an-hood, *n.* The state or qualities of a woman.
Wom′an-ly, *a.* Becoming a woman.
Womb (wōōm), *n.* Place where any thing is generated or produced.
Wom′en (wĭm′en), *n.; pl.* of *Woman.*
Won, *imp.* & *p. p.* of *Win.*
Won′der, *n.* Surprise; astonishment; a prodigy; a marvel. — *v. i.* To be surprised.
Won′der-ful, *a.* Exciting wonder or surprise; astonishing; surprising.
Won′der-ful-ly, *adv.* In a manner to excite wonder.
Won′droŭs, *a.* Wonderful; marvelous; strange.
Won′droŭs-ly, *adv.* In a wonderful manner.
Wont (wŭnt), *a.* Accustomed; habituated; used. — *v. i.* To be accustomed. — *n.* Custom; habit.
Wont′ed (wŭnt′ed), *a.* Accustomed; customary.
Woo (137), *v. t.* [A.-S. *wōgian,* fr. *wōg, wō,* a bending.] To solicit in marriage. — *v. i.* To make love; to court.
Wood, *n.* A collection of trees; substance of a tree; timber; fuel. — *v. t.* To supply with wood. [plant.
Wood′bine, *n.* A climbing
Wood′chuck, *n.* A certain small burrowing animal.
Wood′cŏck, *n.* A bird of the snipe family.
Wood′-cut, *n.* An engraving on wood, or an impression from such an engraving.
Wood′ed, *a.* Covered or supplied with wood.
Wood′en (wood′n), *a.* Made of wood; hard; clumsy.
Wood′-house, *n.* A house or shed for wood.
Wood′land, *n.* Land covered with wood or trees.
Wood′-louse (143), *n.* An insect. [trees.
Wood′man, *n.* One who fells
Wood′-nymph, *n.* A fabled goddess of the woods.
Wood′peck-er, *n.* A bird that pecks holes in trees in pursuit of insects.
Wood′y, *a.* Abounding with, or consisting of, wood.
Woo′er, *n.* One who wooes.

sŭn, ôr, dọ, wọlf, tōō, tŏŏk; ûrn, rụe, pụll; ç, ġ, *soft;* ҫ, ḡ, *hard;* aṣ; eẋist; ŋ *as* ng; this.

Woof, n. Threads that cross the warp in weaving; weft.
Wool, n. The fleece of sheep; short, thick, crispy hair.
Wool'en ⎱ (130), a. Consisting
Wool'len ⎰ of, or pertaining to, wool.
Wool'fell, n. A skin with the wool on.
Wool'li-ness, n. State or quality of being woolly.
Wool'ly, a. Consisting of, or resembling, wool
Wool'-sack, n. A sack of wool; seat of the lord chancellor of England in the house of lords
Word (wûrd), n. Spoken or written sign of an idea; a term; vocable; message; promise; token; tidings; the Scriptures. — v. t. To express in words.
Word'i-ness (wûrd'-), n. Verbosity; verbiage.
Word'ing (wûrd'ing), n. Manner of expressing in words.
Word'y (wûrd'y), a. Using many words; verbose.
Wore, imp. of Wear.
Work (wûrk), v. i. [imp. & p. p. WORKED; WROUGHT.] To labor; to operate; to act; to strain; to toil; to ferment. — v. t. To prepare or form by labor; to effect; to embroider. — n. Labor; toil; employment; a book; any thing made. [who works.
Work'er (wûrk'er), n. One
Work'-house (wûrk'-), n. A house for employing the idle or poor; almshouse. [tion.
Work'ing (wûrk'-), n. Opera-
Work'man (wûrk'-, 143), n. A worker; a skilled laborer.
Work'man-like ⎱ (wûrk'-) a.
Work'man-ly ⎰ Becoming a skillful workman; skillful.
Work'man-ship (wûrk'-), n. Work done; manufacture; manner of making; skill.
Work'shop (wûrk'-), n. A shop where work is done.
World (wûrld, n. The earth; globe; universe; mankind; all which the earth contains.
World'li-ness (wûrld'-), n. State of being worldly; inordinate love of earthly things.
World'ling (wûrld'-), n. One devoted to worldly things.
World'ly (wûrld'-), a. Relating to this world; devoted to worldly enjoyments.
Worm (wûrm), n. Any small, creeping insect; a grub; a reptile; any thing spiral and cylindrical. — v. t. To work slowly and secretly. — v. i. To gain slowly and by secret means.
Worm'-eat'en (wûrm'-), a. Gnawed by worms.
Worm'wood (wûrm'-), n. A plant having a bitter taste.
Worm'y (wûrm'-), a. Abounding with worms; like a worm.
Worn, p. p. of Wear. [ries.
Wor'ri-er, n. One who wor-
Wor'ry (wûr'ry, 135], v. t. To harass with importunity, anxiety, or labor. — SYN. To tease; trouble; vex. — n. Vexation; anxiety; trouble.
Worse (wûrs), a. More bad. — n. A more evil state. — adv. In a manner more evil.
Wor'ship (wûr'ship), n. Religious homage; adoration; a title of honor. — v. t. or i. (130) To pay divine honors to; to adore.
Wor'ship-er ⎱ (wûr'ship-), n.
Wor'ship per ⎰ One who worships
Wor'ship-ful (wûr'-), a. Worthy of honor from character.
Wor'ship-fully (wûr'ship-) adv. With worship or honor.
Worst (wûrst), a. Most vile or wicked; most difficult. — n. The most evil or distressing state. — v. t. To defeat.
Worst'ed (wûst'ed), n. [From the town of Worsted, in England.] Yarn from combed and long staple wool. — a. Consisting of worsted. [herb.
Wort (wûrt), n. A plant; an
Worth (wûrth), v. i. To be; as, woe worth the day. — n. Value; desert; merit.
Wor'thi-ly (wûr'-), adv. So as to deserve well; suitably.
Wor'thi-ness (wûr'-), n. Worth; desert; merit.
Worth'less (wûrth'-), a. Having no worth or value.
Worth'less-ness (wûrth'-), n. Quality of being worthless.
Wor'thy (wûr'thy), a. Having worth; deserving; excellent; meritorious. — n. A man of eminent worth.
Wot, v. To know; to be aware. [Obs. or antiquated.]
Would (wood), imp. of Will.
Wound (woond or wownd), n. A hurt; a cut; a bruise. — v. t. To hurt or bruise. — imp. of Wind.
Wove, imp. of Weave.
Wov'en, p. p. of Weave.
Wran'gle (rång'gl), n. An angry dispute. — v. i. To dispute angrily or noisily.
Wran'gler (rång'gler), n. One who wrangles.
Wrap (råp, 129), v. t. To roll or fold together; to involve.
Wrap'per (råp'per), n. One who, or that which, wraps; a cover. [ering.
Wrap'ping (råp'-), n. A cov-
Wrath (råth), n. Violent anger or exasperation. — SYN. Fury; rage; passion; resentment; indignation.
Wrath'ful (råth'-), a. Angry; enraged; incensed; furious.
Wrath'ful-ly, adv. In a wrathful manner.
Wrath'ful-ness, n. State of being wrathful. [gry.
Wrath'y (råth'-), a. Very an-
Wreak (rēk), v. t. To execute by way of revenge; to inflict.
Wreath (rēth, 96), n. Something twisted; a garland.
Wreathe (rēth), v. t. To twist; to entwine.
Wreath'y (rēth'y), a. Twisted; curled; spiral.
Wreck (rēk), v. t. To destroy or damage, as a vessel, by driving on the shore or on rocks, &c.; to strand; to suffer total loss or destruction. — n. Destruction by sea; any thing wrecked; ruin.
Wreck'er (rēk'er), n. One who causes a wreck; one who searches for wrecks.
Wren (rēn), n. A small bird.
Wrench (rēnch), v. t. To pull with a twist; to wrest. — n. A violent twist; a sprain; an instrument for turning bolts, nuts, &c.
Wrest (rēst), v. t. To take from by force; to distort. — n. Violent perversion.
Wres'tle (rēs'l), v. i. To grapple and struggle; to strive.
Wres'tler (rēs'ler), n. One skilled in wrestling.
Wrest'ling (rēs'ling), n. A wrestle; a struggle; contention.
Wretch (rēch), n. A miserable person; a vile knave.
Wretch'ed (rēch'ed, £7), a. Very miserable. — SYN. Unhappy; afflicted; worthless.
Wretch'ed-ly (rēch'ed-), adv. Miserably.
Wretch'ed-ness (rēch'ed-), n. Misery.
Wrig'gle (rig'gl), v. i. To move to and fro with short motions. — v. t. To move by twisting and squirming.
Wrig'gler (rig'-), n. One who wriggles.

Wright (rīt), *n.* A workman.
Wring (rĭng), *v. t.* [*imp. & p. p.* WRUNG.] To twist; to strain; to distress; to extort.
Wring'er (rĭng'-), *n.* One who wrings; a machine for wringing clothes after they have been washed.
Wrink'le (rĭŋk'l), *n.* A crease; a ridge; a furrow. — *v. i.* or *t.* To contract into furrows.
Wrist (rĭst), *n.* Joint connecting the hand and arm.
Wrist'band (rĭst'-), *n.* The part of a sleeve that covers the wrist.
Writ (rĭt), *n.* A writing; the Scriptures; a legal instrument or process.
Write (rīt), *v. t.* [*imp.* WROTE; *p. p.* WRITTEN.] To form, as letters and words, with a pen; to inscribe; to compose.
Writ'er (rīt'er), *n.* One who writes; an author.
Writhe (rīth), *v. t.* or *i.* To twist; to distort or be distorted.
Writ'ing (rīt'ing, 133, *n.* Act of one who writes; that which is written; a manuscript; a deed; a book; an inscription.
Writ'ten (rĭt'tn), *a.* Expressed in letters.
Wrong (rŏng), *n.* [Allied to *wring.*] Injustice; injury; any violation of right. — *a.* Not right; erroneous. — *v. t.* To injure; to treat with injustice. — *adv.* Amiss.
Wrong'ful (rŏng'-, 139), *a.* Unjust; injurious.
Wrong'ful-ly (rŏng'-), *adv.* Unjustly.
Wrong'-head'ed (rŏng'-). *a.* Wrong in opinion; perverse.
Wrong'ly (rŏng'-), *adv.* Injuriously; unjustly; amiss.
Wrōte (rōt, 19), *imp.* of *Write.*
Wrŏth (rawth), *a.* Full of wrath; very angry; greatly exasperated.
Wrŏught (rawt), *imp. & p. p.* Formed by labor; effected; worked. [of *Wring.*
Wrŭng (rung), *imp. & p. p.*
Wry̆ (rī, 135), *a.* Twisted; distorted; deviating from the right direction.
Wry̆'neck (rī'-), *n.* A small bird allied to the woodpecker.
Wry̆'ness (rī'-, 135), *n.* State or quality of being wry.

X.

Xan'thic (zăn'-), *a.* Yellowish.
Xe'bee (zē'bek, 127), *n.* A three-masted vessel used in the Mediterranean sea.
Xy̆-lŏg'ra-pher (zī-), *n.* An engraver on wood.
Xy̆'lo-grăph'ic } (zī'-), *a.*
Xy̆'lo-grăph'ic-al } Belonging to wood-engraving.
Xy̆-lŏg'ra-phy (zī-), *n.* The act or the art of engraving on wood.
Xy̆-lŏph'a-goŭs (zī-lŏff'a-gus), *a.* Feeding on wood.

Y.

Yacht (yŏt), *n.* A sea-going vessel for pleasure-trips, racing, &c.
Yacht'ing (yŏt'ing), *n.* Sailing on pleasure excursions in a yacht. [its edible root.
Yăm, *n.* A tropical plant and
Yăn'kee (140), *n.* A New-Englander; a citizen of the Northern States.
Yăp, *v. i.* To bark; to yelp.
Yärd, *n.* Measure of three feet; an inclosure; a long, slender piece of timber by which a sail is extended. [yard.
Yärd'-ärm, *n.* Half of a ship's
Yärd'-stick, } *n.* A stick
Yärd'-wand, } three feet in length, used as a measure.
Yärn, *n.* Spun wool, flax, or cotton; a story spun out.
Yăr'row, *n.* A plant having a strong smell and taste.
Yaw, *n.* Temporary deviation of a vessel from her course.—
v. i. To deviate from the line of her course, as a ship.
Yawl, *n.* A small ship's boat, usually rowed with four or six oars. — *v. i.* To yell, as a dog. [of gaping.
Yawn, *v. i.* To gape. — *n.* Act
Y-clēped' (ĭ-klĕpt'), *p. p.* Called; named.
Ye̱, *pron.* Plural of *Thou.*
Yea, *adv.* Yes; verily; certainly; ay. [as lambs.
Yēan, *v. i.* or *t.* To bring forth,
Yēan'ling, *n.* A young sheep.
Yēar, *n.* Time occupied by the earth in revolving around the sun; twelve calendar months, or 365 days. [old.
Yēar'ling, *n.* A beast a year
Yēar'ly, *a.* Annual; coming every year. — *adv.* Annually; once a year.
Yẽarn, *v. i.* [A.-S. *geornan,* from *georn,* desirous.] To feel earnest desire; to long.
Yẽarn'ing, *n.* Strong desire.
Yēast, *n.* Froth of fermenting beer or liquor; barm.
Yēast'y, *a.* Foamy, like yeast.
Yĕlk, *n.* Yellow part of an egg.
Yĕll (123), *v. i.* To utter a sharp, loud outcry. — *n.* A sharp, loud outcry.
Yĕl'lōw, *a.* Being of the color of gold or brass; — *n.* A bright gold color.
Yĕl'lōw Fē'ver. A malignant fever, attended with yellowness of the skin. [yellow.
Yĕl'lōw-ish, *a.* Moderately
Yĕl'lōw-ness, *n.* Quality of being yellow.
Yĕl'lōws, *n. pl.* Jaundice in horses, &c.; a disease of peach-trees. [a dog.
Yĕlp, *v. i.* To bark shrilly, as
Yeō'man (143), *n.* A freeholder; a man free-born.
Yeō'man-ry, *n.* The collective body of yeomen.

Yẽrk, *v. t.* To jerk. — *n.* A jerk.
Yĕs (123, 124), *adv.* Yea; a word that affirms.
Yĕst, *n.* See *Yeast*. [present.
Yĕs′ter, *a.* Last; next before the
Yĕs′ter-day, *n.* The day last past. — *adv.* On the day last past. [night last past.
Yĕs′ter-night (-nīt), *n.* The
Yĕt, *conj.* Nevertheless; however. — *adv.* Besides; at least; still; at all; thus far.
Yew (yū), *n.* An evergreen tree allied to the pines.
Yīeld, *v. t.* To produce; to furnish; to afford.
— *v. i.* To surrender; to comply; to submit. — *n.* Amount yielded; product.
Yīeld′ing, *p. a.* Inclined to give way; compliant.
Yōke (18), *n.* A frame worn on the neck, used to connect oxen for work; bondage; a couple; a pair. — *v. t.* To connect for work; to unite.
Yōke′-fĕl′lōw, } *n.* An associate; a companion; a partner.
Yōke′māte, }
Yōlk (yōlk *or* yōk, 13), *n.* The yelk of an egg.
Yŏn, } *a.* Being at a distance, but within view. — *adv.* At a distance, but within view.
Yŏn′der, }
Yōre, *adv.* Of old time.
Yoụ (yōō), *pron.* Second person singular or plural.
Young, *a.* Not having been long born; juvenile. — *n.* The offspring of animals.
Young′ger (yŭng′ger), *a.* Not so old as another.
Young′gest (yŭng′gest), *a.* Having the least age.
Young′ish, *a.* Rather young.
Young′ling, *n.* A youth; any young creature.
Young′ster, *n.* A young person; a lad.
Your (122), *possessive pron.* Belonging to you.
Your-sĕlf′, *pron.* You only; — used emphatically.
Youth, *n.* The early part of life; a young person; young persons collectively.
Youth′ful, *a.* Young; fresh; vigorous; pertaining to youth.
Youth′ful-ly, *adv.* In a youthful manner.
Youth′ful-ness, *n.* The state of being youthful.
Yule (27), *n.* Christmas.

Z.

ZXF′FER, *n.* Impure oxide of cobalt. [buffoon.
Zā′ny, *n.* A merry-andrew; a
Zeal, *n.* Passionate ardor; earnestness. [zeal.
Zēal′ot (zĕl′ot), *n.* One full of
Zēal′oŭs (zĕl′us), *a.* Filled with zeal; earnest. [ardor.
Zēal′oŭs-ly, *adv.* With great
Zē′brȧ (140), *n.* A South African animal marked with stripes.
Zē′bū (140), *n.* A small quadruped, called also the *Indian bull*, *ox*, or *cow*.
Zĕd′o-a-ry, *n.* A fragrant, aromatic medicinal substance.
Zē′nith, *n.* That point in the heavens which is directly overhead; greatest height.
Zĕph′yr, *n.* A gentle west wind.
Zē′ro (*pl.* Zē′rōṣ, 140), *n.* The cipher, 0; point from which a thermometer is graduated.
Zĕst, *n.* Orange peel cut thin; a relish; taste. — *v. t.* To give a flavor to.
Zĭg′zăg, *a.* Having frequent short, sharp turns. — *n.* Something with short turns. — *v. t.* (130) To form with short turns.
Zĭnc (127), *n.* A bluish-white metal.
Zĭn-çĭf′er-oŭs, } *a.* Containing zinc.
Zĭnk-ĭf′er-oŭs, }
Zĭnck′y (128), *a.* Pertaining to zinc.
Zō′dī-ăc (127), *n.* An imaginary belt in the heavens, which is the sun's path, and contains twelve constellations or signs.
Zo-dī′ac-al, *a.* Pertaining to, or being within, the zodiac.
Zōne, *n.* One of five great climatic divisions of the earth; a girdle; circumference.
Zo-ŏg′ra-pher, *n.* One who describes animals, their habits, &c.
Zō′o-grăph′ic-al, *a.* Relating to the description of animals.
Zo-ŏg′ra-phy, *n.* The description of animals.
Zō′o-lŏġ′ic-al, *a.* Pertaining to zoölogy. [zoölogy.
Zo-ŏl′o-ġist, *n.* One versed in
Zo-ŏl′o-ġy, *n.* [Gr. *zoon*, an animal, and *logos*, discourse.] Science of animals, their structure, habits, &c.; the natural history of the animal kingdom.
Zo-ŏn′o-my, *n.* The laws of animal life.
Zō′o-phȳte, *n.* A body partaking of the nature both of an animal and a vegetable.
Zō′o-phȳt′ic, *a.* Relating to zoöphytes.
Zo-ŏt′o-mist, *n.* One who dissects the bodies of animals.
Zo-ŏt′o-my, *n.* The anatomy of brute animals.
Zouȧve (zwäv *or* zōō-äv′), *n.* One of a body of soldiers wearing an Arab dress.
Zu-mŏl′o-ġy, *n.* See *Zymology*.
Zȳġ′o-măt′ic, *a.* Pertaining to the cheek bone.
Zȳ-mŏl′o-ġy, *n.* A treatise on, or the doctrine of, fermented liquors.
Zȳ-mŏt′ic, *a.* Pertaining to, or caused by, fermentation, or some principle of disease acting like a ferment.

PRONOUNCING VOCABULARY

OF

GREEK AND LATIN PROPER NAMES.

RULES

FOR PRONOUNCING THE VOWELS AND CONSONANTS OF GREEK AND LATIN PROPER NAMES.

RULES FOR THE VOWELS.

1. Any vowel at the end of an accented syllable, and *e*, *o*, and *u*, at the end of an unaccented syllable, have the long English sound; as, *Ca'to*, *Ce'crops*, *Di'do*, *So'lon*, *Cu'mæ*, *Melis'sa*, *Mo-los'sus*, *Tu-lin'gi*; in which words the final vowels of the first syllables have the same sound as the corresponding vowels in the first syllables of the English words *pa'per*, *ce'dar*, *si'lent*, *co'lon*, *du'ty*.

2. *A* ending an unaccented syllable has the sound of *a* in *fa'ther* or in *last*; as, *Ga-bi'na*, *A-re'ne*, pronounced *Gah-bi'nah*, *Ah-re'ne*.

3. *I* ending a final syllable has the long sound, as *To'mi*. At the end of initial unaccented syllables it varies, somewhat indefinitely, between *i* long, as *I-u'lus*, and *i* short (like *i* in *pin*), as in *I-ta'li-a*. In all other cases *i* ending an unaccented syllable has its short sound, as in *pin*.

4. *Y* is pronounced as *i* would be in the same situation.

5. *Æ* and *œ* are pronounced as *e* would be in the same situation.

6. If a syllable end in a consonant, the vowel has the short English sound; as, *Bal'bus*, *Del'phi*, *Cin'na*, *Mos'chus*, *Tus'cus*, in which the vowels have the same sounds as in the English words *man'ner*, *sel'dom*, *din'ner*, *scof'fer*, *mus'ter*.

EXCEPTION. — *E* in final *es* is pronounced as in the familiar proper name *An'des*.

RULES FOR THE CONSONANTS.

7. *C* before *e*, *i*, *y*, *æ*, and *œ*, is pronounced like *s*; before *a*, *o*, and *u*, and before consonants, like *k*; as *Ce'a*, *Cic'e-ro*, *Cy'prus*, *Cæ'sar*, *Cœ'li-a*, *Ca'to*, *Co'cles*, *Cu'mæ*.

8. *G* before *e*, *i*, *y*, *æ*, *œ*, or another *g* followed by *e*, has the sound of *j*; before *a*, *o*, and *u*, and before consonants other than *g*, as above excepted, the hard sound, as in the English words *gave*, *gone*; as *Ge'lo*, *Gi-gan'tes*, *Gyæ'us*, *Ag'ger*; *Ga'bi-i*, *Gor'gi-as*, *Sa-gun'tum*.

9. *Ch* has the sound of *k*, but it is silent before a mute consonant at the beginning of a word; as, *Chtho'nia*, pronounced *Tho'ni-a*.

10. *T*, *s*, and *c*, before *ia*, *ie*, *ii*, *io*, *iu*, and *eu*, preceded immediately by the accent, in Latin words, as in English, change into *sh* and *zh*. But when the *t* follows *s*, *t*, or *x*, or when the accent falls on the first of the vowels following, the consonant preserves its pure sound; as, *Sal-lus'ti-us*, *Brut'ti-i*, *Mil-ti'a-des*, &c. *T* in the termination *tion* also retains its original sound; as, *The-o-do'ti-on*.

11. *S* has, in general, the sound of *s* in *this*. Final *s* preceded by *e*, or a liquid, has the sound of *z*.

12. Initial *x* has the sound of *z*.

13. Initial *ph* before a mute is silent; as, *Phthi'a*, pronounced *Thi'a*. Initial *p* before *s* is silent; as, *Psy'che*, pronounced *Sy'ke*. Initial *p* before *t* is silent; as *Ptol-e-mæ'us*, pronounced *Tol-e-mæ'us*.

14. At the beginning of words we frequently find the uncombinable consonants *mn*, *tm*, &c.; as, *Mne-mos'y-ne*, *Tmo'lus*, &c. These are to be pronounced with the first consonant mute, as if written *Ne-mos'y-ne*, *Mo'lus*, &c.

REMARK. 1. The termination *eus*, derived from the third declension of Greek contracts in εύς, although usually made a single syllable in poetry, is resolved into two syllables in the

(339)

340 GREEK AND LATIN PROPER NAMES.

Table. This is also done by Walker and Trollope, and it is defended by Labbe and Carr. The other syllabication, by which *eus* has the sound of *use*, as in the noun *abuse*, is also given, and is generally to be preferred.

2. The names in Italics are the Anglicized forms of the classical names above them; and each for himself must judge whether to adhere to the classical pronunciation or not.

3. Diacritical marks are used, in this Vocabulary, to indicate the soft sounds of *c*, *g*, and *s*, in some cases, as in *Æ-ac′i-des*, *Æ-ge′ri-a*, *A-chil′les*; also, when *n* has the sound of *ng*, as in *Au′cho-æ*.

The abbreviations *Pw.*, *F.*, *K.*, *Pe.*, *Fac.*, *S.*, *Py.*, *C.*, *L.*, *Lid.*, *B.*, *For.*, *Sch.*, *W.*, *M.*, and *Fr.*, stand, respectively, for the following authorities, viz., *Passow*, *Freund*, *Klotz*, *Pape*, *Facciolati*, *Smith*, *Pauly*, *Carr*, *Labbe*, *Liddell* & *Scott*, *Bischoff* & *Müller*, *Forbiger*, *Scheller*, *Walker*, *Müller*, and *Frijlink*. The figures which follow certain words in the Vocabulary refer to corresponding Rules of Pronunciation. The figure 6, for example, appended to *Abantes*, refers to Rule 6, which shows that the vowel in the last syllable has its long English sound.

A.

Ab′a-lus, C. Py. M.
A-ban′tes, 6
Ab′un-ti′a-des, 6
A-ban′tis
Ab′a-ris
A′bas
Ab′a-tos
Ab′da-lon′i-mus, S. C.
Ab-de′ra
Ab′i-la [W.
Ab′ra-da′tes, 6, C.
A-broc′o-mas
A′bron
A-bron′y-chus C. S. W.
A-bru′po-lis
Ab′u-li′tes, 0, Py. S. W.
A-by′dus
Ab′ys-si′ni, L. W.
Ac′a-cal′lis
A-ca′ci-us, 10, S. W.
Ac′a-de′mi-a
Ac′ar-na′ni-a
Ac′ci-a, 10
A′ce
A-cer′ræ
Aç′e-si′nes, 6
A-chæ′a
A-cha′i-a
A-cha′tes, 6
A ch′e-ron
A ch′i-le′is
A-chil′les, 6
A′era
A′cron
A-crop′o-lis
Ac-tæ′on
Ac-tæ′us
Ac′ti-a, 10

Ac′ti-um, 10
Ad-her′bal
Ad-me′tus, C.
A-do′nis
Ad′ra-myt-te′um, or Ad′ra-myt-ti′um
Ad′ra-myt′ti-um, W. C. M.
Ad′ra-na, *the Oder*.
A-dra′na, B. M. W.
Ad′ras-ti′i Cam′pi
A′dri-an-op′o-lis
A′dri-a′nus
(A′dri-an)
Ad′ri-ne′tum
Æ-aç′i-des, 6
Æ′a-cus
Æ-an′ti-des, 6, W.
Æ-di′les, 6
Æd′u-i
Æ-gæ′um
Æ-ge′ri-a
Æ′ge-us, or Æ′geus
Æg′i-li′a, *an island*.
Æ-gil′i-a, *a demus in Attica*, S.
Æ-gi′na
Æ-gi′ra
Æ′gos Pot′a-mi, or Pot′a-mos
Æ′li-a
Æ′li-a′nus
Æm′i-li-a′nus
Æ-mil′i-us
Æ-ne′is
Æ-o′li-a
Æ′o-lus
Ær′o-pus, *a mountain*, C.
A-er′o-pus
Æs′chi-nes, 6
Æs′chy-lus

Æ-so′pus (Æ′sop)
Æ-to′li-a
A′fer
Af′ri-ca
Af′ri-ca′nus
Ag′a-mem′non
Ag′a-mem-non′i-des, 8
Ag′a-nip′pe
Ag′a-tha
Ag′a-tho
Ag′a-thon
A-ge′nor
A-gen′i-la′us
A′gis
Ag-la′i-a (ag-la′ya)
Ag′o-ra
Ag′o-ran′o-mi [S.
Ag′ri-gas
A′gri-v′ues, 6
A-gric′o-la
A-grip′pa
Ag′rip-pi′na
A′gron
Al′a-ma′ni, or Al′a-man′ni
A-la′ni
Al′a-ri′cus (A′la-ric)
Al-ba′ni
Al-bi′ni
Al′bi-on
Al-cæ′us
Al-can′der
Al-ces′te, or Al-ces′tis
Al′ci-bi′a-des, 6
Al-ci′des, 6
Al-cim′a-chus
Al-ci′o-us
Al′ci-phron, C. W.
Alc-mæ′on
A-lec′try-on
A-le′l-us (a-le′yus)
Cam′pus

Al′e-man′ni, *and* Al′e-ma′ni
A-le′si-a, 10, F. W.
Al′eu-a′dæ, W.
Al′ex-an′der
Al′ex-an′dra
Al-ex′an-dri′a
(Al′ex-an′dri-a)
A-lex′an-dri′na
A-lex′an-drop′o-lis
A-lex′is
Al-lob′ro-ges, 6
Al-phe′us
Al-pi′nus
Al-thæ′a
A-mar′a-cus
Ami′a-ryl′lis
Am′a-ryn′thus
A-ma′zon (Am′a-zon)
A-maz′o-nes, 6 (Am′a-zons)
Am′a-zo′ni-a
Am-bro′si-us, 10 (Am′brose)
A-mil′car
Am′mi-a′nus
Am-phic′ty-on, Pw. Fr.
Am′phic-ty′o-nes, 6 (Am-phic′ty-ons)
Am′phi-ge-ni′a
Am-phi′on
Am-phip′o-lis
Am′phi-tho-a′-trum
Am′phi-tri′te
Am-phit′ry-on
Am-phit′ry-o-ni′a-des, 6
A-myn′tas
A-myn′tor
A-nab′a-sis
An′a-char′sis
A-na′cre-on
[The established

English pronunciation is A-nac′re-on.]
An′ax-ag′o-ras
An′ax-an′der [6
Au′ax-an′dri-des, A-nax′i-man′der
An′ax-im′e-nes, 6
An-cæ′us
An-chi′ses, 6
Ap′cho-æ
An-ci′le
An-co′na
An-do ç′i-des, 6
An′dri-a
An′dro-cles, 6
An-drog′y-næ
An-drom′n-che
An-drom′e-da
An′dro-ni′cus
An-droph′a-gi
Au′ni-bal
An-te′nor
An′thro-poph′a-gi
An-tig′o-ne
Au-tig′o-nus
An′ti-lib′a-nus
An-til′o-chus
An-tim′a-chus
An-tin′o-he
An-tin′o-us
An-ti′o-chus (An′ti-och)
An-ti′o-pe
An-tip′a-ros
An-tip′a-ter
An-tip′a-tris, L. C. W.
An-tip′o-des, 6
An-tip′o-lis
An-tis′the-nes, 6
An′ti-um, 10
An-to′ni-a
An-to-ni′nus
An-to′ni-us
A-nu′bis

GREEK AND LATIN PROPER NAMES. 341

A-pel'la
A-pel'les, 6
Ap'en-ni'nus
  (Ap'en-nines)
Aph'ro-dis'i-a, 10
Aph'ro-di'te, or
  Aph'ro-di'ta
A-pic'i-us, 10
A-pol'lo
Ap'ol-lo'ni-a
Ap'ol-lo'ni-us
Ap'pi-a'nus
  (Ap'pi-an)
Ap'pi-a Vi'a
Ap'pi-i Fo'rum
A-pri'lis
Ap'u-le'i-us (-yus)
Aq'ui-lc'i-a (-le'ya)
Aq'ui-lo
A-qui'nas
Aq'ui-ta'ni-a
A-rab'i-cus
A-rach'ne
A-ra'tus
Ar'ba-ces, 6
Ar-be'la
Ar-ca'di-a
Ar-ces'i-la'us
Ar'che-la'us
Ar'chi-as
Ar'chi-me'des, 6
Ar-chon'tes, 6
Ar-chy'tas
Arc-tu'rus
Ar'e-mor'i-ca
A-re'o-pa-gi'tæ
A're-op'a-gus
A're-op'o-lis
Ar'e-thu'sa
A're-us, or
  A'reus
Ar-gi'vi
Ar-gol'i-cus
Ar'go-lis
Ar'go-nau'tæ
  (Ar'go-nauts)
A'ri-ad'ne
A-ric'i-a, 10
Ar'i-ci'na
A-rim'i-num
A-ri'on
Ar'is-ti'des, 6
Ar'is-til'lus
Ar'is-tip'pus
A-ris'to-bu'lus
A-ris'to-cles, 6
Ar'is-toc'ra-tes,
  S.
A-ris'to-de'mus
A-ris'to-gi'ton
Ar'is-tom'e-ues, 6
Ar'is-toph'a-nes, 6
A-ri'us, or A'ri-as,
  a river, C.
A-ri'us, or A'ri-us,
  the heretic, Fr.
A-ri'us, or
  Ar'ri-us
  Fac.
Ar-mor'i-cæ

Ar-pi'num
Ar'ri-a'nus, Py. S.
  (Ar'ri-an)
Ar'sa-ces, 6, F.
  Fac. M. L. C. K.
Ar-sa'ces, Py. S.
Ar-sin'o-e
Ar'ta-ba'nus
Ar'ta-ba-za'nes, 6,
  S.,
Ar'ta-vas'des, 6
Ar'tax-erx'es, 6
Ar'te-mi-do'rus
Ar'te-mis
Ar'te-mon
Ar-va'les, 6
Ar-ver'ni
As-cal'a-phus
As-ca'ni-us
As'cle-pi'a-des, 6
As-cle'pi-o-do'rus
As'dru-bal
A-sin'i-us
A-so'pus
As-pa'si-a, 10
As-pa'si-us, 10
As'phal-ti'tes, 6
As-tar'te
As-te'ri-a
As-te'ri-on
As-te'ri-us
As-træ'a
As-ty'a-ges, 6
As-ty'a-nax
As-tyd'a-mas, Py.
  S. L.
As'ty-da-mi'a
At'a-lan'ta
A'te
Ath'a-mas
Ath'a-na'si-us, 10
A-the'na
Ath'e-næ'um
Ath'e-nag'o-ras
A-the'ne
A-then'o-do'rus
A'thos
At-lan'tes, 6
At-lan'ti-des, 6
A'tre-us, or
  A'treus
At'ro-pos
At'ti-ca
Au-fid'i-us
Au-gi'as, or
  Au-ge'as
Au-gus-ti'nus
  (Au-gus'tine,
  Au-gus'tin, and
  Aus'tin)
Au-gus'tu-lus
Au-gus'tus
Au-re'li-a'nus
  (Au-re'li-an)
Au-ro'ra
Au'spi-ces, 6
Au-toch'tho-nes, 6
Au-tol'y-cus
Av'en-ti'nus

A-ver'nus, or
  A-ver'na
A-zo'tus

B.

Bac'cha-na'li-a
Bac-chan'tes, 6
Bac'tri-a'na, or
Bac'tri-a'num
Bæt'i-ca
Bai'æ (ba'ye)
Bal-bi'nus
Ba'le-a'res, 6
Bar'a-thrum
Bar'ba-ri
Bar-ba'ri-a
Bar-cæ'i
Bas'i-li'dæ
Bas'i-li'des, 6
Bas'i-li'us, a river.
Bas'i-li'us (St.
  Basil), Py. L.
Ba-sil'i-us, and
  Bas'i-li'us(St.
  Basil), S.
Ba-sil'i-us (St.
  Basil), Fr.
Bas'i-li'us, a Ro-
  man name, For.
Bas'i-lus (also St.
  Basil)
Ba-ta'vi
Bat'ra-cho'my-o-
  ma'chi-a
Bau'cis
Bel'gi-um
Bel'i-sa'ri-us, S. W.
Bel-ler'o-phon
Bc'lus
Ben'e-ven'tum
Ber'e-ni'ce
Be-ro'sus
Bi-brac'te
Bib'u-lus
Bi'on
Bi-thyn'i-a
Bo-ad'i-ce'a
Boc'cho-ris
Bœ-o'ti-a, 10
Bo-e'thi-us
Bo'i-i
Bo-mil'car
Bo're-as
Bo-rys'the-nes, 6
Brach-ma'næ
  (Brah'mans)
Brach-ma'nes, 6
Bri-a're-us, or
  Bri'a-reus
Bri-se'is
Bri-tan'ni
  (Brit'ons)
Brit'o-mar'tis
Brun-du'si-um, 10
Bru'ti-i, 10, or
Brut'ti-i
Bru'tus

Bry'ges, 6
Bu-ceph'a-lus
Bu-col'i-ca
Bu-si'ris
By'blis
By-zan'ti-um, 10

C.

Ca-bi'ri
Cad-me'a
Ca-du'ce-us, 10
Ca-du'ci
Cæs'a-re'a
Cæ-sa'ri-o
Cæs'a-ro-du'num
Ca-i'cus
Ca'i-us (ka'yus)
Ca-la'bri-a
Cal'a-is
Ca-le-do'ni-a
Ca-lig'u-la
Cal'li-cles, 6
Cal-lim'a-chus
Cal-li'o-pe
Cal'li-o-pe'a
Cal-lis'the-nes, 6
Cal-lis'tra-tus
Cal-pur'ni-us
Ca-lyp'so
Cam-by'ses, 6
Ca-mil'la
Ca-mil'lus
Cam-pa'ni-a
Cam-pas'po
Ca-na'ri-i
Can'da-ce
Ca-nid'i-us, S. W.
Ca-nin'i-us
Ca-no'pus
Can'ta-bri
Can'ti-um, 10
Ca-pa/ne-us, or
  Cap'a-neus
Cap'i-to
Cap'i-to-li'nus
Cap'i-to'li-um
Cup'pa-do'ci-a, 10
Ca'pro-æ
Cap'u-a
Car'a-cal'la
Cu-rac'ta-cus
Ca-rau'si-us, 10,
  S. W.
Ca'ri-a
Car-me'lus
  (Car'mel)
Car'pa-thus [see
Car-thag'i-ni-en'-
  sis, or
Car-tha'go
  (Car'thage)
Ca'ry-at'i-des, 6, pl.
Cas-san'der
Cas-san'drn
Cas-si'o-pe, or
  Cas-si-o-pe'a, 10
Cas'si-us, 10
Cas'si-ye-lau'nus

Cas-ta'li-a, or
  Cas-ta'li-us Fons
Cat'i-li'na
  (Cat'i-line)
Ca'to
Ca-tul'lus
Cat'u-lus
Cnu'ca-sus
Ca-ys'ter, or
  Ca-ys'trus
Ce'bes, 6
Ce-cro'pi-a
Ce-crop'i-dæ
Ce'crops
Ce-læ'no
Cel'e-res, 6
Cel'ti-be'ri
Ccl-tos'cy-thæ
Cen'chre-æ
Cen-so'res, 6
Cen-tau'ri
Cen-tum'vi-ri
Cen-tu'ri-a
Ceph'al-le'ni-a
Ce'phe-us, or
  Ce'pheus
Ce-phi'sus, or
  Ce-phis'sus
Cer'a-mi'cus
Cc-rau'ni-a
Cer'be-rus
Ce're-a'li-a
Ce-rin'thus
Ce-the'gus
Chær'o-ne'a
Chal-ce'don
Chal'ce-do'ni-a
Chal-dæ'a
Chal-dæ'i
  (Chal'de-ans)
Chal'y-bes, 6
Cha'os
Cha'res, 6   [W.
Char'i-cles, 6, S.
Char'i-la'us, and
  Cha-ri'lus
Char'i-tes, 6
Cha'ron
Cha-ryb'dis
Chau'bi, and
  Chau'ci
Che'ops
Cher'so-ne'sus, or
  Cher'ro-ne'sus
Chi-mæ'ra
Chi'os
Chlo'e
Cho-roe'bus
Chry-sil'or
Chrys'a-or, C.
Chry-se'is
Chry'ses, 6
Chry'sip'pus
Chry-sos'to-mus
  (Chrys'os-tom)
Chtho'ni-a, 14
Cib'a-læ
Cic'e-ro
Ci-lic'i-a, 10
Cim'bri-cus

GREEK AND LATIN PROPER NAMES.

Cim-me'ri um
Cin'cin-na'tus
Cin'e-as
Cin-get'o-rix
Cir-cen'ses Lu'di
Ci-thæ'ron
Ci-vi'lis
Clau'di-a'nus
  (*Claw'di-an*)
Clau'di-us
Cle'mens
  (*Clem'ent*)
Cle'o-bu'lus
Cle-om'bro-tus
Cle-op'a-tra, *Pw.*
  K. M. Py. C. Fr
Cle'o-pa'tra,* F.*
[This is the
accepted *English* pronunciation.]
Cle-op'a-tris
Clin'i-as, *K. W.*
Clis'the-nes, 6
Cio'a-ci'na
Clo'di-us
Clu-si'ni
Clym'e-ne
Clyt'æm-nes'tra
Coc-ce'i-us
  (-se'yus)
Co'cles, 6
Co-cy'tus
Co'drus
Cœl'e-syr'i-a, and
  Cœl'o-syr'i-a
Col'la-ti'nus
Co-lo'næ
Co-lo'ni-a
Co-los'sus
Col'u-mel'la
Co-lum'næ Her'-
  cu-lis
Co-mit'i-a, 10
Com'mo-dus
Con-cordi-a
Con-stan'ti-nop'o-lis
  (*Con-stan'ti-no'ple*)
Con'stan-ti'nus
  (*Con'stan-tine*)
Co'pi-a
Cor-cy'ra   [*nus*
Cor'cy-ra, *Avie-*
Cor'du-ba
Co-rin'na
Co-rin'thus
Co'ri-o-la'nus
Co-ri'o-li
Cor-ne'li-a
Cor-ne'li-i
Cor'ni-ger
Cor'si-ca
Cor'y-don
Cot'ti-æ
Cran'a-us
Crat'e-rus
Crat'y-lus
Cre-mo'na

Cre'on
Cre-u'sa
Cris-pi'nus
Crit'o-bu'lus
Cro-by'zi, *Py. Sch.*
Croc'o-di-lop'o-lis
Crœ'sus
Cro-to'na
Crus'tu-me'ri-a, or
  Crus'tu-me'ri-um
Cte'si-as, 10, 14
Ctes'i-phon, 14
Cu'ma, or Cu'mæ
Cu-pi'do
  (*Cu'pid*)
Cu'ri-a'ti-i, 10
Cur'ti-us, 10
Cy'a-ne
Cy-ax'a-res, *Py. W.*
Cyb'e-le
Cyc'la-des, 6
Cy-clo'pes, 6
  (*Cy'clops*)
Cyd'o-ne'a
Cyl-le'ne
Cyn'æ-gi'rus
Cyn'e-as
Cyn'o-ar-tes, 6
Cyn'o-sar'ges, 6
Cyn'o-su'ra
  (*Cyn'o-sure*)
Cyn'thi-a
Cyp'ri-a'nus
  (*Cyp'ri-an*)
Cy'prus
Cyr'e-na'i-ci
Cy-re'ne
Cy-ril'lus
  (*Cyr'il*)
Cy'rus
Cy-the'ra
Cyth'e-re'a
Cyz'i-cum

D.

Da'ci-a
Dæd'a-la
Dæd'a-lus
Dal-mat'i-cus
Dam'as-ce'ne
Dam'o-cles, 6
Dan'a-e
Dan'a-i
Da-na'i-des, 6
Da-nu'bi-us
  (*Dan'ube*)
Daph'ne-pho'ri-a,
  S. W.
Dar-dan'i-des, 6
Dar'da-nus
Da-re'us, or
  Da-ri'us
De-cap'o-lis
De-cu'ri-o
De-i'a-ni'ra
De-id'a-mi'a
De-i-ot'a rus

De-iph'o-bus
De'li-a
De'li-us
De'los
Del'phi-cus [*C. W.*
Del-phin'i-um, *S.*
Dem'a-ra'tus
De-me'tri-as
De-me'tri-us
Dem'o-ce'des, 6
De-moch'a-res, 6
De-moc'ri-tus
De-moph'o-on
De-mos'the-nes, 6
Deu-ca'li-on
Di-ag'o-ras
Di-a'na
  (*Di'an*)
[The established
  English pronunciation is
  Di-an'a.]
Dic-ta'tor
Did'i-us
Di'do
Di-es'pi-ter
Di'i
Di-noc'ra-tes, 6
Di'o-cle'ti-a'nus
  (*Di'o-cle'tian*)
Di'o-do'rus
Di-og'e-nes, 6
Di'o-me'de
Di'o-me'des, 6
  (*Di'o-med*)
Di-o'ne
Di'os-cor'i-des, 6
  Py. S.
Di'os-cu'ri
Di-os'po-lis
Dis-cor'di-a
Div'i-ti'a-cus
Div'o-du'rum
Do-do'na
Dol'a-bel'la
Dol'o-pes, 6
Do-mit'i-a'nus, 10
  (*Do-mi'tian*)
Do-na'tus
Do'ri-on
Dra'co
Drep'a-na, or
  Drep'a-num
Dru'i-dæ
  (*Dru'ids*)
Dry'a-des, 6, *Fac.*
  (*Dry'ads*) [*W.*
Dry'o-pes, 6
Du-il'li-us
Du-lich'i-um
Dum'no-rix
Du-um'vi-ri

E.

Eb'o-ra'cum
  Py. Fac. L. For.
  B. Sch.

Ec-bat'a-na, *S. W.*
E-chid'na
E-chi'on
E'cho
E-des'an, *or*
E-de'sa
E'don
E-du'nes, 6, *Thra-*
  cians
E-ge'ri-a
El'a-gab'u-lus
El'a-te'a
El'e-phan'tis
El'eu-sin'i-a
E-leu'the-ræ
E'lis
El'y-ma'is
E-lys'i-um, 10
Em-ped'o-cles, 6
En-cel'a-dus
Eu-dym'i-on
En'ni-us
E'os
E-pam'i-non'das
E-pe'us
Eph'o-ri
Ep'ic-te'tus
Ep'i-cu'rus
Ep'i-dau'rus
E-pig'o-ni
Ep'i-men'i-des, 6
Ep'i-me'the-us, *or*
  Ep'i-me'theus
E-piph'a-nes, 6
E-pi'rus
Eq'ui-tes, 6
Er'a-sis'tra-tus
Er'a-to
Er'a-tos'the nes, 6
Er'e-bus
E-rech'the-us, *or*
  E-rech'theus
E-re'tri-a
Er'ich-tho'ni-us
E-rid'a-nus
E-rig'o-ne
E-rin'nys
E'ros
E-ros'tra-tus
Es-quil'i-æ
Es'qui-li'nus
E-te'o-cles, 6
E-tru'ri-a
E-trus'ci
Eu-bœ'a
Eu-bu'li-des, 6
Eu-bu'lus
Eu-cli'des, 6 [*W.*
Eu-do'ci-a, 10, *S.*
Eu-dox'us
Eu'me-nes, 6
Eu-men'i-des, 6
Eu'pa-tor
Eu-phra'nor
Eu-phra'tes, 6
En-phros'y-ne,
  Lid. S.
Eu-rip'i-des, 6
Eu-ri'pus
Eu-ro'pa

Eu'ro-pæ'us
Eu-ro'tas
Eu'rus
Eu-ry'a-lus
En-ryd'i-ce
Eu-rys'the-us, *or*
  Eu-rys'theus
Eu'ry-tus
Eu-se'bi-us
Eu-sta'thi-us, *S. W.*
Eu-ter'pe
Eu-tro'pi-us
Eux-i'nus Pon'tus
E-vad'ne
E-van'der
E-var'chus
E-vem'e-rus
E-ve'nus
E-veph'e-nus

F.

Fa'bi-i
Fa-bric'i-us, 10
Fa-le'ri-a
Fau'na
Faus-ti'na
Faus'tu-lus
Fav'o-ri'nus
Fe-lic'i-tas
Fe-ra'li-a
Fe-ro'ni-a
Fi-de'na, *or*
  Fi-de'næ
Fla-min'i-a
Flo-ra'li-a
For-tu'na
Fris'i-i, 10
Fu-gu'li-a
Fu'ri-æ
  (*Fu'ries*)

G.

Ga-bi'nus
Ga'des, 6
Gad'i-ta'nus
Gal'a-tæ
Gal'a-te'a
Ga-le'nus
  (*Ga'len*)
Ga-le'ri-us
Gal'li-a
Gal'li-cus
Gal'li-e'nus
Gal-lip'o-lis
Gal'lo-græ'ci-a, 10
Gan'y-me'des, 6
  (*Gan'y-mede*)
Gar-ga'nus
Gel'li-us
Gem'i-ni
Ge-ne'va, *W. L. Fr.*
  K. Sch. M.
Gen'e-va, *For.*

GREEK AND LATIN PROPER NAMES. 343

Gcu'u-a
Ge-or'gi-ca
  (*Geōr'gics*)
Ger-ma'ni-a
  (*Ger'ma-ny*)
Ger-man'i-cus
Go'ry-on, *and*
  Ge-ry'o-neş, 6
Ge'ta
Gla/di-a-to'ri-i
  Lu'di
Gor'di-a'nus
  (*Gor'di-an*)
Gor'di-us
Gor'gi-as
Gor'go-neş, 6
Go'thī
  (*Goths*)
Gra-di'vus
Gra-ni'cus
Gru'ti-æ, 10
Gym-na'si-um, 10
Gym-nos'o-phis'-
  tæ

H.

Ha'dri-a'nus
  (*Ha'dri-an*)
Ha'dri-at'i-cum
Hal-cy'o-ne
Hal'i-car-nas'sus
Ham'a-dry-a-deş, 6
  (*Ham'a-dry-ads*)
Ha-mil'car
Han'ni-bal
Har-mo'di-us
Har-mo'ni-a
Har'pa-gus,
  Py. C. W.
Har-poc'ra-teş, 6
Har-py'i-æ (-ye)
  (*Har'pies*)
Has'dru-bal
He'be
Hc'brus
Hec'a-te
Hec'u-ba
He-ge'mon, *and*
  Heg'e-mon
Heg'e-sip'pus
Hcl'e-na
Hel'i-con
He'li-o-do'rus
He'li-o-gab'a-lus,
  He'li-o-ga-ba'lus,
    C. L.
He'li-op'o-lis
Hel-le'neş, 6
Hel'les-pon'tus
He-lo'tæ, *and*
  He-lo'teş, 6
  (*He'lots or Hel'-
   ots*)
Hcl-ve'ti-i, 10
He-phæn'ti-on, 10
Her'a-cli'dæ
Her'a-cli'tus

Her'cu-la'ne-um
Her'cu-la-ne'um,
  K.
Her'cu-leş, 6
Her-maph'ro-di'-
  tus
Hur-mi'o-ne
Her'mo-do'rus
Her-mog'e-neş, 6
  Pe. S.
Her-mun'du-ri,
  K. Fac. For. F.
He-ro'deş, 6
  (*Her'od*)
He-ro'di-a'nus
  (*He-ro'di-an*)
He-rod'o-tus
Her'o-op'o-lis
Her'u-li
Hc-si'o-dus
  (*He'si-od*)
He-si'o-ne
Hes-pe'ri-a
Hes-per'i-deş, 6
He-sych'i-us
He-tru'ri-a
Hi'e-rap'o-lis
Hi-er'i-chus
  (*Jer'i-cho*)
Hi'e-ro
Hi-er'o-cleş, 6
Hi'e-ron'y-mus
  (*Jer'ome*)
Hi'e-ro-sol'y-ma
  (*Je-ru'sa-lem*)
Hip'pi-as
Hip-poc'ra-teş, 6
Hip'po-cre'ne
  (*Hip'po-crene*)
Hip'po-da-mi'a
Hip-pol'y-te
Hip-pol'y-tus
Hip-pom'e-don
Hip-po'nax
His-pa'ni-a
Ho-me'rus
  (*Ho'mer*)
Ho-ra'ti-us, 10
  (*Hor'ace*)
Hor-ten'si-us, 10
Jo-se'phus
Hy'a-cin'thus
Hy'a-deş, 6
Hy'bla
Hy-das'peş, 6
Hy'dra
Hy-emp'sal
Hy-gc'i-a (-je'ya)
Hy'las
Hym'e-næ'us
Hy-met'tus
Hyp'er-bo're-i, *and*
  Hy-per'bo-re'i
Hyp'e-ri'deş, 6, *or*
  Hy-per'i-deş
Hyp'e-ri'on
  (*Hy-pe'ri-on*)
Hyp'erm-nes'tra
Hyr-ca'ni-a
Hys-tas'peş, 6

I.

I-ac'chus
I-am'bli-chus
I-be'rus
I-ca'ri-a
Ic'a-rus
I-ce'ni, *Fac. W.*
I-co'ni-um
I'da
I-dom'e-neus
Id'u-me'a
Il'i-as
I-li'o-ne, *or*
  I-li'o-na
Il'i-um, *or* Il'i-on
Il-lyr'i-a
Il-lyr'i-cum
Im'a-us
I-ma'us, *K.*
In'a-chus
In'ci-ta'tus
In'te-ram'na
I'o-las, *or* I'o-la'us
I-o'ni-a
I'o-pe
I-phic'ra-teş, 6
Iph'i-ge-ni'a
Ir'e-næ'us
I-re'ne
I-sæ'us
I-sau'ri-a
Is'i-do'rus
I-soc'ra-teş, 6
Isth'mi-a
I-ta'li-a
  (*It'a-ly*)
It'a-lus
Ith'a-ca
It'u-ræ'a
I-u'lus
Ix-i'on

J.

Ja-co'bus
  (*James*)
Jap'e-tus
Jo-se'phus
Jo'vi-a'nus
  (*Jo'vi-an*)
Ju-dæ'a
Ju'li-a'nus
  (*Ju'li-an*)
Ju'li-us
Ju'no
Ju'pi-ter
Jus-tin'i-a'nus
  (*Jus-tin'i-an*)
Jus-ti'nus
  (*Jus'tin*)
Ju've-na'lis
  (*Ju've-nal*)

L.

Lab'da-cus

La'be-o
La'bi-e'nus
Lac'e-dæ'mon
Lac'e-dæ-mo'ni-i,
  or Lac'e-dæm'o-
  neş
  (*Lac'e-de-mo'-
    ni-ans*)
Lach'e-sis
La-cin'i-um
La-co'ni-a, *and*
  La-con'i-ca
Lac-tan'ti-us, 10
Læ'li-a'nus
Læ'li-us
La-er'teş, 6
La'i-us (-yus)
Lamp'sa-cus, *and*
  Lamp'sa-chum
Ian'go-bar'di
La-oc'o-on
La-od'a-mi'a
La-od'i-ce'a
La-om'e-don
La-om'o-don-ti'a-
  dæ
Lap'i-thæ
La'reş, 6
Lar'ti-us, 10, *S. W.*
Lat'e-ra'nus
  (*Lat'er-an*)
La-ti'nus
La'ti-um, 10
Lat'o-bri'gi
La-to'na
La-vin'i-a
La-vin'i-um, *or*
  La-vi'num
Le-an'der
Le'da
Le-ma'nus
Lem'u-reş, 6
Len'tu-lus
Le-on'i-das
Le-on-ti'ni
Le-on'ti-um, 10
Lep'i-dus
Le-pon'ti-i, 10
Le'the
Leu-cip'pus
Leu-co'the-a
Leu-coth'o-e
Li-ba'ni-us, *S. W.*
Lib'a-nus
  (*Leb'a-non*)
Li-ber'tas
Lib'i-ti'na
Li-cin'i-us
Lig'u-reş, 6
Li-gu'ri-a
Lil'y-bæ'um
Lin'go-neş, 6
Lip'a-ra
Liv'i-us
  (*Liv'y*)
Lou-din'i-um
  S. Fac. Sch. For.
  (*Lon'don*)
Lon-gim'a-nus
Lon-gi'nus

Lon'go-bar'di
  (*Lom'bards*)
Lu-ca'nus
  (*Lu'can*)
Luc-cc'i-us (-yus)
Lu'ce-reş, 6
Lu'ci-a'nus
  (*Lu'cian*)
Lu'ci-fer
Lu-cil'i-us
Lu-cre'ti-a, 10
Lu-cro'ti-us, 10
Lu-cul'lus
Lug-du'num
  (*Ly'ons*)
Lu-pcr'cul
Lu'si-ta'ni-a
Lu-te'ti-a, 10
Lyc'i-das
Lyc'o-me'deş, 6
Lyc'o-phron
Ly-cur'gus
Lyn'ceus, *or*
  Lyn'ce-us
Ly-san'der
Lys'i-as, 10
Ly-sim'a-chi'a
Lys'i-ma'chi-a
Ly-sim'a-chus

M.

Mac'e-do
Ma-ced'o-neş, 6
  (*Mac'e-do'ni-ans*)
Mac'e-don'i-cus
Ma-chā'on
Ma'cri-a'nus
Ma-cri'nus
Ma-cro'bi-i
Ma-cro'bi-us
Mæ-an'der
Mæ-ce'nas
Mœn'a-lus
Mæ-o'ni-a
Mæ-on'i-deş, 6
Mæ-o'tis Pa'lus
Mag-ne'si-a, 10
Ma-har'bal
Ma-jes'tas
Mam'er-ti'ni
Ma-mil'i-us
Ma-mu'ri-us
Man-ci'nus
Ma'neş, 6
Man'e-tho
Ma-nil'i-us
Man'ti-ne'a
Man'tu-a
Mar'a-thon
Mar'cel-li'nus
Mar'ci-a'nus, 10
  (*Mar'cian*)
Mar'ci-us, 10
Mar-do'ni-us
Mi'ri-a Lex
Ma-ri-am'ne

GREEK AND LATIN PROPER NAMES.

Ma'ri-us
Mar'sy-as, 10
Mar'ti-a'lis
(*Mar'tial*)
Mas'i-nis'sa
Mas-sag'e-tæ
Mas-sil'i-a
Mau'ri-ta'ni-a
Mau-so'lus
Max-en'ti-us, 10
Max'im-i-a'nus
(*Max-im'i-an*)
Max'i-mi'nus
(*Max'i-min*)
Max'i-mus
Me-de'a
Me'di-a
Me'di-o-la'num
Me-du'sa
Meg'a-cleş, 6, *Py. S.*
Me-gæ'ra
Meg'a-le
Meg'a-ra
Me-gas'the-neş, 6
Mel'a-nip'pi-deş, 6
Mel'a-uip'pus
Me-lan'thi-us
Me'le-a'ger,
K. F. S. Sch.
Me-le'a-ger,
C. Fac.
Me'le-ag'ri-deş, 6
Mel'e-sig'e-neş, 6
Mel'i-bœ'us
Mel'i-ta, *or* Mel'i-te
Me'li-us
Mel-pom'e-ne
Me-nan'der
Me-nec'ra-teş, 6
Men'e-de'mus
Men'e-la'us
Me-nes'the-us, *or*
Me-nes'theus
Mer-cu'ri-us
(*Mer'cu-ry*)
Mer'o-e
Mer'o-pe
Me'rops
Mes-o-po-ta'mi-a
Mes-sa'la
Mes'sa-li'na
Mes-se'ne, *or*
Mes-se'na
Met'a-pon'tum
Me-til'i-l
Met'ro-cleş, 6
Me-zen'ti-us, 10
Mi-cip'sa
Mi'das
Mi-le'si-l, 10
Mi-le'tus
Mil-ti'a-deş, 6
Mil'vi-us
Min'cl-us, 10
Mi-ner'va
Mi'nos
Min'o-tau'rus
Mi-nu'ci-us, 10
Mi-se'num

Mi'thras
Mith'ri-da'teş, 6
Mit'y-le'ne
Mne-mos'y-ne, 14
Mnes'the-us, *or*
Mnes'theus, 14
Mo-des'tus
Mœ'si-a, 10
Mo-los'si
Mo'mus
Mo'na
Mo-ne'ta
Mon'i-ma
Mon-ta'nus
Mor'phe-us, *or*
Mor'pheus
Mul'ci-ber
Mu-sæ'us
Mu'ti-na
Mu-ti'nus
Mu'ti-us, 10
Myc'a-le
My-ce'næ
Myc'o-nus, *and*
My-co'nus
My-ri'na
Myr-mid'o-neş, 6
Mys'i-a, 10
Myt'i-le'ne

N.

Nab'ar-za'neş, 6
L. C. S.
Nab'a-thæ'a
Næ'ni-a
Næ'vi-us
Na-i'a-deş, 6
Nar'bo-nen'sis
Nar-cis'sus
Na-ri'ci
Nar'ni-a
Na-ri'ca
Nan'cra-teş, 6
Ne-æ'ra
Ne-ap'o-lis
Ne-ar'chus
Ne-crop'o-lis
Nec-tan'a-bis
Ne-mæ'a *and*
Ne'me-a, *games*
Ne'me-a, *town and river*
Nem'e-sis
Ne'o-cæs'a-re'a
Ne'o-cleş, 6
Ne'op-tol'e-mus
Ne'pos
Nep-tu'nus
(*Nep'tune*)
Ne-re'i-deş, 6
(*Ne're-ids*)
Ne-re'is, *or*
Ne're-is
Ne're-us, *or*
Ne'reus
Ner'vi-i
Nes-to'ri-us

Ni-cæ'a, *or* Ni-ce'a
Ni-ca'nor
Ni-ceph'o-rus
Nic'i-as, 10
Nic'o-de'mus
Nic'o-la'us
Ni-com'a-chus
Nic'o-me'deş, 6
Nic'o-me-di'a, *or*
Nic'o-me-de'a
(*Nic'o-me'di-a*)
Ni-cop'o-lis
Ni'ger
Ni'o-be
Ni-pha'teş, 6
Nis'i-bis
Noc'ti-lu'ca
Nom'a-deş, 6
No'ni-us
Nu'ma
Nu-man'ti-a, 10
Nu'me-ri-a'nus
Nu-mid'i-a
Nu'mi-tor

O.

O'a-sis
O-a'sis, *Py.*
O-ax'us
O'ce-an'i-deş, 6,
and O'ce-a-nit'i-deş
O-ce'a-nus
Oc-ta'vi-a
Oc-ta-vi-a'nus
Oc-ta'vi-us
O-do'a-cer, *C.* [*M.*
Od'o-a'cer, *W. S.*
Œc'u-me'ni-us, 5
Œd'i-pus, 5
Œ'ne-us, *or*
Œ'neus
Œn-o'e, 6
Œ-no'tri-a
Og'y-geş, 6
O-li'e-ns, *or*
O-i'leus
O-lym'pi-a
O-lym'pi-as
O-lym'pi-o-do'rus
O-lym'pi-us
O-lym'pus
O-lyn'thus
Om'pha-le
Om'pha-lus
On'e-sic'ri-tus
O-nes'i-mus
O-pi'ma Spo'li-a
O-pim'i-us
Op-pi-a'nus
(*Op'pi-an*)
Op'pi-us
Op'ti-mus
Or'ca-deş, 6
Or'do-vi'ces, *C.*
Or-dov'i-ces, 6,
For. K.

O-re'a-deş, 6
(*O're-ads*)
O-res'teş, 6
Or-get'o-rix, *S. Py.*
Or'gi-a
O'ri-enş
O-rig'e-neş, 6
(*Or'i-gen*)
O-ri'on
O-ron'teş, 6
O-ro'pus
O-ro'si-us, 10
Or'phe-us, *or*
Or'pheus
Or-tyg'i-a
O'rus
O-si'ris
O'tho
O-vid'i-us
(*Ov'id*)
Ox'us

P.

Pa-ca'ti-a'nus, 10,
Pac-to'lus [*S. W.*
Pa-cu'vi-us
Pa'dus
Pa-du'sa
Pæ'o-neş, 6
Pa-læ'mon
Pal'æs-ti'na
Pal'a-me'deş, 6
Pal'a-ti'nus
Pa-la'ti-um, 10
Pal'i-nu'rus
Pal-la'di-um
Pal'leş, 6
Pal-my'ra
Pam'me-neş, 6
Pam'phi-lus
Pam-phyl'i-a
Pa-nœ'ti-us, 10
Pan-ath'e-næ'a
Pan'da-rus
Pan-do'ra
Pan'hel-le'neş, 6
Pan-no'ni-a
Pa-no'pe-us, *or*
Pan'o-peus
Pan-the'a
Pan'the-ne, *or*
Pan-the'on
Pa'phi-a, *or*
Pa'phi-a
Paph'la-go'ni-a
Pa'phus
Pa'pi-as
Pa-pin'i-a'nus
(*Pa-pin'i-an*)
Pa-pir'i-us
Pa'ris
Pa-ris'i-i, 10
Par-men'i-deş, 6
Par-me'ni-o, *C. S.*
Par-nas'sus
Par-rha'si-us, 10

Par'the-non
Par-then'o-pe
Par'thi-a
Pa-siph'a-e
Pat'a-ra
Pa-ta'vi-um
Pa-ter'cu-lus
Pat'ro-cleş, 6
Pat'ro-clus
Pau li'nus
Pau-sa'ni-as
Peg'a-sus
Pe-las'gi
Pe-las'gi-o'tis
Pe'le-us, *or*
Pe'leus
Pe-li'a-deş, 6
Pe'li-as
Pe'li-on
Pe-li'on, *son of Peleus*
Pe-lop'i-das
Pel'o-pon-ne'sus
Pe'lops
Pe-lo'rus
Pe-lu'si-um, 10
Pe-nа'teş, 6
Pe-nel'o-pe
Pe-ne'us
Peu-tap'o-lis
Pen-tel'i-cus
Pen'the-si-le'a, 10
Pen'the-us, *or*
Pen'theus
Per'ga-mus
Per'i-cleş, 6
Per'i-pa-tet'i-cl
(*Per'i-pa-tet'ics*)
Per-seph'o-ne
Per-sep'o-lis
Per'se-us, *or*
Per'seus
Pe-ru'si-a, 10
Pe'tra
Pe-træ'a
Pe-tro'ni-a
Pe-tro'ni-us
Phæ'don
Phæ'dra
Phæ'drus
Pha'e-thon
Phal'a-ris
Pha-le'ron
Phar'na-ba'zus, *W. S.*
Phar'na-ceş, 6
Pha'ros
Phar-sa'li-a
Phid'i-as
Phil-dip'pi-deş, 6
Phil'a-del-phi'a
(*Phil'a-del'phi-a*)
Phil'ip-pi'i
Phil-lip'pi
Phi'lo
Phi'lo-cleş, 6
Phi-loc'ra-teş, 6
Phi-lom'bro-tus
Phil'o-me'la

GREEK AND LATIN PROPER NAMES.

Phi-lop'a-tor
Phil'o-pœ'men
Phi-los'tra-tus
Phi-lo'tis
Phi-lox'e-nus
Phin'e-us, or
  Phi'neus
Phin'ti-us, 10, *W. S.*
Pho'ci-on, 10
Pho'cis
Pho'cus
Phœ'be
Phœ-ni'ce, or
  Phœ-nic'i-a, 10
Phœ'nix
Phor'mi-o
Phra-or'tes, 6
Phryg'i-a
Phryn'i-chus
Phthi-o'tis, 14
Piç'en-ti'ui
Pi-ce'num
Pi-o'ri-a
Pi'e-ri'a, or
  Pi'e-re'a, a
  nymph.
Pi-er'i-des, 6
Pi'e-tas
Pin'da-rus
  (*Pin'dar*)
Pi-rith'o-us
Pi-san'der
Pi-sid'i-a
Pis'is-trat'i-dæ
Pi-sis'tra-tus
Pla-tœ'a
Pla-tœ'æ
Pla'to
Plau'tus
Ple'ia-des (ple'ya-
  deez) or Ple-i'a-
  des, 6
Ple-i'o-ne
Plin'i-us
  (*Plin'y*)
Plis'the-nes, 6
Plo-ti'nus
Plu-tar'chus
  (*Plu'tarch*)
Plu'to
Po'li-or-ce'tes, 6
Pol'li-o
Po-ly b'i-us
Pol'y-car'pus
  (*Pol'y-carp*)
Pol'y-cles, 6
Pol'y-cle'tus
Po-lyd'a-mas
Pol'y-dec'tes, 6
Pol'y-do'rus
  (*Pol'y-dore*)
†Pol'y-yg-no'tus
Pol'y-hym'ni-a, or
  Po-lym'ni-a
Pol'y-ni'ces, 6
Pol'y-phe'mus
  (*Pol'y-pheme*)
Po-mo'na
Pom-po'i-i (-pe'yi)

Pom-po'i-us (-yus)
  (*Pom'pey*)
Pom-pil'i-us
Pom-po'ni-us
Po-pil'i-us
Pop-lic'o-la
Pop-præ'a
Por'ci-a, 10
Por-sen'na, *or*
  Por'se-na
Pos'i-de'um
Po-si'don
Pot'a-mus
Pot'i-dæ'a
Præ-nes'to
Prax-it'e-les, 6
Pri'a-mus
  (*Pri'am*)
Pri-a'pus
Pris'ci-a'nus, 10
  (*Pris'cian*)
Pro-co'pi-us
Pro-crus'tes, 6
Pro-me'the-us, or
  Pro-me'theus
Pro-per'ti-us, 10
Pro-ser'pi-na
  (*Pros'er-pine*)
Pro'te-us, or
  Pro'teus
Pro-tog'e-nes, 6
Pru-den'ti-us, 10
Pryt'a-nes, 6
Pryt'a-ne'um
Psam-met'i-chus,
  14, *C. L.*
Psam'me-ti'-
  chus, 14, *K.*
Psy'che, 14
P'tol'e-mæ'um, 14
Ptol'e-ma-e'um
Ptol'e-mæ'us, 14
  (*Ptol'e-my*)
Ptol'e-ma'is, 14
Pub-lic'o-la
Pub'li-us
Pu-te'o-li
Pyg-ma'li-on
Pyl'a-des, 6
Pyr'a-mus
Pyth'e-us, *or*
  Py'theus
Pyth'i-as
Pyth'i-us
Pyth'o-nis'sa

Q.

Quæs-to'res, 6
Quinc'ti-us, 10
Quin'de-cim'vi-ri
Quin'quen-na'les,6
Quin'til-i-a'nus
  (*Quin-til'ian*)
Quir'i-na'li-a
Quir'i-na'lis
Qui-ri'nus
Qui-ri'tes, 6

R.

Ra-mi'ses, 6, *C. W.*
Reg'u-lus
Re'mi
Rem'u-lus
Re-mu'ri-a
Rhad'a-man'thus
Rha'ti-a, 10
Rhe'a
Rhe'gi-um
Rhi-phæ'i
Rhod'o-pe
Rho-do'pis
Rhox-a'ne, or
  Rox-a'ue
Ro-ma'ni
Rom'u-lus
Ros'ci-us, 10
Rox-a'na
Rox'o-la'ni
Ru'bi-con, and
  Ru'bi-co
Ru-til'i-us
Ru'tu-li

S.

Sa-bæ'i
Sa-bel'lus
Sa-bi'ni
Sa'bis
Sa'cæ
Sa-gun'tum, or
  Sa-gun'tus
Sa'is
Sal'a-mi'na
Sal'a-mis
Sa'li-i
Sal-lus'ti-us, 10
  (*Sal'lust*)
Sal-mo'ne-us, or
  Sal-mo'neus
Sa-lo'me
Sa-ma'ri-a, *F. S.*
Sam'a-ri'a
Sam-ni'tes, 6
  (*Sam'nites*)
Sa'mos
Sa-mos'a-ta
Sam'o-thra'ce, or
  Sam'o-thra'ci-a,
  10
San'cho-ni'a-thon
San'eho-ui-a'-
  thon, *Sch.*
Sa'por
Sar'a-ce'ne
Sar'da-na-pa'lus
Sar-din'i-a
Sar'ma-tæ
Sar-mn'ti-a, 10
Sar-pe'don
Sat'i-bar-za'nes, 6, *W. S.*
Sat'ur-na'li-a
Sa-tur'ni-a

Sa-tur'nus
Sat'y-rus
Sax'o-nes, 6
Sçæ'a
Sçæ'va
Sçæv'o-la
Sca-man'der
Scan'di-na'vi-a
Scap'u-la
Scau'rus
Sçi-pi'a-dæ
Sçip'i-o
Sçy'ros
Sçy'thœ
Sçyth'i-a
Sçy-thop'o-lis
Se-bas'te
Seb'as-te'a, or
  Seb'as-ti'a
Se-ja'nus
Se-le'ne
Sel'eu-ci'a, or
  Sel'eu-ce'a
  (*Se-leu'ci-a*)
Se-leu'cus
Sem'e-le
Se-mir'a-mis
Sem-pro'ni-us
Sen'e-ca
Sep-tem'vi-ri
Sep-tim'i-us
Seq'ua-ni
Se-ra'pis
Ser'gi-us
Ser-ri'phus
Ser-vil'i-us
Ser'vi-us
Se-sos'tris
Se-ve'rus
Sex'ti-us, 10
Si-byl'la
Si-ca'ni, and
  Sic'a-ni
Si-chæ'us
Siç'i-nus
Siç'y-on (sish'i-on)
Si-ge'um
Si-le'nus
Sil'i-cen'sæ
Sil'i-us
Si-lu'res, 6
  K. Fac. Sch.
Sil'u-res
  Py. S. For.
Sil-va'nus
Sim'i-lis
Simi'mi-as, *S. Sch.*
Sim'o-is
Si-mon'i-des, 6
Sim-plic'i-us, 10, *W. S.*
Sin'o-e
Si-no'pe
Si-re'nes, 6
  (*Si'rens*)
Si'ris
Sis'i-gam'bis, or
  Sis'y-gam'bis
Sis'y-phus
Sma-rag'dus

Smi'lax
Smin'the-us, or
  Smin'theus
Soc'ra-tes, 6
So'lon
Sol'y-ma
Sop'a-ter
Soph'o-cles, 6
Soph'o-nis'ba
Soph'ro-nis'cus
So-rac'te
So'si-a, 10
So'si-i, 10
So-sis/tra-tus
So'ter
So-zom'e-nus
  (*Soz'o-men*)
Spar'ta-cus
Spar-ta'ni
Speu-sip'pus
Spor'a-des, 6
Spu'ri-us
Sta-gi'ra
Sta-sic'ra-tes, 6
Sta-ti'ra
Sta'ti-us, 10
Sta'tor
Steph'a-nus
Ster'o-pes, 6
Stes'i-la'us, *Sw.*
Stil'i-cho
Stra'bo
Stym'pha-lis
Su-bllc'i-us, 10
Su-bur'ra
Sucs'so-nes, 6, or
  Sues-so'nes
Sue-to'ni-us
Sue'vi
Sui'das, *L. C.*
Sul'o-nes, 6
  For. W.
Sul-o'nes, *K.*
Sul-pit'i-a, or
  Sul-pic'i-a, 10
Sul-pit'i-us, or
  Sul-pic'i-us, 10
Su'o-ve-tau-ril'i-a
Su'sa
Syb'a-ris
Sy'e-ne
Syl-va'nus
Sym'ma-chus
Sym-pleg'a-des,
Sy'phax
Syr'a-cu'sæ
  (*Syr'a-cuse*)
Syr'i-a

T.

Taç'i-tus
Tæn'a-rus,
Tam'e-sis
  (*Thames*)
Tan'a-is
Tan-a-quil
Tan'ta-lus

346 GREEK AND LATIN PROPER NAMES.

Ta-ren'tum, *or*
  Ta-ren'tus
Tar-pe'i-a (-ya)
Tar-pe'i-us (-yus)
Tar-quin'i-us
  (*Tar'quin*)
Tar'ra-ci'na
Tar'ta-rus
Ta'ti-a'nus, 10
  (*Ta'tian*)
Ta/ti-us, 10
Tau'ri-ca
Ta-yg'e-te
Ta'y-ge'ta
Ta-yg'e-tus, *or*
  Ta-yg'e-ta
Te'ge-a
Te'i-us (te'yus)
Tel'a-mon
Tel'e-cles, 6
Te-lem'a-chus
Tem'e-sa, *or*
  Tem'e-se
Ten'ch-te'ri
Ten'e-dos
Te'os, *or*
  Te'i-os
Te-ren'ti-a, 10
Te-ren'ti-us, 10
  (*Ter'ence*)
Te're-us, *or*
  Te'reus
Ter'mi-na'li-a
Ter'mi-nus
Terp-sich'o-re
Ter'tul-li-a'nus
  (*Ter-tul'li-an*)
Te'thys
Te-trap'o-lis
Teu'cer
Teu'cri-a
Teu'to-ni, *and*
  Teu'to-nes, 6 *W.*
Tha'is
Tha'les, 6
Tha-li'a   [*L.*
Tham'y-ris, *S. C.*
Thau-man'ti-as, 10
The'bæ
  (*Thebes*)
Theb'a-is, *C. Fac.*

The-ba'is, *K. F.*
  M.
The'be
The'mis
The-mis'to-cles, 6
The'o-clym'e-nus
The-oc'ri-tus
The'o-do'ra
The'o-do-re'tus
  (*The-od'o-ret*)
The'o-do-ri'cus
  (*The-od'o-ric*)
The'o-do'rus
  (*The'o-dore*)
The'o-do'si-us, 10
The-od'o-ta
The-oph'i-lus
The'o-phras'tus
The'o-phy-lac'tus
  (*The-oph'y-lact*)
The'o-ti'mus
Ther-mop'y-læ
Ther-si'tes, 6
The'se-us, *or*
  The'seus
Thes-pi'a
Thes-sa'li-a
Thes'sa-lo-ni'ca
The'tis
Thra'ci-a, 10
  (*Thrace*)
Thra'so
Thras'y-bu'lus
Thras'y-me'nus
Thu-cyd'i-des, 6
Thu'le
Thy'a-ti'ra
Thy-es'tes, 6
Ti-be'ri-as
Ti-be'ri-us
  (*Tul'ly*)
Ti-bul'lus
Ti-ci'nus, *a river*
Tig'i-nus, *a man*
Ti-gra'nes, 6 [*C.*
Ti'gris
Ti-mæ'us
Ti-mo'le-on
Ti'mon
Ti-mo'the-us
Ti-re'si-as, 10
Ti-sam'e-nus
Ti-siph'o-ne

Tis'sa-pher'nes, 6
Ti-ta'nus
  (*Ti'tan*)   [*W.*
Tith'e-nid'i-a, *S.*
Ti-tho'nus
Ti-tin'i-us
Ti'tus
Tit'y-rus
Tit'y-us
Tmo'lus, 14
Trach'o-ni'tis
Tra-ja'nus
  (*Tra'jan*)
Tre-bel'li-a'nus
Tre'bi-a
Tri-bu'ni
Tri-den'tum
Tri-na'cri-a, *or*
  Trin'a-cris
Trip-tol'e-mus
Tris'me-gis'tus
Tri'ton
Tro'a-des, 6
Tro'as
Trog-lod'y-tæ
  Trog'lo-dy'tæ,
  For.
Trog-lod'y-tes, 6
  Trog'lo-dy'tes,
  For.
Tro'i-lus
Tro'ja
  (*Troy*)
Tro-pho'ni-us
Tu-is'to, *or*
  Tu-is'co
Tul'li-a
Tul-li'o-la
Tul'li-us
Tus'cu-la'num
Tus'cu-lum
Ty'a-næ'us
Tyd'e-us, *or*
  Ty'deus
Tyd'di-des, 6
Tyn-dar'i-des, 6
Tyn-da'ris
Tyn'da-rus
Ty-pho'e-us, *or*
  Ty-pho'eus
Ty'phon

Ty-ran'ni-on
Tyr-rhe'num
Tyr-tæ'us

U.

U-cal'e-gon
Ul'pi-a'nus
  (*Ul'pi-an*)
U-lys'ses, 6
Um'bri-a
Un'de-cem'vi-ri
U-ra'ni-a
U'ra-nus
U'ti-ca

V.

Va'lens
Val'en-tin'i-a'nus
  (*Val'en-tin'i-an*)
Va-le'ri-a
Va-le'ri-a'nus
  (*Va-le'ri-an*)
Va-le'ri-us
Van-da'li-i, *W. Sch.*
Vat'i-ca'nus
  (*Vat'i-can*)
Ve'i-i (ve'yi)
Vel-le'i-us l'a-ter'-
  cu-lus
Ve-na'frum
Ven'e-ti
Ve-no'ti-a, 10
  (*Ven'ice*)
Ven-tid'i-us
Ve'nus
Ver'cin-get'o-rix
Ver-gil'i-a
Ver-gin'i-us
Ve-ro'na
Ver'o-ni'ca, *L. W.*
Ver'tum-na'li-a
Ves-pa'si-a'nus, 10
  (*Ves-pa'si-an*)
Ves-ta'les, 6
Ves-ta'li-a
Vi-ce'ti-a, 10

Vic-to'ri-a
Vim'i-na'lis
Vin-del'i-ci
Vir-gil'i-us
  (*Vir'gil*)
Vir-gin'i-a
Vir-gin'i-us
Vir'i-a'thus
Vi-sig'o-thæ, *K.*
Vis'tu-la
Vi-tel'li-us
Vi-tru'vi-us
Vit'u-la
Vo-lum'ni-a
Vo-lum'ni-us
Vul-ca'nus
  (*Vul'can*)

X.

Xan-thip'pe
Xe-nag'o-ras
Xe-ni'a-des, 6
Xen'o-cle's
Xen'o-cles, 6
Xe-noc'ra-tes, 6
Xe-noph'a-nes, 6
Xen'o-phon

Z.

Za-cyn'thus
Za-leu'cus
Za-ma
Ze'no
Ze-no'bi-a
Zen'o-do'rus
Ze-nod'o-tus
Zeph'y-rus
  (*Zeph'yr*)
Zeux'i-da'mus
Zeux'is
Zo'i-lus
Zop'y-rus
Zor'o-as'tres, 6
  (*Zo'ro-as'ter*)
Zos'i-mus
Zos-te'ri-a, *S. W.*

PRONOUNCING VOCABULARY

OF

SCRIPTURE PROPER NAMES.

THE following Vocabulary contains a careful selection of such Scripture names as present any difficulty of pronunciation; but classical names occurring in the Scriptures, and given in the preceding vocabulary of Greek and Latin names, are for the most part omitted. That mode of pronunciation which is deemed to be best supported, is given first, and any other pronunciation which has, to any considerable extent, the sanction of present and reputable usage, is subjoined as an alternative mode. The names have been accented, divided into syllables, and marked in accordance with the system of notation employed in the previous part of this work. The consulter will not, therefore, require any Rules to guide him to a correct pronunciation of the names here given, but with reference to those which are omitted, it will be well for him to remember, —

1. That, in words of two syllables, the accen is uniformly on the first.
2. That, in words of two syllables in which the accented vowel is separated from the next syllable by only one consonant or by a consonant digraph, the consonant or the digraph generally goes to the following syllables; as, A′din, Jo′tham, &c.
3. That *ch* always has the sound of *k*.
4. That *g* is always hard, as in *go*.
5. That every final *i* forming — with or without a preceding consonant — a distinct syllable, has its long sound; as in A-*bish′a-ī*, Ab′dī.
6. That the terminations *ites* and *enes* (as in Gil′e-ad-ites, Gad′a-renes, &c.), are pronounced in one syllable.
7. That in other respects Scripture names usually follow the analogy of Latin pronunciation. See p. 339.

A.	A-bi′jam	Ăç′i-tho	Ăg′a-rēneṣ′	A-hŏ′ah
	Ăb′i-lē′ne	A-cū′ă	Ăg′e-ē	A-hō′hīte
	A-hĭm′a-el	Ăd′a-dah	Ag-ġē′us	A-hō′lah
Ā′a-lar	A-hĭm′e-lĕch	Ăd′a-ī′ah	A-grĭp′pă	A-hō′li-ăb
Aă′ron (ă′ron)	A-bĭn′a-dăb	A-hăr′ah	A-hŏl′i-bah
Ăb′i-eū́c	Ab′i-ner	Ăd′a-mī	A-bär′hel	Ā′ho-lĭb′a-mah
Ab-ăd′don	A-bĭn′o-ăm	Ăd′a-sȧ	A-hăs′a-ī	A-hū′ma-ī
Ăb′a-dī′as	A-bī′ram	Ăd′be-el	A-hăs′ba-ī	A-hū′zam
Ăb′a-nă	A-bī′ron	Ăd′i-dă	A-hăs′u-ē′rus	A-hŭz′zath
Ăb′a-rīm	Ăb′i-sē′ī	Ā′di-el	A-hă′vă	Ā′ī
Ăb′a-rŏn	Ăb′i-shăg	Ăd′i-nă	Ā′ba-zī′ah	A-ī′ah, *or* Ā′jah
Ăb′de-el	A-bĭsh′a-ī	Ăd′i-no *or* A-dī′no	A-hī′ah	A-ī′ath
Ab-dī′as	A-bĭsh′a-lŏm	Ăd′i-nus	A-hī′am	A-ī′jă
Ăb′di-el	A-bĭsh′u-ȧ	Ăd′i-thā′im	A-hī′an	Ăĭj′a-lŏn (ăj′a-lŏn)
A-hĕd′-ne-gō′, *or* A-bĕd′ne-gō	Ăb′i-shur	Ăd′la-ī	Ā′hi-e′zer	Ăĭj′e-lĕth Shā′har (ăj′e-lĕth)
	Ăb′i-sŭm	Ăd′ma-thă	A-bī′hud	
Ā′bel-bĕth-mā′a-chah	Ăb′i-tăl	A-dŏn′i-bo′zek	A-hī′jah	Ā′in
	Ăb′i-tŭb	A-dŏn′i-căm	A-hī′kam	A-ī′rus
Ā′bel-mā′im	A-bī′ud	Ăd′o-nī′jah	A-hī′ud	Ăj′a-lŏn
Ā′bel-me-hō′lah	Ăb′sa-lom	A-dŏn′i-kăm	A-hī′ma-ă	Ăk′ra-bat-tī′ne
Ā′bel-mĭz′ra-ĭm	A-bū′bus	Ăd′o-nī′ram	A-hī′man	Ăl′a-mŏth
Ā′bel-shĭt′tim	Ăc′a-tăn	A-dŏn′i-zē′dek	A-hīm′e-lĕch	A-lăm′me-lĕch
A-hī′ă	Ăc′ca-ron	A-dŏ′rȧ	A-hī′moth	Ăl′a-mŏth
Ā′bī-ăl′bon	A-çĕl′da-mȧ	A-dŏ′ra′im	A-hĭn′a-dăb	Ăl′çi-mŭs
A-bī′a-săph	A-chā′ĭă (-yă)	A-dŏ′ram	A-hĭn′o-ăm	Ăl′e-mȧ
A-bī′a-thar	A-chă′i-eŭs	A-drăm′me-lĕch	A-hī′o	Ăl′e-mĕth, *or* A-lē′meth
A-bī′dah	Ăch′bŏr	Ăd′ra-mȳt′tī-ŭm	A-hī′rȧ	
Ăb′i-dăn	Ā′chī-ăch′a-rŭs	Ā′drī-ȧ	A-hī′ram	Ăl′ex-ăn′dri-ȧ
A-bī′el	A-chī′as	Ā′dri-el	A-hĭs′a-mach	A-lī′ah
Ā′hī-ē′zer	Ā′chi-ôr	A-dū′el	A-hĭsh′a-hăr	A-lī′an
Ăb′i-ē′zer	Ăch′i-tŏb	Ā′e-dī′as	A-hī′shar	Ăl′lon-băch′uth
A-bī′hu	Ăch′me-thă	Æ′ne-as	A-hĭth′o-phĕl	Al-mŏ′dăd
A-bī′hud	Ăch′sȧ	Ăg′a-bȧ	A-hī′tub	Ăl′mon-dĭb′la-thă′im
A-bī′jah	Ăç′i-phă	Ăg′a-hūs	Ăh′lăi	

ū, ŭ, ī, ō, ŭ, ȳ, *long;* ă, ĕ, ĭ, ŏ, ŭ, y̆, *short;* câre, cär, ȧsk, ąll, whąt; ēre, veil, tẽrm; pīque, fĭrm; sŏn, ôr, do, wọlf, tōō, tŏŏk; ûrn, rẏe, pŭll; ç, g̀, *soft;* e, g, *hard;* aẓ; eẋist; ṇ *as* ng; ṭhis.

(347)

SCRIPTURE PROPER NAMES.

Ăl′na-thăn
Ăl-phœ′us, or Al-phē′us
Ăl′ta-nē′us
Al-tăs′chĭth
A-mād′a-thä
A-măd′a-thus
Ăm′a-lek
Ăm′a-lek-īte
Ăm′a-nä, or A-mä′nä
Ăm′a-rī′ah
Ăm′a-rī′as
Ăm′a-sä, or A-mä′sä
A-mās′a-ī
A-māsh′a-ī
Ăm′a-sī′ah
Ăm′a-thē′is
Ăm′a-thĭs
Ăm′a-zī′ah
A-mĕd′a-thä
A-mīn′a-dăb
A-mīt′tăī
A-mīz′a-băd
Am-mēd′a-thä
Am-mĭd′ī-oī
Ăm′mī-el
Am-mī′hud
Am-mĭn′a-dăb
Am-mĭn′a-dīb
Ăm′mī-shăd′da-ī
Am-mĭz′a-băd
Ăm′o-rīte
Am-phĭp′o-līs
Ăm′plī-äs
Ăm′ra-phĕl
Ăn′a-el
Ăn′a-hä′rath
Ăn′a-ī′ah
Ăn′a-kīms
A-năm′me-lŏch
A-nä′nī
Ăn′a-nī′ah
Ăn′a-nī′as
A-nău′ī-el
Ăn′a-thŏth
Ăn′dro-nī′cus
Ăn′u-e-tŏth′īte
Ăn′ī-ĭm
Ăn′na-äs [nu-üs
An-nū′us, or Ăn′-
Ăn′tī-lĭb′a-nŭs
Ăn′tī-ŏch
Ăn′tī-o-chī′ä
An-tī′o-chĭs
An-tī′o-chŭs
Ăn′tī-päs
An-tīp′a-ter
An-tĭp′a-trĭs
An-tŏ′nī-ä
Ăn′to-thī′jah
A-pā′me
A-pŏl′lĕs
A-phär′sach-ītes
A-phär′sath-chītes

A-phär′sītes
A-phŏ′kah
A-phĕr′e-mä
A-phĕr′rä
A-phī′ah
Āph′sĕä
Ăp′ol-lō′nī-ä
Ăp′ol-lō′nī-us
Ăp′ol-lŏph′a-nĕs
A-pŏl′los
A-pŏl′ly-ŏn (or a-pŏl′yon)
Ăp′pa-īun
Ăp′phī-ä (ĂPfī-ä)
Ăp′phus (ĂPfus)
Ăp′pī-ī Fō′rum
Ăq′uĭ-lä
Ăr′a-bah
Ăr′a-bat-thä′ne (ūr′a-bath-thä′-ne)
Ăr′a-bat-tī′ne
Ăr′a-dŭs   [ĭm
Ä′ram-nä′ha-rā′-
Ä′ram-zō′bah
Ăr′a-rät
Ăr′a-räth
A-rä′thĕs
A-rau′nah
Ar-bā′lä (in Palestine)
Ar-bū′na-ī
Ăr′che-lā′us
Ar-chĭp′pus
Arc-tū′rus
A-rē′lī
Ăr′e-ōp′a-ġīte
Ăr′e-ōp′a-gus
Ăr′e-tās (Gr. 'Αρέτας)
A-rḡ′us
Ä′rī-a-rä′thĕs
A-rīd′a-ī
A-rīd′a-thä
A-rī′eh
Ä′rī-el
Ăr′ī-ma-thē′ä
Ä′rī-ŏch
A-rīs′a-ī
Ăr′ĭs-to-bū′lus
Ăr′ma-ġĕd′don
Ar-mō′nī
Ăr′o-dī
Ăr′o-er
Ar-phăx′ad
Ăr′sa-çĕs
Ăr′sa-rĕth
Ăr′te-mas
Ăr′ij-bŏth
A-rŭ′mah
Äs′a-dī′as
Ăs′a-el
Äs′a-hĕl
Äs′a-ī′ah
Äs′a-nä
A-sär′e-el
Ăs′a-rē′lah

As-bäz′a-rĕth
Ăs′ca-lŏn
A-sē′as
A-sĕb′e-bī′ä
Ăs′e-bī′ä
Ăs′e-nŏth
A-sē′rer
Ăsh′be-ä
Ăsh′che-nåz
Ăsh′er
Ăsh′ī-mä
Ăsh′ke-lŏn
Ăsh′ke-năz
Ăsh′pe-năz
Ăsh′rī-el
Ăsh′ta-rŏth
Ăsh′te-mŏh
Ăsh′to-rĕth
Ăsh′ur
Ăs′ī-bī′as
Ä′sī-el
Ăs′ī-phä
Ăs′ke-lŏn
Ăs′ma-vĕth
Ăs′mo-dē′us
As-năp′par
Ăs′pa-thä
As-phär′a-sŭs
Ăs′rī-el
Ăs′sa-bī′as
As-săl′ī-mŏth
Ăs′sa-nī′as
Ăs′sa-rē′moth
As-shŭr′rim
Ăs′sī-dē′ans
Ăs′su-ē′rus
Ăs′ta-rŏth
As-tȳ′a-ġĕs
A-sŭp′pim
A-sȳn′crī-tus
Ăt′a-rah
A-tär′ga-tīs
Ăt′a-rŏth
Ăt′e-re-zī′as
Ăth′a-ī′ah
Ăth′a-lī′ah
Ăth′a-rī′as
Ăth′e-nŏ′bī-ŭs
Ăth′lāī
Ăt′ī-phä
Ăt′tāī
Ăt′ta-līä
Ăt′ta-lŭs
At-thär′a-tĕs (ath-thär′a-tees)
Au′ġī-ä
Au-rä′nus
Au-tē′as
Ăv′a-rän
Ăv′a-rŏn
Ăz′a-el
Ăz′a-ē′lus
Ăz′a-lī′ah
Ăz′a-nī′ah
A-zä′phī-ŏn
Ăz′a-rä
A-zär′e-el, or A-zä′re-el

Ăz′a-rī′ah
Ăz′a-rī′as
A-zĭ′zel
Ăz′a-zī′ah
Az-bäz′a-rĕth
A-z3′kah
Ăz′e-phū′rith
A-zĕ′tas
A-zī′ä
A-zī′e-ī
Ä′zī-el
A-zī′zä
Ăz′ma-vĕth
A-zŏ′tus
Ăz′rī-el
Ăz′rī-kăm
A-zū′bah
Ăz′u-rän

B.

Bā′al
Bā′al-ah
Bā′al-äth
Bā′a-lē
Bā′al-hā′mon
Bā′al-hā′nan
Bā′al-ī
Bā′al-ĭm
Bā′a-līs
Bā′al-zē′bub
Bī′a-nah
Bā′a-nī′as
Bā′a-rä
Bā′a-sē′iah (-yä)
Bā′a-shä
Bā′a-sī′ah
Bāc′chī-dĕs
Bac-chū′rus
Ba-çē′nor
Ba-gō′as
Bäg′o-ī
Ba-hā′rum-īte
Ba-hū′mus
Ba-hū′rim
Bak-băk′kar
Băk′bu′-ī′ah
Bā′laam (bā′lam), or Bā′la-am
Băl′a-dän
Băl′a-mō
Ba-lăs′a-mŭs
Bal-nū′us
Bal-thä′sar
Bän′a-ī′as
Ban-nä′lä
Ba-rä′ō′bas
Băr′a-chĕl
Băr′a-chī′ah
Băr′a-chī′as
Bar-hū′mīte
Ba-rī′ah
Băr′na-bas
Ba-rō′dīs
Bär′sa-bas
Băr′ta-cus

Bar-thŏl′o-mew
Bär′tī-mē′us
Bä′ruch
Bar-zĭl′la-ī
Băs′a-lŏth
Bäs′ca-mä
Băsh′e-măth
Băs′ī-lĭs
Băs′ta-ī
Băth′-shē′bä, or Băth′she-bä
Băth′-shŭä
Băth′zăch-a-rī′as
Băv′ai-ī
Bē′a-lī′ah
Bĕ′a-lŏth
Bē′an
Bĕb′a-ī
Bē′chor
Be-chō′rath
Bŏc′tī-lĕth
Bĕd′a-ī′ah
Be-dā′iah (-yä)
B3′el-ī′a-dä
Be-ĕl′sa-rus
Bū′el-tĕth′mus
Be-ĕl′ze-bub
Be-ē′rah
Bē′er-ē′lim
Be-ē′rī
Bē′er-la-hä′ī-roī
Be-ē′roth
Bē′er-shē′bä, or Be-ĕr′sbe-bä
Be-ĕsh′te-rah
Bē′he-moth
Bĕl′e-mŭs
B3′lī-al
Bĕl′ma-ĭm
Bel-shăz′zar
Be-nä′iah (-yä)
Bĕn′e-bē′rak
Bĕn′e-jā′a-kän
Bĕn′-hä′dad
Bĕn′-hā′īl
Bĕn′-hā′nan
Bĕn′ī-nū
Bĕn′ja-mīn
Bĕn′-ō′nī
Ben-nū′ī, or Bĕn′-nu-ī
Bĕn′-zō′heth
Bĕr′a-chah
Bĕr′a-chī′ah
Bĕr′a-ī′ah
B3′re-ä, 1 Macc. ix. 4.
Be-rē′ä, 2 Macc. xiii. 4; Acts xvii. 10, 13, and xx. 4.
Bĕr′e-chī′ah
Bo-rī′ah
Be-rī′ītes
Ber-nī′çe
Be-rō′du ch-băl′-dän
Be-rō′thah
Bĕr′o-thāī

ā, ē, ī, ō, ū, ȳ, long; ă, ĕ, ĭ, ŏ, ŭ, ȳ, short; cāre, cär, åsk, ąll, whąt; ẽre, vẽil, tẽrm; pīque, fĭrm;

SCRIPTURE PROPER NAMES. 349

Ber-rŏ'tho	Dĭ-thī'ah	Chĕl'ci-as (-shī-		Ĕg'la-ĭm
Ber-zē'lus	Bī-thy̆n'ĭ-ă	as)	**D.**	Ĕk're-bĕl
Bĕs'o-dē"iah (-yă)	Bĭz-jŏth'jah	Che-lŭ'bāi		Ĕl'a-dah
Bĕt'a-nū	Blō'a-nēr'ḡĕs	Chĕm'a-rĭmṣ	Dăb'a-rĕh	Ĕl'a-sah
Bĕth'-ăb'a-rȧ	Bŏch'e-rṳ	Che-nā'a-nah	Dăb'ba-shĕth	Ĕ'lath
Bĕth'-ā'nath	Bō'chĭm	Chĕn'a-nī	Dăb'e-rāth	Ĕl'-bĕth'-el
Bĕth'-ā'noth	Ilō'oz	Chĕn'a-nī'ah	Dā'brĭ-ȧ	Ĕl'cĭ-ă (ĕl'shī-ă)
Bĕth'a-ny	Bŏẓ'o-rȧ	Chē'phar-ha-ăm'-	Da-cō'bī	Ĕl'da-ah, or El-
Bĕth'-ăr'a-bah	Buk-kī'ah	mo-nāi	Dad-dē'us	dā'ah
Bĕth'-ā'ram		Che-phī'rah	Dăī'ṣȧn	E'lo-ăd
Bĕth'-ā'ven		Chē're-as	Dăl'a-ī'ah	Ē'le-ă'leh
Bĕth'-ăz'ma-vĕth	**C.**	Chĕr'eth-ĭmṣ	Dăl'ma-nū'thȧ	E-lē'a-ṣȧ
Bĕth'-bā'rah		Chĕr'eth-ītes	Dal-mā'ti-ȧ (-mā'-	E-lē'a-ṣah
Bĕth'-bā'sī		Chē'rith	shī-ȧ)	Ē'le-ă'zar
Bĕth'-bĭr'e-ī	Cȧd'mi-el	Chē'rub (a city)	Dăm'a-ris	Ĕ'le-a-zū'rus [e
Bĕth'-dĭb'la-	Çœs'a-rē'ȧ	Chŏs'a-lŏn	Da-măs'cus	Ĕl'- E-lō'he Iṣ'ra-
thā'ĭm	Çă'ia-phas (-ya-	Che-sŭl'loth	Dăn'i-el, or Dăn'-	E-leū'the-rŭs
Bĕth'-ē'den	fas)	Che-thī'im	iel (-yel)	E-leū'za-ī
Bĕth'-ē'mek	Că-ī'nan (Kaïvȧv)	Chet-tī'ĭm	Dăn'-jā'an	El-hā'nan
Be-thŏḡ'dȧ	Căl'a-mŏl'a-lus	Chĭl'e-ăb	Dăth'e-mȧ	Ĕ-lī'ab
Bĕth'-ē'zel	Cal-dū'ȧ	Chī-lī'on	Dăb'o-rah	E-lī'a-dȧ
Bĕth'-gā'der	Căl'i-tăs	Chīn'ne-rĕth	De-căp'o-lis	E-lī'a-dah
Bĕth'-gā'mul	Căl-lĭs'the-nēṣ	Chīn'ne-rŏth	Dē'dan	E-lī'a-dăs
Bĕth'-hăc'çe-rĕm	Căl'va-ry	Chī'os	Dĕd'a-nĭm	E-lī'a-dun
Bĕth'-hā'ran	Că'naan (kā'nan,	Chĭṣ'leū	De-hā'vītes	E-lī'ah
Bĕth'-hŏg'lah	or kā'na-an)	t'hĭt'tĭm	Dĕl'a-ī'ah	E-lī'ah-bȧ
Bĕth'-hō'ron	Cā'naan-īte	Chŏb'a-ī	Dĕl'ī-lah	E-lī'a-kĭm
Bĕth'-jĕṣ'i-mŏth	(-nan- or -na-an-)	Cho-rā'ṣʰan	De-mē'tri-ŭs	E-lī'a-lī
Bĕth'-lĕb'a-ŏth	Căn'da-çē	Cho-rā'zĭn	Dĕm'o-phŏn	E-lī'am
Bĕth'-lĕ'hem, and	Ca-pĕr'na-ŭm	Chŏr'a-shē'us	Dĕṣ'sa-ū (Gr. Δεσ-	E-lī'a-o-nī'as
Bĕth'le-hem	Căph'ar-sȧl'a-mȧ	Cho-zē'bȧ	σαού)	E-lī'a-sȧph
Beth-lō'mon	Ca-phĕn'a-thȧ	Chū'shaṇ-rĭṣh'a-	De-ū'el	E-lī'a-shĭb
Bĕth'-mā'a-chah	Ca-phī'rȧ	thā'ĭm	Deū'ter-ŏn'o-my	E-lī'a-sib
Bĕth'-mär'ca-	Căph'tho-rĭm	Çĭ-lī'cĭ-ȧ (sĭ-lĭsh'-	Dĭb'la-ĭm	E-lī'a-sis
bŏth	Căph'to-rĭm	ĭ-ȧ)	Dĭb'la-thā'ĭm	E-lī'a-thȧ
Bĕth'-mā'on	Căp'pa-dō'ci-ȧ	Çĭn'ne-r"th	Dĭd'y-mŭs	E-lī'dad
Bĕth'-nĭm'rah	(-dō'shī-ȧ)	Çĭn'ne-rŏth	Dĭl'e-ăn	E'li-el
Beth-ō'ron	Căr'a-bā'si-on	Çĭr'a-mȧ	Di-mo'nah	E'li-ē'na-ī
Bĕth'-pā'let	Căr'cha-mĭs	Çī'sāi	Dīn'ha-bah, or	E'li-ē'zer
Bĕth'-pē'or	Căr'che-mĭsh	t lạu'di-ȧ	Dĭn-hā'bah	E-lī'ha-bȧ
Bĕth'phȧ-ḡē	Ca-rē'ah	Çlạu'di-us	Dī'o-nȳ'si-us	Ĕl'i-ho-ē'na-ī
Bĕth'-phē'let	Că'ri-ȧ	t lē'o-pas	(dī'o-nĭzh'ĭ-us)	Ĕl'i-hō'reph
Bĕth'-rā'phȧ	Car-mā'ni-anṣ	Clē'o-pā'trȧ	Dī'os-co-rĭn'thi-	E-lī'hu
Bĕth'-rē'hob	Căr'na-ĭm	Clē'o-phas	us	E-lī'jah
Bĕth'-sā'i-dȧ	Căr'ni-ŏn	Cnī'dus (nī'dus)	Di-ŏt're-phēṣ	Ĕl'i-kȧ, or E-lī'kȧ
Bĕth'-sā'mos	Căr'pha-sȧl'a-mȧ	Dīẓ'a-hăb	Ĕ'lĭm
Bĕth'-shē'an	Car-shē'nȧ	Çœl'o-sȳr'i-ȧ	Dŏd'a-ī	E-lĭm'e-lech
Bĕth'-shē'mesh	Ca-sĭph'ĭ-ȧ	(sēl'-)	Dŏd'a-nĭm	Ĕl'i-o-ē'na-ī
Bĕth'-tăp'pu-ah	Căs'loū	Çol-hō'zeh	Dō'eg	E-lī-ō'nas
Be-thū'el	Căs'la-bĭm	Cō'lī-us	Do-rȳm'e-nēṣ	Ĕl'i-phāl
Bĕth'u-lī'ȧ, or Be-	Ca-thū'ȧ	Co-lŏs'ṣe	Do-sĭth'e-us	E-lĭph'a-lĕh
thū'li-ȧ	Çē'dron	Co-lŏs'si-anṣ (ko-	Dō'tha-ĭm	E-lĭph'a-lĕt
Be-tō'li-ŭs	Çēi'lan	lŏsh'ī-anz)		Ĕl'i-phăẓ, or E-lī'-
Bĕt'o-mĕṣ'tham	Çĕn'chre-ȧ	Cō-nī'ah		phaz
Bĕt'o-nĭm	Çĕn'de-bē'us	Cŏn'o-nī'ah		E-lī'ẓa-bĕth
Beū'lah, or Be-ū'-	Çĕs'a-rē'ȧ	Cō'os	**E.**	Ĕl'i-ṣā'us
lah	Çhā'di-ăs	Cō're		E-lī'ṣha
Bē'zāi	Chæ're-ăs	Cŏr'inth		E-lĭsh'a-mah
De-zāl'e-el	Chal-dē'ȧ	Cou'thȧ (kow'thȧ)	Ē'a-nĕs	E-lĭsh'a-phăt
Bī'a-tăs	Chăn'nu-nē'us	Cū'shan	Ē'bed-mē'leeh	E-lĭsh'e-bȧ
Dĭg'tha-nȧ	Chăr'a-ăth'a-lar	Cū'shī	E-bī'a-sȧph	Ĕl'i-shp'ȧ
Bĭg'va-ī	Chăr-ē'ȧ	Cū'thah, or	E-brō'nah	E-lĭs'i-mus
Bīl'e-ăm	Chăr'a-sim	Cūth'ah	Çȳ'a-mŏn	E-lī'u
Bĭl'ga-ī	Chär'che-mĭsh	Çȳr'a-mȧ	Ec-băt'a-nȧ	E-lī'ud
Bĭn'e-ȧ	Chā're-ȧ	Çȳ-rē'ne	Ec-clē'ẓi-ăṣ'tēṣ	E-lī'ẓa-phăn
Bin-nū'ī, or Bĭn'-	Chăr'ran	Çȳ-rē'ni-ŭs	Ec-clē'ẓi-ăs'ti-cus	Ĕl'i-zē'us
nu-ī	Chăs'e-bȧ		Ĕd-dī'as	Ĕl'i-zur
Bĭr'za-vĭth	Chĕd'or-lā'o-mer		Ĕd're-ī	Ĕl'ka-nah

sŏn, ŏr, dọ, wọlf, tōō, tŏŏk; ûrn, rụe, pụll˙ ç, ġ, soft; c, ḡ, hard; aẓ; eẓist; ɒ as ng; this.

SCRIPTURE PROPER NAMES.

El′la-sar
El-mō′dam
El′na-ăm
El′on-thăn
El′o-hĭm
E-lō′ī
El′pa-ăl
El′pa-lĕt
El′-pā′ran
El′te-kŭh
El′te-kŏn [lăd
El-tō′lad, or El′to-
E-lū′za-ī
El′y-mā′ĭs
El′y-măs
El′za-băd
El′za-phăn
Em-măn′u-el
Em′ma-us
E-nā′ī-bus
E′ne-as (see Æ-
neas)
En′-ĕg′la-ĭm, or
En′-eg-lā′ĭm
En′e-mĕs′sar
E-nū′ni-us
En′-găn′nim
En′-gē′dī
En′-hăk′ko-re
En′-hā′zor
En′-rō′gel
En′-shū′mesh
En′-tap-pū′ah
Ep′a-phrăs
E-păph′ro-dī′tus
E-pĕn′e-tus
E′phăī
Eph′e-sus
Eph′pha-thă
E′phra-ĭm
E′phra-īn
Eph′ra-tah
E-pĭph′a-nēẓ
E-ziā′ias (e-zā′yas)
E′sar-hăd′don
Es′dra-ē′lon
Es-drē′lon
Es′e-bŏn
E-sē′bri-ăs
Esh′-bā′al
E′she-ăn
Esh′ta-ōl
Esh′ta-ul-ītes, or
Esh′tau-lītes
Esh′te-mō′á, or
Esh-tĕm′o-ă
Esh′te-mōh
E-sō′ra
Est′ha-ōl
Es′ther (ĕs′tẽr)
Eth′a-nim
Eth′bā-al
Eū-bū′lus
Eū-ēr′ge-tēẓ
Eū′me-nēẓ
Eū′na-tăn
Eū-nī′çe, or Eū′-
niçe

Eū-ō′di-as
Eū′pa-tŏr
Eū-phrā′tēs
Eū-pŏl′e-mŭs
Eū-rŏc′ly-don
Eū′ty-chŭs
E′vīl-me-rō′dach
Ez′ba-ī
Ez′e-chī′as
Ez′e-rī′as
E-zī′as
E′zi-on-gē′ber

F.

Fōr′tu-nā′tns

G.

Găb′a-el
Găb′a-thă
Găb′ba-ī
Găb′ba-thă
Gă′brī-as
Gă′brī-el
Găd′a-ră
Găd′a-rēneẓ′
Găd′di-el
Gă′ius (gā′yus)
Găl′a-ăd
Ga-lā′tĭă (-lā′-
shĭ-ă)
Găl′e-ĕd
Găl′ga-lă
Găl′ī-lee
Găl′lī-o
Găm′a-el
Ga-mā′lī-el
Găm′ma-dims
Găr′ī-zim
Ga-zā′ră
Ga-zē′ră
Gū′bal
Gŭd′a-lī′ah
Gĕd′e-on
Ge-dī′rah
Gĕd′e-rīte
Ge-dī′roth
Gĕd′e-roth-ā′im
Ge-hā′zī
Ge-hĕn′nă
Gĕl′ī-lŏth
Gĕm′a-rī′ah
Ge-nĕs′a-rĕth
Gĕn′e-sis
Gen-nē′sar
Gen-nē′us
Ge-nū′bath
Gūr′ĝe-sĭneẓ
Gĕr′ī-zim
Ger-rhē′nī-ans
(-rū′-)
Gĕsh′u-rī
Geth-sĕm′a-ne

Ge-ū′el •
Gīb′be-thŏn
Gīb′e-ah
Gīb′e-on
Gĭd-dăl′tī
Gĭd′e-on
Gĭd′e-ō′nī
Gī′a-lāi
Gīl-bō′ă, or Gĭl′-
bo-ă
Gĭl′e-ad
Gĭl′o-nīte
Gĭn′ne-thō
Gĭn′ne-thŏn
Gīr′ga-shīte
Gīt′ta-īm
Gī′zo-nīte
Gnī′dus (nī′dus)
Gŏl′go-thă
Go-lī′ath
Go-mŏr′rah
Gŏr′ĝi-ăs
Gor-tȳ′nă
Gōth′o-lī′as
Go-thŏn′ī-el
Gūd′go-dah
Gūr′-bā′al

H.

Hā′a-hāsh′tă-rī
Ha-ăm′mo-nāī
Ha-bā′iah (-bā′yă)
Hăb′ak-kuk, or
Ha-băk′kuk
Hăb′a-zi-nī′ah
Hăch′a-lī′ah
Hăch′mo-nī
Hăch′mo-nīte
Hăd′ad-ē′zer
Hăd′ar-ē′zer
Hăd′a-shah, or
Ha-dā′shah
Ha-dăt′tah
Hăd′la-ī
Ha-dō′ram
Hăg′a-bah
Hăg′ga-ī
Hăg′ĝe-rī
Hăg-ḡī′ah
Hăg′ḡī-ă
Hăī
Hăk′ka-tăn
Ha-kū′phă
Hăl′ī-car-năs′sus
Hal-lō′esh
Hăm′ī-tăl
Ham-mēd′a-thă
Hăm′me-lĕch
Ham-mŏl′e-kĕth
Hăm′mo-nah, or
Ham-mō′nah
Ha-mū′el
Ha-mū′el
Ha-năm′e-el

Ha-năn′e-el
Ha-nā′nī, or
Hăn′a-nī
Hăn′a-nī′ah
Hā′num
Hăph′a-rā′ĭm
Haph-rā′im
Hăr′a-dah
Har-bō′nah
Hăr′ha-ī′ah
Hăr′ne-pher
Hăr′o-ēh
Hăr′ro-rīte
Ha-rō′shĕth
Ha-rĭl′maph
Hăr′ŭ-phīte, or
Ha-rū′phīte
Hăs′a-dī′ah
Hăs′e-nū′ah
Hăsh′a-bī′ah
Ha-shăb′nah
Hăsh′ab-nī′ah
Hash-băd′a-nă
Hash-mō′nah
Ha-shŭ′bah
Ha-shŭ′phă
Hăs′se-nā′ah
Ha-sū′phă
Hăt′ī-phă, or Ha-
tī′phă
Hăt′ī-tă
Hăt′ti-cŏn
Hăt′ī-lah
Hăz′a-el
Hn-zā′iah (-zā′yă)
Hăz′a-zŏn-tā′mar
Hăz′e-lĕl-pō′nī
Ha-zē′rim
Hn-zē′roth
Hăz′e-zŏn-tā′mar
Hă′zi-el
Hăz′u-bah
Hăz′zu-rīm
Hĕg′a-ī
Hel-chī′ah
Hel-chī′as
Hĕl′da-ī
He-lī′as
Hē′lī-o-dō′rus
Hĕl′ka-ī
Hel-kī′as
Hĕn′a-dăd
Hĕph′zi-băh, or
Hĕph′zi-bah
Her-mŏḡ′e-nēẓ
Hĕr′od
He-rō′dī-as
He-rō′dī-on
Hĕz′e-kī
Hĕz′e-kī′ah
Hŭ′zī-ŏn
Hĕz′rā-ī
Hīd′da-ī
Hĭd′de-kĕl

Hī′el
Hī′e-răp′o-lis
Hī-ĕr′e-el
Hī-ĕr′e-moth
Hī-ĕr′ī-ē′lus
Hī-ĕr′ī-nas
Hī-ĕr′ĭnas
Hī′e-rŏn′y-mus
Hī′e-rĭl′sa-lĕm
Hĭg-gā′ion (-gā′-
yon)
Hĭl-kī′ah
Hĭr-cā′nus
Hīz-kī′ah
Ho-bā′iah (-bā′yā)
Hōd′a-ī′ah
Hōd′a-vī′ah
Ho-dō′rah
Ho-dī′ah
Ho-dī′jah
Hŏl′o-fēr′nēẓ
Hŏr′o-nā′im
Hŏr′o-nīte
Ho-sā′ă
Hōsh′a-ī′ah
Hōsh′a-mă
Ho-shē′ă
Hū′raī
Hū′shaī
Hȳ′dăs′pēẓ
Hȳ′me-nē′us

I.

Ĭb′le-ăm
Ĭb-nē′iah (-nē′yă)
Ĭb-nī′jah
Ĭch′a-bod
Ī-cō′nī-um
Ĭ-dā′lah
Ĭd′u-el
Ĭd′u-mē′ă
Ĭg′da-lī′ah
Ĭg′e-ăl
Ī′im
Ĭj′e-ăb′a-rim
Ī′lăī
Ĭl-lȳr′ī-cum
Ĭph′e-dē′iah (-yă)
Ĭ-rī′jah
Ĭr′-nā′hăsh
Ī′ron
Ĭr′pe-el
Ĭr′-shū′mesh
Ī′gaae (ī′zak)
Ĭ-ṣā′iah (ī-zā′yă)
Ĭs-cār′ī-ot
Ĭs′da-el
Ĭsh′bī-bē′nob
Ĭsh′-bō′sheth
Ĭ-shī′ah
Ĭsh′ma-el
Ĭsh′ma-ī′ah
Ĭsh′me-el-ītes
Ĭsh′me-raī
Ĭsh′u-ah
Ĭsh′u-āi

SCRIPTURE PROPER NAMES. 351

Ĭsh'u-ī
Ĭs'ma-chī'ah
Ĭs'ma-ī'ah
Ĭs'ra-el
Ĭs'sa-char
Ĭs-shī'ah
Ĭs'tal-cū'rus
Ĭs'u-ah
Ĭs'u-ī
Ĭth'a-ī
Ĭth'a-mär
Ĭth'ī-cl
Ĭth're-ăm
Ĭt'ta-ī
Ĭt'u-rē'ă
Ĭz'e-här
Ĭz'ra-hī'ah
Ĭz're-el

J.

Jā'a-kăn
Ja-ăk'o-bah
Ja-ā'lah
Ja-ā'lam
Jā'a-nāī, or Ja-ā'-
 nāī
Ja-ăr'e-ŏr'e-glm
Jā'a-sau
Ja-ā'sī-el
Ja-ăz'a-nī'ah
Ja-ā'zer
Jā'a-zī'ah
Ja-ā'zī-el
Jăb'ne-el
Ja-dā'u
Jad-dū'ă
Jā'el
Ja-hăl'e-lĕl
Ja-hă'zah
Jā'ha-zī'ah
Jäh'da-ī
Jäh'di-el
Jäh'le-el
Jäh'na-ī
Jäh'ze-rah
Jäh'zi-el
Jā'ir
Jā'ī-rus, *Esther*
 xi. 2
Ja-ī'rus, *New Test.*
Jăm'brĕs
Jam-nī'ă
Ja-nō'ah
Ja-phī'ă
Jăph'le-tī, or
 Japh-lē'tī
Jăr'e-sī'ah
Jăr'ī-mŏth
Jär'muth
Ja-rō'ah
Jās'a-el
Ja-shō'be-ăm
Jäsh'ub
Jäsh'u-bī-lē'hem

Jăsh'nb-ītes
Jā'sī-el
Ja-sū'bus
Jăth'nī-el
Jā'zi-el
Jŏ'a-rim
Je-ăt'e-rāī
Jo-bēr'e-chī'ah
Je-bŭ'sī
Jŏc'a-mī'ah
Jĕch'o-lī'ah
Jĕch'o-nī'as
Jĕc'o-lī'ah
Jŏc'o-nī'ah
Jĕc'o-nī'as
Je-dā'iah (-yă)
Jo-dō'iah (-yă)
Je-dē'us
Je-dī'a-cl
Jŏd'ī-däh
Jĕd'ī-dī'ah
Jŏ'di-el
Jĕd'u-thun
Je-ā'lī
Jo-ā'lus
Jo-ē'zer
Jō'gar-sā'ha-dū'-
 thä
Jo-hā'le-el
Jā'ha-lē'le-el
Je-hăl'e-lĕl
Jeh-dē'iah (-yă)
Je-hĕz'e-kĕl
Je-hī'ah
Je-hī'el
Je-hī'e-lī
Jō'hiz-kī'ah
Je-hŏ'a-dah
Je-hŏ'a-hăz
Je-hŏ'ash
Jē'ho-hā'nan, or
 Jē-hō'ha-năn
Je-hol'a-chin
Je-hol'a-dă
Jo-hol'a-kim
Je-hol'a-rib
Je-hŏn'a-däb
Je-hŏn'a-than
Je-hō'ram
Jē'ho-shăb'e-ăth
Jo-hŏsh'a-phăt
Jo-hŏsh'e-bă
Je-hŏsh'u-ă
Je-hŏz'a-băd
Je-hŏz'a-dăk
Jĕ'hu-cāl
Je-hū'dī
Jē'hu-dī'jah
Je-ī'el
Je-kăb'ze-el
Jĕk'a-mē'am
Jŏk'a-mī'ah
Je-kū'thi-el
Je-mī'ma, or
 Jĕm'ī-mă
Jĕm'na-ăn
Je-mū'el
Jc-phŭn'neh

Je-räh'me-el
Jēr'e-chus
Jĕr'e-māl
Jĕr'e-mī'ah
Jĕr'e-mŏth
Je-rī'ah
Jĕr'ī-bāī
Jĕr'ī-chō
Jū'ri-el
Je-rī'jah
Jĕr'ī-mŏth
Jū'ri-ŏth
Jĕr'o-bō'am
Jĕr'o-hăm
Je-rŭb'ba-ăl
Je-rŭb'e-shĕth
Jĕr'u-el
Je-ru'sa-lĕm
Je-ry'shă
Je-sā'iah (-yă)
Je-shā'iah (-yă)
Jĕsh'a-nah
Je-shăr'e-lah
Je-shĕb'e-ăb
Jĕsh'ī-mŏn
Je-shīsh'a-ī
Jĕsh'o-ha-ī'ah
Jĕsh'u-run
Je-sī'ah
Je-sīm'ī-el
Jĕs'su-e
Jĕs'u-ī
Jā'u-el, or Je-ū'el
Jŏz'a-nī'ah
Jĕz'e-bēl
Je-zē'lus
Je-zī'ah
Jō'zi-el
Jez-lī'el
Jĕz'o-ar
Jĕz'ra-hī'ah
Jĕz're-el
Jīph'thah-ĕl
Jō'a-chăz
Jō'a-chim
Jō'a-dā'nus
Jō'a-hăz
Jō'a-kim
Jō-ā'nan
Jō'a-rib
Jō'a-thăm
Jō'a-zăb'dus
Jŏch'e-bĕd
Jo-ē'lah
Jo-ē'zer
Jŏg'be-hăh
Jo-hā'nan
Jo-hăn'nes
Joi'a-dă
Joi'a-kim
Joi'a-rib
Jŏk'de-ăm
Jŏk'me-ăm
Jŏk'ne-ăm
Jŏk'the-el
Jŏn'a-dăb
Jŏp'pe
Jō'ra-ī

Jŏr'ī-băs
Jŏr'ī-bus
Jŏr'ko-ăm
Jŏs'a-băd
Jŏs'a-phat
Jŏs'a-phī'as
Jŏs'e-dĕch
Jo-sū'phus
Jŏsh'a-băd
Jŏsh'a-phăt
Jŏsh'a-vī'ah
Jŏsh-bĕk'a-shĕh
Jŏs'i-bī'ah
Jŏs'ī-phī'ah
Jŏt'ba-thah
Jŏz'a-băd
Jŏz'a-char
Jŏz'a-dăk
Jū'shăb-hē'sed

K.

Kăb'ze-el
Kā'desh-bär'ne-ă
Kăd'mī-el
Kăl'la-ī
Ka-rē'ah
Kăr'ka-ă
Kăr'na-im
Kĕd'e-mah
Kĕd'e-mŏth
Kē'desh Năph'ta-lī
Ke-hĕl'a-thah
Kēl'iah
Ke-lā'iah
Kĕl'ī-tă
Ke-mū'el
Kĕr'en-hăp'puch
Kē'ri-ŏth
Ko-tū'rah
Ke-zī'ă
Kīb'roth-hat-tā'a-
 vah
Kīb'za-ĭm
Kīd'ron
Kīr'-här'a-sĕth
Kīr'-hā'resh
Kir-hē'res
Kīr'ī-ăth
Kīr'ī-a-thā'ĭm
Kīr'ī-ăth'ī-ā'ri-us
Kīr'ī-ŏth
Kīr'jath-jē'a-rīm
Kīsh'ī-ŏn
Kīt'ron
Kŏl'a-ī'ah
Kush-ā'iah

L.

Lā'a-dah
Lā'a-dăn
Lăb'a-nă
Lā'chish

La-cū'nus
La-hāī'rol
La-ŏd'ī-çē'ă
Lăp'ī-dŏth
La-sū'ă
La-shā'ron
Lăs'the-nĕs
Lăz'a-rus
Lĕb'a-nah
Lĕb'a-non
Lĕb'a-ŏth
Lcb-bē'us
Le-bō'nah
Lē'ha-bim
Lĕm'u-el
Le-tū'shim
Lib'a-nus
Lō'-dē'bar
Lō'-ru'ha-mah
Lŏth'a-sū'bus
Lŷc'a-ō'ni-ă
Lȳ-sī'ni-as
Lȳ'sī-as (Ilsh'ī-as
Lȳ-sīm'a-chŭs

M.

Mā'a-chah
Mă-ăch'a-thī
Ma-ăd'āī
Ma-ā'ī
Ma-dī'eh-a-crăb'-
 bim
Mā'a-nī
Mā'a-răth
Mā'a-sū'iah (-yă)
Ma-ăs'ī-āī
Mā'a-sī'as
Mā'a-zī'ah
Măb'da-ī
Mā'e-a-lŏn
Măc'ea-bē'us
Măch'ba-năl
Măch'be-nah
Măch'na-dē'bāī
Mach-pē'lah
Măd'a-ī
Ma-dī'a-bun
Mn-dī'ah
Mă'di-an
Mad-mū'nah
Ma-ē'lus
Măg'da-lă
Măg'da-lē'ne
Măg'di-el
Ma-gīd'do
Măg'pī-ăsh
Ma-hā'lah, or Mă'-
 ha-lah
Ma-hā'la-lē'el
Mī'ha-lath
Ma-hā'le-el
Mā'ha-lī
Mā'ha-nā'im
Mā'ha-neh-dăn

SCRIPTURE PROPER NAMES.

Ma-hăr′a-ī
Ma-hă′zĭ-ŏth
Mä′her-shăl′al-
 hăsh′-băz
Ma-jn′e-ăs
Mak-hē′loth
Mak-hĕ′dah
Măl′a-chī
Mal-chī′ah
Măl′chi-el
Mal-chī′jah
Mal-chī′ram
Măl′chi-shū′ă
Ma-tĕ′le-el
Măl′lo-thī
Ma-mā′ias (-yas)
Mam-nī′ta-nāī′-
 mus
Ma-mū′chus
Măn′a-ĕn
Măn′a-hăth
Măn′as-sē′as
Măn′li-ŭs
Ma-nō′ah
Măr′a-lah
Măr′a-năth′ă, or
 Măr′a-nă′thă
Măr′do-chā′us
Ma-rē′shah
Mĭr′i-mŏth
Măr′i-sa
Măr′se-ná
Mĭs′a-lŏth
Ma-sī′as
Măs′re-kah
Mas-sī′as
Măth′a-nī′as
Ma-thū′sa-lă
Măt′ta-nah
Măt′ta-nī′ah
Măt′ta-thă
Măt′ta-thah
Măt′ta-thī′as
Măt′te-năī
Mat-thī′as
Mat-thī′as (măth-
 thī′as)
Măt′ti-thī′ah
Măz′i-tī′as
Măz′za-rŏth
Me-ă′rah
Me-bŭn′nāi
Mĕch′e-rath-īte
Mĕā′a-bā
Mĕd′e-bā
Me-ā′dā
Me-hĕt′a-bĕl
Me-hī′dā
Me-hū′lah
Me-hū′ja-el
Me-hū′man
Me-hū′nim
Me-jär′kon
Mĕk′o-nah
Mōl′a-tī′ah
Mel-chī′ah
Mel-chī′as
Mĕl′chi-el

Mel-chĭş′e-dĕc
Mĕl′chi-shū′ă
Mā′le-ă
Mŏl′i-cū
Mĕl′i-tă
Me-mū′can
Mĕn′a-hĕm
Me-nĕs′theŭs
Me-ūn′e-nim
Me-ŏn′o-thăi
Mĕph′a-ăth
Me-phĭb′o-shĕth
Mĕr′a-ī′ah
Me-rā′loth (-yoth)
Mĕr′a-mītes
Mĕr′a-rī, or Me-rā′-
 rī
Mĕr′a-thā′im
Mĕr′e-mŏth
Mĕr′i-bah
Mĕr′ib-bā′al
Me-rō′dach-băl′a-
 dăn
Me-rŏn′o-thīte
Me-shĕz′a-beel
Me-shĕz′a-bĕl
Me-shĭl′le-mith
Me-shĭl′le-mŏth
Me-shō′băb
Me-shŭl′le-mĕth
Mĕs′o-bā′īte
Mĕs′o-po-tā′mi-ă
Me-tē′rus
Mĕth′o-är
Mo-thū′sa-el
Me-thū′se-lah
Me-ŭ′nim
Mĕz′a-hăb
Mī′a-min
Mī-cā′iah (-yă)
Mī′cha-el, or Mī′-
 chael (-kel)
Mī-chē′as
Mĭch′me-thah
Mĭg′dal-ĕl
Mĭj′a-min
Mĭk-nē′iah (-yă)
Mĭl′a-lāī
Mī-lē′tus
Mi-nī′a-mĭn
Mĭr′i-am
Mĭs′a-el
Mĭsh′a-el
Mī′she-al
Mish-măn′nah
Mĭsh′ra-ītes
Mĭs′pe-reth
Mĭs′sa-bĭb
Mĭth′re-dāth
Mĭt′y-lē′ne
Mĭz′ra-im
Mnā′son (nă′son)
Mŏ′a-dī′ah
Mŏl′a-dah
Mŏ′o-sī′as
Mŏ′ras-thīte
Mŏr′de-cāi
Mŏr′osh-eth-găth

Mo-rī′ah
Mo-sā′rā
Mo-sē′roth
Mo-sŏl′la-mon
Mȳ′si-ă (mĭzh′i-ă)

N.

Nā′a-mah
Nā′a-man
Nā′a-ma-thīte
Nā′a-mītes
Nā′a-rah
Nā′a-rāi
Nā′a-răn
Nā′a-răth
Na-ăsh′on
Na-a-thus
Năb′a-rī′as
Năb′a-thē′ans
Năb′u-cho-dŏn′o-
 sŏr
Na-dăb′a-thā
Nā′ha-lăl
Na-hă′li-el
Nā′ha-lŏl
Na-hăm′a-nī
Na-hăr′a-ī
Nā′ha-rā′im
Nā′ha-rī
Nā′i-dus
Nā′in
Na-nē′ă
Na-ō′mī, or Nā′o-
 mī
Năph′i-sī
Năph′ta-lī
Năph′tu-him
Na-thăn′a-el
Năth′a-nī′as
Năx′a-rĕth
Nā′a-rī′ah
Nĕb′a-ī
Ne-bā′loth (-yoth)
Ne-bā′joth
Nĕb′u-chad-nĕz′-
 zar
Nĕb′u-shăs′ban
Nĕb′u-zăr-ā′dan
Ne-cō′dan
Nĕd′a-bī′ah
Nĕ′e-mī′as
Nĕg′i-nŏth
Ne-hĕl′a-mīte
Nē′hi-lŏth
Ne-ī′el, or Nĕ′i-ĕl
Ne-kō′dā
Ne-mū′el
Ne-phĭsh′e-sim
Nĕph′tha-lī
Nĕph′tha-lim
Neph′to-ah
Ne-phū′sim
Nĕ′reŭs
Ne-rī′ah
Ne-rī′as

Nĕth′a-nī′ah
Nĕth′i-ninş
Ne-tō′phah
Ne-tōph′a-thī
Ne-zī′ah
Nĭ-cā′nor
Nĭc′o-lāī-tanş
Nĭ-cŏp′o-lĭs
Nĭ′ger
Nĭm′e-veh
Nō′a-dī′ah
No-ē′bă
Nŏm′a-dĕş
Nu-mē′ni-ŭs

O.

Ŏ′ba-dī′ah, or
 Ŏb′a-dī′ah
Ob-dī′ă
Ō′chi-el
Oç′i-nā
Ŏd′o-när′kĕş
Ōl′a-mus
Ōl′i-vĕt
Ŏl′o-fĕr′nĕş
Ōm′a-ē′rus
Ō′me-gă, or O-mĕ′-
 gă
O-nĕs′i-mus
Ŏn′e-sĭph′o-rus
O-nī′a-rĕş
O-nī′as
O-rī′on
Ŏr′tho-sī′as
O-şā′ias (o-zā′yas)
O-xē′ă
Ō-ẓē′as
O shē′ă, or Ō′zhe-ă
Ōth′ni-el
Ōth′o-nī′as
O-zī′as
Ō′zi-el
O-zō′rā

P.

Pā′a-rāi
Pā′āi-ei
Pā′ī
Păl′es-tī′nă
Păl′es-tīne
Păl′ti-el
Pam-phȳl′i-ă
Păr′me-năs
Par-shăn′da-thā
Păr′ŭ-ah
Par-vā′im, or
 Pär′va-im
Pa-sē′ah
Păt′a-rā
Pa-thē′us
Păth′ros

Path-rū′sim
Pāt′ro-bās
Pa-trō′clus
Pā′u
Pĕd′a-hĕl
Pe-däh′zur, or
 Pĕd′ah-zūr
Pe-dū′iah (-yă)
Pĕk′u-bī′ah
Pĕl′a-ī′ah
Pĕl′a-lī′ah
Pĕl′a-tī′ah
Pe-lī′as
Pe-nī′el
Pen-tăp′o-lĭs
Pe-nū′el
Pēr′a-zim
Pĕr′ga-mos
Pe-rī′dā
Pĕr′me-nās
Per-sĕp′o-lĭs
Pe-rū′dā
Pĕth′a-hī′ah
Pe-thū′el
Pe-ūl′thăi
Phāc′a-rĕth
Phāi′sur
Phal-dā′ius (-yus)
Pha-lē′as
Phăl′ti-el
Pha-nū′el
Phăr′a-çim
Phā′raŏh (fā′ro or
 fā′ra-o)
Phăr′a-thō′nī
Pha-rī′rā
Pha-sē′ah, or
 Phā′se-ah
Pha-sū′lis
Phăs′i-rŏn
Phăs′sa-rŏn
Phe-nī′çe
Phe-nī′ci-ă
 (-nish/ī-)
Phēr′e-zīte
Phī-bō′seth, or
 Phĭb′e-sĕth
Phĭl′a-dĕl′phi-ă
 (classical pron.
Phĭl′a-del-phī′ā|
Phī-lär′chēş
Phi-lē′mon
Phĭ-lē′tus
Phī-lĭs′tīne
Phĭ-lŏl′o-gus
Phī′o-mē′tor
Phĭn′e-as
Phĭn′e-has
Phȳ-ġĕl′lus
Pī′-bē′seth, or
 Pĭb′e-sĕth
Pī′-ha-hī′roth
Pĭl′e-hā
Pī-lē′ger
Pĭl-ne′ger
Pīl′tăi
Pīr′a-thŏn
Pī-sĭd′i-ă

sŏn, ôr, dọ, wolf, too, took; ûrn, rụe, pụll; ç, ġ, soft; ċ, ġ, hard; aş; exist; n as nġ; this.

SCRIPTURE PROPER NAMES. 353

Plē'la-dēş (-ya-doez)
Pōch'ez-rĕth
Pŏn'tĭ-us Pī'late (pŏn'shī-us)
Pōr'a-thā
Pōr'cĭ-us (-shī-us)
Pŏw'ī-dō'nĭ-us
Pŏt'ĭ-phar
Po-tĭph'e-rah
Pris-çĭl'lā
Prŏch'o-rus
Ptŏl'e-mā'ĭs (tŏl'-)
Ptŏl'e-mā'us (tŏl'-)
Pu tē'o-lī
Pŭ'tĭ-el

Q.

Quĭn'tus Mĕm'mĭ-ŭs

R.

Rā'a-mah
Rā'a-mī'ah
Ra-ăm'sēş
Rab-bō'nī
Rāb'sa-rĭs
Rāb'sha-kĕh
Rădd'a-ī
Rā'gau
Rī'gĕş
Ra-gū'el
Rā'math-ā'ĭm
Rām'a-thĕm
Ra-mē'sēş
Ra-mī'ah
Rā'phu-el, or Rā'phael (-fel)
Rāph'a-im
Ra-thū'mus, or Rāth'u-mus
Rē'a-ī'ah
Rē'el-ā'ĭah (-yū)
Re-ĕl'ĭ-us
Rec-sā'ĭas (-yas)
Rē'gem-mē'lech
Rē'ha-bī'ah
Rē'ho-bō'am
Re-hō'both
Re'ī
Rĕm'a-lī'ah
Rĕm'mon-mĕth'o-ar
Rē'pha-el
Rĕph'a-ī'ah
Rĕph'a-im
Rĕph'ī-dĭm
Rē'u
Re-ū'el, or Reu'el
Reu'inah
Re-zī'ā
Rhē'gī-um (rē'-)

Rhŏd'o-cūs (rŏd'-)
Rī'bāī
Rŏb'o-ăm
Rŏd'a-nĭm
Ro-gē'lĭm
Rō'ī-mus
Ro-măm'tĭ-ē'zer
Ru'ha-mah

S.

Sā'bach-thā'nī
Sāb'a-ŏth, or Sa-bā'oth
Sāb'a-tē'us
Sāb'a-tus
Sāb'ba-thē'us
Sab-bē'us
Sa-bē'anş
Sā'bī-ē
Sāb'te-chah
Sād'a-mī'as
Sad-dē'us
Sād'du-çēeş
Sā'ha-dū'thā
Sāl'a-mĭs
Sāl'a-sād'a-ī
Sa-lā'thĭ-el
Sāl'la-ī
Sal-lū'mus
Sāl'man-ā'sar
Sal-mō'ne
Sa-lō'me
Sām'a-el
Sa-ma'ins (-yas)
Sa-mā'rĭ-ā (classical pron. Săm'a-rī'ā)
Sām'a-tus
Sa-mē'lus (-yus)
Săm'o-thrā'cī-ā (-thrā'shī-ā)
Sāmp'sa-mēş
Săn'a-băs'sa-rŭs
Săn'a-sĭb
San-bāl'lat
Sāph'a-tī'as
Sap-phī'rā (saf-fī'rā)
Sār'a-bī'as
Sā'raī
Sār'a-ī'ah
Sa-rā'ĭas (-yas)
Sār'a-mĕl
Sar-chĕd'o-nus
Sar-dē'us
Sā're-ā
Sa-rō'thĭ-e
Sar-sē'chim
Sīth'ra-bu-zā'nēş
Sāv'a-rān
Sā'vī-ās
Sçā'va (sē'vā)
Sçy-thŏp'o-lĭs (sī-)
Sĕç'a-cah
Sĕch'e-nī'as

Sŏd'e-çī'as
Sē'ī-rāth
Sē'led
Sĕl'e-mī'ā
Se-leū'cī-ā (-shī-ā, classical pron.
Sĕl'ou-çī'ā)
Se-leū'cus
Sĕm'a-chī'ah
Sĕm'a-ī'ah
Sĕm'e-ī
Se-mĕl'lī-us
Se-nā'ah, or Sŏn'a-ah
Sen-nāch'e-rib, or Sŏn'na-chē'rib
Se-nū'ah
Se-ō'rĭm
Sŏph'a-răd
Sŏph'ar-vā'ĭm
Se-phē'lā
Sēr'a-ī'ah
Sēr'ġī-ŭs
Shā'al-ăb'bĭn
Sha-āl'be-nīte
Shā'a-rā'ĭm
Sha-hāz'ī-math
Shāl'ī-shā
Shāl'le-chĕth
Shāl'ma-ī
Shāl'ma-nē'ger
Shām'a-rī'ah
Shām'ma-ī
Shăm'mu-ah
Shăm'she-ra-ī
Shär'a-ī
Shar-ē'zer
Shār'on
Sha-ru'hen
Shāsh'a-ī
Shā'ul
She-āl'tĭ-el
Shē'a-rī'ah
Shē'ar-jā'shub
Shĕb'a-nī'ah
Shĕb'a-rĭm
Shĕb'u-el
Shĕch'a-nī'ah
Shĕd'e-ur
Shĕl'e-mī'ah
Shŏl'o-mī
Shŏl'o-mith
Shŏl'o-mŏth
Shŏl'mi-el, or She-mā'ah
Shĕm'a-ah
Shĕm'a-ī'ah
Shĕm'a-rī'ah
Shĕm'e-ber
Shē-mī'dā
Shĕm'ī-nĭth
She-mir'a-mŏth

She-mū'el
She-nā'zar
Shŏph'a-tī'ah
She-phū'phan
Shĕr'e-bī'ah
She-rē'zer
Shē'shāī
Shib'bo-lĕth
Shĭg-gā'ĭon (-yon)
Shĭ-ġī'o-nŏth
Shī-lō'ah
Shī-lō'nī
Shī'lo-nīte, or Shī-lō'nĭte
Shĭm'e-ah
Shĭm'e-ăm
Shĭm'e-ăth
Shĭm'e-ī
Shĭm'e-on
Shĭm'shāī
Shĭph'rah
Shĭt'ra-ī
Shō'ba-ī
Shō'cho
Sho-shăn'nĭm
Shŋ'ba-el
Shŋ'the-lah
Sib'be-chāī
Sĭb'ru-ĭm
Sī'çy-on(sĭsh'ĭ-on)
Sī-ġī'o-nŏth
Sī-lō'ah, or Sĭl'o-ah
Sī-lō'am, or Sĭl'o-ăm
Sī-lō'e, or Sĭl'o-e
Sī'mal-cū'e
Sī'nāī
Sĭp'paī
Sĭr'ī-on
Sĭ-sām'a-ī
Sĭs'e-rā
Sŏd'o-mā
Sŏp'a-ter
Sŏph'e rĕth
Sŏph'o-nī'as
So-sĭp'a-ter
Sŏs'the-nēş
Sŏs'tra-tŭs
Sō'ta-ī
Stā'chys
Stŏph'a-năs
Sū'ba-ī
Sū'dī-ăs
Sū'san-chītes
Sy-ē'ne
Sỹ-ĕ'ne
Sy̆n'tī-chē
Sy̆r'ĭ-on
Sy̆'ro-phe-nī'cī-an (-nĭsh'ĭ-an)

T.

Tā'a-năch
Tāb'a-ŏth
Tāb'ba-ŏth

Tā'be-al
Ta'be-el
Tē-bĕl'lī-us
Tāb'e-rah
Tāb'ī-thā
Tāb'rī-mŏn
Tāch'mo-nīte
Ta-hāp'a-nēş
Tāh'pan-hēş
Tāh'pe-nēş
Tāh're-ā
Tāl'ī-thā-cū'mī
Tāl'maī
Tăn'hu-mĕth
Tāp'pu-ah
Tār'a-lah
Tā're-ā
Tăt'na-ī
Tŏb'a-lī'ah
Te-hāph'ne-hēş
Te-kō'ā
Tĕl'-ā'bib
Tĕl'a-ĭm
Tĕl'-ha-rē'shā
Tĕm'a-nī
Thad-dē'us, or Thăd'de-ŭs
Thām'nn-thā
The-cō'e
The-lā'sar
The-ōch-nus
The-ŏd'o-tus
The-ŏph'ī-lus
Thĕr'me-lŏth
Thēs'sa-lo-nī'cā
Thĭm'na-thah
Thŏun'o-ī
Thrā'cī-ā (shī-ā)
Thra-sē'as
Thy'a-tī'ra
Tī-bē'rī-as
Tī-bē'rĭ-us
Tĭg'lath-pī-lē'zer
Tĭl'gath-pĭl-nē'ge
Tī-mē'us
Tĭm'na-thah
Ti-mō'the-us
Tĭr'ha-kah
Tĭr'ha-nah
Tĭr'ī-ā
Tĭr'shn-thā
To-bī'ah
Tō'bī-el
To-bī'jah
To-gär'mah
Tōl'ba-nēş
Tō'phel
Trách'o-nī'tis
Trĭp'o-lis
Tro-ġyl'lī-ŭm
Trŏph'ī-mus
Trỹ-phō'nā
Trỹ-phō'sā
Tū'bī-ē'nī
Tỹch'ī-cus
Tỹ-răn'nus
Tyr'ī-anş
Tỹ'rus

són, ôr, dọ, wọlf, tōō, tōōk; ûrn, rụe, pụll; ç, ġ, soft; c, ġ, hard; aş; exĭst; ṇ as ng;—this.

SCRIPTURE PROPER NAMES.

U.

Ū/la-ī
U-phär/sin
U-rī/ah
Ụ-rī/as
Ụ/ri-el
U-rī/jah
Ū/tha-ī
Ū/zi-ī
Ūz/zah
Uz-zī/ah
Uz-zī/el or Ūz/zi-el

V.

ᵃ Vn-jĕz/a-thà

Va-nī/ah

X.

Xăn/thi-cus
(zăn/-)

Z.

Zī/a-nā/im
Zī/a-năn
Zā/a-năn/nim
Zī/a-văn
Zīb/a-dm/anẓ
Zīb/a-dā/ias (-yas)
Zāb/bāi

Zāb-dȳ/us
Zāb/dī
Zāb/di-el
Zāb/u-lon
Zā/e/ea-ī
Zac-chȳ/us
Zāch/a-rī/ah
Zāch/a-rī/as
Zā/ch/a-ry
Zal-mō/nah
Za-nō/ah
Zär/a-çĕṣ
Zär/a-ī/as
Zā/re-ah
Zär/e-phăth
Zär/e-tăn
Zär/ta-nah
Zäth/o-ē
Za-thū/ī
Zĕb/a-dī/ah

Ze-bā/im
Ze-bī/nå
Ze-boī/im
Ze-bȳ/im
Ze-bū/dah
Zĕb/u-lun
Zĕch/u-rī/ah
Zĕd/e-chī/as
Zĕd/e-kī/ah
Ze-lō/phe-hăd
Ze-lō/tĕṣ
Zĕm/a-rā/im
Ze-mī/rå
Ze/nas
Zĕph/a-nī/ah
Zĕph/a-thah
Zĕr/a-hī/ah
Zĕr/a-ī/ah
Zĕr/e-då
Ze-rĕd/a-thah

Zĕr/e-räth
Ze-rụī/ah
Ze-rŭb/ba-bĕl
Zĕr/u-ī/ah
Zib/e-on
Zīb/i-ah
Zid-kī/jah
Zīl/thai
Zī/phron
Zip-pō/rah
Zo-bȳ/bah
Zō/he-lĕth
Zȳ/phāi
Zȳ/re-ah
Zo-rōb/a-bĕl
Zū/ri-ĕl
Zū/ri-shăd/da-i

ā, ē, ī, ō, ū, y̆, *long*; ă, ŏ, ĭ, ŏ, ŭ, y̆, *short*; câre, cär, åsk, ạll, whạt; ẽre, vẹil, tẽrm; píque, fĩrm.

PRONOUNCING AND EXPLANATORY VOCABULARY

OF

COMMON ENGLISH CHRISTIAN NAMES.

I. NAMES OF MEN.

A.

Aaron (âr'un). [Heb.] Lofty; inspired.
Ā'bel. [Heb.] Breath; transitoriness; vanity.
A-bī'el. [Heb.] Father of strength.
A-bī'jah. [Heb.] To whom Jehovah is a Father. [light.
Ạb'ner.. [Heb.] Father of
Ā'bra-ham. [Heb.] Father of a multitude. [elevation.
Ạ'bram. [Heb.] Father of
Ăd'am. [Heb.] Man; earthman; red earth.
A-dŏl'phus. [O. H. Ger.] Noble wolf, i. e. noble hero.
Ăd'o-nī'ram. [Heb.] Lord of height.
Ăl'a-rĭc. [O. H. Ger.] All-rich: or, noble ruler.
Ăl'bert. [O. H. Ger.] Nobly bright; illustrious.
Ăl'bi-on. [Celt.] Mountainous land; — the ancient name of England.
Ăl'ex-ăn'der. [Ger.] A defender of men.
Ăl'fred. [O. H. Ger.] Elf in council; i. e., good counselor. [ALPHONSO.
A-lŏn'zo. [O. Ger.] Same as
Ăl'phe-us (properly Al-phē'-us). [Heb.] Exchange.
Al-phŏn'so. [O. H. Ger.] Already; willing.
Ăl'vah, } [Heb.] Iniquity.
Ăl'van. }
Ăl'vin, } [O. H. Ger.] Be-
Ăl'win. } loved by all.
Ăm'a-rī'ah. [Heb.] Whom Jehovah promised.
Ăm'a-sả. [Heb.] A burden.

Ăm'brose. [Gr.] Immortal; divine.
Ăm'mĭ. [Heb.] My people.
Ā'mos. [Heb.] Strong; courageous; otherwise, a burden.
Ăn'drew (ăn'dru). [Gr.] Strong; manly.
Ăn'selm. [O. H. Ger.] Protection of God.
Ăn'tho-ny (-to-), } [Lat.]
Ăn'to-ny. } Priceless; praiseworthy.
Ăr'chi-bald. [Ger.] Extremely bold; otherwise, holy prince.
Ăr'te-mas. [Gr.] Gift of Artemis, or Diana.
Ạr'thur. [Celt.] High; noble.
Ā'sả. [Heb.] Healer; physician. [God.
Ăs'a-hĕl. [Heb.] Made of
Ā'saph. [Heb.] A collector.
Ăsh'er. [Heb.] Happy; fortunate. [ness.
Ăsh'ur. [Heb.] Black; blackAu-gŭs'tĭn, } [Lat.] Belong-
Au-gŭs'tĭne, } ing to Au-
Aus'tin. } gustus.
Au-gŭs'tus. [Lat.] Exalted; imperial.
Ăz'a-rī'ah. [Heb.] Helped of the Lord.

B.

Băp'tĭst. [Gr.] A baptizer; a purifier.
Băr'na-bas, } [Heb.] Son of
Băr'na-by. } consolation.
Bar-thŏl'o-mew. [Heb.] A warlike son.
Bar-zĭl'lāi. [Heb.] Iron of the Lord: firm; true.
Băs'il. [Gr.] Kingly; royal.

Bĕn'e-dĭct. [Lat.] Blessed.
Bĕn'ja-mĭn. [Heb.] Son of the right hand.
Be-rī'ah. [Heb.] In calamity.
Bẽr'nard, } [O. H. Ger.] Bold
Bär'nard. } as a bear.
Bẽr'tram. [O. H. Ger.] Bright raven.
Be-zăl'e-el. [Heb.] In the shadow (protection) of God.
Bŏn'ĭ-fāçe. [Lat.] A benefactor.

C.

Cad-wal'la-der. [Brit.] Battle-arranger.
Çæ'ṣar. [Lat.] Hairy; or, blue-eyed; or, born under the cesarean operation.
Cā'leb. [Heb.] A dog.
Căl'vin. [Lat.] Bald.
Cecil (sĕs'il, sĭs'il, or sēs'il). [Lat.] Dim-sighted.
Çē'phas. [Aramaic.] A stone.
Chärleṣ. [O. H. Ger.] Strong; manly; noble-spirited.
Chrĭst'ian. [Lat.] Belonging to Christ; a believer in Christ. [ing Christ.
Chrĭs'to-pher. [Gr.] Bear-
Clăr'ençe. [Lat.] Illustrious.
Clau'dĭ-us, } [Lat.] Lame.
Claude. }
Clĕm'ent. [Lat.] Mild-tempered; merciful.
Cŏn'rad. [O. H. Ger.] Bold in council; resolute.
Cŏn'stant. [Lat.] Firm; faithful.
Cŏn'stan-tīne. [Lat.] Resolute; firm.
Cor-nē'lĭ-us (or kor-neel'-yus). [Lat.] (Uncertain.)

356 COMMON ENGLISH CHRISTIAN NAMES.

Cūth′bert. [A.-S.] Noted splendor.
Cyp′ri-an. [Gr.] Of Cyprus.
Cyr′il. [Gr.] Lordly.
Cy′rus. [Per.] The sun.

D.

Dăn. [Heb.] A judge.
Dăn′i-el (or dănĭyel). [Heb.] A divine judge.
Da-rī′us. [Per.] Preserver.
Dā′vid. [Heb.] Beloved.
De-mē′tri-us. [Gr.] Belonging to Ceres.
Dĕn′is, } [Gr.] Same as DI-
Dĕn′nis. } ONYSIUS. [Fr. form.]
Dĕr′rick. [O. H. Ger.] A corruption of THEODORIC.
Dī′o-nys′i-us (-nĭzh/ĭ-us.) [Gr.] Belonging to Dionysos, the god of wine.
Dŏn′ald. [Celt.] Proud chief.
Dŭn′can (dŭnk′an). [Celt.] Brown chief.

E.

Ĕb′en. [Heb.] A stone.
Ĕb′en-ē′zer. [Heb.] The stone of help.
Ĕd′gar. [A.-S.] A javelin (or protector) of property.
Ĕd′mund. [A.-S.] Defender of property.
Ĕd′ward. [A.-S.] Guardian of property. [property.
Ĕd′win. [A.-S.] Gainer of
Ĕg′bert. [O. H. Ger.] The sword's brightness; famous with the sword.
Ĕl′bert. [O. H. Ger.] The same as ALBERT.
Ĕl′dred. [A.-S.] Terrible.
Ē′le-ā′zer. [Heb.] To whom God is a help.
Ĕ′lī. [Heb.] A foster son.
E-lī′ab. [Heb.] God is his father.
E-lī′as. [Heb.] The same as ELIJAH. [Lord.
E-lī′hu. [Heb.] God the
E-lī′jah. [Heb.] Jehovah is my God.
E-lī′pha-let. [Heb.] God of salvation.
E-lī′sha. [Heb.] God my salvation.
E-lī′zur. [Heb.] God is my rock. [of ELISHA.
Ĕl′lis. [Heb.] A variation
Ĕl′mer. [A. S.] Noble; excellent. [A contraction of ETHELMER.]
Ĕl′nā-than. [Heb.] God gave.
Em-măn′u-el. [Heb.] God with us.

Ĕm′er-y, } [A.-S.] Powerful; rich.
Ĕm′mer-y, }
Ĕm′o-ry.
E′noch. [Heb.] Consecrated; dedicated.
Ē′nos. [Heb.] Man. [ful.
Ē′phra-ĭm. [Heb.] Very fruit-
E-răs′mus. [Gr.] Lovely; worthy to be loved.
E-răs′tus. [Gr.] Lovely; amiable. [powerful.
Ē′ric. [A.-S.] Rich; brave;
Ĕr′nest. [Ger.] Earnest.
Ē′than. [Heb.] Firmness; strength.
Eū′gene, or Eū-gēne′. [Gr.] Well-born; noble.
Eŭs′tace. [Gr.] Healthy; strong; standing firm.
Ēv′an. [Brit.] The same as JOHN. [of God.
E-zē′ki-el. [Heb.] Strength
Ez′ra. [Heb.] Help.

F.

Fē′lix. [Lat.] Happy; prosperous.
Fĕr′di-nand. [O. H. Ger.] Brave; valiant.
Fer-năn′do. [O. H. Ger.] The same as FERDINAND.
Fĕs′tus. [Lat.] Joyful; glad.
Frăn′cis. [Fr.] Free.
Frănk. [Fr.] A contraction of Francis.
Frĕd′er-ic, } [O. H. Ger.]
Frĕd′er-ick. } Abounding in peace; or, peaceful ruler.

G.

Gā′bri-el. [Heb.] Man of God.
Gā′ius (gā′yus). [Lat.] Rejoiced.
Ga-mā′li-el. [Heb.] Recompense of God.
Găr′ret. [O. H. Ger.] Another form of GERALD.
Gĕof′frey. [O. H. Ger.] The same as GODFREY.
Gĕorge. [Gr.] A landholder; husbandman.
Gĕr′ald, } [O. H. Ger.] Strong
Gĕr′ard. } with the spear.
Gĕr′shom. [Heb.] An exile.
Gĭd′e-on. [Heb.] A destroyer.
Gĭl′bert. [O. H. Ger.] Yellow-bright; famous.
Gīles. [Gr.] A kid.
Gĭv′en. [Eng.] Gift of God.
Gŏd′dard. [O. Ger.] Pious; virtuous.
Gŏd′frey. [O. H. Ger.] At peace with God.
Grĕg′o-ry. [Ger.] Watchful; vigilant.

Grĭf′fith. [Brit.] Having great faith.
Gus-tā′vus. [Sw.] A warrior; a hero.
Guy. [Fr.] A leader.

H.

Hăn′ni-bal. [Punic.] Grace of Baal.
Hăr′old. [A.-S.] A champion; general of an army.
Hē′man. [Heb.] Faithful.
Hĕn′ry. [O. H. Ger.] The head or chief of a house.
Hĕr′bert. [A.-S.] Glory of the army. [warrior.
Hĕr′man. [O. H. Ger.] A
Hĕz′e-kī′ah. [Heb.] Strength of the Lord. [merry.
Hĭl′a-ry. [Lat.] Cheerful;
Hī′ram. [Heb.] Most noble.
Hŏr′ace. [Gr.] Same as HORATIO. [Fr. form.]
Ho-rā′ti-o (ho-rā′shī-o). [Gr.] (Uncertain.)
Ho-sē′a. [Heb.] Salvation.
How′ell. [Brit.] Sound; whole.
Hū′bert. [O. H. Ger.] Bright in spirit; soul-bright.
Hūgh (hū), } [D.] Mind;
Hū′go. } spirit; soul.
Humph′rey. [A.-S.] Protector of the home.

I.

Ĭch′a-bod. [Heb.] The glory has departed.
Ig-nā′ti-us (ig-nā′shī-us). [Gr.] Ardent; fiery.
Im-măn′u-el. [Heb.] The same as EMMANUEL.
Ĭn′gram. [Teut.] Raven.
Ĭn′i-go. [Gr.] The same as IGNATIUS. [Sp. form.]
Ī′ra. [Heb.] Watchful.
Ī′saac (ī′zak). [Heb.] Laughter.
Ĭ-sā′iah (ī-zā′ya). [Heb.] Salvation of the Lord. [God.
Ĭs′ra-el. [Heb.] A soldier of
Īv′an. [Brit.] The same as JOHN. [Russian form.]

J.

Jā′bez. [Heb.] He will cause pain.
Jā′cob. [Heb.] A supplanter.
Jā′i-rus. [Heb.] He will enlighten.
Jāmes. [Heb.] The same as JACOB. [ment.
Jā′pheth. [Heb.] Enlarge-
Jā′red. [Heb.] Descent.
Jā′son. [Gr.] A healer.

COMMON ENGLISH CHRISTIAN NAMES. 357

Jăs'per. [Per.] (*Uncertain*.)
Jā'van. [Heb.] Clay; supple.
Jĕd'e-dī'ah. [Heb.] Beloved of the Lord.
Jĕf'frey. [O. H. Ger.] Same as GODFREY.
Jĕr'e-mī'ah,) [Heb.] Exalted
Jĕr'e-my.) of the Lord.
Jĕr'ome (*in Eng.*), Je-rōme' (*in Amer.*). Holy name.
Jĕs'se. [Heb.] Wealth.
Jō'ab. [Heb.] Jehovah is his father. [cuted.
Jŏb. [Heb.] Afflicted; perse-
Jō'el. [Heb.] The Lord is God. [gift of God.
Jŏhn (jŏn). [Heb.] Gracious
Jō'nah,) [Heb.] A dove.
Jō'nas.)
Jŏn'a-than. [Heb.] Gift of Jehovah.
Jō'seph. [Heb.] He shall add.
Jŏsh'u-ȧ. [Heb.] God of salvation.
Jo-sī'ah,) [Heb.] Given of
Jo-sī'as.) the Lord.
Jō'tham. [Heb.] The Lord is upright.
Jū'dah. [Heb.] Praised.
Jū'li-an. [Lat.] Sprung from, or belonging to, Julius.
Jū'li-ŭs. (Gr.] Soft-haired.
Jŭs'tin,) [Lat.] Just; up-
Jŭs'tus.) right.

K.

Kĕn'elm. [A.-S.] A defender of his kindred.
Kĕn'neth. [Gael.] A leader; commander.

L.

Lā'ban. [Heb.] White.
Lăm'bert. [O. H. Ger.] Illustrious with landed possessions.
Lăn'çe-lot. [It.] A little angel; *otherwise*, a little lance or warrior; *or*, a servant.
Lau'rençe,) [Lat.] Crowned
Law'rençe.) with laurel.
Lăz'a-rus. [Heb.] God will help.
Le-ăn'der. [Gr.] Lion-man.
Lĕm'u-el. [Heb.] Created by God.
Lĕon'ard (lĕn'ard). [Ger.] Strong or brave as a lion.
Le-ŏn'ī-das. [Gr.] Lion-like.
Lē'o-pŏld. [O. H. Ger.] Bold for the people.
Lē'vī. [Heb.] Adhesion. See Gen. xxix. 34.
Lew'ĭs (lōō'ĭs). [O. H. Ger.] Bold warrior.
Lī'nus. [Gr.] Flaxen-haired.

Lī'o-nel. [Lat.] Young lion.
Llew-ĕl'lyn (lu-ĕl'lin). [Celt.] Lightning.
Lo-ăm'mī. [Heb.] Not my people.
Lo-rĕn'zo. [Lat.] The same as LAURENCE.
Lŏt. [Heb.] A veil; covering.
Lou'ĭs. [O. H. Ger.] The same as LEWIS. [Fr. form.]
Lū'cī-an (lū'shī-an). [Lat.] Belonging to, or sprung from, Lucius.
Lū'cī-ŭs (lū'shĭ-ŭs). [Lat.] Born at break of day.
Lū'do-vīc. [O. H. Ger.] Same as LEWIS. [Ger. form.]
Lūke. [Lat.] Light.
Lū'ther. [Ger.] Illustrious warrior.
Lȳ-cŭr'gus. [Gr.] Wolf-driver.

M.

Mā'doc. [W.] Good; beneficent. [of the Lord.
Măl'a-chī. [Heb.] Messenger
Ma-năs'seh. [Heb.] Forgetfulness.
Mar-çĕl'lus. [Lat.] Diminutive of MARCUS.
Mar'cī-ŭs (mär'shĭ-ŭs). [Lat.] Same as MARCUS.
Mär'cus,) [Lat.] A ham-
Märk.) mer; *otherwise*—a male; *or*, sprung from Mars.
Mär'ma-dūke. [A.-S.] A mighty noble.
Mär'tin. [Lat.] Of Mars; warlike.
Măt'thew (măth'yu). [Heb.] Gift of Jehovah.
Mat-thī'as (math-thī'as). [Heb.] Gift of the Lord;— the same as MATTHEW.
Mau'rice. [Lat.] Moorish; dark-colored.
Măx'ĭ-mĭl'ĭ-an. [Lat.] The greatest Æmilianus.
Mī'cah. [Heb.] Who is like the Lord?
Mī'cha-el (*or* mī'kel). [Heb.] Who is like God?
Mīles. [Lat.] A soldier.
Mŏr'gan. [Brit.] A seaman; a dweller on the sea.
Mō'şĕş. [Egypt.] Drawn out of the water.

N.

Nā'hum. [Heb.] Consolation.
Nā'than. [Heb.] Given; a gift.
Na-thăn'a-el,) [Heb.] The
Na-thăn'ī-el;) gift of God.

Nēal,) [Lat.] Dark; swarthy;
Nēil,) *otherwise* [Celt.], Chief. [of the Lord.
Nē'he-mī'ah. [Heb.] Comfort
Nĭch'o-las,) [Gr.] Victory of
Nĭc'o-las.) the people.
Nō'ah. [Heb.] Rest; comfort.
Nō'el. [Lat. *Dies Natalis*.] Christmas; born on Christmas day.
Nŏr'man. [Ger.] A northman; a native of Normandy.

O.

Ō'ba-dī'ah. [Heb.] Servant of the Lord.
Ō'bed. [Heb.] Serving God.
Oc-tā'vĭ-ŭs,) [Lat.] The
Oc-tā'vŭs.) eighth-born.
Ŏl'ĭ-ver. [Lat.] An olive-tree. [nineer.
O-rĕs'tĕş. [Gr.] A mount-
Or-lăn'do. [Teut.] Same as ROWLAND. [It. form.]
Ŏs'car. [Celt.] Bounding warrior.
Ŏş'mond,) [O. H. Ger.] Pro-
Ŏş'mund.) tection of God.
Ŏş'wald. [O. H. Ger.] Power of God.
Ōw'en. [Celt.] Lamb; *otherwise*, young warrior.

P.

Păt'rick. [Lat.] Noble; a patrician.
Paul. [Lat.] Little. [PAUL.
Pau-lī'nus. [Lat.] Same as
Pē'leg. [Heb.] Division.
Pĕr'e-grīne. [Lat.] A stranger.
Pē'ter. [Gr.] A rock.
Phĭ-lăn'der. [Gr.] A lover of men.
Phĭ-lē'mon. [Gr.] Loving; friendly. [horses.
Phĭl'ĭp. [Gr.] A lover of
Phĭn'e-as,) [Heb.] Mouth
Phĭn'e-has.) of brass.
Pī'ŭs. [Lat.] Pious; dutiful.
Pŏl'y-cärp. [Gr.] Much fruit.
Pre-sĕrv'ed. [Eng.] Redeemed; saved.

Q.

Quĭn'tin. [Lat.] The fifth.

R.

Rălph (*in Eng. often pron.* räf). [O. H. Ger.] Same as RODOLPHUS. [ing of God.
Răph'a-el. [Heb.] The heal-
Rĕġ'ĭ-nald. [O. H. Ger.] Strong ruler.

sŭn, ôr, dọ, wolf, tōō, tõõk; ûrn, rụe, pu̇ll; ç, ċ, *soft*; ȩ, ġ, *hard*; aẓ; eẋist; ṇ as ng; this.

358 COMMON ENGLISH CHRISTIAN NAMES.

Reu'ben. [Heb.] Behold, a son.
Reu'el. [Heb.] Friend of God.
Reyn'old. [O. H. Ger.] The same as REGINALD.
Rich'ard. [O. H. Ger.] Rich-hearted; powerful.
Rob'ert. [O. H. Ger.] Bright in fame.
Rŏd'er-ic, } [O. H. Ger.]
Rŏd'er-ick. } Rich in fame.
Rŏ'dolph, } [O. H. Ger.]
Ro-dŏl'phus. } Famous wolf, or hero.
Rŏg'er. [O. H. Ger.] Famous with the spear.
Rō'land. [O. H. Ger.] Same as ROWLAND. [Fr. form.]
Rōw'land. [O. H. Ger.] Fame of the land.
Ru'dolph, } [O. H. Ger.]
Ru-dŏl'phus. } Variations of RODOLPHUS.
Ru'fus. [Lat.] Red; red-haired.
Ru'pert. [O. H. Ger.] Same as ROBERT.

S.

Săl'mon. [Heb.] Shady.
Săm'son, } [Heb.] Splendid
Sămp'son. } sun; i. e., great joy and felicity.
Săm'u-el. [Heb.] Heard of God; asked for of God.
Saul. [Heb.] Asked for.
Sē'bȧ. [Heb.] Eminent.
Se-băs'tian (-băst'yan). [Gr.] Venerable; reverend.
Se-rē'no, } [Lat.] Calm;
Se-rē'nus. } peaceful.
Sĕth. [Heb.] Appointed.
Sĭg'is-mund. [O. H. Ger.] Conquering protection.

Sī'las. [Lat.] . A contraction of SILVANUS. [a wood.
Sĭl-vā'nus. [Lat.] Living in
Sĭl-vĕs'ter. [Lat.] Bred in the country; rustic.
Sĭm'e-on, } [Heb.] Hearing
Sĭ'mon. } with acceptance.
Sŏl'ọ-mon. [Heb.] Peaceable.
Stē'phen (stē'vn). [Gr.] A crown.
Sȳl'van, } The same as
Syl-vā'nus. } SILVANUS.
Syl-vĕs'ter. The same as SILVESTER.

T.

Thăd'de-us. [Syr.] The wise.
Thē'o-bald (formerly Tĭb'-ald). [O. H. Ger.] Bold for the people. [of God.
Thē'o-dore. [Gr.] The gift
The-ŏd'o-rĭc. [A.-S.] Powerful among the people. [of God.
The-ŏph'i-lus. [Gr.] A lover
Thē'ron. [Gr.] A hunter.
Thŏm'as (tom'as). [Heb.] A twin. [God.
Tĭm'o-thy. [Gr.] Fearing
Tī'tus. [Gr.] (Uncertain.)
To-bī'ah, } [Heb.] Distin-
To-bī'as. } guished of the Lord.
Trĭs'tam, } [Lat.] Grave;
Trĭs'tram. } pensive; melancholy; sorrowful; sad.
Tȳb'alt. [O. H. Ger.] A contraction of THEOBALD.

U.

U-lȳs'sēṣ. [Gr.] A hater.
Ûr'ban. [Lat.] Of the town; courteous; polished.

U-rī'ah. [Heb.] Light of the Lord. [man.
U'ri-an. [Dan.] A husband-
U'ri-el. [Heb.] Light of God.

V.

Văl'en-tīne. [Lat.] Strong; healthy; powerful.
Vĭc'tor. [Lat.] A conqueror.
Vĭn'cent. [Lat.] Conquering.
Vĭv'i-an. [Lat.] Lively.

W.

Wal'ter. [O. H. Ger.] Ruling the host.
Wĭll'iam (wĭl'yam). [O. H. Ger.] Resolute helmet, or, helmet of resolution; defense; protector.
Wĭn'frĕd. [A.-S.] Win-peace.

Z.

Zăb'di-el. [Heb.] Gift of God.
Zae-chē'us. [Heb.] Innocent; pure.
Zăch'a-rī'ah, } [Heb.] Re-
Zăch'a-ry. } membered of the Lord.
Zā'dok. [Heb.] Just.
Zĕb'a-dī'ah, } [Heb.] Gift of
Zĕb'e-dee. } the Lord.
Zĕch-a-rī'ah. [Heb.] Same as ZACHARIAH.
Zĕd'e-kī'ah. [Heb.] Justice of the Lord.
Ze-lō'tĕṣ. [Gr.] A zealot.
Zē'nas. [Gr.] Gift of Jupiter.
Zĕph'a-nī'ah. [Heb.] Hid of the Lord.

II. NAMES OF WOMEN.

A.

Ăb'i-gail (ăb'ĭ-gel). [Heb.] My father's joy.
Ăch'sȧ. [Heb.] Anklet.
Ā'dȧ. [O. H. Ger.] Same as EDITH. [as ADELINE.
Ăd'a-līne. [O. H. Ger.] Same
Ăd'e-lȧ. [O. H. Ger.] Same as ADELINE. [as ADELINE.
Ăd'e-lāĭde. [O. H. Ger.] Same
.A-dē'lĭ-ȧ. [O. H. Ger.] A variation of ADELA.
Ăd'e-lī'nȧ, } [O. H. Ger.] Of
Ăd'e-līne. } noble birth; a princess.

Ăg'a-thȧ. [Gr.] Good; kind.
Ăg'nĕṣ. [Gr.] Chaste; pure.
Ăl'e-thē'ȧ. [Gr.] Truth.
Ăl'ex-an'drȧ, } [Gr.]
Ăl'ex-an-drī'nȧ, } Feminine of ALEXANDER.
Ăl'ĭçe, } [O. H.
A-lĭç'i-ȧ (-lĭsh'ĭ-). } Ger.] Same as ADELINE. [cess.
Al-mī'rȧ. [Ar.] Lofty; a prin-
Al-thē'ȧ. [Gr.] A healer.
Ăm'a-bĕl. [Lat.] Lovable; amiable. [to be loved.
A-măn'dȧ. [Lat.] Worthy
A-mē'lĭ-ȧ (or a-meel'ya). [O. H. Ger.] Busy; energetic.

Ā'my. [Lat.] Beloved.
An-gĕl'i-cȧ, } [Gr.] Lovely;
An'ge-lī'nȧ. } angelic.
Ănn, } [Heb.] Grace; — the
Ăn'nȧ, } same as HAN-
Ănne. } NAH.
An-nĕtte'. [Heb.] A variation of ANNE. [Fr. form.]
Ăn'toi-nĕtte'. [Gr.] Diminution of ANTONIA. [Fr. form.]
An-tō'ni-ȧ, } [Lat.] Inesti-
Ăn'to-nī'nȧ. } mable.
Ăr'a-bĕl'lȧ. [Lat.] A fair altar; otherwise, an Arabian woman. [of ARIADNE.
Ā'ri-ăn'ȧ. [Gr.] A corruption

ā, ĕ, ī, ō, ū, ȳ, long; ă, ĕ, ĭ, ŏ, ŭ, ȳ, short; cȧre, cär, ȧsk, ąll, whąt; ẽre, vęil, tẽrm; pīque, fĭrm;

COMMON ENGLISH CHRISTIAN NAMES. 359

Au-gŭs'tá. [Lat.] Feminine of AUGUSTUS.
Au-rē'li-á (or aw-reel'yá). [Lat.] Feminine of AURELIUS.
Au-rō'rá. [Lat.] Morning redness; fresh; brilliant.

B.

Bär'ba-rá. [Gr.] Foreign; strange.
Bē'a-triçe, } [Lat.] Making
Bē'a-trix. } happy.
Be-lin'dá. (Uncertain.)
Bĕr'thá. [O. II. Ger.] Bright.
Bĕt'sey. [Heb.] A corruption of ELIZABETH.
Blănçh, } [Teut.] White.
Blănçhe. }
Bridg'et. [Celt.] Strength.

C.

Ca-mĭl'lá. [Lat.] Attendant at a sacrifice.
Căr'o-line. [O. II. Ger.] Feminine of CAROLUS, the Latin of Charles. [Fr. form.]
Cas-săn'drá. [Gr.] She who inflames with love.
Căth'a-rī'nă, }
Căth'a-rĭne, } [Gr.] Pure.
Căth'er-ĭne. }
Çe-çĭl'ĭ-á, } [Lat.] Feminine
Çĕç'ĭ-ly. } of CECIL.
Çe-lĕs'tĭne. [Lat.] Heavenly.
Çē'lĭ-á (or seel'yá). [Lat.] Feminine of CŒLIUS. [It. form.]
Chär'ĭ-tỹ. [Eng.] Love.
Chär'lŏtte. [O. II. Ger.] Feminine of CHARLES.
Chlō'e. [Ger.] A green herb; blooming.
Chris'ti-ăn'á, } [Gr] Fem.
Chris-tī'ná. } of CHRISTIANUS, Lat. for Christian.
Çĭç'e-ly. [Lat.] A corruption of CECILIA.
Clär'á. [Lat.] Bright; illustrious.
Clär'ĭçe, } [Lat.] A variation of CLARA.
Cla-rĭs'sá. }
Clau'dĭ-á. [Lat.] Feminine of CLAUDIUS.
Clĕm'en-tī'ná, } [Lat.] Mild;
Clĕm'en-tīne. } gentle.
Cŏn'stançe. [Lat.] Firm; constant.
Cō'rá. [Gr.] Maiden;—another form of CORINNA.
Cor-dē'lĭ-á (or kor-deel'yá). [Lat.] Warm-hearted.
Co-rĭn'ná. [Gr.] Maiden.
Cor-nē'lĭ-á (or kor-neel'yá). [Lat.] Feminine of CORNELIUS. [Mt. Cynthus.]
Çўn'thi-á. [Gr.] Belonging to

D.

Dĕb'o-rah. [Heb.] A bee.
Dē'li-á (or deel'yá). [Gr.] Of Delos.
Dī-ăn'á. [Lat.] Goddess.
Dī'nah. [Heb.] Judged.
Dō'rá. [Gr.] A contraction of DOROTHEA.
Dŏr'cas. [Gr.] A gazelle.
Do-rĭn'dá. [Gr.] Same as DOROTHEA.
Dŏr'o-thē'á, } [Gr.] The gift
Dŏr'o-thy. } of God.

E.

Ē'dith. [O. II. Ger.] Happiness; otherwise, rich gift.
Ĕd'ná. [Heb.] Pleasure.
Ĕl'e-a-nor, } [Gr.] Light;—
Ĕl'i-nor. } the same as HELEN.
E-lĭṣ'a-bĕth, } [Heb.] Worshiper of God;
E-lĭz'a-bĕth, } consecrated to
E-lī'zá. } God. [of ELEANOR.
Ĕl'lá. [Gr.] A contraction
Ĕl'len. [Gr.] A diminutive of ELEANOR.
El-vī'rá. [Lat.] White.
Ĕm'e-lĭne, } [O. II. Ger.]
Ĕm'me-līne. } Energetic industrious.
Ĕm'ĭ-ly. [O. II. Ger.] Same as EMELINE.
Ĕm'má. [O. II. Ger.] Same as EMELINE.
Ĕr'nes-tĭne. [Ger.] Feminine and dim. of ERNEST.
Ĕs'ther (ĕs'ter). [Per.] A star; good fortune.
Ĕth'el. [O. II. Ger.] Noble; of noble birth;—the same as ADELA.
Ĕth'e-lĭnd, } [Teut.] Noble
Ĕth'e-lĭn'dá. } snake.
Eu-dō'rá. [Gr.] Good gift.
Eu-gē'nĭ-á. [Gr.] Feminine of EUGENE.
Eu-gē'nĭe. [Gr.] Same as EUGENIA. [Fr. form.]
Eu-nī'çe. [Gr.] Happy victory. [report.
Eu-phē'mĭ-á. [Gr.] Of good
Ē'vá. [Heb.] Life.
E-văn'ġe-līne. [Gr.] Bringing glad news.
Ēve. [Heb.] Same as EVA.
Ĕv'e-lī'ná, } [Heb.] Diminutive of EVA.
Ĕv'e-līne. } [It. form.]

F.

Făn'ny. [Ger.] A diminutive of FRANCES.
Faus-tī'ná. [Lat.] Lucky.

Fe-lĭ'cĭ-á (fe-lĭsh'ĭ-á). [Lat.] Happiness. [Faithful.
Fī-dē'lĭ-á (or -deel'yá). [Lat.]
Flō'rá. [Lat.] Flowers.
Flŏr'ençe. [Lat.] Blooming; flourishing. [FRANCIS.
Frăn'çeṣ. [Ger.] Feminine of
Frĕd'er-ī'cá. [O. II. Ger.] Feminine of FREDERICK.

G.

Ġeôr'ġi-ăn'á, } [Gr.] Feminine
Geôr'ġĭ'ná. } of GEORGE. [GERALD.
Ġĕr'al-dĭne. Feminine of
Ġĕr'trŭde. [O. II. Ger.] Spear-maiden.

H.

Hăn'nah. [Heb.] The same as ANNA.
Hăr'ri-et, } [O. II. Ger.] Feminine and diminutive of HENRY.
Hĕl'en, }
Hĕl'e-ná. } [Gr.] Light.
Hĕn'ri-ĕt'tá. [O. II. Ger.] Fem. and dim. of HENRY. [Fr. form.] [light is in her.
Hĕph'zi-bah. [Heb.] My desire,
Hĕs'ter, } [Per.]
Hĕs'ther (hĕs'ter). } The same as ESTHER.
Ho-nō'rá, } [Lat.] Honorable.
Ho-nō'rĭ-á. }
Hor-tĕn'si-á (hor-tĕn'shĭ-á). [Lat.] A lady gardener.
Hŭl'dah. [Heb.] A weasel.

I.

Ī'dá. [O. II, Ger.] Godlike.
Ī'nez. [Gr.] Same as AGNES. [Portuguese form.]
I-rē'ne. [Gr.] Peaceful.
Iṣ'a-bĕl, } [Heb.] The same as ELIZABETH.
Iṣ'a-bĕl'lá. }

J.

Jāne. [Heb.] Feminine of JOHN;—same as JOANNA.
Ja-nĕt' (in Scot. & U. S.),
Jăn'et (in Eng.). [Heb.] Dim. of JANE.
Jăq'ue-lĭne. [Heb.] Feminine of JAMES. [Fr. form.]
Jeăn, } [Heb.] Same
Jeănne, } as JANE or
Jēan-nĕtte'. } JOAN. [Fr. forms.]
Je-mī'má. [Heb.] A dove.
Je-rṳ'shá. [Heb.] Possessed; married.
Jōan (jōn), } [Heb.] Feminine of JOHN.
Jo-ăn'ná. }

sōn, ôr, dọ, wọlf, tọo, tọok; ûrn, rụe, pụll; ç, ġ, soft; c, ġ, hard; aṣ; eẋist; ṭ as ng; tl.is.

360   COMMON ENGLISH CHRISTIAN NAMES.

Jo-sē'phȧ,) [Heb.] Fem. of
Jō'ṣe-phīne.) JOSEPH.
Joyce. [Lat.] Sportive.
Jū'dith. [Heb.] Praised.
Jūl'i-ȧ (or jūl'yȧ). [Lat.] Feminine of JULIUS.
Jū'li-ȧn'nȧ. [Lat.] Feminine of JULIAN.
Jū'li-ĕt. [Lat.] Diminutive of JULIA. [Fr. form.]

K.

Kăth'a-rīne,) [Gr.]   The
Kăth'er-īne.)   same as CATHARINE.
Ke-tū'rah. [Heb.] Incense.
Ke-zī'ah. [Heb.] Cassia.

L.

Lau'rȧ. [Lat.] A laurel.
Lau-rīn'dȧ. [Lat.] A variation of LAURA.
La-vīn'ĭ-ȧ. [Lat.] Of Latium.
Lē'o-nō'rȧ. [Gr.] The same as ELEANOR.
Le-tī'ti-ȧ (le-tish'ĭ-ȧ). [Lat.] Happiness. [LETITIA.
Lĕt'tiçe. A corruption of
Lĭl'ĭ-an,) [Lat.] Lily.
Lĭl'ly.   )
Lō'is. [Gr.] Good; desirable.
Lou-ī'ṣȧ,) [O. H. Ger.] Feminine of LOUIS.
Lou-īṣe'.)
Lū'çi-ȧ (-shĭ-ȧ). [Lat.] Same as LUCY. [It. form.] [CY.
Lu-çīn'dȧ. [Lat.] Same as LU-
Lu-crē'ti-ȧ (-krē'shĭ-). [Lat.] Gain; otherwise, fight.
Lū'çy. [Lat.] Feminine of LUCIUS.
Lȳd'ĭ-ȧ. [Gr.] A native of Lydia, in Asia Minor.

M.

Mā'bel. [Lat.] A contraction of AMABEL.
Măd'e-līne. [Heb.] Same as MAGDALENE. [Fr. form.]
Măg'da-lēne (properly măg'-da-lē'ne). [Heb.] Belonging to Magdala.
Mar-çĕl'lȧ. [Lat.] Feminine of MARCELLUS. [MARCIUS.
Mär'ci-ȧ (-shĭ-). Feminine of
Mär'ga-ret. [Gr.] A pearl.
Ma-rī'ȧ. [Heb.] The same as MARY. [Lat. form.]
Mā'ri-ănne'. [Heb.] A compound of MARY and ANNE.
Mär'i-on. [Heb.] A French form of MARY.
Mär'thȧ. [Heb.] The ruler of the house; otherwise, sorrowful; melancholy.
Mā'ry. [Heb.] Bitter; otherwise, their rebellion; or star of the sea.
Ma-thil'dȧ (-tĭl'-),) [O. H.
Ma-til'dȧ.   ) Ger.] Mighty battle-maid.
Maud. A contraction of MATHILDA, or of MAGDALENE.
May. The month of MAY, or a diminutive of MARY.
Me-hĕt'a-bel,) [Heb.] Benefited of God.
Me-hĭt'a-ble.)
Mĕl'i-çent. [Lat.] Sweet singer; otherwise [Teut.], work-strength.
Me-lĭs'sȧ. [Gr.] A bee. [ener.
Mĭl'dred. [Ger.] Mild threat-
Mī-răn'dȧ. [Lat.] Admirable.
Mĭr'i-am. [Heb.] Same as MARY. [or laments.
Mȳ'rȧ. [Gr.] She who weeps

N.

Năn'çy. A familiar form of ANNE.
Nō'rȧ. A contraction of HONORA, and of LEONORA.

O.

Oc-tā'vi-ȧ. [Lat.] Feminine of OCTAVIUS.
Ŏl'ĭve,) [Lat.] An olive.
O-līv'ĭ-ȧ.)
O-phē'li-ȧ (or o-feel'yȧ). [Gr.] Serpent.
O-lȳm'pi-ȧ. [Gr.] Heavenly.

P.

Pau-lī'nȧ,) [Lat.] Feminine
Pau-līne'.) of PAULINUS.
Pe-nĕl'o-pe. [Gr.] A weaver.
Phē'be. [Gr.] The same as PHŒBE. [of PHILIP.
Phĭ-lĭp'pȧ. [Gr.] Feminine
Phœ'be. [Gr.] Pure; radiant.
Phȳl'lis. [Gr.] A green bough.
Pŏl'ly. [Eng.] A variation of MOLLY, from MARY. [old.
Pris-çĭl'lȧ. [Lat.] Somewhat

R.

Rā'chel. [Heb.] A ewe.
Re-bĕc'cȧ,) [Heb.] Of enchanting beauty.
Re-bĕk'ah.)
Rhō'dȧ (rō'dȧ). [Gr.] A rose.
Rō'ṣȧ. [Lat.] A rose.
Rōṣ'a-bel,) [Lat.] A fair
Rōṣ'a-bĕl'lȧ.) rose.
Ro-sā'lī-ȧ,) [Lat.] Little and
Rōṣ'a-līe.) blooming rose. [Fr. and It. forms.]
Rōṣ'a-lĭnd. [Lat.] Beautiful as a rose.
Rōṣ'a-mond. [Teut.] Horse-protection; i. e., famous protection. [day.
Rox-ăn'ȧ. [Per.] Dawn of
Rȳth. [Heb.] Beauty.

S.

Sa-lōme' (properly sa-lō'me). [Heb.] Peaceful.
Sā'rȧ,) [Heb.] A princess.
Sā'rah.)
Se-lī'nȧ. [Gr.] Parsley; otherwise, moon.
Se-rē'nȧ. [Lat.] Feminine of SERENUS or SERENO.
Sĭb'yl,) [Gr.] A prophet-
Sī-bȳl'lȧ.) ess.
So-phī'ȧ. [Gr.] Wisdom.
So-phrō'ni-ȧ. [Gr.] Of a sound mind.
Stĕl'lȧ. [Lat.] A star.
Sū'ṣan,
Su-ṣăn'nȧ,) [Heb.] A lily.
Su-ṣăn'nah.)

T.

Tăb'i-thȧ. [Syr.] A gazelle.
Thē'o-dō'rȧ. [Gr.] Feminine of THEODORE.
Thē'o-dō'ṣi-ȧ (-dō'zhĭ-ȧ). [Gr.] Gift of God.
The-rē'ṣȧ. [Gr.] Carrying ears of corn.
Thŏm'a-sȧ (tŏm'-),) [Heb.]
Thŏm'a-ṣīne.) Feminine of THOMAS.
Trȳ-phē'nȧ. [Gr.] Delicate; luxurious. [ous; dainty.
Trȳ-phō'ṣȧ. [Gr.] Luxuri-

U.

Ŭl'ri-cȧ. [O. H. Ger.] Rich.
U-rā'ni-ȧ. [Gr.] Heavenly; — name of one of the Muses.
Ŭr'su-lȧ. [Lat.] She-bear.

V.

Va-lē'ri-ȧ. [Lat.] Feminine of VALERIUS.
Vic-tō'ri-ȧ. [Lat.] Victory; feminine of VICTOR. [pure.
Vir-gĭn'ĭ-ȧ. [Lat.] Virgin;
Vĭv'ĭ-an. [Lat.] Lively.

W.

Wĭl'hel-mī'nȧ. [O. H. Ger.] Fem. of WILHELM, German of William. [of peace.
Wĭn'i-fred. [Teut.] A lover

Z.

Ze-nō'bi-ȧ. [Gr.] Having life from Jupiter.

MODERN GEOGRAPHICAL NAMES.

EXPLANATION OF ABBREVIATIONS AND SIGNS.

Ar.	Arabic.	*pron.*	pronunciation.
Dan.	Danish.	*Russ.*	Russian.
Fr.	French.	*Sp.*	Spanish.
Ger.	German.	*Sw.*	Swedish.
Hung.	Hungarian.	*Syn.*	Synonym.
Port.	Portuguese.	*Turk.*	Turkish.

ă, ĕ, ĭ, ŏ, marked with this sign [̮] underneath, have an obscure sound similar to that of short *u*, but are usually considerably shorter, and, indeed, sometimes are almost mute: thus, Grăt'tan might be pronounced grăt'tŭn or grăt't'n; Hĕl'lĕr, hĕl'-lur or hĕl'l'r, &c.

û, ē, ō are similar in sound to ă, ĕ, ō, but are not to be pronounced so long.

ii is employed to denote the long sound of ă.

ö has a sound similar to *e* in *her;* it may be Anglicized by *e*.

ü represents the sound of the German *ü* and the French *u*, which are uttered with the lips in the position for *oo* and the tongue in that for *ee*; it may be Anglicized by the English *u*.

U, small capital, is intended to represent the sound of the French *eu*, which is pronounced nearly like *u* in the English word *fur*.

B, small capital, is used to denote the sound of *b* in Spanish, often nearly approximating that of *v*.

D, small capital, is intended to represent a sound similar to *th* in *this*.

G and K, small capitals, indicate a peculiar guttural sound of the German *ch*, or one similar to it.

H, small capital, has a sound somewhat similar to the preceding, but more resembling a strongly aspirated *h*.

l (*l* liquid) is to be pronounced like *lli* in *million;* it blends the sounds of *l* and *y* consonant.

M and N, small capitals, are used in the respelling of French words, to represent the nasal sound of the preceding vowel, and are not themselves to be pronounced. The French nasal vowels are ăN, ŏN, ōN, ŭN, being similar in sound to *ăng, ŏng, ōng, ŭng*.

ñ is pronounced like *ni* in *minion*; it blends the sounds of *n* and *y* consonant.

R, small capital, has nearly the sound of *rr* in *terror*, but stronger.

ś is used to indicate that the sound of the *s* is very soft, nearly resembling our *z*. In the middle of a word it should be pronounced like a soft *z*.

W has a sound similar to our *v*. The ˘ over the *w* is intended to point out its alliance to our *v*.

y and *ey* at the end of an unaccented syllable sound like *i* in *pin*.

au and *aw* have the sound of *a* in *fall*.

ĕĕ indicates the clear sound of short *i* before *r*, as in the English words *spirit, miracle*, &c.

ow is to be pronounced like *ow* in *cow*, and *ou* like *ou* in *house*. In respelling for pronunciation, *ow* has been replaced by *ou* wherever the former combination would be liable to be pronounced like ō, as in *grow, tow*, &c.

☞ The other marked letters are the same as those used in the body of the Dictionary.

MODERN GEOGRAPHICAL NAMES.

A.

Aa (ä)
Aalborg (ŏl'boRG)
Abbeville (Fr.) (ăb'-vēl')
Ab'be-ville (S. C.)
Ab'er-brŏth'ọck, or Xr'brŏath
Ab'er-deen' [gă'nĭ]
Abergavenny (ăb'ẹr-
Ab'ẹr-ĭst'with (th as in thin)
Abomey (ab'o-mā')
Abookeer, or Abukir (ä-boo-keer')
Ab-se'cọm
Ab'ys-sĭn'ĭ-ạ (ko)
Acapulco (ä-kä-pool'-
Ac'co-mac' [cen'
Ach-een', or Atch-
Acqui, or Aqui (ä'kwoe)
Acquia (ạ-kwī'ạ)
Acre (ä'kr or ā'kẹr)
Aden (ä'dẹn; Arab. pron. ä'dẹn)
Adige (ä'de-jc)
Adlerberg (ä'dlẹr-bĕRG')
Adour (ä'dooR')
Adria (ä'dre-ä)
Adrianople (ad'rĭ-ạn-
Ad'rĭ-at'ĭc [o'pl)
Ægean (Sea) (e-jee'an)
Afghanistan (ăf-găn'-ĭs-tăn')
Ag'ĭn-cōurt (or ä'-zhăN'kooR')
Agulhas (ä-gool'yäs)
Ah'med-nug'gur
Aix (äks)
Aix-la-Chapelle (äks-lä-shä'pel')
Ajaccio (ä-yät'cho)
Akerman (ä'kẹr-män')
Al'ạ-bä'mạ, or Al'ạ-bä'mạ
Alamo (ä'lä-mo)
Aland (ä'land) (Sw. Åland, ō'länd)
A-lap'ạ-hạ'
Al-bä'nĭ-ạ
Albano (äl-bä'no)
Albans, St. (sẹnt awl'-bunz)
Albany (awl'bạ-nỹ)
Al'be-marle (Eng.)
Al'be-marle' (U. S.)
Albuquerque (äl-boo-kĕR/kā or al'boo-kĕrk)
Alcala (äl-kä-lä') [rä]
Alcantara (äl-kän'tä-
Al'dẹr-ney
Alem Tejo, or Alen-Tejo (ä-leN-tā'zho)
Alençon (ạ-leN'sọN'; Fr. pron. ä/lŏN'sŏN')

Alessaudria (äl-ĕs-sän'dre-ä)
Aleutinn (ạ-lu'shĭ-ạn)
Al'ẹx-ạn-drẹt'tạ
Al'ẹx-ạn'drĭ-ạ
Algarve (äl-gaR'vä)
Al-ge'rĭ-ạ [rạs)
Algeziras (al-jẹ-zee'-
Al-gierạ'
Al-go'ạ (usually pron. by the English äl'-go-ạ)
Al-ī-cänt', or Alicante (ä-le-kän'tā)
Allahabad (äl'läh-hạ-
Al'le-ghā'ny [bäd')
Almaden (äl-mä-bĕn')
Almeida (äl-mä'e-dä)
Alnwick, or Alenwick (an'nĭk)
Alsace (äl'säss')
Altai (äl-tī')
Altamaha (awl'tạ-mạ-haw')
Al'tọn
Altona (äl/tọ-nä)
Altorf (äl'toRf), or Altdorf
Am'ạ-zọn
Am-boy'
Am-boy'nạ
A-mĕr'ĭ-cạ
Amherst (am'ẹrst)
Amiens (am/ĭ-ẹnz; Fr. pron. ü/me-ŏN')
Am'mọ-noo'suck
Amoo, or Amou (ä-moo') [moor')
Amoor, or Amour (ä-
A-moy'
Am'stẹr-dam'
An-ạ-deer', or Anadir
Anahuac (ä-nä-wäk')
A-năm' or Au'năm'
Andalusia (an'dạ-lu'-shĭ-ạ; Sp. pron. än-dä-loo-thee'ä)
An'dạ-man'
Andes (an'dēz)
Andorra (än-doR'Rä)
An'do-vẹr
An'dros-cog'gin
Angers (an'jẹrz)
Anglescy, or Anglesea (ang'gl-se)
An-go'lạ [too'rä)
Angostura (än-gos-
An'gus
Anhalt (än'hält)
Anholt (än'hŏlt)
An'jọu (Fr. pron. ŏN'-zhoo')
Annagh (an-nä')
An-nap'o-lis
Ann A-run'del
Annecy (än'se')
Annobon (än'no-bŏn')
Anspach (äns'päg)

Autibes (ŏN'tecb')
An/tĭ-cos'tĭ
An-tiō'tạm
Antigua (an-te'gạ)
Antilles (än-teel' or ŏN'teel')
An'tĭ-och [kce'ä)
Antioquia (än-te-o-
Ant'wẹrp
Apache (ä-pä'chä)
Ap'ẹn-nĭneș
Ap'pạ-lach'ee
Ap'pạ-lach'ĭ-co'lạ
Apurimac (ä-poo-re-mäk')
Aquila (ä'kwe-lä)
Arabia (ạ-rā'bĭ-ạ)
Arad (ŏr'ŏd')
Xr'ạ-gọn (Sp. pron. ä-rä-gōn')
Xr'ạl
Xr'ạ-rat
Ar-cot' [(an'den')
Ar'dẹn, or Ardeunes
Arequlpa (ä-rä-kee'pä)
Argenteuil (aR'zhŏN'-tul')
Ar'gen-tine Re-pub'lic
Argostoli (aR-gos'to-lee) [zĭl')
Argyle, or Argyll (aR-
Arien (ä-re'kä)
Ariége (ä're-āzh')
Xr'ĭ-zo'nạ
Ar-kan'sạs (formerly pron. aR'kạn-saw)
Arles (arlz; Fr. pron. aRl)
Armagh (ar-mä')
Armagnac (aR'män'-
Ar-me'nĭ-ạ [yäk')
A-roos'tŏok
Arpino (aR-pee'no)
Xr'ra-can', or Aracan
Ar-rap'ạ-hōc. Syn. Arapahoe. [räs')
Xr'rạs (Fr. pron. är'-
Artois (ạR'twä')
Xr'un-del (Eng.)
A-run'dẹl (U. S.)
As'ạph
Aschaffenburg (ạ-shaf'fen-burg)
Ascoli (äs'ko-lee)
A-shan'tee, or Xsh'-an-tee'
Asb'tạ-bu'lạ [lŏt)
Ash'ue-lot (ash'we-
Asia (ā'shĭ-ạ, not ā'-zhĭ-ạ)
As-sam'
Assaye (äs-sī or as-sä')
As-sĭn'nĭ-boĭn'
Assisi (äs-see'see)
Asterabad (äs'tẹR-ạ-bäd')
Astl (äs'tee)
Astorga (äs-toR'gä)

As-to'rĭ-ạ [trakhan
As-tra-can', or As-
Asturias (äs-too're-äs)
Atacama (ä-tä-kä'mä)
Atchafalaya (atch-af-ạ-lī'ạ)
Ath'ạ-pes'cōw, or Ath'ạ-bas'cạ
Ath-lone'
Ath'ọl, or Ā'thọl
Athy (ạ-thī')
At'lạs
Aube (ōb)
Auchinleck (af'flek)
Aug.'burg
Augustine, St. (sẹnt aw'gus-teen)
Aurillac (o're'yäk' or ō'rēl'yäk')
Aurungabad (ō-rung'-gạ-bäd')
Aus'tẹr-litz (-lĭts; Gẹr. pron. ows'tẹr-lĭts)
Aus/tral-ā'sĭ-ạ (-ā'-shĭ-ạ)
Aus-trā'lĭ-ạ
Aus'trĭ-ạ
Autun (ō'tŭN')
Auvergne (ō-vĕRn' or ō'vẹRñ')
Aux Cayes (ō kā)
Auxerre (ō'sĕR')
Auxonne (ōks'ōn'), or Aussouc (ōs'sŏn')
Ava (ä'vä)
Avignon (ä/vēn'yŏN')
Avon (ā'vọn)
Ayr (âr)
Ayrshire (âr'shĭr)
Az'of, Azoph, or Azov
Azores (ạ-zōrz' or a-zō'rez)

B.

Bä'bel-man'del, or, more correctly, Bab'-el-man'deb
Badajos (bạd-n-hōs')
Baden (bä'dẹn or bad'ẹn)
Bagdad (bäg-däd' or bag'dad); written also Bagdat.
Bạ-hä'mạs
Bahia (bä-e'ä)
Baïkal (bī'käl')
Baireuth (bī'rụth; Gẹr. pron. bī'roit)
Bal'ạ-ghauts'
Bul'ä-klā'vä
Balaton, more correctly Bálatony (bŏ'-law-toñ) [sel.
Bále (bäl). Syn. Ba-
Bal'e-ār'ic (Islands)
Balize (bä-leez')

MODERN GEOGRAPHICAL NAMES.

Balkan (bäl-kän')
Balkh (bälk); *written also* Bulkh. [spaw]
Ballston Spa (spä or Bal-mŏr'al
Bal'tic [tĭ-mŏr) Bal'tĭ-mōre (or bawl'- Banff (bamf); *sometimes written* Bamff.
Bang'kok' [ğĕr)
Bangor (Eng.) (bang'- Ban'gôr (U. S.)
Ban'nock-burn'
(Ban'tam'
Lapaume (bä'pŏm')
Barataria (bä-rä-tä'- rē-ä)
Barbados, *or* Barbadoes (bar-bā'dōz)
Bar-ce-lo'na (*or* barthā-lo'nä)
Barége (bä'rŭzh')
Barita (bä-ree'tä) *or* Barrita
Barnaul (ban-nowl')
Bar're (*in two syllables*)
Basel (bä'zel) (Fr. Bâle, *or* Basle, bäl)
Ba-ta'vĭ-a (roozh)
Baton Rouge (bat'un Ba-vā'rĭ-a
Bayeux (bä'yuh')
Bayonne (bä'yon')
Bayreuth. *See* Baireuth.
Bel'ed - el - Jer - ced' ; *written also* Beled-el-Jerid, Biled-ul-Gerid, &c.
Bel-fâst' (Ireland)
Bel'fâst (Maine)
Belgium (bel'jĭ-um)
Bel'grade'
Belle Isle, *or* Bellisle (bel-īl')
Belloochistan (belloo'chĭs-tän')
Benares (ben-ä'rĕs)
Bengal (ben-gawl')
Benguela (ben-gä'lä)
Benin (ben-een')
Ben-Lo'mond
Ben-Ne'vis
Berg'en
Berk'shire (bĕrk-leen')
Ber'lin (*Ger. pron.*
Ber-mu'dåz, *or* Bermoo'thes
Bern, *or* Berne (*Fr.*

and Ger. pron. bĕrn *or* bŭrn) [rĭk)
Ber'wick (Eng.) (bĕr'- Ber'wick (U. S.)
Besançon (b'zŏn'sŭn')
Bexar (*Sp. pron.* bāhar'; *often pron. by the Texans,* bęh-har' *or* bar)
Beyroot, Berut, *or* Bairout (bä'root; *Turk. pron.* bī'root)
Bilbao (bil-bä'o ; *often written and pronounced in Eng.*, Bil'bo-a)
Biled-ul-Gerid (bĭl'- ęd-ōōl-jer-eed')
Bil'ler-ic-a
Bing'en
Binghamton (bing'- um-tun)
Bĭr'ma. *Syn.* Burma.
Birmingham (bĭr'- ming-um)
Bis/cay
Blanc, Mont (mŏn blŏn) *or* Mount Blanc.
Blenheim (blen'im)
Bogota (bo-go-tä')
Bo-he'mĭ-a
Bokhára (bo-kä'rä), *or* Bu-cha'rĭ-a
Bo-liv'ĭ-a *Sp. pron.* bo-lee've-ä)
Bologna (bo-lōn'-yä)
Bomarsund (bō'mar- soond')
Bom-bāy'
Bo'na Vis'ta, *or* Bo'a Vis'ta
Bootan (boo-tän'), *or* Bhootan
Bordeaux (bon'dō'), *or* Bourdeaux (boordō')
Borgne (born)
Bor'ne-o
Bor-noo' ; *written also* Bornou [no)
Borodino (bor-o-dee'- Bos'po-rus ; *less correctly written* Bosphorus.
Both'nĭ-a
Boulogne (boo-lōn' ; *Fr. pron.* boo'lōn')
Bourbon (boor'bun ; *Fr. pron.* boor'bōn')
Bourbon (Ky.) (bŭr'- bun)
Bourbonnes-les-Bains (boor-bōn'-lä bāN')
Bourdeaux. *See* Bordeaux.
Bowdoin (bo'dęn)

Brabant (brä'bant *or* brä-bant')
Bra-gun'za
Brah'ma-poot'ra, *or* Bŭr'ram-poo'ter
Bra-zil' (*Port. pron.* brä-zeel')
Bra-zo'rĭ-a
Brazos (brä'zos *or* brä'sōs)
Brĕad-al'bane
Brech'in (brek'in)
Bree'on
Breda (brā-dä')
Brem'en (*or* brā'men) (Europe)
Brem'en (U. S.)
Breslau (brĕs'law *or* brĕs'lou)
Bretagne (brch-tän').
Syn. Brittany.
Breton (brit'un) (Cape)
Briançon (bre'ŏn-sŏn')
Britain (brit'un *or* brit'n)
Brit'ta-ny (Fr. Bretagne, brch-tän')
Brook'line
Brŏok'lýn [brick)
Brück (brük, *almost* Bry'ģęe (*Fr. pron.* brüzh)
Brünn (brün *or* brün)
Bruns'wick
Brus'sels (Fr. Bruxclls, brü'sel')
Bu-cha'rĭ-a. *Syn.* Bokhara. [churest
Bu'chq-rest', *or* Bu- Bu'da (*Hung. pron.* boo'dŭh') [vis'tä)
Buena Vista (bwä'nä Buenos Ayres (bo'nus ä'riz ; *Sp. pron.* bwā'noss ī'rĕs)
Bulgaria (bōōl-gä'rĭ-a)
Bŭlkh. *Syn.* Balkh.
Bur'gun-dy
Bŭr'ram-poo'ter. *Syn.* Brahmapootra.
Bushire (boo-sheer')
Byzantium (bĭ-zau'- shī-um)

C.

Ca-bool' (*called by the natives* Kä'bŭl)
Cä'diz (*Sp. pron.* kä'- dĕth)
Caen (kŏn)
Caermarthen (kęr- mar'then) [von)
Caernarvon (kęr-nar'- Caf-fra'rĭ-a
Cagliari (käl'yä-re)
Ca-haw'ba
Cai'ro (Egypt)

Cäi'ro (U. S.) [bre-ä] Ca-la'/brĭ-a (*or* kä-lä'- Calais (kăl'iss ; *Fr. pron.* kä'lä')
Cal-cut'ta
Cal'ī-cut
Cal'ī-for'nĭ-a
Callao (käl-lä'o *or* käl-yä'o)
Cam-bay'
Cam-bo'dĭ-a, *or* Camboçe'
Cam'bray, *or* Cambrai (*Fr. pron.* brä-dä')
Cambridge (käm'brĭj)
Campagna (käm-pän'- yä)
Campeachy (kam-pee'- che)
Can'a-da
Canajoharie (kan'a-jo- hā're)
Canandaigua (kan'an- dā'gwa)
Canaries (ka-nā'recz)
Ca-nav'er-al
Can-da-har', *or* Kandahar
Cand'ī-a, *or* Crete
Cannes (kän)
Canterbury (kan'ter- ber-e)
Can'ton (China)
Can'ton (U. S.)
Cape Breton (käp brit't'n *or* brit'ŭn)
Cap'u-a
Ca-rac'as, *or* Caraccas
Caramania (kăr'a-mä'- ne-a)
Cardenas (kar'dä'näs)
Cär'ib-be'an Sea
Ca-rin'thī-a
Carlisle (kar-lîl')
Carls'bad, *or* Karlsbad (*Ger. pron.* karls'- bät)
Carlscrona (karls- kroo'na); *or* Carlscroon
Carlsruhe, *or* Karlsruhe (karls'roo)
Car-nat'ic
Carolina (kăr'o-lī'na)
Carpathian (kar-pä'- thī-an)
Car'pen-tā'rĭ-a
Carpentras (kan'pŏn'- trä')
Carrara (kär-ä'rä)
Cartagena (kur'ta-je'- na ; *Sp. pron.* kan- tä-hā'nä)
Cashmere, *or* Kashmire (kash-meer')
Cas'pi-an [k'ree)
Cassiquiari (kä-se-ke- Castile (kas-teel')

da, wolf, too, took ; ŭrn, rue, pull ; ç, ģ, *soft* ; c, g, *hard* ; aṣ ; exist ; n *as* ng ; this (see p. 361).

MODERN GEOGRAPHICAL NAMES.

Castine (kas-teen′)
Cat′a-lo′nI-a
Cat′e-gat, or Kattegat
Caubul (kaw-bool′). *Syn.* Cabool.
Cau′ca-sus
Cayenne (kI-en′)
Cayuga (kā-yoo′ga)
Cebu (se-boo′). *Syn.* Zebn.
Cefalu (chĕf-ä-loo′)
Celebes (sel′e-biz)
Cen′is (or se′ne′)
Ceph′a-lo′nI-a
Cerigo (chĕr′e-go)
Ceuta (sū′tā; *Sp. pron.* thā′oo-tä)
Cévennes (sā′ven′)
Ceylon (see′lon or sī-lōn′)
Chagres (chä′grĕs)
Chaleur (shä-loor′)
Chalons (shä′lōn′)
Chambéry (shŏx′bā′ree′)
Chamouny (shä′moo′-ne′) [päx′]
Champagne (shŏx′-
Champaigne (shampän′)
Chain-plain′
Chandeleur (shan-de-loor′)
Chan′der-na-göre′
Chang-hai. *Syn.* Shang-hai.
Chantilly (shän-tĭl′-lee ; *Fr. pron.* shŏx′tĕl′ye′ or shŏx′te′yā′)
Chapultepec (chäpool-tä-pek′)
Chareute (shä′rŭxī′)
Chartres (shaut·r)
Chat′ta-hoo′che
Chat′ta-noo′ga
Chaudière(shō′de-ĕx′)
Chaumont (N. Y.) (sho′mo′)
Chautauqua (shatäw′kwa)
Chebucto (she-buk′to)
Chelmsford (chemz′-furd) [num]
Cheltenham (chelt′-
Chemung (she-mŭng′)
Chenango (she-nang′go)
Che-raw′
Cherburg (sher′burg or shĕr′boor′)
Cher′o-kee′
Chertsey (ches′se)
Ches′a-peake
Che-sun′cook
Cheviot (chiv′e-ut)
Cheyenne (she-en′)
Chicago (she-kaw′go)

Chick′a-hom′I-ny
Chick′a-mau′ga
Chick′a-pee′
Chick′a-saws
Chihuahua (che-wā′wä)
Chili (chil′le)
Chil′lī-coth′e
Chillon (she′yŏx′ or shil′lon)
Chiloe (che-lo-ā′, *almost* chil-way′)
Chimborazo (chim′borā′zo)
Chi′na
Chinchilla (chin′-cheel′yä)
Chin In′dI-a [num]
Chippenham (chip′-
Chippewa (chip′pe-wä)
Chip′pe-way
Chiswick (chiz′ik)
Chiriqui (che-re-kee′)
Chowan (chō-wän′)
Christiania (kris-te-ä′ne-ä)
Chudleigh (chŭd′lee)
Chuquisaca (choo-kesä′kä) [nah′tI)
Cincinnati (sin′sinCircassia (ser-kash′I-a)
CI′ren-cĕs′ter (*commonly pron.* sis′e-ter *or* sis′in-ter)
Civita Vecchia (chee′vc-tä vĕk′ke-ä)
Clogher (klŏh′ger)
Clon-mell′
Coango (ko-ang′go)
Coblentz (koh′lents) (Ger. Coblenz, ko′blĕnts)
Co′burg (*Ger. pron.* ko′bŭora)
Cochin (ko-cheen′)
Co′chin Chi′na
Cognac (kŏn-yäk′)
Cohahnila, or Coahuila (ko-ä-wee′lä)
Co-im′bra (or ko-eem′-
brä)
Coleraine (kōl-rān′)
Cologne (ko-lōn′)
Colombia (ko-lom′be-ä)
Col′on-sa, or Col′onsay′
Colorado (kol′o rä′do)
Co-lum′bI-a
Com′o-rin
Com′o-ro
Complègne (kŏx′peāñ′) [maw]
Conemaugh (kon′e-
Con′es-to′ga
Congo (kong′go)
Counaught (kon′nawt)
Connecticut (konnet′I-kut)

Con-stan′tI-no′ple
Cooch Bahar(bä-har′)
Coos (ko-os′)
Co′pen-hā′gen (Danish Kjöbenhavn, kyö-ben-hown′)
Cor-dil′ler-as (*Sp. pron.* koR-dĕl-yā′räs)
Cor′do-va, or Cordoba
Co-re′a [fu)
Corfu (kor-foo′ or kor′-
Cŏr′inth
Corpus Chris′ti (kor′pus kris′te)
Corrientes (koR-Recēn′tĕs)
Cor′si-ca
Co-run′na (Sp. Coruña, ko-roon′yä)
Costa Rica (kos′tä ree′kä)
Cotopaxi (ko-topaks′e; *Sp. pron.* ko-to-päh′se)
Coventry (kuv′en-trĭ)
Cŏv′ing-ton
Cowes (kowz)
Cracow (krä′ko)
Crécy (kres′se ; *Fr. pron.* krū′se′)
Cre-mo′uä (*It. pron.* krä-mo′nä)
Crī-me′a (Russ. Krim.)
Croatia (kro-ä′shi-a)
Croix, St. (kroi). *Syn.* Santa Cruz.
Cronstadt (krŏn′stät)
Csongrád (chon-gräd′)
Cu′bä (*Sp. pron.* koo′-
Cul′pep-per [bä)
Cul-rōss′ (or koo′rōs)
Cumana (koo-mä-nä′)
Curaçoa (ku′ra-sō′)
Cŭr′ri-tuck′
Cuzco (koos′ko)

D.

Dahomey (dah′ho-mä′)
Da-ko′ta [le-ä]
Dalecarlia (dä-le-kaR′-
Dalles (dälz) [shI-a)
Dalmatia (dal-mā′-
Dalton (dawl′ton)
Dant′zic (dant′sik) (Ger. Danzig, dänt′sig)
Dan′ube [nelz′)
Dardanelles (dar′da-
Darien (Ga.) (dā′re-en)
Darien, Isthmus of (dä-re-ĕn′)
Darmstadt (daRm′stät)
Dartmouth (dart′-muth)

Dec′can, or Dek′kan
Del′a-go′a
Delaware (del′a-war)
Delft (*every letter should be pronounced*.)
Delhi, or Dehli (Hindostan) (del′lee) [a)
Dem′be-a (or dem-bee′-
Demerara (dem′er-ä′-
ra) [shir)
Denbighshire (den′be-
Deptford (det′furd)
Dĕr′by (or dar′bI)
Derne (dŭr′ng or dŭr′-
nch)
Des Moines (de moin)
Des′sau (Ger. pron. des′sow)
De-troit′
Devises (de-vī′ziz)
Dhawalaghiri (däwol′a-gĕr′re)
Dieppe (dyep or de-ep′)
Dijon (de′zhŏx′)
Dinan (de′nŏx′)
Dinant (de′nŏx′ or denant′)
Dnieper (nee′per ; Russ. pron. dnyĕp′-
er)
Dniester (nees′ter ; Russ. pron. dnyĕs′-
ter)
Do′fra-fl-ĕld′. *Syn.* Dovrefield.
Domingo (do-ming′go)
Dominica (dom′e-nee′-
ka)
Done′as-ter
Donegal (don-e-gawl′)
Dongola (dong′go-la)
Dor′ches-ter
Dor-dogne (dor′dōn′; *Fr. pron.* dor′dōñ′)
Douai, or Douay (loo′-
fi′) : *sometimes written* Doway.
Doubs (doobz or doo)
Douro (doo′ro)
Do′vre-fl-eld′ (Norw. Daavrefjeld, dȳvre-
fyeld′)
Dowlatabad (dow′la-
ta-bäd′)
Drin (dreen), or Drino (dree′no)
Drogheda (drŏh′ue-da)
Drontheim (dront′Im)
Dub′lin
Dubuque (du-bōok′)
Duero (doo-ā′ro or dwä′ro)
Dulwich (dul′Ij)
Dum-blane′ [freess′)
Dumfries (dum-
Dun-bar′
Dundalk (dun-dawk′)
Dun-dass′

ā, ē, &c., *long*; ă, ĕ, &c., *short*; cāre, fär, ăsk, all, what; ēre, veil, tĕrm; pīque, fīrm ; sōn, ŏr,

MODERN GEOGRAPHICAL NAMES. 365

Dun-dee′
Dunfermline (dum-fer′lin)
Dungeness (dun-jg-ness′)
Dunwich (dun′ĭtch)
Duquesne (du-kān′)
Durham (dŭr′um)
Dus′sel-dorf (Ger. Düsseldorf, düs′sęl-doʀf′)
Dwī′na

E.

Ecuador (ek-wä-dōʀ′)
Ediuburgh (ed′ĭn-bŭr-ruh); *written also, but less properly,* Edinboro′.
Ed′ĭs-to
Egypt (e′jipt)
Ekatarinburg (ŭ-kä′tä-reen-booʀg′)
Elbe (elb ; *Ger. pron.* el′bçh)
El-boorz′, or El-brooz′; *written also* Elburz *and* Elbrouz
El′ğin-shire
El Paso del Norte (el pä′ʀo del noʀ′tä)
El′sĭ-nore′, *or* Elsi-neur (el′se-nŭr′)
England (ing′gland)
Entre Douro e Minho (en′trä doo′ro ū meen′yo)
Entre Rios (en′trī ree′-ōs)
Erfurt (ĕʀ′fōbʀt)
Erie (ē′ree)
Essequibo (ĕs-sĕ-kē′-bo)
Estremadura (es-trä-mą-doo′rä) [tĕz)
Euphrates (yṳ-frā′-
Europe (u′rup)

F.

Faeröe (fä′ro *or* fä′rö-ę)
Falkirk (fawl′kirk)
Falkland (fawk′land)
Falmouth (făl′muth)
Falster (făl′stĕr *or* făl′stęr)
Färoe (fā′ro *or* fā′rö-ę)
Fayal (fi-awl′ ; *Port. pron.* fī-ăl′)
Fee′jee. *Syn.* Fiji.
Fermanagh (fęr-man′ą)
Fŭr′ney (*or* fĕʀ′nü′)
Ferrara (fĕʀ-nä′rä)
Ferrol (fĕʀ-ʀōl′)
Fezzan (fĕz′zän′)
Fiji (*pronounced, and*

often written, Fee′-jee)
Finisterre, Cape (fin-ĭs-tĕr′)
Fin′land
Fiume (fyoo′mä)
Flan′derz
Flor′ence
Flo′rës
Flor′ī-dą
Fontainebleau (fōɴ′-tän′blō′)
Fon-te-noy′ (*Fr. pron.* fōɴt′nwä′)
For-mo′są
Fotheringay (foth′er-ing-gā′)
France (fransş)
Frank′fọrt
Freiburg (frī′burg *or* frī′booʀG)
Friä′land
Frio (free′o)
Frische Haff (frish′çh häf)
Friuli (free-oo′lee ; *It. pron.* free′oo-lee)
Frob′ish-ęr′s Strait
Frod′sham
Fulda (fŭl′dä)
Funchal (foon-shäl′)
Fü′nçn

G.

Gaeta (gō-ā′tä)
Galapagos (gal′ą-pā′-gus)
Gal′ą-shiels′
Galatz (gä′läts)
Ga-le′ną
Galicia (gą-lish′ī-ą)
Gal-lip′o-li
Gal′lī-po-lĭs′ (Ohio)
Gal′lo-wāy
Gal′ves-tọn
Galway (gawl′wā)
Gan′gĕs
Garda (gaʀ′dä)
Gardiner (gard′ner)
Garonne (gä-ron′)
Gas′co-nŷ
Gaspe (gäs′pā′)
Gelders, *or* Guelders (ğel′dęrz)
Ģen′ę-see′
Ģe-ne′vą
Ģen′o-ą
Ģeör′ği-ą
Ğer′mą-nŷ
Geysers (ği′sęrz)
Ghauts (gawts)
Ghent (ğent)
Gī-brąl′tąr
Gila (He′lä)
Gilolo (He-lo′lo)
Gizeh (ǵe′zęh *or* ǵee′-zęh)
Glas′gōw

Glen-elg′
Gloucester (glos′tęr)
Glückstadt (glük′stät)
Gmünd (gnŭnt), *or* Gmünden (gmŭn′-dęn)
Gmuud (gmŏönt)
Gol-con′dą
Gona′ves, Les (lā go′-ui′ǵv′ *or* gō-nīv′)
Gon′dar
Görlitz (gŭr′lits, *almost* gŭr′litz)
Gotha (go′tä)
Goth′lạnd
Göttingen, *or* Goettin-gen (ǵet′ting-ęn *or* got′ting-ęn)
Gram′pi-ąn
Granada (grą-nä′dä)
Gratiot (grash′ī-ot)
Grätz, *or* Graetz (grets)
Gravelines (gräv′lĕn′)
Gravesend (grävz′end′)
Great Britain (brit′un *or* brit′n)
Greenwich (grĭn′ŭj)
Grenada (grę-nä′dą)
Grenoble (gręn-ob′l *or* gręh-nō′b′l)
Grisons (grę′zōɴ′)
Gross-Wardein (grōs-ʷaʀ′dīn)
Gro′tọn (Eng.)
Grō′tọn (U. S.)
Guadalajara, *or* Guadalaxara (gwä-dä-lä-Hä′rä)
Guadaloupe (gaw/dą-loop′ *or* gä′dä-loop′)
Gundalupe (gwä-dä-loo′pä *or* gäw′dą-loop′)
Guadalquivir (gaw′-dąl-kwiv′ęr ; *Sp. pron.* gwä-däl-ke-veeʀ′)
Guadiana (gaw′de-ä′-ną *or* gwä-De-ä′nä)
Guarda (gwaʀ′dä)
Guardaful (gwąʀ′dą-fwee *or* gar′dą-fwe′)
Guatemala (gaw′te-mä′lą *or* gwä-tō-mä′lä)
Guayaquil (gwī-ä-keel′)
Guaymas (gwī′mäs)
Guernsey (gĕrn′ze)
Guiana (ge-ä′ną), *or* Guyana
Guienne (ğe′ĕn′)
Guildford (ğil′fọrd)
Guinea (ğin′e)
Gulugamp (găɴ′ɡōɴ′)
Guyandott (ğī-an-dot′)
Gwalior (gwä′lī-or)

H.

Haarlem, Haerlem, *or* Harlem (har′lęm)
Had-rą-maut′
Hague (haig), The
Haïnan (hī-nan′) [dee)
Hakodadi (hä-ko-dä′-
Häleğ-ōw′ęn
Hal′ī-fax
Halle (häl′lęh)
Hallowell (hol′o-wel)
Ham′burg (Ger. pron hām′booʀg)
Hamp′shire [no′ver)
Han′o-ver (Ger. han-
Hartleur (haʀ-flŭʀ′)
Hartz, *or* Hurz (harts)
Harwich (hăr′rij)
Hat′tęr-ąs
Hą-van′ą, *or* Havanna
Haverhill (Eng.) (hav′er-il) [vęr-il)
Haverhill (Mass.) (hā′-
Havre de Grace (hav′çr de gräss)
Hawaii (hä-wī′ee)
Hayti, *or* Haiti (hā′tī)
Hebrides (heb′rī-dēz)
Heel′lą (bēRą′)
Heidelberg (hī′dçl-Heilbronn (hīl-bron′)
Hę-lę′ną (St.)
Helvoetsluys (hel′voot-sloīs′)
Hen-lo′pęn
Hen-rī′ko
Herat (her-ät′)
Hĕr′cu-lā′ue-um
Hĕr′e-fọrd
Hĕr′kī-męr
Herrnhut (bĕʀn′hoot)
Hertford (Eng.) (har′-furd)
Hertford (U. S.) (hŭrt′-furd)
Hesse Cas′sęl
Hesse Darmstadt (hess daʀm′stät)
Highlands (hī′landz) ; *commonly pronounced* hee′landz *by the Scotch.*
Himmaleh (him-mä′-lą), *or* Him-ą-lī′yą
Hin-dọ-stan′, *or* Indo-stan′
His-pan-ī-o′lą
Ho-ang′ho (*pronounced almost* whang′ho)
Hob′ar-tọn *or* Hob′ar-tọn
Ho′bō-kęn
Hochheim (hō′hīm *or* hōk′hīm)
Hofwyl (hof′wīl), *or* Hof-weil (hof′wīl)

---

dọ, wọlf, tōō, tŏŏk; ûrn, rụe, pụll ; ç, ğ, *soft* ; e, ğ, *hard* ; ąz ; eẋist; ɴ *as* ng; this (see p. 361).

Hol'land
Holstein (hŏl'stĭn)
Hol'y-head [rȧs]
Honduras (hon-doo'-
Honfleur (hŏN'flŭʀ' or
  ŏN'flŭʀ')
Hŏn'ī-tŏn [loo]
Honolulu (ho-no-loo'-)
Hoog'ly [tŏn'lk]
Housatonic (hoo'sȧ-
Hué (hoo-ā')
Huelva (wĕl'vä)
Huerta (wĕʀ'tä)
Huesca (wes'kĕ)
Hungary (hung'gȧ-rī)
Hu'rȯn [büd']
Hyderabad (hī'dẹr-ȧ-
Hythe (hīth)

I.

Ice'land
Icolmkill (ĭk'om-kĭl').
  Syn. Ioua.
I'dȧ-ho
Ilfracombe (ĭl'frȧ-
  koom) [-nol']
Illinois (ĭl-lĭ-noiz' or
Il-lȳr'ī-ȧ
Imola (ē'mo-le)
In'dī-ȧ [nȧ]
In'dī-an'ȧ (or in-dī-ä'-
In'dī-an-ap'ȯ-lis
Indies (in'dĭz)
Ingolstadt (ĭng'ol-stät
  or ing'gol-stät')
Innspruck (ĭnss-
  prŏok), or Inns-
  brück (inns'brük)
Interlachen (ĭn'tẹr-
  läx'ẹn)
In'vẹr-ä'ry [lŏg'ī]
Inverlochy (ĭn'vẹr-
In-vẹr-ness'
Ioua (e-o'nȧ)
Ionia (ī-o'nī-ȧ)
I'o-wȧ
Ir-kootsk'
Iroquois (ĭr-o-kwoy')
Isère (e'zĕʀ')
Iṡ'ling-tȯn
Ismail (is-mä-eel'
Ispahan (is-pȧ-hän') or
  Isfahan
Ī'tȧ-ly
I-u'kȧ [or Ibiza
Iviça, Iviza (e-vee'sä),
Ivrea (e-vrā'ä)
Ivry (īv'rī or ēv'rē')

J.

Jacquemel, or Jacmel
  (zhäk'mel')
Jaf'fȧ (or yäf'fä)
Jalapa (hä-lä'pä)

Jalisco (Hä-lees'ko or
  Hä-lĭs'ko)
Jamaica (jȧ-mā'kȧ)
Jȧ-pan'
Japura (Hä-poo'rä)
Java (jä'vȧ or jă'vȧ)
Jeddo (yed'do) [nē]
Jen'ȧ (Ger. pron. yä'-
Jersey (jẽr'zĭ)
Je-rŋ'sȧ-lem
Jesso, or Iesso (yes'so)
Jol'ī-bȧ, or Djoliba
Jonköping, or Jonkö-
  ping (yon'chö-ping,
  almost yon'chep-ing)
Jorullo (Ho-rool'yo ;
  often pron. Ho-roo'-
  yo)
Ju'ȧn Fẹr-nan'dĕz
Ju'ȧn, Saint (Sp. San
  Juan. săn Hoo-än'
  or sän Hwän)
Jungfrau (yōŏng'-
Ju'nī-at'ȧ [frow)
Jut'land

K.

Kal'ȧ-mȧ-zoo'
Kalusz (kä'loosh)
Kamieniec (käm'yen'-
  yets')
Kamt-chat'kȧ, or
  Kamt-schat'kȧ
Kanawha (kȧ-naw'wȧ)
Kan'dȧ-har'
Kankakee (kan-kaw'-
  kee)
Kan'sas
Kara (kä'rä)
Kash-gar', or Cashgar
Kȧ-tah'din
Kä'trine, or Kat'rine
Keighly (keeth'le)
Kelat (kẹl-ät'), or Ke-
Ken'ne-beck' [lath
Ken'ne-bunk'
Ken-tuck'y
Ke'o-kuk' [Land
Kerguelen (kẽrg'e-lẹn)
Kerman (kẹr-män')
Khartoom or Khar-
  toum (ʟar-toom')
Khiva, or Kheeva
  (κen'vä) [sän')
Khorassan (κo'rŭs-
Kiakhta (ke-äx'tä)
Kick'ȧ-poo'
Kief, or Kiew (ke-ef'
  or κī-ev')
Kiel (keel)
Kil-ken'ny
Kil-lar'ney
Kil-mar'nȯck
Kincardine (king-kar'-
  din) [tä'o)
Kingkitao (king-ke-

Kin-ross'
Kin-sale'
Kircaldy (kịr-kawl'dȳ
  or kịr-kaw'dȳ)
Kirkudbright (kịr-
  koo'bree)
Kit'tȧ-tin'ny
Klz'lī Ir'mak [foonT')
Klagenfurth (klä'gẹn-
Klau'ṣẹn-burg (Ger.
  pron. klow'zẹn-
  bōŏʀɢ')
Königingrätz (kö'nig-
  in-gréts'), or König-
  grätz (kö'nig-gréts)
Königsberg (ko'nigz-
  bẹrg), or Koenigs-
  berg (ken'ĭgz-bẹrg ;
  Ger. pron. kö'nigs-
  bĕʀɢ') [(koo-bän')
Kooban, or Kuban
Koordistan, or Kur-
  distan (koor-dis-tän')

L.

Loaland (law'land), or
  Lol'land
Lab'rȧ-dōr'
Lac'cȧ-dives'
Lack'ȧ-wȧn'nȧ
Lad'o-gȧ [läb-ro'nes)
Lȧ-drones' (Sp. pron.
Lago Maggiore (lä'go
  mäd-jo'rā)
Laguna del Madre (lä-
  goo'nä del mäb'rā)
Lahore (lä-hōr')
Laibach (lī'bäx). Syn.
  Laybach.
La Mancha (lä män'-
  chä) [shjr)
Lanark (lẹn'ȧ-tẹr
Lang'ȧs-tẹr
Lan-daff' ; more prop-
  erly Llandaff.
Langres (lŏng'r)
Languedoc (lŏN'Ĕgh-
  dok') [See Plata.
La Plata (lä plä'tä).
La Puebla de los An-
  geles (lä pwĕb'lä dā
  lōs äng'ḥĕl-ĕs)
Lar'sȧ, or Il'lassȧ
  (h'läs'sä)
Latakia (lä'tȧ-kee'ȧ), or
  Ladikia (lä'dc-kee'ȧ)
Lausanne (lō'zän')
Lavaro (lä-vo'ro)
Laybach, or Laibach
  (lī'bäk)
Lĕam'ing-tȯn [horn]
Lẹg-horn' (or leg'-
Lehigh (lee'hī)
Leicester (les'tẹr)
Leinster (lĭn'stẹr or
  leen'stẹr)

Leipsic (līp'sĭk) (Ger.
  Leipzig, līp'tsĭɢ)
Leith (leeth)
Leitrim (lee'trĭm)
Leixlip (läs'lip)
Le'nȧ (Russ. pron.
  lā-nä)
Lenni-Lennappé (len'-
  ne len'nä'pā)
Lĕom'in-+ter (U. S.)
Leominster (Eng.)
  (lem'stẹr) [ōn')
Le'on (Sp. pron. lā-
I.e-pän'to(or lā'pän-to)
Lerida (lĕr'e-dä)
Leucadia (lu-kä'de-ȧ)
  Syn. Sante Maura.
Le-vant'
Lev'en, Loch
Lew'ĭsh-ȧnī
Leyden, or Leiden (lī'-
  dẹn or lā'dẹn)
Lī-be'ri-ȧ
Lich'fĭĕld [fels')
Lichtenfels (lĭx'tẹn-
Liége (leej ; Fr. pron.
  le-āzh')
Lille, or Lisle (leel)
Lima (Peru) (lee'mä)
Lima (U. S.) (lī'mȧ)
Lĭm'ẹr-ick
Limoges (le'mozh')
Limousin (le'moo'säx')
  or Limorin
Lincoln (lĭŋk'un)
Linköpiṇg, or Linkjöp-
  ing (lĭn'chö'ping)
Lin-lĭth'gōw
Lipari (lĭp'ȧ-re or lce'-
  pä-rre) [molt)
Lippe-Detmold (-det'-
Lis'bȯn
Lisic (leel)
Lĭth'u-ä'nī-ȧ
Liv'ẹr-pool
Li-vo'nī-ȧ
Llandaff (lȧn-daf'), or
  Landaff (lȧn)
Llangollen (lan-geth'-
Llanos (lyä'nŏs)
Lcango (lo-ang'go)
Lof-fo'dẹn, or Lȯ-fo'-
  dẹn
Loir (lwär)
Loire (lwär)
Lom'bar-dy
Lomond, Loch (lox
  lō'mund) (lun'd'n)
London (lun'dun or
Londonderry (lun'-
  dun-der'rī) [child]
Loo Choo (ch as in
Lorraine (lor'rän')
Lostwithiel (lost-with'-
  ẹl), or Lestwithiel
Lothian (lo'thī-ȧn)
Lou'don (ou as in
  shout)

ā, ŏ, &c., 'ȯng; ă, ŏ, &c., short; câre, fär, ȧsk, ȧll, whȧt; ēre, vẹil, tẽrm; p"que, firm; sŏn, ȯr,

MODERN GEOGRAPHICAL NAMES. 367

Loughborough (lŭf'-bŭr-ŭh)
Loughrea (lŏH'rä')
Louis, St (sẹnt loo'ĭs or loo'e; *Fr. pron.* sän loo'e') [äd')
Louisiade (loo-ce-ze-
Louisiana (loo'c-zu-ä'nạ)
Louisville (loo'ĭs-vil; *formerly pron.* loo'-
Lŏw'ẹll [ĭ-vil)
Lü'beck
Luc'cạ (*It. pron.* look'kä)
Lucerne (loo-sĕrn')
Lucia, St. (loo-see'ạ, *often called* loo-sce')
Lŭck'now'
Lu'nẹn-burg
Lutzen (lŏŏt'sẹn)
Lux'ẹm-burg (*Fr.* Luxembourg, lüks'-ọN'booR')
Luzerne (Ü. S.) (lu-zĕrn')
Luzon (loo-zōn', *or* Luçon (*Sp. pron.* loo'thōN')
Lỹ-cŏm'ing [jĭs)
Lyme-Regis (līm-ree'-
Lynn-Regis (lĭn-rec'jĭs)
Lỹ'ọns (*Fr.* Lyon, le'ŏN')

M.

Maastricht (mäs'trĭĸt *or* mäs'trĭĸt)
Macao (mä-kä'o *or* mạ-kow')
Mạ-cas'sar
Machias (mạ-chī'ạs)
Mack'ĭ-naw
Mâcon (France) (mä'-kŎN') [(kun)
Macon (U. S.) (mä'-
Mad'ạ-gas'car
Madeira (mạ-dee'rạ, *Port. pron.* mä-dä'-
Mad-ras' [e-rä)
Mad-rid' (*Sp. pron.* mä-preeď, *almost* mädh-reeth')
Mad'rid (U. S.)
Maelstrom (mäl'strum *or* mäl'strum)
Maestricht, *or* Maastricht (mäs'trĭĸt)
Mag'ạ-dox'o, *or* Magadoxa
Mag'dạ-le'nạ
Mag'de-burg (*Ger. pron.* mäG'dẹh-bŏŏRG')
Main, *or* Mayn (mīn)
Maine (France) (män;

Fr. pron. almost mĕn)
Maine (U. S.) (män)
Mạ-jor'cạ
Mal'ạ-bar'
Mạ-lac'cạ
Mal'ạ-gạ (*or* mä/lä-gä)
Mạl'dẹn
Maldives (mal'dīvz)
Malmesbury (mämz'-bẹr-ĭ)
Mal'mö (*or* mäl'mö)
Malta (mawl'tạ; *It. pron.* mäl'tä)
Malvern (maw'vẹrn)
Malwah (mawl'wä)
Man'chẹs-tẹr
Man-dịŋ'go
Mạ-nil'lạ (Sp. Manila, mä-nee'lä)
Mantchooria (man-choo'rẹ-ạ)
Man'tu-ạ (It. Mantova, män'to-vä)
Maracaybo, *or* Maracalbo (mä-rä-kī'bo)
Maranham (mär'ạ-nam'), *or* Maranhão (*Port. pron.* mä-rän-yä'ŏN)
Mar'ble-hĕad' [brŭh)
Marlborough (mawl'-
Mar'mọ-rạ, *or* Mar'-mạ-rạ [säs)
Marquesas (mar-kä'-
Marseilles (mar-sälz')
(*Fr.* Marseille, mar'-säl')
Mar'tạ-ban' [neek')
Martinique (mar'tĭ-
Mä'ry-lạnd
Mä'ry-lẹ-bŏne (*commonly pronounced* mär'ẹ-bun)
Mas'sạ-chu'setts
Mat'ạ-gor'dạ
Mat'ạ-mo'rọs, *or* Matamoras
Mạ-tan'zạs (*or* mä-tän'thäs)
Mauch-Chunk (mawk-chŭnk')
Mạu-mee'
Maurepas (mo're-pä')
Mauritius (maw-rish'-ĭ-us)
Mayence. *See* Mentz.
Mayenne (mä'yen' *or* mĭ'en') [nooth)
Mäy-nooth' (*or* mä/-
Mayo (Ireland) (mä'o)
Mayo (Mexico) mī'o)
Maz'ạt-lan' (*or* ◌ mä-sät-län')
Mechlin (mek'lĭn)
Meck'lẹn-burg (*Ger pron.* mek'lẹn-bŏŏRG')

Medina (Arabia) (me-dee'nạ) [dĭ'nạ)
Medina (U. S.) (me-
Melbourne (mcl'burn)
Mel-rŏẓe' [brĭ)
Mel'ton Mowbray (mō'-
Mem'ịhl (*or* mä'mẹl)
Mcm'phre-mä'gog
Menai (mẹn'ĭ *or* men'-ä) (Strait) [see/no)
Mendocino (mĕn-do-
Mer'ĭ-dạ (*or* mĕr'e-dä)
Mer'ĭ-on'eth
Mer'rĭ-mack
Mersey (mĕr'zĭ)
Messina (mẹs-see'nä)
Mesurado (mä-soo-rä/-do) (*pron.* mäs)
Metz (mĕts; *Fr.*
Meuse (mūz; *Fr. pron.* muz)
Mex'ĭ-co
Miaco (me-ä'ko)
Miami (mī-ä'mĭ)
Michigan (mish'ĭ-g'n, *or* mish'ĭ-gạn)
Milan (mĭl'ạn *or* mĭ-län')
Mĭl-wạu'kee, *or* Milwau'kie
Minas-Geraes (mee'-näs-zhä-rä'ĕs)
Mindanao (min-dä-nä'o)
Min'ne-so'tạ [cạ)
Mĭ-nor'cạ, *or* Mcn-or'-
Miramachi (mĭr'ạ-mạ-shee')
Mis-sĭs/que
Mis'sis-sĭp'pĭ
Missolongbi (mĭs'so-long'ġe)
Missouri (mĭs-soo'rĭ)
Mobile (mo-beel')
Mocha (mo'kạ) [nä)
Mod'e-nạ (*or* mod'ä-
Mo'hawk
Moldau (mol'dow)
Mol-dä'vĭ-ạ
Mo-luc'cạs
Mondego (mon-dä'go)
Mon-go'lĭ-ạ
No-non'gạ-he'lạ
Mon-ro'vĭ-ạ
Mon-tä'nạ [bŏN)
Montauban (mŏN'tō'-
Mont Blanc (mŎN blŏN) *or* Mount Blạnc.
Mont Cenis (mŎN sẹh-nē' *or* sẹh-nĕss')
Montenegro (mon-tä-nä'gro)
Monterey (mon-tä-rä')
Mon'te-vid'e-o (*or* mon-tä-vee'dä-o)
Montgomery (mọnt-gum'er-e)

Mont-pe'lĭ-ẹr
Mont-pel'lĭ-er (*Fr. pron.* mŎN'pĕl'le-ä')
Montreal (mont're-awl')
Mont'sẹr-rat'
Moorzook, Mourzouk, *or* Murzuk (moor-zook')
Mo-rä'vĭ-ạ
Moray; *pron., and often written,* Mŭr'-
Mo-re'ạ [ray.
Morena, Sierra (se-eR/-ä̈ mo-rä'nä)
Mo-roc'co
Mos'cŏw
Moselle (mo-zel')
Mo'sul, *or* Moo'sul
Moy'a-men'sing
Mozambique (mo-zam-beek')
Munich (mū/nik) (German München, mün'ġẹn)
Mŭn'stẹr (Ireland)
Münster (Ger.) (mŭn'-stẹr *or* mŭn'stẹr)
Mur, *or* Muhr (mooR)
Mursuk. *See* Moorzook.
Mus-cat' [teen)
Muscatine (mus'kạ-
Mus-co'ġee
Mus/cọ-vy '[king'gum)
Muskingum (mus-
Mysore (mĭ-sŏr')

N. .

Nacogdoches (nak'o-dō'chĭz)
Namur (nä/mur; *Fr. pron.* nä'mür')
Nan'cy (*Fr. pron.* nŏN'se')
Nangasaki (näng-gạ-sä'ke)
Nan-kĭn', *or* Nanking'
Nantes (nants; *Fr. pron.* nŏnt)
Nan-tuck'ẹt
Naples (nä'plz)
Narbonne (naR'bon')
Nash'u-ạ
Nas'sau (*Ger. pron.* näs'sou)
Natal (nä-täl')
Natch'ĭ-toch'es (*sometimes pronounced* nak'ẹ-tush')
Nav'ạ-hŏe (Indians); *written also* Nabajo.
Navarre (nạ-var')
Ne-bras'kạ
Neck'ạr, *or* Neck'ẹr

dọ, wọlf, tŏō, tŏŏk; ûrn, rụe, pụll; ç, ġ, *soft*; ç, ġ, *hard*; ạṣ; exịst; ṇ *as* ng; this (see p. 361).

MODERN GEOGRAPHICAL NAMES.

Neel'gher'ry, or Nellgherry (neel'gĕr'-ree) [rī-po
Neg-ro-pont', or Eg'-Ne-o'sho
Neots, St. (sẹnt neets')
Ne-paul', or Nepâl
Ngr-bud'dah
Neufchatel, or Neuchâtel (nush/ä'tel')
Neuilly - sur - Seine (nuh'yē'sŭR'sān')
Nense (nūs)
Ne'va (Russ. pron. nä'vä)
Nevada (nä-vä'dä)
Nevers (nẹh-vẽR')
Newfoundland (nu'-fund-land')
New Granada (nu gränä'dä)
New Or'le-ans; often, but less correctly, called New Orleans'.
Ngami ('n-gä'mee)
Niagara (nī-ag'a-ra)
Nicarauga (nik'a-rä'-gwä)
Nice (nees)
Niemen (nee'men)
Niger (nī'jẹr)
Nile [(neem)
Nimes, or Nismes
Ni-phon', or Ni-pon'
Nip'is-sing'
Nizh'nee (or Nijni Nov'go'rod
Norfolk (nor'fọk)
Nor'man-dy
Nor'ridge-wock
Norrköping (nos'chö-ping)
Nor'way [rī)
Norwich (Eng.) (nor'-Norwich (U. S) (nor'-rich or nor'wich)
Nova Scotia (no'va sko'shi-a)
No'va Zem'bla
Nov'go-rod', or No'vo-go-rod'
Nu'bi-a
Nueces (nwā'sēs)
Nu'ren-berg (Ger. Nürnberg, nünn'bēRG)
Nyanza (ne-än'za)
Nyköping, or Nyköping (nü'chö'ping, almost nee'chüping)

O.

Oahu (wäh'hoo)
Oaxaca, or Oajaca (wä-hä'kä)

O'ber-lin
Obi, or Oby (ō'be), or Ob
Oceana (o'she-ā'na)
Oceania (o'she-a'ni-a)
Oceanica (o'she-ǎn'I-ka)
Oc-inul'ḡee
O-co'nee
Odense (ō'dẹn-sẹh)
O-der'sa
Oeland (ö'land)
Ogeechee (o-gee'chee)
O-hi'o
Okhotsk (o-кotsk')
Ol'den-burg (Ger. pron. ol'dẹn-bōoRG')
Olmütz (ol'müts)
Omaha (ō'ma-haw')
Oman (ō-män')
O-ne'ga (Russ. pron. o-nu'gä)
Oneida (o-nī'da)
Onondaga (on'un-daw'ga)
Ontario (on-tā'rī-o)
Op'e-lou'sas
O-por'to
Or'e-gọn
O'ri-no'ko
Orizaba (o-re-sä'bä)
Orkneys (ork'nēz)
Or'le-ans (Fr. pron. oR'lä'ôN')
O'sage'
Os'na-brück'; often called by the English Os'na-burg.
Ost-end'
Os-we'go
Ot'ta-wa (or ot'ta-wä)
Oude (owd)
Ouse (ooz)
Owego (o-wee'go)
O-zark'

P.

Pa-dang'
Pad'u-a
Paisley (pāz'lī)
Pal'em-bang'
Pa-lenque (pä-lenk'ā)
Pa-lẽr'mo
Pal'es-tine
Palmas, or Las Palmas (läs päl'mäs)
Palo Alto (pä'lo äl'to)
Pam'li-co
Pa-mun'key, or Pamun'ky
Panama (păn'a-mä')
Papua (pap'oo-a or pä'poo-ä)
Para (pä-rä')
Paraguay (pä-rä-gwā' or pä-rä-gwī')

Par'a-mĕr'i-bo
Paruna (pä-rä-nä')
Parana-Iba, or Paranahiba (pä-rä-nä-ee'bä)
Parima (pä-rä'mä)
Parina (pä-re-nä')
Paris (pär'is; Fr. pron. pä'Re')
Pascagoula (pas'ga-goo'la)
Paso del Norte (pä'so del noR'tā)
Pas-sä'ic
Pas'sa-ma-quod'dy
Pat'a-go'ni-a
Pavia (pä-vee'ä)
Paw'tuck-et
Pays Bas (pā'e bä)
Pays de Vaud (pā'e dẹh vō)
Paz, La (lä päz; Sp. pron. lä pätu)
Pe-chee-Ice (pä-chee-Pe'dee' [lee')
Pei-ho (pä'hō')
Pe'kin', or Pe'king'
Pe-lew'
Pembina (pẽm'be-na)
Pembroke (pem'-brŏŏk)
Penn'sȳl-vā'ni-a
Pe-nob'scọt
Pen'sa-co'la
Penzance (pẽn-zuns')
Pe-o'rī-a
Perigord (pcr'ē'goR')
Pernambuco (pẽn-näm-boo'ko)
Persia (per'shī-a, not per'zhī-a)
Peru (pe-roo')
Peschiera (pĕs-ke-ā'rä)
Pesth (pest)
Pet-cho'ra, or Petschorn
Pe'ters-burg. Saint
Phil'a-del'phi-a
Phil'ip-pine
Pic'ar-dy
Pictou (pik-too')
Piedmont (peed'mont)
Pilcomayo (pil-ko-nī'o)
Pisa (pee'sä)
Pis-cat'a-qua
Pis-cat'a-quis [mŏn')
Plaqueuine (plak'-Plata, La (lä plä'tä)
Plata, Rio de la (re'o dä lä plä'tä) (ēR')
Plombières (plôN'be-Plymouth (plim'uth)
Poitiers, or Poictiers (poi-teerz'; Fr. pron. pwit'te-ā')
Poitou, or Poictou (poi'too; Fr. pron. pwä'too')

Po'land [shi-a)
Polynesia (pol'i-nce'-Pom'e-rā'ni-a
Pompeii (pom-pā'yee)
Poudicherry (pon'desher'rec)
Pont'chgr-trāin'
Popayan (po-pi-än' or po-pä-yäu')
Po-po-cat'a-pẹtl'
Port-au-Prince (pōrt-ō-prins; Fr. pron. poRt-ō-prăns)
Pōr'to Prin'cī-pe
Porto Rico (pōr-to ree'ko)
Portsmouth (pōrts'-muth)
Pōrt'u-gal
Posen (po'zẹn)
Po-to'mac
Potosi (po-to-see' or po-to'see)
Poughkeepsie (po-kip'si)
Prague (prag)
Prhirie du Chien (prā'. rī du shee n)
Pres'burg, or Press'-burg (Ger. pron. press'bōŏRG)
Presque Isle (presk eel)
Prip'ets (Pol. Prypec, prip'ẽts)
Provence (pro'vōnss')
Prussia (prŭsh'I-a or proo'shi-ä)
Pryth (Ger. pronproot)
Puebla (pwẹh'lä)
Punjab (puu-jäb'), or Pnn-jạnb'
Pyrenees (pir'ẹ-nēz)

Q.

Que-bec'
Quito (kee'to)
Quŏr'ra. Syn. Niger

R.

Raab (räb)
Racine (ras-seen')
Rahway (raw/wā)
Raleigh (raw'li)
Rangoon (rang-goon')
Rap'id-an'
Rap'pa-han'nock
Raritan, or Rariton (rär'it-un)
Rat'is-bon (Ger. Regensburg, rā'gẹns-bōoRG)
Reading (rẽd'ing)
Re-ho'both
Reichstadt (rīk'stät)
Reigate (rī'get)

ā, ē, &c., long; ă, ĕ, &c., short; câre, fär, ásk, ạll, whạt; ēre, vẹil, tẽrm; pīque, fĩrm; sŏn, ŏr,

MODERN GEOGRAPHICAL NAMES. 369

Rei′kĭ-ą-vĭk
R+ims, *or* Rheims (reemz ; *Fr. pron.* rănz)
Resaca de la Palma (rä-sä′kä dä lä päl′mä)
Rhine (rīn)
Rhodes (rōdz)
Rhône (rōn)
Rideau (rŭ′dō′)
Rĭ′gą (*or* ree′gą)
Rio del Norte (rī′o del nort ; *Sp. pron.* ree′o děl noR′tä) ; *called also the* Rĭ′o Grånde (*Sp. pron.* ree′o grän′dä)
Rio Janeiro (rī′o ją-nee′ro *or* ree′o ją-nä′ro)
Ro′ą-noke′
Rochelle, *or* La Rochelle (lä Ro′shel′)
Romagna (ro-män′yä)
Romania (ro-mä′ne-ą *or* ro-mä-nee′ä)
Rome (rōm)   [lia
Roo-une′li-ą, *or* Rumelloth′çr-hįthe (*vulgarly*, red′rĭf)
Rot′ter-dam′
Rouen (roo′ęn ; *Fr. pron.* rwŏN)
Roxburgh (Scotland) (roks′bŭr-rçh)
Rügen (rü′gęn)
Russia (rŭsh′l-ą *or* roo′shĭ-ą)

S.

Saale (sä′lęh)
Sabine (są-been′)
Saco (saw′ko) [halien
Sag-hal′ĭ-en, *or* Sak-Sag′ĭ-naw
Saguenay (sag′çh-nā′)
Sabara (są-hä′rą *or* sab/hä-rä)
Sa′gon (sī′gon′) *or* Sai′gong (sī′gong′)
St. Bernard (sągnt bēr′nąrd)
Saint Germain. *See* Germain, Saint, *and so for all the other names having the prefix of* Saint.
Salado (sä-lä′Do)
Sal-ą-mąnç′ą (*or* sä-lä-mäng′kä)
Saline (są-leen′)
Salisbury (sawlz′bęr-ĭ)
Salvador (säl-vä-dōr′)
Saltz′burg   (sawlts′-burg), *or* Salzburg (*Ger. pron.* sälts′-bōoRa)

Samana (sä-mä-nä′)
Sam′ąr-cand′
Samoa (sä-mo′ä)
San An-to/nī-o
San Diego (sän de-ā′go)
Sand′wich (*or* sand′wij)
San Fran-cis′co (*or* sän frän-sees′ko)
San Joaquin (sän Ho-ä-keen′)
San José (sän Ho-sā′)
San Ju′ąn (*Sp. pron.* sän Hoo-än′ *or* hwän)
Sanquhar (sąnk′ąr)
San Salvador (sän säl-vä-dōr′)
Santa Cruz (san′tą kroos ; *Sp. pron.* sän′tä-krooth), *or* St. Croix (sąnt kroi)
Santa Fe de Bogota (dā bo-go-tä′)
Santa Maria (sän′tä mä-ree′ä)
San′tee′
Santiago (sän-te-ä′go)
Saône (sōn)
Săr′ą-gos′są (Sp. Zaragoza, thä-rä-go′thä)
Sár′ą-to′gą
Sar-din′ĭ-ą   [to)
Sarmiento (sar-me-ĕn-Sas-katch′ą-wąn′
Sault de Sainte Marie (*Fr. pron.* Ro dęh säN mä′re′), *but now usually called* Sault (soo) St. Mä′ry.
Sava (sä′vä)
Są-van′nąh
Sav′oy (*or* są-voī′)
Saxe Altenburg (saks al′tęn-burg)
Saxe Co′burg
Saxe Weimar (saks wī′mąr)
Sax′o-ny
Scan′dĭ-nä′vĭ-ą
Scarborough (skar′-b′rŭb *or* skar′bur-Scheldt (skelt) [rŭh)
Schemnitz (shem′nits)
Schenectady (skę-nek′tą-dẏ)
Schiedam (skee/däm′)
Schiraz (she′räz′)
Schleswig. *See* Sleswick.   [ree)
Schoharie (sko-här′-Schönbruun , *or* Schoenbrunn (shön′broon)
Schoodic (skoo′dik)
Schuyler (skī′lęr)
Schuylkill (skool′kil)
Schwerin (shwä-reen′)
Scigliano (shēl-yä′no)
Scilly (sil′lĭ)
Scinde (sĭnd)

Scio (sī′o *or* shee′o)
Scioto (sī-o′to)
Scituate (sit′u-āt)
Selą-vo′nĭ-ą
Scot′lạnd
Scutari (skoo′tä-ree)
Sebastopol. *See* Sevastopol.
Secunderabad (se-kŭn′dęr-ä-bäd′)
Seine (sān)
Sen′e-cą
Senegal (sen′e-gawl′)
Sen′e-gam′bĭ-ą
Seringapatam (ser-ing′gą-pą-tam′)
Sĕr′vĭ-ą
Setubal (sů-too′bäl), *or* Setuval (sů-too′yäl), *or* St. Ubes (übs)
Sev′as-to′pol (*or* se-vas′to-pol) ; *less correctly*, Sebastopol.
Sev′çrn
Seville (sev′il *or* se-vil′)
Sèvre (sĕv′r *or* säv′r)
Seychelles (sā′shel′)
Sbamo (shä′mo′)
Shang-hai′, *or* Changhai′ (shang′hī′)
Sheerąz, *or* Shiraz (she′räz′ *or* shee′raz)
Sheer-uess′
Shen′an-do′ąh
Shrewsbury   (Mass.) (shrẏz′bēr-ĭ)
Shrewsbury (England) (shrẏz′bçr-ĭ *or* shrōz′bçr-ĭ)
Shrop′shįre
Siam (sī-am′ *or* se′am′)
Sĭ-be′rĭ-ą
Siç′ĭ-lẏ   [ā′nä)
Si-en′ną (It. Siena, se-Si-er′rą Le-o′ne (*Sp. pron.* se-ĕR′Rä lā-o′-nä)
Sierra Madre (se-eR′Rä mäD′rā)
Sierra Morena (se-eR-Rä mo-rä′nä)
Sierra Nevada (se-eR′-Rä nä-vä′dä)
Silesia (sĭ-lee′shĭ-ą)
Sim′plon (*Fr. pron.* säN′plŏN′)
Sinde, *or* Scinde (sĭnd)
Singapore (sing′gą-pōr′), *or* Singapoor
Sin-o′pe
Sioux (*usually pron.* soo ; *Fr. pron.* se-oo′)
Skaneateles (skan′e-at′les) ; *written also* Skeneateles.
Skye (skī)
Sią-vo′nĭ-ą, *or* Sclą-vo′nĭ-ą

Sles′wick (Ger. Schleswig, shles′wĭg)
Sluys (slois)
Smo-lensk′, *or* Smo-len′sko
Smyrna (smĭr′ną)
So-co′trä, *or* Soc′o-trä
Sofala (so-fä′lä *or* so′-fä-lä)
Soissons (swŭs′sŏn′, *almost* swĭ′sŏn′)
Soleure (so′lŭR′) Ger. Solothurn, so′lo-tooRN′)
Solferino (sol-fů-ree′no)
Somauli (so-maw′lee)
Sŭm′çr-set
So-no′rä
Soodan, Soudan, *or* Sudan (soo′dän′)
Southampton (suth-hamp/tun)
Spa (spaw ; *Fr. and Flem. pron.* spä)
Spitz-bęrg′ęn
Staten Island (stat′tn ī′lạnd)   [tun)
Staunton (Va.) (stän′-Staunton (Eng.) (stän′-tun *or* stän′tun)
Stettin (stet-teen′)
Steuben (stu′ben *or* stu-ben′)
Stock′holm
Stŏn′ing-tọn
Stralsund   (sträl′-sound)   [burg)
Strasbourg (straz′-Strasburg (Germany) (sträs′bōoRG)
Stutt′gart, *or* Stuttgard (*Ger. pron.* stŏŏt′gart)
Styria (stĭr′ĭ-ą)
Suez (sŏŏ′ez ; *Arab. pron.* soo-cz′ *or* soo-äz′)
Suffolk (suf′fǫk)
Suir (shụir)
Sumątra (sŏo-mä′trä)
Sŭn′dä
Surat (sŏo-rat′)
Surinam (sŏo-rĭ-nam′)
Sus′que-han′ną
Swe′den
Switz′çr-lạnd (swĭts′-)
Sẏr′ą-cuse
Sẏr′ĭ-ą
Szegedin (sĕg′ed′ĕn′ *or* sĕg′ed′ĭn′)

T.

Ta-co′ny
Taf′ĭ-let′, *or* Tafĭ-lelt′
Tä′gus
Tahiti (tä-hee′te)

---

dǫ, wǫlf, tŏō, tŏōk ; ūrn, rụe, pụll ; ç, ġ, *soft* ; c, ġ, *hard* ; aș ; exist ; ŋ *as* ng ; this (see p. 351)
16 *

MODERN GEOGRAPHICAL NAMES.

Tah'le-quah
Tal'la-has'see
Tal'la-poo'sa
Tampico (tăm-pee'ko)
Tangier (tan-jeer')
Taos (tä'ōs, *almost* Tas-mā'ni-a [towss)
Taunton (Eng.)
   (tawn'ton) [ton)
Taunton (Mass.) (tän'-
Tav'is-tock
Tehran, *or* Teheran
   (teh-h'răn')
Tchuantepec (tä-wän-
   tā-pek')
Teignmouth (tin'-
   muth *or* tăn'muth)
Temesvár (tem-esh-
   vär')
Teneriffe (ten'er-if')
   (Sp. Tenerife, tā-nā-
   ree'fä)
Ten'nes-see'
Ter'ra del Fu-e'go, *or*
   Tierra del Fuego (te-
   ĕa'rä děl fwa'go)
Terre-Bonne (tĕr'-
   bon'; *often pron.*
   tar-bŏn')
Terre-Haute (tĕr'reh-
   hŏt'; Fr. pron. tĕr'-
   hŏt' *or* tĕr-rch-hŏt')
Teviot (tiv'e-ot)
Thames (tĕmz)
Than'et
Thebes (theebz)
Theiss (tīs)
Thes'sa-ly, *or* Thes-
   sā'li-a
Thibet, *or* Tibet (tib'-
   et *or* ti-bet')
Ti'ber
Ti-con'der-o'ga
Tiflis (tif-lees')
Ti'gris
Tim-buc'too [rī)
Tipperary (tip-per-ā'-
Titicaca (tit-e-kä'kä)
Tivoli (tiv'o-le *or* tee'-
   vo-lee)
Tobago (to-bā'go)
To-bolsk'
To-kay'
To-le'do (Sp. pron.
   to-lā'Do)
Tom-big'bee
Tonkin, *or* Tonquin
   (ton-keen')
Toorkistan, *or* Turkis-
   tan (toor'kis-tän')
To-pe'ka
Töplitz, Toeplitz (tŭp'-
   lits), *or* Teplitz
   (tep'lits)
Tor-bay'
To-ron'to
Tortuga (tor-too'ga)
Toulon (too'lŏn')

Toulouse, *or* Thou-
   louse (too'looz')
Touraine (too'răn')
Tournay (toor'nā')
Tours (toor)
Traf'al-gar', *or* Tra-
   fäl'gar
Tran'syl-vā'ni-a
Treb'i-zond'
Trichinopoli, *or* Trich-
   inopoly (tritch'in-
   op'o-le)
Triest, *or* Trieste (tre-
   ěst' *or* tre-ěs'tä)
Trincomalee (trink'o-
   ma-lee')
Trin'i-dad'
Trip'o-li
Trois Rivières (trwä
   re've-ēr')
Trujillo (troo-heel'yo)
Tübingen (tü'bing-en)
Tu'nis
Tur'co-mā'ni-a
Tu'pe-lo
Tu'rin (*or* tn-rin')
Tus'ca-loo'sa
Tus'ca-ny
Tus'ca-ro'ra [rōl')
Tyr'ol (Ger. pron. te-

U.

Ubes, Saint. *See* Se-
   tubal.
Ucayale (oo-kī-ä'lä),
   or Ucayali (oo-kī-ä'-
   lee)
Ukraine (yoo'krän *or*
   oo-krän') [dŏlm)
Ulm (Ger. pron.
Um-bā'gog
Upernavik (oo-pĕr'-
   na-vik)
Up'sal, *or* Upsala (up-
   sä'lä) [räl')
U'ral, *or* Oural (oo-
   U'ri (yoo'rī; Ger. pron.
   oo're)
Uruguay (u'roo-gwā'
   or oo-roo-gwī')
Ushant (ŭsh'ant)
U'ti-ca
Utah (yoo'tä, *less
   properly* yoo'taw)
Utrecht (u'trĕkt)
Uttoxeter (ŭks'e-ter)

V.

Valencia (va-len'shi-a,
   Sp. pron. vä-len'-
   the-ä)
Val'la-do-lid' (Sp.
   pron. väl-yä-Do-
   leeD')

Valparaiso (văl-pā-rī'-
   so) [ver)
Vancouver (van-koo'-
   Van Diemen's (van
   dee'menz)
Vaud (vō), *or* Pays-
   de-Vaud (pā'e-deh-
   vō') [dā')
Vendée La (lä vŏN'-
   Vendôme (vŏN'dŏm')
Venezuela (ven'e-
   zwee'la)
Venetia (ve-ne'shi-a)
Venice (ven'iss)
Vera Cruz (vā'rä
   kroos)
Vergennes (vĕr-jenz')
Ver-mont'
Versailles (ver-sālz';
   Fr. pron. věR'sāl' *or*
   věR-sāy')
Ve-su'vi-us
Vienua (ve-en'na)
Villa (*in Sp.* veel'yä;
   in Port. veel'lä *or*
   vil'lä)
Villa Rica (Sp. Amer-
   ica) (veel'yä rec'kä)
Villa Rica (Brazil)
   (vil'lä, *or* veel'lä,
   ree'kä)
Vincennes (vin'sĕnz';
   Fr. pron. văN'sĕn')
Virginia (ver-jin'i-a)
Vistula (vist'yu-la)
Vitebsk (ve-tebsk'), *or*
   Vitepsk
Vol'ga, *or* Wolga
Vosges (vōzh)

W.

Wabash (waw'bash)
Waday (wä'dī)
Wagram (wä'gram *or*
   wä'gräm)
Wales
Wallachia (wol-lā'kī-a)
Waltham (Eng.) (wŏl'-
   tam)
Waltham (Mass.)
   (wŏl'thăm)
War'saw [rik)
Warwick (Eng.) (wor'-
Warwick (U. S.) (wor'-
   wik *or* wor'rik)
Washita (wŏsh'i-taw')
Wa'ter-ee'
Wa'ter-loo'
Weimar (wī'mar)
Wener (wä'ner), *or*
   Wenner (wen'ner)
We'ser (Ger. pron.
   wä'zer)
West Indies (in'dēz)
West-phā'li-a

Weymouth (wā'muth)
Wil'na, *or* Vilna
Windsor (win'zor)
Win'ne-bā'go
Win'ni-peg
Winnipiseogee (win-
   ne'pis-sok'kī)
Wis-cās'set
Wis-con'sin
Wit'ten-berg [Ger.
   pron. wit'ten-bĕaG')
Woburn (woo'burn)
Wolverhampton
   (wŏŏl'ver-hamp'-
   tun) [*or* wŏŏl'ij)
Woolwich (wŏŏl'itch
Worcester (wŏŏs'ter)
Worms (wŭrmz; Ger.
   pron. wŏrms)
Würtemberg (wŭr'-
   tem-berg; Ger.
   pron. wŭa'tem-
   beaG')
Wy'an-dot'
Wy-o'ming
Wythe (with, *th* being
   sounded as in *thin*)

X.

Xenia (zee'ni-a)
Xenil (hä-neel')
Xingu, *or* Chingu
   (shĕn-goo')

Y.

Yakootsk, *or* Yakoutsk
   (yä-kootsk')
Yang'tse-kiang
   (yang'tse-ke-ang')
Ya-zoo' (do)
Yeddo, *or* Jeddo (yed'-
Yekatarinoslav (yä-
   kä-tä-ree-no-släv')
Yem'en
Yeniseï (yen'e-sā'e *or*
   yen-e-sī') [so)
Yesso, *or* Jesso (yes'-
Yo-semi'-te
Ypres (eep'r) (kä-tän')
Yu'ca-tän' (*or* yoo'-

Z.

Zacatecas (zăk-a-tā'-
   kas *or* sä-kä-tā'käs)
Zaïre (zä-eer') [ze)
Zam-bezo' (*or* zam-bā'-
Zanguebar (zang'gä-
   bar')
Zan'te
Zan'zi-bar'
Zollverein (tsol'fer-īn')
Zürich (zu'rik; Ger.
   pron. tsü'ris)
Zuyder Zee (zī'der zee
   or zoo'der-zee)

ā, ē, &c., *long*; ă, ĕ, &c., *short*; câre, fär, ȧsk, ạll, whạt; ẽre, veil, tẽrm; p:que, firm; sŏn, ôr,

MODERN BIOGRAPHICAL NAMES.

A.

Abdalla (äb-däl′lah), or Abdullah (ạb-dŭl′lah)
Abd-el-Kader (äbd-ẹl-kä′dẹr)
Ăb′ẹ-lard
A-ben′cẹ-rȧġe (Sp. pron. ä-bēn′thū-rä′нȧ)
Abercromby (ăb′ẹr-krŭm/bĭ) [thĭ]
Abernethy (ăb′ẹr-nē-)
Abinger (ăb/n-jẹr)
Abu–Bekr, or Abou-Bekr (ä′boo-bŭkr′)
Adnir (ạ-dâr′)
Adanson (ä′dọɴ′sọɴ′)
Adelung (ä′dẹh-lŏŏng)
Agassiz (ăg′ạ-see or ạ-gns′siz; Fr. pron. ȧ′gǘs′se′)
Ahmed (än′mẹd), or Achmet (äk′mẹt)
Ainsworth (ānz′wọrth)
Akenside (ä′kẹn-sīd)
Aladdin (ạ-lăd/din)
Alaric (ăl′ạ-rĭk) (Lat. A-lar′i-cus)
Alboin (ăl′boin)
Alboni (äl-bo′nee)
Albuquerque (ăl′bu-kẹrk; Port. pron. äl-boo-kĕʀ′kä)
Alciati (äl-chä′tee)
Alcuin (ăl′kwin)
Aldrich (awl′drĭtch or awl-drĭj)
Alembert (ä/lŏɴ′bŭʀ′), or d'Alembert (dä′lŏɴ′bĕʀ′)
Alfieri (äl-fe-ä′rec)
Alford (awl′fọrd) (tee)
Algarotti (äl-gä-rōt′-)
Ali (ä′lee) (ree)
Alighieri (ä-le-ġe-ā′-)
Alison (ăl′ĭ-sọn)
Allston (awl′stọn)
Almack (ăl′mak)
Almeida (äl-mä′e-dä or al-mā′dạ)
Alsop (awl′sọp)
Alston (awl′stọn)
Alton (Eng.) (awl′tọn)
Alvarez (Sp.) (äl′vä-rĕth)

Am′ạ-de′ŭs. Syn. Amadeo.
Amerigo (ä-mā-ree′go or ä-mĕr′e-go). See Vespucci.
Amiot, or Amyot (ä′-me-o′)
Ampère (ŏɴ′pĕʀ′)
Am′u-rnth
Ancillon (Fr.) (ŏɴ′sē′-yŏɴ′)
André (Eng.) (ăn′drā or än/drĭ)
Angelo (än′jä-lo)
Angoulème (ŏɴ′goo′-lĕm′ or ŏɴ′goo′lăm′)
Anquetil-Duperron (ŏɴ′kẹh-tĕl′dd′pĕʀ′-rŏɴ′)
An′strụj-thẹr (popularly an/stẹr)
Xr′a-go (Fr. pron. ȧ′rȧ′go′)
Aram (ā′rạm)
Ar′bŭth-not
Ariosto (Är′ĭ-os′to or ä-re-os′to)
Arminius (ar-mĭn′ĭ-ŭs)
Arnaud (aʀ/nō′)
Arnauld (aʀ/nō′)
Arteveld (aʀ-tạ-vĕlt′), or Arteveld (aʀ-tạ-vĕl/dĕn)
Xr′un-del
Ascham (ăs′kạm)
Ashburnham (ăsh/-burn-ạm)
Xsh′bur-ton, or Ash′-bur′tọn
Atahualpa (ä-tä-hwäl′pä)
Xth′el-stạn
Aubigné (ō′bēn′yā′)
Aubrey (Eng.) (aw′-brĭ)
Auchmuty (ä′mu-tỵ̆)
Au′du-bon (Fr. pron. ō′dü/bŏɴ′)
Augustine (Saint) (sent aw′gus-tin)
Aurungzebe (ō′rŭng-zăb′ or aw′rŭng-zeeb′)
Averroes (ạ-vĕr′ro-ēs or äv-er-rō′ēs)
Avicenna (ăv′e-sĕn′-nạ)
Ayeshah (ä′ẹ-shạ)

Ayscough (ăs′kū)
Ayton, Aytoun (ā′-tun)

B.

Baba, Ali (ä′lee bä′bä)
Bach (bäк)
Bache (bātch)
Bagehot (băj′ut)
Baillie (bä′lee)
Bailly (Fr.) (bä′le or bä′yẹ′)
Bajazet (băj′a-zĕt)
Balboa (bäl-bo′ä)
Balfour (băl′fur; in Scot. bal-fōōr′)
Ballou (băl-loo′)
Balzac (băl/zăk′)
Barbarossa (bar/bạ-ros′sạ)
Barbauld (Eng.) (bar′-bawld or bar-bō′)
Barbour (bar/bur)
Barère (bä′rēn′)
Baretti (bä-ret/tce)
Barham (bär′am)
Baring (Eng.) (bâr′-ing)
Barras (bȧ′rȧ′)
Barrère (bä′ʀĕʀ′). See Barère.
Barth (baʀt)
Barthélemy (baʀ/tāl′-me′ or baʀ′tā′lẹh-me′) [uee]
Bartolini (baʀ-to-lee′-)
Bäth′ŭrst.
Bauer (bow′ẹr)
Baumgarten (bowm′-gäʀ-tẹn)
Bayard (bā′ạrd or bī′-ạrd; Fr. pron. bä′-yäʀ′)
Beatrice (bẹ̆′ạ-treess or Ĭt. pron. bä-ä-tree′-chä)
Beattie (bee′tĭ; Scotch pron. bä′tĭ)
Beauchamp (Eng.) (bee′chạm)
Beauchamp (Fr.) (bō′-shŏɴ′)
Beauclerc (bō′klēʀk)
Beaufort (Eng.) (bō′-fọrt)
Beaufort (Fr.) (bō′-fọʀ′) [nä′]
Beauharnais (bō′äʀ′-

Beaumarchais (bō′mäʀ′shä′)
Beaumont (Eng.) (bō′-mŏnt)
Beauregard (Amer.) (bō′rẹh-gard′)
Bed′dōeạ
Bede (beed)
Bedell (Amer.) (be-dĕl′)
Bedell (Eng.) (bee′dẹl or be-dĕl′)
Beethoven (bä/tō-vẹn)
Behn (bĕn)
Behring (beer′ĭng; Danish pron. bä′-ring)
Belknap (bĕl′năp)
Bellamy (Eng.) (bĕl′-lạ-mĭ)
Bel′len-dẹn
Bellini (bĕl-lee′nee)
Bel′shạm
Belzoni (bĕl-zo′nee)
Ben/bōw
Bentham (bĕn′tạm or bĕn′thăm)
Bentivoglio (bĕn-te-vōl′yo)
Benvenuti (bĕn-vä-noo′tee)
Béranger (bā′rŏɴ′zhä′)
Bĕr′ẹ̆s-fọrd
Bŭrke′ley (formerly baʀk/lĭ̆)
Bernadotte (bĕr-nạ-dot′ or bĕʀ′nä′dot′)
Bŭr′nạrd (Fr. pron. bĕʀ/näʀ′)
Berzelius (bĕr-zee′lĭ-us; Sw. pron. bĕʀ-zĭ/le-us)
Bescherelle (bōsh′rĕl′)
Beth′ạm
Bethune (bẹh-thoon′)
Bewick (bū′ĭk)
Bẽ′zạ
Bilderdijk, or Bilderdyk (bĭl′dẹr-dīk′)
Billaud-Varennes (bẹ′-yō′-vä/rĕnn′)
Biot (be′o′ or be′ot′)
Bligh (blī)
Bliz′ạrd
Blomfield (blŭm′feeld)
Blount (blŭnt)
Blücher (bloo′kẹr; Ger. pron. blü′kẹr)

dọ, wọlf, tụo, took; ûrn, rụe, pụll; ç, ġ, soft; c, ġ, hard; aẓ; exist; ṇ as ng; this (see p. 361)

MODERN BIOGRAPHICAL NAMES.

Blumenbach (bloo'-mẹn-bäk) [yä)
Bobadilla (bo-ba-Deel'-)
Boccaccio (bok-kät'-cho) (*in French and old English* Boccace, bok/käss')
Böckh (bök)
Bode (bo'dẹh)
Boerhaave (bŏr'hȧv; *Dutch pron.* booR'-hä'vẹh)
Böhme (bö'mẹh), *or* Böhm (böm)
Boileau (boi'lo; *Fr. pron.* bwä'lō')
Bojardo, *or* Boiardo (bo-yäR'do)
Boleyn (bŏŏl'in)
Bolingbroke (bŏl'ing-brŏŏk, *formerly* bŏŏl'ing-brŏŏk).
Bolivar (bo-lee'väR; *erroneously pron.* bol'I-var')
Bonaparte (bo'nạ-pärt; *It. pron.* bo-nä-päR'tä)
Bonheur (bo'nUR')
Borghese (boR-gā'zā)
Borgia (bor'jạ *or* boR'-jä)
Borromeo (boR-Ro-mā'o)
Bos-caw'ẹn, *or* Bos'-cạ-wẹn
Bossuet (bos/sü-ā', *almost* bos'swä')
Bossu (bo'sü')
Bossut (bo'sü')
Bos'well
Both'well
Botzaris. *See* Bozzaris.
Boucher (Eng.) (bow'-chẹr)
Boucher (Fr.) (boo'-sha')
Boudinot (boo'de-not)
Bougainville (boo'-gäN'vĕl')
Boulainvilliers (boo'-läN'vē'yä')
Bourbon (boor'bọn); *Fr. pron.* booR'bŏN')
Bourdaloue (booR/dä'-loo')
Bourdon (booR'dŏN')
Bourne (born) [ĕn')
Bourrienne (boo're-Bouterwek (boo'tẹr-wĕk)
Bouvier (Am.) (boo-veer')
Bowditch (bou'ditch)
Bowdoin (bō'dn)
Bowles (bōlz)
Bowring (boor'ing)
Boy'dĕll

Boyer (bwä'yā')
Bozzaris, *or* Botzaris (bot'sä-ris; *popularly called* bọz-zär'is)
Brad'war-dīne
Brahe (brä *or* brä; *Danish pron.* brä'-ĕh)
Brä'mạh
Bramante d'Urbino (brä-män'tä dooR-bee'no)
Brandt (bränt)
Bremer (bree'mẹr; *Sw. pron.* brä'mẹr)
Brissot (bre'so')
Brockhaus (brŏk'-howss)
Broderip (brŏd'rip)
Brodie (bro'dī)
Broeck (brŏŏk)
Brome (brŏŏm)
Brom'ley (brŭm'lī)
Brontë (brou'te)
Brough (brŭf)
Brougham (broo'ạm *or* broo'm)
Broughton (brow'tọn)
Brown Séquard (-sā'-kaR')
Bru-nĕl'
Brunelleschi (broo-nĕl-lẹs'kee)
Brunet (brü'nā')
Buchanan (bŭk-an'-ạn; *often mispronounced* bū-kan'ạn)
Buffon (bŭf'fọn *or* büf'fŏN')
Bulwer (bŏŏl'wẹr)
Bunsen (bŏŏn'sẹn)
Buonarotti (boo-o'nä-rot'tee)
Burckhardt (bŭrk'-hart; *Ger. pron.* bŏŏRk'härt)
Bur-dett'
Bürger (bür'gẹr)
Burgoyne (bur-goin')
Burleigh (bŭr'lī).
Burlamaqui (bür'lä'-mä'ke')
Bussy d'Amboiso (bü'se'dŏN'bwäz')

C.

Cäb'ot
Cạ-do'gạn
Cäd-wọl'lạ-dẹr
Cagliari (käl'yä-ree)
Cagliostro (käl-yos'-tro)
Cairns (kärnz) [tro]
Caius (keez)
Cal'ạ-my
Calderon (käl-dä-rŏn')
Calhoun (käl-hoon')

Calidasa (kä-le-dä'sä)
Cull'cọtt
Cäl'met (*Fr. pron.* käl'mā')
Calvert (Eng.) (käl'-vẹrt) (vẹrt)
Calvert (Amer.) (kŏl'-Cambacérès (kŏN'bä'-sā'rĕs')
Cam'ẹr-on [o-ĕns)
Cạ-mo'ĕns (*or* käm'-Campbell (kăm'ẹl)
☞ Some families of this name call themselves käm'bel.
Canova (kä-no'vä)
Canrobert (kŏN'ro'-bĕR')
Cantemir, *or* Kantemir (kän'tẹh-meer *or* kän'tü-meer')
Canute (kạ-nūt')
Cạp'el
Cä'pet (*Fr. pron.* kä'-pā') roo')
Carew (*generally* ka-Carlisle (kar-līl')
Carlyle (kar'līl *or* kar-līl')
Carmichael (kar-mī'-kẹl *or* kar'mī-kẹl)
Carteret (kar'tẹr-et)
Casaubon (kạ-saw'bọn)
Casimir (käs/e-meer)
Cassini (käs-see'nee)
Castlereagh (käs'sl-rā')
Cavaignac (kä'vĕn'-yäk')
Căv'ẹu-dish
Cecil (sĕs'il *or* sis'il)
Cellini (chĕl-lee'nee)
Cenci (chĕn'chee)
Centlivre (sẹnt-lee'vẹr *or* sẹnt-liv'ẹr)
Cervantes Saavedra (sẹr-vän'tĕz sä-vĕd'-rạ)
Chalmers (chäl'mẹrz; *Scot. pron.* chaw'-mẹrz)
Chamisso (shä'me'so')
Champollion (shäm-pol'le-ọn, *or* shŏN'-pol'lē-ŏN')
Charlemagne (sbar'le-mäN'; *Fr. pron.* sharl'mäN')
Châteaubriand (shä'-tō'bre'ŏN')
Chatham (chǎt'ạm)
Chauncey (chän'sī *or* chawn'sī)
Cherubini (kā-roo-bee'nee)
Chẹs'ẹl-dẹn
Cheyne (chān *or* chīn)
Childebert (chil'de-[bẹrt)
Chīl'dẹr-ic

Chīl'pẹr-ic
Chisholm (chiz'ọm)
Chlopicki (klo-pit/skee)
Cholmondely (chŭm/lī)
Cimabue (che-mä-boo'-ū) [ĕä)
Cimarosa (che-mä-ro'-Cinq Mars (säNk'miRs')
Claverhouse (klav'ẹr-lis *or* klav'ẹrs)
Clotaire (klo'tĕR')
Clough (klŭf)
Clō'vis
Cochrane (kok'rạn)
Cockburn (ko'burn)
Cœur de Lion (kur de lī'ọn)
Coke (kŏŏk *or* kŭk)
Colbert (kol'bĕR')
Cŏl'by
Co-lĕn'so
Coleridge (kōl'rij)
Coligny, *or* Coligni (ko'-lēn'ye', *or* kol'ĕn'-ye')
Cŏl'mạu
Colquhoun (ko-hoon')
Cŏl'tọn
Combe (koom)
Comstock (kŭm'stok)
Condé (kŏN'dā; *Fr. pron.* kŏN'dā')
Confucius (kon-fū'shī-ŭs)
Congreve (kŏng'grēv)
Conybeare (kŭn/l-bēr)
Copernicus (ko-pẹr'-nī-kŭs)
Coquerel (kok/rel')
Corday (kor'dā')
Corneille (kor'nāl' ; *Fr. pron.* koR'nāl'') [lis)
Cornwallis (korn-wŏl'-Correggio (kor-rĕd'jo)
Cor'tẹz (*Sp.* Cortes, koR-tĕs')
Cousin (koo'zăN')
Coutts (koots)
Cowper (kow'pẹr *or* koo'per)
Crăd'ẹck
Crā'h'aw
Crichton (krī'tọn)
Cromwell (krŭm'wel *or* krŏm'wel)
Cunard (ku-närd')
Cuvier (kü've-ā' *or* kü've-ẹr)

D.

Dagobert (dăg'o-bẹrt *or* dä'go'bĕR')
Daguerre (dä'gĕR')
Dalhousie (dăl-hoo'zī)

ā, ĕ, &c., *long*; ă, ĕ, &c., *short*; cāre, fär, ȧsk, ạll, whạt; ēre, vẹil, tẽrm; pīque, fĭrm; sŏn, ôr,

MODERN BIOGRAPHICAL NAMES. 373

Dalton (dawl′tọn)
Dalzell (dā-ĕl′)
Damiens (dä′me-ăN′); *Anglicized* Dā′mi-ẹns.
Dampier (dăm′peer)
Dandolo (dän′do-lo)
Dante (dăn′te; *It. pron.* dän′tā)
Danton (däN′tọn *or* dŏN′tŏN′)
D'Arblay (där′blā)
Daubigné (dō′bēn′yā′)
Dăv′ẹn-ạnt
Dăv′ẹn-pōrt
Davila (dä′ve-lä) [dol′]
De Candolle (dẹh kŏN′-
De-cä′tur
Delaroche (d'lä′rosh′)
Denius (dä-nee′nä) [bī]
Derby (dĕr′bī *or* där′-
Derzhavin (dĕn-zhä′-vin)
Descartes (dā′känt′)
Devereux (dĕv′ẹr-oo)
Dewees (dẹ-weez′)
D'Ewes (dūz)
Diderot (dēd′ro′ *or* dē′dẹh-ro′)
Didot (de′do′)
Diez (deets)
Disraeli (diz-rā′ẹl-ee)
Domenichino (do-mā-ne-kee′no)
Donizetti (don′e-zet′tee *or* do-nū-zet′tee)
Don′o-van
Douce (Eng.) (dowss)
Drouyn de Lhuys (droo′ăN′ dẹh lwee)
Ducange (du-känj′; *French pron.* dü′-kŏnzh′)
Duchesne (dü′shăn′)
Duclos (dü′klo′)
Dudevant (dü′dẹh-vŏN′ *or* düd′vŏN′)
Dumas (dṇ′mā′)
Dumont (dü′mŏN′)
Dun-bar′
Duncan (dugk′ạn)
Dundas (dŭn-däss′)
Dupont (Amer.) (du-pŏnt′)
Durand (Amer.) (du-rănd′)
Dürer (dü′rẹr *or* dü′-rẹr)
Duyckinck (dī′kiṇk)
Dyche (dīch *or* dītch)

E.

Echard (Eng.) (ĕtch′-ạrd)
Egerton (ĕj′ẹr-tọn)
Elgin (ĕl′gịn)

Ellesmere (ĕlz′meer)
Elmes (ĕlmz) [stọn)
Elphinstone (ĕl′fin-
Elzevir (ĕl′zẹh-vịr)
Eneke (ĕnk′ẹh)
Enghien (ŏN′ğe-ăN′)
Epes (eps)
Erasmus (e-răz′mŭs)
Ercilla (ĕn-theel′yä)
Eric (ĕr′ik)
Ericsson (ĕr′ik-sọn)
Erskine (ẽrs′kin)
Estaing (ĕs′tăN′), *or* d'Estaing (dĕs′tăN′)
Este (ĕs′te *or* ĕs′tā)
Esterhazy, *or* Eszter-házy (ĕs′tẹr-hä′ze)
Étienne (ā′te-ĕnn′)
Euler (yoo′lẹr; *Ger. pron.* oi′lẹr)
Ewart (yoo′ạrt)
Ewing (yoo′ing)
Eyre (ăr)

F.

Fabyan, *or* Fabian (fā′bi-ạn) [hīt)
Fahrenheit (fär′ẹn-
Falconer (fawk′nẹr *or* faw′kẹn-ẹr)
Falkland (fawk′lạnd)
Faneuil (fŭn′il)
Faraday (făr′ạ-dā)
Farnese (far-neez′; *It. pron.* far-nā′sū)
Farquhar (fär′kwar *or* fär′kär)
Fatima (fä′tē-mä *or* făt′e-mạ)
Faust (fowst *or* fawst)
Fénelon (fĕn′ẹh-lọn; *Fr. pron.* fān′lŏN′ *or* fā′nẹh-lŏN′)
Fichte (fik′tẹh)
Fingal (fĭng′gạl *or* fing-gawl′)
Firdousi, *or* Firdausi (fir-dow′see)
Flotow (flo′to)
Foix (fwä)
Fontaine (fŏn-tăn′; *Fr. pron.* fŏN′tĕn′)
Fontenelle (fŏn-tẹh-nel′; *Fr. pron.* fŏNt′nel′)
Forbes (Eng.) (fôrbz)
Forbes (Scot.) (fôr′bẹz)
Fordyce (for-dīs′)
Forsyth (fọr-sīth′)
Fortescue (fôr′tẹs-ku)
Fosbroke (fos′brŏok)
Foscolo (fos′ko-lo)
Fothergill (fŏth′er-ğil)
Fouché (foo′shā′)
Foulis (fow′lis; *Scot. pron.* fowlz)

Foulques (fŏok)
Fouqué (foo′kā′). *See* La Motte-Fouqué.
Foureroy (foon′krwä′)
Fourier (foo′re-ẹr; *Fr. pron.* foo′re-ā′)
Francia (South Am.) (frän′se-ä)
Freiligrath (frī′le-grät′)
Frelinghuysen (free′-ling-hī′zẹn)
Frémont, *or* Fremont (Am.) (fre-mŏnt′)
Frŏb′ish-er
Froila (fro′ĭ-lä)
Froissart (frois′särt′; *Fr. pron.* frwä′säR′)
Froude (frood)
Fulton (fŏol′tọn)
Fuseli (fu′sẹ-lī)

G.

Gainsborough (gānz′-b'rọ) [nee)
Galignani (gä-lēn-yä′-
Galileo (găl′i-lee′o; *It. pron.* gä-le-lā′o)
Găl′lạ-tin
Găl′lau-det′
Galt (gawlt)
Galvani (gäl-vä′nee)
Garcilasso (*or* Garcilaso) de la Vega (gan-the-läs′so, *or* gar-se-läs′so, dä lä vä′gä)
Gardiner (gard′nẹr)
Garibaldi (gär-ī-bäl′-dī *or* gä-re-bäl′dee)
Gascoygne, *or* Gascoigne (găs-koin′)
Gasparin (găs′pạ-rin *or* gäs′pä′răN′)
Găv′ẹs-tọn
Gay-Lussac (gā′lüs′-
Geil (jel) [săk′)
Genet (jẹh-net′ *or* zh′nä)
Gengis Khan, *or* Jengis Khan (jĕng′ğis kän *or* kän)
Genlis (zhŏN′le′)
Genseric (jen′sẹr-ik)
Geoffroy (Eng.) (jŏf′-frī)
Gerard (Eng.) *or* (jẽr′ạrd)
Gerry (ğĕr′rī)
Gessler (ğĕss′lẹr)
Ğĭb′bọn
Ğibbs
Ğĭb′sọn
Gifford (ğif′fọrd *and* jif′fọrd) [bẹrt)
Gilbert (Eng.) (ğĭl′-
Gilchrist (ğĭl′krĭst)
Ğĭl-fĭl′lạu

Gillespie (ğĭl-lĕs′pī)
Ğil′mạn
Ğil′mọre
Ğĭl′pin
Giotto (jŏt′to)
Girard (Am.) (jẹ-rard′)
Ğiz′bọrne
Glauber (glaw′bẹr *or* glou′bẹr)
Gleig (gleg)
Glendower (glen′dou-
Glover (glŭv′ẹr) [ẹr)
Go-dol′phin
Goethe. *See* Göthe.
Goldoni (gol-do′nee)
Gonzalo (gon-thä′lo).
Görgei, *or* Gorgey (gŏn′-gä; *Ger. pron.* gör′-oi)
Gortchakov, *or* Gortschakow (gor′chä-kof) [tẹh)
Göthe, *or* Goethe (gü′-
Gough (gof)
Gould (goold) [gör)
Gower (gow′er *and*
Græme (gräm)
Granger (Eng.) (grān′-
Greaves (greevz) [jẹr)
Greenough (green′o)
Gresh′ạm
Griesbach (grees′bäk)
Grisi (gree′see) [ọr)
Grosvenor (gro′vẹn-
Grotius (gro′shi-ŭs)
Grouchy (groo′she′)
Guelph (gwelf) [no)
Guereino (gwĕn-chee′-
Guicciardini (ğwĕt-chän-dee′nee)
Guido Reni (gwee′do rā′nee)
Guise (ğwēz)
Guizot (ğwe′zo′ *or* ğe′zo′)
Günther (gün′tẹr)
Gutenberg (goo′tẹn-bẹng′ *or* goo′tẹn-bĕng)
Guthrie (gŭth′rī)
Guyon (ğī′ọn *or* ge′-
Guyot (ğe′o′) [ŏN′)

H.

Hafiz (hä′fĭz)
Hahnemann (hä′nẹh-män)
Ilăk′lụyt; *written also* Haekluyt.
Hạn-lō′rạn
Hän′dẹl (Ger. Händel, hĕn′dẹl) [kurt)
Harcourt (Eng.) (har′-
Hardicanute (har′de-kạ-nūt′)
Hardinge (här′ding)

dọ, wọlf, tōō, tŏŏk; ūrn, rụe, pụll; ç, ġ, *soft*; c, ḡ, *hard*; ạṣ; exist: ṇ *as* ng; this (see p. 861).

374 MODERN BIOGRAPHICAL NAMES.

Haroun - al - Raschid (hä-roon'äl-räsh'ld)
Haüy (hä'we')
Havelock (hăv'ĕh-lŏk)
Haydn (hä'dn; *Ger. pron.* hī'dn)
Haynau (hī'now)
Hearne (hẽrn)
Heeren (hā'ren)
Hegel (hā'gel)
Heine (hī'neh)
Heintzelman (hīnt'sęl-mạn) [ŭs)
Helvetius (hĕl-vee'shĭ-ĕm'ạns
Hengist (hěng'gĭst)
Herbelot (ĕrb'lo' or ẽr/beh-lo')
Herder (hẽr'dẹr or hĕr'dẹr)
Herrera (ĕa-ra'rä)
Herschel (hẽr'shẹl)
Heylin (hā'lĭn)
Heyne (hī'neh)
Heyse (hī'zęh)
Hoefer (*Ger. pron.* hẽ'fẹr; *Fr.* o'fĕr')
Hogarth (ho'garth)
Holbein (hol'bīn)
Holinshed, *or* Hollynshed (hŏl'inz-hĕd)
Holmes (hōmz)
Houdon (oo'dŏn')
Houghton (ho'tọn)
Houston (*popularly pronounced* hū'stọn)
Hovey (hŭv'ī)
Huger (Am.) (ū-jee')
Hughes (hūz)
Humboldt (hŭm'bōlt; *Ger. pron.* hŏom'-bolt)
Huskisson (bolt)
Huss, *or* Hus (hŭss; *Ger. pron.* hŏoss)
Huyghens (hī'gęnz *or* hoi'gęnz) [lee)
Hyder Ali (hī'dẹr ä'-

I.

Inchbald (ĭnch'bạld)
Inez (ee'nĕz)
Ingelow (ĭn'ge-lōw)
Ireton (īr'tọn)
Iriarte (e-re-ar'tā) *Syn.* Yriarte. [dä)
Iturbide (e-toor'be-
Ivan (Russ.) (e-vän')

J.

Jacobi (yä-ko'bee)
Jamieson (jām'e-sọn *or* jĭ'mĭ-sọn)
Jean Paul (zhŏn powl *or* jeen pawl)
Jellachich (yĕl'lä-ĸĭĸ)

Joan of Arc (*Fr.* Jeanne d'Arc, zhăn dark') [zhwăn'vēl')
Joinville (join'vil *or* Jomini (zho'me'ne')
Joubert (zhoo'bĕr')
Jouffroy (zhoof'frwä')
Jourdain (zhoor'dăn')
Jowett (jō'et)
Juarez (ŏo-ä'rĕs *or* ᴴwä'rĕth)
Junot (zhü'no')
Jussieu (jüs'sū'; *Fr. pron.* zhü'se-ᴜh')

K.

Kantemir (kän'tę-meer)
Kavanagh (kav'ạ-nä' *or* kav'a-näu')
Kearney (kar'nĭ)
Keble (kĕb'l)
Keightly (kīt'lee)
Kneller (nel'lẹr; *Ger. pron.* knęl'lẹr)
Knolles (nōlz; *written also* Knollys (nōlz)
Knowles (nōlz)
Körner (*or* Koerner (kẽr'nẹr) [ko)
Kosciusko (kos-sī-ŭs'-
Kossuth (kosh'shoot')
Kotzebue (kot'sęh-bū; *Ger. pron.* kot'-sęh-boo)
Krummacher (krŏom'-mäĸ-ęr)

L.

Lacépède (lä'sā'pĕd')
Lacroix (lä'krwä')
Laennec (lăn'nĕk')
Ladislas (lăd'ĭs-lạs); *written also* Lad'is-la'us.
La Fayette, *or* Lafayette (lä'fä-ĕt') [fĕt')
Laffitte (lăf'fĭt' *or* lä'-
La Fontaine (lä fŏn'-tĭn'; *Fr. pron.* lä'-fŏn'tăn')
Laing (lăng)
Lally-Tollendal (lăl'-lee' tol'lŏn'dăl')
Lamartine (lä'mar'-tēn')
Lamballe (lŏn'băl')
La Motte-Fouqué (lä mot-foo'kä')
La Pérouse (lä pā'-rooz')
Laplace (lä'plăss')
Las Casas (läs kä'säs)

Las Cases (läs käz)
Lă'thạm
Lavater (lä-vä'ter *or* lä'vä'tĕr')
Lavoisier (lä'vwä'ze-ā')
Layard (lā'ạrd)
Legaré (Amer.) (lẹh-gree')
Legendre (lẹh-zhŏxd'r' *or* lĕh-jĕn'dẹr)
Leibnitz, *or* Leibniz (lĭp'nĭts)
Leigh (lee)
Leighton (lā'tọn)
Lempriere (lĕm'prĭ-er *or* lẹm-preer')
Le Sage, *or* Lesage (lẹh-säzh')
L'Estrange (lĕs-trānj')
Lẽ'vẹr
Leverrier (lẹh-vĕr'rĭ-ẹr *or* lẹh-vā're-ā')
Lewes (lu'ĭs)
Liddell (lĭd'dẹl)
Lieber (lee'bẹr)
Liebig (lee'big)
Lingard (lĭng'gạrd)
Linnæus (lĭn-nee'ŭs)
Linnell (lĭn'nęl)
Liszt (lĭst)
Lloyd (loid) [vä'gä)
Lope de Vega (lo'pā dā
Lopez (lo'pĕs *or* lo'-pĕth) [lo-tĕr')
Lothaire (lo-thĕr' *or* Loudon (lou'dọn)
Louis (loo'is; *Fr. pron.* loo'e')
Lowth (louth)
Loyola ˙(loi-o'lạ *or* lo-Lyford [yo'lä)

M.

Mac-bĕth'
Macchiavelli (mäk-ke-ä-vel'lee). *Syn.* Machiavel.
Mac Culloch (mạ-kŭl'-lŭh) [văn')
Macilvaine (măk'ĭl-Mackay (mạ-kā' *and* mạ-kī')
Mack'in-tŏsh
Mack'lin
Mac-lạu'rĭn
Maclean (mạk-lān')
Macleod (mạ-klowd')
Maclin (mạ-klĭn')
Maclise (mạ-klees')
Macomb (mạ-kōmb')
Macready (mạ-kree'dĭ)
Mad'oc
Magellan (mạ-jẹl'lạn; *Sp. pron.* mä-ᴴĕl-yän')
Maginn (mạ-ɢĭn')

Mahmud, *or* Mahmoud (mäh'mood')
Mahomet (mạ-hom'et, mä'ho-met, *or* mä'ho-met)
Mahon (mạ-hoon' *or* mạ-hōn')
Maimonides (mī-mon'-ẹ-dēz)
Maintenon (mănt'-nōx' *or* män'tẹ-nōn)
Mainwaring (man'nẹr-ĭng) [dä)
Malagrida (mä-lä-gree'-
Malcolm (măl'kọm)
Malesherbes (măl'-zŭrb')
Malone (mạ-lōn')
Malte Brun (mawlt brŭn' *or* mält'ẹ-brŭx')
Marat (mä'rä')
Marie-Antoinette (mä're' ŏx'twä'net')
Marie Louise (mä're' loo'ĕz') [ọn)
Marion (Am.) (măr'e-Marlborough (mawl'-b'ro)
Marlowe (mar'lō)
Martel (maʀ'tel')
Martineau (Eng.) (mar'tĭ-nō)
Masaniello (mä-sä-ne-Mäs'sạ-soit' [el'lo)
Masséna (mäs-sā'nä; *Fr. pron.* mă'sā'nä')
Massillon (măs'sĭl-lŏn *or* măs'se'yŏx')
Massinger (măs'sịn-jẹr)
Mather (măth'ẹr)
Maturin (măt'yoo-rĭn)
Maunder (mawn'dẹr)
Maupertuis (mō'pĕʀ'-twē')
Maurepas (mōʀ'pä')
Maury (Am.) (maw'rĭ *and* mūr'rĭ)
Maury (Fr.) (mō're')
Mazarin (măz'a-reen'; *Fr. pron.* mă'zä'-răx')
Mazzini (măt-see'nee *or* mä-zee'nee)
Meagher (mä'gẹr)
Medici (med'e-chee)
Médicis (mä'de'sēss' *or* med'e-sis)
Meigs (mẽgz)
Melanchthon (mẹ-lăŋk'thọn) [sọn)
Mendelssohn (men'dẹl-Mendoza (men-do'zạ; *Sp. pron.* mĕn-do'-thä)
Metastasio (met'ạ-stä'-sẹ-o *or* mū-tä'-stä'-sẹ-o)

ä, ĕ, &c., *long*; ă, ŏ, &c., *short*; cāre, fär, ăsk, ạll, whạt; ẽre, vẹil, tẽrm; pīque, fĭrm; sŏn, ŏr,

MODERN BIOGRAPHICAL NAMES. 375

Metternich (met/tẽr-nĭk *or* met/tẽr-nĭĸ)
Meyer (mī/ẽr)
Meyerbeer (mī/ẽr-bān/)
Meyrick (mẽr/ĭk)
Mezzofanti (mĕd/sō-făŭ/tee)
Mignet (mēn/yă/)
Mil/līn-ĸẹn
Milne (Scot.) (mĭll)
Milne (Eng.) (mĭln)
Milnes (mĭlz)
Mĭnié (ĭne/ne-ā/)
Mirabeau (mĭr/ạ-bō/ *or* ĭne/rä/bō/) [lä]
Mirandola (me-rän/do-Mo-hăm/mẹd
Moilère (ĭno/le-ẽR/)
Molyneux (mol/ĭ-nooks/)
Moncreiff (mon-kreef/)
Monroe (mọn-rō/)
Monstrelet (mōɴs/-trẹh-lă/) [gŭ]
Montague (mŏn/tạ-
Montaigne (mŏn/tān/ ; *Fr. pron.* mōɴ/tāɴ/)
Montalembert (mōɴ/-tä/lŏx/bêʀ/)
Montcalɪɪ (mŏnt-kăm/)
Montecuccoli (mon/tä-kŏŏk/ko-lee)
Montespan (mŏn/tẽs-păn/ ; *Fr. pron.* mōɴ/tĕs/pŏɴ/)
Montesquieu (mŏn/-tẹs-kū/ ; *Fr. pron.* mōɴ/tās/kẹ-uh/)
Montgolfier (mōɴ/gol/-fe-ā/ *or* mŏnt-gol/fī-ẹr)
Montgomery (Eng.) (mọnt-gŭm/ẹr-ĭ)
Montrose (mọnt-rōz/)
Moore (Eng.) (mōr)
Moreau (mo/rō/)
Morel (ino/rel/)
Morell (mo-rĕll/)
Morrell (Am.) (mŏr/-Mŏr/tọn [rĕl]
Mŏs/by
Mosheim (mŏs/hĭm)
Mottcux (mot-too/)
Moultrie (moo/trī)
Mŭw/ạtt
Mozart (mo-zart/; *Ger. pron.* mot/sart)
Müller (mül/lẹr, *almost* mĭl/lẹr)
Münchhausen (mŭn-chaw/sẹn ; *Ger. pron.* mūnṣ-how/-zẹn) [rät/)
Murat (mü/rä/ *or* mu-Murillo (moo-reel/yo *or* mü-rĭl/lo)
Mylne (miln)

N.

Napier (nā/pe-ẹr)
Narvaez (naR-vä/çth)
Nĕck/ẹr (*Fr. pron.* nĕk/kẽR/)
Ney (nā)
Niebuhr (nee/boor)
Noailles (no/äĭ/ *or* no/-äy/)
Nos/trạ-dā/mus
Novalis (no-vä/lĭs)

O.

Oberlin (o/bẹr-lin)
Ogilby (o/g'l-bĭ)
Ogilvio (ō/g'l-vī)
Öhlenschläger, *or* Oehlenschläger (ö/lẹn-shlä/gẹr) [ŏm/stẹd)
Olmstead (um/sted *or* Orsini (on-see/nee)
Ossian (ŏsh/ạn)
Ossoli (os/so-lee)
Oudinot (oo/de/no/)
Ousely (ooz/lĭ)
Oxenstiern (oks/ẹn-stĭrn/)

P.

Paesiello (pī-ä-se-el/lo), *or* Paisiello (pä-e-se-el/lo, *almost* pī-ze-el/lo)
Palafox (păl/ạ-foks/ ; *Sp. pron.* pä-lä-fŏn/)
Palestrina (pä-lĕs-tree/nä)
Pạll/grave
Palmerston (päm/ẽr-stọn) [lee)
Paoli (pä/o-lee *or* pow/-Pär/ạ-çĕl/sŭs
Pardoe (par/do)
Par/nell
Pascal (păs/kạl ; *Fr. pron.* päs/käl/)
Pearce *and* Pearse
Pēaɪ/sọn *and* Pēar/son
Pellico (pel/le-ko)
Pepin (pĕp/ĭn *or* pip/-ĭn ; *Fr. pron.* pẹh-păx/)
Pepys (pĕps) [sce)
Pestalozzi (pĕs-tä-lŏt/-Petrarch (pee/trärk)
Piccolomini (pĭk-ko-lom/e-nee)
Pichegru (pĕsh/grü/)
Pierce (peerss *or* pĕrss)
Piozzi (pe-ot/see *or* pe-ŏz/zĭ)
Pizarro (pe-zär/ro ; *Sp. pron.* pe-thăR/Ro)

Plantagenet (plăn-tăj/e-net)
Pleyel (plī/ẹl) ; *or* Pleyl (plīl)
Po/cạ-hŏn/tạs
Po/cŏcke
Poln-ʀĕtt/
Polk (polk *or* pōk)
Pombal (pŏm-bäl/)
Pompadour (pŏm/pạ-dōōR/ *or* pŏm/pä/-dōōR/)
Ponce de Leon (pŏn/-thä dä lä-ōn/)
Poniatowski (po-ne-ä-tov/ske)
Porteus (pōR/te-ŭs)
Poussin (poo/sāɴ/)
Powell-(pou/ẹl)
Pow/hạt-tăn/
Praed (prād)
Prichard (prĭtch/ạrd)
Prideaux (prĭd/o *and* prĭd/ŭx)
Priessnitz (preess/nĭts)
Pughe (pū)
Pugin (pū/jĭn)
Pulaski (pū-läs/kce ; *Pol. pron.* poo-läs/-kee)
Pulci (pool/chee)
Pulteney (pŭlt/nĭ)
Pusey (pū/zĭ)

Q.

Quarles (kwärlz)
Quevedo (kä-vä/Do)
Quincy (kwĭn/sĭ *or* kwĭn/zĭ)

R.

Rabelais (rä/bẹh-lä/ *or* räb/lä/)
Rachel (Fr.) (rü/shel/)
Racinc (rä/sĕn/ *or* räs-seen/)
Raffaelle (räf-fä-el/lä) *Syn.* Raphael.
Raleigh (raw/lĭ)
Ranke (räŋk/ẹh)
Raphael (rä/fä-ẹl *or* räf/fä-ẹl) [päx)
Rapin (räp/ĭn *or* rä/-Réaumur (rä/ō/müR/ *or* rō/mur) [bränt)
Rembrandt (rẹm/-Renan (rẹh-nŏɴ/)
Ren/nẹll
Reuchlin (roik/lĭn)
Reynolds (ren/ọldz)
Riccio (rĕt/cho)
Richelieu (rĕsh/ẹh-loo ; *Fr. pron.* rĕsh/le-uh/)
Richter (rĭk/tẹr)
Rienzi (re-en/zee), *or* Rienzo (re-cn/zo)

Rives (Amer.) (reevz)
Rizzio (rĕt/se-o *or* rĭt/-se-o)
Robespierre (ro/bẹs-peer/ *or* rob/ẹs-pẹ-ẽR/) [shŏɴ/bō/)
Rochambeau (ro/-Rochefoucauld (rŏsh/-foo-kō/ *or* rosh/foo/-kō/) [zhä/)
Roget (ro/zbä *or* ro/-Romilly (Eng.) (rom/-jl-ĭ)
Ronge (rong/ẹh)
Rosecrans (rōz/krănts/)
Rothschild (rŏs/chĭld ; *Ger. pron.* rōt/shĭlt)
Rousseau (roo/sō/)
Routledge (rŭt/lĭj)
Rowe (ro)
Rowley (rou/lĭ)
Rutgers (rut/gẹrs)
Rutherford (ruth/ẹr-fọrd)

S.

Saadi. *See* Sadi.
Sabine (săb/ĭn) [ẹr-ẹl)
Sacheverell (sạ-chev/-Saintine (sāɴ/tēn/)
Saint-John (sĕnt/-jŏn *or* sĭn/jẹn) [jẹr)
Saint Leger (sĭl/lĭn-Saint-Pierre (sĕnt-peer *or* sāɴ/pe-ẽR/)
Saint-Simon (sẹnt-sī/mọn *or* sāɴ/se/mōɴ/)
Saladiu (săl/ạ-dĭn)
Sand (Fr.) (sōɴ)
Sän/dỵs (*or* sändz)
Saunderson (sün/dẹr-sọn)
Saussure (sō/sūr/ *or* so/sür/) [il)
Savile, *or* Saville (sav/-Savonarola (sä-vo-nä-ro/lä)
Scaliger (skal/ĭ-jẹr)
Schelling (shel/lĭng)
Schenck (skeŋk)
Schiller (shĭl/lẹr)
Schlegel (shlä/gel *or* shlā/gẹl)
Schleiermacher (shlī/-ẹr-mäk/ẹr)
Schmidt (shmit)
Schuyler (skī/lẹr)
Scoresby (skōrz/bĭ)
Scougal (skoo/gạl)
Scribe (skrĭb) [dü)
Sepulveda (sä-pool/vä-Ṣẹr-ve/tŭs
Sérigné (sä-veen/yä *or* sĕv/ĭn/yä/)
Seward (sū/ạrd)
Seymour (see/mẹr)
Shākes/pēare ; *writ.*

dọ, wọlf, tōō, tŏŏk ; ûrn, ʀụe, pụll ; c, ĝ, *soft* ; c, ĝ, *hard* ; ạs ; exist ; ɴ as ng ; this (see p. 361)

MODERN BIOGRAPHICAL NAMES.

ten *also* Shakspeare and Shakspere.
Sheil (sheel)
Sidmouth (sĭd′mŭth)
Sieyes (se-ĕs′, se-ā′, *or* se-ā′yā′)
Sigel (see′ğel) [mŭnd]
Sigismund (sĭj′is-
Sigourney (sĭg′ọr-ul)
Sismondi (sĭs-mŏn′dĭ; *It. pron.* sēs-mōn′-
Slidell (slī-del′) [dee)
Suorri Sturluson (snor′ree stoor′lŏŏ-
Scane (sŏn) [sọn)
Sobieski (so-be-ĕs′kee)
Socinus (so-sī′nŭs)
Somers (sŭm′ẹrz)
Sontag (sŏn′täg *or* son′täg)
Sotheby (sŭth′ẹ-bĭ)
Soule (sōl) [lā′)
Soulé (soo-lā′ *or* soo′-
Soulouque (soo′lŏŏk′)
Soult (soolt)
Southard (sŭth′ạrd)
Southern (sŭth′ẹrn)
Southey (sowth′ĭ)
Sowerby (sou′ẹr-bĭ)
Soyer (sol′er *or* swä′-yā′)
Spalding (spawl′dĭng)
Spinola (spee′no-lä)
Spinoza (spe-no′zä)
Spurtzheim (spoorts′-him *or* spŭrz′im)
Staël (stäl *or* stawl)
Stanhope (stăn′ọp)
Stanislaus (stăn-is-lā′-ūs *or* stăn-is-lä′us)
Staunton (stän′-tŏn)
Steuben (Am.) (stū′-
Storrs (stŏrz) [bẹn)
Stowell (stō′ẹl)
Strahan *and* Strachan (strawn)
Straparola (st rä-pä-ro′-lä), *or* Sträp′a-röle
Strauss (strouss)[sạnt)
Stuyvesant (stī′vẹ-
Sue (sū; *Fr. pron.* sü)
Suleyman (soo-lā-mān′). *Syn.* Sollman. [sü′ye′)
Sully (sŭl′ĭ; *Fr. pron.*
Suwarrow (soo-ŏr′ro); *written* Souvoroff *or* Suworow (*Russ. pron.* soo-vo′rof)
Swō′dẹn-borg′ (*Sw. pron.* swä′den-borg)

T.

Talbot (tawl′bọt)

Talfourd(tawl′fọrd)
Tallaferro (tŏl′l-vẹr, *sometimes* tĕl′fẹr)
Talleyrand (tăl′lĭ-rănd; *Fr. pron.* tăl′-lä′rŏx′)
Tallmadge (tăl′mŭj)
Tamerlane (tăm′ẹr-lān *or* tăm′ẹr-lān′)
Taney (taw′nĭ) [so)
Tās′so (*It. pron.* täs′-
Tassoni (täs-so′nee)
Tẹ-cŭm′sẹh
Tegnér (tĕng-nēr′)
Teignmouth (tĭn′-mŭth)
Teniers (tĕn′yẹrz; *Fr. pron.* tẹh-ne-ā′ *or* tẹn-yā′)
Thackeray (thak′ẹr-rĭ)
Thalberg (tăl′bĕrg)
Theobald (thee′o-bawld *or* tĭb′bạld)
Thierry (te-ĕr′rĭ *or* te-ā′ree′)
Thiers (te-ĕr′)
Tholuck (to′lŏŏk)
Thom (tom)
Thoresby (thŏrz′bĭ)
Thorwaldsen (tor′-wäld-sẹn *or* tos′-vüld-sẹn)
Tighe (tĭ) [te′ye′)
Tilly (tĭl′le; *Fr. pron.*
Timur, *or* Timour (tee′moor′) [to)
Tintoretto (tēn-to-ret′-
Tippoo Sahib (tĭp′po sä′hĭb; *almost* sā′ĭb)
Tiraboschi (te-rä-bos′-kee) [donf)
Tischendorf (tĭsh′-ẹn-
Titian (tĭsh′ạn)
Tocqueville (tŏk′vĭl; *French pron.* tok′-vĕl′)
Torquato (ton-kwä′to)
Torquemada (tor-kā-mä′pä)
Toucey (tou′sĭ)
Toussaint L'Ouverture (too′săx′ loo′-vĕR′tüR′) [ẹnd)
Townshend (townz′-
Trowbridge (tro′-brĭj)
Tyndale (tĭn′dạl)
Tyrwhitt (tẽr′ĭt *or* tẽr′wit)

U.

Uhland (oo′länt *or* yoo′lạnd)
Ulfilas, *or* Ulphilas (Ŭl′fĭ-las)

Upham (ŭp′ạm)
Urquhart (ûrk′ạrt)
Uwins (yoo′Inz)

V.

Van Buren (văn bū′-rẹn)
Vanbrugh (văn′broo)
Vancouver (văn-koo′-vẹr)
Vandyke (văn-dīk′) (Dutch Vandyck, *or* Vandjik, vän-dĭk′)
Van Rensselaer (văn ren′sẹl-ẹr) (tel′)
Vattel (văt-tel′ *or* văt′-
Vauban (vō′bŏn′)
Vaughan (vaw′n *or* vaw′ạn)
Vaux (Eng. & Amer.) (vawks)
Vega (vā′gä)
Velasquez (vā-läs′kĕz *or* vä-läs′kĕth)
Vernet (vĕR′nā′)
Verplanck (vẹr-plănk′)
Vẹr-sto′gạn
Vĕr′ij-lạm
Vespucci (vĕs-poot′-chee)
Vicente (ve-sen′tä)
Vida (ree′dä)
Vidocq (re′dok′)
Villiers (vĭl′yẹrz)
Vinci (vĭn′chee *or* vĕn′chee)
Vladimir (vlăd′ẹ-mēr)
Volney (vŏl′nĭ; *Fr. pron.* vol′nā′)
Voltaire (vŏl-tĕr′ *or* vol′tĕr′) [ğẹrn)
Vortigern (vor′tẹ-
Voss (Ger.) (foss)

W.

Waldemar (wọl′de-mạr *or* wăl′dẹh-mär) [stĭn)
Wallenstein (wŏl′lẹn-dorf)
War′bur-tọn
Wargentin (wär′ğen-teen) (ing-tọn)
Washington (wŏsh′-
Wattoau (văt′tō′)
Weber (wā′bẹr *or* wā′-bẹr)
Wellesley (wĕlz′lĭ)
Wemys (weemz *or* wīmz)
Werner (wēr′nẹr *or* wĕn′nẹr)
Whalley (hwŏl′lĭ)
Whewell (hū′ẹl)
Whitefield (hwīt′feeld)

Wieland (wee′land; *German pron.* Vee′-länt)
Willoughby (wĭl′lọ-bĭ)
Willughby (wil′lọ-bĭ)
Winckelmann (wĭnk′-ẹl-män)
Windham (wĭnd′ạm)
Wolcott (wŏl′kọt *or* wŏŏl′kŏt) [tọn)
Wollaston (wŏŏl′ụs-
Wollstonecraft (wŏŏl′-stọn-krăft)
Wolsey (wŏŏl′zĭ)
Worcester (wŏŏs′tẹr)
Wordsworth (wûrdz′-wûrth)
Wouverman (wow′vẹr-män)
Wraxall (răks′ạl *or* răks′ạl)
Wycherley (wĭtch′-ẹr-lĭ)
Wycliffe (wĭk′lĭf); *also* Wyclif, Wiclif, *and* Wickliffe. [*thin*)
Wythe (wĭth; *th* as in

X.

Xavier (zăv′ĭ-ẹr; *Sp. pron.* Hä-ve-ār′)
Ximenes (zĭ-mee′nĕz; *Sp. pron.* He-mā′-nĕs)

Y.

Yonge (yŭng)
Yountt (jo′ọt)
Youmans (joo′mạnz)
Yriarte (e-re-aR′tä)
Ysabean (e′zü′bō′)

Z.

Zīm′mẹr-männ (*Ger. pron.* tsĭm′mer-män)
Zinzendorf (tsĭnt′sẹn-dorf)
Zollikofer (Ger.) (tsol′-le-ko′fẹr)
Zŭl′lĭ-kof′ẹr (Amer.)
Zouch (zooch)
Zschokke (tshŏk′kẹh)
Zumala – Carregui (thoo-mā′lä-kăR-Rā′-ḡee).
Zumpt (tsŏŏmpt)
Zuñiga (thoon-yec′gä)
Zwingli (*Ger. pron.* tsWing′lee) (Lat. Zwĭn′gli-ŭs *or* Zulu′gli-us); *written also* Zwingle (zwĭng′gl)

ā, ō, &c., *long*; ŏ, ŏ, &c., *short*; cāre, fŭr, ăsk, ạll, whạt; ẽre, veil, tẽrm; pīque, fĭrm, sŏn, ôr, dọ, wolf, tŏŏ, tŏŏk; ûrn, rụe, pụll; ç, ğ, *soft*; e, g, *hard*; aẓ; exist; ŋ *as* ng; this (*see* p. 831.)

PREFIXES AND SUFFIXES.

*** The "Exercises" given below are designed to furnish material for instruction and practice in the etymological analysis of English words. It is suggested that a certain number of prefixes or suffixes be assigned as a lesson for study, and that the pupil be required to ascertain and explain the literal meaning of the examples appended to them, including the root as well as the formative syllables. To aid in this, the use of Webster's Quarto or Octavo ("National") Dictionary will be necessary.

PREFIXES.

A, a prefix to many English words, is in some cases a contraction of *on*, *in*, *at*, *of*, *to*, *for*; as, *ablaze* for *in a blaze*, *aboard* for *on board*, *afoot* for *on foot*, *aground* for *on the ground*, *ado* for *to do*, *await* for *wait for*. In other cases, it is contracted from the A.-S. inseparable particle *ge-*, which forms verbs from verbs, substantives, adjectives, and is a sort of augment to the past participle. In some cases, it only increases the force of the word, without any essential addition of meaning. — In some words of Greek origin, *a* gives them a negative sense; before a vowel it becomes *an*. In a few words of Latin origin, it is another form of the prefix *ab*.

EXERCISE. — *A*wake, asleep, ahead, aside, afar, aweary; apathetic, amorphous, atheist, abyss, aorist, anonymous, anomaly, anecdote, anarchy; abate, avert.

Ab, a prefix to words of Latin origin, and a Latin preposition, is the same as the Greek ἀπό, Goth. *af*, A.-S. and Eng. *of*. It denotes *from*, *separation*, or *departure*. Before *c* and *t*, it is generally changed into *abs*. See A.

EXERCISE. — *Ab*duct, abject, abjure, abrupt, abrogate, absurd, abuse, abrade, absolve; abscess, abscond, abstemious, abstain.

Ad. [Cf. W. *at*, to, toward, Goth. and Eng. *at*.] A Latin preposition, signifying *to*. In composition, the last letter is usually changed into the first letter of the word to which it is prefixed.

EXERCISE. — *Ad*here, adjoin, addict, adjure, admit, admonish, adorn, advent, acclaim, aggravate, affirm, allege, applaud, arrogate, ascribe, attain.

Al. 1. In Arabic, an article or inseparable prefix, answering to the Italian *il*, and the Sp. *el*. Its use is to render nouns definite, like the English *the*.

EXERCISE. — *Al*cove, alchemy, alembic, almanac, alcohol, alkali.

2. A form of the prefix *ad*. See AD.

Am'bi. [Lat. *ambi*, *amb*, *am*, *an* (as *ambidens*, *ambages*, *amicire*, *anhelare*), Gr. ἀμφί, A.-S. *emb*, *ymb*.] *About*; *around*; — a prefix used in composition in words derived from the Latin.

EXERCISE. — *Ambi*dexter, amblent, ambition, ambiguous; anhelation.

Am'phi, n. [See *supra*.] A prefix in words of Greek origin, signifying *about*, *around*, *on both sides*, *on all sides*, &c.

EXERCISE. — *Amph*ibious, amphitheater, amphibology, amphibrach.

A'na. [Gr. ἀνά.] A prefix in words from the Greek, denoting *on*, *upward*, *up to*, *throughout*, *backward*, *back to*, *again*, *previously*, or *against*.

EXERCISE. — *Ana*logy, analytic, anatomy, anabaptist, anachronism, anagram, anapest, &c.

Ant-, } [Gr. ἀντί, against.]
An'ti-. } A prefix in words from the Greek, meaning *against*, *over against*, or *opposed to*.

EXERCISE. — *Ant*arctic, anthelmintic, antidote, antipathy, antithesis, antifebrile, antipodes, antichristian, antitype.

An'te. A Latin preposition, the Gr. ἀντί, A.-S. & Goth. *and* (cf. ANSWER); used in the composition of English words, esp. in words from the Latin and Greek. It signifies *before in place*, *in front*; and figuratively, *before in time*.

EXERCISE. — *Ante*chamber, antecedent, antediluvian, antemundane, antedate, antepenult.

A'po. [Gr. ἀπό. See AB.] A Greek preposition used in composition, and signifying *from*, *away from*, *off*, or *asunder*. It sometimes has the contracted form *ap*.

EXERCISE. — *Apo*plexy, apothecary, apologue, apostacy, apostrophe, apostle; aphelion, aphorism.

Be, is originally the same word as *by*, A.-S. *be* and *bi* or *big*, Goth. *bi*. It denotes *nearness*, *closeness*, *about*, *on*, *at*, and generally has an intensive force.

EXERCISE. — *Be*set, bedeck, become, bestow, bedim, becalm, becloud, befriend, because, before, betimes.

Bī. [From Lat. *bis*, twice, which in composition drops the *s*.] In most branches of science, *bi* in composition denotes *two*, *twice*, *doubly*. In chemistry, it denotes that the compound contains two parts of the first-mentioned ingredient to one of the other; thus, a *bi*chromate of potash contains two parts of chromic acid to one of potash.

EXERCISE. — *Bi*dentate, biternate, biaxal, bicapsular, bicephalous, bicipitous, bifoliate, bisect, biweekly, binominal.

Bis, *adv.* [Lat. *bis*, twice, for *duis*, from *duo*, two, like *bellum* from *duellum*.] Twice. See BI.

EXERCISE. — *Bis*sextile.

Ca'ta. [Gr. κατά.] The Latin and English form of a Greek

(377)

PREFIXES AND SUFFIXES.

preposition used in composition to signify *down, downward, down upon, downright, completely,* &c. It sometimes drops the final vowel, and is sometimes changed to *cath*.

EXERCISE.—*Cataclysm, catacomb, catalogue, cataract, catarrh, catacaustic, catalepsy, catastrophe; catoptric, category; cathartic, catholic, cathedral.*

Çir′cum. [Accusative of *circus*, a circle, Gr. κίρκος.] A Latin preposition, used as a prefix in many English words. In a few words the *m* is dropped.

EXERCISE. — *Circumscribe, circumspect, circumvent, circumjacent, circumnavigate, circumlocution; circuit, circuitous, circulate.*

Com- or Con-. [The same as *cum*, which is akin to Gr. σύν.] A Latin preposition signifying *with* or *against*, used in composition as an inseparable prefix. The form *com* is used before *b, p,* and *m,* and *con* before the other consonants. Before *l,* however, *con* or *com* is changed into *col;* before *r* into *cor;* while before a vowel or *h*, the *n* or *m* is dropped.

EXERCISE. — *Compose, commotion, commerce, command, compact; connect, concur, construct, convoke, contract; collect; corrupt; coalesce, cohabit, co-operate, coheir, cohere.*

Con′tra. A Latin preposition, signifying *against, in opposition*, entering into the composition of some English words. In old English, it took the form *counter.*

EXERCISE. —*Contradict, contravene, contradistinguish, contravallation: counteract, countermarch, counterpart, countercharm, counterbalance.*

Co. See CON.

Coun′ter. See CONTRA.

De. A Latin prefix denoting a *moving from, separation*. Hence, it often expresses a negative. Sometimes it augments the sense. It coincides nearly in sense with the French *des* and Latin *dis*.

EXERCISE.—*Debark, decline, decease, deduct, decamp, deject, deter, descend, detain, depart, detract, denude, denominate, denounce, derange, deprave, despoil.*

Di. 1. [Gr. δίς, twice.] In chemistry, a prefix denoting two equivalents of the substance indicated by the noun following that of which the prefix forms a part; as, *dichloride of mercury; i. e.,* a compound formed of two equivalents of mercury and one of chlorine. 2. See DIS.

Di′ă. [Gr. διά, akin to Lat. *dis*.] A prefix denoting *through, right through.*

EXERCISE. — *Diameter, diagram, dialogue, diagonal, diacritical, diatribe, dialect.*

Dis. An inseparable prefix, from the Latin (whence Fr. *des*), denoting *separation,* a *parting from;* hence it generally has the force of a negative. It sometimes passes into the forms *di* and *dif.*

EXERCISE. — *Distribute, disconnect, disarm, disoblige, disagree, disorder, dispel, discover; divert; differ, diffuse.*

Dys-. An inseparable prefix, from the Greek δυσ-, hard, ill, and signifying *ill, bad, hard, unlucky, dangerous,* &c.

EXERCISE.—*Dysentery, dyspepsy.*

E. A Latin prefix; the same as Ex.

Em. See EN.

En. A prefix to many English words, chiefly borrowed from the French ; it coincides with the Latin *in*, Gr. *ἐν*. For ease of pronunciation, it is changed to *em*, particularly before a labial.

EXERCISE. — *Enchant, enamor, encore, encamp, engrave, enjoy, enlarge, ennoble, enrich, employ, empower, emboss, embrace.*

Ep, Ep′i. } [Gr. ἐπί. See OB.] A prefix, signifying *on, above, toward, by, to, among, near,* &c.

EXERCISE. — *Epilogue, epithet, epidemic, epitaph, epidermis, epitomize, ephemeral.*

Eŭ. A prefix from the Gr. *εὖ*, well, signifying *well, easy, advantageous, good,* and the like.

EXERCISE. — *Eulogy, euphony, eucharist, euphemism.*

Ex. A Latin preposition or prefix (Gr. *ἐξ* or *ἐκ*), signifying *out of, out, proceeding from.* Hence, in composition, it signifies sometimes *out of;* sometimes *off, from,* or *out;* sometimes *beyond.* In some words, it intensifies the meaning. The *x* regularly remains only before the vowels and before *c, h, p, q, s, t;* it is assimilated to a following *f*, and drops away altogether before the other consonants. In a few words it changes into *ec*. Prefixed to names of office, it denotes that a person has held that office, but has resigned it, or been left out, or dismissed.

EXERCISE. — *Exhale, exclude, excind, excess, exceed, excel, exact, exert, exist, exonerate, exult, exhaust, expend, exquisite, exsiccant, extort; effux, effect, effusion; elect, event, edition, emigrate, eject; eccentric; ex-chancellor,ex-governor, ex-president.*

Ex′trā. [Contr. from *exterâ (parte)*, from *exter*, being on the outside, from *ex*, out of, from.] A Latin preposition, denoting *beyond* or *excess*, often used in composition as a prefix signifying *outside of,* or *beyond the limits or jurisdiction of* that denoted by the word to which it is joined.

EXERCISE. — *Extradition, extravagant, extraneous, extraordinary, extrajudicial.*

For. [A.-S. *for*, allied to Goth. *fair*, Ger. *ver*.] As a prefix to verbs, *for* has usually the force of a negative or privative, denoting *forth, away, out, without.*

EXERCISE. — *Forbid, forsake, forswear, forego.*

Fōre. [A.-S. *fore*, kindred with *for*, prep.] An adjective used in composition, to denote *advancement in place or time.*

EXERCISE. — *Forebode, forefather, foreshorten, foreordain, foresee, foretell, forerunner, foreground, foreshow, forestall, forearm, foreknowledge, forewarn.*

Hȳ′per. [Gr. ὑπέρ, allied to Lat. *super*, Skr. *upare*, Eng. *over*.] A prefix used in composition to denote *excess,* or something *over* or *beyond.*

EXERCISE. — *Hyperbolical, hypertrophy, hyperborean, hypercritical, hyperbole.*

Hȳ′po. A prefix from the Greek preposition ὑπό [allied to Lat. *sub*, Skr. *upar*], *under, beneath*, frequently used in composition to signify *a less quantity*, or *a low state or degree* of that denoted by the word with which it is joined, *position beneath* it, &c. In chemistry, prefixed to the name of a compound con-

PREFIXES AND SUFFIXES. 379

taining oxygen, it designates another compound containing less oxygen; as *hypo-nitrous* acid, which contains less oxygen than *nitrous* acid.

EXERCISE. — *Hypo*chondriac, *hypo*static, *hypo*thesis, *hypote-*nuse; *hyp*hen.

II. The form of *in* when used before words beginning with *l*. See IN.

Ĭm. A prefix from the Latin *in, n* being changed to *m*, before a labial, for the sake of easy utterance. The same prefix is sometimes used in compounds not of Latin origin. For *im*, the French write *em*, which is used in words introduced into English from the French language. See EM.

EXERCISE. — *Im*bibe, *im*mense, *im*partial, *im*moral, *im*port, *im*print, *im*bank, *im*bitter, *im*prison.

Ĭn. 1. [Allied to Gr. ἐν, Skr. *ina*] A prefix from the Latin *in*, often used in composition, and signifying *within, into*, or *among*, or serving to render emphatic the sense of the word to which it is prefixed. — *In* before *l* is changed into *il*; before *r*, into *ir*; before a labial, into *im*. 2. [Allied to Eng. *un*. See UN.] A Latin particle of negation. Before *b* and *p*, it becomes *im*; before *l, m, r*, the *n* assimilates itself to these consonants. In a few words *in* is changed into *ig*.

EXERCISE. — 1. *In*bred, *in*case, *in*ject, *in*spect, *in*duce, *in*-fuse, *in*close, *in*crease; *in*flation, *il*lumine, *il*lusion; *ir*radiate, *ir*-ruption, *ir*rigation; *im*bitter, *im*-mersion, *im*plement. — 2. *In*active, *in*capable, *in*vincible, *in*-tolerable, *in*firm, *im*passable; *il*-licit, *il*limitable, *im*mortal; *ir*-repressible, *ir*resolute; *ig*noble, *ig*-norant.

Ĭn'ter. [From *in*, with an adverbial ending.] A Latin preposition, signifying *among* or *between*; — used as a prefix.

EXERCISE. — *Inter*cept, *inter*-fere, *inter*rupt, *inter*cede, *inter*-pose, *inter*change, *inter*min-gle, *inter*view, *inter*pose, *inter*-vene, *inter*sperse.

Ĭn'tro. [Lat., contr. from *in-tero (loro)*.] A prefix signifying *within, into, in*, and the like.

EXERCISE. — *Intro*duce, *in*-tromission, *intro*vert, *introit*, *in*-trospection.

Mĕt'a. [Gr. μετά, allied to μέσος; Lat. *medius*, Eng. *mid, middle*.] A prefix in words of Greek origin, signifying *in the midst of*; also, *beyond, over, after, behind, with, between, reversely*.

EXERCISE. — *Meta*phor, *meta*-physics, *meta*morphose, *meta*-phrase.

Mis. [A.-S., having the same origin with the verb *to miss*.] A prefix denoting *error, wrong, defect, unlikeness*, &c.

EXERCISE. — *Mis*take, *mis*-manage, *mis*pronounce, *mis*-trust, *mis*behave, *mis*believer, *mis*creant, *mis*demeanor.

Nŏn, *adv*. [Lat. *non*, O. Lat. *nænum, nenum*, from *ne-ænum*, or *ne-unum*, not one.] *Not*; — used in English as a prefix, generally and properly to substantives and verbs only, giving them a negative sense, ordering and varying their meaning, as do the prefixes *un* and *in* those of adjectives; also, in some cases, prefixed to adjectives.

EXERCISE. — *Non*-residence, *non*-performance, *non*-arrival, *non*-intercourse, *non*-intervention, *non*-conductor, *non*-acid, *non*-electric, *non*-existent, *non*-commissioned.

Ŏb. [Kindred with Gr. ἐπί.] A Latin preposition, signifying, primarily, *in front, before*, and hence *against, toward*. In composition the *b* is often changed into the first letter of the word to which it is prefixed. In a few cases the *b* becomes *s*. It means *reversed* or *back* in obovate, occiput, &c.

EXERCISE. — *Ob*ject, *ob*jugatory; *oc*casion; *af*fer; *op*pose; *os*-tentation.

Pā'rá. [Gr., prob. akin to Lat. *præ* and *præter*.] A preposition, used in composition, and signifying *beside, to the side of, to, amiss, wrong, beyond, contrary to*, &c. It is sometimes contracted into *par*.

EXERCISE. — *Para*dox, *para*gon, *para*lysis, *para*site, *para*llel, *para*graph, *para*clete, *para*phrase; *par*ody, *par*oxysm, *par*helion.

Pĕr. A Latin preposition often used in composition as a prefix denoting *through, passing*, or *over the whole extent*. The *r* is sometimes assimilated. In chemistry, it signifies *very, fully*, or *to the ut*-*most extent*; as in *per*oxide, a substance oxidated to the utmost degree.

EXERCISE. — *Per*ambulate, *per*functory, *per*secute, *per*forate, *per*manent, *per*mit, *per*cussion, *per*vade, *per*use, *per*fection, *per*dition, *per*oxide; *pel*-lucid.

Pĕr'i. [Gr. περί, Skr. *pari*.] A prefix used in many words derived from the Greek, and signifying *with, around, about, near*, and the like.

EXERCISE. — *Peri*carp, *pe*-riod, *peri*phrase, *peri*patetic, *peri*phery, *peri*helion, *peri*meter.

Pŏst. A Latin preposition, used in composition as a prefix, signifying *after*.

EXERCISE. — *Post*pone, *post*-script, *post*erior, *post*humous, *post*obit.

Prē. An English form of the Latin prefix, *præ*, *before*. It expresses *priority of time, place*, or *rank*.

EXERCISE. — *Pre*clude, *pre*-dict, *pre*fer, *pre*ponderate, *pre*-cursor, *pre*cede, *pre*fix, *pre*lude, *pre*-eminent.

Prē'ter. A prefix, from the Lat. *præter* (from *præ*, with the adverbial termination *ter*), used in the composition of some English words, and having the signification of *past, beyond*; hence, *beside, more*.

EXERCISE. — *Preter*it, *preter*-mit, *preter*natural.

Prō. [Originally neuter dative for *proi*, Gr. πρό.] A Latin preposition, used in composition as a prefix, and denoting *fore, forth, forward, in front of, in favor of, for, in the place of*.

EXERCISE. — *Pro*duce, *pro*-ject, *pro*fess, *pro*mise, *pro*tract, *pro*noun, *pro*ceed, *pro*voke, *pro*mote, *pro*trude.

Prŏs. [Gr. πρός. Cf. Skr. *prati*.] A Greek preposition, used in composition, and signifying *motion towards, a being on, at, by*, or *beside, a remaining beside*, and hence *connection and engagement with* any thing.

EXERCISE. — *Pros*elyte, *pros*-ody.

Pseū'do (sū'do). [From Gr. ψευδής, lying, false, from ψεύδειν, to belie.] A prefix used in words from the Greek, and signifying *false, counterfeit, pretended*, or *spurious*.

EXERCISE. — *Pseudo*-martyr, *pseudo*-philosophy, *pseudo*nym.

Ra. An inseparable prefix or preposition in words from the French and Italian, coming from the Lat. *re* and *ad* combined. See RE and AD.
EXERCISE. — *Rally, ramble.*

Rĕ. [Lat.] A prefix or inseparable particle in the composition of words, denoting *return, repetition,* or *iteration.* It is abbreviated from *red,* which the Latins retained in words beginning with a vowel.
EXERCISE. — *Recur, reduce, refrain, retract, revert, rebuild, reform, restore, resound, resist, renew, recall, remove, resume, revolve; redeem, reintegrate.*

Rĕ'tro. [Lat., from *re,* and the adverbial termination *ter.*] A prefix in words from the Latin, signifying *back* or *backward.*
EXERCISE. — *Retrocede, retrospect, retrograde, retroact.*

Se. [Original form of *sine.*] An inseparable preposition used in some words from the Latin, and signifying *without, aside, by itself.*
EXERCISE. — *Secure, seduce, seclude, secede, sequester, separate, sedition.*

Sī'ne. A Latin preposition signifying *without,* and used in composition. It drops the final *e* in *sincere,* and also changes the *n* into *m* in *simple.*
EXERCISE. — *Sinecure.*

Stĕp. A.-S. *steóp,* fr. *steópan, stépan,* to bereave.] A prefix used in composition before *father, mother, brother,* &c., to indicate that the person thus spoken of is not a blood-relative, but is a relative by the marriage of a parent.
EXERCISE. — *Stepson, stepsister, stepchild.*

Sŭb. [Allied to Gr. ὑπό.] A Latin preposition, denoting *under* or *below,* used in English as a prefix, to express an *inferior position,* or *intention,* and also a *subordinate degree,* or *imperfect state* of a quality. Before *c, f, g, p, r,* and *m,* the *b* is changed into those letters.
EXERCISE. — *Subscribe, subsequent, submarine, submerge, submit, subtract, subacid, substitute, subside, subordinate, subterranean; succeed, suffer, suggest, suppose, surrogate, summon.*

Sŭb'ter. [From *sub,* and the adverbial termination *ter.*] A Latin preposition, signifying *under,* used as a prefix in English with the same meaning as *sub;* but it is less general in its application.
EXERCISE. — *Subterfuge.*

Sū'per. A Latin preposition (same as Gr. ὑπέρ), used as a prefix, and signifying *above, over,* or *in excess.*
EXERCISE. — *Superfine, superintend, supervise, supernumerary, superadd, superhuman, superfluous, superlative, superstructure.*

Sū'pra. [Orig. *supera,* from *super.*] A Latin preposition, signifying *above, over,* or *beyond,* and used in composition.
EXERCISE. — *Supralapsarian.*

Sŭr. A prefix, from the French, contracted from the Latin *super, supra,* and signifying *over, above, beyond, upon.*
EXERCISE. — *Surcharge, surmount, surprise, surfeit, surmise, surcoat, surface, surplus.*

Sўn. A prefix from the Greek preposition σύν [Lat. *cum,* akin to Lat. *simul,* Skr. *sa-, sam*], *with, along with, together with, at the same time.* Before *b, m, p, ph,* it changes into *sym;* before *l,* into *syl;* and sometimes the *n* is dropped.
EXERCISE. — *Synonym, syntax, synthesis, synod, synopsis, synchronous, synovial, symbol, symmetry, sympathy, symphony, syllogism, system.*

Trăns. A Latin preposition, used in English as a prefix, signifying *over, beyond, through, on the other side.* Hence, in a moral sense, it denotes a *complete change.* It sometimes drops the last consonant, and sometimes the two last consonants.
EXERCISE. — *Transalpine, trans-Atlantic, transport, transfer, transmit, transit, transgress, transform, transcend, tradition, traduce.*

Tri. A prefix, signifying *three, thrice,* from Gr. τρίς, thrice, τρεῖς, τρία, Lat. *tres, tria,* three.
EXERCISE. — *Triangle, trident, triennial, tricennial, tricuspid, triune.*

Ŭl'tra. [Lat., originally fem. of *ulter,* being *beyond.*] A prefix from the Latin, having in composition the signification *beyond, on the other side,* chiefly when joined with words expressing relations of place. In other relations, it has the sense of *excessively, exceedingly, beyond what is common, natural, right,* or *proper.*
EXERCISE. — *Ultramarine, ultramontane, ultramundane, ultratropical; ultra-conservative, ultra-despotic.*

Ŭn. [A.-S *un,* and sometimes *on,* allied to Gr. ἀν, ἀ, Skr. *an, a,* Lat. *in.*] A negative prefix attached at will to almost any English adjective, or participle used adjectively, and to less numerous classes of nouns and verbs. See UN in the Dictionary.
EXERCISE. — *Unable, unfriendly, uncertain, undo, unbar, untruth, unworthy.*

With. [A.-S. *widh, wid,* with, at, against, Icel. *vidh,* against. Compare A.-S. *mid, midh,* Goth. *mith,* Ger. *mit,* with.] An English preposition, used in composition, and signifying *opposition, privation, separation,* or *departure.*
EXERCISE. — *Withdraw, withstand, withhold.*

SUFFIXES.

Ăe. [Gr. -ακός.] A suffix signifying *of* or *pertaining to.*
EXERCISE. — *Demoniac, hypochondriac, cardiac, elegiac, prosodiac.*

Age. [Fr.] A termination of nouns having a collective or abstract meaning.
EXERCISE. — *Advantage, average, herbage, foliage, pillage, vassalage, appanage, homage, parentage, fruitage, anchorage.*

Al. [Lat. *-alis.*] A termination of words from the Latin, denoting *of,* or *pertaining to.* See CAL.
EXERCISE. — *Annual, cordial, final, legal, martial, regal, frugal, filial, carnal, casual, floral, manual, judicial, local, decennial.*

An. [Lat. *-anus.*] A termination of some nouns and adjectives from the Latin, denoting *office, profession,* or *character.*
EXERCISE. — *Christian, comedian, tragedian, elysian, tertian, hyperborean, sylvan, republican, pagan, Roman.*

Ănçe, } [Lat. *-antia.*] Terminations of some nouns having an abstract signification.
Ăn-çy. }

PREFIXES AND SUFFIXES. 381

EXERCISE.—Elegance, abundance, brilliancy, vacancy, dissonance, tolerance, ignorance, circumstance, repentance, infancy, necromancy.

Ant. [Lat. -ans, -antis.] A termination of adjectives from the Latin, expressing quality or habit; and of nouns denoting the doer of a thing.

EXERCISE.—Vagrant, abundant, verdant, extravagant, triumphant, vigilant, dominant, exorbitant; assistant, commandant, dependant, intendant.

Ar. [Lat. -aris.] A termination of adjectives derived from the Latin, and denoting of, or pertaining to.

EXERCISE.—Angular, jocular, perpendicular, similar, linear, familiar, solar, secular, regular.

Ard, the termination of many English words, is taken from the Goth. hardus, A.-S. heard, Icel. & Eng. hard, and appears in proper names; as, Renard, strong in counsel; Goddard, strong in, or through, God, &c. We find it also in appellatives, usually with a bad signification.

EXERCISE.—Drunkard, dotard, bastard, niggard, sluggard, dullard, coward, wizard, laggard, dastard.

A-ry. [Lat. -arius.] A termination of adjectives from the Latin, denoting of, or pertaining to; and of nouns, denoting the doer of a thing.

EXERCISE.—Auxiliary, military, biliary, stipendiary, pecuniary, primary, plenary, ordinary, sublunary, adversary, mercenary, vocabulary, lapidary, boundary, granary.

Ate. [Lat. -atus.] A termination;—1. Of verbs. 2. Of adjectives, implying nature, likeness, quality, agreement, effect, &c. 3. Of nouns, denoting (a.) office or dignity; (b.) the possessor of an office or dignity; (c.) salts containing one degree or more of oxygen.

EXERCISE.—1. Deliberate, initiate, extricate, perineate, suffocate, navigate, ventilate, fascinate, anticipate, venerate. 2. Moderate, ultimate, temperate, obdurate, fortunate, insensate, passionate, effeminate, immaculate. 3. Pontificate, electorate, palatinate; magistrate, delegate, legate, candidate, advocate, laureate, surrogate, sulphate, phosphate.

Ble. [Lat. -bilis.] A termination of adjectives derived from the Latin, or formed on the same model, and signifying capable of being, or worthy to be.

EXERCISE.—Flexible, mutable, sensible, warrantable, capable, curable, blamable, commendable, incredible, accessible, excusable.

Cal. [Lat. -cus.] A termination of adjectives derived from the Latin or following the analogy of such, and signifying of or pertaining to.

EXERCISE. — Anatomical, comical, magical, practical, technical, classical, analytical, botanical, practical, dogmatical, periodical.

Dom. A termination denoting jurisdiction, or property and jurisdiction. It was originally doom, judgment. Hence it is used to denote state, condition, or quality.

EXERCISE. — Kingdom, sheriffdom, dukedom, earldom, Christendom, wisdom, freedom, thralldom.

E-an. [Gr. -αῖος, or -εῖος, Lat. -æus, -eus.] A termination of adjectives derived from Greek adjectives, or formed on the pattern of such adjectives, and denoting of or pertaining to.

EXERCISE.—Cerulean, herculean, hyperborean, subterranean, epicurean, adamantean, tartarean, empyrean.

Ee. A termination of nouns, denoting one on or to whom something is done.

EXERCISE.—Appellee, donee, referee, trustee, lessee, grantee, legatee, patentee.

Eer. See IER.

En. A plural termination of nouns and of verbs formerly in use, as in housen, escapen, and retained in oxen and children. It is also still used as the termination of some verbs, as in hearken, from the Anglo-Saxon infinitive. It is also used to form from nouns adjectives expressing the material of which a thing is made.

EXERCISE. — Glisten, listen; leaden, wooden, golden, birchen, earthen, oaken, hempen, oaten, flaxen, waxen.

Ence,) [Lat. -entia.] A termination of abstract nouns from the Latin, or of nouns that follow the analogy of nouns so derived.
En-cy.)

EXERCISE. — Abstinence, circumference, reticence, innocence, coalescence, diffidence, providence, intelligence, prudence; agency, contingency, presidency, tendency, despondency, exigency, clemency, transparency, solvency.

Ent. [Lat. -ens, -entis.] A termination of nouns from the Latin, denoting the doer of a thing; or of participial adjectives expressing quality or habit.

EXERCISE. — Dependent, recipient, student, president, agent, adherent; fervent, urgent, indolent, esculent, refulgent, incumbent, evanescent, evident, omnipotent.

Er. A termination of many English words, and the Teutonic form of the Latin or. It denotes an agent, and was originally of the masculine gender, but is now applied to men or things indifferently. At the end of names of places, er signifies a man of the place; thus, Londoner is the same as London man.

EXERCISE. — Hater, former, heater, grater, builder, waiter, lover, doer, maker, strainer, poker, ruler, pointer, painter, voter.

Es'cent. [Lat. -escens, -escentis.] A termination of participial adjectives from the Latin, denoting progression, growing, or becoming.

EXERCISE. — Convalescent, putrescent, quiescent, effervescent, phosphorescent, incandescent.

Ess. [Fr., from Lat. -ix.] A termination of nouns feminine, distinguishing them from correspondent nouns masculine.

EXERCISE. — Authoress, lioness, negress, shepherdess, actress, giantess, sorceress, tigress, huntress, countess, priestess, hostess, poetess.

Ful. [The same as full.] A termination of adjectives denoting plenitude or abundance, and generally formed from substantives.

EXERCISE.—Artful, beautiful, peaceful, grateful, careful, useful, bashful, fanciful, painful, powerful, doubtful.

Fy. [Lat. facere, fieri, Fr. fier.] A termination of verbs, denoting to make, to become.

EXERCISE. — Amplify, deify, gratify, liquefy, rarefy, stupefy, pacify, qualify, signify, glorify, ratify, testify, rectify.

Hood. [A.-S. hád, from hád, state, sex, order, degree, per-

son, form, manner, Goth. *haidus*.] A termination denoting *state* or *fixedness*, *condition*, *quality*, *character*, *totality*. Sometimes it is written *head*.
EXERCISE.—Man*hood*, child*hood*, knight*hood*, brother*hood*, boy*hood*, widow*hood*, neighbor*hood*; god*head*.

Ic. [Gr. -ικος, Lat. -*icus*.] A termination of adjectives denoting *of*, or *pertaining to*.
EXERCISE. — Authent*ic*, concentr*ic*, magnet*ic*, seraph*ic*, academ*ic*, dogmat*ic*, per od*ic*, theoret*ic*, botan*ic*, cub*ic*, prosa*ic*, apostol*ic*.

Ics. A termination of nouns, plural in form but singular in signification, applied to certain arts or sciences.
EXERCISE. — Opt*ics*, mathemat*ics*, hydraul*ics*, mechan*ics*, phys*ics*, acoust*ics*, stat*ics*, hermeneut*ics*.

Id. [Lat. -*idus*.] A termination of adjectives denoting *quality*.
EXERCISE. — Ac*id*, liqu*id*, rig*id*, sord*id*, ar*id*, ferv*id*, flu*id*, horr*id*, hum*id*, torp*id*, tim*id*, ranc*id*, torr*id*, viv*id*.

Ier, } [Fr. -*ier*, -*iere*.] A termination of nouns denoting men from their occupations or employment.
Eer.
EXERCISE. — Brigad*ier*, grenad*ier*, financ*ier*, mountain*eer*, volunt*eer*, engin*eer*, auction*eer*, buccan*eer*.

Ile. [Lat. -*ilis*.] A termination of adjectives from the Latin, denoting *of*, or *pertaining to*.
EXERCISE. — Ag*ile*, versat*ile*, doc*ile*, frag*ile*, tac*ile*, puer*ile*, volat*ile*, fert*ile*, host*ile*, fut*ile*, mercant*ile*.

Ine. [Lat. -*inus*.] A termination of adjectives from the Latin, denoting *of*, or *pertaining to*.
EXERCISE. — Adamant*ine*, femin*ine*, prist*ine*, aquil*ine*, can*ine*, clandest*ine*, alp*ine*, serpent*ine*, genu*ine*, equ*ine*.

Ion. [Lat. -*io*, genitive -*ionis*.] A termination of abstract nouns derived from the Latin, or formed after the same analogy.
EXERCISE.—Ambit*ion*, concept*ion*, probat*ion*, evas*ion*, vers*ion*, crucifix*ion*, un*ion*, act*ion*, addit*ion*, compass*ion*, extens*ion*, opin*ion*, vermil*ion*.

Ish. [A.-S. -*ise*, Goth. -*isk*, N. H. Ger. -*isch*] A termination of English words denoting *diminution*, or *a small*

degree of the quality. Ish annexed to proper names forms a possessive adjective. Annexed to common nouns, it forms an adjective denoting a participation of the qualities expressed by the noun.
EXERCISE.—Whit*ish*, yellow*ish*; Swed*ish*, Dan*ish*, Engl*ish*, Span*ish*, Scott*ish*, fool*ish*, rogu*ish*, brut*ish*, child*ish*, dolt*ish*, boor*ish*, slav*ish*, fever*ish*, knav*ish*, girl*ish*, woman*ish*.

Ism. [Gr. -ισμος.] A termination of nouns from the Greek, or of nouns formed on the same model as these, denoting *tenets*, *doctrines*, or *principles*.
EXERCISE.—Athe*ism*, catech*ism*, hero*ism*, mechan*ism*, soph*ism*, skeptic*ism*, archa*ism*, barbar*ism*, heathen*ism*, ego*ism*, magnet*ism*.

Ist. [Gr. -ιστης.] A termination of nouns denoting men from their occupations, pursuits, or principles.
EXERCISE.—Bapt*ist*, chem*ist*, eulog*ist*, the*ist*, ocul*ist*, moral*ist*, novel*ist*, philolog*ist*, soph*ist*, annal*ist*, chem*ist*.

Ite. [Lat. -*itus*.] A termination of nouns and adjectives. It is often used to form collective or gentile names.
EXERCISE.—Appet*ite*, exquis*ite*, favor*ite*, recond*ite*, defin*ite*, oppos*ite*, requis*ite*, bedlam*ite*, Jacob*ite*.

I-ty. See TY.
Ive. [Lat. -*ivus*.] A termination of nouns and adjectives from the Latin, denoting *ability*, *power*, or *activity*.
EXERCISE. — Authoritat*ive*, lucent*ive*, persuas*ive*, vindict*ive*, convuls*ive*, delus*ive*, negat*ive*, format*ive*, conduc*ive*, furt*ive*, deris*ive*.

Ize, } [Gr. -ιζειν.] A termination of verbs from the Greek, or of verbs formed on the same model, and denoting *to make*, *to cause to be*, *to become*.
Ise.
EXERCISE.—Agon*ize*, character*ize*, tantal*ize*, critic*ize*, exerc*ise*, equal*ize*, civil*ize*, enfranch*ise*, exorc*ise*, memor*ize*, organ*ize*, satir*ize*.

Kin. [A.-S. *cyn*, *cynd*, kin, kind, offspring, race; allied to Lat. *genus*, Gr. γενος, γονος] A diminutive termination, denoting *small*, from the sense of *child*.
EXERCISE.—Lamb*kin*, manikin, nap*kin*, pip*kin*, bod*kin*.

Le. A diminutive termination
EXERCISE. — Crumb*le*, bund*le*, gird*le*, jogg*le*, fond*le*, thrott*le*, thimb*le*, cantic*le*, ruff*le*, speck*le*, suck*le*, spark*le*, stopp*le*.

Less. A terminating syllable of many nouns and some adjectives. It is the A.-S. *leás*, allied to Eng. *loose*, from A.-S. *leósan*, to *lose*. Hence, it is a privative word, denoting *destitution* ; as, a wit*less* man, a man destitute of wit, child*less*, without children.
EXERCISE.—Father*less*, faith*less*, penni*less*, law*less*, bound*less*, needle*ss*, life*less*, name*less*, care*less*, hope*less*, nerve*less*, worth*less*, piti*less*.

Let. [French dim. termination *et*, as in isl*et*, eagl*et*, circl*et*, gobl*et*, flow*eret*, baron*et*; with *l* inserted, as in stream*let*, branch*let*.] A termination of diminutives ; as, hamle*t*, a little house ; rivu*let*, a small stream.
EXERCISE.— Eye*let*, front*let*, tab*let*, ring*let*.

Ling. [A.-S.] A termination denoting *condition*, *offspring*, or *progeny*.
EXERCISE. — Hire*ling*, earth*ling*, world*ling*, found*ling*, dar*ling*, first*ling*, under*ling*, star*ling*, ground*ling*, gos*ling*, sap*ling*, change*ling*, fat*ling*, nest*ling*.

Ly. [O. Eng. *lich*, being an abbreviation of A.-S. *lic*, Goth. *leiks*, Eng. *like*.] A termination of adjectives, as in love*ly*, man*ly*, that is, love-*like*, man-*like*. It is also a termination of adverbs [O. Eng. *liche*, A.-S. *lice*].
EXERCISE.— Court*ly*, cost*ly*, priest*ly*, port*ly*, grist*ly*, hill*y*, shelf*y*, brave*ly*, coarse*ly*, pure*ly*, chief*ly*, rash*ly*, tardi*ly*, silli*ly*, augri*ly*, meek*ly*.

Ment. A termination of nouns (formed often from verbs), denoting *condition*, *state*, or *act*.
EXERCISE. — Engage*ment*, manage*ment*, impedi*ment*, embarrass*ment*, judg*ment*, amuse*ment*, invest*ment*, arbitra*ment*, infringe*ment*.

Mo-ny. [Lat. -*monium*, -*monia*.] A termination of nouns from the Latin, signifying *action*, or *an active faculty*, *being*, or *a state of being*, viewed abstractly.
EXERCISE. — Ali*mony*, matri*mony*, testi*mony*, cere*mony*, parsi*mony*, acri*mony*, sancti*mony*, patri*mony*.

PREFIXES AND SUFFIXES. 383

Ness. [A.-S. *-ness, -niss*, Goth. *-nassus.*] A termination of abstract names, denoting state, or quality.

EXERCISE. — Blind*ness*, good*ness*, great*ness*, sweet*ness*, godli*ness*, weari*ness*, stiff*ness*, rush*ness*, boyish*ness*, black*ness*, useful*ness*, zealous*ness*.

Ock. [A.-S. *-ca* or *-uca*.] A diminutive termination of nouns.

EXERCISE.—Bull*ock*, hill*ock*, matt*ock*, padd*ock*, poll*ock*.

Or. A termination of Latin nouns, denoting *an agent*. It is annexed to many words of English origin; as in less*or*. In general, *or* is annexed to words of Latin, and *er* to those of English, origin. See ER.

EXERCISE. — Act*or*, credit*or*, edit*or*, capt*or*, conduct*or*, past*or*, inspect*or*, pret*or*, orat*or*, dictat*or*, profess*or*.

O-ry. [Lat. *-orius.*] A termination of words from the Latin, denoting *of*, or *pertaining to*.

EXERCISE. — Amat*ory*, consolat*ory*, promiss*ory*, satisfact*ory*, compuls*ory*, curs*ory*, prefat*ory*, nugat*ory*, valedict*ory*.

Ose, } [Lat. *-osus, -us.*] A termination of English adjectives (many of which are derived directly from the Latin), denoting *quality* or *property*.

EXERCISE. — Dubi*ous*, consci*ous*, atroci*ous*, conspicu*ous*, oner*ous*, gener*ous*, danger*ous*, popul*ous*, mor*ose*, comat*ose*, oper*ose*, verb*ose*.

Ric. [A.-S. *rice, ric*; fr. the same root as Lat. *regere*, to rule, and *regio*, region.] A termination signifying *jurisdiction*, or *a district over which government is exercised*.

EXERCISE. — Bishop*ric*.

Ship. [A.-S. *scipe, scype*, fr. *scyppan*, to mold, form, shape.] A termination denoting *state*, *office, dignity, profession*, or *art*.

EXERCISE.—Lord*ship*, friend*ship*, chancellor*ship*, steward*ship*, horseman*ship*, copartner*ship*, hard*ship*, clerk*ship*, wor*ship*, scholar*ship*, censor*ship*.

Sion. See ION.

Some. [A.-S. *sum*, Goth. *sama*, like, the same.] A termination of certain adjectives. It indicates *a considerable degree* of the thing or quantity; as, mettle*some*, full of mettle or spirit; glad*some*, very glad or joyous.

EXERCISE. — Blithe*some*, weari*some*, loath*some*, trouble*some*, whole*some*, lone*some*.

Ster. [A.-S. *-estre, -istre*.] A termination denoting *skill* or *occupation*. It was originally applied to denote the female agent in an action. Thus, song*ster* signified, at first, a female who sings; but the ending *ster* having at length, in a measure, lost its peculiar force, the feminine termination *ess* was appended to it; thus, song*ster* became song*steress*, or song*stress*, with a double ending.

EXERCISE. — Drug*ster*, game*ster*, song*ster*, spin*ster*, young*ster*, pun*ster*, malt*ster*, tap*ster*.

T. } [A.-S.] A termination of **Th.** } abstract nouns of Anglo-Saxon origin.

EXERCISE. — Dep*th*, grow*th*, streng*th*, weal*th*, wid*th*, warm*th*, bir*th*, bread*th*, dep*th*, mir*th*, heal*th*, tru*th*; draf*t*, join*t*, fligh*t*, heigh*t*, drif*t*, gif*t*, thef*t*.

Tion. See ION.

Tude. [Lat. *-tudo.*] A termination of abstract nouns from the Latin, signifying *action* or *an active faculty*, *being*, or *a state of being*.

EXERCISE. — Ampli*tude*, forti*tude*, grati*tude*, soli*tude*, infini*tude*, turpi*tude*, alti*tude*, recti*tude*, servi*tude*, apti*tude*, magni*tude*.

Ty. [Lat. *-tas, -tatis*, Fr. *-té.*] A termination of words denoting *action* or *an active faculty*, *being*, or *a state of being*, viewed abstractly.

EXERCISE. — Antiqui*ty*, difficul*ty*, humili*ty*, necessi*ty*, probabili*ty*, luxi*ty*, impie*ty*, socie*ty*, modes*ty*, majes*ty*, liber*ty*, fatui*ty*.

Ure. [Lat. *-ura.*] A termination of words derived from the Latin (often through the Italian or French), and denoting *action* or *an active faculty*, *being*, or *a state of being*, viewed abstractly.

EXERCISE. — Creat*ure*, fract*ure*, legislat*ure*, nat*ure*, superstruct*ure*, lect*ure*, fiss*ure*, flex*ure*, expos*ure*, ten*ure*, junct*ure*, verd*ure*.

Ward, or Wards. [A.-S. *-weard, -weardes*;] Goth. *-vairths*, allied to Lat. *vertere*, to turn, *versus*, toward.] A suffix used in the composition of a large class of words, and denoting *direction*, or *tendency to, motion toward*, and the like.

EXERCISE.—Up*ward*, on*wards*, west*ward*, back*wards*, for*ward*, home*ward*, down*wards*, in*ward*.

Wise. [A.-S. *wise*, allied to *guise*.] A termination of adverbs implying *in the direction* or *manner of*.

EXERCISE. — End*wise*, side*wise*, length*wise*, like*wise*.

ABBREVIATIONS.

(See page xxiv.)

A.

a., or &. (*Ad.*) To *or* at.
ā., or *ăd.* (*ana.*, Gr. ἀνά.) In *med.*, Of each the same quantity.
A. A. G. Assistant Adjutant General.
A. A. S. (*Academiæ Americanæ Socius.*) Fellow of the American Academy.
A. B. (*Artium Baccalaureus.*) Bachelor of Arts.
A. B. C. F. M. American Board of Commissioners for Foreign Missions.
Abp. Archbishop.
A. C. (*Ante Christum.*) Before Christ.
Acc. or *Acct.* Account.
Act., or *act.* Active.
A. D. (*Anno Domini.*) In the year of our Lord.
Ad lib. (*Ad libitum.*) At pleasure.
Adm. Admiral.
Admr. Administrator.
Admx. Administratrix.
Æ., or *Æt.* (*Ætatis.*) Of age; aged.
Agt. Agent.
Al., or *Ala.* Alabama.
Alex. Alexander.
A. M. (*Artium Magister.*) Master of Arts. — (*Ante Meridiem.*) Before noon.
Am. Amos; American.
Amer. American.
Amt. Amount.
An. (*Anno.*) In the year.
Anon. Anonymous.
Ans. Answer.
Apr. April.
Ark. Arkansas.
Asst. Assistant.
A. U. C. (*Ab Urbe Conditâ.*) In the year from the building of the city, *i. e.*, Rome.
Aug. August.
Av. Avenue.

B.

b. born.
B. A. British America; Bachelor of Arts.
Bart., or *Bt.* Baronet.
Bbl. Barrel, barrels.
B. C. Before Christ.
B. C. L. Bachelor of Civil Law.

B. D. Bachelor of Divinity.
Bd. Bond; Bound.
Benj. Benjamin.
Bk. Bank; Book.
B. L. Bachelor of Laws.
Bl. Barrel.
Bp. Bishop.
Br., or *Bro.* Brother.
Brig. Brigade; Brigadier.
Brig.-Gen. Brigadier-General.
Brit. Britain; British.

C.

C. (*Centum.*) A hundred; Cent.
Cal. California; — (*Calendæ.*) Calends.
Cant. Canticles.
Capt. Captain.
Cat. Catalogue.
Cath. Catholic.
C. A. S. (*Connecticuttensis Academiæ Sociæ.*) Fellow of the Connecticut Academy.
C. C. P. Court of Common Pleas.
C. E. Civil Engineer.
Cent. (*Centum.*) A hundred.
Cf. or *cf.* (*Confer.*) Compare.
C. H. Court-House; Custom-House.
Ch. Church; Chapter.
Chap. Chapter.
Chr. Christopher; Christian.
Chron. Chronicles.
C. J. Chief Justice.
Cld. or *cld.* Cleared.
C. M. Common Meter.
Co. Company; County.
C. O. D. Cash (or Collect) on Delivery.
Col. Colonel; Colossians.
Coll. College; Collector.
Comp. Compare; Comparative; Compound.
Con. (*Contra.*) Against; In opposition.
Con., or *Cr.* Contra; Credit.
Conn., *Con.*, or *Ct.* Connecticut.
Const. Constable; Constitution.
Cor. Corinthians.
Cor. Mem. Corresponding Member. [*retary.*
Cor. Sec. Corresponding Secretary.
Cos. Cosine.
C. P. Court of Probate; Common Pleas.

Cr. Credit; Creditor.
Crim. Con. Criminal Conversation, *or* Adultery.
C. S. Court of Sessions. — (*Custos Sigilli.*) Keeper of the Seal.
Ct. Connecticut; Count; Court.
Ct., or *ct.* Cent. — (*Centum.*) A hundred.
Cts., or *cts.* Cents.
Cwt., or *cwt.* (Lat. *Centum*, a hundred, and English *weight.*) A hundred weight.
Cyc. Cyclopædia.

D.

D., or *d.* (*Denarius* or *denarii.*) A penny, *or* pence.
Dan. Danish; Daniel.
D. C. District of Columbia. — (*Da Capo.*) Again, or From the beginning.
D. C. L. Doctor of Civil (or Canon) Law.
D. D. (*Divinitatis Doctor.*) Doctor of Divinity.
Dea. Deacon.
Dec. December.
Deft., or *deft.* Defendant.
Del. Delaware; Delegate.
Del. (*Delineavit.*) He (or she) drew it; — prefixed to the draughtsman's name.
Dep. Deputy; Department.
Dept. Department; Deponent.
Deut. Deuteronomy.
Dft., or *dft.* Defendant.
D. G. (*Dei Gratiâ.*) By the grace of God.
Dict. Dictionary.
D. M. Doctor of Music.
Do., or *do.* (*Ditto.*) The same.
Dols., or *dols.* Dollars.
Doz., or *doz.* Dozen.
Dr. Debtor; Doctor; Dram.
Dwt. (Lat. *Denarius* and English *weight.*) Pennyweight.

E.

E. East; Earl.
Eccl., or *Eccles.* Ecclesiastes; Ecclesiastical.
Ecclus. Ecclesiasticus.
Ed. Editor; Edition.

ABBREVIATIONS.

E. E. Errors excepted; Ells English.
e. g. (*exempli gratiâ*.) For example.
E. I. East Indies, *or* East India.
E. I. C. East India Company.
E. Lon. East longitude.
E. N. E. East-North-East.
Eng. England; English.
Eph. Ephesians; Ephraim.
Esd. Esdras.
E. S. E. East-South-East.
Esq., or *Esqr.* Esquire.
Esth. Esther.
et al. (*et alibi*.) And elsewhere. — (*et alii*, or *aliæ*.) And others.
Etc., etc., or *&c.* (*Et cæteri, cæteræ*, or *cætera*.) And others; and so forth; and the like.
et seq. (*et sequentes*, or *et sequentia*.) And the following.
Ex. Example; Exodus.
Exec., or *Exr.* Executor.
Execx. Executrix.
Exod. Exodus.
Ez., or *Ezr.* Ezra.
Ezek. Ezekiel.

F.

Fahr. Fahrenheit.
F. A. S. Fellow of the Society of Arts.
Feb. February.
Fec., or *fec.* (*Fecit*.) He (or she) did it.
Flor. Florida.
Fo., or *Fol.* Folio.
Fr. France; French.
F. R. G. S. Fellow of the Royal Geographical Society;
Fri. Friday.
F. R. S. Fellow of the Royal Society.
F. R. S. E. Fellow of the Royal Society, Edinburgh.
F. R. S. L. Fellow of the Royal Society of Literature.
F. S. A. Fellow of the Society of Arts.
Ft., or *ft.* Foot, feet; Fort.
Fur., or *fur.* Furlong.

G.

Ga. Georgia.
Gal. Galatians.
Gal., or *gal.* Gallon, gallons.
G. B. Great Britain.
G. C. B. Grand Cross of the Bath.
Gen. Genesis; General.
Gent. Gentleman.
Geo. George.
Geog. Geography.
Gov. Governor.

Gr. Greek; Gross.
Gr., or *gr.* Grain, grains.

H.

H., or *h.* Hour, hours.
Hab. Habakkuk.
Hag. Haggai.
H. B. M. His (or Her) Britannic Majesty.
Hebr. Hebrew; Hebrews.
H. E. I. C. Honorable East India Company.
Hhd., or *hhd.* Hogshead.
H. I. H. His (or Her) Imperial Highness.
H. M. S. His (or Her) Majesty's Steamer, Ship, *or* Service.
Hon. Honorable.
Hos. Hosea.
H. R. House of Representatives.
H. R. E. Holy Roman Empire.
H. R. H. His (or Her) Royal Highness.
Hund. Hundred.

I.

Ia. Indiana.
Ib., *Ibid.* (*Ibidem*.) In the same place.
Id. (*Idem*.) The same.
I. e., or *i. e.* (*Id est*.) That is.
I. H. S. (*Iesus* [or *Jesus*] *Hominum Salvator*.) Jesus the Savior of Men.
Ill. Illinois.
In. Inch, inches.
Ind. Indiana.
incog. (*incognito*.) Unknown.
In lim. (*In limine*.) At the outset.
I. N. R. I. (*Iesus* [or *Jesus*] *Nazarenus, Rex Iudæorum* [or *Judæorum*].) Jesus of Nazareth, King of the Jews.
inst. Instant.
Io. Iowa.
I. O. O. F. Independent Order of Odd Fellows.
i. q. (*idem quod*.) The same as.
Is., or *Isa.* Isaiah.
It., or *Ital.* Italian; Italic.

J.

J. Judge.
J. A. Judge Advocate.
Jan. January.
J. C. JESUS CHRIST.
J. C. D. (*Juris Civilis Doctor*.) Doctor of Civil Law.
J. D. (*Jurum Doctor*.) Doctor of Laws.

Jer. Jeremiah.
Jno. John.
Jona. Jonathan.
Jos. Joseph.
Josh. Joshua.
J. P. Justice of the Peace.
J. Prob. Judge of Probate.
Jr., or *jr.* Junior.
J. U. D. (*Juris Utriusque Doctor*.) Doctor of Both Laws (*i. e.*, the Canon and the Civil Law.)
Jud. Judith.
Judg. Judges.
Jun., *Junr.* Junior.

K.

K. King.
Kan. Kansas.
K. B. Knight of the Bath; King's Bench.
K. C. King's Council.
K. C. B. Knight Commander of the Bath.
Ken., or *Ky.* Kentucky.
K. G. C. Knight of the Grand Cross.
Ki. Kings.
Knt., or *Kt.* Knight.
Ky. Kentucky.

L.

L. Lady; Latin; Lord.
L., *lb.*, or *℔.* (*Libra*.) A pound, in weight.
L., *l.*, or *£.* A pound sterling.
La. Louisiana.
Lam. Lamentations.
Lat. Latin.
Lat., or *lat.* Latitude.
Lb., *lb.*, or *℔.* (*Libra*.) A pound in weight.
L. c. Lower case. — (*loco citato*.) In the place before cited.
L. C. J. Lord Chief Justice.
Ld. Lord.
Lea., or *lea.* League.
Lev. Leviticus.
L. I. Long Island.
Lieut., or *Lt.* Lieutenant.
LL.B. (*Legum Baccalaureus*.) Bachelor of Laws.

☞ The initial letter is doubled to signify the plural.

LL.D. (*Legum Doctor*.) Doctor of Laws.
Lon., *Long.* Longitude.
Lou., or *La.* Louisiana.
Lp., or *Ldp.* Lordship.
L. S. (*Locus Sigilli*.) Place of the Seal.
L. S. D., or *l. s. d.* (*Libra, Solidi, Denarii*.) Pounds, Shillings, Pence.
Lt. Lieutenant.

ABBREVIATIONS.

M.

M. Marquis; Monsieur. — (*Mille.*) Thousand. — (*Meridies.*) Meridian, or noon.
M., or *m.* Mile, miles.
M. A. Master of Arts.
Mac., or *Macc.* Maccabees.
Mag. Magazine.
Maj. Major.
Maj.-Gen. Major-General.
Mal. Malachi.
Mar. March.
Mass., or *Ms.* Massachusetts.
Matt. Matthew.
M. B. (*Medicinæ Baccalaureus.*) Bachelor of Medicine.
M. C. Member of Congress.
M. D. (*Medicinæ Doctor.*) Doctor of Medicine.
Md. Maryland.
Mdlle. Mademoiselle.
M. E. Methodist Episcopal.
Me. Maine.
Mem. Memorandum.
Messrs., or *MM.* (*Messieurs.*) Gentlemen; Sirs.
Meth. Methodist.
Mi. Mississippi.
Mic. Micah.
Mich. Michigan.
Min., or *min.* Minute, minutes.
Minn. Minnesota.
Miss. Mississippi.
Mlle. Mademoiselle.
MM. Their Majesties. — (*Messieurs.*) Gentlemen. See *LL.B.*
Mme. Madame.
Mo. Missouri.
Mo., or *mo.* Month.
Mon. Monday.
Mons. Monsieur, *or* Sir.
Mos., or *mos.* Months.
M. P. Member of Parliament.
Mr. Master, *or* Mister.
M. R. I. Member of the Royal Institution.
Mrs. Mistress, *or* Missis.
MS. Manuscript.
MSS. Manuscripts.
Mt. Mount, *or* Mountain.
Mus. D., *Mus. Doc.*, or *Mus. Doct.* Doctor of Music.

N.

N. North.
N., or *n.* Noun; Neuter.
N. A. North America.
Nah. Nahum.
Naut. Nautical.
N. B. New Brunswick. — (*Nota Bene.*) Note well, *or* take notice.
N. C. North Carolina.
N. E. North-East; New England.
Neb. Nebraska.
Neh. Nehemiah.
Nem. Con. (*Nemine Contradicente.*) No one contradicting; unanimously.
Nem. Diss. (*Nemine Dissentiente.*) No one dissenting.
Neut., or *neut.* Neuter.
N. F. Newfoundland.
N. H. New Hampshire.
N. J. New Jersey.
N. Lat. North Latitude.
N. N. E. North-North-East.
N. N. W. North-North-West.
No., or *no.* (*Numero.*) Number.
Non Pros., or *Non pros.* (*Non Prosequitur*). He does not prosecute; — a judgment entered against the plaintiff when he does not appear to prosecute.
Non seq., or *non seq.* (*Non sequitur.*) It does not follow.
Nos., or *nos.* Numbers.
Nov. November.
N. P. New Providence; Notary Public.
N. S. Nova Scotia; New Style (since 1752).
N. T. New Testament.
Num., or *Numb.* Numbers.
N. W. North-West.
N. Y. New York.

O.

O. Ohio.
Ob., or *ob.* (*Obiit.*) Died.
Obad. Obadiah.
Obt., or *Obdt.* Obedient.
Oct. October.
Olym. Olympiad.
Or. Oregon.
O. S. Old Style (previously to 1752).
O. T. Old Testament.
Oz., or *oz.* Ounce, or ounces.

☞ The z is here used to represent the character ʒ, anciently an abbreviation for terminations.

P.

P., or *p.* Page; Part; Pipe.
Pa. Pennsylvania.
Pass., or *pass.* Passive.
Pd. Paid.
P. E. I. Prince Edward Island.
Penn. Pennsylvania.
Per an., or *per an.* (*Per annum.*) By the year.
Per cent., *per cent.*, *Per ct.*, or *per ct.* (*Per centum.*) By the hundred.
Ph. D. (*Philosophiæ Doctor.*) Doctor of Philosophy.
Phil. Philippians; Philemon.
Phila. Philadelphia.
Pinx., or *Pxt.* (*Pinxit.*) He (or she) painted it.
Pk., or *pk.* Peck.
Plff. Plaintiff.
P. M. Post-Master. — (*Post Meridiem.*) Afternoon.
P. O. Post-Office.
Pos., *pos.*, *Poss.*, or *poss* Possessive.
pp. Pages. See *LL.B.*
Pph., or *pph.* Pamphlet.
P. R. Prize Ring; Porto Rico.
Pres. President.
Prof. Professor.
Pro tem., or *pro tem.* (*Pro tempore.*) For the time being.
Prov. Proverbs.
Prox. (*Proximo.*) Next.
P. S. (*Post scriptum.*) Postscript.
Ps., Psalm, *or* Psalms.
Pt. Pint; Point; Port.
Pwt., or *pwt.* Pennyweight.
Pxt., or *pxt.* (*Pinxit.*) He (*or* she) painted it.

Q.

Q. Question.
Q., or *Qu.* Query; Question; Queen.
Q. C. Queen's Council.
Q. d. (*Quasi dicat.*) As if he should say.
Q. E. D. (*Quod Erat Demonstrandum.*) Which was to be demonstrated.
Q. M. G. Quartermaster-General.
Qr., or *qr.* Quarter (28 pounds); Farthing; Quire.
Qt., or *qt.* Quart; Quantity.
Q. v., or *q. v.* (*Quod vide.*) Which see.
Qy. Query.

R.

R. A. Royal Academy, *or* Academician.
R. E. Royal Engineers.
Rec. Sec. Recording Secretary.
Rev. Revelation; Revolution; Review; Revenue; Reverend.
R. I. Rhode Island.
R. N. Royal Navy.
Rom. Roman; Romans.
Rom. Cath. Roman Catholic.
R. R. Railroad.
Rt. Hon. Right Honorable.
Rt. Rev. Right Reverend.

ABBREVIATIONS. 387

S.

S. South; Shilling.
S. A. South America.
Sam. Samuel.
Sat. Saturday.
S. C. South Carolina.
Sc., or *Sculp.* (*Sculpsit.*) He (or she) engraved it.
Sch., or *Schr.* Schooner.
Scil., or *Sc.* (*Scilicet.*) To wit; namely.
Sculp. or *sculp.* (*Sculpsit.*) He (or she) engraved it.
S. E. South-East.
Sec. Secretary.
Sec., or *sec.* Second; Section.
Sen. Senate; Senator; Senior.
Sep., or *Sept.* September.
Serv., or *Servt.* Servant.
S. H. S. (*Societatis Historiæ Socius.*) Fellow of the Historical Society.
S. J. C. Supreme Judicial Court.
S. *Lat.* South Latitude.
Sld., or *sld.* Sailed.
S. M. Short Meter.
Soc. Society.
Sq. ft., or *sq. ft.* Square feet.
Sq. in., or *sq. in.* Square inches.
Sq. m., or *sq. m.* Square miles.
SS., or ss. (*Scilicet.*) Namely.—(*Semis.*) Half.
S. S. E. South-South-East.
S. S. W. South-South-West.
St. Saint; Street; Strait.
S. T. D. (*Sacræ Theologiæ Doctor.*) Doctor of Divinity.
S. T. P. (*Sacræ Theologiæ Professor.*) Professor of Theology.
Su., or *Sun.* Sunday.
Subj., or *subj.* Subjunctive.

Supt. Superintendent.
Surg. Surgeon; Surgery.
S. W. South-West.

T.

Ten., or *Tenn.* Tennessee.
Tex. Texas.
Theo. Theodore.
Thess. Thessalonians.
Thurs. Thursday.
Tim. Timothy.
Tit. Titus.
Tr. Transpose.
Tu., or *Tues.* Tuesday.

U.

Ult., or *ult.* (*Ultimo.*) Last, or of the last month.
U. S. United States.
U. S. A. United States of America; United States Army.
U. S. M. United States Mail; United States Marine.
U. S. N. United States Navy.
U. S. V. United States Volunteers.
U. T. Utah Territory.

V.

V. Verb; Verse.
V. a., or v. a. Verb active.
Va. Virginia.
Vice Pres. Vice President.
Vid., or *vid.* (*Vide.*) See.
Vis., or *Visc.* Viscount.
Viz., or *viz.* (*Videlicet.*) Namely; to wit. [See *Note* under *Oz.*]
V. n., or v. n. Verb neuter.
Vol., or *vol.* Volume.
V. R. (*Victoria Regina.*) Queen Victoria.

Vs., or *vs.* (*Versus.*) Against, or In opposition.
Vt. Vermont.

W.

W. West; Welsh.
Wed. Wednesday.
W. I. West Indies.
Wis., or *Wisc.* Wisconsin.
W. *Lon.* West Longitude.
Wm. William.
W. N. W. West-North-West.
W. S. W. West-South West.
Wt., or *wt.* Weight.
W. Va. West Virginia.

X.

X., or Xt. Christ.
Xmas. Christmas.

Y.

Yd., or *yd.* Yard.
Yͤ, or yͤ. The.

☞ The y in this abbreviation is a corrupt representation of the Anglo-Saxon þ, or *th*, introduced at the time when the Anglo-Saxon alphabet was superseded by the Old English or Black Letter, in which Ᵹ (y) bore a considerable resemblance in form to þ.

Z.

Zach. Zachary.
Zech. Zechariah.
Zeph. Zephaniah.
Zoöl. Zoölogy.

THE METRIC SYSTEM
OF
WEIGHTS AND MEASURES.

MEASURES OF LENGTH.

METRIC DENOMINATIONS AND VALUES.	EQUIVALENTS IN DENOMINATIONS IN USE.
Myriameter . . . . 10,000 meters,	. . 6.2137 miles.
Kilometer . . . . 1,000 meters,	. . 0.62137 mile, or 3280 feet and 10 inches
Hectometer . . . . 100 meters,	. 328 feet and 1 inch.
Dekameter . . . . 10 meters,	. 393.7 inches.
Meter . . . . 1 meter,	. . 39.37 inches.
Decimeter . . . . . . $\frac{1}{10}$ of a meter,	. . 3.937 inches.
Centimeter . . . . . $\frac{1}{100}$ of a meter,	. . 0.3937 inch.
Millimeter . . . . . $\frac{1}{1000}$ of a meter,	. . 0.0394 inch.

MEASURES OF SURFACE.

METRIC DENOMINATIONS AND VALUES.	EQUIVALENTS IN DENOMINATIONS IN USE.
Hectare . . . . . . 10,000 square meters,	. . . . 2.471 acres.
Are . . . . 100 square meters,	. . . . 119.6 square yards.
Centare . . . . 1 square meter,	. . . . 1,550 square inches.

MEASURES OF CAPACITY.

METRIC DENOMINATIONS AND VALUES.			EQUIVALENTS IN DENOMINATIONS IN USE.	
Names.	No. of liters.	Cubic Measure.	Dry Measure.	Liquid or Wine Measure.
Kiloliter, or Stere	1,000	1 cubic meter . .	1.308 cubic yards	264.17 gallons.
Hectoliter . . .	100	$\frac{1}{10}$ of a cubic meter .	2 bushels and 3.35 pecks .	26.417 gallons.
Dekaliter . . .	10	10 cubic decimeters .	9.08 quarts	2.6417 gallons.
Liter	1	1 cubic decimeter .	0.908 quart	1.0567 quarts.
Deciliter . . .	$\frac{1}{10}$	$\frac{1}{10}$ of a cubic decimeter	6.1022 cubic inches . . .	0.845 gill.
Centiliter . . .	$\frac{1}{100}$	10 cubic centimeters .	0.6102 cubic inch	0.338 fluid oz.
Milliliter . .	$\frac{1}{1000}$	1 cubic centimeter .	0.061 cubic inch	0.27 fluid dram.

THE METRIC SYSTEM.
WEIGHTS.

Names.	METRIC DENOMINATIONS AND VALUES.		EQUIVALENTS IN DENOMINATIONS IN USE.
	Number of grams.	Weight of what quantity of water at maximum density.	Avoirdupois Weight.
Millier, or Tonneau	1,000,000	1 cubic meter	2,204.6 pounds.
Quintal	100,000	1 hectoliter	220.46 pounds.
Myriagram	10,000	10 liters	22.046 pounds.
Kilogram or Kilo	1,000	1 liter	2.2046 pounds.
Hectogram	100	1 deciliter	3.5274 ounces.
Dekagram	10	10 cubic centimeters	0.3527 ounce.
Gram	1	1 cubic centimeter	15.432 grains.
Decigram	$\frac{1}{10}$	$\frac{1}{10}$ of a cubic centimeter	1.5432 grains.
Centigram	$\frac{1}{100}$	10 cubic millimeters	0.1543 grain.
Milligram	$\frac{1}{1000}$	1 cubic millimeter	0.0154 grain.

A. F. Evans

ARBITRARY SIGNS.

I. ASTRONOMICAL.

1. SUN, GREATER PLANETS, ETC.

☉, or ⊙	The Sun.
☾, ☽, or ☪	The Moon.
●	New Moon.
☽, or ☽	First Quarter.
○, or ⊕	Full Moon.
☾, or ☾	Last Quarter.
☿	Mercury.
♀	Venus.
⊕, ⊖, or ♁	The Earth.
♂	Mars.
♃	Jupiter.
♄	Saturn.
♅, or ♅	Uranus.
♆	Neptune.
☄	Comet.
✷, or ✶	Fixed Star.

☞ The asteroids are now designated by numbers indicating the order of their discovery, and their symbol is a small circle inclosing this number; as, ①, Ceres; ②, Pallas; ③, Juno; ④, Vesta; and the like.

2. SIGNS OF THE ZODIAC.

Spring Signs {
1. ♈ Aries, *the Ram*.
2. ♉ Taurus, *the Bull*.
3. ♊ Gemini, *the Twins*.

Summer Signs {
4. ♋ Cancer, *the Crab*.
5. ♌ Leo, *the Lion*.
6. ♍ Virgo, *the Virgin*.

Autumn Signs {
7. ♎ Libra, *the Balance*.
8. ♏ Scorpio, *the Scorpion*.
9. ♐ Sagittarius, *the Archer*.

Winter Signs {
10. ♑ Capricornus, *the Goat*.
11. ♒ Aquarius, *the Waterman*.
12. ♓ Pisces, *the Fishes*.

3. ASPECTS AND NODES.

☌ Conjunction; — indicating that the bodies have the same longitude, or right ascension.
✶ Sextile; — indicating a difference of 60° in longitude, or right ascension.
□ Quadrature; — indicating a difference of 90° in longitude, or right ascension.
△ Trine; — indicating a difference of 120° in longitude, or right ascension.
☍ Opposition; — indicating a difference of 180° in longitude, or right ascension.
☊ Ascending Node; — called also *Dragon's Head*.
☋ Descending Node; — called also *Dragon's Tail*.

II. MATHEMATICAL.

THE RELATIONS OF QUANTITIES.

+ Plus; and; more; — indicating addition.
− Minus; less; — indicating subtraction.
± , or ∓ Plus or minus.
× Multiplied by.
÷, or : Divided by.
= Is equal to; equals.
> Is greater than.
< Is less than.
: Is to; the ratio of; } — used to indicate ge-
:: As; equals; } ometrical proportion.
∴ Hence; therefore; on this account.
∵ Because.
√, or √ Root; — indicating, when used without a figure placed above it, the square root. To denote any other than the square root, a figure expressing the degree of the required root is placed above the sign.
∫ Integral; integral of; — indicating that the expression before which it is placed is to be integrated.
° Degrees.
′ Minutes of arc.
″ Seconds of arc.
′, ″, ‴, &c. Accents used to mark quantities of the same kind which are to be distinguished; as, a', a'', a''', &c., which are usually read *a prime, a second, a third*, etc.
1, 2, 3, &c. Indices placed above and at the right hand of quantities to denote that they are raised to powers whose degree is indicated by the figure.

III. MEDICAL.

āā (Gr. ἀνά), of each.
℞ (Lat. *Recipe*). Take.

APOTHECARIES' WEIGHTS AND MEASURES.

℔ Pound.
℥ Ounce.
ʒ Drachm.
℈ Scruple.
Ō, or O (Lat. *Octarius*) Pint.
♏ Minim, or drop.

IV. MISCELLANEOUS.

&, ⁊, & And. — &c. (*Et cætera.*) And the rest; and so forth; and so on; and the like.

✕, *or* + A character customarily made by persons unable to write, when they are required to execute instruments of any kind, as deeds, affidavits, &c. The name of the party is added by someone who can write; as, John ✕ Smith mark.
       his

4to, *or* 4°. Quarto; four leaves, or eight pages, to a sheet.
8vo, *or* 8°. Octavo; eight leaves, or sixteen pages, to a sheet.
12mo, *or* 12°. Duodecimo; twelve leaves, or twenty-four pages, to a sheet.
16mo, *or* 16°. Sexto-decimo; sixteen leaves, or thirty-two pages, to a sheet.
18mo, *or* 18°. Octavo-decimo; eighteen leaves, or thirty-six pages, to a sheet.

☞ Other sizes are 24mo, *or* 24° (Vigesimo-quarto), 32mo, *or* 32° (Trigesimo-secundo), 36mo, *or* 36° (Trigesimo-sexto), 48mo, *or* 48° (Quadri-gesimo-octavo), 64mo, *or* 64° Sexagesimo-quarto), 72mo, *or* 72° (Septuagesimo-secundo), 96mo, *or* 96° (Nonagesimo-sexto), 128mo, *or* 128° (Centesimo-et-vigesimo-octavo). These sizes are of rare occurrence, and are not commonly known by their Latin names, but are colloquially called twenty-four-mo, thirty-two-mo, &c., or twenty-fours, thirty-twos, &c.

7ber, September; 8ber, October; 9ber, November; 10ber, December.

V. COMMERCIAL.

$ Dollar, *or* Dollars.
¢ Cent, *or* cents.
£ Pound, *or* pounds (sterling).
℔ Pound, *or* pounds (in weight).
@ At, *or* to.
℔ Per.

% Per cent.
%c Account.
XX Ale of double strength.
XXX Ale of triple strength.

A 1 The designation of a first-class vessel; the letter denoting that the hull is well built and sea-worthy, and the figure the efficient state of her rigging, anchors, cables, stores, &c.

VI. TYPOGRAPHICAL.

, Comma.
; Semicolon.
: Colon.
. Period.
— Dash.
? Interrogation.
! Exclamation.
( ) Parenthesis.
[ ] Brackets, *or* Crotchets.
' Apostrophe.
- Hyphen.
´ Acute Accent.
` Grave Accent.
ˆ Circumflex Accent.
~ Circumflex, *or* Tilde.
¯ The Long, *or* Macron.
˘ The Short, *or* Breve.
¨ Diæresis.
¸ Cedilla.
^ Caret.
" " Quotation Marks.
} Brace.
*** Ellipsis.
... Ellipsis; *also*, Leaders.
——— Ellipsis.
* Asterisk.
† Dagger, *or* Obelisk.
‡ Double Dagger.
§ Section.
‖ Parallels.
¶ Paragraph.
☞ Index.
⁂, *or* ⁂ Asterism.

WORDS, PHRASES, PROVERBS, ETC.,

FROM

THE GREEK, THE LATIN, AND MODERN FOREIGN LANGUAGES,

RENDERED INTO ENGLISH.

NOTE. — *L.* Latin; *Fr.* French; *Ger.* German; *It.* Italian; *Sp.* Spanish; *Gr.* Greek.

A.

À la Française. [Fr.] After the French mode; — *la mode*, in fashion; — *l'Anglaise*, after the English fashion.
A fortiori. [L.] With stronger reason; — *mensâ et thoro*, from bed and board; — *posteriori*, from the effect to the cause; — *priori*, from the cause to the effect; — *vinculo matrimonii*, from the tie of marriage.
Abandon. [Fr.] Disregard of self, or of appearances.
Ab extra. [L.] From without; — *initio*, from the beginning; — *intra*, from within; — *uno disce omnes*, from one learn all; from a single instance infer the whole.
Ad eundem (sc. *gradum*). [L.] To the same degree; — *hominem*, to the man; that is, to his interests and passions; — *infinitum*, to infinity; — *interim*, in the mean while; — *libitum*, at pleasure; — *nauseam*, to disgust.
Adscriptus glebæ. [L.] Belonging or attached to the soil.
Agenda. [L.] Things to be done.
Alere flammam. [L.] To feed the flame.
Alis volat propriis. [L.] She flies with her own wings; — motto of Oregon.
Allons. [Fr.] Let us go; come.
Alma mater. [L.] A fostering mother.
Alter ego. [L.] Another self.
Amende honorable. [Fr.] Satisfactory apology.
Amour propre. [Fr.] Self-love; vanity.
Anglicè. [L.] According to the English manner.
Anno ætatis suæ. [L.] In the year of his (or her) age; — *Christi*, in the year of Christ; — *Domini*, in the year of our Lord; — *mundi*, in the year of the world; — *urbis conditæ*, in the year the city (Rome) was built.
Ante bellum. [L.] Before the war; — *meridiem*, before noon.
Appui. [Fr.] Point of support.
Aqua vitæ. [L.] Brandy; spirit; alcohol.
Arbiter elegantiarum. [L.] An umpire in matters of taste.
Argumentum ad hominem. [L.] An argument deriving its force from the situation of the person to whom it is addressed.
Atélier. [Fr.] A workshop, or artist's room.
Au contraire. [Fr.] On the contrary; — *fait*, well instructed; expert; — *revoir*, adieu until we meet again.

B.

Bas bleu. [Fr.] A blue-stocking.
Beau monde. [Fr.] The fashionable world.
Beaux esprits. [Fr.] Gay spirits; men of wit.
Bel esprit. [Fr.] A brilliant mind.
Ben trovato. [It.] Well found; a happy invention.
Bête noir. [Fr.] A bugbear.
Bijou. [Fr.] A jewel.
Billet doux. [Fr.] A love-letter.
Bizarre. [Fr.] Odd; fantastic.
Blasé. [Fr.] Pallid; surfeited; rendered incapable of continued enjoyment.
Bona fide. [L.] In good faith.
Bon bon. [Fr.] A sugar-plum; — *jour*, good day; good morning; — *soir*, good evening.
Bonhomie. [Fr.] Good-natured simplicity.
Boulevard. [Fr.] A public walk or street occupying the site of demolished fortifications.
Bouleversement. [Fr.] An overturning; subversion.
Bourgeois. [Fr.] A man of middle rank in society.
Bourgeoisie. [Fr.] Middle classes of society; traders.
Brochure. [Fr.] A pamphlet.
Brusque. [Fr.] Rude; blunt.
Brutum fulmen. [L.] A harmless thunderbolt.

C.

Cacoëthes loquendi. [L.] A rage for speaking; — *scribendi*, an itch for scribbling.
Cæteris paribus. [L.] Other things being equal.
Café. [Fr.] A coffee-house.
Calèche. [Fr.] A half-coach or calash.
Calembour. [Fr.] A pun.
Canaille. [Fr.] The rabble.
Cantatrice. [It.] A female professional singer.
Caput mortuum. [L.] The worthless remains.
Casus belli. [L.] That which involves or justifies war.
Catalogue raisonné. [Fr.] A catalogue of books arranged according to their subjects.
Caveat emptor. [L.] Let the buyer beware. [say.
C'est-à-dire. [Fr.] That is to
Chanson. [Fr.] A song.
Chapeau bas. [Fr.] Hats off; — *bras*, a military cocked hat.
Chargé d'affaires. [Fr.] An inferior diplomatic representative at a foreign court.
Charivari. [Fr.] A mock serenade of discordant music.
Châteaux en Espagne. [Fr.] Castles in Spain, the land of romance; castles in the air. [piece.
Chef-d'œuvre. [Fr.] A master-
Chère amie. [Fr.] A dear friend; a mistress.
Chevalier d'industrie. [Fr.] One who lives by persevering fraud. [former.
Ci-devant. [Fr.] Formerly;
Circa, or *Circiter.* [L.] About.
Citoyen. [Fr.] A citizen; a burgher.
Concierge. [Fr.] A porter; a door-keeper.
Coiffeur. [Fr.] A hair-dresser.

WORDS PHRASES, PROVERBS, ETC. 393

Comme il faut. [Fr.] As it should be.
Compos mentis. [L.] Of a sound mind.
Con amore. [It.] With love; earnestly.
Confrère. [Fr.] A brother; an associate.
Congé d'élire. [Fr.] A leave to elect. [seur.
Conoscente. [It.] A connois-
Contretemps. [Fr.] An awkward mishap or accident.
Conversazione. [It.] A meeting of company for conversation.
Cordon sanitaire. [Fr.] A line of troops to prevent the spreading of pestilence.
Corps diplomatique. [Fr.] A diplomatic body.
Corpus delicti. [L.] The substance or foundation of the offense.
Corrigenda. [L.] Typographical errors to be corrected.
Coup d'état. [Fr.] A stroke of policy in public affairs; — *de grace*, a finishing stroke; — *de main*, a sudden enterprise or effort; — *de soleil*, a stroke of the sun.
Crescite, et multiplicamini. [L.] Grow, or increase, and multiply; — the motto of Maryland.
Crevasse. [Fr.] A deep crevice; a breach.
Crimen læsæ majestatis. [L.] High treason.
Crux criticorum. [L.] The puzzle of critics; — *mathematicorum*, the puzzle of mathematicians.
Cui bono? [L.] For whose benefit? *Colloquially, but erroneously*, of what use?
Cuisine. [Fr.] A kitchen; cookery.
Cum grano salis. [L.] With a grain of salt; with some allowance; — *privilegio*, with privilege.
Currente calamo. [L.] With a running or rapid pen.
Custos rotulorum. [L.] Keeper of the rolls.

D.

Débutant. [Fr.] A person who makes his first appearance before the public.
Débutante. [Fr.] A woman making her first appearance before the public.
De gustibus non est disputandum. [L.] There is no disputing about tastes; — *jure*, from the law; by right;
17*

— *mortuis nil nisi bonum*, say nothing but good of the dead; — *novo*, anew; — *profundis*, out of the depths.
De trop. [Fr.] Too much, or too many; not wanted.
Dei gratiâ. [L.] By the grace of God.
Demi-monde. [Fr.] Disreputable female society; abandoned women.
Denouement. [Fr.] The unraveling or discovery of a plot; catastrophe.
Deo gratias. [L.] Thanks to God; — *volente*, God willing.
Dernier ressort. [Fr.] A last resource.
Deus ex machina. [L.] A god descending from a machine (in a theater); an unexpected and fortunate occurrence.
Dies iræ. [L.] Day of wrath; — *non*, a day on which judges do not sit.
Dieu défend le droit. [Fr.] God defends the right; — *et mon droit*, God and my right.
Dirigo. [L.] I direct or guide; — the motto of Maine.
Disjecta membra. [L.] Scattered limbs or remains.
Distingué. [Fr.] Distinguished; eminent.
Distrait. [Fr.] Absent in thought.
Dolce far niente. [It.] Sweet doing-nothing; sweet idleness.
Dominus vobiscum. [L.] The Lord be with you.
Double entente. [Fr.] Double meaning; a play on words.
Douceur. [Fr.] A bribe.
Dramatis personæ. [L.] Characters represented in a drama.
Dulce et decorum est pro patriâ mori. [L.] It is sweet and honorable to die for one's country.
Dum vivimus, vivamus. [L.] While we live, let us live.
Durante beneplacito. [L.] During good pleasure; — *vitâ*, during life.

E.

Eau de vie. [Fr.] Water of life; brandy.
Ecce homo. [L.] Behold the man; — applied specifically to any picture representing the Savior up to the people by Pilate, and wearing the crown of thorns.
Editio princeps. [L.] The first edition.
Égalité. [Fr.] Equality.

Elève. [Fr.] A pupil; a foster child.
Elite. [Fr.] A choice or select body of persons. [tion.
Éloge. [Fr.] A funeral ora-
Embonpoint. [Fr.] Plumpness; fleshiness.
Émeute. [Fr.] A riot; a mob.
Employé. [Fr.] One who is employed.
En arrière. [Fr.] In the rear; — *famille*, in a domestic state; — *passant*, in passing; by the way; — *rapport*, in a condition or relation of sympathy; in a condition to admit of free communication; — *route*, on the way.
Enceinte. [Fr.] Pregnant.
Enfans perdus. [Fr.] Lost children; a forlorn hope.
Ennui. [Fr.] A feeling of weariness and disgust; tedium.
Ensemble. [Fr.] The whole.
Ense petit placidam sub libertate quietem. [L.] With the sword she seeks quiet peace under liberty; — the motto of Massachusetts.
Entente cordiale. [Fr.] Evidences of good will, exchanged by the chief persons of two states. [ourselves.
Entre nous. [Fr.] Between
Entrée. [Fr.] Entry; first course at table.
Entrepôt. [Fr.] A bonded warehouse; a free port.
E pluribus unum. [L.] One out of many; one composed of many; — the motto of the United States.
Ergo. [L.] Therefore.
Esprit de corps. [Fr.] The animating spirit of a collective body. [perpetual.
Esto perpetua. [L.] Let it be
Et cum spiritu tuo. [L.] And with thy spirit; — *id genus omne*, and every thing of the sort; — *sic de similibus*, and so of the like; — *tu, Brute!* and thou also, Brutus!
Eureka (εὕρηκα, hū-rā'ka.) [Gr.] I have found it; — the motto of California.
Ex animo. [L.] Heartily; — *cathedrâ*, from the bench; with high authority; — *officio*, by virtue of his office; — *parte*, on one side only; — *pede Herculem*, we recognize a Hercules from the size of the foot; that is, we judge of the whole from the specimen; — *post facto*, after the deed is done.
Excelsior. [L.] Higher; more elevated; — the motto of New York.

Excerpta. [L.] Extracts.
Exempli gratiâ. [L.] By way of example.
Exeunt omnes. [L.] All go out.
Exposé. [Fr.] An exposition.

F.

Facile princeps. [L.] Evidently pre-eminent; the admitted chief.
Faubourg. [Fr.] A suburb.
Fauteuil. [Fr.] An easy chair.
Faux pas. [Fr.] A false step.
Fecit. [L.] He made it.
Femme couverte. [Fr.] A married woman; — *de chambre,* a chambermaid.
Festina lentè. [L.] Hasten slowly. [festival.
Fête champêtre. [Fr.] A rural
Feu de joie. [Fr.] A firing of guns in token of joy; a bonfire.
Feuilleton. [Fr.] Bottom part of a French newspaper, separated by a line from the rest, and devoted to light literature, criticism, &c.
Fiacre. [Fr.] A hack.
Fidei defensor. [L.] Defender of the faith.
Fille de chambre. [Fr.] A chambermaid; — *de joie,* a prostitute.
Flagrante bello. [L.] During hostilities; — *delicto,* in the commission of the crime.
Fortiter in re. [L.] With firmness in acting.
Friseur. [Fr.] A hair-dresser.
Fuit Ilium. [L.] Troy *has* been.
Fusillade. [Fr.] A simultaneous discharge of fire-arms.

G.

Gallicè. [L.] In French.
Garçon. [Fr.] A boy, or a waiter.
Garde du corps. [Fr.] A body guard; — *mobile,* a guard liable to general service.
Genius loci. [L.] The genius of the place. [police.
Gens d'armes. [Fr.] Armed
Gloria in excelsis. [L.] Glory to God in the highest; — *Patri,* glory be to the Father.
Γνῶθι σεαυτόν (*Gnothi seauton*). [Gr.] Know thyself.

H.

Haud passibus æquis. [L.] Not with equal steps.
Haut gout. [Fr.] High flavor; fine or elegant taste.

Haute nouveauté. [Fr.] A great novelty.
Hic et ubique. [L.] Here and everywhere; — *jacet,* here lies; — *labor, hoc opus est,* this is labor, this is work.
Hoc age. [L.] Do this; — *anno,* in this year; — *loco,* in this place; — *tempore,* at this time.
Honi soit qui mal y pense. [Fr.] Shame on him who evil thinks. [always time.
Hora è sempre. [It.] It is
Hors de combat. [Fr.] Out of condition to fight.
Humanum est errare. [L.] To err is human.

I.

Ich dien. [Ger.] I serve.
Id est. [L.] That is; — *genus omne,* all of that sort.
Imprimatur. [L.] Let it be printed; — a license to print a book, &c.
Improvvisatore. [It.] An impromptu poet.
Improvvisatrice. [It.] An impromptu poetess.
In æternum. [L.] Forever; — *articulo mortis,* at the point of death; — *commendam,* in trust; — *curiâ,* in the court; — *equilibrio,* in equilibrium; — *esse,* in being; — *extremis,* at the point of death; — *flagrante delicto,* taken in the fact; — *formâ pauperis,* as a poor man; — *foro conscientiæ,* before the tribunal of conscience; — *futuro,* in future; henceforth; — *hoc signo vinces,* in this sign, or under this standard, thou shalt conquer; — *limine,* at the threshold; — *loco,* in the proper place; — *loco parentis,* in the place of a parent; — *medias res,* into the midst of things, or affairs; — *medio tutissimus ibis,* you will go most safely in the middle; — *memoriam,* in memory; — *nubibus,* in the clouds; — *perpetuum,* forever; — *posse,* in possible existence; — *propriâ personâ,* in person; — *puris naturalibus,* quite naked; — *re,* in the matter of; — *rem,* against the thing; — *sæculâ sæculorum,* for ages on ages; — *situ,* in its original situation; — *statu quo,* in the former state; — *terrorem,* as a warning; — *toto,* in the whole; entirely; — *totidem verbis,* in so many words; — *transitu,* on the passage; —

usum Delphini, for the use of the Dauphin; — *utrumque paratus,* prepared for either event; — *vacuo,* in empty space; — *verba magistri jurare,* to swear to, or by, the words of another; to adopt opinions on the authority of another: — *vino veritas,* there is truth in wine.
Infanta. [Sp.] A princess of the blood royal in Spain and Portugal.
Infante. [Sp.] Any son of the king, except the eldest, or heir apparent.
Insouciance. [Fr.] Indifference; carelessness.
Inter alia. [L.] Among other things; — *nos,* between ourselves.
Invitâ Minervâ. [L.] Without genius. [said it.
Ipse dixit. [L.] He himself
Ipsissima verba. [L.] The very words.
Ipso facto. [L.] In the fact itself; — *jure,* by the law itself.

J.

Je ne sais quoi. [Fr.] I know not what.
Jeu de mots. [Fr.] A play on words; a pun; — *d'esprit,* a witticism.
Jupiter tonans. [L.] Jupiter the thunderer.
Jure divino. [L.] By divine law; — *humano,* by human law.
Jus civile. [L.] Civil law; — *divinum,* divine law; — *et norma loquendi,* the law and rule of speech; — *gentium,* law of nations.
Juste milieu. [Fr.] The golden mean.

L.

Labor ipse voluptas. [L.] Labor itself is pleasure; — *omnia vincit,* labor conquers every thing.
Laissez faire. [Fr.] Let alone.
Lapsus linguæ. [L.] A slip of the tongue.
Laus Deo. [L.] Praise to God.
Le beau monde. [Fr.] The fashionable world; — *diable boiteux,* the lame devil; — *roi le veut,* the king wills it; — *roi s'avisera,* the king will consider or deliberate.
Lèse majesté. [Fr.] High treason.
L'étoile du nord. [Fr.] The star of the north; — the motto of Minnesota.

WORDS, PHRASES, PROVERBS, ETC. 895

Lettre de cachet. [Fr.] A sealed letter; a royal warrant.
Lex non scripta. [L.] The common law; — *scripta, statute law; — talionis,* the law of retaliation.
Liaison. [Fr.] An alliance; an illicit connection. [trial.
Lite pendente. [L.] During
Loco citato. [L.] In the place cited.
Locum tenens. [L.] A deputy or substitute; a proxy.
Locus in quo. [L.] The place in which; — *sigilli,* place of the seal.
Longo intervallo. [L.] By or with long interval.
Lucus à non lucendo. [L.] A *jeu d'esprit* in etymology, which, assuming that *lucus,* a dark wood or grove, is derived from the verb *lucere,* to shine, supposes it must be *à non lucendo,* from its not being light.
Lusus naturæ. [L.] A sport or freak of nature.

M.

Macte virtute. [L.] Proceed in virtue. [faith.
Ma fois. [Fr.] Upon my
Magnum opus. [L.] A great work.
Magnus Apollo. [L.] Great Apollo; one of high authority.
Maître d'hôtel. [Fr.] A house-steward.
Mal à propos. [Fr.] Ill-timed.
Malgré nous. [Fr.] In spite of us. [itself.
Malum in se. [L.] Bad in
Mare clausum. [L.] A closed sea; a bay.
Matériel. [Fr.] Materials or instruments employed (opposed to *personnel*).
Mauvais goût. [Fr.] Bad taste; — *honte,* false modesty.
Me judice. [L.] I being judge.
Mélange. [Fr.] A medley.
Mêlée. [Fr.] A hand-to-hand fight; a riot.
Memento mori. [L.] Remember death.
Memorabilia. [L.] Things to be remembered.
Mens sana in corpore sano. [L.] A sound mind in a sound body.
Mésalliance. [Fr.] Improper association; marriage with one of lower station.
Meum et tuum. [L.] Mine and thine.
Mirabile dictu. [L.] Wonderful to be told; — *visu,* wonderful to be seen.
Mittimus. [L.] We send; — a writ to commit an offender to prison.
Modus operandi. [L.] Manner of operation.
Montani semper liberi. [L.] Mountaineers are always freemen; — the motto of West Virginia.
Monumentum ære perennius. [L.] A monument more durable than brass.
Multum in parvo. [L.] Much in little.
Mutatis mutandis. [L.] The necessary changes being made.
Mutato nomine. [L.] The name being changed.

N.

Naïve. [Fr.] Having native or unaffected simplicity.
Naïveté. [Fr.] Native simplicity.
Ne plus ultra. [L.] Nothing further; — *quid nimis,* not any thing too much or too far; — *sutor ultra crepidam,* let not the shoemaker go beyond his last.
Née. [Fr.] Born; as, Madame de Staël, *née* (that is, whose maiden name was) Necker.
Négligée. [Fr.] An easy, unceremonious attire; undress.
Nemine contradicente. [L.] No one speaking in opposition; — *dissentiente,* no one dissenting.
Nemo me impune lacessit. [L.] No one wounds me with impunity; — the motto of Scotland.
Nil admirari. [L.] To wonder at nothing; — *desperandum,* never despair.
N'importe. [Fr.] It matters not.
Noblesse oblige. [Fr.] Rank imposes obligation; much is rightly expected of one of high birth or station.
Nolens volens. [L.] Whether he will or not. [touch me.
Noli me tangere. [L.] Don't
Nolle prosequi. [L.] To be unwilling to proceed.
Nom de plume. [Fr.] A pen name; an assumed title; — *de guerre,* a war name; a traveling title; a pseudonym.
Non compos mentis. [L.] Not in sound mind; — *est inventus,* he has not been found; — *obstante,* notwithstanding; — *omnis moriar,* I shall not wholly die; — *sequitur,* it does not follow; an unwarranted conclusion.
Nosce teipsum. [L.] Know thyself.
Nota bene. [L.] Mark well.
N'oubliez pas. [Fr.] Don't forget. [see.
Nous verrons. [Fr.] We shall
Novus homo. [L.] A new man.
Nuance. [Fr.] Shade; gradation; tint.
Nudum pactum. [L.] A contract made without any consideration, and therefore void. [or never.
Nunc aut nunquam. [L.] Now

O.

Obiit. [L.] He, or she, died.
Obsta principiis. [L.] Resist the first beginnings.
Odium theologicum. [L.] The hatred of theologians.
Ohe! jam satis. [L.] O, now there is enough.
Οἱ πολλοί (Hoi polloi). [Gr.] The many; the rabble.
Omnia vincit amor. [L.] Love conquers all things; — *vincit labor,* labor overcomes all things.
On dit. [Fr.] They say; flying rumor.
Onus probandi. [L.] The burden of proving.
Ora e sempre. [It.] Now and always.
Ora pro nobis. [L.] Pray for us.
Ore rotundo. [L.] With round, full voice.
O! si sic omnia. [L.] O that he had always done or spoken thus.
O tempora! O mores! [L.] O the times! O the manners!
Otium cum dignitate. [L.] Ease with dignity; dignified leisure.
Oubliette. [Fr.] Dungeon of a castle.
Oui dire. [Fr.] Hearsay.
Outré. [Fr.] Out of the common course; extravagant.
Ouvrier. [Fr.] A workman; an artisan.

P.

Papier mâché. [Fr.] Chewed or mashed paper; a hard substance made of a pulp from rags or paper.
Par exemple. [Fr.] For example; — *excellence,* by way of eminence.
Pari passu. [L.] With equal pace.

WORDS, PHRASES, PROVERBS, ETC.

Par nobile fratrum. [L.] A noble pair of brothers; two just alike. [of honor.
Parole d'honneur. [Fr.] Word
Particeps criminis. [L.] An accomplice.
Parvenu. [Fr.] An upstart; one newly risen into notice.
Pas d pas. [Fr.] Step by step.
Passé. [Fr.] Past; out of use; faded; worn out.
Passe-partout. [Fr.] A master-key.
Pâté de foie gras. [Fr.] Goose-liver pie.
Paterfamilias. [L.] The father of a family.
Pater noster. [L.] Our Father; the Lord's prayer; — *patriæ*, father of his country.
Patois. [Fr.] Dialect of the lower classes.
Patres conscripti. [L.] Conscript fathers; the Roman senators.
Peccavi. [L.] I have sinned.
Peine forte et dure. [Fr.] Strong and severe punishment. [liking.
Penchant. [Fr.] Inclination;
Pendente lite. [L.] Pending the suit.
Pensée. [Fr.] Thought.
Per annum. [L.] By the year; — *capita*, by the head; — *centum*, by the hundred; — *contra*, contrariwise; — *se*, by itself considered.
Perdu. [Fr.] Lost.
Personnel. [Fr.] Body of persons employed in some public service.
Petitio principii. [L.] A begging of the question.
Petit maitre. [Fr.] A dandy; a coxcomb.
Peu de chose. [Fr.] A trifle.
Pirouette. [Fr.] A whirl on the toes, as in dancing.
Pis aller. [Fr.] The last shift.
Più. [It.] More.
Pleno jure. [L.] With full authority. [web.
Plexus. [L.] A network;
Poco à poco. [It.] Little by little.
Poeta nascitur, non fit. [L.] The poet is born, not made.
Point d'appui. [Fr.] Point of support; prop.
Pons asinorum. [L.] Bridge of asses.
Post mortem. [L.] After death; — *obitum*, after death.
Pot-pourri. [Fr.] A hotchpotch: a medley.
Preux chevalier. [Fr.] A brave knight.
Prima facie. [L.] On the first view.

Primus inter pares. [L.] Chief among equals.
Principia, non homines. [L.] Principles, not men.
Pro aris et focis. [L.] For our altars and firesides; — *bono publico*, for the public good; — *et con*, for and against; — *formâ*, for the sake of form; — *hâc vice*, for this turn or occasion; — *ratâ*, in proportion; — *tempore*, for the time.
Procès verbal. [Fr.] A written statement.
Profanum vulgus. [L.] The profane vulgar.
Proh pudor. [L.] O, for shame.
Propria quæ maribus. [L.] Those things which are appropriate or peculiar to men, or to husbands.
Punica fides. [L.] Punic faith; treachery.

Q.

Quantum libet. [L.] As much as you please; — *meruit*, as much as he deserved; — *mutatus ab illo!* how changed from what he was!; — *sufficit*, a sufficient quantity; — *vis*, as much as you will.
Quasi. [L.] As if; in a manner.
Quelque chose. [Fr.] A trifle; something; any thing.
Quid pro quo. [L.] One thing for another; an equivalent: — *rides?* why do you laugh?
Qui facit per alium, facit per se. [L.] He who does a thing by the agency of another, does it himself.
Quis custodiet ipsos custodes? [L.] Who shall guard the guards themselves?
Qui tam? [L.] Who as well?
Qui transtulit, sustinet. [L.] He who transplanted, still sustains; — the motto of Connecticut.
Qui vive? [Fr.] Who goes there? — hence, on the *qui vive*, on the alert.
Quo animo? [L.] With what mind or intention? — *jure?* By what right?
Quod erat demonstrandum. [L.] Which was to be demonstrated; — *vide*, which see.

R.

Rara avis. [L.] A rare bird.
Recueil. [Fr.] Collection.
Reductio ad absurdum. [L.] A reducing a position to an absurdity.

Regnant populi. [L.] The people rule; — the motto of Arkansas. [Properly, *Regnat populus.*]
Religio loci. [L.] The religious spirit of the place.
Renommée. [Fr.] Renown; fame.
Requiescat in pace. [L.] May he rest in peace.
Res angusta domi. [L.] Narrow circumstances at home; poverty. [the end.
Respice finem. [L.] Look to
Résumé. [Fr.] A summing up; recapitulation.
Resurgam. [L.] I shall rise again.
Revenons à nos moutons. [Fr.] Let us return to our sheep; let us return to our subject.
Rifacimento. [It.] Renewal; re-establishment.
Robe de chambre. [Fr.] A dressing-gown or morning-gown.
Rouleau. [Fr.] A little roll.
Rudis indigesta moles. [L.] A rude and undigested mass.
Ruse de guerre. [Fr.] A stratagem of war.
Rus in urbe. [L.] The country in town.

S.

Salle. [Fr.] A hall.
Salon. [Fr.] An apartment for company; a fashionable party; or fashionable society.
Salus populi suprema est lex. [L.] The welfare of the people is the supreme law; — the motto of Missouri.
Sanctum sanctorum. [L.] Holy of holies.
Sans cérémonie. [Fr.] Without ceremony; — *peur et sans reproche*, without fear and without reproach.
Sauve qui peut. [Fr.] Save himself who can.
Savoir faire. [Fr.] Ability; — *vivre*, good breeding.
Scandalum magnatum. [L.] Defamatory speech or writing to the injury of persons of dignity.
Scire facias. [L.] Cause it to be known. [session.
Séance. [Fr.] A sitting or
Secundem artem. [L.] According to rule; — *naturam*, according to the course of nature.
Semper felix. [L.] Always fortunate; — *fidelis*, always faithful; — *idem*, always the same; — *paratus*, always ready.

WORDS, PHRASES, PROVERBS, ETC. 397

Senatûs consultum. [L.] A decree of the Senate.
Se non è vero, è ben trovato. [It.] If not true, it is well feigned.
Sesquipedalia verba. [L.] Words a foot and a half long.
Sic itur ad astra. [L.] Such is the way to immortality; — *passim*, so everywhere; — *semper tyrannis*, ever so to tyrants, — the motto of Virginia; — *transit gloria mundi*, so passes away earthly glory; — *vos non vobis*, thus you do not labor for yourselves.
Sicut ante. [L.] As before; — *patribus, sit Deus nobis*, as God was with our fathers, so may he be with us.
Similia similibus curantur. [L.] Like things are cured by like.
Si monumentum quæris, circumspice. [L.] If you seek his monument, look around.
Simplex munditiis. [L.] Of simple elegance.
Sine curâ. [L.] Without charge or care; — *die*, without a day appointed; — *qua non*, an indispensable condition.
Si quæris peninsulam amœnam, circumspice. [L.] If thou seekest a beautiful peninsula, behold it here; — the motto of Michigan.
Sit tibi terra levis. [L.] May the earth lie lightly upon thee.
Soi-disant. [Fr.] Self-styled.
Soubrette. [Fr.] An intriguing woman.
Stans pede in uno. [L.] Standing on one foot.
Stat magni nominis umbra. [L.] He stands the shadow of a mighty name. [which.
Statu quo. [L.] The state in
Stet. [L.] Let it stand.
Suaviter in modo, fortiter in re. [L.] Gentle in manners, but resolute in deed
Sub judice. [L.] Under consideration; — *rosâ*, under the rose; privately.
Sui generis. [L.] Of its own kind.
Summum bonum. [L.] The chief good.
Suum cuique. [L.] Let each have his own.

T.

Tabula rasa. [L.] A smooth or blank tablet.

Tant pis. [Fr.] So much the worse.
Tapis. [Fr.] A carpet; also, the cover of a council-table; hence, *to be on the tapis* is to be under consideration.
Tempora mutantur, et nos mutamur in illis. [L.] The times are changed, and we are changed with them.
Tempus fugit. [L.] Time flies.
Terræ filius. [L.] A son of the earth; that is, a human being.
Terra firma. [L.] Solid earth; a safe footing; — *incognita*, an unknown country.
Tertium quid. [L.] A third something; a nondescript.
Tiers-état. [Fr.] The third estate; commons or commonalty.
Tò καλόν (To kalon). [Gr.] The beautiful; the chief good.
Totidem verbis. [L.] In just so many words.
Toties quoties. [L.] As often as.
Toto cælo. [L.] By the whole heavens; diametrically opposite.
Tout-à-fait. [Fr.] Entirely; — *au contraire*, on the contrary; — *ensemble*, the whole taken together.

U.

Uberrima fides. [L.] Superabounding faith.
Ubi supra. [L.] Where above mentioned.
Ultima ratio regum. [L.] The last argument of kings; war; — *Thule*, utmost limit.
Una voce. [L.] With one voice.
Uno animo. [L.] With one mind; unanimously.
Usque ad aras. [L.] To the very altars; — *ad nauseam*, to disgust.
Usus loquendi. [Lat.] Usage in speaking.
Utile dulci. [L.] The useful with the pleasant.
Ut infra. [L.] As below; — *supra*, as above stated.
Uti possidetis. [L.] As you possess; state of present possession.

V.

Vade mecum. [L.] Go with me; a constant companion.
Væ victis. [L.] Woe to the vanquished.
Vale. [L.] Farewell.

Valet de chambre. [Fr.] An attendant; a footman.
Veni, vidi, vici. [L.] I came, I saw, I conquered.
Verbatim et literatim. [L.] Word for word and letter for letter.
Verbum sat sapienti. [L.] A word is enough for a wise man.
Vetturo. [It.] A hack.
Vetturino. [It.] A hackman.
Vexata quæstio. [L.] A disputed question.
Via. [L.] By the way of.
Via media. [L.] A middle course.
Vice. [L.] In the place of; — *versâ*, the terms being exchanged.
Vide ut supra. [L.] See what is stated above.
Vi et armis. [L.] By force and arms; by main force.
Vincit amor patriæ. [L.] Love of country prevails; — *omnia veritas*, truth conquers all things.
Vis à vis. [Fr.] Opposite; facing.
Vis a tergo. [L.] A propelling force from behind; — *inertiæ*, the power of inertia; resistance; — *vitæ*, the vigor of life.
Vitam impendere vero. [L.] To stake one's life for the truth.
Vivat regina. [L.] Long live the queen; — *rex*, long live the king.
Vivâ voce. [L.] By the living voice; by oral testimony.
Vive la république. [Fr.] Long live the republic; — *la bagatelle!* success to trifling; — *le roi*, long live the king. — *la reine*, long live the queen.
Vivida vis animi. [L.] The lively vigor of genius.
Voilà. [Fr.] Behold; there is, or there are.
Vox, et præterea nihil. [L.] A voice, and nothing more; — *populi, vox Dei*, the voice of the people is the voice of God.
Vraisemblance. [Fr.] Appearance of truth.
Vulgò. [L.] Commonly.

Z.

Zonam solvere. [L.] To loose the virgin zone.
Zollverein. [Ger.] A union among the German states for the collection of custom-house duties.

A CLASSIFIED SELECTION OF ILLUSTRATIONS

FOR

WEBSTER'S HIGH-SCHOOL DICTIONARY.

☞ Any words in the following grouping of Illustrations not found in the body of the work, may be found explained in Webster's Unabridged Dictionary.

BIRDS.

400 A CLASSIFIED SELECTION OF ILLUSTRATIONS

BIRDS.—Continued.

FOR WEBSTER'S HIGH-SCHOOL DICTIONARY.
DEAF AND DUMB ALPHABET.

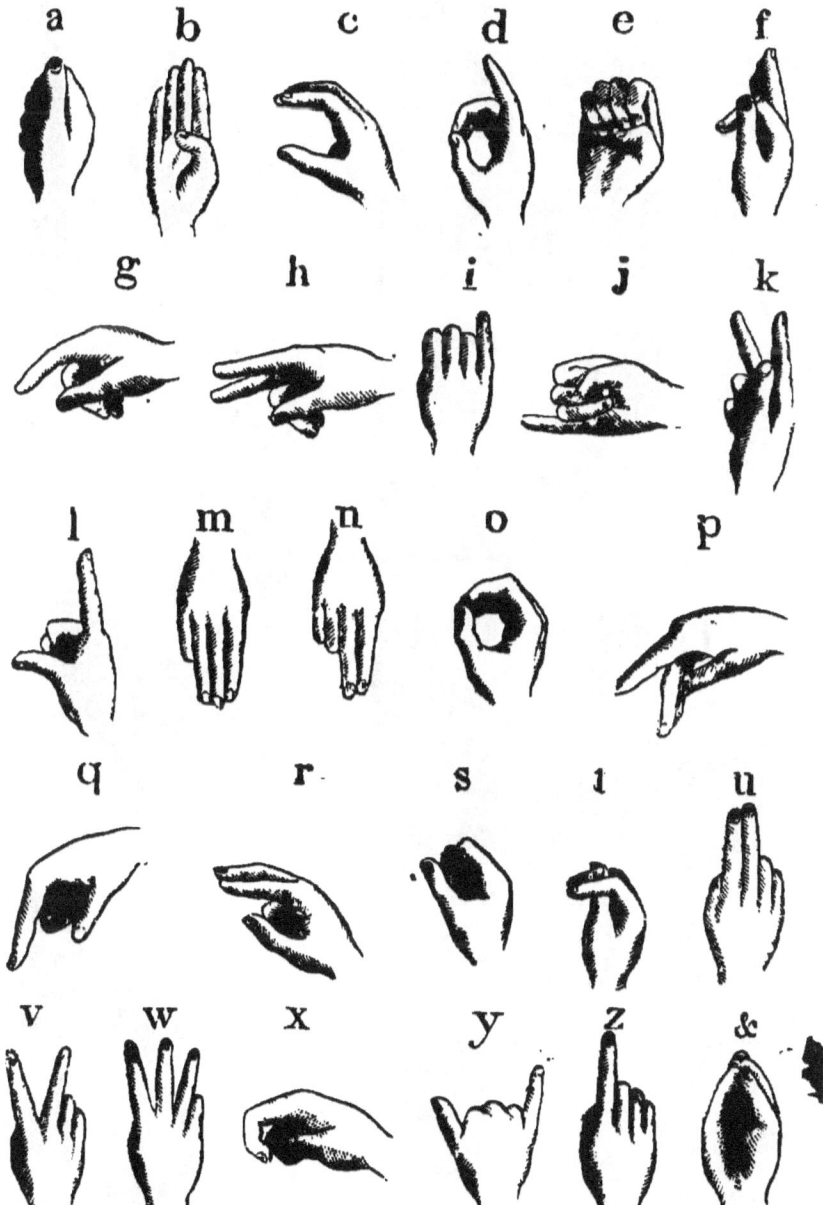

402 A CLASSIFIED SELECTION OF ILLUSTRATIONS

FLAGS, BANNERS, &c.

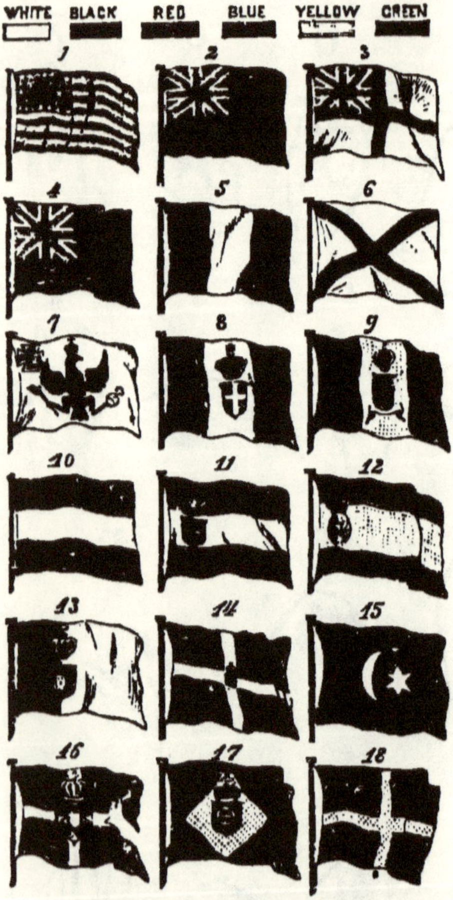

Flags of Principal Maritime Nations.

1, United States; 2, Great Britain, red Ensign; 3, Great Britain, white Ensign; 4, Great Britain, blue Ensign; 5, France; 6, Russia; 7, Prussia; 8, Italy; 9, Belgium; 10, Holland; 11, Austria; 12, Spain; 13, Portugal; 14, Greece; 15, Turkey; 16, Denmark; 17, Brazil; 18, Sweden.

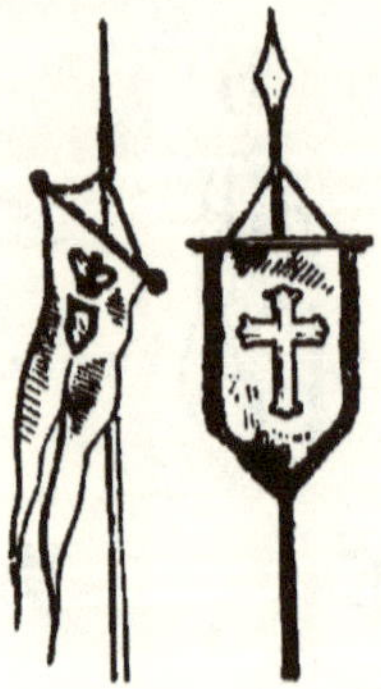

Banners.

Colors.

Oriflamme.

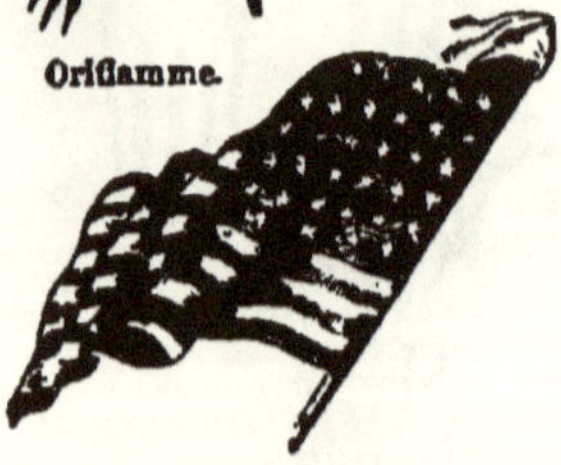

Flag.

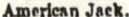

American Jack.

English Jack.

Standard.

NATURAL PHILOSOPHY, OPTICS, &c.

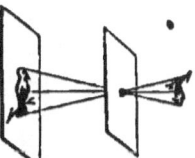

Camera Obscura, Exterior and Interior.

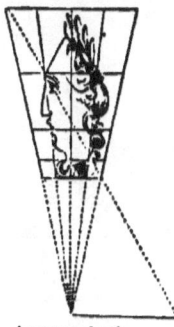

Anamorphosis.

Accidental point.

Convex.

Convexo-concave.

Convexo-convex.

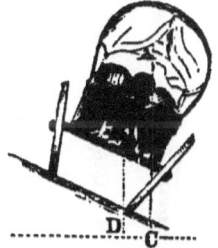

Center of Gravity.

Meniscus.

Prism.

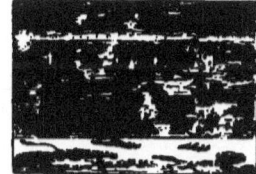

Mirage.

Pencil of Rays.

Light, separated by a Prism into the seven primary Colors.

a, prism; *c, d,* spectrum; *v,* violet; *i,* indigo; *b,* blue; *g,* green; *y,* yellow; *o,* orange; *r,* red.

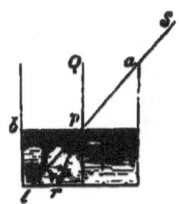

Refraction.

a, b, vessel, lower part filled with water; *s l,* ray of light in straight line; *r p s,* ray of light refracted; *q,* perpendicular.

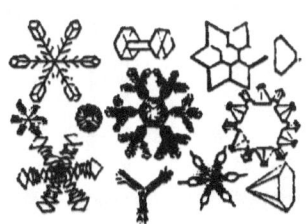

Snow Crystals.

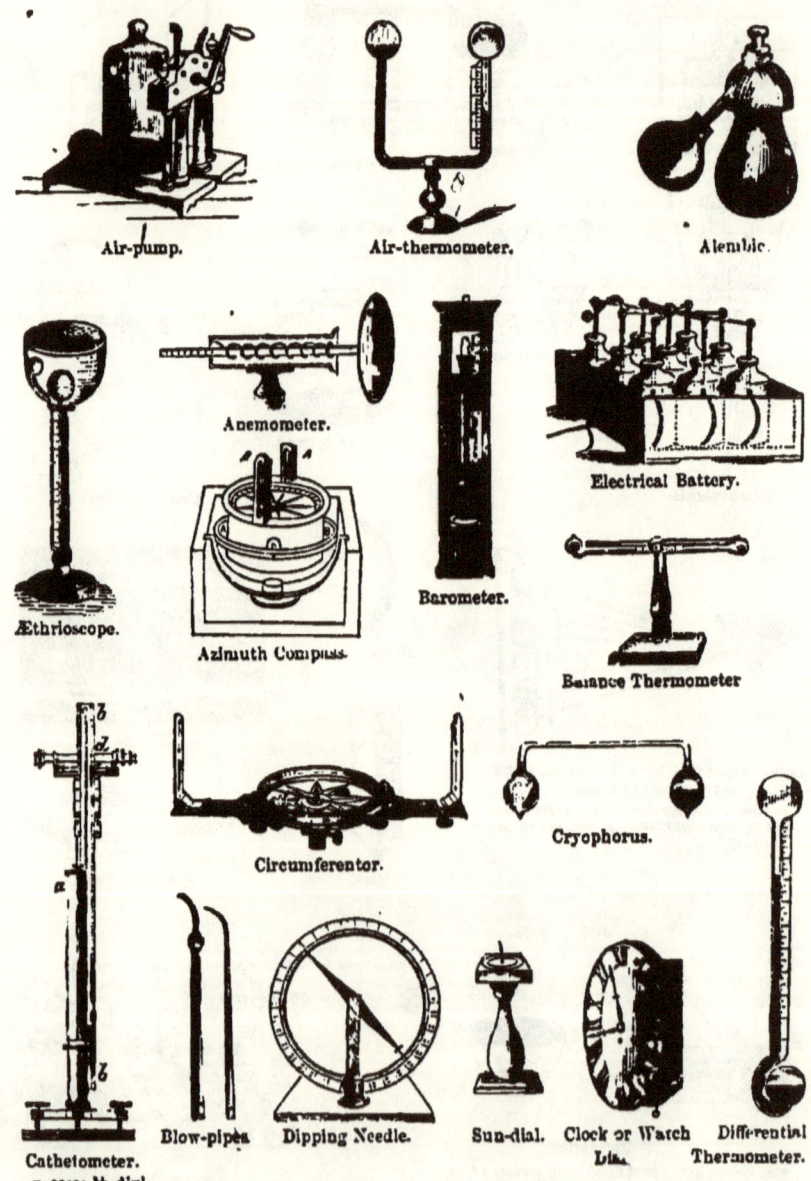

PHILOSOPHICAL INSTRUMENTS. — Continued.

Hour-glass.

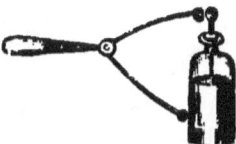
Discharger, and Leyden Jar.

Galvanic Battery.

Hadley's Quadrant
i, index-glass; *h*, horizon-glass; *s*, sight.

Eudiometer.

Galvanic Pile.

Hydrometer.
A, scale; *B*, ball; *C*, stem; *D, F*, weights.

Safety Lamp.

Theodolite.

Reflecting Goniometer.

Hydrostatic Balance.

Magic Lantern.

Opera-glass.

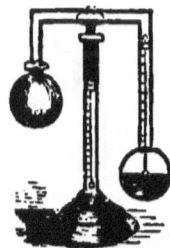
Daniell's Hygrometer.

Gunner's Quadrant.

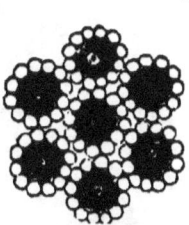
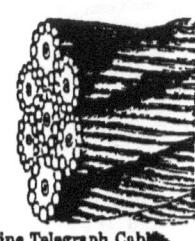
Sections of Submarine Telegraph Cable.

A CLASSIFIED SELECTION OF ILLUSTRATIONS

PHILOSOPHICAL AND SCIENTIFIC INSTRUMENTS.—Continued.

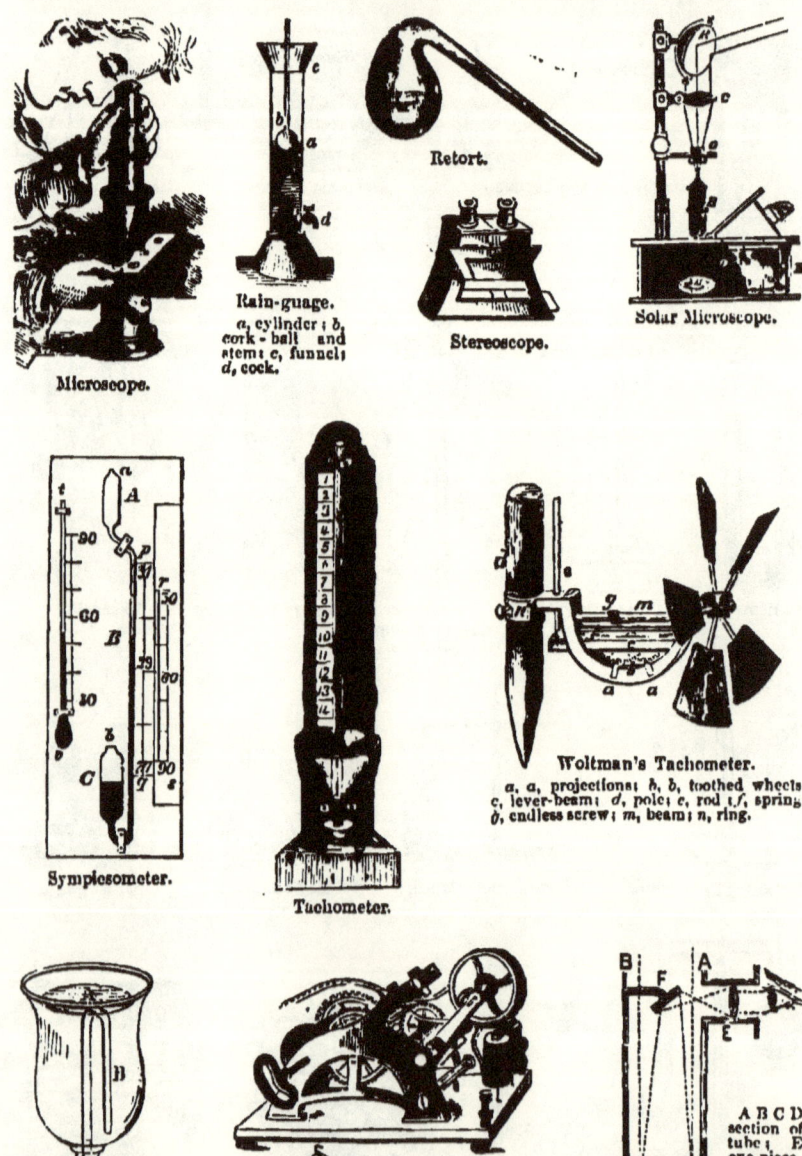

FOR WEBSTER'S HIGH-SCHOOL DICTIONARY. 407

PLANTS, SHRUBS, FLOWERS, AND FRUITS.

Acacia.

Ananas (Pine-apple.)

Anona (Sour-sop).

Agave, or American Aloe.

Sugar-cane.

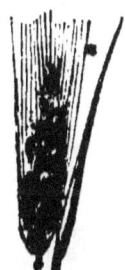
Barley.

Barometz.

Cactus (Melon-thistle)

Cockscomb.

Coffee.

Cotton-plant.

408 A CLASSIFIED SELECTION OF ILLUSTRATIONS
PLANTS, FLOWERS, FRUITS, &c. — Continued.

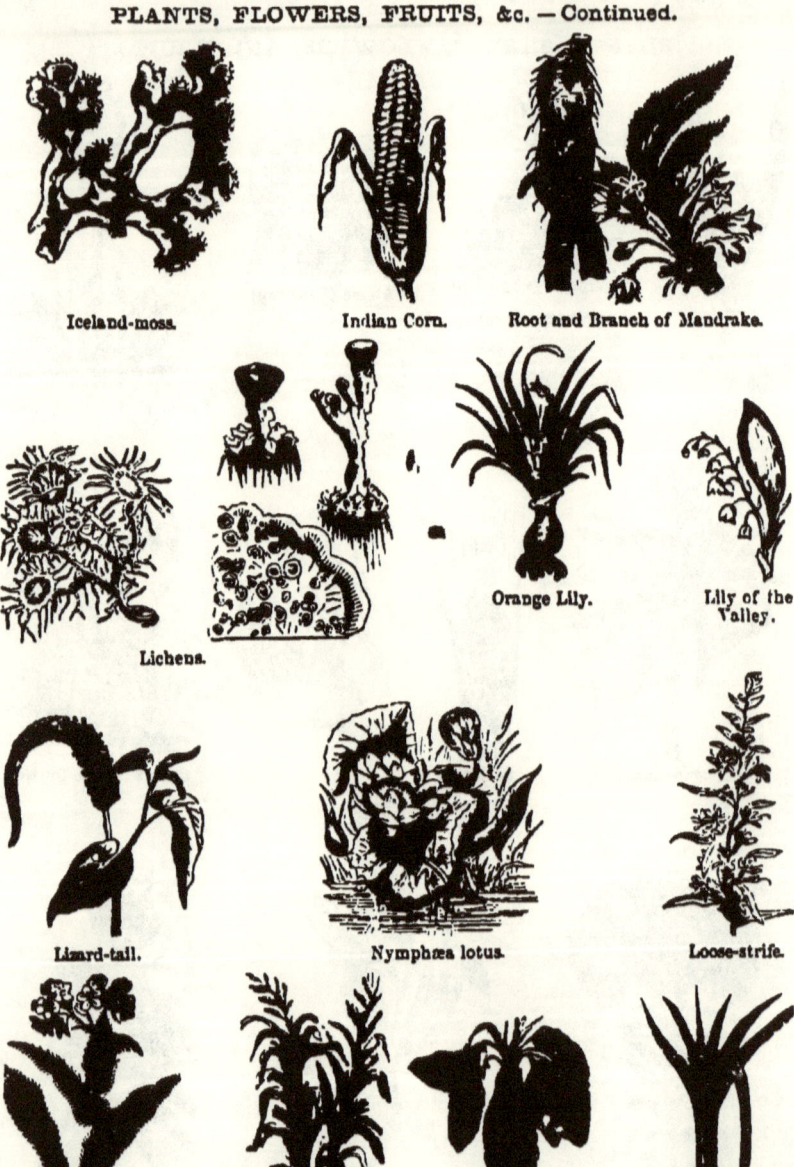

FOR WEBSTER'S HIGH-SCHOOL DICTIONARY.

QUADRUPEDS.

Aard-vark.

Agouti.

Antlers of Fossil Elk.

Ant-bear (Great Ant-eater).

Ape.

Armadillo.

Aye-aye.

Baboon.

Ass.

Aurochs.

Alpaca.

QUADRUPEDS. — Continued.

Babiroussa.

Black Bear.

White Bear.

Indian Badger.

Beaver.

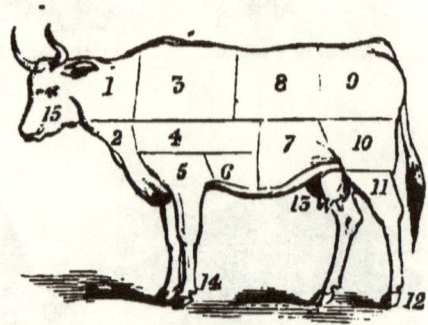
Beef.
1, neck; 2, shoulder-piece; 3, chine; 4, ribs; 5, clod; 6, brisket; 7, flank; 8, loin, sirloin; 9, rump; 10, round; 11, leg; 12, foot; 13, udder; 14, shin; 15, cheek.

Bison.

Cuban Blood-hound.

Buck, or Fallow Deer.

FOR WEBSTER'S HIGH-SCHOOL DICTIONARY. 411

RELIGION. — UTENSILS, DRESS, &c., USED IN WORSHIP AND RELIGIOUS CEREMONIES.

412 A CLASSIFIED SELECTION OF ILLUSTRATIONS
RELIGION.—UTENSILS, DRESS, &c.—Continued.

REPTILES.

414 A CLASSIFIED SELECTION OF ILLUSTRATIONS

TREES AND THEIR FRUITS.

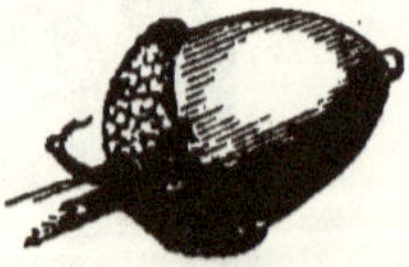

Acorn.

Baobab Tree.

Banana.

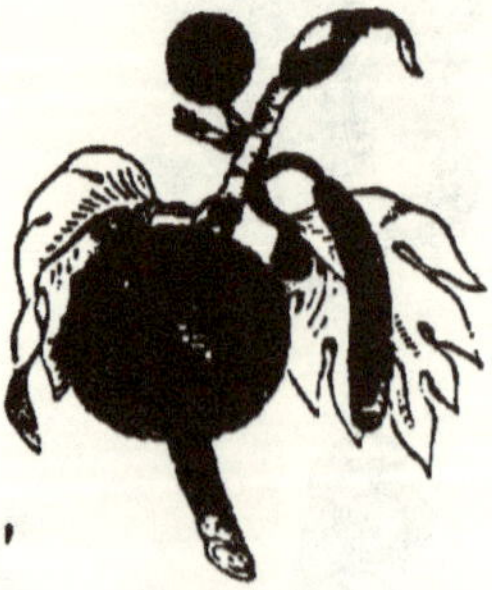

Bread-fruit.

Cedar of Lebanon.

Banyan Tree.

Cashew, and Fruit.

Cinnamon, Leaf and Blossom.

Cocoa.

Dragon-tree.

FOR WEBSTER'S HIGH-SCHOOL DICTIONARY.

TREES AND THEIR FRUITS. — Continued.

www.ingramcontent.com/pod-product-compliance
Lightning Source LLC
Chambersburg PA
CBHW030604300426
44111CB00009B/1096